Acclaim for the Pulitzer Prize winner *Parting the Waters*

"In remarkable, meticulous detail, Branch provides us with the most complex and unsentimental version of King and his times yet produced."
—Robert C. Maynard,
The Washington Post Book World

"Endlessly instructive and fascinating, thorough, stupendous. Now the source and standard in its field."
—David Levering Lewis,
The Philadelphia Inquirer

"A compelling story, masterfully told."
—Richard John Neuhaus,
The Wall Street Journal

"A masterpiece . . . remarkably revealing. . . . The past, miraculously, seems to spring back to life."
—Jim Miller,
Newsweek

"Already, in this chronicle, there is the material of *Iliad* after *Iliad*. . . . There is no time in our history of which we can be more proud."
—Garry Wills,
The New York Review of Books

D0047260

"Superb history."

—Robert Wilson,
USA Today

"A wide-ranging, monumental tapestry. Branch recounts the turbulent era with feeling and insight."

—David Anderson,
United Press International

"A brilliantly written saga that breathes life into the people and passions of the King years."

—Harold C. Fleming,
The News and Observer Book World

"A book that excites as the best history ought to . . . a notable achievement."

—Roger Harris,
Newark Star-Ledger

"A dense, elegant narrative that ranges from the back of the bus in Montgomery, Alabama, to the Oval Office. Branch has reconstructed an era that changed America forever."

—Kim Hubbard and Linda Kramer,
People

Also by Taylor Branch

Pillar of Fire
Blowing the Whistle: Dissent in the Public Interest (with Charles Peters)
Second Wind (with Bill Russell)
The Empire Blues
Labyrinth (with Eugene M. Propper)

TAYLOR

BRANCH

SIMON & SCHUSTER PAPERBACKS
New York London Toronto Sydney

PARTING

America

in the

King Years

1954–63

THE

WATERS

Simon & Schuster Paperbacks

Rockefeller Center
1230 Avenue of the Americas
New York, New York 10020

SIMON & SCHUSTER PAPERBACKS and colophon are registered
trademarks of Simon & Schuster, Inc.

For information about special discounts for bulk purchases,
please contact Simon & Schuster Special Sales:
1-800-456-6798 or business@simonandschuster.com.

Designed by Mary Beth Kilkelly/Levavi & Levavi
Picture research: Natalie Goldstein

Manufactured in the United States of America

17   19   20   18   16

The Library of Congress has cataloged the hardcover edition as follows:

Branch, Taylor.
Parting the waters: America in the King years, 1954–63 / Taylor Branch.
p.   cm.
Bibliography. Includes index.
1. Afro-Americans—Civil rights.   2. Civil rights movements—
United States—History—20th century.   3. King, Martin Luther, Jr.,
1929–1968.   4. United States—History—1953–1961.   I. Title.
E185.61.B7914   1988   88-24033
973'0496073—dc19   CIP
ISBN-13: 978-0-671-46097-6
ISBN-10:   0-671-46097-8
ISBN-13: 978-0-671-68742-7 (Pbk)
ISBN-10:   0-671-68742-5 (Pbk)

We are grateful for permission to quote from "Listen, Lord—A Prayer"
in God's Trombones *by James Weldon Johnson. Copyright 1927 by*
The Viking Press, Inc. Copyright renewed 1955 by Grace Nail Johnson.
Reprinted by permission of Viking Penguin Inc.

For the Choir of
All Souls Unitarian Church, Washington, D.C.

And in memory of
Septima Poinsette Clark

CONTENTS

PREFACE

Almost as color defines vision itself, race shapes the cultural eye—what we do and do not notice, the reach of empathy and the alignment of response. This subliminal force recommends care in choosing a point of view for a history grounded in race. Strictly speaking, this book is not a biography of Martin Luther King, Jr., though he is at its heart. To recreate the perceptions within his inherited world would isolate most readers, including myself, far outside familiar boundaries. But to focus upon the historical King, as generally established by his impact on white society, would exclude much of the texture of his life, which I believe makes for unstable history and collapsible myth.

To overcome these pitfalls of race, I have tried to make biography and history reinforce each other by knitting together a number of personal stories along the main seam of an American epoch. Like King himself, this book attempts to rise from an isolated culture into a larger history by speaking more than one language.

The text moves from King to people far removed, at the highest and lowest stations. By seeking at least a degree of intimacy with all of them —old Mother Pollard and also President Eisenhower, Bob Moses of SNCC and also J. Edgar Hoover of the FBI, with the Kennedys and also King's rivals within the black church—I hope to let the characters define each other.

My purpose is to write a history of the civil rights movement out of the conviction from which it was made, namely that truth requires a maximum effort to see through the eyes of strangers, foreigners, and enemies. I hope to sustain my thesis that King's life is the best and most important metaphor for American history in the watershed postwar years.

The chosen structure—narrative biographical history—has influenced several elements of style. For example, the word "Negro" is employed here in narrative covering the years when that term prevailed in common usage. Far from intending a political statement, I merely hope to recreate the feeling of the times, the better to capture the sweep of many changes including the extraordinary one in which the entire society shifted from "Negro" to "black" almost overnight. Because of the length of this work, for which I beg the reader's indulgence, that shift falls within the span of a second volume.

On another matter of housekeeping, I regret having to leave the record on Stanley Levison slightly ajar. Since 1984, I have sought the original FBI documents pertaining to the Bureau's steadfast contention that King's closest white friend was a top-level Communist agent. On this charge rested the FBI's King wiretaps and many collateral harassments against the civil rights movement. In opposing my request, the U.S. Department of Justice has argued in federal court that the release of thirty- to thirty-five-year-old informant reports on Levison would damage the national security even now. Almost certainly there is bureaucratic defensiveness at work here—and also, I suspect, some petty spy rivalry with the CIA—but so far the logic of secrecy has been allowed to reach levels of royalist absurdity.

Other evidence, including David Garrow's pioneering work on the FBI investigation of King, has convinced me that Levison's character and historical contributions are established beyond significant doubt. Nevertheless, the material being withheld denies the American public a common ground for historical discussion. This stubborn wisp of mystery allowed President Reagan, even while honoring King with a national holiday, to state publicly that a charge of fundamental disloyalty hangs over him. I deeply regret that a democratic government still labors to keep such allegations alive through state secrecy. It is all the more sad this year, when Soviet authorities canceled history examinations throughout their country on the admission that their national heritage has become lost among the lies and official secrets of the past.

Baltimore, Maryland
August 1988

PARTING THE WATERS

ONE

FORERUNNER:
VERNON JOHNS

Nearly seven hundred Negro communicants, some wearing white robes, marched together in the exodus of 1867. They followed the white preacher out of the First Baptist Church and north through town to Columbus Street, then east up the muddy hill to Ripley Street. There on that empty site, the congregation declared itself the First Baptist Church (Colored), with appropriate prayers and ceremonies, and a former slave named Nathan Ashby became the first minister of an independent Negro Baptist church in Montgomery, Alabama.

Most local whites considered the separation a bargain, given the general state of turmoil and numb destitution after the war. Governor Robert M. Patton and the new legislature, in a wild gamble based on Andrew Johnson's friendliness toward prominent ex-Confederates, openly repudiated the Fourteenth Amendment's recognition of Negro citizenship rights, only to have a Union brigadier walk into the Montgomery capitol to declare that he was superseding the state government again until its officials saw fit to reconsider. White spirits fell; Negro spirits soared. The town's population had swelled to fourteen thousand, with Negroes outnumbering whites three to one. Refugees of both races were fleeing the crop failures and foreclosures in the countryside and streaming into Montgomery, where they often lived in clumps on the streets and entertained themselves by watching the outdoor sheriff's sales.

Under such conditions, and with the U.S. Congress threatening a new Fifteenth Amendment to establish the right of Negroes to vote and govern, most whites were of no mind to dispute the Negro right to religion. Many were only too happy to clear the throngs from the church basement, even if it meant that their previous items of property would be conducting their own church business at the corner of Columbus and Ripley—offering motions, debating, forming committees, voting, hiring and firing preachers, contributing pennies, bricks, and labor to make pews and windows rise into the first free Negro institution. The Negro church, legal in some respects before the Negro family, became more solvent than the local undertaker.

Ten years later, a dissident faction of the First Baptist Church (Colored) marched away in a second exodus that would forever stamp the characters of the two churches. Both sides would do their best to pass off the schism as nothing more than the product of cramped quarters and growing pains, but trusted descendants would hear of the quarrels inevitable among a status-starved people. Undoubtedly some of the tensions were the legacy of slavery's division between the lowly field hands and the slightly more privileged house servants, the latter more often mulattoes. These tensions culminated when "higher elements" among the membership mounted a campaign to remodel the church to face the drier Ripley Street instead of the sloping Columbus, where they were obliged to muddy their shoes on Sundays after a rain. Their proposed renovation, while expensive, would afford cleaner and more dignified access.

Most members and some deacons considered this an unseemly and even un-Christian preoccupation with personal finery, but a sizable minority felt strongly enough to split off and form the Second Baptist Church (Colored). Although the secessionists shared the poverty of the times and of their race—and held their organizational meeting in the old Harwell Mason slave pen—the world of their immediate vision was one of relative privilege. At the first baptismal services, conducted by a proper British minister, guests included three equally proper white Yankee schoolmistresses from the missionary legions who were still streaming south to educate and Christianize the freedmen. In January 1879, the new church paid $250 for a lot and a building that stood proudly in the center of town on Dexter Avenue, little more than a stone's throw from the grand entrance of the Alabama state capitol. The all-Negro congregation renamed itself Dexter Avenue Baptist Church. Its first minister, a former slave named Charles Octavius Boothe, wrote that the members were "people of money and refinement" and boasted that one of the members, a barber named Billingslea, owned property worth $300,000. This claim, though widely doubted, entered the official church history.

From the beginning, Dexter Avenue operated as a "deacons' church," meaning that the lay officers took advantage of the full sovereignty claimed by each Baptist congregation. They were free to hire any preacher they wanted—trained or untrained, fit or unfit—without regard to bishops or other church hierarchy. The Baptists had no such hierarchy at all, nor any educational requirements for the pulpit, and this fact had contributed mightily to the spread of the denomination among unlettered whites and Negroes alike. Anyone with lungs and a claim of faith could become a preacher. And as the ministry was the only white-collar trade open to Negroes during slavery—when it was a crime in all the Southern states to teach Negroes to read or allow them to engage in any business requiring the slightest literacy—preachers and would-be preachers competed fiercely for recognition. Religious oratory became the only safe marketable skill, and a reputation for oratory substituted for diplomas and all other credentials. For most of the next century, a man with a burning desire to be a saint might well find himself competing with another preacher intent only on making a fortune, as all roads converged at the Negro church. It served not only as a place of worship but also as a bulletin board to a people who owned no organs of communication, a credit union to those without banks, and even a kind of people's court. These and a hundred extra functions further enhanced the importance of the minister, creating opportunities and pressures that forged what amounted to a new creature and caused the learned skeptic W. E. B. Du Bois to declare at the turn of the twentieth century that "the preacher is the most unique personality developed by the Negro on American soil."

Not surprisingly, these powerful characters sorely tested the ability of congregations to exercise the authority guaranteed them in Baptist doctrine. As a rule, the preachers had no use for church democracy. They considered themselves called by God to the role of Moses, a combination of ruler and prophet, and they believed that the congregation behaved best when its members, like the children of Israel, obeyed as children. The board of deacons at Dexter Avenue Baptist Church was one of the few to defend itself effectively against preachers who regularly tried to subdue the membership. Indeed, the board's very identity seemed rooted in the conviction that the church's quality lay as much in the membership as in the pastor. And because those same deacons also made it a tradition to choose the best trained, most ambitious ministers, titanic struggles after the fashion of those between European monarchs and nobles became almost a routine of church life at Dexter. Nearly a dozen preachers came and went in the first decade.

By contrast, the First Baptist Church (Colored) remained a "preacher's

church," with only three pastors during its first fifty-seven years of existence. The exalted preachers tended to reign in a manner that provoked
another mass exodus in 1910, not long after the church burned to the
ground. The minister at that time, Andrew Stokes, was a great orator and
organizer who had baptized an astonishing total of 1,100 new members
during his first year in the pulpit. Stokes made First Baptist the largest
Negro church in the United States until the great migration of 1917
created larger congregations in Chicago. He was also a money-maker. If
white realtors had trouble selling a house, they often advanced Stokes
the down payment, letting him keep his "refund" when white buyers
mobilized to keep him out of their neighborhood. Stokes would joke with
his deacons about the justice of making the whites pay for their prejudice, and he donated a portion of the proceeds to the church. This was
fine, but a controversy erupted when Stokes proposed to rebuild the
burned church a few hundred feet to the northeast on a corner lot that
he owned and to take title to the parsonage in exchange for the property.
Many irreparable wounds were inflicted in the debate that followed.
Stokes went so far as to promise to make the new church entrance face
Ripley Street, as the wealthier members had demanded more than thirty
years earlier, but the unmollified elite among the deacons led a fresh
secession down to Dexter Avenue Baptist.

It was said that Dexter actually discouraged new members, fearing that
additions above the peak of seven hundred would reduce the quality of
the whole, and several Dexter deacons predicted in public that Stokes
would never be able to rebuild First Baptist without their money and
influence. Undaunted, Stokes continued preaching to the impoverished
masses who stayed with him, meeting outdoors when he could not borrow a church, and he laid down his law: those who were too poor to meet
the demands of the building fund must bring one brick each day to the
new site, whether that brick was bought, stolen, or unearthed from Civil
War ruins. At the dedication ceremony five years later, Stokes led the
great cry of thanks that went up for what became known as the "Brick-
a-Day Church."

Over the next thirty years, the friction between the two churches
diminished to the point of religious, if not social, cooperation. Small
meetings of important community leaders tended to take place at Dexter,
larger meetings in the spacious sanctuary at First Baptist. The congregations and their contrasting traditions were remarkably stable. Officers at
both churches tended to be grandchildren of those who had marched out
of the white church in the first exodus, and children of those who had
separated over issues of mud and class. Moreover, their personalities
tended to reflect these differences. William Beasley, church secretary at

First Baptist, was genial, strong, and outgoing, from a long line of working people. R. D. Nesbitt, church clerk at Dexter, was wiry and erect, an insurance executive of light tan skin, well dressed and professional, reserved with strangers and even some of his friends. A further difference between them was that Nesbitt and his pulpit committee were about to begin a run of hard luck that would stand out as an ordeal even in the contentious history of Dexter's relations with its pastors.

In the late summer of 1945, Nesbitt traveled for the first and only time in his life to the annual meeting of the National Baptist Convention, its five million members making up the largest association of Negroes in the world. As always, the five-day meeting was an extravaganza unnoticed by whites except the hotel managers who appreciated the attendance records consistently set by upwards of fifteen thousand Negro preachers, choir members, and church officials. The conventioneers lost themselves in preaching, singing, and electioneering. Processions of singers in brightly colored robes filled great halls. The father of gospel music, Thomas Dorsey, often made a celebrity appearance to lead renditions of his own compositions, such as "Precious Lord, Take My Hand." Unemployed choir directors hustled jobs and old friends reunited along countless tables heaped with fried foods and delicacies. Amid the din, the inspiration, and the consumption, church pulpits were traded and filled.

That year Nesbitt went home with the name of a prestigious, highly trained candidate for the vacant pulpit at Dexter—a man further recommended to the church's tastes by his attendance at no less than five colleges, and by the possession of four names, Alfred Charles Livingston Arbouin. Six months later, after Dexter's usual painstaking selection process, Arbouin assumed his duties.

Among the deacons, worry spread privately but quickly when Reverend Arbouin arrived in Montgomery with a wife, whose existence had somehow escaped the background investigation. Matters worsened when inquiries turned up other Arbouin wives. When Arbouin took leave to attend the 1946 National Baptist Convention, the church slipped into the kind of nightmare that chills a deacon's bones. In the minister's absence, Mrs. Arbouin began so flagrant a friendship with a soldier from Maxwell Air Force Base that the deacons called her in for a private meeting even before Arbouin returned. Mrs. Arbouin interrupted their courtly, painfully ornate inquiry to administer a profound shock to the deacons—baring her bruised shoulders and legs, telling them that she was the victim of beatings in her own home, and declaring herself firmly unrepentant.

Confronted with a demand for his resignation, Reverend Arbouin refused and responded that his private affairs were his own business. He dared the deacons to take the sordid matter before the entire congregation, which he knew was the last thing they wanted. Arbouin, however, had not taken the measure of these deacons, who fought back with a lawsuit seeking his removal under a judicial order of secrecy. Not a word of the case reached the newspapers, Negro or white.

Raising a powerful defense, Arbouin claimed that the Constitutional separation of church and state barred the judge from entering an ecclesiastical argument, and that in any case the deacons had failed to obtain his dismissal by vote of the entire congregation, as required by Baptist practice. The deacons, for their part, used their connections to summon no less a personage than Rev. D. V. Jemison, president of the National Baptist Convention, to testify about proper procedures in such sensitive cases. When the closed trial was over, the decision rested with the white judge. No doubt impressed with Jemison, and swayed by the deacons' lack of support for Arbouin, the judge ordered the Reverend to leave his pulpit by a certain date. Until then, he further ordered, R. D. Nesbitt and the four other deacons who had brought the suit were not to speak, sing, or even pray within the walls of Dexter Avenue Baptist Church, on pain of having the entire order rescinded. Thus the deacons managed to save the church from their own misjudgment, and Arbouin managed to escape without public scandal. He went on to spend seventeen years as the pastor of a church in New York. Dexter's official history noted that his "entire ministerial career [was] God-blessed."

Nesbitt and the Dexter Avenue deacons waited nearly a year before seeking a new minister. Fortune fell to them when they did, in the form of a recommendation from a new music professor at Alabama State College—the Negro school that had been founded in Dexter's basement and from whose faculty the church membership was largely drawn. Altona Trent Johns was a pianist and music teacher of some renown, daughter of a college president, member in good standing of the Atlanta Negro aristocracy from its early twentieth-century flourishing on "Sweet Auburn" Avenue, and, most important to Nesbitt, wife of one of the most brilliant scholar-preachers of the modern age, Vernon Johns. Negroes placed him in the foremost triumvirate of their preachers, along with Mordecai Johnson and Howard Thurman.

Through Mrs. Johns, Nesbitt invited the eminent preacher to deliver a trial sermon. The church was packed when the imposing figure of Vernon Johns rose to the pulpit, recited a long passage of Scripture without looking at the Bible, and then held the congregation spellbound for half an hour without a pause or benefit of notes. Dexter's stolid deacons were accustomed to quality, but in Johns they recognized a mind of a higher order altogether. Upon learning that Johns wanted to join his wife in Montgomery, they suspended precedent for the first time in Nesbitt's memory and offered Johns their pulpit without an investigation or a second trial sermon. Johns moved into the parsonage on South Jackson Street in October 1948. His behavior pitched the entire church into four years of awe, laughter, inspiration, fear, and annoyance. For Nesbitt, the responsible deacon, Johns became the most exquisite agony he had ever known in the church.

Vernon Johns was merely another invisible man to nearly all whites, but to the invisible people themselves he was the stuff of legend. The deepest mysteries of existence and race rubbed vigorously together within him, heating a brain that raced constantly until the day he died. His ancestry was a jumble of submerged edges and storybook extremes. During slavery, his father's father was hanged for cutting his master in two with a scythe, and even eighty years later it was whispered in the Johns family that the hunting dogs would not approach the haunted spot where the murder had occurred.

Johns's maternal grandfather was a white man named Price, of Scottish descent, who maintained two entirely separate families—one white, one Negro. This type of bi-patriarchy, though fairly widespread, was never publicly acknowledged in either culture. The Negro children handed down stories about how Price became one of the first inmates at the new Virginia State Penitentiary for killing another white man he caught trying to rape his slave mistress. He protected the mistress "just like she was a white woman." For this he was admired by some Negroes, but he was by nature a mean, violent, complicated man. When his Negro wife died in the 1870s, he took all his Negro children into the other household to be raised by his childless white wife, "Miss Kitty." Vernon Johns's mother, Sallie Price, made this transfer as a little girl, and years later she told her family how the taboos had been respected against all opposing reality, even in the intimacy of the home. She never called her father "father," for decency required the Negro children to be orphans and the white couple to be missionary dispensers of foster care. When Price died about 1900, Sallie Price Johns went to the funeral with her young son Vernon and her husband Willie, son of the hanged slave, and sat through the burial services in a separate-but-equal family section, just across the gravesite from Miss Kitty and the white relatives.

Willie Johns died not long afterward, and in due course Sallie Johns married her dead husband's younger brother. So Vernon Johns finished his youth as the stepson of his uncle, and grandson of a slave who killed his master and of a master who killed for his slave. Only in the Bible did he find open discussion of such a tangle of sex, family, slavery, and violence.

Born in 1892, Vernon Johns grew up outside Farmville, in Prince Edward County, an area so remote that its inhabitants preserved a distinctive speech pattern from the early Scots who settled there. Outsiders found the accent faintly Elizabethan and the country correspondingly backward. It lay at the extreme northern boundary of the rich agricultural Black Belt, and Vernon Johns always clung to the belief that farming was the base line of independence and prosperity, even long after the twentieth-century marketplace had reduced his home region to something like a ghost of nearby Williamsburg.

Johns had a square head and jaw, flaring nostrils, a barrel chest, and huge hands that he joked were like Virginia hams. He looked like the farmer he was, except that he always wore scholarly horn-rimmed glasses. Poor eyesight caused him to vow as a youth that he would read the small print of the Bible only once. Usually he listened to others read out loud, and he first displayed extraordinary gifts by reciting from memory long passages he had heard only once or twice. In grammar school, scolded for erasing a blackboard filled with the week's assignments, Johns reproduced every word from memory. He soon moved on to more substantial feats, memorizing long biblical passages, including the entire Book of Romans. This greatly pleased his father Willie, who left the farm on Sundays to earn extra money as a "saddlebags preacher."

Like most Negro parents, Sallie Johns and her husbands invested what meager educational funds they had in their eldest daughter, keeping Vernon on the farm. There his gifts seemed to multiply in the process of self-education. He would recite poetry behind the plow and scrounge books to read at night. He used these skills and his gumption to talk his way into several schools, including the Virginia Seminary at Lynchburg. Tossed out for rebelliousness, he ran away from home to Oberlin College in Ohio, pushed his way into the dean's office, and announced his readiness to begin classes. The dean replied, as politely as the erudite dean of a famous liberal white college could speak to a rude Negro youth during World War I, that Oberlin had already turned Johns down because of his worthless credits.

"I got your letter, Dean Fiske," Johns replied. "But I want to know whether you want students with credits or students with brains."

As both Fiske and Johns told it later, the dean rather impatiently handed Johns a book written in German and demanded that he read it—and was surprised when he did. He soon dispatched Johns to see Dr. Edward Increase Bosworth, the eminent dean of Oberlin Seminary. Bosworth tested Johns with a book of Greek scripture, and Johns smiled. In later years, he would discard his Latin and Hebrew on aesthetic grounds, but he would always collect histories and poems in his beloved Greek. By the end of the day, Bosworth was impressed enough to enroll Johns as a provisional student, and by the end of the term he had taken on the young phenomenon as his protégé—making him a full-fledged member of the graduate seminary and helping him find work as a part-time preacher to support himself. Within the year, Johns displaced Robert M. Hutchins as class leader in scholarship. Hutchins, a liberal Midwesterner in the abolitionist tradition, found himself pushed beyond the limits of tolerance, and he remarked that no country Negro could make the grades Johns was making without cheating. When Johns got word of the insult, he promptly sought out Hutchins on the campus, called him a son of a bitch, and punched him in the mouth. (The two later became good friends and remained so throughout Hutchins' long tenure as president of the University of Chicago.)

Just before his graduation ceremonies in the spring of 1918, Johns was chosen to deliver the annual student oration at the Memorial Arch, dedicated to the Oberlin students killed in China's Boxer Rebellion. After graduation, he enrolled in the graduate school of theology at the University of Chicago, headquarters of the Social Gospel theologians. Then he stepped back into the restricted universe of jobs open to Negroes, where his fame as a religious scholar and preacher quickly brought him offers of the best pulpits and teaching jobs in the 1920s, though his temperament caused him to lose or leave them just as quickly and make his way back to the family farm in Virginia. From there, he earned small lecture fees at Negro churches and schools up and down the East Coast. He would catch the Richmond train and rumble off, wearing a tattered suit with books stuffed in the pockets. On his return, his brother would often meet him at the station with a fresh horse, and Johns would farm for a few days before his next lecture.

This was the era of the Scopes trial, when theological liberals and fundamentalists battled not only in churches and colleges but also in courtrooms and legislatures and on the front pages over issues ranging from creationism and the Virgin Birth to the social obligations of Christians. Each side had its own pamphlets, journals, conventions, and rooting sections. Johns, an ardent exponent of liberal theology, was more than a little irritated by the failure of the liberals to include any works by Negroes in their annual book of best sermons. He sent the theologians in charge of the publication several sermons by Mordecai Johnson and Howard Thurman. When these were rejected, Johns sat down and wrote out a sermon of his own, "Transfigured Moments," which in 1926 became the first work by a Negro published in *Best Sermons*. This analysis of the symbolism of mountains in the lives of Moses, Elijah, and Jesus Christ would be studied by Negro theology students for the next generation. "It is good to be the possessor of some mountain-top experience," wrote Johns, in a long passage on the need to tie the inspiration of leaders to the experience of the common people. "It is a heart strangely un-Christian that cannot thrill with joy when the least of men begin to pull in the direction of the stars."

Within the insulated but resonant world of Negro church people, Johns was already as famous as Mordecai Johnson, then president of Howard University in Washington, D.C., and Howard Thurman, already an internationally known mystic theologian on his way to breakthrough posts at both Negro and white universities. (Johns had courted the woman who married Thurman, and succeeded Mordecai Johnson as pastor of the First Baptist Church of Charleston, West Virginia.) They were his friends and peers, but here the similarities ceased. Whereas Johnson and Thurman were polished men who hailed from the Negro aristocracy and did the things respected scholars are supposed to do—publish regularly in the leading journals, retire into positions of responsible administration, and leave behind an orderly correspondence with other luminaries in the field —Johns was a maverick who seldom wrote anything down and who thought nothing of walking into distinguished assemblies wearing mismatched socks, with farm mud on his shoes.

Having married a daughter of a college president in 1927, he mingled thereafter in those circles only as a tourist. During the Depression his eccentricities carried him beyond maverick status into more or less the life of a bohemian. He would jump into the car with a friend and leave the family for months at a time, preaching here and there, hawking old books at ministers' conventions, selling subscriptions to fledgling magazines. Most of the people he saw on these tours knew nothing of his intellectual attainments. Among those who did, Johns did not bother to answer when they wondered why he eschewed the relative security of a college for life on the road. Johns loved to travel. Because Negroes had trouble finding motels and restaurants to serve them in the segregated South, he would pack blocks of cheese and quarts of milk in ice and take off on drives of non-stop poetry recital. Fellow travelers knew him to finish all of Keats in Alabama and get through Byron and Browning before hitting Farmville. Johns calculated distances in units of poetry, and if he tired of verse he waded into military history.

When the economy recovered in the 1940s, Johns went back on the college lecture circuit—speaking to chaplains, historians, and even economists, plus the usual run of theologians—but his manner never approached conventionality. University officials would answer a summons to his "office" only to find him at a phone booth in the bus station. Student emissaries, on chauffeuring Johns to the president's guest residence at the university, would ask for his bag and be handed just that— a paper bag from a grocery store, filled with books, underwear, and a semi-fresh shirt. Usually, the very brilliance of his lectures would make people forget such eccentricities, which, if remembered at all, tended to be regarded as amusing. Many members of the Dexter Avenue church in Montgomery were to find, however, that there was a biting side to Johns's iconoclasm.

At first, his differences with the Dexter congregation involved no more than subtleties, for in many respects the pastor and the members were agreed. All abhorred the slightest displays of emotionalism in a church congregation, for example. There was no shouting at Dexter, nor even any responsive "Amens" during the sermon. At their most demonstrative, the members might allow a quiet murmur of approval to run through them. This restraint pleased Johns. He did not believe in marathon prayer meetings or revivals or the hyperactive church auxiliaries that were so prevalent in many churches. Neither did Dexter, which did not even have Sunday evening services.

But Johns loved Negro spirituals—the music developed during slavery —believing them to contain both a historical and a spiritual authenticity that belonged in the church. Unfortunately, Dexter did not allow spirituals, either. Johns objected that the church mistook the form of dignity for its essence and campaigned to change the Dexter hymnal, which at that time contained no musical scoring for the songs—only the words, like a book of poetry. Johns argued that the hymnal was an affectation that made singing painful to the ear. And certainly the hymnal should include the spirituals. He tried to schedule spirituals at numerous planning meetings, only to be told that it was "not done at Dexter." Finally, Johns went to the extreme of inviting the congregation to sing a spiritual that was not on the printed order of service. He beckoned Edna King, the church organist, to begin. She, a true Dexter member, failed to follow her pastor's wishes even under such pressure. Muscles twitched in his jaw and in hers, but she refused to play "Go Down, Moses," "We'll Soon Be Free," "I Got Shoes," or any other spiritual. In response, Johns would lecture the congregation on the important differences between dignity, pride, and vanity. In time, he would do worse.

One of his first acts in Montgomery was to replace the tiny bulletin board atop the steps at the church entrance with a much larger one on the sidewalk facing Dexter Avenue. In 1949, all Montgomery read there that Vernon Johns would preach the following Sunday on the topic "Segregation After Death." No doubt many whites cherished a private hope that the races would be separated in the afterlife, but the public notice also invited suspicion. Local leaders found it mildly unnerving that a Negro minister planned to address so volatile and worldly a topic as segregation in the first place, and the police chief guarded against the possibility of an incendiary trick by inviting the minister to explain himself down at the station.

Johns told the chief and his men that the sermon would be open to everyone but that he would be happy to give a preview on the spot, in case they were too intimidated to attend a Negro church. Soon Johns was reciting his text from memory, beginning with Luke 16:19, which is Christ's parable of the beggar Lazarus and the rich man Dives. Having ignored Lazarus all his sumptuous life, Dives was shocked to look up from hell to see him in heaven. He implored father Abraham to send Lazarus down to hell with some cool water to ease his torment, but Abraham replied that a "great gulf" was fixed between them. The great gulf, preached Johns, was segregation. It separated people and blinded them to their common humanity—so much so that Dives, even in the midst of his agony, did not think to speak directly to Lazarus or to recognize his virtues, but instead wanted Abraham to "send" Lazarus with water, still thinking of him as a servant. It was not money that sent Dives to hell, said Johns, since after all Dives was only a millionaire in hell talking to Abraham, a multimillionaire in heaven. Rather Dives was condemned by his insistence on segregation, which he perversely maintained even after death. After he preached on this theme for a few minutes, Johns later boasted, there was "not a dry eye in the station house." But his sermon that Sunday brought mixed comfort at best to his own congregation, as he made it clear that it was not only whites who sought to segregate themselves. "What preacher wouldn't love to have a church full of members like Dives?" he asked, going on to describe Dives's "purple raiment" in graphic terms that made it remarkably like the fine clothes assembled before him. Having said bluntly that the social attitudes of most white churchgoers rendered them no more Christian than "sun worshippers," he said practically the same thing of the "spinksterinkdum Negroes" who paraded in the "fashion show" at Dexter. "Spinksterinkdum" was a term of his own invention, which he steadfastly refused to define, but most of his listeners discerned that it had to do with a pronounced rigidity among the elite.

Johns directed harsh pronouncements to both whites and Negroes, but the whites were cushioned initially by post–World War II attitudes.

Their superior status was relatively secure then; the notion of drastic change for the benefit of Negroes struck the average American as about on a par with creating a world government, which is to say visionary, slightly dangerous, and extremely remote. The race issue was little more than a human interest story in the mass public consciousness. This was Jackie Robinson's second season with the Brooklyn Dodgers. Satchel Paige made his Major League debut that summer at an age somewhere between thirty-nine and forty-eight, treating 78,000 Cleveland fans to his famous "hesitation pitch," the legality of which was hotly debated. In the biggest race story of the year, Southern politicians walked out of the Democratic Convention and ran a presidential ticket of their own, but even that was treated as something of a menacing joke, as evidenced by the fact that the Southerners accepted their "Dixiecrat" nickname, and newspaper editors across the South expressed considerable chagrin over the spectacle.

In Montgomery, the only racial development that pierced through symbolism was President Truman's executive order of July 26, 1948, ending segregation in the armed forces. This touched Montgomery in a sore spot. The regional economy was heavily dependent on two Air Force bases, Maxwell and Gunther, which poured nearly $50 million a year into the area. Though most citizens were loath to admit it, this federal money had revived a local economy that had been failing since the glory days before the Civil War. There was even a touch of romance to it. F. Scott Fitzgerald and Zelda had found each other in Montgomery, drawn there by the novel flying machines. During the 1930s, Claire Chennault and Billy McDonald used to fly over the city in two airplanes with the wings tied together by silken cords that never broke—to demonstrate the precision of the aircraft to skeptical military chieftains. After World War II, Air Force spending brought back enough prosperity for old Montgomery families to recall the days when Montgomery County itself stretched through most of central Alabama and when its aristocracy was the envy of the state. Reestablished Montgomery still looked down on a steel town like Birmingham as a crude, belching monster, and on pretentious old cotton towns like Selma (just downstream on the Alabama River) as impostors. (A common graffito in the bathrooms of Montgomery high schools read, "Flush the toilet: Selma needs the water.")

Truman's order reminded everyone that the source of Montgomery's new identity was the Yankee government itself, which was imposing a regimen of full-fledged race-mixing at the two huge air bases. The city was helpless to stop it, but its council could and did make sure that such practices did not spread into the city. It was against the law in Montgomery for a white person and a Negro to play checkers on public property, nor could they ride together in a taxi. The ordinances governing the public bus system were tougher than those in other Southern cities, where Negroes sat in the back and whites in the front of the bus, coming together as the bus filled up. In Montgomery, the bus drivers were empowered to impose a "floating line" between the races as they considered necessary to keep a Negro man's legs from coming too close to a white woman's knees. In practice, this meant that the driver would order Negroes to vacate an entire row on the bus to make room for one white person, or order them to stand up even when there were vacant seats on the bus. Negroes could not walk through the white section of the bus to their own seats, but were instead required to pay their fares at the front and then leave the bus to enter through the rear door. Some drivers were spiteful enough to drive away before the riders could reboard.

For Vernon Johns, the practical import of the Montgomery atmosphere was that while he could say things to and about the whites that had never been said so publicly, his deeds were strictly circumscribed. His strident denunciations only brought him Negroes seeking redress that he could not provide. Of the Negro women who came to him with stories of being raped and beaten by white men, Johns was especially moved by the stories of two young girls. Each time, he drove the girl to the Tuskegee hospital in the dead of night for a medical examination, and each time he questioned the victim at length to satisfy himself that she was telling the truth. Each time, he went with the victim to file charges at the police station—in one case against a storekeeper who had broken into a home to rape the babysitter; in the other, against six white policemen. The first case actually went to trial, but the storekeeper was acquitted on the testimony of his wife, who said she was pregnant and had therefore given her husband permission to seek sex outside the home. The second case went nowhere, as the local authorities refused to order policemen to stand in a lineup.

Johns was no more effective in cases when the victim was himself. Once when he paid his fare on a bus and was told to get off for reboarding at the back, he refused and took a seat in the front. The driver refused to move the bus, whereupon Johns demanded and got his money back. The refund itself was unprecedented, but when Johns invited all the Negroes and whites on the bus to follow him off in protest, no one followed. One Dexter member on the bus remarked that he "should know better" than to try something like that. On another occasion, Johns walked into a white restaurant and ordered a sandwich and a drink to take home with him. His request immediately produced a tense silence in the entire restaurant, but there was something about his size and his fearless manner that caused the attendant to make the sandwich. Then he fixed the drink and, perhaps under pressure from the onlookers, poured it slowly onto the counter in front of the minister. Johns ordered another drink, saying, "There is something in me that doesn't like being pushed around, and it's starting to work." With that, a gang of customers ran to their cars for guns and chased him out of the restaurant. "I pronounced the shortest blessing of my life over that sandwich," he said later. "I said, 'Goddam it.' "

No pliable façade stretched over Johns's brooding, irascible nature. Sometimes people wondered whether the inner Johns was vexed more by the human nature of the whites than the cosmic nature of the universe, but they never had to guess about the content of his criticism. He was unsparing in his disdain for politeness, flattery, and other forms of ordinary protection for the fragile personality, believing them to be invitations to unreality. Humor was the only salve he allowed. One day on the streets of Montgomery, he ran into a prominent Dexter member named Rufus Lewis—a strapping man with a clear eye and the voice of authority, a funeral director known among Negroes as a football coach and pioneer in voter registration. Johns called to him and drew a crowd as he quizzed Lewis about the registration campaign. From Johns, this very attention was the supreme compliment. When he finished, he said, "Lewis, this is fine, but you don't come to church. You better hope you don't die while I'm here, because if you do you'll have a hell of a funeral." On a Sunday, all heads in the Dexter congregation turned as Dr. H. Councill Trenholm—president of Alabama State College, the largest employer of Montgomery Negroes generally and of Dexter members in particular—eased himself into a pew. "I want to pause here in the service," Johns intoned from the pulpit, "until Dr. Trenholm can get himself seated here on his semi-annual visit to the church." Trenholm never returned to Dexter while Johns was in Montgomery. Rufus Lewis did, but not very often.

Johns shocked his congregation more profoundly on other occasions. When Dr. R. T. Adair shot his wife to death on the front porch of their home, on suspicion of adultery, no Negro in town was surprised to hear that the eminent physician did not spend a night in jail. But when Adair next took his customary seat at Dexter, Johns sprang quickly to the pulpit. "There is a murderer in the house," he announced to a stunned congregation. "God said, 'Thou shalt not kill.' Dr. Adair, you have committed a sin, and may God have mercy on your soul." Johns stared down at Adair in solemn judgment, with one eye in a menacing twitch caused by a childhood kick from a mule. Then he sat down. Although his public rebuke carried no further sanction, it was a shockingly bold fulfillment of another special role of the Negro preacher: substitute judge and jury in place of disinterested white authorities.

His most consistent pulpit campaign concerned the image and eco-

nomic status of Montgomery Negroes. Johns excoriated Dexter members
for their attachment to status and prestige above work. The Negro professional class in Montgomery was pitifully small: one dentist and three
doctors for 50,000 people, as opposed to 43 dentists and 144 doctors for a
roughly equivalent number of whites. More than half the employed Negroes were laborers and domestic workers. Even salesclerk was considered too good a job for Negroes, as whites outnumbered them 30 to 1
behind the counters. The backbone of the Negro middle class was its
educators—the faculty at Alabama State and the public school teachers
—but they were utterly dependent on the goodwill of the white politicians who paid their salaries. Under these oppressive conditions, Johns
thundered from the pulpit, it was almost criminally shortsighted for
educated Negroes to cling to titles and symbolic niches instead of building an economic base from which to deal more equally with whites as
well as among themselves. He named the Alabama State business professors and challenged the congregation to name an actual business to
which any of them had ever applied himself. Business was beneath them,
Johns said derisively. And farming was too dirty. "If every Negro in the
U.S.A. dropped dead today," he declared, "it would not affect significantly any important business activity." In order to make something
worthwhile, they would have to take risks and immerse themselves
among the common people, and this, he said, was the step they were
least willing to take. He scolded his listeners for being eager to sell off
their few productive assets in exchange for articles of prestige. "You say
you want a definition of perpetual motion?" he asked. "Give the average
Negro a Cadillac and tell him to park it on some land he owns."

Combined with his political views, these doctrines made Johns a kind
of hybrid of the schools of thought that had been contending among
Negroes since the Civil War. Like Booker T. Washington, he espoused
hard, humbling work in basic trades, as opposed to W. E. B. Du Bois's
"talented tenth" strategy, which called first for an assault on the leadership classes by an educated Negro elite. Like Du Bois and Frederick
Douglass, Johns advocated a simultaneous campaign for full political
rights. He rejected as demeaning and foolhardy Washington's accommo-
dationist strategy of offering to trade political rights for economic ones.
Like Du Bois, he believed fiercely in the highest standards of scholarship
and never suffered fools at all, much less gladly. But like Washington, he
believed that the dignity and security of a people derived from its masses,
and that without stability and character in the masses an elite could live
above them only in fantasy.

These were words—words to argue and fill books with, words to deliver from pulpits, but words nevertheless—and the most acidic of lec-

tures alone could never have brought Johns and R. D. Nesbitt to grief at Dexter Avenue Baptist Church. After all, churchgoers were accustomed to being called sinners of one sort or another. Although Johns prided himself on sermons that created an anger the members had to take out the door, rather than guilt that resolved itself in soggy contrition right there in the service, he knew that even anger dissipated in time. The members could have remembered what they wanted to remember, his poetry and eloquence, had it not been for the minister's shocking business enterprises. He did something that esteemed preachers like Mordecai Johnson and Howard Thurman would never do, any more than they would preach a sermon like Johns's classic "Mud Is Basic." Du Bois would never have dreamed of doing it—not in his Vandyke beard and his spats, with his gold-topped cane. And even Booker T. Washington, with his chauffeurs and secretaries and attendants, never gave the slightest indication that he himself intended to cast his bucket down into industrial work. But Vernon Johns would preach and scold and cajole about the importance of practical work, and then he would go right outside the church and sell farm produce on the street there, under the brow of the state capitol, with Dexter men milling about in their best suits and the women in their best hats, and with the white Methodists spilling out of the church down the street. Johns peddled hams and onions, potatoes and watermelons, cabbages and sausage. Many Dexter members were mortified by the sight of their learned pastor wearing his suit on the back of a pickup. Among the milder reactions was that it "cheapened" the church.

All this spurred Johns to sharper criticism. The congregation liked to eat good food and buy consumer goods, so why should they dislike associating with those who provided them? He accused them of persisting in the white man's view of slavery—that labor was demeaning—when Negroes should know that it was oppression, not labor, that demeaned them. On the contrary, the desire to avoid labor had enticed whites into the corruption of slavery.

Johns's three daughters soon noticed that the Montgomery atmosphere and the congregation's resistance had put a harder edge on his arguments and soliloquies, and he seemed to lose himself less often in the sheer pleasure of his musings. This pushed his temper closer to the surface, even within the family, as was frightfully demonstrated one night at home when he kept calling on his wife to support him in one of his observations. Mrs. Johns, who took delight in her husband's crusades but was as serene as he was volatile, was playing the piano. She decided to let him know that he was being repetitious by ignoring the third or fourth invitation to discuss the same point. This annoyed Johns, who began to

shout, and Mrs. Johns showed her displeasure over the shouting by continuing to ignore him. Johns went berserk, shouting louder and louder,
and finally, to the horror of his niece and daughters, ripping the sleeve
off his wife's dress in a rage. The children would never forget how Mrs.
Johns kept playing the Bach, never missing a note, saying nothing. Vernon Johns held the torn piece of dress in his hand for a few seconds, then
dropped it and walked silently out the door. He returned a few minutes
later with some steaks and a bubbly new mood, as though the fit had
never occurred.

Johns cultivated a garden in the yard behind the parsonage on South
Jackson Street and set many worshippers' teeth on edge with a running
description of the cultivation process. Then one Sunday, "just to show
you what can be done on a tiny patch of land," he pulled a huge cabbage
and a plump onion from behind the pulpit and held them up for the
congregation to inspect. "I left the roots on them just to prove they
weren't bought in the store," he announced mischievously. Another Sunday he arrived for the service without shoelaces, probably because he had
misplaced them, but when he noticed the stares of the congregation,
Johns casually told them, "I'll wear shoestrings when Negroes start making them."

But it was the fish that first got him hauled before the board of deacons.
One Sunday he had a load of fish iced down on the back of a truck, and
the odor, together with the traditionally low estate of the fishmonger,
created a rebellion within the church. Johns complied with a formal
letter requesting his presence before the deacons. When he learned the
nature of their complaint, he intimidated them with a fully annotated
lecture on the importance of fish and fishermen to the Christian religion,
world history, and nutrition. He paid them a backhanded compliment by
remarking on the summons as a sign that he was finally getting the
church's attention. And he defended himself. "Gentlemen, I have a duty
to provide you with the Gospel," he said, "and I have a right to provide
you with food. As far as I'm concerned, I will sell anything except whiskey and contraceptives. Besides, I get forty calls about fish for every one
about religion." When the deacons failed to endorse this license, Johns
abruptly resigned and walked out the door. Nesbitt was detailed to seek
him out and arrange a truce.

He succeeded, but the net result was to worsen positions all around.
Nesbitt himself was further compromised. As a deacon known to be
personally sympathetic to Johns, and as a member of the minority "non-
teacher clique" that was less hostile toward the preacher, Nesbitt found
himself under attack for failing to control Johns, who went on selling
produce. Some members wanted to get rid of the pastor and had been

heartened by his resignation. This stiffened their resistance to his wishes, which in turn made Johns pound on the big Bible in the pulpit. He never opened the pulpit Bibles during his tenure at Dexter, but he wore out at least three of them with his fists. On several occasions, the organist's continued refusal to play anything but the most conservative hymns made Johns walk out of the church in anger. Nesbitt was obliged to chase him several blocks down Dexter Avenue, begging him to return to the service.

Had it not been for the fact that visitors were still coming to Montgomery from great distances to listen to Johns and to praise him afterward, church opinion might have solidified against him sooner. As it was, the membership was divided over an exasperating problem: Johns was both the highest and lowest, the most learned and most common, the most glorious reflection of their intellectual tastes and most obnoxious challenge to their dignity. He enjoyed reminding them that the same Moses who talked to God on Mount Sinai also rejected his status as the adopted grandson of Pharaoh to lead the Hebrew slaves out of Egypt. Like Moses, Johns received from his people a tumultuous vacillation between the extremes of veneration and rebellion. Unlike Moses, he worked no political miracles to sustain his leadership. Another resignation was tendered and refused in 1950.

Johns often loaded the milk and cheese into his car and disappeared, driving up to the family farm in Virginia to spend a few days behind the plow. The animals or the equipment frequently dealt him some minor injury—he was nearing sixty now, and had not been a real farmer for thirty years.

In the spring of 1951, he drove to Virginia again. This time it was a crisis: the Ku Klux Klan had burned a cross in his brother's yard to intimidate the Johns family over a school strike. The trouble had begun on the morning of April 23, 1951, at Farmville's R. R. Moton High School (named for Booker T. Washington's aide and successor), when the school's principal was informed by telephone that the police were about to arrest two of his students down at the bus station. Failing to recognize the call as a ruse, he had dashed off for town. Shortly thereafter, a note from the principal was delivered to each classroom, summoning the whole school to a general assembly. All 450 students and twenty-five teachers filed into the auditorium, and the buzz of gossip gave way to shocked silence the instant the stage curtain opened to reveal not the principal but a sixteen-year-old junior named Barbara Johns. She announced that this was a special student meeting to discuss the wretched conditions at the school. Then she invited the teachers to leave. By now it had dawned on the teachers that this was a dangerous, unauthorized situation running in the direction of what was known as juvenile delinquency. Some of them moved to take over the stage, whereupon Barbara Johns took her shoe off and rapped it sharply on a school bench. "I want you all out of here!" she shouted at the teachers, beckoning a small cadre of her supporters to remove them from the room.

This was Vernon Johns's niece, the daughter of his brother Robert. She had lived with her uncle from time to time—taking piano lessons from Aunt Altona, coping with Uncle Vernon's strict winter regimen in which all the children were required to play chess or read a book and to answer questions he might fire at them at any time on any subject. Barbara had rebelled by hiding a comic book between her knees; of all the Johns clan she was regarded as the one with a fiery temperament most like her uncle's. Now she reminded her fellow students of the sorry history since 1947, when the county had built three temporary tar-paper shacks to house the overflow at the school—how the students had to sit in the shacks with coats on through the winter; how her history teacher, who doubled as the bus driver, was obliged to gather wood and start fires in the shacks in the mornings after driving a bus that was a hand-me-down from the white school and didn't have much heat either, when it was running; how the county had been promising the Negro principal a new school for a long time but had discarded those promises like old New Year's resolutions; and how, because the adult Negroes had been rebuffed in trying to correct these and a host of related injustices, it was time for the students to protest. Even if improvement came too late to benefit them, she said, it would benefit their little brothers and sisters. With that, she called for a "strike," and the entire student body marched out of the school behind her.

Before the Negro adults had decided what to do, and before most of the local white people had noticed the controversy at all, Barbara Johns and her little band sent out appeals to NAACP lawyers, who, completely misreading the source of the initiative, agreed to come to Farmville for a meeting provided it was not with "the children." When the lawyers told a mass gathering of one thousand Negroes that any battle would be dangerous and that the strike was illegal, it was the students who shouted that there were too many of them to fit in the jails. When the skeptical lawyers said that the NAACP could not sue for better Negro schools—only for completely integrated ones—the students paused but briefly over this dizzying prospect before shouting their approval. A few more days into the strike, an almost surreal tide swept through the entire Negro community, overwhelming the solid conservative leadership that had always held sway. A young preacher, who called himself a lifelong "disciple" of Vernon Johns, delivered a thunderous oration at a mass meeting. "Anybody who would not back these children after they stepped out on a limb is not a man," he declared, and the assembly voted to proceed with an attack on segregation itself. The NAACP lawyers filed suit on May 23, 1951, one month after the students had walked out of school. Consolidated with four similar suits, it was destined to reach the U.S. Supreme Court as part of the historic *Brown* v. *Board of Education of Topeka.*

Had the student strike begun ten or fifteen years later, Barbara Johns would have become something of a phenomenon in the public media. In that era, however, the case remained muffled in white consciousness, and the schoolchild origins of the lawsuit were lost as well on nearly all Negroes outside Prince Edward County. This was 1951. In Montgomery, Vernon Johns learned of the controversy by letter, as the Johns households in Farmville still had no telephones. Television was an infant, and the very word "teenager" had only recently entered common use. The idea that non-adults of any race might play a leading role in political events had simply failed to register on anyone—except perhaps the Klansmen who burned a cross in the Johns yard one night, and even then people thought their target might not have been Barbara but her notorious firebrand uncle.

There was a tense scene in the kitchen when Vernon Johns arrived from Montgomery. His brother Robert, a farmer twenty years younger than he, who had always been meeker and more practical, made no secret of his fear. Nor did his wife. Both of them were consumed with worry over the safety of their headstrong daughter—now banished to her room during the summit conference—and with all the violence and risk, they did not welcome the fact that Uncle Vernon was so plainly "tickled" by the trouble in his native county. They asked him to take Barbara home with him to Montgomery until tempers calmed. Vernon agreed, and Robert begged him to be careful on the long trip. He had always believed that his older brother was a terrible driver, especially when he was quoting all that poetry.

Barbara Johns changed from student leader to student exile the very next morning, as her parents piled her into Uncle Vernon's green Buick with the cheese and the milk and a very large watermelon, but without a word of explanation. It embarrassed her that her legendary uncle stopped on the side of the road to eat the watermelon, like the stereotypical Negro, and her resentment grew as he failed to say anything or ask a single question about her astonishing achievement. She speculated furiously about his silence. Perhaps he exhorted Negroes to stand up for

themselves but really wanted to take all the risk himself. Perhaps he
wanted to protect her as a family member, or as a young girl—though
either would violate her image of him. She listened to the poetry and
wondered whether she could ever comprehend what a person of such age
and presence was really like. Finally, she decided that the most likely
explanation for his silence was that he was proud of her but simply
refused to compliment her, as he had refused to compliment people all
his life, for fear of implying that he had ever expected less. This theory
caused her pride to overtake her resentment, and she resolved never to
mention her feats in Farmville to anyone in Montgomery.

The first thing Barbara Johns noticed was that pressures on her uncle
were building. Rumors of plots and defections within the Dexter Avenue
congregation arrived almost daily, and it was considered a bad sign that
ever fewer churchwomen favored the pastor's house with cooked dishes
from their kitchens. Johns, still selling produce on the street, escalated
his criticism of his members for being insulated in their own individual
worlds. "You don't even know each other's names!" he would exclaim
from the pulpit, and he called on the congregation to repeat the names of
new members out loud. If they were so separated from each other even
among their own class, he argued, how could they ever hope to pull
together as a race? He became obsessed with this insulation because he
believed Negroes went so far as to follow the lead of the white newspapers, objectifying Negroes—especially the victims of police violence—
as a faceless category apart from them. This was a violent time in Alabama—an era when a judge and jury sentenced a Negro man to death for
stealing $1.95 from a white woman (commuted later by Governor Fol-
som) and when police officers often meted out harsher justice informally,
beyond the meager restraints of a court. One Montgomery case stuck in
Johns's mind: officers stopped a man for speeding and beat him half to
death with a tire iron, while Negroes watched silently nearby.

Not long after this incident, Johns summoned his oldest daughter,
Altona, and said gravely, "Come with me, Baby Dee. I'm going to preach
a sermon." His manner so frightened her that she said nothing as they
walked out of the parsonage, across the capitol grounds, and down the
hill to Dexter Avenue. Johns opened the glass case of the church bulletin
board and handed the box of metal letters to his daughter. She spread the
letters on the sidewalk. As was his habit, Johns thought for a moment
and then directed her to post a new sermon title for the following Sunday: "It's Safe to Murder Negroes in Montgomery." She fumbled with
the letters in the bright sunshine, and when it was done she followed her
father back up the hill as wordlessly as she had come.

The phone began to ring that night. Hostile white callers threatened to burn the church down unless Johns removed the sign, and anxious Dexter members passed along tips about whites who were angry and church members who were upset. A police officer came to the church with a summons for Johns. He answered it, and was escorted to the circuit courthouse by a handful of policemen, including the chief. Charges of inciting to riot, slander of the police department, and disturbing the peace were mentioned, but nothing so formal came of the hearing, which amounted to an examination of Johns by the judge, the police chief, and a few influential citizens who had gathered there to take the measure of this bizarre Negro. Having asked why such a sign had been placed outside the church, the judge nodded slowly when Johns replied that he had placed it there to attract attention to his forthcoming sermon. When the judge suggested that he might do well to take it down, Johns replied with a brief lecture on the meaning of signs in history—how civil authorities had pressured men to take down their signs in ancient Greece and Egypt, in Rome, and in Europe during the Reformation. Then the judge asked why anyone would want to preach on so inflammatory a subject as murder between the races. "Because everywhere I go in the South the Negro is forced to choose between his hide and his soul," Johns replied. "Mostly, he chooses his hide. I'm going to tell him that his hide is not worth it." The judge soon dismissed Johns with a warning that he would bring trouble on himself if he persisted.

The Klan burned a cross on the church lawn that Saturday night, but it did not prevent a large crowd from assembling to hear what Johns would say. He went on at some length contrasting the murder of Negroes with the "lynching of Jesus," making points at the expense of each set of killers and victims, and he concluded with a prediction that violence against Negroes would continue as long as Negroes "let it happen." When he finished, the crowd that spilled into the street fairly hummed with mixed dissension and determination.

Unexpectedly, the white judge called Johns at home the next week to express his regret over the cross-burning. He wanted to discuss certain of the references in classical history that Johns had cited in his courtroom. Then he asked if there was anything he could do for Johns personally. Perhaps there was, said Johns: he had heard that the judge owned a copy of the memoirs of Union general William T. Sherman, which, if true, was a rare possession for a white Southerner, inasmuch as Sherman had burned much of Georgia and South Carolina, but in any case Johns would like to borrow the book. The judge laughed and said he would be happy to send it over. Then he asked to speak frankly, and confided that he had insisted the police allow Johns to deliver his sermon, arguing that it would cause less trouble to the community to let the man talk than to stop him. This remark incensed Johns, who invited the judge to attend his sermon the next Sunday. The judge sent Sherman's memoirs but did not show up. Johns preached on the topic "When the Rapist Is White" and heard no more from the judge, but he returned the book.

These and other sermons further complicated the internal politics of Dexter Avenue Baptist Church. Some members who were upset by Johns's pronouncements on race pretended to like them but worried out loud that his "antics" with the fish would undermine his endeavors. Some reconsidered the fish and would have happily bought some if only Johns would quit preaching such dangerous sermons, while others were proud of his courage in the race sermons and blamed the political timidity of other members for driving the preacher into odd pursuits like the fish. Johns, of course, saw his two campaigns as part of the same larger truth, but few others did. He resigned two more times early in 1952.

Both resignations related not to politics but to minor changes in marketing techniques. One came when Johns began storing his Sunday wares in the church itself, for the convenience of his Dexter customers. From the pulpit, he would append to a *tour de force* sermon some remarks on his bargain prices and the quality of the produce in the basement. Sales increased, but a number of the members believed that Johns had crossed the threshold of defilement. In particular, some of the leading women of the church were incensed. This put Johns in serious trouble, as women made up the majority of church membership. They also provided nearly all the initiative for regular church functions, from music and meals to flowers, and the matriarchal tendencies in Negro society magnified their actual power far beyond their auxiliary listings in the church roster.

The second, decisive incident occurred when Johns and Rufus Lewis actually drove onto the campus of Alabama State College with a truckload of watermelons. In so doing, they violated the home territory of leading church members, opening them and their church to ridicule from colleagues who were riveted by the sight of the learned Vernon Johns selling watermelons on a campus that was the spearhead of Negro advancement and prestige in the area. The deacons told him so in a stormy meeting. Johns walked out again. Nesbitt later carried out his duty by informing him that the board of deacons had recommended that the church accept this latest resignation, his fifth. In a tense meeting, the Dexter congregation agreed by majority vote.

Vernon Johns left Montgomery in advance of his family, working his way north on a lecture tour of churches and Negro colleges. He was back home in Farmville, Virginia, by December 1952, when Thurgood Mar-

shall and Spottswood Robinson, among other NAACP lawyers, rose in
the Supreme Court to tell the Justices of school conditions in Johns's
native county. Barbara Johns and her uncle followed reports of the landmark *Brown* case, but neither they nor anyone else dreamed that as a
result of it the white authorities in Farmville would close the entire
public school system for five years, rather than compromise the practice
of racial segregation. Long before it was over, Barbara Johns would begin
carrying a permanent sense of guilt for stirring up the trouble on principle
but then leaving others to bear the consequences of the movement. She
thought it was a fault she shared with her uncle.

R. D. Nesbitt's problems were more immediate. He needed to find a
new pastor for Dexter Avenue Baptist Church, and to rescue himself
from heavy criticism over his two previous choices, Arbouin and Johns.
Some members held him responsible for seven consecutive years of pastoral controversy. Nesbitt could not help feeling jealous of William Beasley, his long-standing counterpart over at First Baptist Church, to which
their common ancestors had migrated after the Civil War. Beasley had
just gone through another smooth transition, installing Rev. Ralph D.
Abernathy as the seventh pastor of "Brick-a-Day Church" in its history
—since the exodus from the white church in 1867.

It was never so easy at Dexter. The deacons and members had always
been fastidious about new preachers—letting weak candidates suffer humiliation, keeping the strong ones guessing—and now they were more
determined than ever to be careful. They rejected preachers young and
old for more than a year. From the standpoint of church image, they
reestablished themselves as a congregation that was hardly desperate for
a new preacher, and then, as usual, they delayed still longer, until Nesbitt
and others feared the church seemed faction-ridden and indecisive. After
all, no church was really a church without a preacher. So Nesbitt stepped
up his scouting efforts.

One day in December 1953, about a year and a half after Johns's departure, Nesbitt had finished auditing the books of the Pilgrim Life Insurance Company's Atlanta district office and was talking with W. C. Peden,
the local manager. Peden knew about the Vernon Johns ordeal, and was
a good enough friend that Nesbitt began confiding in him about his
troubled search for a new pastor, about how difficult it was to satisfy the
Dexter members. What he needed, he said, was a more traditional pastor
—an educated and trained one, to be sure, in the Dexter tradition, but
someone more conventional than Johns in dress, manner, and behavior,
someone less controversial, perhaps a younger and less established man
who could not give the deacons such a battle.

Peden bolted upright with an idea. "Nesbitt, I think I have your man," he said. He was thinking of a young man of impeccable habits, just coming out of the finest schools, the son of a wealthy, established pastor. Peden knew the family well enough to be aware that the young man was in Atlanta on vacation. So he arranged for Nesbitt to meet Martin Luther King, Jr.

TWO

ROCKEFELLER AND
EBENEZER

The King whom Nesbitt sought out had been born into a most unusual family, which had risen from the anonymity of slavery to the top of Atlanta's Negro elite within the short span of three generations, attached to a church named Ebenezer. Their story was one of determination and romance, inspiring though not always pretty. One odd white thread ran through the whole of it: insofar as the Kings encountered anything better than obstruction in the white world, it could be traced more often than not to the influence of a most unlikely source, John D. Rockefeller.

Rockefeller's impact upon Negro Atlanta can be dated from a Sunday service in June 1882 at the Erie Baptist Church in Cleveland, Ohio, which he attended with his wife and in-laws. The church allowed two visiting women to make a plea from the pulpit in behalf of the Atlanta Female Baptist Seminary, a school for Negro girls they had started the year before. It was a pitiful tale. Nearly a hundred unschooled, poorly clothed girls were crammed into the basement of an Atlanta church, on a floor of dirt and mud, the only private classroom being the coal storage area. There were four strong-willed teachers, all of them white, college-educated spinsters from the North. As it turned out, the two who came to Cleveland had taught Rockefeller's wife back before the Civil War, when women were first pushing their way into schools and the abolitionist societies. Mrs. Rockefeller was fiercely proud of her former teachers. At the close of the service, the Atlanta visitors took up a collection for their school, netting $90.72. Rockefeller quietly came forward to pledge another $250. It was his first gift to Negro education.

Son of an itinerant salesman of quack medicines, Rockefeller had already come a long way from the fruit and vegetable merchant who had married Laura Spelman. He was rich, but he was not yet the colossus of the robber barons. Only he and a few partners knew that he had invented that very year the secret network of interlocking stock pledges—called a trust—through which he would levy a monopoly fee on the industrial development of the entire country. Rockefeller himself would scarcely change. He would always be reticent and quiet, yet ferocious—an Old Testament man so secure in his purpose that he could, like Jehovah, crush his rivals and their women and children without the slightest qualm. He would always teach Sunday school in the Baptist faith he had sought out on his own when a penniless boy. The Baptists were descended from the Anabaptists of sixteenth-century Germany, who had rebelled against Martin Luther for not going far enough in his break with the Catholic Church. They were the extreme democrats, hostile to complex theological doctrines and to any church practice that fostered the authority of the clergy. For this, Catholic and Protestant clergymen alike had considered them dangerous enough to burn. Rockefeller himself always loathed the weakness of the poor and the messy obstructions of democracy, but he would cling to the church of the common people.

He would cling also to the Spelmans. When he married Laura, he took her sister Lucy into his home, where she would live as a spinster for almost sixty years. When the sisters' father died in 1881, he took in their mother as well. From what little is known of their private life, it appears that the Spelmans as a group exercised considerable influence on Rockefeller outside the office. They were better educated than he, enthusiastic about far-flung causes, and independent of spirit. Laura Spelman's senior essay in high school was titled "I Can Paddle My Own Canoe." John D. Rockefeller's classroom recitation at the same school was called "I'm Pleased Although I'm Sad."

Two years after Rockefeller's gift to the Female Seminary, the mighty clan took the train all the way to Atlanta and walked in on the ceremonies celebrating the third anniversary of the humble school for Negro women. All the surprise guests, including young John junior, were called upon to speak, but only Mrs. Spelman offered an address of any length, recalling the days when her Cleveland home was a stop for Sojourner Truth and her runaway slaves on the Underground Railroad. The only meals she ever remembered cooking herself had been those served to young Negro runaways, she said proudly. Before the end of the ceremony, the trustees announced that henceforth the college would be called Spelman, after the Rockefeller in-laws. The news made the students burst into cheers, and the proper headmistress—always distressed by emotional displays of any kind, especially those common to Negro religious gatherings—rose to hush them. She called on the students to pledge solemnly that they would remain loyal to the school and never bring reproach upon its new name.

On his own and through Dr. Henry Morehouse of the Baptist Home Mission Society in New York, Rockefeller began buying up large tracts of land on Atlanta's West Side. He housed the Spelman students in an old Union Army barracks pending the completion in 1886 of Rockefeller Hall, the first brick building on the new Spelman campus. He gave adjacent lands to two Baptist colleges for Negro men, including a college named after Dr. Morehouse, who became president of the Spelman board. Soon there were a Packard Hall and a Giles Hall at Spelman, named for the two women who had come to Cleveland in search of funds, followed in 1900 by a Morehouse Hall. That same year, John D. Rockefeller, Jr., announced that his family would donate enough money to build four more structures along the tree-lined quad at Spelman. Still, it was only a beginning. The three schools remained land-rich, owning scores of undeveloped acres for future growth. At the time, no one realized that this strategic acquisition would make the twentieth-century demographics of Atlanta unique among American cities. As the town grew, these holdings caused white developers to avoid most of the southwest quadrant of the city, and the Negro educational complex provided a pool of professional people to expand outward into that territory along stratified class lines. As a result, Atlanta would not develop along the usual pattern of a Negro inner city surrounded by whites. The two races would move outward into their own suburbs.

Through all the early years, the three Spelman women visited the college frequently and kept up a steady correspondence with its officials. Their interest made Spelman the prettiest and richest of the Negro colleges in Atlanta, which nettled some officials at the schools for men. New presidents—always single women from New England—were known progressively less for their educational skills and more for their ties to the Rockefellers. All the headmistresses were strict disciplinarians who pushed their charges toward the twin extremities of Victorian refinement and Booker T. Washington–style practicality. Until the 1920s, Spelman required its students to rise at four thirty in the morning to wash and iron their clothes. The school always demanded proficiency in both homemaking and the classics. As late as the 1940s, students

could not leave the campus without special permission, and they had to
wear gloves and a hat even in the summer.

Male students crowded into ramshackle buildings at the two Baptist
colleges next to the elegant Spelman campus. Although Atlanta University counted among its faculty one of the nation's finest sociologists, in
W. E. B. Du Bois, it was Morehouse College that acquired a special aura
of prestige. The "Morehouse man" became a social and civic model, and
was conceded the advantage in courtship battles for the highly prized
Spelman women. By the mid-1890s, each school had elevated its curric-
ulum above the grade-school equivalencies of Reconstruction and was
awarding full-fledged college degrees. Morehouse awarded its first three
in 1897. Among its graduates the next year was a Rev. A. D. Williams,
who married Jennie C. Parks of Spelman on October 29, 1899. Alberta,
their only child who survived infancy, became Martin Luther King's
mother.

Williams was a slave preacher's son who ran away from a country home
to Atlanta as a small boy, became a preacher himself, and in 1894 had no
better prospects than the pastorate of the eight-year-old Ebenezer Baptist
Church, which had only thirteen members and a tiny, incomplete, heavily mortgaged building, against which the bank was threatening foreclosure.* Accepting the challenge, Reverend Williams mounted a series
of revivals and other fund-raisers that paid off the mortgage. His recruits
quickly pushed the membership above one hundred, so that the church
began looking for a larger property. He attended college in his spare time,
married Jennie Parks, and otherwise acquitted himself as a worthy
Morehouse man. By 1900, Ebenezer was prosperous enough to swallow
up a larger church by buying its building, which was threatened with
foreclosure. A few years later, Reverend Williams himself was able
to give his only child, Alberta, then a toddler of three, a Ricca & Son
"upright grand piano" for her lessons.

His successes over the next dozen years went against the larger tides
of the early progressive era, when Social Darwinism was rising to full
strength in American politics. For race relations, this meant a rush backward, as whites in the South and North generally agreed that there were
more important things to do in the world than to contend with each

---

* Ebenezer, meaning "the stone of help," was derived from the Old Testament,
like the names of many Negro churches. "Then Samuel took a stone, and set it
between Mizpeh and Shen, and called it Ebenezer, saying, Hitherto hath the Lord
helped us." (I Samuel 7:12)

other over the status of the Negro, which was then fixed by science as lowly. By concerted agitation and widespread violence, Southern whites had revolted against the political structure of Reconstruction, first establishing that Negroes would not be allowed to dominate any legislative body by numerical majority. From there, a march by degrees eliminated Negroes from governing coalitions, then from the leverage of swing votes on issues that divided the whites (such as populism and the recurring proposals to ban the sale of alcohol), and finally from any significant exercise of the vote.

Northerners acquiesced in the renewed hegemony of Southern whites. The reigning idea was that racial quarrels, while accomplishing nothing since the Civil War, had interfered with business, diverted reform campaigns from more productive fields, and hindered America's new efforts to win a commanding position in the battle for global influence. Indeed, some liberals spoke of racism as the linchpin of the progressive movement, meaning that progress could be made only when white supremacy mooted the race question in politics. Old pro-abolitionist journals like the *Atlantic Monthly* published articles on "the universal supremacy of the Anglo-Saxon." Best-selling books of the time included Charles Carroll's *The Negro, A Beast*, published in 1900 by the American Book and Bible House in St. Louis, and Robert W. Shufeldt's *The Negro, A Menace to American Civilization*, published in 1906. Thomas Dixon's *The Clansman: A Historical Romance of the Ku Klux Klan* was published in 1905, and ten years later became *The Birth of a Nation*, the feature film whose stunning success established Hollywood and motion pictures as fixtures of American culture.

In Washington, the last Negro congressman was sent home to North Carolina in the spring of 1901. When President Theodore Roosevelt invited Booker T. Washington to dinner at the White House later that year, Democrats denounced the President on the front pages for nearly a week. Political professionals, reported *The New York Times*, faulted the President because he "did not reflect" before making the move. Even Roosevelt's defenders tended to see the controversy in the light of the new era. "The sun shines on the American citizen, down to the heathen Chinese," a New Yorker wrote to the *Times*, "and God's glories cannot be hid from a poor outcast negro, whom God sent into the world for the wise and just to civilize." That same year, manager John McGraw tried to circumvent the ban on Negro players in professional baseball by passing off his second baseman Charlie Grant as an Indian, but it didn't work.

The ugliest side of this mood visited the Williams neighborhood in 1906, in the form of the Atlanta race riot. With that year's gubernatorial primary coming up, and with the candidates pledging to complete the disfranchisement of Negro voters, newspapers accompanied the political stories with accounts of rapes and insults against white women. The relatively liberal Atlanta *Constitution* often had several of these on a single front page, culminating in one story headed "Negro Menaced Miss Orrie Bryan." There was a formal portrait of Miss Bryan beneath a four-column photograph of her father calling on a large crowd to help him lynch one Luther Frazier, who allegedly had accosted, but not touched, Miss Bryan. White mobs killed nearly fifty Negroes over the next three days. The *Constitution*'s banner headlines included "Governor Calls All Troops Out," "Chased Negroes All the Night," "Too Much Talk Was His Doom," "Riot's End All Depends on Negroes," "He Used a Dead Body to Ward Off Bullets," and a sidebar from Delaware called "Whip with Nine Thongs Avenges White Women Assaulted by Negro."

The 1906 riot, along with a similar one two years later in Abraham Lincoln's hometown of Springfield, Illinois, provoked Atlanta University's Du Bois to join with white Northern philanthropists to create the NAACP in 1909. Young Reverend Williams, whose accomplishments at the Ebenezer church were making him a community leader, became the first president of the Atlanta chapter. For him, the riot's aftermath brought an unexpected blessing in the flight of prominent white families from Victorian homes near the downtown riot area. He bought one of them at a bargain price. Its location on Auburn Avenue, only a few blocks from Atlanta's first cluster of Negro businesses, was a great advantage to him in church recruitment. Even better, there were sites available along that same street, between the house and the businesses, that would make an ideal permanent home for a new church. These considerations of price and location outweighed the fact that the two-story Queen Anne–style house—with its five bedrooms, wraparound porch, twelve-foot ceilings, and modern coal furnace in the basement—was far too big for the Williams family of three. By taking in boarders, they earned money toward the payments.

In 1909, they moved into the new house at 501 Auburn Avenue with their young daughter, Alberta. From childhood, she was homely in appearance, with blunt features and a rather squat frame, yet always known for her sweet shyness and humility. Neighbors considered her the kind of person who would not be noticed in a small crowded room, and relatives would even say she was "kind of fearful." She lacked the assertiveness of her parents, perhaps intimidated by her father's achievements and by her mother's stature as the "First Lady of Ebenezer." But she became an astute observer of church politics, as taught to her by both parents, and she developed an enormous strength—passive, absorptive, sure of herself—on her own ground, which was always church and family. Her refinements and talents were directed there. In both places, she would be a creature of refuge—organizer, comforter, facilitator. All her life she would be the official organist at Ebenezer and also at one of the auxiliaries of the National Baptist Convention.

Ebenezer members considered Reverend Williams an able preacher, but his reputation and influence outside the church derived primarily from his skills in real estate and civic action. He was the type who convened meetings, identified community goals, and got elected to chair committees he himself proposed. He became president of the Atlanta Baptist Ministers' Union, then floor leader of the Georgia delegation to the National Baptist Convention. Later, as the NBC's national treasurer and a member of both its foreign and home mission boards, Williams held some of the most influential positions of trust and patronage in the church of his time. For his community service, Morehouse conferred an honorary doctorate upon him in 1914, before he had even begun to build the new Ebenezer church. At the end of World War I, he sent Alberta to her mother's alma mater, Spelman.

By then, John D. Rockefeller was employing phalanxes of lawyers, bodyguards, and bureaucrats to protect him from those trying to beg or claim his money. In the spring of 1914, the "Ludlow massacre" secured his reputation as a principal villain in the history of labor unions, when Colorado militiamen attacked and burned a tent city of workers on strike against Rockefeller mining interests, killing six men by gunfire and thirteen women and children in the flames. A year later, Laura Spelman Rockefeller died, and the old man was obliged to keep her body in storage for three months until his lawyers worked out a truce with Ohio officials who threatened to arrest him under a $311 million tax judgment if he set foot in Ohio to bury her. Meanwhile, under pressure of old age, the new income tax law, inheritance taxes, and the U.S. government's antitrust case against Standard Oil, Rockefeller accelerated his charitable contributions, giving $100 million to the new Rockefeller Foundation and another $50 million to his General Education Board, which supported Baptist colleges. Of the latter amount, $10 million went to build a new chapel and expand the divinity school at the University of Chicago. Other Rockefeller donations created stately new buildings along the landscaped quad at Spelman. The Bessie [Rockefeller] Strong Building and the Laura Spelman Rockefeller Memorial Building were completed by 1918, in time for the education of Alberta Williams. Mike King, later known as Martin Luther King, Sr., and still later as Daddy King, met her while she was studying there.

·   ·   ·

Mike King gazed at Alberta Williams from a considerable distance before he talked with her. To him, the gap between himself and the eminent minister's daughter was greater than the social distance between her and John D. Rockefeller. The latter two dressed in fine clothes and spoke proper English, whereas Mike King described himself as a semiliterate country bumpkin. Although he schemed to meet Alberta Williams for weeks, and planned to put on what airs he could, the first words he said in response to her greeting were, "Well, I'se preaching in two places." He was wise enough to know that this would never do.

Born in December 1899, the second of ten children on a sharecropper's farm outside Stockbridge, Georgia, King had grown up currying mules, plowing fields, skipping most of what little school there was, and always living in fear of his father James. Late one night, a highly intoxicated James King began beating his wife Delia after starting an argument over whether she should cook a fish. Young Mike King was only fourteen, but he was barrel-chested and strong for his age. Somehow he managed to pull his enraged father off his mother and survive the desperate fight that ensued. When it was over, his father repeatedly vowed to kill him. Mother King eventually sold enough of the family livestock to buy a used Model T Ford for her son's escape to Atlanta. To Mike King, working as a laborer in an Atlanta tire plant, the car was a prize almost beyond imagination. Aside from status and mobility, the Model T gave him the means to pursue the most coveted profession open to unschooled Negroes, the ministry. The car allowed him to keep his regular job while seeking Sunday work at tiny churches that might hire any untrained circuit preacher who sounded all right and could get himself to their remote meetinghouses in the country. King found two such churches before he was twenty. He became a professional preacher in the time-honored manner of the ambitious former slaves, before he had been inside a church that could afford an organ.

He and thousands of preachers like him made up the rank and file of the National Baptist Convention. Immediately, young King began attending its local meetings, once driving out to Jonesboro, Georgia, to hear a scheduled address by the national treasurer, Rev. A. D. Williams. Williams failed to appear, but other speakers gave him the treatment customarily afforded NBC dignitaries anyway, praising him to the skies, not failing to mention the Christian attributes of all his family members, including the daughter at Spelman who had already organized a new choir at Ebenezer church. The description so struck young King that, by his own account, he told friends that very night that he would marry Alberta Williams, whom he had never met. The friends laughed at him.

By virtue of a coincidence that would later be called providential, King knew where Alberta Williams lived. His older sister, who had come from Stockbridge ahead of him, was one of the boarders at the Williams house. Still, her presence in a room of the target household was not much of an advantage. This was 1920, and the daughter was living in a dormitory at Spelman. Even polished Morehouse students from prominent families were allowed to call on Spelman women only on Saturdays at a specified hour, for a cumulative time not exceeding twenty minutes a month as punctiliously recorded by Spelman faculty supervisors. And such a glimpse of courtship was possible only if the Spelman student responded favorably to the man's calling card. On other days, Spelman rules allowed no visitors, nor any messages.

Fortunately for King, Alberta Williams broke her ankle and was obliged to spend several weeks convalescing at home. During that time, he visited his sister as often as possible, but even then he did not attempt to enter the sanctum of the house. The Williams family was strict, his sister advised, and to be the slightest bit forward was to risk not only his banishment from the premises, but hers. As a result, Mike King spent a lot of time polishing his Model T on Auburn Avenue, hoping Miss Williams would chance to sit on the front porch. Whenever she did, he watched her as much as he dared, while trying to think of a socially acceptable excuse to speak to her. His first venture ended quickly in disastrous retreat after his comment about preaching in two places. He thought the sound of his own voice condemned him as a farmhand. He also thought, however, that she had not emitted as much disapproval in those few seconds as she might have. In the postmortem, his sister warned him for the hundredth time that he could never enter the world of Alberta Williams without some education. King believed he had been preaching fairly well on common sense, fervor, and Sunday school memories, but now he began to see the social practicality of her advice.

After taking some tests at a local school for Negroes, he was stunned to learn that he could be admitted no higher than the fifth grade. He was twenty years old. Suddenly, years of humiliating pain loomed ahead of him, as he realized that he would have to shed his preacher's dignity to make a fool of himself in classrooms of children, working at night and studying in his sleep, just to finish high school. College—Alberta's level —lay somewhere beyond that, and marriage was nowhere in sight.

Mike King's determination was such that he resolved to push his way through the humiliation rather than avoid it. In an oversized desk among the younger students, he took up his studies, learning how to form words correctly in his mouth. Some months later, still a beginner, he came into luck on one of his regular spare-time patrols along Auburn Avenue. Alberta Williams was walking up the street, coming home from Spelman for an overnight visit. King tried to approach her boldly, now that his education was under way, but he faltered, muttering something about how she probably didn't remember who he was. "Oh, I couldn't forget meeting a preacher," she replied, smiling. "My father wouldn't allow it."

These were the first words from her that he would remember. They opened a whole world of church politics. To Reverend Williams, unlettered preachers like Mike King were his constituents in the outside realm of national Baptist affairs, just as the people who lived near Ebenezer were his constituents at home. They should be recognized, respected, and cultivated, not only by Williams himself but by his entire household. This was social justice and a family enterprise together, God's business and their business. His daughter knew her part well.

King asked her on the spot to consider opening a courtship with him. There was something about her reaction—shocked nearly to the edge of her poise, but not displeased—that made him sense the truth: no one had ever asked her to court. The Morehouse men had sent in no calling cards to her. When King pressed the matter, standing there on Auburn Avenue, she agreed to seek her father's permission. Soon they commenced a courtship in the old style—six years of teas, church socials, and chaperoned Sunday-afternoon rides in the Model T.

On those rides, they watched with admiration as workers built Reverend Williams' imposing new Ebenezer Baptist Church, which was completed in 1922. King told Alberta that he would have a church like that one day. He was full of plans. When they passed Atlanta Life Insurance Company and the other new businesses that were making Auburn Avenue a showplace of Negro enterprise, he would announce his intention to be part of that, too. He preferred to be part of a bank, such as the new Citizens Trust Company. Practically everybody in town followed the accumulation of its assets; barbers could tell you the current figure as a matter of common knowledge. Most of all, King would say, he wanted a big brick house like the ones on "Bishops' Row," where the Methodist bishops who ran Morris Brown College lived. He would lay claim to these future possessions with the utmost authority and confidence, like Jehovah: let there be a brick house. This was his character, no doubt fortified by what he learned as an apprentice student of the Williams family. Success was a mixture of common sense, rigid adherence to a few well-chosen proverbs, and the projection of a successful image. The subtleties of Reverend Williams' approach to church politics all made sense to King, as did his moral rule that no preacher can prosper long by fleecing his people, as many tried to do. Finally, King understood why a preacher must embellish and polish himself to some degree, to pull the people behind him. Williams was known as Dr. Williams, possessed of two

Morehouse degrees, but King found out that he had attended More-house only one year. Even the mighty were not that far removed from a lowly past like his own.

Reverend Williams, not unmindful that some Ebenezer members thought young King was aiming to marry the coveted Ebenezer pulpit along with his only daughter, withheld permission for the marriage. He sent Alberta away to Virginia for further schooling, but King waited loyally for her return a year later. For his part, King was so busy catching up on his education that for a number of years he didn't mind being tested. When he completed his high school equivalency in 1926 and permission still was not forthcoming, King knew what was lacking. He marched into the office of the Morehouse registrar and took a battery of entrance tests, which he failed miserably. The registrar told him to his face that he was "just not college material." There was some schooling in him now, but he was still rough and plain. King's forte was power and bluster, as he demonstrated by walking out of the registrar's office, past an alarmed secretary, and into the office of Dr. John Hope, the Morehouse president. Hope, the best friend and benefactor of W. E. B. Du Bois, was so admired as an educator that Negro parents had been naming their children after him for years.* He said almost nothing as King blurted out a speech about how he had always done things that people said were beyond him, that only five years earlier he couldn't even read but now he could, that he wanted to go to Morehouse no matter what the tests said, and if given the chance he would prove again that people underes-timated him. Finally stopping himself, King waited vainly for a reply and then retreated from the office in despair. It was all over. A secretary caught up with him as he was leaving the campus. Back in the office, Hope wordlessly handed him an envelope and told him to take it to the registrar, who made no attempt to hide his disgust a few minutes later when he read the order to admit the bearer to classes at Morehouse.

Mike King and Alberta Williams were married at Ebenezer Baptist Church not long thereafter, on Thanksgiving Day of 1926. Reverend Williams arranged for three of the most prominent ministers in Atlanta to conduct the ceremony, and he gave away the bride. On returning from their honeymoon, the newlyweds moved into the middle upstairs bed-room in the Williams home on Auburn Avenue. The elder Williams couple were disposed to celebrate their only daughter's marriage but not yet her departure from the home—certainly not to the kind of place Mike King could afford as a part-time student and preacher. In later years, it

---

* One such child, John Hope Franklin, would become a prominent historian and the author of *From Slavery to Freedom*.

would become evident that factors other than money kept Alberta William King in her childhood home, as she would live there for many years after her husband became the highest-paid Negro minister in Atlanta. He was a powerful man who nevertheless bent to the personal domination of another family, particularly its women. Like John D. Rockefeller, King lived with his in-laws until they died.

John D. Rockefeller, Jr., now managing the family interests in place of his eighty-eight-year-old father, headed the Rockefeller entourage at the dedication of Sisters Chapel at Spelman College on May 19, 1927. This was front-page news even in the white newspapers. In one of his rare speeches, Rockefeller eulogized the Spelman sisters—his mother and his aunt Lucy—whose estates had paid for the chapel and for whom it was named. The tone of the ceremony was proud and festive, though mindful of racial politics. Every effort was made to foster the notion that Negro education was benign, posing no threat to the social or political order. Observers did not fail to note that the many white dignitaries on the program included the son of the chief chaplain to General Robert E. Lee himself. One of only two Negro speakers was a minister who had co-officiated at the marriage of Mike and Alberta King six months earlier.

Rockefeller returned to a Baptist project far larger than the chapel—the construction of Riverside Church in New York. The second generation Rockefeller was shifting his interest to theological disputes that would touch the next generation of Kings. With growing alarm, he watched the pitched battles of the Harry Emerson Fosdick controversy, which paralleled the Scopes trial and shaped the world of theology for several decades to come. Fosdick was a preacher of such stature that the prestigious First Presbyterian Church of New York called him to its pulpit even though he was a Baptist. All had gone well until 1922, when Fosdick preached a sermon titled "Shall the Fundamentalists Win?" In it he defended the efforts by liberal theologians such as Albert Schweitzer to reconcile religious faith with both science and modern historical scholarship. The Christian faith did not require strict adherence to such doctrines as the virgin birth of Jesus, he declared, pointing out that virgin birth was not unique to Christianity or even to religion but was common to many great figures of antiquity—claimed for Pythagoras, Plato, and Augustus Caesar, as well as for Buddha, Lao-tze, Mahavira, and Zoroaster. He also spoke against other elements of doctrine, such as the belief that Jesus' death was "a sacrifice to satisfy divine justice," theologically necessary as "substitutionary atonement" for the sins of believers.

Fosdick's sermon provoked a nationwide movement to have him tried for heresy by a Presbyterian synod or at least expelled from the First Presbyterian Church. (Young John Foster Dulles represented Fosdick with a legalistic defense, arguing that the Presbyterian Council could not try a Baptist for heresy.) One New York pastor called Fosdick "the Jesse James of the theological world." By October 1924, *The New York Times* was following developments almost daily, with headlines such as "Jam Fifth Avenue to Hear Dr. Fosdick—Crowds Tie Up Traffic." When the campaign finally forced Fosdick to leave the church in March 1925, Rockefeller asked the exiled minister whether he would be interested in coming to Park Avenue Baptist, where he taught the men's Bible class. Fosdick, who drew from a well of spiritual and intellectual pride at least as deep as Rockefeller's bank account, was not awed in the slightest. He declined, saying he could not acquiesce in the strict Baptist requirement that all church members be baptized by full immersion. What if that were dropped, Rockefeller persisted. Still no, said Fosdick, because he did not want to be known as the minister of another elite church in the swankiest part of New York. Well, said Rockefeller, what if the church were moved? Now slightly unnerved, Fosdick dodged the question, saying that would be almost incredible, as the Park Avenue church had been completed only three years before at no small cost to Rockefeller. Anyway, said Fosdick, he did not wish to be known as the pastor of the richest man in the United States. "I like your frankness," Rockefeller said after a brief pause, "but do you think that more people will criticize you on account of my wealth than will criticize me on account of your theology?" Rockefeller's persistence soon acquired a new pastor for the Park Avenue congregation, which met Fosdick's conditions that they abandon their new building on Park Avenue, build a new one nearer the poor neighborhoods of New York, and discard the Baptist label from the church name. Rockefeller bought up a large tract of land on upper Riverside Drive in an intermediate zone, near Harlem but buffered by the campus of Columbia University. He razed the apartment buildings and contributed approximately $4 million toward the construction of the huge Riverside Church, in thirteenth-century Gothic style. On October 5, 1930, more than six thousand people tried to cram their way in to hear Fosdick's first sermon in the new church, where two generations later Dr. Martin Luther King, Jr., would deliver some of the most important sermons of his life.

Young King, who was still in diapers when Riverside Church was built, had been born in his parents' bedroom at the Williams home on January 15, 1929. His father named him Michael Luther King, Jr., but everyone called him "M.L." or "Little Mike." He was the middle child of three, sixteen months younger than his sister Christine, and seventeen months older than his brother A.D., who was named for the patriarch, grandfather Williams. The great stock market crash split the interval between the births of M.L. and A.D., bringing on conditions so hard that church members often paid their pastor with food instead of money.

Reverend Williams died suddenly of a heart attack in March 1931. Even in the mourning period that followed the funeral, the members of the family were grounded enough in the practicalities of the church to know that they had come to an important crossroads. The rock of Ebenezer was gone, at a time when the ravages of the Depression had shrunk church membership to about two hundred and reduced contributions more than proportionately to the loss. Seriously delinquent in its mortgage payments, the church faced the certain loss of its home, and possible extinction, unless a new pastor—someone stronger and more respected than the late Reverend Williams, if that were possible—could reverse its fortunes.

These adverse circumstances caused more confusion than usually attends the filling of a pulpit. Both the church and the deceased pastor's family were divided. Most of the deacons wanted to find someone older and more experienced than Mike King, who had pastored only minor-league country churches, but such pastors tended to be ones who already had churches and were clinging to them during this time of extreme adversity. Within the family, Alberta Williams King expressed the strongest opinion. "King," she said—she would always call her husband by his last name—"I don't want you to go to Ebenezer. I'll never be the First Lady there, but at Traveler's Rest I am the First Lady." By this she meant that at Ebenezer she could never take the place of her mother. Mrs. Williams wanted her son-in-law to take Ebenezer, for reasons that ran in the opposite direction. Without her husband, she faced the loss of her church role unless the pulpit stayed in the family. Mike King, for his part, tried to straddle the positions of the two Williams women.

After seven months of indecision at Ebenezer, Mrs. Williams finally abandoned the woman's normal church role of offstage persuasion and took the floor. Still the First Lady, she declared that Mike King was destined to succeed her husband as pastor. Her speech swayed the membership, which caused the deacons to reverse themselves and recommend King as the new preacher, and King accepted the call after assuaging the hurt feelings of his wife.

By the time the new pastor assumed his duties at Ebenezer in January 1932, a local bank had prepared a rude introduction for him by putting a court-sanctioned padlock on the church's front door. His first job was to negotiate enough credit to get the padlock removed, so that he could hold services in the hope of raising enough money to make the church solvent. His career was at stake, as was his well-being in the delicate mix of cross-currents within his own family. Seldom if ever was a preacher's nature better suited to the critical challenge of his life. As a preacher, Mike King was everything Vernon Johns was not—practical, organized, plainspoken, and intensely loyal to the things and people at hand. His talents, like the task before him, had little to do with rebellions or with the theological battles over fundamentalism. Instead, they were harmonious with the theme of the most popular religious book of the 1920s, *The Man Nobody Knows*, by advertising executive Bruce Barton, who added the subtitle *Wist ye not that I must be about my father's* BUSINESS?

King was an earthbound preacher, bursting with energy. At a time when Negro evangelists like Father Divine and Daddy Grace were attracting great crowds on the strength of their ability to feed hungry people, he advanced the notion that Ebenezer must help its people prosper financially as well as spiritually. They must pull together, help each other, and establish the church as a place not only of refuge in a hostile world but as a group of people who were going places. His sermons mixed straightforward Christian fundamentalism with boosterism. If a barber joined Ebenezer, he would urge from the pulpit that the members patronize that barber. If the barber prospered, he would soon be reminded to make it known through his reciprocal contributions to the church.

Well aware that some people belittled him as a man who preached in his father-in-law's church while living in his mother-in-law's house, King risked everything on a message that promised at once to establish his authority and rescue the church's finances: the members would reap great rewards if they pulled together behind him, their leader, on call to his word. Accordingly, he moved swiftly to centralize the control of the church. His first and most radical move was to abolish the independent budgets of the various smaller units at Ebenezer—the Sunday school, the Baptist Training Union, the clubs and auxiliaries. Henceforth, the new pastor decreed, all these scattered fiefdoms would contribute their money to the central treasury of the church. A corollary of King's drastic reorganization was his break with the tradition of anonymous giving. There would be no more collection plates passed at church suppers or club functions, because he believed that the practice of anonymous giving made possible the practice of anonymous nongiving. To insure the greatest measure of control over the contributions of individual members, King established an open record system. Each member's contributions were recorded in the official church ledger, and the ledger was available for inspection at all times. Anonymous donations, though welcome, received no credit in the ledger.

This new system shocked the sensibilities of many church members.

There would be no more memberships "on the cheap," no more "talking big and giving small." No longer would the church clubs raise and spend money on their own favorite functions while letting the church fend for itself. Now Reverend King had exposed everything. Doubtless his gamble would have been impossible in better times, but King took over Ebenezer just as the Depression was changing from temporary hardship to permanent nightmare. After the shock of exposure, church members realized that the hard times were affecting everyone, not just themselves. The church ledger proved to be a powerful instrument in breaking down the social distances between people, as the members now knew one another as never before. From the pulpit, King praised every mite and every dollar in plain but thunderous sermons, promising that once they had torn down the walls that separated them, they would rebuild the figurative walls of Ebenezer Baptist Church into a mighty structure.

Having seized control of church finances by centralizing the budget, King created a whole new system of clubs—twelve of them, after the months of the year. All church members born in January were members of the January Club, and so on. He looked upon them as something like the twelve tribes of Israel. The clubs elected their own officers, sponsored their own events, and nominated their own entrants for such contests as Prettiest Baby and Best School Achievement. When a member contributed to the church, the amount would be credited not only to his or her individual account but also to the club's total. The clubs made special donations and undertook special projects for the church. King encouraged any competition among them that would benefit Ebenezer.

One of King's shrewdest innovations was based on his observations of the Negro insurance companies on Auburn Avenue, which were being hailed as a national showpiece of Negro capitalism. Most Negroes, not being large property owners, had no need of fire or automobile insurance. Negro insurance companies created their own market by inventing policies tailored to their clientele—small ones, designed to pay for funerals and doctor's bills, occasionally for education. The companies hired armies of sales agents to collect premium payments from poor people in the most practical way: in small amounts, very frequently, often no more than a nickel a week. King recognized that this kind of payment schedule was precisely what a church should strive for in the hard times of the Depression. More creatively, he saw that if an insurance company could go door to door for its money rather than wait for customers to bring it to the office, so could a church. Therefore, King made every effort to recruit insurance salesmen and executives for membership at Ebenezer.

As always, his sales pitch envisioned many kinds of cross-pollenation: the salesmen would find new customers among the Ebenezer membership, while the members could handle their insurance needs within the church. Moreover, the shut-ins and sick people could make their church contributions directly to the insurance salesman on his rounds. A salesman born in March might well visit his fellow March Club members every week, returning with one nickel for Atlanta Life and another for Ebenezer. In yet another dimension, King saw how such an extension program could minister to members in their homes as well as collect from them. The salesmen on their rounds could read Sunday school lessons to the shut-ins and sick people, or, more practically, their wives or other Ebenezer members could come along behind them to read the lessons. Out of this notion grew one of the early church outreach programs.

From the beginning, Mike King projected his own dreams of prosperity and happiness onto the church as a whole, always speaking of himself as the essential, central leader. He boasted openly of the number of loans he had secured, the number of votes he controlled, the amount of money he had brought into the church building fund, of the advertisers he had found for the local Negro newspaper, the *Daily World*, and of the students he had gotten into Morehouse or Spelman. Few people seemed to resent his manner, partly because it was common to ministers and mostly because he produced. His bluster was the heart of the leadership for which he was loved and respected. If anyone suspected that part of it was compensatory, growing out of his humbler position within his own household, no one made an issue of it. He was simply Mike King—always shaking hands, encouraging and demanding, making himself the center of attention in any room, full of claims for the past and promises for the future. The key to his multiple roles and identities was always Ebenezer church, and King preached to the members as though they were one person: "I want to tell you this morning, Ebenezer. You can do it."

He could safely say that he rescued Ebenezer Baptist Church from bankruptcy within his first few months as pastor. Membership increased geometrically from two hundred toward a Depression peak of four thousand. His gamble paid off so handsomely that the church made him the highest-paid Negro minister in Atlanta at the end of his first year. His second year at Ebenezer was FDR's first in the White House, and while he might not have made quite as much noise in his world as Roosevelt made in Washington during the Hundred Days, he made considerably more headway in reversing economic calamity. In the spring of 1934—a little more than two years after taking the pulpit at Ebenezer—Mike King asked his membership to send him on a summer-long tour of Europe, Africa, and the Holy Land. It was a trip that the richest of people might have envied in those hard times, and for a Negro sharecropper's son to step right up to such a fantasy so soon after landing his first full-time job, so soon after attaining basic literacy, stretched even the bounds of the American Dream.

Young Mike King was only five years old when his father said good-bye to his church, his three children, his wife, and his mother-in-law and set off to board an ocean liner bound for France. From Paris, Reverend King took a train to Rome, and later crossed the Mediterranean to Tunisia, making his way from there across North Africa to Cairo. After touring Egypt, he crossed the Nile and soon entered the Holy Land. There he visited biblical sites in Jerusalem, Bethlehem, and elsewhere, before catching a ship back to Europe for the week-long Baptist World Alliance meeting in Berlin. This was a fitting end to a glorious trip for King, who took his seat among the delegates from nations scattered around the globe. The Berlin conference bristled with the excitement of past and present history. King and his fellow ministers heard rumors about the fiery new German leader, Adolf Hitler, and they toured historic sites in the land of their religious heritage, where Martin Luther had defied the Catholic Church and where the Anabaptists later had defied Luther.

Reverend King's triumphant homecoming in late August 1934 was announced to Negro Atlanta in a banner headline in the *Daily World:* "Rev. King Is Royally Welcomed on Return from Europe." The story listed all the speakers who had paid tribute to him at the Ebenezer reception, as well as all the dishes served. This was King's moment, the watershed of his life, and he honored the occasion by changing his name from Michael to Martin, becoming Martin Luther King. For consistency, he also changed the name of his older son to Martin Luther King, Jr.

The change of name was one of the most important events in the younger King's early life. For him it would be the mark of great expectations, a statement of identity that honored traditions in both religion and race. Name changes have always been part of religious history, used to announce the existence of a "new person." Jacob became Israel, Saul of Tarsus became Paul, Simon became Peter, and the first act of every new pope is to choose a special name for his reign. During the civil rights movement the most obtuse white person would be obliged to learn the difference between a nigger and a Negro, later between a Negro and a black person. Subtle arguments took place about the difference between a Negro-American and an American Negro. The ado over name distinctions during the years of acute political crisis may have obscured a pattern that had run deep in the culture through many generations. The collective and individual identity of slavery's descendants never was a settled matter, but fluctuated with circumstances, resulting in frequent shifts of name.

Under slavery, a name was the property of the master and not of the slave, so that a slave's name frequently changed at the auction block and sometimes on the whim of the master. Among the joyous feelings most frequently mentioned by freed or escaped slaves was the freedom to choose a name. A name was no longer incidental. "For it is through our names that we first place ourselves in the world," Ralph Ellison wrote. After the war, the new publications of the former slaves quickly took up the issue of what to call themselves as a race. The terms "black" and "negro" (the latter traceable to the earliest slave traders, who were Spanish and Portuguese) were widely disparaged because the slavemasters had preferred them, and also because their literal meaning excluded hundreds of thousands of mulattoes, whose color was not black. "Colored" was thought to be more inclusively accurate, but among other drawbacks it failed to distinguish the former slaves from Orientals and Indians. Moreover, the term "colored" implied that whites were not colored, or that coloring was a property added somehow to basic human qualities. Alternatively, some argued for the word "African," but this only raised a continuing dispute as to whether the term referred to race or the place of origin. By the late nineteenth century, the term "Negro" came to be widely accepted, after newspapers in New Orleans mounted a campaign to capitalize the first letter. (White newspapers were slow to adopt this dignifying practice. *The New York Times* did not begin to capitalize "Negro" until 1950.)

The name question was never settled to everyone's satisfaction. The NAACP adopted the respectable-sounding "colored people" at its founding in 1909, but the next year the first Negro-owned daily newspaper to circulate throughout the nation tossed out all the contending names in favor of its own invention, the word "Race," which was the semantic equivalent of a placebo. In the Chicago *Defender,* "colored men" became "Race men," and "Negro achievement" became "Race achievement." This novel practice was mainly the product of extreme color sensitivity on the part of the *Defender*'s founding tycoon, Robert Abbott. Born into slavery and then adopted into a white family after his mother married a German, Abbott hated the word "Negro" and anything associated with the color black—to the point where he refused to wear black, married women white enough to "pass," and, when greeted by white people at the Chicago Opera, often gave a pathetic mumbo-jumbo reply in the hope that he would be taken for an African diplomat instead of an American. Yet Abbott became a great champion of "the Race."

The name debate touched the deepest dilemmas of esthetics, values, and identity, sometimes in the most prosaic forms. One method Negroes used to keep whites from calling them by their first names was simply to have none. Moses "Cap" Meredith named his son simply J. H. Meredith. This required some courage, because many whites who asked the boy's name did not like being told that it was "just J.H.," which deprived them of the diminutive uses of a first name. Not until he enlisted in the Air Force in 1950 did the son bow to regulations and choose names to go with the initials, becoming James Howard Meredith. Only when he became nationally known as the Negro Meredith who applied to the University of Mississippi did lawyers and reporters ferret out the formal names and make them, by the sheer power of fame, the ones Meredith would use.

King acquired his given name Martin in the context of this history. There remains much reticence and confusion as to exactly how and why Reverend King changed the names, as inconsistencies plague the only two accounts released. The first version appeared in L. D. Reddick's excellent 1959 biography of King Jr., which was written with extensive cooperation from the King family.* According to Reddick, Reverend King's parents disagreed on his name from the time he was born, with the stronger Delia King's choice, Michael, prevailing until she died in 1924. Then King began calling himself Martin, the name his father had always preferred.

Reddick himself recognized the problem with this story, which was to explain why Reverend King named his son Michael Luther King, Jr., in 1929, five years after King himself had switched to Martin. The family answer he recorded was that "Michael" appeared on the birth certificate because of a communications mix-up between the father and the doctor who delivered the baby. Furthermore, Reddick reported, King discovered the error a few days after the birth and made a special trip to the hospital to make sure the first name on the certificate was changed to "Martin." This was not done, because of still another mix-up at the hospital, Reddick reported, which was not rectified until 1934.

In his own 1980 autobiography, Reverend King recalled that he had continued to use his mother's preferred "Michael" until sometime after his father's death in 1933, when he changed his name and his son's from Michael to Martin in keeping with his father's deathbed wish. This version has the advantage of eliminating the ten-year delay and the hospital mix-ups, but the conflict between the two stories tends to cast doubt on both of them. The import of Reverend King's version is that he changed

---

* Reddick used the byline L. D. Reddick, but his full name was Lawrence Dunbar Reddick—after Paul Lawrence Dunbar, a celebrated turn-of-the-century poet.

the name by which he and his son had been known for thirty-five years and five years, respectively, solely on the request of his alcoholic father, with whom his relations had varied between murderous estrangement and chilly civility, and that he did this in spite of his beloved mother's lifelong campaign to call him Michael.

These accounts seem implausible, or incomplete, partly because the particular name chosen evokes the founder of the Protestant faith. One fact that Reddick and King seem to agree on is that the change was formalized in 1934, the year King went to Europe. (Of this there is independent confirmation. King Jr.'s birth certificate remains a family secret, but State Department records indicate that it was filed on April 12, 1934, in the name "Martin Luther King, Jr." This indicates that King Jr.'s name was recorded officially when he was five years and three months old.) This trip was the culmination of King's stupendous feat of will, by which he had raised himself out of illiteracy into Morehouse, into a prominent marriage, and finally into stunning success at Ebenezer against the tides of the Depression. For Mike King, who had come to Atlanta smelling like a mule, the switch to Martin Luther King caught the feeling of his leap to the stars.

Changing his name meant a lot of trouble for King. On the legal formalities, he had to deal with Atlanta's white bureaucracy. Then he had to tell his friends, his church members, and countless people with whom he did business. There are many indications of ambivalence on his part, resistance on the part of those around him, or both. In 1934, he changed his listing in the Atlanta phone book from the previous "King, Michl L., Rev." to "King, M. L., Rev." In 1936, he switched back to "King, Michl L., Rev." Not until 1937 was he listed as "King, Martin L., Rev." His listing on the bulletin board of Ebenezer, as well as his signature on letters and legal documents, remained the same, "Rev. M. L. King." To friends, he and his son remained "Big Mike" and "Little Mike," or "Reverend King" and "Mike," or later "Daddy King" and "M.L." The son never would list himself in the phone book by his formal name.

If Reverend King did intend to make a proud statement with the new name, it is historically fitting that his peers and his son refused to bring it prematurely into common usage. To claim kinship to Martin Luther was characteristically overbearing of the senior King. His son shrank from it, commenting publicly only once, after the Montgomery bus boycott, that "perhaps" he had "earned" his name. Reverend King supplied the wish and the preparation, but it remained for strangers in the world at large to impose Martin Luther King's new name upon him.

In Depression Atlanta, roughly two-thirds of all adult Negro males were unemployed, and M.L.'s earliest recorded memories were of the long bread lines that stretched around many a corner in his neighborhood. Less than twenty years later, as a graduate student, he would begin an autobiographical sketch with his impressions of the bread lines, stating that the sight of them contributed to "my present anti-capitalistic feelings."

He also remembered his intense desire to imitate his older sister, Christine. In 1934, when a guest minister at Ebenezer made a strong pitch for the salvation of young souls, M.L. watched his sister rise to make the first profession of faith. Impulsively, as he later confessed, "I decided that I would not let her get ahead of me, so I was the next." He wryly observed that he had no idea what was going on during his subsequent baptism. He knew the feeling of being special, and the intense pressure of churchly expectation, long before he had the slightest grasp of religion. His eagerness to keep up with Christine was so strong that he pestered his way into first grade with her that September, a year ahead of schedule. He remained there until the day he gave the teacher a vivid description of his last birthday party, showing five fingers for the five candles that had been on the cake. Thus undone by his own enthusiasm, he was sent home as too young. The next year he managed to skip a grade to catch up with Christine, but she skipped one too, and young M.L. would chase her all the way through high school.

Christine, taking after her mother, was a quiet girl who possessed considerable strength of character and mind. A far better student than either of her brothers, she had gifts that greatly enhanced her stature in the eyes of young M.L., who aspired to her learning but would always trip over his bad grammar and spelling. Even as an adult, he would laugh about his jumbled spelling and seek guidance from Christine or a secretary. The youngest child, A.D., shied away from the precocity of his siblings, preferring to distinguish himself by daredevil feats of adventure and rebellion. He was a rock thrower and a bike crasher. M.L. much preferred to play than to fight, but he did once knock his brother cold by hitting him over the head with a telephone after A.D. harassed Christine beyond the point of endurance.

A.D. once slid down a bannister at high speed into grandmother Williams, knocking her into a heap on the floor. As her relatives raced to her from all points in the house, and were shouting and moaning and wondering how to tell whether she was alive, a far deeper panic seized M.L. He ran upstairs to his room at the back of the house and threw himself out the window. A new round of cries from the children brought horror to the elder Kings, when, just as Mrs. Williams was beginning to revive, they had to run outside to their older son, who did not move until he heard that his grandmother was alive. Only gradually did it sink in that the shock of harm to the grandmother had driven M.L. blindly toward suicide.

All the grandchildren felt something special for Mrs. Williams. As small children and later as adults, they called their own mother "Mother dear," which was affectionate but formal and slightly humorous. They reserved the primal "Mama" for grandmother Williams. She and M.L. took this closeness a step further, and she let it be known that he was her favorite grandchild.

In 1934, the year of M.L.'s baptism and Reverend King's trip to Europe, the NAACP split asunder in an ugly public controversy that revealed once again the trick mirrors around the issues of race and racial identity, where perspective was so central as to affect vision itself. At the center, as usual, was W. E. B. Du Bois, a founder of the NAACP and editor for twenty-four years of its magazine, *The Crisis.* The brilliance of his attacks on Booker T. Washington's policy of racial accommodation and his call for full-scale protest of all injustices against Negroes had positioned him to succeed Washington in national leadership after the latter's death in 1915. As a scholar and essayist without peer, Du Bois was known for prose that gracefully mixed cold, unsparing analysis with lyrical passages on the noble heritage of the Negro people and the justice of their cause. As a political leader, however, he suffered all the liabilities of an elitist intellectual. Even his supporters described his personality as difficult at best, and his haughtiness was so extreme as to inspire collections of Du Bois stories. Once complimented on the honor of being Harvard's first Negro Ph.D., Du Bois is said to have icily replied, "The honor, I assure you, was Harvard's."

A variety of frustrations had swelled within Du Bois during the 1920s, and during the Depression he had come to focus most of his ire upon his nominal boss, Walter White. Since witnessing the 1906 Atlanta race riot as a frightened teenager, White had gone on to become a famous investigative reporter of lynchings—using his light complexion to infiltrate lynching areas in the guise of a white journalist. A gifted publicist and lobbyist who called several Supreme Court Justices and more than a score of U.S. senators by their first names, White was as vain as Du Bois and made no secret of his belief that the grand old man was too eccentric to play a constructive role in the NAACP's new drive for legislation against lynching and Jim Crow. Du Bois, though ever more dependent upon White and the NAACP as the circulation of *The Crisis* fell steadily, refused to promote the NAACP's programs in the magazine. He considered the programs mundane, and he made matters worse by commenting that White had no brains. In 1932, White brought the showdown nearer by hiring a young man named Roy Wilkins to control Du Bois within the New York NAACP office.

The grandson of Mississippi slaves, Wilkins had been abandoned by his father as a small boy, shortly after his mother died. Taken in by a Minnesota uncle who had achieved solid status in the turn-of-the-century Negro upper class as the butler to the president of the Northern Pacific Railroad, Wilkins grew up happily in Duluth until his vagabond father turned up a number of years later to claim him, obliging his aunt and uncle to defeat the father in a custody battle. Thereafter, at the University of Minnesota and as a successful editor at the Kansas City *Call*, Wilkins applied himself diligently to the task of becoming a self-made aristocrat. At the newspaper office during the day, he was a supreme practical realist who was not above crime stories or the corny headlines of the circulation drive, but at night he put on his tuxedo and broke into the tiny glittering world of Kansas City's Negro upper class. He met his future wife at a fashion show sponsored by one of the exclusive women's clubs, and "married up" splendidly after overcoming the strenuous objections of her parents, who, as light-skinned Catholics who counted both Booker T. Washington and Du Bois among their houseguests (at separate times), wanted little to do with an ink-stained lowbrow like Wilkins. But he succeeded then and later on the strength of his savvy versatility, always plainspoken and laconic in the style of actor Jimmy Stewart. He measured political choices by the standards of the common man, conceiving of the NAACP's goal as the achievement of ordinary fair play between the races. Unflappable, he could speak of "the cards we have to play" in the middle of a riot. He would devote his life to the NAACP, but when the call came from New York he also was powerfully attracted by the idea of getting into an apartment at 409 Edgecombe Avenue, which he knew all the way from Kansas City as "the finest address in Harlem."

In New York, Wilkins swiftly recommended a number of changes—all of which were anathema to Du Bois—that he thought would turn *The Crisis* into a mass magazine capable of supporting itself financially. The first contribution out of Wilkins' own typewriter was a sports story about Negro track stars, which, Wilkins dryly recalled, the beleaguered Du Bois allowed to run "tucked among the most august literary and sociological thinkers of the race." After that, Du Bois tried to isolate Wilkins at the magazine, looking upon him with utmost condescension as a newspaperman and obvious bureaucratic ally of Walter White. Wilkins was obliged to create his own role as a publicist. In his first major campaign, after Will Rogers used the word "nigger" four times in his premiere broadcast over the new NBC radio network, Wilkins orchestrated a bombardment of protest telegrams directed at Rogers, NBC, and Gulf Oil, the program's sponsor. Network officials stated that they were helpless to interfere, citing Rogers' First Amendment rights, but two weeks later NBC Radio censored all mention of race, segregation, or lynching from a show about the twenty-fifth anniversary of the NAACP. Wilkins cranked up the telegrams again, but NBC found a way out of the crossfire: Will Rogers switched to the more acceptable term "darky," and shows dealing with the NAACP ceased to be heard on NBC.

By 1934, Du Bois had come to a rather bitter turn. His fame did not change the fact that he was sixty-six years old, with no savings, and being overtaken by younger, more practical men. In addition to these problems, he faced his own growing pessimism—telling himself that the South was just as segregated, and the North more so, than they had been before he and the NAACP began their labors. Such thoughts boiled up into his shattering editorial for the January 1934 *Crisis,* in which he turned the entire NAACP philosophy on its head. Negroes should face the fact that they would die segregated, he declared, in spite of all justice and their best efforts. Therefore, to hate segregation was inevitably to hate themselves, and it would be far better to embrace voluntary segregation in schools, colleges, businesses—both for reasons of psychic well-being and to build concentrated strength for later fights.

This editorial touched off a storm not only within the NAACP but throughout the Negro press. Du Bois received very little support, as even his long-standing admirers believed his comments would bolster the old white racist argument that Negroes fared better under segregation. His bureaucratic enemies within the NAACP denounced him for the heresy of proposing to "embrace Jim Crow." Roy Wilkins—even forty-five years later, after Du Bois's reputation was revived by the black power movement—would always attribute the shocking editorial to childish frustration, claiming that Du Bois "picked up a brick and tossed it through the biggest plate-glass window he could see." A scholar who knew and admired Du Bois would find evidence that his real motive was to say something nice about Negro colleges so that his friend John Hope would be able to hire him back at Atlanta University. (His attacks on Booker T. Washington had rebounded sharply against Du Bois among the white philanthropists who supported Negro education.) Then and later, people found it easier to dismiss Du Bois personally than to dismiss his arguments. Walter White and other NAACP officials knew that they could not denounce all segregated institutions without appearing to criticize the Negro church and the Negro college, and they did not want to support some kinds of segregation while opposing others, for fear of sounding inconsistent. In bringing these contradictions to the surface, Du Bois tied the NAACP in knots. NAACP board chairman Joel Spingarn decreed that the anti-segregation policy ruled out all meetings in Negro churches and schools and all fund-raising events at nonintegrated institutions. This policy would have shut down the organization entirely had it not been quietly reversed.

Du Bois fought passionately on the pages of *The Crisis* during the first six months of 1934. Spurning all talk of appearances and strategies, he marshaled the raw prose for which he was famous: "We have got to renounce a program that always involves humiliating self-stultifying scrambling to crawl somewhere where we are not wanted, where we crouch panting like a whipped dog . . . No, by God, stand erect in a mud-puddle and tell the white world to go to hell, rather than lick boots in a parlor." From there, he went on to insult his boss in print with the charge that White was really a white man anyway, who fought segregation because he wanted to be with white people. He published personal attacks on other NAACP officials and announced that his campaign sprang from internal politics as well as the merits of segregation. Privately, he demanded that a number of people be fired—Roy Wilkins first, then Walter White. But Du Bois, whose idea of bureaucratic craftiness was to speak to his confederates in French, was no match for his opponents. They counterattacked with stories about Du Bois's own yearnings to enter the white world, and the affectations he borrowed from it. They tried to embarrass him by quoting his own attacks on Marcus Garvey's nationalist arguments, and they even spread rumors about his sex life, stressing his preference for very light-skinned women.

Out of phase with his times, Du Bois wound up the year out of the NAACP and back on the faculty of Atlanta University, where he commenced a long-running battle with Florence Matilda Read, the Spelman president and Atlanta University treasurer installed in 1927 by John D. Rockefeller, Jr. In New York, Roy Wilkins took over *The Crisis* and tried to make the best of the Du Bois scandal by publishing an article in which H. L. Mencken complimented Negroes above all other ethnic groups for their willingness to criticize each other in public. The net result on NAACP doctrine was that the organization repledged itself to fight segregation and reburied the fundamental contradictions in the face of white hegemony. At another level, the controversy showed, like others before and after, that racial isolation and racial outreach can each be taken as foolish and cowardly or as wise and brave, depending on historical mood and circumstance. Practically, Du Bois's outbursts meant that local

NAACP groups were freer for a time to choose targets without fear of censure, for no one at the New York office wanted to reopen the poignant debate with which Du Bois had said good-bye to the better part of his career.

Down in Atlanta, Reverend King ventured into politics on both sides of the Du Bois issue. In 1935, he led several hundred people to the courthouse, where they registered to vote. The success of this traditional NAACP activity was marred, however, by the small numbers and by factionalism among the leadership. Many Negroes said openly that they would not register for fear of economic reprisals. Others opposed the march because it would "make trouble," and still others because they believed it was part of a deal with white politicians. The march was not repeated. In 1936, King became the spokesman for a group of Negro schoolteachers who wanted to force the city to raise their salaries to the level of teachers in the white schools. This campaign was more in keeping with the thrust of Du Bois's new challenge, and some people opposed it for that very reason, arguing that improvements in segregated institutions only strengthened segregation. Some of the poorer Negroes in Atlanta objected to the idea of making the relatively privileged schoolteachers a primary concern, when so many people had no work at all, and some of the teachers themselves shied away for fear of their jobs. All this, plus negative actions of various kinds by white liberals and conservatives alike, added up to more conflict than the teachers cared for, and King abandoned the project after a few meetings.

Although there was no dramatic civic progress in those years, Reverend King was at the forefront of what movements there were, propelled by his continued success at Ebenezer. With great fanfare, the minister capped a fund-raising drive with an installation ceremony for a new Wurlitzer organ that featured two manuals and two thousand pipes. It became the pride of Alberta King, the church organist. Remarkably, the expansion at Ebenezer accelerated until the church caught and passed its older and more established rival on Auburn Avenue, Wheat Street Baptist, where the building program for a new church stalled and then collapsed in mid-construction. The renowned Rev. J. Raymond Henderson of Wheat Street finally resigned in despair, leaving his members to quarrel with one another over alleged embezzlement of church funds by insiders.

Reverend King was master of Auburn Avenue less than six years after taking over a bankrupt Ebenezer, but his preeminence lasted only a matter of months. Wheat Street hired as its new pastor Rev. William Holmes

Borders, who was in many respects a twin of Reverend King—a preacher's son from rural Georgia who had begged President John Hope personally for permission to attend Morehouse, who believed so strongly in money as a measure of church and pastor that he listed the value of church real estate in worship programs. The principal difference between the two ministers was that Borders had obtained seminary and master's degrees at Northern white colleges. Wheat Street hired him off the Morehouse faculty. His wife taught at Spelman. In degree-conscious Atlanta, the Borders family was several steps ahead of the Kings on the refinement index, and Borders highlighted the distinction by becoming the first Negro minister in Atlanta to have a regular radio program, "Seven Minutes at the Mike." The show helped spread his reputation for polished sermons filled with commanding language and perfect diction. To the consternation of Reverend King, Borders became one of the preachers young Mike listened to in his eagerness to learn big words.

What became a forty-year rivalry between Borders and King started briskly, as Borders promptly borrowed money to tear down the old scaffolding at Wheat Street and renew construction. Breathless newspaper stories followed progress on the building, until, only nineteen months later, huge crowds jammed Auburn Avenue trying to gain entry to the dedication service at the newly completed church. (King would not finish rebuilding Ebenezer for another two years.) Borders did not hesitate to compare himself favorably to his fellow pastor up the street. Nor did he shrink from public criticisms of King's politics and morals, as evidenced later that year in a clash over *Gone With the Wind.*

In 1939 Hollywood marked the attainment of full maturity the same way it had marked its birth a quarter-century earlier—with a milestone film touching the subject of race and the Civil War. Like *The Birth of a Nation, Gone With the Wind* contributed heavily to a national consensus that for sixty years had been building on a foundation of nationalism, Social Darwinism, and psychological avoidance. The result was that no remotely accurate history of post-Reconstruction race relations survived in the majority culture, even in advanced scholarship. Gone were the odysseys of Spelman and dozens of schools like it, along with the stories of hundreds of lesser schools, thousands of missionary educators, and scores of Negro statesmen whose forbearance was recorded in unknown speeches of florid Victorian eloquence. Gone also was unbecoming realism about the reestablishment of legal white supremacy. The national consensus became so strong that the very subject of race was reduced to distorted subliminal images—as captured in the two films—and sophisticated white Americans took it for granted that the Civil War sprang from causes that had little if anything to do with race. After uncomfortable reality was bleached from recognized history, what remained, ironically, was the very thing the new film claimed was gone with the wind —the romance.

The opening of *Gone With the Wind* swept aside ordinary life. Even the theater critic of the *Daily Worker* wanted so badly to praise the film that the U.S. Communist Party had to fire him for capitalist heresy, as *The New York Times* rather gleefully reported. In Atlanta, Clark Gable led the grand parade up Peachtree Street as Army technicians installed the antiaircraft spotlights that would bathe the arriving stars at the next evening's premiere. The parade made its way to the City Auditorium, where the Junior League was holding a Gone With the Wind Ball for the film stars, gathered celebrities, and selected Atlantans. The City Auditorium was the center of the universe that evening, and Reverend King found a way to be part of it as the only Negro preacher there. The Ebenezer choir, under the direction of Mrs. King, performed four stirring spirituals for the guests.

The following Tuesday, at the regular meeting of the Atlanta Baptist Ministers' Union, Borders and several other ministers launched a ferocious attack on King for allowing his choir to appear at a function that was not only segregated but also plainly sinful, inasmuch as its advertised purpose was to dance and drink whiskey in violation of Baptist doctrine. The more militant ministers decried the indignity of Negro choir members dressed in aprons and Aunt Jemima bandanas to serenade an all-white audience that not even Hattie McDaniel, who played "Mammy" in the film, was allowed to join. More conservative ones stressed the evils of dancing. Hemmed in on left and right, King argued that the extraordinary circumstances justified this one association with sin, but he could not stave off a resolution of censure.

This embarrassment, though it did nothing to improve relations between King and Borders, had little impact outside the argumentative world of preachers. King's string of tangible successes grew longer. His community service and economic influence were such that Morehouse College elected him to its board of trustees, as did the Citizens Trust Bank. More important, the year of *Gone With the Wind* was also the year that the Baptist World Alliance brought its worldwide convention to Atlanta. This was the same event King had attended five years earlier in Germany. As one of relatively few Atlanta ministers of either race with experience in the World Council, King served prominently as an organizer. For race relations, the week's crowning achievement occurred when a Negro preacher, Rev. J. H. Jackson, addressed a crowd of some 35,000 cheering Baptists jammed into previously segregated Ponce de Leon Park. Jackson was pastor of the Olivet Baptist Church in Chicago, which had succeeded Ralph Abernathy's First Baptist in Montgomery as the largest Negro Baptist church in the United States. Jackson also was considered a prince of the national Negro church. During the convention, he lived with the King family on Auburn Avenue, and would return there frequently as a houseguest in later years, when he reigned at the National Baptist Convention and King served as one of his lieutenants. Young M.L. knew and revered Jackson from the time he was ten years old, unaware that the famous orator was destined to crush him within the church as a blood enemy.

As a Morehouse trustee, Reverend King knew Dr. Benjamin Mays, a former Morehouse teacher who had earned such a reputation as a theologian that Reinhold Niebuhr and Paul Tillich included him in the private brain trust they had created to address the great issues of God and mankind. Mays, who had distinguished himself during the 1930s as head of the School of Religion at Howard University in Washington, D.C., was the leading candidate to become president of Morehouse when a vacancy occurred in 1940. A conspiracy intervened briefly when a Rockefeller associate, who was a vice president of the University of Chicago and board chairman of Spelman College, offered Mays instead a chance to become the first Negro president of Spelman. The Rockefeller associate wanted to oust the dictatorial Florence Read, saying that she was anything but a professional educator and had been only a Rockefeller secretary. He appealed to Mays to take Spelman, which was a much bigger job than Morehouse. This introduction to the intrigue within the Rockefeller camp caused Mays to stall for time. In the end, he declined the Spelman offer, not wishing to stake his whole career on winning what was certain to be a bitter battle on ground that was unfamiliar to him, and chose Morehouse.

Young M. L. King and Benjamin Mays arrived at the campus together— King as a seventh-grader at the Atlanta University Laboratory School, Mays as president of Morehouse. M.L. saw President Mays fairly often that year, as it was his father's custom to attend concerts and lectures at Morehouse or Spelman with all three children in tow. After the events, Reverend King always made his way to the stage or dressing room to congratulate the performers, adults and students alike, never failing to introduce himself and each of his children. The tenor soloist of the Morehouse Quartet was struck by the directness and energy of this powerful preacher who made pointed comments of encouragement to everyone, and who took such obvious pride in his children.

To reach the Lab School each morning, young King rode a segregated city bus from Auburn Avenue through downtown Atlanta to the sprawl-ing campus that Rockefeller and the Northern Baptists had bought in the previous century. Some mornings he took his violin to school for lessons, and the violin case, together with his proper dress, must have made him a prim sight for the passengers. The violin was his mother's idea, to which M.L. responded with a sullen obedience that never advanced his violin music much beyond a scratchy whine. A.D. did better, according to family legend. M.L. showed relatively more promise on the piano, but his impatience with fundamentals and his desire to make impressive sounds quickly pushed him out of step with his lessons. As an adult, he would occasionally sit down among trusted friends and play snatches of the "Moonlight Sonata" and nothing more, professing it to be the only piece he knew.

One Sunday afternoon in May, at the end of M.L.'s first year at the Lab School, grandmother Williams served as the Women's Day speaker at Mount Olive Baptist. Back home, her grandchildren went upstairs to study, but sometime later M.L. slipped off to walk down Auburn Avenue for a downtown parade. This was a time of Lend-Lease and war news from Europe, and children could sense the rising excitement—the many military uniforms, the martial music, the parades. M.L. was watching the marchers when a young friend tapped him on the shoulder with the news that he'd better get home fast: his grandmother was dead.

A heart attack had struck the family matriarch as she sat on the plat-form at Mount Olive. In the blur of tears and helpless grief that he found at home, young King discovered unforgettable feelings of anguish that went to the very bottom of him. His first blind reaction was to blame himself: if he had not sneaked off without permission to indulge his curiosity at the parade, Mama would still be alive. His special feelings for her collided with the first cold rush of human finality, so overwhelm-ing him that once again he threw himself out the upstairs window. The family gathered him up again, but this time there was no good news to relieve him. For days he fell into long crying spells, and he could not sleep. His grief had been so pronounced that neighbors and relatives were surprised to witness his dignified composure at the funeral. People said he became a young man overnight.

In his autobiographical sketch of a decade later, King identified the death of his grandmother as a childhood event having "tremendous effect on my religious development." He recalled the personal impact at great length, with unreserved emotion that swept over gaping contradictions. In one passage, he wrote that his grandmother's death provoked his first serious discussions "on the doctrine of immortality," during which his parents assured him that "somehow my grandmother still lived." "I guess this is why today I am such a strong believer in personal immortality," he concluded. In the same sketch, however, he described a prolonged slide into religious skepticism that began about the time his grandmother died and reached the point of extreme public heresy at Ebenezer the next year, when at the age of thirteen, "I shocked my Sunday School class by denying the bodily resurrection of Jesus." Such a statement from the preacher's favored son in a fundamentalist church doubtless created a stir. King recorded nothing further of what he had said out loud, but he wrote that from then on, "doubts began to spring forth unrelentingly," until, by his second year of college, he "regretted going to church." The stress of his grandmother's death, combined with his own questioning nature, put too much pressure on the fundamentalist edifice, which collapsed under him. His grandmother's death brought young King for the first time to both belief and unbelief, and therefore to the sharp edge of religious inquiry. Her death also deprived him of the one person in the household who seemed to combine pure love with natural, unforced authority.

For Daddy King, the loss of his mother-in-law was partially offset by the freedom it gave him to realize his lifelong goal of owning his own home. Shortly after the funeral, he bought a yellow brick house, "the kind I had been dreaming about," only a few blocks away from the Williams home on Auburn Avenue, where his wife had spent nearly all her life and where their children had been born. Mrs. King, displaying some of her late mother's independence, declined to sell or mortgage the house and apply the proceeds toward the purchase of the new home on Boulevard. As executor and sole heir to her mother's estate, she took possession of the house in her own name and rented it out for the income. The family lived in the new King house, but she kept the old house in the Williams family.

The new brick house was located on "Bishops' Row," where the Negro bishops had lived before the Methodist college moved across town to the Atlanta University campus in a further consolidation of that educational complex. It was no longer fashionable to live downtown near the Auburn Avenue business district, as moneyed pioneers were building modern houses on large wooded lots out beyond the combined Negro college campus, in an area known as Hunter Hills. Later it would be called simply the West Side. At the Lab School, M.L. came to know many of the sons and daughters of the Negroes living there, and the experience helped further sensitize him to social conditions. The prevailing rule was that the West Side was better than the East Side, with jokes running about how special an East Side boy had to be to get a date with a West Side girl. There were cross-cutting strata of income, family history, skin color, and religious denomination—running from the ultra-elite First Congregational Church, where extremely light-skinned Negroes sometimes held services with neither music nor preaching but only their own thoughts, which were assumed to be profound, down to the primitive Baptists and other churches for the illiterate. Negro society of that era was preoccupied with numerous gradations among the minority of the race that was healthy, working, and otherwise able to address such matters. Young King wrote defensively of his neighborhood as "a wholesome community, notwithstanding the fact that none of us were ever considered member[s] of the 'upper upper class.' " A Negro writer characterized the area as "mostly lower middle class, and upper lower class." One of King's best friends in high school broke it down even further as "upper lower class and lower middle and middle middle class."

That same friend concocted the first nickname that stuck to M.L., "Tweedie," in tribute to his penchant for tweed suits. Young King was something of a dandy—meticulously groomed and fastidious about his clothing. From grade school on, he had a reputation for elaborate, Victorian-style courtship—full of letters, gentlemanly maneuvers, and shameless panegyrics of love poetry. He pursued his finery and big words with such natural panache that he brought no scorn upon himself. Always unassuming, he slipped easily from tweeds to dungarees. His enormous social range meant that "Tweedie" was simply incorporated into the nickname pool of his neighborhood clique, along with "Shag," "Rooster," "Sack," and "Mole."

World War II quickened the pace of his education. The Atlanta University Laboratory School, which had been created as an experiment to prove that high-quality teachers could turn out Negro graduates every bit as skilled as white ones, folded when the war drained off much of the student body at Atlanta University. As a result, young King had to attend the city's only public high school for Negroes, which was also located on the West Side. His bus rides continued. After tests showed that the Lab School had pushed him ahead of his class at the public school, he entered Booker T. Washington High School in the fall of 1942 as a thirteen-year-old tenth-grader. He was there when the Allies landed in North Africa. By the following spring, Reverend King and his fellow Morehouse trustees faced something much worse than the usual financial crisis. The war was taking a high percentage of the students who might have gone to Morehouse, and not even the superhuman fund-raising efforts of President Mays—already known as "Buck Benny" for his practice of mercilessly hounding Morehouse men for fees and donations—could halt the losses that were pushing the college near bankruptcy. The board chairman suggested that Morehouse close for the duration of the war, but

Mays devised an alternative that might allow it to scrape by: the college lowered its standards and its entrance age in order to admit younger freshmen. Later, King stated forthrightly that he was reading on no better than an eighth-grade level when he enrolled that fall, at the age of fifteen.

At about this time, Spelman's President Read finally triumphed in her ten-year guerrilla war against the chairman of the Atlanta University sociology department, Dr. Du Bois. Although she was neither a scholar nor an educator, her informal position as the Rockefeller representative gave her an overriding strength at all the schools, since she was also a Morehouse board member and the treasurer of Atlanta University, signing all its checks. Grumbling Negro faculty members nicknamed her Rockefeller's white "overseer." Her *coup de grâce* on Du Bois was simple and quiet: his name failed to appear on the faculty payroll list for the fall of 1944. The seventy-six-year-old Du Bois, who had written three books and dozens of scholarly articles since his noisy departure from the NAACP in 1934, came rudely to the end of yet another career. Nearly twenty years of writing and political turmoil still lay ahead of him when Atlanta University set him adrift without notice or ceremony.

Earthshaking events—as spectacular as Hiroshima and as subtle as the early research on the birth control pill—generally failed to disturb the self-absorption of King and his peers at Morehouse, where it had become traditional to say that there were only two kinds of students: those at Morehouse and those who wished they were. President Mays, in his weekly address to the student body, harnessed all his authority and eloquence to the task of arousing student interest in the issues of the outside world. By his own admission, he failed. Using one of many sayings that became part of his legend, Mays chided the students regularly for not getting excited about "anything larger than a hamburger."

Most of the close friends King made at Morehouse were in private rebellion against the ministry. Bob Williams, the tenor soloist who had met King years earlier and was now back at Morehouse after a stint in the Army, came from a family of preachers but was intent on becoming an opera star like his idol, Roland Hayes. Young Samuel Cook—only fifteen, like King—had determined not to follow his father in the pulpit, and Walter McCall was an Army veteran who had preached for money and decided that he hated it. McCall's career plan was to support himself as a part-time minister but channel his considerable idealism toward his goal of becoming a lawyer like Thurgood Marshall, who could help his people. He considered it far easier to make ends meet as a preacher than as a lawyer, and easier to serve humanity as a lawyer than as a preacher. McCall's perception—that idealists must look to the law, breadwinners to the church—would have baffled white students. This stark cultural reversal was part of the natural landscape for Negroes. So was the fact that some two-thirds of Negro college students always had been female, which meant that every male college graduate could expect at least two marriageable women among his peers.*

King entered Morehouse planning to become a doctor, but he soon dropped the idea after deciding that the biological sciences were too cold and mathematical to suit him. Then he, like his friend Walter McCall, set his sights on the law. Dirt poor, McCall toiled in the basement of Groves Hall as the unofficial campus barber, cutting students' hair for a dime. He subjected all his customers to complaints about a host of physical ailments, especially arthritis, and about his financial plight. When King once told him after a haircut that he could not pay his dime right away, McCall became enraged that this privileged, suave, and polished kid professed to have money troubles. The two of them "went to the grass" outside, drawing a crowd, and King prevailed in the wrestling match even though he gave away many pounds and five years to the Army veteran. Having won McCall's respect, King convinced him that his parents really did not give him very much spending money. He soon paid his dime, and the two antagonists became almost inseparable friends, known to everyone as "Mac and Mike." They were a humorous pair of opposites. The gruff, confrontational McCall seemed possessed of a harder rebellion in what he later called a "revolutionary stage." He abhorred religious tastes—especially the happy chatter about heaven and the cross—and looked upon religious ideas as a point of departure. When he and King and other members of their small group went to church, they always sat in the balcony and looked down on the proceedings like anthropologists.

King would remember being startled by Morehouse and its reverberations on his own racial identity, when "for the first time in my life, I realized that nobody there was afraid." This realization is paradoxical in two respects: it contradicts his own memory that Reverend King had always shielded him at home and at Ebenezer from racial cowardice and most racial humiliation; and it is literally untrue. Morehouse students had hardly escaped racial fear, which was a component even of their subordinate relationship to the white Miss Read. Few if any students felt

---

* The sex ratio among Negro college students would remain stable even through the generation after King's death, when a dramatic influx of females would move the white student ratio toward the historic Negro norm.

comfortable with whites or challenged Atlanta's segregation laws, and everyday episodes of fear often intruded upon King's dormitory bull sessions. What was new to King at Morehouse was not an absence of fear but a willingness to question the fear that was there.

He had never known such an attitude at home. Reverend King was not disposed to discuss the race issue. On the few occasions when segregation openly challenged his dignity, he had defended himself bravely in episodes destined to become part of the King legend—as when he indignantly walked out of a shoe store after a clerk insisted on serving him and young M.L. in a segregated section. While boasting of his own fearlessness, the elder King had devised a philosophy and a daily routine that avoided precisely that sort of episode, whose emotional charge was always rooted in fear. He made the race issue simple: he was right, segregation was wrong, and the hatefulness of white people was a mystery best left to God. His son had grown up with this attitude, but was startled to find that Morehouse people freely undertook to solve the mystery themselves. King had his first frank discussions about race on the Morehouse campus. Many of the countless theories about it emanated from the sociology department, whose professors thought of race behavior as a subcategory of all social behavior. They tried to reduce racial fear from a taboo to a branch of knowledge, penetrable by logic. King decided to prepare himself for a legal career by majoring in sociology. Walter Chivers, his adviser and primary teacher in the department, conceived of racism in vaguely Marxist terms as a necessary byproduct of an economic system that benefited whites.

As to religion, much of the pressure King felt was a deepening of the denial that had begun to overcome him when grandmother Williams died three years earlier. He recalled a few years later that his first two years of college pushed him steadily into a "state of scepticism," during which he regretted his church background. He made it clear that this was extremely painful, but it was also liberating. At Morehouse, he wrote, "the shackles of fundamentalism were removed from my body." The Morehouse atmosphere initiated King to the mixed thrills of freethinking. In his case, the growing pains were compounded by factors personal to him —the unusual bond to his late grandmother, and the convergence of both racial and religious fears in the person of his father, whose attempts to banish them on the strength of his own naked authority seemed alternately fraudulent and all too human. In the cycles of perception, Reverend King appeared now and then as one whose strengths transcended his fundamentalism. He was still the father, who had shown how to run a church and make his way in the world, daring to dispense answers that thousands found serviceable.

These pressures, which introverted King in the classroom and at home, never threatened to paralyze him in the company of his new friends. He and McCall spent a lot of time experimenting with some of the tamer sins against Baptist doctrine, such as dancing and card-playing. They would sneak out of church early to play cards. At Morehouse, King worked hard to develop the accouterments of urbanity. One of his campus models was Professor Gladstone Chandler, who smoked a pipe, wore a smart tweed jacket, and invented ingenious games to help his English composition students learn new polysyllabic words. This was one course in which King was no underachiever, because the flamboyant pedantry of the word games brought him no end of fun. If Professor Chandler called on King with a simple "How are you?" he would reply, "I surmise that my physical equilibrium is organically quiescent." To friends around the Mac and Mike clique, King was an affable personality resting on a foundation of decency, moving politely but steadily away from the religious straitjacket of his youth toward the Morehouse ideal of the successful, fun-loving gentleman. When Bob Williams, who finished Morehouse at the end of King's second year, heard some time later that his young friend had decided after all to become a preacher, his first reaction was to laugh out loud in disbelief.

During the summer of 1946, King quit his job as a laborer at the Atlanta Railway Express Company because the foreman insisted on calling him "nigger." Whites were using the epithet with greater frequency then, as increased racial hostility was merely one of many new rumblings when the whole world began to adjust to the meaning of the great war. Amid runaway inflation and fears of a return to the Depression, economic warfare broke out into a chaos of general labor strikes, company goon squads, and emergency government programs. The Soviet Union and the United States began to split the globe into two warring camps, each claiming to represent idealism against an empire of evil ambitions. Colonized peoples in Asia and Africa denounced the hypocrisy of the democratic nations that doggedly reasserted sovereignty over them, and in a similar spirit America's Negro soldiers demanded that they be given at home the rights they had fought for overseas. Whites resisted these demands, especially in the South, with a ferocity that put lynchings back into the headlines. Mobs assassinated no fewer than six Negro war veterans in a single three-week period that summer. In Georgia's first multiple lynching since 1918, one of those six veterans died when a group of hooded men pulled him, his wife, and another Negro couple out of a car near Monroe, lined the four of them up in front of a ditch, and fired a barrage that left a reported 180 bullet holes in one of the four corpses. In the aftermath, state investigators in Monroe complained that "the best people in town won't talk about this," but they and the FBI would compile enough evidence to take before a grand jury, which declined to return an indictment. Local Negroes called in Rev. William Holmes Borders from Atlanta to conduct the funeral.

The story of the Monroe lynching was one of many that the NAACP's Walter White told to President Truman in the Oval Office that September. "My God!" exclaimed Truman. "I had no idea it was as terrible as that." He promised to do something, and soon thereafter appointed a special commission to recommend legislation dealing with all deprivations of Negro citizenship rights. At a time when Negro leaders had trouble getting themselves into the White House at all, much less getting a delivered promise out of it, Truman's action made him an overnight hero. King's friend Samuel Cook helped organize the first campus chapter of the NAACP, which was soon sponsoring debates on such questions as whether Negroes should protest segregation by refusing to serve in the armed forces. The campus mood changed drastically that fall with the major influx of returning war veterans, who, having seen combat in foreign lands, now mingled with the "babies" Morehouse had recruited in their absence. Cook, though only seventeen, faced the challenge of serving the amalgamated student body as its president, having been elected the previous spring on the strength of his popularity as a football star.

King showed little interest in the campus agitation about public affairs. Now a junior, he was spending more and more time in the company of Larry Williams and Walter McCall, studying preachers. It was a tight little trio. As time and practicality seasoned their religious rebellions somewhat, they sought to answer the question of whether the ministry could be cut to the shape of their ambitions. They could be found in the Wheat Street balcony as often as three Sundays a month that year, studying Borders' mannerisms, his organizational style, and above all the high-toned sermons in which he aroused his congregation without merely repeating the homilies of eternal life. Not surprisingly, Borders welcomed their attendance a great deal more than Reverend King appreciated their absence. When Larry Williams, an Ebenezer member, grew so close to Borders over the year that he asked to be apprenticed to him as a Wheat Street assistant, Reverend King took it as proof of intrigue. He asked his son to cut off his friendship with Williams.

M.L. refused, which made his position in the jumble of private belief and family harmony more delicate than ever. Actually, his gropings toward a conscionable brand of preaching made him look beyond Borders toward something much less orthodox, but he could not say so to his father. Reverend King's dissatisfaction was real and close to him personally. In addition, he could not ignore the possibility that any religion vague and secular enough to satisfy him would be too mushy to sustain a church. Reverend King always talked about sustaining the church. M.L. was trying to steer through treacherous psychological waters in many respects. By the end of his junior year, he had given up talk of becoming a lawyer and was noncommittal when asked about his future.

Pressures at home were so severe that King rejoined the Morehouse tobacco program for the summer of 1947. As a fund-raising venture during the war, the college had contracted to supply Connecticut growers with student laborers for the harvest. King had made the trip three years earlier, mostly to get out of Atlanta, but this time it was less of an adventure, more of a work gang. Having been voted one of the two laziest workers before, King now channeled his natural exuberance into playful but determined resistance. There was beer around the barracks at times, and for King the antics culminated abruptly when a policeman accosted him during a nighttime foray. As scrapes go, it was rather civilized; he did not see the inside of a cell. Still, for any young person, let alone Reverend King's son, the mere thought of explaining such an incident at home caused great consternation. Reports were sure to reach his father.

Back in Atlanta, he told some of his closest friends that he had decided to soften the blow by first telling Reverend King what he most wanted to hear: he would follow him into the ministry. The news overjoyed the patriarch, who made a show of weighing the sincerity of his son's intentions but then scheduled M.L. for an immediate trial sermon. He told the news to the Ebenezer congregation in the only acceptable way—that his son had been "called by God to the pulpit." The younger King's friends knew he was too sensitive to be teased about these circumstances at the time, but later they joked about how it was really the "hot sun of the tobacco field" that had called him.

On the appointed Sunday afternoon, a sizable crowd filed into the church basement, where trial sermons were traditionally held. Then others came, and still more, until Reverend King, in his glory, finally shouted, "It won't hold 'em! It won't hold 'em!" and waved everyone upstairs into the main sanctuary. Young M. L. King did not have the commanding presence of his much larger father in the pulpit, as some noticed, but he already spoke with an authority that made people forget his small stature. Although he talked less of Jesus and used more big words than many of his listeners would have liked, the trial was a great success. The boy was only eighteen, they said, and youngsters always talk more about living a good life than about heaven. Clearly, he was gifted, for he seemed to project his entire being in the expression of his

sentiments, the sonorous baritone making music of his convictions. The
Ebenezer congregation rose up in celebration. On a word from Reverend
King, young M.L. was quickly ordained as a full-fledged minister and
made assistant pastor of the church. No one but young King and a few of
his Morehouse friends knew that his first pulpit oration had been borrowed from "Life Is What You Make It," a published sermon by Harry
Emerson Fosdick of the Riverside Church in New York.

The last year at Morehouse was a heady one for King. He and Larry
Williams, now assistant pastor to Borders, walked around the campus
like young lords. Whenever Borders asked Williams to conduct one of his
funerals, Williams would ask King to stand in with him. If the two of
them were not preaching sermons, they were marrying and burying people, while still going to classes and doing homework, and basking in fresh
admiration from local females. Walter McCall teased his friends for getting carried away at times, but he was on the same path. All three of
them felt the honor of being an out-of-town guest preacher at the
churches of King's uncle Joel in Shade Grove, South Carolina. King once
flew home from his uncle's church, becoming the first member of the
family to travel by airplane. He and Williams made the trip so often that
they gave each other new nicknames. King became "Shady" and Williams "Grove." Morehouse students called the two of them "The Wreckers," in tribute to their reputations as ladies' men. King's friends still
saw fit to call him Tweedie, noting the affectation in his habit of closing
his sermon folder just as he stepped into the pulpit—so that everyone
would know he was preaching without notes. This practice greatly annoyed Reverend King, who wanted his son to preach from a manuscript.
    The big news during King's last year at Morehouse came out of Wash-
ington. Truman became the first American President to address an
NAACP convention, and when the commission he had appointed the
previous year released its report, "To Secure These Rights," most observers expressed shock that Truman allowed publication of an agenda so far
in advance of public opinion. The report brought the phrase "civil rights"
into common political parlance, replacing "the Negro question." There
was even greater shock the following February, just three days after the
assassination of Mohandas Gandhi in Delhi, when Truman sent a special
civil rights message to Congress asking for a federal anti-lynching law,
among other things. Atlanta *Constitution* editor Ralph McGill, the
South's most responsible liberal on the race question, attacked the legislation as too radical for the white South, which stimulated the
NAACP's Walter White to call McGill a "weasel." These two men then

felt obliged to go through a minuet of apology and redefinition on liberalism's shrinking territory of comfort. At Morehouse, a majority of realists saw the new bill as a desperate effort to revive Truman's reelection
hopes in the North. They predicted correctly that the bill would go nowhere, but still there were distant rumblings indicating that the postwar
world might become an altogether new age. The new mood was an old
battered faith, now buttressed by the goodwill that follows a war and by
the harsh realities of a shrinking globe.

King took his first public stands that winter on issues far removed
from the dominant ones, beginning with an article for the campus newspaper titled "The Purpose of Education." Most Morehouse students, he
wrote, were in danger of pursuing education as an "instrument of exploitation so that they can forever trample over the masses." Properly conceived, he argued, education provides "noble ends rather than a means
to an end" and rescues learning from the moral vacuum of "efficiency."
"The most dangerous criminal may be the man gifted with reason, but
with no morals." As an example of such a creature, he cited no less a
figure than former Georgia governor Eugene Talmadge, who, King wrote,
had a Phi Beta Kappa key and "one of the better minds of Georgia, or
even America . . . yet he contends that I am an inferior being."

The article was vintage early King—taking a broad swipe at a topic of
his own choosing, making provocative connections (in this case linking
the selfishness of Morehouse students with the racism of Talmadge),
working toward a synthesis of religion and intellect, and struggling
against himself to express original ideas while indulging a fondness for
platitudes. Education was very much on his mind that year. Now that he
had made a career choice, there was indeed a purpose to his own education. He knew that he needed big ideas to go with his big words if he
wanted to elevate his ministry above fundamentalism without sinking
into permanent skepticism. In this crucial respect, his training had only
begun. He wanted to go to seminary, as had Borders, Fosdick, and Johns,
among the finest of the preachers he had studied. He wanted to go specifically to a white seminary, so that while answering the burning questions he could also prove to himself what he had always been taught—
that he was as good as anyone. Finally, he wanted to get out of Atlanta
for a while, and away from Reverend King. By entering the ministry, he
had taken a step or two back under his father's control. That year, Reverend King did with his new assistant pastor what he could not have
done a year earlier with the politely rebellious student: he made M.L.
apologize publicly to the Ebenezer congregation for the sin of going to a
YWCA dance with Larry Williams. King also tried but failed to prevent
his son from joining a new interracial council of students from Atlanta's

white and Negro colleges, arguing that M.L. should stay among his own and not risk "betrayals" from the white students. King thought this was absurd.

Before the school year ended, Morehouse observed a traditional celebration of student oratory that made it unique among Negro colleges. Each academic department, and most clubs and associations, selected an outstanding student to give an annual address to the student body on its behalf. The procession of speeches continued for weeks—one a day at the compulsory chapel services in the basement of Sale Hall—culminating in the Senior Sermon. President Mays and the faculty chose King to speak for his class at that event. Some of his classmates would retain vivid memories of being startled by King's passion and clarity—especially when he declared that "there are moral laws of the universe that man can no more violate with impunity than he can violate its physical laws."

That spring he applied to Crozer Theological Seminary in Pennsylvania and told first his mother, then his sister, then his brother, and finally his father that he wanted to go there. Reverend King snorted in protest for a few days. Seeing no need of further education, he did not want to lose his son, or his assistant pastor, and he was extremely suspicious of Crozer as a white seminary noted for its liberal leanings in theology. In the end, as always, he not only relented but agreed to foot the bill. Neither he nor his son had any idea of the enormous impact Crozer would have on young King's life, but one of them, at least, was eager to find out.

Christine King and her brother graduated in separate ceremonies at Sisters Chapel in June 1948. She was twenty; he was nineteen. As he preached through the summer and made ready to leave home, King was especially happy that his best friend, Walter McCall, was going to Crozer with him. Together they moved the Mac and Mike show into the great Northland to match wits with the smartest white folks they could find.

THREE

NIEBUHR AND THE
POOL TABLES

Late in the summer, King arrived at Chester, Pennsylvania, a small industrial town outside Philadelphia that was the home of Crozer Theological Seminary. It was 1948, a year of surprises—the Berlin blockade, the first sensational charges against Alger Hiss, Truman's upset victory over Thomas Dewey—but to King and his fellow students nothing would match the first few days on the Crozer campus. Most of them expected an atmosphere of modestly progressive religion, of biblical belief tempered by modern knowledge. Their idea of liberalism was more or less along the line of one white student who arrived with a satchel full of research he hoped would prove his thesis that it was biologically possible for Jonah to have lived three days and nights inside the belly of a whale, as the Bible says he did.

What the students encountered was an atmosphere of unorthodox freethinking that went far beyond the rebellions of youth in that taut era. There were signs of it in the naked children who played outside their home with the full approval of their father, M. Scott Enslin, a New Testament scholar of world renown. Student rumors quickly established that Enslin observed neither Christmas nor Easter, believing them to be historically inaccurate perversions of the religious spirit. Some students labored to control their surprise over such things as the enormous gold cross on the table at the front of the Crozer chapel, a display that would be prohibited in most Baptist churches as idolatrous. And although they might not admit it, nearly all the students were shocked by what was directly beneath the chapel: a recreation room with three pool tables and a shuffleboard court. King, like most of them, thought he was modern to approve of dancing, but he had always shunned pool halls as the lowlife setting for knife fights and shootouts. Now he confronted the reality of a poolroom beneath his seminary chapel. Students in practice preaching class would occasionally hear the heathen clatter of a new rack being broken below.

The Negro students in the entering class had selected Crozer precisely because it was a white school of high reputation. Each one had steeled himself in anticipation of an alien environment, expecting to be one of a handful of Negroes at most, and perhaps the only one. What they found instead was almost as big a surprise as the pool tables. There were ten of them in a class of thirty-two. When Walter McCall arrived later in the year—he had been working to save tuition money—they would make up a full third of the class. Their classmates included three Chinese students, several Indians, a Japanese student who was refined and quite popular, a Negro from Panama, and assorted other foreigners. They were all stirred in among the white students in classes, dormitories, and the cafeteria, where a white student from Mississippi stunned everyone by blessing the food with a prayer that began, "Oh Thou whom we've been led to call Buddha, Yahweh, Christ, Zoroaster . . ." and on through the pagan deities. No major seminary of any denomination had achieved such a racial mix, and none would do so again, even after the black revolution of the next generation.

The Crozer administration was making valiant efforts to instill egalitarianism among the students. They had removed all the locks from the dormitory doors, for instance, which to the Negro students meant that the Crozer philosophy excluded not only racial separation but also racial security. Students could wander freely in and out of each other's rooms at any hour of the day or night. This arrangement modified notions of physical safety and even private property, so that nearly everything came to depend on community trust. To clean up the students' rooms, Crozer provided a staff of polite and efficient maids who, like the faculty, were all white.

Crozer president Edwin Aubrey, who years earlier had taught Benjamin Mays at the University of Chicago, called the new students together in the chapel early in the year and told them bluntly that they were the largest and least intelligent class he had known at the seminary. He had grudgingly yielded to financial pressure to increase enrollment, he said, but he refused to relax standards of performance. Aubrey correctly predicted that many of the students gathered there soon would be gone—less than half the entering class, including six of the eleven Negroes, would graduate in 1951—but he did not say that he himself was preparing to resign the presidency.

Like Crozer itself, Aubrey was something of a theological anachronism, a bulwark of classical liberalism on increasingly conservative terrain. Religious liberals, having won control of most of the nation's institutions of higher learning twenty-five years earlier, after the Scopes and Fosdick trials, could no longer sustain both academic excellence and mass appeal. Religious thought was becoming vaguer and more secular, no longer commanding the intense public interest that had once put Fosdick on the front page of the *Times*. Religious conservatives, meanwhile, had established their own seminaries and were perfecting simpler messages of great popular appeal in a troubled, complex age. King's graduate school career would witness the rise to national prominence of Billy Graham and Norman Vincent Peale. Against these trends, Crozer failed to compete successfully for students.

Aubrey, a native of England, first held out to make Crozer a small school of elite scholars, and then, facing extinction, tried to hold on to the seminary's liberal image by recruiting an expanded class in 1948 that included an unprecedented number of Negroes and Southern whites together. This experiment put Aubrey under considerable strain, as a number of Crozer trustees already believed that the liberal image was part of the recruitment problem. Aubrey would resign that year and be succeeded by a caretaker president whom the students called "Creeping Jesus" for his habits of walking slow and saying little. The Crozer president during King's third and final year would be a hard-preaching moderate from Wake Forest, Sankey Blanton, who, by raising money and toning down the school's image, would help squeeze out another two decades of life for Crozer. In retrospect, King's class at Crozer was a desperate racial gamble in an isolated pocket of theological history, but to the students it was a culmination of American idealism, at a time when there was much confident talk of conquering poverty and disease, of ending colonialism and establishing an international brotherhood within the empire of liberty.

Two required courses occupied most of King's time during the first year: M. Scott Enslin on the New Testament and James B. Pritchard on the Old. Both teachers were accomplished linguists who used the original Greek and Hebrew manuscripts to sort out the historical mysteries within the Bible. Enslin addressed the many contradictory accounts of quotations ascribed to Jesus—such as "he that is not against us is for us" in the Gospel of Mark, as opposed to "he that is not with me is against me" in Matthew—always drawing upon larger lessons about the differing purposes and historical circumstances of the biblical authors. A radical biblical critic in the tradition of Albert Schweitzer, Enslin did not hesitate to dispute what he regarded as historically fanciful biblical statements—declaring, for instance, that Jesus and John the Baptist never met each other. Pritchard taught a similarly unsparing course about the prophets of ancient Judaism. He was just finishing the preparation of *Ancient Near Eastern Texts,* a huge volume that would become a standard reference work. An archeologist and historian of the ancient Near Eastern cultures, Pritchard taught his students that neither Moses nor the great Israelite exodus from Egypt was mentioned anywhere in the contemporary literature of the region—not by the Persians, the Hittites, the Sumerians, or the Egyptians themselves. Pritchard's conclusion, which he shared with four or five of the other leading Western scholars in the field, was that Moses was an uncorroborated historical figure, quite possibly a legendary one, and that the Exodus itself was probably a much smaller and more symbolic event than the one described in the Bible.

The standing joke among the Crozer students who survived these courses was that Pritchard destroyed the biblical image of Moses in the first term and Enslin finished off Jesus in the second. King not only survived but flourished academically as never before. He earned a B— in Pritchard's course, which put him near the top because Pritchard gave out only two grades of A— above him. (The other four Negroes who would graduate with King all received D's.) Pritchard was surprised to find that a Southern Baptist like King adjusted so quickly to Crozer. King was not only undaunted by the subject matter of his course but also socially precocious around professors of musty old subjects. He soon became a regular babysitter for the Pritchard daughters, presenting himself for duty in a suit and tie, carrying a stack of books under his arm.

When Walter McCall arrived for the winter term, he found his friend utterly transformed. The indifferent student of the Morehouse years was replaced by one who was utterly absorbed in course work and already earning grades that would make him valedictorian of his class. As the most abrupt and perhaps most pronounced character change in King's life, this transition at Crozer was partly the result of his intense desire to distinguish himself in a white culture. Competing for the first time against white students, many of whom had superior college training, King wanted fervently to prove that he could not only succeed but excel. This desire, and his heavy sense of racial duty, entangled him in a paradox of identity that Du Bois had made famous among Negro intellectuals more than forty years earlier: "One ever feels his twoness, an American, a Negro; two souls, two thoughts, two unreconciled strivings . . ." For King, this meant that to represent his race nobly he had to behave more like his idea of white people and less like white people's idea of Negroes. In particular, he was driven to escape the white stereotype of the Negro who was, in his words, "loud and always laughing . . . dirty and messy." At Crozer, he was "morbidly conscious" of being late. He dressed more immaculately than ever, and he was "grimly serious" in the classroom. In short, he gave the Tweedie side of himself the appearance of a dedicated scholar.

These concerns hardly made King unique among the Negro students, however, and his sudden excellence was supported by an enthusiasm of much deeper substance. Unlike many of his fellow students, he welcomed the skeptical rigor of Pritchard and Enslin. Crozer's approach to seminary training was to tear down the students' religious belief system and start over, building a body of religious knowledge as rationally as possible, reducing the "leap of faith" to the tiniest arc of reverence. Crozer tried to do for its students what boot camp did for marine recruits, but with a drastically less fixed idea of what the finished product would be. In this difficult process, King enjoyed a large head start over most of his fellow students. Having muscled his way into a state of religious skepticism some years earlier against the combined weight of his heritage and his father's authority, he found Crozer's idea of religion no less liberating than the racially mixed classes, the unlocked dorms, and the white maids. He was on his own, six hundred miles from home, immersed in a world of religious, moral, and historical ideas he knew he loved in a way he could not yet define, with no prior obligation to buy any of it. He became suddenly and permanently fascinated. The floor of his room was soon piled high with books, and he would sometimes read all night.

Among the theologians and philosophers King studied during his first year at Crozer was Walter Rauschenbusch, a German Lutheran-turned-Baptist whose experiences as a minister in the Hell's Kitchen area of New York at the close of the nineteenth century led him to write *Christianity and the Social Crisis*, the publication of which is generally regarded as the beginning of the Social Gospel movement in American churches. (The book was among the few King would ever cite specifically as an influence on his own religious beliefs.) Rauschenbusch rejected the usual religious emphasis on matters of piety, metaphysics, and the supernatural, interpreting Christianity instead as a spirit of brotherhood made manifest in social ethics. He saw the Christian ministry as an extension of the Old Testament prophets, who denounced pride, selfishness, and oppression as transgressions against the divine historical plan, which was to culminate in the Christian ideal of "love perfection" among all people. Rauschenbusch was not the first theologian to see the similarity between the Second Coming and Marx's vision of a classless, stateless society, but he was the first to tie them together boldly as both the essence of biblical religion and the goal of Enlightenment progress. The minister's job, he declared optimistically, is "to apply the teaching functions of the pulpit to the pressing questions of public morality." Critics denounced him as a utopian or a Communist. But to generations of followers, Rauschenbusch rescued religion from sterile otherworldliness by defining social justice as the closest possible human approximation of God's love.

George W. Davis, the professor who introduced King to Rauschenbusch, was the son of a union activist in the Pittsburgh steel mills. He was also the only strict pacifist on the Crozer faculty, and the strongest admirer of Gandhi. It was Davis' personal copy of *That Strange Little Brown Man of India, Gandhi* that King read in the seminary library, responding positively to its message and to its overtly racial characterization of Gandhi. King never accepted pacifism at Crozer, and in fact wrote a paper attacking A. J. Muste's notion that the atomic bomb had transformed the essential moral questions of war and peace, but he did otherwise adopt Davis as a mentor and faculty adviser, taking nearly one-third of his Crozer courses from him. The pairing made sense, as Davis was the embodiment of Rauschenbusch's Social Gospel, and King, in his own words, "found it easy to fall in line with the liberal tradition" at Crozer. He also warmed to Davis as a kind and accessible man.

Not all Crozer professors carried their modern biblical criticism into liberal politics. Enslin, most prominently, made no secret of his disdain for Rauschenbusch and the entire Social Gospel movement. To Enslin, as to Albert Schweitzer, the Sermon on the Mount teachings that Rauschenbusch considered the essence of religion were intended only as an "interim ethic" pending the imminent establishment of a heavenly order that Jesus expected but that never came. Thus he dismissed the exaltation of the humble in the Sermon on the Mount, along with the troublesome blanket condemnations of worldly attachments. Those teachings were irrelevant to ordinary human affairs, he said, and the concerns of the Social Gospel were essentially political squabbles far beneath religion's proper focus on the nature of ultimate reality. Enslin's criticisms were brilliant and acidic, his behavior eccentric, and his private beliefs well concealed. He alone appeared to understand them, and students puzzled as to why such a man always attended at least three Baptist church services a week, where he was obliged to listen to banalities that he would not tolerate for an instant on the campus. The faculty considered him its leading Tory in politics, and most students thought of him as something of a bigot. In his letter recommending valedictorian King to graduate schools, Enslin would express surprise that a colored man from the South had done so well at Crozer.

Crozer students were more divided than the faculty in their social beliefs. The great racial experiment of 1948 dismayed some of the new white students as much as it gratified the Negro ones. An undercurrent of tension shortened some meals in the cafeteria, and the open-door dormitories led to inevitable difficulties that occasionally flared up into hostility. Forgiveness was the school's specific reaction and racial harmony its recommended prescription. Fully in keeping with the approved Crozer attitude, King expressed the belief that love and reason could bring out in all people a basic goodness that was deeper than racial hatreds or personal animosities. All but one of his graduating Negro classmates generally agreed with him. The exception, Joseph Kirkland, was the only Northerner among them and also the only preacher's son other than King. Streetwise and tough, Kirkland had rebelled against his authoritarian, intellectual father—holder of three Ph.D.'s, pastor of Philadelphia's largest Negro Baptist church—at an early age, becoming a numbers runner and bootleg whiskey dealer in the ghetto underworld. His idea of the Social Gospel was to drag Crozer professors into boozy strip joints, exposing them directly to the common folk they normally analyzed from a distance. Kirkland believed that the Social Gospelers were naïve about the social chasms within each race. He teased the Southerners for being so impressed by the racial integration in the North generally—reminding them that such policies did not extend a single foot off the campus into downtown Chester. He teased King in particular for being sheltered. At Crozer, King was the only Negro and one of the very few students of any race who did not have to work at an outside job to support his studies. King "works with his checkbook," laughed Kirkland, who was rather proud of himself for having spurned his own father's support. When King first visited Kirkland's room and objected to the beer kept there in coolers, saying that they all had "the burdens of the Negro race" on their shoulders, Kirkland replied, "So what?"

King's oratory was among his chief distinctions at Crozer. His peers so admired his preaching technique that they packed the chapel whenever he delivered the regular Thursday student sermon, and kibitzers drifted into practice preaching classes when King was at the podium. A generation later, some of the white students who remembered very little else about King would remember the text, theme, and impact of specific King practice sermons. There was a chapel sermon on the text "They have a zeal, but not according to knowledge," for example, and a talk to the women's group of a white Baptist church on the theme of Christianity and communism. King perfected minute details of showmanship, such as tucking away his notes at the podium in a manner just unsubtle enough to be noticed, and his general style was extremely formal. He called his orations "religious lectures" instead of sermons, in fact, but the conflict inside him over such issues as knowledge versus zeal—with all their underpinnings of race, class, and theology—generated enough heat to make his sermons interesting. At Crozer, practice preaching courses brought King some of his best grades and highest approval. During the three seminary years, he took no fewer than nine courses related to the art of pulpit oratory.

His homiletics professor, Robert Keighton, brought to the classroom a preoccupation with style and the classical form of argument, which suited King perfectly. A "high" Baptist—accused by some of the "low" or "snake stomping" Baptists on campus of being an Episcopalian at heart—Keighton favored understatement, dry humor, tightly structured presentations, and a liberal sprinkling of illustrative quotations from poets and playwrights. He had organized, and still coached, the Crozer drama club. In class, Keighton remarked that he wished he knew his Bible as well as he knew Shakespeare, and it was rumored among the students that he had been offered a curatorship at the Shakespeare Museum in England. Keighton's taste in more modern poets ran to W. H. Auden and T. S. Eliot, but as a concession to the romantic yearnings of preachers, he introduced King to some of the English-language poets he would quote throughout his public career, among them James Russell Lowell and William Cullen Bryant. Perhaps less fortunately, he also introduced the rhetoric of Saint Augustine, who was given to dramatic pairings of night-and-day clichés ("muddied the clear spring of friendship with the dirt of physical desire and clouded over its brightness with the dark hell of lust"), especially when speaking of sin or evil. Keighton, like Augustine, emphasized that a large part of religion was public persuasion, as can occur when speakers of the highest gifts address the most difficult questions. King came to accept the shorthand description of oratory as "the three P's": proving, painting, and persuasion, aimed to win over successively the mind, imagination, and heart.

In lectures dealing with the preacher's tradecraft, Keighton taught that a preacher should first prepare an outline based on one of the proven sermon structures. There was the Ladder Sermon, the Jewel Sermon, the

Skyrocket Sermon, the Twin Sermon, the Surprise Package Sermon, and many others. The Ladder Sermon climbed through arguments of increasing power toward the conclusion the preacher hoped to make convincing. The Jewel Sermon held up a single idea from many different angles, as a jeweler might examine a precious stone. The Skyrocket Sermon usually began with a gripping human interest story leading to a cosmic spiritual lesson, followed by a shower of derivative lessons falling back to earth among the congregation. Keighton's method was to lecture on such methods and then direct his students to try them. More than a few students left Crozer because of stage fright in Keighton's homiletics. King thrived on both the setting and the pressure. Keighton's homiletics imposed order and style on his childhood desire to use big words, in an art form he had studied all his life.

Preaching class was the laboratory of the seminary. It was also a vital part of campus social life, because public speaking exposed each student's personality and facilitated friendships to a degree far beyond the likely results of coffee hours or other social conventions. The Negro students shared much merriment in contrasting Keighton's archly formal structures with their own homemade preaching formulas. Keighton might have his Ladder Sermon, they joked, but they had Rabbit in the Bushes, by which they meant that if they felt the crowd stir, they should repeat the theme, just as a hunter shoots into the shaking bush on the assumption that a rabbit might be there. Keighton might have his Classification Sermon, but they had Three Points in the Palm of a Hand. King and Walter McCall liked nothing better than sneaking in to hear their Negro classmates preach in real churches off campus. Both of them were accomplished mimics. To the mortification of the classmate, McCall would shout out a countrified parody of what they had heard, full of emotional fireworks about Jesus as the Holy Spirit incarnate, and then King would deliver the "correct" versions in equally exaggerated spiels of Enslin's rational historicism, speaking of Jesus as a gifted Jewish prophet with a lot of personal problems.

With Horace "Whit" Whitaker, a Southern Negro who was generally considered the second-best preacher in the class, King and McCall spent many evenings at the home of Rev. J. Pious Barbour, a local pastor who had been the first Morehouse graduate to attend Crozer. Barbour was a raconteur and amateur philosopher of some renown, and the influx of Negro students at Crozer in 1948 gave him a steady audience for his favorite pastime, Socratic dialogues, which he hosted after sumptuous home-cooked meals prepared by Mrs. Barbour. Boasting of himself as "the deepest theologian in the Baptist Church," Barbour sometimes slipped into outright nonsense, as in his quotation-laden warnings against letting a Catholic priest into one's house, but he was never dull. He enjoyed making the students uncomfortable with the latest ideas about almost anything. "Tillich is all wet," he later wrote King. "There is no 'being itself' . . . Kant proved that." Barbour welcomed the mental jousting as a relief from his less stimulating duties in the church. The students turned his ample hospitality into a social mainstay, taking dates there for extended evenings that allowed them to enjoy the good food and show off their learning before young ladies who were impressed enough or patient enough to listen.

One of King's dates that first year was Juanita Sellers, an Atlantan whom he had known since high school. Attractive, poised, and intelligent, she was doing graduate work at Columbia University along with Christine King and a few other friends from Spelman. Sellers had grown up in the new elite West Side of Negro Atlanta, daughter of the city's most prominent Negro mortician. Her social standing was such that when people carped about "social climbing" when she and her group of friends all pledged the Delta sorority at Columbia, they replied airily that such a motive was impossible for them because they had nowhere to climb. This attitude, in addition to her other qualities, made her precisely the sort of woman Daddy King was anxious for his son to marry. There was some rejoicing in Atlanta, therefore, when King visited Sellers in New York several times that year and invited her to spend weekends at Crozer. Sellers and Christine King traveled down to the seminary together, spending more than one evening with King and his friends at the feet of Pious Barbour.

During his first summer vacation from Crozer, while serving again as more or less the full-time pastor at Ebenezer, King saw Sellers enough to spark a rumor that their longstanding friendship was turning into a romance. While entertaining her one afternoon in the King home on Boulevard, he announced suddenly that there was someone he wanted her to meet. He urged her to brush her hair and freshen her makeup that very moment, to look her best. Without further explanation he escorted her to the Liberty Baptist Church, not far from Ebenezer. There King rang the doorbell at the church office and was invited in for tea with the pastor. It was all very pleasant, though churchy and formal. Afterward, King thanked Sellers for obliging him and said no more about the visit. It took a somewhat perplexed Sellers several days to find out from Christine King that the visit had been an exercise in ministerial diplomacy. King's previous steady girlfriend had been an "East Sider" and a member of the Liberty church. By calling on her pastor in the company of Sellers, King was announcing his change of heart and implicitly offering him an opportunity to object. Moreover, the visit was a courtesy to the Liberty pastor, so that he would be well informed if the previous girlfriend asked him as her pastoral counsellor what had become of King, as was entirely possible. These and a thousand other calculations made up the preacher's code, in which King was an advanced student.

Daddy King looked proudly on his son's mastery of the political and social graces, but the moral standards he absorbed at Crozer were another matter entirely. By the second year, King was so imbued with the Social Gospel that he dared to drink beer, smoke cigarettes, and play pool openly in the presence of his father, whenever Reverend King visited Crozer. He went so far as to usher his father into the poolroom beneath the chapel, inviting him to play, trying to act as though it were perfectly normal, taking pride in his hard-earned skill as a player. He knew Reverend King would object violently, which he did, but he trusted excessively in the persuasive powers of the liberal Christian teachings that defilement comes only from within (as in Matthew 15:11). When he pointed out to his father that it was not the smoke-filled poolroom itself that was sinful but rather the plan sometimes hatched there to rob the liquor store, Reverend King brushed it aside as a book-learning excuse for sin. In what was to become a permanent pattern of conversation between them, King gently teased his father about being old-fashioned, and Reverend King defended his methods by pointing to his own time-tested success in the world.

The underlying battle of wills was a stalemate, the insurrectionary potential of which was not lost on relatives such as Rev. Joel King. With the senior King, he visited his nephew at Crozer several times, never failing to ask why King permitted M.L. to smoke and play pool while forbidding such vices to everyone else, including Joel, who was a grown man almost old enough to be M.L.'s father. Reverend King seethed under this line of questioning. Joel, for his part, decided he was not getting a satisfactory answer. Finally, after one long drive back to Atlanta from Crozer, he decided to try some of his nephew's boldness himself. As he and Reverend King walked toward the house on Boulevard, Joel lit a cigar. King walked wordlessly ahead of him up the steps to the front door. Then, just as Joel was beginning to think that the crisis had passed, King whirled and crushed the lighted cigar with the back of his hand, sending sparks into his brother's hair and down his suit. Joel King never figured out how M.L. managed to defy Reverend King with impunity.

Between father and son, ideological differences erupted again during the Christmas holidays of 1949, when young King decided to divide his time between preaching at Ebenezer and studying the works of Karl Marx

at home. Communism was a subject of feverish public interest at the
time, with the second Alger Hiss trial under way in New York and a
Communist government celebrating its recent victory in China. Harry
Emerson Fosdick had preached a widely publicized sermon at New
York's Riverside Church earlier that year in which he argued that the
Communist movement had stolen two dormant aspects of traditional
Christian appeal: the psychology of conversion, and the Social Gospel's
commitment to the oppressed. King read *The Communist Manifesto* and
some interpretations of Marx and Lenin before framing an objection to
communism that would serve him the rest of his life. In a suitably erudite but pat phrase, he came to reject communism because of its "historical materialism and ethical relativism," meaning Marx's doctrine that
economic forces alone determine the path of history and Lenin's teaching
that what was good in politics was to be defined continuously by the
vanguard party according to the needs of the revolution. King objected
that these cold, scientific doctrines left no room for moral forces to act
in history, or for moral standards to rise above the Machiavellian, tyran-
nical tendencies of politics.

To Reverend King, M.L.'s fancy phrases were no better than quibblings
over alien notions. No good preacher needed to read a lot of books to
decide that communism was un-Christian, he declared, fulminating
against having all that Communist propaganda in his house. This would
remain a sore point. For the younger King, it was all the more difficult
because some of his most faithful intellectual mentors constantly urged
him in the opposite direction. Melvin Watson, chairman of the Morehouse School of Religion, was one of a generation of Negro intellectuals
—many of them stalwart Baptist preachers—who quietly amassed expertise on Communist doctrine because of explicit Soviet promises on race
and the downtrodden. "The Communist theorists were definitely not
materialistic after the fashion of the Greek atomists," wrote Watson,
after listening to King preach against communism at Ebenezer. "Marx's
. . . variety of materialism is very difficult to refute and is a very disturbing phenomenon." Watson sent King a number of sophisticated but avuncular critiques, always with the cheery salutation "Dear Little In-
Coming Doctor!" He urged King not to be discouraged by the Ebenezer
congregation's response to his lecture on dialectics. "Some people did
sleep," Watson noted, "but some would have slept regardless of the
theme."

The elder King took a new approach when he delivered his son for his
final year at Crozer. No longer the stern figure who recoiled from the
pool tables and departed as quickly as possible, Daddy King arrived in his
finest three-piece suit, a gold watch chain dangling from his vest pocket,

and made his presence known—shaking hands gregariously, complimenting the professors on their learning and the students on their prospects, telling everyone how proud he was that M.L. was finishing up his Bachelor of Divinity degree and would be joining him permanently at Ebenezer the next year. The seminarian himself stoically endured this performance, later telling his friends that his father was prone to exaggeration. He did not intend to join Ebenezer at the end of the year, nor any other church. Early that fall he wrote an open letter to the Ebenezer congregation, thanking the members for their support the previous summer "in the absence of our pastor," stressing the fact that his father was still master of the church. He also sat down with his adviser and favorite Social Gospel professor, George Davis, to discuss the first-rank graduate schools at which he might obtain a doctorate in the philosophy of religion. His first choice was Yale, Davis' own school. By November, he had applied to Yale, to Boston University, and to the Divinity School at Edinburgh University in Scotland. Yale turned him down in spite of his exemplary record at Crozer, but the other two schools accepted him before the Christmas holidays. This left King with a decision to make, and also with the familiar task of discussing with his mother how best to tell his father.

King already was aiming for further graduate study when he first read Reinhold Niebuhr during his last year at Crozer. The experience did not change his plans, but it appears to have changed nearly everything else, including his fundamental outlook on religion. Before Niebuhr, King wanted to pursue his doctorate for reasons of pleasure, inertia, and prestige. He had enjoyed Crozer beyond all expectation. He wanted to keep studying, especially since his future and its inevitable clash with Reverend King's agenda was not yet resolved in his mind. He wanted a doctorate because it would place him in rarefied company. (Drawn to distinguished titles, he and his friends wrote letters to each other playfully appending long strings of advanced degrees to each other's names, in the manner of British scholastics.) After Niebuhr, King experienced for the first time a loss of confidence in his own chosen ideas rather than inherited ones. The Social Gospel lost a good deal of its glow for him almost overnight, and he never again fell so completely under the spell of any school of thought, including Niebuhr's. Although the Niebuhr influence went to the heart of the public and private King and affected him more deeply than did any modern figure, including Gandhi, the connection between King and Niebuhr would be obscured by complicated twists of time, race, and popular imagery.

The publication of Niebuhr's *Moral Man and Immoral Society* in 1932, when King was three, marked the beginning of the end of classical liberalism in American theology. Niebuhr had come to teach at Union Theological Seminary in New York in 1928, by way of Yale Divinity School and a thirteen-year ministry in Detroit, having achieved considerable fame as a champion of the auto workers and Negro migrants struggling to survive in Henry Ford's town after World War I. He was also an internationally prominent pacifist who had served several terms as president of the Fellowship of Reconciliation.* For that reason, *Moral Man and Immoral Society* caused a howl of betrayal among practically all nonfundamentalists interested in religion, because Niebuhr attacked the Social Gospel's premise that the steady advance of reason and goodwill in the modern age was capable of eradicating social evils. His chief target was the eminent John Dewey, the last American philosopher to have a large popular following. Niebuhr ridiculed Dewey's notion that ignorance was the principal cause of injustice, stating instead that it was "our predatory self-interest." There was no evidence, said Niebuhr, that human beings became less selfish or less predatory as they became better educated. War, cruelty, and injustice survived because people were by nature sinful.

Niebuhr accused the liberal world of being "in perfect flight from the Christian doctrine of sin." Intellectuals winced at the sound of the word itself, and modern theologians expressed shock that one of their idols was debunking the central idea of progressive history . To admit evil as a permanent aspect of the human character, as Niebuhr did, was to confound the theologian again with the question of what kind of God would permit such suffering, and why, and to cast doubt on the prevailing intellectual notions about the meaning of history. Such an idea threw Christians back to hard realists like St. Augustine, who believed that each person had to choose "love of God in contempt of one's self," or to Martin Luther, who held that man was a craven sinner in desperate need of divine grace.

Niebuhr did not go quite that far, although he did later admit to an

---

* The Fellowship, which would be headed by A. J. Muste during King's public career, had been founded shortly before World War I by Henry Hodgkin, an English Quaker, and Sigmund Schultze, Kaiser Wilhelm's chaplain, who vowed not to participate in any war that might result from the rabid nationalism of their respective countries. Their vow was regarded as a sentimental quirk at the time, but the fruitless carnage of the Great War transformed them into sages. For the generation between the world wars, pacifism was a thoroughly respectable mass movement not only in Europe but also in the United States, where a 1935 poll of undergraduates found that 39 percent would fight in no war at all and another 33 percent would fight only if the United States itself was attacked.

unfashionable respect for Augustine as a man who "saw very clearly that it was not the mind which governed the self, but the self which governed the mind." What Niebuhr did was to invent his own distinction between the character of people acting in large social groups as opposed to their character as individual people. Human nature was such that individuals could respond to reason, to the call of justice, and even to the love perfection of the religious spirit, but nations, corporations, labor unions, and other large social groups would always be selfish. Society, Niebuhr argued, responded substantively only to power, which meant that all the forces of piety, education, charity, reform, and evangelism could never hope to eliminate injustice without dirtying themselves in power conflicts. He ridiculed, for example, the notion that moral suasion would ever bring fundamental economic and political rights to the American Negro in Detroit or anywhere else. "However large the number of individual white men who . . . will identify themselves completely with the Negro cause, the white race in America will not admit the Negro to equal rights if it is not forced to do so. Upon that point one may speak with a dogmatism which all history justifies."

Having committed heresy against the Social Gospel, and against the doctrine of progress itself, Niebuhr turned upon the Marxists, whose ideas had influenced him profoundly since his ministry in Detroit. Acknowledging that the Marxists understood the need for power to establish justice, he attacked them for pretending to have discovered a science of history even though Marx offered only an "apocalyptic vision" of triumph over selfishness and oppression, "in the style of great drama and classical religion." Believing unreservedly in their false science, Niebuhr wrote, Marxists fell easily into blind tolerance of the injustice inherent in their creed, which, "charged with both egotism and vindictiveness," proclaimed it the destiny of Marxists to speak for the poor and to exact vengeance upon the non-poor. According to Niebuhr, the inevitable result was a naïve credulity as well as "a policy of force and fear." * He denounced Stalin's "policy of 'liquidating' foes"—in a book published in 1932, years before most observers in the United States realized that such a policy really existed.

Moral Man and Immoral Society created a sensation in intellectual circles, transforming Niebuhr into a stark iconoclast. Mainstream liber-

---

* Niebuhr hinted privately that his target was his own department head at Union Theological Seminary, Harry Ward, whom he described as "a naïve Christian Marxist." Ward had returned from the Soviet Union to write *In Place of Profit*, which Niebuhr called "a glorification of Russian society as having gotten rid of selfishness."

als, such as the editor of the *Christian Century*, were disturbed by the
Marxist themes that remained in his work, while Marxists hated him for
criticizing Stalin. One Communist reviewer, after denouncing Niebuhr
for spreading "the sauce of Christianity" on his political analysis, decided that he was "worse than a thug." Horrified Social Gospel reviewers
implied that Niebuhr's emphasis on sin made him a traitor to progress,
or even a fundamentalist. That same emphasis might have endeared him
to religious conservatives, but they could not bring themselves to compliment a man who routinely questioned the literal truth of the Bible
and who criticized Franklin Roosevelt as too conservative.

By the time King read *Moral Man and Immoral Society* in the fall of
1950, Niebuhr was transformed yet again and had risen in stature to
become a weighty public figure. During the intervening eighteen years,
Hitler had changed Niebuhr's theory of immoral society and implacable
evil from a theologian's semantic invention to the most hotly debated
topic on the globe. Niebuhr worked personally to help intellectuals escape from Germany, bringing Paul Tillich to teach with him at Union,
and he founded *Christianity and Crisis* during World War II, primarily to
counteract the influence of the American pacifists he once had led. After
the war, he joined Eleanor Roosevelt, Hubert Humphrey, and other
prominent liberal politicians in creating Americans for Democratic Action, whose purpose was to promote anti-communism among liberals—
a theme that would help put John Kennedy in the White House. In the
Cold War, as in the war against the Nazis, Niebuhr's thought to some
degree followed his fame.

In the book, King came fresh upon the earlier Niebuhr—a great theologian with an inner drive very much like his own, who had shocked the
religious world in 1932 and now King in 1950 by declaring that the evil
in the world was bigger than either the Social Gospel or Marxism. Both
creeds hoped to see the meek inherit the earth, said Niebuhr, but the
spiritual forces were too shy or too pure to fight the harsh world of evil,
and the materialistic forces were too mechanical or too conspiratorial to
allow the humanity which justice needs to breathe. The Social Gospel
avoided the grit of politics; Marxism abhorred the church and all forms
of idealism. To Niebuhr, they represented together the overriding tragedy
of the age—"modern man's loss of confidence in moral forces." By
"moral," he meant the mediating unscientific realm of justice, which
combines love and politics, spiritualism and realism. Morality was a
compromise of religion and politics, necessitated by the special character
of the immoral society.

This talk of morality pushed a number of buttons inside King. Morality
was the preacher's traditional fallback position. In moments of religious

doubt, which King had experienced and always would, a preacher who could not talk about salvation could always talk about the Ten Commandments or the Sermon on the Mount. If racial justice was not God's cause, it was at least a moral one. It did not bother King a great deal to hear religious conservatives say that the Social Gospel was too secular to be religious, but it was quite another matter to hear Niebuhr say that the Social Gospel did not touch the evil in the world and was therefore not moral. Hitherto, King and his Negro friends at Crozer had been able to drift along toward their degrees, thinking that if they performed as well as whites in school, preached the Social Gospel, helped as many Negroes as possible to rise to full skills behind them, and all the while encouraged the racial enlightenment of progressive white people, then they could make a contribution toward social justice whether or not their religious qualms subsided. If Niebuhr was correct, however, any Social Gospel preacher was necessarily a charlatan, and the Negroes among them were spiritual profiteers, enjoying the immense rewards of the Negro pulpit while dispensing a false doctrine of hope. Such a prospect deeply disturbed King, who already felt guilty about his privileges compared with the other Negro students at Crozer. Daddy King's unabashed pursuit of success embarrassed him, and he would always be extremely sensitive about money. The shocking implication of Niebuhr's book was that Daddy King was correct in his emphasis on sin and honest in his belief that the minister should try as hard as anyone else to get ahead. By this light, the Social Gospel offered King little more than the chance to become a hypocrite.

Niebuhr was turning against a strain of political and religious idealism that had been building since the epiphany of Count Leo Tolstoy, whose eyes had locked on three familiar words from the Sermon on the Mount: "Resist not evil." "Why had I always sought for some ulterior motive?" asked Tolstoy. " 'Resist not evil' means never resist, never oppose violence; or, in other words, never do anything contrary to the law of love." In his old age, the great Russian novelist was transformed into the intellectual father of modern pacifism. His book *The Kingdom of God Is Within You* had a profound influence on young Mohandas Gandhi when he was a student in England. Toward the end of Tolstoy's life, Gandhi corresponded with him and named his first commune, in South Africa, Tolstoy Farm.

In his book, Niebuhr attacked pacifists and idealists for their assumption that Gandhi had invented an approach that allowed religious people to be politically effective while avoiding the corruptions of the world. For Niebuhr, Gandhi had abandoned Tolstoy the moment he began to resist the color laws in South Africa. Gandhi's strikes, marches, boycotts, and demonstrations were all forms of coercion, which, though nonviolent, were contrary to the explicit meaning of "Resist not evil." Niebuhr applauded what Gandhi was doing but not the sentimental interpretations that placed Gandhians above the ethical conflicts of ordinary mortals. For Niebuhr, such a belief was dangerously self-righteous as well as unfounded.

While Gandhi's methods were political and promised only a slight chance of improvement in the world, Niebuhr said bluntly, they belonged to "a type of coercion which offers the largest opportunities for a harmonious relationship with the moral and rational factors in social life. . . . This means that non-violence is a particularly strategic instrument for an oppressed group which is hopelessly in the minority and has no possibility of developing sufficient power to set against its oppressors." Niebuhr amplified this gleam of hope as it might apply to the cause of the American Negro. If Gandhi's methods were somehow adapted to American conditions and then employed in a difficult, protracted campaign, they could make headway toward justice even against the selfish forces of the immoral society. After making several suggestions as to how a Negro nonviolent movement might proceed, Niebuhr concluded that "there is no problem of political life to which religious imagination can make a larger contribution."

Like Niebuhr, King allowed his religious and political thoughts to run along the same moral edge. Questions about the existence and nature of God seemed to merge with a simpler, more existential question: Is the universe friendly? Although Niebuhr distinguished sharply between the realms of love, perfection, and God on the one hand and justice, reality, and man on the other, he tried with his theory of moral man and immoral society to place them along a single continuum. As King would paraphrase him in a student paper, "Justice is never discontinuously related to love. Justice is a negative application of love. . . . Justice is a check (by force, if necessary) upon ambitions of individuals seeking to overcome their own insecurity at the expense of others. Justice is love's message for the collective mind."

For King, another immediate attraction in Niebuhr's book was its tension. Niebuhr combined an evangelical liberal's passion for the Sermon on the Mount with a skeptic's insistence on the cussedness of human nature. While giving free rein to his own internal battle on these issues, Niebuhr saw far more promise in Gandhi than most religious liberals, and he honed the Gandhian method to its most defensible combination of religion and politics. Both the linkage and the tension appealed to King, whose own small world had been a blend of opposites—serenity and ambition, knowledge and zeal, church and state, Negro and white.

His most heartfelt speeches would always pit the sunny skies of justice against the midnight storms of oppression, in warring Augustinian phrases. Implicitly, a step toward or away from justice could affect his present judgment about whether the universe was friendly and therefore about the nature of God. Even as a student, King believed that religion was alive only at its edges, and that doubt was as important as belief. In a paper obviously influenced by Hegel and Niebuhr, King wrote that "if a position implies a negation, and a negation a position, then faith carries disbelief with it, theism, atheism, and if one member of the pair comes to be doubted the result may be disastrous to religion itself."

In later years, King never tried to stem the rivers of ink that described him as a Gandhian. Part of his acquiescence was a product of public relations, as he knew that within the American mass market there was a certain exotic comfort in the idea of a Gandhian Negro. King mentioned buying a half-dozen books about Gandhi in a single evening, but he never bothered to name or describe any of them. He almost never spoke of Gandhi personally, and his comments about Gandhism were never different than his thoughts about nonviolence in general. By contrast, he invoked Niebuhr in every one of his own major books, always with a sketch of *Moral Man and Immoral Society*. He confessed that he became "enamored" of Niebuhr, who "left me in a state of confusion."

"Niebuhr's great contribution to contemporary theology," King wrote, "is that he has refuted the false optimism characteristic of a great segment of Protestant liberalism, without falling into the anti-rationalism of the continental theologian Karl Barth, or the semi-fundamentalism of other dialectical theologians." This meant a great deal to King, but doubtless very little to most of his readers. He said little more in public. In private, however, he came to describe Niebuhr as a prime influence upon his life, and Gandhian nonviolence as "merely a Niebuhrian stratagem of power." King devoted much of his remaining graduate school career to the study of Niebuhr, who touched him on all his tender points, from pacifism and race to sin.

On November 25, 1950, three days after King took his final exam in American Church History 153 (in which he was asked to discuss the evangelical campaigns between 1500 and 1760 to spread Christianity among American Indians), the Communist Chinese Army entered the Korean War in mass wave attacks. This intervention raised fears that the conflict would spread into a new world war, only six years after Hitler's defeat, and in the United States the new Chinese enemy fueled a hatred of communism as a global, inhuman conspiracy. The Justice Department, apparently spurred by Secretary of State Dean Acheson's outrage over a peace petition drawn up in Sweden, obtained a criminal indictment against W. E. B. Du Bois for circulating the petition in the United States without having registered as an agent of the Soviet Union. *The New York Times* vaguely identified Du Bois as "an author widely known in connection with Negro movements," but the eighty-two-year-old founder of the NAACP and *The Crisis* was arraigned in handcuffs and faced trial more or less anonymously. Harry Belafonte—then an unknown New York actor of twenty-four, some two years older than King—was among those walking a scraggly picket line outside the courthouse. Belafonte had become enamored of Du Bois, and awakened to politics, by reading some of the Du Bois books that Negro sailors passed around during World War II. The Du Bois indictment pitched the NAACP into convulsions, even after a federal judge dismissed the case. Roy Wilkins straddled the issue by engineering one NAACP resolution condemning the indictment as an affront to Negroes, and others that warned Negroes of "so-called peace organizations" and empowered NAACP chapters to conduct internal purges against Communist infiltration.

Wars, conspiracies, and witch-hunts little affected the pace of student life at Crozer. Scott Enslin's teachings about the historical Jesus still shocked the incoming freshmen, who still pretended to be pool sharks as they brutalized the three tables under the chapel. One of the student leaders who helped them adjust to the Crozer atmosphere as it affected faith and recreation was M. L. King, who served that year as president of the student body. Mike and Mac still played pool until three o'clock on many mornings, often joined now by a new white friend named Snuffy. Professor Kenneth Lee "Snuffy" Smith, a Virginia Baptist, had just returned from graduate study at Duke to join the Crozer faculty. He was about McCall's age, just five years older than King, and so short that even King at five feet seven inches towered over him by half a foot. It was Smith who taught Niebuhr in one of his courses, and noticed the impact upon King. King wanted to read more Niebuhr, but the pace of his studies left him little time.

In the middle of the year, King grew fond of Professor Smith's steady girlfriend, Betty, the daughter of a German immigrant woman who served as the cook for the Crozer cafeteria. At first, the incipient competition between the two male friends—student and teacher, Negro and white—was absorbed in banter and professions of goodwill. After all, Smith had just returned from Duke on fire with the spirit of the Social Gospel, and the living of that creed ruled out jealousy. Nevertheless, an ugly tension deadened the camaraderie around the pool table soon after King openly began pursuing Betty. When he won her over, tempers flared.

King's friends nervously enjoyed the story of the seminary love triangle until he ruined it for them by turning serious. He said he had fallen in love, and that Betty was in love with him. Friends tried to make jokes about whose theological and racial liberalism was being most sorely tested—his, Smith's, or Betty's—but nothing worked. King was not laughing, and in time no one else was either. Making no secret of his distress over what to do, King asked for advice. Kirkland said bluntly that he should know better than to consort with the daughter of a mere cook, Negro or white. Marcus Wood cautioned him more diplomatically about the difficulties of finding a church that wanted a racially mixed family in the parsonage. Whitaker, older and perhaps wiser than the others, let King talk himself out. He listened as King resolved several times over the next few months to marry Betty, railing out in anger at the cruel and silly forces in life that were keeping two people from doing what they most wanted to do. Late one night, his clothes rumpled from an evening of romance on the campus grounds, King knocked on Whitaker's window, wanting to talk again. Whitaker led him through questions that were familiar by now, and King finally broke down. He could take whatever Daddy King might say, he told Whitaker, but he could not face the pain it would cause his mother.

King forced himself to retreat, and struggled against bitterness. Even as he did, a crude, literal trial of flesh and spirit threatened his best friend, Walter McCall, whose girlfriend charged him with bastardy. When all attempts to mollify her failed and it appeared that court could not be averted, a mortified McCall had to make a pained, confidential approach to a Crozer professor, asking him to testify that he was a seminary student in good standing, of such character and promise to the clergy as to make it extremely unlikely that he was the father of the child, or that he would abandon the child if he was. The professor so testified, and the court ruled in favor of McCall. The ethical ramifications of the case for McCall and for Crozer dictated that everything be handled as quietly and as delicately as possible. Snuffy Smith, among the few liberal professors who knew of it, seized on the not-guilty verdict, believing that it cleared everyone. Inasmuch as McCall all but acknowledged paternity in a later letter to King, however, the verdict may have meant, on the contrary, that Crozer's reputation for religious authority helped convince the court of a lie, thereby allowing McCall to escape his responsibilities to the woman and to his child.

This sort of morally radioactive situation has always given religious institutions a powerful incentive to seek quiet, private solutions in matters of sex and the clergy. When race is added as a third factor—as it was in this case by the fear that a McCall scandal would give ammunition to those who opposed Crozer's recruitment of Negro students—the combination becomes so unbearably sensitive that discretion and hypocrisy govern almost instinctively. Historically, such avoidance would help explain how some four million mulattoes came into being in the United States with practically no recorded cases of legal or ecclesiastical disgrace ever attached to members of the dominant white culture.

At Crozer, King came hard to the judgment that the price of a mixed marriage was higher than he was willing to pay for the love of one woman or the dream of the beloved community. He knew that the responsible course was to follow the unwritten family guidelines of the profession: that a minister must marry, that he must marry sooner rather than later, that his choice of a wife was important not only personally but also as it would affect his career, and that he must look for certain objective qualities in prospective mates. Among Negro ministers—who enjoyed enormous advantages over their white counterparts because of the preacher's greater prestige within the culture, and also because of a relative plenitude of female peers—the selection process seemed elevated at times to a minor affair of state. An underlying sense of urgency strained against a host of practical calculations that were almost political in nature. King told Whitaker he would be married by the end of his first year out of Crozer, even though at the time he had not settled on the bride.

In the summer of 1951, Reverend King was less happy with his son's decision to seek a doctorate than he had been three years earlier with his desire to go to Crozer. Seminarians might be overeducated to Daddy King's way of thinking, but at least they tended to preach in a church, whereas Ph.D.'s tended to teach in a university. This indeed was young King's plan. "For a number of years I have been desirous of teaching in a college or a school of religion," he wrote in his application to Boston University. "The teaching of theology should be as scientific, as thorough, and as realistic as any other discipline. In a word, scholarship is my goal." Reverend King pressed all his objections to the fullest but, as always, relented when young King insisted that he needed further learning. Then the father circled from surrender to generosity, agreeing to pay all his son's expenses in graduate school. He also gave him a new green Chevrolet for finishing at the top of his Crozer class. The Chevy had "Power Glide," just like Horace Whitaker's car that King admired so much.

It helped somewhat that King decided to pursue his doctorate at Boston University instead of Edinburgh. The decisive factor was the presence at Boston of Edgar S. Brightman, who for years had been the leading exponent of a school of theology known as Personalism. King's adviser at

Crozer, George W. Davis, was a follower of Brightman, as were many other Crozer professors. Even Enslin respected him highly as a religious philosopher. Brightman's school harked back to the intensely personal God of the Jewish scriptures and to early Christian theologians such as Augustine, who sometimes described God using only a long list of human emotions, modified to remove any objectionable qualities and raised to infinite strength. Led by Brightman, the Personalists had been defending themselves against the drift of theology. Religion, like everything else in the modern age, was succumbing to its envy of science. Most of the advanced schools of theology, feeling less adequate in a time of science's empirical miracles and permanent, mathematical truths, protected themselves with scaled-down promises and vague imitations of the scientific method. Karl Barth called God the "wholly Other." Tillich was defining God with his own intricately technical language of symbolism. Henry Nelson Wieman, whom King would compare with Tillich in his Ph.D. dissertation, called God "that something upon which human life is most dependent . . . that something of supreme value which constitutes the most important condition." Even Niebuhr told an audience at Yale that Jesus was "a revelation of the mystery of self and of the ultimate mystery of existence." Theology, which had once ruled all science as well as all being, was resorting to more and more elaborate shrugs. King himself shared this propensity to vagueness on the crucial questions, but, in much the same way that a doubting preacher fell back from the afterlife to morality, he embraced Personalism's teaching that there was rich, empirical meaning in religious experience.

In September 1951, King packed the green Chevrolet for the long drive from Atlanta to Boston. The Korean War was in prolonged, bloody stalemate. President Truman had just appeared in the first coast-to-coast television broadcast, addressing the Japanese Peace Treaty Conference in San Francisco. Willie Mays was finishing his first season with the New York Giants, and the telephone company was preparing to introduce direct long-distance dialing in New Jersey. On his way north, King stopped in Brooklyn to preach a guest sermon at Gardner Taylor's Concord Baptist Church, which was competing with Adam Clayton Powell's Abyssinian Baptist of Harlem for the distinction of being the largest Protestant congregation in the United States. Guest appearances in Taylor's pulpit were hotly coveted by Negro preachers of any denomination. The honor came to King when he was only twenty-two, on the strength of his preaching reputation and his father's connections to Taylor as a fellow power in the National Baptist Convention.

Two days after his Brooklyn sermon, listening to his first Boston University lecture by the master, Edgar S. Brightman, King scribbled across

the top page of his notebook: "Hartfort Luccock says that the only proof
of immortality is 'a life worth preserving.' " To the formal Brightman,
this amounted to nothing more than a crackerbarrel quip, but King liked
it. He also liked Brightman, and would take ten of his fifteen Ph.D.
courses from him or his main Personalist protégé on the faculty, L. Harold DeWolf. King almost immediately established a personal bond with
Professor DeWolf, a kindly Nebraskan who remained active in the Methodist Church. Before Christmas, DeWolf returned the first of many papers King would write for him, this one entitled "The Personalism of
J. M. E. McTaggart Under Criticism." It earned an A and the comment
"excellent, incisive criticism, a superior paper." King quickly became
one of his favorite students.

At Boston, the collegial atmosphere of a small seminary like Crozer
was gone, replaced by the mass bustle of a large urban university. Graduate students often moved in a tireless circuit between class, library,
apartment, and off-campus job. Weyman McLaughlin, the Negro student
of systematic theology considered closest to King in scholarship ability,
worked evenings as a skycap at Logan Airport. He studied late at night
by the light inside his closet, so as not to wake his apartment mates.

King continued to wear tailored suits whenever he stepped out of his
apartment, and he worked consciously to develop habits befitting an
intellectual. Doodling on the back of a notebook, he practiced increasingly ornate signatures, until the "g" in King looped all the way back to
the "M" in Martin. Like many of the other students, he tamped, smoked,
and fiddled with a pipe almost constantly, spoke with an air of detached
reserve, and developed the far-off look of a philosopher. Technically, King
was a philosopher, as he was registered in the philosophy department
and planned to seek his degree in the philosophy of religion.

He took no preaching courses at all, as Crozer had taken him beyond
the classroom, but he kept up a lively correspondence on advanced pulpit
tradecraft, sometimes complete with stage directions. " In the sermon I
used the silent conclusion," a friend wrote King in 1952, "and it seemed
to be quite effective. I used an illustration and when I concluded appeared
as if I was to continue[,] then abruptly, 'Let us pray.' " On his own, King
began to create a repertoire of written sermons. Several of his earliest
models were inspired by classroom ideas, which he expanded by adding
his own illustrations and spiritual twists within one of the classical
sermon structures taught by Keighton. From Spinoza's epistemological
theory that there are three levels to knowledge, which can be related to
three levels of moral life, King wrote a sermon entitled "The Three
Dimensions of a Complete Life," which he would use throughout his
career. Another of his standard sermons, "What Is Man?", was inspired

by his study of the complete works of Niebuhr during his first year at Boston. Niebuhr also inspired "The Answer to a Perplexing Question," a sermon on the persistence of evil.

King himself fostered much of what passed for social life among roughly a score of Negro graduate students at Boston University, by organizing what was called the Dialectical Society or Philosophical Club. Graduate students interested in philosophy or religion gathered one evening a week to share a potluck supper and a rarefied discussion about God or knowledge. One student read a formal paper, and the others then jumped in to criticize or support it. The club lasted throughout King's student life in Boston, becoming so popular that white students dropped in occasionally and Professor DeWolf once delivered the paper for discussion. A rather stiff decorum prevailed early in the evening, as pipe smoke and abstract jargon mingled in the air, but the hard core of participants usually settled into a bull session late at night.

"Well, I had a big funeral last weekend," King announced during one of the meetings. "We buried Jim."

"Jim who?" someone asked.

"Jim Crow," King replied.

Laughter broke out as the others realized King was joking about the slang name for segregation. "Yeah, we did Jim up real good," King drawled. "We put him to rest."

George Thomas was one of a tiny minority of Negro students who lost interest in the Dialectical Society precisely because Jim Crow and other political matters were relegated to the joke period. With Douglas Moore, his only steadfast ally among the Negro graduate students, Thomas organized what they called "spiritual cell movements" to further the cause of world peace. They fasted together against the Korean War, denounced the atomic bomb at campus rallies, and drove to New York to march against Franco's Spain. In later years, Moore became a mentor of the Southern student sit-in movement. At Boston, he and Thomas occasionally landed a fellow divinity student for an attempt to integrate a clerks' union at Sears or for a protest against McCarthyism, but they never landed King himself. He remained aloof, absorbed in course work. At the Dialectical Society, discussions of politics were largely confined to the issue of whether it was wise for them to choose "race-related" topics for papers, theses, and doctoral dissertations. King concurred with the general consensus that to do so might cheapen their work in the eyes of influential Negroes as well as whites. That was realism. The mainstream Negro students considered activists like Thomas and Moore somewhat "up in the clouds," as one of them wrote King, adding that "the world is not going to be converted overnight." King left virtually no references to race or politics among his student papers at Boston University. He took some courses from professors who were known as crusaders for racial justice, such as Alan Knight Chalmers and Walter Muelder, but he did most of his work with sympathetic non-activists like DeWolf.

Students who visited King at his apartment on Massachusetts Avenue, across from the Savoy Ballroom, usually found him surrounded by a stack of books four feet high. Roommate Philip Lenud, a friend from Morehouse, did the cooking; King washed the dishes. Visitors came to learn that King thought nothing of phoning home and talking for two or three hours at a time—always with the long-distance charges reversed, always with his mother. King told her about everything—his friends and professors, bank overdrafts, lost silverware, preaching assignments, clothes, Dialectical Society meetings, food problems, and girlfriends. Almost always, the conversation worked its way to the subject of courtship, as this was a prime concern not only of mother and son but also of Reverend King, who made no secret of his desire to see his son married soon. He had been uneasy since the previous summer of 1951, when the romance with Juanita Sellers inexplicably had failed to mature.

King was doing his best to marry. He and Philip Lenud double-dated frequently, and King met other possibilities in the churches where he preached. He had long since invented a coded rating system for eligible women, calling an attractive woman a "doctor" and a stunning one a "constitution," saying that she was "well-established and amply endowed." Along with the other Negro students, he was keenly interested in the drama of one student who was "passing" for white at BU. They admired, castigated, and laughed at her endlessly—but always keeping a safe distance, as no one really wanted responsibility for exposing her gambit. Otherwise, King's bachelor style fit the postwar fashion. He elbowed his male friends in the ribs if a "constitution" went by, collected phone numbers, and began each contact with a promising new lady by trying out his lines. Early in 1952, he called a woman blindly on the recommendation of a friend. After passing along a few of the friend's compliments as reasons why he had obtained the phone number, King threw out his opening line. "You know every Napoleon has his Waterloo," he said. "I'm like Napoleon. I'm at my Waterloo, and I'm on my knees."

"That's absurd," Coretta Scott replied. "You don't even know me."

Unabashed, King continued with the melodrama and poetry, throwing in some comments about his course work that identified him quickly as a man of substance. His come-on crisscrossed between directness and caricature, authority and humor. When Scott did not hang up on him after his opening flourishes, it was only a matter of minutes until he persuaded her to have lunch with him the next day. He picked her up in his Chevrolet and took her to a cafeteria. There he learned that she had grown up on a farm in rural Alabama, daughter of a man who feared whites but who did not shrink from building a fine house with his own hands. By strength and perseverance, Obadiah Scott had accumulated several hundred acres, placing him among the elite yeomen of the poor Negro farmers. His daughters had picked cotton in the fields and scrubbed clothes in a washtub, but they had acquired enough of the family grit to seek their education at a private school in a nearby town, which had been established by Congregationalist missionaries after the Civil War and run ever since as a church school. From there, Coretta Scott had followed her older sister north to Antioch College, and after graduation she had come to Boston's New England Conservatory of Music on a small scholarship.

She aspired to become a classical singer, but her prospects were uncertain at best. Even if she possessed the rare talent to make the great leap between the level of a good church soloist and that of a full-time professional, she lacked the financial backing to give her career much of a start. She survived by working alongside the Irish maids at a fashionable Beacon Hill boardinghouse in exchange for room and board. Thus far, her college degree, her social connections among cultured Negroes, and her ladylike comportment—which she could stretch at will into the regal posture of a diva—had brought her little more than the chance to starve at one of the most fashionable addresses in Boston. Suffering from the compounded insecurities of race, poverty, and the competitive world of music, Scott struggled to keep her dignity and her optimism above her acute sense of realism. "The next man I give my photograph to is going to be my husband," she told herself. Nearly two years older than King, she would turn twenty-five that spring and was already past the prime marrying age of that era. In the absence of a career break or a prosperous suitor, she would soon be obliged to scale back her ambitions.

King knew all this. It would become one of his stinging jokes to tease her with the remark that she would have wound up picking cotton back in Alabama had he not come along. At their first lunch, however, he praised her looks, especially her long bangs, and launched into discussion of topics from soul food to Rauschenbusch. To Coretta Scott, who had been put off at first sight by King's lack of height, he seemed to grow as he talked. As he drove her back to the Conservatory, he shocked her again by declaring that she would make him a good wife. "The four things that I look for in a wife are character, intelligence, personality, and beauty," he told her. "And you have them all. I want to see you again." She replied unsteadily that she would have to check her schedule.

Their courtship became an odd mixture of romance and pragmatism. King spoke in poetic cadences and treated her to elegant evenings of concerts and theater, but he made no secret of the fact that he was consciously selecting a wife and that she and the other women under consideration had to meet certain conditions. With the help of her older sister, Coretta cooked a meal in the King-Lenud apartment that King said "passed" his cooking test. She replied in the affirmative when he asked whether she could bring herself, as a preacher's wife, to treat the uneducated "Aunt Janes" of a Negro Baptist congregation without condescension. Unexpectedly, she met another test when King asked her to detour through Atlanta that summer to visit him at his home. When she replied offhandedly that she probably would not come, King exploded. "Forget it," he told her. "Forget the whole thing." Unlike Juanita Sellers, who had defied King in a similar dispute, Scott reconsidered under the pressure.

She arrived in Atlanta that August, a few weeks after the Republican Party nominated Dwight D. Eisenhower for President at its Chicago convention—the first ever to be televised. Her first exposure to King's world —the big church, big house, big city, the elite Negro social clubs and powerful connections—intimidated her. She thought Mrs. King treated her coolly, and Reverend King practically ignored her. To the master of Ebenezer, she was merely another of his son's many girlfriends, and a country girl to boot. Anyone could claim to be a concert singer, but very few had much to show for it. Reverend King's aloofness did not surprise her, because she already knew from M.L. and from her Atlanta confidants that the patriarch was determined that his son marry into one of the socially prominent West Side families. She had even heard that M.L. would not be allowed to make such a strategically important choice on his own, that the "final decision" lay with Daddy King. All this was unnerving enough as a rumor, but the reality of meeting the King family was worse—so imposing and yet so friendly, so polite and yet so cold. Not surprisingly, she found that the most human and endearing member of the King world was her boyfriend himself.

Back in Boston, King showed signs of having his mind on things other than his studies. One of his first philosophy papers that fall came back with a grade of D+ and covered with acidic comments from the professor, such as "let's not get wordy," "obviously," and "why?", with circles drawn around numerous grammatical errors. Recovering, King earned three consecutive A's from the same professor on papers about Descartes, William James, and Mahayana Buddhism. Then, almost as if there were a plan to keep him off balance, old friends descended upon him with worries about his prolonged bachelorhood. His old Crozer friend Horace "Whit" Whitaker chided him in a letter for failing to meet the marriage deadline he had set for himself two years earlier. Whitaker guessed that "one-time wreckers" were still distracting King. A few weeks later, King received a letter from W. T. Handy, Jr., a future Methodist bishop who had left Boston University after King's first year. "I know you are still galivanting [sic] around Boston, the most eligible and popular bachelor in town," Handy wrote. "I wonder how you are progressing with my steadying influence gone. Remember M.L., 'we are expecting great things from you.' The only element to restrain our expectations from bearing fruit will be M.L. himself. However I know that he will not allow himself or influences to bring failure about him or embarrasment [sic] to his beloved Father and Mother."

King's parents visited Boston that fall. Now that their son was calling home less frequently, and after the summer visit from Coretta Scott, they were distressed enough to seek some answers in person. Both elder Kings immediately noticed the tidiness of the apartment on Massachusetts Avenue, and, knowing neatness to be uncharacteristic of either their son or Philip Lenud, they attributed it to a feminine presence. Their suspicions focused all the more on Coretta Scott, who seemed to be with their son constantly. Reverend King, with his customary bluntness, began asking M.L. about the status of his other girlfriends in her presence, calling them by name. M.L. shrugged them off one by one, but he did not respond to the challenge with a profession of interest in Coretta. Satisfied to have her there among them during teas and meals, he had no wish to press the challenge further. Reverend King did. When he could elicit no statement of intention from his son, he bored in directly on Coretta. He suggested that the career she planned in secular music was hardly fitting for the prospective wife of a Baptist minister. When she said nothing, he switched to a jovial mood and said he figured her romance with M.L. was just a college infatuation anyway, and probably would not last out the year. Again, she did not respond.

Reverend King abruptly shifted to his Jehovah voice: "Let me ask you very directly. Do you take my son seriously, Coretta?"

Utterly nonplussed, she tried to make a joke of it. "Why, no, Reverend King," she said. "Not really."

At last he had forced his opening. Good, he said, and he went on to make himself plain in a thunderstorm of words. He was glad Coretta had no serious designs on his son, because the elder Kings knew for a fact that he had already proposed marriage to a number of women in Atlanta and elsewhere. He named some of them. Coretta was merely another one. The elder Kings had not yet given their permission for him to marry, and when they did, the bride would be someone better suited to him than was Coretta Scott. "M.L. has gone out with the daughters of some fine, solid Atlanta families," said Daddy King. "Folks we've known for many years, people we respect, and whose feelings we'd never trample on. I'm talking, Coretta, about people who have much to share and much to offer."

This outburst was more than Scott could bear. "*I* have something to offer, too," she interjected defiantly.

Daddy King, giving no sign that her flash of anger had impressed him, continued with a glowing description of Juanita Sellers. "We love that girl," he said. "I don't know what M.L. is going to decide. But I'm glad to hear you say you don't take him seriously, because unless you know my son better than I do, I would advise you not to."

All this time M.L. said nothing, much to Scott's dismay. He drew his mother into another room and told her that he planned to marry the woman his father had just blistered unmercifully. He knew the message would get through. He told Coretta so as he drove her home. The news consoled her, but King wounded her in the next breath by criticizing her for having failed to make a good impression on his father.

Mrs. King's message worked on her husband's nerves. Later during their visit, he was trying to endure polite conversation among the four of them when suddenly it became too much for him. Without warning, he slammed his fist on the table, terrifying the others. "You-all are courting too hard!" he shouted. "What's this doing to your studies?"

This shook the words out of his son. "I'm going to get my doctorate," he said quietly. "And then I'm going to marry Coretta."

A moment later, Daddy King slammed the table again. "Now you two had better get married!" he commanded, as though he had just conceived of the idea himself.

A few weeks after King achieved the painful marriage truce with his father, Professor DeWolf lectured for six hours on the theology of Augustine, the North African bishop who, after nearly thirty years of ribald womanizing, became the first great genius of comprehensive Christian theology. Augustine had made Christianity at least as respectable philosophically as Manicheanism, Neo-Platonism, and astrology, its chief rivals among Mediterranean intellectuals in the early fifth century A.D. His doctrines of church authority helped the Vatican survive the Middle Ages, the eight hundred years that followed the destruction of the Roman Empire. In a January examination, DeWolf asked his class to explain

Augustine's complex theory of evil, in which the great saint sought to reconcile God's authority over evil with His infinite benevolence. "The problem of evil baffles the theist, not the atheist, " King began. His essay received an A.

King composed an outline for a sermon entitled "How a Christian Overcomes Evil." It was a Ladder Sermon of three ascending steps, each divided into parts. "The first step in overcoming evil is to discover what is worst in us," he wrote, going on to specify the evil in unorthodox fashion as "that sin to which we are most frequently tempted." This he followed with a call for honesty with oneself, using language overlaid with so many psychological turns as to render it opaque: "The hidden fault must be called by its right name, otherwise we miss seeing our pride under fear of an inferiority complex." After a second step on using God's grace to begin combat with the evil, King came to his crucial third step: "Concentrate not on the eradication of evil, but on the cultivation of virtue." By way of illustration, he contrasted the technique of Ulysses, who fought the temptation of the sirens by putting wax in the ears of his sailors and by strapping himself to the mast of his ship, with that of Orpheus, who resisted those same sirens by playing his harp so beautifully as to make the siren song seem unappealing. King recommended the approach of Orpheus. "Evil is not driven out, but crowded out," he concluded. "Sensuality is not mastered by saying: 'I will not sin,' but through the expulsive power of something good." Only in this final sentence did King introduce sensuality as the specific sin to which he was directing his method.

His focus on sensuality added to the mystery of the difficult sentence he wrote about the need for honesty to overcome evil. In that context, "fear of an inferiority complex" could mean fear of being unmasculine, of being unloved, and King could have been warning that such an obsession would lead people to overlook their own pride of conquest. For Augustine, as well as for Niebuhr and Martin Luther and most other theologians of note, human pride was the principal door to sin, including sexual ones. Alternatively, King could have been referring to an inferiority complex in the more common usage of the time, meaning racial inferiority—warning that such a handicap in a Negro could make him blind to his own racial pride, or to the pride that lies beneath all considerations of race. Or, finally, he could have meant some combination of sensuality and race, as they merge into powerful interior forces. In any case, numerous logical pitfalls worked against King's formula for combatting such sins. If the harp of Orpheus played the same kind of music as did the alluring sirens, only better, then, King implied, virtue and sensuality were of the same nature. By setting good and evil in a kind of competition, rather than in opposition, King changed the nature of the contest from a tug-of-war into a race. The two forces might move side by side, covering much the same ground, and thus would be in danger of becoming indistinguishable. Perhaps because of the obvious flaws in his formula, King never expanded his outline for "How a Christian Overcomes Evil" into a complete sermon. It remained among his papers as an unfinished outline.

Professor Brightman died that April after a long illness, leaving King without a faculty adviser. Soon afterward, he shifted his registration from the graduate school's philosophy department to the School of Theology, and with DeWolf as his new adviser sought to finish his Ph.D. course work within one more school year. He had to petition the faculty to allow him to take a heavy course load pending success on a second round of the required German-language competency test. While King struggled with his German, the outside world rushed through what the movie newsreels would call a "Year of Change." Stalin died in March. England celebrated the coronation of Queen Elizabeth in June. Eisenhower, the new President, felt so optimistic about the prospects for a truce in Korea that he restored the traditional Easter egg roll for children on the White House lawn. Ethel and Julius Rosenberg, convicted of giving atomic secrets to the Soviet Union, were executed at Sing Sing on June 19, the day after King's wedding.

King had kept up the meetings of the Dialectical Society through the spring of his engagement. In the bull sessions, he endured more than his share of ribbing for having agreed to submit to the harness of matrimony. It made him stiffer, they said, and several of them grumbled among themselves that Coretta Scott was too "bourgie," their word for "bourgeois." Coming from a self-constituted assembly of dialecticians, this criticism was audacious in the extreme, but some of them sensed that she was different. When King's friends relaxed after their exertions, they preferred women who would jitterbug with them, as had most of his other girlfriends. Scott refused to do so. Her idea of music was strictly classical. When performing, her tastes ran to hoop-skirted formal gowns, and she clasped her hands in front of her at shoulder level, gazing as far off into the clouds as any philosopher. Such affectations provoked some of King's colleagues at Boston University to think of her as one who "tried too hard," and to some degree her manner would injure King's future relations with earthy friends like Walter McCall. There was, however, some countervailing opinion within the male caucus. King's friends considered her an intelligent, strong-willed woman, skilled in the social graces, "not down with it, but no dummy." She had a gift for remembering names, always put newcomers at ease, and never failed to be polite

—all of which would serve her well as the wife of a minister. Moreover, she was ambitious and fiercely loyal.

Most of these traits came into play on her wedding day, June 18, 1953. She had planned to have a small private ceremony in the front yard of her parents' home, not far from Selma, but wound up with what she called the largest wedding in the history of those parts. She fretted intensely that the urbane King clan would look down on her solid country folk as mere farmhands, but at the same time she did not want to appear to be trying to impress them. This was more than enough to knot the stomach of any bride, and Reverend King did not help her nerves by sweeping her and the bridegroom off for a private talk just before the ceremony. It was not too late to back out, he said, strongly advising them not to go through with the ceremony unless they simply could not help it. "I preach because I can't help myself," Reverend King declared, "and when you get married you should think of it like that, as something you are impelled to do. Think about this for a few moments and decide if this is the way you feel." Scott persevered through this bizarre speech and through the bollixed details common to most weddings. Years ahead of her time, she wanted the promise to obey her husband removed from the wedding vows as inequitable, and she was strong enough to get Reverend King to agree. When the reception was finally over and the newlyweds were allowed to escape, King fell exhausted into sleep and she did the driving. Because resorts, motels, and hotels in Alabama were prohibited by law from serving Negroes, they were obliged to spend their wedding night at the closest thing to a public accommodation within reach of Negroes—a funeral parlor, owned by a friend of the Scott family.

Fully within the King tradition, Coretta Scott King found herself swept immediately into the world of her in-laws. Reverend King baptized her at Ebenezer on the Sunday following the wedding. She and her husband lived in the King home on Boulevard for the remainder of the summer, and Daddy King arranged a teller's job for her at the Citizens Trust Bank, of which he was a director. At summer's end, the entire family went to Miami for a historic meeting of the National Baptist Convention. President D. V. Jemison, who had ruled the convention for years without serious opposition, even though he had gone blind and had to be led around by the hand, was retiring on the inducement of a large cash settlement and a special pension. There was much excitement among the preachers over the prospect of a new election. Daddy King's old Atlanta rival, William Holmes Borders, was running on a ticket headed by Jemison's vice president and likely successor, but a strong challenge was mounted by Rev. J. H. Jackson, the renowned orator and friend of Daddy King, who in 1939 had broken Atlanta's color barrier before a mass audience of the World Baptist Alliance. In a spirited campaign, Jackson mobilized the younger preachers by engineering an anti-dictatorial amendment to the NBC constitution, prohibiting self-succession by the president. Daddy King was a floor manager of Jackson, and young King served as a lieutenant. Joel King came down from his new church in Michigan. Most of King's Negro classmates from Crozer attended, as did some ten thousand other preachers from churches great and small. They would all remember the wild insurgency that elected J. H. Jackson and how they "stayed up all night" to do it, standing on chairs, waving brooms to sweep out the older order.

After the convention, Coretta Scott King accompanied her husband as he preached his way north to Boston, stopping in Washington and Baltimore for guest sermons. Once settled in their new apartment, King resumed discussions with Professor DeWolf about the Ph.D. dissertation he would write after a final year of course work. In the end, King selected a topic—comparing Paul Tillich's idea of God with that of Henry Nelson Wieman—that promised credit without substantial risk. Tillich and Wieman led two rival schools at the pinnacle of liberal Protestant theology—Union Seminary and the University of Chicago, respectively—but in the sense most fundamental to DeWolf and King, their ideas of God were virtually identical. Both Tillich and Wieman were Transcendentalists, as opposed to Personalists. To King, therefore, the conclusion of his dissertation was never in doubt: he would criticize both Tillich and Wieman for having ideas of God that were too arid, speculative, and cerebral to answer human yearnings in the province of religion. His dissertation would be an academic exercise for the most part, born of a tactical choice to use Personalism as a tool of criticism rather than a subject. Although DeWolf pressed him at times to spell out his Personalism against all the standard tests of theology, King was wise enough to know that Personalism was better as a creed than as a system.

King wrote to Tillich, asking whether he knew of other dissertations on the subject King proposed. Tillich replied from sabbatical in Switzerland on September 22, saying that he knew of none. "PS," he added, "I am very much interested." Later that year, for some reason, King put the same question to Niebuhr, whose secretary answered for him in the negative. Inasmuch as King already had his protocol clearance from Tillich himself, and as his topic had nothing to do with Niebuhr's work, it appears that King wrote this second letter solely out of respect for Niebuhr.

While in correspondence with the masters of theology over his dissertation, King put out feelers to his contacts on the faculties of Negro colleges, where Morehouse men were heavily represented. On the church side, he already knew which major Baptist pulpits were vacant across the country. That winter, he allotted one month for a job-hunting trip to the South. He planned to talk with Dr. Mays about a possible teaching post at Morehouse, visit other colleges, and preach wherever he could get into a vacant pulpit that interested him. Through his friend Melvin Watson, he obtained an invitation to preach a trial sermon at the First Baptist Church of Chattanooga, Tennessee, and he scheduled a sermon at the chapel of Alabama State College in Montgomery, whose dean was a Morehouse man. All the while, he would work on his father, slowly and deliberately, to make him see that it was best for the son to go out on his own rather than to Ebenezer. With these plans made, and the new Mrs. King left behind in Boston, he set out on December 18 with a fellow member of the Dialectical Society. On the drive south, King talked apprehensively about First Baptist of Chattanooga. It had a reputation as a fastidious congregation, and had recently sent a friend of theirs packing without explanation after what the friend thought was a brilliant trial sermon.

Just before the new year, Tuskegee Institute announced that it was ceasing publication of its annual Lynching Letter, which the college had issued every year since 1912. There had been no reported lynchings in the United States for the past two years, said the announcement, and only six since 1949. Henceforth, Tuskegee would report each year on Negro jobs and income figures instead of lynchings. When the news came out, King was in Atlanta, preparing to preach his trial sermon in Chattanooga on January 3. One of his father's insurance friends called to make sure he would be at the house for a while, to meet someone about a church matter. King agreed, and was sitting over an afternoon plate of pork chops when Reverend King escorted R. D. Nesbitt into the kitchen. Nesbitt knew none of the Kings, nor they him. He was wearing an expensive business suit with wide dress suspenders and carrying a briefcase. Making his introductions, he advised King that he had been recommended as a possible new pastor for the Dexter Avenue Baptist Church in Montgomery, of whose pulpit selection committee Nesbitt was chairman.

Although King knew that Dexter was vacant because of the troubled departure of Vernon Johns, he had made no scouting effort toward the church—probably because he considered it too small. He thanked Nesbitt but put him off, saying that he had already promised to give his answer to First Baptist of Chattanooga when he visited there the next Sunday, which was long before he could possibly have a trial at Dexter.

"Well, Brother King, I'm an old Baptist man," said Nesbitt. "I've been in this before. If they want you, they will wait for you. You do not have to give them an answer Sunday when you go there, and I would love for you not to until you have preached to Dexter."

Reverend King's unhappiness over the recruitment attempt moved him to interrupt. "You don't want to go to Dexter, M.L.," he said. "That's a *big* nigger's church." He called off the names of several influential Dexter members who had reputations for making a preacher's life miserable.

Nesbitt, eyeing the senior King warily, replied that several of the members he mentioned were already dead, and that the church had a reputation for attracting some of the finest preachers in the country.

King looked up from his pork chops, making his calculations. He was already committed to preach in Montgomery on the afternoon of January 17. To preach at Dexter that morning could do no harm. If he decided to take the job in Chattanooga before then, he could simply say so. He told Nesbitt that he could preach a trial sermon at Dexter on the morning of the seventeenth, if that was convenient.

By Saturday, January sixteenth, all that had changed was King's assessment of his prospects in Chattanooga. He had received fulsome praise but no concrete offer. He was waiting to hear further from the church, but his instincts told him his chances had already expired. His mind was on other possibilities, and on Tillich and Wieman.

A phone call came to him at the house. "Young King," rasped a scratchy voice, "this is Vernon Johns. I hear you're going to preach at my former church in Montgomery tomorrow. I'm supposed to preach myself at First Baptist, but I'm sort of stranded here in Atlanta. You think I could hitch a ride over to Montgomery with you?"

"It would be an honor, Dr. Johns," King replied. "Where are you?"

"I'm downtown at the bus station."

"Well, you wait right there, Dr. Johns. I'm leaving in a few minutes, and I'll pick you up on the way out of town."

FOUR

FIRST TROMBONE

Take him, Lord—this morning—
Wash him with hyssop inside and out,
Hang him up and drain him dry of sin.
Pin his ear to the wisdom post,
And make his words sledge hammers of truth—
Beating on the iron heart of sin.
Lord God, this morning—
Put his eye to the telescope of eternity,
And let him look upon the paper walls of time.
Lord, turpentine his imagination,
Put perpetual motion in his arms,
Fill him full of the dynamite of thy power,
Anoint him all over with the oil of thy salvation,
And set his tongue on fire.

JAMES WELDON JOHNSON, *GOD'S TROMBONES*

King collected the legendary old man and set out on the four-hour drive to Montgomery. It was a cold day, but the farmland of central Georgia and Alabama looked beautiful to both of them, especially to Johns the farmer. King tuned the radio to a Metropolitan Opera performance of Donizetti's *Lucia di Lammermoor,* one of his favorite operas. Arriving in Montgomery late in the afternoon, King dropped Johns off at the parsonage of the First Baptist Church, where he would be staying with the family of the pastor, Ralph Abernathy. King knew Abernathy only vaguely from Baptist conventions and from student gatherings in Atlanta, but he perceived immediately that Johns was no stranger to the Abernathys, who embraced and fussed over him like their long-lost uncle. Johns sniffed the air and drew himself up in delight. "Juanita, bless you," he said to Abernathy's wife. "I believe you are making the prophet's dinner for me. Is it ready?"

"Yes, Dr. Johns. I have it," she replied.

"Well then, young King, I thank you," said Johns, bowing hastily to King. "I have something very important to do." He proceeded directly to his customary seat at the dining table.

The Abernathys pressed King to join them for the meal. "Well, thank you, but Dr. Brooks has prepared a meal for me at his house," said King. Then he hesitated. The prophet's dinner, having baked and simmered most of the day, had saturated the parsonage with the aroma of steak and onions, turnip greens and cornbread, and a dozen kindred delights. "I *believe* Mrs. Brooks has prepared something," said King, less sure. "But, Lord, that food is smelling so good. Well, I believe I will join you, if you don't mind." Laughing, he was shown to a seat next to Johns.

The two preachers praised Juanita Abernathy's handiwork lavishly as they consumed it, and the gregarious Abernathy played host. "Brother King, I want to assure you of something," he said. "Everybody at Dexter had been mad at me this week, because they think I invited Dr. Johns here just to conflict with your trial sermon. They're all talking about how the promising young Ph.D. from Boston is coming to Dexter, and now Abernathy is trying to cut into his audience by putting Johns into First Baptist on the same Sunday. Well, it's not true. In the first place, I didn't know you were coming. In the second place, I didn't invite Dr. Johns to preach. He sent me a letter saying he was coming through here on his way to New Orleans, and he would be pleased to preach for me. And I said I would be honored to have him in my pulpit, which I always am. Isn't that right, Dr. Johns?"

Johns said it was. He told King not to worry about the Johns loyalists who would worship at First Baptist instead of Dexter in the morning, because the "important" Dexter members, who he said were also the "mean" ones, would be in King's audience, not Johns's, and they were the ones King would have to win over. Johns said that he did not envy King. "If you take my church and a nigra named Randall is still there on the Board, you'd better be very careful," he advised.

This prompted Abernathy to introduce one of his favorite subjects—the differences between the Dexter and First Baptist congregations. "I describe it like this, Brother King," he said grandly. "And I know Dr. Johns agrees, because I heard him say it first. At my church, you may talk about Jesus. You may preach about Jesus from the pulpit. But at Dexter, they would prefer that you not mention his name."

The preachers began to laugh. "They would prefer that you talk about Plato or Socrates or somebody like that," Abernathy continued. "And if you just *have* to mention Jesus, they would like you to do it just as quietly and briefly as possible. Isn't that right, Dr. Johns?"

"That's true," said Johns, "but it doesn't mean they know the first thing about Plato."

"That's right," said Abernathy. "Now in my pulpit, you can talk all you want to about Jesus, but you will be the only one preaching. The congregation is not going to help you out. Very rarely will anyone say anything at First Baptist, any more than at Dexter. Ever since old Reverend Stokes ran the church, the preacher preaches and the congregation listens. If one of his guest preachers started whooping or hacking or zoning, Stokes would jump up and interrupt him: 'Don't take my people backward.' That's what he'd say. The same as Dexter. Isn't that right, Dr. Johns?"

Johns agreed, although he probably thought Abernathy, in his eagerness to portray the two churches as twin sisters of the aristocracy, exaggerated the refinement of his own congregation. Most Dexter members thought of First Baptist as a "shouting" congregation, pure and simple.

Abernathy launched into a series of stories whose purpose was to flatter Johns and to provoke him to recitation. He told, for instance, of the ghosts at the two churches—of Dr. Adair's murder of his wife and of the murder inside First Baptist during a power struggle after old D. V. Jemison had defeated the home pastor, Reverend Stokes, in elections of the National Baptist Convention. He told how Johns had scandalized Dexter by interrupting the wedding service of the daughter of Montgomery's most prominent Negro physician to announce that he and Abernathy would be selling watermelons during the reception. He told the full story of Johns's "It Is Safe to Murder Negroes" sermon, and recalled first hearing Johns about six years earlier, when he was a student at Alabama State College and Johns was the new pastor at Dexter. Even as a loyal member of First Baptist, and later as its pastor, Abernathy had made himself something of a protégé of Johns's. They conducted revivals together. Among Johns's cadre of street salesmen, Abernathy was the champion peddler of women's lingerie, a distinction that regularly sparked merry yarns among the preachers.

"Brother King," said Abernathy, "I remember the first time I met you, too. And I bet you don't remember. It was in the summer of 1950, when I was a student at Atlanta University. And your father had turned the pulpit over to you for the summer. So I went over to Ebenezer one Sunday to see if you could preach. You preached a fine sermon on the nature of faith. And when I went through the line after the service, you shook my hand and said, 'Were you pleased with the sermon?' And I said, 'Yes, I want to thank you. You blessed my soul.' Do you remember that?"

King made some noncommittal remarks, and Abernathy rescued him quickly from his discomfort. "And do you know what?" he continued with a grin. "The *very next day*, the young lady I was going to escort to a play at Sisters Chapel called me on the phone to say that she was not feeling well and wouldn't be able to go. Well, I didn't know what to do. I already had the tickets, but I couldn't find anybody else to go with me. So I went to the play by myself, and do you know what I saw? I saw that same young lady who told me she was sick walking into the play on the arm of the young preacher who had just blessed my soul. That was you, Brother King."

This story pleased King as much as it embarrassed him. "Well, those days are over, Brother Abernathy," he said. He told them of Coretta, congratulated Abernathy on his marriage to Juanita, added further praise of the fine dinner he had just hastily consumed, and took his leave. It was still early in the evening. King made his way into what passed for the Negro business district in Montgomery: a gas station and a few carry-out stores on the fringe of the Alabama State campus. As he called the Brooks home from a pay phone in the Regal Café, he saw one of his old Morehouse friends walk through the door. It was Robert Williams, the tenor soloist, who had gone on to Juilliard and the Union Seminary School of Sacred Music before postponing his career indefinitely for lack of support funds. Now he was teaching at Alabama State. While catching up on the eight years since they had seen each other, Williams teased King about becoming a preacher. King replied that he really was not one yet, and asked whether he should consider coming to Dexter.

Williams shook his head over the prospect. "I don't know, Mike," he replied with a grin. "They've got a lot of tough old buzzards in that church. But if anybody can pastor them, you can." King thanked Williams for the confidence and then teased him for not joining Dexter or going to church regularly.

After an evening at the Brooks home, King rose in the Dexter pulpit the next morning to deliver "The Three Dimensions of a Complete Life," his most polished composition. The setting fitted him well—a small, handsome, wooden church on the only remaining piece of Negro-owned real estate along the central thoroughfare of Montgomery, just down from the whitewashed state capitol—and it appeared that Vernon Johns drained off very little of his crowd. Dexter members turned out in good number to hear King, partly because his reputation had already fed rumors that he might be the one to fill the pulpit at last. They received his demeanor and his message enthusiastically, so much so that Robert Nesbitt led a small group of Dexter officials to call on King that very afternoon at the Brooks home for what amounted to preliminary negotiations.

King told them that he was very impressed with Dexter but that he had a number of options and was taking things slowly. Nesbitt said pretty much the same thing to King. Among Dexter's options, they all knew, was King's best friend and old schoolmate Walter McCall, who had preached a highly successful trial sermon at Dexter some weeks earlier. The board of deacons had already favored McCall with a rare invitation to preach a second trial sermon. If successful again, McCall would be in line for the job. McCall wanted Dexter badly, as he had narrowly lost several other prestigious pulpits and was painfully bored as dean of men at a small college in Georgia. It was most awkward for King to enter the prolonged Dexter screening process in the midst of his friend's promising effort, but he and Nesbitt smothered the tension with mannerliness and propriety.

That evening, King returned to Abernathy's for another supper. Johns had left for New Orleans on the afternoon train, and his absence freed Abernathy to speak more candidly about the painful controversy at Dexter. Johns, he said, had never dreamed that Dexter would accept any of his resignations, including the fifth one, and the sudden firing had confronted him with the unpleasant reality that he had nowhere to go. His wife had taken a teaching job in Virginia, but Johns simply refused to vacate the Dexter parsonage. He had holed up there for the better part of a year, blithely ignoring the orders of the Dexter board members who had engineered his dismissal. The dispute had grown nasty when the deacons disconnected the gas, electricity, and finally the water at the parsonage. Gamely holding out, Johns read by candlelight, carried his water, and kept warm by burning his huge inventory of old newspapers. All along, the public reality was that the esteemed Vernon Johns was residing at the parsonage until Dexter selected a new pastor, but the private reality was that Johns, cornered by old age and his own temperament, desperately resisted the board's campaign to starve him out.

"That Johns is a mess," Abernathy concluded, laughing. Still, he knew enough of Johns and Dexter to offer King two bits of practical advice. First, it was better in the long run to be a pastor than a prophet. Brilliant, lonely, romantic, and impractical, the prophet was the highest form of the preacher without a church, but, according to preacher folklore, he inevitably wound up a tragic and rather ridiculous creature, like a king without a kingdom. Second, King should be mindful of the fact that Dexter never expected to keep preachers long, and should avoid the trap of trying to be the kind of preacher Dexter wanted—an intellectual in the pulpit who gave little attention to the organization of the church itself. To survive at Dexter, a preacher needed to pitch himself headlong into the committees, finances, and personalities—in short, into the guts of church control. Otherwise, the most eloquent preacher would be no match for the entrenched powers.

Back in Boston, King put his career options up for discussion at the Dialectical Society. He was still considering Benjamin Mays's offer to teach at Morehouse, but the little church in Montgomery grew larger in his mind. Dexter's elite reputation appealed to the King whose graduate studies were bringing his enthusiasm for gilded pedantry to its youthful crest. (In a letter thanking the chaplain of Alabama State for allowing him to preach there, King wrote that he had enjoyed the "ontologically real" fellowship. The chaplain's reply teased King for his rhetorical flourish.) Also, King was drawn to the challenge of succeeding a prophet like Vernon Johns. Primarily, this meant conquering the notorious baronies at Dexter. King was still very much his father's son, and Reverend King made no attempt to hide his ideas of pastoral authority—once telling a conference of Baptist ministers how, when an Ebenezer member dared to stand up in church and ask to see a report of expenditures, he had silenced the member's disloyalty by threatening to hit him over the head with a chair if he pursued such a question.

Within a few weeks, events pushed King toward Dexter. Walter McCall went back to Montgomery for his second trial sermon, which he called "The Four Dimensions of a Complete Life." This transparent embellishment of King's own sermon reflected McCall's keen competitive desire to top his friend, and perhaps that very focus injured his performance. In any case, his second trial was as much a failure as the first had been a success. Meeting afterward with Nesbitt, McCall was deeply distressed. "I can't touch King," he said with resignation. It was an uncomfortable day for everyone. Nesbitt and practically everyone else at Dexter liked McCall personally, but the church was clearly moving toward King because of his class and originality. McCall did not need to be told. He and King talked on the phone to reassure each other that they were still friends.

About that time, King himself tasted rejection when the First Baptist Church of Chattanooga passed him over to call another minister. This fulfilled King's premonition that his tryout had not gone well, but he could not figure out whether he had been too young, too intellectual, too political, or perhaps tainted by some obscure grudge traceable to his father or even his grandfather. Almost nothing was too paranoid or petty to influence pulpit selection committees, which preachers regarded as dangerous, fascinating mistresses. After consultations with his adviser, Melvin Watson, King moved cautiously toward Dexter, advising Nesbitt by phone that he was willing to preach a second trial sermon and to meet with the full board of deacons, if the church so desired, but that he was still considering other alternatives. In the ensuing negotiations by phone, Nesbitt made a bold move to pressure King for an early decision: he would break with church precedent by dispensing with further trials, and he offered a salary of $4,200 a year. In church parlance, this worked out to $100 for each first (or communion) Sunday of the month and about $75 for all other Sundays, and it would make King—straight out of school—the highest-paid Negro minister in Montgomery.

Nesbitt's offer put King in a strong position to bargain for anything except delay. On April 14, 1954, he wrote a letter to Nesbitt accepting the call. "However," he added, "I find it necessary to predicate my acceptance upon the following considerations." He asked that the parsonage be put into good living order, that the church pay for his commutation between Boston and Montgomery until he completed research for his Ph.D. dissertation at the end of that summer, and that the church understand his expectation of salary increases "as the Church progresses." King's approach was businesslike, but he probably did not drive as hard a bargain as Dexter would have allowed. After a quick meeting with the selection committee on April 18, Nesbitt accepted his terms in full. The church had ended one of the longest pulpit vacancies in its history.

King underwent a complete physical examination at Boston's Lahey Clinic. Dr. Rosemary Murphy measured him at 5'6½", 166½ pounds, pulse 70, normal and strong in all respects. He was fit and confident, which was fortunate because he needed all his strength to overcome objections to Dexter on the part of his wife and father. Segregated, backward Alabama was among the last places Coretta wanted to live, as she had spent her entire life struggling to get away. In Boston, while King negotiated with Nesbitt, the New England Conservatory presented her as one of the soloists in the premiere of Cuban composer Amadeo Roldan's "Motivos de Son," with orchestra. She sang regularly in the choir of a white Presbyterian church. In Montgomery, she knew, both these distinctions lay beyond the realm of dreams, and therefore she lobbied strenuously to get her husband to choose a position in the North more in keeping with their attainments. Although King tried to reassure her that the Dexter position would be temporary, she forced him to invoke what he called his authority as head of the household. King's idea of the wife's role in a marriage was traditional, much like his father's, and he reminded his wife that he had made this clear before she accepted his marriage proposal. Even so, Coretta did not resign herself to Montgomery for months after she was physically there.

Reverend King, still wounded because his son was rejecting his natural succession at Ebenezer, tried to strike fear in him. The notorious barons of Dexter would trample him, he warned; nothing but danger, humiliation, and career disaster lay ahead in Montgomery. To this, King responded with more than his usual mixture of filibuster, charm, and stubbornness. Dexter was his first test, and he would master that church the way Reverend King had mastered Ebenezer. "*I'm* going to be pastor," he told his wife and his father, "and I'm going to run that church."

King began his career at the age of twenty-five, in the year that witnessed the invention of the TV dinner and the microchip, the marriage of Joe DiMaggio and Marilyn Monroe, and the closing of the immigration center on New York's Ellis Island. The first news films of a hydrogen bomb test showed shirtless American engineers smoking pipes and wearing pith helmets as they adjusted the rigging for a blast far out in the Pacific Ocean. At a ceremony for the official insertion of the words "under God" into the Pledge of Allegiance, President Eisenhower commented that the American form of government makes no sense without a "deeply felt religious faith—and I don't care what it is." This statement annoyed liberal and conservative intellectuals alike, but the general public seemed to approve. A Gallup poll showed that 94 percent of Americans believed in God, 68 percent in an afterlife.

On May 17—two weeks after King's first sermon as pastor-designate of Dexter—Chief Justice Earl Warren handed down the Court's decision in the *Brown* case, without advance notice. News hunger on the matter was so intense that the Associated Press issued a flash bulletin at 12:52 P.M. noting simply that Warren was issuing the opinion, another at 1:12 P.M. saying that he "had not read far enough into the court's opinion" for reporters to discern its conclusion, and a final bulletin at 1:20 declaring that the Court had struck down school segregation as unconstitutional by a vote of 8–0.

The earth shook, and then again it did not. There were no street celebrations in Negro communities. At Spelman College in Atlanta, sophomore Barbara Johns continued her longstanding silence about her role in the case, sensing muted apprehension among her fellow students. They seemed to worry that the great vindication might mean the extinction of schools like Spelman. The day after Warren's announcement, President Eisenhower informed the District of Columbia that he wanted the nation's capital to set an example of compliance with the law by desegregating in advance of specific court orders. James Reston of *The New York Times* attacked the *Brown* decision as a venture into sociology, saying that "the Court insisted on equality of the mind and heart rather than on equal school facilities." Southern politicians first announced that they would obey the Court and then changed their minds.

Sherman Adams, Eisenhower's chief of staff, was preoccupied with political images, wanting to make sure that the Democrats could not blame Republicans for the decision by pointing to Ike's appointment of Warren. Experts in various fields were unsure of themselves, largely because the gap between the two races was so wide as to preclude vision, or even imagination, across it. Ironically, Americans seemed surer of what they wanted foreigners to think of the *Brown* decision than of what they thought themselves. The Voice of America immediately translated Warren's opinion into thirty-four languages to broadcast the good news overseas, but some domestic media outlets fell silent. Universal Newsreels never mentioned the most important Supreme Court decision of the century. It was too controversial.

Ten days before the *Brown* decision, the French command at Dien Bien Phu had surrendered, causing an extraordinary wave of emotion across the United States. Its focus was a young French nurse who had been stranded amid the battle as the lone woman within the doomed garrison. After the victorious Vietnamese rebels—still commonly called "natives" or "Reds" in news dispatches—released her to French-held Hanoi, no one was more surprised than Geneviève, daughter of the Viscountess Oger de Galard Terraube, to discover that she had become a rallying symbol in the West. The story of the fresh-faced French nurse had everything—heroics, war, sex, purity, noble birth, political and ethnic symbolism. When she arrived in New York two months later, *The New York Times* hailed her on page one as the "Angel of Dienbienphu," and a quarter-million New Yorkers turned out for a ticker-tape parade up Broadway. Still somewhat dumbfounded by it all, the reluctant heroine proceeded to Washington, where she received the Medal of Freedom from President Eisenhower. She became the first foreign citizen invited to address a joint session of Congress since General Lafayette, hero of the American Revolution.

King was preparing to move to Montgomery. From Fort Valley State, a small Negro college in Georgia, Walter McCall wrote to complain of a record-breaking heat wave that was drying up lakes and rivers all across the South. The drought seemed to compound a touch of self-pity in

McCall, who told King that "all things seem to be going your way." "I thought that you had forgotten the Ole Boy," he added, before turning to the main subject on his mind, which was "the lady angle." McCall announced that he intended to marry a young woman from South Carolina, and asked King to serve as his best man. But McCall was a restless man, as King and his friends well knew, and two sentences later he was describing for King his "other chick" from North Carolina. "She works in N.C. and holds residence in Albany, Ga.," he wrote. "Doc., really she is beautiful, but she does not have what this girl has. I hate to break off from her, but I am ready to be married, so I am not willing to continue playing the field."

McCall turned to the painful matter of the woman he had refused to marry and the child he refused to support. He had sent the woman fifty dollars to help with the child, which turned out to be a mistake because it gave her "a ray of hope" for marriage. "She has already worried the very daylight out of me by long distance phone calls and a host of letters," McCall fretted. "So, instead of continuing that support, I have cut it off already. Never do I expect to help in any fashion. Man, [she] will harass me to death if I give her the least o' consideration. Hate to take that attitude, but I think I am wise in so doing." He closed with a bare "hello to Coretta," who was too formal for his taste.

The letter itself was pure McCall—exposed, hot and cold, sentimental and also hard as porcelain, vexed by the nature of women. King knew well that the wedding announcement was far from definitive. In a letter to McCall ten weeks later, he would inquire discreetly about "the marriage situation." By then he was living in Montgomery and preaching at Dexter. His chief purpose in writing McCall—as in writing almost everyone else he knew—was to seek help in the campaign to take his new church by storm.

On September 5, 1954, when King rose to the Dexter pulpit for the first time as resident pastor, he held in his hand a surprise document: "Recommendations to the Dexter Avenue Baptist Church for the Fiscal Year 1954–1955." He announced to the congregation that he was going to distribute copies of his recommendations for their prayerful consideration, to be acted upon at a subsequent business meeting. After the worship service, members took their copies and saw from the very first sentence that the boyish-looking young man in the pulpit did not intend to become another victim of the church fathers. "When a minister is called to the pastorate of a church," King declared, "the main presupposition is that he is vested with a degree of authority." From there, he

proclaimed himself on the single theme of authority in a ringing preface
worthy of Moses, Augustine, or Luther.

> The source of this authority is twofold. First of all, his authority originates
> with God. Inherent in the call itself is the presupposition that God directed
> that such a call be made. This fact makes it crystal clear that the pastor's
> authority is not merely humanly conferred, but divinely sanctioned.
>   Secondly, the pastor's authority stems from the people themselves. Im-
> plied in the call is the unconditional willingness of the people to accept the
> pastor's leadership. This means that the leadership never ascends from the
> pew to the pulpit, but it invariably descends from the pulpit to the pew.
> This does not mean that the pastor is one before whom we must blindly
> and ignorantly genuflect, as if he were possessed of some infallible or su-
> perhuman attributes. Nor does it mean that the pastor should needlessly
> interfere with the deacons, trustees or workers of the various auxiliaries,
> assuming unnecessary dictatorial authority. But it does mean that the pas-
> tor is to be respected and accepted as the central figure around which the
> policies and programs of the church revolve. He must never be considered
> a mere puppet for the whimsical and capricious mistreatment of those who
> wish to show their independence, and "use their liberty as a cloak for
> maliciousness." It is therefore indispensable to the progress of the church
> that the official board and membership cooperate fully with the leadership
> of the pastor.

Had it stood alone, King's preface would have sounded defensively audacious. Most probably, he could have gotten the congregation to adopt
it as a resolution, but the church powers on whom he served notice
would have bided their time and in the long run the resolution would
have had little effect. King did not take that chance. He followed his
preface with thirty-four specific recommendations toward a complete
financial and organizational mobilization of the church. The first one he
borrowed directly from Reverend King's invigoration of Ebenezer in
1932: all church members shall belong to one of twelve clubs, according
to the month of their birth. "Each club shall be asked to make a special
contribution to the church on the last Sunday of the month for which it
is named," wrote King. "Also, on the Church Anniversary each club shall
be asked to contribute at least one hundred dollars ($100.00)." Next, he
proposed that the church begin a "four year renovation and expansion
program." He named specific goals, from a new carpet and "electric cold
water fountain" for 1955 to an entire new religious education building
for 1959.

After these two financial shockers, King recommended the establishment of a host of new committees, boards, and councils. A social and
political action committee would promote membership in the NAACP
and sponsor "forums and mass meetings" before elections to discuss the

issues. "Every member of Dexter must be a registered voter," he wrote, at a time when less than 5 percent of Negroes in Alabama were registered. One new committee would raise money to give a Dexter high school graduate a small college scholarship, another would establish a nursery so that parents of small children could attend church more easily, a third would seek new members. Contented Dexter had never done such things.

His final dozen recommendations returned to the pivotal subject of finance and church control. He proposed that each deacon be assigned twenty-five church members who lived near him ("It shall be the duty of the deacon to persuade the member to catch up his or her pledge"), and he outlined the same centralized treasury and budget that his father had used so successfully at Ebenezer. Henceforth, there would be no more ad hoc rallies, special collections, or anonymous giving. "I recommend that all money in the treasury of each auxiliary be turned over to the general church treasurer by November 1, 1954," he wrote. Dexter would operate by check instead of cash. The pastor alone, and not the deacons or the trustees, would decide how much to pay guest ministers. No one would take collections home to count them; all money would be deposited in the bank immediately. If all this and more were done, King concluded with a flourish, "Dexter will rise to such heights as will stagger the imagination of generations yet unborn."

His plan was to claim leadership and to demonstrate it in one swift stroke. In perhaps the most critical and daring tactic, King named specific people for all the appointments to his plethora of committees. He showed that on the first day he already knew his congregation well enough to take a huge risk in one of the minister's most delicate areas, personnel assignments. Among those he appointed were Dr. Adair, whom Vernon Johns had denounced for murdering his wife, Dr. Pettus, whose daughter Johns had embarrassed by selling watermelons at her wedding, and Rufus Lewis, the funeral proprietor and former football coach who had accompanied Johns on his fateful watermelon run to the Alabama State campus.

The list, along with the whole package, would be voted up or down. By listing the names in advance, King gave a large number of the most influential church members a vested interest in his reform. By tying both the committees and the finance plan to Moses' definition of pastoral authority, King gave the members a clear choice: they could validate his authority along with his recommendations, or could challenge them both. It was Thermidor, a royalist counterattack, with implicit warning that if the nobles resisted, King would leave Dexter before they could celebrate his arrival.

King was proud of his coup. He had spent months preparing his recommendations, going so far as to consult the organizational reports of successful Negro churches around the country. Even after Dexter capitulated, he sent copies to other clergymen for their comments and advice. Those who responded singled out for applause King's description of the pastor's preeminence. Melvin Watson referred to the preface as "beautifully and appropriately formulated." Another friend wrote simply that King had done "a very good job" on the authority question. There was little disagreement among pastors on this point. Their one common criticism was that King might be taking things too fast, with too much organization, too many overlapping committees, too much busywork. "Hectic activity in the church is not necessarily an indication that the cause of the Kingdom is being promoted," cautioned Watson.

King believed that hectic activity could bond him to the congregation and to the town. He had more than enough energy. Every morning he was up by five-thirty to work for three hours on his dissertation. Then he was off to the church, where he might preach at a funeral, supervise the painting of the basement, or play musical chairs with the members of the June Club. He went to NAACP meetings, made social calls on the other Negro ministers in town, and joined the local Morehouse Club. Montgomery was a haven for Morehouse alumni—so much so that one of Alabama State's nicknames was "Little Morehouse"—and King soon discovered that Elliott Finley, a Morehouse acquaintance, had a pool table in his home. He played pool there in the evenings ("Old Finley thought he could whip me at Eight Ball, so I had to give him a lesson"). Late at night, he often worked another few hours on the dissertation. That first year at Dexter, he made two trips back to Boston to confer with DeWolf and to defend his dissertation before the Ph.D. examining committee, attended no less than ten conclaves of the National Baptist Convention, preached forty-six sermons at Dexter, and delivered twenty addresses at churches and colleges from New York to Louisiana. Proud of his blinding schedule, King reported to the church that on top of everything else he had read exactly twenty-six books and 102 magazines.

Even the stolid R. D. Nesbitt was telling the deacons that the new pastor had "revolutionized" Dexter within the first two months. King kept committee members so busy working on projects they liked that they had no time to oppose those they disdained. Six weeks after making his recommendations, King was able to report the collection of more than $2,100 on a single Sunday. This amounted to half his annual salary and was considered by his fellow clergymen to be an amazing feat for a church with only three hundred members on the books. Predictably, King encountered the most foot-dragging, the most ingenious delay pattern of missed deadlines and slipped minds, against his dictum that all monies from the bank accounts and cigar boxes of the scattered church auxiliaries be surrendered to the new central treasury by November 1. But he collected it all on time, on the strength of his mandate and his persistence.

The deadline was of more than passing significance to the new pastor, because on the last day of October Reverend King led a caravan of Ebenezer members down the highway to Montgomery—including Mother King and her choir, and supporters numbering nearly a hundred—for the formal ceremonies in which young King was installed in the Dexter pulpit. King was able to report to his father that he had established financial control of Dexter's legendary baronies.

King already had written Paul Tillich to ask for a personal interview. In November, Tillich replied from Aberdeen, Scotland, where he was delivering the Gifford Lectures. Tillich was working feverishly on the second volume of his *Systematic Theology,* with new ideas and definitions coming to him so rapidly that he often muttered to colleagues or himself, "I must revise my system." Despite his burdensome schedule, Tillich advised Ph.D. candidate King that he would be happy to talk with him for his dissertation on Tillich's ideas of God but regretted to say that he would not be at Harvard during any of King's trips to Boston, as King had hoped, because he would be writing, traveling, and lecturing for another year before taking up new duties at Harvard. He gave dates when he would be available in Chicago or New York.

Although King would finish his dissertation before the interview could be arranged, the mere fact that he had been welcomed by the most eminent Protestant theologian in the world was satisfying. He began his career near the summit of both the white and Negro church worlds. His "twoness" seemed to translate into sturdiness and balance, as his interest in Tillich's abstractions did not crowd out his instinct for power within the practical confines of Dexter Avenue Baptist Church. Beneath his genteel, aristocratic manner—never without his big words or his dress fedora—there were only hints at first that King was balanced, holding within himself contending forces of great power. One hint was his rapport with Dexter's less sophisticated members, who noticed that King never greeted them with the dreaded question, "What are you doing?" This password was an invitation for the person so greeted to mention some sabbatical, club project, upcoming convention, or other delicious burden of professional status. It offended those who would have to reply that they were just farming or ironing the white folks' laundry, as they always had. Even an old farmer like Vernon Johns had asked people what they were doing, and was capable of that satisfied tone of voice when he did—but not King. The new pastor always looked his members squarely in the eye and asked them *how* they were doing, usually following with a personal question about their health or the kids. Moreover, he would linger over such conversations against all competing obligations. It was a small thing except to those who treasured the difference.

Another hint was the way he preached. At first some of the older members complained that Pastor King was "not a God man," meaning that he did not dwell on salvation or describe the furniture in heaven. Soon those complaints died away, however, as the congregation grew accustomed to King's passion. In keeping with Dexter's heritage, he sprinkled classical quotations within his lectures on the hidden meaning of the universe, but he also released a good deal of controlled heat through the cracks in Keighton's sermon types. And his listeners responded to the passion beneath the ideas, to the bottomless joy and pain that turned the heat into rhythm and the rhythm into music. King was controlled. He never shouted. But he preached like someone who wanted to shout, and this gave him an electrifying hold over the congregation. Though still a boy to many of his older listeners, he had the commanding air of a burning sage. He began to come into full power that first year on his own, at Dexter and also at some of the largest Negro churches in the country, where he "brought down the house."

Late in November 1954, he preached a guest sermon at Atlanta's Friendship Baptist Church that sent aftershocks of recognition through the church world of his hometown. King was becoming a phenomenon, and the magnitude of his success put Reverend King into his usual jumble of emotions—pride, worry, envy, love, and fear. On December 2, he wrote his son a letter, enclosing young King's checkbook, which he had balanced and corrected. (Though King was married and gone, his father handled such chores because he was good at them and because he was a power in Atlanta banking. There were no Negro banks in Montgomery.) Beginning "My dear M.L.," the elder King passed along some preacher news from Ebenezer. "Sister Luella Allen lost her husband yesterday," he wrote. "I am sure you remember her, she is the little Sister that usually sits on the left side of the church, shouts up against the wall. With the exception of that, everything seems to be moving on very well around the church." Then, noting that he had just gotten another phone call "about how you swept them at Friendship Sunday," he delivered a thunderous message to his son, warning that success threatened not only temptation and sin but annihilation. "You see, young man, you are becoming very popular. As I told you, you must be very much in prayer. Persons like yourself are the ones the devil turns all of his forces aloose to destroy."

On March 2, 1955, a handful of white people sought to board a city bus as it chugged up Dexter Avenue to the Court Street stop. Peering into the rearview mirror, the driver saw that the white section was full of whites and that both the Negro section and the "no-man's-land" in the middle were full of Negroes. The driver turned around and pointed to a row in the middle section. "Give me those seats," he said to the four Negro women seated there. Two of them moved obediently to stand in the aisle, but two of them pretended not to hear and stared into the middle distance. The driver, having committed himself to secure the seats, cajoled and warned the two recalcitrant women. Then he stepped outside to hail a foot policeman, who in turn hailed a squad car with two other policemen. Soon the policemen began pressuring some of the Negro men to give their seats to the holdout women. Seeking the point of least resistance, they tried to turn a segregation dispute into a question of chivalry. One man complied, but no one would move for the last holdout, a feisty high school student named Claudette Colvin, who defended her right to the seat in language that brought words of disapproval from passengers of both races. One white woman defended her to the police, saying that Colvin was allowed to sit in no-man's-land as long as there were no seats in the Negro section, but another white woman said that if Colvin were allowed to defy the police, "they will take over." Colvin was crying and madder than ever by the time the policemen told her she was under arrest. She struggled when they dragged her off the bus and screamed when they put on the handcuffs.

Four days later, the *Advertiser* published a letter in which one of the white passengers commended the policemen for handling the bus incident without violence, without even raising their voices. Montgomery Negroes, by contrast, disputed the need to handcuff a high school girl. To them, Colvin had been entitled to her seat even under the hated segregation law, and for her to have been insulted, blamed, and arrested on the whim of the driver and by force of law was a humiliating injustice not only to her but to all the Negro passengers who had witnessed the arrest in helpless, fearful silence. Prosecutors had thrown the book at Colvin, charging her with violating the segregation law, assault, and disorderly conduct. She might be going to jail instead of to Booker T. Washington High School.

Privately, E. D. Nixon consulted Clifford Durr about the Colvin case. The two men made an unlikely pair: Nixon, a Negro railroad porter with fists as big as eggplants and a coal-black face, and Durr, a white lawyer and Rhodes scholar from the Alabama gentry. Between them, they had connections that reached high and wide among the quixotic groups that for decades had tried to build a network of support for civil rights. E. D. Nixon was a union man. For nearly half of his fifty-six years, he had served as president of the Alabama branch of A. Philip Randolph's Brotherhood of Sleeping Car Porters. Nixon almost worshipped Randolph, who in his legendary career had dared to attack Du Bois for urging Negroes to fight in World War I, then had fought the Pullman Company for twelve years before winning recognition of the first major Negro trade union. Randolph was an old lion—tall, white-haired, and dignified, speaking elegantly with a slight British accent—and Nixon was a homespun Alabama copy of him. He was famous to Montgomery Negroes as the man who knew every white policeman, judge, and government clerk in town, and had always gone to see them about the grievances of any Negro who asked him for help. Nixon seldom got anything close to justice, but he usually got something. Once, he pushed his way into the governor's office, and he was the first Negro since Reconstruction to put himself on the ballot for local office. He was not an educated or cultivated man, however, and many of the town's more educated Negroes sniped at him for his imperfections.

Clifford Durr, for his part, was a grim harbinger to white Southern liberals on the race issue. He retained many influential contacts from his glowing past as a second-echelon braintruster of the New Deal. The Johnsons, Lyndon and Lady Bird, were old friends, for example, and Durr was related by marriage to Supreme Court Justice Hugo Black. But these surviving ties counted for very little when Durr rebelled against the most sensitive taboos of the Cold War era. First he had resigned his post as FCC Commissioner to represent some of the early victims of the Truman loyalty program. To Durr, the loyalty hearings were un-American inquisitions in which innocent people were branded as perverts or subversives on the word of anonymous FBI informants. His cases isolated him from mainstream politics, and things grew worse when he returned home to practice law.

With Aubrey Williams, a fellow New Dealer from Montgomery, Durr sponsored the Highlander Folk School in Tennessee. For more than twenty years, Highlander had functioned as a unique "workshop" of the Social Gospel, being one of the few places in the South where Negroes and whites mixed freely. Its founder, Myles Horton, had been a student of Reinhold Niebuhr at Union Theological Seminary. Niebuhr was chairman of the Highlander advisory board that at times had included Eleanor Roosevelt, Norman Thomas, and Harry Emerson Fosdick. Durr tried to defend Highlander as a sensible, patriotic experiment in racial democracy, but during the passions of the Joseph McCarthy hearings and the

Brown case his associations landed him, his wife Virginia, Myles Horton, and Aubrey Williams before James Eastland's Senate Internal Security Subcommittee. On television, Eastland let it be known that he considered Highlander freakish, mongrelized, and basically Communist. The normally judicious Durr exploded in rage, challenging Eastland to a fist-fight, and photographs of guards restraining him landed on the front page of *The New York Times*. After that, Durr lost most of his remaining clients in Montgomery. He became a threadbare patrician, explaining patiently why he thought the confluence of events had reduced him to such a state. His wife was far less tolerant. She combined the background of a Southern belle with the sharp tongue of an early feminist, and had called Eastland a "nasty polecat" long before the Highlander hearings.

After the Colvin arrest in Montgomery, Nixon and Durr conferred with Colvin, Colvin's relatives, witnesses from the bus, and Fred Gray, a young Negro lawyer only one year out of school, who moonlighted on weekends as a preacher. Durr considered Gray bright, aggressive, and promising. He had been advising the younger man on the eccentricities of the Montgomery courts, and now they weighed the prospects of turning the Colvin defense into an attack on segregation. Gray agreed to represent Colvin and was eager to make a run at it.

Nixon's first move was to try negotiation. He called for an appointment with Police Commissioner Dave Birmingham, a man he knew to be an amiable populist in the style of Governor James "Kissin' Jim" Folsom. Shortly thereafter, with an ad hoc Colvin committee that included the new Baptist minister in town, Rev. M. L. King, Jr., Nixon arrived in Birmingham's office for talks, which led quickly to a tentative agreement. Bus drivers should be courteous to everyone, and bus seats should be filled by Negroes from the back and whites from the front, eliminating the no-man's-land where passengers could be removed or inserted by the driver. If the bus company adopted such a policy, said Birmingham, he would instruct the police to act accordingly.

The plan sailed along until it reached the desk of Jack Crenshaw, the bus company's lawyer, whose instincts ran quickly to objection. What would happen if whites tried to board a bus completely filled with Negroes? Would they stand in the aisle? If so, where would be the white section required by state law? Crenshaw said the bus company would not endorse something that could be construed as illegal, especially not with its operating license soon up for renewal. This was sneaky, he said. If the police wanted to change the segregation laws, they should change them outright. Stung, Nixon's committee went back to Birmingham and asked him to implement the plan on his own, but the police commissioner retreated painfully.

Meanwhile, Claudette Colvin had been found guilty at a brief trial. On May 6, Judge Eugene Carter crossed up the Colvin supporters with an appeal ruling worthy of a fox. He dismissed the segregation charge, nullifying their plans to take that issue into federal court on constitutional grounds. Dismissing the charge of disorderly conduct, he showed a willingness to forgive. Upholding the charge of assault—the most preposterous of the three—he let it be known that he would tolerate no challenge to authority. Finally, he sentenced Colvin to pay a small fine—a sentence so much lighter than anticipated that it ruined her martyr status. Many Negroes who supported her cause nevertheless came to believe she was lucky.

Fred Gray wanted to press an appeal anyway, but Durr and Nixon believed that the case had already lost its momentum. There was much internal turmoil among Negro leaders. Members of the influential Women's Political Council—most of whom served on the social and political affairs committee at King's church—had completed a discouraging canvass of the likely witnesses in the case. Most of them were frightened, and might at any moment deny what they had said. Colvin herself would not recant, they reported, but she was immature—prone to breakdowns and outbursts of profanity. Worse, she was pregnant. Even if Montgomery Negroes were willing to rally behind an unwed pregnant teenager— which they were not—her circumstances would make her an extremely vulnerable standard-bearer. Some of Colvin's friends resented this assessment as condescending. Women leaders criticized the local ministers for failing to press the segregation issue harder and more eloquently during the negotiations, which the women stressed above the lawsuit, and the ministers defended themselves by recalling the lawyers' advice against poisoning the trial atmosphere with too much excitement. In the end, E. D. Nixon made the decision. Although Nixon was sensitive about his country dialect and often asserted his worth defensively against the airs of the more educated Negroes, saying, "You won't find *my* car parked out in front of no loan shop," his practicality prevailed. Colvin would not do, he decreed. Her family agreed and paid the fine.

That July, one month after getting his doctorate, King flew to New Orleans to explore a special new job at Dillard University. Dillard, founded by Congregationalists shortly after the Civil War, had enjoyed the patronage of Chicago philanthropist Julius Rosenwald and his heirs. Its campus of whitewashed classical buildings laid out on a vast tree-lined lawn was as handsome as Spelman's, and its reputation was the equal of any coeducational Negro college in the South. The Dillard president, A. W. Dent, a Morehouse man from Daddy King's class, wanted King to become dean of the new Lawless Memorial University Chapel.

In that post, he would be allowed to teach courses in the religion and philosophy departments without being lashed to the full schedule of a regular faculty member. He would preach in the chapel, but he would escape the more tedious duties of a church pastor. The combination was ideal for King. From Dent's point of view, the job's only drawback was that construction of the chapel would not be completed by September, and it was complicated to start anything at a college in the middle of the school year. King welcomed the delay, however, as he thought he should stay at Dexter at least another year. He would also have to figure out how to tell Dr. Mays and his father, among others.

To search so soon for a teaching job was a departure from King's plan to preach for a number of years, like Mordecai Johnson, Niebuhr, and Howard Thurman, before rising to life in the academy. He was advancing the schedule because he was impatient—not because of failure at Dexter but by the very fact of his success. His father's budget system had worked; Dexter had already paid off a debt of nearly $5,000 from the Johns era, hired new staff, and paid $1,000 into the new building fund. King had made the church into a beehive, and now he saw the only catch: the hive could get no bigger. The legendary Stokes had baptized a thousand a year during the heyday of Montgomery's First Baptist, and Daddy King had baptized enough to build Ebenezer from two hundred souls to four thousand, but King would finish his banner year having baptized only twelve. Fewer than thirty new members joined the rolls, and many of those were part of the annual turnover at Alabama State. The only way for Dexter to grow larger was to transform itself into a mass church of all classes, and the only way to do anything substantial with the new building fund was to move away from the prestigious but tiny site there beneath the state capitol. King knew his congregation would do neither.

Restless, King decided to step up his activity in the local chapter of the NAACP. He gave a stirring speech at one of its small gatherings and then accepted a position on the executive committee. His letter of appointment came from Rosa Parks, secretary of the chapter. A seamstress at a downtown department store, Parks made extra money by taking in sewing work on the side. She had come into the NAACP through E. D. Nixon, who had served as chapter president for five years before stepping aside for a friend. Her background and character put her firmly astride the class fault that divided the politically active Negroes of Montgomery. Had the professionals and the upper strata from Alabama State taken over the organization—as they were threatening to do now that the *Brown* case had brought fresh excitement to the NAACP—Parks might well have been replaced by one of the college-trained members of the Women's Political Council. As it was, she remained the woman of Nixon's circle most congenial to the Council members. She wore rimless spectacles, spoke quietly, wrote and typed faultless letters on her own, and had never been known to lower herself to factionalism. A tireless worker and churchgoer, of working-class station and middle-class demeanor, Rosa Parks was one of those rare people of whom everyone agreed that she gave more than she got. Her character represented one of the isolated high blips on the graph of human nature, offsetting a dozen or so sociopaths. A Methodist herself, she served as teacher and mother figure to the kids of the NAACP Youth Council, who met at a Lutheran church near her home.

That church, Trinity Lutheran, was an oddity in itself. To Negroes, a principal attraction of Trinity Lutheran had always been its affiliated private school, which was supported as a mission by the World Lutheran Council. For years it had been the only decent school available to Negroes, and many ambitious families had swallowed their distaste for the staid Lutheran liturgy in order to educate their children. Along with an even tinier Congregational church, Trinity was high church in doctrine and worship. Dexter got most of the college professors; Trinity got a few of the high school teachers.

For several years, the minister at Trinity had been Nelson Trout, a Negro Lutheran who felt somewhat excluded as the head of a minuscule congregation outside the mainstream of Negro religion. His peers from the big Baptist and Methodist churches took neither Trinity nor its pastor very seriously, Trout believed, and it was all he could do to get some of them to turn out for the ceremony that marked the crowning achievement of his work in Montgomery—the dedication of the new parsonage, next door to the church. Ralph Abernathy arrived with King. The two young Baptists attended such functions together so frequently that Trout had come to think of them as a team—Mr. Rough and Mr. Smooth. Abernathy tended to lead King through the crowds, introducing him to selected new people, in a manner that offended Trout because Abernathy was at once so deferential to King and so lordly toward everyone else. Trout found it much easier to talk informally with King, and in a private moment once felt enough at ease to ask as a Lutheran how King, a Negro Baptist, had acquired the name Martin Luther. King looked searchingly at Trout for some time, then smiled and parried with a question of his own: how did a Negro like Trout come to be a Lutheran? Trout laughed. The competition was too rough among the Baptist preachers, he replied, and the Lutherans were begging for Negroes.

Many years later, Trout would become the first black Lutheran bishop

in the Western Hemisphere. On leaving Montgomery in 1955, he failed
to anticipate the social friction that his new parsonage would cause—
mostly because he assumed that his successor would be a Negro. Lutheran policy changed again, however, and when a white minister named
Robert Graetz finished his seminary training that year in Ohio, he found
his name on the missionary assignment list among those of his colleagues going to Africa and South America—posted to Trinity Lutheran
down in Alabama. Dutifully, Graetz had personal stationery printed up
bearing a biblical quotation: "And the angel of the Lord spoke unto Philip
saying, 'Arise, go toward the South.' " Along with his wife and their two
toddlers, Graetz headed for Montgomery, where they became the first of
Trinity's white pastoral families to live in Trout's parsonage among the
Negro parishioners.

The Graetzes discovered instantly that the social effects of the new
location were severe. Previously, Montgomery whites had allowed Trinity pastors to live among them and preach to Negro Lutherans, on much
the same social calculus that allowed doctors to visit a brothel in a
medical emergency. Now that they were living in the brothel, however,
the Graetzes forfeited their modicum of acceptability. Local whites
shunned them everywhere from the laundromat to the supermarket. In
most respects, the Graetz family lived as though they were Negroes, but
their white skin produced some unprecedented legal contortions. Because they always chose to sit in the upstairs Negro section of movie
theaters, for instance, theater owners worried that to sell them tickets
might bring down Alabama's legal sanctions against establishments that
"sponsored" interracial public meetings. (Those same laws made it technically illegal for Graetz to preach in his own church.) The theater owners' solution was to let them in free. Montgomery's ticket takers soon
learned the face of every Graetz and knew to whisk them all rapidly into
the theater, so as to minimize the ire of paying white customers. Reverend Graetz tried repeatedly to pay, believing that he should not profit
from his Christian witness. The owners would not hear of it.

The Graetzes almost never got to laugh at such absurdities. There was
too much tension. Besides, the daily ostracism caused too much hurt
within the family for its excesses to be funny. Not all the hostility came
from whites. Many of Trinity's members had been happier with Negro
pastors like Trout. Some of them said out loud that they did not need a
white man to tell them how to live. At first, even those who tried hardest
to welcome them were saddled constantly with awkwardness, as nothing
came naturally to the Graetzes. In most situations outside the Lutheran
worship service, they did not know what to eat, say, or do. Drawing on
their best natural defense, they became sincere—too sincere, even by the

standards of the clergy. At sessions of the Montgomery Human Relations Council, Reverend Graetz met most of the others who made up the town's handful of white liberals, including the Durrs. Like him, they were all sincere, and some were timid, or brilliant, or damaged. Juliette Morgan, the kindly city librarian, was a recluse by night who shut herself up in a dark house with her mother. Of the Negro ministers in town, Reverend King often attended, though he usually arrived late. Graetz found King easily approachable, always supportive of him in his difficulties as a racially isolated newcomer and curious about the details. As they became better acquainted, Graetz decided that King's own experience as a Negro student among whites in the North gave him a feel for life at Trinity Lutheran.

In October, while King was off in Georgia for a week, living and preaching with Walter McCall, a white woman boarding the Highland Avenue bus asked the driver to make Mary Louise Smith vacate a seat for her. Smith refused, was arrested, convicted, and fined nine dollars under the segregation law. Negro activists pitched themselves into another flurry of battle preparation, except that it was foreshortened this time by a pronouncement from E. D. Nixon. Smith, he decided, was no better suited to stand at the rallying point than was Claudette Colvin the previous spring. Her father was an alcoholic. She lived in one of those see-through clapboard shacks out in the country. If a legal fight started and newspaper reporters went out to interview the Smith family, said Nixon, "we wouldn't have a leg to stand on." In the end, Smith paid her fine. Nixon's judgment prevailed, but leaders of the Women's Political Council grumbled that Smith's shortcomings were irrelevant to the principles of the case.

Returning home to the afterbuzz of the Smith arrest, King prepared a formal report to his congregation at Dexter, looking back on his first year and forward to the second. This time there were no new recommendations. His brief cover letter was devoted to the subject of money. "May I close," he wrote, "by asking you to consider this question: Where else in all the world can a dollar buy so much?"

A big baby girl—weighing more than nine and a half pounds—was born three weeks later. Mother King arrived swiftly from Atlanta to take up her station. Dr. Pettus, the attending physician, was of the old school that required confinement of the mother both before the birth and for a month thereafter. He exempted Mother King from the semi-quarantine he imposed around the baby, but the new father initially had the status of a special visitor who came and went by the rules. Generally, King's role was to peek happily, to crow, to embrace, to entertain and restrain callers, and to pass along what he had heard from Dr. Pettus and the women.

Two minor disagreements intruded on the domestic excitement within the first few days. First, King told the family that he was thinking of running for president of the local NAACP chapter. Coretta objected strenuously, and Mother King supported her. The timing of the sudden announcement made it look suspiciously like one of the senior King's attention-getting maneuvers. King's wife and mother told him that the last thing he needed with a new baby was a demanding new office, especially since his church and his outside preaching already kept him constantly in motion. They were not impressed by King's reason for wanting to run, which was primarily that Rufus Lewis had been pushing him to do so and predicting that he could win. There was a good deal of discussion within the household, during which time King kept in contact with Lewis and with R. D. Nesbitt, in whose offices the NAACP held many of its meetings. His interest soon came to the attention of E. D. Nixon, who called upon King to advise him that he had controlled the NAACP for many years and was already committed to another candidate. He liked King but would have to oppose him if he ran. This warning, combined with the home-front opposition, finally made King back away, but he liked to tease his wife and mother by remarking that he might change his mind.

The second disagreement had to do with the baby's name. Coretta, seeking the unusual and distinctive, wanted to call her Yolanda Denise. King wanted something simpler, arguing that Yolanda was too difficult to pronounce, and too redolent of the tendency among middle-class Negroes to reach out for status in a name. Coretta won. King made himself happy with the nickname "Yoki," saying that if they had another daughter he would like to give her a plain name, like Mary Jane.

On December 1, 1955, the day Yolanda became two weeks old, Rosa Parks left the Montgomery Fair department store late in the afternoon for her regular bus ride home. All thirty-six seats of the bus she boarded were soon filled, with twenty-two Negroes seated from the rear and fourteen whites from the front. Driver J. P. Blake, seeing a white man standing in the front of the bus, called out for the four passengers on the row just behind the whites to stand up and move to the back. Nothing happened. Blake finally had to get out of the driver's seat to speak more firmly to the four Negroes. "You better make it light on yourselves and let me have those seats," he said. At this, three of the Negroes moved to stand in the back of the bus, but Parks responded that she was not in the white section and didn't think she ought to move. She was in no-man's-land. Blake said that the white section was where he said it was, and he was telling Parks that she was in it. As he saw the law, the whole idea of no-man's-land was to give the driver some discretion to keep the races out of each other's way. He was doing just that. When Parks refused again, he advised her that the same city law that allowed him to regulate no-man's-land also gave him emergency police power to enforce the segregation codes. He would arrest Parks himself if he had to. Parks replied that he should do what he had to do; she was not moving. She spoke so softly that Blake would not have been able to hear her above the drone of normal bus noise. But the bus was silent. Blake notified Parks that she was officially under arrest. She should not move until he returned with the regular Montgomery police.

At the station, officers booked, fingerprinted, and incarcerated Rosa Parks. It was not possible for her to think lightly of being arrested. Having crossed the line that in polite society divided Negroes from niggers, she had reason to expect not only stinging disgrace among her own people but the least civilized attentions of the whites. When she was allowed to call home, her mother's first response was to groan and ask, "Did they beat you?"

Deep in panic, the mother called E. D. Nixon's house for help. Mrs. Nixon absorbed the shock and promptly called her husband at the downtown office he maintained more or less as a place to talk civic business when he was not riding the trains.

"What was it she was arrested about?" asked Nixon.

"I don't know," Mrs. Nixon replied impatiently. "Go and get her."

Nixon sighed. It was just like his wife to give him orders as though he could always tell the white authorities to do things, such as to release prisoners. Still, he shared her urgency, because he knew Rosa Parks was in danger every minute she remained in jail. If anything happened to her there, Parks would be utterly without recourse or remedy. Nixon called Fred Gray's office, but he was gone for the day. After leaving messages for Gray all over town, Nixon summoned the courage to call the jail directly. What were the charges against Rosa Parks, he asked the desk sergeant—only to be told they were none of his damned business. Nixon hung up. This was serious. The normal courtesies he received as the universally recognized Negro leader were suspended, which must mean that the race laws had been transgressed.

Nixon called Clifford Durr and told him what he knew. Durr promised to find out what he could from the jail, and soon called back with a report: Rosa Parks was charged with violating the Alabama bus segregation laws. That was all. When he volunteered to accompany Nixon to make bond for Mrs. Parks, Nixon accepted the offer readily. In fact, he told Durr to wait for him to come by. They would convoy to the city jail. When Nixon pulled up at the Durr home, Virginia Durr was waiting outside with her husband, ready to go too. She had first known Rosa Parks as a seamstress she hired to hem dresses for her three daughters, and had thought well enough of Park's NAACP work to recommend that she spend a vacation week at one of Myles Horton's interracial workshops at the Highlander Folk School. Parks had done so, returning to say that her eyes had been opened to new possibilities of harmony between the races. Virginia Durr was indignant that the fearful humiliation of jail had now fallen upon such a person.

Officers fetched Parks from the cellblock as Nixon was signing the bond papers. She and Nixon and the Durrs were soon inside the Parks home with her mother and her husband Raymond, a barber. The atmosphere was as charged as the taciturn Rosa Parks could ever allow it to become, with much storytelling and rejoicing that the immediate danger, at least, had passed. Nixon read the mood of the Parks family well enough that he spoke business to Durr only in asides, out of their hearing. He asked for Durr's legal opinion: was this the case they had been waiting for? Could they use it to win a victory over segregation on appeal? Durr replied in snippets as he could, mindful of the Parks family. The only flaw with the case as he saw it was that the charges would first be heard in state court rather than federal court. But there were ways to move cases. Otherwise, the circumstances were highly favorable. There were no extraneous charges to cloud the segregation issue, and Rosa Parks would make a good impression on white judges. This was enough for Nixon, who already knew instinctively that Rosa Parks was without peer as a potential symbol for Montgomery's Negroes—humble enough to be claimed by the common folk, and yet dignified enough in manner, speech, and dress to command the respect of the leading classes.

Nixon asked the husband and mother to excuse Rosa briefly, so that she could speak privately with him and the Durrs. He put the question to her: would she be willing to fight the case, the way she knew they had wanted to fight earlier with Colvin and Smith? Rosa Parks did not have to be told twice what he meant, but she knew that it was a momentous decision for her family. She said she would have to approach her relatives with the idea privately, and chose to talk first alone with her mother and then with her husband. The proposal upset both of them. Raymond Parks came nearly undone. Having just felt primitive, helpless terror when his wife had been snatched into jail, he could not bear the thought that she would reenter that forbidden zone by choice. Now there was hope that the arrest could be forgiven as an isolated incident, but if she persisted, it would be deliberate. It would be political. "The white folks will kill you, Rosa," he said, pleading with her not to do it.

Rosa Parks finally announced her decision. "If you think it will mean something to Montgomery and do some good, I'll be happy to go along with it," she said. The Durrs and then Nixon soon left. It was late on a Thursday evening. Before going to bed, Nixon pulled out his portable tape recorder and reeled off a long list of people he needed to call. Meanwhile, Fred Gray had received the message about the arrest. After talking with Parks and agreeing to represent her, he had called several of his friends on the Women's Political Council, including Jo Ann Robinson. A divorced professor of English at Alabama State, Robinson had grown up the last of twelve children on a one-hundred-acre Georgia farm, which her father had told her was a gift from his own father, a wealthy white farmer. The only one of her siblings to finish college, Robinson had come South again from Cleveland in 1949. She was among the leaders of the women's group who served on Reverend King's new political affairs committee at Dexter Avenue Baptist Church. Like most professional women among the Negroes of Montgomery, she had no trouble identifying with Rosa Parks, even though she herself drove a car and seldom rode the buses. As soon as she heard from Gray that night, Robinson called her closest friends on the council. All of them responded like firefighters to an alarm. This was it.

Casting off the old rules about how Negro women should never travel alone at night in Southern towns, Robinson and her friends met about midnight at their offices at Alabama State, each under the pretext of grading exams. They drafted a letter of protest. "Another Negro woman has been arrested and thrown into jail because she refused to get up out of her seat on the bus and give it to a white person," they began. They revised the letter repeatedly, as ideas occurred to them. "Until we do something to stop these arrests, they will continue," the women wrote. "The next time it may be you, or you or you. This woman's case will come up Monday. We are, therefore, asking every Negro to stay off the buses on Monday in protest of the arrest and trial." As they worked, the women felt urgency closing in upon them. They realized that the best way to notify Montgomery Negroes, given their lack of access to newspapers or radio, was to leaflet the town through the churches and the contacts of the Women's Council. The best place to get copies of such an incendiary letter printed, they realized, was precisely where they were— at Alabama State, on the mimeograph machines. This would require stealth, because the college was funded largely by the Alabama legislature. If white people ever learned that state-employed teachers had used taxpayer-owned facilities to plot a revolt against segregation laws, heads would roll and budgets would surely be cut. So the women resolved to finish the mammoth task before daylight and never to speak of what they had done. They soon lost all thought of going to bed that night.

Robinson decided to call E. D. Nixon to let him know what they were doing. To her great surprise, the voice that came on the line was alert and full of news about the Parks case at three o'clock in the morning. Nixon was already bustling about his house getting ready to arrange the Parks defense before leaving on his morning Pullman run through Atlanta to New York and back. He instantly approved Robinson's idea of the one-day bus boycott, saying that he had something like that in mind himself. He told her that he planned to summon Montgomery's leading Negroes to a planning meeting the very next day, at which both the legal defense and the boycott would be organized. Robinson was the first to know.*

Nixon began his calls about five o'clock that morning. He called Ralph Abernathy first, then his own minister, then King. He was in a hurry. When King came on the line, Nixon did not bother to ask whether he

---

* This point, marking the origins of the Montgomery bus boycott, would become hotly contested ground to future generations of civil rights historians. King himself would divide the credit between Nixon and the Women's Political Council, citing Nixon for taking the first steps to fight the Parks case and the women for conceiving of the boycott. Nixon himself would later claim credit for both, stating that he had told his wife—after leaving the Parks home but before hearing from Robinson a few hours later—that there would be a boycott. King's partisans would dismiss Nixon's assertion with more than a hint of condescension, but Nixon's side of the story would be taken up later by various kinds of revisionists. Roy Wilkins stressed Nixon's longtime service to the NAACP, whereas black power activists stressed Nixon's proletarian origins to show that the boycott sprang from the masses. Some white chroniclers seemed to stress Nixon's role because he was a colorful character whose contribution had been overlooked. Years after the pro–E. D. Nixon revisionists, new feminist versions, largely unpublished, would stress the role of the upper-class women of the Women's Political Council.

All sources, including E. D. Nixon, agree that the long discussion at Rosa Parks's home that first night was confined to the prospect of a legal challenge to the arrest, without mention of a boycott, and no one denies that before morning the women had written an independent letter calling for a boycott. These facts support King's original division of the credit. Some of the more subjective arguments deriving from this central dispute retain their validity, however. Nixon has been slighted by popular history and patronized by supporters of King. Openly wounded by this treatment, Nixon has probably exaggerated his role in response. And the Montgomery women have been ignored to a greater extent even than Nixon.

had awakened the new baby, or even to say hello. Instead he plunged directly into the story of the Parks arrest, telling King of his determination to fight the case and his plan to stay off the buses on Monday. He asked King for his endorsement.

"Brother Nixon," King said quickly, "let me think about it and you call me back."

Nixon said fine. He'd make some other calls, but he wanted King to know that he wanted to use Dexter for the meeting that afternoon. Its central location made the church convenient for people working in downtown offices. Of course, said King—he just wanted to think before endorsing Nixon's specific plan. By the time he talked to King again, King had himself talked with Abernathy and other ministers. After endorsing the general plan, he helped Abernathy call the remaining names on Nixon's list.

One of Nixon's last calls was to Joe Azbell, the city editor of the Montgomery *Advertiser*. Promising "the hottest story you've ever written," Nixon asked Azbell to meet him at the train station. Azbell did. Nixon, wearing his white coat and porter's cap, told him the whole story as a confidential informant, mentioning no names except that of Rosa Parks, then hopped on his Atlanta-bound train.

While he was gone, about fifty of the Negro leaders assembled in the basement of King's church, where, after a protracted and often disorderly argument about whether or not to allow debate, they approved the plans more or less as Nixon had laid them out in advance. All undertook to spread the word. King and others retired as a committee to draft a new leaflet that was essentially a condensation of the one already being circulated by the thousands by the Women's Political Council. "Don't ride the bus to work, to town, to school, or any place Monday, December 5 . . ." it said. "If you work, take a cab, or share a ride, or walk." There was a final sentence with new information: "Come to a mass meeting, Monday at 7:00 P.M., at the Holt Street Baptist Church for further instruction." The meeting continued amid a good deal of chaos, as some worked to print up the leaflet on the Dexter mimeograph machine, while others phoned to warn Montgomery's eighteen Negro taxi companies that they would be called upon to be heroes on Monday, and still others huddled over countless details. The meeting broke up about midnight.

By the next day, Saturday, thousands of Montgomery's Negroes had either seen the leaflets or heard the news by word of mouth. Reverend Graetz of Trinity Lutheran had heard rumors, but his persistent questioning of his own church members brought poor results. He was still a white man, after all, and no one wanted to be the one who triggered a general alarm in Montgomery by telling him. Frustrated, Graetz decided to phone the best friend he had in town outside his congregation, the woman who used his church building for meetings of the NAACP Youth Council. "Mrs. Parks," he said, "I keep hearing that somebody was arrested on the bus and there's going to be a boycott. Is that true? Who was it?"

There was a long pause. "It's true," Parks said, almost sheepishly. "It was me, Pastor Graetz. I was the one arrested."

"*You?*" Graetz exclaimed. He rushed over to the Parks home to learn the details. The next morning, from the pulpit of Trinity Lutheran, he delivered what he called a Christian analysis of the Rosa Parks arrest. Then he announced that he and his family would observe the boycott, and he urged his members to do likewise. A murmur of approval went through the congregation. At Dexter, King made a similar announcement, as did Abernathy at First Baptist and all the others.

Nixon returned from his train run that day to find that Joe Azbell had written a story in the morning *Advertiser*, headlined "Negro Groups Ready Boycott of Bus Lines." It was not the dominant race story in the paper. That distinction went to the sensational lead item from Georgia, about how "a howling mob of Georgia Tech students" had broken through police lines at the state capitol in protest of Governor Marvin Griffin's recent statement that Georgia Tech should not be allowed to play in the upcoming Sugar Bowl because its opponent, the University of Pittsburgh, was discovered to have a lone Negro on the team as a reserve running back, and because Sugar Bowl officials had agreed to allow Pittsburgh fans to be seated on a nonsegregated basis. The Georgia governor, who since the *Brown* decision had enjoyed much favorable publicity from swashbuckling defenses of segregation, discovered that they did not fare so well against an emotional tradeoff in the sports area. He soon backed down, somewhat shaken by the experience of having the sons of his finest constituents smashing the windows and doors of his office.

Azbell's Montgomery story seemed much tamer. "A 'top secret' meeting of Montgomery Negroes who plan a boycott of city buses Monday is scheduled at 7 P.M. Monday at the Holt Street Baptist Church," he began, going on to quote liberally from both the first and second leaflets, which had been relayed into the hands of the authorities by white women who had gotten them from their maids. The story reported that Montgomery had been "flooded with thousands of copies" of the leaflets, and that the Holt Street minister said the mass meeting would be open to people of all races. Azbell never bothered to explain how a meeting so advertised and described could be called "top secret" in the newspaper. He did not need to. White people would not attend, and the purpose touched upon the possibility of revolt against segregation. Any such meeting was self-evidently "top secret," as the import of the situation overturned the literal meaning of the words. E. D. Nixon cared little about inaccuracies or the fact that the story was clearly intended as a warning to white readers. To him, the story was effective advertising. It would get the word out to more Negroes.

He was up before dawn on Monday morning. So were the Kings, M.L. drinking coffee and Coretta keeping watch at the front window, nervously waiting to see the first morning bus. When she saw the headlights cutting through the darkness, she called out to her husband and they watched it roll by together. The bus was empty! The early morning special on the South Jackson line, which was normally full of Negro maids on their way to work, still had its groaning engine and squeaky brakes, but it was an empty shell. So was the next bus, and the next. In spite of the bitter morning cold, their fear of white people and their desperate need for wages, Montgomery Negroes were turning the City Bus Lines into a ghost fleet. King, astonished and overjoyed, jumped into his car to see whether the response was the same elsewhere in the city. It was. He drove around for several hours, watching buses pass by carrying handfuls of white passengers.

Police cars, manned by officers with helmets and shotguns, followed many of the buses on the orders of the new police commissioner, Clyde Sellers. His theory, which he had announced personally on the radio in special police bulletins, was that only violence by Negroes could motivate other Negroes to stay off the buses. "Negro 'goon squads' reportedly have been organized here to intimidate Negroes who ride Montgomery City Line buses today," began Joe Azbell's front-page story. The Sellers plan called for roving police squads to intimidate the Negro goons before they could intimidate Negro bus riders. It backfired. Confused Negro passengers took a look at the heavily armed white policemen swarming around their bus stops and shied away, wanting no part of such a scene. The plan, having frightened into the boycott some of the very Negroes whom Sellers hoped to reassure, proceeded to do worse. The policemen felt bureaucratic pressure to arrest the goons. Now that practically *all* the Negroes were boycotting the buses, their boss's theory suggested that entire armies of goons must be at work. But where were they? At 7:15 P.M., police arrested a nineteen-year-old college student as he was helping an old Negro woman into his car. The officers said the student was offering the woman a ride as an alternative to the bus, but they knew this was not the kind of goon activity Commissioner Sellers had in mind. They made no more arrests.

After Rosa Parks was convicted that morning, and after Fred Gray filed notice of appeal, E. D. Nixon walked out of the courtroom to post bond for her release. The sight that greeted him in the courthouse hallway shocked him almost as much as the empty buses at dawn: a crowd of some five hundred Negroes jammed the corridor, spilling back through the doors and down the steps into the street. Nixon, who was accustomed to find there only a few relatives of the accused, knew then that the empty buses had been no fluke. The jostling, and the sight of still more worried-looking policemen with shotguns, rattled even Nixon temporarily. He tried to disperse the crowd, promising to bring Rosa Parks outside unharmed as soon as the bond was signed. Some voices shouted back that the crowd would storm the courthouse to rescue both Parks and Nixon if they did not emerge within a few minutes. Something was new in Montgomery.

All the Negro leaders knew it long before they reassembled that afternoon to plan for the evening's mass meeting. Nixon, Abernathy, and a leading Methodist minister named French had met to draw up a list of negotiating demands for the bus boycott, reasoning, as usual, that if the demands were not prearranged they would never escape the chaos of debate. No sooner had the presiding officer presented the Nixon-Abernathy-French ideas to the group as a general proposition than another clique of two or three suggested that the proposals be mimeographed and handed to all those attending the mass meeting. That way, Negroes could vote on the proposals without discussing them out loud, which would conceal their plans from any white reporters present. Another person from this group proposed that the names of the leaders also be kept secret, including all those present. They discusssed the fine points of stealth and security until E. D. Nixon rose in anger. "How do you think you can run a bus boycott in secret?" he demanded. "Let me tell you gentlemen one thing. You ministers have lived off these wash-women for the last hundred years and ain't never done nothing for them." He threatened to expose the ministers as cowards before the mass meeting if they tried to hide. He scolded the ministers and everyone else for letting the women bear the brunt of the arrests and then backing down like "little boys." "We've worn aprons all our lives," he said. "It's time to take the aprons off. . . . If we're gonna be mens, now's the time to be mens."

King arrived late at the meeting, just as Nixon was spewing out the last of his taunts. Perhaps to defend himself as the conspicuous newcomer who had drawn the crowd's eye, or perhaps to quiet what threatened to become a disastrous war of pride, he spoke before anyone could answer the tirade. "Brother Nixon, I'm not a coward," he said easily. "I don't want anybody to call me a coward." All the leaders should act openly, he said, under their own names.

Rufus Lewis seized the moment. He and Nixon had never liked each other much, having been personal and class rivals for decades. Lewis feared that Nixon's intimidating speech was a preplanned signal for someone to propose that Nixon himself head the new boycott organization, and in that light it was quite fortunate that King had arrived just then to speak in a manner that both challenged Nixon and agreed with him. All this went through Lewis' head in a flash, and he quickly took the floor to move that Dr. M. L. King be elected president. By prearrangement with Lewis, a Reverend Conley jumped up to second the motion. A momentary silence followed this challenge, as the members of various small caucuses eyed each other. There was hesitation and some discussion, but in the end no one else was nominated—not Nixon, nor Abernathy, nor any of the powerful senior ministers. Idealists would say afterward that King's gifts made him the obvious choice. Realists would scoff at this, saying that King was not very well known, and that his chief asset was his lack of debts or enemies. Cynics would say that the established preachers stepped back for King only because they saw more blame and danger ahead than glory. No leader had promised all Montgomery to secure justice for Claudette Colvin, and what would have become of his reputation if he had? In the long run, what was a fourteen-dollar fine levied on Rosa Parks to a community that had calmed down after lynchings?

After the election of other officers and the selection of a name for the organization—the Montgomery Improvement Association—someone rose to suggest that the bus boycott should be suspended during the upcoming negotiations over the demands. As of that day, he said, the boycott was a stunning success, but if they tried to go on with it people would get tired sooner or later and filter back onto the buses, which would make the white people laugh at the new MIA and grant no concessions. Other speakers supported this argument, observing that it would be better to preserve the boycott weapon as a threat than to spoil it by overuse. On the verge of approval, the proposal was suspended so that the ministers could select hymns, prayers, and speakers for the mass meeting. Then it was finessed altogether in haste. The leaders would wait to see how many people turned out that night.

King raced home to his wife and new baby sometime after six. Hesitantly, he informed Coretta that he had been drafted as president of the new protest committee. Much to his relief, she did not object to the *fait accompli* and in fact said quietly that she would support him in whatever he did. King said he would have no time for supper. He had to leave for the mass meeting within half an hour, and after that he had to address a banquet sponsored by the YMCA, one of the only integrated organizations in Montgomery. Most on his mind was the speech at Holt Street— his first appearance as the new protest leader, the first words most of the audience would have heard from him. He went into his study and closed the door, wondering how he could possibly create such an important speech in a few minutes, when he required fifteen hours to prepare an ordinary sermon. His mind raced. He knew from his conscience that he wanted to answer one peevish charge that had apeared in both newspaper articles thus far—that the Negroes had borrowed the boycott tactic from the White Citizens Councils, which had openly adopted a policy of harsh economic reprisal against Negroes who fought segregation. King searched for the correct words by which he might distinguish the bus boycott from un-Christian coercion. He had written only a few notes on a piece of paper, when it was time to go.

Elliott Finley, King's Morehouse friend with the pool table, drove him to the rally. King had a few minutes to think in the car. A traffic jam on the way to Holt Street extended the time a bit, and then a bit more, until they realized they could go no farther—the church was surrounded. The hostile press later estimated the crowd at five thousand people; Negroes put it at two or three times that figure. Whatever the exact number, only a small fraction of the bodies fit inside the church, and loudspeakers were being set up to amplify the proceedings to an outdoor crowd that stretched over several acres, across streets and around cars that had been parked at all angles. Clifford and Virginia Durr never got within three blocks of the church door. Reverend Graetz was the only white supporter inside—the only white face seen there other than reporters and cameramen. "You know something, Finley," said King, as he prepared to abandon the car. "This could turn into something big." It took him fifteen minutes to push his way through the crowd. Shortly thereafter, the Holt Street pastor called him to the pulpit.

King stood silently for a moment. When he greeted the enormous crowd of strangers, who were packed in the balconies and aisles, peering in through the windows and upward from seats on the floor, he spoke in a deep voice, stressing his diction in a slow introductory cadence. "We are here this evening—for serious business," he said, in even pulses, rising and then falling in pitch. When he paused, only one or two "yes" responses came up from the crowd, and they were quiet ones. It was a throng of shouters, he could see, but they were waiting to see where he would take them. "We are here in a general sense, because first and foremost—we are American citizens—and we are determined to apply our citizenship—to the fullness of its means," he said. "But we are here in a specific sense—because of the bus situation in Montgomery." A general murmur of assent came back to him, and the pitch of King's voice rose gradually through short, quickened sentences. "The situation is not at all new. The problem has existed over endless years. Just the other day—just last Thursday to be exact—one of the finest citizens in Montgomery—not one of the finest Negro citizens—but one of the finest citizens in Montgomery—was taken from a bus—and carried to jail and arrested—because she refused to give up—to give her seat to a white person."

The crowd punctuated each pause with scattered "Yeses" and "Amens." They were with him in rhythm, but lagged slightly behind in enthusiasm. Then King spoke of the law, saying that the arrest was doubtful even under the segregation ordinances, because reserved Negro and white bus sections were not specified in them. "The law has never been clarified at that point," he said, drawing an emphatic "Hell, no" from one man in his audience. "And I think I speak with—with legal authority—not that I have any legal authority—but I think I speak with legal authority behind me—that the law—the ordinance—the city ordinance has never been totally clarified." This sentence marked King as a speaker who took care with distinctions, but it took the crowd nowhere. King returned to the special nature of Rosa Parks. "And since it had to happen, I'm happy it happened to a person like Mrs. Parks," he said, "for nobody can doubt the boundless outreach of her integrity. Nobody can doubt the height of her character, nobody can doubt the depth of her Christian commitment." That's right, a soft chorus answered. "And just because she refused to get up, she was arrested," King repeated. The crowd was stirring now, following King at the speed of a medium walk.

He paused slightly longer. "And you know, my friends, there comes a time," he cried, "when people get tired of being trampled over by the iron feet of oppression." A flock of "Yeses" was coming back at him when suddenly the individual responses dissolved into a rising cheer and applause exploded beneath the cheer—all within the space of a second. The startling noise rolled on and on, like a wave that refused to break, and just when it seemed that the roar must finally weaken, a wall of sound came in from the enormous crowd outdoors to push the volume still higher. Thunder seemed to be added to the lower register—the sound of feet stomping on the wooden floor—until the loudness became something that was not so much heard as it was sensed by vibrations in the lungs. The giant cloud of noise shook the building and refused to go away. One sentence had set it loose somehow, pushing the call-and-response of the Negro church service past the din of a political rally and on to something else that King had never known before. There was a rabbit of awesome proportions in those bushes. As the noise finally fell back, King's voice rose above it to fire again. "There comes a time, my friends, when people get tired of being thrown across the abyss of humiliation, where they experience the bleakness of nagging despair," he declared. "There comes a time when people get tired of being pushed out of the glittering sunlight of life's July, and left standing amidst the piercing chill of an Alpine November. There . . ." King was making a new run, but the crowd drowned him out. No one could tell whether the roar came in response to the nerve he had touched, or simply out of pride in a speaker from whose tongue such rhetoric rolled so easily. "We are here —we are here because we are tired now," King repeated.

Perhaps daunted by the power that was bursting forth from the crowd, King moved quickly to address the pitfalls of a boycott. "Now let us say that we are not here advocating violence," he said. "We have overcome that." A man in the crowd shouted, "Repeat that! Repeat that!" "I want it to be known throughout Montgomery and throughout this nation that we are Christian people," said King, putting three distinct syllables in "Christian." "The only weapon that we have in our hands this evening is the weapon of protest." There was a crisp shout of approval right on the beat of King's pause. He and the audience moved into a slow trot. "If we were incarcerated behind the iron curtains of a communistic nation —we couldn't do this. If we were trapped in the dungeon of a totalitarian regime—we couldn't do this. But the great glory of American democracy is the right to protest for right." When the shouts of approval died down, King rose up with his final reason to avoid violence, which was to distinguish themselves from their opponents in the Klan and the White Citizens Council. "There will be no crosses burned at any bus stops in Montgomery," he said. "There will be no white persons pulled out of their homes and taken out on some distant road and murdered. There will be nobody among us who will stand up and defy the Constitution of this nation."

King paused. The church was quiet but it was humming. "My friends," he said slowly, "I want it to be known—that we're going to work with grim and bold determination—to gain justice on the buses in this city. And we are not wrong. We are not wrong in what we are doing." There was a muffled shout of anticipation, as the crowd sensed that King was moving closer to the heart of his cause. "If we are wrong—the Supreme Court of this nation is wrong," King sang out. He was rocking now, his voice seeming to be at once deep and high-pitched. "If we are wrong— God Almighty is wrong!" he shouted, and the crowd seemed to explode a second time, as it had done when he said they were tired. Wave after wave of noise broke over them, cresting into the farthest reaches of the ceiling. They were far beyond Rosa Parks or the bus laws. King's last cry had fused blasphemy to the edge of his faith and the heart of theirs. The noise swelled until King cut through it to move past a point of unbearable tension. "If we are wrong—Jesus of Nazareth was merely a utopian dreamer and never came down to earth! If we are wrong—justice is a lie." This was too much. He had to wait some time before delivering his soaring conclusion, in a flight of anger mixed with rapture: "And we are determined here in Montgomery—to work and fight until justice runs down like water, and righteousness like a mighty stream!" The audience all but smothered this passage from Amos, the lowly herdsman prophet of Israel who, along with the priestly Isaiah, was King's favorite biblical authority on justice.

He backed off the emotion to speak of the need for unity, the dignity of protest, the historical precedent of the labor movement. Comparatively speaking, his subject matter was mundane, but the crowd stayed with him even through paraphrases of abstruse points from Niebuhr. "And I want to tell you this evening that it is not enough for us to talk about love," he said. "Love is one of the pinnacle parts of the Christian faith. There is another side called justice. And justice is really love in calculation. Justice is love correcting that which would work against love." He said that God was not just the God of love: "He's also the God that standeth before the nations and says, 'Be still and know that I am God—and if you don't obey Me I'm gonna break the backbone of your power—and cast you out of the arms of your international and national relationships.' " Shouts and claps continued at a steady rhythm as King's audacity overflowed. "Standing beside love is always justice," he said. "Not only are we using the tools of persuasion—but we've got to use the tools of coercion." He called again for unity. For working together. He appealed to history, summoning his listeners to behave so that sages of the future would look back at the Negroes of Montgomery and say they were "a people who had the moral courage to stand up for their rights." He said they could do that. "God grant that we will do it before it's too late." Someone said, "Oh, yes." And King said, "As we proceed with our program—let us think on these things."

The crowd retreated into stunned silence as he stepped away from the pulpit. The ending was so abrupt, so anticlimactic. The crowd had been waiting for him to reach for the heights a third time at his conclusion, following the rules of oratory. A few seconds passed before memory and

spirit overtook disappointment. The applause continued as King made
his way out of the church, with people reaching to touch him. Dexter
members marveled, having never seen King let loose like that. Abernathy
remained behind, reading negotiating demands from the pulpit. The boycott was on. King would work on his timing, but his oratory had just
made him forever a public person. In the few short minutes of his first
political address, a power of communion emerged from him that would
speak inexorably to strangers who would both love and revile him, like
all prophets. He was twenty-six, and had not quite twelve years and four
months to live.

FIVE

THE MONTGOMERY
BUS BOYCOTT

A few days after the Holt Street mass meeting, one of the teachers at a Methodist missionary school near Nagpur, India, rushed outside to investigate a bellowing noise that had pierced the early morning stillness. In the hut next door, he found his colleague James Lawson still in a fit of shouting and clapping and foot-stomping. Such joyous abandon was almost as alarming to the teacher as the violence he had feared, because he knew Lawson as the essence of the cerebral personality—a man who had worn spectacles since the age of four, whose superior manner and precise articulation smothered any hint of emotionalism in his character. Yet now, even after Theopolis burst through the door, Lawson was still dancing, and could only point to a story in the English edition of the Nagpur *Times* about how thousands of Negroes were refusing to ride segregated buses in a small American city.

This was the beginning, cried Lawson. This was what he had been dreaming about, what he had gone to prison for, what he had come halfway around the world to find at its source, only to discover that Gandhism without Gandhi was dissolving into power politics and petty quarrels. Lawson was overwhelmed by the ironic news that the spirit of the Mahatma was breaking out only six or seven hundred miles south of his home in Ohio. He sensed immediately that he would come to know M. L. King, who was described in the Nagpur *Times* as a man of exactly Lawson's age, race, and profession.

In Montgomery, Juliette Morgan, the reclusive city librarian, watched the empty buses roll for a few days and then penned a letter to the Montgomery *Advertiser*. "Not since the First Battle of the Marne has the taxi been put to as good use as it has this last week in Montgomery," she wrote. "However, the spirit animating our Negro citizens as they ride these taxis or walk from the heart of Cloverdale to Mobile Road has been more like that of Gandhi than of the 'taxicab army' that saved Paris." Morgan declared that the bus boycotters had "taken a lesson from Gandhi, and from our own Thoreau, who influenced Gandhi." She recommended that her fellow white citizens read Edmund Burke's speech "Conciliation with the American Colonies," and warned them against "pharasaical zeal." "One feels that history is being made in Montgomery these days, the most important in her career," she concluded.

These last words confirmed her status as something of a ninny, even among those white people who admired the grandeur of her learning. Who of sound mind could write that a shift by Negro maids in their common mode of transportation was more important than all the past glories of Montgomery? Morgan's letter brought down upon her a prolonged harassment by young people who threw rocks through her windows, insulted her on the streets, and played tricks on her in the library. Her flighty sensitivity only provoked them to do worse. A little more than a year later, she would be found poisoned in her house, an apparent suicide. By way of explanation, whites would stress her emotional vulnerability or alleged mental problems, while Negroes remained certain that she had been persecuted to death on account of the "Battle of the Marne" letter.

Only the rarest and oddest of people saw historical possibilities in the bus boycott. Of the few people who bothered to write the *Advertiser* at first, most were white women who saw it as a justifiable demand for simple decent treatment. One woman correspondent did speculate that there must be a Communist hand behind such strife, but the great mass of segregationists did not bother to address the issue. In its first editorial, the *Advertiser* described the principal MIA demand—for bus seating by race, with Negroes from the back of the bus and whites from the front, eliminating the reserved section—as a compromise within the principles of segregation. Editor Grover Hall, Jr., advised white Montgomery simply to accept the proposal and be done with it. The very moderation of the demands led civil rights groups such as the national NAACP to frown upon the boycott as a wildcat movement for something less than integration.

As for the boycotters themselves, the religious fervor they went to bed with at night always congealed by the next morning into cold practicality, as they faced rainstorms, mechanical breakdowns, stranded relatives, and complicated relays in getting from home to job without being late or getting fired or getting into an argument with the employer, then getting home again, perhaps having to find a way to and from the grocery store, and cooking and eating supper, dealing with children and housework, then perhaps going back out into the night for a mass meeting and finally home again, recharged by the "rousements" of Abernathy and the inspiration of King, and then at last some weary but contented sleep before the aching chill of dawn started the cycle all over again. To a largely uneducated people among whom the most common occupations were maid and day laborer, the loss of what was for many their most important modern convenience—cheap bus transportation—left them with staggering problems of logistics and morale.

The bus boycott was a day-to-day operation. When the Montgomery police commissioner dropped hints during the first week that he would order the arrest of any taxi drivers who charged less than the minimum forty-five-cent fare, it became clear that the emergency ten-cent fare— and therefore the "taxicab army"—was doomed. King immediately called his college friend T. J. Jemison, who, as secretary of the National Baptist Convention, was a prince of the national church on a much higher level than the Kings.* Jemison, who knew King well enough to call him Mike, had led a bus boycott in Baton Rouge during the summer of 1953 and organized a car pool after the authorities banned the use of cut-rate and unlicensed taxi service. King gleaned from Jemison every useful detail within memory about how to organize a massive car pool. That very night he took the pulpit at a mass meeting to explain why they had to maintain the boycott without benefit of the eighteen Negro taxi companies. The good news, King announced bravely, was that they could organize a car pool similar to the one in Baton Rouge. To do this, car owners must volunteer cars, and drivers must volunteer to drive. No money could change hands directly, but passengers could make contributions to the MIA, and the MIA could in turn subsidize the costs of the car pool.

King described his proposal in the most glowing terms possible, but he knew that the complicated new system would introduce a host of prac-

---

* In a dynastic compromise of the kind often made in the baronial politics of the National Baptist Convention, Jemison was serving under President J. H. Jackson, who had ousted Jemison's blind father at Miami in 1953. It would take the younger Jemison twenty-nine years to oust Jackson.

tical problems. Cars lent to the boycott by the wealthier Negroes doubtless would be wrecked, worn, soiled, and abused by student drivers or by
passengers. The automobile was still among the prime status symbols in
the United States, and therefore to volunteer one's car as public transportation was a radical act of togetherness. Passengers, for their part,
might resent becoming dependent on the largesse of their betters. Knowing such things, King was stunned once again when the crowd greeted
his proposal with a church-rocking roar of approval. Whatever it took,
they would do it. That first night, more than 150 car owners signed up
to lend their cars to the boycott. The fractious classes of Montgomery's
Negroes now promised to blend their daily lives. Several thousand of
them floated from the mass meeting of December 8 on a buoyant new
cloud of optimism, leaving the harsh arithmetic to the future, or to God.
Between 30,000 and 40,000 Negro fares were being denied to the buses
every day. Subtracting generously for walkers and for people who were
simply staying at home, the car pool would have to supply 20,000 rides,
which worked out to more than 130 rides a day for each of the volunteered cars. By herculean efforts, King knew, Jemison had kept his boycott going in Baton Rouge for two weeks before it fell apart.

At the first negotiating session, on December 8, the three co-equal city
commissioners parried King's arguments before a large crowd of reporters, boycotters, and white spectators. Commissioner W. A. "Tacky"
Gayle (who was designated mayor because he supervised the employees
at city hall) finally suggested that the negotiating parties retire to talk
more frankly in private, and there the bus company's lawyer, Jack Crenshaw, performed the stickler's role, as he had in the Colvin case. He had
no objection to the rather vague MIA demand for greater courtesy on the
part of bus drivers, but he rejected the demand that the bus company hire
Negro drivers for predominantly Negro routes. This, said Crenshaw, was
a matter of private enterprise. As to the third and principal demand—bus
seating—Crenshaw said the MIA plan was illegal. When Crenshaw
leaned back to huddle with the other white negotiators, King thought he
heard him whisper that if the whites gave in on this point the Negroes
would go around boasting of a victory, which would be unacceptable.
Some time later, Crenshaw recalled objecting that under the MIA plan a
Negro man could be "practically rubbing knees" with a white woman.
Pride and deep feeling stalemated the talks, which were adjourned after
four hours.

    At their next meeting, on December 17, King opened with a conces-
sion. The MIA was no longer asking that the bus company hire Negro

drivers immediately, only that the company accept applications from qualified Negroes, with the intention of hiring them when job positions became available. Three eminent white ministers dominated the awkward, exploratory deliberations in the Chamber of Commerce conference room. A Methodist preacher, whom negotiator Jo Ann Robinson described as "stately, reverential, almost godly," sought to cut through the tension with an eloquent speech stressing the common religious values of the two races. In the end, however, he disappointed the MIA delegation by portraying the boycott as an exaggerated response to the frailties of human nature. Yes, he was sure that bus drivers had behaved discourteously toward Negro passengers, but he was also sure they had mistreated white ones too. The province of the soul was much larger and more spiritual than bus seats, and for that reason he was especially sorry to see ministers of the gospel leading a political campaign. When he finished, a Presbyterian minister (brother of Senator Richard Russell of Georgia) observed that it was nearly impossible to conduct discussions in good Christian faith while one side was inflicting damage on the other. Therefore, he proposed that the MIA leaders first call off the boycott to establish an atmosphere conducive to negotiations. This remained Dr. Henry "Jeb" Russell's position from start to finish.

Rev. Henry Parker of the First Baptist Church, out of which Abernathy's church had been born eighty-eight years earlier, attempted to bridge the substantive differences. The problem, said Parker, was a narrower one than most people believed, and from what he could tell most of the bus incidents could be traced to uncertainty among the Negro passengers as to just where the reserved white section ended. To eliminate this confusion, he proposed that signs be installed in all buses designating the first ten seats for whites and the last ten seats for Negroes, with those in between to be filled by overflow passengers of either race. King and the other Negroes objected vehemently to the detested "White Only" signs, which had been eliminated from Montgomery buses twenty years before. The whites replied that they were open to any other proposal that promised to eliminate the confusion. They drew the attention of the Negro delegation to technical flaws in the MIA proposal. Suppose that a bus filled completely with Negroes seating themselves from the back, as the MIA wanted, and then, at a certain stop, ten Negro passengers left the bus from scattered seats while ten white passengers boarded. Where would the white passengers sit? How could they call such a bus segregated, in compliance with state law? On such hypotheticals, the delegations circled to exhaustion.

Six days before Christmas, a newcomer took a seat on the white side of the conference table at the Chamber of Commerce. Someone whispered to King that he was Luther Ingalls, secretary of the Montgomery White Citizens Council. When Ingalls rose to speak, King jumped up to object that he was not a member of the committee. "Furthermore," King said rather testily, "we will never solve this problem so long as there are persons on the committee whose public pronouncements are anti-Negro." When someone replied that the mayor had approved Ingalls' presence, King said the mayor had acted unfairly by adding to the committee without consulting the MIA representatives.

King's statement provoked Reverend Parker of First Baptist to defend Ingalls. "He has just as much right to be on this committee as you do," Parker said heatedly. "You have a definite point of view, and *you* are on it." Some of the other whites, following Parker's lead, criticized King for introducing hostility and mistrust into the meeting before Ingalls had spoken a word. These comments set off an acrimonious exchange between white and Negro delegates over what was objective and who had cast the first stone. Each side moved to adopt its own proposals, and the other side always voted as a bloc to stop them. Some of the whites criticized King for dominating the discussion on the Negro side. He was inflexible, they said, an obstacle to negotiation. This accusation hung in the room until Abernathy stood up to say that Dr. King spoke for him and all the other Negro members. From there, negotiations resumed in a rather bitter mood. Finally, King made a motion to recess. The whites, he said, had come to the meeting with "preconceived ideas."

This time there was no need for Reverend Parker to lead the counterattack. Mrs. Logan A. Hipp, a white woman who had been serving as secretary for the meeting, rose to speak. "You are the one who has come here with preconceived ideas," she told King, trembling with indignation. "I resent very deeply the statement that we have come here with preconceived ideas. I most certainly did not." As proof, she mentioned that she had come to the conclusion that she would vote in favor of hiring Negro bus drivers. Negroes already served as chauffeurs, she said, and therefore could no doubt adapt to the buses. A white man seconded Mrs. Hipp, saying that he had come prepared to vote for some of the MIA proposals.

A few hours later, King left the utterly unproductive meeting burdened by what he called a "terrible sense of guilt." He had come to the negotiations expecting to find that the more enlightened whites would acknowledge the soundness of his moral claims, like the whites at Crozer and Boston University, and that the less enlightened ones would expose themselves in defensive hatred, like the more abusive segregationist whites he had encountered in his life. Instead, he found that the whites sincerely believed that morality was neutral to the issue, that the White

Citizens Council was more or less a natural counterpart of the MIA as a racial interest group. The whites had spoken as the diplomats of a large country might defend their interests to diplomats from a small one. Their technical approach had deprived King of the moral ground he had occupied all his life. Frustrated, King had spoken in anger and resentment, which had served only to ruin the negotiations and convince the more reasonable whites that if there was indeed a moral battle at hand, they and not King held the advantage. Filled with self-reproach, King called Reverend Parker on the telephone to apologize for any of his comments that had given offense. Parker seemed taken aback by the very sound of King's voice, and by the unprecedented overture that was at once humble and gentlemanly, suggesting equality. He fell into a nervous, perfunctory recitation of the points he had made earlier in the day.

Parker called no more meetings, and the pressure of continuing the boycott fell heavily on the MIA. They passed the Baton Rouge car-pool record and struggled onward. Every day's transportation brought slightly less chaos but more strain and fatigue; every mass meeting brought renewal. Speakers built morale at the predominantly female meetings by singling out some of the walking women as heroes. One of the more conservative ministers told the crowd about a group of women he had seen walking to work early one morning. They were walking in pride and dignity, he declared, with a gait that would "do justice to any queen." The same preacher quoted an elderly woman who had told him that if her feet gave out she would crawl on her knees before riding the buses. Another preacher told the crowd of his effort to give a ride to an ancient woman known to almost everyone as Mother Pollard. She had refused all his polite suggestions that she drop out of the boycott on account of her age, the preacher announced. He inspired the crowd with a spontaneous remark of Mother Pollard's, which became a classic refrain of the movement: "My feets is tired, but my soul is rested."

King took to the pulpit to say that he knew everyone was worrying about how to do their Christmas shopping. He proposed that they all rally to the boycott and to the original meaning of Christmas at the same time by refusing to shop at all. They should take the money they were planning to spend on presents and divide it into thirds—putting one part into their savings account, giving another part to charity and the third to the MIA. If they had to go somewhere, they should visit someone in need or go to church or a mass meeting. By restoring the true spirit of Christmas, they could give each other a lasting gift that no amount of money could buy.

A sharp decline in Christmas purchases by Negroes caused Montgomery store owners to wince, but they were not greatly alarmed. Negro

purchasing power accounted for a small fraction of their business, and
the effect of the drop-off was spread among a large number of merchants.
City Bus Lines enjoyed no such cushion, however. Its financial distress
reached quickly to Chicago, headquarters of the parent company, and the
men running the Montgomery subsidiary spoke the blunt, empirical language of financial pain. From the beginning, their public statements that
the boycott was 99 percent effective gave no comfort to the Montgomery
politicians who were minimizing the boycott to the same news reporters.
In the first week of 1956, bus company managers told the three city
commissioners that they faced imminent bankruptcy. White people were
not even beginning to make up the loss of Negro riders, they said.
No matter how much the mayor and the White Citizens Council
urged whites to patronize the buses, most of them drove cars and
could not bring themselves to climb aboard a bus. Therefore, the bus
company demanded an emergency fare increase. The commissioners
had no choice but to approve, but they felt a strong political incentive to make sure that if there was to be blame, the voters would lay it
elsewhere.

Three days after the increase was approved, a crowd of some 1,200
people gathered at the Montgomery City Auditorium for a rally of the
White Citizens Council. The first of two guest speakers from Arkansas
told the audience of the *real* boycott, the white boycott, in which Arkansas council members were cooperating to cut off credit, supplies, sales,
and all other forms of economic sustenance to Negroes identified as anti-
segregation activists. Just as the speaker was making sarcastic remarks
about the few fainthearted Arkansas businessmen who were afraid of
alienating Negro customers, a booming voice rang out from the back of
the auditorium. "*I* don't have any Negro customers!" shouted Clyde
Sellers, the Montgomery city commissioner in charge of police. Sellers
walked grandly down the aisle to the stage, and as the hushed crowd
recognized him they erupted row by row into a prolonged standing ovation. Lifted to the podium and introduced, Sellers assured the crowd that
he would never "trade my Southern birthright for a hundred Negro
votes." This brought a roar of applause that was topped only by his
dramatic pledge to join the White Citizens Council that very night. A
large photograph of Sellers shaking hands with one of the Arkansas
speakers appeared the next day at the top of the *Advertiser*'s front page,
above the headline "Sellers Draws Applause at White Citizen Parley."
The story said he "stole the show."

Daddy King, arriving on January 8 to preach at Dexter, found his son
under nearly unbearable pressure. The boycott had lasted a month.
Transportation chairman Rufus Lewis had dragooned nearly every

Negro-owned vehicle into the car pool—between 275 and 350 a day—and there were no replacements for those who wanted to drop out. The MIA treasury was exhausted, which meant that Lewis relied increasingly on goodwill, and the inspiration of the mass meetings was wearing down under the hardships of another day's resistance. Accordingly, the day after Daddy King's sermon, the MIA leaders sued for peace. They asked for a fourth negotiating session, this time with Sellers and the two other city commissioners. Fred Gray, not King, presented a new MIA plan. This was a conciliatory gesture in itself, and Gray's legal presentation made it clear that the MIA was bending to the city's technical view of the seating problem. He announced that the MIA was now willing to make a major concession: Negroes would move voluntarily to fill seats that became vacant toward the back of the bus, and white passengers would move forward to fill vacancies toward the front. This meant that under busy conditions the passengers would be resegregating themselves continuously, and, as a practical matter, the Negroes would be doing nearly all the moving. On a full bus, many Negro riders would never be able to relax in their seats. They would be obliged to keep looking to the rear to see if they had to move. But at least they would not have to stand up over empty seats in the white reserved section, nor would they have to vacate seats on the order of bus drivers who anticipated the arrival of whites.

The city commissioners rejected the new offer categorically. There were remote technical objections, such as what would happen if disagreement arose among the passengers as to which of them needed to move, but the more powerful objections were political and psychological. Under the new proposal, white passengers would be obliged to move forward to fill vacant seats to make room for Negroes standing in the back. This was unheard of—the law had never required whites to move for Negroes. The commissioners held fast to the whites-only section as a requirement of the segregation laws. Their position was hardening, the more so because they saw the MIA weakening.

At the next MIA executive board meeting, the members admitted gloomily that they had misconstrued the nature of the contest. It was no longer—if indeed it ever had been—a question of finding the proper wording for the best possible compromise. According to the official minutes of the meeting, the board agreed that the negotiations had broken down into a siege, testing "which side can hold out the longer time, or wear the other down." This new strategic situation boded ill for the MIA. It could hold fast until forced to surrender, or it could try to reverse its retreats by taking a wild gamble to offset the steady erosion of strength. Ironically, the Montgomery Negroes faced a strategic disadvantage not unlike that of the Confederates in 1862, when daring counterstrokes made Southern legends of Robert E. Lee and Stonewall Jackson.

This kind of historical twist was just the thing to appeal to Grover Hall, Jr., the editor of the Montgomery *Advertiser*. Hall was anything but a conventional white citizen of the town. Scorning piety and most social orthodoxy, he cultivated his own eccentricity to the point of decorating his apartment with mynah birds and large stands of camellias. Hall was a dandy. He seemed to enjoy the stories that circulated of his elegant bachelorhood—of his wry humor and his scotch and his music collection, and the effects of the combination upon a succession of fine young women who possessed just a touch of wildness. Hall cherished the image of himself as a self-taught historian and *philosophe*, who had inherited the editorship despite his lack of college training. His idol was H. L. Mencken, notwithstanding Mencken's celebrated satires on the South as a land filled with pretentious buffoons. In fact, Hall took a rather perverse pleasure in tweaking his fellow Southerners with Mencken-like observations on their peculiarities. When Clyde Sellers made his Hollywood entrance at the City Auditorium, Hall wrote derisively that "in effect, the Montgomery police force is now an arm of the White Citizens Council."

In January, concluding reluctantly that the boycott had endured long enough to require special journalistic attention, Hall summoned a young reporter named Tom Johnson to his office for an assignment: find out "who is behind the MIA." Perhaps the Negroes would talk with him. Johnson received the challenge with trepidation. Never before had the *Advertiser* approached Negro life as a subject for serious journalism. As the paper had no reliable news sources among Montgomery's Negroes, Johnson talked first with the police and with every knowledgeable white leader in town. The most common opinion he found was that the NAACP was secretly directing the boycott. This was everywhere, but it was vague. Probing further, Johnson found an intriguing current of suspicion pointing toward a man who worked ceaselessly for the boycott but professed to have little to do with its direction. The suspect's humility, it was thought, might be the perfect disguise. After discussing his preliminary findings with Hall, Johnson wrote the first article of his boycott series about Reverend Graetz, who, as a white man, seemed uniquely qualified for the role of hidden mastermind. With this thesis, Hall and Johnson bravely took their readers across the racial barrier.

Johnson's story, "The Mechanics of the Bus Boycott," appeared on January 10 and gave white citizens their first specific news about the inner workings of the MIA—its budget (nearly $7,000 spent so far), the number of cars in the car pool (up to 350 daily), and the ideas of the leadership. Johnson wove these facts into a profile of Graetz, but he did not write explicitly that Graetz was the "brains behind the boycott." He had come to disbelieve the rumors himself, partly because he found Graetz to be almost suicidally ingenuous. Unfazed by interrogation, Graetz volunteered stories animated by a childlike faith and utter disregard of political reality. He recalled, for instance, that he had once been introduced to the NAACP's Walter White, and that White had complimented young white people for doing so much to advance the NAACP cause. "Naturally, I just beamed," Graetz told Johnson, "because that really fit me." Such statements floored Johnson (who regarded White as an "incendiary"), convincing him beyond doubt that Graetz was incapable of the deviousness required to run the boycott covertly.

The next Saturday morning, Johnson kept his appointment at the Dexter Avenue pastor's office, where King was finishing work on his sermon for the next day, "How to Believe in a Good God in the Face of Glaring Evil." It was the day before King's twenty-seventh birthday. Johnson, who was about King's age, was among the first of many reporters who found that King looked and acted much older than his years. He spoke slowly and formally, seeming to protect himself with a great wall of dignity. Johnson returned to the *Advertiser* offices with a notebook full of information, including the full title of the dissertation on Tillich and Wieman. He told Hall that he was "relatively unimpressed." For the editor's benefit, he read notes of King's quotations on Tillich and Kant, even Nietszche, which Johnson interpreted as evidence of King's eagerness to use philosophical patter to impress people. Maybe it worked on the Montgomery Negroes, he conceded, because Johnson had seen some of the oldest Negro ministers in town treat King with extraordinary respect, bordering on sycophancy. King spoke with authority on the boycott and might well be the leader. Unlike Graetz, he seemed to have the capacity for tactical maneuver. King had told Johnson that although as MIA leader he was seeking concessions within segregation, he was personally for "immediate integration" because as a minister of the gospel he believed segregation to be evil. This candor supported what Montgomery whites had been saying all along—that the radical Negro leaders were not really for segregation, that they were lying.

Johnson wrote up many of the pertinent facts of King's history, including the exact number of years that grandfather A. D. Williams had been pastor of Ebenezer, and went so far as to search out Will Durant's *Story of Philosophy* to give his readers a definition of "dialectics," about which King talked so much. The publication in the *Advertiser* of a full-scale

portrait of a Negro was a historic event in itself. And while hostile readers could draw from it inferences that King was uppity and devious, as
Johnson himself believed, the tone of the article was generally neutral.
Hall wanted it straight. If angry whites objected, Hall would tell them
that the city fathers had bollixed things up in pretending to know everything about the local Negroes. Perhaps it was time to learn something
about those inciting this rebellion. In the article, Johnson committed
himself to only one judgment about King, in the headline: "The Rev.
King Is Boycott Boss." Then he hedged. "There seems to be uncertainty
in the minds of the white community of Montgomery over the identity
of the director of the bus boycott," he began. "Who is the acknowledged
boycott leader? He seems to be the Rev. Martin Luther King, Jr."

The *Advertiser* published Johnson's article on January 19, just in time
for it to be stirred into the cycles of frustration and mistrust that were
rising in Montgomery. Ignorance and fear in various combinations gave
rise to the possibility of a blind man's brawl. That same week, Police
Commissioner Sellers told the Jaycees that the boycott was continuing
only because white citizens were "sitting by." Ninety percent of the
Negroes wanted to ride the buses, he declared, but were intimidated by
goon squads under the command of the Negro elite, which had never
ridden the buses and never would. The Sellers speech made the front
page. In combination with the Johnson article, it inspired a rumor campaign directed personally against King. He was an outsider, whites said
to each other and to Negroes they knew. He had never even been on a
bus in Montgomery. He was a highfalutin preacher who was mainly
interested in getting his name in the newspaper. Whites repeated among
themselves what became the standard joke, purporting to quote one of
the poor foot soldiers of the boycott: "Those Negroes are making things
awful tough on us niggers."

Myths circulating between and within the races reinforced one another
to produce bizarre, unintended effects. Some of the white women who
needed the services of their maids badly enough to drive them to and
from Rufus Lewis' car-pool pickup spots seized upon the commissioner's
story, saying that they transported the maids only to protect them from
the goon squads—not, of course, to support the boycott. Some Negroes,
frightened by the rising white anger against the boycott, rallied to the
conservative NAACP idea of bringing the case to court, even though that
meant the radical step of challenging segregation, while others rallied
more strongly to the boycott precisely to avoid the tinderbox of the
NAACP. The city commissioners, meanwhile, focused their attention
on the fact that practically none of the former bus riders would tell a
white person that they thought the boycott was a good idea. Ordinary

Negro folk would tell even known MIA supporters like the Durrs that their regular bus had "broken down" that day, or that they were walking for medical reasons, or, in a pinch, that they "just stays off the buses and leaves that boycott alone." The commissioners, blinkered by myth and deception, devised a brazen political gamble to put the Negroes back on the buses.

On Saturday night, January 21, a reporter named Carl Rowan saw an item moving on the AP wire in Minneapolis: the Sunday *Advertiser* would break the news that the Negroes had agreed to end the boycott. All Negroes would return to the buses Monday morning, said the story, which spelled out settlement terms including more courtesy from the bus drivers, special "all-Negro" buses during rush hours, and preservation of the existing seating arrangements on normal bus runs. Rowan already had been to Montgomery to cover the boycott. Finding it difficult to believe that the MIA leaders would accept such a minimal settlement, he called King in Montgomery to find out whether the story was true.

Listening to Rowan read the AP ticker, King felt the bottom fall out of his composure. He admitted that he knew nothing of such a deal. Privately, he feared that some of his MIA colleagues might have betrayed him behind his back. It was possible, King knew, for rivals to plot privately with the white people, especially because he was so exposed as a young outsider. Now that there was scant hope of negotiating an honorable settlement or of holding out long enough to force one, he was the natural scapegoat for almost certain humiliation. Compressed tensions could have caused a hemorrhage within the MIA leadership—but who? Rowan told him that the *Advertiser* story identified no one on the Negro delegation, saying only that it included "three prominent Negro ministers." King asked Rowan to call Commissioner Sellers to find out if the story was really true and, if possible, to learn the names of the ministers.

Rowan agreed. King hung up and waited. The timing of the story was clever. It would spring upon Montgomery just in time to cause mass confusion in the Negro churches at Sunday morning services. Many of the boycotters would be angry with the meager terms, while others would be happy that the ordeal was over and proud that they had given the white folks a run for their money. The fragile psychology of the boycott would be broken. And the MIA leaders would face the impossible choice of endorsing the settlement or admitting that it was not theirs.

Rowan called back. Sellers had confirmed the story, he reported, but had refused to name the three ministers on grounds of confidentiality. The most Rowan could pry out of Sellers was their church affiliations:

one was a Baptist, one a Presbyterian, and the third the pastor of a Holiness church. King's mind pounced on these clues. A Holiness church? Was Rowan sure? There was no such thing as a "prominent" Holiness minister among Montgomery Negroes—nor were there any Holiness preachers among the MIA leadership. A crack of hope appeared to King. With Rowan's clues, he thought he might find out who the conspirators were, if they existed. The Baptist preacher could be any one of a multitude, but there were very few Negro Presbyterians to investigate.

Fortified by such hope, King placed calls to the MIA leadership. His tone and his words put this crisis so far above all the other ones attendant to the 20,000 daily rides of the car pool that the essential preachers were all sitting in his living room within half an hour. King told them the shocking news of the story that would be in the paper the next morning. The immediate response of his colleagues brought great relief to King. No one rallied to the settlement as inevitable. They all denounced it. Everyone was alarmed, but no one wanted to give in to the destructive potential of the story without a fight. In short, they reacted as King himself had reacted, which confirmed his belief that the conspirators were not among them.

The first thing to do was to identify the three preachers in league with the commissioners. They learned all three names before midnight, and the results were as favorable as the King group could have wished. The three preachers who had met with the city commissioners were neither MIA members nor influential citizens. They were country preachers, who said Mayor Gayle had called them to city hall to discuss unspecified "insurance matters" and then handed them a copy of the bus settlement when they got there. That was it. The audacity of the city commissioners registered: they were engineering a naked hoax on the calculation that it would dissolve the boycott instantly or, failing that, at least divide the Negroes so that the boycott could never last. The ministers in King's home faced the calamitous prospect that the ruse might work. The commissioners had surprise and authority working for them, and the Negroes lacked a means of mass communication that could compete with the *Advertiser*.

They decided to wake up every single Negro minister in Montgomery, plus Graetz, in the hope that all of them would from their pulpits denounce the *Advertiser* story as a fake. Half the ministers went back to the telephones for this task, while King went off into the night with a group that admitted knowing the locations of the country "dives." This was Saturday night. By virtue of Rowan's warning, they had a chance to catch large numbers of their fellow citizens at the only traditional Negro meeting places other than the churches. A few of them, such as Rufus

Lewis' Citizens Club, approached the atmosphere of a ballroom, but the masses gathered at unmarked spots far out in the country, where people of King's dress and demeanor were never seen. There the laborers, farmers, and maids, often still in their work boots and dirty uniforms, came to lose themselves in loud music and strong drink and hugging and sweaty dancing. King and his coterie of prim preachers must have made quite a sight as they shouldered their way into the flesh and the noise, got the music to stop as it did only for police raids and major fights, cleared their throats, and finally introduced themselves to say that the white people were trying to call off the boycott with a trick, that the boycott was still on no matter what the *Advertiser* said in the morning, and that they should tell everybody that Reverend King and the others said in person to stay off the buses and come to the mass meeting Monday night. Then, after a few cheers and some grunts, and perhaps a question or two, the preachers moved out across the back roads to the next juke joint.

On Monday morning, the day after the *Advertiser* announced that the boycott had been settled, empty buses rolled through the streets once again. The bus company manager announced tersely that there was "no noticeable increase on the Negro routes." The city commissioners were of no mind to accept stark physical realities that contradicted their public assurances of the previous day. Cornered, faced with public ridicule, they fought back in all directions at once. Mayor Gayle immediately issued what Joe Azbell, on the next day's front page, called a "dynamic statement." He first blamed the collapse of the weekend agreement on the duplicity of the three Negro ministers he said had approved it. The commissioners had tried "with sincerity and honesty to end the boycott," but now it was "time to be frank." The government had "pussyfooted around long enough." The Negroes believed they had "the white people hemmed up in a corner," said the mayor, but the whites "have no concern" and "do not care" and "are not alarmed" about Negro bus riders. "It is not that important to whites that the Negroes ride the buses," he repeated. "When and if the Negro people desire to end the boycott, my door is open to them. But until they are ready to end it, there will be no more discussions."

Hard upon this statement came the announcement from city hall that Commissioner Frank Parks and Gayle were following Sellers into the ranks of the White Citizens Council, making it unanimous. The next day, Mayor Gayle was back on the front page urging the white women of the city to stop helping their servants. "The Negroes are laughing at white people behind their backs," he said. "They think it's very funny and amusing that whites who are opposed to the Negro boycott will act

as chauffeurs to Negroes who are boycotting the buses." Commissioner
Sellers announced at the same time that he was instructing the Montgomery police to toughen up on Negroes standing around on the streets
waiting for rides. Commissioner Parks announced that dozens of businessmen had volunteered to lay off employees who supported the boycott. All three commissioners said they were surprised by the outpouring
of public support for their new hard line. Mayor Gayle held up a thick
stack of congratulatory telegrams. Sellers said people had walked into
his office volunteering to help the police. The city hall switchboard operator said she was swamped with calls praising the mayor, and Joe
Azbell found excited white people all over town. "I hope the Negroes
walk until they get bunions and blisters," one man told him.

Among MIA leaders, gratification over the success of the weekend
rescue mission was restrained severely by fear. It was one thing to defy
the city authorities for eight weeks, and still another to humiliate them
and call them outright liars from every pulpit in town. A grim King
offered his resignation to the MIA board that same Monday. Now there
was no chance at all of a negotiated settlement with him as the MIA
leader, but his offer lay on the table. No one would pick it up, as the
other prospective leaders knew that to change was to split, and to split
inevitably was to lose. Rev. S. S. Seay, one of the most respected of the
senior ministers, was moved to call King back to duty in the language of
the Messiah. "You are young and well-trained in the spirit," he told King.
"I will drink my portion of this cup, but you can drink of it deeper."

The executive board gave King a unanimous vote of confidence. Then
it turned to the more difficult task of devising a new strategy. One faint
hope was that the city would allow a group headed by Rufus Lewis to
operate a Negro-owned bus line, which would take the pressure off the
car pool. The city would almost certainly deny Lewis' application for a
franchise, however, lest it be accused of donating the economic benefits
of segregation to the Negroes. Assuming that the Lewis plan would fail,
the board members discussed their ultimate weapon—a federal lawsuit
against bus segregation. Fred Gray, knowing that white Alabama would
react to such a step as the social equivalent of atomic warfare, had been
quietly seeking advice on the possibility since the first week of the boycott, when he wrote to NAACP lawyers in New York. Also, he had talked
extensively with Clifford Durr and with several of the more experienced
Negro lawyers in the state. All agreed that the federal suit offered the
best hope of a court-ordered solution, certainly much better than the
Rosa Parks appeal, which was bogged down in the state courts. Durr
warned Gray to be sure of his plaintiffs, saying that if the white authorities could bring enough pressure to make a plaintiff back out of a suit,

they could then bring criminal prosecution against Gray himself on the obscure charge of "barratry," or false legal representation. Durr knew of a Negro lawyer who had been driven from the state by such means.

A thousand pitfalls lay in the path of the federal suit, some technical and others political. Gray reported to the board that he was having trouble locating potential clients—people who had been mistreated on the buses and were willing to stand firm as plaintiffs. He had been unable to find a single Negro male in Montgomery willing and able to be a suitable plaintiff. But he had found several women, including Claudette Colvin and her mother. He told the board that he could be ready to file a case in a matter of days. Legally, the case appeared to be sound, but it would take many months, if not years, to resolve. This presented the MIA leaders with unpleasant choices. If they called off the boycott pending the outcome of the legal proceedings, they might as well not have had the boycott in the first place. If they continued it, they would face for the first time the likelihood of a more or less permanent car pool, at a time when strain was putting new cracks in the operation every day. Under pressure, the MIA board members were second-guessing themselves even as they voted to direct Fred Gray and the strategy committee to prepare final recommendations on the lawsuit by the next week. There was no celebration. The white people across town were doing the celebrating that Monday. By the peculiar jujitsu of the boycott, the white people were excited after their weekend fiasco, while the Negroes were bemoaning the implications of their successful rescue mission. Every action seemed dwarfed by reaction in the next round. It had been so since the bus driver's first words to Rosa Parks.

From the next day forward, Montgomery policemen stopped car-pool drivers wherever they went—questioning them, checking their headlights and windshield wipers, writing traffic tickets for minute and often imaginary violations of the law. Car-pool drivers crept along the road and gave exaggerated turn signals, like novices in driving school. Policemen ticketed them anyway. Jo Ann Robinson, known as a stickler in everything from driving to diction, would get no less than seventeen tickets in the next couple of months—some for going too fast, others for going too slow. Traffic fines mounted, diverting into the city treasury money that might have gone into the MIA car-pool fund. Drivers feared that their insurance would be canceled or their licenses suspended. Backbiting increased, with some people saying that Rufus Lewis was too dictatorial to run the car pool and others saying that he sympathized too readily with the drivers as opposed to the riders.

On Thursday afternoon, January 26, King finished his day at the Dexter church office and started home with his secretary and Bob Williams, his friend from Morehouse. King was driving. When he stopped to pick up a load of passengers at one of the downtown car-pool stops, two motorcycle policemen pulled up behind him. All the passengers in King's car tried to behave normally, but three blocks down the street the motorcycles were still close behind. Williams told King to creep along; maybe they would go away. Nothing happened during the drive to the next pickup station, but when the passengers started to leave the car, one of the motorcycle policemen pulled up next to the driver's window and said, "Get out, King. You're under arrest for speeding thirty miles an hour in a twenty-five-mile zone."

Stunned, King did not protest. Telling Williams to notify Coretta, he stepped out of the car and soon found himself in the back of a radio-summoned police cruiser, whispering to himself that everything would be all right. King said nothing to the policemen, even when he realized that the cruiser was heading away from downtown. Panic seized him. Why weren't they going to the jail? The farther they went, past strange neighborhoods toward the country, the more King gave in to visions of nooses and lynch mobs. When the cruiser turned a corner on a dark street and headed across a bridge, his mind locked onto a single fear of the river. He was trembling so badly that it took him some time to absorb the meaning of the garish neon sign ahead, "Montgomery City Jail." He felt a tumbling rush of emotions—first joy that he was not going to be killed by a mob, then embarrassment that he had never even known where the city jail was and had assumed it was downtown, then guilt that he had blocked the jail out of his mind so thoroughly even when some of the boycotters were going there, then a colder though less piercing fear again as he realized he was going there, too. This last fear swelled up inside him in the corridor as he smelled the foul cell long before he got there, and when the jailer said, "All right, get on in there with all the others," he stood numb. King heard the iron door clang shut for the first time on him and a lifetime of distinctions.

The moment did not last forever, though, and before he finished staring at the wood-slat bunks and the toilet in the corner, the other prisoners recognized his face. Then King himself recognized a schoolteacher from the bus boycott. The teacher joined the drunks and common criminals who rushed up to King wanting to hear his story. Jail was not the end of the world to them, of course, and every new prisoner had a story. Before King could finish his, one of the prisoners interrupted to ask his help in getting out. Another did the same, and then others, until King finally shouted out, "Fellows, before I can assist in getting any of you out, I've got to get my own self out." At this, the entire cell erupted in laughter. King was such a mixture of the exalted and the common—the formal "assist" of the educated leader and the plaintive "own self" of all prisoners. For him, the shock of his first arrest was already over.

Abernathy was the first to arrive at the jail after Williams and Coretta spread the alarm. His frantic urgency to get King out ran smack into the bureaucracy of the constabulary, and after finally accepting the fact that it was too complicated and too late in the evening to get King out on a property bond, Abernathy raced off to scrounge up enough currency to make a cash bond. Leaving, he passed carloads of Dexter members and MIA supporters who were converging on the jail. On the inside, King thought he was being bailed out when the jailer came after him. So did the prisoners, one of whom shouted, "Don't forget us when you get out." King shouted back that he wouldn't, but soon found himself rolling his fingers across an inkpad. Fingerprinted, hopes dashed, he was soon back in the cell. By the time the jailer came for him again, he had already learned to expect nothing. He held himself in check even when he began to realize that now it was the jailer, not he, who was frightened—a large crowd of Negroes had practically surrounded the building. The jailer hurried King out the front door on his own recognizance, and King, who had entered the jail in the grip of terror a couple of hours earlier, walked out to address a huge throng of well-wishers. It was some time later, at that night's mass meeting, before Abernathy caught up with the switches and reversals that rendered his cash unnecessary.

Word of King's arrest radiated through all of Negro Montgomery, stimulating rumors, horror stories, and vows of retribution. A restive crowd gathered outside the packed mass meeting. Inside, King and the other MIA leaders feared that the latecomers who could not squeeze into the meeting might do something violent. Besides, they wanted to share King's story and the joyous unity of the mass meeting with everyone possible. So the leaders took the unprecedented step of sending criers outside to announce that there would be a second mass meeting at another church immediately after the present one. With this news, the outside crowd moved off, mostly on foot, to the second church, which they filled, then to a third one.

This phenomenon repeated itself that night until there had been no fewer than seven mass meetings. Many people attended more than one of them. No one could believe it. In a floating conversation among several of King's friends and peers, mostly Dexter members, it was decided that it was too dangerous to let King drive anymore. To protect him, they would form themselves into a corps of drivers and bodyguards. It was agreed that they must override any objections from King and start that very night. Richmond Smiley went off to fetch his little .25-caliber Baretta. Bob Williams, another of those who would be a driver for the next few years, was so moved by the night's events that he went back to his studio and worked until morning, arranging what would become his first published choral work, "Lord, I Just Can't Turn Back." His choir at Alabama State performed the composition that week.

King woke up the next morning to a fresh day of pressure. For him, time was fluctuating too rapidly between moments of deep fear and those of high inspiration. Late the next night, his mind was turning over as he lay in bed. Coretta had fallen asleep. The phone rang again. "Listen, nigger," said the caller, "we've taken all we want from you. Before next week you'll be sorry you ever came to Montgomery." King hung up on the angry voice. Hope of sleep receded further. He paced the floor awhile before giving in completely to wakefulness, which drove him to the kitchen to make a pot of coffee. Some of the Negro callers were just curious about his arrest, while others wanted to complain about the car pool. He never knew what to expect. The sensations of the incoming images pressed in upon him—the hatred of the whites, the burdened, offended rectitude of the middle-class Negroes, the raw courage or neediness of the plain folk. He associated the Negro voices with the sea of enraptured black faces he had seen from the pulpit at mass meetings. The pressure of the Negro callers worked against this image, as did the white callers against his memories of Crozer. There was no idea nor imaginable heart large enough to satisfy all of them, or to contain them. The limitless potential of a young King free to think anything, and therefore to be anything, was constricted by realities that paralyzed and defined him. King buried his face in his hands at the kitchen table. He admitted to himself that he was afraid, that he had nothing left, that the people would falter if they looked to him for strength. Then he said as much out loud. He spoke the name of no deity, but his doubts spilled out as a prayer, ending, "I've come to the point where I can't face it alone." As he spoke these words, the fears suddenly began to melt away. He became intensely aware of what he called an "inner voice" telling him to do what he thought was right. Such simplicity worked miracles, bringing a shudder of relief and the courage to face anything. It was for King the first transcendent religious experience of his life. The moment lacked the splendor of a vision or of a voice speaking out loud, as Vernon Johns said they did, but such differences could be ascribed to rhetorical license. For King, the moment awakened and confirmed his belief that the essence of religion was not a grand metaphysical idea but something personal, grounded in experience—something that opened up mysteriously beyond the predicaments of human beings in their frailest and noblest moments.

The next day, a Saturday, King worked until early evening at the MIA and at the Dexter office. Among other chores, he wrote a letter to thank Roy Wilkins for the NAACP's "fine contribution" to the MIA, which had arrived not long after King publicly criticized the NAACP for scorning the boycott. Appropriately to their long future together, this first exchange between King and the famous civil rights leader, whom he addressed as "Mr. Wilkins," was concerned with money, tinged slightly with suspicion, and smothered with politeness. Among the day's crises, the one commanding the most attention was a rumor that the police were going to raid the MIA offices at Rufus Lewis' Citizens Club. King worked the phones to find an alternate site, which was not easy to do given the scarcity of centrally located, Negro-owned real estate in Montgomery. Intelligence reports of an imminent raid came so thickly that King and the other MIA leaders spirited away the MIA records that night in the trunks of the automobiles of trustworthy Citizens Club patrons. The next morning, they transferred them stealthily to the basement of the First Baptist Church while Abernathy was conducting the morning service upstairs. Some weeks later, E. D. Nixon secured permanent space for MIA headquarters in a building owned by the all-Negro Bricklayers Union.

At the Monday executive board meeting, members voted to proceed with the federal suit against bus segregation in Montgomery. They all knew it was a fateful step. For reasons of tactical consistency, they resolved to tell both the city fathers and their own followers that the boycott would continue as a separate matter. If the city agreed to the MIA's current segregation reform proposal, Negroes would return to the buses on those terms pending the outcome of the lawsuit. If the city tried to combine the two matters, offering to modify segregation on the buses if the MIA would drop the lawsuit, the MIA would consider such offers as they came. Frankly, King and his colleagues expected no such offers, anticipating correctly that their NAACP-style lawsuit would bring down nothing but increased hostility from the city. Against the punishment ahead, the MIA leaders offered the vision of a great victory over all bus segregation—no more technical hypotheticals about who might have to move where on the bus under what conditions. Freedom would be so simple. People could sit anywhere there was a seat.

King tried to explain this at the mass meeting that night in Abernathy's church, which was packed with a crowd of two thousand people. He tried to rally everyone's courage behind the lawsuit decision and the boycott, pulling the distant hopes nearer while dispelling the fears close by. It was not one of his best speeches. After he finished, old Mother Pollard got up and made her way slowly to the front of the church. This was not un-heard of. Since being enshrined as walking heroes of the boycott, some of the more outspoken old people were moved to speak from the floor at the mass meetings. Their folk wisdom and their tales of daily life inside the homes of powerful white people—how the boss lady had slipped them five dollars for the boycott with a warning not to tell the boss man, and later that same day the boss man had slipped them another five with a warning not to tell the boss lady—had become a special treat at the mass meetings, bringing both entertainment and inspiration.

Mother Pollard drew a hush of recognition and the automatic right to speak. "Come here, son," she said to King, and King walked over to receive a public, motherly embrace. "Something is wrong with you," said Pollard. "You didn't talk strong tonight."

"Oh, no, Mother Pollard," King replied. "Nothing is wrong. I am feel-ing as fine as ever."

"Now you can't fool me," she said. "I knows something is wrong. Is it that we ain't doing things to please you? Or is it that the white folks is bothering you?"

Pollard looked right through a smiling but flustered King. Before he could say anything, she moved her face close to his and said loudly, "I done *told* you we is with you all the way. But even if we ain't with you, God's gonna take care of you." With that, Mother Pollard inched her way back toward her seat, as the crowd roared and King's eyes filled with tears. Later, King said that with her consoling words fearlessness had come over him in the form of raw energy.

He first noticed that something was wrong a few minutes later when a messenger slipped in to Abernathy, who rushed down into the base-ment and then returned, looking worried. King was standing in the front of the church as the collection plate was being passed. He saw Abernathy whispering furtively with other MIA preachers. More messengers came and were dispatched. Perhaps the MIA records had been seized. The organ played and King watched calmly. A couple of the messengers seemed to start toward him and then to hesitate and retreat. Finally, one of the ushers waved King to the side of the platform to give him a message, but S. S. Seay stepped between them, shaking his head in the negative. This caused King to wave Abernathy over to him. "What's wrong?" he whis-pered.

Abernathy and Seay looked at each other, stalling. "Your house has been bombed," said Abernathy.

"Are Coretta and the baby all right?"

"We are checking on that now," said a miserable Abernathy, who had wanted to have the answer before telling King.

In shock, King remained calm, coasting almost automatically on the emotional overload of the past few days. Nodding to Abernathy and Seay, he walked back to the center of the church, told the crowd what had happened, told them he had to leave and that they should all go home quietly and peacefully, and then, leaving a few shrieks and a thousand gasps behind, walked swiftly out a side door of the church.

Near his house, King pushed his way through a barrage of ominous sights and sounds. Little boys dashed around carrying pop bottles broken in half for a fight. Negro men brandished guns and knives, and some confronted the barricade of white policemen shouting for them to disperse. One berserk man, struggling to break the grasp of a policeman, challenged whites to shoot it out with .38s. Shouts of anger and recognition competed with sirens and the background noise of earnest Negro women singing "My Country 'Tis of Thee." Flanked by MIA leaders, King walked across the broken glass on his front porch and into the living room, which was jammed with Dexter members. Among them was an isolated group of first-time visitors to the King home, including several white policemen, reporter Joe Azbell, Mayor Gayle, Commissioner Sellers, and the fire chief. King brushed by them and into a back room, where a group surrounding Coretta and little Yoki, now ten weeks old, parted to make way for him. King hugged Coretta, and gave thanks that they were all right. Then he assumed the remote calm of a commander. There was much to do. Bombers were loose, and a riot was threatening to erupt outside. He leaned forward and whispered, "Why don't you get dressed, darling?" to Coretta, who was still in her robe.

King moved back into the front room to receive a crime scene report from Sellers and the mayor, both of whom assured him that they condemned the bombing and would do everything in their power to punish the bombers. "Regrets are fine, Mr. Sellers," an authoritative voice called out from behind King's shoulder. "But you created the atmosphere for this bombing with your 'get tough' policy. You've got to face that responsibility." It was C. T. Smiley, King's board chairman at Dexter and the older brother of the driver with the Baretta. More important to every Negro in the room, Smiley, as principal of Booker T. Washington High School, was utterly dependent on the city commissioners for his continued livelihood.

Sellers and Gayle said nothing. Joe Azbell and a couple of other white reporters wanted to leave the house to file their stories. They worked as stringers for national publications, and they knew this bomb story would sell. But they could not get out of the house, which was surrounded by angry, armed Negroes. A policeman rushed in huffing and said that some people in the crowd were saying they wouldn't leave without assurance from King that everything was all right.

King walked out onto the front porch. Holding up his hand for silence,

he tried to still the anger by speaking with an exaggerated peacefulness
in his voice. Everything was all right, he said. "Don't get panicky. Don't
do anything panicky. Don't get your weapons. If you have weapons, take
them home. He who lives by the sword will perish by the sword. Remember that is what Jesus said. We are not advocating violence. We want to
love our enemies. I want you to love our enemies. Be good to them. This
is what we must live by. We must meet hate with love." By then the
crowd of several hundred people had quieted to silence, and feeling
welled up in King to an oration. "I did not start this boycott," he said. "I
was asked by you to serve as your spokesman. I want it to be known the
length and breadth of this land that if I am stopped, this movement will
not stop. If I am stopped, our work will not stop. For what we are doing
is right. What we are doing is just. And God is with us."

King stepped back to a chorus of "Amens," but as soon as Sellers
stepped forward to speak, the mood vanished as suddenly as it had arrived. The mob booed him. When policemen tried to shout them down,
they booed even louder.

King raised his hand again. "Remember what I just said," he cried.
"Hear the Commissioner."

Sellers began anew, promising full police protection for the King family. Mayor Gayle seconded him and announced that the city would pay a
$500 reward for information leading to the arrest of the bombers. When
they finished, King urged the crowd to disperse. "Go home and sleep
calm," he said. "Go home and don't worry. Be calm as I and my family
are. We are not hurt. I am all right and my wife is all right."

"Show her to us!" cried a voice in the crowd, and Coretta came outside
to stand with him. The crowd began to trickle away, followed by the
reporters and white officials. Everyone took with them yarns that would
be repeated throughout the city the next day, including the white policeman who said he would sure enough be dead if it hadn't been for that
nigger preacher. Many of the Negroes would liken the sight of King with
his hand raised to the famous poses of Gandhi or to Jesus calming the
waters of the troubled sea. And the story of C. T. Smiley raced from
mouth to mouth: imagine a Negro school principal telling off the police
commissioner like that in front of everybody. For many, this was the
most shocking event of the long night.

King took his rattled family to the Brooks home—where he had spent
his first night in Montgomery two years earlier after eating the prophet's
dinner with Vernon Johns. Long before dawn, both Daddy King and Coretta's father Obadiah Scott showed up there separately, each pounding
on the door, scaring the sleepers inside. The two fathers had come to
take their children away from bombings. Daddy King in particular was

all thunder. "Well, M.L.," he said, "you just come on back to Atlanta." King, stalling, said that the bomb had not done much damage and that he had to think of the important principles at stake there in Montgomery. Daddy King cut him off. "It's better to be a live dog than a dead lion," he said. They argued for several hours, both afraid, with Daddy King stressing that the movement had gotten out of hand, that the danger was all out of proportion to Rosa Parks, and his son saying yes, it was bigger than bus seats now. Meanwhile, Coretta resisted her own father's command to go home with him. After the fathers retreated, King took his wife aside and emotionally thanked her for being such a soldier. She was deeply moved to hear that King, with all his strength, needed her.

Fred Gray filed the papers in federal court the next day, February 1, just as President Eisenhower asked Congress to raise the price of first-class postage stamps by a penny, to four cents. Both actions made the front pages of newspapers across the country, as had the King bombing two days earlier. Ike's news was bigger news, of course, but the boycott was rising to consciousness outside Montgomery.

February dawned cold and dangerous. The night of February 1, a bomb exploded in E. D. Nixon's yard, drawing another angry crowd. Three days later, the *Advertiser* reported that one of Gray's clients said she "was surprised" to see herself listed as a plaintiff, and that she had told Mayor Gayle, "You know I don't want nothing to do with that mess." Jeanatta Reese, who worked as a maid for one of the mayor's relatives, broke down under the pressure as visitors of both races trampled a path to her door, urging her to stick to the contrary assurances she had given them. The police car that had been parked outside King's house since the bombing disappeared and then reappeared for continuous station outside the ex-plaintiff's house. MIA boycotters took this as a telltale sign that the woman was in great fear, which under the circumstances meant that she was throwing in with the whites, who promptly decided that she was more deserving of police protection than was King. Fred Gray was in trouble, as Durr had warned.

Three days later, white students rioted at the University of Alabama against the court-ordered admission of the first Negro student in the school's history. Rumors circulated that the violence had been triggered by the angry reaction of a few whites to the sight of Autherine Lucy's arrival in a Cadillac, or to a report that she had paid her registration fee with a hundred-dollar bill. In reaction, the university trustees suspended Lucy, citing reasons of her own safety. She and the NAACP, which had litigated her case for three years, expressed shock that the university held her rather than the mob responsible for the riot, and promptly went to court seeking reinstatement. Outraged and bewildered, Roy Wilkins said in New York that he never dreamed anything like a riot would occur. It had been "a routine case" like many others, he said, and therefore he had "figured it was a well-established principle, it's oiled, it's greased, it's going."

In Montgomery, Fred Gray's draft board revoked his minister's deferment on the day after the riot. Four days after that, the Mississippi and Alabama White Citizens Councils drew ten thousand people to the Montgomery Coliseum for what was described as the largest segregation rally of the century, with all three Montgomery city commissioners on the stage as featured stalwarts. "I am sure you are not going to permit the NAACP to control your state," declared the star speaker, Senator James Eastland of Mississippi, whose "one prescription for victory" was for Southern white people to "organize and be militant." Three days after the rally, a Montgomery judge impaneled a special grand jury to investigate racial unrest in the city, and local prosecutors summoned before the jury more than two hundred Negro witnesses to testify about who was leading the boycott. Word leaked out that the grand jury was preparing criminal indictments against MIA leaders under a 1921 statute prohibiting boycotts "without just cause or legal excuse." During the parade of witnesses, police arrested, booked, and fingerprinted Fred Gray on the charge of barratry. In the *Advertiser*, Joe Azbell wrote that the city was on the verge of a "full scale racial war."

King escaped on February 20 to preach at Fisk University's Religious Emphasis Week. He was still in Nashville when Bayard Rustin made his appearance in Montgomery. Of those outsiders who would be drawn prominently into King's life, Rustin was the first to show up in person. He opened up two-way traffic with movement tacticians of the outside world, bringing with him experiences and influences far beyond the confines of the Negro church spirit that had sustained the boycott thus far. Rustin was an internationally respected pacifist, as well as a vagabond minstrel, penniless world traveler, sophisticated collector of African and pre-Columbian art, and a bohemian Greenwich Village philosopher. Nearly forty-six years old when he got to Montgomery, he had lived more or less a hobo's life, committed to the ideals of world peace and racial brotherhood. Abernathy and E. D. Nixon could tell from the first sight of him—tall and bony, handsome, animated, and conspiratorial, full of ideas that spilled out in a high-pitched voice and a proud but squeaky West Indian accent—that Rustin was a colorful character. It would have taxed the creative powers of Dickens or Hugo to invent him.

Born in 1910, the last of nine children in a family of Negro caterers,

Rustin grew up in a sixteen-room mansion on one of the broad, tree-lined streets of West Chester, Pennsylvania. Unlike its grimy sister city of Chester, site of Crozer Seminary, the town had all the advantages of enlightened wealth. It was the home of an influential Quaker meeting, to which the Rustins belonged, and of experiments in progressive, integrated education. Rustin knew that his family did not own the enormous house in which they lived, but he never found out exactly how they got there. The usual answer was that the white folks "didn't need it" and liked having their favorite cook and caterer nearby. There were also stories that Rustin's mother's family had sued the town long ago to repossess properties once owned by an Indian tribe from which the family was descended, but Rustin could never figure out to his satisfaction how or whether the stories related to his house.

As a precocious eleven-year-old when Harding was President, Rustin won one too many school contests and provoked jealous students to taunt him, saying he didn't know who his mama was, or his daddy. This made no sense to Rustin, but more taunts and a few questions at home turned his entire world upside down. The woman he had always known as his older sister Florence was in fact his mother. His mother and father, the uneducated caterers, were actually his grandparents, and his other brothers and sisters were actually his aunts and uncles. Since his birth, all the family members had created the fiction that an illegitimate grandson was a legitimate son. Among the greatest leaps young Rustin faced when attempting to realign his emotions was to take notice of the man who before had been only Florence's controversial and inconsequential boyfriend, whom Rustin suddenly beheld as a kind of stepfather. This man, like the one Rustin learned was his long-vanished natural father, was controversial because he was a West Indian. American Negroes tended to dislike the West Indian immigrants, because of their arrogance and their British accents and their extreme color consciousness. Rustin, having grown up hearing Negroes call them "monkey chasers," struggled to control his prejudice against them, including the one in his house. His first shocked response was to listen more carefully to his new stepfather, and within a few weeks he had picked up a pompous West Indian accent that he kept all his life.

When the Depression and family poverty forced him out of college, Rustin went to live with a relative in Harlem. There he waited tables, sang on street corners, talked jazz and revolution, catered private meals for white people, went to free night classes at City College, and otherwise practiced his own art of survival. During 1931, the year he arrived, the hottest political story in Harlem was the Communist International's "show trial" of an immigrant Finn named August Yokinen, charged with acting discourteously toward three Negroes at a Harlem nightclub run by the Communist Party. The trial, attended by 1,500 spectators and covered on the front page of *The New York Times*, proved spectacularly successful in advertising the International's strict policy of brotherhood on the race question. The Communist Party ran the only integrated social clubs in Harlem. Rustin attended them regularly. Although as a Quaker he had been inclined toward the gentlemanly pacifism more associated with the Socialists, he was bitterly disappointed by the official Socialist position that racism would disappear automatically upon the establishment of socialism. By a corollary of this doctrine, the Socialists ruled out as wasteful any special agitation on the race issue. As a practical matter, it meant that white Socialists stayed out of Harlem. Disgusted with the Socialists, Rustin joined the Young Communist League.

His musical talents flourished during the thirties. Faithful to the spirit of the International, Rustin learned an amazing assortment of workers' songs, English madrigals, and folk classics. He earned jobs singing backup for folk singer Leadbelly in New York cafés, and he traveled for nearly two years with Josh White. Everywhere he went, he recruited for the Young Communist League. His qualities made him an ideal organizer. He could entertain crowds with speeches or songs, write pamphlets skillfully, and run a meeting. Fearless, unattached, able to get along with whites and Negroes alike, Rustin rose quickly as a youth recruiter for the Communist Party.

Within days after Hitler invaded the Soviet Union in June 1941, the party's Central Committee ordered Comrade Rustin to shut down his Jim Crow work immediately. Policy had shifted overnight. Now comrades were to stop anything that might divert the attention of the United States from the menace of Hitler. Stunned, Rustin asked for a night to think it over. The past few years had been the happiest of his life. He had crisscrossed the country many times, speaking at colleges and high schools and union halls. Having found himself, he could not quit his work just because the party cared more about the Soviet Union than about race. On the other hand, he could not leave the party without giving up most of his friends and his most stable point of reference over the past decade. The next morning, Rustin went back to the Central Committee and resigned, cutting himself adrift again.

Some weeks later, he secured an appointment with A. Philip Randolph, president of the Brotherhood of Sleeping Car Porters. Until recently, the Communist Rustin had scorned Randolph as a lifelong Socialist. Now, suddenly, it was Randolph who was the most militant of the Negro leaders, having threatened publicly to lead a massive march on Washington unless President Roosevelt issued an order banning racial discrimination in defense industries. Randolph's most vociferous critics were American Communists, including the Negro Communist leader who had just shoved Rustin out of the party. They called Randolph a traitor for attempting to interfere with American war preparations. In Randolph's office, Rustin confessed blindness for having worked so long for the Communists, and the ever tolerant Randolph told him to forget it. Recognizing his talents, Randolph gave him temporary work in his March on Washington movement. When Roosevelt capitulated, signing the order on defense jobs, Randolph made an appointment for Rustin to see A. J. Muste at the Fellowship of Reconciliation.

As FOR's youth secretary, Rustin began his career as an itinerant Gandhian. FOR leaders, recognizing that pacifist recruitment was going nowhere so long as Hitler was making war, decided to emphasize the anti-colonial aspects of Gandhian nonviolence. By the seesaw habits of ideological politics, activists for Negro rights came suddenly to the fore in Gandhian circles even as they became taboo in Communist ones. The FOR developed during the war a new organization called the Congress of Racial Equality. Rustin worked both for FOR and CORE, as did a young Negro aristocrat named James Farmer. Together they sat at the feet of a traveling Gandhi disciple named Krishnalal Shridharani, author of *War Without Violence*. This book became the semiofficial bible of CORE, and by example the hard-drinking, cigar-smoking, woman-chasing Shridharani taught the wide-eyed young Americans that Gandhian politics did not require a life of dull asceticism.

It did require sacrifice, however, and in 1943 Rustin renounced as an unconscionable privilege his right to Quaker war duty in a hospital, spending the remainder of World War II in Lewisburg Penitentiary. Upon his release, he headed a Free India Committee and was frequently arrested for picketing outside the British Embassy in Washington. In 1947, Rustin joined a CORE-sponsored bus ride through the South to test a new Supreme Court ruling that Negro passengers on interstate routes could not be forced to sit in the back of the bus. White opponents met the challenge with beatings, and Rustin was among those convicted under local segregation laws. A showcase appeal proceeded until the day Roy Wilkins called the freedom riders to his office to say that the NAACP lawyers had misplaced their interstate bus tickets, which was essential evidence. Therefore, the appeal could not go forward. "You boys have got to go on the chain gang," said Wilkins. Amid the instant recriminations, in which some of the riders charged that the local NAACP officials were crumbling under pressure, Rustin took the Gandhian position that cheerful acceptance of punishment might make a better witness for the cause than lawful evasion. "If we got to go, we got to go," he told Wilkins with a smile. After the chain gang, he went to India for six months on the invitation of Gandhi's Congress Party, and later to Africa, where he worked with young African anti-colonists like Kwame Nkrumah and founded the Committee to Support South African Resistance. Stories of his travels became legend within the restricted circles of Gandhian intellectuals.

Rustin welcomed more jailings and a few beatings, including one in New Orleans that left him without some of his front teeth. On June 25, 1951, he led a motley group of religious idealists, Marxists, and FOR activists on a march from Central Park to Times Square in protest against the Korean War. One of the passersby was so infuriated by the speeches that he seized a picket sign, ripped off the placard, and rushed toward Rustin with the stick, screaming that they were a bunch of Commies. Rustin calmly handed the man a second stick, inviting him to strike with them both. Nonplussed, the man threw both sticks on the ground, but later he decked another marcher with his fists, while Rustin shouted excitedly to passersby that there was nonviolent power in the acceptance of the blows.

He could make such a solemn speech and then abruptly break into a grin of delight and say he needed to go "Gandhi" somebody into giving some money for a march. He had a strong sense of the absurd and a gift for parody, both of which were enhanced by his modified Cary Grant accent. These charms were appreciated in the bohemian culture of Greenwich Village. He drank at the White Horse Tavern along with Dylan Thomas, Norman Mailer, and other literati, and entertained people by singing obscure ditties back at his apartment, accompanying himself on the harpsichord. His personal life was generally a mystery, even to most of his friends, but it was widely assumed that he was a homosexual. This proclivity would suit or explain some of the eccentricities of Rustin's life—his hobby of cooking gourmet meals for rich people on Park Avenue, his sponsors who kept him going at times with gifts of money or art. In the Village of those years, homosexuality caused little stir, but when Rustin began to get into public trouble, his political colleagues worried that there might be a self-destructive urge at the core of him.

After several such incidents threatened to engulf the FOR in public scandal, A. J. Muste told Rustin and the top leaders of FOR that he loved Rustin like a son but that he would have no choice but to dismiss him if anything happened again. Not long thereafter, on January 21, 1953, Rustin and two other men were arrested in the back of a parked car in Pasadena, California, convicted on morals charges, and sentenced to thirty days in jail. Rustin resigned from the FOR staff the next day. Upon his release, he went back to New York a much reduced man, having lost the confidence of Muste's circle of leaders, which included all those capable of employing Rustin in what he regarded as the struggle of the century. This made the third time that Rustin had been crushed—once by his family, once by the Communist Party, and now by his own inner drives. Unemployed, a bastard, a Negro, an ex-Communist, an ex-con, and a homosexual, he was a misfit by any social standard, but Rustin still believed that he could not only rescue himself but also have a positive moral impact on the entire country. To him, this was cosmic logic and the romance of the ages. He saw a chance in the Montgomery bus boycott before anyone else.

Rustin left New York for Montgomery by car on the same day that King began Religious Emphasis Week at Fisk University in Nashville. His timing was exquisite. That morning, Ralph Abernathy received from the city commissioners and a group of white businessmen what was billed as an ultimatum: if the Negroes promptly accepted the settlement terms they had previously rejected, there would be "no retaliation whatsoever" against those taking part in the boycott; if they did not, the law would take its course. Abernathy did not have to guess what this meant, as the whole town was abuzz with the news that the grand jury had returned a fistful of criminal indictments. He bargained without result and then walked outside to tell reporters that the city was offering nothing more than segregation and increased bus fares. "We have walked for eleven weeks in the cold and rain . . ." he said. "Now the weather is warming up. Therefore we will walk on until some better proposals are forthcoming from our city fathers."

That was for public consumption. Abernathy proceeded directly to a tense meeting of the executive board. It was all very well to say they were going on, it was agreed, but could they continue the boycott if the leaders and the car-pool drivers were all in jail? What were the white people really going to do? The general consensus was that the whites wanted to "cut off the head" of the boycott. They wanted to get King first. No one said outright that this was a reassuring idea, but several did say that they could keep going even if King were lost. Avoidance was in the air. Few if any of the people in the room had ever been arrested. Finally, S. S. Seay rose to speak as though possessed. "We all know they're gonna try to separate Dr. King from the rest of us," he said. "He knows it, too. He's talked about it, and I have seen that disturbed look in his face. I'd know it anywhere. I say let's all go to jail!"

These words snapped through the room. One minister headed for the door, caught himself, and then broke the silence with "How we gonna do that?" It was a logical question, but met with an emotional response. Board members and observers jumped to their feet to second Seay, and all the meandering talk of tactics and procedure was washed over by a tide of bravado. That night they took a unanimous recommendation to a huge mass meeting at St. John's A.M.E. Church. Of four thousand people in attendance, only two voted to end the boycott on the city's terms.

The next morning, Abernathy formally notified the city of the MIA's decision by telegram. Not long thereafter, Bayard Rustin knocked on his door. Abernathy recognized some of the references Rustin offered, but otherwise he did not know quite what to make of him. Citing the chaos of the moment, which was evident by the constant flow of messengers and the guards posted on the porch, Abernathy begged off a long discussion about the boycott. He advised Rustin to draw the shades on the windows and bolt the door of his hotel room.

E. D. Nixon accorded Rustin a lengthier reception, being less busy than the acting MIA leader. Besides, he struck up an instant bond of trust and rapport with Rustin because of Philip Randolph, their common mentor. Randolph had raised the money for Rustin's trip to Montgomery. The reason for the nearly martial state of preparation around Abernathy, Nixon explained, was that they all expected the deputy sheriffs to start rounding up the indicted people any day now. If that was so, said Rustin, then the MIA leaders might be making a tactical mistake by waiting anxiously for the deputies to come after them. Such behavior reinforced the psychology of the crusading lawman and the skulking criminal. Rustin gently suggested a more Gandhian response—something on the order of handing an attacker a stick. That evening, after leaving Nixon's, Rustin walked up to South Jackson Street to take a look at King's house. Floodlights had been strung around the roof to illuminate the perimeter for security. Volunteer guards stood outside even though, as Rustin had learned to his disappointment, King and his family were out of town.

Abernathy was on the phone to Nashville that night, finally telling King that it was certain. The grand jury had returned the largest wholesale indictment in the history of the county. Deputy sheriffs, prosecutors, and white reporters had been busy around the courthouse all day, and now were saying that the dragnet operation would begin the next day. King promised Abernathy he would return to Montgomery first thing in the morning. He made airline reservations to fly back through Atlanta, where he had left his wife and daughter for the week, then skipped the rest of the schedule in Nashville. As his early morning flight touched down in Atlanta, he knew that he must weather a family ordeal before he could step off into the unknown abyss of prison in Montgom-

ery. His mother had been confined to bed for most of the three weeks
since the bombing. As for Daddy King, who had never thought his son
should go to Dexter in the first place, King was aware that this final crisis
could not have come on a worse day. By a telling coincidence, Daddy
King was to sign the legal instruments securing a loan of $150,000 for
the Ebenezer building program. Few preachers anywhere had the standing to borrow such a sum in 1956. The dollar amount of this ambition
had been for some time the centerpiece of Daddy King's self-description
in church programs, and it would remain so until he did something even
bigger. King, approaching his parents on the concourse of the Atlanta air
terminal, knew by their downcast expressions and slow, trudging walks
that he had already ruined what would otherwise be a proud day in their
lives.

Daddy King opened his attack during the drive home to Boulevard.
M.L. should not go back to Montgomery at all, he said. Their phone had
been ringing all morning with calls. The morning *Advertiser* said that an
incredible 115 Negroes had been indicted and that deputies were beginning a massive roundup, and the news was being broadcast over the radio,
even in Atlanta. The elder King said that he had already talked with his
friend Herbert Jenkins, the Atlanta police chief, and learned that Montgomery detectives had come to Atlanta in the hope of finding an old
charge on which King could be arrested. Jenkins said the Montgomery
authorities wanted to get King out of Alabama. That was how serious it
was, said Daddy King. Until things cooled down, at least, M.L. should
stay in Atlanta, where he had the support of powerful Negroes and even
of some powerful whites, like Chief Jenkins and Mayor Hartsfield.

As usual, King let his father's monologue run its course. Daddy King
said he was sure he was right, but just in case his son had any doubts, he
had invited Dr. Mays and some of the other men M.L. most respected to
come by the house that afternoon. These men of stature and proven
judgment all cared personally for M.L., having known him since he was
a small boy. M.L. could hear for himself what they had to say. When the
question was put, King agreed to stay for the summit meeting, although
the delay meant that he missed his connecting flight to Montgomery.

At the appointed hour, Dr. Mays was there in the King home, along
with President Rufus Clement of Atlanta University, the local bishop of
the A.M.E. church, the editor of the Atlanta *Daily World*, and a half-
dozen of the most influential money men on Auburn Avenue. Daddy
King repeated his speech for their benefit. If anything, it was more emotional than the one he had made in the car. At its conclusion, those
present murmured their assent. This came as no surprise to King, who
realized that, given his father's shrewd willfulness, anyone who disagreed

would not have been invited. One by one, the assembled leaders began their own speeches in support of Daddy King, until King finally interrupted in pain. "I must go back to Montgomery," he said. His friends were being arrested and hauled off to jail at that very moment. How could he hide here in Atlanta?

The silence that hung in the room was broken only when Daddy King burst into tears, in front of the same men with whom he was to swap six-figure securities that day. His sobs made the stillness all the more excruciating. King looked pleadingly at Dr. Mays, who soon spoke up to say that perhaps young King had a point, that perhaps those in the room would do well to turn their influence toward defending him in Alabama. His words broke the tension in many respects, not least by giving people something to do. One of the lawyers ran off to place a call to no less a personage than Thurgood Marshall. He returned shortly with the good news that Marshall promised to throw the entire weight of the NAACP Legal Defense Fund behind young King's defense. This and other assurances helped Daddy King recover, and soon he was saying that he was going back to Montgomery himself. He was going to stick by his son. He would accompany him to the jailhouse. Daddy King was himself again, but at the same time he was stalling—at least by the urgent timetable that was beckoning his son. Daddy King was going, but he had the loan business to take care of. And he did not want to fly. He wanted to go by car, but he did not want King or himself or either of the wives to drive. It was too dangerous. He would find a driver for them. They would leave in the morning.

All this delay in Atlanta caused King to miss a different kind of drama in Montgomery. E. D. Nixon, the first to be arrested under the boycott indictment, did not wait for the deputies to come for him. On Bayard Rustin's suggestion, he walked inside the county courthouse to the sheriff's office and said, "Are you looking for me? Well, here I am." The deputies looked quizzically at each other and then welcomed Nixon to jail. Within a short time, he was booked, fingerprinted, photographed, and released on bond. No sooner had a smiling Nixon walked past a few Negroes milling around the courthouse than word of his feat began to spread through Negro Montgomery. Nixon had turned the dreaded process of being apprehended into something quite different—quicker and less painful than a trip to the dentist. Soon Nixon's dignified old pastor walked into the courthouse, and the news flashed that he had actually traded jokes with the deputy who arrested him.

Such behavior set off a chain reaction. Word of what was happening went everywhere, drawing more indictees and more spectators. Some of the arriving smiles were forced, but the ones on leaving jail were always genuine. As the crowd grew into the hundreds, applause and words of encouragement began to lift the mood. Those already out on bail advised the others on ways to post the $300 bond as quickly as possible. Those picked up by deputies, like Abernathy, passed through the crowd waving and hugging people. Soon the deputies out on the dragnet were coming up empty because so many of the Negroes were on their way downtown voluntarily. Laughter began to spread through the crowd. A joke went around that some inquiring Negroes were upset upon being told by phone that they were not on the arrest list. Some of the white deputies, infected by the good humor, began to enjoy themselves too. Sheriff Butler, exasperated by this perversion of the penal spirit, came outside to shout, "This is no vaudeville show!" But he had little effect. The jailhouse door, which for centuries had conjured up visions of fetid cells and unspeakable cruelties, was turning into a glorious passage, and the arriving criminals were being celebrated like stars at a Hollywood premiere.

Rustin worked joyfully in the background. When it developed that a shortage of bondable property might pose a threat to the swift release of boycotters yet to be arrested, he persuaded a friend to wire him a loan of $5,000, which he turned over to Nixon. At the end of the day, Rustin took his second consecutive night walk, ignoring repeated warnings from boycotters who said the Montgomery authorities were itching to find an "outsider" upon whom to blame all their troubles. This time he went to the home of Jeanatta Reese, the embattled woman who had withdrawn from the MIA lawsuit. Two police cars still sat outside. Rustin marched up to the officers on sentry duty and asked breezily to see Mrs. Reese. The officers, doubtless having never seen or heard anyone like Rustin, eyed him warily. At first they questioned him on the suspicion that he might want to hurt Mrs. Reese, but the more he talked, the more they simply wanted to know who he was. Their questions posed a threat, as his true identity might expose the MIA to scandal. "I am Bayard Rustin," he said, drawing himself up to full height. "I am here as a journalist working for Le Figaro and the Manchester Guardian." The officers wrote that down, as Rustin explained to them something of the importance of the French and British papers. It took Rustin ten minutes of persistent conversation to talk his way to Mrs. Reese's door for a conversation that turned out to be hardly worth the effort. "I had to do what I did or I wouldn't be alive today," she told him.

The King family pulled up to the Montgomery parsonage at nine the next morning, to be greeted by television cameras and a contingent of boycotters still exuberant over the jailings of the previous day. Within a few minutes, King, Daddy King, and Abernathy were off to the courthouse, trailed by a small caravan of Dexter members. On the way, Abernathy briefed them about procedures at the county jail (as opposed to the city jail, where King had been booked a month earlier). He also described his own arrest as one of the best things that had ever happened to him. King, facing jail again, struggled to believe him, and an utterly mystified Daddy King did not believe him at all until he experienced for himself the holiday atmosphere around the courthouse. The crowd cheered all three of them. King was processed again—photographed this time, with jail number 7089 hanging under his chin—and released back into the embrace of his followers. He was the twenty-fourth minister to be booked.

On the recommendation of Nixon and Abernathy, King invited Rustin to a meeting of the strategy committee afterward, at which it was decided to change the mass meeting into a prayer meeting from that night forward. The idea was to foster spiritual commitment for the long ordeal ahead. Each meeting's agenda would be organized around five prayers, including one for the strength of spirit to be nonviolent, one for the strength of body to keep walking, and a "prayer for all those who oppose us." Rustin was impressed by the intuitive Gandhian method at work in the plan. Privately, he told King that he had been all over the world and not seen a movement that could compare with what he had seen already in Montgomery. He wanted to help spread the word, particularly among believers in nonviolence. There were articles to be written, funds to be raised, specialized techniques to be taught. He realized the dangers involved with "outside agitators," particularly Northerners, but he would work behind the scenes if King thought it wise. King, beholding Rustin for the first time, said they needed all the help they could get.

Rustin drifted by Abernathy's church, site of that night's mass meeting. To his amazement, he found that the church started filling up at four o'clock, and he watched the crowd sing hymns and pray on their own for three hours. The meeting began when all ninety of those arrested thus far walked out onto the church podium. Instantly, the audience of mostly plainer folk rose to its feet, and parents brought their children forward to touch them as the ovation rolled on. King said that the spirit of the boycott was for "all people, black and white." Abernathy declared that the solidarity of the movement during King's absence proved that the boycott was "not a one-man show." The leaders, feeling a superabundance of support, called for a day of thanks—no car pool, no taxis, no private cars. Everyone would walk tomorrow on "Double-P Day," the day of prayer and pilgrimage.

What distinguished this meeting from all previous ones was not so much its fervor or content but the presence of some thirty-five reporters from all over the country. For the first time, the Montgomery bus boycott had drawn a press contingent of accredited correspondents. Unfortunately for Rustin, none of these reporters knew him as the man from *Le Figaro*, but several of them did know of him as a resplendent figure in Greenwich Village. As they talked with the host reporters at the *Advertiser*, who were constantly in touch with the local police, further doubts sprang up about his identity. These became serious enough that there was talk of calls being placed to Paris and London to check up on him.

Rustin knew the baleful signs. He called John Swomley, executive director for the FOR, in New York, with an urgent message for Muste and the others. Rustin described what he had seen in Montgomery, saying that the MIA people were at once gifted and unsophisticated in nonviolence. (As an exhibition of the latter, Rustin had in mind his first visit to the King home, when he shouted to stop someone from sitting on a loaded pistol that was lying on the couch.) These people *must* have somebody come in who was qualified to teach nonviolence. There were only four or five such people in the country, including Rustin, and he told Swomley sadly that he would not be staying long. He knew he had no claim on his old organization, but he implored Swomley to trust his judgment and send someone in on the next plane.

Rustin attended Dexter services that Sunday and then spent the evening in the King home, going over the history of the boycott in some detail. Coretta remembered hearing Rustin give a speech at Antioch some years earlier. Neither she nor King expressed any objection to Rustin's long history in left-wing politics, and King spoke knowledgeably of figures like Muste. He was trying to practice nonviolence, he told Rustin, but he did not subscribe to Muste-style pacifism because he believed no just society could exist without at least a police power. Rustin quibbled some, but nevertheless these were not the views he had expected of a Montgomery preacher.

It was the worst of worlds for Rustin. His affection for the MIA people and his vision of the role he could play expanded even as his position deteriorated by the hour. Word came that the white people were saying *Le Figaro* had never heard of him and was offering a reward for the identification of the impostor. About that time, an influential Negro reporter from Birmingham got word that Rustin was in town. Knowing Rustin's background, he burst into a leadership huddle to announce that the white people were sure to find out about him and would use the information to discredit everything the boycott had accomplished thus far. Now Rustin was in a cross fire. On Monday, word came that the whites might arrest him for fraud or for inciting to riot, and the Negro reporter clinched things by threatening to expose Rustin in his newspaper if MIA leaders did not get him out of town. Rustin stalled. He had become fixated on a desire to transfer his informal role personally to the new nonviolence tactician from the FOR staff. The ensuing scenes could have been condensed from a Western movie. Glenn Smiley, the replacement, came into town and received a hurried, rather sad briefing from the departing Rustin, whom he had known for fifteen years. Then Rustin introduced Smiley to King and managed chipper good-byes before King was obliged to have him smuggled to Birmingham in the back of a car.

Like Rustin, Smiley had traveled on the FOR staff since his own imprisonment for pacifist resistance to service in World War II. By appearance and temperament, however, the two friends were utterly different. Smiley was a mild-mannered white Methodist preacher from Texas, who looked and sounded like one until he spoke on the subject of violence or race. His first act was to trade in his New York license plates for Georgia ones. His first advice to King was to get rid of the guns around his house. Smiley thought King's most striking quality was his stubbornness—how he would give in to fears and then almost angrily sweep them aside as irrelevant to the choices at hand. "Don't bother me with tactics," he said more than once. "I want to know if I can apply nonviolence to my heart." At such times, Smiley was much burdened by the inadequacy of his Gandhian advice. For four years, he would go in and out of Montgomery on call, often arriving for midnight MIA strategy sessions. Invariably, King would jump up at two or three o'clock in the morning to say that the work of the Lord could not go forward unless they sent out for some soul food, and Smiley, to the astonishment of himself and his relatives, learned to love pig's-ear sandwiches. So did the Lutheran missionary, Robert Graetz.

Within a week of King's second arrest in Montgomery, cabinet secretary Maxwell Rabb summoned E. Frederic Morrow, the first Negro professional ever to serve on the White House staff, for an old-fashioned chewing out. Rabb was tired of getting Morrow's memos urging the President to speak out in favor of desegregation, he said, and what galled him most was that Negro voters still seemed to prefer the Democratic Party of Eastland and Byrd in spite of all Eisenhower had done in civil rights, such as the desegregation of nearly all public facilities in the nation's capital and the official support for the NAACP position in the *Brown* case. Negro voters were ungrateful, Rabb charged. He said he was disgusted with the whole issue and would not stick his neck out anymore.

Morrow swallowed his disagreement in retreat, as he often did. A public relations expert on leave from CBS-TV, the son and grandson of preachers, Morrow had obtained a secretary from the White House pool only after a tearful woman from Massachusetts volunteered, citing the obligations of her Catholic faith, and now staff women were under strict orders to enter and leave his office in pairs, so as to allay suspicions of sexual misconduct. Morrow walked softly. He had been working at the White House nearly nine months but had not yet been sworn in for duty. This was another uncomfortable subject. Morrow and everyone else knew that the Administration had already gotten credit in the Negro media for his presence, and that the traditional ceremony would only generate negative results among white voters. (Morrow would not be sworn in for another three years. A private, unannounced ceremony— without the President—made his prior service retroactively official.)

A few days after being lectured by Rabb, Morrow was called into the office of the man who hired him, Sherman Adams, Eisenhower's chief of staff and alter ego. Adams was worried about race again. The previous year it had been Mississippi—the sensational Emmett Till lynching and a rash of lesser atrocities that had generated political pressure to hire Morrow. This year it was Alabama. A federal judge had revoked Autherine Lucy's suspension from the University of Alabama, only to have the trustees expel her permanently the next day. The case was a bundle of lunacy; Lucy had been suspended and expelled before she had ever enrolled. What worried Adams was the prospect of violence. Alabama whites were crowing about how the riot had "worked"; it had restored segregation. As for the Negroes, the latest FBI intelligence reports revealed that the Communist influence was pervasive, Adams said, and the Negro leaders were not sophisticated enough to control planted insurrectionists. Morrow did not argue. He valued Adams for his personal kindnesses, not for his advanced views on civil rights. In fact, Morrow knew that Adams was the most powerful figure among those urging that Eisenhower do as little as possible in civil rights.

Practically speaking, the fight within the Eisenhower Administration over civil rights was a contest for the President's ear between Sherman Adams and Attorney General Herbert Brownell. The President asked FBI Director J. Edgar Hoover to present a classified briefing about race on March 9, 1956, for the cabinet meeting at which the Administration would decide whether to approve, modify, or cancel Brownell's plans to ask Congress for a new civil rights bill. No such legislation had passed since Reconstruction.

Hoover arrived with a brace of aides, easels, and display charts. His peek into the inner world of Negro protest, though couched in the language of secret revelation, was superficial and riddled with error. Cursory remarks on Montgomery, for instance, misstated several dates and laws while distorting the nature of the bus boycott. No one in the Cabinet Room knew better, however, and the facts were of secondary importance anyway. Politically speaking, Hoover cut masterfully along the fault line of the Administration. He expressed no sympathy for civil rights and painted an alarming picture of subversive elements among the integrationists. As an example of a clearly subversive development, Hoover informed the cabinet that Chicago mayor Richard Daley had come close to public criticism of President Eisenhower for not taking stronger action in the Emmett Till lynching case. "I hasten to say that Mayor Daley is not a Communist," Hoover added gravely, "but pressures engineered by the Communists were brought to bear upon him." These comments hinted at political danger, but Hoover stopped short of saying that Republican civil rights legislation would reflect Communist influence. Instead, he put the imprimatur of the FBI upon some of the worst allegations of anti-Negro brutality by militant segregationists, particularly in Mississippi. He described the White Citizens Councils ambiguously as new organizations that "either could control the rising tension or become the medium through which tensions might manifest themselves." Overall, his performance left just enough political room for Brownell's program, minus any anti-lynching legislation. One of the FBI charts showed that the number of lynchings had dropped from twenty to less than three per year since the FBI had begun informal investigations in 1939. Hoover wanted no formal legal responsibility in this area.

Brownell promptly gave the cabinet a speech defending his plan to submit legislation to create an independent Civil Rights Commission to gather facts about voting rights violations and economic reprisals against Negroes. Also, the bill would create a Civil Rights Division in the Justice Department, and strengthen the Attorney General's legal standing to seek enforcement of voting rights in the federal courts. When Brownell finished, Secretaries Ezra Taft Benson of Agriculture and Marion Folsom of Health, Education and Welfare spoke up in opposition. Benson wanted to wait until there was a Republican Congress. Folsom said that anything beyond the fact-finding commission would be imprudent because it would "anticipate" its results.

The President interrupted. "Where do you think that the Attorney General's suggestions are moving too rapidly?" he asked. "They look to me like amelioration." As always, his word shifted the tone of the debate. A few objections as to the practicality of the legislation followed, but Brownell soon asked permission to proceed. "Okay," said Ike. "But put into your presentation a statement that what is needed is calmness and sanity. The great mass of decent people should and will listen to *these* voices, rather than to the extremists. Make your statement like your brief to the Supreme Court. Don't take the attitude that you are another Sumner."

The most Sherman Adams could win at the cabinet meeting was a delay: Brownell must bring the historic legislative package back to the

White House for final clearance. In the interim, Adams benefited by the release of the "Southern Manifesto," which equated integration with subversion of the Constitution and pledged the entire region to fierce resistance. The document was signed by some ninety Southern congressmen and all the senators except the two Tennessee mavericks, Estes Kefauver and Albert Gore, and the Senate Majority Leader, Lyndon Johnson of Texas. Johnson was saying privately that the manifesto's only effect would be to push Negro votes into the Republican column in key swing states of the North. In the White House, Adams was hoping just that. He managed to weaken a few of Brownell's proposals and to make sure that when the bill was submitted to Congress, it came from the Attorney General and not, as was customary for major bills, from the President.

Advertiser editor Grover Hall pronounced the mass indictments "the dumbest act that has ever been done in Montgomery." From the standpoint of local whites, the move backfired immediately by recharging the boycotters' morale and severely weakening the time-honored stigma of jail as a weapon of social control against Negroes. This was just the beginning of the miscalculation. As days went by, the hordes of reporters attracted to town by the mass indictment wrote stories that stimulated a great shower of public support—and money—upon the MIA from across the nation and even from distant lands. The city fathers, showboating as they delivered what they believed would be a crushing blow, had blithely ignored the possibility that their show would not play well to audiences beyond the horizon. "Everybody now concedes that this was dumb," Hall wrote.

For the puckish editor, who found himself serving as "duenna and Indian guide to more than a hundred reporters of the international press," the media influx caused an intense, personal exposure to the vagaries of the race issue on both its grand and prosaic stages. One early effect was that Hall ventured inside Dexter Avenue Baptist to meet King, in his role as escort to reporter Peter Kihss of *The New York Times*. To Hall, King was "largely inscrutable," a self-possessed man without humor, in whose statements about death, suffering, and violence Hall found a "conspicuous thread of thanatopsis." Still, Hall admitted that King was an "authentic intellectual," and not a polysyllabic charlatan with cereal-box degrees. King's discourse on philosophy, Hall found, was "comprehending, forceful exegesis." He committed these judgments to print, along with many others that offended his white readers. When he asked one frantic caller how she knew that the Communists were running the boycott, she replied, "It just stands to reason." This comment amused Hall enough to publish it too.

By the time the boycott case went to trial, the encampment of Negro reporters and domestic "war correspondents" had been augmented by journalists from more than ten foreign nations, including Japan, Italy, the Netherlands, Germany, and Australia. There was M. K. Kamath of the Press Trust of India and Daniel Morgaine of *France-Soir.* From England came Keith Kyle of the London *Economist* and, eventually, the distinguished Alastair Cooke of the *Manchester Guardian.* (Ironically, in view of that paper's leftist perspective and Rustin's invocation of its name, Cooke may have been the foreign journalist most sympathetic to the local segregationists. He wrote of King as "the cat's-paw of the NAACP.") Of these, Hall's favorite seemed to be Morgaine of France, who once called just before a scheduled cultural briefing at the *Advertiser* saying, "I am so soree, Meester Hall. I must break ze appointment, for I have achieved an appointment with the Reverend King." For Hall, this fawning attention made King like yesterday's bee sting—a tiny, throbbing thing that tickled and hurt at once, and above all that he could not leave alone. Local prosecutors concentrated the attention into an exclusive preoccupation by announcing that they intended to hold eighty-nine of the indictments in abeyance. They prosecuted King alone as a test case.

Eight lawyers sat around King at the defense table when the four-day trial opened on March 19, 1956. One part of the legal team guided King and other MIA witnesses through a line of defense testimony that flirted with perjury. The minister of Holt Street Baptist could not recall seeing King at his church on the night the boycott began. Graetz testified that he could not remember ever hearing King urge people to boycott the buses. Fear and legalism combined to produce a defense based on evasive denial that King had anything to do with any boycott, if there was one. Other King lawyers tried to establish that the boycott was "not without just cause" by summoning a stream of Negro women to the stand to testify about cruelties they had seen and endured on the buses.

Neither of the legal strategies mattered very much to the outcome of a trial that had become symbolic to all sides. The judge, who taught a men's Bible class at a church across the street from Dexter, pronounced King guilty immediately at the conclusion of the summations. He sentenced the defendant to pay a $500 fine or serve a year at hard labor. Newspapers recorded the exact moment, 4:39 P.M., when King emerged from the courthouse to tell a cheering crowd that the bus protest would continue. "Behold the King!" shouted someone, and others answered "Hail the King!" and "King is King!" Returning that evening to Holt Street, where it had all begun, King was presented to the first of that night's series of enormous mass meetings with the words, "Here is the man who today was nailed to the cross for you and me." King declared,

"This conviction and all the convictions they can heap on me will not diminish my determination one iota."

He had been a public figure among Montgomery's Negroes for nearly four months, but now fame spilled into the outside world. W. E. B. Du Bois himself, who had known Negro leaders stretching back to Frederick Douglass, wrote that if passive resistance could conquer racial hatred, which he doubted, then Gandhi and Negroes like King would have shown the world a way to conquer war itself. *Jet* magazine put King on its cover, calling him "Alabama's Modern Moses." *The New York Times*, in a "Man in the News" profile published during the trial, described King as a man who believed that "all men are basically good," and whose pulpit oratory "overwhelms the listener with the depth of his convictions. . . . He is particularly well read in Kant and Hegel."

King learned immediately that the astonishing personal impact of the trial reached far beyond Montgomery. At his first Northern fund-raiser since the boycott began, he received in New York what one newspaper called "the kind of welcome [the city] usually reserves for the Brooklyn Dodgers." Some ten thousand people tried to crowd into Gardner Taylor's Concord Baptist Church to hear him. Collection plates gathered $4,000 for the MIA. The president of the City Council made an appearance at the church. Mobs of admirers pressed upon King, and the Negro press reported sighs among groups of doting women.

The phenomenon of mass adulation far from home struck like a sudden bolt, but King had to work for other support gained on the New York trip. Harry Belafonte responded cautiously to his invitation for a private meeting at Adam Clayton Powell's church in Harlem. Belafonte could be temperamental. He had recorded but not yet released the calypso album that would make him an international star—the first solo album ever to sell a million copies—and he wondered why King insisted that they meet alone. He was wary of preachers and established Negro leaders, partly because he thought they never had supported his idols Du Bois and Paul Robeson. Only curiosity about this new kind of preacher lured him to the church. King said he had heard that Belafonte cared deeply about the race struggle, quite apart from his career in show business. This flattered Belafonte's political side, but what broke down his resistance was King's air of humility, in sharp contrast with the circus of adulation surrounding him. While he found King sophisticated, clearly not the hick or holy roller he had feared, King's offstage personality struck him as a mixture of determination and almost doe-like vulnerability. "I need your help," King said repeatedly. "I have no idea where this movement is going."

Within a week of the mass arrests in Montgomery, King and the NAACP's Roy Wilkins had entered what would become a long-standing quarrel over money. King protested in a letter to Wilkins that the NAACP seemed to be gathering money for itself "in the name of our movement." Wilkins defended his instructions that all proceeds from the boycott fund-raisers be routed through his office, saying that the NAACP expected to absorb many of the MIA legal expenses, but he did not specify which ones. He added a warning to King: "I am certain I do not need to stress that at this time it would be fatal for there to develop any hint of disagreement as to the raising and allocating of funds." NAACP officials, who saw themselves in the climactic stages of a twenty-year legal battle to integrate public institutions such as the schools, were reluctant to endorse the radically new approach of a mass boycott. Negotiations over legal support stalled further, so that by the time of King's trial only one of his eight lawyers came from Thurgood Marshall's legal staff. During the trial itself, the NAACP issued a droll statement that it would await the final outcome of the boycott before deciding whether passive resistance techniques could be useful.

Wilkins became more accommodating when the trial established King as a national symbol. Three weeks after the conviction, he notified King that the NAACP would pay all costs for its attorneys to represent King and any of the other mass-indictment defendants brought to trial, as well as the MIA in its federal suit against bus segregation and Rosa Parks in her own ongoing case. In addition, Wilkins offered to pay half the $9,000 fee charged by one of the local Alabama firms in the King case. Oddly enough, Wilkins extended this generous offer at a time when fame had made the fledgling MIA wealthier than the national NAACP, and King accepted the offer even though he did not need the money at the time. The MIA cases might wind up in the U.S. Supreme Court, King reasoned, where the NAACP lawyers had an unsurpassed record in civil rights cases. "We are quite conscious of our dependence on the NAACP," King wrote Wilkins in a conciliatory letter, mentioning that his church had just purchased a $1,000 life membership in the NAACP. Within a week, Wilkins invited King to address the NAACP's annual convention in San Francisco.

On June 1, 1956, some weeks before the NAACP convention, Alabama attorney general John Patterson obtained an extraordinary court order banning most NAACP activities within the entire state of Alabama, including fund-raising, dues collection, and the solicitation of new members. Patterson based his request for the order on the assertion that the NAACP was "organizing, supporting, and financing an illegal boycott by Negro residents of Montgomery." The order transformed this old rumor into the factual predicate for effectively outlawing the organization, and when the NAACP resisted a corollary order to surrender its membership and contribution lists to Patterson, the judge imposed a $100,000 contempt fine as well. It took the NAACP eight years and several trips to the U.S. Supreme Court to void these sanctions. During all that time, the Alabama NAACP was disbanded. On one level, this shocking development threw King and Wilkins together as common defendants. But Wilkins could hardly forget that it was King's boycott that had put the NAACP out of business in an entire state, at a critical time in the school desegregation cases, and this handicap would grow more serious as other Southern states tried to follow Alabama's example.

One hidden effect of the Patterson order was to drive some of Alabama's former NAACP leaders into closer alliance with King. The most unusual and significant of them was Fred Shuttlesworth in Birmingham, a volatile, rough-cut man who had been raised in the backwoods of Alabama. Convicted of running the family still in 1941, Shuttlesworth had wandered around Alabama as a truck driver and cement worker, discovering in the process that the natural gift his mother so prized in him, his memory, was well suited to the work of a country preacher. Accepting the "call," Shuttlesworth bought a cow to help support him and his young wife while he pitched himself into colleges and seminaries, built a house out of World War II scrap materials, and preached as many as five times each Sunday. At his first full-time pulpit in Selma, Shuttlesworth had quarreled ceaselessly with his deacons over the prerogatives of the minister, finally receiving what he called a vision from God telling him to persevere and subdue them.

Only a few days after the Patterson court order, Shuttlesworth received another divine message, saying, "Ye shall know the truth and the truth shall make you free." He interpreted this to mean that the demise of the faction-ridden NAACP was a blessing in disguise, and that he should replace it with his own organization, like King's in Montgomery. He knew King, having gone to Montgomery several times to deliver contributions, and the idea of an organization free of the NAACP bureaucracy appealed strongly to him. His public summons to create a new group attracted publicity in the white press as a blatant circumvention of the court order banning Negro agitation, as well as an unprecedented challenge to Birmingham's pugnacious police commissioner, Eugene "Bull" Connor. One troubled Negro preacher went so far as to tell Shuttlesworth that he had received his own vision from heaven, in which God told him to tell Shuttlesworth to cancel the meeting. "When did the Lord start sending my messages through you?" Shuttlesworth hotly replied. "The Lord has told me to call it on." Ordinary folk, drawn by the tension and

the publicity, packed the church on the night of June 5 to hear Shuttlesworth announce the formation of his own Alabama Christian Movement
for Human Rights. This deed first singled him out as the preacher courageous enough or crazy enough to defy Bull Connor.

In Montgomery, King and the other MIA leaders were celebrating a
tangible victory. On June 4, a panel of three federal judges ruled in the
MIA's favor in the suit Fred Gray had filed back in February, two days
after King's house was bombed. By a 2–1 vote, the judges struck down
Montgomery's bus segregation ordinances as unconstitutional. Attorneys for Montgomery and for the state of Alabama immediately appealed
the decision to the U.S. Supreme Court. Although the segregation laws
remained in effect pending that ruling, which for the boycotters meant
that months of walking and car-pooling stretched ahead, thousands of
hallelujahs were raised at mass meetings in Montgomery. For the first
time, they were on the winners' side in a white man's forum, and now
would go into the Supreme Court seeking to sustain the ruling of three
white Southern judges. The odds for ultimate legal victory shifted heavily in their favor.

Optimism broke out like an epidemic. Every hardship, every funeral of
a faithful walker who had died, became grist for inspiration to keep
walking another six months if necessary. Everybody knew that the first
six months had been the hard ones. They were cresting. The MIA was
rich. It was buying and operating its own fleet of more than a dozen new
station wagons, sparing much of the wear on the cars of private volunteers. At the time of the court victory, the MIA had stowed away deposits
totaling more than $120,000 in banks scattered from New York to Okla-
homa—outside Alabama and therefore safe from legal raids by Attorney
General Patterson. King decided that the MIA was secure enough for him
to take a vacation. With Coretta and the Abernathys, he vanished by car
toward the coast of California, planning to make his way to San Francisco
for the NAACP convention.

Shortly after they left, MIA secretary Uriah J. Fields held a press conference in Montgomery to charge that the boycott leadership was riddled
with corruption. It involved thousands of dollars in misappropriated
funds, he said, and leaders who had become "too egotistical and interested in perpetuating themselves." "I can no longer identify myself with
a movement in which the many are exploited by the few," Fields declared. His public resignation created the most sensational news since
the mass arrests. Fields was an outspoken, unconventional, bootstrap
leader, about King's age. He had worn a goatee since his student days at
Alabama State, which marked him as an outsider among the more image-
conscious leaders. Campaigning as a rebel, Fields had defeated in a stu-

dent election the heavily favored fraternity candidate, who was now a protégé of King's at Dexter Avenue. Fields believed that on their records as activists he, and not King, should have been elected MIA president, and he openly begrudged Abernathy his growing role as second in authority. It galled him that King was in demand for speaking engagements all over the country, whereas he had landed only one out-of-town appearance in Pittsburgh.

By timing his gambit to coincide with the absence of King and Abernathy, Fields hoped other disgruntled leaders would rally to demand a restructuring of the executive board. However, he grossly underestimated the bond between King and the great masses of Montgomery's boycotters. Ordinary people called Fields a traitor, and his own church voted without dissent to strip him of the pastorate. By the time King landed in Montgomery, having aborted his California vacation to face the insurrection at home, Fields already was so thoroughly discredited that King's task was more to protect than to prosecute him. At a mass meeting, King made a long speech denying the charges but calling on the MIA membership to forgive Fields as a prodigal son. Defending his leadership was easy for King—too easy, in a sense, because he did not have to address the elements of truth in Fields's charges. Thousands of dollars had in fact been misappropriated out of the MIA treasury, as car-pool drivers and assorted hustlers were charging the MIA for oceans of gasoline and truckloads of imaginary spare tires. A reorganized transportation committee was trying to plug the holes in the reimbursement system. As for the alleged high-handedness and egotism of the MIA leadership, there was a good deal of it, and it was resented not only by Fields. Some, like E. D. Nixon, believed they were being shunted aside for lack of polish or education, and a few of the lay people thought they were out because they were not preachers. Now such criticism would be confined forever to privacy. The defection and swift decapitation of Fields demonstrated that public criticism of the MIA would not only be seized upon by white opponents but also taken as a personal criticism of King, which would not be tolerated.

King flew back to San Francisco to address the forty-seventh NAACP convention. Hundreds of delegates pressed upon him to shake his hand, including Medgar Evers, the NAACP field secretary in Mississippi. Evers invited King to Mississippi, saying that "your presence would do more . . . than any" to raise hopes in his state. The idea of a mass movement by nearly fifty thousand Negroes in a single city captivated the delegates, whose customary role in the NAACP was limited to support of the lawyers fighting segregation in court. Delegates on the convention floor drafted numerous resolutions in favor of the nonviolent methods of the bus boycott. Wilkins and Thurgood Marshall opposed them in a protracted struggle that put King in the awkward position of the insurrectionary guest. He tried to make himself as scarce as possible, but when reporters cornered him with questions about whether he thought nonviolent methods might help desegregate the schools, he replied that he had not thought about it much but that they probably could do so. This comment prompted an annoyed Thurgood Marshall to declare that school desegregation was men's work and should not be entrusted to children. Some reporters quoted him to the effect that King was a "boy on a man's errand." Wilkins worked more diplomatically to smother the threat of a runaway convention, finally engineering passage of a resolution calling merely for the executive board to give "careful consideration" to the use of the Montgomery model.

In July, sensitive to criticism that he had been neglecting his church, King started a newsletter, the *Dexter Echo*, to keep in touch with his members. He devoted his own column, "From the Pastor's Desk," mostly to problems of church finances. To offset slow collections during the summer months, King supervised the second annual Prettiest Baby Contest, which netted more than $2,000. The winning baby, on the strength of the $645.60 raised by the sponsoring August Club, was King's daughter Yoki, now eight months old.

King was off on a speaking tour of the Midwest. In his absence, the *Echo* published a FLASH bulletin announcing that his photograph was on display at the Brussels World's Fair. When King went on to Canada to address a convention of Negro morticians, E. D. Nixon called to say that A. Philip Randolph had secured an invitation for King to testify before the platform committee of the Democratic National Convention in Chicago. King, more conscious than ever of seniority and protocol among leaders, told Nixon that he did not want to testify unless Roy Wilkins approved. Nixon called Wilkins, who said, "I agree with you, Brother Nixon. He ought to be there, although it will take some of the spotlight off me." With this clearance, Nixon then made the arrangements for King to tell the Democrats that civil rights was "one of the supreme moral issues" of the age. Perhaps because he was so intent on soothing leaders of national stature, such as Wilkins, King neglected to give enough credit for his convention appearance to E. D. Nixon—or so Nixon came to believe. Thereafter, he spoke to King only when necessary, and the coolness between the two of them became the subject of private gossip. This was to be King's portion—new realms of success, blurred by aggravations striking randomly on all sides.

On August 25, two or three sticks of dynamite exploded in Reverend Graetz's front yard, shattering the windows in nearby homes. Graetz returned from out of town to find that the police had confiscated personal records and correspondence from his home as part of the bombing investigation. Detectives promptly interrogated Graetz himself, in a manner that provoked the two-year-old Graetz boy to shout, "Go away, you bad policemen!" The ever-repentant Graetz later confessed to a fleeting surge of pride in his son's combative spirit. The next day's *Advertiser* reported Mayor Gayle's suspicions that Graetz had bombed his own home in order to stimulate out-of-state contributions to the MIA. "Perhaps this is just a publicity stunt to build up interest of the Negroes in their campaign," he said. Two days after the bombing, King composed his first letter of protest to the White House, telling Eisenhower that Montgomery Negroes were living "without protection of law." Cabinet secretary Maxwell Rabb replied perfunctorily for the President that "the situation in Montgomery has been followed with interest."

Adlai Stevenson, the Democratic candidate for President, worried about the Negro vote, especially after Roy Wilkins sharply criticized his desire to keep the civil rights issue out of the campaign. "We must recognize that it is reason alone that will determine our rate of progress," Stevenson replied to Wilkins, who proceeded to denounce the candidate's blithe vagueness in such blistering language that Stevenson's friend Eleanor Roosevelt threatened to resign from the board of the NAACP. In October, Stevenson's concern over the issue prompted his appearance at a rally in Harlem, where he criticized as too passive Eisenhower's statement that it "makes no difference" what he thought personally of the Supreme Court's school desegregation decision. "I support this decision!" cried Stevenson. His supporters argued that his statement set him apart from Eisenhower as more friendly to Negroes, while his detractors replied that it meant little for a candidate to say he supported the law of the land, as did Eisenhower, while refusing to say what he would do to enforce it.

Eisenhower campaigned differently. On October 10, he attended a World Series game between the Brooklyn Dodgers and New York Yankees at Ebbets Field. Sitting with him as a guest in the presidential box was E. Frederic Morrow. There was no official announcement of his presence, but word spread immediately through the Negro press, which noted that Stevenson could not afford to socialize with Negroes for fear of alienating Southern Democrats. The next day, Eisenhower invited Harlem congressman Rev. Adam Clayton Powell, Jr., to the White House for a private meeting that became big news when Powell, a Democrat, emerged to endorse Eisenhower for reelection, saying that he would do more for civil rights.

The Negro issue was lost for the remainder of a campaign that finished memorably in the grip of two major world crises, the Hungarian revolt against Soviet domination and the combined effort of Israel, Great Britain, and France to take the Suez Canal from Egypt by war. Eisenhower made scathing private remarks about the "mid-Victorian style" of the Suez attack. If the United States supported such blatant colonialism, he said, the reaction "might well array the world from Dakar to the Philippine Islands against us." His implicit threat to cut off American oil supplies to Europe helped rescue Nasser, a man Eisenhower loathed, and made a fiasco of Britain's last effort to salvage an empire.

Fear of war turned a probable Eisenhower reelection into a landslide margin of nearly 10 million votes. On election night, an aide danced joyfully into Eisenhower's hotel suite with the news that the Republican ticket had carried the city of Montgomery, Alabama, for the first time in history. No one quite knew why, since Montgomery's white citizens were known to be furious over the Administration's private efforts to help Negroes in their eleven-month boycott of the bus system.* Post-election analysis showed that Negroes had voted Republican in substantial numbers for the first time since the New Deal, giving Eisenhower about 60 percent of their votes. Republican strategists looked forward to a major realignment of American politics, in which fiscal conservatives, educated suburbanites, and Negroes would combine to form an enlightened majority. This was among the many aspects of the election results that disheartened Stevenson. "I am quite bewildered about the Negroes," he said.

In Montgomery, city officials petitioned a state court for an injunction banning the MIA car pool as an unlicensed municipal transportation system. The injunction was the legal weapon King's lawyers had feared most, knowing that court orders had the power to regulate behavior in advance of substantive court decisions. A prime illustration of such power was Attorney General Patterson's order that outlawed the Alabama NAACP pending the outcome of protracted litigation. A similar injunction in Montgomery would mean that boycott leaders who persisted in operating the car pool would be subject to peremptory jailing on contempt charges. It would shift all the advantages of judicial delay from the MIA to the city.

---

* General Lewis B. Hershey, director of the National Selective Service System, repeatedly blocked attempts by the Montgomery draft board to induct MIA attorney Fred Gray into the Army. Local draft board members across Alabama resigned in protest against "political interference" by the Eisenhower Administration, as did George C. Wallace, then a judge handling draft appeals near Montgomery. Shortly before the election, both U.S. senators from Alabama called for a congressional investigation of the Fred Gray draft case.

At the *Advertiser*, Grover Hall fulminated that the move came almost a year too late, being just "another blunder" now that the issue of segregation itself was before the U.S. Supreme Court. Hall wanted to prod the city fathers into thinking about more fundamental lines of defense. His purpose was not to give solace to King, of course, and King took none. To him, the Supreme Court decision lay somewhere in the unpredictable future, whereas the dreadful impact of the proposed injunction could be only hours away. It threatened to destroy all the accrued benefits of the car pool—the MIA-owned station wagons, the entire support budget, and the organized driver system. The boycotters would have to walk into their second winter, which was fast approaching.

On Tuesday, November 13, one week after the Eisenhower landslide, King sat glumly at the defendant's table as city lawyers told Judge Eugene Carter why he should not only ban the car pool by injunction but also impose a $15,000 fine on the MIA to compensate the city for lost tax revenues. A surprise city witness testified that the MIA had deposited $189,000 in his Montgomery bank, a sum that city lawyers used to ridicule King's contention that the car pool was a voluntary, "share-a-ride" cooperative. Both sides mounted arguments that seemed highly ironic even at the time. Conservative city lawyers charged that the car pool was a "private enterprise" and therefore should be regulated or banned; King renewed his amnesiac defense that the boycott occurred spontaneously and without any organization or leadership that he could remember very well.

During a recess, an AP reporter slipped to the front of the courtroom and handed King a note. Inside was a bulletin the reporter had ripped off the AP ticker: "The United States Supreme Court today affirmed a decision of a special three-judge panel in declaring Alabama's state and local laws requiring segregation on buses unconstitutional. The Supreme Court acted without listening to any argument; it simply said 'the motion to affirm is granted and the Judgment is affirmed.' "

It was over. With blood pounding in his ears, King rushed to the back of the courtroom to tell Abernathy, E. D. Nixon, and Coretta. There was commotion at the plaintiff's table, as word was reaching the city lawyers. The news sprinted through the courtroom on whispers, until one Negro, unable to bear the silence any longer, rose to declare, "God Almighty has spoken from Washington, D.C.!" Judge Carter was obliged to bang his gavel many times to restore order, and he handed down his injunction against the car pool even though the Supreme Court decision made it irrelevant.

Montgomery's Negroes did not care about the injunction now. They were celebrating. That night, at the first of two enormous mass meetings,

S. S. Seay reported that the Ku Klux Klan was preparing to march on Montgomery. No matter, he cried out, "we are not afraid, because God is on our side." Seay burst into tears at the pulpit, and, said the *Advertiser*, "several women screamed with what appeared to be a religious ecstasy." The newspaper noted that King entered the meeting at precisely 7:23 P.M., touching off a standing ovation that lasted until Abernathy managed to quiet the crowd for the reading of the Scripture. A hush settled tentatively over the assembly as Robert Graetz walked to the pulpit. The skinny, jug-eared white preacher began to read from the famous love chapter of I Corinthians: "When I was a child, I spake as a child, I understood as a child, I thought as a child: but when I became a man I put away childish things." Before he finished the sentence, everyone in the church rose en masse to cheer the passage, which struck the chord of their new self-respect with the force of an epiphany.

Legal technicalities delayed the implementation. The Supreme Court decision would not take effect until appropriate orders reached Montgomery, King learned, whereas the spiteful injunction banning the car pool was in operation already. This meant that during the interim, bus segregation remained the law and the MIA could provide no alternative transportation system. To endure this delay without provoking the whites to legal harassments, MIA leaders summoned up the last reserves of energy within their followers to keep boycotting the buses until the integration orders arrived. They would walk. In effect, they would struggle through a victory lap.

Euphoria propelled them. The statement King issued after hearing word of the decision was filled with the youthful enthusiasm that sometimes overran the bounds of his rhetoric. "Often we have had to stand amid the surging murmer [sic] of life's restless sea," he said. "Many days and nights have been filled with jostling winds of adversity." But he recommended the prudent course: "For these three or four days, we will continue to walk and share rides with friends." This time estimate from King's legal experts proved highly optimistic, as slow Court paperwork extended the victory lap through five arduous weeks.

Celebrities called King from the first day. Mahalia Jackson wanted to come to Montgomery to sing in celebration. Several Negro seminary presidents offered to deliver theological evaluations of the boycott's Christian spirit. Such a flurry of impressive offers inspired King to organize an entire week of seminars and church services, which he called the Institute on Nonviolence and Social Change. Reporter Carl Rowan, novelist Lillian Smith, and white Unitarian leader Homer Jack agreed to participate, as did the most powerful national figures in the Negro Baptist Church. Daddy King's rival William Holmes Borders came from Atlanta to speak. Gardner Taylor came from his enormous "million-dollar" Concord Baptist Church in Brooklyn, and T. J. Jemison came up from Baton Rouge.

King opened the Institute program on December 3 with an address at the Holt Street Baptist Church, where his speech almost exactly a year earlier had electrified the first mass meeting. He announced that the last year had taught six lessons: "(1) We have discovered that we can stick together for a common cause; (2) Our leaders do not have to sell out; (3) Threats and violence do not necessarily intimidate those who are sufficiently aroused and non-violent; (4) Our church is becoming militant, stressing a social gospel as well as a gospel of personal salvation; (5) We have gained a new sense of dignity and destiny; (6) We have discovered a new and powerful weapon—non-violent resistance."

To King, the lessons of leadership and unity came first, the militancy of the church next, and the "discovery" of nonviolence last. His list was aptly chosen and properly ordered as a distillation of the boycott experience. Nonviolence, like the boycott itself, had begun more or less by accident. The function of the boycott leaders had been to inspire, to react, and to persevere. Not until Birmingham, more than six years later, would King's idea of leadership encompass the deliberate creation of new struggles or the conscious, advance selection of strategies and tactics. For now, his notion of leadership emphasized the display of learning. He said many wise things in his address—on technology, colonialism, the pace of time, but the speech as a whole went sprawling. King quoted notables from Heraclitus to Bob Hope. His anthem was a yearning for justice, and he extolled the value of martyrdom in a meditation on courage, but his oratory suffered markedly from abstraction once he was cut loose from the specific pressures of the boycott.

Sunday, December 9, was a banner day for King. In the morning, he turned over his Dexter pulpit to Vernon Johns, who preached a sermon commemorating the seventy-ninth anniversary of the church's secession from First Baptist. In the afternoon, King presided at First Baptist over a huge service culminating the events of the Institute week. Visiting choirs warmed up the crowd with an hour of music. Vernon Johns, swallowing his pride and his distaste for the National Baptist Convention, offered up the invocation in his inimitable growl. Then, after a solo by King's friend Bob Williams, J. H. Jackson made his entrance. He never had openly endorsed the boycott, and he said almost nothing of it that day. Nevertheless, his presence as the titular head of the largest and most powerful organization controlled by American Negroes guaranteed an enormous, respectful crowd, estimated at up to eight thousand people. His was the kind of power King and Abernathy dreamed about when they spoke of spreading the movement through the instruments of a militant church. At the last NBC convention, in September, Jackson had bestowed a sign of recognition on King by inviting Coretta to give a solo recital at his church in Chicago. Now Jackson acknowledged King among the few royal figures of the Negro Baptists—Jackson, Gardner Taylor, the Jemisons, and, to a lesser extent, Adam Clayton Powell, Jr. King had surpassed his father within the ranks of the organized Negro clergy. In the long Institute program, King's name and everything about him was spelled entirely in capital letters. This was also true of Jackson but of no one else.

On December 20, Supreme Court notifications arrived at the federal courthouse in Montgomery, and deputy U.S. marshals served notices on city officials. That night, King told a mass meeting that the walking was over. He stressed reconciliation, saying that the boycott had brought a victory for justice that would benefit both races. It was not a victory over the white people, he said, but most white politicians seemed to believe otherwise. Mayor Gayle and Police Commissioner Sellers managed to be out of town, unavailable for comment. A local judge who was forced to dissolve his pro-segregation decrees denounced the Supreme Court decision as based on "neither law nor reason" but an "evil construction."

King, in his suit and dress hat, followed by Fred Gray, Abernathy, Glenn Smiley, and a flock of cameramen and reporters, boarded a city bus before dawn the next morning. "We are glad to have you," the bus driver said politely as he rumbled off down the street. Photographers on board took pictures of King sitting next to Smiley near the front of the bus. The integrated group achieved a convivial banter with the driver, who went so far as to make an unscheduled stop to pick up Reverend Graetz. Summoned outside by the bus horn, Graetz was treated to the sight of Smiley leaning casually out the front door of a city bus. "What time do you want me for dinner tonight?" Smiley shouted grandly, as though he had transformed the bus into a personal limousine. Graetz joined King and all those on the bus in laughter. It was a moment of innocence, dearly paid for.

King asked Bayard Rustin to come to Montgomery. Only the extraordinary burst of post-victory activity produced the invitation, as both men knew Rustin's physical presence could be a dangerous matter. Local whites still remembered the mysterious impostor from Le Figaro, and King felt a greater political threat from his own colleagues, especially the preachers, among whom tolerance for homosexuals was shunned as the wedge of evil. Some of the Negroes around King remembered Rustin less than fondly as the bizarre, imperious man who had caused a great alarm in their camp back in February. Even worse, Rustin had just arranged the publication in his Socialist magazine, *Liberation*, of an article by E. D. Nixon, in which Nixon claimed more than his share of credit for the creation of the boycott.* The article earned Nixon a fresh burst of ridicule from some of King's more intellectual friends. King's desire to hide Rustin from practically everyone was so strong that he asked him to fly into Birmingham instead of Montgomery. Bob Williams met Rustin there and put him face down in the backseat of his car. King's instructions were that Rustin was not to raise his head until the car was parked safely at the Dexter parsonage.

Rustin arrived on Sunday, December 23, in time to inspect the damage from a shotgun blast fired into King's home early that morning. Everyone was scared, but no one was hurt. King huddled privately with Rustin on a host of matters, including New York fund-raising, Randolph's efforts to facilitate better relations between Wilkins and King, future publications by King, a possible King trip to meet with Gandhians in India, and, most important, King's response to the Negroes across the South who were besieging him for help in their desire to integrate their bus systems. King and Rustin had just finished one of their strategy sessions when Daddy King burst through the front door of the parsonage like a G-man leading a raid. The shotgun news had propelled him to Montgomery in high dudgeon. Coretta asked him if he would like something to eat.

"I have not come to eat," Daddy King declared. "I have come to pray." He commanded M.L. to get down on his knees and then prayed out loud. Rustin retreated into an adjoining room, from where he heard Daddy King talking to God in such a way that God seemed to be telling the younger King that the boycott was over and that God now had things for him to do outside of politics. The prayer went on for some time. At its conclusion, Daddy King spoke more directly on the same theme, and the tension of the ensuing argument soon reduced his son to tears of anger and frustration. The younger King said little in his own defense until the end, when he blurted out that he would just have to do what he felt he had to do. Somehow this ended it. The force of the moment was such that Rustin felt he had witnessed a unique crisis between the Kings.

The next day, Christmas Eve, a car pulled up to a Montgomery bus

---

* In the same issue of *Liberation*, A. Philip Randolph endorsed the activism of nonviolence, and the aged Harry Emerson Fosdick, pastor emeritus of New York's Riverside Church, called the boycott a "godsend." Fosdick quoted one of King's favorite lines, from the abolitionist preacher Theodore Parker: "The arc of the moral universe is long, but it bends toward justice."

stop where a fifteen-year-old Negro girl was standing alone, and five men jumped out, beat her, and quickly fled. In Birmingham, Fred Shuttlesworth announced that he would lead a group onto the front of the buses the day after Christmas. He was preparing himself for the test on Christmas night, sitting in his parsonage with one of his deacons, when some fifteen sticks of dynamite exploded beneath them, virtually destroying the house. Investigating police shining flashlights through the dense clouds of smoke heard shouts from the basement, where Shuttlesworth and his deacon had fallen. "I'm not coming out naked!" cried the preacher, who was dressed for bed. The police draped Shuttlesworth with blankets, pulled fallen lumber off the deacon, and pronounced it a miracle that either was alive. When several officers advised Shuttlesworth to leave town, he proclaimed loudly that he would never do it. "God erased my name off that dynamite," he declared, his sense of destiny renewed. The next day, he led two hundred of his followers into the white sections of Birmingham buses. More than a score of them were arrested and convicted on charges of violating the segregation laws.

In Montgomery, after shotgun snipers fired on an integrated bus, King issued a statement calling on city authorities to "take a firm stand" against such violence. City Commissioner Parks, one of the few whites to speak up in response, announced that the city would have to suspend bus service if the shootings continued—a statement that dismayed King's followers because they believed that stopping the only integrated public institution in Alabama was precisely what the snipers wanted to accomplish. Two days later, bushwhackers fired another volley at an integrated bus, this time sending a pregnant Negro woman to the hospital with bullet wounds in both legs. The city commissioners halted night bus service.

King sent out invitations to what he called the first Negro Leaders Conference on Nonviolent Integration. Sixty preachers from ten Southern states responded, gathering in Atlanta at Ebenezer early in January of 1957. They represented a pitifully small portion of the Negro preachers in the region, but their ranks included many of the most influential mavericks. Fred Shuttlesworth came from Birmingham, and Rev. C. K. Steele from Tallahassee, Florida, where he was leading a Montgomery-inspired campaign to integrate the buses. William Holmes Borders attended from Atlanta, where his own nonviolent bus demonstration provoked Georgia's governor to put the state militia on standby alert just before the conference. Bayard Rustin came down from New York to work quietly on drafting resolutions and an organizational charter.

Abernathy stayed with King in the Atlanta family home. At 2:30 A.M. on January 10, the day the conference was to begin, Mother King shook

Abernathy awake to take an emergency phone call. "Ralph, they have bombed our home," said a shaky Juanita Abernathy from Montgomery. "But I am all right and so is the baby." She reported that the porch and front room of the house were practically demolished, and that the arriving policemen seemed frightened too, because other blasts had been heard since. They said the Hutchinson Street Baptist Church was destroyed, its roof caved in. People were calling or driving around the street in dumb panic, some too afraid to go outside and others too afraid to stay home.

The King home in Atlanta was lit up and buzzing as Abernathy relayed the news. The preachers offered prayers, and then Abernathy worried out loud about First Baptist. "I don't want Reverend Stokes's church bombed," he said plaintively. Daddy King was pacing the floor angrily. "Well, they are gonna bomb it," he said. Abernathy grew so agitated that he tried repeatedly to get a call through to his wife. When he finally succeeded, he learned that the panic in Montgomery was growing worse. There had been another blast, loud enough to be heard all over town. It was definite that Hutchinson Street Baptist had been hit—people had seen the ruins—and the Graetz home had been bombed again. Mrs. Abernathy went off the line briefly and came back to say that another one had just gone off, close to their home. She felt the rumble. And another church had been hit. She was not sure which church and had no idea yet about where the latest bomb had struck.

Later reports confirmed Abernathy's fears that it was First Baptist. He and King, leaving Coretta and Rustin to run the Atlanta conference, departed before dawn for Montgomery, where they surveyed the night's total of four bombed churches and two houses. Of the churches, First Baptist was the least severely hit, as the bomb had torn apart the basement but done little damage to the sanctuary above. Still, city authorities condemned it as structurally unsound for use.

King returned hastily to Atlanta, where the assembled preachers voted to form an organization that, after several name changes, would be called the Southern Christian Leadership Conference. They elected King president. In the name of the new organization, he sent telegrams to President Eisenhower, Attorney General Brownell, and Vice President Richard M. Nixon. Sherman Adams replied for the President that it was not possible for Eisenhower to schedule a speech in the South against segregationist violence, as King had requested. An aide to Brownell replied that the Justice Department would look into the bombings and other incidents but that the primary authority for the maintenance of law and order was lodged in state governments. Nixon did not reply.

Abernathy stayed in Montgomery, supervising church volunteers who worked frantically on Friday and Saturday to shore up the basement beams and sweep out the debris at First Baptist. City inspectors, granting Abernathy's desperate wish to hold Sunday services there, stipulated wisely that no one was to go upstairs, as their weight might cause the temporary beams to collapse. Abernathy agreed. A piano was hauled in, a makeshift pulpit erected, and on Sunday the members took seats on chairs in the basement. They cast anxious looks toward the fresh carpentry above them and the grit on the floor. A pall hung over the service until Mrs. Beasley, mother of church clerk William Beasley and one of the oldest members of the congregation, rose to speak. "I don't like what I see here today," she said. "Brother Pastor, you can't leave no church worried and troubled. I remember in 1910, when this church was just a big hole in the ground after the fire. And two fine ladies from Dexter walked by and said, 'What is *this*? Unborn generations will say this hole is where the First Baptist Church was *supposed* to be.' But they were wrong! Dr. A. J. Stokes built this church, and I want you to have a vote of confidence that we will build it again!" As the congregation jumped to its feet, church pianist Dorothy Posey spontaneously began to play the "Hallelujah Chorus."

The inspiration that surged through First Baptist derived in part from community rivalries, and MIA leaders discovered to their dismay that a new and uglier side of crisis psychology emerged simultaneously with the most inspired goodwill. Even those who had lived through the boycott could not explain it, except to say that the MIA community was suffering a natural letdown. Once the endeavor was behind them, crisis emotions slipped easily into depression or jealousy. Some resented the fact that Abernathy's prestige rose dramatically because he was the only leader bombed both at church and at home. Graetz's stature grew because on the most recent night of terror his home had been the target of two bombs, one of which did not go off. (An intrepid neighbor snipped the smoldering end off a fuse leading to eleven sticks of dynamite.) When the rumor mill passed the word that one of the Graetz bombs had been meant for a Methodist preacher within the MIA, that preacher actually became consumed with regret that he had not been bombed—to the point that he later had a mental breakdown. Rev. Uriah J. Fields, the "traitor" of the previous summer, was temporarily restored to leadership because the church he had regained, Bell Street Baptist, suffered the most destruction on the night of the bombs.

E. D. Nixon, who was not bombed this time, became openly hostile to King's manner and importance. Not long after the bombing, Nixon resigned as MIA treasurer with a bitter "Dear Sir" letter to King, in which he complained of being "treated as a child." Some of King's partisans looked upon Nixon with the same tart condescension that moved one of them publicly to refer to Rosa Parks as "an adornment of the movement." In this spirit, the most sophisticated leaders around King agreed that the next desegregation target should be the Montgomery airport. Graetz, Fred Gray, and a few others objected to this notion as absurd and selfish, inasmuch as only a tiny fraction of MIA members ever had been on an airplane. But the leaders, including Abernathy, wanted to hit the airport. They had moved up from the bus.

A roiling undertow ensured that the MIA would never again play a major part in American racial politics. Although the force of the boycott would reach the country by delayed reverberation, Montgomery's contribution was already history. King himself suffered a corresponding letdown. He was fearful of the bombs, saddened by the backsliding on bus integration, hurt by criticisms within the MIA that he traveled too much and received too much attention, and depressed by the carping disunity among the MIA leadership. Instinctively, he took the fears and failures upon himself, feeling guilty and miserable, and the overload of guilt spilled over into self-reproach. On the Monday night after Abernathy's basement church service, King took the pulpit at an MIA mass meeting. Praying publicly for guidance, he said, "Lord, I hope no one will have to die as a result of our struggle for freedom in Montgomery. Certainly I don't want to die. But if anyone has to die, let it be me!" His outcry threw the audience into pandemonium. Shouts of "No! No!" clashed with a wave of religious ecstasy. In the midst of it, King became overwrought. He gripped the pulpit with both hands, unable to speak. He remained frozen there long after the crowd stilled itself, which produced an awkward silence and then a murmur of alarm as the seconds went by. King never spoke. Finally, two preachers draped their arms around him and led him to a seat.

Two weeks later, Bob Williams was on Saturday night duty at the Dexter parsonage. Coretta and Yoki were in Atlanta. There was the usual mix of friendly and hateful phone calls, but something disturbed King so much that he got up from his bed to wake Williams. "Bob, I think we better leave here tonight," he said. The two of them promptly went to Williams' house. Several hours later, before dawn, a bomb exploded on the corner nearest the parsonage. The blast crushed the front part of a house, damaged an adjacent Negro taxi stand, and shattered the windows of three taxis parked there, sending the drivers to the hospital with cuts. During the alarm that followed, someone went to the empty parsonage to check on King and found twelve sticks of dynamite lying on the front porch, the fuse giving off an acrid smell. An hour later, after a tense drama inside the police cordon and a near riot on the outside, the state of Alabama's chief munitions expert defused the bomb. Two Negroes who denounced the police for failing to catch any of the bombers were arrested and later convicted for incitement to riot. King, summoned by telephone, arrived to quiet the crowd with a speech.

That morning, from the Dexter pulpit, King told the congregation of his experience in his kitchen exactly one year earlier, just before the first bombing. He had heard an inner voice telling him to ignore the confusions and fears swirling about him and do what he thought was right. An *Advertiser* reporter was attending the service that morning because of the bomb, and his report set off a venomous delight within Grover Hall. In the pages of the *Advertiser*, Hall ridiculed what he called the "vision in the kitchen speech," distorting it to imply that King's will to fight segregation had come to him from an alleged kitchen conversation with God. A few days later, Hall came across a passage in an obscure newsletter from a Methodist college outside Alabama, in which a professor wrote that King's nonviolent bearing during the boycott had been worthy of Christian saints. Hall developed this item into a scathing editorial entitled "Dr. King Enters Hagiology of Methodist Church," which touched off a heated controversy throughout the South. Some Alabama churches voted to cut off all financial support for Methodist higher education.

A few days after the taxi-stand bombing, Montgomery police charged seven white men with that crime as well as most of the prior bombings. Hopes for justice swelled within the MIA, until a jury acquitted the first two defendants in spite of their signed confessions. About the same time, the Alabama Supreme Court ruled against King's appeal of his "illegal boycott" conviction. It was a technical ruling—Fred Gray had missed a procedural filing deadline—and King ruefully decided not to press the case to the U.S. Supreme Court for fear of losing on the same technicality. He paid his $500 fine painfully, hating to lose, hating especially to be blocked from getting a substantive ruling on the legality of the protest. He hoped that one of the eighty-nine remaining defendants might be vindicated on constitutional grounds, or on the strict finding that the boycotters had "just cause," but Montgomery prosecutors closed off this avenue by dismissing all these cases. Simultaneously, the prosecutors dropped charges against the remaining white bombing defendants.

King deplored the import of this twin amnesty, which Judge Carter accepted as a package, because it perversely equated the boycott with the bombings, many of which were capital crimes under Alabama law. He did not attack the linkage publicly, however. Doing so would have accomplished nothing practical, and it would have risked further separating him from the eighty-nine MIA leaders now spared prosecution. King's helplessness was evidence of the political shrewdness of the prosecutors' move. Segregationists could take solace from the fact the Negro leader stood proven wrong—tried, convicted, given every chance to appeal, and deemed finally a criminal. They had his money to prove it. The Negro population at large had just absorbed a historical reminder of local law and random violence. What little had been lost to the segregationists in the boycott case had since been avenged many times over. Nighttime bus service was quietly restored, and the bombing attacks ceased.

E. Frederic Morrow marched in Eisenhower's second inaugural parade on January 20, 1957. Later that day, by special invitation, he and his wife became the first Negroes ever to sit in the presidential reviewing stand. Clare Boothe Luce—the first female ambassador in U.S. history, and wife of *Time* founder Henry Luce—introduced herself to King in a fan letter that January. A Republican globalist who had just returned from duty in Italy, she wrote King that "no day passed but the Italian communists pointed to events in our South to prove that American democracy was a 'capitalistic myth.'. . . Our enemies abroad have profited greatly from the efforts of these Americans who would deny their own Constitution. No man has ever waged the battle for equality under our law in a more lawful and *Christian* way than you have."

Within a few weeks of Luce's letter, a *Time* correspondent was assigned to write the story of Montgomery in the form of a sympathetic, full-length profile of King. *Time*'s New York editors objected to a mention in the story draft that "Onward Christian Soldiers" was sung at MIA mass meetings, saying that the song's warlike spirit clashed with *Time*'s Gandhian slant on King. "Above all," said *Time* in describing King's education, "he read and reread everything he could find about India's Gandhi." Many adjustments of image were crammed into the frantic revision period attendant to major stories. An artist prepared a strikingly handsome, close-up portrait of King to fill most of the space within the celebrated red borders of *Time*'s cover.

The *Time* story established King as a permanent fixture of American mass culture. *The New York Times Magazine* soon followed with a history of the boycott, which was mostly about King, and NBC's Lawrence Spivak invited him to become the second Negro ever to appear on "Meet the Press." After the boycott, the mantle of fame fell ever more personally on King, who told *Time* that he and his father had chosen to call themselves after Martin Luther, the founding Protestant, and that "perhaps we've earned our right to the name." It was a proud but tentative "perhaps." The boycott had touched him indelibly—astonished, battered, broadened, and inflamed him. Now that it was over, the turmoil within his own world at home served only to drive him more quickly toward a larger constituency.

In February, just before the *Time* cover story hit the stands, he spent an evening at Oberlin College in Ohio, where Vernon Johns had gone to school forty years earlier. A campus YMCA official named Harvey Cox, himself fresh out of seminary, arranged for King to address a general convocation. Afterward, Cox hosted a private dinner, at which the invited students and faculty behaved somewhat shyly around King. During the meal, King found himself isolated, with no one sitting on either side of him, but a student did move nonchalantly to sit directly across the table. Introducing himself as James Lawson, he said he had looked forward to this meeting since first reading King's name in the Nagpur *Times* more than a year earlier. King's interest perked up instantly. He asked about India, saying he hoped to go there soon, and Lawson replied with a description of his Methodist missionary work. Lawson had returned by way of Africa, spending a month there with some of the leaders of the independence movements. King brightened again; he told Lawson he had just received an invitation from Kwame Nkrumah to attend the ceremonies marking the end of British colonialism in Ghana.

The two men fell headlong into conversation. They discovered in a rush that they had similar histories and interests. They knew many people in common and had read many of the same theology books. Lawson had grown up the son of a Republican minister who preached the gospel of love but also wore a .38 on his hip as a precaution against harassment from white people. His mother, said Lawson, was the love influence in his life. As a champion debater in high school and college, he had argued in 1946 that preventive atomic warfare against the Soviet Union was justified to stop the threat of Communism—a memory that made him wince slightly. Two years later, Lawson had decided that the law of love as demonstrated by Jesus did not permit violence except to lay down one's life for another, and had developed theories linking the conscription and segregation laws in principle as denials of religious conscience. In 1951, while serving as national president of the United Methodist Youth Fellowship, he had refused induction into the Army on pacifist grounds, for which he served more than a year in federal prison. Bayard Rustin had come to Ohio to counsel him. So had Glenn Smiley.

These names, like almost everything else Lawson said, struck sparks of recognition in King. The affinity between them was such that they could almost anticipate each other even while first getting acquainted. They were two different personalities on the same quest. In many respects, Lawson was ahead of King as an activist, but King had already realized Lawson's dream of starting a nonviolent mass movement. Now,

King said, he was trying to figure out how to extend the Montgomery model across the South. His best idea so far was to work through the Baptist Convention or the NAACP, but he was not sure what that would mean in practice. Most probably nothing, said Lawson, remarking caustically that the NAACP was by nature an organization of lawyers and banquets, limited by the small numbers and cautious temperament of the Negro middle class. King said ruefully that he was probably right, but how could you build something out of nothing to attack the segregation practiced daily by millions of whites and Negroes?

By the end of the dinner, King was recruiting Lawson to come South to find or create an answer. Lawson said he planned to do just that as soon as he finished the graduate work he had interrupted for prison and India.

"We need you now," King implored him. "We don't have any Negro leadership in the South that understands nonviolence." Lawson promised to hurry. The two men began an association that lasted until Lawson invited King to Memphis to help the sanitation workers in 1968, but now they shared a vision of destiny unmixed with fate.

SIX

A TASTE OF THE
WORLD

As the boycott dissolved in memory to a quaint story of tired feet and empty buses, King groped on a number of fronts to spread what he called the "Montgomery experience" across the South. Deluged with speaking invitations and cheered by enraptured audiences, he hoped that the power of his speech might fuel a mass conversion, like the Great Awakening of the 1740s. More realistically, he knew that oratory could aspire only to enlightenment, and that enlightenment was not enough. Power was required. Toward that end King devised a number of plans. While trying to build his own organization, he labored also to register several million new Negro voters, enlist the organs of mass communication, harness the influence of the organized clergy, gain the endorsement of the highest white leaders, and mobilize a "nonviolent army" of witnesses. When segregationist resistance threatened these efforts, King tinkered incessantly with strategy, trying many combinations of tactics. He consulted the few professed specialists in racial politics, who, since the prospects for overturning the everyday arrangements of the entrenched white majority were dim, tended to be eccentrics of assorted varieties—pietists, incendiaries, one-worlders, Communists, and other ideologues. King learned gradually to distinguish between kooks and quixotics of promise.

Among the strangers who had descended on King during the bus boycott was Harris Wofford. A New Yorker of distinguished Southern lineage, Wofford had been educated at Yale Law School, but his interest in the World Federalist Movement dated from childhood. After World War II, his political idealism had driven him to spend several years observing Gandhism in India, where he and his wife Clare wrote a book called *India Afire*. The couple had returned home filled with the conviction that the proper focus for Gandhians in the United States was the race issue. To the horror of his family, Wofford enrolled for two years at Howard University Law School in Washington, becoming the first white student there since the female suffragists of the 1910s.* Then he found a job at Covington and Burling, Dean Acheson's blue-chip law firm in Washington, where he divided his time between corporate clients and the few scattered souls agitating for integration, such as Myles Horton at the Highlander Folk School. "I wish some of the Gandhian techniques could be used," he wrote Horton in 1954. Wofford's personal contacts ranged from the Luces of *Time* and Senator John F. Kennedy of Massachusetts to the eminent Negro preacher Mordecai Johnson. He was something of an enigma within both circles.

Wofford began his campaign for King's attention in 1956, mailing him a Gandhian analysis of the bus boycott, along with a copy of his book and a pamphlet he had written on nonviolence. When this brought no response, he sent off another letter, reintroducing himself as "your arm chair strategist" and posing the question: "Isn't this the time for some straight Gandhian civil disobedience?" One of King's aides wrote "Please read this" across the second letter. This earned a hurried "Thanks for your letter" scrawled by King, meaning that the aide should compose a letter of thanks. Undaunted, Wofford began looking out for advance word of King's appearances in the North and finally ran across him in New York. He made his pitch on the run: King should go to India to meet the real Gandhians, and Wofford thought he could raise the travel funds.

Intrigued, King invited Wofford to pursue the idea aboard his orator's road show, and, shortly after the bus boycott, the Woffords accompanied the Kings to the Baltimore "national conclave" of a Negro fraternity, Omega Psi Phi. Coretta sang in the fraternity's talent contest, and King delivered a blistering attack on the assembled Omegas for devoting themselves to the pursuit of liquor and luxuries. Turning to what was already his standard theme when addressing the Negro middle class, he dared them to make alliances with, rather than shun, the less fortunate mem-

---

* Wofford's Southern grandmother literally collapsed when she heard the news that he would attend a Negro school, and as she was being carried upstairs shouted, "If God made them equal, I hate God! I hate God! I hate God!"

bers of the race. The Woffords were struck first by the effrontery of the
message and then by the warmth of the reception. The Omegas applauded and cheered, taking no offense at being scolded for their secular
sins. King was a hero, and as he spoke, representatives of other Negro
organizations were rapping on the door. Unable to resist, King squeezed
in quick visits to the local Freemasons and a couple of churches. The
Woffords demonstrated the mettle of their interracial experience by be-
having naturally on a whirlwind tour of Negro establishments.

Also in Baltimore, King and Wofford met with officials of the Libby
Holman Reynolds Foundation, who were interested in putting up the
money for King to tour India. On advance information from King, Bayard
Rustin appeared at the interview as King's protector. Rustin wanted
badly for King to go to India, but not necessarily under the guidance of
Wofford, with whom he had quarreled intermittently since a World Federalist meeting in 1942, when high school student Wofford attacked Rustin's argument that nonviolence precluded resistance even to Hitler.
Rustin and Wofford, independently recognizing King's immense potential for nonviolence, competed for the role of Gandhian mentor. To offset
Wofford's foundation contacts, Rustin brought with him from New York
his own "money man," Stanley Levison.

Levison became King's closest white friend and the most reliable colleague of his life. They were introduced in an offbeat situation that was
typical of "Negro work" in that era. Libby Holman Reynolds, who controlled the foundation which bore her name, had made a reputation in
show business as a sultry torch singer and companion of actor Montgomery Clift. She inherited her fortune only upon winning acquittal on
charges that she had murdered her husband, a tobacco tycoon. Her be-
clouded image hardly suited King's or Gandhi's, but her bohemian tastes
produced philanthropy that was available nowhere else. King discussed
India with her, the dueling Gandhians Wofford and Rustin (one in pin-
stripes, the other practically a fugitive), and Levison himself.

A leftist radical since his college days during the Depression, Levison
nevertheless had a firm capitalist side to him. He was a forty-four-year-
old socialist who had grown rich off real estate investments, a lawyer
who shunned law books and had never practiced law. He had owned car
dealerships but never learned to drive. As a longtime official of the American Jewish Congress, the smaller and more liberal counterpart to the
American Jewish Committee, Levison had specialized in fund-raising for
the AJC and for a host of civil libertarian and radical causes—to save the
Rosenbergs, to abolish as unconstitutional the McCarran Act and other
restrictions on political expression from the McCarthy era, to assist the
defendants in the Smith Act "show trials." Since 1949, nearly a hundred

top officials of the U.S. Communist Party had been jailed or deported under the Smith Act. Working closely and often clandestinely with defense committees, Levison had served in effect as a financial pillar of the Communist Party during the height of its persecution.

Levison was a fiercely independent thinker, of eclectic political interests. After Joseph McCarthy's power was broken by Senate censure in 1954 and the Justice Department reduced Smith Act prosecutions, he joined with A. Philip Randolph and others to support the beleaguered Southern Negroes trying to integrate public schools under the *Brown* decision. Communists officially scorned such efforts, as they had scorned Randolph for decades. In the prevailing Marxist jargon, as laid down from Moscow, integration was a "revisionist" pursuit based on the false hope of progress without world revolution. Moreover, the ideal of integration contradicted the official Moscow goal of "separate national development" for American Negroes, modeled on the Soviet republics. This arcane line made for private Communist derision toward the *Brown* decision and the Montgomery bus boycott, but it also isolated the party from the aspirations of most American Negroes. None of this was new, nor was Levison bound by such disputes. Early in 1956, after the lynching of Emmett Till, he and Rustin—plus Randolph, Dr. Harry Emerson Fosdick, the NAACP, and a host of religious and civic groups—formed an emergency organization called In Friendship, which raised money to support the victims of segregationist vigilantes, mostly in Mississippi. In Friendship had included the Montgomery boycotters among the beneficiaries of its Madison Square Garden rally in May 1956, and Levison personally had raised most of the advertising funds for a Coretta King–Harry Belafonte–Duke Ellington concert a few weeks before Rustin introduced him personally to the Kings.

King's revealing directness deeply impressed Stanley Levison, who resolved at that moment to get to know him better. As for King, he found nothing objectionable about Levison, least of all his radical connections. Although King largely rejected Communist doctrine, he never wavered in support of the victims of McCarthyism or in his sympathy with Communist advocacy for the oppressed. He also gave the American Communists enormous credit for their record on the race issue. Regardless of their doctrinal contortions, the Communists advocated and practiced racial equality far beyond any other political organization in the country. King knew of wealthy white Southerners who, converted to communism in the 1930s, had given their lives working among Negroes in textile mills and union shops. It was said that FBI agents spotted white Communists by their ease and politeness around Negroes, or by the simple fact that they socialized with Negroes at all. To Negroes, this was all part of heaven's mystery—why only the Communists? Even King's most conservative teachers had drilled into him the minutiae of Communist history on the color question—that Stalin, for instance, had written into the Soviet Constitution a provision that discrimination by color was a national crime. "I think there can be no doubt about it that the appeal of Communism to the Eastern nations today can be traceable to a large degree to the Soviet attitude toward *race*," a Morehouse professor wrote to King in 1952.

Levison and King both knew Ben Davis, who for twenty years had been one of the four or five most powerful Communists in the United States. Davis was a Morehouse man. In the early 1920s, when all Morehouse students were required to have jobs, Davis had claimed the position reserved for the richest, most promising young man on campus: chauffeur to the college president. Every morning, Davis arrived ceremoniously in his own chauffeur-driven Pierce-Arrow, then jumped out, donned a chauffeur's cap, and assumed driving duty in President John Hope's brand-new green Dodge. After finishing Harvard Law School, Davis had lived quietly at the pinnacle of the Negro aristocracy in Atlanta until 1933, when he defended Angelo Herndon. A teenaged Communist from Chicago, Herndon faced a death sentence—reduced to eighteen years on a chain gang—for distributing to Negroes a leaflet proclaiming that the Communist Party could end segregation and unemployment. On appeal, the Herndon sedition case became second only to the Scottsboro rape case as the most sensational and prolonged racial trial of the Depression. Davis, shattered by direct exposure to primitive hatreds, official and nonofficial, embraced the heresy that American democracy and his own insular Negro prestige were no better than illusions. He renounced them both, along with the blessings of his family, to join the Communist Party in New York, and his name had been whispered among Atlanta Negroes ever since. As a member of the Central Committee, Davis had dismissed Howard Rushmore from the Communist newspaper for succumbing to the "plantation" blandishments of *Gone With the Wind*, and had personally imposed upon Bayard Rustin the Kremlin's order to cease anti-segregation work during World War II.* Running openly on the Communist ticket, Davis won regular election to the New York City Council. He served there during and after World War II, until his own 1949 conviction in the first and largest Smith Act trial. After completing more than three years in Atlanta Penitentiary for

---

* As often happened among ideologues of that era, Rushmore turned violently against the Communists. He took up a second career as an anti-subversion specialist for the Hearst newspapers.

subversive conspiracy, Davis, with the help of Stanley Levison, raised money to defend dozens of fellow Communists on related charges.

Levison met King just as the U.S. Communist Party faced extinction. The year of the Montgomery boycott had also been the year of Soviet Premier Khrushchev's secret speech denouncing Stalin as a tyrant, murderer, and traitor to Communist principles. Endorsement of these revelations by the Kremlin caused massive psychological trauma among American Communists. Some beat their hands bloody against the wall. Despair only deepened in the fall of 1956 when Khrushchev himself sent Soviet tanks to crush a rebellion by Hungarian workers whom the Kremlin had portrayed as blissfully socialist and free. The steady drain of disillusioned party members swiftly became a flood. By the end of the year, party membership was down from a postwar high of 80,000 to some 5,000. So many of this remnant were FBI informants that J. Edgar Hoover briefly entertained a proposal to take control of the party by throwing the votes of informants behind one faction at the upcoming party convention in February 1957.

Before the convention, a tiny caucus of the three warring factions debated alternatives to the dissolution of the party. John and Lillian Gates represented the liberals, who wanted to break loose from subservience to the Soviet Union and "Americanize" the party, taking Communist principles into mainstream politics. Ben Davis represented the hard-liners, who scorned such proposals as reformist surrender. Against the evils he had known, Davis could imagine no cure less cataclysmic than another Russian Revolution, and, having given up everything to follow the Kremlin, he snarled at the suggestion that he retreat to Atlanta and join a timid little NAACP picket line. Albert "Doc" Blumberg represented a middle faction loyal to Communist Party leader Eugene Dennis. Blumberg, a former philosophy professor at Johns Hopkins, also functioned as the party's expert on relations with sympathetic or cooperating external groups, and in that capacity he brought Stanley Levison to the caucus. The leaders solicited Levison's opinion as to the effect of various compromises on prospects for friendly relations with labor and civil rights organizations and for raising money to defend indicted party members.

Levison excused himself during the debate to place a phone call to Martin Luther King in Montgomery. In the few weeks since Baltimore, he had been sending King suggestions and draft strategies for expanding the integration movement. As the nature of Levison's call registered on the people in the adjoining room, a new debate erupted. The Gateses argued furiously that Levison was subjecting King to needless, unconscionable danger. If a spy or an FBI wiretap revealed such a call from a gathering of top national Communists, King might be destroyed. King had enough problems already, they said, and party people should stay away lest they ruin him—as they had ruined Paul Robeson—by encouraging him to endorse the Soviets. All this infuriated Ben Davis, who retorted that the Gates faction always blamed the party instead of the reactionaries. America needed a hundred Robesons, he insisted, and if Levison could make one of King, so much the better. The argument raged until Levison returned to shrug it off. King was not a Communist, he said, and he could take care of himself.

The national convention gathered shortly thereafter, on February 9, in New York's East Village. Bayard Rustin attended as an observer, guessing correctly that many dedicated people would be available for pacifist and integrationist work as soon as they threw off Communist discipline. The convention itself was filled with bitterness and gallows humor, with informants circulating in conspicuous droves. Resolutions of the liberal Gates faction were passed by temporary majorities but doomed by inescapable logic: the most effective way to democratize and Americanize the party was simply to leave. A last mass defection soon left the party an empty shell, more authoritarian and blindly pro-Soviet than ever. All the leaders from the pre-convention caucus left the party with the exception of Ben Davis, who was too old and hardened to change. To King, Levison, Rustin, and many others, Davis was an object lesson more telling than Robeson. Davis welded himself to the contortions and reversals of Soviet strategy for the remaining six years of his life, growing more dogmatic and irascible than ever. Hounded and prosecuted to the end— New York even tried to deny him a driver's license—he became to the pragmatic King an example of Communist futility and waste. Nevertheless, he considered Davis a figure of supreme tragedy rather than supreme evil.

That same February, King, Levison, and Rustin pursued strategies far removed from the labyrinth of Communist doctrine. King's foremost idea was that power derived from the stature and prestige of leaders. Seeking the recognition of the highest American leaders for his cause, he fixed his sights on the White House. Shortly after meeting Lawson at Oberlin, he reconvened the ministers whose Atlanta conference had been interrupted by the night of church bombings in Montgomery. In the midst of a lurching, long-winded debate over what to call themselves, their chief business was to send out urgent telegrams drafted by Stanley Levison and Bayard Rustin. The most important of these implored President Eisenhower to reconsider his earlier response that it would not be possible for him to make a speech in the South urging law and order. It also called for a White House conference on compliance with integration rulings. "In the absence of some early and effective remedial action," said the wire, "we will have no moral choice but to lead a Pilgrimage of Prayer to Washington. If you, our president, cannot come South to relieve our harassed people, we shall have to lead our people to you in the capital in order to call the nation's attention to the violence and organized terror."

Eisenhower was in Newport, Rhode Island, prior to heading for a two-week hunting vacation in southern Georgia. On his way out of a church service in which he heard a sermon on the need for new civil rights laws, Ike shook hands with the Navy chaplain and said, "You can't legislate morality." News of this instantly famous comment crossed the ministers' telegrams. Although it dismayed King, the remark provided him with the grist for numerous sermons about how the President misconstrued the essential function of law. Eisenhower was correct that racial brotherhood was ultimately an issue of conscience and morality, King said, but the purpose of law was to establish justice in the lesser realm of ordinary life. All laws, whether seeking to prohibit murder or income tax evasion, governed external behavior rather than subjective attitudes. Therefore, King argued, the proper purpose of the desired civil rights laws was to take down "Whites Only" signs and to secure the ballot for Negroes who wanted to vote. "A law may not make a man love me," said King, "but it can stop him from lynching me."

King wanted to make his case to Eisenhower personally—and to be seen doing so—but the President ducked. Eisenhower supported the basic citizenship rights of Negroes, which was why he allowed the resubmission in 1957 of his proposed voting rights legislation, but he bridled at the company of Negroes. This discomfort extended to school desegregation laws and to any other proposals that would foster more than minimal contact between whites and Negroes, even in public places. Forty years in a segregated Army conditioned Eisenhower to think of Negroes as inherently subordinate. His condescension was so natural and paternal as to seem nearly well-meaning. Only his private secretary winced with embarrassment when he passed along the latest "nigger jokes" from his friends at the Bobby Jones golf course in Augusta. During his vacation at Thomasville, Georgia, where King's telegram reached him, Ike shot his first wild turkey. His hunting party rode around Treasury Secretary Humphrey's farm in wicker carriages pulled by white mules and driven by what a friend called "the old colored retainers." Eisenhower never had received a Negro delegation at the White House to discuss civil rights, and he did not reply to King's telegram.

The first head of state King met turned out to be an African, Kwame Nkrumah. He rushed off with Coretta to the ceremonies that transformed the Gold Coast into Ghana, the first independent nation of sub-Saharan Africa. Judged by the deference and attention granted him, his stature grew in proportion to the distance he put between himself and his Montgomery home. In New York, reporters singled him out among the large entourage of Negroes making the journey, paying scant attention to more established leaders such as Ralph Bunche, Adam Clayton Powell, Mordecai Johnson, and A. Philip Randolph. Out over the Atlantic, members of the flight crew recognized King from the *Time* cover. They invited him into the cockpit, and the captain let him take a playful turn at the airliner's controls. In Accra, capital of the new nation, the Kings were treated to a private luncheon with Nkrumah. During the rounds of receptions, dinners, and balls, King ran across Vice President Nixon, head of the official U.S. delegation. Nixon had not bothered to answer King's telegrams, but he was shrewd enough to recognize that the joy he witnessed at the birth of Ghana was part of an imminent world change. There were three billion people in the world, he grew fond of saying—roughly a billion each in the Soviet and Western blocs, and a third billion in the emerging poorer nations such as Ghana. Nixon said that whites were only a tiny minority of the third billion which held the balance of world influence. In Accra, where Nixon treated his Negro countryman with the courtesy due an ambassador, he invited King to come to Washington for private talks on civil rights. Having traveled halfway around the world to secure the audience that had eluded him at home, King did not miss the political lesson. The logic of diplomacy gave him a stature that he lacked as a political nonentity in the South. His experiences in Ghana helped secure his belief that the *Zeitgeist,* or spirit of the age, was rising to the defense of oppressed peoples. Everything he saw tended to confirm it.

As fresh world travelers, he and Coretta returned through Rome, Geneva, Paris, and London, hearing everywhere a clatter about what would become of restive colonies on the southern portion of the globe. In April, King entered the Dexter pulpit to report on his journey. His congregation had made the trip possible with a bonus of $2,500—the equivalent of more than a half-year's salary—and King, like his father, did his best to reward his church members with a reenactment of the high moments of the journey they had made possible. This time he preached a sermon that went far beyond diary or travelogue. He achieved in oratory a prescient self-awareness that ran ahead of his deeds.

Beginning simply, King reminded his listeners where Africa was, how many people it contained, and listed the names of some of its countries. He sketched the history of the Gold Coast as a colony down to the

moment of triumph on March 5, 1957, when some five hundred international dignitaries watched the close of the British-ruled parliament.
"The thing that impressed me more than anything else that night," King
told his congregation, "was the fact that when Nkrumah walked in with
his other ministers who had been in prison with him, they didn't come
in with the crowns and all of the garnish of kings, but they walked in
with prison caps and the coats that they had lived with for all of the
months that they had been in prison." He told of one sight that particularly impressed him: Nkrumah dancing with the Duchess of Kent at the
state ball. They had whirled about the floor in each other's arms—the
new prime minister dancing with the representative of the British crown.
For King, who was plainly enchanted with the notion of Nkrumah and
the duchess—"dancing with the lord on an equal plane"—the return trip
through London had become almost a journey of temptation. "I never
will forget the thoughts that came to my mind when we went to Buck-
ingham Palace," King continued. "And I looked there at all of Britain, at
all of the pomp and circumstance of royalty. I thought about all of the
queens and kings that had passed through here. Look at the beauty of the
changing of the guards, and all of the guards with their beautiful horses.
It's a beautiful sight." He dwelled fondly on descriptions of grandeur, but
then haunting thoughts of colonialism overtook him by ambush. "I
thought of many things," he said. "When I stood there in Westminster
Abbey, with all of its beauty, I thought about all of the beautiful hymns
and anthems that the people would go into there to sing, yet the Church
of England never took a stand against this system. The Church of England sanctioned it. The Church of England gave it a moral stature. And
all of the exploitation perpetuated by the British Empire was sanctioned
by the Church of England. Something else came to my mind. God comes
into the picture even when the Church won't take a stand. God . . . has
said that all men must reflect the dignity and worth of all human personality. . . . Seems this morning that I can hear God speaking."

   In a fit of oratory, he tried to tear himself from the lures of power and
distinction, cutting his own path between the ancient poles of worldly
glory and spiritual triumph. "Then I can hear Isaiah again," he said,
"because it has a profound meaning to me. That somehow 'every valley
shall be exalted, every hill shall be made low, the crooked places shall be
made straight, and the rough places plain. The glory of the Lord shall be
revealed, and all flesh shall see it together.' And that's the beauty of this
thing. *All* flesh shall see it together. Not some from the heights of Park
Street * and others from the dungeons of slum areas. Not some from the
pinnacles of the British Empire and some from the dark deserts of Africa.

---

* The street on which the wealthiest of Montgomery's white citizens lived.

Not some from inordinate, superfluous wealth and others from abject, deadening poverty. Not some white and some black, not some yellow and some brown, but all flesh shall see it together. They shall see it from Montgomery! They shall see it from New York! They shall see it from Ghana! They shall see it from China! For I can look out and see a great number, as John saw, marching into the great eternity, because God is working in this world and at this hour and at this moment. And God grants that we will get on board and start marching with God, because we got orders now to break down the bondage and the walls of colonialism, exploitation, and imperialism, to break them down to the point that no man will trample over another man, but that all men will respect the dignity and worth of all human personality. And then we will be in Canaan's freedom land. Moses might not get to see Canaan, but his children will see it. He even got to the mountain top enough to see it, and that assured him that it was coming." King closed the service by asking the congregation to sing the traditional Baptist hymn of invitation, and the members of the prim little church filed out to the strains of the organ postlude, having sampled not only London and Ghana but King's own vision of apocalypse.

Out of the pulpit, King still pursued influence by guile. He delayed following up on his invitation to visit Nixon because he was afraid the audience might jeopardize the Prayer Pilgrimage to Washington, which was predicated upon the Administration's refusal to hear Negro grievances. King wanted to have the march. He and Randolph had discussed it in Ghana, and in New York they proposed it to Roy Wilkins in a way that forced him to go along. For Wilkins, who did not like marches, the Pilgrimage was acceptable because it was couched primarily as a mass supplication in support of the Administration's voting rights bill. King agreed to speak to the crowd about voting, leaving the preeminent issue of school desegregation to the exclusive attention of Wilkins and the NAACP.

To prepare for the Pilgrimage, the leaders relied heavily on the new coalition, In Friendship. Stanley Levison concentrated on money matters, contracts, and advertising, while Bayard Rustin drafted strategy memos and delivered organizational pep talks in church basements. Wilkins worked the inside game in Washington, where he alone had a staff. His people petitioned the government for permission to use the steps of the Lincoln Memorial. The Administration stalled, on the belief that to allow thousands of discontented Negroes to gather in the heart of the capital was a formula for annoyance, if not disaster. Wilkins and his

Washington representative, Clarence Mitchell, convinced White House aides that they had headed off a plan by King to march on Washington in protest against Eisenhower's "failure." This line, along with private remarks by NAACP counsel Thurgood Marshall that King was an "opportunist" and a "first-rate rabble-rouser," helped ingratiate the NAACP with the Administration as the more responsible, businesslike wing of the Negro movement. Maxwell Rabb assured his superiors in the White House that the "entire character" of King's plan had been modified so that the President "will not be adversely affected." The NAACP campaign advanced parochial interests in the process of achieving the common goal of White House clearance for the Lincoln Memorial permit. This was inside politics.

King worked on his speech, knowing that he would be addressing the largest live audience of his career. On one of his speaking tours before the Pilgrimage, he honed his text with his private editors, Rustin and Levison. Rustin objected strenuously to the most important line in King's draft—"Give us the ballot!" In a working draft, he substituted the refrain "When we have achieved the ballot . . . "

King studied the changes in frowning silence. "Bayard, this just doesn't sit right on my tongue," he said.

"Well," said Rustin, "tell me exactly what you want to say."

"Give . . . us . . . the . . . ballot," said King, between long pauses. He practically sang the words, as though to emphasize that his concern was how they sounded as opposed to how they looked on paper.

Taking a deep breath, Rustin explained his criticism. "Martin, colored people don't want to have somebody 'give' them anything anymore," he said. "Why don't you say, 'We demand the ballot!'? Something like that. 'Give us' just sort of falls like a pile of dirt."

King put on what Rustin called his gentle stare. "Well, Bayard," he said, "I don't mind your criticizing my ideas. But I don't like your criticizing my words, because I'm better at words than you are." This ended the argument. Rustin, unconvinced, feared that King's mistake would cause pundits to brand him weak and ineffective.

The Prayer Pilgrimage took place on May 17, 1957, the third anniversary of the *Brown* decision. A crowd of some thirty thousand people gathered at the Lincoln Memorial for a high-spirited program that lasted more than three hours. Randolph presided. Mahalia Jackson sang. A military helicopter buzzed overhead during Wilkins' speech and then vanished during Adam Clayton Powell's, prompting jokes about the influence Powell had earned by endorsing Eisenhower in the previous election. Most of the other speakers were preachers—Mordecai Johnson, William Holmes Borders, and Fred Shuttlesworth among them—or ce-

lebrities from a new crop of entertainers who were breaking out of the
Negro market: Sammy Davis, Jr., Ruby Dee, Sidney Poitier, and Harry
Belafonte. King came last. By the time Randolph presented him, the
crowd had long since forgotten the injunction to maintain a prayerful
decorum. Coretta, listening on the radio down in Montgomery, heard
them roar when her husband hit his stride in protest of the nearly total
disfranchisement of Southern Negroes. An astonished, somewhat chastened Bayard Rustin heard King roll out "Give us the ballot!" refrains
like cannon bursts in a diplomatic salute. The crowd cheered lustily even
when King strayed from his text to explain the distinctions between *eros,
filios,* and *agape,* the three Greek words for "love." Rustin decided that
he had overestimated the importance of content. Press commentators
would say that King's performance proved that his Montgomery leadership was no fluke. Rustin already knew that, but he puzzled over King's
ability to move widely divergent audiences with material that seemed
suited to a college student's notebook.

King wrote his letter to Vice President Nixon so that it would arrive
on the day of the Pilgrimage. Reminding Nixon of his invitation in
Ghana, King suggested four dates for a meeting in Washington. Nixon
promptly confirmed what became, in the popular parlance of the new
nuclear age, the first "summit conference" between a Negro leader and
Nixon or Eisenhower. Still more promising results came from King's
performance at the Pilgrimage, when, only three days after the speech,
cabinet secretary Maxwell Rabb tracked King down at the Statler Hotel
in New York to say that Eisenhower himself would be pleased to see him
soon.

Rustin and Levison prognosticated, debated, and drilled King on what
he should say to Nixon and to the reporters who would question him
afterward. They went so far as to draft long memoranda that included
questions anticipated at post-meeting press conferences and recommended responses. "If there is one concept of dominating importance it
is that of the non-partisan approach," they wrote King, concerned that
Nixon might lure him into making public statements favoring the Republican Party. The two advisers knew that King was vulnerable to blandishments from the Republicans, because Daddy King and nearly all the
most powerful preachers of the National Baptist Convention were lifelong Republicans. By force and repetition, they urged on King a "superhuman vigilance" against partisanship, citing "the extreme importance
of this conference for race relations."

Accompanied by Abernathy, King arrived at the Formal Room of the
U.S. Capitol on June 13, 1957, to keep his appointment with Vice President Nixon, who was seconded by Labor Secretary James P. Mitchell.

Photographers were allowed inside to take pre-meeting shots of the four men posing in various combinations. When the doors were closed, King followed the pleasantries with a long monologue on the oppression of Negroes in the South. He repeated his request that President Eisenhower come South to deliver a speech calling for compliance with the Supreme Court's school desegregation ruling and for the implementation of Negro voting rights. If the President could not come, King said, Nixon should. Nixon replied that he could perhaps arrange to attend a meeting of the President's Committee on Government Contracts somewhere in the South. He invited King and Abernathy to help him choose the best site, and the three of them finally settled on New Orleans or Atlanta. During the discussion, Nixon established a tone of alliance between himself and the two preachers. The three of them were pitted against the powerful Southern Democrats in the Senate, who wanted no speeches, no hearings, no school desegregation, and no new civil rights bill. The liberal Democrats, he said, were prone to "grandstand" for extreme bills that had no chance of beating a Southern filibuster, while some Republicans were careless or lazy because they had negligible civil rights constituencies.

The Vice President got so caught up in the politics of passing the Administration's civil rights bill that he lost track of time. Two hours went by, with seventy reporters still waiting outside. Flashbulbs lit up the faces of King and Abernathy when they finally emerged. As reporters crushed in upon them with questions, Bayard Rustin appeared from the wings to announce that Dr. King would not answer any questions. Shouting above the hubbub, he managed to maneuver King and Abernathy out the door and into a waiting car, leaving some of the Negro journalists especially angry to be left quoteless. King never gave them anything more than the vaguest accounts of the talk with Nixon. Rustin's logic, to which King acceded, was that King could not discuss the meeting without sounding partisan or risking contradiction from the Administration.

Privately, King told Rustin that Nixon was a mixture of enthusiasm with pragmatism, whose general stance was that he would help the cause of civil rights if he could do so without getting hurt politically. King's major reservation about the Vice President was that his relish and conviction seemed so evenly applied to all subjects as to mask his interior substance. Nixon was "magnetic," King wrote a year later, in a public letter that darted between flattery and suspicion. "I would say that Nixon has a genius for convincing one that he is sincere. When you are close to Nixon he almost disarms you with his apparent sincerity. . . . And so I would conclude by saying that if Richard Nixon is not sincere, he is the most dangerous man in America."

Nixon, for his part, privately told his colleagues at the White House that King had promised to launch a massive voter registration drive if the voting rights bill became law. Both King and Abernathy confided that they had voted Republican in 1956, he said, and they believed most new Negro voters would vote Republican too. In a separate message, Nixon said he thought Eisenhower would enjoy talking with King. He assured the President that King was not "a man who believes in violent and retaliatory pro-Negro actions."

Senate debate on the first civil rights bill in 82 years consumed 121 hours and 31 minutes, with South Carolina's Strom Thurmond breaking the filibuster record by holding the floor for a little more than 24 continuous hours. Aside from such dedicated segregationists, the legislative tangle defied conventional political labels. Majority Leader Lyndon Johnson of Texas worked conspicuously to engineer passage of a bill that would appear more his than Eisenhower's. Careening around the Senate floor, often waving his arms in a giant windmill motion to spur the pace of Senate business, Johnson whittled the bill down to minimal form on what he thought was the political center of gravity. Then he argued inevitability to both sides, telling liberals that it was as potent as possible and Southern Democrats that it was as weak as possible. Johnson bludgeoned, wheedled, and horse-traded for votes. His opponent, cast in the unlikely role as chief crusader for the strongest possible bill, was the archconservative Republican leader William Knowland of California. Knowland's family owned the Oakland *Tribune*, a newspaper notoriously unfriendly to Negroes.

Organized labor further complicated the political alignments by weighing in largely on the side of the Southerners. Because too many strikes had been broken, they argued, by state militia acting on the authority of a single judge's injunction, labor leaders supported an amendment that guaranteed the right of a jury trial to state officials accused of violating court orders on voting rights. Wilkins argued vehemently that such an amendment effectively would nullify the voting rights provision, as it was generally accepted that no Southern jury would return convictions against state officials in Negro voting rights cases. Nevertheless, many labor leaders joined the anti-labor South, and Wilkins sided with an old nemesis, Senator Knowland.

The climactic moment came just after midnight on August 2. Johnson, having deleted from the bill a provision empowering the Justice Department to sue for the enforcement of school desegregation, brought the jury trial amendment up for a final vote. A few liberal Democrats and

Republicans—squeezed between Negroes and Eisenhower on one side and Johnson, the Southerners, and organized labor on the other—sided with Johnson. Senators Henry Jackson and John F. Kennedy went with Johnson at the last minute, a defection that civil rights leaders would not soon forget, and the jury trial amendment passed by a vote of 51–42. Reporters who swarmed onto the Senate floor heard Vice President Nixon denounce the Senate's action as "a vote against the right to vote." Nixon collared Johnson in the cloakroom and conceded only temporary defeat, vowing to pass a stronger bill the next year. The NAACP's Clarence Mitchell was astonished to see the tough old-guard Minority Leader, William Knowland, break into tears in his office because of the setback to civil rights. At a cabinet meeting later that morning, Eisenhower called the jury trial amendment one of the worst political losses of his Administration. Having been rebuffed on voting rights, the one area in which he strongly supported the Negro movement, Eisenhower faced renewed pressure from Negroes on issues where his private sympathies lay with the Southerners.

The amended civil rights bill passed the Senate less than a week later. Once again, the occasion itself was more important than the content. Former Secretary of State Dean Acheson praised the bill as "one of the great achievements since the war," and *The New York Times* called it "incomparably the most significant domestic action of any Congress in this century." Such enthusiasm strained the bounds of credulity, certainly in the minds of civil rights leaders themselves. Roy Wilkins convened a meeting in the Washington office of Joseph Rauh—a well-known white labor lawyer and founder, with Reinhold Niebuhr and others, of Americans for Democratic Action—at which the sole topic of discussion was whether to urge Eisenhower to veto the weakened measure as worthless. The argument raged all day in the crowded room, as coffee cups and phone messages piled up on the desks. When Wilkins finally decided to take the bill, and King announced later that he agreed, leading Negro newspapers attacked both of them for their moderation. "How silly can you get?" the Chicago *Defender* asked of King. Wilkins defended the decision in his customary style. "If you are digging a ditch with a teaspoon and a man comes along and offers you a spade," he said, "there is something wrong with your head if you don't take it because he didn't offer you a bulldozer."

Although King and Wilkins both endorsed the Civil Rights Act of 1957, the effect of the law was to highlight the differences between them. To Wilkins, the law meant that the NAACP's legislative campaign was making its first meager gains. Civil rights was no longer a "virgin," he said. To King, the lesson of the bill was that Negroes should place less reliance on white institutions and take more responsibility upon themselves. On the same day that the Senate finally passed the Johnson bill, King called his council of preachers together in Montgomery for another meeting. The preachers changed the name of their new organization for the fourth and last time, becoming the Southern Christian Leadership Conference. On King's recommendation, they adopted a permanent structure that was carefully designed to minimize friction with the NAACP. King's SCLC was established as a consortium of institutional affiliates—mostly churches and civic groups. Unlike the NAACP, the SCLC had no individual memberships, and therefore the two organizations would not compete for members. SCLC leaders emphasized that theirs was a supplementary body whose purpose was to enable the region's Negro leaders to plan activities parallel to those of the NAACP. Their first goal was to register two million new Negro voters before the 1960 presidential election.

This diplomatic mimicry was small consolation to Wilkins, who realized that the preachers around King represented prominent Negro churches in the South, which were the principal source of NAACP revenue. "What sound reason is there for having two organizations with the same goal when one has been doing such an effective job?" asked the Pittsburgh *Courier* a few days after the Montgomery SCLC meeting. Wilkins saw the SCLC moving into a vacuum that was partially King's own creation. The NAACP was entangled in twenty-five separate lawsuits challenging its right to operate in the South, most of them filed by hostile states and municipalities. The pioneer action, which had effectively abolished the NAACP in Alabama, had been aimed at King's Montgomery bus boycott. Wilkins feared that mass actions of the sort proposed by King might put the NAACP out of business in the South altogether. It was mass action by hostile white people that NAACP strategists saw as the greatest threat to their long struggle for school desegregation. They saw the Little Rock crisis as a timely demonstration of their point.

On September 4, Arkansas governor Orval Faubus ordered the National Guard to prevent nine Negro students from enrolling in previously all-white Central High School. School administrators, who had been preparing for this day since the *Brown* decision three years earlier, were patrolling the school corridors urging unruly students to refrain from "incidents" and to think of themselves, the school, and the nation at all times. Some faculty members grumbled about having to cook their own meals and sweep their own classrooms, after Faubus' troops barred Negro service workers as well as the nine new students, but most teachers behaved with scrupulous rectitude. So did most of the white students. Nearly all of them opposed integration, but those who shouted out the window about "getting the niggers" generally came from the same minority of troublemakers who refused to tuck in their shirts.

The day's events opened the spectacular public phase of what became known as the Little Rock crisis. An ever larger mob of angry white adults gathered outside Central High each morning to make sure the troops turned the Negro students away, and a corresponding corps of reporters arrived to write about the troops, the mob, the students, the governor, and, eventually, President Eisenhower. The prolonged duration and the military drama of the siege made Little Rock the first on-site news extravaganza of the modern television era. Faubus became the center of national attention as he sparred with federal courts over their authority to make him rescind his orders to the troops. Legal experts agreed that Faubus, by using the armed forces of a state to oppose the authority of the federal government, had brought on the most severe test of the Constitution since the Civil War. King and Wilkins were among those sending telegrams calling for the President to take a firm stand.

Ten days into the crisis, Faubus flew to Newport, Rhode Island, for a private conference with Eisenhower. To the President and his aides, Faubus seemed to have a split personality. One moment he was an anguished politician searching for a way to end a confrontation that had gotten out of hand, and the next moment he was a publicity genius ranting about federal plots to have him dragged off in chains. White House aides puzzled over the governor's personal psychodrama, which seemed to weave in and out of the public arena. Faubus' own father, who was attacking him for racism in pseudonymous newspaper letters, was said to believe that the governor's true motive was to embarrass the white patricians who had fled to the Little Rock suburbs, leaving him with the race problem. Whatever his motives, Faubus annoyed Eisenhower by agreeing to a draft statement but then changing the words before he released it back home. Eisenhower stated repeatedly that the law must be obeyed but that he could think of few things worse than using federal force to overpower Faubus' troops. Faubus seized upon the statements to claim that the President was working secretly with the segregationists.

After another week of mounting crisis, the federal court finally cornered Faubus with an ironclad contempt citation, and the governor, negotiating furiously with congressmen, lawyers, White House aides, and other intermediaries, appeared willing to shift the mission of his Guardsmen: instead of protecting the white school from the nine Negro children, they would protect the nine Negro children from a white mob that had reached the size of a battalion. "Now begins the crucifixion!" the governor declared in a dirge of surrender that made headlines, but on Monday, September 23, he crossed up the White House again by simply withdrawing the National Guard from the scene, leaving the school to the mob. By midmorning, angry whites had beaten at least two Negro reporters, broken many of the school's windows and doors, and come so close to capturing the Negro students that the Little Rock police evacuated them in desperation. Central High was segregated again before lunch, and students joined the mob in cheers of victory.

Eisenhower's patience snapped when Faubus allowed the mob to run free again the next morning. No longer denying the crisis, he convinced himself that Little Rock was not an issue of racial integration but of insurrection, like Shays's Rebellion. "Well, if we have to do this, and I don't see any alternative," he told Attorney General Brownell, "then let's apply the best military principles to it and see that the force we send there is strong enough that it will not be challenged, and will not result in any clash." Brownell never forgot the surge of adrenaline he felt at the President's words. Eisenhower phoned General Maxwell Taylor at the Pentagon and told him to scrap plans to use U.S. marshals. He wanted riot-trained units of the 101st Airborne Division, and ordered Taylor to show how fast he could deploy them at Central High School. Taylor put a thousand soldiers into Little Rock before nightfall.

School integration in Little Rock resumed the next morning, when the presence of the U.S. Army settled the military question without casualty or engagement. What little resistance there was occurred inside the school, student style, in a campaign of Negro-baiting that produced a year-long ordeal for school administrators as well as the new students. Outside the school, the heat of the postmortem rhetoric varied inversely with the speaker's capacity for action. As Governor Faubus was reduced to utter ineffectuality, his pronouncements reached at once for the heights of fantasy and the depths of racial fear. In a wild radio speech, he accused white soldiers from the "occupation forces" of following the female Negro students into the girls' bathrooms at Central High. Faubus had failed by his own standards and brought international ridicule down upon his state, but Arkansas politicians conceded that his performance made him unbeatable in the next election.

On October 4, 1957, the Soviet Union launched into space the world's first man-made satellite, named Sputnik. News of the achievement produced a tremor of fear and wounded pride in American politics. Overnight, nearly everything about America was deemed second-rate—its scientists, its morals, its math teachers, even its road system. Edward Teller, the hydrogen bomb scientist, told Eisenhower that Sputnik was a worse defeat for the United States than Pearl Harbor. A blue-ribbon commission reported shrilly that the West was indefensible without a drastic increase in weapons spending and a crash program to build underground "fallout shelters" for every American citizen. "Control of space," declared Lyndon Johnson, "means control of the world." When the first American attempt to match the Soviet feat exploded two seconds after takeoff, in full view of the television cameras, the national humiliation was complete. Reporters asked Eisenhower questions on practically no other subject. Faubus disappeared from the news as suddenly as he had appeared, and the entire race issue receded proportionally.

As King struggled against the tide, competition from the NAACP was hardly the sole obstacle he encountered among his own allies. Tactically, he knew that he must carry the cause beyond bus segregation, but how could Negroes boycott facilities—libraries, schools, parks, restaurants, and others—from which they were already excluded? The bus system had provided political leverage to the great mass of Montgomery's Negroes, and the boycott had allowed them to exercise it effectively through an action—staying off the buses—that did not require face-to-face, illegal confrontations with white authority. No other segregated institution offered such advantages.

Lacking ready answers, King applied himself with a vengeance to his most obvious talent, speaking at the rate of four events per week, or two hundred a year. After interviewing King, one magazine estimated his annual travel at 780,000 miles—a staggering total, which, even if only a quarter true, put him on propeller-driven commercial airplanes steadily enough to circle the globe eight times a year. He acquired a reputation as the complete evangelist, who could preach integration to the humble as well as the elite, to the erudite and the ignorant, to the practical and the idealistic. As he did so, however, he contracted the evangelist's curse. No matter how many cheers he received or how many tear-streaked faces assured him that lives were transformed, tomorrow's newspaper still read pretty much like today's. Segregation remained in place. People listened wholeheartedly but did nothing, and King himself was surer of what they should think than what they should do. Under these conditions, oratory grew upon him like a narcotic. He needed more and more of it because he enjoyed the experience, yet was progressively dissatisfied with the results.

One idea for improvement was to amplify his message through the public media. "All we need is the sponsor to give us a half hour weekly," Levison wrote King, half seriously. "We already have the star." Television was beyond the reach of Negroes, and the best Levison could do was to help King obtain a contract from Harper & Brothers to write a book about Montgomery. This venture held out the prestige of authorship and the promise of a mass audience, but cultural and commercial pressures inhibited the project. King's publishers wanted him to sound intellectual but not too dry, inspirational but not too "Negro." One editor wanted to make sure that in listing the grievances of Negroes he never said anything that might be construed as favorable to communism. All the editors cautioned King against projecting familiarity or identification with the readers. He was to be billed explicitly as "a leader of his people," addressing himself to whites. These complexities of voice and tone proved difficult even for King. He fell badly behind in meeting the deadline set by the publishers, to whom King was an unproven writer with a perishable story to tell.

The pressure built steadily until a New York editor flew to Montgomery and ordered King to stop preaching. "To prepare and preach sermons is to use up creative energy that your soul and body wants to use on this book," he wrote in a follow-up letter. King ignored the order, but he finally accepted an ultimatum that he pay $2,000 of his $3,500 royalty advance to a Harper's staff employee, Hermine Popper, in return for her guidance as a writer and editor. Within days, Popper was functioning at the hub of an editorial network that kept updated revisions flying back and forth between her, King, Levison, Rustin, Harris Wofford, and MIA historian L. D. Reddick. King confided to Levison that the book project "has been the most difficult job that I have encountered."

In the first year of their acquaintance, King came to rely upon Levison as a counsellor, business manager, guide to big-time New York politics, and above all as a friend who made no demands. All King's other advisers pressed personal yearnings, ambitions, or pet theories upon him, even when they tried not to, but Levison seemed to shun frivolity and stargazing, contributing his time freely so long as he was working efficiently. He and King seldom discussed the grand questions, as agreement on such things was largely unspoken between them. Levison did advise King in great detail about his personal investment strategy, observing that "bonds do better when common stocks weaken," and even pitched himself into King's tax records. To King, Levison was living proof that a crusader need not be a chump, a victim, or a failure, and in that respect it was gratifying that Levison got along so well with King's parents. When Levison first visited King in Atlanta, Daddy King brought him home to dinner. Mother King served him her son's favorite lemon pie. Such a festive interracial occasion was a noteworthy event in Atlanta, where even Daddy King's white friends in the mayor's office did not come home with him to share a meal. The Kings received Levison more warmly than they received Negro advisers such as Rustin, whom they regarded as possibly dangerous to their son. And Daddy King had a known weakness for rich men.

Not long after meeting "a most extraordinary young minister" in Baltimore, Levison had stunned his wife by telling her that Martin King was his only true friend in the world. Levison liked nothing better than to talk politics with King. It was usually after midnight when King called, and they talked for hours, always blunt but friendly. King did not pretend to admire Levison's taste in clothes, and Levison did not pretend to like the boiled cabbage served him when he went South. Their relationship seemed to be grounded in a neutral zone of corny ideals, beyond race. King refused to accept Levison's profession of agnosticism. "You don't know it, Stan," he teased, "but you believe in God."

King pursued two alternative methods of spreading the movement by mass communications. It might be possible, he thought, to attack segregation in a specified city or town by means of a planned series of mass meetings, rallying night after night around the ideals he had put forward in Montgomery. His model, oddly enough, was the "crusade" developed by evangelist Billy Graham, whose skilled organizers prepared each target area for months—compiling mailing lists, enlisting church sponsors and volunteer groups, arranging publicity campaigns and special bus routes—before Graham arrived for two weeks of nightly mass meetings. The revival-style format held great promise for King, who, like Graham, was still above all else a proselytizer.

Graham, for his part, thought enough of King's purpose to invite him to deliver a prayer during the sixty-eight-night Madison Square Garden Crusade in 1957. The evangelist was acquiring a reputation among Negroes as an enlightened white fundamentalist. During the Little Rock crisis, one of Graham's Negro staff members published an article titled "No Color Line in Heaven," in which he compiled Graham's views opposing segregationist dogma. Graham held rallies in Harlem, and his crusade committee included Gardner Taylor and Thomas Kilgore of In Friendship, two of King's closest and most influential friends. At their suggestion, Graham held three private strategy meetings with King in New York, after which he became one of the few whites to call King by his birth name, Mike. The two men shared enormous optimism over the potential of serial crusades to advance the power of evangelism through mass organization and communication. On King's side, there were even dreams about a Graham-and-King crusade that would convert racially mixed audiences first in the North, then in border states, and finally in the Deep South. These dreams foundered, however, on the question of emphasis between politics and pure religion. Kilgore and Taylor found Graham increasingly unwilling to talk about the worldly aspects of the race issue, without which the drama of interracial revivals would be lost. Furthermore, racial polarization was making it more difficult for Graham to hold interracial meetings at all. Like countless Southern moderates, he was being forced to choose, and within a year King would be writing to "Brother Graham" pleading with him not to allow segregationist politicians on the platform of the San Antonio Crusade. The two preachers tacitly agreed to confine their cooperation to privacy.

King did not retreat so easily from his plans for the National Baptist Convention. With five million members and more than twenty thousand preachers, it dwarfed the NAACP and made the hundred or so founding preachers of the SCLC seem numerically insignificant. King's goal—to turn the mammoth, unwieldy, politically inert National Baptist Convention into a reform vehicle—was a challenge to the most astute preacher politicians. He discussed it obsessively before the September 1957 convention, when J. H. Jackson had promised to step down. As many preachers suspected, however, Jackson developed second thoughts about his constitutional obligation. When the moment was ripe, a Jackson lieutenant sprang up, called for a suspension of the rules to keep him on as president, and led a great shout of acclamation. It was over more quickly than a Teamsters election. Afterward, Jackson moved steadily to consolidate power against active involvement in civil rights, growing more autocratic and more conservative. The preachers close to King, joking that Billy Graham was more likely to embrace the civil rights cause than was Jackson, drifted toward insurrection within their own church.

King pushed doggedly to concoct the formula for a new movement. On October 18, at the first executive board meeting of the Southern Christian Leadership Conference, he presented to the assembled preachers detailed plans for a campaign he called the Crusade for Citizenship, a modified version of a Billy Graham crusade to be directed toward the goal of Negro registration. There would be mass meetings, evangelical appeals to the unregistered, then registration classes and support committees for those making the attempt. Acutely aware that nearly all his board members were also NAACP officials, King tried to assure everyone that Roy Wilkins approved of the crusade, but the skeptical preachers told him that, if so, the word was not getting down to the local NAACP chapters.

Almost desperate with haste, King announced plans to begin the Crusade for Citizenship simultaneously in at least ten cities by February.

Quite apart from the NAACP's skepticism, such a schedule was ambitious to the point of being foolhardy at a time when the fledgling SCLC consisted of nothing more than the preachers there in the church with King. Those men behaved like a council of barons. They were given to long-winded speeches of cross-pollinated tribute, to deliberative posturing, and to a work process consisting largely of decrees, delegations, and postponements. Recognizing that the SCLC did not even have an office, King appointed a committee (which included Daddy King) to discuss the best city of location. Then, after most of those present spoke of the personal qualities they would most like to see in the SCLC's first paid staff person, King appointed a committee to select a director. After a few motions on minor housekeeping matters, the members moved to adjourn.

Five days later, King presided over the annual business meeting of his Dexter congregation. The occasion marked the third anniversary of the bold coup by which he had first centralized and commanded the proud congregation. In spite of the renown he had brought upon the church since then, he spoke in a tone of apology. Confessing that he had "fallen behind in my church responsibilities," he reported that only a handful of new members had been added to the congregation. He spoke retrospectively for the most part, recommended no new programs, and established only two new church committees. Amid painful descriptions of "this almost unbearable schedule under which I am forced to live," he struck a note of pathos as he thanked the congregation for its uncritical, consoling support. "When my critics, both white and Negro, sought to cut me down and lessen my influence," he said, "you always came to me with the encouraging words: 'We are with you to the end.' " During his report, a courier brought exciting news from the hospital: Coretta had given birth to their second child, Martin Luther King III. King announced the tidings but cut short the spontaneous celebration to resume the business meeting. A group of the church's most influential women huddled outside in disapproval. They believed it was unseemly for their pastor not to have gone to the hospital long before, but they could not bring themselves to interrupt. Finally, one of the women called the hospital to say that Dr. King was detained.

King's oratory indicated that he was passing through a spell of melancholy. His sermons were more poignant than usual—personal to the point of self-pity, and yet stubborn, refusing to give in. Early in December, at the Montgomery Improvement Association's second annual Institute on Nonviolence and Social Change, King reminisced about the classless spirit of unity that had strengthened the boycott, and then turned to the greatest obstacle to racial unity—the universal stigma of being branded a Negro. Whites had relied for centuries on a perversion of "Aristotle's logic," he said. "They would say, now, all men are made in the image of God. That's the major premise. Then comes the minor premise: God, as everyone knows, is not a Negro. Then comes the conclusion: therefore, the Negro is not a man." King dismissed the syllogism along with the "curse of Ham" argument, pointing out that Noah was drunk when he pronounced the curse, and moved on to what he called the more modern defense of segregation: that the "temporary" inferiority of Negroes was an established fact, from which followed the judgment that commingling of the races would retard the progress of whites. This argument bothered King. While he rejected the notion of justifying future segregation on the basis of its past pernicious effects upon Negroes, he called upon Negroes to improve their conduct. They may not be able to buy perfume in Paris, he said, but they could all afford a nickel bar of soap. He recited statistics on Negro crime, welfare, and illegitimacy. Oppression was no excuse for these, he declared, because "the first thing about life is that any man can be good and honest and ethical in morals, and have character."

He followed a tirade against the flaws of the Negro underclass with an attack upon the professionals. "I have met more school teachers recently who . . . wouldn't know a verb if it was as big as that table," he said. ". . . For a college graduate to be standing up talking about 'you is,' there is no excuse for it! And some of these people are teaching our children, and crippling our children." Shedding all reserve, he shouted, "I'm gonna be a Negro tonight!" and directed a vituperative tongue at his own peers. He told the audience of having attended a convention of his fraternity, Alpha Phi Alpha, at which it was boastfully announced that the members spent $500,000 for liquor. "A handful of Negroes," King said acidly, ". . . spent more money in one week for whiskey than all of the 16 million Negroes spent that whole year for the United Negro College Fund and for the NAACP. Now that was a tragedy. That was a tragedy. . . . I know this is stinging . . ."

It was an unsettling, almost unhinged speech, in which the sharp realities that dominated his private struggles for once overwhelmed the diplomacy of his public speech. The war-torn nostalgia of the Institute itself may have dragged down his mood. Historian L. D. Reddick, King's friend and intellectual companion in Montgomery, described the week unsparingly as a "flop" that left King "distraught." Immediately afterward, the results of his leadership recruitment drive for the Crusade for Citizenship did nothing to improve his state of mind. In carefully drafted letters pointing out that the registration drive was not in conflict with the goals of the NAACP, King invited Nobel laureate Ralph Bunche,

J. H. Jackson, and other nationally prominent Negroes to lend their names to the Crusade's national advisory committee. Most of them refused. Bunche told King he did not want to cause any "misunderstanding in the public mind" about his wholehearted support for the NAACP. The Urban League's Lester Granger declined King's invitation with a transparently disingenuous remark about the need to draw the line in giving out his signature—"one more drink pushes the inebriate over the edge." Roy Wilkins warned King that he planned his own national drive a few days before King's in February, and advised that he had just ordered the NAACP's Southern field secretaries to make voter registration the "number one activity for 1958." Lacking a ready response to these daunting, disheartening letters, King told a secretary to write Wilkins that he would reply later. On that evasive note, he ended what a college friend called his "year of disagreement."

Early in the new year, Stanley Levison and Bayard Rustin contrived to rescue the Crusade for Citizenship by implanting a very special person as an ad hoc staff commander. They arranged to meet King alone during one of his flight layovers at New York's La Guardia Airport, where they delicately proposed that he authorize them to recruit Ella Baker for the job. Baker, their partner in a working triumvirate at In Friendship, had joined the NAACP in 1940 and become something of a legend for her prowess in organizing youth chapters in the South. After resigning in 1946 as national director of branches, she had served for a time as president of the New York chapter, the first woman to hold such an office. Since then, she had patched together a meager living as a freelance civil rights consultant, on grants from the YWCA and kindred groups.

As Rustin and Levison expected, King balked at their proposition. He was not sure that a woman could be effective. He thought the SCLC board might be more comfortable with a preacher, and in any case he wanted to talk things over with his selection committee. Levison and Rustin brushed aside all such objections. This was an emergency, they said. The crusade was scheduled to open simultaneously in twenty-one Southern cities on February 12, Lincoln's Birthday, but as yet the SCLC had no central office. The plain fact was that the SCLC was muddling toward disaster. Its selection committee had been dancing a roundelay with various preacher candidates for the SCLC job, all of whom wanted to keep their pulpits at least part-time. Baker, by contrast, had no family or job encumbrances. She would cost the SCLC nothing because her living expenses could be raised in New York, and she was much more experienced in the work than anyone the SCLC could hope to find. Levison and Rustin told King that while they were not sure Baker would accept the job, he must let them try to persuade her. King finally agreed, on the condition that Baker be promised no SCLC money and only an "acting" director's title.

Leaving the airport with this limited mandate, Levison and Rustin congratulated themselves for having had the foresight to exclude Baker from the initial presentation. They knew that she would have been put off by all the elliptical talk of church protocol and by King's condescension toward professional women. Baker was sensitive on both issues. Only to close friends did she entrust the confession that long ago she had been married briefly and painfully to a preacher. Now, she said proudly, she belonged to no man. Although a faithful member of Kilgore's church in New York, Baker often expressed herself tartly about the self-preoccupation of preachers, whom she called "glory-seekers." It was no surprise to Levison or Rustin that she resented news of being "volunteered," without her knowledge, for an onerous task, and they were obliged to spend many hours lobbying against her misgivings.

Ella Baker flew to Atlanta sooner than she had promised and checked into the Savoy Hotel on Auburn Avenue. She began with nothing—not even a telephone or a typewriter—but by the crusade's opening day a month later she had compiled a list of events in all twenty-one places, produced and distributed literature, collected information on the various states' registration laws, and established herself as a master of stratagems for surmounting the legal obstacles to Negro registration. The events on opening day consisted essentially of church rallies, for which the SCLC's leading preachers swapped pulpits. King himself appeared in Miami, where he announced the crusade's purpose in an impassioned but unusually lean address. "We want the right to vote now," he said. "We do not want freedom fed to us in teaspoons over another 150 years."

The simultaneous rallies were generally enthusiastic and well attended, but by the hard measure of registration statistics they led to very little gain. A month later, the Associated Press released a story that the SCLC's crusade had produced negligible increases in Negro registration. Ella Baker, who was staying on in Atlanta, defended the program in a report citing ongoing registration drives in a dozen cities, but privately she agreed with the criticism. The SCLC ministers showed little interest in following up the great exhortations with efforts to identify, instruct, transport, and otherwise support potential registrants, she believed. One SCLC preacher went so far as to tell King that he had "packed the church" on Crusade Day himself and therefore did not need Baker's "superfluous printing." To Baker, this complaint exemplified the worst of the pulpit mentality. She told King that he needed to work harder to set an example for the other ministers, to convince them that the great emotional events were just the beginning, not the end, of a perilous movement such as voter registration. Baker was careful not to disagree too sharply with King, but subtle sparks flew between them within weeks of her arrival in Atlanta. She had no better luck than anyone else in locating him by telephone, and King's secretary reported that Baker was "a little abrupt" after being told that he was not available to take one of her calls.

Baker's emergency stint at the SCLC stretched through the spring with no end in sight, as negotiations for a permanent director remained mired in the selection committee. She sent information on the persecution of would-be voters in the South to Levison for inclusion in the In Friendship newsletter, and she conducted an SCLC voters' conference in Clarksdale, Mississippi. Fewer than two hundred people showed up for the public rally there, on one of the few occasions when King addressed a half-empty house. He delivered a stirring speech on the right to vote, and the SCLC representatives sent off another in their series of telegrams requesting an audience with President Eisenhower.

Back in Montgomery, King found the usual enormous backlog of correspondence. A man serving a 198-year sentence in New Mexico for statutory rape pleaded for help, declaring his innocence. A girl from South Carolina wrote asking, "is dancing a sin and is Rock and Roll songs a sin when I sings them?" A preacher and part-time college professor wondered why King had not responded to his two previous letters, both of which concerned his application on May 11 to become the first Negro to enroll at the University of Mississippi. This last matter became urgent when Mississippi authorities committed the professor to the state mental institution on the explicit ground that only an insane Negro would seek admission to Ole Miss. King issued a statement of protest, and Ella Baker asked an SCLC representative to visit the new inmate at the sanitarium. In the midst of all this, King received his first call from the White House. A presidential aide asked whether he could come to Washington to discuss a possible meeting with Eisenhower. "When?" asked King. "I can come day after tomorrow."

Shifts in the White House bureaucracy facilitated King's breakthrough. Sherman Adams had asked Rocco Siciliano, an oil-company labor lawyer serving as the President's special assistant for personnel management, to take over the civil rights duties of cabinet secretary Maxwell Rabb, who had just resigned. Siciliano did not welcome the assignment. His primary mission in the White House was to push for legislation granting higher pay to federal employees in the upper ranks. He also supported the controversial "long weekend" proposal by which President Eisenhower later ordered some federal holidays to be observed on Mondays. Any identification as a "liberal" hurt Siciliano's advocacy of both causes, and he knew nothing of civil rights. Still, he could not refuse Adams.

Going through Rabb's civil rights files for the first time, Siciliano noticed that for five years White House officials had fended off the persistent requests of Negro leaders for a presidential meeting. Moreover, the President's standing on civil rights had been battered lately by the indictment on income tax charges of his chief Negro supporter, Congressman Adam Clayton Powell. Siciliano decided to explore ways of getting Eisenhower off the defensive. He called King, the Negro preacher down in Alabama whose name currently aroused no special animus among Republicans.

As usual, ferocious infighting preceded the presidential audience. When King walked into the White House alone on June 9, Siciliano and E. Frederic Morrow quickly made it plain that there were only two issues: which of the many Negro leaders should see Eisenhower, and what they would say to him. They preferred only King and Randolph, and wanted pointedly to exclude Powell and Wilkins. King made an issue only of Wilkins, saying that it would be "impossible" for him to see Eisenhower without the NAACP leader. Over the next two weeks, King pressed the White House aides to add Lester Granger, executive director of the Urban League. Sherman Adams tried to block the meeting, or at least Wilkins, but then a House subcommittee set off the most spectacular personal scandal of the Eisenhower presidency by accusing Adams of petty corruption. The "vicuna coat" scandal ruined Adams, who soon resigned his office in a nationally televised address. Although his troubles lowered White House resistance, the proposed meeting came under rearguard attack from Adam Clayton Powell. Furious that he was to be excluded, he issued a face-saving statement that it was all his idea and that he himself had named the Negroes who would attend. White House press secretary James Haggerty rebuked Powell with a terse denial, and the ensuing protest grew so intense that E. Frederic Morrow left Washington to escape his phone. King, being pressed for support by his embattled, volatile fellow preacher, asked Rustin and Levison to compose for him a letter of vague but careful endorsement.* The advisers "conditioned" a discreet statement on Powell's "adherence to principle," as

---

* Powell wanted money as well as political endorsements. He sent King a form letter of characteristic bluntness: "If you desire to [contribute] anonymously, let me know or you can place cash in an envelope marked PERSONAL-CONFIDENTIAL."

Levison wrote King. He hoped the veiled warning would "help Adam mature."

King, Randolph, Wilkins, and Granger arrived at the White House early on the morning of Monday, June 23, 1958, having stayed up most of the previous night to compose a joint statement. They were greeted by Siciliano, Morrow, and the new Attorney General, William P. Rogers, who would accompany them to see the President. The three Administration officials left the four Negroes in Siciliano's office while they gave Eisenhower his final advance briefing. As they talked, Siciliano looked anxiously to his two colleagues to remind them of a delicate point they had agreed to make. When neither Rogers nor Morrow responded, a slightly annoyed Siciliano summoned his courage and said, "Mr. President, there are two words that generally cause some negative reaction that I might suggest you not use when you talk with them. These two words are 'patience' and 'tolerance.' "

Eisenhower frowned. "Well, Siciliano, you think I'm going to avoid good English words?" he replied.

"No, sir," Siciliano said uncomfortably. "I was just trying to point out that there are certain things that might cause the wrong reaction."

The prearranged format of the meeting gave King an advantage, as he was the only preacher on his side. His three colleagues were skilled bargainers, but Eisenhower was far from ready to bargain with them. He wanted only to listen. After Randolph read the text of a nine-point plan for increased White House leadership in civil rights, King preached a short sermon on the powers of moral leadership. He struck a positive tone, painting vivid pictures of the beneficial effects the President could set in motion with gestures such as speeches, White House conferences, and simple statements on the moral imperatives of racial integration. His role was to try to lure Eisenhower into greater activity by summoning up feelings of duty and glory. Wilkins followed in support of the three legislative recommendations, and Lester Granger closed with an uncharacteristically blunt report, telling Eisenhower that bitterness among Negroes was stronger now than ever in his lifetime. Granger said Eisenhower's calls for patience made leadership more difficult for Negro moderates, and that more divisive leaders would emerge if the current ones could not soon point to greater progress.

As soon as Granger finished, Attorney General Rogers spoke up to defend the Administration. As the Negroes were speaking, he had been skimming through the preface to their nine-part plan, which spoke of anger, failure, and despair, and contained Wilkins' favorite line that the government could not hope to cure segregation "by prescribing an occasional tablet of aspirin and a goblet of goodwill." Rogers did not like it.

Fearing that it would be released to the press, he complained to Randolph that the preface was nothing like the oral presentation he had just delivered to the President. Rogers spoke authoritatively, as he considered the race issue to be his province within the Administration.*

Eisenhower seconded his Attorney General, saying he was extremely dismayed to hear that after five years' labor by his Administration, bitterness among Negroes was at its height. If bitterness was the result of progress, he wondered out loud, was it wise to push forward? Like Rogers, Eisenhower cast himself as the aggrieved party, matching his own vexations against the sufferings of Negroes as described by the four leaders. His tone moved Granger to reassure him that the bitterness of Negroes was not directed at him personally, nor at the Administration. Except for Eisenhower's endorsement of the need for stronger voting rights legislation, nothing was concluded beyond a general agreement that the meeting had been constructive.

King and his three companions strode briskly to the Fish Room of the White House to face the assembled White House press corps, augmented by at least a dozen Negro correspondents. "May I say that we were received graciously . . ." said Randolph. "The President manifested a profound interest in this whole question." Paralyzed by the same logic that had silenced King after his Nixon meeting, the leaders refused to say anything that might alienate the government or that the White House might later deny. They took refuge in political babble, for which they suffered the punishment of irritated reporters. Wilkins parried increasingly barbed questions about why he was refusing to say anything critical about Eisenhower only a month after blasting him for insensitivity and inaction. Finally, when the first Negro member of the Washington Press Club demanded to know whether Eisenhower had "brainwashed" him and the others, Wilkins hastened to terminate the press conference.

Publicly, the Eisenhower meeting remained an empty still-life, framed but devoid of substance. This was considered a blessing in the White House, and Siciliano reported to Eisenhower that the meeting had been "an unqualified success—even if success in this area is built on sand." Privately, Siciliano took his own forebodings to heart. He decided that

---

* Rogers dated his own interest in civil rights to his wartime service aboard an aircraft carrier, when he watched Negro sailors fire exposed .50-caliber machine guns as the last line of defense against Japanese kamikazes, and then, when the fight was over, those same Negro sailors went below decks to serve meals to Rogers and the other white officers of a segregated Navy. Among other endeavors, he had worked on the Justice Department's supporting brief in the *Brown* case and had pushed through the appointments of fair-minded Republican judges in the South who themselves were to make history in civil rights.

the civil rights assignment was hazardous to his career when *Business Week* published a photograph of the post-Adams White House staff with a caption identifying him as "Rocco Siciliano—Minorities." Furious, Siciliano marched into the office of General Wilton Persons, the new chief of staff. "I can't do this any longer," he said. Persons, a native of Montgomery, did not object, and the Eisenhower White House never again assigned anyone to the civil rights portfolio.

In mid-August, a group of prominent Indians led by R. R. Diwakar, chairman of the Gandhi Memorial Trust, made a pilgrimage to Montgomery to see King. While the Indians were happy to hear that he was still planning to visit India, Diwakar in particular took it upon himself to warn King about hardships ahead. Pointing to lessons from Gandhi, he advised King to prepare not just to talk about suffering but to endure physical sacrifice himself. The path of his life dictated such a course. King said he was ready. But for the moment his attention was diverted by the latest enhancement to his reputation. After the Indians departed, he sent an inscribed copy of his new book to Indian Prime Minister Jawaharlal Nehru. Stanley Levison wrote him on August 15 with the good news that Harper & Brothers already had ordered a second printing, even though the book would not be published for another month.

Troubles continued to hound Ralph Abernathy. The dispute within the MIA over its next desegregation target was nineteen months old, having already outlived the campaign to repair the bomb damage to Abernathy's church. One leadership faction still wanted to attack the segregated facilities at the local airport, while Graetz and a group of lay leaders wanted to integrate the parks, playgrounds, and other municipal properties. In spite of much fanfare and preparation, neither plan produced results. Among many other effective countermoves, the city commissioners firmly declared that they would close all the parks before they would integrate them. Pressure to devise a new strategy fell heavily on Abernathy, as King was so frequently out of town, and Abernathy found no relief in his parallel duties as treasurer of the SCLC. In August, Ella Baker was reminding him yet again that the office still lacked a secretary and a mimeograph machine. These elementary deficiencies reflected poorly on an organization that claimed to be running voter registration drives in ten states.

Late on the afternoon of Friday, August 29, 1958, Abernathy was working in his basement office at First Baptist when the husband of one of his church members walked in unannounced. "I guess you know why I have come," said Edward Davis. "I have come to kill you." With that, he pulled a small hatchet from his shirt and struck Abernathy with the handle. Terrified, Abernathy reached for the phone during the struggle that followed. Davis then stuck a pistol into his back, but when he hesitated to fire, either by plan or because inhibitions still checked his rage, Abernathy bolted out of the office screaming, "He wants to kill me!" He ran past his secretary, Alfreda Brown, up the stairs, and out the door.

Davis was right behind him, brandishing the hatchet high in the air as he chased Abernathy down the middle of Columbus Avenue for two blocks. Among the astonished witnesses were two officers in a Montgomery police cruiser, who managed to catch Davis before he overtook Abernathy. Davis threw the hatchet when he saw them coming. There were conflicting reports as to whether he threw it down to get rid of it, or at Abernathy in a final burst of anger, but there was no doubting the pandemonium and shock. Davis, still almost berserk, flung his pistol out of the back of the police car. It went off when it hit the pavement, frightening and then enraging the policemen, who had been sloppy in their arrest procedure. At the station, Davis gave them an even bigger surprise by declaring that he had attacked Abernathy because the preacher had been having a sexual affair with his wife since she was fifteen years old. This stunning accusation against the second most important civil rights leader in Montgomery soon led to the interrogation of Vivian McCoy Davis, who, mortified by the news of what her husband had done and said, pitched such a fit of indignation that the police arrested her too, on a charge of disorderly conduct. Meanwhile, back at the police station, a shaken Abernathy, who had suffered bruises and minor cuts, refused to sign a complaint warrant against Davis, who was denying that he had ever touched the gun found in the street. A police officer signed a warrant based on his own eyewitness statement, and both Davises were bound over for arraignment.

By morning, Montgomery was saturated with talk of the scandal. Every undisputed detail of the story—the hatchet-waving chase out of the church and down a city street in broad daylight—was so spectacular and so irretrievably public as to let loose a torrent of gossip on the most taboo of subjects, sex and the clergy. Davis, known to nearly every Negro in town as "Big Two," a nickname of obscure origins, had been the star halfback on the Alabama State football team a few years earlier. After college, he had served a hitch in the Air Force, and had just returned home to become a schoolteacher. His career pattern placed him squarely in Montgomery's Negro middle class, but many doubted that his personality was suited to the decorum expected of a teacher. "Big Two" had a reputation for flamboyance, womanizing, and fits of jealousy. Many remembered his famous reply to a request by his Alabama State coach that he give up an extravagant romance in order to conserve his strength for football. "Hey, she's giving me a house and a car," Davis was said to have told the coach. "What are *you* doing for me?" For this sort of attitude, Davis was appreciated as a character, but not taken too seriously, certainly in comparison with a preacher of Abernathy's stature. This weighed against the credibility of his accusation. On the other hand, he was precisely the kind of person who, if he believed someone was cuckolding him, might do something as crazy as a hatchet-and-gun assault inside the city's oldest Negro Baptist church.

Some years later, King confided to a colleague that he not only had known of Abernathy's extramarital liaisons in Montgomery but had joined in some of them himself. This confession, if true, dated King's own infidelities back to his tenure in Montgomery, and thus the Davis scandal must have touched some of the deepest secrets and most piercing fears in his own life.

Early on the morning of September 3, King went to the Montgomery Recorder's Court at city hall for the preliminary hearing in the Davis case. The courtroom was jammed by a predominantly Negro crowd, with lines of jostling would-be spectators backed up through the corridors and onto the sidewalk. Inside, a white judge tried to preserve order and a white prosecutor prepared to outline a case brimming with salacious facts, while the audience waited eagerly to hear what the Negro antagonists would say about each other under oath, in a contest that pitted Montgomery's only two Negro lawyers against each other. Abernathy, although formally a prosecution witness, had retained Fred Gray to defend him against Davis' anticipated testimony, and Davis had hired Charles Langford to defend him against the criminal charges. King and Coretta, arriving just behind the Abernathys at the courtroom, found that policemen would admit only Abernathy, who waved a subpoena commanding him to appear. "I'm waiting to see my lawyer, Fred Gray," King told a police sergeant, hoping Gray could get them a seat inside.

"If you don't get the hell out of here, *you're* going to need a lawyer," said the sergeant.

When King peered into the courtroom to see if Gray was coming to help, the sergeant's patience snapped. "Okay, boy, you done done it now," he said, and beckoned to two officers. They seized King roughly from behind, shoving him toward the door. Negro bystanders gasped in horror at the sudden violent treatment of King, which only made the officers tighten their grip. On tenterhooks as they manhandled King down the corridor, the policemen snarled at Coretta not to make a sound of protest: "Just nod your head, and you'll go to jail, too."

A photographer walking toward city hall happened upon an extraordinary scene of King—wearing a gold wristwatch, a tan suit, and a broad-banded snap-brim fedora—grimacing in pain as one policeman pushed him forward and the other twisted his right arm so far around that his hand was positioned behind his shoulder. A procession of Negroes followed in the distance, as the news of what was happening to King drained some of the people and much of the interest from Judge Loe's courtroom. The photographer kept clicking his shutter as the policemen pushed King up the steps of the police station and pinioned his shoulder to the booking desk. One of them shouted that King was charged with loitering. Minutes later, back in the holding cells and out of the camera's sight, one of the policemen reached inside King's shirt collar from behind and pulled backward, choking him while the other officer searched him. Then one put a foot into King's back and shoved him into an empty cell. King tried to compose himself as he wondered what would happen next. He was grateful when a lieutenant he knew walked by and said quietly that he would not allow anybody to bother King while he was there.

Allowed soon thereafter to post bond pending trial, King walked out of the police station to find his wife and friends amid a large crowd of supporters, some of them weeping. He addressed them briefly from the steps, saying that he would continue to stand up for the right to be treated fairly, "even if it means further arrest, or even physical death." Then he told the crowd to go in peace, that he was all right. There was talk of a mass meeting. It was a scene reminiscent of the bus boycott, and the spectators experienced a return of that era's sensory overload. The news soon arrived from the courtroom that Vivian Davis had stood significantly at her husband's side. Convicted and fined $25 on her own disorderly conduct charge, she indicated to the court that she would support Edward Davis' plea of not guilty by reason of provocation. Abernathy, summoned to speak, confirmed that Davis had made the accusations but said they were not true. The judge scheduled for November a full trial on the disputed facts.

To outside news organizations, the Davis trial was at once steamy, murky, legally perilous, and an unimportant local story. What moved instantly on the news wires were photographs and stories of King's arrest, which struck with such speedy impact that the next day's *Advertiser* carried the text of Roy Wilkins' outraged telegram from New York. International wire services also picked up the photographs, and messages from everywhere began pouring into Montgomery in volume not seen since the mass arrests two and a half years earlier. The MIA's executive board convened more or less continuously in special session. King met with roving caucuses of his closest advisers to discuss how he should react to his anticipated conviction.

Early the next morning, King was quickly tried, convicted, and sentenced to pay a fine of $14 or serve fourteen days in jail. After the pronouncement of the sentence, Fred Gray informed a clearly startled Judge Loe that King elected to serve out the time. King rose briefly to confirm his decision. When the judge agreed to receive a full explanation of his reasons, Abernathy supplied a copy of a prepared text. In tone and substance, King's statement bore a striking resemblance to Gandhi's famous declaration before Justice Broomfield on March 18, 1922, in Ahmedabad, during Gandhi's first (and last) trial by a British court in India. "Your Honor, you have no doubt rendered a decision which you believe to be just and right," King began. ". . . My action is motivated by the impelling voice of conscience."

The courtroom buzzed in reaction to King's decision. Reporters and spectators clamored for copies of the statement, which Abernathy handed out freely. Together with Coretta, Abernathy then made his way to the street, where a large crowd voiced disappointment over not seeing King himself. Abernathy tried to explain why King was not coming, but the police would not allow him to make a speech. Abernathy then shouted out, "Let's walk to Dexter!" This march of seven blocks to King's church had been planned to recapture the old "walking city" spirit of the boycott, and Abernathy was as expansive in that role as he had been subdued two days earlier. He presided over an impromptu mass meeting of testimonials to King, including one from Coretta, then announced plans for MIA members to maintain a vigil outside the city jail in continuous shifts throughout the fourteen days of King's sentence.

These solemn plans contributed to what was later called a logistical comedy. Back at city hall, King sat in the holding area making friends with his fellow defendants of the day who were heading for jail, but when the paddy wagon pulled up to transport the first load, an officer barred King from entering. Nonplussed, King went back to the holding pen and waited for a second group to accumulate, only to be turned away again. This time, he was told to go home—someone had paid his fine. King insisted that there had been a mistake. He questioned people back up through the court hierarchy until he finally protested to Judge Loe himself in chambers, saying that he wished to serve the time. Shrugging, the judge replied that he was powerless to change the fact that an anonymous person had paid the $14. Locked out instead of in, King soon found himself standing outside city hall alone—blocked from entering the same forbidding place outside town that had so terrified him after his first arrest, and frightened him still. Now, somewhat deflated by the role reversal, he rushed to the Dexter meeting but arrived too late. The crowd had dispersed to take up the vigil outside the jail. Meanwhile, back at city hall, reporters finally cornered Police Commissioner Clyde Sellers with reports that it was he who had paid King's fine. Sellers admitted it. He had paid the fine out of his own pocket, he declared, to save the taxpayers the expense of feeding King for fourteen days. Calling King's courtroom statement "just another publicity stunt," Sellers quipped that King was trying to boost sales of his forthcoming book.

The mass meeting that night at Bethel Baptist Church drew five hundred people—a modest crowd by boycott standards, but a sizable one given the day's confusion. Laughing uproariously at word that Sellers had paid the fine, the crowd showed good news sense, as the novelty of a Southern police commissioner paying the debts of a Negro he plainly loathed, just to keep him out of jail, featured prominently in news accounts about King's decision to choose a jail sentence over a minor fine. The laughter relieved an otherwise grim mood about racially skewered measures of Alabama justice. People at the mass meeting told of seeing the officer nearly break King's arm, and of other brutalities rumored and real, and their impact was magnified by King's extraordinary emotional bond with his MIA supporters. Even the Edward Davis case folded into this emotional solidarity. Charles Langford was withdrawing as defense counsel, leaving Davis to substitute the white lawyer who had represented the city of Montgomery during the boycott. The chemistry of the case was being realigned so that Davis was perceived to be the lone stooge allied with the prosecutor, the judge, and other white powers against Abernathy, the victim. At the mass meeting, the crowd gave Abernathy a standing vote of confidence without dissent. King rose shortly thereafter to deliver a speech of passion and yearning tinged with self-reproach. "I am happy that I could suffer just a little bit," he declared. "I am happy that I could suffer . . . It makes me feel a closer part of you."

Illustrious preachers in King's world took a more professional view of the tribulation. A few days later, at the National Baptist Convention in Detroit, J. Raymond Henderson cornered both Abernathy and King for serious pastoral counseling. Henderson, who had been Daddy King's first rival at Wheat Street twenty-seven years earlier, and who of late had brought money and support to the bus boycotters, feared that the famous young preachers did not appreciate the degree of their risk. His first night back home in Los Angeles, worries about them kept Henderson from sleeping, and before dawn he wrote a letter to each of them warning against a host of dangers—plots, tax scandals, violence, and especially the "damning influence" of women. "They themselves too often delight in the satisfaction they get out of affairs with men of unusual prominence," Henderson wrote King. "Enemies are not above using them to a man's detriment. White women can be lures. You must exercise more than care. You must be vigilant indeed." Henderson wrote with a sense of urgency, calling King "a marked man" and recommending that he move himself and his family out of Montgomery. He was friendly, even tender, and yet hard-headed. His letter ignored a preacher's Christian duties, let alone the feelings of the women who might be hurt. All its warnings looked narrowly to the issue of King's public reputation.

King flew to New York to celebrate the publication of *Stride Toward Freedom*, which marked the end of a literary ordeal. He sent autographed books to Eisenhower, Nixon, Chief Justice Warren, Harry Truman, and Reinhold Niebuhr, and asked Stanley Levison to send complimentary copies to a number of other prominent people—including Dwight Macdonald, George Meany, Helen Gahagan Douglas, and Harry Emerson Fosdick, pastor emeritus of the Riverside Church—and to assorted preachers, congressmen, and the members of the new Civil Rights Commission. Harris Wofford, who finished reading his copy on the day he saw news photographs of King being manhandled by Montgomery police, wrote Levison that the segregationists might make a bestseller of a book Wofford found too tepid.

On September 17, King promoted the book in New York, appearing live on network television with Dave Garroway of the "Today" show. That weekend he appeared at Blumstein's department store in Harlem to inscribe buyers' copies. It was an unusual book-signing party in that Blumstein's did not sell books. King was set up behind a desk in the back of the shoe department. To this rather humble setting flocked a number of New York's civic leaders, mostly Negroes and Jews, nearly all of them dressed smartly in their best clothes, hats, and jewels. A photographer hired by King's publisher had just taken a picture of NAACP president Arthur Spingarn standing next to King and was steering others into position when a woman wearing baubly earrings, sequined spectacles, and a blue raincoat stepped out from the milling crowd of some fifty people. "Is this Martin Luther King?" she asked.

"Yes, it is," King replied easily, as though greeting a fan.

The woman's hand came from under her raincoat and flashed in an arc. King reflexively yanked his arm up just enough for the razor-sharp blade to cut his left hand as it plunged deep into his chest. A quick-witted woman next to King knocked the attacker's fist from the handle before she could pull it out for a second stab. The attacker stepped back, making no effort to flee, and shouted, "I've been after him for six years! I'm glad I done it!"

Her shriek cracked the instant of silence. Pandemonium erupted with shouts of "Grab her!" and "What happened?" rising above the grunts of

those trying to subdue the woman, who was spitting out shrill obscenities about King and the NAACP. Nettie Carter Jackson, Grand Daughter
Ruler of the Elks and one of the sponsors of the promotion, spoke sharply
to those whose attention was riveted on King. "Don't touch that knife!"
she ordered. Its hilt protruded from King's chest at a point a few inches
below and to the left of the knot in his tie. King sat down in the chair
behind him. "That's all right," he said in a stony calm. "That's all right.
Everything is going to be all right." Nettie Jackson told him to hush, he
should not talk. Then, as security guards hustled the attacker outside to
the police and the screams and shouts died down, Jackson daubed the
blood from the minor wound on King's left hand. A score of bystanders
who had nothing else to do with their residual panic concentrated furiously on her every movement.

Forty-five minutes later, police detectives escorted the attacker—now
identified as Izola Ware Curry, a forty-two-year-old native of a tiny Georgia town called Adrian—into the emergency room of Harlem Hospital,
where King lay waiting on a gurney with the blade still in his chest.
Fearing that he might die of the stab wound, the detectives wanted to get
his identification of the woman on record. They negotiated successfully
with the nervous doctors and then maneuvered the woman cautiously
within King's view. Before he could speak, Curry cried out, "That's him!
I'll report him to my lawyers!" She stood rigidly erect and haughty, proud
as a queen. Such behavior worsened the detectives' other fear—that they
might lose their criminal case to the asylum. Curry had been raving
incoherently about persecution and torture and her anger at King for
having undermined her Roman Catholic faith. If she was a loony, the
detectives knew, she was a dangerous one. A police matron had discovered a fully loaded Italian automatic inside her blouse. King, still calm
and lucid though growing weaker, identified Curry before she was hustled off again.

King was still awaiting treatment an hour later when New York governor Averell Harriman, then in the heat of a losing reelection contest
against Nelson Rockefeller, arrived at Harlem Hospital. As Harriman
patted the victim softly on the hand, King gamely assured him that
everything would be all right. The delay, Harriman learned from the
doctors, was caused by the critical position of the blade, which X rays
showed to be lodged between the heart and a lung. A team of surgeons
was being assembled to remove it. The governor waited in the corridors
more than four hours, until doctors advised him that the delicate surgery
had been successful. They had to remove two ribs and portions of King's
breastbone before they could safely extract the instrument. It had grazed
the aorta, they said. One of the surgeons later told King that even a
sneeze could have punctured the aorta and killed him.

Prosecutors arranged an unusual Sunday arraignment for Izola Curry. She stood defiantly through Magistrate Vincent Rao's recitation of the pertinent facts until he stated that she was alleged to have stabbed King with a knife. "No," she interrupted sharply. "It was a letter opener." Detectives sustained her correction. She had used an instrument quite different from the kitchen knife common to urban stabbings: a slender Japanese penknife with a gently curved blade and a handle of inlaid ivory. Like her Italian automatic, it was a stylish weapon. As a would-be assassin, Curry had expensive foreign tastes jarringly at odds with her low station as an itinerant Negro maid who had drifted alone for many years since leaving a broken home and a failed marriage. Shortly after the magistrate resumed his presentation, Curry interrupted again to announce that she was accusing King of "being mixed up with the communists," adding that she had "reported the case to the FBI and it's being looked into." These statements landed her at Bellevue Hospital, where she was diagnosed as a paranoid schizophrenic. Upon order of indefinite commitment to the Matteawan State Hospital for the Criminally Insane, Curry disappeared permanently, leaving behind only a single deed of mysterious, unfathomable horror.

Recovering at home, King settled into a period of relative stillness unique to his entire adult life. He delivered no speeches or sermons outside the Dexter pulpit for many weeks. Nor did he travel. From Virginia, where white leaders locked twelve thousand white and Negro children out of public schools that fall under the state's new "massive resistance" laws, an old seminary acquaintance named Wyatt Tee Walker appealed to King to lend his presence in a protest march. "What we really need now, Mike, is your support," he wrote. King begged off Walker's march, citing his health. He also canceled his appearance at Randolph's Youth March for Integrated Schools, in which Harry Belafonte and a jaunty Bayard Rustin led a thousand students from New York to Washington, in a novel protest that drew praise from the normally reserved Stanley Levison. "If the young people are aroused from their lethargy through this fight," he wrote King, "it will affect broad circles throughout the country as well as vertically through the different economic stratifications. In this sense there is a great similarity to the student movement which emerged in the thirties in support of the great liberal issue of that day—the right to trade union organization. . . . Since I see this emerging around civil rights in that area, I am greatly encouraged."

The Edward Davis trial lasted all day on November 21 and well into the night. Complications of race, sex, and religion left every word of testimony subject to contrary interpretation, as many Negro spectators believed that the white prosecutors were really helping the defendant, Davis, and that the defense was really prosecuting the victim, Abernathy. Vivian Davis broke down on the stand as she testified about both "natural and unnatural" sexual acts with Abernathy at the home of a relative, and, pressed for an explanation, she described as unnatural what others called oral sex. Her husband testified that she had admitted the affair to him, and that he had warned Abernathy the previous May to stay away from her.

In rebuttal, Abernathy offered a radically different account of his conversation with the defendant. Davis actually had come to him offering to kill white opponents of the MIA for money, Abernathy testified, and he had refused to entertain the idea. This testimony served to discredit Davis without going so far as to embrace the theory—widely believed by Negroes but unpalatable to the prosecutors and the all-white jury—that whites hostile to the MIA had hired Davis to ruin Abernathy by means of a spectacularly slanderous hoax. Some Negroes in the courtroom laughed when Davis hotly denied Abernathy's story, but defense lawyers chipped away at its plausibility. Neither Davis' character nor his wild daylight attack on the preacher seemed to fit Abernathy's portrait of a spurned killer-for-hire, they suggested. And, in the absence of evidence that Davis had been paid anything at all, it seemed unlikely that money had induced him to take actions guaranteed to land him in jail, to destroy his wife's reputation, and to mark him as a political traitor among his own people. The defense case rested on the theory that Davis' motive was blind, irrational jealousy, which fit the crime.

The jury required only thirteen minutes to agree, acquitting Davis on all charges. Its verdict surprised no one and proved nothing, as even a white defendant well might have escaped conviction on equivalent facts. Outside the courtroom, the social effects of the case offered a truer test of its impact. Davis soon divorced his wife, and she moved away from Montgomery to seek a new start. Abernathy, who had not wanted to bring charges against Davis at all, delivered a prepared statement to local newspapers branding the case as "another futile attempt on the part of the evil forces in our community to conquer by dividing." He thanked "friends throughout the nation for the profound and unshakeable confidence which they have expressed in me and their abiding loyalty throughout this trying ordeal."

With King and other friends, Abernathy went to the Dexter basement that night to allow the pressure to drain. He was on edge and distraught, Vivian Davis' testimony having obliterated his normal jocular mood. His friends sought to encourage him with observations that he had fared well, that nobody in his church or the community believed the Davises' word over his. They predicted correctly that it would all soon be forgotten. Many factors, including the prestige of the pulpit and a gale-force crosswind of politics, helped protect Abernathy among Montgomery's Negroes. In the great gulf between the races, there was no ground firm enough to support anything resembling an objective opinion. The Abernathy scandal illustrated the power of avoidance more strongly than anything in King's experience, including the Walter McCall paternity dispute at Crozer. King was soon teasing Abernathy about the nasty things Vivian Davis had said about him.

In Atlanta, personal strains of a different sort prolonged the ineffectiveness of the SCLC's Crusade for Citizenship. John Tilley, the elderly Baltimore preacher finally hired as the SCLC's executive director, was proving to be a disappointment. Tilley drew for King schematic charts of the SCLC's primary functions and "the secondary functions which will make the primary or basic functions possible." His gifts in this area had impressed the SCLC selection committee, but they registered few voters and exacerbated Ella Baker's resentment of the preacher fraternity. Maddeningly to Baker, King was at once the antithesis of the preacher type and its epitome. In private, he was personable, self-effacing, willing to listen, to serve, and to work hard—all qualities that had induced Baker to extend her volunteer SCLC work for a full year, under adverse conditions. Within the SCLC, however, King was a preacher's preacher, which brought him a degree of adulation that few institutions outside the Negro church could approach. At the third MIA Institute on Nonviolence in early December, the printed program called for a "Testimonial to Dr. King's Leadership" during the main meeting, with formal speeches from six different preachers and a half-hour reserved for "General Expressions from the Floor." To Ella Baker, frustrated by the SCLC's bare solvency and its paralyzed registration campaign, this sort of activity was not mere froth but a harmful end in itself. She finally asked King directly why he permitted all the circular praise—the meetings of his friends to plan the literature that would be distributed at the conference in his honor. "Well, I don't want to," King told Baker. "The people want to do this."

King's choices seemed to fuse. To do nothing was to accept praise. To act, to expose himself to further danger, was to seek praise. Even an act of criminal madness had brought him praise, and Abernathy's private scandal had achieved the same result indirectly. King felt that he did not deserve what he was receiving and that he needed to change somehow. During his semi-withdrawal in the winter of 1958, his wife described him as a "guilt-ridden man" who was fearful of making the slightest mistake and obsessed with his notion of personal redemption through suffering. His friend L. D. Reddick, who was then finishing the first biography of King, wrote that the stabbing was a "natural turning point in his life," and made so bold as to recommend a "thoughtful reordering" of King's priorities. Reddick called for more discipline and restraint in King, more political organization and more renunciation of worldly concerns. In short, he wanted King to remake himself in the service of his cause.

In Washington that January of 1959, one of the more conspicuous changes involved the decor of Senator Lyndon Johnson's office. The Majority Leader, buoyed by the twenty-eight-vote majority the Democrats had gained in the 1958 elections, annexed spacious new quarters and hired a New York decorator to furnish them in a style advertising a man comfortable with power. The result was a shimmering mixture of green and gold, soon nicknamed the Taj Mahal. From there, Johnson moved quickly to place his personal stamp on the new Senate by controlling its most volatile institutional issue—the cloture rule, which governed the chances of civil rights bills. One by one, he summoned the incoming senators to flatter, cajole, or intimidate them. No matter how many liberals had been elected in 1958, Johnson told each one, he would never permit the radical relaxation of the cloture rule that reformers now thought possible. It would ruin the party in the South, he said, and worse, it would play into the hands of Vice President Nixon, who was using liberal Northern Democrats in a scheme to win Negro votes for the Republicans. In an impressive display of personal influence, Johnson induced many supporters of civil rights to help him crush the cloture reform movement in the new Senate.

On February 4, Attorney General William Rogers told a White House meeting of Republican leaders that the Administration must submit a new civil rights bill in spite of the cloture defeat. There were technical flaws in the Voting Rights Act of 1957, he said, and at the very least a new proposal would reduce political resistance to the present law. Most Republican leaders, especially House Minority Leader Charles Halleck, wanted no part of a new civil rights bill. They reminded President Eisenhower of his speculation that the 1957 act would be the last for a decade or two, but Eisenhower said that he was friendly to any new bill addressing proven subterfuge against Negro voting rights. Chief of Staff Persons advised Rogers that no bill could go to Congress anytime soon, because the President had promised privately to give ample notice to Senate Majority Leader Johnson.

This news visibly alarmed Rogers. "Excuse me, Mr. President," he said quickly. "I think it would be a terrible mistake to tell Lyndon Johnson what we're going to do. He'll steal our bill and make it sound like the whole idea was his. I think he's setting you up."

Eisenhower frowned. "Do you really think Lyndon is doing that?" he asked. He sent a message asking Johnson to come immediately to the White House. The Republican leaders drifted away, leaving Rogers and the President gossiping alone until the Majority Leader arrived. "Bill, if Lyndon tries to get around my desk, block him off," Eisenhower said. "I can't stand it when he grabs me by the lapel." Sure enough, not long after bursting into the President's office, Johnson jumped to his feet and began to circle the desk, and Rogers quickly interposed himself, absorbing the shoulder-thumping and finger-jabbing with which Johnson characteristically supplemented his conversation. By meeting's end, Eisenhower was satisfied that Johnson would take only as much credit for the civil rights bill as was necessary to get it through the Senate. Such assurances became moot when the bill languished all year in committee.

The civil rights issue intruded widely upon Eisenhower's political dealings, including his uneasy alliance with Vice President Nixon. In disastrous campaign performances the previous fall, Nixon had tried an unusual rhetorical mix. Prevented by Eisenhower from advocating defense increases in the wake of Sputnik, he had courted the hardshell vote with diatribes calling the Democratic Party a "haven for socialists" and worse. At the same time, prevented by Eisenhower from being too specific about civil rights, he had sought liberal and Negro votes with vague promises in race relations. Each of his pitches was faulted for excessive partisanship, and they clashed so sharply in tone as to renew doubts about Nixon's sincerity. The 1958 elections had forced him into a career reappraisal.

At a political meeting that winter, Nixon suggested that the Administration push strongly to enact tax credits for tuition paid to private schools. The idea, he explained, was to reach out to the growing number of families that would like to send their children to private schools but were pained by the cost. He wanted the Republicans to run on what he called "the erosion of the middle class," by appealing to resentment against social leveling and a perceived loss of privilege. Nixon's presentation moved Eisenhower to contradict him in the presence of the other Republican leaders. The middle class was *not* disappearing, said the President. It was more prosperous and far larger than ever in history. What was disappearing were the laboring classes, who were sending their children to college in staggering numbers. Eisenhower emphasized the astonishing breadth of progress during his own lifetime, but Nixon held his ground through an increasingly personal debate. New professionals and others rising to the middle class felt threatened, he insisted. Middle-class people believed they were "sinking." Politically, Nixon was beginning to depend less on theory and more on the status desires of people like himself. He was becoming less of a civil rights man, more grasping, more of a demographer. Comparatively speaking, Eisenhower was an idealist.

Early that February in New York, King met his traveling companions for the India trip: Coretta and L. D. Reddick. *Crusader Without Violence*, Reddick's biography of King, was just coming off the press, which added to the excitement of departure. At a final rendezvous, Rustin provided a new stack of materials about India that included an essay on Gandhi's *shanti sena*, or "nonviolent army," which Rustin called "the latest thinking on the latest concept in the Gandhi movement." King wanted time to absorb Gandhism as a discipline that might help him escape a drift toward stagnation as a glorified after-dinner speaker. Personally, he wanted to study Gandhi's lifelong struggle to harmonize his own life with his philosophy. King found much to tease himself and Coretta about on these accounts. Embarking on a trip to study Gandhi, a man who had renounced wealth, sex, and all clothing except his loincloth, the Kings carried trunks stuffed with suits and dresses to wear at the most elegant of the hotels built during the British Raj. Their first act on the trip was to pay a large tariff for excess baggage.

This was the sort of thing that annoyed Reddick, who was devoted to King but prickly by nature and highly independent of mind. Reddick thought King was too passive. Ironically, Reddick himself proposed a distraction that nearly wrecked the trip at the outset. He persuaded the Kings to abort their stay in London to spend a few days in Paris with Reddick's old friend Richard Wright, author of *Native Son*, then catch their scheduled London–New Delhi flight during a stopover in Zurich. All went well until the King party learned that their plane from London had been ordered to bypass Zurich's dense fog and head straight toward Delhi. Geography, weather, and foreign languages combined against them, with the result that they found themselves on a train through the Swiss Alps when the plane that was supposed to be carrying them was passing over Iran. In Delhi, a crowd of some five hundred people gathered at the airport, many bearing garlands. By the time investigators established that King never boarded his ticketed flight in London, the airport crowd had dissolved in confusion.

King tried desperately to reach Delhi by the second night of his India tour, but he failed. At the hour when he was supposed to be entering Prime Minister Nehru's sandstone palace for dinner, he had given up for the night in Bombay. Alone on the airport bus, like ordinary tourists, he and his companions recoiled from the sight of emaciated people densely packed on the sidewalks and in doorways along Bombay's narrow streets —an immense human carpet of homelessness. Sudden exposure to India's starkest extremes did little to console them for the disaster of missing Nehru.

A small replica of Sunday's crowd convened two days late to greet the embarrassed King party at Delhi's Palam Airport. Each of the two organizations sponsoring the visit had assigned a guide for the duration of the trip—James Bristol for the American Friends Service Committee and Swami Vishwananda for the Gandhi Memorial Trust. The two guides gave King a piece of extraordinary good news: Nehru had agreed to reschedule the King dinner for that very night. Government experts considered this nothing less than a miracle, given the ramifications likely to befall Nehru for being willing to shift his schedule to benefit a man without diplomatic rank.

The Prime Minister greeted the King party wearing the white jacket that had made him famous in world fashion, with a rose pinned to the breast. Nehru's daughter, Indira Gandhi, served as hostess. The other guests were Nehru's confidante Lady Mountbatten and Pamela Mountbatten, the wife and daughter of Lord Mountbatten, the last British Viceroy of India, with whom Gandhi and Nehru had negotiated the details of Indian independence a dozen years earlier. At dinner, Nehru impressed King with knowledgeable remarks about the Montgomery bus boycott and King's subsequent career. He strongly defended India's foreign policy of "nonalignment," arguing that it was not passivity in the face of the ideological struggle between the United States and the Soviet Union, but rather an aggressive strategy to induce the superpowers to see each other through eyes less blinded by hatred and pride. King spoke so often about his desire to learn more of Gandhi's nonviolence that Nehru felt obliged to remind him that it was impossible to say how the surprisingly pragmatic Mahatma might have dealt with the concrete problems of modern India, let alone the problems King faced in the United States. His replies disappointed King slightly, but the two men discussed race, colonialism, Gandhi, communism, and nonviolence largely without interruption for nearly four hours. The other guests listened politely but somewhat restlessly; Coretta retained vivid memories of the splendor and the parlor courtesies.

Two days later, after a continuous blur of speeches and teas, the pilgrims rose early enough to make a six o'clock flight to Patna, where they joined Jayaprakash Narain, a famous disciple of Gandhi. On the way to Narain's remote ashram, or spiritual village, the seer explained his conviction that Indian industry and all other centralized organizations should be abolished because of their pernicious effects on religion and country life. Narain opposed Nehru, who believed that India must become a modern industrial state. King listened politely, charmed by the odes to purity, but he remarked that Narain depended upon factory-made jeeps to get to his ashram. As the travelers made their way to Calcutta and on down the east coast of India, they noticed that it was not so easy to correlate shades of color with grades of social prestige. The wretched Untouchables did not have the darkest skin, for instance, and street beggars came in all hues. It was clear to the Kings that the Indians were celebrating them partly for their color, as fellow dark people struggling against white domination, but the meaning of color internally among the Indians was much harder to determine. One of the few indications they noticed was that newspaper advertisements for brides commonly specified a preference for light skin.

They pushed on to the All-India Cattle Auction as well as to a meeting of angry labor leaders. King talked with Gandhians of various types and eccentricities—Muslims, mystics, rich industrialists, Communist governors, and cynical bureaucrats. He discussed economic development with the chief minister of Bangalore and debated with a conclave of African students who believed unanimously that the nonviolent way of Nkrumah never could remove colonialism from the Congo or apartheid from South Africa. The party worked back up the west coast to Bombay, where the Kings had made their unscheduled entrance to the country. King stayed instead at Mani Bhavan, the home Gandhi himself had used whenever in Bombay. There was no heat, hot water, or shower, and only two Indian-style toilets, which were basically holes in the floor. Nor was there furniture to speak of. Nevertheless, the Kings did not complain. Their host, S. K. De, who gave them use of his room at Mani Bhavan, found that King complained only of Bombay's emaciated, homeless beggars. His reaction reminded De of a previous guest, Arthur Koestler, who had featured haunted descriptions of Bombay in one of his novels.

On March 1, the King party reached Ahmedabad, site of the ashram from which Gandhi had commenced the Salt March. Then, in the remote northern village of Kishangarh, King kept a rendezvous with Vinoba Bhave, India's "walking saint" and most revered Gandhian. Gentle, bearded, and otherworldly, Vinoba had no home, no real organization, and no regard for discipline beyond the appeal of his own morality. For years he had been walking back and forth across India, stopping to ask rich landowners to contribute one-fifth of their holdings to his Bhoodan movement, which aimed to redistribute the acreage to landless peasants. King encountered the Vinoba phenomenon in the countryside—a cloud of dusty meditation at the center of a moving gaggle of pilgrims and celebrity-seekers. Breaking through, King was dismayed to find Vinoba impossibly vague. Like a Western caricature of an Eastern guru, Vinoba spoke in riddles, answered questions with questions, and escaped randomly through the corners of sentences. To King, whose mind was always transposing his Indian experience to the United States, Vinoba summoned up the word "kook," which activated some of the deepest fears of middle-class American Negroes. Who remembered the educated, eccentric man committed to a mental asylum only last year for the simple act of applying to the University of Mississippi? Even among civil rights activists, Clennon King was slipping away—a kook not worth fighting for.

King's anxieties did not help his upset stomach, and neither condition made him look forward to the next morning's scheduled "walk with Vinoba," a rite that had come to be almost obligatory for Gandhian pilgrims. Vinoba, he learned, always commenced his daily walk at three thirty in the morning, so that he could cover a nine-mile stretch in time to begin prayers and meetings by seven or eight. The prospect of a long moonlight trudge with the inscrutable mystic moved King to ask for an "Americanized" walk. The next morning, he and Reddick overtook Vinoba in a car.

To make the best of the strolling audience, King put to Vinoba questions that had been tugging at him as he listened to the tangled theories of various Gandhians: should not India, as the first nation to come to life on nonviolent principles, set an example for the world in foreign affairs by disarming itself? What were the risks? Would any modern country dare to exterminate the world's first nonviolent nation? On this subject, King felt he made contact. Suddenly the great man became quite enthralling, at least in flashes, and King ran up against the unsettling dilemma of any observer who decides that a madman is a genius. Where was the line that stood between the two qualities, and was King or Vinoba drawing it? Although unilateral disarmament was no less visionary a proposal than anarchy or anti-industrial communalism, its possibilities took hold of King as home spindles, ashrams, and other forms of economic primitivism could never do. It was the inspiration he had been seeking—how to extend the spirit of the Montgomery bus boycott as far as religion and politics would allow. He could advocate international nonviolence as a Negro and as a human being, as a Gandhian and as an American, as a minister and as a student of war.

At his farewell press conference on March 9, King was careful to say that he was presenting "a suggestion that came to me during the course of our conversations with Vinoba." He explained that his suggestion was a consequence of the failure by the United States and the Soviet Union to have the "faith and moral courage" to stop the arms race. The reporters nodded vigorously in assent, as denunciations of the superpowers for militarism were a rhetorical staple in India. "It may be," King continued, "that just as India had to take the lead and show the world that national independence could be achieved non-violently, so India may have to take the lead and call for universal disarmament, and if no other nation will join her immediately, India should declare itself for disarmament *unilaterally.*"

The mood of the press conference soured instantly. Reporters rained hostile questions on King, making the point that disarmament was absurd for India because of the threat from its mortal enemy, Pakistan, which the United States was busily rearming. How could Dr. King fail to see that the bloodthirsty Pakistanis would love nothing better than to slaughter nonviolent Indians? King tried to calm their fears, to minimize the risk, to remind them that the true test of Gandhian nonviolence came in the severest trials of one's own life. Most of the reporters kept repeating that King did not understand the Pakistanis, and they glossed over his strange ideas in generally buoyant dispatches on the departure of the Negro Gandhian.

Returning by way of Egypt and Greece, the Kings landed in New York on March 18. They spent a pleasant social evening in what King called the "palatial apartment" of Harry and Julie Belafonte, who treated them to a private home screening of a new Hollywood film, *The Diary of Anne Frank.* Belafonte offered to give another benefit concert for the SCLC, which sweetened King's homecoming because the singer's concert receipts from a single evening could raise the SCLC budget several times over. Four days later, King stepped into the Dexter pulpit to report on his adventures in India. From a description of the Salt March, he distilled for his listeners those qualities of the Mahatma he had found most arresting. Foremost among them was Gandhi's "absolute self-discipline," which King believed was the key to Gandhi's sainthood. The Mahatma had criticized himself mercilessly in his published journals, demonstrating what King hailed repeatedly as an "amazing capacity for internal criticism."

"Most of us have an amazing capacity for *external* criticism," King said wryly. "We can always see the evil in others. We can always see the evil in our oppressors." The Indian people had felt keenly the injustices of British colonialism, he said, but Gandhi had forced them to acknowledge also the injustice of their own caste system, which had developed long before the first Englishman set foot on Indian soil. He tried to dispel the gloom of Gandhi's martyrdom with an emotional flight about the greater power of his spiritual example, then he closed with an ecumenical prayer much like the one with which the unhinged Mississippi white student had shocked the diners in the Crozer cafeteria a decade earlier. "O God, our gracious heavenly father," King intoned. "We thank thee for the fact that you have defined men and women in all nations, in all cultures. We call you this name. Some call thee Allah, some call you Elohim. Some call you Jehovah, some call you Brahma. Some call you the Unmoved Mover."

Just now thirty years of age, King returned from India in the spring of 1959, when portentous events were occurring rapidly but almost always in quiet good order. Secretary of State John Foster Dulles died in May. Shortly thereafter, the world's first nuclear-armed Polaris submarine slipped into the Atlantic Ocean down the coast from Newport, where teenager Joan Baez, a native of Staten Island, was about to leap to notice in the world of folk music with her bell-clear soprano voice, singing songs of noble causes and hard times. In Palm Beach, Florida, on April 1, tycoon Joseph P. Kennedy hosted the first private strategy session toward the nomination of his son John for President in 1960. The presence of pollster Louis Harris at the Kennedy conclave gave proof that marketing specialists were advancing from advertising into politics. Also in Florida, the Pentagon demonstrated the growing power of public relations when it introduced the first team of prospective astronauts, successfully passing off seven high-strung and often cantankerous test pilots as specimens of a new American personality type—bland heroes. All seven were white Protestant men from small towns; six had crew cuts. A steady diet of propaganda created the historically dubious impression that it was the wholesome, well-rounded types who stepped off into the unknown.

From New York, Bayard Rustin organized A. Philip Randolph's second Youth March on Washington. At the head of the solemn parade of marchers making their way into the capital, the irrepressible Rustin violated his own rules of silence by muttering witticisms about the kooks with him in the column as well as the gawkers on the side of the road. "Social dislocation," Rustin chanted merrily, pronouncing the first word "so-see-all." It was his personal formula for social change. When the marchers reached Washington, King appeared at the rally to make another speech about voting rights. "Do you realize what would happen . . . if three million Negro voters were added to the rolls in the South?" he asked the crowd. But the gathering was not large enough to command much interest outside civil rights circles.

Significantly, one outsider who did take notice was FBI Director J. Edgar Hoover, who saw FBI reports that A. Philip Randolph publicly thanked Stanley Levison for his help with arrangements. This news seemed to rekindle Hoover's interest in Levison, whom the Bureau had labeled some years earlier as a member of the Communist Party. One of Hoover's assistants drafted a memo suggesting that Levison's assistance to the march "may have been at the direction of the CP as we do know that the CP was extremely interested in the demonstration." Bureau documents also noted that Levison was "closely associated" with King, who was described as "one of the motivating forces behind this demonstration." The implication was clear—Levison was strategically placed to be orchestrating both the Washington march and King's career on Communist orders. Hoover directed the New York FBI office to report on the details of Levison's involvement. His order commingled King, Levison, and racial demonstrations under the poisonous heading of subversion.

There was more to Hoover's reaction than either his hostility to communism or his prejudice against Negroes, both of which were strong. Above all else, the Director was a consummate bureaucrat, sensitive to deep historical tides. Twenty years earlier, the FBI had mushroomed in size to guard against Nazi espionage. From a mid-Depression force of fewer than five hundred agents, the Bureau had more than tripled by Pearl Harbor, then tripled again by D-Day. Hoover never needed further education on the advantages of an intelligence agency over a law enforcement department. An intelligence agency enjoyed greater prestige, less danger of public failure, greater freedom and power through the mystique of secrecy, and an enhanced role for shaping national values and symbols. To avoid postwar retrenchment at the FBI, he fought a protracted bureaucratic war to become chief of the new worldwide intelligence apparatus —even though he spoke no foreign languages and never then or later set foot outside the United States. On losing out finally to the newly created CIA, a vengeful Hoover had extracted from President Truman a major consolation prize: responsibility for "background checks" and other loyalty investigations of federal employees. Such work not only sustained the Bureau's manpower levels through the McCarthy era but vastly increased Hoover's political influence as the defender and oracle of domestic security.

Since the final collapse of the U.S. Communist Party after 1956, Hoover had anticipated a bureaucratic danger similar to the end of World War II: a completed mission. The Party's demise coincided with constitutional rulings from the courts and the Justice Department that all but ruled out lawful prosecutions of Communists, except for espionage. Hoover, facing the logical superfluity of thousands of his agents, immediately authorized a new campaign to keep them occupied in extralegal harassments of Communists and other protest groups. From 1956 onward, the formal COINTELPRO operations took the FBI deeper into domestic spying. Through covert operations and blatantly political investigations, the Bureau became more of a classical intelligence agency, like the CIA. Hoover kept COINTELPRO highly secret, as it violated basic constitutional restrictions on internal police power. On reviewing the files years later, his best biographer concluded that Hoover's lack of clear legal ground for the majority of the FBI's work "made him violently defensive whenever the Bureau's authority for its secret operations was questioned." That happened rarely, however, and COINTELPRO helped maintain the Director's desired allocation of agents. In 1959, while carrying out the renewed investigaton of Stanley Levison, the New York FBI office assigned four hundred special agents to internal security squads and only four to organized crime.

For the time being, the Levison matter was a farsighted precaution on Hoover's part. As yet there was no public knowledge of the heavily skewed deployment of Bureau personnel, let alone any serious political challenge to Hoover's command. If politicians ever tried to show that Communists were effectively extinct, and that Hoover therefore had miscast the FBI as a giant horde of buffalo hunters, the Director was prepared to cite threats such as Levison. Until then, Levison did not particularly bother him. In fact, later that year he authorized agents to recruit Levison as an informant. After several attempts, ever sensitive FBI officials assured Hoover that although Levison turned them down, he had said nothing unfriendly to the Bureau.

Hoover's antagonism toward King remained similarly subdued, as civil rights threatened no imminent divisions within the FBI's constituency. The mood of the era was still such that King and Hoover could arrive independently on the same side of the civil rights crisis, as in the Mack Parker lynching. In April 1959 a band of hooded men abducted Parker from the Mississippi jail cell where he was being held on charges of raping a white woman. King sent a telegram to Attorney General Rogers the next day urging a federal investigation of the disappearance. The few known facts, stated King, made it "almost appear as though mob action was invited." Rogers agreed, and so did Mississippi's governor, James P. Coleman. In the kind of act that doomed him as a "moderate" by the standards of Mississippi politics, Coleman asked for FBI help.

Hoover dispatched a team of sixty agents to Poplarville about the time Parker's mangled body was found floating in the Pearl River. Working the most sensational lynching case since Emmett Till's in 1955, the agents extracted confessions from three of the lynchers, identified the others, and established the complicity of a law enforcement official in the abduction. When the local prosecutor refused to allow the grand jury to see the FBI report, Hoover authorized agents to volunteer their testimony to the state grand jury. When the jury snubbed the FBI witnesses, Attorney General Rogers publicly branded the Mississippi investigation "a travesty on justice, flagrant and calculated." The Justice Department sought indictments under weaker federal statutes, but a federal grand jury of Mississippians refused to comply. An excellent FBI investigation was utterly wasted, leaving the killers at large and all the evidence hidden under seal.

Less spectacular injustices were pressing steadily on King. In Louisiana, state officials crushed an SCLC registration drive by conducting a review the effect of which was to *remove* ten thousand Negroes from the small number on the rolls. This reversal made little news, but it so disheartened local civil rights workers that Ella Baker left her New York home again, on her own volition. Although squeezed out of the SCLC, and long since discouraged by its slow preachers' methods, Baker kept extending her emergency visit to Shreveport until it consumed five weeks. She got along well with C. O. Simpkins, a dentist who was the only non-preacher heading an SCLC operation, but their best efforts to rally the crusade brought only 250 people to the courthouse. Stalling registration officials talked to only forty-six of them, and registered only fifteen. At this rate, it would take decades just to regain the meager registration totals predating the crusade.

Similar failures had been accumulating for some time across the South. When King returned from India, he reacted to the situation with a deed that was alien to his character and almost unique in his entire career: he fired someone. He demanded the immediate resignation of SCLC executive director John Tilley, stating that the crusade "has not had a dynamic program commensurate with the amount of money that it is spending." The SCLC board began searching again for a replacement with the same impossible combination of qualities—a preacher of sufficient stature to merit their confidence, and who was also willing, unlike any of the board members including King himself, to quit his church for full-time civil rights work. In the meantime, King asked Ella Baker to come back to the SCLC, this time as the paid executive director. The board agreed, provided that Baker's status was considered "acting" rather than permanent, allowing the search to continue. Baker moved back into the Atlanta office and resumed official correspondence on familiar subjects—the leaky roof, the lack of an air conditioner—made all the more difficult by the sad state of the SCLC treasury.

King fired Tilley because he was impatient. Nothing—not his near martyrdom, or his White House audience, or his thousand speeches—had rekindled the movement spirit of the boycott. King returned home determined to make a fresh start with the lessons of India. In April, he wrote William Stuart Nelson,* one of his mentors among Negro theologians, expressing the belief that the SCLC "had failed to get the philosophy over to many persons in the South because we had not taken the time to give serious study to it." He proposed convening a three-day Institute on Nonviolence that summer in Atlanta. King wanted to organize an American Salt March. To do that, he decided it would be well to move the annual Institute out of Montgomery. "Since returning from India," he wrote Nelson, "I am even more keyed up over this idea."

The Institute on Nonviolent Resistance to Segregation gathered at Spelman College in July. There was disappointment in the registered attendance of fewer than a hundred people, and particularly in the virtual absence of representatives from Atlanta itself, but the speakers included nearly every one of the small band of nonviolence leaders. Bayard Rustin, James Lawson, and Glenn Smiley all led workshops, as did King and Abernathy. Gandhian author Richard Gregg led a group discussion. L. D. Reddick reported on the Gandhian campaign against the caste system in India. Melvin Watson, King's Morehouse adviser on subjects ranging from pulpit-hunting to Stalinism, led a prayer service. Dr. C. O. Simpkins of Shreveport presided over one session, and Wyatt Tee Walker, a quotable newcomer since his enormous New Year's Day march in Richmond, presided over another. Ella Baker shared a panel with Will Campbell, a liberal white Southerner of some stature both as a preacher and author.

They were seeking a new instrument, a breakthrough. Experience in civil rights had taught them that Christianity needed to be modified for politics, and Gandhism modified for American culture. The two systems had to be synthesized, molded, and adjusted—but exactly how, no one knew. The problems were as plain as the word "nigger" and the solutions as vague as "Americanized nonviolence." A hundred semantic distinctions emerged. The speakers turned nonviolence into a social science, speaking of it as an attitude that had complex effects on practitioners and targets alike. There was much talk of how human beings respond to violence, and how Gandhians had prepared themselves to absorb beatings. Rustin, Smiley, and others told of some of the disarming nonviolent

---

* Dean of the faculties at Howard University in Washington. King had hoped to be guided through India by Nelson, who had spent the last six months of 1958 there on a Fulbright scholarship, but Nelson had been unable to extend his visit long enough.

tricks they had discovered in the past twenty years. In attacking what he called some common myths of nonviolence, Lawson stated that most violent segregationists were only made more angry by the sight of passive demonstrators curled in the fetal position. This was a way to get livers kicked in and backs broken, he said, recommending that resisters try to maintain eye contact with those beating them.

Lawson believed that the theoretical discussions needed to be "balanced with practical application to concrete situations." Since moving from Ohio to Nashville at King's beckoning, he had been testing his ideas about nonviolence with student volunteers. He called his Nashville seminars "workshops" instead of classes, and made it a point always to be working on a "project." It could be a demonstration, a march, a picket line, or some combination of the three against a segregated theater or recalcitrant voting registrar. Lawson was planning test demonstrations against some of the segregated department stores in Nashville for that fall. CORE's Gordon Carey, who had helped Wyatt Tee Walker organize his Richmond march, was planning sit-down demonstrations in Miami.

Lawson and the other new American Gandhians approached their projects with the care of a chemist. Each step was meticulously planned, executed, and evaluated, with an eye toward isolating behavior and controlling response. The precision of the training developed confidence, but it also made nonviolence an esoteric specialty. Only the tiniest fraction of those who opposed segregation could be expected to spend months preparing themselves for demonstrations, and that tiny fraction would be drawn from people considered kooks even by their own supporters. Much of the nonviolent activity in the state of North Carolina was traceable to the influence of Douglas Moore, the radical from whom King himself had kept his distance at Boston University. In North Carolina, Moore had been leading a sit-in campaign and legal battle against a segregated ice cream parlor. Amazed by King's performance during the bus boycott, he had written King a wrenching letter about "the things that are on my heart," proposing that King organize a cadre of Gandhian shock troops. "I have maintained for years that one hundred well-disciplined persons could break the backbone of segregated travel in North Carolina in less than a year," Moore wrote. He had received only a token reply from King's secretary. Now, less than two years later, Moore was the North Carolina representative on King's SCLC board. No other preacher from that state cared enough to make the long lonely drives to conferences on nonviolence.

King, moving inevitably into alliance with people like Douglas Moore, confronted the paradox of nonviolence. How could the new Gandhians hope to assemble an army of nonviolent kooks and visionaries, and how

could such a painstaking discipline be transmitted efficiently to masses
of recruits even if they could be found? By seeking those with the gumption to specialize in taking beatings and the patience to do so in a protracted campaign, nonviolence seemed to be a self-limiting doctrine.

One clue to the solution appeared in Montgomery one day that summer, when Abernathy asked King to stop by First Baptist right away.
King soon walked into a meeting of Abernathy, Fred Gray, and a young
boy of eighteen who was introduced as John Lewis. The boy, Abernathy
advised, was a seminary student in Nashville and had become a devoted
member of Lawson's nonviolence workshops. Determined to become the
first Negro student to enroll at a white college in Alabama, Lewis wanted
to sue for the right to enter Troy State College, in his home county. The
sincerity of his letters and phone calls had impressed Abernathy and
Gray enough to pay Lewis' bus fare from Nashville, so that they could
measure him in person against his hazardous ambition.

King encountered a young man somewhat like himself in appearance
—small, sturdy, dark-skinned, with a rounded face built for warmth
more than looks—but completely lacking in refinement. Lewis spoke
with a stammer, and could barely complete a full sentence even when
the stammer gave him peace. He said he had "come up" so far back in
the country that he could not remember even *seeing* a white person in
his youth. This made him decidedly not the type the NAACP lawyers
had been choosing for integration test cases, because he appeared to be a
Negro whom no amount of education could polish. Yet there was an
incandescence in Lewis that shone through all his shortcomings. He said
he was ready to die to go to Troy State but that he could probably avoid
such fate if he followed nonviolent principles. The meeting ended with
the two preachers agreeing to find the money somehow to finance a
lawsuit. Gray agreed to take the case provided that Lewis, still a minor,
obtained his parents' consent.

On the return bus to Nashville, a starstruck Lewis kept telling himself
that he had met and talked with Dr. Martin Luther King, Jr. Lewis was
proud of the fact that he had discovered King before the bus boycott made
him famous. By chance, he had listened in 1955 to a radio sermon entitled "Paul's Letter to the American Christians," in which King assumed
the style and theology of St. Paul to criticize Christians for selfishness
and failures of brotherhood. Lewis still remembered being heartshaken
in front of the radio. Within the space of an hour, his dreams of becoming
a preacher had focused upon a new idol.

Lewis' fantasy life had marked him early as a peculiar child. Growing
up on a small farm without plumbing or electricity, he had vexed his
parents by ducking out of work in the fields. He said he disapproved of

farm work because it was like gambling with nature. The parents at first considered this a bizarre excuse for laziness, but when they learned the intensity of his will they could only wish that laziness was the cause. Young Lewis lived in a world of his own. He had no feeling whatsoever for hogs, dogs, or most farm animals, but endless hours of study convinced him that chickens were worthy of adoption as the world's innocent creatures. Whenever a chicken was killed for dinner, Lewis cried hysterically and boycotted meals. He refused for days to speak to anyone in his family. Instead of growing out of his chicken fixation, he grafted it to the religious fervor that came over him about the age of eight.

Soon young Lewis was preaching to his chickens, sneaking out to the henhouse whenever he could to holler and pray for them in long incoherent sermons, loosening the stammer from his tongue. Bedtime became a religious ritual in the henhouse, with Lewis in contemplation of his clucking congregation as he preached them to a peaceful roost. He developed a full ministry by the age of ten. If a small chicken died, Lewis buried it in a lard can and made sure flowers grew on the site. He also baptized the new chicks. Once he got carried away in his prayers and baptized one too long, which became one of his worst childhood memories. The horror of pulling the lifeless chick from the water gave him lasting nightmares.

Lewis' preaching remained a farm boy's dream until 1957, when he became the first member of his family ever to finish high school. Hoping to follow Dr. King to Morehouse, he had sent off for a catalog, only to discover at a glance that its tuition was far beyond the family's means. Lewis wound up at the only school he could find that charged no tuition, Nashville's American Baptist Theological Seminary. For a country boy whose outstanding memory from his only city visit was the miracle of an elevator ride, independent college life in Nashville was a mixed assault of intimidation and adventure. Somehow it made perfect sense to hear in church that a man was offering classes on Dr. King's philosophy of nonviolence. James Lawson had arrived in Nashville the same time as Lewis. By the fall of 1958, while traveling as a field secretary for the Fellowship of Reconciliation, Lawson was leading classes in nonviolence on a weekly basis. If he happened to be out of town, his colleague Glenn Smiley often filled in. No one attended these unique classes more faithfully than Lewis, who found them far more engaging than his regular seminary work. He drank in knowledge of Gandhi, Thoreau, and the pioneers of American religious freedom before he finished remedial work in English and math. Seasoned by two years in Nashville, inspired by King and trained by Lawson, Lewis rode the bus home from Montgomery all aglow, ready to take risks for the Social Gospel.

Lawson sent a busload of Nashville students to the Highlander Folk School that fall. Lewis made sure to drag along James Bevel, one of his hallmates at the seminary dorm. Bevel had refused to attend Lawson's workshops for more than a year, but he consented to visit Highlander because it sounded more like a vacation. Bevel was recognized as the natural leader of the seminary. He had grown up in a split family, shuttling between a mother in the Mississippi Delta and a father in Cleveland, where Bevel worked as a teenager in the steel mills. Brash, quick-tongued, and sociable, he had just signed a rock-and-roll recording contract with his brothers when a sudden religious conversion propelled him to the Nashville seminary instead. One rumor held that he was fleeing an unwanted new son. Regardless, he became a preacher of budding genius, famous on the hallway for nonstop shower preaching at the top of his voice, trying out wild theories and bizarre improvisations, telling dazzling stories and working himself into such a frenzy that, as the joke went, Bevel needed a shower after his shower. He had no interest in the Social Gospel or in Lewis' nonviolent theories. Lewis, the tireless proselytizer, lured him to Highlander in hope of support.

Of the Highlander speakers, it was Myles Horton who first cracked Bevel's sense of mastery. Horton questioned the claims of students who said they had separated themselves from segregation's assertion that they were inferior. He made them doubt who they were, what they were saying. Bevel had never heard a white man speak so bluntly and yet so deftly. He seemed like Socrates, always challenging assumptions, boring deeper toward the core. The effect put Bevel on edge. He began to feel an oppressive weight. At a later session, he sizzled when another speaker berated the students for cowardice. "Just look at the Polish students," said the speaker. "They are busy helping to get the government of their country straightened out, and you are all here winding around the maypole, and going up the side steps to see a movie, and playing bridge. How do you feel?" Bevel's temper snapped. He walked out on the heavy-handed speech and slammed the door.

Lewis stayed behind for classes with Septima Clark. She was another of King's improbable hopes, percolating out of sight at Highlander. Clark was sixty years old, daughter of a slave owned by South Carolina's Poinsette family (from whom a species of winter flower took its name). She specialized in teaching illiterate adults to read and barely literate ones to become teachers. Her extraordinary gifts in that field inspired Myles Horton to put her in charge of an experimental "citizenship school" at Highlander. In a compressed week's workshop, Clark promised to turn sharecroppers and other unschooled Negroes into potential voters, armed with basic literacy and a grasp of democratic rights. There was even hope

that she might design a system of geometric growth whereby gifted illit-
erates could be quickly trained as teachers in the field. Her character was
a miraculous balance between leathery zeal and infinite patience. Clark
was a saint even to many of the learned critics who predicted she would
fail. A professor visiting Highlander complained that John Lewis was not
a suitable leader—he stuttered, split his infinitives, had poor reading
patterns. "What difference does that make?" she asked. All that would
come, she said. Besides, the people he needed to lead already understood
him, and so did Bevel. She predicted Bevel would be back. Clark counseled patience. As always, she worked both sides of the gaping class
divide without letting the friction ruin her spirits.

That fall, Ella Baker made a special trip to Highlander to explore the
idea of coupling Clark's citizenship-school program with the SCLC's
faltering Crusade for Citizenship. She had heard that Clark was drawing
her teachers almost entirely from a group that Baker considered the most
promising human resource in the South—Negro women—and also that
her program was aimed at plain unlettered Negroes, who made up the
overwhelming bulk of the population that needed registering. Baker
knew, however, that these very factors would raise instinctive doubts
among the SCLC preachers. Literacy schools involved tedious work, outside the daily interest or control of the clergy. Also, being openly predicated upon widespread Negro ignorance, they presented image problems
to leaders still struggling to build public recognition of a "new Negro" of
proper manners. For these reasons, Baker downplayed her enthusiasm for
the schools when she got back to Atlanta. She asked only that she be
"authorized to explore this field further."

King himself was discouraged after the Institute on Nonviolence. At the
SCLC's annual convention, he went before his board with a straightforward admission that the Crusade for Citizenship had failed. Fund-raising
and registration totals fell dismally short of the goals announced at the
outset, eighteen months earlier. "Honesty impels us to admit that we
have not really scratched the surface in this area," said King. His diagnosis was that the SCLC and the NAACP had paralyzed each other; his
remedy was to call a regional meeting in the hope of reaching cooperative
agreements with the South's NAACP chapters and other local groups in
voter registration. In effect, he wanted to bypass the NAACP national
office, but realists at the meeting pointed out that the plan would never
escape Wilkins' attention.

In desperation, King looked to public relations. Complaining that "the
SCLC has not been publicized through the press or otherwise," he rec-

ommended hiring a professional publicist for a minimum period of six months. The person he had in mind was Bayard Rustin, but he did not mention Rustin's name at first, for fear of rekindling the sort of controversy that had driven Rustin out of Montgomery during the boycott. King knew well that it would be difficult to sell a homosexual ex-Communist to a group of Baptist preachers, and he wanted first to win approval of the idea itself. The assembled ministers voted to begin the search for a publicity assistant, and otherwise they respectfully discussed King's ideas into limbo. Not long afterward, *Jet* magazine published an unsigned gossip item saying that "the clergy-based Dixie vote campaign has almost come to a halt." It mentioned the departure of Tilley, the pitiful registration totals as measured against the SCLC's announced goals, and other signs of failure that King himself had just acknowledged to his colleagues. "Meanwhile," concluded *Jet*, "the NAACP quietly has expanded its southern vote registration force and is marking up gains in many states. The moral: headlines won't do it."

Here was the Wilkins line on King in concentrated form, made public. The words stung King so sharply that he called *Jet*'s Washington bureau chief to register a strong protest. A week later, he steamed into an SCLC meeting with a list of proposals designed to "counteract some false ideas that have been disseminated." Nearly all of them looked to the field of public relations. He called for a press release stating that the SCLC was "expanding its activities," a newsletter "mailed to at least five thousand persons" that would say the same thing and appeal for funds, and, "after prayerful and serious consideration," he recommended Bayard Rustin by name for the public relations job. The crisis at the SCLC was so pressing that King dispensed with the usual politesse and bluntly urged his colleagues to take "the risk." Recognizing the "possible perils involved," he assured them that Rustin would "quietly resign" in the event of embarrassing public reaction.

In addition, King recommended that yet another SCLC peace-seeking mission be dispatched to NAACP headquarters in New York to "clear up what appears to be seeds of dissention [*sic*] being sown by persons in the top echelon in the NAACP." King wanted to bargain with Wilkins, but the SCLC preachers were quick to point out that he would reduce his leverage if he hired Rustin, whose background was well known to Wilkins. As always, it seemed, one of King's goals was hostage to another. The recommendations were postponed indefinitely—at least until Rustin returned from his latest excursion, a political caravan deep into French colonial Africa.

Limits finally overtook King at the end of the decade. He decided to apply himself directly to strengthening the SCLC, which had been floundering for nearly three years. Almost inevitably, the decision required him to move to SCLC headquarters in Atlanta. This meant the elimination of months of aggregate time spent waiting at the Atlanta airport during layovers. Almost anything moving in or out of the South had to go through Atlanta, and King was no exception. Of course, Atlanta also meant Ebenezer and Daddy King. The elder King, just now turning sixty, had never ceased to remind his son that he looked forward to his return to the pulpit that had been in the family throughout the twentieth century.

King knew that to return to Atlanta without returning to Ebenezer would grieve his father beyond repair. He also knew that Ebenezer's membership was falling off—partly, he suspected, because Daddy King was getting tired and was taking the congregation for granted, often preparing his sermons on the church platform during the services. King's younger brother was just leaving a stint as assistant pastor there, having grown out of his rebellion enough to enter the ministry but not enough to tolerate the daily supervision of Daddy King. King believed that he, unlike A.D., could make a symbiotic co-pastorate work. Daddy King could continue to manage the church; King could draw large new crowds. Indeed, the greater part of the family burden caused by a move to Atlanta would seem to fall on Coretta. She would become co-First Lady of Ebenezer with her mother-in-law, and would live in dependence on Daddy King, who had vociferously opposed King's marriage to her.

For some months, King had been cajoling Abernathy to go with him to Atlanta to become the SCLC's full-time executive director. Abernathy resisted. He loved his job at historic First Baptist, and he liked the prospect of succeeding King in Montgomery as president of the MIA. Most of all, he could not bear to face life in Atlanta without a pulpit. No matter how many times King guaranteed that he could preach somewhere in Atlanta every Sunday—and might even make more money in guest fees than as a permanent pastor—Abernathy protested that it would never be the same. He wanted to follow King almost anywhere, he said, if he could figure out a way to remain captain of a ship.

King finally lost patience. "Make up your mind," he said sharply. "I can't wait on you forever."

Abernathy was hurt. "You've never talked to me that way before, Michael," he said. (He and King had fallen into a habit of calling each other by their "real" first names in private matters.) It was unfair, Abernathy complained, to expect him to leave the pulpit when King himself was planning to move to Ebenezer.

King seemed to be overcome at once by remorse. After a long silence he said, "David, I told you that I remember watching my daddy walk the benches when I was a little boy."

"I know," Abernathy said quietly. "Walking the benches" referred to ministers who leaped from the pulpit in mid-sermon to preach ecstatically as they danced up and down the pews, literally stepping over the swooning bodies in the congregation. Abernathy knew that King considered it the most vaudevillian, primitive aspect of his heritage.

"He walked the benches," King repeated, in humiliation and wonder. "He did it to feed and educate his family. Now I've got to help him. Don't you see that?"

"I know, Michael, I know," said Abernathy. He protested no more, but neither did he agree to go to Atlanta. When the difficulty passed and they regained their humor, King gave him two weeks to decide.

King's own decision, while wrenching in its formation, was carried out with the utmost formality. He called R. D. Nesbitt, the deacon who first had found him as a student six years earlier, eating a plate of pork chops at Daddy King's house. The two of them sat on the front porch of the Dexter parsonage as King told Nesbitt he would resign on the last Sunday of November, effective the last Sunday in January, 1960. In making the announcement from the Dexter pulpit on Sunday, November 29, King tried first to heap upon himself all the burdens of fame and responsibility, saying that he had been doing the work of "five or six people," traveling, speaking, laboring under the demands not only of Montgomery but of the entire nation, suffering "the general strain of being known." By always "giving, giving, giving, and not stopping to retreat," he said, he had reduced himself almost to a "physical and psychological wreck." King exposed in himself all the grand, raw self-pity of the unpolished martyr. Two days later, he revealed the flip side of his mood in an expansive declaration for the press. "The time has come for a broad, bold advance of the southern campaign for equality," he said. " . . . I am convinced that the psychological moment has arrived. . . . We must train our youth and adult leaders in the techniques of social change through nonviolent resistance. We must employ new methods of struggle involving the masses of the people."

That same Tuesday, Georgia governor Ernest Vandiver responded publicly to reports that King was moving to Atlanta. "Wherever M. L. King, Jr., has been there has followed in his wake a wave of crimes including stabbing, bombings, and inciting of riots, barratry, destruction of property and many others," Vandiver declared. "For these reasons, he is not welcome to Georgia. Until now, we have had good relations between the races."

King worried about the diplomacy of his return to Atlanta, the South's

most visible and self-conscious city. Atlanta was perhaps the only metropolis in America where the members of an enlightened white oligar-
chy spoke frankly and easily of themselves as "the power structure." The
Negro leaders did pretty much the same in their own sphere. Consequently, King knew that his every move was under close scrutiny. *Constitution* editor Ralph McGill said that Atlanta whites were on guard,
like "citizens of medieval walled cities who heard that the great plague
was coming." King was returning to the city of "Sweet Auburn" Avenue,
Negro banks, and the comfortable homes spreading out through the West
Side beyond the Atlanta University complex. His parents had made the
move to the West Side, and were now enduring the long commutes across
town to and from Ebenezer, but King decided to move his family into a
small rented home on the less fashionable East Side, not far from the
church. This raised some eyebrows, as did his old 1954 Pontiac, and
when word spread through Negro Atlanta that King was thinking of
buying a house in the barely respectable Vine City area, which was dotted with slum housing, there was talk that the Kings were too conspicuously humble. They did no lavish entertaining. King drew a token salary
of only $1 a year from the SCLC and a middling $6,000 from Ebenezer.
His standard of living was perceived to be jarringly beneath his stature
in the world.

King told Negro reporters that he was not coming to take over the
Negro leadership but to "render any assistance" he could. In this and
other ways, he downplayed his homecoming in order to placate Atlanta's
established Negro leaders, most of whom had known him as a small boy.
"I grew up with those people," he told an SCLC colleague. "They'll eat
me alive if I make a mistake." But his sensitivities about what he called
bourgeois living standards ran deep. The toddler who wanted to "get me
some big words" was the same one whose earliest memories were of
bread lines in the Depression. He was ambivalent—a humble prince. He
stopped to chat amiably with the poorest people he encountered on the
street, but he had the SCLC issue a special press release announcing that
he had been invited to speak in the chapel of Harvard University. Coretta
shared his political values, but she brought her cook with her from Montgomery, and her early moves in the new city established her as adept in
the way of the Atlanta aristocracy. To find a babysitter and errand-runner
in the new town, she called the wife of the Spelman College president
and asked her to send over a suitable student.

King's shift back home to Atlanta marked a transition between decades. In Nashville, on successive Saturdays, James Lawson sent a dozen
of his most disciplined student Gandhians, John Lewis among them, into
the segregated areas of downtown department stores. Their refusal to

move on as ordered caused some disruption, but their unfailing politeness and the novelty of their method reduced the tension to about the level of a party-crashing. The students returned to Lawson's workshops for evaluations of their test demonstrations.

In San Francisco, at the annual convention of the AFL-CIO, A. Philip Randolph spoke from the floor three times in a single day, each time seeking action against official segregation within member unions. This was one time too many for AFL-CIO president George Meany. "Who the hell appointed you the guardian of all the Negroes in America?" he shouted from the podium. The affront stimulated Randolph to organize a Negro labor federation outside the AFL-CIO in order to bring pressure on Meany.

At the White House, President Eisenhower brooded about the property confiscations and other anti-American actions taken by the revolutionary government in Cuba. "Castro begins to look like a madman," he fumed to his aides, and he briefly entertained a plan to strangle Cuba with a naval blockade. As always, however, Eisenhower kept his alarm to himself. Having used his avuncular patience and his military steadiness many times over the past decade to muffle crises that threatened renewed world war, he was not about to change over a small island. Similarly, he restrained his burning fury against those he considered responsible for creating an atmosphere of feverish demand to spend more money on weapons. The demand had more to do with greed and anxiety than with military judgment, he believed, and was subverting both politics and military professionalism. Entering his last year as President, he denounced as "damn near treason" the behavior of military officers who lobbied through politicians and reporters for weapons that had been rejected with the government.

With Stanley Levison, King confronted the last hurdles blocking the move to Atlanta: nettlesome tax audits by both the IRS and the state of Alabama. An auditor ordered King to prove that the money that passed through his bank account in excess of his declared income was not taxable—a challenge that hit King's weak spot. Having routed all expense monies and donations through his own accounts, he found it almost impossible to substantiate those sums as legitimate deductions. He was especially hard pressed to satisfy the Alabama auditor, who refused to accept donations to the SCLC or the MIA as nontaxable contributions. King found it easier to pay under protest than to fight. He settled with the IRS for nearly $500 in back taxes, and his parting gift to Alabama was a check for $1,667.83.

The King family returned to Montgomery at the end of January 1960 for King's last official service at Dexter. They received from the congregation an engraved silver tea service and countless tender expressions of farewell. On the following night, Abernathy hosted a much more extravagant "Testimonial of Love and Loyalty," at which the extreme sentiments of humility and royalty bathed each other in a warm harmony that was attainable almost nowhere else. The packed crowd rocked with "Amens" when told that Negroes in Montgomery remained psychologically and politically downtrodden—that too many of them still filed to the back of the bus in disregard of their boycott victory, that there were still no Negro bus drivers and not a single Negro policeman "to escort our children across the streets at the school as the white children are escorted." Very few in the audience were allowed to vote, and even King himself could not get the "White" and "Colored" signs removed from the entrances to public places. These laments only highlighted the contrasting adulation of King, who, like Jesus, was praised as a savior on a donkey. No fewer than nine church choirs performed before the service began with a processional hymn called "The Integration Song," in which the traditional Baptist refrain "When we all get to heaven" was changed to "When we all know justice."

During the service itself, five additional choirs saluted King. Representatives of Montgomery's major Negro guilds and associations—the barbers, merchants, beauticians, doctors, preachers, and others—came forward in succession to pay tribute to King before he formally transferred the MIA's official gavel to Abernathy. At the end, bearers came forward to present King with a last expression of homage: a wooden box filled with cash, as broad and deep as King's shoulders, reaching from his midsection to his chin. King accepted all this like a monarch, but then, in the sort of gesture that made people shake their heads in wonder, he directed that the money be divided between the MIA and the SCLC. "And I mean every penny of it," he quipped, in a backhanded tribute to the clergy's reputation for accounting tricks. "I cannot claim to be worthy of such a tribute," he added seriously. When he finished, they all sang "Blest Be the Tie That Binds" and received the benediction.

King severed his last connections to Montgomery. In many respects, the first phase of his career had brought years of frustration. Even his trips abroad, like his White House audience, brought vexations, and the prodigious energies he had thrown into a thousand speeches had exposed as an illusion the hope that his larger purpose could be accomplished by political evangelism. These things were more troublesome to King than most people around him could have guessed, and yet they had benefited him more than he could know. The stale glories chipped away at the headiness and false wisdom attendant to early fame. They strengthened his already remarkable steadiness. The oratorical illusion had propelled him so rapidly around the country that he made in only a few years a lifetime supply of acquaintances, some of historic importance. The speeches also helped King learn to read audiences of every composition and above all to acknowledge the limits of his own special gift, oratory.

Fate could have designed no better culmination of these lessons than events occurring simultaneously with the Testimonial of Love and Loyalty. That same night of Monday, February 1, students at the Negro colleges around Greensboro, North Carolina, were electrified by reports of what four freshman boys had done that day. Even the words that had started it all were the stuff of new myth. At a bull session, one of them had said, "We might as well go now." Another had replied, "You really mean it?" The first had said, "Sure, I mean it," and the four of them had gone to the downtown Woolworth's store and slipped into seats at the sacrosanct whites-only lunch counter. The Negro waitress had said, "Fellows like you make our race look bad," and refused to serve them, but the four freshmen had not only sat there unperturbed all afternoon but also promised to return at ten o'clock the next morning to continue what they called a "sit-down protest." That night, the four instantly famous students on the campus of North Carolina A&T were meeting with elected student leaders, and rumors spread that others were volunteering to join them in the morning. With telephones buzzing between campuses, word flashed that even some white students from Greensboro College wanted to sit in with them. The student leaders were arranging it so that students could sit down in shifts so as not to miss classes. Nineteen students sat with the four freshmen at Woolworth's on Tuesday. On Wednesday, the number swelled to eighty-five as the "sit-in" became a contagion.

SEVEN

THE QUICKENING

No one had time to wonder why the Greensboro sit-in was so different. In the previous three years, similar demonstrations had occurred in at least sixteen other cities. Few of them made the news, all faded quickly from public notice, and none had the slightest catalytic effect anywhere else. By contrast, Greensboro helped define the new decade. Almost certainly, the lack of planning helped create the initial euphoria. Because the four students at Woolworth's had no plan, they began with no self-imposed limitations. They defined no tactical goals. They did not train or drill in preparation. They did not dwell on the many forces that might be used against them. Above all, they did not anticipate that Woolworth's white managers would—instead of threatening to have them arrested—flounder in confusion and embarrassment. The surprise discovery of defensiveness within the segregated white world turned their fear into elation.

The spontaneity and open-endedness of the first Greensboro sit-in flashed through the network of activists who had been groping toward the same goal. On the first night, the first four protesters themselves contacted Floyd McKissick, who, as a maverick lawyer and NAACP Youth Council leader, had joined Rev. Douglas Moore in the Durham ice cream parlor case and other small sit-ins. McKissick and Moore rushed to nearby Greensboro. Simultaneously, the news traveled along parallel lines of communication with such speed that a vice president of the mostly white National Student Association was in Greensboro on February 2, the second day, before any word of the sit-in had appeared in the public media.

On the third day, when the number of protesters passed eighty, Douglas Moore called James Lawson in Nashville with a volley of bulletins. The protest would continue to grow, he reported, as enthusiastic student volunteers were only too eager to absorb the organizing discipline of the adults who had arrived to work in the background. The sit-in "command center" at North Carolina A&T was operating with crisp, military efficiency—briefing new protesters on nonviolence, quashing rumors, dispatching fresh troops as needed. Most important, Moore reported, sympathetic sit-ins were about to begin in Durham, Raleigh, and other North Carolina cities. Moore, who knew already that Lawson had been preparing for new Nashville protests, urged him to speed up the schedule so that the movement could spread into other states. Lawson promised to try. Moore then made other calls, including one to the FOR's Glenn Smiley. McKissick called Gordon Carey, the CORE official who had worked on Wyatt Walker's Richmond march and the Miami sit-ins the previous year. Carey flew from New York to Durham at the end of the first week. By Saturday, the Greensboro sit-in counted some four hundred students, and Kress, the other big downtown dime store, had been added to the target list. A bomb scare that day interrupted the demonstrations. Later, Klansmen and youth-gang members crowded inside the stores to menace the protesters. Store managers who had been desperately polite all week now threatened to call in legal force.

Before serious reprisal fell upon Greensboro, fresh sit-ins broke out the following Monday in the surrounding North Carolina cities of Raleigh, Durham, and Winston-Salem. Three days later in nearby High Point, students assembled at a church before marching downtown to the segregated lunch counters, and as it happened, Fred Shuttlesworth had come in from Birmingham to preach the midweek service for the minister of that church. Shuttlesworth became the first eyewitness from the tough Deep South states below North Carolina. He saw the well-dressed students step off in good order, like soldiers in the joyous early stages of a popular war, and he heard that it was the same in the other North Carolina towns—only bigger. Shuttlesworth promptly called Ella Baker at the SCLC office in Atlanta. He was not the first to report to her about the sit-ins, but he was the first voice of authority from the inner circle of SCLC preachers. This is it, he told Baker. "You must tell Martin that we must get with this," said Shuttlesworth, adding that the sit-ins might "shake up the world."

The movement first leaped across state lines on the day after the High Point sit-in. An SCLC preacher in Rock Hill, South Carolina, reported by phone to McKissick that his charges were "ready to go." They went from his church to the lunch counters on Friday, the same day police arrested forty-one students sitting in at the Cameron Village Woolworth store in Raleigh. In handcuffs, the Raleigh students swept across the threshold of the jail with eyes closed and hearts pounding, and, like the bus boycotters four years earlier, they soon re-emerged on bail to discover that their identities had not been crushed. They were unharmed and did not feel like trash. A flood of relief swelled their enthusiasm.

In Nashville that Friday night, Lawson presided over what turned out to be the first mass meeting of the sit-in movement. About five hundred new volunteers crowded into the First Baptist Church along with the seventy-five veterans of the nonviolence workshop. Lawson and the other adults argued for delay, on the grounds that only a small fraction of the students had received any training. This was not a game, they said. Sooner or later the city would put demonstrators in jail, and their organization—the Nashville Christian Leadership Conference, a local affiliate of King's SCLC—had less than $100 in reserve. They needed time to raise a bail fund. These and other words of caution gave way to a tide of student sentiment, however, and Lawson found himself giving a crash course on nonviolence late into the night. He told the crowd how to behave in the face of a hundred possible emergencies, how to avoid violating the loitering laws, how to move to and from the lunch counters in orderly shifts, how to fill the seats of students who needed to go to the bathroom, even how to dress: stockings and heels for the women, coats and ties for the fellows. When in doubt, he stressed, the newcomers should take their cue from the behavior of the workshop members who had demonstrated before.

They broke up that night amid nervous prayers and whispers of "Good luck," and Lawson's logistical plan worked smoothly the next morning. Church cars traveled a circuit between the First Baptist Church and designated pickup spots near Nashville's four Negro colleges—Fisk University, Tennessee State, Meharry Medical, and the Baptist seminary. When all were assembled at the First Baptist staging area, Lawson moved them out five hundred strong. White Nashville, which had changed hands nearly a dozen times during the Civil War, awoke slowly to a kind of invasion force it never had encountered before, as rows of neatly dressed Negro college students filed into the downtown stores to wait for food service.

The Nashville students—destined to establish themselves as the largest, most disciplined, and most persistent of the nonviolent action groups in the South—extended the sit-in movement into its third state. Their success helped form the model of the student group—recruited from the campuses, quartered in the churches, and advised by preachers. Elated with the early results, Lawson called King, Ella Baker, and Douglas Moore, among others, to exchange reports. Each of them in turn called acquaintances who might help open other fronts. By the end of February, sit-in campaigns were under way in thirty-one Southern cities across eight states. News attention remained scanty for the most part in both white and Negro media, largely because people were conditioned to think of student antics as transient events. Moore predicted that the sit-ins soon would put an end to such complacency. "If Woolworth and the other stores think this is just another panty raid," he told reporters, "they haven't had their sociologists in the field recently."

The earliest wave of student protests spanned the two weeks preceding King's first two sermons as the new co-pastor at Ebenezer. More ominously for King, they coincided with the arrival of ugly rumors that Alabama officials were not satisfied with the back taxes they had extracted from him on January 18. Talk filtered out of the courthouse to the effect that lawyers for the state were putting King's name before a grand jury on charges that could send him to prison for a decade or more. The growing intensity of the rumors alarmed King enough to seek legal and financial help in advance. He sent urgent telegrams to Harry Belafonte and actor Sidney Poitier, and he asked Roy Wilkins to help him find the best criminal defense lawyers in the country. Wilkins recommended two of his NAACP board members. King wrote a guarded letter to one of them, Judge Hubert T. Delaney in New York, asking him to receive his "special assistant," Bayard Rustin, for a briefing about a confidential matter. As the third week of sit-ins began, King himself conferred with potential defenders in New York.

On the way home, he stopped off in North Carolina to see Douglas Moore. Abernathy, up from Montgomery, joined him for a visit to the F. W. Woolworth lunch counter in downtown Durham, which company officials had closed in the vain hope that delay would make the students forget about the protest. That night King spoke at a rally in support of the continuing sit-ins in the clustered cities of central North Carolina. "Men are tired of being trampled over by the iron feet of oppression," he said, repeating the trigger line of his first speech during the bus boycott. "The underlying philosophies of segregation are diametrically opposed to democracy and Christianity, and all the dialectics of all the logicians in the world cannot make them lie down together."

These were familiar King themes. A significant departure lay in his unequivocal early endorsement of the protest, which he said was "destined to be one of the glowing epics of our time." Alone among the established leaders of either race, he praised the students as a mature force in adult politics: "What is fresh, what is new in your fight is the fact that it was initiated, led, and sustained by students. What is new is that American students have come of age. You now take your honored places in the world-wide struggle for freedom." The respectful tone of his remarks was highly unusual in an era when student achievements of any kind were customarily relegated to a junior, preparatory role in the public mind—and the novel, extralegal sit-in method was mainly attracting puzzled frowns and widespread suspicion. Even the major Negro newspapers were reporting the sit-ins cautiously. They registered as a newfangled teenage rumble with a partially redeeming purpose. They were not controlled or approved by the adult civil rights organizations, and for that reason alone the NAACP Legal Defense Fund refrained from defending the first students arrested.

King embraced the students for taking the step he had been toying with for the past three years—of *seeking out* a nonviolent confrontation with the segregation laws. He had traveled halfway around the world to wrestle with obscure Gandhian conundrums, and declared countless times that he was prepared to die for his beliefs, but he had never been quite willing to follow his thoughts outside the relative safety of oratory. With a simple, schoolboyish deed, the students cut through all the complex knots he had been trying to untie at the erudite Institutes on Nonviolence. His generosity of spirit made it easy for him to give the students credit for their inspiration, and his own lingering fears no doubt added to his admiration of their courage. Even now, King himself was not ready to join them at a lunch counter or otherwise force a test of the segregation laws with his person. He made no pledge to do so at Durham, but the pull of it fueled his exhortations to the assembled students. "Let us not fear going to jail," he declared. "If the officials threaten to arrest us for standing up for our rights, we must answer by saying that we are willing and prepared to fill up the jails of the South. . . . And so I would urge you to continue your struggle." "Fill up the jails" was a new battle cry for King, an incendiary one by the standards of both races.

No sooner had King warmly embraced the student protest movement than his forebodings of danger came to life in another quarter. Two Georgia sheriff's deputies appeared at the Ebenezer church office on the day after the Durham speech, armed with a warrant for King's arrest on Alabama perjury charges. King surrendered to them and was led off as a prisoner to the county courthouse, leaving behind a wave of shock and rumor that quickly radiated from Auburn Avenue to the West Side. Daddy King rushed to the courthouse. He led a gathering crowd of lawyers and other prominent Negroes trying to fathom the nature of King's alleged crimes. The news that they were felonies was received, doubted, confirmed, and finally accepted as a stinging blow. The further news that they grew out of King's Alabama tax problems puzzled and then outraged the lawyers, some of whom knew that King had already paid the disputed back taxes for the years in question. It was almost unheard of for a taxpayer who accepted and paid the state's assessment to be prosecuted as a criminal, and even then the normal procedure was for the state to bring charges of tax evasion—a misdemeanor. King was the first citizen in the history of Alabama to be prosecuted for felony tax evasion, the technical charge being that he had perjured himself in signing his tax returns for 1956 and 1958. Governor John Patterson, who as attorney general had led the fight against the bus boycott and the state NAACP, did nothing to contradict speculation that Alabama was stretching state power to its limits in order to make a political example of King. While signing the papers requesting King's extradition from Georgia, Patterson made a merrily sarcastic public statement. "If you dance," he quipped, "you must pay the fiddler."

The confluence of the sit-ins and the perjury indictment slapped King with a cruel irony. Just as he was deciding that he should aim his political influence at filling the jails with idealistic young protesters, Alabama struck at the most sensitive spot of such resolve. If convicted on tax charges, even in the white courts, he would take to prison the tarnished public image of a lying, greedy, sham preacher. This was everything King had resolved most devoutly not to be himself and to change in his church if he could. His entire life's struggle as a preacher had begun in rebellion against what he saw as the cynical pabulum and exploitative uses of fundamentalist doctrines. For Governor Patterson to make a mockery of all that threatened not only to extinguish his own identity but to impugn the foundation of his beliefs. Never before or after was King so distraught about his future. Returning home from his arraignment on the day of the arrest, he canceled speaking engagements in Chicago and California. He felt he could not face an audience, hold his head up, or be sure of his courage. Then he decided that if he did not keep going, he would have lost already. In a fit of energy, King rebooked his speeches and caught a later flight to Chicago that same afternoon.

Although the tax indictment was not a front-page story in the nation's leading newspapers, word of it spread rapidly through communities friendly to civil rights. Roy Wilkins declared publicly that the NAACP would do everything in its power to defend him. Negro newspapers de-

nounced the indictment as political. King, though buoyed enormously
by the outpouring of support, recognized its limits. Even those who extolled his character could not unequivocally assert his innocence of the
charges. There was a tiny seam of doubt—even if King *had* slipped up a
little on his taxes, they temporized, he was being persecuted as a leader
of his race. This was the crevice that King would fall through if convicted
and sent away to prison. Desperately, he sought to create an alternative
tribunal that might stand against the full judgment of the Alabama
courts. He tried to recruit a blue-ribbon commission of prestigious white
leaders—the deans of the Harvard law and divinity schools, the head of
the National Council of Churches, the president of the Southern Baptist
Convention—to examine his tax records, but the efforts failed.

On the same day that Atlanta's most distinguished Negro preachers
met to formulate a statement deploring King's indictment—an event
that received banner headlines in the Negro press—a parallel group of
the city's leaders met more quietly with the express purpose of heading
off the threat of student sit-ins in Atlanta. The Rev. Dr. Samuel Williams
—King's Morehouse philosophy professor, who doubled as a Baptist
preacher and was also a charter officer of the SCLC—joined all six presidents of the colleges in the Atlanta University complex at the latter
meeting. Benjamin Mays of Morehouse warned the students that any
"flare-ups" in Atlanta would be blamed on King, and the students eventually agreed to draw up a statement of their grievances, patterned after
the Declaration of Independence. This was the proper way to do things
in Atlanta, which was different from the other cities. The compromise
remained vague as to whether the manifesto would be a prologue to or a
substitute for a sit-in. Julian Bond of Morehouse—son of an Atlanta
University dean and former president of two Negro colleges, whose own
childhood had been favored not only with his scholarly initiation by
W. E. B. Du Bois himself but also by an audience with Albert Einstein—
undertook to draft most of the manifesto, for submission to the college
presidents.

In Nashville, the students in Lawson's workshop had completed their
second week of daily sit-ins on Friday, February 26, when the chief of
police let it be known that their grace period was over. He warned that
the downtown merchants had requested trespassing or disorderly conduct arrests if the demonstrations continued. This was the challenge for
which the students had braced themselves. John Lewis stayed up all
night composing a list of nonviolent "do's and don'ts" to guide the students through the trauma of being arrested. The secretary to the semi-

nary's president typed them on a mimeograph stencil, ending with Lewis' earnest admonition: "Remember the teachings of Jesus, Gandhi, Thoreau, and Martin Luther King, Jr."

Each student carried one of the mimeographed sheets the next day as the column marched silently back downtown to the designated stores. Hostile white teenagers shouted "Chicken" and "Nigger." The police allowed some of the whites to attack Lawson's unresisting troops with rocks, fists, and lighted cigarettes before moving in to arrest seventy-seven Negroes and five white sympathizers—to the applause of several hundred white onlookers. When a policeman said "You're under arrest" to John Lewis, a lifetime of absorbed taboos against any kind of trouble with the law quickened into terror. He tried to blot out everything but his rules as the police frisked, cuffed, and marched him to the paddy wagon. Then, riding to jail with the others, his dread gave way to an exhilaration unlike any he had ever known. They had held steady through the worst, he believed, and by the highest standards they knew there was no doubt that they had been in the right. Their fervor rose to such heights that Lewis and some of the other workshop veterans made a pact that weekend to escalate their Gandhian witness.

At their trials on Monday, the twenty-ninth, their chosen speaker stood up in court to interrupt the monotonous drone of guilty verdicts and fines. Diane Nash—a Chicago native as dedicated as Lewis and much more articulate—informed the judge that a group of the defendants had decided to choose jail instead of a fine. "We feel that if we pay these fines we would be contributing to and supporting the injustice and immoral practices that have been performed in the arrest and conviction of the defendants," she announced nervously. Nash, Lewis, and fourteen others were soon led off to jail, making good on the Gandhian gesture King himself had tried unsuccessfully in Montgomery a year and a half earlier. The emotional force of their example was so strong that more than sixty of their fellow defendants changed their minds, pocketed their fine money, and joined them in jail. Outside the courtroom, many Negroes were shocked at the news that their city, forced to choose, had imprisoned some of the finest students in the area instead of the white hoodlums who had attacked them. Some also felt shame at remaining aloof from the protests while such treatment was being meted out to the nonviolent students. Among those most deeply affected was James Bevel, who came down from his bathroom soliloquies to lead the next wave of demonstrators by the same route to jail, where he was greeted by an overjoyed John Lewis.

The spectacle of the sit-ins had worked the critical degree of conversion in Bevel, and similar changes spread so rapidly through an aroused

Negro population that Mayor Ben West made a conciliatory move. In exchange for a halt in the demonstrations, he offered to release the jailed students and appoint a biracial committee to make recommendations about segregation at downtown stores. Nash, Lewis, Bevel, and the other students emerged from jail as heroes who had forced a Southern city to grant one of the long-denied requests of the established civil rights groups. Hard upon the news of this victory, however, came the news that the trustees of Vanderbilt University had summarily expelled James Lawson from the Divinity School without a hearing or the approval of the faculty. The expulsion was reported on the front page of *The New York Times*, beginning national coverage of the onrushing clash between the university and the Vanderbilt faculty. About four hundred Vanderbilt teachers came to resign in protest, ultimately forcing Lawson's reinstatement. Meanwhile, the intrepid Diane Nash led a band of protesters to the lunch counter at the Greyhound bus terminal, which was not covered by the truce with the mayor. There, to the surprise of the entire city, the management served the students without incident. Segregation was broken at Greyhound even as the Vanderbilt trustees were counterattacking against Lawson. The pattern of the early sit-ins was established: constant surprises, all-night meetings, serial victories, and setbacks, with the elders of both races often on the defensive against their young.

On February 25, after a planning session at Abernathy's home in Montgomery, thirty-five Alabama State students walked into the basement cafeteria at the state capitol, asked for food service, were refused, and walked out again. This rather tame incident nevertheless aroused a ferocious reaction that suggested a difference between Montgomery and Nashville, which by Alabama standards was a metropolis nearing borderstate flexibility. Almost immediately after the students left the state capitol, Governor Patterson summoned Alabama State president H. Councill Trenholm, the dignified pillar of the Negro community whom Vernon Johns had shamed many years earlier for paying "his semi-annual visit" to church. The governor bluntly ordered Trenholm to identify and expel all the Negro students who had requested service at the white cafeteria. Patterson did not fret about touching off nationwide sensitivities over academic freedom, as in the Lawson case at Vanderbilt. In fact, he underscored his tough line by calling in reporters to make himself clear. "The citizens of this state do not intend to spend their tax money to educate law violators and race agitators," he recalled telling Trenholm, "and if you do not put a stop to it, you might well find yourself out of public funds." Trenholm, who with his father had run Alabama State for more than fifty years, gave reporters but a single line of response: "I have no alternative but to comply." The next day, angry student leaders protested the governor's public humiliation of their president, saying that they had done no more than to ask to buy food at a public building. Fred Shuttlesworth came in from Birmingham to announce that Patterson's threat was "totalitarian in spirit."

Nearly four thousand Negroes, including most of the Alabama State student body, rallied that Friday night at the Hutchinson Street Baptist Church. It was the largest crowd since the bus boycott. Student leader Bernard Lee found himself standing on the platform with Shuttlesworth, Abernathy, and Martin Luther King—who had just arrived in town from Atlanta to surrender on his perjury indictment. The crowd applauded for Lee almost as loudly as for the three most famous Negroes in Alabama. Basking in adulation, Lee felt lightheaded from the effects of his sudden elevation. Until that week, he had been just another college student—a married father of three, veteran of Air Force duty at a Strategic Air Command base in Montana, where he cared for, as he was fond of saying, nuclear weapons so awesome that they would make World War II seem like "a little picnic." His nickname was "Jelly," in tribute to his love of food. This quality, plus his relatively advanced age, had propelled him into leadership of the campus cafeteria protests for the past two years, and that experience had pushed him in turn to the forefront of the capitol protest two days earlier. Now he was the one who had signed the press release answering Governor Patterson, and his name was praised unanimously by his fellow students. Their deafening approval of his remarks at the rally swept Lee up into the theater of the new movement. "Boy, they really love you here, don't they?" laughed King.

That night Lee received an equally memorable initiation into the habits of preacher politics when the three ministers invited him to share their private feast at Abernathy's house. He glowed in the presence of offstage conversation that bounced from Scripture and pulpit banter to high-level nonviolent tactics, and he marveled at the vast quantities of fried chicken the three preachers managed to consume between words. Lee was transformed. It occurred to him for the first time that he might become a preacher. Nearly four years' work toward an accounting degree began to fade inexorably from his mind, along with his former plans and his attachments to wife and family. He began to move toward his future role as King's valet and shadow—toward an identification so complete that Lee came to boast that his moods and whims, even his health cycles, moved in perfect concert with King's.

Emotions in Montgomery ran high that Saturday, the day of the first mass arrests in Nashville. Rumors of student sit-ins at Montgomery's downtown lunch counters attracted roving bands of angry white people armed with small baseball bats. There were no sit-ins, but exchanges between the white vigilantes and ordinary Negro shoppers occasionally flashed into violence. While one white man scuffled with a Negro woman on the sidewalk, his companion bludgeoned her from the blind side. There was little doubt about the nature of the encounter or the names of the people involved, because Sunday's *Advertiser* carried a photograph with a caption naming the attacker. The white photographer and reporter at the scene both said that the police had stood by passively, and that the crack of the baseball bat on the woman's head could be heard from half a block away. Governor Patterson announced that he would leave the investigation to local officials. Police Commissioner L. B. Sullivan—who had replaced Clyde Sellers since the bus boycott—blamed the Negro students for causing the original disturbance and the *Advertiser* for publishing the photograph. Editor Grover Hall, while dividing the larger blame between "rash, misled young Negroes" and "white thugs," defended his newspaper against the police commissioner. "Sullivan's problem is not a photographer with a camera," he wrote. "Sullivan's problem is a white man with a baseball bat."

On the Monday following the attacks, King surrendered at the Montgomery County Courthouse on the income tax charges. Booked, fingerprinted, and released on $4,000 bond, he walked six blocks through the downtown shopping area, past the spot where the woman had been struck on Saturday. His purpose, he told the small number of Negroes following him, was to demonstrate at once his rededication to nonviolence and his conviction that Negroes could not allow themselves to be intimidated. King then returned to the heated strategy sessions at Abernathy's house. The students wanted to have sit-ins in order to live up to the performance of their peers elsewhere in the South, but most of the adult Negroes in town feared for the very survival of Alabama State. President Trenholm was nearly hemorrhaging from the pressure of trying to maintain both the support of the state and the respect of his students. In the end, the students compromised by agreeing to hold a prayer service on the steps of the capitol.

More than half the student body walked downtown the next day. Bernard Lee made a short speech. A student soprano's rendition of "The Lord's Prayer" so moved her voice teacher, King's old friend Robert Williams, that he vowed to himself not to flunk her that term in music theory. The students all sang "The Star-Spangled Banner" and marched back to campus. Alabama's State Board of Education expelled Bernard Lee and eight other "ringleaders" the next day, ignoring President Trenholm's plaintive request that they merely be placed on probation. From the march and the expulsions, the challenges escalated at a quickened pace.

King went back to Atlanta to prepare for his trial, but he was bombarded with bulletins from Nashville, Montgomery, and the newly erupting campuses across the South. At Orangeburg, South Carolina, on the day of the Montgomery prayer service, some four hundred students from South Carolina State and Claflin College marched downtown to sit at the segregated lunch counters. Forewarned, local police and units of special state agents intercepted them with massed force, firing tear gas and water hoses before they arrested 388 of the student marchers. Doused, choking students, herded into an enclosed park, found themselves as stunned by their own calm as by the ferocity of the police rebuff. Charles McDew, leader of the Orangeburg march, would always recall looking back at the melee from a police car after his arrest, to see one of the hulking local football stars, David "Deacon" Jones, holding in his arms a crippled female student who had been knocked down by the firehoses. The expression on Jones's face was one of peaceful sadness instead of rage. The sight of it haunted McDew. Although he had little use for nonviolence or even for Christianity, he became convinced that an inescapable power could be buried in doctrines of meekness and humanity.

Orangeburg was the first of some forty new cities that experienced student demonstrations in March, as the sit-in movement spread into Georgia, West Virginia, Texas, and Arkansas. In Montgomery, the Alabama State student body pledged at a mass meeting not to register for spring classes until their nine expelled peers were reinstated, whereupon the administration, under relentless pressure from the state, banned unregistered students from the cafeteria. In response, Abernathy pledged to lead a prayer march from the city's Negro churches in support of the students, and in response to that, Police Commissioner Sullivan publicly warned of police reprisals "if the Negroes persist in flaunting their arrogance and defiance by congregating at the Capitol." Abernathy, trying to lead his march out of Dexter across the short distance to the capitol, found his way blocked by police, fire trucks, and a sizable vigilante mob from the outlying counties. He retreated. The students tried to pick up the campaign the next day by marching around the campus with placards, but the Negro administrators, whipsawed mercilessly between their bosses and their bus boycott memories, tried to protect the school by herding the students off campus. No sooner did the students step off campus, however, than police units arrived in force to make sure they did not demonstrate in the city itself. The students, trapped in a street along the campus border, milled around as police reinforcements arrived with tear gas cannisters, carbines, and even a couple of submachine guns. Finally, the police hauled off thirty-five students in the first of the Montgomery arrests. A woman professor, torn by conflict as to whose behavior was most improper, lectured some of her female students in frustration. "Don't all of you pile on top of each other," she said to five of them who had been ordered into the back of a patrol car. "Let them get another car for you." For this, the officers promptly arrested the professor too, on charges of interference.

With the Montgomery student movement temporarily throttled, and the white authorities thoroughly mobilized, Abernathy found himself isolated among the city's Negro leadership. In spite of his best efforts to rally them, his own MIA board refused to sanction any statement or mass meeting in support of the students. Unlike the bus boycott, the student sit-ins were openly subject to physical repression and extremely dangerous to the Negro community's economic center at Alabama State. Nerves frayed under the pressure. When Shuttlesworth privately criticized Abernathy for failing to control the MIA board only five weeks after receiving the gavel from King, Abernathy snapped, "Fred, I'm not a dictator." He also pointed out that Shuttlesworth himself had been unable to command much adult support for student sit-ins in Birmingham.*

In mood and method, the Southern cities opposing the sit-in movements varied as widely as the sit-in movements themselves. The demonstrations highlighted the divisions among the Negroes as well as those between the races. Abernathy was not the only local leader caught between the urgency of the student protest and the balky hesitation of the most influential Negroes. For King, still traveling constantly, the pressures accumulated on both sides of this internal division. Adding to the strain was his imminent criminal trial in Alabama, for which he desperately needed precisely those commodities least controlled by students and most controlled by the traditional elders: money, lawyers, and accountants.

King tried to go in both directions at once, by a path of his own inven-

---

* Police Commissioner Bull Connor had suppressed Birmingham's one tentative student demonstration. When a dozen Negro college students carried placards with religious slogans into a park in a Negro section of the city one night, police officers seized, fingerprinted, photographed, and thoroughly intimidated them at the police station before releasing them with instructions to "be good." Connor issued a terse press release stating that he would not permit such activities. Confident that the local students were not a threat, he worried only about Shuttlesworth and possible threats from afar. "Keep your eyes open for this negro, Lawson," Connor wrote his chief of detectives. "He has been kicked out of Vanderbilt, and I understand he is a Birmingham negro, or an Alabama negro. [Here Connor was in error. Lawson never lived in Alabama.] He may come down here to start some trouble. If he does, you will know what to do with him."

tion. On March 5, he offered Ella Baker's SCLC post to Wyatt Tee
Walker. In so doing, he signaled his refusal to wait any longer for Aber-
nathy. He was accommodating the preachers of the SCLC board, many
of whom had never recognized Baker as anything more than a clerical
caretaker,* but he was insisting that the job be filled by someone of
Baker's activist views and King's own generation. Walker was a hotspur.
As a New Jersey high school student in the 1940s, he had heard Paul
Robeson say that if being for freedom and equality meant being a Red,
then he was a Red. Walker promptly joined the Young Communist
League. One of his high school papers was a five-year plan for a Soviet-
type economy in the United States, and he dreamed of carrying out technically ingenious assassinations against leading segregationists. In college, he acquired dark-rimmed glasses that gave his face the look of a
brooding Trotskyite. No single obsession could contain his ambitions,
however, as Walker identified with the richest industrialists and the best
painters as well as the fiercest revolutionaries. Whatever he did, he
boasted to his peers, he would make a million dollars along the way.

Walker's college advisers steered him toward the pulpit, and his gifts
landed him the historic Gillfield Baptist Church of Petersburg, Virginia.
Organized in 1797, Gillfield was a regional center for the Negro aristocracy, much like Dexter in Montgomery. Until shortly before Walker's
arrival in 1952, the Gillfield congregation had segregated itself by skin
color, with the lighter Negroes sitting on one side and the darker ones
on the other. To preach against the class divide, Walker sought the advice
of Vernon Johns when the renowned preacher drifted to Petersburg upon
his downfall in Montgomery. Walker fell under Johns's spell. He copied
his preaching style, borrowed his books, and sold eggs for one of Johns's
farm cooperatives. The news of the *Brown* decision flashed on the radio
when Walker was chauffeuring Johns to a co-op meeting, and the two
preachers knelt on the shoulder of Virginia's Highway 460 to offer a
prayer of thanks.

Six years later, Walker proved his own enthusiasm for the sit-ins by
going to jail before King's job offer reached him in Petersburg. Spurning
the role of supervisor, he took his wife, his two children, a few other
preachers, and several students to the all-white Petersburg public library.
His budding media consciousness inspired him to appear wearing a clerical collar for the first time in his life. His flamboyant admiration of
Vernon Johns inspired the peculiar act by which he violated the segregation laws: before the eyes of the gathered police and reporters, Walker

---

* Including Wyatt Walker himself, who would always maintain that he succeeded John Tilley instead of Baker.

asked the librarian to give him the first volume of Douglas Southall Freeman's biography of Robert E. Lee. Johns, who admired some of Lee's qualities while despising his cause, often had cited Freeman's book to Walker in his Civil War discourses, and it tickled Walker to think that white Southerners would arrest him for trying to read about their most cherished hero. The Petersburg police chief came forward politely with an offer to post bond for Walker and the others there at the library and thus spare them the indignity of jail, but Walker asked to be treated no differently than normal prisoners. They all spent three days in jail before accepting bail.

Complications of salary and pulpit arrangements delayed Walker's answer to the SCLC offer for months, but the arrest itself only whetted King's desire to hire him. He sent Walker and his companions a telegram of support. Not long thereafter, he sent a similar telegram to Fred Shuttlesworth on his arrest in Birmingham, and he welcomed the invocation of his name by students who escalated the "jail-in" movement in mid-March. From her cell in Tallahassee, having led a march of one thousand students, Pat Stephens issued a public statement: "We could be out on appeal, but we strongly believe that Martin Luther King was right when he said, 'We've got to fill the jails in order to win our equal rights.'" Stephens and four other students became the first to serve out their full sentence, which was sixty days. King praised them, declaring that there was "nothing more majestic and sublime" than their willingness to suffer for a righteous cause.

Only in Atlanta did King mute his praise of the sit-in movement. On March 9, the same day he sent a telegram to Eisenhower protesting what he called a "reign of terror" in Montgomery, King said nothing about the publication of "An Appeal for Human Rights," which had been composed by the Atlanta students. Nor did he comment six days later when the students rebelled against the counsel of the university presidents and mounted sit-in demonstrations. The students, the police, and even the gawking bystanders were almost uniformly courteous. Spelman women wore stockings and gloves as they rode off to be booked. Nearly all the seventy-seven students arrested identified themselves on the police blotter merely by the name of their college.

The Atlanta protest lasted only one day before being smothered under the combined influence of the Negro and white power structures, who appealed for reason and negotiation. Some student leaders complained bitterly of vanity and obstructionism on the part of their elders. C. A. Scott, editor of the Atlanta *Daily World*, had required them to pay the full advertising rate to print their manifesto—either out of greed, they said, or out of a desire to protect himself with the white people against charges of aiding the protest. The students also resented Scott's patronizing editorials, which praised them for having a worthwhile objective but consistently urged them to quit making trouble and leave things in steadier adult hands.

These disputes cut close to King. C. A. Scott was not only an old friend of Daddy King's but also a trustee at Ebenezer, and thus technically one of King's bosses. Furthermore, as editor and controlling partner of the only Negro daily in the South, Scott helped regulate the light in which King himself would be presented to his primary constituents. King had been reared to look at the world through the eyes of established figures like Scott, and he was practical enough to recognize his dependence on them. Jesse Blayton, another pillar of Ebenezer, raised a more pointed reminder to King of his difficult position. Over the years, Blayton had built an accounting business into a parallel career as president of the Citizens Bank, of which Daddy King was a trustee. Since King's indictment in Alabama, Blayton had been going through King's financial records in order to help prepare a defensible accounting. To King's discomfort, Blayton viewed these services more or less the way Scott viewed the publication of the student manifesto—as a commercial transaction. Off the top, he billed King $1,000 for "two weeks studying thesis of case in order to decide patter[n] of working paper procedures," and before he was through he had charged King nearly as much to audit two tax returns as King earned from Ebenezer in an entire year.

Even the lawyers thought Blayton was milking King's predicament with an eagerness ill-suited to a longtime family friend. Their sentiments were little consolation to King, however, especially in light of his financial troubles with the lawyers themselves. He had five of them, led by the NAACP board members Wilkins had recommended. William Ming of Chicago and Judge Hubert Delaney of New York were, respectively, a courtroom lawyer and an appeals expert of high reputations. Arthur D. Shores of Birmingham, the senior man among King's three Alabama lawyers, had been the NAACP's principal lawyer in the state before the NAACP banning order of 1956, which was still in effect. Fred Gray and S. S. Seay, Jr., were the younger men who were supposed to do the bulk of the preparatory work. Each member of the defense consortium was considered legally or politically indispensable, but they made an unwieldy team. Several of the lawyers were strangers to each other. They came from five different firms in four different cities in three different states. At King's expense, they duplicated each other's research and quarreled over the division of responsibility. Worse, they bickered over fees, with the Northerners complaining that the Southerners were charging beyond their competence, and the Southerners complaining that the high-powered Northerners refused to disclose their rates even to their co-counsel. Among the few areas of consensus was a general feeling that King stood almost no chance of winning the tax case before an Alabama jury. This judgment rendered the facts of Blayton's accounting essentially irrelevant and his exorbitant fees that much more painful. The lawyers tried to conjure up a legal issue that might entice an appeals court to overturn a perjury conviction growing out of the tax laws.

King found himself soliciting encouragement from any expert who offered hope, no matter how farfetched or expensive. The dire circumstances of the case stretched his pliant nature to its limits, until he felt that he could not afford to alienate anyone who might conceivably be of help. He realized that the fees he was incurring, while larger than he could reasonably hope to pay, were still smaller than the most important professionals felt entitled to charge for their most important cases. Therefore, King felt a keen mixture of victimization and gratitude, helplessness and faith. He lacked the blunt, personal assertiveness of Stanley Levison, who told the assorted lawyers to their faces that they should be ashamed of themselves for letting their concern over fees cloud King's defense against persecution. Levison lobbied quietly and persistently, protected against resentment by the strength of his own example as the most steadfast and selfless of the professionals who devoted themselves to King. These qualities endeared Levison to King, but King himself was too shy to make demands directly or to equate his interests with those of the civil rights movement. On the contrary, King astonished Levison and Harry Belafonte alike by taking them through long philosophical discussions on the distinction between personal and political obligations. Insisting that he could never allow a penny of "movement money" to be applied to his own personal expenses, King tried to devise unimpeachable guidelines. A traffic ticket was clearly a personal obligation, he stated, but what about the income tax indictment? What circumstances made it political? How could he justify using movement money to defend himself? Belafonte and Levison grew impatient with these quibbles, arguing that Governor Patterson's statements alone put the tax indictment squarely into politics.

In New York, the Committee to Defend Martin Luther King and the Struggle for Freedom in the South, of which Bayard Rustin was executive director, collected enough hard currency by the end of March to pay for a full-page ad in *The New York Times*. Rustin sat down with Harry Belafonte to draft the fund-raising appeal. Entitled "Heed Their Rising Voices,"* the ad followed capsule descriptions of official reactions

---

* A phrase taken from a *Times* editorial of March 19, 1960, which endorsed the sit-in movement as "something new in the South, something understandable."

against the sit-ins with a brief history of the efforts to prosecute and intimidate King. "In Montgomery, Alabama," it read, "after students sang 'My Country 'Tis of Thee' on the State Capitol steps, their leaders were expelled from school, and truckloads of police armed with shotguns and tear gas ringed the Alabama State College Campus . . . " King's perjury indictment, the ad continued, was part of a Southern strategy "to behead this affirmative movement, and thus to demoralize Negro Americans and weaken their will to struggle."

The appeal ran in the *Times* on March 29, after which contributions poured into the King defense committee in sums many times greater than the cost of the ad. A week later, the attorney general of Alabama announced that Governor Patterson had instructed him to examine the possibility of suing the *Times* and the signatories of the ad for libeling the official representatives of Alabama. On April 8, Police Commissioner Sullivan of Montgomery wrote identical letters to each of the four Alabama preachers listed in the endorsement section of the ad—Abernathy, Shuttlesworth, Joseph Lowery of Mobile, and S. S. Seay, Sr.—demanding "a full and fair retraction of the entire false and defamatory matter." This notice came as a chilling surprise to the four ministers, none of whom had known of the ad's existence, much less that their names had been used.

Instantly, fear and alibis began chasing each other through the telephone lines. The four ministers complained bitterly to King that they had not consented to the use of their names. Fearfully, they pointed out technical errors in the text of the ad. The Montgomery students had sung "The Star-Spangled Banner," they said, not "My Country 'Tis of Thee," and the police never had "ringed" the Alabama State campus, in the sense of surrounding it. Instead, the police had massed along one border. The pressure shifted quickly to Rustin, who replied tersely to King that the errors were minuscule. They most certainly were not libelous by any standard. Besides, said Rustin, the four ministers who were complaining about being listed in the paper were the very ones who, in the absence of a threatening letter, would have complained most loudly as SCLC board members if they had *not* been listed. In its preliminary stages of bluster and petty bickering, *Sullivan* v. *New York Times* showed little promise of a landmark Supreme Court case. For King, the most discouraging aspect of the fracas was the pattern: whenever he appealed for help, a reaction seemed to follow that put him deeper into trouble and made help harder to find.

At Highlander Folk School, Myles Horton had been fighting his own desperate legal battle since the previous summer, when a Tennessee prosecutor led a surprise raid on one of Septima Clark's workshops. The deputies hauled away a score of prisoners and a truckload of evidence including a washtub full of ice, soft drinks, and beer, plus a jar of coins. With charges of Communist subversion blocked by facts and the Constitution, prosecutor Ab Sloan fashioned a legal noose out of the washtub and the jar. To Highlander, they merely encouraged visitors to chip in for their drinks, but to the state of Tennessee they were critical proof that Highlander was selling alcoholic beverages without a license. Therefore, Sloan argued, Highlander's charter as a nonprofit corporation should be revoked, and furthermore, since Horton had drawn up the charter without stockholders, under Tennessee law all Highlander property—the land, buildings, even the library—would be forfeit to Tennessee upon dissolution of the charter. It was a confiscation scheme worthy of the Sheriff of Nottingham. Describing Highlander in court as an "integrated whorehouse," Sloan obliterated the facility within two years.* In a parallel case, he managed to obtain a criminal conviction against teetotaler Septima Clark under the moonshine laws.

With these gloomy judgments postponed briefly under appeal, Clark hosted the first regional conference of students involved in the sit-in movement. Nearly a hundred students from nineteen states spent the first weekend of April at Highlander, where they exchanged phone numbers, philosophies, and their favorite tips about how to run a demonstration. A Nashville quartet led by James Bevel performed "You Better Leave Segregation Alone" and other original compositions in close harmony "do-wop" style, drawing great enthusiasm from the audience. The students were suffused with energy, frankly amazed by their introduction to one another and to Highlander. Guy Carawan, Highlander's resident folksinger, taught them old songs that had evolved through the 1930s labor movement into the Highlander repertoire: "We Shall Not Be Moved," "Keep Your Eyes on the Prize," "This Little Light of Mine," "I'm Gonna Sit at the Welcome Table," and "We Shall Overcome."

All this was new, and the spirit of discovery ran so strong that many of the same students journeyed to North Carolina less than two weeks later for a second conference, organized by Ella Baker. She persuaded King to guarantee the expenses with $800, even though the costs of his upcoming criminal trial had drained the SCLC treasury nearly to the bottom.†

* Highlander was first padlocked on September 26, 1959, by order of Judge C. C. Chattin, on charges of selling beer. With the padlocks removed pending appeal, the judge revoked Highlander's corporate charter on February 16, 1960, and when the U.S. Supreme Court refused to intervene, all Highlander property was auctioned under state receivership on December 16, 1961.
† Early in April, King took the drastic step of pledging a $600 contribution to the

With Glenn Smiley and Douglas Moore, Baker made the arrangements with her own alma mater, Shaw University in Raleigh. The trio agreed that James Lawson would serve as "dean" of the conference, with Moore as his assistant.

On April 15, nearly 150 students from nine states poured into North Carolina, where the first sit-ins had erupted ten weeks earlier. Very few of them had heard of Lawson, but his keynote address on the first night created a mass of instant disciples. He spoke in a manner as learned and idealistic as King's. "Love is the central motif of nonviolence," he declared. "Love is the force by which God binds man to Himself and man to man. Such love goes to the extreme; it remains loving and forgiving even in the midst of hostility. It matches the capacity of evil to inflict suffering with an even more enduring capacity to absorb evil, all the while persisting in love." In the same speech, however, Lawson balanced these lofty statements with trenchant realism. "Most of us will be grandparents before we can lead normal lives," he said. He directed withering criticism at the NAACP as "too conservative," charging that *The Crisis,* Du Bois's NAACP journal, was no more than "the magazine of the black bourgeoisie." Lawson denounced the NAACP for its preoccupation with fund-raising and lawsuits. Such a strategy unjustly and unwisely exposed the courts to disrepute, Lawson insisted, by heaping upon them tasks that were inherently political. He attacked the NAACP for begging, for failing to develop what he called "our greatest resource: a people no longer the victims of racial evil, who can act in a disciplined manner to implement the Constitution."

This was strong stuff. Lawson lifted the taboo against NAACP criticism much more directly than did King, who was content to praise the students for "moving away from tactics which are suitable merely for gradual and long-term change." Like Lawson, King swept away the crowd with his speech. He remained the conference's celebrity, but Lawson's frankness carried the appeal of revealed secrets. Many of the students adopted Lawson as their own private discovery. Together, the two leaders inspired an enthusiasm for nonviolent activism such as neither had ever seen. It was the defining, animating zeal of the conference, so readily accepted that the students put the word "Nonviolent" into the name they chose for themselves: Student Nonviolent Coordinating Committee. They were the first civil rights group ever to do so.

This religious fervor coexisted with boisterous student politics. After a vigorous contest between a Morehouse man from Atlanta and a Wyatt Tee Walker protégé from Virginia, the presidency of the new organization

---

SCLC from his own pocket—a tithe of his Ebenezer salary—and challenged all the SCLC board members to do likewise.

went to Marion Barry, who was the most politically skillful of Lawson's Nashville delegation.* Further jockeying broke out over a plan to send SNCC (pronounced *snick*) representatives to the Democratic and Republican conventions that summer. Ella Baker and King wrangled briefly over who the student delegates should be and how they should travel to the Democratic Convention in Los Angeles. In fact, the mild undercurrent of tension between Baker and King became a subject of wonder and gossip at Shaw. Some of the students were astonished to see a woman contradict a man of King's stature. Her character itself was a cultural revelation. As for Baker, who was on her way out of the SCLC again after chafing for more than two years beneath the indifference and condescension of its commanding preachers, she embraced the sit-in movement with the special fervor of a rescued victim. She began to devote herself singlemindedly to the cause of the students, encouraging their independence, warning them against ceremony, educating them on the foibles of their elders.

In later years, a SNCC historian would write that Baker "smashed" King's plans to dominate the students at the Shaw conference. This melodramatic pronouncement greatly exaggerated the sectarian divisions at that time. It was Baker, not King, who drafted testimony for the students to deliver before the platform committees of the two mainstream political parties, and it was Baker who tried to smooth over Lawson's criticisms of the NAACP. "There is no fight," she told reporters, asserting that only a "difference in emphasis" separated the NAACP from the SCLC and the student movement. In philosophy of leadership, Baker was much closer to King than either was to James Lawson, who vigorously opposed all forms of status distinction within the movement, even elections. Lawson, an extreme communalist, believed that leadership hierarchies were invidious—similar in nature to the racial caste system against which they were struggling. Under his influence, the Nashville student movement was structured so that the role of spokesperson rotated among all those who desired to serve.

At Shaw, the prevailing spirit dissolved rather than swelled leadership divisions. Just before King left Raleigh for Washington, where he defended the sit-ins on the "Meet the Press" television show, Lawson and Douglas Moore drew him off for an isolated conference in the bleachers of the Shaw gymnasium. Lawson made an announcement in hushed tones. If King was still serious about the offers he had made over the years, he and Moore would drop everything to work as full-time SCLC staff members.

---

* Barry would be elected mayor of Washington, D.C., eighteen years later.

King responded emotionally. "Oh, yes!" he exclaimed. "That's the best news I've ever heard." It was clear that he recognized the magnitude of the sacrifice his two friends had decided to make. They were willing not only to leave their own pulpits but also to serve under King, their age peer, who had come to nonviolent activism long after they did.

When Lawson asked about Wyatt Walker, whom he knew to be negotiating for Ella Baker's job, King replied that it did not matter. What was important, he said, was to get Lawson and Moore teaching nonviolence to student recruits all over the South. He would find the money somewhere, he said. Lawson and Moore could go into new cities, train nonviolent brigades, and launch demonstration campaigns. King could come in to rally the support forces. Perhaps they could hit two new cities at once. The three of them let loose some of their fantasies before Moore started teasing King about the SCLC board. Would all those Baptists really put two troublemaking Methodists on their payroll? It was well known, quipped Moore, that while Baptists understood kingship, it took a good sober Methodist to build a sound structure. A buoyant King soon left them with a promise that he would make the arrangements within two weeks.

Back in Atlanta, all five of King's lawyers privately delivered a grim appraisal of his chances of spending the new decade outside of prison. As yet they had not settled on a defense strategy. Worse, as they had become acquainted with one another and with the case, none of the five had committed himself to a recommendation as to the most favorable line of argument. They were in a bind. The constitutional issues that the NAACP lawyers had developed in civil rights cases over the years did not apply well to criminal cases involving the tax code. As to the plain facts of the case—whether or not King's income had exceeded what he reported on his tax forms—the lawyers expected the jury to go against them, and they all agreed that King had little chance of getting an appeals court to overturn a jury verdict. This was the dismal picture.

William Ming, an eminent Chicago trial attorney, carried out a delicate mission for the defense team.* The lawyers desperately needed to know how bad things were—how much unreported income King actually had enjoyed—but they despaired of ever learning from Blayton, who seemed happily awash in check stubs and bank statements. Ming privately intro-

---

* In 1947, Ming had helped W. E. B. Du Bois draft a petition urging the new United Nations to recognize that the human rights claims of American Negroes were similar to those of the colonized peoples around the world.

duced to King a young lawyer named Chauncey Eskridge, whom he had brought along from his firm. Explaining that Eskridge was a tax specialist with training as an accountant, Ming asked King's help in getting Blayton to accept help from Eskridge. Ming needed all the diplomacy he had ever used in a courtroom just to make this request of his client. Not only was he asking King to bear the expense of a second accountant, he was also asking him to help push aside Daddy King's friend and benefactor Jesse Blayton, a touchy man certain to resent the intrusion. The lawyers already were fretting among themselves about the harm that a resentful Blayton might do to them on the witness stand, and their sensitivity about such matters raised the tension that permeated Ming's request: he was pressuring King to establish his own innocence. Even in the privacy of consultations with his lawyers, King was still maintaining that he had not diverted to his own use any of the tens of thousands of dollars that passed through his hands every year. Yet he had conceded to newspaper reporters that there "may be some little unintentional mistake[s] in my returns."

Eskridge, who had already heard some of the lawyers laughing among themselves at King's claims of innocence, was left alone with his new client in King's Ebenezer study. He asked how King had prepared his tax returns, and King replied rather sheepishly that he had relied almost exclusively on his diaries. Under prodding, he explained that he always wrote his daily receipts and expenditures into the pocket diary that contained his schedule. Blayton had expressed no interest in the diaries, saying they were not financial records. Hearing this, Eskridge perked up instantly. Diaries could be admissible as tax evidence, he said, although defendants rarely submitted diaries, which were usually more rather than less damaging to them. This was all news to King. When Eskridge asked where his old diaries were, King said he had no idea but that Coretta would probably know. He called home, and when Coretta said she thought the diaries were buried away in an old trunk, he relayed Eskridge's request that she find and deliver them to the church right away.

Soon Eskridge was leafing through the little books. Sure enough, there were notes in King's handwriting on every page, recording travel expenses, contributions, and speaking fees in meticulous detail. For every check received, King had written down what portions he planned to give to the SCLC or the MIA or Dexter, and what portion, if any, he planned to keep. When Eskridge expressed amazement that a person could have such messy and confused bank records and yet keep such a precise diary, King replied that the diary was a habit that had been drilled into him from childhood by Daddy King, who taught that keeping a penny-conscious budget was the first rule of frugality. King readily consented to let Eskridge study the diaries, and as the five principal lawyers gathered for a marathon session with King, the young tax lawyer headed back to the hotel to face an endless day with the diaries, his adding machine, and his work sheets.

King's grueling consultations were interrupted by a series of telephone bulletins from Nashville and Montgomery. The first news was that dynamite had exploded with enough force to demolish the home of Nashville attorney Alexander Looby, damage the two adjoining houses, and blow out 147 windows at the nearby Meharry Medical College. Looby and his wife, asleep in the rear of the house, survived without serious injury. The Nashville police chief was calling the attack the work of killers. "You don't throw that much dynamite to scare somebody," he said. The viciousness of the blast unified Nashville in a flash of trauma so strong that more than three thousand people, including many whites, marched about ten miles through town that very morning.

Mayor Ben West met the enormous crowd of marchers at city hall. He pledged to enforce the law impartially and to do everything possible to catch the bombers, and he defended his leadership in the sit-in crisis by saying that he lacked the power to tell the store owners what to do. "We are all Christians together," he said in the end. "Let us pray together." At this, a student shouted out, "How about eating together?" After the prayer, Diane Nash pushed her way to the microphone to ask the mayor whether he would appeal to all citizens to stop racial discrimination. "I appeal to all citizens to end discrimination, to have no bigotry, no bias, no hatred," West replied.

"Do you mean that to include lunch counters?" asked Nash, pressing the issue. She was standing face to face with the mayor. Her bravado hushed the crowd into silence.

"Little lady," West replied, trying to be genial, "I stopped segregation seven years ago at the airport when I first took office, and there has been no trouble there since."

Nash bored in relentlessly. "Then, Mayor, do you recommend that the lunch counters be desegregated?"

West, a moderate white politician skewered in public before an emotional crowd, answered the crucial question with a single word, "Yes." This drew cheers. The mayor tried desperately to equivocate by reminding everyone that the decision rested with the store owners, but Nash paid no attention. She had her answer.

That same afternoon, crossing the Nashville bulletins, news reached King that Montgomery police commissioner L. B. Sullivan had filed a $500,000 libel suit against *The New York Times* and the four SCLC preachers from Alabama whose names had appeared in Rustin's ad. Governor Patterson, Mayor James, and former commissioner Clyde Sellers were said to be right behind Sullivan with similar suits. These were bizarre cases. None of the plaintiffs had been mentioned by name in the *Times* ad, and each alleged only trivial errors in the narrative facts described in the text. Nevertheless, they took umbrage at the ad, saying that it defamed them by implication. They based their libel claim primarily on Rustin's general characterization of the Southern law enforcement officials as "violators of the Constitution" in their actions to suppress the sit-ins.

From its beginning, the *Sullivan* case confronted the American court system with a delicate political dilemma, and the unbearable sensitivities of race pushed judges into almost surreal extremes of irony. Eventually, the Justices of the U.S. Supreme Court avoided the racial content of the facts by inventing a new standard of law. To do so, they redefined the legal concept of defamation in a case that mentioned no names, and based the standard of allowable news reporting on a paid advertisement that was touched by no reporter and never passed through a newsroom. All this would grow out of a fund-raiser for King's tax trial, but he faced crueler, more immediate ironies. He was meeting with lawyers who did not quite believe him, and who were not even sure whether they would be paid, when word came that the same Alabama officials who were behind his prosecution on the tax case were filing for punitive damages against those cooperating to pay for King's defense. The instant effect of the libel case was to make it even harder for King to raise money. The white authorities of Alabama were serving notice that newspapers willing to publish King's paid messages had to fear that Alabama might haul them into court. For the lawyers, the discouraging news meant that they faced a second troublesome, multiyear case before they had formulated a defense to the first one, and that they stood less chance of collecting fees in either.

By the flinty machismo of those who gamble with lives for a living, King and his counsel managed to eat a good supper and to get off a funny story or two about the calamities of the day. Early the next morning, a tired but clearly awed Chauncey Eskridge cornered some of the lawyers at the Waluhaje Hotel. "Fellas, I got news for you," he declared, holding up his work sheets. "Dr. King didn't take any of that money."

This announcement took the breath of William Ming in particular, who could not believe that any criminal defendant might be less guilty than he had already admitted to the newspapers. Eskridge explained that he had compiled all the figures from King's 1956 diary, and that the income figures netted out to a paltry $368 more than the outside income reported on King's tax return. Even that discrepancy might be explained by minor errors, he said. Eskridge told his colleagues that while it would take much work to verify that King actually did with the monies what the diary said he intended, he, for one, was utterly convinced that King was telling the truth. In fact, he was convinced that King was more honest than anyone he ever hoped to meet.

Leaving the stunned lawyers at the Waluhaje to reassess their strategy, the freshly converted Eskridge hastened to Ebenezer with the exciting result. King maintained his reserve until he was sure he understood the full impact of the report, then suddenly rushed across his study to hug Eskridge like a long-lost cousin. The Chicago tax lawyer dated his interest in politics from that moment. His devotion to King began to grow, splitting him apart from his family and consuming his life with the movement. He would be standing beneath the Memphis balcony at the instant King was shot down.

Much renewed, King excused himself at midday to catch a flight to Nashville, where he was to address an enormous evening rally in the gymnasium at Fisk University. A substantial minority of the crowd was white. Bomb threats intervened before he could speak, causing the police to evacuate the gym for a search. This consumed hours and would have ruined any normal gathering, but in the wake of the Looby bombing, emotions were running too high. Loudspeakers were set up for those left standing outside, and great roars went up when King saluted Lawson's troops as "the best organized and the most disciplined in the Southland." The spirit of their campaign, he declared, was stronger than the ill will in all the bombers and segregation laws arrayed against them. Segregation was surely finished, he said, though he could not say exactly when it would expire. (As it turned out, the Nashville movement broke segregation at six of the major downtown lunch counters only twenty days later.) "No lie can live forever," he said. "Let us not despair. The universe is with us. Work together, children. Don't get weary."

Fortunately for King, he was conditioned not to trust high moments, just as he fought against succumbing to low ones. Scarcely had he returned home from the optimism of Nashville than internecine warfare broke out elsewhere. The first shot landed in the form of a blistering letter from Roy Wilkins. "We were puzzled and greatly distressed at the criticism of the NAACP voiced by the Rev. James Lawson at the Raleigh meeting," Wilkins began. Giving notice that "we feel aggrieved over this unwarranted attack," Wilkins threatened King with responsibility for causing a historic rupture. "I know that you join me in the determination not to have a break between our groups," he warned. "We seek the same goals and have the same enemies. Those enemies would be happier than they have been for forty years if a split should develop." In closing, Wilkins demanded that King make amends, and said there were "other disturbing elements in the picture" that could be discussed only in private conference. The "other elements," as King probably guessed, were his plans to hire Lawson and Moore.

Lawson received the blow secondhand. Just as he was beginning to wonder why he had not heard anything further from King about joining the SCLC, he received a mysterious phone call from the venerable A. J. Muste of the FOR. Muste asked Lawson to meet him at Boston's Logan Airport to receive a message that could not be delivered by telephone. At the airport rendezvous, Muste said that he had been in frequent contact with Martin Luther King lately regarding events in Africa,* and that King had implored him to deliver a most disagreeable message: Roy Wilkins had vetoed Lawson's employment at the SCLC. King said Wilkins had stated flatly that the NAACP would "have no dealings with SCLC, ever," if King allowed Lawson or Moore to join the SCLC staff.

Lawson had trouble believing the news. Furious, deflated, and sad, he asked Muste why he thought King would let Wilkins dictate SCLC hiring policy out of something so petty and misguided as Wilkins' anger about a speech to a student meeting. If Wilkins was so stung by charges that his organization was bourgeois and timid, Lawson fumed, he should make it better. Instead, he was forcing King to make the SCLC more like the NAACP. Muste replied that he could only guess from the way he talked that King did not believe Wilkins was bluffing. Perhaps it was because he had so many prominent NAACP people on his own board, Muste speculated, or perhaps it was because he believed he could not sacrifice NAACP goodwill when he was defending two expensive legal cases that would probably go to the Supreme Court.

---

* Two days after police fired into a crowd of people demonstrating against apartheid in Sharpeville, South Africa, Muste and Bayard Rustin pressured King to attend an upcoming conference in Ghana, which had been called to protest French plans to test atomic bombs in Africa. Muste feared that the worldwide outrage over the "Sharpeville massacre" would push the African anti-colonial movement into violence. "There is probably no one in the world today who can speak more convincingly about nonviolence to Africans than yourself," Muste wrote King, observing shrewdly that increased visibility in Africa would benefit King indirectly in the struggle against segregation at home by making it "harder for any elements here to attack or stop you and your people." King decided not to attend the Ghana conference, sending Abernathy in his place. (Abernathy and Muste were the only two Americans at the meeting.) But King did continue to work with Muste and Rustin to support the anti-colonial movement. On May 5, for instance, he welcomed Kenneth Kaunda—a pro-independence leader of Northern Rhodesia and future president of Zambia—to Ebenezer.

"I think Martin underestimates his strength," Lawson said wearily. In the end, he and Muste decided that his best course was to let it pass. Lawson thanked Muste, saying he knew it was a tortured gesture of kindness on King's part to send someone Lawson respected so much, and he resolved never to speak to King about the episode. But the upshot of the stinging rebuke was to make Lawson more of a loner. Douglas Moore, for his part, heard the news directly from King, who said miserably again and again that he had no choice. Bitterly disappointed, Moore began to disengage from the miracle liftoff of the sit-in movement. By the next year, he had secured a position as a missionary in the Belgian Congo.

King had no time to nurse his regrets. While struggling with legal bills and trial preparations, he made it his first priority to end the chronic confusion over the staff leadership of the SCLC. He stepped up recruitment pressure on Wyatt Tee Walker, whose brash demands quickly confronted King with the first crucial personnel decision of his public career. In substance and in character, Walker offered the prospect of a sharp break with the SCLC's lethargic past. He was prepared to take the fateful leap out of the ministry. If selected, he promised to work a revolution of discipline. Secretaries would not be allowed to have coffee at their desks. He would demand to hear their typewriters humming by nine o'clock in the morning. If the SCLC needed more secretaries, he would find the money. Walker would not mind being known as the one who threatened and insulted people to advance the SCLC's interests. "In fact," he told King, "I'm just mean enough to like it."

He spoke of himself as King's agent, master administrator, and private "son-of-a-bitch." A leader like King, who was accommodating by nature, desperately needed such a person, observed Walker, who offered to assume responsibility for disasters, to promote King's image, and to go so far as to stay out of photographs with King. He would see to it that King reaped the glory. In return, he demanded complete authority within the organization. King must grant him the uncontested right to hire and fire people as he saw fit. King's lieutenants, particularly Bayard Rustin in New York, must cease issuing public statements in King's name unless first cleared with Walker. Ella Baker could stay on in the Atlanta headquarters if she wished, so long as she understood that she would be working for Walker. In addition to this authority, Walker wanted the SCLC to hire two of his friends from Virginia—you cannot run an organization, he said, without having your own people on the staff—and to pay him a salary of $8,000, which was twice what he was making as pastor at Gillfield. It did not bother him in the slightest that this sum

exceeded what King himself earned from Ebenezer. King's income limitation was self-imposed, Walker explained, and he did not share King's
qualms about money.

To King, the chief drawback to Walker's package was Walker himself.
He abounded with brains and zeal, but he embodied little more of the
nonviolent spirit than a locomotive. Also, Walker's military idea of authority was certain to clash with the realities of the SCLC. It was essentially a charismatic organization, and the influences on King's decisions
extended far beyond the SCLC preachers. Somehow King convinced himself that he could have all Walker's virtues while controlling any adverse
effects of his abrasive nature. His only countermove was a subtle one: he
asked Walker to meet privately with Stanley Levison and Bayard Rustin
before taking the job. Walker objected strenuously, saying that Levison
and Rustin were not even on the SCLC board. Why should he meet with
them? Just talk with them, King gently replied, and the result was a two-
day meeting early in May at New York's Sheraton Atlantic Hotel. At its
conclusion, Walker was satisfied that he had established his line of authority. Rustin and Levison were satisfied that they had headed off some
of Walker's moves for power, such as his idea to abolish all of King's
support organizations in New York and to centralize all fund-raising
operations in Atlanta. These were impractical notions, they said, because
most of the money was coming from New York. In the end, the three of
them compromised. When the agreement was sealed, King sent out a
flock of letters to his board members and other key supporters, almost
begging them to contribute at least an extra $100 to the SCLC. The
payroll was about to double in August. "It would be most embarrassing
to bring a man from a substantial church and not be able to pay his
salary," King wrote.

His resignation settled, Walker continued to preach slashing, dazzling
sermons throughout Virginia in support of the sit-ins. His anthem was a
call for unity. Supporters of the sit-ins needed to unify in courage and in
action, he declared. Above all, they needed to unify behind one leader,
and that leader was Martin Luther King. He spoke of King's persecutions,
his needs, his example, his teachings, and his tactics, hailing him as
Moses. (In private, Walker addressed King simply as "Leader.") The
crowds invariably roared in approval. After one rally, in Newport News,
a spectator pushed his way forward to shake hands. Thoughtful concern
was written all over the face of the young man, who had been trained in
philosophy at Harvard. It was all he could do to assert himself among the
jostling crowd of Walker's well-wishers. "Rev. Walker," he said, when
his chance came, "why do you keep saying one leader? Don't you think
we need *a lot* of leaders?"

This was Bob Moses—then a New York high school teacher on a visit to his Virginia uncle. Moses possessed a character almost wholly at odds with his biblical namesake, the original lawgiver of Israel. He was spiritual but not religious, political but not ambitious. The question he put to Walker accurately foretold the axis that always would divide him most sharply from King. They both believed in the spirit of brotherhood, but King believed in the necessity of gods, as interpreted by leaders of rank. Moses did not. His perspective was so alien to that of the Negro church in general, and of Wyatt Walker in particular, that Walker gave him only a quizzical look and passed on without making a reply. Moses shrugged. Having written down during Walker's speech the name and address of the Committee to Defend Martin Luther King, he went back to New York to present himself to Bayard Rustin as a volunteer.

Meanwhile, King stepped into the Montgomery courthouse on May 16 to face arraignment on his income tax charges. Sheriff's deputies on horseback supplemented a phalanx of state troopers and city policemen stationed outside as a precaution against a recurrence of racial demonstrations. Inside the tense courtroom, King joined his five attorneys of record at the defense table, while the new legal assistant, Chauncey Eskridge of Chicago, sat behind them in the special section reserved for Negroes. King's lawyers protested this courtroom segregation itself in one of many legal objections they placed on the record for appeal. They won a postponement, but a barrage of phone calls from Atlanta ruined their strategy meetings that night. Now that King was not to be in court the next day, he became the prize of a fierce lobbying campaign. Atlanta college students wanted him to help them commemorate the sixth anniversary of the *Brown* decision. They had planned to march from Atlanta University to the state capitol for a rally, but Governor Vandiver had just announced that he would use state troopers to prevent any Negro from setting foot on the capitol lawn. Vandiver's warning caused tremors within Atlanta's Negro leadership. The six presidents of the Atlanta University colleges were asking what good could come of it. The students, who had remained mere observers of the sit-in movement since their one-day demonstration in March, pleaded with King to support them, but their elders argued that it would be sheer folly for King to cross the governor of Georgia over something so trivial as an aborted student march. Vandiver's antipathy for King was a matter of public record.

Students gathered the next morning not knowing whether they would march or King would come. Dr. Brawley of Clark College took the most extreme position of the six presidents: he ordered the doors of the gymnasium locked from the outside in an effort to keep the students from marching. But someone slipped out a window to spring the locks, and the Clark students joined an immense tide of students that prayed, caucused, and sang, then surged into the streets 1,500 strong. They marched from the West Side to the perimeter of the capitol grounds, where they found that the governor indeed had posted state troopers with orders not to let them pass. From there, the main body of students retreated eastward through downtown Atlanta—reversing the historical path of Negro migration from the city—toward Auburn Avenue. Borders had agreed to let them hold their rally at Wheat Street Baptist Church. The students had heard radio bulletins that King was flying in from Montgomery expressly to join them, but conflicting rumors buzzed until the head of the column came into sight of Borders and King together at the top of the Wheat Street steps. Waving and beaming, the two preachers greeted the students like victorious pilgrims. A great shout of triumph went back through the line of march, and when the rally began, King commended the students for their nonviolence and for having the courage to take a stand. King praised Borders, Borders praised King, and everyone praised the students—even the college presidents who had urged them not to march. All six turned up on the dais during the rally, giving thanks that their fears had been proven wrong. The goodwill was so pervasive that no one thought ill of the presidents or begrudged them their places of honor.

During the Atlanta student march, white pedestrians stood silently for the most part, gawking at the endless procession. A bewildered woman matter-of-factly said, "I didn't know there were that many niggers *in* college." Her comment, which made the newspapers, was fairly representative of the national state of mind. For the vast majority of Americans who were not directly threatened or inspired by the demonstrations, the very existence of large masses of Negro college students came as a revelation. Hitherto, whites had been able to categorize Negroes as both a class and a race of laborers, because the educated ones they knew tended to be famous, idiosyncratic by definition and set apart from ordinary life. Even in the North, white-collar Negroes were an uncommon sight in the downtown business districts. Now, suddenly, their presence in sufficient numbers to clog streets or fill up jails began to register, and more than a few members of the majority culture wondered how they would fit into the greater scheme of things.

For those millions who did not happen to witness a live march, the civil rights issue remained a distant cause, arousing variously curiosity, foreboding, or hope. Sit-in stories from anywhere outside one's hometown played on the inside pages along with the wildcat coal strikes and the news that the government had approved an invention called the birth control pill. In the spring of 1960, the stories that dominated the front pages tended to reverberate homeward from overseas. Even the most prominent race stories came not from Dixie but from Africa. When police in Sharpeville, South Africa, opened fire on a crowd of blacks demonstrating peacefully against the hated identity-card laws of apartheid—killing sixty-nine people, most of whom were shot in the back—dispatches shocked readers all over the world. The Eisenhower Administration denounced the South African government for its repression. Foreign capital began fleeing South Africa in multimillion-dollar chunks. Photographs of Africans burning their identity cards appeared on American front pages above stories featuring riots and predictions of the final rebellion. The tension faded, however, as the South African government simply jailed 13,000 suspicious Africans without trial. Neither the African blacks nor their white liberal supporters had an answer to state power unchecked by law or qualm.

In May, not long after the Sharpeville massacre, secret agents snatched former S.S. colonel Adolph Eichmann out of Argentina for transport to Israel, where his trial for Nazi war crimes against Jews made him world famous as the man in the glass booth, on his way to the gallows, and intellectuals debated how this bland technocrat fit with the global image of evil incarnate that had fastened upon the Nazis in the fifteen years since Hitler's death. Across that same span, the world had struggled to comprehend a successor evil that was, like Eichmann, too real to be comprehensible: the specter of thermonuclear war. In early May, all 160 million Americans participated in a national air-raid alert, the seventh since U.S. officials had acknowledged that the Russians might be capable of raining nuclear warheads down on the Western Hemisphere. As before, schoolchildren crawled under their desks, Wall Street closed, television screens went blank, and American leaders set examples by scurrying into underground bomb shelters. The consumption of electricity in New York dropped 90 percent for half an hour.

On May 5, as devilish Civil Defense officials were putting government executives through a surprise repeat of the national air-raid drill, word reached Eisenhower in his top-secret North Carolina command bunker that Khrushchev was claiming publicly that the Soviets had shot down an American spy plane. Reacting instinctively to protect the secrecy of the U-2, and on the assumption that both the CIA pilot and his plane were destroyed, Eisenhower ordered release of the cover story that a weather plane must have strayed off course. The next day, when the President was back in Washington to sign the Civil Rights Act of 1960 into law, he confirmed the weather plane story to reporters, and the day after that Khrushchev sprang his trap, announcing that the Soviets had captured Francis Gary Powers alive and would prove to the world that he had been flying no weather plane. This should have finished the tale, but Eisenhower, reeling in shock, authorized another cover story. The State Department admitted that it was a spy plane but blamed Powers as a renegade, asserting that he had no orders to fly over the Soviet Union. When this flimsy claim did not last a single day, the White House acknowledged the bare essential truth, but Eisenhower could never bring himself to admit that he had personally approved each U-2 flight. "I would like to resign," he said despondently in the White House. In public, he never lost confidence. A week later, he flew to Paris for a summit meeting, only to watch a sputtering, sarcastic Khrushchev brand the United States a pirate nation and walk out. Eisenhower flew home again on May 17, as King was greeting Atlanta's marching students at the Wheat Street Church.

The U-2 was so important an event that millions denied its importance, rallied to the flag, and routinely denounced the Russians. What lingered beneath were memories of Ike's humiliation, of the first great lie, the public debut of the CIA in a vaguely sinister context, and the first serious puncture in the American innocence that had swelled up since Eisenhower's war.

In spite of the unnerving headlines from abroad, the country exhibited a mood of tranquil optimism. Distant crises were exciting, after all, and at home the United States left behind the bitterness of the McCarthy years while building its "economic miracle" through an unbroken generation, with no sign of slowdown in sight. Americans had licked polio. Cancer was next. A majority of employees wore white collars, and economists puzzled over the enigma of surplus, wondering what else people could want. "Gone for the first time in history is the worry over whether a society can produce enough goods," *Time* had announced. Automobiles were everywhere, and those who turned on their car radios were most likely to hear the strings of the Percy Faith orchestra playing the winsome "Theme from *A Summer Place*," which was the number one song that spring. By the end of the year, adults and kids alike were trying the new dance craze called "the twist," introduced by an orphan singer from Philadelphia named Chubby Checker. There was a rapprochement between age groups. Adults were cooler, teenagers less wild.

Building all through the year—laid down along the heart of the culture somewhere between the threats of holocaust and the gurgle of pop entertainment—was the presidential campaign. The contest for the Democratic nomination drew a host of candidates, each of whom was perceived to have a fatal flaw. Senate Majority Leader Lyndon Johnson enjoyed the

support of nearly every leading Democrat in Congress, but he and everyone else knew that no pure Southerner had run successfully for President
in more than a hundred years. Adlai Stevenson, the best-known Democrat, was a two-time loser to Eisenhower. Like Johnson, he was loath to
expose himself to loss and therefore played Hamlet in public as to
whether he would run at all. Senator Hubert Humphrey of Minnesota
suffered no such restraint, but he was not very well known, and his
reputation as a champion of civil rights and labor unions was thought to
confine the range of his appeal. Senator John Kennedy of Massachusetts
began with a limited political network as a result of his run for the vice
presidency at the 1956 convention, but he was young and he was Roman
Catholic.

Early bickering among the Democrats seemed to work to the advantage
of Vice President Nixon, who was all but assured of his party's nomination. He faced no Republican opponent except possibly New York governor Nelson Rockefeller, who wanted to run but could not bring himself
to say so. Possessed of broader experience than any of the Democrats,
and with the mantle of Eisenhower at least formally on his shoulders,
Nixon was shrewd enough to warn against the sort of complacency that
had led to Dewey's upset by Truman in 1948. Theirs was still a minority
party, he kept reminding his supporters, and he was not Eisenhower.
"Anyone who does not recognize that we are in for the fight of our lives
must be smoking opium," he told Nebraska Republicans.

Kennedy eliminated Humphrey from the race by winning early primaries in Wisconsin (next door to Humphrey's home state) and in the
Protestant stronghold of West Virginia. The unannounced candidates
grumbled that Kennedy's wit and glamour were seducing the party toward defeat, and the leading Democrats looked on the new front-runner
with distaste. Only two senators endorsed him for the nomination.
Eleanor Roosevelt continued to campaign for Stevenson, making scathing remarks about Kennedy as a puppet of his millionaire father and a
coward in the battle against McCarthyism.* Adam Clayton Powell continued to support Johnson, the Southern wheeler-dealer. Former president Harry Truman said he was for Senator Stuart Symington or for
Johnson—anybody but Kennedy—and he felt so strongly as to scold Kennedy on television just before the convention. "Senator, are you certain
that you are quite ready for the country, or that the country is ready for
you?" he asked.

---

* Kennedy had been the only Democratic senator who neither voted for nor
announced his support of the historic censure resolution against McCarthy in
1954.

Race played a large role in the campaign, less because of the civil rights movement than because the polls were showing the Negro vote to be divided and volatile. The candidates competed intensely for Negro votes, but they tried to do so in ways that would generate as little controversy as possible among whites. Subtle-minded readers of *Jet* magazine knew Lyndon Johnson was serious about running for President when they saw the "exclusive" posed photograph of LBJ with a Negro leader in the March 3 issue. The hypersensitive Johnson never had allowed such a photograph to be published, for fear of losing votes in Texas. Two months later, Johnson wore brand-new contact lenses on a "non-candidate" campaign tour of three primary states, and all the while he was welcoming Negroes into his Taj Mahal along with everyone else he could corral.

Johnson had many endorsements but few convention delegates. Kennedy had the reverse problem, which proved to be the better one, but the candidate himself worried that his strategy might not win him certain blocs of voters, including Negroes. His insecurities peaked when he allowed a campaign aide to talk him into attending an NAACP dinner, only to have Jackie Robinson refuse to have his picture taken with Kennedy on the grounds that he was a Republican. Stung and embarrassed, Kennedy left, saying he thought Robinson was for Humphrey. This was true, he learned, but Robinson considered himself a Republican for Humphrey, and if Humphrey did not win the nomination, the former Dodgers star might support Nixon. Hard on this intelligence came the rumor that even Roy Wilkins felt misgivings about Kennedy, and sympathized privately with Lyndon Johnson. "We're in trouble with the Negroes," said campaign manager Robert Kennedy. He assigned Harris Wofford, the white Gandhian lawyer whom King had known since the boycott, to work full time on the Negro vote.

Senator Kennedy himself was so alarmed by his lack of feel for race politics that he decided to investigate personally. One night late in May, he carved a hole in his campaign schedule, jettisoned his retinue of advisers, planners, and noisemakers, and instructed his driver to wait for him outside Harry Belafonte's apartment building on New York's West End Avenue. After introducing himself to Belafonte and thanking him for agreeing to the hastily arranged visit, Kennedy came straight to the point. He said he knew Belafonte was for Stevenson. That was all right, he could understand it. But Kennedy was looking ahead to the fall campaign against Nixon. He was worried about Jackie Robinson, and he had two favors to ask. Could Belafonte explain to him how someone like Jackie Robinson could ever endorse Nixon for President, and would Belafonte consider organizing Negro stars for Kennedy, to offset the political damage of Robinson's likely defection?

Belafonte, who remained convinced that Stevenson would win the Democratic nomination, made small talk as he absorbed the many surprises of his first few seconds with Kennedy—the candidate's assumption so early in the contest that he would win the nomination, his sharp intuition that Jackie Robinson was a political problem that he must address forcefully, his capacity to ask penetrating questions and request brash favors under cover of his charm. Belafonte replied that he could understand why Robinson and other prominent Negroes did not prefer Kennedy among the Democratic candidates. Kennedy was an unknown to them, without friendships or even acquaintances, and he had no record of sympathy with the cause of civil rights. Belafonte confessed, however, that he had no better idea than Kennedy why Jackie Robinson might endorse Nixon. He considered Nixon anathema for his role as a leader of the McCarthy witch-hunts, during which Du Bois had been arrested, Paul Robeson driven from the country, and Belafonte himself partially blacklisted. On civil liberties grounds alone, said Belafonte, he would do everything he could to help Kennedy defeat Nixon, if Kennedy won the nomination. In the course of the long strategy session that followed, Belafonte recommended above all that Kennedy establish a close relationship with Martin Luther King.

"Why do you see him as so important?" Kennedy asked. "What can he do?"

Belafonte paused. It was clear to him that Kennedy was not being snide or argumentative. The senator saw King as an unfamiliar preacher who had once led a bus boycott in Alabama and was now facing trial on income tax charges. What was King in comparison with the nearly universal appeal of Belafonte or Jackie Robinson, who could sway Negro voters without alienating white ones? Belafonte tried to explain to Kennedy his belief that the Negro vote no longer could be contested on the basis of popularity, because civil rights was building to the status of a sacred cause. He said he was not a religious man himself but had seen and felt King's impact. Its strength was not reflected in either the white or Negro press. "Forget me," he advised Kennedy. "Forget Jackie Robinson and everybody else we've been talking about. If you can join the cause of King, and be counselled by him, then you'll have an alliance that will make the difference."

Kennedy, always nodding, asking more questions, thanking Belafonte for the information, made no commitments and disclosed no plans. At the end of nearly three hours' discussion, he made his way back downstairs to his car. Belafonte called King almost immediately with a report on Kennedy, whom he described as unschooled and unemotional but very quick. He recommended that King make every effort to get to know

Kennedy. King was receiving the same advice from Harris Wofford, who was promoting Kennedy to King and King to Kennedy. Like Belafonte, Wofford was a Stevenson man. Even after joining Kennedy's staff, in fact, he kept up his contact with the reluctant candidate from Illinois. He wrote a letter commending King to Stevenson, a copy of which he sent King "in strictest confidence," hoping to make sure that no one in the Kennedy camp would discover that he was still consorting with the enemy.

On May 22, King took his seat at the defendant's table in Judge James J. Carter's Montgomery courtroom, charged with perjury. There were legal motions and futile skirmishes over segregation in the spectator area as well as the jury box, but the prosecutors managed to introduce by the third day a mountainous pile of 999 exhibits—mostly copies of deposit slips and checks payable to King. The state's case built smoothly until King's strutting Chicago barrister, William Ming, cross-examined the chief prosecution witness, Lloyd D. Hale, the state revenue auditor who had appeared at the Dexter parsonage back in January to demand payment of back taxes. Ming tried to make the prosecution's blizzard of numbers backfire by asking Hale how the state had arrived at its own estimate of King's income. Hale admitted that he had made his calculations pretty much spontaneously, on the same day he had visited King. Furthermore, Hale testified, the state of Alabama was *still* not sure how much money King had earned in 1956, the year in question. These answers were highly favorable to the defense. Ming studied Hale, a clearly troubled man who seemed to make an effort to be objective in his characterization of King, and decided to pose an extremely dangerous question. Did Hale remember telling King that day at the parsonage that there was no evidence of fraud in the tax return, he asked. Hale said he did. This testimony drew gasps from spectators, who were shocked to hear a white Alabama civil servant give comfort to a Negro in Alabama's most visible, and blatantly political, trial.

The prosecutors seemed agitated as they rested their case; the defense remained subdued. The facts lay somewhere in a maze of numbers, and King had never won a case in an Alabama court. The defense lawyers put R. D. Nesbitt on the stand to tell the jury how fiercely King had resisted the salary increases the Dexter trustees tried to force upon him, and Morehouse's President Mays led a string of distinguished character witnesses. Still, defense hopes for a mistrial were so dim that King's lawyers, after furious internal argument, took the ultimate risk of putting King himself on the stand. As expected, the prosecutors in cross examination ridiculed King's descriptions of the daily financial notations in his little diaries and battered him with questions designed to maximize the jury's political hostility. This high price the defense lawyers were willing to pay so that King could corroborate Hale's testimony about their conversation in the parsonage on the day of the tax ambush. After King stepped down, the defense lawyers called as their final witness the accountant and Ebenezer trustee J. B. Blayton, who told incomprehensible tales of accounting inventions such as the geographic-median-airfare method he had used to estimate King's legitimate travel deductions for 1956. Somehow, from all the numbers he threw into the air, Blayton pulled the precise figure of $235.16 as the paltry amount of King's undeclared income. Even that, Blayton testified, could be explained by an alternative expense formula. Throughout Blayton's testimony, Chauncey Eskridge muttered to himself that Blayton was merely grafting bowdlerized accounting jargon to the results of Eskridge's own calculations. Eskridge knew, however, that Blayton's expostulations might be helpful, because the defense had an equal right to lay claim to the benefits of confusion.

The courtroom bristled with acrimony on Saturday, May 28, the morning of closing arguments. Extra reporters jammed in for the climax of the trial, including one Negro reporter who touched off the day's first controversy by taking a seat in the white spectator section. Bailiffs ordered him to move. The jury deliberated for some three hours and forty-five minutes, nearly every moment of which was the occasion for new speculative interpretations by someone in the anxious crowd. When the words "Not guilty" were pronounced, Daddy King and Mother King burst into tears along with Coretta, and Delaney's emotion overcame him as he rose to praise the judge for his conduct of the trial. Judge Carter banged his gavel against the rising tide of hallelujahs, sobs, and moans of relief, and then he ordered the bailiffs to evacuate the courtroom row by row and march the predominantly Negro crowd out of the courthouse in single file in order to forestall demonstrations of joy. Outside, special units of highway patrolmen prevented any clusters or huddles, with the result that the Negroes, too happy or too shocked to do otherwise, marched single file all the way to Dexter Avenue Baptist Church. King, who had received the verdict passively, having prepared himself to be marched off to jail, rearranged himself enough to speak a single sentence to the reporters who surrounded him outside the courthouse: "This represents great hope, and it shows that there are hundreds of thousands of white people of good will in the South, even though they may disagree with our views on integration." Judge Delaney could only say that the acquittal was "the most surprising thing in my 34 years as a lawyer."

King joined the long procession back to Dexter for a spontaneous church service, during which he and Abernathy asked the young people to lead them in singing a song called "We Shall Overcome." It was a Negro hymn dating to the pre-gospel era of the early twentieth century that had been transported by South Carolina tobacco workers to Highlander Folk School, where it had been adapted for protest.* Since Septima Clark's Highlander workshop in April, the song had been spreading rapidly among the students of the sit-ins. Simple strains and dogged sincerity made the hymn suitable for crisis, mourning, and celebration alike, as many adults discovered when they heard the song for the first time that day.

On leaving Dexter, Coretta and Abernathy split off to keep church speaking engagements, while King rode home to Atlanta with his mother and father. To the homecoming crowd that filled Ebenezer the next morning, King preached a revealing sermon entitled "Autobiography of Suffering." He had not spoken out previously about all his persecutions, he said, for fear that people might think he was playing for sympathy. Now he reviewed them in detail—from the bombings of the bus boycott and the near-fatal stabbing in Harlem to all the outrages of the trial just ended. The sermon was a cry of complaints let loose, but the litany was so sweet and self-focused that King seemed to be engaged, if not enlivened, by the record of his own ordeals. This was not a new theme with him. It reached toward the innocent pathos of a messiah, but King did not give in completely to somber melodrama, and he certainly did not entertain the belief that the acquittal was the result of his own mystical powers. He joked about how the state of Alabama had fought to provide him with free housing for a few years, and he described the verdict as a quirk. Perhaps the twelve jurors had discovered a point of identity with King as a common victim of the loathsome tax audit that was stronger even than the separation of the races. Or perhaps this jury, unlike pre-

---

* "We Shall Overcome" is generally traced to "I'll Overcome, Some Day," which was written in the World War I era by Rev. C. A. Tindley of Philadelphia. Tindley was a prime influence on Thomas A. Dorsey, the father of modern gospel music. The gospel rhythms, along with the quartet styles and other modes of religious music pioneered by Tindley and Dorsey, became so popular that they burst out of the black churches into concert halls and even nightclubs during the Depression. Later, through pop music and the civil rights movement, they registered strongly among millions in the majority white culture who remained ignorant of the origins in black sacred music. One small indication of the astonishing range of early gospel is the fact that Tindley wrote not only the model for the anthem of the civil rights movement but also "Stand By Me," a title which Ben E. King of the Drifters adapted to puppy romance and made into a hit rock 'n' roll song.

vious ones, had seen some truth too glaring to overlook. In any case, segregation remained. King gave thanks for the welcome verdict without pretending to explain it. "Something happened to the jury," he told his congregation.

EIGHT

SHADES OF POLITICS

On the Monday after King's acquittal, Governor Patterson sent a strong message to anyone who may have doubted that the pride of Alabama had been invested in the perjury prosecution: he filed a $1,000,000 libel suit based on the *New York Times* advertisement that Rustin had written to raise funds for the King defense. Patterson's suit differed from the one filed earlier by Police Commissioner Sullivan of Montgomery in that he named King himself as a defendant, even though King's name did not appear as a sponsor of the advertisement. The governor sued the *Times* in spite of the fact that the newspaper had published, in response to his formal demand, a full retraction of all assertions that may have given offense to Alabama officials. Simultaneously, Patterson launched a retribution that King felt even more closely: he ordered President Trenholm of Alabama State to fire a dozen of King's friends and supporters on the faculty, including his biographer L. D. Reddick, his old friend Robert Williams, and Jo Ann Robinson, who had helped draft the women's boycott petition on the night of the Rosa Parks arrest. Reddick was fired outright, and the others resigned in order to spare Trenholm the agony of his decision.

Aside from hurting King personally and threatening the extinction of his organization, the vendetta compounded the difficulties of his political objectives in the presidential election. Patterson supported Senator

Kennedy for President, having formed a political acquaintance at the 1956 Democratic Convention. In fact, Patterson had endorsed Kennedy in 1959, so early and so enthusiastically as to embarrass Kennedy. King was trying to move Kennedy and the Democrats away from Patterson's segregationist demands. To do so, he needed to find pressures that were strong enough not to compromise his own principles and yet not so strident as to leave the presidential candidates room to cultivate the millions of voters who felt more in common with Patterson than with King. The task was at once delicate and grossly brutal. Most of King's lobbying was as clandestine as Patterson's was public.

Among the Democrats, King had a well-positioned ally in Congressman Chester Bowles, the former governor of Connecticut and ambassador to India. Bowles was chairman of the platform committee for the Democratic Convention, and as such possessed considerable influence over the party's civil rights plank. He was enough of a regular politician to be on Harry Truman's approved list of presidential candidates, but he shared with King a passion for Gandhian nonviolence as well as a long-time acquaintance with Harris Wofford. The three of them, in concert with Bayard Rustin and many others, worked to draft an "ideal" civil rights plank for the Democratic platform, and to advance it against Southern opposition with tactics that included plans for a picket line outside the Los Angeles Convention Center. The conspirators worked secretively. Wofford especially did not want his Kennedy bosses to know that he was working with King and Bowles, because he knew they harbored a dislike for Bowles as an egghead. Worse, the top Kennedy aides believed Bowles was a rival for the nomination, using the civil rights issue to establish himself as the liberal dark-horse candidate.

Wofford operated from an insecure position within the Kennedy campaign, roughly analogous to that of E. Frederic Morrow in the White House. He held what was traditionally a separate and minor portfolio in national political campaigns, tasked with "getting out the black vote" by whatever means necessary. Although Sargent Shriver, his immediate boss, was married to a sister of John and Robert Kennedy, Shriver was merely an in-law, teased for being too liberal. His nickname within the family was "Boy Scout." Ted Sorensen, Senator Kennedy's closest aide, advised Wofford at their first meeting not to become too closely associated with Shriver, because the insiders thought of him as the "house Communist." As always, it was said partly in jest, but the attitude was daunting to Wofford. Those closest to Senator Kennedy were driving hard to reach the average voter in the fifty-first percentile of victory. If they thought of Sargent Shriver—the highly successful manager of patriarch Joseph Kennedy's Chicago Merchandise Mart, himself the scion of a pre-

Revolutionary Maryland family—as sentimental, impractical, and pink-ish, they were not likely to be enamored of King.

It was all Wofford could do to schedule a meeting between Kennedy and King, as Harry Belafonte had suggested. This was finally arranged for breakfast on June 23, in the New York apartment of Kennedy's father. It turned out to be a hurried introduction and a general talk. In Washington, Wofford waited as anxiously as any matchmaker, hoping the two of them would like each other. When it was over, he chose to put a positive interpretation on the rather neutral reports he received from the two sides. All Kennedy had to say was that he felt he had "made some prog-ress" in winning King's support. King, who was rushing to go overseas, told Wofford that the meeting had been pleasant but that Kennedy lacked a "depthed understanding" of the civil rights issue.

Shortly after meeting King, Senator Kennedy made his most direct campaign statement on the lunch counter sit-ins, telling a group of Afri-can diplomats that "it is in the American tradition to stand up for one's rights—even if the new way to stand up for one's rights is to sit down." Such favorable comments may have been partially the result of King's lobbying, but Kennedy seemed to aim them more pointedly at Jackie Robinson. A week after the King breakfast, Kennedy held a summit meeting with Robinson, the result of which was a publicly released letter from Kennedy promising full support for Negro rights. Robinson told reporters that he was "not nearly as critical as I have been," but he stopped short of endorsing Kennedy.

By then, King had flown to the convention of the Baptist World Alli-ance in Rio de Janeiro, where he urged his fellow Baptists to recognize the religious context of political freedom. More than a few conservative ministers were uncomfortable with King, but evangelist Billy Graham supported his church ambitions by hosting a banquet in King's honor. While in Rio, King received a nasty introduction to the underside of presidential politics. An emissary from Congressman Adam Clayton Powell contacted him with the message that if King did not call off his plans to picket the Democratic Convention in Los Angeles, Powell would tell the press that King was having a homosexual affair with Bayard Rustin. In a panic, King decided to call A. Philip Randolph, his co-sponsor for the picket lines, but Randolph was out when the inter-national call came through, and the person who picked up the phone in New York was none other than Rustin, who frequently worked out of Randolph's office. King, in acute discomfort, gradually disclosed to Rus-tin the substance of the threat. The two men kept asking each other if the threat was real. Both knew that the mercurial Powell was capable of bizarre deeds of political intimidation, but this was stretching the bounds. If Powell did carry out his threat, however, it would matter very little that his charge was untrue. The mere assertion would be extremely damaging, especially since many reporters and most of the active Negro preachers knew of Rustin's homosexual "problem," which lent credence to the charge.

Randolph's first reaction was to find out what Powell was up to. He knew that Powell was under enormous stress. Some of his congressional aides had been convicted of kicking back part of their government salaries to Powell, who had just been saved by a hung jury himself at another of his tax trials. Powell faced others, including imminent libel action by a Harlem woman he had denounced on television as a "bag woman" for corrupt police.* Worst of all, Tammany Hall Democrats, still bitter over Powell's endorsement of Eisenhower in 1956, were working through their alliances in the national Democratic Party to deny Powell his chairmanship of the House Education and Labor Committee. By seniority, Powell was in line to become the first Negro chairman of a major standing committee in the history of the U.S. Congress.

All across the board, Randolph figured, Powell was moving to protect himself with the regulars, while King and Randolph were plotting with the mavericks. Powell favored Lyndon Johnson or Stuart Symington, the presidential candidates supported by the congressional leadership. He was courting organized labor, which he would need for his chairmanship, at the same time that Randolph's quarrel with AFL-CIO president George Meany over union racism was growing into a public standoff. Powell also remained friendly with J. H. Jackson. In the end, Randolph decided not to delve into the mess or talk with King at all. His method was simple: he instructed Rustin to call King in Rio with the message that Randolph

---

* This was the famous Esther James case, which would hound Powell for the rest of his life. Over the next decade, more than eighty judges in ten different courts would be called upon to rule on such questions as whether the House of Representatives had the constitutional power to expel Powell for standing in contempt of court orders to pay Mrs. James. As often happened with Powell, his own flamboyance and the race issue publicly overwhelmed the substantive origins of the dispute. His attack on Mrs. James, first delivered in a speech to the House and then repeated on March 6, 1960, on television, was but a small part of an extremely detailed investigation of police corruption in Harlem. New York police officers were taking payoffs to protect the numbers racket and other vices, he said, naming Mrs. James almost incidentally as one of those helping to collect the payments. Ironically, his charges of corruption would be substantiated in spectacular police scandals that developed after his death. But most New York politicians and newspapers dismissed his original campaign as a political slur on the New York police department. From there, the popular fiction grew that Powell's troubles started with a capricious ad hominem attack on Mrs. James.

was going ahead with the plans he announced, and that if King pulled out, Randolph would have no choice but to say King had done so at the request of Powell. In effect, this was friendly counter-blackmail.

Rustin made the call, which was at least as difficult for him as for King. He was still very much a closeted homosexual. Moreover, Rustin knew that his personal liabilities were once again burdening not only King but possibly the cause itself. This was not a pleasant thought for him. King received the message with a stoic acknowledgment that bordered on approval. He flew from Rio to Los Angeles as planned. Nothing changed except for the personal feelings among the four men, which never fully recovered.

In Los Angeles, the frantic machinations of an undecided contest boosted the normal convention chaos to a hyperkinetic state. Kennedy was picking up delegates by the handful and was said to have nearly enough to win, but his front-runner status failed to win over the stalwarts of the party. Eleanor Roosevelt and Walter Lippmann publicly urged him to step aside in favor of the more seasoned Adlai Stevenson. Negro voters disliked Kennedy, Mrs. Roosevelt declared, adding that he would do better "to grow and learn" as Stevenson's running mate. A spokeswoman for Lyndon Johnson charged that Senator Kennedy suffered from Addison's disease, which was true, and "would not be alive today if it were not for cortisone," which was probably not true, but the Kennedy campaign, running hard on youth and vigor, flatly denied it all. Lyndon Johnson himself attacked Kennedy by alluding to the reputation of Joseph Kennedy as an appeasing isolationist during his prewar service as U.S. ambassador to Great Britain. "I wasn't any Chamberlain umbrella policy man!" he shouted. "I never thought Hitler was right!"

The hotels surrounding the convention hall swarmed with dealmakers and rumors of deals. A few minutes after non-candidate Hubert Humphrey first arrived at the Statler-Hilton, his longtime supporter Joseph Rauh rushed up puffing to the door of his suite. Rauh, the ADA founder and veteran civil rights lobbyist, pushed partway inside before being firmly repulsed by unseen doorkeepers. "I've got to see Hubert!" Rauh shouted, pounding the door in flustered surprise. He had an urgent deal to propose: if Humphrey would endorse Kennedy immediately, securing his nomination, Kennedy might make Humphrey his running mate. Rauh ran around to another door. This time he heard the unmistakable belly laugh of Lyndon Johnson—arch-foe of Kennedy, civil rights, and Rauh alike—but before Rauh could force his way inside to find out what Johnson was doing there, a Humphrey aide shoved Rauh back into the

hallway and decked him with a punch to the jaw. It dawned on Rauh
even as the concussion rattled through his head that he was too late.
Humphrey would endorse Stevenson as part of a convoluted three-step
scheme just sealed with Johnson. In step one, Humphrey would hold his
small bloc of delegates for Stevenson long enough to deny Kennedy the
nomination on the first ballot. Realistic delegates would then desert both
Kennedy and Stevenson to nominate Johnson in step two, and step three
was that Johnson would name Humphrey as his running mate.

At the Shrine Auditorium, Wilkins, Randolph, King, and Adam Clayton Powell presided harmoniously over a meeting of some 250 Negro
delegates. Each of the presidential candidates was invited to appear in
person, or to send a message to the group. Kennedy came himself and
was booed so lustily on making his entrance that the NAACP's Clarence
Mitchell had to shout for decorum. Kennedy's witty candor earned scattered applause at his exit, but it could not match the reception accorded
Hubert Humphrey, who declared that he would rather stand up for civil
rights than attain any political office in the land, including the presidency. When the candidates had departed, Adam Clayton Powell outdid
them all. He began to preach, and all the delegates jumped to their feet
in cheering applause as he called for "a revolution of passive, massive
resistance." Then came King, speaking in his deeper tones and slower
rhythms but building to the same heights. "We have a determination to
be free in this day and age," he declared.

The three student sit-in leaders who had been selected at the Raleigh
conference back in April were allowed to testify before the platform
committee, reading a statement drafted mostly by Ella Baker. King also
testified, then disappeared in the company of Clarence Jones and Michael
Harrington, the two men Bayard Rustin had recruited to staff the civil
rights agenda for the convention. Jones, a California entertainment lawyer married to a wealthy white publishing heiress, most reluctantly had
provided some paid legal research for King's defense on the perjury
charge. In manner and appearance, he and his working partner were an
odd pair—Jones with his handsome ebony face, sports car, tailored suits,
colognes, European accessories, and brisk executive style, and Harrington with the weathered impish face of an Irishman who had been discussing socialism every night for ten years in the same New York bar,
wearing blue jeans and a Dodgers baseball cap. Together, they briefed
King about the past month's infighting among the local civil rights activists.

On Sunday, July 11, the day before the convention officially began,
King, Randolph, and Wilkins led a march of about five thousand people
—two or three times the expected number—through the streets of Los

Angeles to the Sports Arena. They all gathered on the grounds for an NAACP-sponsored rally, at which a surprise guest appeared in the person of Democratic National Committee chairman Paul Butler, who welcomed the marchers and promised that the party would soon enact a civil rights plank to meet their approval. Cheers went up for Butler. King and Wilkins addressed the crowd, as did Adam Clayton Powell, who vanished before the picket lines were set up at the conclusion of the rally.

Organized into teams and shifts, the picketers vowed to keep up a round-the-clock vigil until the delegates inside approved the Bowles civil rights plank. The motley line, numbering anywhere from a few dozen up to a few hundred at a time, came to include a carload of white Cornell students who drove cross-country from New York, as well as church groups and off-duty members of Randolph's Brotherhood of Sleeping Car Porters. Through the long days and nights ahead, the spectacle developed as a minor feature story for journalists. King himself took several shifts on the line, where, buffeted by mixed crowds of reporters, well-wishers, and hostile segregationists, he impressed Harrington with his equanimity. After the first day of the convention, Harrington and Jones took turns escaping with King to hideaways, where Harrington found himself in long soulful dialogues on Hegel and Max Weber. King's discourses on such topics as the similarities between the Social Gospel and the ethical principles of socialism convinced Harrington that he was talking with someone who was essentially a socialist. This drastically altered Harrington's expectations of a Negro Baptist preacher from the South.

Clarence Jones was more impressed by King's lighter side. King teased Jones about his California-paradise lifestyle, including the tropical tree in his living room that grew through the retractable roof of his canyon-side ranch house. Introduced to Jones's wife Ann, King liked her so much that he quickly began calling her "Doctor," the honorary title he had bestowed since high school on women he found classy and attractive. "Attorney Jones and Doctor Jones," he would say grandly, extolling the couple as a Hollywood match. "Aren't you something?"

At the Biltmore Hotel, Robert Kennedy stood on a chair to give one of his many briefings to his campaign workers. In such crowd scenes, he seemed to lose the crisp authority and flashing temper for which he had become known in politics. For the moment both his voice and his frame seemed thinner than usual. "Remember," he shouted out among his commands for the day, "all the way with the Bowles platform." As the campaign workers dispersed to their tasks, Harris Wofford swallowed his amazement that Robert Kennedy had endorsed the platform in its entirety, including the far-reaching civil rights plank. Having been unable thus far to get Kennedy even to read the civil rights plank, Wofford feared that perhaps he did not realize what he had just done. Or perhaps he had made a calculated decision that supporting the plank would help hold Northern delegates against the threat of Lyndon Johnson. Or perhaps Kennedy had given the order simply because its brevity was worth more at the moment than all the political benefits he could imagine from more complicated alternatives. In any case, Kennedy campaign workers pushed their delegates to support the platform as drafted. A coalition of Southern delegates in hot rebellion presented a minority civil rights plank to the full convention, but it was voted down. Many battles later, Kennedy won the presidential nomination on the first ballot by holding nearly two-thirds of the delegate votes outside the South.

Into the early hours of Thursday morning, while the corks and flash-bulbs were still popping and the huzzahs being raised in hotel corridors, the new nominee and his advisers debated the selection of a Vice President. Early the next day, Senator Kennedy decided to pay a surprise call on Lyndon Johnson to offer the nomination, which was not expected, so that he could take credit for having done so when Johnson refused. Kennedy did not quite offer the job; he merely took the idea a few inches outside his pocket and flashed it in front of Johnson, as he put it. Moments later, a breathless Kennedy took his brother aside in another hotel room. "You just won't believe it," cried John Kennedy. "What?" said Robert. "He wants it," said the nominee, in utter disbelief. "Oh, my God!" said Robert. "Now what do we do?"

All sides waffled through a day of apoplectic indecision. Senator Johnson and his wife, along with Washington *Post* publisher Philip Graham, were "about as composed as three Mexican jumping beans" as they sat on a bed waiting to hear whether Kennedy would announce his offer of second place on the ticket. Robert Kennedy arrived on a diplomatic mission of the utmost delicacy, suggesting to Johnson that he might want to remove himself because of the ferocious opposition in the North. Instead, the Johnson camp put through an anguished call to Senator Kennedy himself, who backed off, saying, "Bobby is not up to date." Johnson handed the phone to Robert Kennedy so that he could hear the decision from his brother. These climactic moments humiliated both Johnson and Robert Kennedy, sealing a personal enmity between them. Kennedy, who assumed blame for the confusion so that his brother could remain more presidential, protected himself by telling friends that Johnson had begged him tearfully to be allowed on the ticket. Johnson protected himself with stories about how "that little shitass" Robert Kennedy had tried to jettison him without his brother's knowledge.

Most of the rancorous passions had been stuffed out of sight by the following night, when Adlai Stevenson introduced young Senator Kennedy as the one who "will lead our people into a new and spacious era, not for us alone, but for our troubled, trembling world." The smiling young face that came onto the screen was still new to millions of American viewers. So was the Boston accent. His oration was primarily a display of mood and taste, revealing Kennedy to be an ardent Anglophile with a hunger for noble romance. In his brief address, Kennedy mentioned eight American presidents, four British kings, and two British prime ministers. Citing Lloyd George's remark that a tired nation is a Tory nation, Kennedy declared that the United States could afford to be neither. He summoned the nation not so much from pessimism as from complacency. "The New Frontier is here whether we seek it or not," he said. "Beyond that frontier are uncharted areas of science and space, unsolved problems of peace and war, unconquered pockets of ignorance and prejudice, unanswered questions of poverty and surplus." Kennedy concluded with a quotation from Martin Luther King's favorite Old Testament prophet, Isaiah: "They that wait upon the Lord shall renew their strength; they shall mount up with wings as eagles; they shall run, and not be weary."

Unlike Kennedy, whose personality held attention as far and wide as broadcasts and the printed word could carry it, King created a sensation that was confined almost entirely to his immediate surroundings. In Los Angeles, he went nowhere without drawing a crowd, but in the news accounts from the convention he was only a part of the civil rights sidelight. When King returned home to Atlanta, his mail from the public focused on such topics as his use of the word "Negro." One correspondent, like others before him, chastised King for using a name originating in slavery, and after rejecting the term "black" as inappropriate for people of mixed color, informed King that the proper term was "Afro-American." (A committee had been formed in New York to promote public education on racial nomenclature.) Another correspondent, Malcolm X, objecting to one of King's attacks on racial separation, invited him to hear Black Muslim leader Elijah Muhammad at a Harlem rally "and then make a more intelligent appraisal of his teaching." Malcolm X was gaining a reputation in the white media as an incendiary anti-white orator at the same time that his debating skills were bringing him lecture dates in prestigious theology schools, such as King's own alma mater in Boston. Rather oddly, he addressed his letter to King at the NAACP office in New York, and King instructed his secretary to decline the invitation with a polite letter beginning "Dear Mr. X."

Although moving in relative obscurity, King kept up a travel pace nearly as grueling as that of a candidate. From Los Angeles, he flew home to preach at Ebenezer and then to Buffalo for another of the National Baptist Convention's week-long preliminary meetings, during which he received the good news that Alabama prosecutors were dropping a second perjury charge against him. After preaching at Ebenezer again, he flew to Oklahoma for two SCLC fund-raisers and on to Chicago for the Republican National Convention. There Randolph's agenda was virtually transplanted from Los Angeles, complete with the march, the rally, and the round-the-clock picketing. Rustin had sent out two advance organizers from New York, and King spent most of the week under the escort of Chauncey Eskridge, the lawyer-accountant who had deciphered his diaries for the Montgomery perjury trial.

For the civil rights people, everything about Chicago was bigger. The march drew twice as many people as the one in Los Angeles, and the picket lines were correspondingly fuller. On the day before the convention opened, there were two NAACP-sponsored rallies instead of one—both of them in Negro Baptist churches. New York governor Nelson Rockefeller was the featured attraction at the first rally. He had just concluded an extraordinary eight-hour negotiating session with his rival, Vice President Nixon, the result of which was an alliance behind Nixon and a joint statement of principle. The two of them vowed publicly to strengthen the civil rights plank of the Republican platform. Their last-minute pact was being denounced by conservative leader Barry Goldwater as "the Munich of the Republican Party," as "immoral politics," and as a "surrender" by Nixon to "the leader of the Republican left."

Goldwater's hostility helped make Rockefeller a hero to nearly six thousand people who jammed in and around the Liberty Baptist Church for the afternoon rally. Introduced by Roy Wilkins as the man who "made a backbone plank out of a spaghetti plank," Rockefeller delivered a rousing speech that the crowd interrupted thirty-three times with applause. King and Fred Shuttlesworth of Birmingham addressed an even larger crowd that night. The leading Republicans seemed to be on their side. "Nixon Says Rights Plank Must Be Made Stronger," announced the lead headline in The New York Times, above a story quoting Nixon in favor of the sit-ins and against "balancing" his ticket with a Southerner. The next day's lead headline read "Nixon Wins Civil Rights Fight."

President Eisenhower arrived in Chicago for a ticker-tape parade and a televised speech to the convention. By far the most popular man in the United States, Eisenhower was the secret weapon of the Republican Party. However, the Nixon-Rockefeller pact four days earlier had compounded his personal doubts about Nixon's capacities. What troubled the

President was not so much the civil rights provision as the call for increases in the defense budget. ("There must be no price ceiling on America's security," Rockefeller and Nixon had declared in their joint statement.) Disgusted, Eisenhower protested to Nixon by telephone. How could Nixon expect to run on the Eisenhower record of peace and prosperity and also pander to Kennedy's charges that Eisenhower was betraying the nation's security? How could he run as a fiscally sound Republican and also run up deficits to buy new weapons without military justification? A squirming Nixon replied that Rockefeller had slipped the weapons into the statement on his own. This was Nixon's dilemma. He needed the support of both Rockefeller and the President, but he knew that Eisenhower held Rockefeller in even lower personal regard than he did. The President disdained the New York governor as a weak-minded spendthrift who promoted himself with idiotic schemes such as building a federally subsidized bomb shelter in every American basement.

Nixon tried to patch over the differences, but Eisenhower made his triumphal entry into the Chicago Amphitheater still steaming over the Rockefeller pact, the U-2 disaster, and other accumulated insults to his military expertise. In his televised address, he scarcely mentioned Richard Nixon or the Republican Party. Instead, he declared that "just as the biblical Job had his boils, we have a cult of professional pessimists, who . . . continually mouth the allegation that America has become a second-rate military power."

Rockefeller promptly supported Eisenhower's dim view of his competence by misintroducing the new nominee as the "man who'll succeed Dwight D. Eisenhower next January—Richard E. Nixon." Gasps sounded through the Amphitheater before an alert bandleader covered them up with music. Richard M. Nixon, ignoring the slip, came to the podium to deliver an acceptance speech no doubt taxing to his listeners—about twice as long as Kennedy's and devoid of classical allusions or witty quotations. Nixon lengthened and diverted his argument with his style of chatty self-debate.* He also felt obliged to straddle the gap between Eisenhower's pride and Kennedy's charges that "American prestige is at an all-time low," repeating at length that "a record is not something to stand on but something to build on." In spite of these forensic drawbacks, Nixon's speech was one of the most successful of his life. Thorough and responsible, without grudges or threats, his survey of government prob-

---

* "Now we come to the key question: what should our answer be? And some might say, why, do as they do. Outpromise them, because that's the only way to win . . . And I serve notice here and now that whatever the political consequences, we are not going to try to outpromise our opponents."

lems conveyed a workmanlike comprehension, and he evoked the traditional idealism of the plain people: "And I know, my fellow Americans, I know tonight that we must resist the hate. We must remove the doubts, but above all we must be worthy of the love and the trust of millions on this earth for whom America is the hope of the world."

Nixon came out of the convention with a lead over Kennedy in the polls. Privately, Eisenhower criticized him for choosing U.N. ambassador and former senator Henry Cabot Lodge as his running mate. Lodge was too liberal on civil rights and too genteel to be an effective campaigner, thought the President, who had lobbied for a rich Texan and for a general on the grounds that they had proven they could manage people and dollars in the millions. Still, Eisenhower occasionally found himself outraged over signs of racism at the convention. He sat proudly in the VIP lounge at the Amphitheater as E. Frederic Morrow, who had flown with him to the convention aboard Air Force One, strode to the platform to make a brief but historic televised speech. "One hundred years ago my grandfather was a slave," Morrow began. "Tonight I stand before you a trusted assistant to the President of the United States." By the time he uttered these words, Eisenhower was cursing his television screen because the network producers had chosen to cut away. The networks had blacked out Negro speakers at both conventions for fear of offending Southern stations. Although the race issue was bubbling up strongly enough to make both political parties take platform stands of unprecedented clarity, it was still too sensitive for television.

King returned home to Atlanta thinking there was not much difference between Kennedy and Nixon on civil rights. Both on principle and on the relative merits of the candidates, King was inclined to be neutral in the fall election. This put him at odds not only with the highly partisan Daddy King but also with the Atlanta *Daily World*, which was run by family friend and Ebenezer trustee C. A. Scott. The *World* scarcely waited for the conclusion of the Republican Convention before declaring in a headline, "Nixon and Lodge Are Best to Fight World Communism."

On the Morehouse campus, King joined student leaders who had been meeting periodically since their SCLC conference back in April. Their spirits were high, and with good reason, as the sit-ins of the previous spring had been reverberating through the adult world all summer. City officials in Durham, North Carolina, were taking steps to end segregation "quietly" in many downtown stores. Two drugstore chains based in Virginia had agreed to end lunch counter segregation—which news, announced at the NAACP convention, inspired jubilant youth delegates to lift Roy Wilkins to their shoulders like a triumphant football coach. The U.S. Attorney General, William Rogers, had represented Vice President Nixon during the civil rights battles at the Republican Convention and then proceeded directly into negotiations with the owners of chain stores across the South. News stories out of the Justice Department indicated that the owners were willing to integrate their lunch counters if they could do so all at once; their fear was that Southern legislatures would enact more laws *requiring* segregation. Meanwhile, Trailways officials announced that they would desegregate the restaurants in their bus terminals throughout the South. The company would continue to maintain separate lunch counters and restrooms as a public service, said the beleaguered officials, but customers of all races would be free to sit anywhere.

Victories and rumors of victory swelled the hopes of the student leaders. Their movement had not only captured the attention of the highest officials in the land but also pushed segregationists into defensive, ridiculous compromises. At their Atlanta meeting, the students discussed ambitious plans to push into new areas and attack other segregated institutions, such as churches and public parks. Their crying weakness, everyone agreed, was that the organized student movement was of negligible size in proportion to the vast opportunities created by the sit-ins. The Student Nonviolent Coordinating Committee's office was merely a corner of King's SCLC office, which itself was no bigger than a three-man barber shop. The sole SNCC staffer was a volunteer student on leave from Union Theological Seminary. Only nine student delegates could be mustered for the Atlanta conference, one of whom represented both the District of Columbia and the entire state of Florida. There were no delegates at all from rural areas or from the tough states of Mississippi and Louisiana, and the SNCC delegates were outnumbered at their conference by observers such as King, reporter Carl Rowan, and the recently fired professor L. D. Reddick. In the face of all these deficiencies, the SNCC delegates borrowed a maneuver from the SCLC: they resolved to recruit more people for yet another conference two months hence, at which time they hoped to establish SNCC as a permanent organization. They boldly invited Senator Kennedy and Vice President Nixon to attend.

Privately, some of the leaders of the Atlanta student movement went to King with a worry that was emblematic of the times. They feared that one of their supporters might be a Communist. In particular, they suspected a New Yorker who was coming to their meetings, joining their picket lines, making friends with their friends. He was older and more sophisticated than most of them, with strange habits and a volunteer spirit that seemed too good to be true. After much internal debate, the Atlanta students had called him in for what amounted to an interrogation. When this settled nothing, they decided to pass their doubts along to King, because the man in question said he had come South to work as a summer volunteer for the SCLC. Promising to look into the matter, King summoned the suspect to his study at Ebenezer.

King and Bob Moses were introduced to each other under these unfortunate circumstances. Alone together in the study, they said little and moved slowly. There were long silences. A mutual distaste for the subject at hand—a loyalty investigation—accented each man's natural reserve. King, distracted by the rush of greater events, retreated into the formality of his preacher's role, and Moses, too self-assured to fall into hero-worship of King and yet too respectful to assert any of his complaints about the way the movement was being run, waited patiently for King to challenge him. King was slow to do so. Though frail, bespectacled, and soft-spoken to the point of whispering, Moses carried about him the strong presence of an Eastern mystic. There was something odd about him, yet he also managed to communicate a soothing, spiritual depth.

Ostensibly, the two of them met as world-famous leader and obscure volunteer, judge and accused, Baptist preacher and suspected Marxist, but beneath the trappings of rank the two men were natural competitors in the realms of politics and religion, destined to become opposing symbols for the holy wars within the civil rights movement. Their personalities struck deep notes that were so close together as to be unbearably dissonant. Never—and certainly not at their first strained meeting— were they to acknowledge the range of similarities between them.

At twenty-five, Moses was only six years younger than King. Born and raised in Harlem, he had been marked as an extremely sensitive child. He was admitted to Stuyvesant High School, a school for gifted students, and even there he distinguished himself by developing a taste on his own for the works of the Chinese philosopher Lao-tze. His grandfather had been an early leader of the National Baptist Convention, a distinguished but overbearing preacher who had moved his family to New York just in time to be struck by a mortal illness and the hard times of the Depression. As a result, the invalid grandfather Moses had been unable to educate or support the last few of his many children. Moses' father, one of those left out, retained a lifelong bitterness over his lack of education or professional accomplishment. Together with his wife, he encouraged his son's bookish proclivities and inculcated in him an ambition to succeed at one of the better white colleges, as opposed to the traditional Negro ones, which they dismissed as too "social." They were thrilled when he won a scholarship to enter Hamilton College in upstate New York, for the fall term of 1952.

Suddenly, as one of only three Negroes in the student body, Moses had

entered a new universe of white middle-class culture. Excluded by race
from the all-important fraternity social system, he gravitated toward an
integrated Christian study group, whose members, still reeling from the
apocalypse of World War II, embraced a Last Judgment fundamentalism
as a shield against the vanity-glutted world they saw around them. Moses
joined some of them who commuted to New York City to preach in the
streets. On many a Saturday night, he stood beneath the lurid bright
lights of Times Square and took his turn among the hillbilly preachers
and West Indian soothsayers and the other student evangelists—holding
up his Bible and urging streams of tourists to repent. His voice was much
too soft for the task, however, and a few of his Hamilton professors
perceived that his zeal was connected to a more eclectic curiosity about
the cosmic questions. Moses became a philosophy major. He read Camus
in French, renewed his study of Eastern philosophers, and took an interest in pacifist thought on the issues of war and peace. Admiring professors placed Moses in Quaker workshops held overseas. He spent one
Hamilton summer vacation in France living among pacifists whose beliefs had been tested by the Hitler occupation, and he spent the next
summer in Japan, dividing his time between a Quaker workshop and the
home of a Zen Buddhist monk. His writings about these experiences,
plus his mastery of the great metaphysical philosophers, established him
as the kind of oddity that was much more respectable to faculty tastes
than were street preachers. In 1956, Moses was accepted into the Ph.D.
program of Harvard's graduate department of philosophy.

Still deeply insecure about his ability to compete with white students
at a Harvard level, Moses arrived in the Boston area two years after King
had departed. Much had changed in those two years. Paul Tillich, the
world-famous theologian on whom King had written his dissertation at
Boston University but whom he had never met, was now a professor of
philosophy and religion at Harvard. Moses attended his lectures, but his
perception of Tillich was affected deeply by a historic shift in the prevailing world view of professional philosophers. Tillich was more than
out of vogue; his focus on the old questions of truth and being made him
irrelevant to modern analytic philosophy. Generally speaking, the analytic philosophers had put aside the ancient riddles until they could find
a way to make words as precise and scientific as numbers. Their papers
bristled with equations and notations of symbolic logic. Mathematical
proof came to replace persuasiveness as the test of good philosophical
work. Soon Moses joined the small cliques of graduate philosophy students who sat disapprovingly through Tillich's lectures. "It was all
poetry," they said derisively, meaning that Tillich was just playing with
words. Moses absorbed enough of the analytic school to understand all

this, but part of him yearned to hear the religious and philosophical poetry.

He was well along toward his doctorate when, in February 1958, the news came that his mother had died suddenly. In shock, he went to New York for the funeral. Afterward, his father packed his bags and left for a short trip of escape and recovery. Before Moses could leave for Harvard, the police called with the news that they had picked up Mr. Moses on the street. He had gone mad, apparently. Police officers found him raving, hurting himself, shouting that he was movie star Gary Cooper. They took him to the Bellevue psychiatric unit, where he remained under treatment for many months. He was released not long before police officers brought Izola Ware Curry to the same hospital for evaluation after she stabbed King.

Moses left Harvard and went home to take care of his father. To support the two of them, he took a job as a teacher of mathematics at the Horace Mann High School in New York. He was still there in 1960 when the sit-ins began in the South. At the New York office of the Committee to Defend Martin Luther King, Moses worked as a volunteer for Bayard Rustin. He had met Rustin years earlier to discuss conscientious objection to the military draft, but Rustin did not remember it. Now Moses found himself engaged again on the issues of moral philosophy that had absorbed him before the interruption of his education at Harvard. On the recommendation of Bayard Rustin to Ella Baker, he took a bus South to work for Dr. King.

Atlanta, like the Harvard philosophy department, was not quite what Moses expected. There were only three people in the SCLC office, and one of them—Ella Baker—was preparing to return again to New York to make way for the incoming Wyatt Tee Walker. The second was Dr. King's secretary, Dora McDonald, who spent her time answering the phone, logging King's phone calls and correspondence, and typing stencils for fund-raising appeals. The third was Jane Stembridge, the SNCC volunteer from Union Seminary. King was away at the political conventions, and no one could quite think of anything for Moses to do every day. At first he kept looking for a "work force" somewhere—for the rooms where volunteers must be stuffing envelopes, canvassers preparing to knock on doors, organizers training to go out into the field—but the New York–style beehive simply did not exist.

As the reality sank in that the SCLC was but a church office with three frantic telephones, Moses made friends with Stembridge and consumed long hours with her debating the merits of Paul Tillich. Through her, he met some of the leaders of the Atlanta student movement, who were engaged almost daily in picket lines and planning meetings. Moses, hungry for something to do, joined them on picket lines outside Atlanta supermarkets that refused to hire Negro clerks. On some days, when the students were otherwise engaged in lengthy meetings, Moses was the only one on the line. For the sake of company, he found and joined another picket line in town, and one day the police arrested him and his fellow demonstrators. He was identified in news accounts as Robert Moses of the SCLC. When the Atlanta students called him in shortly thereafter and asked how he had managed to locate an alternative picket line, Moses replied that he had heard about it while attending a mathematics lecture entitled "Ramifications of Goedel's Theorem." His answer did nothing to allay the students' suspicions that this hyper-intellectual Yankee volunteer might be a Communist.

In King's church study, Moses' passive nature rendered useless one of King's most valuable traits—his patience as a listener and resolver of conflicts. Forced into the offensive, King recounted what he had heard about the picket line, the arrest, and Moses' identification as an SCLC volunteer. When Moses offered no challenge to the account, King explained that the group sponsoring that picket line, the Southern Conference Education Fund, was a spin-off of one of Eleanor Roosevelt's old interracial groups, sponsored by Aubrey Williams and Myles Horton, among others, and now run by Carl and Anne Braden. It was the group Senator Eastland had been investigating for Communist ties back in 1954, when Clifford Durr had gone berserk in the New Orleans hearing room.* "I'm not saying that any of that is true," King told Moses, "but I advise against any more demonstrations with the SCEF people. Some people think it's Communist, and that's what matters. We have to be careful."

Moses did not agree, but he did not object. As an SCLC volunteer, he considered himself bound to follow its policies. His only reply was a question on a completely different topic: did Dr. King mind if Moses took the fund-raising appeal over to the Butler Street YMCA so that he could assemble volunteers for collating, addressing, and stuffing? He thought he could get the appeal into the mail much faster that way. King heartily endorsed the idea, and the brief meeting closed on an artificial note of agreement.

King himself was on friendly terms with the leaders of the SCEF, against which he had just warned Moses. So were Ella Baker and Rustin. There was an element of expediency, even hypocrisy, in the way King handled the controversy over Moses, but for King it was but a small reflection of much larger and more painful conflicts of pragmatism, be-

---

* See p. 122.

lief, and personal loyalty. Most troublesome was the purging of Rustin. Ever since King had demanded that his SCLC board hire Rustin as its coordinator and publicist, the internal resistance had been building again among preachers who were put off by Rustin's homosexuality and Communist past. Pressure against him had increased after the crippling lawsuits were filed over Rustin's *New York Times* ad—the preachers conceded that it was not really Rustin's fault, but they criticized him anyway—and shortly thereafter had come the grotesque blackmail threat from Adam Clayton Powell. These things, added to the memories of smuggling Rustin in and out of Montgomery during the boycott, supported the argument that Rustin would always be a liability. Against these cold facts, King felt loyalties of principle and personal feeling for Rustin, which were only made worse by his awareness that Rustin, nearing fifty years of age, was counting on King for a regular job. Squeezed, King finally appointed an SCLC committee under Rev. Thomas Kilgore —Ella Baker's pastor and one of King's preaching mentors in New York —and Kilgore, with King's blessing, informed Rustin of the committee's conclusion that Rustin should break off contact with King. Deeply wounded, Rustin faulted King for delegating such a personal matter to a committee and for failing to tell him face to face. He resigned from the Committee to Defend Martin Luther King. Fund-raising for the *New York Times* libel cases fell off drastically as a result, and lawyers were hounding King for fee payments.

Moses knew nothing of this strife when he came to Atlanta on Rustin's recommendation. His quick friendship with Ella Baker might also have made the introduction uncomfortable for King, as Baker was leaving again, crowded out of the SCLC by the noisy arrival of Wyatt Tee Walker. On August 1, Walker moved decisively to establish himself by evicting the one-woman SNCC office from the premises—though he helped Stembridge find space across the street. Even before reaching Atlanta, Walker got King to send out over his signature letters praising Walker's talents to correspondents across the South. The publicity brochures for Walker's first SCLC conference touted Walker and King alike as "internationally known" civil rights leaders. On balance, King believed that Walker's talents greatly outweighed his faults, but for Moses the new Walker regime only accentuated his estrangement from King and the Atlanta students.

When Jane Stembridge proposed that he escape the discomfort of Atlanta by going on a recruiting trip through the states unrepresented in SNCC, Moses jumped at the chance. He wanted to see the rural South, and he actually preferred to go alone. The idea took hold in a quick spin of preparation. Wyatt Walker provided bus tickets; Moses agreed to pay all other expenses himself. Ella Baker gave briefings on helpful contacts between Atlanta and the Texas border. Stembridge combed through the SCLC mailing lists and sent out letters asking people to take Moses in. After a last flurry of excitement that included "kneel-ins" at seven white churches in Atlanta, Stembridge put Moses on a Greyhound bus on Saturday, August 13, and he disappeared from the innards of Alabama. "SNCC now has a Field Representative," she wrote proudly.

Moses and Stembridge were not the first nor the last to be smitten by the romance, religion, and danger of the movement. From Talladega, from Shuttlesworth's house in Birmingham, from Alabama country churches and on into Mississippi, Moses reported his recruitments to her in letters of giddy impressionism. "I plooped on front lawns, lawn chairs, kitchen chairs, back porches, straw and purple velvet with a high back," he advised in his first dispatch. Moses typed out the names and addresses of dozens of people he had met who expressed interest in SNCC.

"You are doing mucho great job," Stembridge replied. Her letters kept Moses abreast of the growing excitement over the October SNCC conference. Ella Baker, proving that she would not abandon the students even after leaving the SCLC, had visited from New York just to help with the planning. A. J. Muste was coming, and so was Bayard Rustin. "If there is ANY capacity in which Bayard can work," Stembridge wrote Moses, "he will do so."

Moses met his future in Cleveland, Mississippi, in the person of Amzie Moore, a World War II veteran and gasoline station entrepreneur. Moore's voter registration efforts, and the opposing campaign to strangle his businesses, had been dramatic enough to gain the attention of faraway J. Edgar Hoover in 1956, and the support of his cause had been one of the prime reasons for the founding of In Friendship that same year, by Rustin, Ella Baker, and Stanley Levison. Four years later, Moore still had the filling station, and he had an amiable business relationship with his ex-wife, whose beauty shop was partitioned off inside the mechanic's area. "Amzie is the best I've met yet," Moses wrote Stembridge, "but then I should have known from Miss Baker; I would trust him explicitly and implicitly, and contact him frequently. He works in the Post Office, two hours a day for the last two years, and lives like a brick wall in a brick house, dug into this country like a tree beside the water."

Amzie Moore took Moses' recruitment pitch and turned it backward. It was fine for SNCC to recruit young people from Mississippi, he said, but it would be better for SNCC to send a work force of students *into* Mississippi to register voters under the protection of the new civil rights laws. "Amzie thinks, and I concur, the adults here will back the young folks but will never initiate a program strong enough to do what needs to be done," Moses wrote Stembridge. Sentence by sentence, the intoxication of his letters grew into clear-headed fantasy or revelation. "Amzie thinks he can lay his hands on a bus if we can gas it up," he wrote. "The idea is to tackle the 2nd and 3rd Congressional Districts, about 25 counties in all. . . . The main thrust is to take place next summer. . . . Nobody starry eyed, these are nasty jobs but we're going to find some nasty people to do them, so put me down 'cause I'm not only getting mean I'm getting downright nasty."

"I cannot believe your letters," Stembridge replied. ". . . I got so excited that things almost happened to my kidneys. This VOTER REGISTRATION project is IT!" She was telling Ella Baker, Rustin, and everyone else she could find that Moses, who had left on the Greyhound hoping to find a carload of students for the conference, now had her scrambling to find money to print some 200,000 copies of the Mississippi state constitution, the better to educate the would-be new voters.

On August 26, during a campaign stop in Atlanta, Vice President Nixon was greeted at the airport by a dozen of the most influential Negroes in the city. Moses slipped back into the city by Greyhound a few days later, laden with more addresses and ideas. His return was an occasion for both celebration and regret. As much as he ached to stay on in the South, he told Stembridge, he could not renege on the last year of his teaching contract nor yet leave his father. He headed North to meet his math classes after Labor Day, promising to be back.

That same summer, a white lawyer from a small town in Wisconsin embarked on a parallel odyssey of revelation. John Doar was lanky, taciturn, and plainspoken. In 1960, still building a general courthouse law practice, he counted it as a small step of success that a client paid him to go all the way to California to work on a paternity suit. He was there when Harold Tyler, chief of the Justice Department's Civil Rights Division, tracked him down by telephone.

Attorney General William Rogers had hired Tyler for the express purpose of stepping up the enforcement of the 1957 and 1960 Civil Rights Acts. It was a sign of the times that not a single politically connected Republican, nor any friend of Tyler's, expressed interest in the high-ranking position of first assistant in the Civil Rights Division. Tyler's only connection to Doar was that the two of them had overlapped at Princeton, and that some of his friends, after scratching their heads, recalled Doar as a good lawyer who was not on the fast career track and therefore might be interested in the job. Tyler offered the job to Doar over the phone, sight unseen.

Doar thought it over. All he remembered from Princeton was that the Southern students were always saying it would be a terrible mistake for outsiders to inject themselves into the complicated Negro problem. On the other hand, he had grown up resenting the South's one-party system because it allowed unchallenged Southern committee chairmen to dominate Congress, penalizing his home state. Having been taught that perpetuation of Southern oligarchs in Congress was related somehow to the exclusion of Negroes from politics, Doar resolved that it would be a service to history and to Wisconsin if he helped create an honest, Wisconsin-style two-party system in the South. He called Tyler from California at six o'clock in the morning and said tersely, "I'll do it."

Doar arrived in Washington in July 1960 and plunged immediately into the two bureaucratic struggles that would mark his career. The first one pitted legal thinking against political calculations. When Doar assumed his duties, the Civil Rights Division had only three pending voting rights cases under the 1957 Civil Rights Act.* Each was a landmark case, and the lawyers for the defendants had resisted with a host of tactics. Most fundamentally, they had persuaded Southern federal judges to declare portions of the new act to be unconstitutional infringements on the rights of the states, which forced the Justice Department to win contrary opinions on appeal before the cases could go forward. This was taking years, and meanwhile the Southerners were discovering other methods of avoidance and delay. For instance, some of the officials charged with refusing to register Negroes to vote simply resigned their offices, whereupon their lawyers moved to vacate the Justice Department suits on the grounds that there was no properly situated defendant. The 1960 law mended this defect by allowing the Justice Department to include the states themselves as defendants, but the constitutional challenges to the new law were just beginning and promised to stretch well into the decade.

Facing this gauntlet of defenses, Tyler's predecessor had decided to pursue only the three test cases doggedly to victory—no matter how long it took—in order to establish a legally tested avenue toward binding court orders. Only then, hypothetically, would the government come to the task of enforcing such court orders, and here the famed "jury trial" amendment of the 1957 act would work to the advantage of defendants who refused to obey them. Pending the outcome of the three original suits, Tyler's predecessor had refrained from filing others, as redundant suits only risked adverse precedents in weaker cases. This reasoning

---

* In Terrell County, Georgia; Macon County, Alabama; and Washington Parish, Louisiana.

would have prevailed in arid classrooms, but it flew headlong into the political urgency of Attorney General Rogers. To Rogers, the test-case strategy was vulnerable to political attack as a "do nothing" policy on civil rights enforcement. He wanted more suits.

Doar perceived quickly that politics in the Justice Department gave four sides to every issue instead of the lawyer's proverbial two. He soon encountered a second bureaucratic obstacle in the way of the Attorney General's civil rights plans: a sluggish FBI. Doar began to learn the subtleties of FBI work in the case of Haywood County, Tennessee, one of two predominantly Negro counties outside Memphis where voting disputes attracted widespread publicity in 1960. When the Civil Rights Division first asked the FBI to investigate complaints that white Haywood County farmers were systematically evicting Negro sharecroppers who tried to register to vote, Hoover first tried to scuttle the matter in advance by pointing out that it was very difficult to prove a connection between evictions and attempts to register, as required under the 1957 act. The Civil Rights Division asked for the investigation anyway, and Hoover complied promptly and efficiently with the official request, as he always did. The resulting report was practically useless to the Justice Department lawyers, however, because the local FBI did nothing more than interview the original Negro complainant and obtain a repetition of the story that had appeared in the newspapers.

The Bureau was not inherently or inevitably slow. Agents could move with intelligent, concentrated force, even in civil rights cases, as they had demonstrated in the Mack Charles Parker lynching a year earlier. But lawyers in the Civil Rights Division concluded that Hoover's attitude could fine-tune the hypersensitive FBI bureaucracy to produce anything from galloping initiative to tarpaper resistance—all within a pose of eager cooperation. The Haywood County case was getting the tarpaper. To several more Justice Department requests into the summer of 1960, the FBI replied with reports that invariably contained the narrowest conceivable answers to the questions specifically posed, and nothing more. On July 22, just after Doar arrived in Washington, a white woman in Haywood County gave the FBI copies of two lists she said were circulating among the white people. The lists named those Negroes marked for eviction, credit squeezes, or other forms of reprisal; the woman thought it was wrong. The FBI report to the Justice Department merely noted the woman's claim without forwarding the lists as evidence or making the slightest effort to verify her information. These omissions necessitated still more requests from the Civil Rights Division. Privately, supervisors at FBI headquarters called Tyler and other supervisors at Justice to recommend that the investigation be curtailed or postponed, especially on registration days. The presence of FBI agents at tense scenes only increased the chances of hostility toward the agents. J. Edgar Hoover, as every graduate of the FBI Academy knew, had built his Bureau explicitly on the role model of the small-town banker. This worked splendidly for the agents' usual work of tracking car thieves, bank robbers, Communists, and other outcasts, but the image made it wrenchingly difficult for the agents to take the side of the outcasts themselves.

Lawyers at Doar's level, dependent on the Bureau for basic information, determined that they had no alternative but to play by Hoover's rules. Taking up the game, the lawyers invented elaborate "coaching" or "box" memos, which were designed to eliminate every vestige of discretion left to FBI field agents. They directed that specific questions be asked of specific people, and then, guessing at the possible responses, directed that a range of specific follow-up questions be posed. These requests soon approached the structure of giant latticework molecules. In time, a single one of them ran to nearly two hundred pages in length.

Doar remained enough of a country lawyer to sense that this bizarre coaching process demeaned both sides and was unlikely to produce realistic information about what was going on in Haywood County, Tennessee, or anywhere else. Accordingly, he decided that summer to go poke around a little himself, talk to a few people. This was what he had always done in Wisconsin, and perhaps he was too new to Washington to realize how zealously the FBI regarded its dictum that "prosecutors prosecute; the FBI investigates." Almost casually, Doar ventured outside the policymaking sanctum of Washington. In Haywood County, he sought out a Negro schoolteacher and asked how he could see for himself what was going on in the county. Quickly Doar found himself agreeing to drive far into the back country to attend some of the regular church meetings. On the first night, he walked into a dimly lit clapboard church packed with Negro sharecroppers who had tried to register to vote. Called to the front, Doar announced nervously that he was from the Department of Justice and was there to help. He asked, as a matter of curiosity, whether any of the people there had received notices of eviction. Nearly every hand in the church went up.

It was a moment of shock that Doar never forgot. Staring into all those faces, he doubted that the drive to prevent Negro voting could be so widespread, until he collected fifty affidavits from sharecroppers who had saved their written eviction notices and were willing to testify. Doar poked around the county some more, and located other white people who were willing to testify that the organized whites had gone so far as to obtain legal opinions on how best to prevent Negro registration without getting caught in federal violations. Doar soon added the names of nearly fifty white defendants to the U.S. complaint in District Court. He returned to Washington knowing that he still needed the FBI and still would have to speak the bureaucratic language of policy. Nevertheless, he had opened a new eye, learning more from a few days on his own than he had gleaned from thousands of pages of memos. His pioneering trademark thereafter was to act partly as his own FBI agent. Like Bob Moses, he was being drawn into the rural South as his own "work force," and the experience would make it impossible for him ever to go home to Wisconsin.

On the Tuesday after Labor Day, more than 35,000 anxious National Baptists crammed into Philadelphia's Convention Hall for a pre-convention musical extravaganza. The crowd, hailed as the year's largest gathering of Negroes under one roof anywhere in the world, was enormous even by the fantastic standards of the NBC, as delegates flocked in from all over the country to witness the great showdown with J. H. Jackson. This presidential election, not the contest between Kennedy and Nixon, absorbed King's partisan energies in 1960. The challenge to the NBC president, which King had been contemplating for several years and planning feverishly since sealing an agreement with his fellow conspirators in January, was the most daring political risk a preacher could take within the profession. If successful, the Northern insurgents agreed to establish the SCLC—the only church-based civil rights organization—as an "official auxiliary" of the Convention. By winning over the institutional Negro church, King believed, he could break out of the crippling parochialism of the tiny SCLC and bypass the internecine conflicts with the NAACP.

King himself was not the candidate who would challenge J. H. Jackson, of course. He was much too young to have a chance, and a politically fatal number of preachers would have voted against him simply because he lacked sufficiently impressive credentials. Ebenezer was a powerful church, but it was far beneath the league of the titanic congregations from which Convention presidents had sprung. King's candidate was Gardner Taylor, whose reputation was such that white clergymen had elected him president of the New York State Council of Churches, and whose thunderous sweet preaching had attracted more than 11,000 members into his congregation at Concord Baptist in Brooklyn. (It was there, in Taylor's newly completed $2.5 million church, that King had preached to 10,000 people on his first trip to New York during the boycott.) All the preachers knew it was no idle matter to plot a coup against Old Jack, who already had purged state presidents from the Convention

for lesser acts of disloyalty, and had once packed several preachers off to
jail. In the event of failure, every overt Taylorite would become a marked
man. Swirling apprehensions meant that much of the campaigning was
clandestine and furtive, spoken in code words of "Alabama" leaning one
way and "Ohio" another.

Mahalia Jackson maintained a regal presence in both warring camps of
preachers. As the queen of gospel, she personified much of the Convention's identity, including the great World War I migration of Negroes up
the Mississippi River to Chicago. A food lover, she described her life's
journey as a transfer from New Orleans, where she had learned to cook
baby alligators, to Chicago, where her generation of Negroes taught the
Chicago stockyards that it was better to make chitlins of hog guts than
to throw them away. In Chicago, young Mahalia Jackson had promptly
fallen in with Thomas A. Dorsey, the father of gospel music, and the two
of them were stigmatized within the established church for "hollering"
and wild rhythms that degraded the race and upstaged the preacher.
Jackson had been muffled and hidden for twenty years at her beloved
National Baptist Convention meetings, where she had diapered young
Aretha Franklin and gotten to know Mother King from Atlanta at the
music planning sessions. Finally, shifts in Convention politics and her
1950 breakthrough to fame on the Ed Sullivan television show made her
an institution among Baptists as the "official soloist" of the National
Baptists.

Determined to preserve that status as a key to her livelihood, Mahalia
Jackson arrived as a known friend of King, who had stayed in her home
during the Republican Convention weeks earlier, and also as the loyal
vassal of Old Jack. Her retinue included a new lawyer, Chauncey Eskridge, who was reeling from his first exposure to the bizarre atmosphere
of the Convention, where charged politics surged under and around the
central balm of what amounted to a continuous church service. From
the singer, Eskridge learned what could safely be said to whom, as he
watched her trying to maintain her neutrality. The impending battle
touched deep beliefs of religion, politics, and race, with personal follow-
ings of a strength bordering on idolatry. Schism was in the air. Secretary
T. J. Jemison—son of Jackson's predecessor, leader of the Baton Rouge
bus boycott of 1953, King's old friend and first adviser as a protest leader
—believed privately in everything Taylor and King stood for, but he
decided painfully that his own presidential ambitions were best served
by remaining a Jacksonite. Or so believed the Taylorites, who said they
did not trust Secretary Jemison to count the votes for president.

Pennsylvania governor David Lawrence, who had delivered Lyndon
Johnson's vice presidential nominating speech in Los Angeles under instructions from Senator Kennedy, officially welcomed the National Bap-

1

The early civil rights movement grew from Montgom-
ery, Alabama, where (1) bus
boycotters, led by Dr. Martin
Luther King, Jr., gained the
world's attention, to the 1963
March on Washington (2),
where more than 250,000
protesters came together for
the cause of freedom.

2

7

Among the Rockefeller family's contributions to King's heritage were New York's Riverside Church (3), where worshippers lined up in the 1930s to hear Rev. Harry Emerson Fosdick. Today, the golf course has been replaced by the Martin Luther King, Jr., Wing, and 120th Street (in the foregound) is now Reinhold Niebuhr Place. The Rockefellers also heavily subsidized the black colleges in Atlanta attended by King and his forebears, including his mother and father (4), pictured with a grandchild in the King family home. Among other early King influences were NAACP founder W. E. B. Du Bois (5), who was succeeded at *The Crisis* magazine by the young Roy Wilkins (6). The esteemed Vernon Johns (7) preceded King in his first pulpit at Montgomery's Dexter Avenue Baptist Church (8).

5

6

3

4

After Montgomery blacks rallied behind
seamstress Rosa Parks (9), who dared to defy
segregation laws on city buses, local whites first
suspected Rev. Robert Graetz (10) as the
organizer of the bus boycott. King, pictured with
Bayard Rustin (11) after a mass arrest of boycott
leaders and addressing a mass meeting at the

13

10

"Brick-a-Day" First Baptist Church (12), labored for a year to keep the local buses nearly empty (13) by arranging a voluntary carpool system to take workers to and from downtown pick-up stations (14).

14

15

16

17

A public man at twenty-seven, King posed
on the Dexter church steps (15) in 1956 with
his wife, Coretta, daughter Yolanda, and the
Alabama Capitol in the background. All that
year, during the boycott, sentinels and
searchlights guarded the King family home
(16).

18   19

King addressed a national prayer pilgrimage at Washington's Lincoln Memorial in April 1957 (17) with Roy Wilkins (seated, bottom left). That same month, in an attempt to enlist the aid of powerful Americans, the Kings met Richard and Pat Nixon in Ghana (18). After the Little Rock school desegregation crisis of 1957 (19), King finally achieved his first meeting with a U.S. President on June 23, 1958 (20). Participants included (left to right) Lester Granger, King, E. Frederick Morrow, President Eisenhower, A. Philip Randolph, Attorney General William Rogers, Rocco Siciliano, and Roy Wilkins.

King's years of frustration and relative obscurity in the late 1950s were interrupted in September 1958, when police seized him outside the Montgomery courthouse (21, 22) and later in the year when he was stabbed in a New York department store. A bystander nursed King's hand (23) as the weapon protruded from his chest. Later, a silk-robed King recuperated with the help of his wife and mother (24). Relocating to Atlanta in 1960, the Kings received a farewell tribute at Dexter (25) on the night before the sit-in movement began in Greensboro, North Carolina.

23

24

21

22

25

26   27   28

> "The growing movement of peaceful mass demonstrations by Negroes is something new in the South, something understandable.... Let Congress heed their rising voices, for they will be heard."
>
> —New York Times editorial
> Saturday, March 19, 1960

Heed Their Rising Voices

As the whole world knows by now, thousands of Southern Negro students are engaged in widespread non-violent demonstrations in positive affirmation of the right to live in human dignity as guaranteed by the U. S. Constitution and the Bill of Rights. In their efforts to uphold these guarantees, they are being met by an unprecedented wave of terror by those who would deny and negate that document which the whole world looks upon as setting the pattern for modern freedom. . . .

In Orangeburg, South Carolina, when 400 students peacefully sought to buy doughnuts and coffee at lunch counters in the business district, they were forcibly ejected, tear-gassed, soaked to the skin in freezing weather with fire hoses, arrested en masse and herded into an open barbed-wire stockade to stand for hours in the bitter cold.

In Montgomery, Alabama, after students sang "My Country, 'Tis of Thee" on the State Capitol steps, their leaders were expelled from school, and truckloads of police armed with shotguns and tear-gas ringed the Alabama State College Campus. When the entire student body protested to state authorities by refusing to re-register, their dining hall was padlocked in an attempt to starve them into submission.

In Tallahassee, Atlanta, Nashville, Savannah, Greensboro, Memphis, Richmond, Charlotte, and a host of other cities in the South, young American teenagers, in face of the entire weight of official state apparatus and police power, have boldly stepped forth as protagonists of democracy. Their courage and amazing restraint have inspired millions and given a new dignity to the cause of freedom.

Small wonder that the Southern violators of the Constitution fear this new, non-violent brand of freedom fighter . . . even as they fear the upwelling right-to-vote movement. Small wonder that they are determined to destroy the one man who, more than any other, symbolizes the new spirit now sweeping the South—the Rev. Dr. Martin Luther King, Jr., world-famous leader of the Montgomery Bus Protest. For it is his doctrine of non-violence which has inspired and guided the students in their widening wave of sit-ins; and it is this same Dr. King who founded and is president of the Southern Christian Leadership Conference—the organization which is spearheading the surging right-to-vote movement. Under Dr. King's direction the Leadership Conference conducts Student Workshops and Seminars in the philosophy and technique of non-violent resistance.

Again and again the Southern violators have answered Dr. King's peaceful protests with intimidation and violence. They have bombed his home almost killing his wife and child. They have assaulted his person. They have arrested him seven times—for "speeding," "loitering" and similar "offenses." And now they have charged him with "perjury"—a felony under which they could imprison him for ten years. Obviously, their real purpose is to remove him physically as the leader to whom the students and millions of others—look for guidance and support, and thereby to intimidate all leaders who may rise in the South. Their strategy is to behead this affirmative movement, and thus to demoralize Negro Americans and weaken their will to struggle. The defense of Martin Luther King, spiritual leader of the student sit-in movement, clearly, therefore, is an integral part of the total struggle for freedom in the South.

Decent-minded Americans cannot help but applaud the creative daring of the students and the quiet heroism of Dr. King. But this is one of those moments in the stormy history of Freedom when men and women of good will must do more than applaud the rising-to-glory of others. The America whose good name hangs in the balance before a watchful world, the America whose heritage of Liberty these Southern Upholders of the Constitution are defending, is our America as well as theirs. . . .

We must heed their rising voices—yes—but we must add our own.

We must extend ourselves above and beyond moral support and render the material help so urgently needed by those who are taking the risks, facing jail, and even death in a glorious re-affirmation of our Constitution and its Bill of Rights.

We urge you to join hands with our fellow Americans in the South by supporting, with your dollars, this Combined Appeal for all three needs—the defense of Martin Luther King—the support of the embattled students—and the struggle for the right-to-vote.

Your Help Is Urgently Needed . . . NOW !!

Stella Adler
Raymond Pace Alexander
Harry Van Arsdale
Harry Belafonte
Julie Belafonte
Dr. Algernon Black
Marc Blitzstein
William Branch
Marlon Brando
Mrs. Ralph Bunche
Diahann Carroll

Dr. Alan Knight Chalmers
Richard Coe
Nat King Cole
Cheryl Crawford
Dorothy Dandridge
Ossie Davis
Sammy Davis, Jr.
Ruby Dee
Dr. Philip Elliott
Dr. Harry Emerson Fosdick

Anthony Franciosa
Lorraine Hansberry
Rev. Donald Harrington
Nat Hentoff
James Hicks
Mary Hinkson
Van Heflin
Langston Hughes
Morris Iushewitz
Mahalia Jackson
Mordecai Johnson

John Killens
Eartha Kitt
Rabbi Edward Klein
Hope Lange
John Lewis
Viveca Lindfors
Carl Murphy
Don Murray
John Murray
A. J. Muste
Frederick O'Neal

L. Joseph Overton
Clarence Pickett
Shad Polier
Sidney Poitier
A. Philip Randolph
John Raitt
Elmer Rice
Jackie Robinson
Mrs. Eleanor Roosevelt
Bayard Rustin
Robert Ryan

Maureen Stapleton
Frank Silvera
Hope Stevens
George Tabori
Rev. Gardner C. Taylor
Norman Thomas
Kenneth Tynan
Charles White
Shelley Winters
Max Youngstein

We in the south who are struggling daily for dignity and freedom warmly endorse this appeal

Rev. Ralph D. Abernathy
(Montgomery, Ala.)

Rev. Fred L. Shuttlesworth
(Birmingham, Ala.)

Rev. Kelley Miller Smith
(Nashville, Tenn.)

Rev. W. A. Dennis
(Chattanooga, Tenn.)

Rev. C. K. Steele
(Tallahassee, Fla.)

Rev. Matthew D. McCollom
(Orangeburg, S. C.)

Rev. William Holmes Borders
(Atlanta, Ga.)

Rev. Douglas Moore
(Durham, N. C.)

Rev. Wyatt Tee Walker
(Petersburg, Va.)

Rev. Walter L. Hamilton
(Norfolk, Va.)

I. S. Levy
(Columbia, S. C.)

Rev. Martin Luther King, Sr.
(Atlanta, Ga.)

Rev. Henry C. Bunton
(Memphis, Tenn.)

Rev. S. S. Seay, Sr.
(Montgomery, Ala.)

Rev. Samuel W. Williams
(Atlanta, Ga.)

Rev. A. L. Davis
(New Orleans, La.)

Mrs. Katie E. Whickham
(New Orleans, La.)

Rev. W. H. Hall
(Hattiesburg, Miss.)

Rev. J. E. Lowery
(Mobile, Ala.)

Rev. T. J. Jemison
(Baton Rouge, La.)

COMMITTEE TO DEFEND MARTIN LUTHER KING AND THE STRUGGLE FOR FREEDOM IN THE SOUTH
312 West 125th Street, New York 27, N. Y. UNiversity 6-1700

Chairmen: A. Philip Randolph, Dr. Gardner C. Taylor; *Chairmen of Cultural Division:* Harry Belafonte, Sidney Poitier, Shelley Winters; *Treasurer:* Nat King Cole; *Executive Director:* Bayard Rustin; *Chairmen of Church Division:* Father George B. Ford, Rev. Harry Emerson Fosdick, Rev. Thomas Kilgore, Jr., Rabbi Edward E. Klein; *Chairman of Labor Division:* Morris Iushewitz

29

30

In Nashville, lunch counter protests led to arrests for Diane Nash (26, third from left) and her Gandhian mentor, James Lawson (27). With the encouragement of Ella Baker (28), groups across the South formed the Student Nonviolent Coordinating Committee (SNCC). When King tried to raise money to defend himself against a perjury indictment, Alabama officials secured million-dollar judgments against a *New York Times* ad (29) designed to encourage financial support. *Sullivan* v. *New York Times* became a landmark Supreme Court case. King joined the student sit-in movement in Atlanta on October 19, 1960 (30), with Lonnie King (left), beginning what would become a decisive subplot in the presidential campaign of Senator John F. Kennedy (31).

31

President Kennedy and Mrs. Kennedy review the Inaugural Parade.

32

33

President Kennedy with civil rights aide Harris Wofford.

Attorney General Robert Kennedy with assistants John Seigenthaler and Byron "Whizzer" White.

34

Robert Kennedy with J. Edgar Hoover.

35

Harry Belafonte and Stanley Levison in the late 1960s.

37

36

Stanley Levison (middle), King's best white friend and Hoover's chief target, with King and an unidentified man at a New York reception in 1961.

Alabama officials confiscate Rev. Fred Shuttlesworth's car in January 1961, during the *Sullivan* v. *New York Times* investigation.

38

39

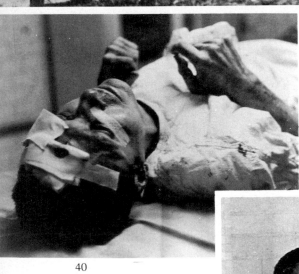

40

41

42

Civil rights made national news in the early days of the Kennedy administration, when the first freedom bus was attacked and burned outside Anniston, Alabama, on May 14, 1961 (39). Freedom Rider Jim Peck (40) was among those hospitalized after beatings that same day in Birmingham. Six days later, new Freedom Riders reached Montgomery, where another vigilante ambush left John Lewis and James Zwerg battered (41). After an all-night siege inside Ralph Abernathy's church (42), the Freedom Riders finally left Montgomery—under heavy martial escort (43).

43

44

Soldiers guarded the Freedom
Rider bus during a stop on the
way to Mississippi (44),
where Bob Moses worked
alone that summer in an attempt to register black voters
(45).

45

tists to Philadelphia on Wednesday. The balloting for president took place the next day, and on Friday a small wire-service story appeared on page 60 of *The New York Times*, one of the only white newspapers to mention the event at all. "Negro Baptists Pick a Brooklyn Pastor," said the *Times*, which quoted a Gardner Taylor victory statement that the election would put the National Baptists "in the forefront of the civil rights struggle." The story represented fairly accurately the political hopes of the Taylor wing, but it bore only a superficial relation to actual events.

What happened at the convention was bedlam. The noise began when Old Jack made his entrance to the hall for the Thursday morning business session, surrounded by swarms of his supporters. As the cheers finally died down, the Taylorites, who had prepared for the moment by hiring at least two uniformed bass drummers from a parade band, struck up a counterdemonstration to prove they could not be intimidated. When J. H. Jackson's gavel hammered down enough order to begin business, Taylorites moved to "qualify the house," meaning to separate the visitors from the voting delegates, and to tally the votes for president by a roll call of the states. They cheered when Jackson recognized the motions, contrary to most expectations, and cheered again when they carried. Some Jacksonites wondered whether the president might be giving up, but then the president of the Kansas chapter made a surprise announcement that his nominating committee found Dr. Jackson to be preeminently qualified over Dr. Taylor, and he moved that the Convention adopt the committee's recommendation that Jackson be reelected unanimously. All order ceased as of that moment, as shouts of approval competed with cries of "No!" Frantic parliamentarians debated whether such a motion could supersede the roll-call election.

When Jackson, above the din, ruled out of order a motion to separate the nominating committee report from the election itself, Taylorites surged toward the podium in huge numbers. The bass drums resumed. Rival caucuses paraded through the hall bearing placards for Taylor or Jackson. Two preachers and a woman banged a piano with their forearms. Roars of "We want Jackson!" and "We want Taylor!" and "Qualify the house!" and "Khrushchev!" occasionally rose above the deafening noise. Jackson tried to call for a voice vote on the motion, but someone yanked the plug on the public address system. Reporters standing under the podium less than six feet away from Jackson's head later wrote that they could not hear a word he shouted nor anything else but noise for the next full hour. A plea by a Philadelphia police inspector restored enough order for the delegates to join in singing "Glory to His Name" and "Oh Lord, Stand By Me," but the chaos resumed on the first mention of business. Finally, Jackson banged a silent gavel and made his way out of Convention Hall back to the Benjamin Franklin Hotel, surrounded by a squad of white policemen.

In his wake, Jacksonite lieutenants announced that Dr. Jackson had been reelected by voice-vote approval of the nominating committee motion, and that Jackson had adjourned the convention for the day. Jubilation, relief, and outrage followed, as thousands streamed out of Convention Hall to analyze these stupendous proceedings. Inside, the Taylorite lieutenants reached a crisis decision to go forward as though Jackson's exit had been nothing more than a temper tantrum. They managed to find a Convention vice president who could claim to have the authority to preside in the absence of the president, and the Taylorites struggled to go forward with the roll call against impediments of confusion, noise, and hostility. Some three hours later, the tabulation was announced: Taylor had won by a vote of 1,864 to 536.

On the floor, King rose immediately to speak, hushing the crowd with his presence. Making his sympathies irreversibly public, King moved for the election of the Taylorite slate of NBC officers. It was a shrewdly politic list. T. J. Jemison and some of the most recalcitrant Jacksonites were purged, but several Jacksonites were retained in an effort to promote reconciliation. King's list was approved by a shouted voice vote, and only then did Gardner Taylor himself make an entrance to the hall. By then the Jacksonites were returning in great numbers to prevent the consummation of the ouster, and they raised such a clamor that the triumphant Taylor was forced into helpless silence on the stage, where he was fanned by supporting preachers. Some time later, J. H. Jackson marched back into the hall within a phalanx of Jacksonites. He managed to reach the podium with the evident intent of expelling the usurper, but Taylor clung fast to the microphone. The two rivals faced each other in a frozen pose for hours, until city officials began turning out the lights at ten thirty. On his way out of Convention Hall, King talked with reporters. "The people voted overwhelmingly for Dr. Taylor," he said. "It is really unfortunate that Dr. Jackson will not honorably give up." A reporter noted sadly that the delegates had savagely beaten a concert grand piano, among other noisemakers, for a cumulative total of nearly five hours.

The next day, a battery of Taylorite lawyers persuaded a U.S. District Court judge to sign an injunction ordering all Convention records and monies to be turned over to Gardner Taylor as the duly elected president.* About the same time, Jackson's lawyers served Gardner Taylor with an injunction from a different federal judge, ordering Taylor to cease

---

* Taylor's lawyers included Benjamin Hooks, a preacher-lawyer from Memphis who served on King's SCLC board, the daughter of J. Pious Barbour, King's philosopher-host at Crozer Seminary, and Chauncey Eskridge of Chicago.

all disruptions against the Convention's duly elected president, J. H. Jackson. The program ceased, and for all practical purposes the eightieth convention of the National Baptists was aborted two days early—leaving sermons unpreached, Sunday-school lesson books unsold, well-rehearsed choirs unheard, and prepaid hotel rooms unoccupied. In the federal courts, where the struggle continued for weeks, two white judges who clearly had no idea what they were doing when they signed their opposing injunctions desperately called for the advice of Philadelphia's first and only Negro judge in the Court of Common Pleas. There was no resolution to the ecclesiastical dispute within man's law, however, as all the judges eventually found ways to renounce their jurisdiction. Jackson retained control of the board, the treasury, and all Convention property; he was angry and unbent. Chauncey Eskridge went home to Chicago and soon perceived that all his legal business from Baptist preachers was drying up in Jackson's hometown. King's dream of appropriating the power of the Convention for the civil rights movement would have to wait at least another year.

In Baltimore, after nearly a decade of persistent negotiations, the city's white and Negro Baptist preachers came together to discuss the role of the church in a time of racial tension. The meeting itself was a historic event, a gathering of uneasy strangers, and for the occasion the preachers of each race selected a representative to speak about their common religious heritage. The Negro preachers chose Vernon Johns, hoping that he would dazzle the white preachers with his learning. Indirectly, Johns was an employee of some of the white Baltimore preachers. His Maryland Baptist Center, which offered adult education to Negro preachers, was a kind of missionary program sponsored jointly by the white Southern Baptists and the National Baptist Convention.

On the appointed day, some 150 preachers met for lunch at the Seventh Baptist Church. There were no disputes over seating arrangements, the blessing of the food, the singing of "Jesus Keep Me Near the Cross," or the meal itself. But as the chosen white preacher developed his sermon on the theme of Christian salvation, of being "washed in the blood of the Lamb," Vernon Johns began to twitch noticeably in his seat. When the white man finished, Johns stood up abruptly. He did not wait to be introduced, nor did he begin with the effusive salutations that had been established as the order of the day. "The thing that disappoints me about the Southern white church is that it spends all of its time dealing with Jesus after the cross, instead of dealing with Jesus before the cross," he growled, and a number of the Negro preachers already were sinking inwardly toward oblivion.

Johns turned to the white preacher who had just sat down. "You didn't do a thing but preach about the death of Jesus," he said. "If that were the heart of Christianity, all God had to do was to drop him down on Friday, and let them kill him, and then yank him up again on Easter Sunday. That's all you hear. You don't hear so much about his three years of teaching that man's religion is revealed in the love of his fellow man. He who says he loves God and hates his fellow man is a liar, and the truth is not in him. That is what offended the leaders of Jesus's own established church as well as the colonial authorities from Rome. That's why they put him up there."

To a stunned audience, many of whom seemed to be leaning backward, Johns sputtered through quick explanations of Dives and Lazarus, and a story about how God rebuked Abraham for driving a stranger from his tent. "There is a world of disparity between the idealism of Jesus and the practices of men," he said. "But Jesus is not crazy. We are crazy. The church has not formally denounced the Sermon on the Mount. It has merely let it slide. I want to deal with Jesus before the cross. I don't give a damn what happened to him after the cross."

With that, Johns sat down again, having consumed no more time than normally allotted to opening jokes and bromides. Faces were red. Appetites were lost. The tentative brotherhood of Negro and white Baptist preachers in Baltimore was stifled as a collective movement, and Johns soon was asked to resign his position at the Maryland Center. He drifted off again to the sermon and lecture circuit. In his own gruff, impolitic way, the old man had spoken up for the same idea of worldly religion that King supported at the Philadelphia convention, with similarly disastrous results.

The Johns debacle, the journeys of Bob Moses and John Doar, and the civil war among the National Baptists were obscure events to nearly everyone who was not directly involved. The national focus of religion and politics was the presidential campaign, specifically the controversy that erupted when Norman Vincent Peale and a committee of prominent Protestant clergymen questioned the wisdom of allowing a Roman Catholic in the White House, saying "our American culture is at stake." Senator Kennedy responded directly to the challenge in a formal address to Protestant clergymen in Houston, endorsing "an America where the separation of church and state is absolute—where no Catholic prelate would tell the President (should he be a Catholic) how to act, and no Protestant minister would tell his parishioners for whom to vote—where no church or church school is granted any public funds or political preference . . . " Kennedy's Houston speech effectively drove the religious issue underground for the remainder of the campaign, where it joined the equally explosive issue of civil rights. Both candidates considered themselves overextended on race by pre-convention promises and formal party platforms. They downplayed the issue in the first of the four historic Kennedy-Nixon television debates on September 26. Focusing by agreement on domestic affairs, the two candidates agreed that America was wealthy, powerful, and free—but needed to be much more of each in order to fulfill itself and to compete with the mortal threat of worldwide communism.

On the Kennedy campaign staff, the civil rights people kept a profile in keeping with their issue—low and tucked away. Campaign manager Robert Kennedy put them in a K Street office building, physically separated from the national headquarters on Connecticut Avenue, and there was much internal controversy over the desire of Sargent Shriver and Harris Wofford to call their section the "Office of Civil Rights." Among those close to the Kennedy brothers, Colorado attorney Byron R. "Whizzer" White argued most persistently that the proposed title was inflammatory to marginal white voters. In the end, a compromise was reached. In return for keeping their office name, Wofford and Shriver agreed not to use the phrase "civil rights" in the one major public event for which they had been promised the candidate's presence. Their Harlem conference on civil rights became the Democratic National Conference on Constitutional Rights.

For Shriver and Wofford, the status of their office was further diminished by unseemly infighting between two Negro groups competing for stationery privileges, office space, and public visibility with the candidate. A husband-wife team staked a claim based on the social relationship they had struck up with Senator Kennedy by mentioning their vacation home on Martha's Vineyard. However, Robert Kennedy scorned the couple as socialite ornaments even before he found out that the husband was one of the lawyers for Jimmy Hoffa's Teamsters union.* Kennedy hired a Negro lawyer away from the Humphrey campaign, but the new choice only occupied himself in petty rivalry with the socialites before causing a full-alarm crisis in Oklahoma, where he was seen bringing a white woman onto the campaign plane during a stopover. None of this helped Wofford and Shriver, who considered all the rivals to be useless reflections of the Kennedy brothers' haphazard disregard. The Negro campaign workers might as well have been off in a minstrel show.

Shriver knew enough to appeal to Louis Martin—first to mediate the

---

* Unbeknown to Kennedy or Shriver, the lawyer also represented J. H. Jackson in his battle to control the Negro Baptists. For King, this was another indication that the Kennedys picked their Negroes ineptly.

dispute and then to supplant all the rivals. Martin was no ordinary fixer. Hard-headed, fun-loving, and rich, he had bought and sold insurance companies, founded a newspaper in Michigan, edited the Chicago *Defender* for twelve years, presided over the Negro Newspaper Association, and worked in presidential campaigns since 1944. Shriver admired his bluntness so much that he asked what Martin recommended as the single most important step the Kennedy campaign could take to win Negro votes. "Well, as an old newspaper man I may be prejudiced," Martin replied. "But I think you've got to go after the Negro newspapers. They lynched Sparkman and Kefauver * as Southerners, and they'll lynch Lyndon Johnson the same way if you don't do something about it. And I *know* those papers aren't going to do a damn thing for you unless you pay us some money."

This remark struck Shriver as cold-blooded and cynical, but he knew it was precisely what the civil rights staff needed more of to be taken seriously. The watchword inside the Kennedy campaign was "tough." Those who let their idealism or anything else get ahead of their toughness were downgraded as losers. Shriver recognized instantly that Louis Martin understood the inner workings of the Negro world in a way that could be communicated effectively to Robert Kennedy, Lawrence O'Brien, Whizzer White, and the other insiders of the Kennedy campaign. Martin knew how to transfer the money safely—through the purchase of advertising space—and he seemed to know precisely how much money each editor needed to temper his hostility toward Lyndon Johnson. These were areas across the racial divide where even Harris Wofford felt hopelessly at sea.

Shriver decided that Martin was a godsend. From the day he first talked with Martin about the campaign job, he did not rest until he had persuaded him to move to Washington. "I'll get the money for you," he promised. The new staff man arrived just in time to solve the delicate problem of William Dawson of Chicago, dean of the Negro congressmen, whom Robert Kennedy had made the titular chairman of the campaign on the recommendation of Chicago's Mayor Daley. On Dawson's first day in the campaign, he complained about the civil rights name as offensive to "our good Southern friends" and refused to work until the K Street office was upgraded to suit his dignity. This put Shriver and Wofford into a quandary over how they, as white people, should respond to a well-connected Negro who was much more conservative on the race issue than they were. Martin told them not to fret about Dawson, whom he

---

* Senator John Sparkman of Alabama and Senator Estes Kefauver of Tennessee, Adlai Stevenson's running mates in 1952 and 1956.

described as a corrupt old ward politician from the Daley machine. On Martin's advice, they built Dawson a specially partitioned private office, nicknamed "Uncle Tom's Cabin," and left him alone except for ceremonial occasions.

Louis Martin did not always produce miracles, however, as glaringly demonstrated by his failure to persuade Jackie Robinson to endorse Kennedy. As Senator Kennedy had feared months earlier, the most widely admired living Negro announced his support for Nixon early in September. He went on the road almost full time to campaign for the Republican ticket. Inside the Kennedy campaign, this was a disaster that grabbed the attention of the advisers close to the candidate. To them, the single most important endorsement after Robinson would be Adam Clayton Powell. Since the Democratic Convention in Los Angeles, Congressman Powell had been cruising on a yacht in the Mediterranean amid well-founded rumors in the Negro press that he was laying plans to divorce singer Hazel Scott, his second wife. From his cruise, which lasted nearly two and a half months, Powell sent radiophone instructions for an emissary to open negotiations with the Kennedy people. The emissary made his way to Sargent Shriver, who discerned that remuneration in the form of hard cash was involved. A hasty series of meetings among top Kennedy aides produced a decision to pass off the negotiations to Louis Martin.

When Powell's emissary, Ray Jones, laid out the terms—$300,000 cash in advance to buy a complete, nationwide Powell organization for turning out the Negro vote—Martin laughed out loud, as if to remind Jones that he was not dealing with some skittish white novice. Martin knew that there would never be any nationwide organization, that the money was for Powell himself, and that the elaborately described infrastructure was a sham. He and Jones quickly established a flinty, adversarial rapport that enabled them to reach a tentative agreement on the sum of $50,000 for ten Powell endorsement speeches. A temporary impasse then developed because Jones did not trust the Kennedy campaign to pay the money if Powell delivered the speeches first, and Martin did not trust Powell to give the speeches if he delivered the money first. This problem was solved by arranging for New York's mayor Robert Wagner to act as a middleman. Kennedy brother-in-law Stephen Smith would pay the money to Wagner, who would pay it out to Powell in $5,000 chunks on the completion of each scheduled speech. As a final touch, Martin tried to get Powell to agree to delay the announcement of his divorce until after the election, but Powell promised only to delay until after his first speech for Kennedy.

Powell ratified the arrangement on his return from the Mediterranean. Everything was in place before the two-day National Conference on Con-

stitutional Rights opened in Harlem on October 11, at which Senator
Hubert Humphrey, Eleanor Roosevelt, and some four hundred civil rights
leaders gathered to prepare a report on how a Democratic president
should approach the civil rights issue. Senator Kennedy drew cheers with
a declaration that President Eisenhower should have called such a conference after the *Brown* decision six years earlier, and more cheers with
his bold campaign promise to end racial discrimination in federally subsidized housing by presidential executive order, "with the stroke of a
pen." Caught up in the euphoria of the moment, he declared that racial
freedom was an American idea, not a Russian one. He shouted out that
in Africa there were no children named Lenin or Marx or Stalin, or, for
that matter, Richard Nixon. All this brought roars of approval. "But there
are children called George Washington," Kennedy continued. "There are
children called Thomas Jefferson! There may be a couple called Adam
Clayton Powell!"

"Careful, Jack," Powell called out devilishly from behind, and a peal
of laughter went up in tribute to Powell's playboy reputation.

Ten days later, the announcement of Powell's divorce became the biggest story in the Negro press. Kennedy's advisers were still delaying the
release of the promised report from the big civil rights conference, and
King, most unexpectedly, was in jail.

King missed the New York conference because of his annual SCLC board
meeting, which was held that year in Shreveport, Louisiana. It marked
the third consecutive year in which the SCLC ventured to Mississippi or
Louisiana around the opening of the school year. Coincidentally, for the
third year, Mississippi authorities supplied grim news to the Negro
preachers. Two years after Clennon King was institutionalized for applying to attend Ole Miss, and a year after Clyde Kennard was arrested on
the premises of Mississippi Southern College as he left his admissions
interview, police in Hattiesburg arrested Kennard for stealing five bags
of chicken feed, which were found in his barn. The young Negro boy
who admitted stealing them and putting them there said it was Kennard's idea—for which testimony the boy was returned to his job on
probation. With Medgar Evers denouncing the trial as a transparent
frame-up, Kennard was hauled off to serve seven years on the Mississippi
chain gang. Henceforth, as a convicted felon, he was ineligible to apply
to any of Mississippi's all-white colleges.

In Atlanta, King found himself the target of three opposing pressures.
Students wanted him to join them in sit-ins. His father and many of the
city's Negro leaders wanted him to endorse Nixon. Harris Wofford and
Louis Martin, among others, wanted him to help Kennedy. So did Frank

Sinatra. These forces converged upon him at the time of the October SNCC conference, which opened on October 14 at Atlanta's Mount Moriah Baptist Church with King delivering an address on the philosophy of nonviolence. More than two hundred people attended the three-day session. Bayard Rustin was scheduled to speak, but the students withdrew his invitation after AFL-CIO officials threatened to cancel a funding grant if Rustin appeared on the program. The Rustin controversy became the most rancorous internal issue of the weekend. Moses' correspondent Jane Stembridge argued vehemently that the motives were irrelevant to the basic principles of free association, and she quit SNCC in protest when she was overruled on grounds of financial necessity. Rustin also retreated in the face of a personal rejection that came hard upon the Adam Clayton Powell blackmail that summer. He had little to do with King or with the Southern movement for the next three tumultuous years.

Amzie Moore arrived from Mississippi to make his novel proposal for nonviolent SNCC students to encamp in Mississippi and register Negro voters. He received only polite interest, however, as the abstract idea of lonely registration work was lost in the excitement over mass demonstrations. Diane Nash outlined the Nashville movement's plans for a succession of campaigns against segregated stores, restaurants, theaters, and public facilities. James Lawson relentlessly pressed the students to deepen their commitment to nonviolence, arguing that they had squandered their "finest hour" by coming out of jail the previous spring. "Instead of letting the adults scurry around getting bail," he declared, "we should have insisted that they scurry about to end the system which had put us in jail. If history offers us such an opportunity again, let us be prepared to seize it."

Once again, Lawson matched or exceeded King's impact upon the students. His "jail, no bail" speech helped create a vanguard spirit that stayed on to churn up the relationship between King and the leaders of the Atlanta student movement. At the Atlanta University complex, they drew upon the largest and most respected concentration of Negro students in the South, and yet their cumulative protest seemed almost trivial in comparison to the nonviolent wars of attrition elsewhere. They still had only one day's jailing—and no desegregation victories—to their credit. As Bob Moses had discovered, the Atlanta students were impeccably organized and well equipped for nonviolent combat. They had amassed a cache of two-way radios, projectile-proof parkas, and laminated picket signs that would not wash out in the rain, but they had not quite broken through their inhibitions. They were an uncomfortable elite in a time of shifting standards.

Atlanta student leaders implored King to go along with them on a sit-in aimed toward jail. His presence would boost their strength, guarantee headlines, and generate political pressure beyond the capacity of the students alone. King's own brother A.D., who was trying to finish his Morehouse degree at the age of twenty-nine, put the request to him, along with Lonnie C. King (no relation) and Spelman president Herschelle Sullivan, the co-leaders of the Atlanta student movement. So did Bernard Lee, whose expulsion from Alabama State made him such a hero that the student body of Morris Brown College in Atlanta elected him president shortly after he transferred in as a senior.

Objections of pride, fear, and politics gorged up within King. If he went along, he warned them, much of the publicity would be diverted from them to him, and, worse, some important civil rights leaders might be less likely to help student groups simply because they were too closely associated with King. That was a reality, he said. Perhaps they should remain independent, as SNCC leaders often suggested. The students argued in rebuttal that Atlanta was King's hometown. Rich's—the city's largest department store and chief target of the planned campaign—was a place where King and his parents and Ebenezer members had shopped all their lives. One of the most prized possessions in Atlanta was a Rich's charge plate, which the students were now urging Negroes to surrender in protest against the store's segregation. No, said the students, King never could be an intruder here. Rich's was a symbol of Atlanta, which was a symbol of the hopes of the South, and King was a symbol of the hopes of the Negro people.

"Well, maybe I should do it," said King, but he was not sure. The students snatched bits of time with him at home, at Ebenezer, at the SNCC conference, and points in between. When he left town for a speech, a delegation of them followed him to the airport and huddled with him on the concourse before takeoff. Glenn Smiley, the FOR field secretary King had known since the boycott, came through the airport at the same time, headed in a different direction, and happened upon the sight of King surrounded by a half-dozen students. King was on the verge of tears, holding his face in his hands. Smiley interrupted, calling out a greeting, and the departing flight extended King's reprieve.

In Washington, the pressure of a presidential election only three weeks away was weighing on Louis Martin and Harris Wofford. The Kennedy campaign as a whole was scoring on the race issue at the expense of Henry Cabot Lodge, Nixon's running mate. Lodge, caught up in the spirit of a Harlem rally just after Kennedy's, had either promised or predicted that a Nixon Administration would appoint a Negro to the cabinet. Senator Kennedy pounced on this statement as "racism at its worst." He and Lyndon Johnson each pledged that a Kennedy Administration would not consider race or religion at all in cabinet appointments—they would consider only "qualifications." Vice President Nixon took the same public stance, in what was taken as a mild rebuke of Lodge, and Lodge could not extricate himself from the dispute for nearly two weeks. Although the episode worked to Kennedy's advantage, Wofford and Martin winced at the underlying reality that this was really a pitch to white voters. Lodge had given Kennedy and Johnson a safe way to attack the Republicans for excessive sympathy for Negroes.

Wofford and Martin searched for an offsetting gesture to Negro voters. Martin's constant refrain at the office was "Let's get all our horses on the track!"—newspapers, the NAACP, churches, Powell, Negro celebrities. One horse not quite on the Kennedy track was King. They had been approaching an agreement with King for some time. Although King told them that he could not formally endorse either candidate, he had been hinting at a willingness to say something favorable about Kennedy's commitment to civil rights, *if* Kennedy would do something mildly dramatic to justify it. What King had in mind was for Kennedy to visit him, possibly at an SCLC meeting, in the South. The site of the meeting was vitally important, said King, because Negro voters were becoming sensitive to political hypocrisy. In an era of unenforced court decisions and showcase civil rights planks, it would mean almost nothing for King and Kennedy to meet in New York or Chicago, but it would mean a great deal in Atlanta or Montgomery.

King talked by phone with Martin and Wofford about the pros and cons of various cities and particular statements. This was the zone of negotiation. The Kennedy men, knowing that they would have to sell any proposed deal to hostile superiors, and ultimately to the candidate himself, tried to talk King into a compromise city such as Louisville or St. Louis. They argued that the Kennedy people would not be overly impressed with the kind of "nonpartisan statement" King had in mind—that to their bosses, people were either for Kennedy or not—and that King should be flexible on the city if he refused an outright endorsement. While bargaining, Louis Martin warned King that major civil rights demonstrations before the election would almost certainly ruin any possible agreement. Demonstrations were anathema to Kennedy campaign strategists, who did not want to remind Negro voters in the North that Kennedy was aligned with the Southern officeholders who would repress the demonstrators. At the same time, demonstrations would make it impossible for Kennedy to meet with someone like King, which would risk losing an enormous bloc of Southern white votes. Opinion polls showed that Kennedy might become the first Democrat to lose the South in more than a hundred years.

Kennedy pressure was also reaching King from Hollywood. Through the contacts of Harry Belafonte and Clarence Jones, King had persuaded Frank Sinatra, Sammy Davis, Jr., and other entertainers from the Sinatra clique to perform for a civil rights fund-raiser in Carnegie Hall, scheduled for January. Sinatra, whose rendition of "High Hopes" had been the Kennedy campaign song since the early primaries, was unhappy that King was refusing to return the favor by appearing at a Kennedy rally in California. Through Sammy Davis, he sent an ominous message that King should not count on the help of Sinatra if he snubbed Sinatra's friend Senator Kennedy. Against this veiled threat, Stanley Levison joined Belafonte in supporting the commitment to nonpartisanship. "One point might be stressed with Sammy [Davis]," Levison advised King by letter. "Since you are concentrating on getting the vote in the South, the effectiveness of your efforts would be diminished if you were identified as an adherent of one party. . . . Sometimes I think these people see you too much as a personality of glamour, not as a leader whose responsibilities will continue over decades and through changes of great magnitude. . . . Frank, Sammy and the others are not intellectual leaders nor moral leaders[,] so their decisions can be more easily arrived at without the singular weight that attaches to a decision or stand by you."

King received Levison's letter during the SNCC conference, which coincided with the Lodge controversy over hypothetical Negro cabinet members and King's roving ordeal with the Atlanta students, including his brother. When he returned from his speaking trip, the students caught up with him again at his parents' home, where Mother King nearly always had some turnip greens on the stove. He was munching the greens, dipping bread into the juice, as the students pressed him toward consent, saying they were ready to move within forty-eight hours, their plans couldn't wait. Before they got very far, Daddy King burst into the kitchen wearing a glower of disapproval. "M.L., you don't need to go!" he said urgently. "This is the students, not you."

Daddy King scattered the students like bowling pins. King put up his usual soft defense against his father's arguments, agreeing whenever he could, and maintained a similar attitude when the students circled back to renew their urgent pep talks. All the while, King took phone calls from Harris Wofford in Washington. At one point, Wofford thought he had clearance to offer a Kennedy-King meeting in Nashville, which was "Southern enough" for King but "too Southern," as it turned out, for Kennedy's top strategists. The Southern politicians within their telephone networks howled so loudly in opposition that the Nashville plan was revoked. A hundred phone calls and many white lies later, Wofford called King again to offer Miami instead of Nashville, the next afternoon or evening. King was not very happy about the switch. Wofford repeated the Kennedy arguments that Miami was a "Deep South city," but he did not do so very forcefully. He said it was the best he could do.

King thought it over, then told Wofford frankly that one reason he was inclined to accept Miami was that it would overlap with a student demonstration just now boiling up in Atlanta. "I don't want to have to be there," he said. Wofford replied that the Kennedy people would not be happy to hear of a demonstration whether King was there or not. He thought it best not to tell them, for fear they would back off the Miami plan. King said he had tried to get the students to delay the new sit-in until after the election, but his heart was not in it. Wofford understood this. His firm Gandhian belief in civil disobedience occasionally shined through the corporate lawyer persona he was stressing for the Kennedy campaign. Louis Martin had seen through it already, and teasingly advised Wofford to become a priest.

"I'll do it," King told Wofford. "But you should tell Mr. Kennedy that I will be obliged to issue a pro forma invitation to Mr. Nixon."

Wofford's heart sank. "Do you really feel you have to do that?" he asked.

"Yes," said King. "I don't think Mr. Nixon will accept, but I have to give him the chance."

When King hung up, it appeared that he had maneuvered himself into a choice of safe, prestige politics over the gritty, dangerous protest. The students would be angry, but they would have to accept a meeting with one or both of the presidential candidates as a legitimate reason for missing a demonstration. Daddy King, on the other hand, would be relieved that his son was out of the sit-in but unhappy that he was moving toward Kennedy.

When Wofford hung up, he decided that this latest twist was something he should take directly to Senator Kennedy himself, if possible, because his aides would certainly shoot it down. He squeezed in a minute or two with Kennedy, who was getting ready to leave for Miami, to explain the condition of a parallel invitation to Nixon. "The hell with that," Kennedy replied instantly. "Nixon might be smart enough to accept. If he does, I lose votes. I'm taking a much greater risk in the South than Nixon, but King wants to treat us as equals. Tell him it's off."

The next day, Tuesday, October 18, Daddy King joined the leadership of the Atlanta Baptist Ministers' Union in an endorsement of the Nixon-Lodge ticket. These were the city's senior Negroes, for the most part—men who had grown up with a loyalty to the "party of Lincoln" and whose status within their community as relatively big businessmen reinforced that identity against the Democratic encroachments since Franklin Roosevelt. This year, there was an additional factor binding them as conservative Baptists to the Republicans: Kennedy's Catholic faith. Perhaps for that reason they took the unusual step of signing their names to a declaration of Republican support.

In Miami that day, both Kennedy and Nixon made headlines with addresses to the national convention of the American Legion. Nixon called for a full economic quarantine against the "intolerable cancer" of communism in Cuba, but Kennedy drew more applause by charging that Nixon's preference for economic solutions indicated a lack of military resolve. "I have never believed in retreating under fire," said Kennedy. He ridiculed Nixon for having said to Khrushchev, in the famous kitchen debate, "You may be ahead of us in rockets, but we are ahead of you in color television." Kennedy drew laughs and cheers from the legionnaires when he added, "I think I'll take my television in black and white."

Also that day, Atlanta student movement leader Lonnie C. King called his pastor at Ebenezer to make a final plea for the demonstration. "You are the spiritual leader of the movement, and you were born in Atlanta, Georgia," he told King. "And I think it might add tremendous impetus if you would go."

"Where are you going to go tomorrow, L.C.?" asked King.

"I'm going to be on the bridge down at Rich's."

"Well, I'll meet you on the bridge tomorrow at ten o'clock," said King. With these words, he took his first deliberate step toward prison.

NINE

A PAWN OF HISTORY

Eighty demonstrators, their watches synchronized, requested service in eight different segregated establishments at precisely eleven o'clock the next morning, October 19. King's group was refused service at a snack bar in the covered bridge that connected buildings of the Rich's complex on either side of Forsyth Street. Company officials did not ask the foregathered police officers to arrest them, however, and the demonstrators then took an elevator to the sixth-floor Magnolia Room, the store's most elegant restaurant for shoppers. There the board chairman of Rich's interceded personally. Failing to persuade the demonstrators to leave, he had them arrested under a state anti-trespass law.

As the first to be arrested, and the only nonstudent among the defendants, King was first to speak in court that night before Judge James E. Webb, who set bond at $500 pending trial. "I cannot accept bond," said King. "I will stay in jail one year, or ten years." In a brief, nervous courtroom oration, King explained that he did not want to go to jail, nor to "upset peace," but that his decision to choose jail was in accord with the principles of a movement that went "far beyond" dining room segregation and other Southern folkways. He urged the judge to vacate the charges. When Webb refused, King was hustled off to spend the first night of his life behind bars. Thirty-five students followed him in quick succession.

Tension gave way to euphoria shortly after the new prisoners found themselves in a special cell block of the county jail, in the care of Negro guards who supplied games, books, and phone messages. The first prison meal—steak smothered in onions—wiped out any lingering doubts that these particular prisoners had been marked for favorable treatment. The high quality of the food quickly seduced them out of plans for a prison fast. The students, realizing that the worst was over, turned with enthusiasm to the task of creating a communal regimen that would see them through weeks, even months, in jail together. Bernard Lee eagerly claimed the bunk just above King's. He noted with scarcely concealed pleasure that their co-prisoners in the female cell block were sending messages envious of the males for having King among them. King was a special prize to the students generally and to Lee in particular. He joined with them in organizing a prison routine—sang with them, participated in their workshops, and addressed them in sermonettes on nonviolence. Lee was delighted to find that he could beat King regularly at checkers, and King, pondering the checkerboard, vowed playfully that he would get even as soon as he could catch Lee around a pool table.

Boredom had no chance to penetrate the cell block, especially since news filtered in hourly about how their arrest was gripping the city of Atlanta and beyond. Mayor William Hartsfield was holding meetings. Atlanta police chief Herbert Jenkins was giving the demonstrations his personal attention. Reporters counted as many as two thousand Negro student picketers around segregated targets on Thursday, the second day. Three more prisoners came into the cell block, and twenty-two others went into the city jail. No nerves failed—no one bonded out.

On Friday, jail authorities allowed King and student leaders to hold a press interview, at which King spoke quietly, almost shyly, about his reasons for joining the student protest. "I had to practice what I preached," he said. He spoke proudly of the fact that his fellow prisoners included five of the six student body presidents from the Atlanta University complex, plus two "college queens" and a number of honor students. Of his own sacrifices, King mentioned only the loss to the SCLC of revenue from his scheduled speeches during the most lucrative quarter of the year. "I was to have been in Cleveland on Sunday," he said. The Cleveland preachers had guaranteed the SCLC $7,000 from the event.

That night, 85 million Americans watched the fourth and final debate between Kennedy and Nixon. Confined by agreement to issues of foreign policy, the debate was an unrecognized milestone of American politics in that it featured the clandestine preoccupations that had been growing within the U.S. government since World War II. Kennedy, who later maintained that his CIA briefings had not covered the subject, criticized the Republicans for not doing precisely what they were doing: helping Cuban exiles prepare to overthrow Castro by covert warfare. Nixon, who already had helped launch this plan, decided he must protect the operation's secrecy by opposing his own policies. He criticized Kennedy in the debate for making "probably the most dangerously irresponsible recommendations" of the campaign. If the United States followed Kennedy's prescription for secret warfare, Nixon declared, we would violate no fewer than five treaty commitments prohibiting intervention in the internal affairs of Latin American nations. All through the debate, Kennedy and Nixon attacked each other in coded language that was not always clear to each other—let alone to most viewers, who still knew little more about the CIA than they had known about the Manhattan Project before Hiroshima.

Although he worked in the Kennedy campaign, Harris Wofford responded to the surface realities like almost everyone else, and he found himself in the uncomfortable position of agreeing with Nixon. At his home the next morning, Wofford heard radio reports that the Ku Klux Klan was marching in opposition to student picketers on the streets of Atlanta. King was spending his fourth day in the county jail. Wofford, as one of King's few friends outside Atlanta who knew how badly he had wanted to avoid this ordeal, chastised himself for doing nothing to help. Wofford impulsively started calling Atlanta contacts, among them a prominent attorney named Morris Abram, who agreed to talk with Mayor Hartsfield about getting King out of jail.*

Abram found Hartsfield in the center of a maelstrom at city hall. Telegrams for and against King were arriving hourly in stacks from all over the country. Police officials were rushing in with reports about the growing threat of violence between white and Negro picketers. Hartsfield, negotiating in the city council chamber with many of the city's most influential Negro leaders, was offering to begin intensive negotiations toward the desegregation of all downtown stores, and to say so publicly, if the Negroes would come out of jail and refrain from demonstrations during a truce period. The sticking point, Abram learned from the mayor, was that King and the students were refusing to accept release on bail. They would come out of jail only if the charges against them were dropped. This stand entangled mediator Hartsfield in bureaucracy as well as racial politics. As mayor, he could arrange to drop the charges against

---

* Abram's subsequent high positions would include terms as president of the Field Foundation, of the American Jewish Committee, and of Brandeis University, and, two decades later, appointment by President Ronald Reagan to the U.S. Civil Rights Commission.

those in the city jail, but he had no jurisdiction over King and the others held in the county jail pending trial on state charges. These could be dropped only by the state prosecutor or by the criminal complainant, Rich's department store. Its owner, Richard Rich, was consumed by fear that if he gave in, Negroes would descend on his stores with demands for nothing less than complete desegregation, which would drive white business to Rich's competitors. This was a fate only slightly worse to Rich than his current one of being exposed in an ugly racial conflict. Rich had broken down in tears on hearing that his board chairman could get King and the demonstrators out of the Magnolia Room only in handcuffs.

To a wily old politician such as Hartsfield, the best way to run such a formidable gauntlet was to announce the desired settlement before the diverse parties agreed to it. This required more than a little fudging, with its attendant political risk, and the mayor was casting about for a way to avoid taking all the political responsibility for the gambit. When Abram mentioned the call he had just received from Harris Wofford, whom Hartsfield knew as a Kennedy campaign aide, lights seemed to flare up in the mayor's head. It occurred to him that he might accomplish a great deal by announcing that Senator Kennedy had asked him to get King out of jail. Not only would this buttress the truce with a name of national importance, making it harder for Governor Vandiver and other state Democrats to denounce, but the move might also win Negro votes for Kennedy in closely contested Northern states. The more Hartsfield thought about the brainstorm, the better it seemed to him. He might not only extricate his city from a dangerous, embarrassing racial conflict but perhaps even elect a president of the United States.

Soon Abram was calling Wofford from the Mayor's office to broach Hartsfield's bold proposal. Wofford almost fainted when he heard it. He was feeling even more on the political fringe of the Kennedy campaign, and he knew from hard personal experience that the last thing his bosses wanted was to be associated with King in a Southern racial confrontation. Frantically, Wofford begged Abram and Hartsfield not to go forward with the plan unless Senator Kennedy approved, and he reminded Abram that his own call earlier that morning had been strictly personal, not political. Wofford promised to seek Senator Kennedy's permission, but, being extremely reluctant to subject himself to further ridicule, he made only halfhearted attempts to locate the candidate, who was barnstorming through Kansas. Then Wofford called the Atlanta mayor's office again to report that it was impossible to make contact and that therefore the plan was off. By this time, however, a battered Hartsfield was desperate for a solution. He grabbed the phone from Abram and said, "Now, Harris, I'm just so certain that his taking a position will help him with this doubtful

Negro vote all over the nation that I'm going to take it on myself to tell this group that Senator Kennedy is asking me to intervene. That he has asked me to turn Martin Luther King loose. Why should he be ashamed of that? I'm going to turn him loose anyway."

Wofford's panic returned instantly. He poured into the mayor's ear all the arguments that had been thrown at him inside the campaign, about how Kennedy was in danger of losing Georgia, the South, and the entire election because of his association with civil rights. Hartsfield did not believe this, but he promised Wofford that he would contact Kennedy himself. Using Wofford's private numbers, Hartsfield tracked Kennedy from telephone to telephone in Kansas—now hearing bands playing in the background, now hearing a policeman say Kennedy had just left. Finally, Hartsfield gave up and returned to the city council chamber to bargain with Daddy King and the others. There, under pressure, he invoked Kennedy's name behind his own truce conditions. A reporter who had sneaked into the chamber quickly put the story of Kennedy's involvement on the national wires.

Very shortly, enraged Southern politicians, including Kennedy's Georgia campaign strategists, called Hartsfield demanding to know exactly how and why the Democratic nominee had been dragged into the King controversy. The mayor dissembled adroitly and then called Wofford with a warning. "Now, I know that I ran with the ball farther than you expected, Harris, my boy," he said, trying gamely to be casual, "but I needed a peg to swing on and you gave it to me, and I've swung on it." Hartsfield told Wofford not to let Kennedy disavow Hartsfield's announcement under pressure from Southern governors. In this new emergency, Wofford did manage to reach the Kennedy campaign plane in Kansas City. His report caused shock—"Hartsfield said *what?* You did *what?*"—followed by curses and fury. When Pierre Salinger, Ken O'Donnell, and other top aides signed off to draft a statement protecting Kennedy, a chastened Wofford waited to see whether they would call Hartsfield a liar. As it turned out, the statement released was vague and noncommittal: " . . . Senator Kennedy directed that an inquiry be made to give him all the facts on that situation and a report on what properly should be done. The Senator is hopeful that a satisfactory outcome can be worked out." This accomplished the primary objective of minimizing the story, which received practically no attention in the press.

Hartsfield spent the rest of that Saturday trying to sell his plan to the Negro conclave in the city council chamber. After many urgent messages to and from the county jail, it turned out that King and the students would not accept bail on Hartsfield's promise to get the state charges dropped. Sticking to their "jail, no bail" slogan, they insisted that they could wait until the charges actually were dropped, or until their trials. It was nightfall before the mayor bypassed this last obstacle. He ordered the unconditional release of the students held in the city jail, pledged to have King and the others out of the county jail by Monday morning, and declared victory. There would be no demonstrations on Monday by either Negroes or Klansmen, he said, and he would begin desegregation talks with the downtown merchants that same day. Speaking for the Negro delegation, Reverend Borders praised the agreement, the mayor, and the city. "This was the best meeting we've ever held in the city of Atlanta," he told reporters, adding that "the shortest route to heaven is from Atlanta, Georgia." All that remained was for Hartsfield to visit Richard Rich and the state prosecutor, separately, and to tell each of them that the other had agreed to drop the charges.

The next day, Governor Nelson Rockefeller preached Sunday sermons at four different Negro churches in Brooklyn, wearing a gray tie with a little pink elephant on it. Rockefeller managed to endorse the Republican ticket without mentioning Richard Nixon by name. Leaving the hard partisan pitch to his pulpit companion, Jackie Robinson, the governor gave his "fellow Baptists" a talk on the love verses of I Corinthians. "We've got to make love a reality in our own country," he said. "When the great spiritual leader, the Rev. Dr. Martin Luther King, finds himself in jail today because he had the courage to love, we have a long way to go in America." One of his hosts that day, Daddy King's old friend Sandy Ray, told the congregation that he was sticking with the Republicans again in the upcoming election, although he was not that happy about the ticket. "To be frank," said Ray, "most of us wanted the Governor to be the nominee."

Daddy King outpreached Rockefeller that same day in Cleveland. Filling in for his jailed son, he preached six different sermons at the SCLC fund-raisers and then flew home to Atlanta in time to join the jubilant crowd outside the county jail Monday morning, waiting for the release of the prisoners.

The sense of crisis returned in new form when jail officials notified Negro lawyers that they had received a bench warrant ordering them to hold King in jail on other charges. Cries of betrayal went up. The lawyers eventually established that the warrant was issued on the authority of a judge in neighboring De Kalb County, where Emory University was located. The previous May, King and Coretta had driven writer Lillian Smith to Emory Hospital there for her cancer treatments, and a De Kalb policeman had stopped them for questioning—as was frequently done when patrol officers spotted interracial groups of travelers. The officer, finding that King was still driving on his Alabama license some three months after moving to Georgia, had charged him with the misdemeanor of driving without a proper permit, and Judge Oscar Mitchell had sentenced King to a twelve-month sentence, which he suspended, plus a $25 fine. Now Judge Mitchell asked Fulton County to keep King in jail pending a hearing on whether the Rich's arrest violated the terms of his suspended sentence in the May traffic case.

King's cellmates mutinied over the news. While jail officials were processing their release papers under the Hartsfield agreement, the students were banding together in a pledge not to leave the jail without King. They accused Hartsfield of bad faith, and it took some time for the mayor to convince them that he was as upset about the bench warrant as they were. He suspected political machinations on the part of Governor Vandiver, who held a press conference that morning to announce that he had talked personally with Senator Kennedy and received assurances that the candidate had "no authority, intention or desire" to intervene in Georgia's criminal processes. Even as Hartsfield was countering this move with his own press conference, in which he made fuzzy statements about just who had urged him on Kennedy's behalf to release King, he was scrambling to persuade angry Negroes not to renounce the deal. He argued that Judge Mitchell had no case against King. The traffic charge was a minor misdemeanor in the first place, and the charges were now dropped in the Rich's case. King's lawyers sustained him with a dozen technical arguments, saying the De Kalb matter could be cleared up quickly. To reassure King's cellmates, Daddy King and other adult leaders were permitted into the cell block to make speeches. "M.L. will be all right," he said. King himself made a speech urging his cellmates to abide by the agreement, and when the other thirty-seven marched out regretfully, but peacefully, to freedom, he spent his first night in jail alone.

The students reassembled outside the Fulton County jail early Tuesday morning in a vigil of support, waiting for King to be transferred to De Kalb County for Judge Mitchell's hearing. A group of white theology students, in Atlanta on a mission to encourage the sit-ins, joined them in quiet prayers until the first sight of King turned all their hopeful apprehension into cold fear. Emerging from the jail between two De Kalb County detectives, King wore not only handcuffs but also leg and arm shackles. The students fell silent enough to hear the clang of metal as King was marched briskly to a squad car and put into the backseat next to a police dog. The car sped away, leaving the students behind, helpless. As for King, who was trying not to look at the ferocious German shepherd beside him, it was a sudden return to the terror of his first arrest nearly five years earlier in Montgomery, when visions of lynching had undone him. Now that he had given the white authorities a tiny legal opening at the Magnolia Room, it was they and not he who would control his exposure to danger.

Nearly two hundred King supporters—including Roy Wilkins, who was in town, and four presidents from the Atlanta University complex— crowded into Judge Mitchell's hearing. The De Kalb County territory was alien to the Atlantans. Worse than unfamiliar, it was fearful, as everyone knew that county officials recently had sanctioned a Ku Klux Klan parade through the corridors of that same courthouse. The hearing was permeated with an atmosphere of latent race violence, and with survival instincts more suited to a murder trial than a traffic case. Solic- itor Jack Smith demanded a harsh penalty, saying that King had shown "no sign of penitence or remorse." Donald Hollowell, King's chief attor- ney, presented character witnesses and a host of arguments, but Mitchell banged the gavel, revoked King's probation, and ordered him to serve four months at hard labor on a state road gang, beginning immediately. The spectators gasped in shock. Hollowell jumped to his feet to ask that King be released on bond pending appeal of both the current ruling and the original traffic sentence, but Judge Mitchell denied the motion. He ordered the sheriff's deputies to take King away.

The emotion in the courtroom was such that the dignified Samuel Williams—Morehouse philosophy professor, preacher, SCLC board member, Atlanta NAACP president—flung himself forward to cry out against the injustice. Deputies wrestled him to the floor and soon pitched him into the holding cell with King. When Williams recovered his com- posure, he was brought back into court for a lecture from Judge Mitchell and then released. The judge allowed the King family a parting visit in the holding cell. As King saw his wife and his sister Christine approach- ing the cell in tears, he said, "Corrie, dear, you have to be strong. I've never seen you like this. You have to be strong for me." His pleading tone, and the tiredness that had crept into his face after six days in jail, only made Coretta collapse further into weeping. Daddy King was so upset that he scolded her for it. "You don't see me crying," he said. "I am ready to fight."

King tried to make peace. "I think we must prepare ourselves for the fact that I am going to have to serve this time," he said. There was not much to say, and the family soon left him behind. Coretta, who was six months pregnant, gave way to self-pity as she contemplated bearing their third child with her husband in jail.

In the aftershock outside, Mayor Hartsfield worked diligently to dissociate his city from the De Kalb proceedings. "I have made requests of all the news agencies that in their stories they make it clear that this hearing did not take place in Atlanta, Georgia," he announced. Governor Vandiver's press spokesman, on the other hand, warmly praised Judge Mitchell's decision. "I think the maximum sentence for Martin Luther King might do him good," he said, "might make a law-abiding citizen out of him and teach him to respect the law of Georgia." At the SCLC, Wyatt Tee Walker fended off Negro reporters who wanted to know why he had not responded to the sentence by setting up protest pickets around the De Kalb County courthouse. There was "too much tenseness," he said, and it was too dangerous to operate away from "home ground."

Instead, Walker spread an alarm by telephone in advance of headline news. For the time being, he forgot partisanship, protest, and even segregation, believing that the only issue now was King's life. The state road gang meant cutthroat inmates and casually dismissed murders. King had to be freed or he would be dead. This was the emergency message that Walker and a band of colleagues sent to every person they could think of who might conceivably have influence. Stanley Levison called lawyers, union leaders, Rockefeller aides, politicians. Harry Belafonte called every entertainer he knew, as well as aides on both sides of the presidential race—Robert Kennedy, Sargent Shriver, E. Frederic Morrow, Jackie Robinson. All the while, Donald Hollowell was hurriedly preparing a writ of habeas corpus, arguing that Georgia law did not permit a judge to withhold bail in a misdemeanor case. This was unassailable legal ground, but those around King had lost faith in the law.

In Washington, Harris Wofford responded to the alarm that same day by drafting a dignified statement of protest for Senator Kennedy to make. His draft was promptly buffeted around inside the Washington campaign headquarters and over the wires to the Chicago suburbs, where Kennedy was making speeches. Inevitably, phone calls buzzed down into Georgia and back by the dozens, and Wofford was soon hearing that Governor Vandiver had promised to get King out of jail on the condition that Kennedy make no public statement about the matter. Vandiver wanted to send out a strong, clear signal of segregationist resolve in Georgia; he made the Gestapo tactics Wyatt Walker was describing sound like a small tactical maneuver. The governor and his allies won the quick round of infighting within the Kennedy campaign, which earned the loser, Harris Wofford, a quick mollifying call from Senator Kennedy that night. "What we want most is to get King out, isn't it?" Kennedy asked.

Wofford agreed. Still, he was miserable when Coretta King called soon thereafter wanting to know if he could help. He could not tell her about the Vandiver agreement, for fear that public news of it would make

Vandiver renege on his promise, and he had no other good news to offer. Disconsolate, Wofford went out for an after-work beer with Louis Martin. The two of them groped for ideas. They wanted to do *something* to help, but it had to be something that would not run them into the political buzz saw inside the campaign. Out of these constraints came their idea of getting an important personage to call Coretta with encouragement. This was only a small gesture, but it was something that would make them feel better. Politically, they knew that there might be some advantage if they could keep the gesture beneath the threshold of white attention. If Vandiver and his allies were not aroused in anger, the Kennedy campaign might be able to spread the word privately among Negro voters.

Recharged by this idea, Wofford managed to reach his old mentor Chester Bowles, who, as it happened, was entertaining Adlai Stevenson at his home for dinner. Bowles readily agreed to call Coretta King at once with his personal good wishes and the best assurances he could give her that all was being done to free King. This he did, and after Stevenson went home Bowles reported to Wofford that his call seemed to lift her spirits. The only hitch, he told Wofford, was that Stevenson had refused to take the phone even to say hello to Coretta, saying it was not proper as he had not been introduced to her. Bowles and Wofford puzzled over their friend's skittishness. It might be traced to political caution—Stevenson hoped to be Secretary of State if Kennedy was elected—or, as Wofford thought more likely, to Stevenson's simpler, more personal discomfort in the presence of Negroes. This trait, which Wofford had observed firsthand, was one of the factors that had moved him to switch from Stevenson to Kennedy early in the election year.

These and countless other phone calls went on until after midnight. By then, King and eight other prisoners had divided up the bunks inside a crowded cell at the De Kalb County jail and King had dropped off to sleep, only to be wakened by a voice calling "King! Get up!" Seconds later came more shouts and a flashlight shining into his eyes. Grabbing his suit, he stumbled out into the hands of sheriff's deputies, who wordlessly handcuffed and shackled him. He was led clanking through the cell block out into the night, then deposited inside a police car. When he received no answers to his questions about where they were taking him, he fell silent.

Hollowell called the jail just before eight o'clock that Wednesday morning to advise the authorities that he was on the way with his writ of habeas corpus. The writ would do no good now, he was told, as King had been transferred to Reidsville, the maximum-security prison. Hollowell recoiled in shock. His news swept through Negro Atlanta within the hour, and the alarm calls went out again. Coretta King was nearly hysterical by the time she reached Harris Wofford. She had just received the one phone call King was allowed on arrival at the Reidsville state prison. They had yanked him out of jail in the middle of the night without warning, she said. No one had any idea what would happen next.

Wofford went to Louis Martin with the latest details, which further undermined their faith in the Vandiver promise. A few retellings of the Reidsville story revealed to them, however, that the Negro and white perceptions of the event were growing ever farther apart. Those who identified with King felt the terror of the shackles and the tough cops, the quick bang of the gavel, and the unscheduled nighttime ride 230 miles out into rural Georgia. Those with more detachment saw the case as a matter of Southern ignorance that would be reversed sooner or later, and to them the issue of how and when King was transferred to Reidsville was relatively unimportant. Morris Abram argued that King actually was safer at Reidsville than he had been at the De Kalb County jail. Such nonchalance undercut Wofford's efforts to stir up new interest within the Kennedy campaign. In fact, Kennedy's aides were neglecting to return his phone calls, the better to avoid his nagging.

Wofford called his own boss, Sargent Shriver, who had been spending most of his time lately in his crucial home state of Illinois, running Businessmen for Kennedy and Johnson. Shriver was in Chicago, where the candidate's entourage was passing through like a storm. Senator Kennedy had just finished a campaign breakfast with about fifty Illinois businessmen at O'Hare Airport and was huddled with his advisers in a special holding suite near the runway, waiting for his plane to leave. Wofford's call found Shriver there, and Shriver gave him the kind of flyspeck attention lower aides usually get from officials standing within thirty feet of a candidate for President. In emergency shorthand Wofford blurted out the headlines—King snatched off to state prison, no release from Vandiver, Coretta hysterical, the campaign civil rights office swamped with calls. He said he and Louis Martin had given up the idea that Kennedy should make a public statement, but they had something simpler and less controversial in mind. "If the Senator would only call Mrs. King and wish her well," said Wofford, "it would reverberate all through the Negro community in the United States. All he's got to do is say he's thinking about her and he hopes everything will be all right. All he's got to do is show a little heart. He can even say he doesn't have all the facts in the case . . ."

"All right, all right," Shriver said hurriedly. "You've got to give me some good numbers." After money and publicity, accurate phone numbers were the most precious commodity in a campaign.

Wofford quickly rattled off numbers for Hartsfield, Morris Abram, and others, assuming Shriver would want to lay the groundwork for a call. "No, no," said Shriver. There wasn't time for all that. "Where is she? Give me *her* number." He took down the King home number in Atlanta, put it in his pocket, and rejoined the huddle around Kennedy.

Shriver waited, hoping that Sorensen, O'Donnell, Salinger, Lawrence O'Brien, and the other members of Kennedy's kitchen cabinet would rush off to telephones and typewriters. He did not want to mention Wofford's idea in their presence. If they did not strangle the idea on sight, the aides, who liked to speculate about how contemplated moves might play in *The New York Times*, would object that Kennedy could not possibly do anything quiet in the King case, which was on that morning's front page. Finally, Senator Kennedy said he was not feeling well and went into the bedroom to lie down. Shriver alone followed him. Gently but urgently, he repeated Wofford's proposition, stressing what he called King's "lousy treatment" in jail and Mrs. King's emotional breakdown. "I think you ought to give her a call, Jack," he concluded.

Kennedy sat up wearily on the bed. "What the hell," he said. "That's a decent thing to do. Why not? Get her on the phone."

Shriver quickly pulled the paper from his pocket and dialed the number. The phone rang in the King bedroom, where Coretta was dressing to keep an appointment with Morris Abram. Daddy King, who had decided that this situation was grave enough to require the influence of a white lawyer like Abram, instead of Hollowell, was on his way to take her with him. When Coretta identified herself, Shriver said, "Just a minute, Mrs. King, for Senator Kennedy," and handed the phone to the candidate on the bed.

After greeting her, Kennedy said, "I know this must be very hard for you. I understand you are expecting a baby, and I just wanted you to know that I was thinking about you and Dr. King. If there is anything I can do to help, please feel free to call on me."

"I certainly appreciate your concern," said Coretta. "I would appreciate anything you could do to help."

It was over within two minutes. Coretta called Mother King fairly bursting with the news, and Shriver sneaked out the back door of the suite before the aides arrived to whisk Senator Kennedy to the plane.

At Reidsville state prison, clad in striped prison garb, King was being held in solitary confinement until the custodians finished processing him into prison duties. His presence already had attracted the special attention of the inmates. Some Negro prisoners sent messages reminding him that they had written him for advice about how to appeal convictions for various heinous crimes; other messages informed him that there was a movement to stage a hunger strike in his honor. King discouraged the idea.

That afternoon, he wrote his first letter from prison, to Coretta. "Hello Darling," it began.

Today I find myself a long way from you and the children . . . I know this whole experience is very difficult for you to adjust to, especially in your condition of pregnancy, but as I said to you yesterday this is the cross that we must bear for the freedom of our people. . . . I have the faith to believe that this excessive suffering that is now coming to our family will in some little way serve to make Atlanta a better city, Georgia a better state, and America a better country. Just how I do not yet know, but I have faith to believe it will. If I am correct then our suffering is not in vain.

. . . I understand that everybody—white and colored—can have visitors this coming Sunday. I hope you can find some way to come down. . . . Also ask Wyatt to come. There are some very urgent things that I will need to talk with him about. Pleas[e] bring the following books to me: *Stride Toward Freedom*, Paul Tillich's *Systematic Theology* Vol. 1 and 2, George Buttrick *The Parables of Jesus*, E. S. Jones *Mahatma Gandhi, Horns and Halo*, a Bible, a Dictionary and my reference dictionary called *Increasing Your Word Power*. This book is an old book in a red cover and it may be in the den or upstairs in one of my bags. Also bring the following sermons from my file[:] "What is Man" "The Three Dimensions" "The Death of Evil" . . . [He listed fifteen more sermons.] Also bring a radio.

Give my best regards to all the family. Please ask them not to worry about me. I will adjust to whatever comes in terms of pain. Hope to see you Sunday. Eternally yours, Martin.

On the campaign flight to Detroit, Senator Kennedy mentioned casually to Pierre Salinger that he had made a personal call from Chicago to Mrs. Martin Luther King. It was not quite a confession and not quite a warning, but Salinger and the others had no trouble figuring out that Shriver had slipped something past them, probably on the urging of the pesky Wofford. Salinger was concerned enough to call Robert Kennedy on the radiophone.

In general, Kennedy aides were admired for just what Salinger now feared of Wofford: daring, unorthodox maneuvers to unearth political treasure. The biggest hero inside the campaign was the lawyer who had pried out of the Eisenhower State Department a secret poll showing U.S. prestige to be in decline around the world because of the U-2 incident and the crises in Cuba and the Congo. In order to protect Kennedy from charges that he was using classified information for partisan purposes, the lawyer helped leak the poll to *The New York Times* with assurances that the campaign would not be identified as its source. Then, citing the *Times* story, Senator Kennedy was free to demand release of the poll and to hammer away on what he called "a threat to survival." In the last month of the campaign, Kennedy made more headlines with the prestige issue than with any other. What Salinger and his colleagues feared was that Wofford was just enough of a Kennedy man to apply these hard-headed tactics to a softheaded issue.

This was precisely what Wofford and Louis Martin had in mind. To protect himself inside the campaign, Wofford first called Coretta King and told her that it was vitally important for her not to tell any reporters about Senator Kennedy's call without Wofford's consent. Then he and Martin began to guide reporters toward a story in Atlanta, moving delicately and indirectly, mentioning Abram and others who knew of the call while trying to keep themselves hidden as sources. The game ended abruptly when a *New York Times* reporter called Wofford wanting to know why Coretta King was saying that she would not talk to reporters without clearance from Wofford. (Wofford had neglected to tell her that she must not only follow his instructions but keep the instructions themselves confidential.) Shrugging, he called her back and told her it was all right to talk now.

At the Kennedy campaign headquarters in Washington, Robert Kennedy's first move after hearing that reporters were onto the story was to call Sargent Shriver in a quiet fury. When Shriver disclosed the facts of the phone call from the Chicago airport, Kennedy tongue-lashed and belittled him in a tirade that permanently strained the family relationship between them. "You bomb-throwers have lost the whole campaign," he said. When he hung up on Shriver, he sent orders for Wofford and Martin to report to his office at once.

The summons was received in the civil rights office as a calling card from the executioner. "Well, I think you're the best one to tell Bobby what happened," Wofford said to Martin.

"He said both of us," Martin protested, trying to laugh. He agreed, however, that Wofford was much more exposed as the culprit, and finally went to Kennedy's office a few minutes ahead of Wofford, hoping to soften the blow.

Robert Kennedy picked up with Martin where he had left off with Shriver, in a stream of curses delivered in an ominously quiet manner. As Martin waited for an opening to defend himself, it seemed to him that Kennedy's outburst was strangely disconnected from the facts—that his ranting was the nervous frustration of a campaign manager only thirteen days from the election, burdened by a million problems. "Well, one reason we did it," Martin interjected at first chance, "was that they took Dr. King out of Atlanta on an old traffic charge of driving without a license. Then they sentenced him to four months on the chain gang, denied bail, and took him off in the middle of the night to the state prison. All in one day."

"How could they do that?" Kennedy asked doubtfully. "Who's the judge? You can't deny bail on a misdemeanor."

Martin decided that Kennedy may have lost sight of the essential fact that King was a Negro—a detail Southern politicians carefully avoided in their protests against interference in the King case. "Well, they just did it," said Martin. "They wanted to make an example of him as an uppity Negro. That's why it's so dangerous to us in the campaign. I've heard that Jackie Robinson is trying to get Nixon to hold a press conference and blame the whole thing on the Democrats. Those are all Democrats running things down there." Martin stopped. For all he knew, the Jackie Robinson story, which he had invented on the way to Kennedy's office, might be true.

Kennedy paused for a number of seconds and then said, "Uh, goddammit," in a weary expletive that could have cut in many directions.

When Wofford joined them, Kennedy chewed him out for insubordination, for pushing Senator Kennedy into a politically explosive controversy. He commanded the civil rights office to do nothing else controversial for the duration of the campaign—no literature, no press conferences, no little schemes, nothing that might get into the newspapers—and then dismissed them curtly. After they left, Kennedy asked his aide John Seigenthaler to drive him to the airport to catch a plane to New York for a speech. On the way, he wondered out loud if there was something he could do to draw fire away from his brother in the King case. His anger darted furtively toward all those involved, except for Senator Kennedy. Seigenthaler advised him to do nothing.

Later that night, the Kennedy campaign plane also landed in New York. As the candidate stepped off the plane, a reporter asked him if it was true that he had called Mrs. King earlier that day. "She is a friend of mine," said Kennedy, who had never met Coretta and never would, "and I was concerned about the situation." As he brushed past the reporter, he said something softly about having a traitor in his camp.

Still, the reporter had a confirmation. The next morning's *New York Times* contained a two-inch item on page 22 noting that Senator Kennedy had made a sympathy call to Mrs. King, and that a Republican spokesman said Vice President Nixon would have no comment on the King case. The *Times* played it as a minor story, and most of the nation's major news outlets gave it even less attention. Politically, this was just what Wofford and Martin had wished. They would have had an opening to publicize among Negro voters an event that went practically unnoticed among whites. But now, under Robert Kennedy's explicit gag order, they ruefully let the opportunity pass.

In Atlanta, Donald Hollowell dispelled a far more intense gloom that morning when he trumpeted the news that Judge Mitchell had changed his mind and signed an order to release King on $2,000 bond. In a mad scramble of joy, Wyatt Tee Walker raided the SCLC treasury to charter a private plane, grabbed Ralph Abernathy, and took off for Reidsville ahead of three other private planes filled with lawyers and reporters. It was soon recorded that King emerged from the prison at 3:46 P.M., free after eight days and nights in three different prisons. The rest of the King family met the caravan of planes outside Atlanta at 5:57 P.M. A reporter who was seeing King for the first time as he tumbled out of the plane and hugged Coretta wrote that he "had a look of vulnerability about him —not softness, naivete, but somehow hurtable."

Daddy King escorted his son into a Cadillac limousine big enough to hold the entire family, including the children and Christine's husband, and the caravan of planes turned into a triumphal procession of automobiles. A hundred sit-in veterans were waiting in cars at the Fulton County line, on the way into Atlanta. King's caravan pulled over to the side of the road on sight of them. People spilled joyfully out of the cars into the road, where they sang "We Shall Overcome." Then the combined line of cars made its way to Ebenezer for a spontaneous mass meeting. King was the object of thanksgiving, but Daddy King was the master of the overflow crowd. He spoke of God and courage and fear, and then chose that moment to make the announcement he had promised Harris Wofford earlier that day. "I had expected to vote against Senator Kennedy because of his religion," he declared. "But now he can be my President, Catholic or whatever he is. It took courage to call my daughter-in-law at a time like this. He has the moral courage to stand up for what he knows is right. I've got all my votes and I've got a suitcase, and I'm going to take them up there and dump them in his lap."

The crowd roared approval, and roared again when Ralph Abernathy said it was time to "take off your Nixon buttons." But King himself, almost visibly compressed by the sudden shift from prison to politics, spoke more personally about jail as a test of faith. "We must master the art of creative suffering," he said. All he said about the presidential election was that he would never let a candidate's religion determine his vote.

About the time King's plane from Reidsville touched down near Atlanta, David Brinkley of NBC's "Huntley-Brinkley Report" called Harris
Wofford to verify a wire service story that "a brother of Senator Kennedy"
had called Judge Mitchell personally to secure King's release. Wofford
denied the story, telling Brinkley that it was so implausible as to defy
belief. The press office at campaign headquarters was also denying the
story, on the orders of John Seigenthaler.

When Robert Kennedy checked in by telephone that night, Seigenthaler told him about the press rumor: "Guess what that crazy judge says
in Georgia? He says you called him about King not getting bail."

There was a long pause on Kennedy's end of the line. "Did he say
that?"

"Yes," replied Seigenthaler. "But don't worry. I . . . put out a denial."

After another long pause, Kennedy said, "Well, you better . . . retract
it." To Seigenthaler's astonishment, he admitted rather sheepishly that
he had made the call to the judge from New York. Kennedy explained
that he had gotten steamed up on reflecting that the act of a lynch-law
judge was "screwing up my brother's campaign and making the country
look ridiculous before the world."

Very shortly, Seigenthaler summoned Harris Wofford to help him draft
a press statement about why Kennedy had called the judge. The stunning
news made a number of powerful emotions collide within Wofford. Personally and politically, he was overjoyed that Kennedy's radical about-
face may have contributed to King's release, but as a corporate lawyer
and former law professor he disapproved strongly of Kennedy's call to a
sitting judge as a clear violation of the legal canon of ethics. Over the
phone, Kennedy groped with him for an alibi. "Can't we just say I was
inquiring about Dr. King's constitutional rights to bail?" he asked. Wofford stayed on into the night writing a statement that vacillated between
pride and apology.

Still later that night, a phone call awakened Louis Martin at his home
in Washington: "This is Bob Kennedy. Louis, I wanted you especially to
know that I called that judge in Georgia today, to try to get Dr. King
out."

Martin was jolted out of bed, instantly awake. "What's that again?" he
said. Kennedy repeated himself. He had called Judge Mitchell from a
phone booth in New York to register his opinion that any decent American judge would release King on bond by sundown.

Martin decided not to ask what had made Kennedy change so from his
tirade of the previous day. "You have just become an honorary brother,"
he laughed.

The next morning, Martin walked into a briefing at campaign head-

quarters and heard Kennedy press spokesmen still denying the story of
Robert Kennedy's call to Judge Mitchell. They were doing so in spite of
the fact that *The New York Times* featured the call in that morning's
story on the King release, mercifully omitting any mention of the Kennedy campaign's denials. To Martin, such confusion was all in a day's
work. Eventually, the press office caught up with the statement Wofford
had helped draft for Kennedy. With King no longer in jail, the entire
matter quickly dropped out of the nation's white newspapers for lack of
a compelling focus. The aftermath ran strong in the Negro press, however. The Pittsburgh *Courier* cited as a "universal consensus" the opinion of an observer who said, "These white folks have now made Dr.
Martin King, Jr. the biggest Negro in the United States."

Inside the Kennedy campaign's civil rights office, Martin and Wofford
reported to Shriver that the acute sensitivity to the King case was causing
a phenomenal "sea change" within the Negro electorate. Now that Robert Kennedy had broken his own ban against campaign involvement with
the case, they were seeking permission to exploit the change. Their
scheme—designed explicitly to flood Negro voters with the Kennedy
side of the King case in a way that minimized the danger of a backlash
among white voters—was to print a pamphlet for mass distribution
within the Negro churches of the nation on the last Sunday before the
presidential election. They would run no newspaper ads, even in Negro
papers, nor do anything else likely to filter into the white press. They
would establish a "dummy committee" of preachers to protect the Kennedy campaign against being identified as the sponsor of the pamphlet.
They would include no statement from a Kennedy spokesman. In fact,
the pamphlet would consist of nothing more than statements by the King
family and Negro preachers about Senator Kennedy's phone call to Coretta. It would not mention Robert Kennedy's call to the judge. The proposed pamphlet would be titled *"No Comment" Nixon Versus a
Candidate with a Heart, Senator Kennedy.*

The pamphlet loomed as an enormous gamble. To compose, print,
ship, and distribute it in such a short time would certainly preclude all
the civil rights office's scheduled efforts for the balance of the campaign,
but Martin gave assurances that it could be done. Shriver, facing the
choice between the pamphlet and everything else, instantly chose the
pamphlet. Moreover, he ordered Wofford and Martin to say nothing of it
to Robert Kennedy. Shriver promised to take the responsibility and to
find the money without going through the campaign manager. His decision flung Wofford and Martin pell-mell into the production of a logistical miracle. Their first decision was not to seek an explicit endorsement
of Kennedy from King. They used King's published statement that he

was "deeply indebted to Senator Kennedy, who served as a great force in making my release possible." That was good enough in the emergency.

Most of the political pressure on King was coming not from the Kennedy or Nixon campaign but from his own father. Having broken with the old guard of Republican Negro leaders, he was under severe criticism for confusing politics with personal emotion. Daddy King defended his change of allegiance like a battlefield commander, calling it the only honorable path. Kennedy's gestures to his son *demanded* repayment, he argued, by the preacher's time-honored code that one kindness deserves another. Having taken this exposed ground, Daddy King was vexed by the fact that his own son, who was the recipient of the kindness and a man much more favorably disposed toward Kennedy than he was, declined to join ranks with him. And he was nettled beyond endurance that some of his son's advisers who were working for Kennedy nevertheless urged King to remain officially neutral in the presidential campaign. Daddy King did not like neutrality. He intercepted one of Harry Belafonte's many calls on the weekend after the release and refused to let his son hear any more daffy New York thinking. "You just don't understand," Daddy King told Belafonte. "You can't have a man do what Kennedy did and not pay your debt."

"I agree," said Belafonte. "My point is about how the debt is paid. I don't think Martin should ever be put in the position of becoming an advocate for any candidate. He shouldn't play the game like a politician, on a lesser level."

"You are too young for these things," Daddy King replied, and abruptly said good-bye.

King himself escaped the brunt of these family pressures by flying to Chicago that weekend to resume his speaking schedule. He tried to resolve them when he returned by issuing a formal statement in which he explained that he could not endorse a candidate because "the role that is mine in the emerging social order of the South and America demands that I remain non-partisan. . . . But for fear of being considered an ingrate, I want to make it palpably clear that I am deeply grateful to Senator Kennedy for the genuine concern he expressed in my arrest." King's official neutrality displeased his father as too weak, while his pro-Kennedy messages struck the city's Republican establishment as heresy. Almost simultaneously with King's statement, William Holmes Borders and the leading Baptist ministers except for Daddy King joined in "firmly re-endorsing" Nixon. The preachers explained that this second extraordinary gathering was necessary in light of "recent political developments in Georgia, and in Atlanta in particular."

That Sunday, Harris Wofford met Senator Kennedy at Washington's

National Airport for a quick bit of business before the candidate embarked on his final week of campaigning. Kennedy had promised to sign for release to the press the final document of resolutions passed in Harlem three weeks earlier, but now he asked Wofford directly if he really needed to sign the document to get elected. Wofford admitted that the resolutions were probably superfluous, without saying that a prime reason for his confidence was the new pamphlet on the King case, the first 50,000 copies of which were rolling off the presses that day. The "blue bomb," as the pamphlet was known because of its cheap blue paper, was still secret from the Kennedys.

Kennedy decided not to release the civil rights promises until after the election. Handing the unsigned paper back to Wofford, he said, "You can consider me on record—with you." Then he put his three-year-old daughter Caroline on his back and headed toward the campaign plane. On the way, he spoke the only words Wofford ever heard him say publicly or privately about the King case. Referring to Daddy King's "suitcase of votes" declaration that he would vote for Kennedy in spite of his Catholicism, Kennedy mused to Wofford, "That was a hell of a bigoted statement, wasn't it? Imagine Martin Luther King having a bigot for a father." He grinned and added, "Well, we all have fathers, don't we?"

Not entirely by coincidence, Police Commissioner L. B. Sullivan's libel suit against *The New York Times* and King's four SCLC associates came to trial that week in Montgomery. Abernathy, Shuttlesworth, Joseph Lowery, and S. S. Seay sat at the defense table near Harding Bancroft and other *Times* executives. Defense lawyers had forbidden King to be in the courtroom, or even in Montgomery, fearing that his presence would serve only to inflame the jurors against the defense, but King was very much there in absentia. The suit, which had grown out of the Alabama perjury indictment just after the outbreak of the sit-in movement, was coming to trial nine months later in the wake of a similar effort to make an example of King in the Reidsville prison sentence.

The trial began inauspiciously for the defense when an all-white jury was selected. There followed an unceremonious argument over courtroom use of the word "nigger," which was won in the end by a plaintiff's lawyer who told the judge that he was merely following the customary pronunciation of a lifetime. Montgomery *Advertiser* editor Grover Hall, taking the stand as the plaintiff's first witness, testified that although he did not particularly like Commissioner Sullivan, he did conclude as an expert observer that most Montgomery citizens would consider the "Gestapo" charges in the *Times* ad to be defamatory of Sullivan had they believed the charges. On this point, the *Times* lawyers tried to get Hall to admit that the ad, far from injuring Sullivan, had made him a hero throughout the state of Alabama.

It was a bizarre trial. Neither side bothered to address the substantive truth or falsity of the ad's statements. Both sides agreed that Bayard Rustin was the chief culprit—the defense disclaiming responsibility for what he had written, the plaintiff saying the defendants should have questioned Rustin's assertions that Alabama authorities were persecuting King. Fred Gray and the *Times* lawyers portrayed their clients as innocent bystanders to a dispute between Rustin and Alabama, while Sullivan's lawyers portrayed Sullivan as the victim of powerful corporate interests in the North. On the third day, the jury brought in a verdict of guilty and an award to Sullivan of $500,000 in damages. Sullivan and his lawyers posed triumphantly for photographs that appeared on front pages across the South. The defense lawyers appealed to the Alabama Supreme Court.

The Montgomery trial, like the King cases in Atlanta, played out along a hidden geological fault within Democratic politics. The paradoxes of race made it possible for controlled racial conflict between the South and the national party to benefit both sides. At the Democratic Convention of 1940, the national Democrats helped gain Franklin Roosevelt's first heavy Negro vote simply by inviting a Negro minister to deliver a prayer. During this invocation, Senator "Cotton Ed" Smith stalked out of the convention to a hero's welcome at home in South Carolina, where he delighted crowds with lightheartedly hateful speeches denouncing the Northerners for inviting a "thick-lipped, blue-gummed, nappy-headed Senegambian" to pray before the party of John C. Calhoun. Now, twenty years later, national Democrats could hope that two Kennedy phone calls about the King case might deliver the Negro vote in the North. At the same time, governors Vandiver and Patterson, by acting resolutely on the anti-Negro side, not only enhanced their own political popularity but also, paradoxically, helped convince white Southerners that it was still safe to vote the traditional Democratic ticket for President.

These were fatefully unstable combinations, as everyone knew. Neither Nixon nor Kennedy mentioned the King arrests, the Sullivan trial, or related matters in public. In fact, during the closing days of the closest presidential race in the twentieth century, they moved farther and farther away from sensitive issues such as race. Instead, Nixon asked his secret weapon, President Eisenhower, to go on the road for him, and Ike defended the Republican record of the 1950s—his record—before enormous crowds around the country. Nine million new homes had been built, he declared. College enrollment was up by 75 percent, the economy by 45 percent. There was peace. Along with Nixon, Eisenhower attacked Kennedy for "bewailing America's strength," for "talking loosely about relative military strength," and for "wringing his hands" about the nation's prestige in the world. Nixon flew more than 7,000 miles on the last day of the campaign before collapsing, utterly exhausted, in the Royal Suite of the Ambassador Hotel in Los Angeles.

Kennedy was making his way eastward from California, where he unveiled his plan to establish a Peace Corps of unarmed American volunteers in the poor nations of the world, warning that "the enemy advances now by non-military means." On reaching Connecticut, he said, "I run as a candidate for the Presidency with a view that this is a great country but it must be greater." He repeated a quotation from Lincoln about the coming storm—"I know there is a God, and I know he hates injustice" —then flew on to Boston and finally, exhausted, arrived at the family compound at Hyannis Port.

Far removed from these twin storms of political attention, beneath the notice of campaign professionals, the Kennedy campaign's "blue bomb" was spreading through the Negro culture by means of the most effective private communications medium since the Underground Railroad—the church. Nearly two million copies were being shipped by bus, train, and airplane—duplicated and bundled, picked up and unbundled, praised from ten thousand pulpits and handed out. The confines of race made it easy for the civil rights office to keep the operation secret within their own organization, but even the secret-keepers did not know all the secrets that made their logistical miracle possible. Neither Wofford nor Shriver knew—and Louis Martin was only dimly aware at first—that their main distribution network was drawn almost entirely from the Gardner Taylor faction of the National Baptist Convention, which was still in a death struggle with J. H. Jackson for control of the national church. The Kennedy "dummy committee" was located in Philadelphia, site of the riotous church schism in September. Its co-chairman was one of the preachers J. H. Jackson had expelled from the Convention and sent off to jail three years earlier,* and the cover endorsement on the "blue bomb" was a quotation from Gardner Taylor himself. Taylor's nationwide telephone apparatus was reactivated for the Kennedy-King emergency.

---

* Rev. Marshall L. Shepherd. The other co-chairman, Dr. William A. Gray, was the father of future congressman and House Budget Committee chairman William Gray, Jr.

Not all the Taylor preachers had been Kennedy supporters, nor had all the Jackson preachers been inclined to Nixon. But all had taken special notice when J. H. Jackson publicly denounced the sit-ins shortly after King's arrest at Rich's, saying that some Negroes "talk too much about racial integration and not enough about racial elevation." * Then, in quick succession, came news of a manacled King being hauled off to Reidsville and of Kennedy's expression of sympathy. The force of the sudden blows sheared off not just Daddy King's Republicanism but a host of cross-cutting affiliations within the Negro Baptist clergy. A fissure within the Negro Baptist church shifted into line with the racial fault underlying American politics, producing a seismic rumble.

Sargent Shriver and Louis Martin felt it on Sunday, November 6, the mass-distribution day for the "blue bomb." Both were home in Chicago, working frantically for the last two days of the campaign, and by now Martin had told Shriver something of the Negro church battles affecting their work. They ventured that morning to Olivet Baptist Church—J. H. Jackson's pulpit, the largest congregation in the city—curious to see what the worshippers were doing. Shriver stood with his children across the street from the entrance, transfixed by the sight of all the church-goers carrying the blue pamphlets. They were not bringing them out of the church, as expected; somehow they had gotten hold of them in advance and were taking them *into* church, along with their Bibles. They were taking pamphlets praising J. H. Jackson's mortal enemies into his own church. Given the current level of ecclesiastical hostility, this was something like taking the Bill of Rights into the Kremlin or Lutheran tracts into the College of Cardinals.

Nearly all those who passed by seemed to be talking about what King had suffered and what Kennedy had done. Shriver realized in a rush that the pamphlet touched something transcendent, beyond campaign machinations and the most bitter preacher politics. It put him in awe to witness such a silent tremor among the common people of a culture different from his own, and to feel it shaking something as close to him as the Kennedy campaign.

King took no active part in the campaign. On Monday, snugly within his own world, he addressed fifteen hundred beauticians at the Bronner Brothers Fall Beauty Clinic on Auburn Avenue. On Election Day, the Atlanta *Daily World* urged Negroes one last time to vote Republican.

---

* King told Negro reporters that he "felt very badly" after reading newspaper accounts of Jackson's remarks while confined in the Fulton County jail.

Vernon Johns's old friend John Wesley Dobbs declared on the front page that Kennedy's Boston had fewer Negro policemen than segregated Atlanta—a deficiency he blamed on the Catholic Church. Dobbs said he could not understand how any self-respecting Negro could vote Democratic in view of the state party's refusal to allow a single Negro to become a member, "not even Mr. Walden or M. L. King."

King himself was not permitted to vote that day. Georgia officials ruled that he had not established residency long enough to vote in Atlanta, and Alabama officials said that it was too late for him to pay the $1.50 poll tax required to vote by absentee ballot in Montgomery. Like the two candidates and millions of groggy TV viewers, he went to bed not knowing who would be the next President. Toward dawn the next morning, electoral votes were still shifting from one column to the other. In fully one-third of the states, the Kennedy and Nixon totals were hovering between 48 and 52 percent. When Senator Kennedy emerged from his bedroom at nine o'clock, his aide Ted Sorensen greeted him with the news that he had won California and therefore the presidency. As it turned out, Sorensen was wrong about California but right about the election. Nationally, Kennedy had received 34,221,463 votes to Nixon's 34,108,582, for a popular margin of two-tenths of one percent. The tiniest of changes—5,000 votes in Illinois and 28,000 in Texas—would have opened the White House to Nixon instead of Kennedy.

A dejected President Eisenhower, stunned by what he regarded as a "repudiation" of his eight years, first blamed Henry Cabot Lodge for promising a Negro cabinet member. By "sticking his nose into the make-up of the cabinet," Eisenhower fumed privately, Lodge "cost us thousands of votes in the South, maybe South Carolina and Texas." Soon, however, the President reversed himself to say that the Nixon campaign had been too little concerned with Negro votes, not too much. He then blamed the loss on "a couple of phone calls" by John and Robert Kennedy in the King case.

What happened between Eisenhower's instinctive reaction and his considered one was a nationwide detective search for the secret of the 1960 election. Everyone seemed to have a private theory about what had been the decisive factor—whether stolen votes in Chicago or Nixon's makeup man for the first debate. As legions of analysts sifted the results, it did not take them long to discover that the most startling component of Kennedy's victory was his 40 percent margin among Negro voters. In 1956, Negroes had voted Republican by roughly 60–40; in 1960, they voted Democratic by roughly 70–30. This 30 percent shift accounted for more votes than Kennedy's victory margins in a number of key states, including Michigan, New Jersey, Pennsylvania, Illinois, and the Carolinas. On the day after the election, Republican National Chairman Thruston B. Morton declared that his party had taken the Negro vote too much for granted.

The crucial switch was easier to identify than to explain. Kennedy had entered the election year as the declared Democratic contender *least* popular among Negroes—certainly less popular than the Republican opponent, Nixon, whose civil rights record was generally considered creditable. In the summer, Nixon had insisted upon a strong civil rights plank in the most visible dispute at the Republican Convention, whereas Kennedy angered Negroes by choosing Lyndon Johnson as his running mate. During the campaign itself, neither candidate had said anything dramatic about civil rights. Kennedy might have pulled closer to Nixon on the strength of his looks and polished demeanor, analysts figured, but to have trounced him so soundly begged for a cause of glaring, magical strength.

The King case leaped to national attention during the postmortem as the overlooked master clue. Most people in the country first learned of the saga retrospectively, as capsule summaries of the Kennedy phone calls were told and retold to establish the difference between the two candidates on civil rights: Kennedy had acted in response to King's plight, whereas Nixon had not. Some reporters unearthed the essential facts of the Kennedy pamphlet. Others wrote stories clarifying that there had been two separate Kennedy calls—one by Senator Kennedy to Coretta King and another by Robert Kennedy to Judge Mitchell. *The New York Times*, still pursuing both sides of the story a month after the election, published a statement that had been drafted but never released by the Eisenhower White House, calling King's Reidsville sentence "fundamentally unjust."

It turned out that many people inside the Nixon campaign—Attorney General Rogers, E. Frederic Morrow, and Republican Negroes in Georgia, among others—had implored Nixon to say something supportive of King, but Nixon had declined. When news of King's Reidsville sentence had broken, Nixon had been on his way to South Carolina in the hope of an upset there and elsewhere in the Deep South. His response had been to hide Rogers within his entourage, as a man unpopular among Southern whites because of the Justice Department's voting rights suits, and to say nothing about King. For Nixon, the unfortunate result was that he still did not carry South Carolina, Georgia, or Alabama, but he lost enough Negro votes to suffer defeats in larger Northern states. In later statements, Nixon implied that the Eisenhower White House had been at fault for failing to issue a statement drafted by the Justice Department. Such an authoritative but indirect response, said Nixon, would have neutralized Kennedy's call without risking Nixon's white vote in the

South. His explanation was faulty, however, because the statement to which he referred was not even drafted until four days after King was released from Reidsville, by which time it was already useless.* Politics and personal beliefs aside, the Nixon campaign was fatally encrusted with the incumbent Eisenhower bureaucracy in Washington. It moved by memo, letter, and clearance, whereas the Kennedy people moved by telephone.

As the political side of the King arrests gained historic notoriety, pride and other human factors spurred those close to the events to embrace interpretations favorable to themselves. Kennedy's inner circle of advisers—the realists who had resisted all suggestions of intervention in the King case, who had not known of either Kennedy call in advance, nor anything of the "blue bomb"—downplayed the importance of the entire matter. So great was their need to deny having been outsmarted by the softheaded bomb-throwers in the civil rights section that they argued, obstinately and fatuously, that Kennedy would have won a landslide victory among Negro voters even without the King affair, "as the result of economic issues." Meanwhile, the staunchly Republican Ebenezer members who ran the Atlanta *Daily World* announced joyfully that Nixon had carried the Negro precincts of Atlanta in spite of the Kennedy-King dramatics. The editors offered these results in refutation of the theory that Kennedy fever had swept up those Negroes best informed about the King case, but the results more likely showed that King was less honored in his hometown than elsewhere, and that prestige Republicanism was strong enough in Negro Atlanta to survive one last election.

Both Morris Abram and Daddy King warmed to a technicality that mattered to few others in the country besides King Jr.: that the younger King had declined to endorse Kennedy formally whereas Daddy King had agreed. Both Abram, who had engineered the endorsement, and Daddy King, who had delivered it, came to imply by either omission or emphasis that King's suffering could not have influenced Negro votes on its own, as King had not instructed his followers how to vote. To the end of his life, Daddy King would attribute Kennedy's victory to his own "suitcase full of votes" statement.

In Washington, the hindsight attention to the King story troubled the President-elect, who worried that the new perception of him as a man beholden to Negro voters would impair his ability to govern the divided country. Within days of the election, Kennedy adjusted to this adjust-

---

* The unreleased statement was drafted by Deputy Attorney General Lawrence E. Walsh, who would become Special Counsel for the Iran-Contra investigation in 1987.

ment of his image by sending out word that his administration did not contemplate seeking new civil rights legislation or supporting challenges to the filibuster rule in the Senate. This reassured his Southern supporters but punctured the enthusiasm of Roy Wilkins, who promptly criticized Kennedy for surrendering the Democratic platform before taking office.

The President-elect said nothing publicly about how the King case might have affected his victory. Robert Kennedy—every bit as competitive by nature, but possessed of a confessional, self-deprecating humor that lacked his brother's hard deflective irony—said with a laugh some years later that he had called Judge Mitchell on the suggestion of Georgia governor Ernest Vandiver, King's most aggressive political enemy of the moment. This revelation appeared to clash with both the Machiavellian and the humanitarian interpretations of the Kennedy calls. It made sense only if Vandiver, shrinking from his promise to get King out of Reidsville, had talked Robert Kennedy into assuming the political risk. Kennedy's motivation remained a mystery, perhaps even to himself. After the election, his public comments on the matter reflected a keen ambivalence, as though the bizarre rebounds of the King case had put into question the entire relationship between winning and being decent. Asked by a journalist if he was glad he had called Judge Mitchell, Kennedy replied enigmatically: "Sure I'm glad, but I would hope I'm not glad for the reason you think I'm glad."

In the midst of the post-election excitement, *Time* correspondent Theodore White sat down to write *The Making of the President, 1960*. A spectacular success, the book sold more than four million copies and caused fundamental changes in campaign reporting, if not in the conception of the American presidency itself. White captured the swell of postwar confidence with his central thesis that the presidency had acquired the glow of a sacred romance. In the modern revolutionary age, he argued, the awesome responsibilities of the office overwhelmed the traditional American skepticism of power and royalty. "A hush, an entirely personal hush, surrounds this kind of power," he wrote, "and the hush is deepest in the Oval Office of the West Wing of the White House, where the President, however many his advisers, must sit alone." White's inventive use of capital letters for the Oval Office swept into standard usage in many languages, becoming a symbol of the modern United States.

"In the sixties, the office of the Presidency, which John F. Kennedy held, was above all an intellectual exercise," wrote White. More scientifically than most, he verified the Negro vote and the Kennedy-King calls as the critical ingredient in the outcome of the election. Having isolated the key to a seminal event at the gate of history, he was almost obliged to soar away upon his thesis, in safe disregard for the contrary facts of his own central illustration. White's celebration of power had no room for the wrongheaded, race-wrapped disorder that stumbled through the King episode from start to finish. Discarding most of his evidence from Shriver, Wofford, and others, he described the expression of sympathy for King as the "master stroke." Robert Kennedy's call became an execution of "the command decision" by the Kennedy organization in the pursuit of the Negro vote. Going still further, White appraised the King maneuver as "the most precise response of result to strategy" in the entire 1960 campaign. A final, rhapsodic description of the King calls slipped all bounds of fact: "Decisions now not only followed crisply and unfalteringly in sequence, but where decision pointed, the organization followed —and the various parts of the organization had all passed through their break-in period, had been road-tested, and purred in the comforting hum of human machinery intermeshing with the same complete efficiency that one remembers of the American bomber crews flying out of Tinian and Saipan."

Many clouds distorted or obscured interpretation of the pivotal election, which emerged as a kind of mythological puberty rite for the United States as a superpower. Still, one plain fact shined through everywhere: two little phone calls about the welfare of a Negro preacher were a necessary cause of Democratic victory. This fact mattered dearly to Republican county chairmen as well as Democratic mayors, to students of politics as well as crusaders on both sides of the civil rights issue. That something so minor could whip silently through the Negro world with such devastating impact gave witness to the cohesion and volatility of the separate culture. That at the heart of this phenomenon was not just any preacher but Martin Luther King gave his name a symbolic resonance that spilled outside the small constituency of civil rights. Before, King had been a curiosity to most of the larger world—unsettling and primeval in meaning, perhaps, but as remote as the backseats of buses or the other side of town. Now, as a historical asterisk, a catalytic agent in the outcome of the presidential election, he registered as someone who might affect the common national history of whites and Negroes alike.

TEN

THE KENNEDY TRANSITION

On the day after the election, playing touch football at Hyannis Port under the mass scrutiny of freshly encamped reporters, President-elect Kennedy received a telegram from the old lion of the British Empire. "On the occasion of your election to your office, I salute you," wired Sir Winston Churchill. While tributes poured in from lesser figures, Kennedy presided over a family dinner giddy with triumph and exhaustion, during which the guests imagined how they might rearrange the world. One favored idea was to get rid of Allen Dulles at the CIA and J. Edgar Hoover at the FBI, on the grounds that these entrenched founding bureaucrats were incompatible with the Kennedy spirit of change. The President-elect enjoyed the sportive dinner talk, but the next morning he promptly announced his intention to reappoint Dulles and Hoover. Then, surrounded by Secret Service agents, he flew off to Palm Beach for a vacation.

As the Kennedy plane headed south, John Lewis and two companions sat down with their ten-cent hamburgers at a Nashville restaurant called The Krystal, a pioneering chain of the fast-food industry. A visibly distressed waitress poured cleansing powder down their backs and water over their food, while the three Negroes steadfastly ate what they could of their meal. Lewis returned to the restaurant two hours later with his friend James Bevel, the new chairman of the Nashville student movement. Their request to speak with the manager met with the reply that the place was being cleared for emergency fumigation, whereupon the manager locked the front door, turned on a fumigating machine, and exited to the rear, leaving Bevel and Lewis alone amid the rising spray. The two of them endured for some time, with Bevel preaching quietly about the deliverance of Shadrach, Meshach, and Abednego from King Nebuchadnezzar's fiery furnace. Outside, the commotion and the escaping smoke soon attracted a roaring fire engine. A Negro preacher was pleading with the firemen to smash in the door, and a news photographer was snapping pictures of the two gasping figures inside, when the nervous manager reappeared with the door key. He tried to make light of the episode, but the fumigation dramatized his association of Negroes with insects and other vermin. For Lewis and Bevel, it was but another day of witness.

King experienced both the energized glamour of the Kennedy victory and the morally transcendent humiliation of Bevel and Lewis. He tasted of both worlds, and knew both sets of people. During the transition between administrations, he called both John and Robert Kennedy on behalf of Morris Abram, urging that he be made Solicitor General. Similarly, he asked the Kennedys to appoint Benjamin Mays to the Civil Rights Commission or to an ambassadorship, and he wrote private letters of protest on hearing that Georgia's senators had blocked such an appointment. King did not succeed in these patronage requests, but the consultation itself was a lofty new role that he never had approached with Eisenhower.

After the election, he crossed the Atlantic again—this time as a guest of the Nigerian government on the occasion of its independence from Great Britain. He returned to New York to defend sit-in demonstrations in a nationally televised debate against Richmond *News Leader* editor James J. Kilpatrick. "Truly America faces today a rendezvous with destiny," King said nervously, "and I think these students, through their non-violent, direct, courageous action, have met the challenge of this destiny-paced moment in a very majestic way." Kilpatrick, who had risen to prominence since the *Brown* decision by espousing Virginia's right to "interpose" its sovereignty against federal integration orders,* asserted that the hidden goal of the sit-ins was sexual—universal miscegenation. "We believe it is an affirmatively good thing to preserve the predominantly racial characteristics that have contributed to Western civiliza-

---

* "Interposition," as defined by Kilpatrick, was essentially a modernization of John C. Calhoun's "nullification" doctrines, developed more than a century earlier.

tion over the past two thousand years," Kilpatrick told the NBC audience, "and we do not believe that the way to preserve them lies in fostering any intimate race mixing by which these principles and characteristics inevitably must be destroyed." In addition to sex and civilization, Kilpatrick cited a host of legal precedents against the sit-ins and then denounced them as a "boorish exhibition" of "plain bad manners." One of his subtler ploys was to speak of King in the third person, as though he were not there. King left the studio believing he had failed to parry the full range of Kilpatrick's explicit and implicit attacks.

He returned home to find his father marching in picket lines outside Atlanta's downtown department stores. Time having expired on the truce that Mayor Hartsfield had negotiated before the election, Daddy King and the other Negro elders felt obliged to admit to the students that progress seemed to stall without the pressure of demonstrations. Daddy King, wearing a JIM CROW MUST GO! placard, took up marching alongside rock 'n' roll singer Clyde McPhatter. They made an unlikely pair. For a brief period, nearly all the elements of Negro society in Atlanta—hotheaded youth, academics, even the Republican stalwarts such as John Wesley Dobbs—were united in protest.

During the changeover of administration, King and the Kennedy people had virtually no face-to-face contact, even privately. King was not invited to the Inauguration, nor was he, like Roy Wilkins, granted a private audience with the President-elect to present his civil rights agenda. King's name was too sensitive at the time, too associated with ongoing demonstrations that were vexing politicians in the South. As it happened, the two sides drifted into collusion more or less independently around two gritty requirements of politics: votes and money.

Wyatt Walker noticed that a number of the country's more aggressive, liberal philanthropists were expanding their commitments in the civil rights field, which was becoming recognized as a kind of institutionalized crisis. Responding eagerly to the prospect of large stipends, Walker and King quickly learned a whole new vocabulary: grant proposals, funding conduits, advance budgeting, program reviews. With the active encouragement of Stanley Levison, they met in New York with the heads of the Taconic and Field foundations, among others, and talked with numerous college deans about scholarship replacement funds for expelled sit-in students. From Highlander, Myles Horton suggested that the SCLC take over the endowment of Septima Clark's thriving citizenship school. Horton wanted to protect Clark against the likelihood of Highlander's demise.

King and Walker were drawn to the vision of a multifaceted attack on segregation in a targeted town—with Clark training the registration workers and teachers, SNCC students sitting in, King preaching, and Walker coordinating the attack. More immediately, they liked the fact that some influential foundation officials already were devoted to Clark. If they sponsored her through the SCLC, they might also come to subsidize other SCLC projects, such as the money-starved voter registration drives. By January, Walker was at the center of several scholarship funds through which the SCLC was supporting the education of scores of arrested students.* Complex arrangements were begun to transfer Septima Clark's citizenship school to the SCLC, and two major proposals were filed for voter registration money.

Meanwhile, the Kennedy people were approaching a voter registration strategy from the top down, by way of Robert Kennedy's post-election reviews. The civil rights constituency was volatile, politically cheap, and potentially decisive. Such was the lesson of the King phone calls in the campaign, and the advisers were shrewd enough to recognize another sign hidden among the election results. In Fayette County, Tennessee— one of the two counties in Tennessee where John Doar of the Eisenhower Justice Department had sued to protect Negroes—twelve hundred new Negro votes helped turn the county Republican for the first time since Reconstruction. This landslide, going against the general Kennedy landslide, was interpreted to mean that Negroes in the South would reward those who helped them gain the right to vote.

For Robert Kennedy and his political aides, the circumstances dictated a conscious strategy of "appoint and appoint, elect and elect"—as expressed by Harris Wofford in a political memo. The repetition was deliberate. The idea was to keep appointing Negroes to jobs and to register enough Negroes to render Southern officeholders more sympathetic to their legislative proposals. It was a policy of accretion, with nothing so sweeping or grand as to touch off a segregationist backlash against them. In school desegregation, as in voter registration, the Kennedys planned to work "Negro by Negro," one by one, in lawsuits and registration campaigns. "The years go by," wrote a friendly journalist, lamenting the tactical concession to time, "yet there can be no other strategy."

Harris Wofford remained a Kennedy insider without portfolio, slightly tainted but possessed nevertheless of a unique blend of contacts that helped King and the Kennedy Justice Department alike. During the

---

* SCLC scholarship students included Bernard "Jelly" Lee of the Montgomery sit-ins and Stokely Carmichael, a freshman at Howard University in Washington, D.C.

changeover of administration, he learned from King of the SCLC's ambition to acquire foundation grants, and Wofford recommended foundation executives he thought might help. Then he advised some of his foundation friends that the best political brains in the Kennedy Administration had decided to push Negro voter registration, and he completed the circle by telling his Kennedy contacts that King was seeking foundation grants for that very purpose. As a catalyst, Wofford found that people from each of the three sides were happy to hear about the enthusiasm of the other two. King's people were pleased that the nervy Kennedy types were determined to "make things happen" in voter registration. The foundation people swelled with the prospect of helping the New Frontier and Southern Negroes at the same time, under the implicit protection of the federal government. And the Kennedy people were attracted to the idea of a quiet, well-financed coup. All three sides realized that they stood to lose heavily if the partisan Kennedy role came to public attention. Tax exemptions and political reputations were at stake, as was the new Administration's duty to act impartially in the sensitive area of voting. Consequently, the exploratory meetings took place in an atmosphere of secrecy.

In the glare of a crisp, snow-blanketed day, John F. Kennedy delivered an inaugural speech that from its first phrase—"We observe today not a victory of party but a celebration of freedom"—was a paean to liberty. The speech defined an American identity by looking outward, projecting a new battle cry of freedom into the Cold War struggle against communism—all set dramatically within an era of ultimate risk in which "man holds in his mortal hands the power to abolish all forms of human poverty and all forms of human life." As a liberal, Kennedy tempered militancy with sentiments of moral grace mixed with pragmatism—"If a free society cannot help the many who are poor, it cannot save the few who are rich"—and he dreamed that even the Communists might join the free world to "explore the stars, conquer the deserts, eradicate disease." No American president had ever surveyed such a vast domain with such an urgent sense of mission. "In the long history of the world," Kennedy declared, "only a few generations have been granted the role of defending freedom in its hour of maximum danger."

The speech struck the country with a bolt of energy, as Kennedy projected the image of a daring sailor in a gale wind. Some of his excitement reached down among King's colleagues. In Birmingham, where criminal trials from sit in cases had pitched Negroes into a continuous crisis, Fred Shuttlesworth walked into the weekly mass meeting at the St. James

Baptist Church and paid tribute to Kennedy from the pulpit. "What a wonderful President we have now!" he exclaimed, reminding the crowd that he and the freedom movement had helped put Kennedy into office. The moment inspired Shuttlesworth to come down to sit next to two men who were highly conspicuous as the only white people in the congregation. The bantam preacher made a fuss over welcoming them, shaking their hands warmly, and then he introduced them with relish as members of the police intelligence squad sent by Bull Connor into all the mass meetings. "This is Detective Jones," he announced. "He voted for Nixon along with the other white people." Shuttlesworth made a speech breaking all allegiance with the Republicans. "Ike never did nothing for the Negroes in the eight years he was in there," he said. "No Negro ever played golf with Ike." He turned the meeting over to a minister who began preaching so fervently from Ezekiel about the dry bones of the faithless that more than a dozen people had to be carried out in fits of uncontrollable excitement, and the deacons finally covered the preacher himself with an overcoat and several scarves, to calm him. This was an old ritual of religious ecstasy that was just being introduced to white teenagers through the performances of rock stars, most notably James Brown.

For King himself, it remained to be seen how much Kennedy's ideas of freedom overlapped with his. Kennedy never mentioned segregation, civil rights, or race in his inaugural address, and to some degree the new President was using his political gifts to make his summons to freedom intoxicating to both Negroes and white Southern Democrats. Still, King had to find it encouraging that Kennedy occasionally condemned racial prejudice as "irrational," and that he seemed so much more comfortable in the presence of Negroes than had Eisenhower. Kennedy danced with Negro women on Inauguration night and included Louis Martin and his wife among the members of his political "family," as introduced on the platform of the inaugural gala.

These were signals. And certainly Kennedy and King connected in the visible sphere of glitter and stardom. By and large, Kennedy's celebrities supported King, and vice versa. Frank Sinatra produced and starred in the Kennedy gala, bringing to the stage an interracial cast that included Nat "King" Cole, Jimmy Durante, Mahalia Jackson, Sidney Poitier, Leonard Bernstein, Ella Fitzgerald, Peter Lawford, and Harry Belafonte. Lawford, married to the new President's sister Patricia, was part of Sinatra's casino-hopping, moviemaking "Rat Pack," whose extravagances were splashed regularly in the tabloids and fan magazines. The only member absent from the gala was Sammy Davis, Jr. His recent interracial marriage to a Swedish actress made him, like King, too controversial for a mainstream political gathering.

Exactly a week after the Inauguration, Sinatra reassembled the celebrities for a five-hour tribute to King at New York's Carnegie Hall. Sammy Davis, Dean Martin, Count Basie, Tony Bennett, Nipsey Russell, and other popular entertainers joined Sinatra's cast. Although the event attracted no national attention, it raised $50,000 for the SCLC and established King as the possessor of a celebrity drawing power that ambitious politicians could not ignore. Advisers to New York governor Nelson Rockefeller built up a thick file of memos debating the fine points of Rockefeller's participation. Worries that Rockefeller might become tainted by association with the racy, gangsterish Sinatra crowd, for example, were dismissed with the observation that the Rat Pack was "already firmly associated in the public eye with Jack Kennedy." The advisers decided that Rockefeller could get away with buying a $400 box of tickets unless the benefactors were listed by name and category in the program, in which case political considerations required him to buy the top box at $800. In the end, Rockefeller paid the $800. He also sent a cordial telegram to Carnegie Hall, as did President Kennedy.

From New York, King flew on to Chicago, Philadelphia, and Salt Lake City for speeches on successive days. In Chicago, he stayed with Mahalia Jackson, who was about to sing for Pope John XXIII on another of her European tours. They consumed a lavish soul-food feast, during which word came that Coretta had gone into labor with her third child. "You *better* name it Mahalia," laughed Jackson. As King shuttled between the dinner and the phone, receiving bulletins from the Atlanta hospital, she kept up such banter that King agreed in a show of surrender to let Jackson or one of her best friends name a baby girl. If it was a boy, he said, the name would be Dexter, after his former church in Montgomery. A few calls later, he came back with a happy announcement: "It's Dexter."

On January 28, the new President held an unusual Saturday meeting in the Cabinet Room of the White House. All staff aides were barred from the top-secret review of plans to overthrow Fidel Castro's Cuban government by clandestine invasion. The Pentagon leaders pressed for greater force to insure the success of the military mission, while Secretary of State Dean Rusk pressed for either no operation at all or a much quieter one, the better to protect the U.S. diplomatic position in the world from charges of illegal intervention. President Kennedy kept saying he wanted to achieve both goals at once—success and anonymity. CIA officials proposed to do so by derring-do and deception. This was the first of ten White House meetings that led to the Bay of Pigs invasion in April. Although the United Nations already had debated and voted on formal Cuban charges that an American-sponsored invasion was imminent, war preparations remained a non-subject in public simply because the government treated them as such.

In King's world, scattered crusaders were as intent upon gaining recognition for their freedom plans as Kennedy was determined to conceal his. James Bevel and his student group announced a nonviolent campaign for desegregation of Nashville's movie theaters on February 1, the anniversary of the first Greensboro sit-in. Other student groups across the South were preparing "jail-ins." *The New York Times*, reviewing the year of "stand-ins at theatres, kneel-ins at churches and wade-ins at public beaches," declared that Negro protests threatened to "assume the proportions of a national movement." In Birmingham, where Fred Shuttlesworth was running out of appeals on one conviction for which he faced a sentence of sixty to ninety days at hard labor, Alabama authorities gained court permission to seize his automobile in partial settlement of the libel judgment against him in the Sullivan case, which also was still on appeal. The same authorities seized personal property of the three other Negro defendants in the suit, including Abernathy's car and some land he had inherited. The car brought $400 at auction, the land $4,350. King protested these actions as blatant persecutions by Alabama officials, but the stories played no better than blurbs. The race issue remained generally avoidable, as measured by the public mood. Reporters asked President Kennedy no questions on the subject at his first televised press conference.

Still less known was a letter written on the second day of the Kennedy presidency by an obscure Air Force veteran in Mississippi named J. H. Meredith. Inspired by a broadcast of the Kennedy inaugural speech, Meredith decided that his best contribution to democratic rights was to seek admission to the University of Mississippi. He wrote for an application and then promptly sought the counsel of Mississippi's NAACP field secretary, Medgar Evers. Evers, who felt wounded personally by the gruesome fates of the last two Negroes who had tried to integrate Mississippi's white universities, was none too happy to hear of Meredith's ambition. But he recognized the stubborn, military precision with which Meredith was pursuing his goal, and put him in touch with Thurgood Marshall's NAACP lawyers.

When the President insisted on the appointment of his brother Robert as Attorney General, the younger Kennedy added to the worries of a political manager the duties of the cabinet officer most directly responsible for progress in civil rights. Kennedy sent a terse directive—"tell me what you're doing"—down into the various parts of the Justice Department, including the Civil Rights Division. John Doar, his boss having resigned, replied for the division as the senior Republican holdover, though he had only seven months' experience himself. Doar was just back from a successful series of court appearances in which he had convinced judges that eviction notices served on Negro sharecroppers in Tennessee were illegal reprisals against them for registering to vote. On behalf of the U.S. government, Doar had won court orders vacating the eviction of some three hundred sharecroppers. Others, evicted already, were encamped in tent cities known as "Freedom Villages," whose struggle to exist was being chronicled daily in Negro newspapers across the country. Mahalia Jackson sang a song over the telephone for a rally benefiting the embattled sharecroppers, who repaid her by naming a strip of mud "Mahalia Jackson Avenue."

Doar was only slightly less a hero to the inhabitants. Voting records from counties all over the South, recently obtained under the new Civil Rights Act of 1960, had been wheeled into his office on dollies and stacked high against the walls. As Doar and his staff pored through the records, he put pins in a map of the South indicating counties practicing the most egregious, systematic, and effective repression against Negro voters. Some lawsuits were filed already; many others were in preparation. Doar's summaries of them made the most compelling reading of the report he sent to Robert Kennedy, who, like his predecessors under Eisenhower, came quickly to the conclusion that voting rights were the strongest political and moral opportunity for the Justice Department in the field of civil rights. Squeezing Doar into one of his planning meetings, Kennedy said briskly, "I want to move on voting." He asked Doar to stay on in the new Administration even though he was a Republican.

The search for a Democrat to replace Doar's boss passed through the Kennedy talent-scouting operation, headed by Sargent Shriver, where Harris Wofford screened candidates for the government job he wanted most himself. To Shriver's mind, Wofford was by far the most qualified person available to head the Civil Rights Division—based on his legal education and experience, his service to the Kennedy campaign, and his voluminous personal knowledge of the people and issues of civil rights. Unfortunately for Wofford, however, Shriver's recommendation ran into the opposition of Byron R. "Whizzer" White, the All-American football player from Colorado, Rhodes scholar, and national chairman of Citizens for Kennedy. Robert Kennedy made White deputy Attorney General over Wofford's objection that he was stubborn and humorless. White returned Wofford's low opinion in full measure. He convinced Robert Kennedy that Wofford could never conceal from hostile Southern congressmen his long history of sympathy for Gandhi, King, and the doctrines of civil disobedience.

Shrewdly, White recommended to Kennedy as a neutral candidate Wof-

ford's friend and law partner Burke Marshall, whom White had known at
Yale Law School. Marshall was a highly respected corporate lawyer who
had represented Standard Oil, the Du Ponts, and other powerful clients
in some of the biggest antitrust cases of the previous decade. Only two
items in his career—both traceable to Wofford's recruitment—jarred
slightly against the popular image of the gray-flannel lawyer: he had once
taught a course on corporate law at the predominantly Negro Howard
University Law School, and he had once read Arnold Toynbee in an
executive reading group led by philosopher Scott Buchanan. Marshall
knew none of the civil rights leaders and had contributed to none of the
civil rights organizations, nor had he ever shown any interest in race
issues. To Byron White, it was precisely his lack of expertise in the
substance of civil rights that recommended Marshall to head the Civil
Rights Division. In no other legal field was ignorance a qualification, but
the race issue was so controversial that any history of personal interest
was tantamount to a political statement. Wofford himself half agreed,
and he put Marshall's name on the recommendation list in spite of his
antipathy for White.

Robert Kennedy invited Burke Marshall to his office for a talk that
soon became legendary in the Justice Department as the "silent interview." Like Kennedy, Marshall was slight of build, wispish and reedy of
voice, though much less rumpled and windblown than the thirty-five-
year-old Attorney General. Also like Kennedy, he could be extremely
sparing of words. When they met, Marshall knew he was being considered for a post, but he had no idea which one. He presumed that it
would be in the Antitrust Division, in which event he planned to decline.
The Civil Rights Division was mentioned in passing, but neither man
had much to say about the issue except that there were laws which must,
of course, be enforced. And since both men preferred silence to small
talk, they divided the better part of half an hour into long silences broken
by mumbled civilities. When the interview was over, Marshall believed
he had blown his chance for any job in the Justice Department, but
Kennedy, to the surprise of his aides, decided he had found just the man
for the Civil Rights Division. To him, Marshall was an elite lawyer too
smart to make mistakes, too self-possessed to blunder compulsively into
controversy, too honest to claim he had all the answers.

King wrestled with offices and appointments during his own period of
transition, relying heavily on Gardner Taylor at the juncture of politics
and religion. With Harry Belafonte, Taylor helped King design a voter
registration plan that would bypass the foundations and other large fund-

ing sources with a direct, "dollar per person" appeal to Negro church-goers. When Alabama officials continued to confiscate the property of King's colleagues, Taylor raised and delivered personally to Atlanta a $5,000 contribution for the defense in the *New York Times* libel case. At the same time, Taylor gently told King that if Abernathy and Shuttles-worth felt so oppressed in Alabama that they must abandon the South for safer pulpits in the North, King must let them go with his blessing. Early in 1961, Taylor sponsored Abernathy in a trial sermon at the Mount Lebanon Baptist Church in Brooklyn.

King and Abernathy were "Taylor men" in the church schism whose outcome would determine their stature in the national clergy. When in January Taylor lost his last appeal for court recognition of his election in Philadelphia, J. H. Jackson had the national church board declare the Taylor preachers to be an illegitimate, secessionist group. In response, Taylor publicly denounced the resolution as a "veiled dagger" aimed at church democracy, and pledged to launch a nationwide "truth saturation program" to vindicate his claim at the next general convention that September, in Kansas City. Thomas Kilgore and several others took leave of their church duties for a full thirteen weeks to tour the country, lining up votes and money for Taylor. King did the same—quietly—at scores of church stops on his speaking schedule.

As a member of the National Action Council of the Congress of Racial Equality, Taylor was looking for a new national director. The consensus of his selection committee was that CORE, as a pioneer of Gandhian direct action in pursuit of racial integration, should not have faded into obscurity at a time when the student sit-ins were bringing national publicity to such techniques. The CORE leaders dispatched an emissary to Atlanta to offer King the position. King replied that he was already over-extended and would consider the job only if he could merge the predominantly white, Northern intellectuals of CORE with the Southern Negro preachers of the SCLC. The impracticalities of this notion were so manifest that he declined the offer almost immediately.

With King out of consideration, the maneuverings within CORE centered on one of the founding members from 1942, James Farmer. He was a large hulking man of forty-one, nine years King's senior, whose father had been the first Negro to earn a Ph.D. degree in the state of Texas. Young Farmer had grown up something of a prodigy, well-connected enough to have secured a White House audience with FDR as a teenager. His earliest memories were idyllic scenes of his erudite father sitting under a tree reading books in Latin, Greek, German, French, and Aramaic. Since leaving CORE in the mid-1940s, partly because of chronic bureaucratic clashes with Bayard Rustin and A. J. Muste, Farmer had lived for a time at a Gandhian ashram in Harlem and bounced around between union organizing jobs before finally settling in at the NAACP. There was a note of personal tragedy in his past—his first wife had miscarried and divorced him shortly after finding a love note from the white mistress who became Farmer's second wife—but it was his parvenu ambition that marked him at the staid NAACP. Feeling blocked from advancement within the hierarchy there, Farmer worked eagerly with old friends to secure the opportunity at CORE, once King had declined. Gardner Taylor made the official selection.

Roy Wilkins, with his fine ear for gossip, summoned Farmer for a conference before he had worked up the courage to resign. To Farmer's immense relief, Wilkins did not seem to resent the defection. Farmer's first thought was that Wilkins must consider CORE, with its tiny membership and dingy offices, too small to be a threat to the NAACP, but the more Wilkins talked nostalgically about fresh starts and small organizations, the more Farmer came to believe that even the comfortable Wilkins felt a bit hemmed in after thirty years at the NAACP. Wilkins advised him to be ruthless at the beginning of his tenure. "I should have listened to Minnie," * said Wilkins. "She said, 'Roy, clean house. They're all Walter White's people, loyal to him. Get them out and put your own people in.' " Wilkins told Farmer he had come to regret his leniency, now that he was surrounded and paralyzed by people he could not afford to fire. "The second thing is this," Wilkins said with a wan smile. "You're going to be riding a mustang pony, while I'm riding a dinosaur."

The prophecy began to come true at once. At Farmer's first CORE staff meeting, Gordon Carey proposed that CORE undertake a second Journey of Reconciliation, similar to the bus ride taken by Bayard Rustin and others in 1947. He had more than historical commemoration in mind. The earlier ride had been conceived as a nonviolent test of a Supreme Court decision banning segregation aboard buses in interstate travel, and that ruling had just been extended in a new case† prohibiting segregation in the waiting rooms and restaurants serving interstate bus passengers. Neither Court decision was widely enforced in the South. Carey's idea was that CORE, though unable to compete with the huge number of students in the sit-ins, could send an interracial cadre of people well trained in nonviolence on a bus ride through the entire South, testing bus facilities, and that publicity about their courage in the face of almost certain violence by segregationists would advance CORE's principles on many fronts. Farmer endorsed Carey's idea, then changed the name of his first project from Journey of Reconciliation to Freedom Ride.

---

* Minnie Badeaux Wilkins, Roy Wilkins' wife.
† *Boynton* v. *Virginia*, handed down in December 1960.

.   .   .

On February 1, 1961, a second libel trial against *The New York Times* and the four SCLC preachers from Alabama ended in Montgomery. The city's mayor, Earl James, had sought damages separate from those awarded Police Commissioner Sullivan the previous November. Defense lawyers, noting that Mayor James and five members of the jury were wearing beards in preparation for centennial celebrations of the Civil War, had objected that these conspicuous Confederate symbols created an atmosphere prejudicial to the defendants. Judge Walter B. Jones, who had been chosen to administer the oath of office to a Jefferson Davis stand-in at a ceremony marking the Confederacy's hundredth birthday, overruled the objection.* He also enforced strict segregation at the trial, ordering Bernard Lee removed from the white side of the courtroom. After rejecting various mistrial motions, Judge Jones moved the case swiftly to the jury, which assessed another $500,000 libel penalty against the defendants. Three similar suits were still pending, including one filed by Governor Patterson.

That same day, Negro students all across the South staged demonstrations honoring the first anniversary of the Greensboro sit-in. Some of these events were purely ceremonial. Others, like the pickets raised by the Nashville nonviolence workshop outside the city's segregated movie theaters, were opening moves of carefully planned, protracted campaigns. The anniversary sit-ins were noted here and there in the press, but what made electrifying news within the loose network of the protesters themselves came out of Rock Hill, South Carolina. Police there arrested ten students sitting in at a McCrory's lunch counter, and when the local judge imposed sentences of $100 or thirty days' hard labor on the road gang, nine of the ten students carried out their solemn pledge to take the hard labor. One of them had carried a toothbrush to the sit-in to be prepared for the chain gang. Another had written a letter to pained, disapproving parents: "Try to understand that what I'm doing is right. It isn't like going to jail for a crime like stealing or killing, but we are going for the betterment of all Negroes."

The "Rock Hill Jail-In" was an emotional breakthrough for the civil rights movement. Its philosophical rationale—on the Gandhian notion that cheerful suffering for a principle makes effective political witness—was familiar enough to students who had read or heard the speeches of James Lawson. What made the Rock Hill action so timely, however, was that it responded to a tactical dilemma that was arising in SNCC discus-

---

* Jones's 1956 injunction outlawing the Alabama NAACP was still in effect, pending appeal.

sions across the South: how to avoid the crippling limitations of scarce bail money. The obvious advantage of "jail, no bail" was that it reversed the financial burden of protest, costing the demonstrators no cash while obligating the white authorities to pay for jail space and food. The obvious disadvantage was that staying in jail represented a quantum leap in commitment above the old barrier of arrest, lock-up, and bail-out. There were primal fears of chain gangs, of claustrophobia, and of assault by guards or hostile inmates, not to mention the lost college credits.

As it happened, SNCC convened a three-day meeting at the Butler Street YMCA in Atlanta two days after the jail-in began. The nine student representatives were heavily outnumbered by observers and advisers, among whom the most commanding presence was Ella Baker. The meeting was interrupted one evening by a call from the York County jail in Rock Hill. Tom Gaither used one of his allotted jail calls to make a plea for support. All nine would make it through the rest of the thirty days on the chain gang, he promised, but he believed that the impact of their example would be dissipated unless someone reinforced them. Gaither's call sliced through whatever contemplative distance remained for the students gathered comfortably in Atlanta. To those who had made "putting your body on the line" the trademark of their movement, the appeal was irresistible. Ideas of launching sympathetic "jail-ins" in other cities were rejected on grounds of delay and difficulty. It soon occurred to them that the best form of support was the most direct one: they could go to Rock Hill themselves and join the nine prisoners in jail. One by one, four of the nine students present in Atlanta pledged to do so immediately. Diane Nash was the first, followed by Ruby Doris Smith of Spelman, Charles Sherrod of Virginia Union Seminary, and Charles Jones of Johnson C. Smith College in North Carolina. With the others, they drafted a press release praising those already jailed in Rock Hill, ending "we feel that in good conscience we have no alternative other than to join them."

With Ella Baker's blessing, the four students drove to Rock Hill, sat in at the same dime store, and told the judge they would serve their time. Their deed made them the stuff of instant legend among SNCC sympathizers. Tidbits of their stories slipped out of the jail to be highly prized —of jailhouse freedom-singing so fervent and affecting that the warden tried to stifle it by putting them all in solitary, of Jones and Sherrod, who already were preachers, proselytizing among the regular prisoners on the chain gang, of singing freedom songs down at the edge of a river bottom as they shoveled sand double time into dump trucks. The hateful guard eventually came to brag about what amazing workers they were. Their zeal overflowed so freely, it was said, that the students bent the leaden habits of jail to their own convictions. The Rock Hill jail-in was destined to be a failure by some standards, in that no stores were desegregated nor any further recruitments made. It was an unforgettable vicarious triumph for thousands of sit-in veterans, however, because the thirteen Rock Hill prisoners set a new standard of.psychological commitment to be debated and matched. More important, they introduced the idea of roving jail-goers and mutual support. As students began to think of any jail in any town as potentially their own, a new kind of fellowship took hold on the notion that the entire South was a common battlefield.

The first connection between Rock Hill and the Freedom Ride was established upon the completion of Tom Gaither's jail term. Gaither, having joined the CORE staff the previous year, was invited to New York as a hero, and Farmer selected him to make a scouting trip by bus between Washington, D.C., and New Orleans, making plans and contacts, reconnoitering the defenders of segregation in bus terminals along the way. Gaither made sure to include Rock Hill on the route. He predicted violence at Anniston, Alabama, which he described in a report as "a very explosive trouble spot without a doubt."

In Atlanta, King was preoccupied with political casualties among his peers. The latest $500,000 libel judgment convinced Fred Shuttlesworth and Ralph Abernathy to think more seriously of escaping to the North. At the first Birmingham mass meeting after the seizure of his car, Shuttlesworth went so far as to announce that he had a job offer from a church in Cincinnati. This prompted his alarmed followers to take up collections to buy him a new car, which they planned to register "in the name of Jesus" for legal protection against further seizures, and King privately tried to persuade Shuttlesworth to stay in Birmingham. He was so worried about losing Abernathy to New York that he wrote a private letter to a deacon at the West Hunter Street Baptist Church in Atlanta, where the pulpit was vacant, practically begging West Hunter to make an offer to Abernathy.

Seeing his friends so shaken, King recognized the significance of the thirteen jailed students in South Carolina all the more. On February 17, he sent a letter of tribute "to the freedom fighters," care of the prisoners he knew best, Nash and Sherrod. "You have inspired all of us by such demonstrative courage and faith," he wrote, adding a hopeful pronouncement on the nonviolent dynamics at work: "You transcend the judgments of evil men who decry the powerful weapon you are using. Every day that you remain behind bars sears the conscience of that immoral city. You are shaming them into decency."

The Nashville sit-in veterans, inspired by the sacrifice in Rock Hill of their compatriot Diane Nash, gradually escalated their protests against movie theater segregation. James Bevel sent groups marching downtown nightly to picket the theaters that refused them entry. Some white customers shied away from the scenes of potential conflict; some expressed support for the Negroes; many tried to pretend nothing unusual was happening. Anxious theater owners tried to preserve their business without appearing to give in to pressure. They wanted the pickets to leave, but they did not want to have them arrested for fear of bad publicity. Night by night, Bevel's squads marched off not knowing whether they would be attacked or not, and if so whether it would be by the police or the hostile white teenagers, whom they called "hoods." The hoods wore ducktail haircuts and menaced the picketers in growing numbers.

In James Lawson's absence, King's friend Rev. Kelly Miller Smith served as the leading adult adviser at the strategy sessions, which were held in Smith's First Baptist Church. By the time incipient violence had progressed to the point of near riot, with punches and flying rocks mixed in with the tomatoes, Smith had called a number of friends for assistance, including the prominent white clergyman Will Campbell. Painfully, Smith, Campbell, and the other adults recommended at one meeting that the picketing be suspended in favor of negotiations. As James Bevel and other articulate students debated the proposal, John Lewis sat stoically in a corner. Whenever asked a question, he ignored the fine points of whatever theory was being put forward and said simply, "We're gonna march tonight."

Theologian Campbell, who was deeply preoccupied with the question of whether the demonstrators would bear responsibility for provoking the violence inflicted upon them, had known Lewis from the previous year's sit-ins as an unpolished student who stuttered badly. Finally, exasperated by the deference the monosyllabic Lewis seemed to command from the other students, Campbell lost his patience. "You know there's very apt to be violence, serious violence, tonight if there's another demonstration," he said sharply to Lewis. "And I can only conclude that it's just a matter of pride with you. And bullheadedness. You're refusing to agree with us because of your own pride and your own sin."

The room went silent under the sting of Campbell's rebuke. Lewis smiled warmly at Campbell, as though taking pity on him. "Okay, I'm a sinner," he replied softly. "We're gonna march."

Campbell found no words to engage such directness. The students followed Lewis' lead and Bevel's tactics. They kept the pressure on the theater owners and endured the nightly shower of abuse. On February 20, the Nashville police began to make spot arrests of the demonstrators. They found Lewis in a picket circle in the snowy street outside Loew's Theater and took him off to jail. It was his fourth arrest.

Refusing to post bail, Lewis was unable to deliver his senior sermon at the seminary. He rescheduled it after his release, at which time he rejoined the line of theater marchers. In the March issue of the new SNCC newsletter, *The Student Voice,* Lewis read that theater campaigns were continuing in ten other cities from Dallas to Charlottesville, Virginia. He saw in the same issue CORE's first advertisement seeking volunteers for "Freedom Ride, 1961." Lewis promptly responded. Undaunted by a CORE application form emphasizing violence and prolonged incarceration as possible hazards, Lewis stated that he would willingly sacrifice his graduation from the seminary and anything else required. "This is [the] most important decision in my life," he wrote, "to decide to give up all if necessary for the Freedom Ride, that Justice and Freedom might come to the Deep South."

In Atlanta, where student demonstrators still were trying to match the lunch counter victories attained in Nashville the previous year, continuing sit-ins and boycotts caused the white owners of thirteen corporations to close more than seventy of their downtown stores for three months, through February 1961. With business paralyzed and all employees, including some five hundred Negroes, laid off, pressure for settlement built on both sides. Mayor Hartsfield, still feeling injured politically by his inability to broker an agreement after the fall elections, stepped aside when white businessmen agreed to negotiate directly with Negro leaders. In the opening round, Chamber of Commerce president Ivan Allen, Jr., received A. T. Walden, an elderly lawyer and dean of the Auburn Avenue business fraternity, at his office supply company. Walden was a fixture of the old guard, known by honorary titles such as "Colonel" and "Judge." There was a sticky moment when Walden asked to be shown to a bathroom. Allen hesitated briefly. He knew he could not ask a man of Walden's rank to use the unkempt separate restroom for Negroes, but he also knew that his white employees would rebel if he allowed Walden to use the restroom reserved for them. Allen, quick-witted and instinctively gracious, invited Walden to use his own private bathroom.

Many of the students maintaining the boycott against segregated stores might have taken the bathroom episode as an allegory of Negro leadership in Atlanta. They believed that the entrenched old leaders like Walden had made a lifetime habit of being satisfied with executive treatment for themselves alone. The elders believed that the young people were trying to undercut them in public, and strains worsened dramatically on March 7, when terms of a proposed deal were revealed at a climactic meeting of the negotiating teams. A joint statement, released by the Atlanta Chamber of Commerce, made front pages in the North as well as the South. Carefully written to protect the signatory white merchants from charges of capitulating to the Negroes, its central premise was that "the fine relationship which has existed between the races for a long number of years in Atlanta should be reinstated in every way." The statement concealed the obligations of the white parties in a convoluted sentence that avoided any explicit mention of integration, promising only to adopt "the same patterns . . . as are finally decided upon in the public school issues in Atlanta." No such ambiguity shielded the ten Negro signatories, who pledged immediately to "eliminate all boycotts, reprisals, picketing, and sit-ins, and to bring back a condition of complete normalcy as soon as possible."

Whatever soothing effect this unbalanced language may have had on Atlanta's whites, it carried an offsetting political cost among Negroes. Speakers at campus rallies denounced the provisions making lunch counter integration hostage to successful integration of the public schools, warning that if whites found a way to hang on to segregated schools, as they had done for almost seven years since the *Brown* decision, they could delay lunch counter integration not just six months but indefinitely. One student-body president advocated continued demonstrations, saying that the Negro leaders who engineered the agreement had not really supported the protest in the first place. With substantial numbers of adult Negroes falling under the sway of student objections, as measured by the buzz of street talk, Daddy King, Walden, and Borders searched under duress for a way to explain themselves, to keep their traditional authority from being proved hollow. The front page of the next day's *Daily World* advertised their next move in a blaring headline: "Clarification Mass Meeting at Warren Church Tonight."

An apprehensive Ivan Allen was one of the few whites in the manifestly tense crowd of two thousand that jammed into the Warren Methodist Church for a heated debate of the settlement. When Borders tried to give assurances that the lunch counters would be desegregated in September regardless of what happened in the schools, citing his own private understandings with the white business leaders, student and adult speakers alike challenged the value of his word and ridiculed an agreement that failed to say on its face what it meant. After the two student negotiators—the presidents of the Morehouse and Spelman student bodies—refused to defend the settlement, Daddy King strode to the pulpit for the unaccustomed purpose of justifying himself before a sea of skeptical teenagers. "For the first time in years, as far back as I can remember, the Chamber of Commerce agreed to take it upon itself the responsibility of working with the merchants to agree and settle this thing," he said. "We've got to give and take." At first there were only scattered rumbles of dissatisfaction, but when he said, "I've been around this kind of thing for thirty years," a student shouted out, "That's what's wrong!" The church erupted in laughter. Boos greeted Daddy King's next words. As he became flustered, he tried more persistently to invoke the weight of his experience, but this tactic only provoked his hecklers to drown him out in showers of catcalls and hisses.

The younger King was in town for an SCLC meeting about foundation grants for voter registration. As was his habit, he arrived late for the mass meeting, just in time to witness his father's humiliation. He was not scheduled to speak, but he began to make his way through the crowded aisles. Recognition of him ran through the church, quelling the noise, and when he reached the pulpit he slowly and deliberately surveyed the faces before him, with a pained look on his own face that imposed an expectant silence. There were tears in his eyes.

"I'm surprised at you," he said, beginning a soft lamentation against what he called the surrender of a nobly struggling people to "the cancer of disunity." Slowly, King waded into an extemporaneous speech praising the wisdom of the elders, the innovations of the young people, and the courage of everyone. He knitted the contending factions together with a passionate description of their purpose, which to him was larger even than freedom and dignity because they had a chance to show the world that strength and morality could rise together above primordial hatred. After a peroration on the fullness of his vision, he returned finally to the relatively small matter of the dispute over a settlement he called "the first written contract" Atlanta's whites had deigned to make with them. "If this contract is broken, it will be a disaster and a disgrace," he declared, in a voice close to fury. "If anyone breaks this contract, let it be the white man." With that, he vanished from the hushed church, leaving Daddy King rescued, Lonnie King relieved (though suffering from a bleeding ulcer), Ivan Allen in awe, and the settlement effectively ratified.

The race issue was intruding on Kennedy's early presidency so persistently as to be irksome. Even before the inauguration, he had been forced to pass over his first choice for Secretary of State, Senator William Fulbright of Arkansas, because of Fulbright's segregationist voting record. Similarly, he dropped plans to make Governor Ernest Vandiver Secretary of the Army after aides realized that the press was sure to make sport of Vandiver's ceremonial duties as head of an integrated army in contrast with his highly publicized battle to thwart integration. Fortunately for Kennedy, plans to announce the Vandiver nomination were set aside shortly before white students rioted over the court-ordered admission of the first two Negroes at the University of Georgia, putting Vandiver on television as the central figure in a controversy that Kennedy believed detracted from the world image of the United States.

The President believed that segregation, like colonialism, was an anachronistic addiction curable by the steady advance of modern attitudes. To him, this required the exercise of cool, detached reason in an atmosphere of public calm, which was incompatible with emotional demonstrations by either whites or Negroes. Like any President, Kennedy responded instinctively against "unrest" within his domain, but in the area of civil rights especially he stressed calm as a condition of progress. Such a posture necessarily placed civil rights on the periphery of his ambitions in the White House, inasmuch as no President, and certainly not one so romantic as he, could or wanted to accomplish his major goals in seclusion.

On February 7, still in his first round of appointments, Kennedy received John Hannah and Father Theodore Hesburgh, two of the leading Eisenhower appointees to the Civil Rights Commission. His goal was to persuade them to remain in office during his term, as he considered them to be highly qualified and did not wish to see expectations of new civil rights policy raised by their resignation and replacement. The two men agreed to stay on, but they asked the President's help in correcting several minor impediments to their work. One of them was the absence, since Rocco Siciliano's abrupt resignation in 1958, of a White House staff person formally in charge of civil rights. They wanted someone to make sure the President was receiving the commission's views. Kennedy dismissed this request before they could list the next one. "I already have a special assistant who is working full time on that," he said. "Harris Wofford."

Hannah and Hesbergh said nothing more about the matter until they left the White House, when they promptly called Wofford. They both knew him well, as Wofford had worked at the commission and once taught at Notre Dame under Hesbergh, who was president of the university. In fact, they had consulted with Wofford only minutes before going in to see President Kennedy, at which time Wofford had still been a talent searcher without position in the Administration, planning to work with Sargent Shriver in the creation of the Peace Corps. When Hannah passed along what the President had just said, a stunned Wofford assured Hannah that he did not know anything about a White House job. Minutes later, he received an urgent summons to Kennedy's office, and as he sat outside waiting to be shown in, a strange man thrust a book before him and said, "Are you Mr. Wofford? Please raise your right hand and repeat after me."

"What for?" asked Wofford.

"I'm supposed to swear you in," the man replied.

"But I don't know what the job is, and I haven't talked to the President yet," said Wofford. When the man dismissed the questions as irrelevant to his orders, Wofford asked plaintively, "Do *you* know what the job is?"

"That doesn't matter," the man said crisply. "The President knows. All you do now is swear to uphold the Constitution. Is there anything wrong with that?"

A shrugging Wofford swore the oath just before he was shown in to see the President, who told him briskly that he needed him on the staff, working under the general mandate of "minimum civil rights legislation, maximum executive action." Kennedy, already late for an urgent foreign policy meeting, brushed aside Wofford's questions about his authority with a general instruction to work with Sorensen at the White House and with the Justice Department. "You're the expert," he said with a smile. "Get going." He told Wofford to search the Executive Office Building and commandeer "the best office that's left."

Theoretically, Wofford occupied the ideal government position for a man of his convictions: the one in the White House, closest to the power emanating from the President, with an exclusive civil rights portfolio. As a practical matter, however, he knew he enjoyed little rapport with Sorensen or any other central figure on the White House staff, and less with Byron White at the Justice Department. White believed that the passions of race politics would undermine respect for law if handled at Justice, while Kennedy's closest aides feared they would hurt the President if publicly associated with the White House. All these people were much closer than Wofford to President Kennedy. They would soon learn of the ad hoc, almost flippant manner in which Kennedy had appointed him, and react accordingly. Wofford began his tenure in grave danger of becoming an ornament at the White House.

Quite apart from the political dangers perceived, those closest to the President shied away from civil rights because they considered the racial controversies being publicized too prosaic, too small and quirkishly human, for the President's attention. The Iowa legislature was debating a bill that would require the state's barbers to know how to cut Negro hair. In baseball, the annual rash of spring training disputes featured a running story out of Bradenton, Florida, where owners of the best hotel agreed, after a long battle, to give rooms to Milwaukee Braves star outfielder Hank Aaron and other Negro players, provided they consented to take their meals behind a special partition in the dining room. Such entanglements of segregation were always being presented for comment in Washington, only to be brushed aside by the savviest advisers as inherently belittling to the President.

Only once that first winter did President Kennedy allow himself to take sides in a public squabble over civil rights, and he came to regret it. On the approach of the Civil War Centennial, trouble stirred in Charleston, South Carolina, where reporters learned that a Negro delegate to the National Civil War Commission would not be permitted to stay in the hotel hosting the commemoration of the battle of Fort Sumter. When the legislature of New Jersey, home state of the Negro delegate, passed a resolution urging all states to boycott the opening ceremonies, President Kennedy bowed to pressure and wrote a letter to General Ulysses S. Grant III, chairman of the commission, stating that all delegates deserved equal treatment as officials of a government body. This venture earned him only scorching rejoinders from Southern delegates, who maintained that the President had no authority over the private affairs of South Carolina hotels.

The controversy escalated rapidly. General Grant supported the South against Kennedy, declaring through a spokesman that the commission's business was to commemorate the war and not to interfere in "racial matters." New York, California, and Illinois joined New Jersey in calling for a boycott. Administration officials, scrambling now that the authority of the President was publicly at issue, eventually conceded that they could not force any suitable Charleston hotel to integrate for the occasion. To save face, they did muster the votes to move the ceremonial banquet out of the segregated hotel to a U.S. Naval Base three miles outside Charleston, only to have Southerners gleefully notify reporters that the Navy still segregated its own personnel on the base. Then, on the eve of the Fort Sumter ceremony, a Southern delegate made a speech to the commission containing what Northern delegates called slurs on the ancestry of President Abraham Lincoln, racial and otherwise. After an escalating exchange of insults, the commission delegations acted out an upside-down parody of Civil War politics. Northerners called on President Kennedy to "relieve" General Grant for failing to preserve the honor of the federal government, while Southerners rallied to support the grandson of the man whose troops had mowed down their forebears from Shiloh to Appomattox.

From the point of view of the White House advisers, the second battle of Fort Sumter was a farcical tempest over the hotel accommodations for a single Negro woman, proving that the President would probably look foolish and impotent if he tried to act nobly in racial politics. Mercifully for Kennedy, the political damage from the affair was limited by the low level of public interest in the Civil War itself. Centennial history began a four-year trek through the back pages. Charleston officials reported that the city's tourist traffic was down by half on the day of the ceremony. News from Fort Sumter was overshadowed by the opening of the Eichmann trial in Jerusalem and even more so by Soviet cosmonaut Yuri Gagarin's first manned space flight, which shocked Americans as a kind of reprise on Sputnik. Five days later, these sensational stories were swept away by the real-life military disaster at the Bay of Pigs.

Beyond geopolitics and ideology, President Kennedy felt a keen antipathy for Fidel Castro as a man who personified many qualities he himself cherished—youth, vigor, daring against impossible odds. Castro lived gaily on the edge of survival, ruthlessly suppressing his internal enemies and then stopping by to gossip with common folk on the street. Called simply "Fidel" by worshippers and revilers alike, Castro had the sort of Hemingway "ballsiness" that the Kennedys so admired, along with the awareness to present himself to the Western world in the proper mixture of idealism and existentialism.

When this same Castro not only crushed the surprise invasion at the Bay of Pigs but also exposed as a clumsy lie the entire CIA cover story of American noninvolvement, the sting of President Kennedy's humiliation spread instantly to millions of citizens. U-2 pilot Francis Gary Powers remained in the Soviet Union on charges of capital espionage even as Castro's triumphant army imprisoned more than a thousand surviving soldiers of the Bay of Pigs brigade. For the second time in a year, an American President went before the nation for the politically torturous act of public apology. Although the President gracefully assumed responsibility, and his allies diverted blame elsewhere, no Kennedy defender developed a cogent rationale for his decisions—most especially for his persistent reductions of the invasion's military power in the hope of secrecy.*

Still, the President did not recoil from the international struggle against Communist rivals, nor change his definition of its terms. On the contrary, he became ever more immersed in foreign affairs, more deter mined to energize the entire Western defense network with the new doctrines of flexible response, counterinsurgency warfare, and economic assistance. Having initiated a $17 billion nuclear missile program a

---

* Four years later, Kennedy's closest aide and explicator still would cling to the bizarre notion that the military result at the Bay of Pigs was essentially a matter of noise. "The President thought he was approving a quiet, even though large-scale, reinfiltration of fourteen hundred Cuban exiles back into their homeland. He had been assured that the plan as revised to meet his criteria was an unspectacular and quiet landing of patriots plausibly Cuban in its essentials, of which the air strike was the only really noisy enterprise that remained."

month before the Bay of Pigs, he returned a month afterward to deliver a special State of the Union address in which he called for twelve thousand new Marines, the training of new anti-guerrilla units that came to be known as Special Forces or Green Berets, and a tripling of funds for fallout shelters and other civil defense programs. Moreover, he made the electrifying announcement that the United States was undertaking to place a man on the moon "before this decade is out."

In the struggle against communism, Kennedy officials displayed ambivalence or avoidance only about the issue of subversion at home. There the swirling contradictions between democratic freedoms and the suppression of subversives had been demonstrated painfully in the career of Senator Joe McCarthy, and both John and Robert Kennedy, still vulnerable to charges of abetting or tolerating McCarthy's witch-hunts, knew better than to repeat his rampage against vaguely defined security risks. Nevertheless, it was difficult to rally the entire nation for a showdown with communism without taking measure of the alien threat at home. This was a delicate matter for Robert Kennedy, who was J. Edgar Hoover's nominal boss even though Hoover had been FBI Director longer than Kennedy had been alive. He tried to soothe Hoover with flattery and other personal attentions while establishing his prerogatives as Attorney General, to acknowledge Hoover's immense power as the nation's expert on internal security while also advancing the New Frontier's post-McCarthy attitudes.

The personal relationship between Hoover and Robert Kennedy was an Oriental pageant of formal respect, beneath which played out a comedy of private insults and mismatched quirks. From the beginning, Kennedy's people spoke of the Director's "good days" of crisp, brilliant efficiency and his "bad days" of cartoonlike lunacy. During John Seigenthaler's first private visit, Hoover punctuated a tirade against newspapers with a listing of known Communists on the copy desk of the New York *Herald-Tribune*, then lurched into a long description of Adlai Stevenson as a "notorious homosexual." Seigenthaler blinked in amazement, not least because other FBI officials were using the same details of the same episodes to ridicule former diplomat Sumner Welles. When Seigenthaler returned to the Justice Department, Attorney General Kennedy took one look at him and said, "He was out of it today, wasn't he?" Hoover's quicksilver moods became a running joke, which was made all the more surreal by the assumption that Hoover himself was homosexual in style if not in performance. On learning that the Director's associate and bachelor housemate, Clyde Tolson, had been hospitalized for an operation, the Attorney General quipped to his aides, "What was it, a hysterectomy?" Against all that, however—and against the wildly conspiratorial tips from disgruntled FBI agents that Hoover had his office bugged—Kennedy insisted that all his subordinates spare no effort to cooperate with the Bureau. It was more than a matter of political necessity for him. His father had once offered Hoover $100,000 a year to become chief of security for the Kennedy interests, he said. To Robert Kennedy, his father's assessment of Hoover's worth meant something, and it was a measure of Hoover's devotion to the Bureau that he had turned the offer down.

From the FBI, the Kennedy Justice Department received a similar mixture of outward respect and private derision. Even lowly field agents often referred to Robert Kennedy's office as the "playpen" or "rumpus room," making sport of the Attorney General's stocking-footed work style, his touch-football parties, and the splashes of children's art on his office walls. Such informalities offended the punctilious Hoover, who resented all the more Kennedy's efforts to function as his boss in substance as well as title. When Kennedy broke the cherished FBI tie to the White House by getting his brother's aides to refuse Hoover's calls, Hoover retaliated by becoming unavailable to receive the Attorney General's calls. Kennedy countered by installing a direct telephone line into Hoover's office. Down the line at the Bureau, agents resented the effrontery to Hoover but also laughed at the war of manners. The Old Man still could make Kennedy jump through hoops, they said, as in the matter of the Negro agents. When Kennedy gently urged the Director to integrate his elite work force, Hoover first claimed it was an internal FBI matter, then that the Bureau already was integrated. Over nearly two years, Hoover strung out the Attorney General's suspicious and increasingly annoyed campaign to learn the specifics of the integrated Bureau. Hoover's masterly bureaucratic retreat was a source of proud merriment within the FBI, where it was widely known that the "Negro agents" consisted of Hoover's Washington driver, his white-coated doorman, his all-purpose messenger, plus chauffeurs attached to the Miami and La Jolla FBI offices to be available for the Director's vacations. All five Negro retainers had been made Special Agents to exempt them from civil service protections as well as military service, making them personally dependent on Hoover.

J. Edgar Hoover's top officials at the FBI first took personal notice of King only two weeks after the Kennedy inauguration, when *The Nation* magazine published an article by King titled "Equality Now." Deep within a long list of recommendations for the incoming Administration was a parenthetical reference to the FBI: "If, for instance, the law-enforcement personnel in the FBI were integrated, many persons who now defy federal law might come under restraints from which they are presently free." This one sentence rocketed up through that portion of the FBI bureaucracy keeping watch for the appearance of criticism in the public domain. Internal defenders branded King "in error," apparently on the theory that even one "Negro agent" technically invalidated charges of segregation. A memo to Assistant Director Cartha "Deke" DeLoach, Hoover's political guardian, recommended that the Bureau not "call his hand on this matter as he [King] obviously would only welcome any controversy or resulting publicity that might ensue."

By any reasonable measure, the substance of King's article was a much greater threat to the incoming Kennedy Administration than to Hoover. Its publication served notice that King was not disposed to trim his expectations in the face of harsh political realities, nor even to hold his peace during the "honeymoon" normally allotted a new President. Beginning simply with the assertion that "the principle is no longer in doubt," King brushed aside all qualifiers to the moral imperative of racial integration, along with the claims of segregation laws in more than a dozen states. For all that, King substituted a single question—how can the new President most rapidly and effectively bring about integration? "We must face the tragic fact that the federal government is the nation's highest investor in segregation," wrote King. His tone was unfailingly positive, as usual, and he presented his agenda as an "opportunity" for the Administration. Still, for fresh Kennedy officials, the article could be perceived only as a warning shot across the Administration's bow, or, more accurately, across its stern.

King was not invited to the first large meeting of civil rights leaders in the Attorney General's office on March 6, at which the petitioners suggested the appointment of a roving federal prosecutor for the South, and Kennedy in turn stressed the importance of voting. King, threatened with exclusion, responded by seeking access at a higher level. Ten days later, after the "clarification mass meeting" in Atlanta, he wrote the White House to seek a private appointment with President Kennedy himself. Appointments secretary Kenneth O'Donnell turned him down on March 25, citing the squeeze of the "present international situation" on the President's time. Communist guerrillas were overrunning Laos; Portuguese troops were suppressing a revolt in Angola; the Congo remained in turmoil following the assassination of the new country's deposed premier, Patrice Lumumba; new Soviet demands imperiled the nuclear test ban talks in Geneva.

The King problem became a running subtopic of conversation among the half-dozen top Kennedy officials most concerned with civil rights. At

Harris Wofford's weekly interagency meeting at the Civil Rights Division, hesitations and calculations were swapped at some length, with the more conservative men worrying generally about the dangers of establishing a political relationship with someone like King. Louis Martin, installed after the inauguration as assistant chairman of the Democratic National Committee, finally suggested a way out of the impasse: they should invite King to Washington for a secret, "off the record" meeting. If King agreed to come under such conditions, and fulfilled his pledge to keep the event out of the newspapers, that in itself would be a reassuring sign of how he operated. If the scheme worked, Martin argued, the Kennedy people would get a chance to take their measure of King in a political setting, and to make the case to him for their civil rights plans, without publicity. If it did not work, they needed to find out sooner rather than later, and it would be easier to limit the political damage from a secret meeting than from a public one.

Not until after the Bay of Pigs invasion were the arrangements completed, with secrecy permeating every detail. King was permitted to bring only one aide. The setting was a private dining room of the Mayflower Hotel rather than a government office building, and the luncheon was laid out on a buffet table rather than served by waiters, who had been known to pass on tidbits of conversation to reporters. One by one the parties arrived—Wofford and Kenneth O'Donnell from the White House, Louis Martin from the DNC, Attorney General Kennedy, John Seigenthaler, Burke Marshall and two or three others from Justice, plus King and his aide—no more than a dozen people in all. There were no formal introductions. When the Attorney General arrived, the men served themselves and sat down for a Kennedy-style meeting over lunch.

By prior designation, Burke Marshall did most of the talking for the Kennedy side. He explained to King his view of the severe constraints on the federal government imposed by constitutional federalism, as applied more rigidly in federal laws governing civil rights than in other fields. The Justice Department had little power to intervene in school desegregation cases or even police brutality cases except in very narrowly defined circumstances, Marshall explained, and its widest latitude by far lay in the protection of voting rights. There the Justice Department was, in the watchword of the Administration, "moving" by both conventional and unconventional methods. Attorneys from the Civil Rights Division were filing suits to enjoin Southern counties from harassing or discouraging Negro registrants. John Doar, for example, had just come back from an undercover assignment in Hattiesburg, Mississippi, on such a case, and he was working to develop another in Selma, Alabama. By Marshall's presentation, all roads in civil rights led to voter registration, where the federal government's most explicit legal authority could protect the most significant political opportunity for Southern Negroes. Attorney General Kennedy and others chimed in on this central theme.

When Kennedy made a second trip to the buffet table, Harris Wofford made a point of falling in behind him, smiling in the warmth of a minor satisfaction. "You remember that fellow you were worried about my having associations with, that I didn't remember?" he whispered.

"Who's that?" Kennedy replied.

"Stanley Levison," said Wofford. To Kennedy's noncommittal look, he added, "Well, you better remember him now, too, because that's him you're sitting next to."

"Oh, really," Kennedy said drily. "That's interesting." Without another word he returned to his seat next to Levison, the companion King had chosen to bring to this highly unusual introductory meeting with the Kennedy people. Wofford, for his part, was pleased that the Attorney General seemed to have appreciated the irony of the situation as well as Wofford's implied message that the mild-mannered white man with King did not seem so dangerous in the flesh.

Levison did not say very much during the meeting, nor did King. To the Kennedy people, in fact, the most noticeable aspect of King's private behavior was his quietness. He did not preach, bargain, or strike postures. When called upon for response, he heartily endorsed all the Administration's plans in the field of voting rights, promised to step up the SCLC's registration work in tandem with the lawsuits, and indicated his full understanding of the need to conceal the Administration's facilitating role in the registration work itself. Although King did say that voting was not the only avenue of progress toward Negro rights—and that sit-ins, mass meetings, legislation, boycotts, and a host of other tactics could make contributions—he stressed no point of difference. With his slow cadences of speech, his lofty expressions, and his amiable demeanor, King struck the Kennedy people as a saint or a pushover, or both. He was not the type they would think of asking out for a beer, but he was reasonable. Louis Martin, who had known King only slightly, would never waver from the opinion formed that day that King was "the most self-effacing national leader I have ever known." In later years, Burke Marshall revised his opinion of King's political abilities upward, saying that he was "easy to underestimate."

King noticed that Louis Martin grabbed the bill for the lunch, and as the meeting began to break up he made his way to Martin's side. Nodding toward the papers Martin was handling for the payment, he dropped his formality just long enough to ask, "Whose tab?"

Martin hesitated for an instant, taken aback to hear King ask so directly about such housekeeping. "Mine," he replied. "My account at the DNC."

"Thank you," said King, shaking his head in approval and giving Martin a quick smile that was almost a wink. Martin took it to mean that King was pleased to see him handling the money himself, rather than performing the usual retainer role for one of the white bosses. Martin said simply, "You're welcome," together with a quick nod of recognition, which he hoped would say that he was equally pleased to learn that King paid attention to such small but significant details. This passing moment marked the first germ of friendship between the only two Negroes in the room.

King's overall performance so relieved and reassured the Kennedy officials that they moved almost by group instinct to cultivate him politically rather than to disengage. Attorney General Kennedy set the tone with his response to King's remark that harassed and endangered voter registration workers often had trouble reaching the FBI for assistance. Kennedy wrote down the telephone numbers of John Seigenthaler and Burke Marshall and handed them to King. "Any hour of the day or night," he said, "you call." From the Mayflower, Wofford found a reason to take King back to the White House for a chat and a tour, during which the President "discovered" that King was there—almost certainly upon the report of Ken O'Donnell, who had been much more skeptical of King before the meeting—and popped out to pay his respects. "It's good to see you," said President Kennedy, shaking King's hand for the first time since their campaign meeting seven months earlier. Kennedy said he had been keeping up with King's work through the Attorney General. He alluded briefly to the confidential plans to promote Negro registration in the South and promised his support. To King's polite inquiries about how he was doing, Kennedy replied that everything was fine except that the world had fallen in on him since the disaster in Cuba.

In honor of his pledge to keep the Mayflower meeting secret, King made no public reference to it then or later, and he did not even acknowledge his chance meeting with President Kennedy until after the assassination in Dallas. The only news King generated was a small item in a Negro gossip column, stating accurately that he planned to "join the colony at Oak Bluff" on Martha's Vineyard for a month that summer, to relax among exclusive company on the grounds of a nineteenth-century Methodist camp meeting. King still had a powerful appetite for prestige and for luxuries, but competing against it was an ego strong enough that he did not need to chatter about his attentions from the Kennedys. That ego, in the crucible of the Freedom Rides, would blow apart the Administration's hopes for a cozy, private partnership.

John Doar faced new competition inside the Justice Department. On the political recommendation of Southern Democrats, Burke Marshall hired an Arkansas lawyer named Jerome Heilbron, who came into the Civil Rights Division representing the thesis that persuasion was more effective than lawsuits. Heilbron argued that Southerners had never been approached correctly, by people who knew their language and habits. They could be won over with honeyed threats, he said, whereas lawsuits would backfire.

Doar knew better than to scoff. He was the outsider, the Republican in a Democratic Justice Department. The Attorney General already had begun to tease him, saying, "You're the best weapon the Republicans have," by which he meant that Doar's civil rights suits alienated Democratic Southern voters. Doar knew that there were substantial legal reasons to take Heilbron seriously. Even the most ardent civil rights liberals conceded that the Justice Department faced crippling handicaps in litigation, of which the most vexing was the *Screws* precedent. Over countless cups of coffee, the Doar school of lawyers agreed with Heilbron's on one legal point: there was no easy way around *Screws*. Aptly named, the case was a monster on their shoulders.

Fortified with alcohol, Sheriff Claude Screws went one night with two retainers to the home of a Negro named Robert Hall, arrested him, and took him in handcuffs to the courthouse yard in Baker County, Georgia. There, in public view, Screws beat Hall with fist and blackjack for at least fifteen minutes, then dragged his lifeless corpse feet-first into a jail cell. Although no state murder charges were brought, federal prosecutors presented evidence of such egregious brutality that an all-white jury convicted the sheriff under a Reconstruction statute designed to protect the civil rights of Negroes. After that, Screws pursued an appeal in which, conceding that he had intended to kill Hall, he argued that the Constitution protected him from any charge except the appropriate one of murder, under Georgia law. ("The defense is not pretty," wrote Supreme Court Justice Rutledge.) The Supreme Court reversed Screws's conviction by a twist of reasoning that even the defense lawyers had not offered. The government had failed to prove that Screws had attacked Hall with the specific intent to deprive him of his civil rights, the Court ruled. Prosecutors had shown merely that Screws intended to kill him. This was the Court's strict interpretation of the word "willfully" in the statute. Incredibly, it meant that henceforth federal prosecutors in such cases had to prove that the defendants were thinking about constitutional violations while they committed heinous, primordial crimes. This was the *Screws* precedent, from a decision written by liberal Justice William O. Douglas in 1944. Within the tiny fraternity of civil rights prosecutors, the decision was an unpleasant echo of *Dred Scott.* And no matter how badly they wished to discard the case as a wartime aberration, like the Japanese internment cases, it was controlling law still.

The same standards of specific intent applied to civil actions on the intimidation of voters under Section (b) of the 1957 Civil Rights Act. Civil rights prosecutors called them "b-suits" for short, and Doar knew better than most that the *Screws* case made b-suits nearly impossible. They were nightmares that required objective proof of a subjective intent. For the protection of voting rights, this left prosecutors with "a-suits," which were nightmares of tedium. Under Section (a) of the 1957 act, federal prosecutors could obtain injunctions against local officials if they could prove that racial discrimination existed. Practically speaking, this meant that they had to obtain and present to the court the actual voter registration applications, then prove to the court that individual Negroes were denied registration whereas whites of equal or lower competency were not, and that no factor other than race explained the discrepancy, and then prove that such discrepancies occurred in sufficient numbers to constitute a "pattern" of discrimination. This had to be done slowly through the courts, against obstruction and delay by the opponents, on a county-by-county basis. There were 159 counties in Georgia alone.

Doar saw no alternative to this laborious scheme. He fully understood why a newcomer to the field such as Burke Marshall would welcome Heilbron's alternative, or any other. Certainly Heilbron's plan would be quicker if it worked, and Doar could not quarrel with the severity of the chosen test, as Heilbron volunteered to try out the honeyed-threat idea in the remote and forsaken home county of the *Screws* case itself. He negotiated for Negro voting rights in "Bad" Baker County, where the retired Sheriff Screws had been succeeded in recent years by Sheriff L. Warren "Gator" Johnson. Negroes did not vote in Baker County.

Doar continued along the path he already had chosen: the relentless production of a-suits. Having learned that the local federal prosecutors would not help at all in the South, and that the FBI was a blunt instrument, Doar and his colleagues invented their own system to expedite the process in spite of the handicaps. The first principle was that they had to meet the Negroes personally. They had to establish trust. They had to learn how to tell a reliable witness from one who would crumble under the fear. They had to learn which counties to choose first and how to go about looking for supporting witnesses. They had to do these things and many others without the slightest assistance from the established local institutions. In fact, they had to avoid local whites altogether. By the spring of 1961, Doar had seen enough to know that he could not do his job from behind a desk in Washington. To be a regular legal bureaucrat was to be blind and helpless.

In early April, Doar and a colleague named Bob Owen flew into Jackson, Mississippi, incognito. They wore khaki pants, work shirts, and old boots. They would prefer that the FBI not know they were there, lest the Bureau get huffy about trespass on its investigative territory, but the disguises were mostly to fool the local whites. To minimize the chances of provoking curiosity, they drove out into the remote countryside and checked into a flophouse motel. Before dawn the next morning they introduced themselves to Medgar Evers. Sitting at his kitchen table, Doar explained their purpose, and soon Evers, who knew almost every Negro on their list of those who had complained about voting discrimination over the years, was marking spots on their special-issue large-scale maps. Doar and Owen used the marks as guides to a dirt-road farm in one county and a back-alley house in the next. They drove down to Natchez, over to Hattiesburg, then up to Clark County—knocking on doors, poking their way out into cornfields, interviewing rejected Negro voters, asking each one for the names of others. They would send the new names to the FBI for interview.

The scouting trip through Mississippi was the first of many that helped them refine an assembly line for a-suits. They did not need to interview white voters; Bob Owen could scan the handwriting on approval forms, subpoena twenty or so with the poorest literacy, select witnesses on the basis of one-minute interviews outside the courtroom, and send the best ones to the stand for questioning by Doar. They learned quickly that they needed predominantly rural counties, with lots of farmers, because teachers and other middle-class urban Negroes felt too much economic pressure to testify. Large counties offered a higher pool of potential witnesses than small ones, and the degree of discrimination tended to vary directly with the proportion of Negroes in the county.

Using these and other makeshift guidelines, Doar and Owen surveyed a county map of the South with a view toward initiating an a-suit in each federal court district. In Alabama, the maps led them to stick a pin in Dallas County. By this selection method, the Justice Department went to work in Selma, the local county seat, long before SNCC or Martin Luther King. From testimony before the Civil Rights Commission, Doar and Owen had the name of Amelia Boynton of the Dallas County Voters League, and on their next trip they went promptly to see her. Boynton ran a small insurance office. On her wall, the lawyers found a plaque with stars next to the names of Dallas County Negroes who had *tried* to register. Boynton's honor roll was a bounty of witnesses, which enabled the Civil Rights Division to move swiftly. Doar filed an a-suit before the end of April.

These were the days, Robert Kennedy later said wistfully, "when we thought we were succeeding because of all the stories on how hard everybody was working." In early May, Dallas County registrar J. P. Majors resigned to avoid turning over his registration records to the federal prosecutors, forcing Doar to return to Selma to modify his pleading so as to keep the a-suit alive. Doar did not see the avalanche ahead that was to sweep him into nearby Montgomery. Nor did King, who flew off to address the annual convention of the United Automobile Workers in Detroit, on the invitation of union president Walter Reuther. Nor did Robert Kennedy, who, while trying to figure out what had gone wrong at the Bay of Pigs, decided to give a major civil rights speech at the University of Georgia. John Lewis had by far the clearest premonition of the upheaval that would bring them all to Montgomery, and he thought he was going to New Orleans.

ELEVEN

BAPTISM ON WHEELS

When John Lewis missed his bus in Nashville, his seminary friends James Bevel and Bernard Lafayette drove him at high speeds to overtake the bus in Murfreesboro, Tennessee. From there, Lewis rode alone to Washington to begin Freedom Ride training on May 1, joining James Farmer and eleven recruits. It was a motley collection—three white females, three white males, and seven Negro males, ranging in age from twenty-one to sixty. There were two students and a folk singer, several CORE staff members, a retired Michigan professor and his wife, a preacher, and a free-lance writer. There was James Peck, an heir to the Peck & Peck clothier fortune, who, since silencing the Harvard Freshman Dance of 1933 by arriving with a Negro date, had spent more than three years in prison, and endured numerous arrests, for ignoring laws and social conventions that conflicted with his idealism. There was also strapping, square-jawed Albert Bigelow, a Harvard-trained architect and former Navy captain, whose World War II experience had converted him into so ardent a pacifist that he had skippered his protest craft *Golden Rule* into atomic test zones out in the Pacific. Lewis was the youngest rider and one of two SNCC students in the group. The other was Henry Thomas of Howard University in Washington.

Official Washington took no notice of them. The CORE press office had interested only three reporters, all Negroes, in covering the Freedom

Ride. Simeon Booker of *Jet* magazine tried to ease his qualms by notifying the FBI of CORE's hazardous project. Then Booker slipped into the Justice Department for one of those thirty-second, bob-in conversations, telling the Attorney General and his aide John Seigenthaler that there would probably be trouble. "Okay, call me if there is," Kennedy replied briskly, adding, "I wish I could go with you." It reassured Booker to know that the Attorney General of the United States knew in advance of his trip with this quixotic band of Freedom Riders, but the glib tone of Kennedy's remark made Booker wonder whether his apprehensions had registered fully. Kennedy promptly forgot all about the Freedom Ride.

The thirteen riders embarked on the morning of May 4 in two groups, one on Greyhound and the other on Trailways. According to plan, they scattered throughout each bus in various combinations—some whites in the back and Negroes in the front, with at least one interracial pair of seatmates and a few riders observing less conspicuously from traditional seats. Fifty-two miles south of Washington, the buses pulled into the first rest stops at Fredericksburg, Virginia. "White" and "Colored" signs still guarded the waiting rooms and restaurants, but the riders endured nothing more illegal than icy looks. Reboarding, they pressed on with similar results to Richmond and then to Petersburg, where they were applauded at a mass meeting in Wyatt Walker's former church before spending the night in guest homes. Thirteen days, fifteen hundred miles, and scores of bus stations stretched between them and their destination in New Orleans. Most of the bus stations were located in parts of town where the Supreme Court and Gandhi were seldom discussed.

On the second day they passed through Farmville in Prince Edward County—home of the Vernon Johns family and the Virginia portion of the *Brown* case. To avoid compliance with the integration ruling, the county government had transferred most of its school property to hastily organized private schools for white children. Nearly all the Negro children had gone without schooling for two years. The impasse in Prince Edward had attracted national publicity, with issues drawn so starkly that the Kennedy Justice Department recently had filed its first school desegregation case there, in an attempt to force a reopening of the public schools. When the Greyhound and Trailways buses pulled into Farmville, the Freedom Riders found that the local "Colored" signs had been freshly painted over at the stations. All thirteen riders obtained service without incident, as the powers of Prince Edward County declined to extend their "massive resistance" to interstate transportation. By nightfall, the riders had passed through Lynchburg to Danville, where, for the first time, bus station officials turned them away. There were no arrests, however, and no violence.

High above, Alan Shepard and Robert Kennedy were in transit, too, pioneers as visible to the world as the Freedom Riders were unknown— Shepard on the first American manned space flight, Kennedy on his way to give his maiden civil rights speech at the University of Georgia. "Western Nations Rejoice," beamed one of the half-dozen Shepard head-lines in the next day's *New York Times*, celebrating the fifteen-minute space flight as a tonic against Bay of Pigs and Sputnik blues. President Kennedy held a spirited news conference as soon as Shepard was safely down.

Robert Kennedy's ordeal was similarly packed with tension. He and his aides had been working on his speech for five weeks, since Kennedy had decided that it would be hypocritical of him not to set forth his civil rights policies where they would be most applied and least welcome. With his hands trembling slightly, as was his fate at public events, Kennedy thanked Georgia for giving his brother "the biggest percentage majority of any state in the Union," and then he introduced civil rights as a part of the battle against communism abroad. At home, he told the Georgians, "We, the American people must avoid another Little Rock or another New Orleans. We cannot afford them. . . . Such incidents hurt our country in the eyes of the world." On this point, he declared that the graduation of the two Negro students just admitted to their university on pain of riot "will without question aid and assist the fight against Communist political infiltration and guerilla warfare."

Kennedy maintained this hard line on the civil rights issue itself. "Southerners have a special respect for candor and plain talk," he said. ". . . You may ask: will we enforce the civil rights statutes? The answer is: yes, we will." He volunteered as a matter of personal belief that he agreed with the *Brown* decision, and he pledged to desegregate his own Department of Justice at least as rapidly as he pressed for desegregation anywhere else. Of the department's Prince Edward County suit, much criticized in the South, Kennedy told the Georgians that the larger interests of the nation would require any of them to take the same action if holding his position. "For I cannot believe," he said, "that anyone can support a principle which prevents more than a thousand of our children in one county from attending public school—especially when this step was taken to circumvent the orders of a court." Promising action tempered by fairness, he offered a deliberate contrast with the Eisenhower image. "We will not stand by and be aloof," he said. "We will move."

The sixteen hundred Georgians in the audience remained quiet as Kennedy shyly took his seat at the end, and then they broke into applause for a full thirty seconds, as measured by one reporter, in tribute to his persuasiveness or his courage, or both. This reception was noted, along

with the absence of ranking Georgia politicians, in news accounts praising Kennedy's "resolute speech" on civil rights. It appeared, at least for
the remainder of that weekend, that the Attorney General had worked a
miracle by articulating a truly national policy. On Tuesday, however,
White House press secretary Pierre Salinger announced that the President was disowning two legislative versions of the Democratic platform
he had promised to support during the campaign, and almost simultaneously Georgia's Governor Vandiver was announcing that John Kennedy had given him a campaign pledge never to use federal force to
support desegregation laws in Georgia. Rancorous debate over political
deals sprang up on the back pages, where Roy Wilkins likened Kennedy's
disowning of the civil rights bills to "an offering of a cactus bouquet."

The first Freedom Rider bus pulled into the Greyhound terminal at
Rock Hill, South Carolina, on the morning of Salinger's announcement.
This being the site of the "jail-in" that was already legendary among
SNCC students, John Lewis made an effort to rotate into the position of
first tester. As he made his way from the bus toward the whites' waiting
room, the usual tensions seemed to coil rather than abate. The Rock Hill
terminal was more of a "hangout" than most, filled with pinball machines played by white youths of a type that had become the scourge of
the sit-in movement. One of them was leaning on either side of the door,
with about twenty more behind.

The first two stepped in front of Lewis to block the entrance. One of
them said, "Other side," jerking his thumb toward the Colored entrance.

Lewis drew himself up for the standard speech. "I have a right to go in
here on grounds of the Supreme Court decision in the *Boynton* case," he
said.

There was a pause, followed by a reply of "Shit on that" and a shoving
of Lewis back and forth in the doorway. One of the attackers threw a
punch that caught Lewis in the mouth, making the first loud pop of fist
against flesh on the Freedom Ride. Lewis sank to the ground. More
whites surged toward the primitive sounds of violence. Albert Bigelow,
next in line behind Lewis, stepped forward to put his body between Lewis
and those kicking him. Bigelow's erect posture and determined passivity
—such an alien sight in a fistfight—did not keep the attackers from
darting in to strike him on the head and body. Three or four thudding
blows dropped Bigelow to one knee, and as one of the attackers lunged
toward Bigelow he knocked Genevieve Hughes, the third Freedom Rider
in line, sprawling to the floor.

Several Rock Hill policemen shouted the fracas down to a sullen lull,
and the police captain waded in to extricate Lewis and Bigelow, who
were bruised and bleeding but fully conscious. Pointing around disgust-

edly at the attackers, as though knowing them well from previous juvenile cases, the captain asked Lewis and Bigelow whether they wanted to press assault charges. Both said no—this was not in the spirit of nonviolent resistance. Their refusal displeased the captain, who seemed upset that his politically risky offer to arrest local white boys was going to waste. He waved all the suspects away, and the Freedom Riders filed into the waiting room to place their food orders unmolested.

The Trailways bus arrived two hours later to find the terminal closed, locked up tight. Local contacts informed the second group of the attack as they drove them to an evening mass meeting at Friendship Junior College, where the students of the Rock Hill jail-in were enrolled. The Freedom Riders were saluted that night for maintaining their composure and goodwill through their first crisis. John Lewis, the first casualty, received that very night an urgent message from Nashville: the American Friends Service Committee had declared him a finalist in competition for a two-year grant to live and work among Gandhians in India, on the same scholarship James Lawson had won in 1954. The catch was that Lewis had to drop out of the Freedom Ride and fly immediately to Philadelphia for a personal interview; the Friends had wired money for a plane ticket. It was a bittersweet dilemma for a person of Lewis' convictions, but the next morning, after soldierly farewells, he headed north alone while the other dozen riders rolled south toward Columbia and Augusta.

King was in Montgomery for an SCLC board meeting. The occasion marked the first time he had returned to the city since his income tax trial a year earlier. In an effort to show that the steady bombardment of official persecution—the libel suits, criminal prosecutions, and firings at Alabama State—had failed to deter his movement, King presided over two days of meetings in Governor Patterson's capital city. He sent a telegram to Attorney General Kennedy in praise of his speech at the University of Georgia, and he announced the formation of an eighteen-member National Council of Attorneys to help defend the four SCLC preachers in their libel cases. Privately, he talked with the Alabama defendants—Abernathy, Shuttlesworth, Lowery, and Seay—about whether they should endure the continued seizure of their personal assets or leave the state. Shuttlesworth had just accepted a new pulpit in Cincinnati. Abernathy had all but decided to move to West Hunter Street Baptist in Atlanta, but he could not yet bring himself to tell his congregation in Montgomery.

King and Wyatt Walker returned to Atlanta in time to have dinner on

Saturday night, May 13, with the Freedom Riders. They celebrated a successful journey through nearly seven hundred miles of upper Dixie, and King spoke glowingly of their example and their willingness to continue on through the fiercest segregationist states of the Deep South. After giving them what inspiration he could, however, King took the reporter, Simeon Booker, aside and told him that he had just come from Alabama, where the public mood was ugly and where just enough publicity had appeared to make people aware that the Freedom Riders were coming. "You will never make it through Alabama," King whispered emotionally, and Booker, not knowing what to say, tried to make light of it by telling King that he was keeping close to the hulking Farmer. "He's the only one I can outrun," quipped Booker, adding that they planned to leave Farmer behind to occupy any white hoodlums who might chase them.

Farmer had scarcely fallen asleep that night when he received an emergency phone call from his mother. His father, the professor he remembered sitting under a tree reading books in Greek back during the Coolidge era, had asked to see "Junior's itinerary" that night in his Washington hospital bed and, noting that Junior would cross into Alabama the next day, had promptly fallen into a coma and died. Mrs. Farmer would always insist that the old man had willed his own death in order to save his son's life by forcing him to come home for the funeral. Farmer, hating himself for feeling relieved to be spared what lay ahead, took leave of his colleagues, who chose unanimously to keep to the schedule. A handful of student reinforcements joined them in Atlanta. In Farmer's absence, Michigan student Joseph Perkins became group captain on the Greyhound bus, with James Peck in charge on Trailways. Both buses headed west on U.S. 78. Alabama plainclothes investigators mingled unannounced among the passengers.

After the Tallapoosa and Heflin stops, the Greyhound driver confided to group leader Perkins that drivers from buses heading east were warning of a mob up ahead in Anniston, where CORE scout Tom Gaither had predicted certain trouble. These were not idle rumors. When the bus eased into its berth at Anniston, new terminal signs reading "White Intrastate Passengers" and "Negro Intrastate Passengers" gave evidence that subtle legal minds had prepared to meet the constitutional challenge of the Freedom Rides. (The Supreme Court had banned segregation at facilities serving passengers traveling across state lines.) Still, the signs offered slight deterrence compared with the large crowd of men bearing clubs, bricks, iron pipes, and knives. The nine Freedom Riders and five regular passengers sat frozen to their seats as the mob shouted for the Freedom Riders to come out. Some tried to force open the door. This brought the two Alabama state investigators out from under cover—they ran to the front of the bus and braced themselves against the pull lever, holding the door shut. Enraged, the mob began pounding on the bus with pipes and slashing the tires. Those inside shouted that the driver should leave before the bus was disabled. The driver did not argue. He revved the engine and backed up. The numb, terror-stricken passengers watched Anniston policemen move in from positions on the fringe of the crowd to direct the bus out of town, as though they had suddenly awakened to a traffic problem.

The Greyhound escaped down Highway 78 at a high rate of speed, spurred on by reports from the back that the mob was in hot pursuit. About fifty cars, containing as many as two hundred men, soon were stretched out behind them as the Freedom Riders headed for Birmingham. Not far outside Anniston, the bus began to list to one side, and the driver realized that some of the slashed tires were going flat. Helpless, he pulled the bus off the highway, shut down the engine, and scampered off into the countryside. The sounds of slamming doors and shouts from the converging posse were amplified in the quiet of the bus.

This time the mob used bricks and a heavy ax to smash the bus windows one by one, sending shards of glass flying among the passengers inside. The attackers ripped open the luggage compartment and battered the exterior again with pipes, while a group of them tried to force open the door. Finally, someone threw a firebomb through the gaping hole in the back window. As flames ran along the floor, some of the seats caught fire and the bus began to fill with black, acrid smoke. When the choking passengers realized that the fire could not be contained, they gave way to panic. In the front, state investigator E. L. Cowling saw that the mob was no longer trying to force entry but now was barricading the door to seal them in the fire. Desperate and weak from the smoke, Cowling brandished his revolver and the attackers fell back. When he managed to get the door open, Albert Bigelow and others herded the passengers to the exit. The mob, frenzied by the sight of them but made panicky by Cowling's gun, danced around the perimeter of the smoke billowing through the door, taking swings at those escaping. Henry Thomas, the SNCC student from Howard, staggered into the clear and was felled by a blow to the head. The others tumbled out behind him, and the attacks continued until arriving Alabama state troopers fired warning shots into the air. The mob retreated to their cars, and the troopers eventually ferried the passengers to Anniston Hospital. A photographer took a shot of the flames leaping out the front window of the abandoned bus, with a thick column of smoke rising from windows all along the sides. By evening, this photograph would move on both the national and international wires for distribution around the world.

The Trailways bus pulled into Anniston an hour behind the Greyhound. Jim Peck and the other Freedom Riders encountered an eerie silence as they walked through the terminal to buy sandwiches in the whites-only restaurant. Most of the bystanders averted their eyes. A few mumbled something about a "race riot." The Freedom Riders reboarded the bus with their sandwiches, noting that this was the first time the local whites seemed to be more on edge than they were. Charles Person, a Morehouse freshman, and Herbert Harris, a Morris Brown sophomore, sat back down in the front seat of the bus. When they did, the bus driver exited for a quick series of huddled conversations with Anniston police officers and with a small group of tough-looking men. Eight of them jumped on the bus just ahead of the driver and stood in the aisle as he flipped on the tour-guide microphone. "We have received word that a bus has been burned to the ground and passengers are being carried to the hospital by the carloads," he announced nervously, giving the first report on the fate of the Greyhound. "A mob is waiting for our bus and will do the same to us unless we get these niggers off the front seats."

One of the Freedom Riders broke the fearful pause with the dutiful reply that they were all interstate passengers with a legal right to sit anywhere on the bus, but the sentence was not yet completed when one of the whites standing over the front seat crashed his fist into Person's face. Another reached over to hit Herbert Harris. The whites yanked the two students into the aisle, kicking and slugging them from both ends of the confined space. As they did, group leader Peck and Walter Bergman, the retired professor from Michigan, jumped out of their seats at the back and ran forward, horrified, to protest. They did not get very far. One of the white men turned from the two students and hit Peck with a blow that knocked him backward over two seatbacks. Another fist dropped Bergman to the floor. Suddenly, the fury of the mob turned on the two downed white Freedom Riders. Some lifted Peck from the seat to rain blows on his bloodied face, while others stomped on the chest of the prostrate Bergman.

"Don't beat him any more!" cried Mrs. Bergman. "He's my husband!"

Some of the mob responded by snarling at Mrs. Bergman as a "nigger lover," while others warned their friends not to kill Bergman, who lay unconscious on the floor. They soon stopped pounding long enough to drag Person and Harris back through the aisle, over Bergman, and to toss them across the backseat, on top of other passengers. They threw Peck on top of the two students, dragged Bergman to the back, and then, grisly work done, sat down in the middle seats to make sure no Negroes moved up front for the ride. The bus driver, who had disappeared during the fight, reboarded along with a policeman. A brief, silent survey of the new seating arrangement seemed to satisfy them, whereupon the policeman

jumped off and the driver went tearing out of town on back roads, hoping
to sneak around the mob waiting on the highway to Birmingham. Simeon
Booker, sitting in the backseat amid the groans, shock, and blood, fumbled for a way to distract the whites from their unbearable leering stares.
All he could think of was to offer them a copy of *Jet* magazine's preview
story on the Freedom Ride.

There were few secrets in Birmingham. For two weeks, Fred Shuttlesworth had been telling King and others of rumors that the Ku Klux Klan
would ambush the Freedom Riders at the bus terminal there. Gary
Thomas Rowe, an FBI informant within Klavern Palace 13, had told his
FBI handlers that the Birmingham police agreed to give the Klansmen
fifteen unmolested minutes to beat the integrated riders. The SAC (Special Agent in Charge) of the FBI's Birmingham office had reported the
details of the police-Klan agreement to FBI headquarters in Washington
several times, beginning on May 5. He had also alerted the police department at least five times to the Klan's impending attack—never mentioning the police department's own complicity in the reported plans, on the
usual security grounds, for fear of exposing Rowe as an FBI informant to
the police, and through the police to the Klan. The Birmingham SAC
kept a record of the many warnings he had passed along, as though the
official notices conveyed responsibility to the police. It was an uncomfortable exercise for a law enforcement officer with advance knowledge
of a crime. With almost transparent chagrin, he informed Director Hoover in Washington that he had been obliged to deliver his last warning
on Sunday, May 14, to Detective Tom Cook, an officer he knew to be an
active collaborator with the Klan, as Cook was "the only man on duty."

Rev. John Rutland, Bull Connor's Methodist pastor, was down at city
hall that morning, pleading with Connor not to let them beat up the kids
on the buses. Among white newsmen, anticipation was so strong that
half a dozen reporters, photographers, and television crews were gathered
near the downtown bus terminals by midafternoon. CBS commentator
Howard K. Smith, passing through Birmingham on his way back to New
York, picked up rumors grave enough to make him drive downtown to
investigate personally.

Actors in the impending drama played multifaceted roles, under various legitimate poses, but most of their actions worked to the immediate
benefit of the Klan. Police detective Cook, Bull Connor's most trusted
intelligence officer, told three reporters of the imminent arrival of an
integrated bus group and then abruptly walked away toward the police
station, leaving the reporters baffled about his retreat. At the Greyhound

station, where the first Freedom Rider bus was scheduled to arrive, Gary Thomas Rowe learned by telephone from police headquarters that the first bus would come into the Trailways terminal instead. Rowe sounded an alarm to scores of Klansmen posted nearby, and they all dashed four blocks from Greyhound to Trailways.

When the Trailways bus pulled into the Birmingham terminal, the eight white men who had boarded in Anniston exited first—seemingly to lose themselves in the terminal crowd, forestalling any detection or questioning by the authorities. Charles Person and Jim Peck, the latter's face and shirt caked with blood, stepped first from the bus to the landing. As the designated testers for Birmingham, they stood quietly for a moment, surveying avenues of escape that appeared little more promising than the terminal itself. Peck, deciding that he could not bring himself to ask Person to carry on with the objectives of the Freedom Ride, glanced at his partner for a sign of his intent. "Let's go," Person said simply, heading slowly for the white waiting room as planned. Peck fell in behind him. Walter Bergman and some of the others followed.

They walked into a corridor brimming with Klansmen, reporters, and witnesses transfixed by the premonition of violence. On their approach, a confused Klansman muttered that they should kill the Negro, Person, because he must have hurt the obviously wounded white man, Peck, but as they came forward Peck said they should not hurt Person. This gesture of cross-racial friendship ignited the crowd's rage, and the Klansmen roughly shoved Person back toward the Negro waiting room. When he turned and tried to walk through them once more, a Klansman shoved him sideways against a concrete wall. Others came up behind him. "Hit him," someone shouted, and a Klansman obliged with a fist to Person's face. Person rose with a bloodied mouth, only to be hit again. This time he fell back into the arms of a Klansman, who held him to receive a third blow, after which he fell to his knees. Peck moved to help him up and was flattened by a rain of five or six punches. Then about a dozen Klansmen surrounded the two men and pummeled them with kicks, pipes, and objects that looked to one horrified bystander, Howard K. Smith, like heavy key rings. FBI informant Rowe contributed lustily to the beatings.

The Freedom Riders entering behind the lead pair tried to retreat from the mayhem, only to find their path blocked by Klansmen. When reporter Simeon Booker looked into the terminal a few seconds later, he saw a bloodied Walter Bergman on his hands and knees crawling desperately among the legs of the men beating him, groping for a door. Recoiling, Booker held a newspaper up in front of his face, punched a small hole in the middle of it for vision, and edged his way around the exterior of the building. Luck probably helped him more than this camouflage, but

Booker did manage to find a Negro cabdriver who was as eager to leave the scene as he was. He jumped in the back and gave the driver Fred Shuttlesworth's home address.

The violence at the terminal was contagious, furtive, and often blind. A Birmingham white man, who had been in the men's room for some time, emerged with a look of innocent shock that provoked the mob. He became one of seven bystanders hurt badly enough to be hospitalized. A Negro man arriving to pick up his girlfriend was set upon, as were several reporters. A white photographer from the Birmingham *Post-Herald,* who had the presence of mind to remove the film from his camera after shooting the attack on Peck, was clubbed with a lead pipe and his camera smashed. Outside—where a hysterical woman passenger who had been caught on the Trailways ride from Anniston was shouting, "It started on the bus! It started on the bus!"—a handful of Klansmen came upon one Negro Freedom Rider * and knocked him repeatedly into a pile of trash boxes. Then, seeing a man talking into the car radio of a vehicle marked WAPI News, they smashed all the windows of the car, dragged news director Clancy Lake away from his live broadcast out into the street, ripped out his microphone, and fled. By the time the allotted fifteen minutes were up, and a phalanx of Birmingham policemen had trotted briskly into the Trailways terminal, the Klansmen were well dispersed and in a triumphant, surly mood. One retreating carload, a mile away from the terminal, came upon two Negro men talking on a street corner. They stopped abruptly, jumped the Negroes, and beat them.

When reporter Booker brought the first grim news to Shuttlesworth's house, the preacher summoned his deacons and some stalwart members of his Alabama Christian Movement for Human Rights. Before he could organize volunteer patrols to rescue the Freedom Riders, several of the victims straggled to his house in taxis. Charles Person arrived with a swollen face and open cuts on his head but remarkably coherent for one who had been beaten both in Anniston and in Birmingham that day. A frightened Negro doctor refused to treat Person's wounds, and while a woman was giving him first aid, Jim Peck, miraculously, spilled alone from a taxi with a crimson head and jagged broken teeth, and hunched over from the pain of blows to his ribs. "You need to go to a hospital," Shuttlesworth said by way of a greeting. As they waited for the ambulance, Peck struggled over to Person and shook his hand.

Among the alarms to reach Shuttlesworth's house in the next hour was a call of distress from Anniston Hospital, where Freedom Riders

---

* Probably Isaac Reynolds of Detroit.

from the burned Greyhound bus were besieged. A large contingent of the white mob had pursued them there, and hospital personnel, intimidated by the mob, ordered the Freedom Riders to leave, saying their presence endangered other patients. Trapped between the mob's anger and the hospital's nerves, without means of transportation, the Freedom Riders huddled in one hospital corner after another, being told repeatedly to go somewhere else. In Birmingham, Shuttlesworth issued another call for volunteer drivers, saying he would lead a caravan on the sixty-mile mission to Anniston Hospital and back. There would be no weapons allowed, he declared, "not even a toothpick." Soon there were eight drivers, all of whom made a fuss over Shuttlesworth, insisting they could not allow a recognizable leader like him to expose himself to the danger. Their concern was genuine, but some of it may have been born of the judgment that nonviolence was an unaffordable luxury in this emergency. Soon eight cars of Negro churchmen, brimming with shotguns and rifles, took off down Highway 78 to pick up the enervated but immensely grateful pacifists in Anniston.

From Shuttlesworth's home, Booker after many attempts finally reached John Seigenthaler, the Attorney General's special assistant. After reminding Seigenthaler of his predictions of trouble, Booker told him of the day's bloody events and of his fears that the Freedom Riders would not get safely out of Birmingham. Seigenthaler took Shuttlesworth's number and called back shortly with an encouraging report. The Justice Department would be in touch first thing Monday morning, he promised, and would make sure that the right to safe interstate travel was protected. When Seigenthaler suggested that the job would be easier if Booker and other reporters downplayed the story for a while, Booker replied that this would be impossible. The story was too big. White reporters were milling around everywhere. Some of the reporters had themselves been assaulted.

That evening in Shuttlesworth's Bethel Baptist Church, a battered Walter Bergman explained to the small crowd that CORE was a nonviolent action group that believed in racial equality. Shuttlesworth told them about the frantic efforts to locate the lost, scattered riders, and about Bull Connor's threat to have him arrested for harboring interracial gatherings in his home. Still, Shuttlesworth's tone was defiant as he cried out that they had gone through the worst of it. "When white men and black men are beaten up together," he declared, "the day is coming when they will walk together."

The ambulance bearing Jim Peck had been turned away from Carraway Methodist Hospital, and he now lay under the surgery lights in the Hillman Hospital emergency room. It took fifty-three stitches to patch his six head wounds, most prominently a four-inch horseshoe-shaped gash on his forehead. Photographers standing behind the doctors took pictures of the gore for the local newspapers, and a clutch of reporters tossed questions to the woozy and nauseated patient. Peck answered questions coherently, though weakly, sometimes pausing in the effort to distinguish the attack in Anniston from the one in Birmingham. To a final series of questions about his plans, and whether the ferocious attack had been worth it, he replied simply, "The going is getting rougher, but I'll be on that bus tomorrow headed for Montgomery." Reporters looked incredulously at Peck and then at one another. As they broke up, a policeman remarked that Peck did not even have one penny on his person. On hearing this, a well-dressed Negro—one of Shuttlesworth's men —slipped up to the operating table and folded Peck's hand around a dime. "Call us when they get through with you, and we'll come get you," he said quietly.

At two o'clock on Monday morning, jittery hospital officials peremptorily discharged Jim Peck into the night. Shuttlesworth came to retrieve him, and they drove through an equally jittery Birmingham, heavily patrolled by police cars. Stopped once for interrogation, Shuttlesworth finally made it home and put Peck to bed on a couch.

In Nashville, James Bevel presided over a glorious Sunday picnic in celebration of a victory settlement in the movie theater campaign. Noting that there had been some forty days and forty nights of demonstrations since February, Bevel was preaching happily about the Great Flood, the temptations of Jesus, and other famous "forty stories" from the Bible, while otherwise letting go of the tension by eating, flirting, and having a good time, when someone heard a radio report about the burned Greyhound bus. Almost immediately, Diane Nash suggested that Bevel, as temporary chairman of the Nashville movement, call an emergency meeting to discuss a student response. Bevel replied that there was nothing they could do or say about distant Alabama that could not wait until they had finished their picnic, but Nash was insistent. The movement was about selflessness, she said. Individual people didn't matter, and neither did distance, time, or picnics. She kept up a running attack, picturing the Freedom Riders waiting for help in a burning bus somewhere while the Nashville veterans lingered over their fried chicken and cakes. Bevel withdrew to consult with his closest friends. "She's going to keep talking nasty about us," he lamented. Concluding forlornly that the picnic was ruined anyway, Bevel moved the proceedings to the First Baptist Church.

Everyone knew about the Freedom Ride. John Lewis, just back from his interview in Philadelphia, was with them that day, having stopped off in Nashville on his way to rejoin the CORE group. The initial question among the Nashville students was whether the bus-burning presented another Rock Hill. Were the Freedom Riders going to jail? Should they go and join them? As grimmer and grimmer reports filtered in from Birmingham, however, the issue became death instead of jail. Would the Freedom Ride produce the first martyrs to nonviolence? If so, would it help or hurt the movement? Should the Nashville students welcome such a risk for themselves, even seek it out? A marathon debate ensued as to whether the adult supervisors of the Nashville Christian Leadership Council, who controlled the organization's funds, would agree to support a venture that might well lead to the deaths of the young people.

The Nashville debate lasted all night and continued into Monday, overlapping with the regathering of the Freedom Riders at Shuttlesworth's house in Birmingham. A jolt of publicity greeted the new day. Shuttlesworth marveled to see the local papers filled with sympathetic accounts of the attacks, written by reporters he had always viewed as segregationists. The Birmingham *News* published a pained front-page editorial headlined "People Are Asking: 'Where Were the Police?'" Beneath it, alongside graphic pictures of the beatings, appeared Police Commissioner Connor's statement: "I have said for the last 20 years that these out-of-town meddlers were going to cause bloodshed if they kept meddling in the South's business. . . . It happened on a Sunday, Mother's Day, when we try to let off as many of our policemen as possible so they can spend Mother's Day at home with their families." The *News* dismissed Connor's explanation as lame and all but accused him of conspiring with the Klan. Birmingham's leading businessman told *The Wall Street Journal* that the violence gave the city "a black eye." In New York, where the story played on the front page, the *Times* editors decided to run a separate article about the "eyewitness account" that Howard K. Smith had broadcast on CBS Radio. In Washington, seeing the photograph of the burning Greyhound on the front page of his morning *Post*, James Farmer called his CORE staff in New York and instructed them to superimpose that shot over one of the Statue of Liberty to form a new emblem for the Freedom Ride.

In faraway Tokyo, the morning newspapers shocked no one more than Sidney Smyer, the incoming president of the Birmingham Chamber of Commerce. Smyer, leading the city's business delegation at the International Rotary Convention, could not read the Japanese writing, but he could recognize the ugly photographs of the bus station riot. The *Post-Herald* photographer's carefully preserved roll of film had survived his beating to move on the international wires. As a result, Smyer found himself the object of cold stares and perplexed questions from his Japanese hosts and the assembled international businessmen, who had suddenly lost interest in Birmingham's climate for investment. Words failed Smyer and his Birmingham friends as they tried to explain that the incident was grossly unrepresentative of their city. They felt like zoo specimens on display. Smyer, though a stout segregationist and a Dixiecrat from 1948, told his Birmingham colleagues that something must be done about Bull Connor.

At the Shuttlesworth home, fame struck at ten o'clock that morning with the announcement that the Attorney General of the United States was on the telephone, asking to speak with Simeon Booker. The *Jet* reporter told Kennedy that the Freedom Riders considered themselves "trapped" in Birmingham by hostile mobs that were reported to be forming near the bus station. Booker gave the phone to some of the group leaders and then to Shuttlesworth, who told Kennedy that their most urgent need was for police protection on the ride to Montgomery. Kennedy's first suggestion was that they consolidate into one bus. Crisply, he promised to arrange bus security and call back. There was great rejoicing when Shuttlesworth recounted this conversation to the assembled Freedom Riders, who, with their swollen faces, surgical stitches, and lungs still burning with smoke, sagged at the prospect of facing another mob.

In Washington, Kennedy was working under a severe handicap—his chief civil rights man, Burke Marshall, was confined to his apartment at the end of a two-week case of the mumps. Kennedy established a telephone network between his office, Marshall's apartment, liaison people at FBI headquarters, and Shuttlesworth's house, and was soon back on the line with the Birmingham preacher. "Okay," he told Shuttlesworth, "Mr. Connor is going to protect you at the station and escort you to the city line." This was a concession relayed through the FBI from Connor, under pressure from Birmingham leaders angry over the previous day's violence.

Shuttlesworth thought it over. "They were escorted to the city line in Anniston," he replied, as politely as he could. "That's where the bus burned." He and Kennedy quickly established that they needed protection as far as the Alabama line.

"Wait," said Kennedy. "I'll call you back." This was a problem for Governor Patterson, whom Kennedy had known as a political supporter since the 1956 Democratic Convention. The Attorney General initiated a series of calls to Patterson and his aides, during which Patterson complained that the Freedom Riders were not "bona fide" interstate travelers, and that as governor he could not help people violate the Alabama segregation laws. Kennedy and Burke Marshall kept arguing that the federal government would have to protect the riders from violence if the state could not, and that since nobody wanted federal intervention, all sides should cooperate to get the Freedom Riders out of Alabama as quickly as possible.

Surrounded by reporters, policemen, supporters, and darting carloads of hostile whites, Shuttlesworth led the eighteen Freedom Riders down to the Greyhound terminal, across the street from Bull Connor's jail, to catch the three o'clock bus to Montgomery. They listened en route to nearly continuous radio bulletins on their exact position, on the size of the mob waiting at the station, and on the latest reports of the personal diplomacy between Governor Patterson and Attorney General Kennedy, which itself was big news. At the terminal, they made their way to the bus landing and braced themselves for the wait. Birmingham policemen dutifully kept angry whites away from them, but hate and violence were again close enough to touch, even before their arrangements began to come undone. Radio reports announced that Governor Patterson was correcting previous statements attributed to him. "I refuse to guarantee their safe passage," he said, soon adding that "the citizens of the state are so enraged that I cannot guarantee protection for this bunch of rabble-rousers." A spokesman for the governor said that angry whites had been spotted all along the highway from Birmingham to Montgomery.

These reports put Shuttlesworth back on the telephone with Kennedy, and so did notice from Greyhound clerks that the bus drivers were refusing to drive. "Get a Negro to drive it," Kennedy told Greyhound officials, and, impatient with their recital of obstacles and impossibilities, he said he might have to send an Air Force plane down for the Freedom Riders —he could have it there in two hours—if Greyhound failed to find a white bus driver brave enough to do his job. Shuttlesworth, hoping to maintain pressure on the various officials, said the Freedom Riders would sit there peacefully at the terminal until the impasse was resolved.

The Freedom Riders felt the pressure, too, and their resolve began to fray under cumulative exposure to dread. Trapped again, public targets more than ever, the eighteen riders began to talk among themselves of diminishing returns. Already, they had called national attention to racial hatred more dramatically than they had ever hoped. Further beatings would not accomplish anything, and further delays would make it impossible for them to reach New Orleans on Wednesday, May 17, for the big rally on the seventh anniversary of the *Brown* decision. They notified Shuttlesworth that they had decided to jump over their opponents by taking an airplane directly to New Orleans. No sooner had they made flight reservations and begun their retreat from the terminal than radio reports of the change signaled a general stampede. Elements of the mob reached the airport ahead of them, transplanting the siege.

In Nashville, where a revolving mass of sit-in veterans had been debating the Freedom Ride almost continuously for twenty-four hours, the discussion shifted when they got word that the CORE group was abandoning the buses. Suddenly, the issue was not one of reinforcing the riders but replacing them, not boosting the ride's success but preventing its failure. Diane Nash soon traced James Farmer to Washington, where he was attending his father's funeral. She asked him whether CORE would object if Nashville students went to Birmingham and took up where the original riders left off. Her request left Farmer temporarily speechless, but he gave his consent.

In Washington, Robert Kennedy returned to the Justice Department from Burke Marshall's apartment, where he had gone for the last volleys of the Greyhound negotiations. Marshall came with him, pronouncing his mumps officially over. The two of them met with Roy Wilkins, urging him to support their voter registration plans, and then Kennedy walked into the office of John Seigenthaler, the only Southerner on his immediate staff. "Look," he said, "they're at the airport and they can't get off the ground. It's going to be about seven o'clock before we get them out of there. Do you think you can get down there and help them?"

Seigenthaler blinked. "What sort of help do they need?" he asked.

"I think they primarily need somebody along just to hold their hand and let them know that we care," said Kennedy. The urgency in his voice moved Seigenthaler to leave instantly for the airport. Two hours later, on a brief layover in Atlanta, he checked in with Kennedy by telephone and learned that the Freedom Riders were still in Birmingham, delayed indefinitely by a bomb threat.

While Seigenthaler was in transit, 350 Negroes filed into the Kingston Baptist Church for a mass meeting. Before Shuttlesworth arrived, a preacher cajoled the crowd to contribute to another special collection to replace the Shuttlesworth automobile that had been confiscated in the *Sullivan* libel case. A man in the audience rose to speak, acutely aware of the Birmingham movement's new visibility. "Supposing *The New York Times* heard it took us six months to pay for his car?" was all he said. Shuttlesworth was their representative. Most of them swelled vicariously with every minute enlargement of his stature, and believed that he earned every bit of it with raw courage. There was hope that he could be dissuaded from his move to Cincinnati.

Shuttlesworth made his entrance shortly after nine o'clock and delivered a speech filled with the day's wonders as well as its trials. "I talked

to Bob Kennedy six times," he announced, to great effect, and he recounted in detail all the courtesies and solicitude he had received that
day from the nation's chief law enforcement officer, a white man. Interrupted by a whispered message, he told the audience, "Excuse me, I have
a long-distance call from Bob," * rushed off, and came back with a full
report. "They got plenty of police out at the airport tonight simply because Bob talked to Bull," he concluded. "The police didn't bother me at
the bus station. . . . Bob told me, 'If you can't get me at my office, just
call me at the White House.' That's what he said."

When he stepped down, another preacher dismissed the meeting with
a rhetorical cry: "Don't we have a great president, who has courage and
conviction? There is only one F. L. Shuttlesworth!"

Across town from the mass meeting, Seigenthaler found a pathetic
huddle of casualties at the Birmingham airport, suffering as much from
battle fatigue as from their wounds. Held there into the night by repeated
bomb threats, some of them had given way to paranoid ranting and had
to be restrained by their companions. Seigenthaler talked with Simeon
Booker and then identified himself to the head of the police detail. "We
don't want any trouble," he said. "We just want to get these people out
of here."

"We want them out just as much as you do," replied the policeman,
citing his orders from Bull Connor. He took Seigenthaler to meet the
manager of the airline, who was distraught over bomb threats that were
coming in like clockwork every time a flight to New Orleans was announced. The three of them concocted a scheme that included diversions
in the airport, a departure without announcement, and, most critically,
an order to airline personnel not to answer the telephone until the plane
was off the ground. Seigenthaler soon boarded with the Freedom Riders,
as the police unit sealed off the gate behind them, and the plane lifted off
the ground near midnight. The CORE group, after two days in Alabama
and eleven days in the South, found safety in the air.

Four hours later, a telephone call from Burke Marshall woke Seigenthaler in his New Orleans hotel room. "You know Diane Nash in Nashville?" snapped the usually collected Marshall.

"Yes, I know who she is," said Seigenthaler.

"Well, you come from that goddam town," said Marshall. "They
started another group down to Birmingham to take over by bus where

---

* The Attorney General preferred to be called "Bob" instead of the diminutive
"Bobby" by everyone except his older brother. The President said "Bob" in an
exaggerated way that had the reverse effect of tweaking his younger brother for
wanting to seem older.

those others left off. . . . If you can do anything to turn them around, I'd appreciate it." When Seigenthaler responded groggily, Marshall said, "Diane Nash is at this number."

Seigenthaler roused himself to call the Nashville church where the crisis meeting was approaching its second consecutive dawn. The line was busy. Then, as newspaper presses rolled with morning headlines announcing the end of the Freedom Ride, and early-bird newscasters talked of President Kennedy's departure that morning on a two-day state visit to Canada, Seigenthaler began waking up people he knew in Nashville who might conceivably bring pressure on Nash, telling them about the grim realities of Birmingham. "I came through there," he said. "All hell is going to break loose. She's going to get those people killed."

In Nashville, maddening details consumed all of Tuesday, May 16. The smallest questions of logistics—should they ride segregated from Nashville to Birmingham, or should they stick to their principles at the risk of being stopped even before they could begin to take up the Freedom Ride?—opened large questions of philosophy and personal belief, and just when one issue seemed to be settled someone would confess an old doubt or a new fear. Phone calls from Seigenthaler, and from sobbing or angry parents who had just seen gruesome news footage of Jim Peck disembarking from the plane in New Orleans, destabilized the emotions beneath a wobbly consensus. That evening, with the divided Nashville adults agreeing to donate $900 from the sit-in treasury without explicitly endorsing the student plan, Diane Nash pushed ahead with a call of final notice to Shuttlesworth. "The students," she told him, "have decided that we can't let violence overcome. We are going to come into Birmingham to continue the Freedom Ride."

"Young lady," Shuttlesworth replied in his most authoritative voice, "do you know that the Freedom Riders were almost killed here?"

"Yes," Nash said tersely. Her patience was almost spent. "That's exactly why the ride must not be stopped. If they stop us with violence, the movement is dead. We're coming. We just want to know if you can meet us."

She returned to the student group for the final and most difficult decision: which of the volunteers would be chosen to make the ride. It was treated as a life-or-death matter. There was money to buy ten bus tickets and retain a marginal reserve, they decided, and they left it to their chairman, James Bevel, to select the ten. Bevel first chose John Lewis, for leadership and for continuity with the original Freedom Ride. He said that he would not appoint Diane Nash, because she was too valuable as the focal person in Nashville. In all, Bevel chose six Negro male students and two Negro females, plus a white student of each sex—all proven veterans of what Bevel called a "nonviolent standing army." He did not appoint himself, he explained, because he had made a commitment to drive to New York to pick up furniture to help a friend set up house after his upcoming wedding. This was precisely the kind of bourgeois attachment of which Nash and others were so scornful, but their disapproval did not reach to Bevel's other choices.

Nash relayed the details to Shuttlesworth, who began to speak in a crudely improvised security code—of different "chickens," some speckled and others Rhode Island Red, to be delivered to Birmingham at a specified time. FBI agents had informed him that the police were tapping his telephone. It was ten o'clock when the Nashville students finally dispersed. The selected riders received emotional farewells from the others. Some of them wrote out their wills. Some notified relatives, friends, teachers, and college deans. All of them went home exhausted to pack and try to sleep.

Selyn McCollum missed the Greyhound bus at dawn, and the lone white female overtook the group by car more than fifty miles down Highway 31, in Pulaski, Tennessee. There were no further disturbances —other than a whispered running argument over the insistence of Jim Zwerg, white, and Paul Brooks, Negro, on sitting together in violation of the generally accepted plan—until Birmingham police flagged down the bus at the city limit, nearly two hundred miles south of Nashville. Officers summarily arrested Zwerg and Brooks for their obvious violation of Alabama segregation law. Then some officers remained sternly at attention on board while others drove patrol cars in escort formation toward the terminal. More officers jumped inside on arrival. They guarded the front door, taped newspapers over all the windows, and then examined the ticket of each passenger wishing to leave. All those whose tickets originated in Nashville and called for travel to New Orleans by way of Montgomery and Jackson, Mississippi, were identified as Freedom Riders and told to stay on the bus. Those who insisted on their right to leave were treated roughly, pushed back into seats by billy clubs in the stomach. Selyn McCollum, seeing that the Freedom Riders were being isolated within the darkened bus, took advantage of the fact that her ticket read Pulaski instead of Nashville. "I'm not with this group," she said, holding out her ticket, and when she was permitted to exit, she ran through the gathering mob to call Diane Nash back in Nashville. Nash then called Burke Marshall's office at the Justice Department, asking why the Freedom Riders were being held against their will at the terminal.

Inside the bus, the Freedom Riders maintained the discipline they had learned from Jim Lawson. They kept insisting on their right to leave, pushing up from their seats to the point of physical repression by the police, and at the same time they tried to make human contact with the officers. They asked them one by one if they were World War II veterans, and if so, what they had fought for. They asked them if they were Christians, and if so, did they believe that Christ had died for all people. There were few memorable conversations, but the Freedom Riders did establish over time the limits of the police orders, which were to intimidate them but not to harm them. After an hour's stalemate convinced the police commanders that these nine riders were not going to retreat to the airport like the ones two days earlier, new orders came down that the Freedom Riders were to be allowed to leave the bus. Soon they stepped out to behold a jeering crowd gathered in the terminal parking lot. The Nashville students walked within a corridor formed by two rows of blue-helmeted policemen, billy clubs crossed like a Roman guard, through the crowd into the terminal, where Selyn McCollum and Fred Shuttlesworth were waiting for them.

Monday's siege at the Birmingham Greyhound terminal was essentially re-created on Wednesday. Police commanders, straddling the thin edge between protection and repression, between maintaining peace and preserving segregation, now emphasized to the Freedom Riders that the police, as they could see, were protecting them from a mob of angry white people. It would make their task much easier, they advised, if the Freedom Riders would not mingle interracially there in the white waiting room. To this argument, and to a host of similar blandishments, the Freedom Riders steadfastly replied that they intended to wait there in accordance with the Supreme Court's *Boynton* decision and to catch the five o'clock bus to Montgomery.

The stalemate lasted three more hours, during which time some of the crowd's hostility was redirected toward the police officers who were constantly pushing them back. Finally, Bull Connor himself appeared at the terminal, and as the Freedom Riders moved to board the Montgomery bus he ordered his men to arrest them. Cheers went up from the bystanders as the police officers handcuffed the ten riders and dragged them to the paddy wagons. When Connor's nemesis, Fred Shuttlesworth, demanded to know why this was being done, he too was arrested, which drew more cheers. Connor, having satisfied the segregationists by deed, now moved to placate the image-conscious city fathers by telling reporters that he was placing the Freedom Riders under "protective custody." The students sang freedom songs as they were transported to the Birmingham jail. They tried to calm themselves by saying that this was no worse than another night on the Nashville picket line.

President Kennedy returned from Canada as the Freedom Riders went off to jail. Early the next morning, unannounced and unrecorded by the official schedule, Robert Kennedy walked into the White House and up to the President's private quarters, accompanied by Byron White and Burke Marshall. The trio from Justice caught the President in his pajamas, with his breakfast sitting in front of him. The Attorney General greeted his brother as though they were resuming an interrupted business meeting. "As you know, the situation is getting worse in Alabama," he began. The new batch of Freedom Riders were refusing to eat in the Birmingham jail, demanding to be put back on the bus. Greyhound officials, upset about their firebombed bus, were refusing to transport any Freedom Riders without guarantees of police protection, and Governor Patterson was refusing to repeat the guarantee he had made and then half-repudiated on Monday. In fact, the governor was hedging and equivocating—almost hiding, Kennedy reported—for fear of being caught in a political trap. If Patterson declared that he would protect the Freedom Riders as interstate travelers, then Alabama voters might say that he had knuckled under to the federal government, sacrificed Alabama's segregation laws, and accepted the unmanly role of nursemaid to the hated group of interracial troublemakers. If, on the other hand, Patterson declared he could not or would not protect the Freedom Riders, he would be admitting limits to state sovereignty and all but inviting the federal government to assume police power in his state. To Patterson, either course was political suicide.

The result thus far was a stalemate, which was the outcome least tolerable to the federal government. The Attorney General did not say— he did not have to—that his own highly visible role in getting the first Freedom Riders out of Birmingham had helped elevate the drama into a major national story, with reporters still waiting in Alabama for the federal government to resolve this second crisis. For Robert Kennedy, the dilemma already was a humbling demonstration of the race issue's mystifying, unconventional powers. A handful of faceless, nameless, half-suicidal pacifists had seized his attention by the simple act of riding a bus. Less than two weeks after Kennedy's sweeping rhetorical commitment to activist law enforcement in civil rights—"We will move"— reality contrived for him a cruel test in which the Administration's reputation hung on whether he could empower a single bus to move out of the Birmingham station.

They had come to the White House, said the Attorney General, to report that they had begun contingency planning for direct federal intervention in Alabama. The President himself might be required to act publicly, if things went badly. All three Justice officials were agreed that the most drastic and least desirable course was the "Little Rock method" —the use of Regular Army troops to guard the Freedom Riders' bus. Among the many drawbacks of this option were President Kennedy's campaign statements faulting Eisenhower for allowing the 1957 Little Rock school crisis to deteriorate to the point that federal troops had been required. Kennedy had promised a more vigorous, farsighted presidential leadership to spare the country such traumas. To falter now, so early in his Administration and so soon after the Bay of Pigs, might raise questions about the President's elementary competence. It would certainly bring the wrath of the South down on him, and Kennedy, unlike Eisenhower, rested his thin governing margin upon solid electoral support in the South.

Compounding these negative prospects was the most absorbing, dramatic new fact of the President's political life: the White House had disclosed only two days earlier that President Kennedy would meet Soviet Premier Khrushchev in Vienna within the month for personal negotiations on the full range of issues dividing East and West. It was bad enough that Kennedy had to prepare for these fateful talks weakened by the Bay of Pigs. To face Khrushchev against the backdrop of racial strife within the bosom of the free world, while commanding troops against his own people, would open Kennedy to ridicule from the Soviet leader. Clearly, the Army option threatened multiple disaster and was a dreaded last resort. Calling out the National Guard, Kennedy's next choice down the military scale, was not much better. By far the most palatable alternative was to protect the Freedom Riders' bus with a force of U.S. marshals and other civilians within the federal service.

Very little of this needed to be said to President Kennedy, whose mind was quickest when cutting through multi-shaded calculations. Robert Kennedy asked Byron White to review for the President his efforts to assemble a conglomerate force of civilian officers. White named the agencies he had contacted in addition to the Marshal Service, including the U.S. Border Patrol, the Treasury Department's Bureau of Alcohol, Tobacco and Firearms (known among moonshiners as "the revenooers"), and even the Bureau of Prisons, which had agreed to lend some prison guards to the emergency detail. White reeled off the numbers of agents available from different units in different locations, along with the distances from Montgomery, the estimated time required to concentrate them for action, and plans for deploying the men along the road between Birmingham and Montgomery.

Speaking like the makeshift general he had become overnight, White briefed the President about how he would make a unified command from so many disparate bureaucracies. The Army had agreed to help solve the staggering problems of transport and logistics, lending planes, trucks, barracks, and rations, he reported, adding frankly that such cooperation was traceable almost entirely to the relief of the commanders on learning that their own soldiers were not slated for domestic riot duty. The overall task was impossible, White concluded wryly, but it could be done. He hoped the force would never be used. Toward that end, the preparations already undertaken were being advertised to Governor Patterson in order to reinforce the credibility of the Administration's ultimatum: if Patterson failed to use state power to protect lawful travelers from violent mobs, the federal government would have no choice but to step in.

When White finished, Robert Kennedy asked Burke Marshall to outline the President's authority under the law. Marshall was nervous, having never met the President before, but Kennedy's alert manner reassured him, recalling for Marshall the sense of putting a complex legal argument before a manifestly skilled judge. He told Kennedy that the law required the President to issue a proclamation announcing a breakdown of public order before implementing either of the two military options, the Army or the National Guard. Therefore, these alternatives bore the added disadvantage of risking the President's own prestige by what amounted to an admission of national crisis. Happily, Marshall's reading of the United States Code—Title 10, Sections 331, 332, and 333—convinced him that use of Byron White's army of deputy marshals required only a written notice from the President to the Attorney General, recognizing the threat to public peace and ordering the Attorney General to use all powers at his disposal to enforce federal laws. This notice need not be released to the public, said Marshall, which meant that the Administration had the legal authority to carry out White's plan without invoking the President's name. In addition, Justice Department lawyers were preparing to ask a strong federal judge in Alabama, Frank Johnson, Jr., for an injunction ordering the Alabama Klan not to interfere with the right of the Freedom Riders to travel unmolested, and also ordering the Alabama police departments to provide adequate protection to the Freedom Riders in light of the public threats against them. This injunction, if obtained, would provide another leg of authority for the use of the deputy marshals.

President Kennedy asked only a few questions, mostly about timing. For his own unstated reasons, he asked Marshall whether it was likely he could get by without making a decision until Monday. Marshall replied that the stalemate probably would not hold that long. The Freedom Riders were being held illegally, without charges, and lawyers were demanding their release. The President, switching to the preferred way out, wondered how they could move most effectively to induce Governor

Patterson to take responsibility. He knew Patterson personally. Was it time for direct contact by him? If so, should it be by telephone, telegram, or letter? It was decided to place a call to Patterson's office in Montgomery. Moments later a chagrined operator reported that the governor was said to be on a fishing boat somewhere far out in the Gulf of Mexico. Patterson was unavailable even to the White House. This egregious snubbing of the President introduced the Kennedys to a far different John Patterson from the one they had known.

There was to be no word of the President's involvement. The Attorney General would say only that he was meeting with his own advisers in an effort to maintain law and order in Alabama, and the three Justice Department men would push forward with the contingencies outlined that morning. With these orders understood, the President excused himself to dress for the day. Burke Marshall, looking back into the room as he made his exit, was struck by the sight of the breakfast tray on the table, still untouched.

The three men plunged into a day of chaos at the Justice Department. They built the secret army of marshals out of nothing, aided only by a riot-training course that Attorney General Rogers had initiated after Little Rock. Lawyers walked briskly through the corridors carrying what they called "field maps" of Alabama. They discussed weaponry, tactics, and the apparel of the new civilian soldier. They fended off reporters. The top officials quibbled with commanders of the Army Quartermaster Corps.

Shuttlesworth was convicted on obstruction charges at a boisterous evening trial in Birmingham. Justice Department telephones were still ringing after midnight when notice arrived of Bull Connor's miracle cure. His men were dragging the limp, protesting Freedom Riders out of their cells into unmarked police cars. Connor himself assured federal officials that no harm would come to them, saying that he was taking two reporters along as witnesses. His compromise, he said, would protect the Freedom Riders in a manner consistent with Alabama law and the opinions of Alabama voters. He was going to "escort" them personally through the state, under cover of darkness, and dump them into Tennessee. His plan, relayed instantly through the Justice Department and down to Seigenthaler, was received as an unorthodox and illegal but thoroughly effective remedy for the nightmarish stalemate. The crisis in Alabama was over. Connor laughed off a cautionary question from Washington about how he would justify the forced release of the Freedom Riders from his jail. "I just couldn't stand their singing," he quipped.

·   ·   ·

Heading north on U.S. Highway 31, John Lewis sat behind Bull Connor in one of the police cars. His fears of police beatings, even a prearranged lynching, gradually receded as Katherine Burke, one of the more outspoken Freedom Riders, launched into a friendly conversation with her fearsome captor, offering to cook him breakfast and smother him with Christian kindness if he would accompany her back to Tennessee State in Nashville. Connor responded with good-natured yarns about how much he would appreciate her cooking. As the miles rolled by, the two of them settled into a rather jolly conversation, much to the wonder of Lewis and the others.

Connor halted the police caravan abruptly at the tiny border town of Ardmore, Tennessee. As his officers stacked the Freedom Riders' luggage on the side of the road, he pointed through the darkness at the railroad track running beside them and to what he said was a station up ahead. "You all can catch a train back to Nashville from here," he said, then roared off. The Freedom Riders huddled alone in the pre-dawn silence, a little more than a hundred miles from Birmingham and a little less than a hundred from Nashville.

There were seven of them now, they discovered. Jailhouse segregation had prevented them from learning earlier that Selyn McCollum's father had flown down from Buffalo, New York, to demand personal custody of his daughter, and that Jim Zwerg and Paul Brooks had been released separately. Amid tentative hugs and celebrations, it required very little conversation to establish that none of them knew anyone in or near Ardmore. Or that they were ravenously hungry, not having eaten in two days. Or that they felt more imperiled now, as seven infamous Negroes stranded by night in the middle of nowhere, than in the cells of the Birmingham jail. A party of them finally dared to venture toward the buildings, where they feared Klansmen might be waiting for them. They found no train station, nor anyone yet stirring, but they did find a pay telephone, from which they placed a collect call to the Nashville movement headquarters.

The sleepless Diane Nash scarcely absorbed their bizarre news before she raised urgent business. "Eleven other packages have already been shipped to Birmingham by other modes of transportation," she said. This meant that eleven other students had been recruited to take up the ride, on the assumption that the ten ahead of them might stay in jail. "What are you going to do now?" asked Nash. Awkwardly, the Freedom Rider in Ardmore promised to call back again soon, as neither he nor his companions were thinking much beyond food and rescue.

The seven of them agreed that their first objective was to reach shelter. Clutching their luggage, they went trekking single file down the railroad track in search of a "Negro home" in the country. They found one after first morning light. The elderly couple answering a scout's knock turned out to be simple, isolated farm people, who did not know much about the outside world. Every Negro in the South had heard of the Freedom Riders by now, however, and the sudden realization that these revolutionaries were at the door, seeking help, put fear into them no less than would a Martian invasion. The old man cried out and blocked the door. It took much pleading along with some recitation of Scripture to gain entry, but the jittery couple eventually warmed to the Freedom Riders, finding in themselves more protective instinct than fear, more pride than suspicion. The spirit of the adventure filled the old man with such courage, in fact, that he agreed to go out and buy food for them. Craftily, to minimize suspicion, he went to several different stores for portions of the large order. He said all the white merchants knew that he and his wife never bought two dozen eggs or two pounds of bologna at once.

From the humble refuge, John Lewis placed a call to inform Diane Nash of their collective decision. All seven packages were ready to return to Birmingham, he announced, as soon as transport could be arranged. Nash already had found a volunteer driver, Leo Lillard, who left within minutes. Waiting for him, the seven stiffened their resolve by self-catechism in nonviolence. If they fled home to Nashville, they kept saying, they would be doing exactly what the segregationists wanted them to do: retreating out of fear. They had to return. When Lillard's car roared up to the agreed-upon rendezvous point, they all squeezed in—making four in the front and four in the back—and told him to keep heading south for Birmingham, over the same roads they had just traveled with Bull Connor. Dazed by fatigue, yet brimming with zealous optimism, they were consumed by the belief that the hatred of mobs could not prevail, having seen, after all, sparks of humanity even in Connor, the archracist. When they heard the first bulletin in which a white Alabama radio announcer declared with relief that the "so-called Freedom Riders" were gone, sent packing to Nashville by Bull Connor, a thrill shot through them. The laughter in the car gave way to intermittent pauses of awed silence, as it was all becoming too dazzling to believe. Suddenly, they were not only in the news but ahead of it. They were stealing a march on segregation.

In Washington that Friday morning, Burke Marshall was trying to catch up with the backlog of routine work that had accumulated during his bout with the mumps. His office cleared a draft of a Robert Kennedy letter to Martin Luther King, thanking him for sending a telegram in praise of the Attorney General's speech at the University of Georgia. "I hope you will continue to make your views known to me," said the letter, at the bottom of which Kennedy scratched a more personal "Many thanks to you."

Another piece of Marshall's work was a long letter to Montgomery's mayor, Earl James. Marshall reviewed for James the results of three federal investigations begun during the Eisenhower Administration, all involving blatantly illegal racial persecutions by the Montgomery police force. In two of the cases, policemen had entered the homes of whites stationed at Maxwell Air Force Base, upon receiving reports that Negro Air Force officers were visiting in white neighborhoods, and had arrested all the occupants on charges of disturbing the peace. In the third case, a squad of policemen had arrested on disorderly conduct charges a white Illinois professor, his wife, and thirteen of his students, who were having lunch in a Negro café near Alabama State while on a sociology field trip through the South. "We do not wish to take any federal action, and do not wish to make any public issue of the matter," Marshall informed Mayor James, "if it can satisfactorily be worked out." What the federal government wanted, he added, was "some assurance . . . that incidents will not be repeated and that federal action in these cases and resulting adverse publicity to your city can be avoided. It is toward that end that I am writing you on this informal basis."

Marshall's letter was an application of the Administration's policy of quiet persuasion, by which the Attorney General wanted to give Southern officials some latitude along the tense line between federal and state laws on race. The policy was premised on the hope that Southerners would find it less embarrassing to abandon the excesses of segregation in private than to defend them in public. However, Marshall could not avoid signaling that the federal government was preoccupied with political comfort, too. The very reasonableness of Marshall's letter was grounded in reluctance born of politics, which gave Mayor James a glint of hope that there was a mirror image to the federal threat: he could hope that Kennedy and Marshall would prefer to tolerate the excesses of segregation in private than to attack them in public.

Diane Nash had remained quiet about her reinforcements at first, for tactical reasons, but it became too much for her when her own allies around the South seemed to lose heart upon learning the news of Bull Connor's victory in Alabama. She began dropping hints along her telephone network that there was a big surprise in store for Mr. Connor. Her prediction spread so quickly that it achieved bulletin status before Leo Lillard's car reached Birmingham. The eight students speeding down the highway heard on the radio that the Freedom Riders—themselves—were not retreating to Nashville after all but were making their way back to Birmingham in a private car to renew the fight. Suddenly, instead of stealing a march, they were heading into a manhunt. Unnerved, Lillard's passengers stacked themselves on the floorboards in hiding. In their fear, they decided it would be safer to roll up all the windows, so they soon became piles of sweating apprehension. Lillard ducked off the main highway and angled into town by back roads, through Bessemer. Eyeing all cars with suspicion, he announced that he would try to outrun anyone who followed them.

At last at Shuttlesworth's house, the students had a joyous reunion with the reinforcements who had arrived ahead of them. Among these was Ruby Doris Smith of Spelman, famous to all of them as one of the four SNCC students who had answered the call to the Rock Hill jail. The sight of her made their whole quest feel much larger. Now that they were in Birmingham, any pain ahead would fulfill the purpose of the Freedom Ride, and their shrinking fears were transformed into a heady eagerness to return to the bus station. They gulped down sandwiches around Shuttlesworth's table, and then, amid prayers and final instructions, headed downtown to catch the five o'clock Greyhound to Montgomery.

When reporters within the milling crowd saw John Lewis and other familiar faces, they realized that all the crazy reports indeed were true. Negroes, whom Bull Connor had cowed into silent submission for years, were not only defying him but outwitting him under the most searing public scrutiny. This was high drama—a third attempt to move the Freedom Ride forward from the spot of the Mother's Day beatings. The Freedom Riders pushed their way stoically through the crackling anger of the crowd to the bus, which was idling at the loading platform, but Greyhound officials soon canceled the trip for lack of a driver. A round of cheers went up from the crowd as the Freedom Riders filed back into the station, saying they would wait there for a bus to Montgomery, however long it took. Birmingham officials made the wait as difficult as possible by disconnecting the public telephones and closing the snack stands, while police officers arrested Shuttlesworth again, this time on Bull Connor's complaint that he had "conspire[d] with unknown persons" to cause a mob to gather in Birmingham on Mother's Day.

While officers hauled Shuttlesworth away, police riot units found that their no-violence orders required increasingly stern measures against a milling white crowd they soon estimated at three thousand. At first, officers merely reprimanded stray whites who walked across the feet of the seated Freedom Riders or deliberately spilled drinks into their laps, but canine units eventually moved the whites back out of the terminal building. The Freedom Riders sang "We Shall Overcome." John Lewis and others began to preach in tandem. One of the more devout students could not help noting with satisfaction that fear seemed to deepen the reverence of a few skeptics who had been perfunctory about earlier religious devotionals. As night fell, bystanders tossed occasional rocks over the heads of policemen through the terminal windows.

The crisis was fully revived in Washington. Those who had been de-alerted were realerted. Robert Kennedy, stepping up pressure to get the Alabama governor off his "fishing boat," had President Kennedy himself place another call. This time, Patterson did not bother to use the fishing excuse. He simply refused to take a phone call from the President of the United States. Word of the snub soon reached reporters, and *The New York Times* and other newspapers would print page-one headlines such as "President Can't Reach Governor." An angry Robert Kennedy told Patterson's aides that the President would issue a public ultimatum threatening federal intervention unless the governor emerged to discuss protection for the Freedom Riders. This brought Patterson to the tele-phone for a long, rancorous conversation with the Attorney General. Kennedy proposed instant solutions to all Patterson's political objec-tions: if the governor could not afford to announce that Alabama would protect the Freedom Riders, said Kennedy, he could say he was protecting "the highways." These facile suggestions only enraged Patterson, who, convinced that the Attorney General was paying only superficial respect to the realities of the governor's political career in Alabama, launched into a tirade. He had sworn an oath to preserve racial segregation, he said. "You're making political speeches at me, John," Kennedy interjected. "You don't have to make political speeches at me over the telephone." Patterson feared that he was being pushed into a deal whose meaning would be twisted into an abandonment of segregation. He declared that he would discuss the matter only face to face, with a personal represen-tative of the President.

John Seigenthaler soon found himself tearing down the highway from Birmingham to Montgomery with a White House telegram in his pocket. On this, the fifth day of what had begun as an ad hoc goodwill trip, he was pressed into higher service as an emissary of the President. He rushed directly to the Alabama capitol. Escorted into the governor's of-fice, he confronted not only Patterson but the wary faces of all the Ala-bama cabinet members, convened around a long table for an extraordinary night session.

"Glad to see you. You're a Southerner," Patterson remarked on hearing Seigenthaler's Tennessee accent. He followed this hearty welcome with an angry oration, which Seigenthaler decided was largely for the benefit of the assembled Alabama politicians. "There's nobody in the whole country that's got the spine to stand up to the goddamned niggers except me," Patterson declared, using the word "nigger" with casual defiance. "And I'll tell you I've got more mail in the drawers of that desk over there congratulating me on the stand I've taken against what's going on in this country . . . against Martin Luther King and these rabble-rousers. I'll tell you I believe that I'm more popular in this country today than John Kennedy is for the stand I've taken." Some time later, after more rhetoric and some earnest bargaining over the best way to get the Freedom Riders out of Alabama, he invited Seigenthaler to use his personal telephone, there in sight of the Alabama witnesses, to report the results to Robert Kennedy.

"He's given me this statement," Seigenthaler told Kennedy, looking at his notes: " 'The State of Alabama has the will, the force, the men, and the equipment to give full protection to everyone in Alabama, on the highways and elsewhere.' He says he does not 'need or expect assistance from the federal government.' "

"Does he mean it?" Kennedy asked Seigenthaler.

"I think he does," Seigenthaler replied. Then he turned to Patterson. "Governor, he wants to know if you mean it."

"I've given my word as governor of Alabama," said Patterson, and he repeated his statement so loudly that Kennedy could hear it through the receiver in Seigenthaler's hand. After relaying further details of the assurances, Seigenthaler was soon talking on the governor's phone with the president of the Greyhound bus company, who was as anxious about protection as Kennedy. Governor Patterson apologized profusely to the Greyhound president for the bus burned in Anniston the previous Sunday. As the agreements were being finalized, Seigenthaler developed an affinity for Alabama Public Safety Director Floyd Mann. Mann was operating under severe constraints—the governor's insistence that Mann's highway patrol officers not be too visible in protecting the Negroes, for example, and the jealously guarded prerogatives of the city police forces —but he impressed Seigenthaler as a sympathetic, professional officer who was determined to protect the Freedom Riders from ambush on the open road.

Federal and state officials haggled late into the night. Governor Patterson, even while making grudging concessions to protect the Freedom Riders, was maneuvering by other channels to stop them. His own attorney general, MacDonald Gallion, obtained from Montgomery's Judge Walter B. Jones a state injunction forbidding "the entry into and travel within the state of Alabama, and engaging in the so-called 'Freedom Ride' and other acts or conduct calculated to promote breaches of the peace." The injunction was formally addressed to James Farmer and CORE, even though Farmer was still in Washington and no CORE people had been on the rides since Monday, but these imperfections were immaterial to the plan. For the state's purposes, the injunction would serve as a legal basis for contempt-of-court arrests that would stick, at least temporarily, and would transfer the entire dispute into the labyrinth of the court system, along with the five-year-old ban on the NAACP. State lawyers hurried to perfect binding copies of the injunction for serving on the Freedom Riders.

At 6:05 the next morning, before the injunctions reached Birmingham, Greyhound driver Joe Caverno stepped forward to address a large press contingent and the nineteen bleary-eyed Freedom Riders—two of the fourteen reinforcements had dropped out during the long night—gathered on the loading platform next to a split-level bus marked "St. Petersburg Express." "I'm supposed to drive this bus to Dothan, Alabama, through Montgomery," Caverno said nervously, "but I understand there is a big convoy down the road. And I don't have but one life to give. And I don't intend to give it to CORE or the NAACP. And that's all I have to say." With that, he disappeared through the "Drivers Only" door of the terminal, leaving his audience bewildered by his fearfully eloquent repudiation of the high-level arrangement that was on everyone's lips. No other driver appeared. Confusion seeped outward from the inert bus, with Bull Connor's policemen no less puzzled than anyone else. The Freedom Riders decided to remain on the platform, singing hymns and Negro spirituals. Jim Zwerg, the only white male among them, sang a solo in "Oh, Lord, Keep Your Eyes on the Prize."

The latest snarl ruined Robert Kennedy's Saturday morning in Washington. He called the Greyhound superintendent in Birmingham to demand an explanation. "Drivers refuse to drive," said an exasperated George Cruit.

"Do *you* know how to drive a bus?" asked Kennedy, in an ominously quiet voice.

"No."

"Well, surely somebody in the damn bus company can drive a bus, can't they?" Kennedy said. ". . . I think you should—had better be getting in touch with Mr. Greyhound or whoever Greyhound is, and somebody better give us an answer to this question. I am—the Government is—going to be very much upset if this group does not get to continue their trip."

This last sentence—intercepted by eavesdroppers on the phone line in Alabama—soon appeared in newspapers all across the South in support of the argument that Robert Kennedy was working surreptitiously for the Negroes. More conspiratorial Southerners came to believe that Kennedy had been the mastermind behind the entire Freedom Ride. Far beyond any other word or deed of his tenure at Justice, the remark would erode Kennedy's political standing in the South, making the name

"Bobby" a regional epithet.* The immediate effect of Kennedy's words
was to cause blunter, more heated words to fly between the interested
parties. Bull Connor arrived at the bus station to join the private negotiations. Finally, without warning, an unhappy-looking Caverno bolted
through the door along with the president of the local bus drivers' union
and the chief Greyhound dispatcher. Policemen herded the startled Freedom Riders behind the three of them onto the bus, and, as reporters
dashed to their cars to follow, the St. Petersburg Express raced through
downtown Birmingham, escorted by police cars with sirens wailing. The
highway patrol picked them up at the city line, and the entire convoy—
shadowed by FBI observers, plainclothes state detectives, and a highway
patrol airplane, plus the trailing reporters—headed for Montgomery at
speeds nearing ninety miles per hour.

The Freedom Ride, paralyzed since the Mother's Day beatings, resumed at 8:30 A.M. on Saturday, May 20. In the interim, John Lewis and
the other Nashville students had endured six days and nights on a roller
coaster between joy and fear, exhilaration and boredom—largely uninter-
rupted by sleep—and several of them reacted to the moment of triumph
by dozing off. Attorney General Kennedy, relieved at last, went out for a
long horseback ride through the Virginia countryside.

The Special Agent in Charge (SAC) of the Montgomery FBI office sent
word to headquarters, and from there the message reached Marshall at
the Justice Department, that he did not believe a word of Police Commissioner Sullivan's promise to protect the Freedom Riders on their arrival in the capital. Back from Washington came orders to remind
Sullivan of the governor's assurances. The SAC complied, telling Sullivan that the bus was on its way from Birmingham. Floyd Mann, equally
skeptical of the Montgomery police, called Sullivan to make sure there
could be no disputes about proper notice. Mann told Sullivan he had just
received a radio report from his highway patrol airplane that the bus was
fourteen miles outside Montgomery. Highway patrol units, forbidden to
work within city limits, would be dropping off soon. Sullivan replied that
there were plenty of Montgomery police at the bus terminal. This was
true at the time, but the policemen promptly began to vanish.

Elsewhere in Montgomery, Seigenthaler finished breakfast with John
Doar, who had been working on his voting rights a-suit in nearby Selma.

---

* "I never recovered from it," Kennedy said in an oral history in 1964. In a lighter
vein, he always remained amused that his agitation had led him to speak of "Mr.
Greyhound."

Seigenthaler eagerly sought the experienced counsel of Doar, but he also knew to avoid public identification with him. Because Doar's lawsuits already marked him as an enemy to segregationist officials in Alabama, Burke Marshall had ordered Doar to stay clear of the Freedom Ride crisis. Accordingly, the two Justice Department colleagues had avoided all personal contact until the completion of Seigenthaler's visit to Patterson the previous night, and even now they were wary of being seen together. They decided to split up before the arrival of the Freedom Riders. Doar wanted to work on his Selma case. Seigenthaler, wearing a set of sports clothes he had borrowed from Doar, dropped him off at the downtown Federal Building, which overlooked the Greyhound terminal, and then, driving alone, began circling the block to look for a parking place. Figuring mistakenly from the regular bus schedule, he thought he had a half hour before the arrival of the St. Petersburg Express. In fact the high-speed bus was pulling into the terminal already, just out of sight. Seigenthaler saw a motorcycle policeman leaving the area in a hurry.

John Lewis, selected to speak for the group, stepped first off the parked bus and paused before a semicircle of reporters on the platform. As other reporters rushed up in front of him, and the Freedom Riders filled in behind, Lewis surveyed a terminal area that was familiar to him from scores of bus rides home to nearby Troy, where he had preached to the chickens. Now all the platforms and streets and parking lots were deserted. Aside from the drivers of a few taxis parked in the distance, the only people he could see beyond the reporters were a dozen or so white men hidden in a shadowy entrance to the terminal. Lewis felt an eerie foreboding. "It doesn't look right," he whispered to a companion.

Facing a battery of cameras, microphones, and notepads, Lewis got halfway through an answer to the first press question before falling strangely silent, transfixed by what he saw coming up behind the reporters. Norman Ritter, the Time-Life bureau chief from Atlanta, reacted to Lewis' face by turning to confront the dozen white men who had been standing in the door. He held out both arms to create a boundary for the interview, but the men, brandishing baseball bats, bottles, and lead pipes, pushed past him. One of them slapped Moe Levy of NBC News, and this first act triggered a seizing and smashing of cameras and equipment.

"Let's all stand together," said Lewis, as the Freedom Riders retreated backward along the enclosed loading platform. Hemmed against a railing that ran along a retaining wall, they stood helpless as the white men barreled into them. Some of Lewis' group jumped, some were pushed, and some were literally thrown over the railing onto the roofs of cars parked in the Post Office lot below. Those who did not take their luggage with them were soon pelted with their own suitcases. Above, on the platform, reporters who objected, or who tried to take photographs of the attack, were set upon by a small mob whose full fury was now released. The enraged whites smashed *Life* photographer Don Urbrock repeatedly in the face with his own camera. They clubbed Norman Ritter to the ground, beat a Birmingham television reporter, and chased the reporters who escaped.

Down below, the Freedom Riders realized that whites who had been secluded at various observation posts were closing in on them from all directions. Some stalked and some charged, egged on by a woman in a yellow dress who kept yelling "Get those niggers!" Fighting panic, the Freedom Riders made their way to two nearby Negro taxis and tried to send the seven females away to safety. Four of the five Negroes jumped into the backseat of the first taxi, whose driver had a little boy with him on the front seat. "Well, I can't carry but four!" cried the driver, when he saw that he was drawing the attention of the onsurging whites. There was no time to argue. The Freedom Riders shoved the fifth female Negro into the front seat anyway. "Well, I *sure* can't carry them!" shouted the driver, eyeing Susan Wilbur and Sue Harmann, the two white students. Doors slamming, he drove off as the two whites were pushed inside the other taxi. Before the second driver had a chance to say that it was illegal for him to transport whites, the mob yanked him and his keys outside to prevent the car from leaving, then dragged the two women from the back. Others chased the male Freedom Riders, some of whom were trying futilely to act on John Lewis' shouted directions about how to zigzag to Columbus Street and climb the long hill toward the refuge of Ralph Abernathy's church.

The first taxi, filled with screams and shouts, found one of the two exits from the parking lot choked off by a stream of angry whites. Swerving around, bombarded with conflicting advice, the driver found the other exit blocked by cars. This was too much for him. He told the Freedom Riders that he was going to abandon the taxi. While some of his passengers tried desperately to calm him, others looked back in horror at the loading platform. They, along with several Alabama reporters standing closer, saw a dozen men surround Jim Zwerg, the white Wisconsin exchange student at Fisk in Nashville. One of the men grabbed Zwerg's suitcase and smashed him in the face with it. Others slugged him to the ground, and when he was dazed beyond resistance, one man pinned Zwerg's head between his knees so that the others could take turns hitting him. As they steadily knocked out his teeth, and his face and chest were streaming with blood, a few adults on the perimeter put their children on their shoulders to view the carnage. A small girl asked what the men were doing, and her father replied, "Well, they're really carrying on." The Freedom Riders in the nearby taxi turned away in sickened hysteria.

Upstairs at a window of the Federal Building, observer John Doar, his renowned dour composure already dissolved, was describing the sudden disaster over the telephone to Burke Marshall. "Oh, there are fists, punching!" he cried. "A bunch of men led by a guy with a bleeding face are beating them. There are no cops. It's terrible! It's terrible! There's not a cop in sight. People are yelling, 'There those niggers are! Get 'em, get 'em!' It's awful." One of Robert Kennedy's secretaries was taking notes on an extension phone. Marshall, still listening to Doar, asked another one to track down the Attorney General. Less than five minutes after the bus door opened in Montgomery, official Washington knew that pipes and bare knuckles nullified all the painstaking federal-state agreements.

Seigenthaler, driving slowly toward the scene through a mass of bystanders, first saw suitcases flying upward in the distance. He did not yet know that this was the Freedom Riders' luggage being thrown into the air—smashed open as trophies—but he could sense the contagion of a riot. As he moved within sight of the loading platform, a swarming mass of several hundred people came into view, running in all directions, to and from scattered pockets of violence. To Seigenthaler, it looked like a close-up of a giant anthill. He caught sight of one well-dressed Negro darting ahead of his pursuers, and then, closer to his car, he saw a cluster of people moving around a young white woman. This was Susan Wilbur, struggling to escape after being pulled from the Negro taxi. White women were beating her from behind with pocketbooks, and a teenager was jabbing her from the front, dancing like a prizefighter.

Seigenthaler decided to try to rescue her. He drove up on the curb and jumped out. As he did, a woman with an especially heavy shoulder bag knocked Wilbur across the right front fender of his car, and by the time Seigenthaler reached her lying there, the crowd of screaming, angry whites jammed in so tightly upon them that he could not push his way to the car's back door. He grabbed Wilbur by the shoulders, managed to pull the right front door open, and, shouting "Come on, get in the car," began to slide across to the driver's seat. He saw in a flash that another white student—Sue Harmann, whom he had not seen before—had dived into the back.

Wilbur balked. Still absorbing blows, she shouted, "Mister, this is not your fight! Get away from here! You're gonna get killed!"

Seigenthaler jumped back outside, where people were climbing over his car. "Get in the damn car!" he shrieked at Wilbur.

Wilbur, not sure who Seigenthaler was, kept insisting during the struggle that she was nonviolent and did not want to get anybody hurt. As she did, two men stepped between Seigenthaler and the car door, one of them shouting "Who the hell are you?" With Seigenthaler frantically telling them to get back, that he was a federal agent, the other men brought a pipe down on the side of Seigenthaler's head. Then the crowd, crushing in to seize Sue Harmann, kicked his unconscious body halfway under the car.

His was not the only prostrate form littering the scene as the rioters kept scurrying, shouting, and celebrating. Zwerg was face-down in a patch of warm, gooey repair tar on the pavement. John Lewis lay unconscious near the retaining wall, felled by a blow from a wooden Coca-Cola crate, and his seminary schoolmate, William Barbee, lay some distance away. Barbee had been overtaken and knocked to the pavement, and was still being stomped and kicked by a taunting swarm of rioters when Floyd Mann suddenly appeared among them. "Stand back!" he shouted above the din, showing his drawn revolver. "We are going to keep law and order." He cleared the attackers from Barbee and moved on to pull others from a television cameraman. Mann, a state official within city jurisdiction, was acting alone, without support or legal authority.

Police Commissioner Sullivan arrived with a squadron some ten minutes after the first violence. By then the Freedom Riders were either down or gone, but the milling crowd was still growing by the hundreds, gawking or looking for new targets. Behind Sullivan came Alabama Attorney General Gallion in the company of his assistants and a deputy sheriff. They made their way to John Lewis, who was pointed out to them as a Freedom Rider, and stood over him to read Judge Jones's injunction.

Struggling to his feet, Lewis managed to locate and revive Barbee and Zwerg. For safety, the three of them huddled near the same state officials who were serving them with an injunction that held them responsible for the riot. All three Freedom Riders were bleeding. Zwerg in particular was a hideous sight, moving Lewis and several reporters to beg the officials to have him taken to a hospital. Police officers kept saying that Zwerg was free to leave. Lewis and Barbee placed him gingerly into the backseat of a white cab, which was promptly abandoned by the driver. The deputy sheriff read Judge Jones's injunction to Zwerg as he sat motionless, uncomprehending. Some time later, a Negro taxi driver volunteered to take Lewis and Barbee to a hospital, but the segregation laws forced Zwerg to remain behind. Commissioner Sullivan told inquiring reporters that all the ambulances for whites were out of service with breakdowns. One reporter ventured to the taxi where Zwerg was sitting and tried to explain why it was taking so long to evacuate him. "You can't get me out of here," Zwerg replied vacantly. "I don't even know where I am or how I got here."

Some fifteen or twenty minutes later, a police lieutenant came upon the partially hidden form of Seigenthaler, who was just beginning to stir. "Looks like you got some trouble, buddy," he said.

"Yeah, I did," said Seigenthaler, waking to pain. "What happened?"

"Well, we had a riot."

"Don't you think you better call Mr. Kennedy?"

"Which Mr. Kennedy?"

"The Attorney General of the United States."

The lieutenant frowned. "Who the hell are you?" he asked.

"I'm his administrative assistant," groaned Seigenthaler, in a manner that convinced the lieutenant he was talking with a bona-fide big shot. He ran for help, carrying news that reporters picked up instantly. Seigenthaler passed out again. He awoke in the X-ray room of a hospital, lying beside a doctor who was talking on the telephone with Byron White in Washington.

By that time, police had allowed Zwerg to be taken by a Negro ambulance to a Catholic hospital, which agreed to receive him. At the riot scene, the crowd swelled to upwards of a thousand people, still breaking into sporadic violence. A handful of whites ambushed two stray Negro teenagers half a block from the bus terminal, setting one briefly on fire with kerosene and breaking the other's leg with a stomping. Other rioters built an enormous bonfire from the scattered contents of the Freedom Riders' suitcases. Police began to make arrests, eventually hauling off seven people charged with disorderly conduct and two alleged drunks. In the midst of all this, Commissioner Sullivan sat on the back of a car, fielding press questions about police preparedness and the causes of the riot. "I really don't know what happened," he said. "When I got here, all I saw were three men lying in the street. There was two niggers and a white man."

Susan Wilbur and Sue Harmann, pounded upon continuously as they fled, had pushed their way inside a church and called police officers, who eventually put them on a train bound for Nashville. "I don't know why they let us go," Wilbur told reporters. "Maybe it was because we are girls." Meanwhile, the five Freedom Riders in the stalled taxi had barged into a Negro home in Montgomery and called Shuttlesworth in Birmingham. Other Freedom Riders, stranded in hiding places all over the city, called Diane Nash with reports on their location and condition. Under her long-distance instruction, the scattered Freedom Riders began showing up one by one at the home of Rev. S. S. Seay—a defendant in the *New York Times* libel suits and the preacher who, at a climactic early moment of the bus boycott five years earlier, had risen in a fit of courage to bid all the Negro preachers go to jail.

Now Seay hosted a euphoric rebirth of the Freedom Ride. Each newcomer who came through his door was embraced as a survivor—purged of sufferings and picked clean of tales about when he or she had last seen everyone else at the terminal. Spirits swelled with each new arrival, and there were constant bulletins from Nash about how they were shaking up the outside world. Shuttlesworth and Abernathy were on the way to help, she said. She was leaving for Montgomery herself, and so was Jim Lawson, who had been on the way to visit his sick mother in Ohio. Martin Luther King might come. President Kennedy's personal representative had been beaten at the terminal too, and the Kennedys might send in the Army. Newspapers like *The New York Times* were sending in their own correspondents, no longer content to rely on wire service reports. The Freedom Riders had broken out of Birmingham at a terrible price, but nothing could stop them now. John Lewis walked into Seay's house fresh from the hospital, with a bandaged head, and received an emotional welcome in proportion to his wounds and his determination. He announced that even the two students left in the hospital were ready to go on. William Barbee soon made this message public with a statement to reporters at his bedside. "As soon as we're recovered from this, we'll start again," he said. One floor above him, in the white section of St. Jude's Hospital, Jim Zwerg cleared enough concussion from his head to tell reporters essentially what they had heard from Jim Peck in the Birmingham operating room six days earlier. "We will continue our journey one way or another," said Zwerg. "We are prepared to die."

TWELVE

THE SUMMER OF FREEDOM RIDES

The Attorney General, who was said to have gone from horse-back riding to an FBI baseball game, had been difficult to locate. He was still wearing shirtsleeves and a baseball cap when he walked into his office late Saturday to join the emergency conclave of Byron White, Burke Marshall, and ten other Justice officials. His feelings of betrayal personalized by the brutal attack on Seigenthaler, Kennedy called Governor Patterson to demand an explanation for the absence of police protection that morning. Patterson's aides put him off, saying the governor could not be reached, and this evasion put Kennedy into such a fury that he decided it was time to send in the marshals. After notifying President Kennedy at his weekend retreat in Middleburg, Virginia, he dispersed staff lawyers to activate the makeshift army they had been preparing all week. Then he called Seigenthaler's hospital room in Montgomery. "How are you doing?" he asked.

"This is a terrible headache," Seigenthaler replied.

"Well, we're sending the marshals there."

"I'm sorry to hear that," said Seigenthaler, who knew this meant trouble, and he signed off with a weak joke, advising Kennedy never to run for governor of Alabama.

Given Seigenthaler's medical condition, which was listed as serious though not life-threatening, only an extreme emergency could have induced the Attorney General to call him back the same afternoon on business. But Kennedy did precisely that only an hour or two later. By then, the implications of sending the marshals were rumbling ominously. In Alabama, where Patterson was stating publicly that the state already had restored order, Kennedy's decision to send federal marshals after the riot, uninvited, was denounced as a political insult that invited the Freedom Riders to continue or even escalate their actions under federal protection. Kennedy realized that his forces would arrive too late to stop the first Montgomery riot but in time to be blamed if a second one occurred. To compound the pressure on him, word came that Martin Luther King was about to fly into Montgomery to encourage the Freedom Riders. The Attorney General knew that King's name, like the federal intervention, would attract reporters and increase the danger of renewed attacks by white mobs. Worse, Kennedy's lawyers were telling him that since the U.S. marshals were going in on a mission to protect interstate travelers, and since King himself would be an interstate traveler, he had little choice but to have the marshals protect King too. In effect, King would be coming into Alabama to support the Freedom Ride under armed federal guard, and no one had to tell Kennedy how Governor Patterson would react. Kennedy tried by phone to convince King not to go to Alabama. So did Marshall. When they failed, Kennedy was not above trying a little manipulation; Seigenthaler's wounds might soften a firm resolve.

"I was wondering if you think it would help any if you talk to King," he inquired awkwardly, knowing that he was asking Seigenthaler to play on King's sympathies, in a lobbying campaign to make King choose a course favored by Patterson over one pressed upon him by the Freedom Riders. Seigenthaler gamely volunteered to make the phone call, but the plan was abandoned before he could reach King. Floyd Mann, appearing later at his hospital room, broke down weeping in sympathy and frustration.

From Washington that night, James Farmer ordered his New York staff to begin recruiting an emergency team of CORE members to take up the Freedom Ride in Alabama, lest the Nashville students assume complete command of a crusade that was catapulting CORE into national recognition for the first time in its history. About midnight, John Doar drove fifty miles north of Montgomery, then puttered across the water in a little boat to Judge Frank Johnson's lakeside cottage. He carried a sheaf of affidavits supporting the Justice Department's petition for a temporary restraining order against Alabama Klan groups. Johnson declined Doar's request to include Birmingham in its scope—even though Doar's best evidence of Klan conspiracy in the riots came from Birmingham—but he agreed to sign the order as it applied to Montgomery. This being a bold and hazardous act for an Alabama judge, Johnson then accepted Doar's offer of U.S. marshals to protect his own life.

King flew into Montgomery about noon the next day, Sunday, May 21, a little more than a week after he had warned that the original Freedom Riders would never make it through Alabama. U.S. marshals—about fifty of them by the count of state agents—met King at the airport and escorted him to the familiar confines of Abernathy's house, where King had first lighted in Montgomery with Vernon Johns more than seven years earlier. While he made plans for a mass meeting that night, the marshals outside refused to tell reporters or state agents why they were there. Everyone knew they were guarding King, of course, and to Governor Patterson it was an act of sneaky, cowardly treachery on the part of Attorney General Kennedy. Patterson also realized his sudden political opportunity. Having had little to gain when pitted against the lowly, mostly Negro Freedom Riders, whose stature rose in every clash with white Alabama, Patterson seized the new underdog role in a battle against the federal government itself. He summoned Byron White to the capitol for what amounted to a public council of war.

"We don't need your marshals," Patterson told White, as the two of them stood there before the Alabama cabinet and a host of reporters. "We don't want them, and we didn't ask for them. And still the federal government sends them here to help put down a disturbance which it helped create."

White responded to the governor's anger with the calm argument that they shared a common mission of preserving public order. "Everything seems very peaceful this morning," he said. "Yet yesterday's violence showed how fast it can erupt."

Patterson told White that the Freedom Ride was inspired by Communists. With some sarcasm, he asked White if the federal marshals, in their devotion to law and order, would assist state agents in executing Judge Jones's order to have the Freedom Riders arrested for violating his injunction. ("I cannot guarantee that," White replied. "I am not familiar with your injunction.") Patterson bore in on the issue. "Will you make available all the information you have about the Freedom Riders who came in yesterday?" he asked.

"No," said White.

"You know where some of these Freedom Riders are, don't you?"

"Yes," White replied. "In the hospital."

"Do you know where the others are?"

"No, I don't."

"If you knew where some of these people are, would you inform us?"

"I will never know where these people are," White replied evasively.

Patterson warned White that Alabama regarded the U.S. marshals as "interlopers" without special rights or privileges in the state. "Make especially certain," he said gravely, "that none of your men encroach on any of our state laws, rights, or functions, because we'll arrest them like anybody else." The governor dismissed White after forty-five tense, unpleasant minutes.

These words crackled out over the airwaves, along with news that King and his supporters would meet in Abernathy's church that night. The Freedom Riders already were hiding in the basement library of the church, hoping that police would not dare to arrest them there. Governor Patterson, who could be sneaky himself, received an intercept report that Byron White called Washington immediately after their confrontation to recommend that the marshals be pulled out of Alabama. Patterson was especially encouraged that White chose to call his old friend President Kennedy rather than his boss, the Attorney General. By going out of channels to express doubts about the wisdom of using the marshals in Alabama, White signaled a warning that the younger Kennedy might be out of his depth.

People began trickling into Abernathy's "Brick-a-Day" church about five o'clock, more than three hours before the mass meeting was scheduled to begin. Without a preacher, an organist, or a pianist, they sang and prayed among themselves, relying buoyantly on the familiar hymns. This early ritual was a sign of the old spirit in Montgomery, gone since the bus boycott, but this time students were involved as heroes, victims of mobs, and the governor and even the President were arguing about them in the newspapers. Those making their way into the church could see a dozen or so white men standing outside First Baptist with nightsticks and yellow armbands stenciled "U.S. Marshal," guarding the church.

There was a small cluster of whites across the street, in a city park that had been closed under threat of an MIA integration suit, and another around the corner on the fringes of Oakwood Cemetery. A woman standing on the corner of Jefferson and Ripley recruited a third group from the passing traffic with come-on waves and shouts of "Get out of that car!" Among the Negroes, the elderly and the most devout were first to arrive, as usual, often with a bit of food in one hand and a grandchild's hand in the other, and they had little trouble steering past glares or occasional profanities. As the white crowd grew larger and bolder, however, some Negro families hesitated to run the gauntlet of jeers, and those who did often moved at a brisk trot into the sanctuary of the church. By nightfall, fifteen hundred people jammed First Baptist, with at least twice that many whites gathered outside and around the block.

Between hymns, Rev. S. S. Seay told the congregation stories about the Freedom Riders' courage—how they had appeared one by one at his home the previous night, beaten but unbowed. He introduced Diane Nash, who was sitting on the platform in a place of honor, and he revealed that the Freedom Riders themselves were right there among them. He could not introduce them, or even allow them to sit together, because he wanted to reduce their vulnerability to arrest. John Lewis and the others were scattered among the choir members in the loft, but they could not conceal themselves completely, nor did they want to. Whenever Seay pointedly introduced a bandaged young stranger to say a few words or to lead them in singing "We Shall Overcome," the open secret sent emotional waves of tribute through the church, lifting songs and "Amens" that smothered the ominous noises from the street.

King had not yet made an entrance. Downstairs in Abernathy's office, he tinkered with the program, fretting about backstage details. Abernathy, Shuttlesworth, and Wyatt Walker slipped up and down the pastor's back stairs with late reports on the mood of the crowd. Ushers brought progressively fearful messages from latecomers to the church, who told of seeing broken car windows outside or of dodging rocks. Pockets of whites were raising "nigger chants," daring the Negroes to come out of the church. Shuttlesworth, observing that James Farmer would not be able to make it through that crowd, volunteered to meet his flight from Washington and bring him personally from the airport. Waving aside all objections, Shuttlesworth ventured out into the mob just as Negroes outside were giving up hope of getting in.

"We've got to go out and see what's happening," King announced sometime later. A chorus of dissent went up instantly among those around him. Fred Bennett, a young SCLC aide from Atlanta, told King that it would be suicide for him to face a mob in Montgomery, where his face was so well known. Bernard Lee, who had grown ever more devoted to King in the year since his expulsion from Alabama State, told King he was too valuable to take such risks. When King persisted, runners went upstairs to fetch Walker and Abernathy, in the hope that they could dissuade him. In whispers, the leaders debated several different theories of King's purpose. Some said he simply wanted to see for himself how bad the mob was before charting his next move. Others said he wanted to attempt the miracle of shaming the mob with his presence, demonstrating in the flesh that he and the other clergymen inside were not afraid. A still more dramatic reading had it that King wanted to give his own life to the mob in order to save the congregation. Walker and Abernathy did not have time to clarify all this when they pushed through to King at the basement door. King was in an emergency mode, tuning out all the clatter around him. "Let's go," he told them. "Leadership must do this."

A handful of preachers stepped outside, with Bennett and Lee circling watchfully around King, like bodyguards. They moved slowly around the square block of the property to survey a mob that now surrounded them in a continuous line, held back on the far side of the street by the fragile inhibitions of mobs—perhaps by the sight of the marshals and their radios, or the church steeple, or perhaps for lack of a spark. The jeers and the occasional thuds of thrown missiles carried clearly through the early evening air, and soon there rose above them the cry of someone who recognized King. "Nigger King!" it rang out. "Come over here!" King moved slowly toward the challenge, but rocks began to land around him. Then a metal cylinder skidded to a stop at King's feet. Fred Bennett pounced on the object and threw it toward a vacant spot on the grounds. The entourage pulled King in retreat during a frantic debate about whether the cylinder had been a bomb or a tear gas cannister, and if tear gas, where it had come from since there were no police in sight, and whether the police might be in collusion with the mob. Back in the church, King went upstairs to the pulpit. Stressing the positive, he announced that the marshals were still there and that the people outside remained behind a perimeter across the street. The mood inside rose up as though in contest with the shouts of the mob, as a baritone soloist led them all in singing "Leaning on the Everlasting Arms."

In Washington, the Attorney General's office was transformed into a weekend command post, from which Robert Kennedy—clad informally after a Sunday game of touch football—established a permanent open line with Byron White's staging area at Maxwell Air Force Base outside Montgomery. The staging area was in chaos. White had about four hundred men, including eighty off-duty guards from the maximum-security federal prison in Atlanta, but no sooner did guards arrive from Atlanta and other prisons, it seemed, than their shifts changed and the wardens began to complain about the risk of prison riots in their absence. Some of the guards were leaving already, to be replaced by Immigration and Border Patrol employees due in from Texas and the Gulf Coast. White's assistants were swearing in the arrivals as deputy U.S. marshals. William Orrick, a San Francisco lawyer serving as Assistant Attorney General for the Civil Division, had checked in with the office that morning upon reading of the assault on Seigenthaler, and only a few hours later he had been commandeered to Alabama himself. Now he was racing around Byron White's staging area trying to organize the marshals into instant platoons as he remembered them from the Army. With alarming reports coming in by radio from the marshals at First Baptist, Orrick and his colleagues improvised madly. When Army commanders refused, in the absence of orders from their superiors, to allow Army trucks to transport the marshals into an active civil conflict, the Justice team tracked down the local postmaster and demanded the use of mail trucks.

Byron White was not communicating with the Negroes in the church, more or less because he did not want to appear to be aiding the Freedom Riders. White and Kennedy, acutely sensitive to Governor Patterson's strident declarations that Alabama was maintaining order, had sent out only token forces of marshals to likely trouble spots around the city. They knew that the need to reinforce them in great numbers was growing critical—not a single city policeman had been sighted at First Baptist during the three hours that the mob had been swelling, and the only state officials were two plainclothes detectives slipped in by Floyd Mann—but they did not want to move in without a request from Patterson. State officials were riding a sharp edge between refusal to protect the Freedom Riders and refusal to ask for federal help; federal officials were caught between willingness to protect the Freedom Riders and a need to be asked.

During the war of nerves, the only communication Byron White received from Alabama authorities was an abrupt telephoned question from Police Commissioner Sullivan: if all Montgomery policemen and firemen went on strike that night to protest federal intervention, Sullivan wanted to know, would the federal marshals assume responsibility for traffic control and fire alarms? This tricky question soon ensnarled Justice staff lawyers in Kafkaesque puzzles about whether intervention at the church might open the federal government to millions of dollars in liability if Montgomery citizens allowed parts of their city to burn.

Fred Shuttlesworth found a much more unruly mob on his return to the church than he had warned Farmer to expect. A block from First Baptist, as they were pushing gently through the crowd jamming a side street, the whites surrounded their car and rocked it from side to side. The driver threw the gearshift into reverse and peeled out backward. On the advice of a Negro taxi driver, they abandoned the car to approach the church on foot through Oakwood Cemetery, only to come up behind yet another swirling wall of angry people. "They've got the church hemmed in," said Shuttlesworth after a moment's hesitation. "All right, Jim, follow me." With that, the wiry, diminutive Shuttlesworth bellowed, "Out of the way! Come on! Let him through! Out of the way!" He wafted the startled white people out of his path with wild arm motions, as Farmer cringed behind him through the parting mass.

Safely inside the church basement, where they were fussed over like reinforcements at the Alamo, the two of them went up the pastor's staircase into the church. King joyfully presented Farmer to the congregation as the national director of CORE and author of the original Free-

dom Ride. Farmer was introduced to Diane Nash, then embraced John
Lewis, the only veteran of both legs of the journey. After hearing tributes
to the symbolic moment of union and giving a brief speech, Farmer was
excused to join the leadership conclave downstairs in Abernathy's office.
There he listened to Southern preachers in hurried analyses of various
distant white men—Kennedy, Patterson, White, Sullivan, Mann—who
might control their safety that night.

Farmer was a leader without a staff, a newcomer among people who
worshiped King and had never heard of CORE, by and large. Having
scorned the pulpit and abandoned the South twenty years earlier for a
life among bureaucrats, bohemians, and intellectuals, he was quickened
but detached at the eye of the crisis, with much to represent but little to
do. As he listened to the excited talk of strangers against a background
of hymns about salvation through Jesus and Rebel yells from outside,
fear loosened its grip on him, routed by disordered reality. Only days
after burying his father and an hour after in-flight meal service, Farmer
was still almost hypnotized by images of Shuttlesworth's lunatic charge
through the mob.

Not long after eight o'clock, King and the others rushed to investigate
chilling reports that a car had been overturned near the corner of Ripley
and Jefferson. Glances through windows confirmed that it was true: the
car lay wheels-up on the street, circled by triumphant rioters who fled
when an old man threw a lighted match near the gas tank. The car soon
exploded into flame, illuminating the scene in the primeval light of a
bonfire. By then, there was a flutter of panic around King, as the same
message was coming from all directions: fear was infecting the congregation. People were saying that one destroyed car would never satisfy a
mob that size. Much smaller mobs had burned one bus and beaten two
groups of Freedom Riders that week, and now the congregation was
trapped inside what amounted to an enormous bus without wheels.

Scattered members of the mob darted across the no-man's-land of
Ripley Street to throw rocks at closer range, from church property. Each
of them retreated quickly, but soon the crowd began to inch forward
along the whole line of Ripley Street to the rallying cry "Let's clean the
niggers out of here!" In response, the U.S. marshals ran briskly to positions spread thinly—every twenty feet or so—along the church side of
Ripley Street. They held up their nightsticks in a barrier pose as the two
state detectives ran along the mob line ahead of them, pushing people
back toward the curb. Against thousands of people worked up by hours
of hate-mongering and spurred on by the flaming car, they knew the
armbands and nightsticks were nothing more than a tissue of restraint.
The marshals radioed distress to Byron White, who summoned Chief

U.S. Marshal James McShane after a tense conversation with Robert Kennedy. "Get those marshals in cars and get down there!" White ordered. McShane, a puckish ex-cop who had been rewarded with his present job for campaign work as John Kennedy's bodyguard and chauffeur, roared off for the church with three mail trucks, followed by straggler groups in whatever cars could be grabbed.

Inside the church, they were singing "Love Lifted Me," an old hymn of refuge:

> *Love lifted me.*
> *Love lifted me.*
> *When nothing else could help,*
> *Luuuuuhhhhhve lif—ted meeeeee.*

Chorus after chorus rang out as the marshals fired their first tear gas cannisters into the advancing crowd. Each round offered a few minutes' reprieve while the coughing rioters retreated pell-mell, but then the marshals themselves retreated as an angrier crowd came on again. Rocks began to fly, and one of the marshals went down when a brick hit his shin. Crudely fashioned Molotov cocktails, lobbed toward the church, burned themselves out on the open ground behind them. Byron White, hearing the mounting turmoil on the radio, asked for Robert Kennedy on the open phone line. "It's going to be very close," he said. "Very touch and go."

From the pulpit, Reverend Seay stopped the hymn periodically to exhort the crowd to remain calm. Then he called for another chorus. "I want to hear everybody sing, and mean every word of it!" he shouted, and most of them did. From the outside, the church seemed to lift off the ground in song, but some of the men who had prepared for this moment were slipping out of the pews, reaching for knives, sticks, and pistols in their coat pockets. There were heated whispers in the wings as some of them told the preachers that they were not about to let the mob burn or bludgeon their families without a fight, even in church. Reports of considerable arms within the congregation reached King along with the news that skirmishers from the mob had reached the locked doors of the church. "All right, I'll call him," King said.

Wyatt Walker's sense of protocol, finely honed within the National Baptist Convention, dictated that he, as the number-two man under King, should address Robert Kennedy so that King could be reserved to speak with his parallel officer within the government, the President. Accordingly, Walker placed an emergency call to Robert Kennedy at the Justice Department in his own name, "acting for Dr. King," and when

the Attorney General came on the line Walker told him that only immediate federal action could save their lives.

"I know," said Kennedy. "We are doing everything we can. Is it possible for me to speak with Dr. King?"

Walker surrendered the phone. As King was ticking off the signs of
grave peril—the burned car, the firebombs—Kennedy interrupted. "The
deputy marshals are coming," he said repeatedly. Seeking a point of
identity with King, he recalled hearing stories from his grandfather, John
"Honey Fitz" Fitzgerald, about how anti-Catholic mobs had burned nun-
neries in nineteenth-century Boston.

King excused himself to ask Walker and Abernathy to rush upstairs
with the glad news that Attorney General Kennedy himself promised
help. Then he asked when the help would arrive, and Kennedy, who had
no idea, could only maintain a posture of hopeful government authority.
Soon, he assured King. Very soon. Hearing the hymns being sung in the
background, he changed the subject with the trademark gallows humor
of his family. "As long as you're in church, Reverend King, and our men
are down there, you might as well say a prayer for us," he suggested.

King did not laugh.* He excused himself to receive the latest alarms
from lookouts, who had spotted no rescuers. With defenders brandishing
weapons at points of entry to the church, King addressed Kennedy in a
voice of taut urgency. "If they don't get here immediately, we're going to
have a bloody confrontation," he said. "Because they're at the door now."

Within moments, runners arrived with the news that reinforcements
had been sighted. McShane's men from the mail trucks were waving
nightsticks and pushing their way single file through the mob. King
dashed off to verify and then back to the phone with profuse thanks.
"You were right," he told Kennedy. "They're here."

Massing in front of the church, the new marshals fired an enormous
volley of tear gas that sent the rioters cursing and stumbling backward
in flight. Shouts of joy went up from the congregation, followed by
prayers and a hymn of praise. It was a dramatic rescue straight out of
Hollywood, except that the giant cloud of tear gas drifted slowly back
over the church. Some of Abernathy's deacons were obliged to block
panicky people from fleeing into the hands of the mob, while others
rushed to close windows. The sudden absence of ventilation, combined
with an unusually warm May night and the body heat of fifteen hundred
frightened people, quickly turned First Baptist into an acrid sauna. Outside, the marshals fell prey to the gas too, as few of them had face masks.

---

* "He didn't think that that was very humorous," Kennedy recalled three years
later in an oral history.

They retreated around the corner of the church and down the muddy hill on the Columbus Street side, out of the drifting fumes.

Advance commandos of an enraged, regrouped mob were dashing back across the field as it cleared. The attackers battered against the front doors, and some of the marshals, hearing cries from within that the doors had been breached, gained entry through the back door of the basement. They ran through the clogged corridors in time to push the rioters back outside with nightsticks and shoulders. A new round of tear gas stopped the main body of rioters, but one of them managed to heave a brick through a large stained-glass window, scattering the terrified occupants under a shower of broken glass. The brick hit an old man on the head, and while a corps of nurses materialized to care for him, Reverend Seay's thundering voice labored to contain the pandemonium everywhere else. He asked deacons to take the children to the basement, and he asked everyone who could to lie down on the floor. Rocks shattered smaller windows, and tear gas, pouring through all the holes, literally choked off the hymns. Each round of gas, fired nearer and nearer the church, did less harm to the attackers and more to the defenders themselves. The euphoria of the rescue was reduced to a cruel memory.

Through Cyrus Vance at the Pentagon, Robert Kennedy ordered Army units placed on alert at Fort Benning, Georgia. In the agony of deciding whether to commit them, he maneuvered more diligently than ever to obtain some sign of state consent to the federal presence. He sent messages through Patterson's aides without result. His only friendly communications with a state official were with Floyd Mann, who was nearly crushed by conflicting duties. Mann, having already violated the governor's strict refusal to cooperate with federal officials in protecting the Freedom Riders, did take it upon himself to call Byron White at the Maxwell staging area and request that he "commit any reserves."

"We've committed all we have," White replied. "They are at your disposal." This exchange was interpreted in the Attorney General's office as a breakthrough. Although Mann had not asked for troops on behalf of the governor, he had asked for something, at least, and the significance of his call was magnified with each grave new report from Montgomery. A brick hit a marshal on the head, gashing his forehead. Gunshots were fired into Negro homes on four different streets near the church. A Molotov cocktail bounced off the roof of the church. Tear gas was running low.

When word of a renewed mass charge came to Byron White, he reported almost plaintively that he did not know whether this one could be contained. His tone helped push Robert Kennedy over the edge. "That's it," he said; he would call the President. A legal argument ensued over a technicality concerning the presidential proclamation that was required for the use of the armed forces. They had the proclamation there in the office, but President Kennedy was in Middleburg, out in the horse country of northern Virginia. Would it be legal for them to start the troops moving from Benning to Maxwell before a helicopter could get the proclamation out to Middleburg for the President's signature?

Kennedy hesitated on Marshall's advice. Word soon came that another volley of tear gas was driving back the mob, and during the reprieve came the dramatic news that Governor Patterson had proclaimed a state of martial law. Montgomery policemen were running toward the church in a phalanx, with their commanders shouting "All right, let's move out of here!" Behind them, the first fifteen white-helmeted soldiers of the Alabama National Guard marched double-time with bayoneted rifles. Another hundred came up shortly. The Guardsmen took positions around the front of the church as policemen chased the rioters out of the area. On orders from Byron White, Chief Marshal McShane promptly sought out the colonel in charge of the first Guard unit and placed the federal forces under state command. The colonel ordered the marshals to withdraw from the scene. Elsewhere near the church, Police Commissioner Sullivan made his first appearance of the night. White teenagers pelted his car with bricks.

Inside the church, hosannas went up on the first sighting of the soldiers, who were assumed to be U.S. troops sent in by President Kennedy. Reverend Seay and other speakers came to the pulpit to say that it was truly a historic, divinely blessed night of deliverance when the federal government sent marshals and then soldiers expressly to protect Negro citizens against a white mob. This time the reprieve lasted, and although there remained in the church the broken glass, frayed nerves, overwrought children, and a strong residue of tear gas, these badges of the ordeal only made the congregation more determined to receive what they had come for. After hymns and introductions further bonded them to the Freedom Riders, King began to deliver his main address sometime after ten o'clock.

His prepared speech followed standard King themes of history, love, and injustice, but the crisis prompted him to chastise Governor Patterson for his performance since the Freedom Riders first entered Alabama. "Ultimate responsibility for the hideous action in Alabama last week must be placed at the doorstep of the governor of the state," he declared. "His consistent preaching of defiance of the law, his vitriolic public pronouncements, and his irresponsible actions created the atmosphere in which violence could thrive." This departure from his text was preserved by reporters; others were lost. The general impact upon the congregation was what might be expected from a preacher of King's ability under conditions that seemed drawn from a biblical tale. He and his audience had faced fire, stones, fists, and tear gas for a cause grounded in their beliefs. As midnight approached, some seven hours after the first congregants had arrived, the faces he looked down upon were still wet with perspiration but drained nearly dry of emotion.

In the Attorney General's office at that hour, his judgment perhaps dulled by exhausted relief, Robert Kennedy made what he came to regret as the biggest political miscalculation of the week: he permitted a UPI photographer to take a shot of him in his informal clothes with his feet on the desk, talking on the telephone. The picture would accompany national stories on the Alabama siege and provoke a flood of indignant letters criticizing Kennedy for looking sloppy and undignified on the job. Thereafter he avoided work photographs except when wearing a business suit.

By that time King was plunged once again into despair. The latest shock occurred when the crowd fairly bolted for the doors upon dismissal, only to discover that the troops would not allow them to leave. The National Guard soldiers had their bayonets pointed inward toward the church doors as well as outward toward the departed mob. Although this turn of events completed a certain symmetry in the madness of the night, the congregants were far too tired to appreciate it. To them, their liberators had turned into their guards. All the men protecting them turned out to be under the command of their arch-tormentor, Governor Patterson, and none of the federal men was anywhere in sight. Some who tried to push their way out were repulsed by rifle butts. Some said it was a plot by the state to trap and imprison the Freedom Riders. Some said it was a twist too bitter to be sanctioned by God. There was some cursing and much harsh talk before King went out to parley with the martial law commander, Adjutant General Henry V. Graham.

To all King's pleas that the people locked inside the church desperately needed to go home—to eat, to bathe, to take medicines, to recover, to reassure worried relatives—Graham replied that the situation was too volatile. His news was so bad that King maneuvered to have Graham deliver it himself, and the general eventually marched inside the church at the head of a column of aides, one of whom read Governor Patterson's proclamation of martial law to the congregation. Like all Patterson's public statements, it was relentlessly hostile to their cause.* General Graham followed it with his own announcement that the congregation

---

* "Whereas, as a result of outside agitators coming into Alabama to violate our laws and customs, outbreaks of lawlessness and mob action have occurred. . . . Whereas, the Federal Government has by its actions encouraged these agitators to come into Alabama to foment disorders and breaches of the peace . . . "

would be held in the church "for the time being, probably until morning."

As Graham marched out with his entourage, King rushed downstairs to place another emergency call to Robert Kennedy, who excused himself from a post-midnight interview with a *Time* reporter. "You shouldn't have withdrawn the marshals," King protested, with such force that Kennedy held the phone away from his ear. King's distress spilled over as he said that Kennedy had abandoned his people to the hostilities of Patterson's National Guard, acting now under plenary powers. There might be heart attacks or strokes, with so many people stuffed into the church under such stress. He asked what kind of justice there could be in a land where the authorities permitted churchgoers to be terrorized and then forced them to huddle all night under inhuman conditions. He said he felt betrayed.

Kennedy—weary of being asked to do more, and sensitive about having deferred instantly to Patterson in spite of the governor's record of manifest contempt for the rights of the Freedom Riders—lost his patience. "Now, Reverend," he said. "Don't tell me that. You know just as well as I do that if it hadn't been for the United States marshals, you'd be dead as Kelsey's nuts right now!"

There was a long silence on the telephone. King no doubt puzzled over the meaning of "Kelsey's nuts," an obscure term Kennedy had heard in Boston politics. There was no question about the force of Kennedy's sentiment, however, and King, after swallowing dozens of rejoinders, collapsed in resignation. "All right," he sighed. "All right." He signed off and returned to help Seay organize the most cheerful possible submission. A one-minute rule was established for the hundreds of people lined up to call home over the church's one phone line. Children were to sleep on tables in the basement, and old people received preference on Abernathy's burgundy pew cushions.

Governor Patterson called Kennedy shortly after King hung up, breaking two days of phone silence now that he had been forced to act. "Now you got what you wanted," he said heatedly. "You got yourself a fight. And you've got the National Guard called out, and martial law. And that's what you wanted." He blamed Kennedy for all the violence. Kennedy insisted that he had acted only with reluctance, to prevent violence. During their raging argument, Kennedy managed to ask whether the Negroes would be allowed to leave the stifling church building now that Patterson had everything under control. The governor replied that the National Guard could guarantee the safety of all the Negroes except for King. They could not guarantee King's safety.

"I don't believe that, John," said Kennedy. "Have General Graham call me. I want him to say it to me. I want to hear a general of the United States Army say he can't protect Martin Luther King."

Patterson shrieked into the telephone that Kennedy was missing the point. The issue was not military capability but the public perception that Patterson was giving succor to the most despised name in Alabama. "You are destroying us politically," he said.

"John, it's more important that these people in the church survive physically than for us to survive politically," Kennedy said, clinging to the high ground that he had previously abandoned to King.

Toward dawn, Byron White sent William Orrick to the field headquarters of the National Guard's Dixie Division to seek a truce with General Graham. Ushered into a room full of tension and Confederate flags, Orrick felt as though he were a Russian officer suing for peace. "General, I came over here to negotiate," he said, "and we want to know whether your troops are going to leave that church and let the people go home." Graham replied that this was a matter for the governor to decide, but after Orrick blurted out that he was tired and had to have an answer to prevent a war between federal and state authorities, a compromise was soon reached.

The first groups left the church at four thirty that morning in National Guard trucks. To the irrepressible Shuttlesworth, the lesson of the night was that Alabama had been forced to protect Negroes in the very act of fighting Alabama segregation. Mixing mirth and gall, Shuttlesworth began calling Governor Patterson "Pat" in honor of their new partnership. "When I left the church this morning," he boasted to a congregation later that day, "Pat's soldiers carried me home."

Monday morning found an aching John Seigenthaler home in Washington, ordered to bed for two weeks by his doctors. Other participants in the ongoing siege held positions near telephones, mostly in Montgomery. Elsewhere, millions of people who had spent the May weekend in ordinary activities learned of the conflict down in Alabama through news stories heavily influenced by public relations. Byron White told reporters that the Sunday riot had "not nearly" reached the point at which he would consider the use of U.S. troops. Attorney General Kennedy built a rosy story of federal-state cooperation around Floyd Mann's single phone call for reserves, and *The New York Times* accepted Kennedy's version in a page-one account headlined "Alabama Asks U.S. Help As New Violence Erupts." Governor Patterson, at a triumphant day-after news conference, held up stacks of telegrams running 75-to-1 in favor of his stand against both federal intervention and the Freedom Riders. "Congratulations!" wired a group of Princeton students, and segregationist encouragement flooded the Alabama capital from as far away as California and Canada.

Because the beaming Patterson made no mention that his National Guard units were still dispersing whites loitering around the bus station and still patrolling Negro neighborhoods to guard against bomb throwers, it remained for the iconoclastic Grover Hall to raise these unsettling facts for Montgomery readers. "Patterson started out by saying that he would not nursemaid the agitators and he might arrest the U.S. marshals," Hall wrote in the *Advertiser.* "But before it was over Patterson was baby-sitting the agitators all night in a church and the highway patrol was working in harness with the federal troops." Hall heaped sarcasm upon the governor for making Alabama the only state in the South to have "a problem" with the Freedom Riders. Roy Wilkins, taking a wildly different slant on the same point, told the Negro press that the Freedom Riders did not run into trouble until they arrived in the state where the NAACP was banned.

The Freedom Riders themselves were all secluded in the home of Montgomery pharmacist Richard Harris. King was there, too, along with Wyatt Walker, James Farmer, and Diane Nash. By nightfall, James Bevel and James Lawson arrived from Nashville, the former having aborted his New York furniture-hauling trip. In all, more than twenty people from the major strains of American nonviolent protest were gathered together under one roof in the city of the bus boycott, just across the street from the Dexter parsonage where King had lived for five years. What kept the Freedom Riders publicly muted for the better part of two days was not the arrest warrants or the mobs, nor even the leadership mechanics of a new coalition. Instead, the silence masked a renewed student campaign to have King join them in witness. "Where is your body?" they asked in their standard refrain. Wyatt Walker, Bernard Lee, and others close to King objected that King was too valuable in his present role. He was needed for fund-raising speeches, high-level negotiations, and other functions that could not be done from a bus seat.

Diane Nash called Atlanta almost hourly to consult with Ella Baker, who had left her unhappy tenure at the SCLC to develop a warm and deepening role as confidant to the sit-in students. Baker's interpretation of King's reluctance to join the Freedom Ride was consistently that of a disappointed mother. "Oh, he's just worried about his little group," she said, meaning that King was preoccupied with the image and financial health of the SCLC. Baker said the same thing about Farmer, who was declaring that the ride would continue immediately with five CORE volunteers from New Orleans. The Nashville students knew, however, that no volunteers had arrived yet, and Farmer's references to the Free-dom Ride as "my show" stunned them as empty and parochial. The Nashville students were already there twenty strong, ready to ride, suf-fused with an egalitarian zeal that made fund-raising, posturing, and political calculation cheaply profane to them. Even the mild-mannered John Lewis recoiled from Farmer as pompous and worldly. The Nashville students did not even bother to ask Farmer whether he intended to join the ride.

King was different. Diane Nash, once Ella Baker had coached some of the awe out of her, asked King point-blank to go with them. He would set an example of leadership that might raise the standard of nonviolent commitment everywhere, she said. King replied that he agreed with her. He wanted to go but was not sure, he said. Daddy King and others on the SCLC board had pelted him with caution by then, and his aides, having talked with the lawyers in Atlanta, jumped in with the argument that King was still on probation from his 1960 traffic arrest in Georgia—the sentence that the judge had reimposed on him just before the Kennedy-Nixon election. If arrested now on the Freedom Ride, King faced an additional six months in a Georgia prison, said Walker and the others, and what would the movement gain by having King in jail on a traffic charge?

The students, following Nash, made light of this objection. "I'm on probation, and I'm going," said one. "Me, too," said another. King with-ered visibly under the pressure, as he had done the previous October when the Atlanta students implored him to join the Rich's sit-in. In a final, tortured retreat, he said, "I think I should choose the time and place of my Golgotha." Some of the students recoiled from this naked identification with Christ himself, rather than with Christian mortals. Both King and the students drew back from the unbearable tension of the personal revelation, and King, alone with Walker, said, "I am the one who has to answer for what I do, and I'm not going!"

Walker soon went back to the students, and when the issue welled up again, he cut them off. "Look," he said sharply, "if Dr. King decides he's not going, that's it. He don't have to have no reason." The fire in his eyes stifled all further dissent. So did his abrupt switch to the double negative of street jargon, which Walker used to signal straight talk—all Negro, no polish, no nonsense.

The students generally resented Walker's imperious manner, but they were divided on King. Among the young preachers, James Bevel sup-ported King's decision on the grounds that he could carry the message of the Freedom Ride to tens of thousands around the country. He cautioned his fellow students against making badges of their commitment. Paul

Brooks, who had been arrested outside Birmingham on the first bus of Nashville reinforcements, said he wished King had simply acknowledged his fear. "I would have respected him more," Brooks confided. John Lewis bridled at any overt criticism of King, but even he found himself defensively repeating Lawson's teaching that in nonviolence you do not badger people or force them beyond their commitment. He was looking gently but painfully back on King, patronizing the man he revered.

These nicks and bruises were tucked out of sight when they all left Dr. Harris' house on Tuesday afternoon to face a press conference. There was still martial law in Montgomery, with a thousand helmeted Guardsmen on the streets, and a large contingent of the nation's press corps was assembled there to find out whether the Negroes would press the battle. Farmer, Abernathy, and Lewis made brief statements before King read a joint declaration that the ride would go on through the heart of Mississippi, martial law or not, protection or no protection. This was dramatic enough, but then King put the prepared text aside. "Freedom Riders must develop the quiet courage of dying for a cause," he said, chocking back the emotions that had torn at him in the private debates. "We would not like to see anyone die. . . . We all love life, and there are no martyrs here —but we are well aware that we may have some casualties. . . . I'm sure these students are willing to face death if necessary."

At about midnight during the Sunday siege in Abernathy's church, Robert Kennedy had passed along to his brother a complaint from Assistant Attorney General Orrick about the sluggish performance of FBI agents in Montgomery. President Kennedy, finally given an opportunity to do something other than sign the dreaded troop proclamation, had relayed the complaint to FBI Director Hoover that same hour, and within minutes the Montgomery SAC had appeared in front of Orrick at Maxwell Air Force Base, pledging eager cooperation and begging Orrick not to criticize the Bureau again.

On the Monday morning after he had received the presidential nudge, Hoover ordered up an instant report—on King, whom he perceived to be the proximate cause of the Montgomery crisis. The sketchy document rushed to his desk that same day was a jumble of obscure suspicions. It noted that King had thanked Ben Davis, the Communist ex-city councilman from New York, for donating blood to him when King was stabbed in 1958. It recorded correctly that King had delivered the closing speech at Highlander Folk School in 1957, but branded Highlander a "Communist Party training school." In language, detail, obsession with communism, and pervasive enmity toward King, the FBI report strongly resembled a report produced a year earlier for Bull Connor by Detective Tom Cook, Connor's Klan-connected security chief. Scanning the FBI document, Hoover learned that the Bureau had not fully investigated King, and he scrawled a commanding "Why not?" in the margin.

Hoover's agents arrested four men that Monday morning for burning the Greyhound bus in Anniston. After Orrick's complaint, they were working diligently to secure affidavits in support of Judge Johnson's injunction. These were valuable functions, for which the FBI was indispensable, but the top officials of the Kennedy Justice Department sensed enough of Hoover's attitudes to know that he would resist any new assignment in the emergency. In particular, if the Freedom Riders continued on from Montgomery, he would dig in against having his men protect them directly, as the U.S. marshals were doing. Hoover's stated reason was that the FBI could not be objective in its investigative role if associated with the Freedom Riders. His deeper reason was that the FBI was an intelligence agency, like the CIA, and did not perform menial "guard duty" even for the President, much less Negro rabble-rousers.

That left the marshals to protect the Freedom Riders, but Robert Kennedy was reconsidering that idea even before Byron White flew back to Washington for emergency consultations. He decided they were too poorly trained and organized to be effective against determined rioters; also, their presence handed Patterson and other Southern governors a popular cry of resistance. The nightmarish experience in Montgomery left Byron White worrying about how to withdraw the marshals, not how to use them again, and Burke Marshall was saying that while the federal government could not contemplate establishing a permanent force to protect all interstate bus passengers, neither could it protect some and not others. In review, therefore, Kennedy's first move was to rule out the use of White's marshals or the Army on the journey to Mississippi. He would rely on the states. This was a most "difficult decision," Marshall recalled. Robert Kennedy met with the President for forty-five minutes on Monday, agonizing over his decision not to defend the Freedom Riders even as King was agonizing over his decision not to join them.

Kennedy then faced the seemingly impossible task of inducing the Alabama and Mississippi authorities to perform police duties they had resolutely spurned—and to do so without being able to make credible threats of using federal marshals to fill the breach. Needing extraordinary, novel tactics, he developed during dozens of conversations with them a critical distinction between force and violence. In effect, Kennedy agreed to let state officials defend segregation by making forcible, unconstitutional arrests of the Freedom Riders so long as those officials did not let mobs accomplish the same purpose by violence. Byron White gave public support to the deal on Monday by telling reporters that the United States would stand aside if the Freedom Riders went to jail. "That would be a matter between the Freedom Riders and local officials," he said. "I'm sure they would be represented by competent counsel." Years later, in a confidential oral history, Kennedy remained uncomfortable about the arrangement. "So I, in fact, I suppose, concurred [in] the fact that they were going to be arrested," he said, "though I didn't have any control over it."

All that Tuesday night, the Alabama and Mississippi authorities worked themselves into a state of feverish cooperation with Kennedy in devising for the Freedom Riders' bus an armed escort worthy of a NATO war game. Kennedy wanted a display of power that would serve to intimidate ambushers reportedly gathered along the 258-mile highway between Montgomery and Jackson, Mississippi, the designated arrest point. The state officials, once they agreed to forestall violence, wanted to stage an extravagant show in order to advertise that interracial travelers could not survive with anything less. By midnight, Mississippi governor Ross Barnett was so enthusiastic about the cooperative arrangement that he jokingly invited Byron White to ride in the escorted bus over to Jackson and have dinner with him. "You'll have the nicest ride," Barnett chortled over the phone to White. "You'll be just as safe as you were in your baby crib."

The Freedom Riders themselves did not know of these plans. For them, Tuesday was a night of tension, exhortation, and occasional celebration. A carload of Nashville reinforcements arrived, as did some of the CORE recruits from New Orleans. Later that night, a group of sit-in veterans came in all the way from Washington, D.C., where the original Freedom Ride had begun nineteen days earlier. This group included Howard University students John Moody, William Mahoney, and Stokely Carmichael, along with a white divinity student named Paul Dietrich. They all piled into Dr. Harris' house, where the central topic of debate was whether they would make it out of the Montgomery bus station. Since the Saturday riot, mobs had reappeared periodically on rumors of encountering the Freedom Riders again. Some of the students wrote personal testaments and notification lists, while others deposited their valuables with those staying behind. Paul Dietrich entrusted his imperial jade ring to James Farmer, who had decided not to go.

When the Freedom Riders left the house at dawn, an Alabama National Guard jeep appeared to escort their cars. At the bus station, more than one hundred Guardsmen held small clumps of bystanders at bay some distance from the terminal building. These were the first welcome signs of protection, but they were taken for nothing more than a signal that the authorities had decided not to permit a repeat of the Saturday riot. Abernathy, Walker, King, and King's brother A.D., who had come in from Atlanta, all marched with the riders into the whites' waiting room and ordered coffee or snacks from the lunch counter. The bus station manager told reporters flocking in behind that they were the first Negroes ever to receive service. Even these small acts, though recently sanctioned by the federal courts, were illegal under the criminal statutes of Alabama. As such they made King subject to rearrest for violating the conditions of his probation in Georgia, but King was determined to share at least a small part of the day's risk. He followed the group outside to the Trailways loading platform, where they were surprised to find the seven o'clock bus to Jackson empty of other passengers. Soldiers were refusing entry to anyone except Freedom Riders and newsmen with credentials. There were sixteen reporters aboard. In the end, only twelve Freedom Riders stepped forward, nearly all from Nashville. They chose their mentor in nonviolence, James Lawson, as group leader for the trip.

Suddenly, behind the dozen Freedom Riders, came an equal number of National Guard soldiers in full battle dress, carrying bayoneted rifles, and behind them came their commander, General Graham. Addressing the Freedom Riders from the front of the bus, he seemed radically different from the stern antagonist who had marched into First Baptist Church. "This may be a hazardous journey," Graham said softly. "We have taken every precaution to protect you. And I sincerely wish you all a safe journey." As he stepped off the bus, several of the students thanked him emotionally for the whiff of reconciliation. Outside, just before the bus pulled out at 7:06 A.M., King reached up to an open window and shook the hand of Paul Dietrich to wish him good luck.

A squadron of motorcycle policemen helped the bus push its way through the congestion around the station. The policemen dropped off at the city limits to leave the bus in the midst of an extraordinary procession numbering some forty-two vehicles—mostly highway patrol cars, their sirens wailing, with several dozen more reporters bringing up the rear. Supplementing the main convoy were FBI spotter cars at strategic checkpoints, helicopter escorts, and U.S. Border Patrol airplanes in high-altitude reconnaissance—providing reports to Attorney General Kennedy's office via Byron White's staging area back in Montgomery. After the procession hurtled past the first scheduled stop, at Selma, the Guard commander on board revealed that all intermediate stops had been canceled. There would be no terminals, no snack bars, no rest rooms during the entire seven-hour trip to Jackson.

The caravan maintained speeds of nearly seventy miles per hour except for two brief delays. When fear and indigestion made a Freedom Rider violently ill, vigilant Guardsmen formed a tight circle around him while he vomited on the side of the highway. The second stop occurred at the border town of Scratch Hill, Alabama, where the crest of a hill brought into view a long line of Mississippi Guardsmen and state police units, poised to take over. The Mississippi escort was even longer than Alabama's. As the Scratch Hill transfer was being made, a distraught James Lawson jumped from the bus to hold an impromptu press conference with the milling reporters. He protested that the enormous military escort was contrary to the Freedom Riders' entire philosophy. It was unnecessary, he told the reporters, many of whom, terrified themselves by news tips of dynamite ambushes ahead in Mississippi, thought Lawson was out of his mind. "We would rather risk violence and be able to travel like ordinary passengers," Lawson added. ". . . We will accept the violence and the hate, absorb it without returning it."

By then it was late morning, and a second group of fourteen Freedom Riders had bought tickets for the 11:25 Greyhound out of Montgomery. Among them were two CORE students from New Orleans, Jerome Smith and Doris Castle, and Henry Thomas, a veteran of the Anniston bus-burning ten days earlier, who had returned for a second ride. Group leader Lucretia Collins, a Nashville student who had been with the ride since Birmingham, conducted nonviolence workshops en route.

News of this second busload came as a seismic shock to Robert Kennedy. All the cajoling and commandeering for the two-state armored caravan had been predicated on the assurance that they would have to pull it off only once. Instead, the fragile trust of the Alabama and Mississippi authorities was shattered again. Their motivation for cooperating with Kennedy, in what they regarded as a compromise of segregationist principle, was to end the crisis in a way that discouraged further bus riders. With new riders at the station even before the Alabama fleet returned to Montgomery, they felt betrayed, ridiculous. Kennedy himself, scrambling madly to keep the agreement patched together this one more time, was angry enough to issue his first formal statement. His aides in Washington told reporters that this second busload had "nothing to do with the Freedom Riders."

Kennedy's statement moved toward the position of the Alabama and Mississippi authorities. He complimented them for maintaining order so far and then made public to integrationists everywhere his warning that there would be no federal protection. "The leaders of the student groups testing segregation laws," he announced, ". . . today were informed that no Federal marshals would accompany them." The focal point of Kennedy's appeal for normalcy was his brother's imminent trip to Europe for talks with Charles de Gaulle and Nikita Khrushchev. President Kennedy was about to ask Congress to put an American on the moon and to boost U.S. spending on nuclear weapons—partly to bolster his strength for the summit meeting—and in this charged context, continuing international publicity about ugly race riots in the South would send the leader of the free world into European palaces with mud on his shoes. "I think we should all keep in mind that the President is about to embark on a mission of great importance," the Attorney General concluded. "Whatever we do in the United States at this time which brings or causes discredit on our country can be harmful to his mission."

From his office, Kennedy monitored the progress of the first bus into Mississippi. Byron White, James McShane, Kennedy aide Joe Dolan, Burke Marshall, and FBI assistant director Al Rosen reported almost continuously from scattered posts. They exchanged rumors—Martin Luther King reported leaving Montgomery for Atlanta on Eastern Airlines at 2:25 P.M., then reported to have postponed until the next day, twenty-five cars waiting in apparent ambush, a man with a homemade bomb in Jackson—and reports on the size of the waiting crowds at various bus stations. The crowd at Meridian was so angry-looking and the police so uncooperative that Kennedy ordered the convoy to bypass the city altogether.

In Montgomery, James Farmer picked at an early lunch in the bus terminal, with the fourteen Freedom Riders sitting near him and fully armed Alabama soldiers standing guard just behind. The Attorney General's public warning that there would be no federal marshals registered fully upon them, as did the noise outside from a hostile crowd that had swelled to upwards of two thousand people. Battalions of National Guardsmen were holding them back, but portents of the journey ahead further weakened the knees of the Freedom Riders as Farmer escorted them to the Greyhound. When they boarded, Farmer walked down the length of the bus on the outside, shaking hands through the windows as King had done earlier. Doris Castle of New Orleans, a college student of nineteen who looked much younger, took Farmer's hand with a look of puzzlement on her face.

"My prayers are with you, Doris," said Farmer.

She stifled her alarm enough to cry out in a whisper, "You're coming with us, aren't you, Jim?"

Farmer told her all the things he had been telling himself—about how he had been away from the office for four weeks, and the mail was stacked high, and how somebody had to go out and find the money to keep the buses rolling—but even as he did so he sensed that his own booming voice was vacant of heart, and it seemed to him that Castle's eyes dilated into enormous globes of doelike terror. Farmer broke away from her look in a rage. "Get my luggage!" he shouted at a newly arrived CORE retainer standing by his car. "Put it on the bus! I'm going." Somehow he remembered to give Paul Dietrich's ring to Wyatt Walker before he jumped on the bus. With soldiers ordered aboard and reporters joining them, and with reserve helicopters moving into formation at the last minute, the second caravan took off down the highway some four hours after the first.

The departure did not end the day's dramatics at the bus station, however, nor its rude surprises for Robert Kennedy. Before the Montgomery crowd could disperse, rumors ran through it that a bus was approaching the city from the east with an interracial team of riders who had been testing facilities at all the little towns on the way in from Atlanta. Not far behind the rumors came another Greyhound, and from it stepped a group of men in the telltale manner—wearing expressions of worn nerves, huddling together, looking rather lost. There were two professors of Religion from Wesleyan University in Connecticut, two clergymen from Yale (including university chaplain William Sloane Coffin, Jr.), and three Negro students, including Charles Jones of SNCC. Wyatt Walker and Fred Shuttlesworth greeted them, and the sight of the nine men trapped there seemed to destroy the tolerance of the crowd, who for twenty minutes lobbed rocks and other missiles over the restraining lines of soldiers. Finally, two cars pushed their way into a space cleared by the National Guard units. Abernathy jumped from one of them and shepherded the men inside. One of the reporters who converged upon the cars shouted questions to them about the Attorney General's statement, which was being read on the radio, that the Freedom Ride should be stopped because it was embarrassing the United States before the Khrushchev summit meeting. Abernathy, leaning out his car window, replied, "Well, doesn't the Attorney General know we've been embarrassed all our lives?" Bystanders shook their heads in disbelief at the sight of Alabama troopers escorting yet another mixed group, this time right into town. "That's a damn shame," one of them declared.

Farmer's group was heading into Jackson, Mississippi, behind Lawson's, which had been hauled out of the whites-only rest rooms of the Jackson bus terminal and off to the city jail. The Coffin group was meeting with King at Abernathy's house in Montgomery, deciding whether to press on toward Jackson, too, and Burke Marshall was receiving alarming intelligence of new student groups forming all over the South to go in behind them. To Kennedy, the Coffin group represented a distressing change in the composition of the protesters. No longer confined to Quakers, kooks, students, pacifists, or even Negro Gandhians, the ranks of the Freedom Riders suddenly included prominent Ivy League professors. With the crisis stretching endlessly ahead, an angry Robert Kennedy released his second press statement of the day, which was designed to head off the favorable publicity such people might attract. "Besides the groups of Freedom Riders traveling through these states, there are curiosity seekers, publicity seekers and others who are seeking to serve their own causes," Kennedy declared. "A cooling-off period is needed," he added, warning riders to "delay their trips." Governor Patterson praised the statement as "the first time the federal government has displayed any common sense in some days."

Kennedy grew even angrier over the next few hours. As Farmer's group was joining Lawson's in the Jackson city jail, he learned that all twenty-seven of the Freedom Riders were refusing bail and were planning to stay in jail after conviction rather than pay fines or secure appeal bonds. When Burke Marshall and Byron White failed to obtain satisfactory explanations, Kennedy called King that night, demanding to know why the Freedom Riders would not accept bail.

"It's a matter of conscience and morality," said King, more formal under attack. "They must use their lives and their bodies to right a wrong. Our conscience tells us that the law is wrong and we must resist, but we have a moral obligation to accept the penalty."

"That is not going to have the slightest effect on what the government is doing in this field or any other," Kennedy snapped. "The fact that they stay in jail is not going to have the slightest effect on me."

"Perhaps it would help if students came down here by the hundreds—by the hundreds of thousands," said King.

"The country belongs to you as much as to me," said Kennedy. "You can determine what's best just as well as I can, but don't make statements that sound like a threat. That's not the way to deal with us."

King pulled back instinctively, fearing that his leverage on Kennedy was backfiring. "I'm deeply appreciative of what the Administration is doing," he said. Then, despairing of argument, he collapsed into a preacher's cry: "I see a ray of hope, but I am different than my father. I feel the need of being free now!"

Kennedy let it pass. "Well, it all depends on what you and the people in jail decide," he said wearily. "If they want to get out, we can get them out."

"They'll stay," said King, and there was nothing more to say.

Kennedy called Harris Wofford to vent his anger against the Freedom Riders in jail. "This is too much," he said. "I wonder whether they have the best interest of their country at heart. Do you know that one of them is against the atom bomb?" Wofford mumbled a soothing reply. His known sympathies for civil disobedience had all but excluded him from the phone loop during the Administration's first crisis in his field of duty.

In Montgomery, King returned to Abernathy's living room after his jolting conversation with Kennedy. "You know," he said, "they don't understand the social revolution going on in the world, and therefore they don't understand what we're doing." His report did nothing to dispel the gloom hanging over William Sloane Coffin and six other new Freedom Riders. Aside from fear, some of them were upset by Robert Kennedy's suggestion that their mission was unpatriotic, that it would weaken the President at the very moment he was trying to negotiate world peace with the Soviet Union. These were sobering, intimidating thoughts for people who were accustomed to life on the campus. "We're really just faced with a simple issue," said King. "Do you want to go on?" He led them all in a prayer for guidance. Some wept openly under the crush of fear and conflicting loyalties, and in the end they passed out slips of paper to vote by secret ballot. When the tally came up unanimous in favor of going on—rejecting the Attorney General's advice—there was much hugging and rejoicing as they steeled themselves for the trip to the bus station.

Abernathy, Walker, Shuttlesworth, and Bernard Lee accompanied them for what turned out to be a short journey. While they were sitting at the lunch counter, surrounded by Guardsmen during their pre-trip integrated meal, Sheriff Mack Sim Butler walked behind their stools and counted off all eleven of them for arrest. The sheriff later stated that he had exhausted his forbearance protecting the original Freedom Riders. "I was so furious," he said, "because I thought if I finally got that first bunch of roughnecks out, it would be all over!"

Attorney General Kennedy pulled five hundred of the six hundred federal marshals out of Montgomery that afternoon. To trusted reporters, he made public some of the complaints he had been making privately to King—attacking the wisdom, the motivation, and even the physical courage of the new Freedom Riders. "It took a lot of guts for the first group to go," he told The Washington Post, "but not much for the others." Lashing out, he called the Freedom Riders "the safest people in America" and derided their decision to remain in jail as "good propaganda for America's enemies." The Attorney General, summarized the Post, "does not feel that the Department of Justice can, at these times, side with one group or the other in disputes over constitutional rights." Gone, only eighteen days after his speech at the University of Georgia, were the grand words about how the department would move swiftly to enforce federal court decisions guaranteeing the constitutional rights of Negroes.

Kennedy's anger failed to dampen enthusiasm at CORE headquarters in New York. On the day after Farmer's arrest in Jackson, a CORE spokesman announced that contributions were pouring in through the mail and that more than a hundred people had volunteered to take up the ride. "We believe we can end segregation by the end of this year," he told reporters.

In the education building at Ebenezer, King presided over the founding meeting of the Freedom Ride Coordinating Committee. Gordon Carey of CORE represented Farmer, who remained in the Jackson jail. Two Nashville preachers represented Bevel and Lawson, who were with Farmer, and an SCLC assistant sat in for Wyatt Walker, who was in the Montgomery jail. With a SNCC representative and an officer of the National Student Association, these six people pledged to "intensify" the Freedom Ride until bus segregation crumbled across the South. They planned to open recruiting offices in four Southern cities. They would raise money to pay for bus tickets and lawyers. They would request an audience with President Kennedy. They would seek a "strong ruling from the Attorney General in clearly establishing the rights of interstate travelers (possibly) through an order to the Interstate Commerce Commission." They would "fill jails in Montgomery and Jackson in order to keep a sharp image of the issues before the public."

That was on Friday, May 26, three weeks after the original CORE Freedom Riders had left Washington in utter obscurity. After an odyssey that had changed many lives and come to the attention of millions, they were allied formally with the heirs of the Montgomery bus boycott and the student sit-ins, maneuvering along a collision course with the federal government as well as the Southern states.

Then the Freedom Rides dropped precipitously and permanently from the headlines. The idea seemed to spread by osmosis that the South's best course, under the truce with the Justice Department, was to defend segregation quietly, under the color of law. Accordingly, the new Freedom Riders came to be funneled efficiently, almost protectively, into the Mississippi prison system. Their fate receded as an old story.

As the second wave of riders reached Mississippi, President Kennedy delivered an extraordinary second 1961 State of the Union address to a joint session of Congress. "I am here to promote the freedom doctrine," he declared on May 25. "The great battleground for the defense and expansion of freedom today is the whole southern half of the globe— Asia, Latin America, Africa, and the Middle East, the lands of the rising peoples. Their revolution is the greatest in human history. They seek an end to injustice, tyranny, and exploitation." But the President's address never mentioned racial injustice at home, let alone the Freedom Rides. He asked Congress for nearly $2 billion to "almost double the combat power of the Army" and to begin the race to the moon. Just after a contentious summit meeting with Khrushchev in Vienna, Kennedy had tripled draft calls and sought from Congress another $3.2 billion for weapons and fallout shelters. In short, he had moved the country toward a war footing over the disputed territory of Berlin, and in such a mood he was less inclined than ever to recognize the distracting problem of the Freedom Riders. At his press conference late in June, when the number of jailed Freedom Riders was approaching two hundred, the President volunteered nothing on the subject. Nor was he questioned about it.

Public opinion leaders seemed only too eager to oblige the President by disengaging from the strife down in Mississippi. *The New York Times*, which gave King and the civil rights movement generally sympathetic coverage, opposed the extension of the ride. "They are challenging not only long-held customs but passionately held feelings," the paper declared. "Non-violence that deliberately provokes violence is a logical contradiction." A news story that same day, headlined "Dr. King Refuses to End Bus Test," cast the issue in a most negative light. "Some liberal Southerners of both races joined moderates and others today in asserting that the Freedom Riders should be halted," it began, consigning the renewed campaign to the far fringes of public support. This was the last page-one story on the Freedom Rides to appear in the *Times*. A Gallup poll in June showed that 63 percent of all Americans disapproved of the Freedom Rides.

Robert Kennedy, having denounced both King and the Freedom Rides in the most scathing terms on Thursday and Friday, arrived at the Justice Department on Monday morning, May 29, in an entirely different mood. He announced to his staff that King's suggestion of seeking a ruling from the Interstate Commerce Commission might not be so naïve after all, in spite of that agency's notoriously encrusted bureaucracy. In fact, the idea seemed so good upon reconsideration that Kennedy sent Justice Department lawyers scrambling into unfamiliar territory. They came up with the novel idea of a "petition" by the Attorney General to the nominally independent ICC. They researched, drafted, and cleared the document for Kennedy's signature—all on that same day. Justice teams gave ICC commissioners and assorted bureaucrats no peace until they issued the ruling Kennedy wanted, handed down that September. In so doing, they had telescoped a process that normally took years—even if the commissioners liked the proposal, which in this case they did not—into less than four months. Experts considered the lobbying feat a bureaucratic miracle.

The difference, after the early Freedom Rides, was that Justice Department officials pursued the private strategy with a vengeance. They im-

mediately stepped up efforts to create a well-financed, tax-exempt organization to register Negro voters in the South. On the tax side, the clandestine pursuit resembled the campaign to secure tax benefits for those
who helped ransom the Bay of Pigs prisoners. Kennedy himself intervened with IRS Commissioner Mortimer Caplan to help secure a tax
exemption for the new Voter Education Project, housed in Atlanta's
Southern Regional Council. When that organization's director, Leslie
Dunbar, went to the IRS to negotiate for his exemption, Burke Marshall
and other Kennedy officials went with him.

Marshall, Harris Wofford, and foundation executive Stephen Currier
worked simultaneously to bring the various civil rights groups under
uniform rules and a central budget. This task had been delicate enough
earlier in the spring, given the touchy history between Roy Wilkins and
King, but now the complications rose geometrically with the addition of
CORE and the SNCC students. Logically, neither organization seemed
promising for registration work. CORE had few members in the South;
SNCC was not really an organization, having only one full-time staff
member. Both organizations were deeply engrossed in the Freedom
Rides. None of these objections mattered to the Justice Department,
however. CORE and SNCC must be recruited, whatever it took, because
one of Kennedy's goals was to coax them out of precisely the kind of
confrontational actions around which they were shaping their identities.

In early June, Marshall attended a small conference that included several of the SNCC and CORE leaders not in Mississippi jails. At the
Capahosic, Virginia, plantation once owned by Booker T. Washington's
successor, R. R. Moton, Marshall sat under a live oak tree on the banks
of the York River and made the case for voter registration. His most
receptive listener among the students was Timothy Jenkins, who was
bound for Yale Law School in the fall. Jenkins was deeply critical of what
he called the "pain and suffering school" within SNCC. He did not share
their religious zeal, and he thought direct action was a dead end. Whenever the zeal died out, he predicted, the movement would be left with no
political protection, and to Jenkins all such protections were grounded in
the vote. He believed this so strongly that he had already set out to win
over three people he thought could swing the balance of power within
SNCC. The "three Charlies," he called them: Sherrod, Jones, and
McDew. There were not three more dissimilar people in the SNCC leadership—Sherrod the country mystic, deeply religious with a stubborn
streak; Jones the sophisticated dandy, son of a prominent Southern
preacher, with his fancy clothes and a modulated baritone, a junior version of King; and McDew the Northern athlete, daring and "cool," with
a subtle appreciation of both labor history and Jewish prophets. To Jen-

kins, it was immensely hopeful that the same movement could attract
three such people, and it was even more hopeful that they came to see
the merits of voter registration after many all-night discussions.

On June 16, Attorney General Kennedy received in his office a delegation from the Freedom Ride Coordinating Committee. It included the
"three Charlies," plus Wyatt Walker, who had bailed out of the Montgomery jail, and Diane Nash, whom Jenkins had written off as "addled
by piety" and "hopelessly committed" to nonviolence. They all hoped to
secure some additional federal help for the Freedom Rides, but what they
received instead was a counterpoint from the Attorney General. The
Freedom Rides were no longer productive, he said. The committee members could accomplish more for civil rights by registering Negro voters,
and if they would agree to move in that direction he would do everything
he could to make sure they were fully supported and protected. He mentioned the confidential work already under way to secure a tax exemption and large foundation grants.

This was too blunt for Charles Sherrod, who was on his feet, nervous
but angry, sputtering indignantly against what he regarded as a bribe to
lure him from righteous work. "You are a public official, sir," he said.
"It's not your responsibility before God or under the law to tell us how
to honor our constitutional rights. It's your job to protect us when we
do." Sherrod moved toward the Attorney General as he began preaching,
and Wyatt Walker, fearing that he might attack Kennedy in the frenzy of
his sermon, pulled him back toward his seat by the pocket of his pants.
When the tension passed, Kennedy resumed his argument, pacing stocking-footed. By educating and registering Negro voters, he said, they might
not make immediate headlines but they could alter the politics of the
South.

Kennedy and his aides pressed their points then and later. They went
so far as to extend confidential promises that the Administration would
arrange draft exemptions for the students—so long as they confined
themselves to quiet political work. Harris Wofford put the choice to
them most graphically: they could have jails filled with Freedom Riders,
or jails filled with white Southern officials who tried to obstruct federally
protected voting rights. They could be persecuted or protected. To those
who expressed interest in voter registration went phone numbers for
Burke Marshall or John Doar, along with assurances that they could call
the Justice Department collect anytime they got in trouble down South.

These arguments proved to be telling. They were made at a time when
Robert Kennedy was being credited by Negro leaders for forceful inter-
vention in the early Freedom Ride, when Shuttlesworth was telling
Negro church crowds about the progress made already under the Ken-

nedy Administration, shouting "We thank Jack, Bob, and God!" And even to those aware of Kennedy's abrasive criticisms, or those suspicious of his political motives, the Attorney General was appreciated for his combative involvement. He did not stand aloof, and he seemed to feel that if he shortchanged the civil rights groups in one way, he needed to compensate them in another.

On his wedding anniversary, Kennedy invited Harry Belafonte out to his Hickory Hill home and asked him once again to use his considerable influence among the SNCC students to encourage voter registration. Belafonte promptly invited a delegation of Freedom Riders to visit him in Washington, where he was performing. On the eve of the latter meeting, Kennedy and Marshall advertised their ability to make things happen by generating a front-page article in *The New York Times*, "Negro Vote Surge Expected in South—Administration Experts Sure of a Political Breakthrough." In effect, the article summarized Kennedy's side of the private arguments. "The Rev. Dr. Martin Luther King, Jr. and other leaders of the new militant movements—the sit-ins and the Freedom Riders —have come around to agree that the vote is the key," it said. ". . . Confidence that the Government will do its best to protect those who try to register and vote also encourages Negroes to make the attempt." Belafonte encouraged the students to dismiss as politics the article's suggestion that "Negro apathy" and a bad "attitude" among Negro leaders had held back the voting revolution in the past. In the end, the students said they would be willing to convene the Freedom Riders to propose the voter registration plan. Belafonte gave them $10,000 of his own money to get started.

Kennedy allowed no doubts to grow. By the end of July, the heads of all the major civil rights organizations were interested enough to attend an all-day meeting in New York, with Wofford and Burke Marshall representing the Administration. Farmer, just out of jail in Mississippi, had to be convinced that he was not abandoning CORE's entire purpose at its moment of glory. Roy Wilkins had to be convinced that the NAACP would not appear to be abandoning its banner of school desegregation. These were among the least of the problems. Nevertheless, a month later these same people were back in the Fifth Avenue offices of the Taconic Foundation, this time with "working papers." They divided the territory of the South and resolved acute differences over the proportional allocation of funds. They recruited the Field Foundation and the Stern Fund to supplement the Taconic Foundation's money. They searched for administrators and conduits who were acceptable to all the various grantees, grantors, and intermediaries. They hammered out a hundred compromises. Within another month, foundation executives translated the deals into fuzzy language, and lawyers checked organizational flow charts against the tax code.*

The Voter Education Project was created essentially by a forced march in the opposite direction from the Freedom Rides, in spirit if not in purpose. To accomplish the march that same summer of 1961, with the Freedom Rides still going on, was a tribute to the willfulness of the Kennedy Justice Department and a feat even more impressive than the bus order wrenched from the Interstate Commerce Commission. Both deeds had far-reaching implications for Southern politics. Insiders soon argued that these machinations were the significant events of the entire period, and dialectical disputes reminiscent of the Montgomery bus boycott arose as to whether the essential ingredient of progress was law or confrontation, reason or shock, decrees or changes of spirit.

Down in Mississippi, a very different transformation was taking place among the Freedom Riders. For some of the prisoners, survival was a letdown. Having absorbed so many mob beatings, or stories of them, and having passed so many angry crowds and imaginary ambushes, the Freedom Riders hyperventilated with religious fervor, in a sense, so that a few of them seemed to collapse of disappointment when they passed unscathed into custody. Others tore anxiously at their hair. All of them, once they recovered in the lower-floor cell block of the Hinds County jail, began to sing. Hank Thomas led them in "We Shall Overcome," so loudly that the female prisoners across the way took up the same song. They ran through the repertory of movement songs, and when the singing finally died down into conversation between the cells, James Bevel could be heard preaching out loud from Acts 16, about how God sent an earthquake to shake open the foundations of the jail holding Paul and Silas in Philippi, and how He would send a similar earthquake to Jackson, Mississippi, within two days to liberate the Freedom Riders.

Bevel preached lyrically and almost continuously, leaving those within earshot alternately inspired, amused, and worried over his growing expectation of a divine jailbreak. When the deadline passed and Bevel seemed to fall into despondency, James Farmer and others feared that he might be cracking up. Most of the Freedom Riders did not know Bevel well, and those who did, like his fellow seminarians John Lewis and

---

* The Southern Regional Council went so far as to assert that its interest in the political revolution was wholly academic, in keeping with its tax-exempt charter. It would administer the project "in order that, by empirical evaluation of the results accruing from the programs which you will carry on with funds allocated under the grant, SRC can subsequently draw publishable conclusions."

Bernard Lafayette, knew that he lived on the wispy edge between religious genius and lunacy. As it happened, a trusty left Bevel's cell without fully locking the sliding steel door, and Bevel, seeing his chance, asked Lafayette to pray again for a sign that their cause would prevail. During the prayer, Bevel slipped quietly out of his cell to stand in front of Lafayette's, and Lafayette, opening his eyes to this vision of freedom, shrieked in terror and dived headlong under his bunk. Bevel rejailed himself, laughing uproariously. He and Lafayette explained the shrieks and fits with various versions of the story, leaving their fellows in other parts of the cell block uncertain of their ballast. There was no question, however, that Bevel had moments of lucid practicality. When the jailers cut off cigarettes and snacks to the Freedom Riders because of their loud singing, he devised a clandestine exchange system with other parts of the jail.

Other prisoners revealed themselves to be variously meek, truculent, stolid, or hysterical in adapting to jail life. Some pledged grandly to stay "until hell freezes over" but then bailed out after a few days behind bars. Those behind remained roughly two-thirds college students, three-quarters male, and more than half Negro, with Quakers and Jews, including several rabbis, represented disproportionately among the whites. James Lawson, whose experience a decade earlier made him the recognized expert on prison culture, gave them advice about how to get along with the thieves and drunkards in the jail, and warned them against getting too attached to anything except their own inner strengths, because all their routines were beyond their control. Very soon, jail authorities sorely tested them by transferring most of the Freedom Riders to the Hinds County prison farm, out in the country. There the young prisoners were crammed by the dozen into thirteen-by-fifteen-foot cells with stopped-up toilets. The food was bug-ridden. For their singing they were stuffed into claustrophobic "sweatboxes." Their only consolation was that there were not nearly boxes to hold all the singers at once.

Shortly after midnight on June 15—the day before their representatives were meeting with Attorney General Kennedy worlds away in Washington—guards herded forty-five of the male prisoners from their cells into closed truck trailers. The trucks lurched out of Jackson with the prisoners sealed in darkness. When finally they tumbled out blinking into the dawn light, they found themselves standing beneath an observation tower just inside the barbed-wire gate of an enormous compound, surrounded by guards with shotguns. The warden welcomed them to Parchman Penitentiary. "We have bad niggers here," he warned. "Niggers on death row that'll beat you up and cut you as soon as look at you." He ordered them to follow him in a line of march to a cement-block processing building.

As they moved out, the guards discovered two young white men from

Chicago still lying in the back of a truck. "We refuse to cooperate, because we've been unjustly imprisoned," said Terry Sullivan, in a speech that Lawson and the others had counseled him to shelve. The guards dumped the two Chicagoans out of the truck and dragged them by their feet through mud and grass and across concrete into the receiving room, where the prisoners were ordered to take off their clothes. When the two of them still did not move, guards shocked them with cattle prods until they writhed on the floor, screaming in pain. The guards finally tore off their clothes.

The prisoners were left waiting there for what seemed like an eternity before being marched to shower rooms, where they bathed under the gaze of shotguns. More than one of them felt stabbing rushes of identification with the prisoners of the Nazi concentration camps. Then they went on another naked march along cement corridors to the maximum-security wing, where, locked two to a cell, they endured another long wait before the guards brought their only prison clothes—a T-shirt and a pair of pea-green boxer shorts. Left alone at last, they shouted out their relief in complaints about the skimpy, ill-fitting garments. "What's all this hang-up about clothes?" James Bevel cried out above the noise. "Gandhi wrapped a rag around his balls and brought the whole British Empire to its knees!"

Their hymns, spirituals, and freedom songs once again became the principal issue of contention with the jail authorities, who, to regain control of the prison atmosphere, threatened to remove all the mattresses from the cells if the Freedom Riders did not fall silent. Hank Thomas soon exploded with zeal, rattling the bars as he shouted for the guards. "Come get my mattress!" he cried. "I'll keep my soul!" The outburst inspired the entire cell block to sing "We Shall Overcome," and one prisoner after another flung his mattress against the cell door for the guards to collect.

Not all the Freedom Riders willingly accepted the sacrifice. One of them had to be pried away from his mattress by the guards. Nor did all share the religious ethos of the cell block. Stokely Carmichael, among others, remained aloof from the religious devotionals, and many of the Freedom Riders envied or resented the advanced Gandhism of the Nashville students. There were abstruse Gandhian arguments about whether the decision to fast in jail should be determined by the inner convictions of the prisoner or by the political effects upon the outside world. There were also less lofty disputes, such as fistfights through the bars when non-fasting prisoners aggressively slurped their food in front of those trying not to eat.

For all the frictions, the Freedom Riders maintained an astonishing *esprit* as their number swelled in Parchman Penitentiary. Only a few asked to have their mattresses back. They lay on the steel springs at night, and they sang steadfastly through all the punishments devised to break them. When normal prison intimidations failed to work, frustrated authorities tried dousing them with fire hoses and then chilling them at night with giant fans. They also tried closing all the windows to bake them in the Mississippi summer heat. None of these sanctions had the desired effect, and many of them backfired. When the original group of Freedom Riders bailed out for appeal on July 7, they nearly floated out of the cells in the knowledge that they had gone into the heart of the beast and survived.

From the Montgomery bus boycott to the confrontations of the sit-ins, then on to the Rock Hill jail-in and now to the mass assault on the Mississippi prisons, there was a "movement" in both senses of the word —a moving spiritual experience, and a steady expansion of scope. The theater was spreading through the entire South. One isolated battle had given way to many scattered ones, and now in the Mississippi jails they were moving from similar experiences to a common experience. Students began to think of the movement as a vocation in itself. From jail, John Lewis notified the Quakers by letter that he was withdrawing from the India program because he wanted to work full time in the South.

When James Farmer flew home to New York, he was met at the airport by television cameras and crowds of admiring CORE supporters chanting "Farmer is our leader!" This reception was not so surprising, inasmuch as Farmer's role in the Freedom Rides had placed him instantly on the covers of Negro magazines as a national leader. More surprising by far were the similar greetings for those who went home to Los Angeles, Chicago, Boston, and small towns scattered in between. The usual small gatherings of the faithful were overrun by strangers who came out in huge numbers to pay tribute to a Freedom Rider—any Freedom Rider.

The emotional wave of the Freedom Rides collided with the Kennedy registration plan. At a SNCC meeting exactly one week after their release from Parchman, student Freedom Riders were shocked to hear some of their colleagues propose that SNCC adopt as its "top priority" the voter registration drive being discussed with Harry Belafonte. They were talking of a mammoth operation of some 200,000 student workers—a force a thousand times larger than the Freedom Riders. Passionate arguments erupted. Those just out of prison objected that there was nothing Gandhian about voter registration, which they saw as conventional, political, and very probably a tool of the Kennedy Administration for getting "direct action" demonstrators off the streets. Voter registration advocates replied that they were ready to undertake the drudgery of registration work, intimating that the Freedom Riders had been seduced by the allure of martyrdom. In the end, the factions could agree only to postpone the fateful decision until a showdown conference at Highlander Folk School a month later. "In a very real sense, this is an emergency call and we are expecting representatives from each state," field secretary Charles Sherrod wrote in his convening circular. "The outcome of this meeting may determine the direction of the civil rights fight for years to come!"

As it happened, Bob Moses was on his way to Mississippi that month to begin a new life. As the Harvard-trained philosopher who had undertaken SNCC's first recruiting trip into the Deep South and then volunteered to spend "two or three years" working for SNCC in the forbidding state of Mississippi, Moses had become a minor celebrity in SNCC circles before the Freedom Rides. Because the work he planned was known to center on voter registration, SNCC chairman Charles McDew, Charles Jones, Tim Jenkins, and other leaders of the registration faction sought his endorsement for their side in the internal struggle. Baffled by the intrigue, Moses said his own voter registration plans had nothing to do with grand schemes or philosophy. They were simply a response to Amzie Moore's analysis of what would work best in Mississippi. Moses declined to attend the Highlander meeting or otherwise take part in the dispute, but he did ask the SNCC leaders to include his Mississippi registration project in any recruitment programs they developed. McDew and the others were happy to provide him with John Doar's private telephone number at the Justice Department. After Moses had gone, Jenkins remarked that he seemed far too meekly intellectual to have the slightest chance against Mississippi segregationists.

Arriving at last at Amzie Moore's house in Cleveland, Mississippi, Moses found his host in an unusually distracted state. All Mississippi was agitated by the Freedom Rider arrests going on down in Jackson, Moore said, and this was not the best time to begin registration work. His reasons for delay stretched out daily before giving way to avoidance, and Moses, while not wishing to question the judgment of his mentor as to the local chemistry of race, did not wish to sit indefinitely in Moore's spare room. Moore finally suggested a way out of the awkwardness growing up between them. An NAACP leader from McComb, a small town near the southern border of the state, had written him after seeing a report in the Negro press, wanting to know if Moore would send a few of his "teams of students" to register voters in McComb. Moore suggested to Moses that things were not as tight—not as touchy—in McComb as they were in the Delta towns nearby. Perhaps he should get started down there. Moses painfully took his leave. A bus ride of nearly two hundred miles due south put him in McComb, where he explained to NAACP leader C. C. Bryant that he alone was the first team.

At Highlander, three days of rancorous debate produced nothing more than a deadlock among the state delegations within SNCC. Charles McDew announced dramatically that he was going to break the tie by casting the chairman's vote in favor of the voter registration plan. Several direct-action advocates stalked out in anger. Ella Baker, trying desperately to keep her prized students from surrendering to the leadership preoccupations that had so vexed her at the NAACP and the SCLC, proposed that SNCC operate for a time as two cooperating wings—direct action under Diane Nash and voter registration under Charles Jones. Her compromise won grudging acceptance from everyone except a few direct-action diehards. Bernard Lee left SNCC permanently, as did the former leader of the Atlanta sit-in movement, Lonnie King. By the end of the conference, a grim joke went around that SNCC should have two doors for its dingy office, so that the rivals would not cross each other's path.

Neither side's project began smoothly. The direct-action wing adopted a proposal called "Move on Mississippi," authored by the Nashville student-preacher Paul Brooks. It envisioned a protracted nonviolent assault beginning in the capital city of Jackson, which, like Montgomery, had a Negro college and a large portion of the state's middle-class Negro citizens. James Bevel and Bernard Lafayette did manage to find some local students willing to demonstrate, but city police countered them shrewdly. Instead of arresting the demonstrators, they arrested the SNCC leaders for "contributing to the delinquency of a minor" by urging students under eighteen to break the segregation laws of Mississippi. Tried, convicted, and sentenced to up to three years, they bailed out on appeal and visited Amzie Moore in Cleveland to regroup. These sentences, by far the harshest yet meted out to students in the movement, were among the signs of rising white anger that were making Amzie Moore jittery.

As for voter registration, SNCC leaders went directly to the Justice Department for discussions on targeting, demographics, law, and strategy. From a map on the wall in John Doar's office, they noted pins stuck into the Southern counties judged most ripe for registration lawsuits. By Doar's reckoning, two of the most promising areas were Dallas County, Alabama (Selma), and Terrell County, Georgia, where the Eisenhower Administration had won the first voting rights suit under the 1957 Civil Rights Act. Charles Sherrod migrated to Georgia to begin a pilot project in Terrell County, but he soon discovered that most of the Negroes there were fearfully mistrustful of anyone who discussed civil rights. When he dared to propose demonstrations and registration drives, even his few hard-won acquaintances refused to talk with him. Sherrod was obliged to retreat to the nearby city of Albany and start over.

These troubled beginnings went almost unnoticed even within the magnified vision of the civil rights network. There were too many layers of activity. Sherrod was talking with Doar and a hundred others; Moses and Bevel were at work in Mississippi; the Freedom Rides were still going on. Students were hearing about beatings administered to friends and relatives in Parchman Penitentiary. Millions of dollars were being discussed in foundations even as tears of grief and inspiration were flowing. In miniature, the Freedom Riders were compressing into one summer the psychology of the first three centuries of Christianity under the Roman Empire. Perpetually on the brink of schism, apostles of nonviolent love were fanning out into the provinces to fill jails, while their confederates were negotiating with the emperors themselves for full citizenship rights, hoping to establish their outlandish new faith as the official doctrine of the state.

King contained these divergent strains within himself. Drawn to both the martyrs and the rulers, he was exposed during the Freedom Rides to extremes of scorn and admiration that were unprecedented even for him. His relations with the SNCC students suddenly became intimate but touchy and complex, as did those with Robert Kennedy. So sensitive was King's name in public debate that the white Southern Baptist Convention—which was trying to make peace with President Kennedy after its shrill warnings against putting a Catholic in the White House—forced its seminary to apologize publicly for allowing King to discuss religion on the Louisville campus. Within the church, this simple invitation was a racial and theological heresy, such that churches across the South rescinded their regular donations to the seminary. "Steps have been taken to help prevent the recurrence of this kind of error," announced Rev. J. R. White of the Southern Baptist Seminary's board of trustees. White, pastor of First Baptist of Montgomery, had been at loggerheads with King since the bus boycott negotiations.

Governor Rockefeller, on the other hand, went out of his way to associate with King as a political celebrity. On a single day in June, he took King aboard his private plane to Albany, brought him to his private quarters for dinner, introduced him at a Freedom Ride rally in the capitol, ordered his staff to use the Rockefeller fortune to disseminate the passion of King's oratory, and sent King to his next New York speech in the company of a Rockefeller-hired film crew. Rockefeller later produced a film and a long-playing phonograph record (King's first) of the address.

He sent copies to Ebenezer, and, just in case the church was not equipped to view the film, he included a sound projector in the gift package. The governor wrote King that he was using the film "to interest the television networks in doing a thoughtful study of your work." Rockefeller's motivation for this sudden shower of attention was at least partly political: his strategy for the 1964 election was to attack President Kennedy on both flanks by taking more liberal stands on civil rights and more aggressive ones on military policy. Still, there was much common ground between Rockefeller and King. One of the governor's sons-in-law had been arrested as a Freedom Rider. Rockefeller was a frequent speaker at Negro colleges and a Sunday school teacher at Harry Emerson Fosdick's Riverside Church. His unique heritage put him far closer to King's world than any other national politician, and it was remarkable in a sense that the affinity between them was not more pronounced.

King flew back to Atlanta for a day or two between the high-level foundation meetings and Freedom Ride speeches in Indianapolis, Pittsburgh, St. Louis, Hartford, San Francisco, Miami, Syracuse, and Whitewater, Wisconsin—in the breakneck pattern so familiar that he claimed he could recognize airports around the country by their distinctive smells. He ventured into Jackson, Mississippi, on July 6 to welcome Farmer, Lawson, Bevel, Lewis, Doris Castle, Jerome Smith, and the others out of Parchman Penitentiary. "We will wear you down by our capacity to suffer," he advised white Mississippians, adding that "segregation is dead" and that the only remaining question was "how expensive" they would make Jim Crow's funeral. In all his talk of martyrdom and death, he pictured himself not as a victim but as an orator presiding over the last rites.

King still yearned for a life of prestigious, intellectual repose such as he had tasted in his pipe-smoking graduate-school days. Two weeks after the Jackson rally, he added to his schedule for the coming year a commitment to teach a Morehouse seminar on his favorite philosophers— Plato, Aristotle, Augustine, Locke, Kant, Hegel, and Nietzsche. In a letter marked CONFIDENTIAL, the dollar-conscious Benjamin Mays instructed King not to tell anyone except Coretta of the college's $1,500 fee, lest Mays face a revolt of Morehouse professors paid less generously per classroom hour. Then King broke away to spend his first August vacationing on fashionable Martha's Vineyard, in a cottage arranged for him by Stanley Levison. The versatile Levison was working diligently with Harry Belafonte to help King push on both sides of the Freedom Ride controversy. They were encouraging the Kennedy-sponsored voter registration drive, which would siphon energy from demonstrations, but they were simultaneously raising money to continue the Freedom Rides. "I deposited a check of one hundred dollars in the SCLC account," Levison wrote King that summer, "because the maker died suddenly and I wanted the check to clear before the bank froze the account." For the sharp-eyed, practical Levison, death inspired thoughts of probate courts instead of funeral orations.

Yet it was Levison to whom King entrusted the task of presenting his personal interpretation of the Freedom Rides to the readers of *The New York Times Magazine*. This particular task required a penetrating cross-cultural sensitivity, because King wished to build his message around the class character of the Negro protesters. Levison's draft opened with King's memory of Mother Pollard saying "My feet is real tired" during the bus boycott and then, jumping ahead five years, pointed out that the contemporary Freedom Rider was not "an elderly woman whose grammar is uncertain" but students who were "college-bred, Ivy League clad, youthful, articulate, and resolute."

Many readers doubtless puzzled over this as an odd point to single out, and perhaps a snobbish one besides. But King did not wish merely to marshal credentials for himself or his cause—he wanted desperately to communicate how much those protesters were willing to sacrifice. Unlike similarly educated whites, their hold on middle-class respectability was extremely tenuous. Any slip—a lost job, a scrape with the law, a psychological breakdown, a personal scandal—could easily send them sliding back into the oblivion of the Negro underclass. Against such sharp risks, Negroes had poured generations of rigid training and lifetimes of effort into slavish imitations of white refinements. They had made themselves into what sociologist Gunnar Myrdal described as the "exaggerated American," dedicated to conspicuous consumption and status symbols, as King told the *Times* readers.

This cultural context was what made the Freedom Rides so revolutionary to King. "Today the imitation has ceased," he said. For the first time in history, white students were imitating Negroes. "I am no longer surprised to meet attractive, stylishly dressed young girls whose charm and personality would grace a Junior Prom," King went on, almost in amazement, "and to hear them declare in unmistakably sincere terms, 'Dr. King, I am ready to die if I must.' " By risking identities and attachments that had come to seem more precious than life itself, the students were discovering something that King believed truly was more precious.

Such preoccupations were close to King's heart as he rested on Martha's Vineyard for the upcoming church battle against J. H. Jackson. He stayed there on August 3, sending Wyatt Walker to the emergency meeting when the state of Mississippi tried to collect some $300,000 of Freedom Rider bail bonds as forfeit. He was there on August 7, when Moses and a Freedom Rider volunteer opened their first voter registration school in Mississippi, on August 9, when the Southern Baptist Seminary apologized to its constituent churches for letting him speak, and on August 11, when the SNCC students began their clash at Highlander. On August 13, as the exhausted students were accepting Ella Baker's compromise, King made a day trip to New York to preach in Riverside Church. East German shock troops were throwing down barbed wire as the first line of a Berlin Wall, sealing off West Berlin. Full attention of the superpowers made that Cold War drama eclipse all other freedom stories of the year.

THIRTEEN

MOSES IN McCOMB, KING IN KANSAS CITY

C. C. Bryant was a practical, plainspoken leader in the mold of Montgomery's E. D. Nixon. Like Nixon, he was a railroad man who drew his paycheck from the faraway mecca of Chicago, which guaranteed him a measure of freedom from the local white economy of McComb. Although Bryant worked as a laborer, operating a loading crane for the Illinois Central, his independent stature rose above the teachers and preachers and the few other local Negroes from the traditional leadership positions. He was a deacon, a Sunday school teacher, a Boy Scout leader, and president of the Pike County NAACP chapter. He was also a high official of the Freemasons, and in this capacity he gained permission for Bob Moses to use the second floor of the all-Negro Masonic Temple as a voter registration school. The first floor was rented out to a butcher.

Moses knocked on doors through the blistering August days, telling all those who would listen that he was C. C. Bryant's voter registration man. His studies at Amzie Moore's house already had made him an expert in Mississippi's arcane registration laws, which, among other tests, required applicants to interpret a section of the state constitution to the satisfaction of the county registrar. This obstacle alone put voting out in the wild yonder of dreams among Mississippi Negroes, and Moses counted it as an initial victory if he could get someone in a McComb household even to imagine being inside the registrar's office in the county courthouse, where few Negroes dared to venture. Behind that psychological barrier lay fears of being branded a renegade, plus piercing doubts of literacy, self-worth, and entitlement. Moses addressed all these each night in his class at the Masonic Temple. Voter registration, as Amzie Moore and C. C. Bryant had perceived, was a full-time job.

Hollis Watkins, a teenager from the tiny hamlet of Summit, Mississippi, poked his head into Moses' office one day and said he'd heard a rumor that Martin Luther King was in town working on some big mysterious project—was he Martin Luther King? Moses, sensing that there was a hard kernel of grit behind Watkins' youthful naïveté, said he didn't know anything about Martin Luther King coming to McComb but that there was a new class in town to teach Negroes how to vote so they could become first-class citizens. Watkins was interested. He had "plans" to go to college but no money or job. Living with his parents, staving off the inevitable plunge into adult worries, he had plenty of time. Very shortly he and a similarly situated teenager named Curtis Hayes became the project's first two volunteers. They distributed leaflets advertising the registration classes.

Luckily for Moses, a few of those attending his first classes on August 7 were people who had been promising Bryant that they would try to register. Four of them pronounced themselves willing after the first night's class. Moses accompanied them to the county courthouse in the nearby town of Magnolia the next day, and three of the four were registered. Three people came forward after the second night's class, of whom two were accepted by the registrar the next day. Their success and another night's class produced nine more volunteers on the third day. By then the registrar was alerted to the possibility that this surge of Negro traffic through his office was not incidental, and he approved only one of the nine applicants.

Pike County's racial barometer was sensitive enough that the appearance of sixteen Negroes in the courthouse on three successive days was a development worthy of a story in the McComb *Enterprise-Journal.* While warning local segregationists, the news generated excitement among the Negroes scattered through the depressed farm-and-timber country of southern Mississippi. Within days, farmers from the surrounding countryside made their way into McComb and up to Moses' corner of the Masonic Temple. After listening to his talks on nonviolence, elementary civics, and the Mississippi constitution, they beseeched him to expand his fledgling project into two of the adjacent counties, where not a single person from the Negro majority population had voted within memory. Relative to the rural wilderness of Amite and Walthall counties, McComb's 12,000 people and 250 registered Negro voters made it a progressive metropolis.

Moses could not bring himself to tell them that it was too dangerous,

or that it was tactically unwise for him to divert attention from Mc-
Comb. After discussions with Bryant, he also decided that he could not ·
earn the trust of the unregistered populace if he avoided what he called
the "tough areas." Accordingly, Moses addressed the logistical problems
of working without money outside McComb. To cover large distances in
the countryside he would need to borrow a car, and he needed a place to
stay in remote areas. It took time and patience to arrange such things in
a region where spare cars were scarce and an educated Northerner suspect. Sometimes he spent half the day arranging where he would spend
the night. But soon a farmer in Amite County named E. W. Steptoe
offered to put him up. Steptoe and his wife had nine children, all but two
of whom were grown. He had been a leader of the county NAACP chapter
until the sheriff had confiscated the membership rolls two years earlier.
The NAACP had been defunct in Amite County since then.

On the morning of August 15, Moses and the first three Amite County
volunteers drove to the county courthouse in the town of Liberty, some
twenty-five miles from McComb. A plaque on the lawn proclaimed that
it was the oldest courthouse in Mississippi, built in 1839, and boasted
that Cecil Borden's condensed milk had been invented in Liberty, as had
Dr. Tichener's antiseptic powder. The four Negroes passed the plaque
and the Confederate memorial statue, entered the enormous white brick
structure, and made their way to the office of the county registrar, who
asked rather sternly what had brought them there.

A very old Negro man waited helplessly for one of the two women
volunteers to reply, but both of them also stood speechless with fear.
Moses finally spoke up from behind. "They would like to try to register
to vote," he said. The registrar questioned Moses about his interest in
the matter and then told them all to wait. While they did, curious officials came by for silent looks at the oddities who were making themselves the chief topic of the day's conversation. The sheriff stopped in,
followed by deputies, clerks from the tax office, and an examiner from
the driver's license bureau. A Mississippi highway patrolman sauntered
in and took a seat.

Six hours later, Moses finally escaped the tension of the courthouse.
His three volunteers knew they would be rejected as voters, but they
were elated anyway, because they had been allowed to fill out the forms.
This was a first for them, and they celebrated until they noticed the
highway patrolman from the registrar's office coming up behind them.
He followed them at bicycle speed for ten miles down Highway 24 toward McComb. Fear grew steadily among the Negroes as they pulled off
the highway, took side roads, and did everything they could think of to
salvage the hope that the tail was a coincidence. The patrolman matched

every maneuver. At last he turned on his flashers, pulled them over, and ordered them to follow him. Now there were moans of apprehension and regret in their car, as the Amite County volunteers vowed never again to set foot in the registrar's office.

In McComb, Moses alone was placed under arrest. The Pike County attorney rushed down from Magnolia that same evening. At first he proposed booking Moses for the crime of interfering with an officer in the act of making an arrest, but he changed his mind upon reflecting that Moses was the only one who had been arrested. He substituted the vaguer charge of interfering with an officer in the discharge of his duties. Then he notified the local justice of the peace and asked Moses if he was prepared to stand trial. Moses requested the proverbial one phone call.

When permission was granted, he fished an emergency number from his wallet. He had never spoken to John Doar, and had no idea whether Doar would be in his office so late at night. For effect, he amplified his instructions to the operator: Washington, D.C., he said, the United States Department of Justice. When Doar not only came on the line but also agreed to accept a collect call, Moses felt a surge of relief. Noting the surprised looks on the faces around him, he gave Doar a description of the day's events. It was detailed, clinical, and neutral in all but his conclusion that his arrest was fraudulent of purpose and clearly designed to discourage voter registration by acts under the color of law, as prohibited by the Civil Rights Acts of 1957 and 1960. After conferring with Doar about the prospects for a federal investigation, Moses signed off and pronounced himself ready for trial.

The justice of the peace found Moses guilty that night and fined him $50. Perhaps sensitive to the prisoner's obvious connections with the U.S. Justice Department, he offered to suspend the fine if Moses would pay $5 in court costs—what amounted to a nominal fee for pulling the judge away from his supper. Moses quietly explained that he could not pay the fee, because it was part of an unjust prosecution, whereupon the judge sent him to the Pike County jail. Moses spent his first night behind bars. His was the first SNCC jailing in Mississippi other than the Freedom Riders, who were still landing in prison by way of the Jackson bus station.

Two days later, an NAACP lawyer came down from Jackson to secure Moses' release by paying the full fine. He did so with the grudging approval of NAACP superiors who considered this another case of getting stuck with legal bills for activities that were neither sponsored nor approved by the NAACP. The bruised feelings of NAACP officials were not assuaged any by the fact that Moses was less than totally grateful for their generosity. He was happy to be out of jail, but he had refused on principle to pay the fine himself and was ambivalent about whether others should have done so.

Moses went into McComb and found that the Masonic Temple had been transformed during his brief absence. Nearly a dozen Freedom Riders had come into town from Jackson, where the convictions of Bevel and Lafayette on contributing to the delinquency of minors had halted sit-in recruitments temporarily, and several SNCC leaders had made their way into McComb after the fractious debates at the Highlander Folk School. The news of Moses' arrest had blurred the sharp distinctions drawn at Highlander between "safe" voter registration and "dramatic" nonviolent demonstrations. Overnight, McComb became the summer's new magnet town. Ruby Doris Smith, one of the four SNCC veterans of February's Rock Hill jail-in, arrived in a Freedom Rider group, and Charles Sherrod came in from his fledgling registration project in Georgia. Charles Jones was on his way, as was former SNCC chairman Marion Barry. Picking up on Moses' door-to-door registration work, they added a twist from Jackson by recruiting local high school students to help them.

Moses missed most of the new excitement in McComb. He returned quickly to Steptoe's farm out in Amite County, hoping to repair the damage caused by the harrowing experience of his first three volunteers. Word of his arrest had spread through the county. Steptoe reported that Negroes working around the courthouse had overheard whites talking about how the Moses project was being discussed at meetings of the White Citizens Council. With such fearful news on the Negro grapevine, it took days for Moses and Steptoe to persuade anyone to go near a registration class. Steptoe himself, though bold enough to give lodging to Moses, was not quite ready to try registering. Nor did he want too many people to be seen coming and going near his farm, which sat directly across the road from the home of Mississippi state representative E. H. Hurst. As Steptoe explained it to Moses, Hurst was a pillar of segregation, but the real threat was his daughter's husband, Billy Jack Caston, whose name had a fearful ring to the ears of Amite County Negroes. Caston had a reputation as a wild, violent ruffian.

Steptoe did not rest until he had arranged for Moses to hold his registration classes in a one-room Baptist church, way out in the woods—the same church into which the sheriff had burst to confiscate the Amite County NAACP records. (The sheriff, in another touch of Faulknerian reality, was Billy Jack Caston's cousin.) A few of the boldest Amite County Negroes appeared at the nightly meetings to hear Moses talk about registration. He refrained from pressuring them, to the point of never asking whether anyone wanted to try to register. The unspoken question was left hanging. Finally, nearly two weeks after the first attempt, a farmer named Curtis Dawson volunteered to go down, and an old man known only as Preacher Knox jumped up to join him. Though their offer was applauded heartily in the meeting, Moses and Steptoe discussed it long into the night. Dawson was solid, they agreed, but Preacher Knox was flighty, voluble, and sometimes daft—given to random enthusiasms and endorsements of all opinions. Moses worried about whether it would be correct to refuse Knox's offer, and if he did, whether it would be fair to let Dawson go alone. Moses decided to take his chances on Knox.

The next morning, August 29, the three of them found the sidewalk near the courthouse blocked by three young white men. Dawson recognized the one in front as Billy Jack Caston; the second was another of the sheriff's cousins, and the third was the sheriff's son. There was very little talk. Caston asked Moses where he was going. To the registrar's office, Moses replied. Caston said no he wasn't and struck a quick, swiping blow to Moses' forehead with the handle of his knife.

In a mystical discovery even more vivid than the pains shooting through his head, Moses felt himself separating from his body as he staggered on the sidewalk. He floated about ten feet up in the air so that he could watch the attack on himself comfortably. His fears became as remote as Caston's grunts, and time slowed down so that he could hear Preacher Knox running away on the sidewalk before he saw Caston slapping and shaking him. In peaceful surrender, he saw Caston hit him again behind the right temple, saw himself sink to his knees, saw Caston drive his face to the pavement with a crushing blow to the top of the head. Through waves of concussion, he distinctly heard Curtis Dawson pleading with Caston to stop the beating.

His first thoughts, upon hearing the feet of his attackers depart were that he could function in spite of his wounds and that it was urgently important to reach the courthouse. "We've got to go on to the registrar," he said, as Dawson struggled to overcome his horror at the sight of the blood flowing down from the gashes in Moses' head. Preacher Knox returned to help him to his feet. "We can't let something like this stop us," said Moses. "That's the whole point." Dawson replied bravely that he was ready; Preacher Knox agreed. Moses was deeply moved by their decision, and most especially by Preacher Knox's unexpected courage, but as the three of them crossed the street toward the courthouse he wondered whether Knox, with shock compounding his scrambled ways, really knew what he was doing.

The county registrar reserved a practiced, well-what-have-we-got-here look for Negro customers, but it vanished in a gasp at the sight of Moses, whose bloody head and shirt combined with his serene, quiet voice to give him a presence as eerie as Banquo's ghost. The registrar gamely sought refuge in bursts of businesslike indifference, excessive politeness, and put-upon impatience, before all his bureaucratic poses collapsed under the weight of his nerves. He said he was closing the office and asked the three Negroes to leave.

They retraced their steps from the courthouse, watched by scattered clumps of bystanders. Dawson drove out to the Steptoe farm, where Moses' weakening condition caused a great stir of mumbled anguish, and then, as there was no Negro doctor in Amite County, they drove back to McComb to visit one newly arrived from Fisk University in Nashville. The doctor, who had taken no part in the voter registration previously, talked with Moses while putting nine stitches into three head wounds. Before he finished, he offered the registration project the use of his car.

Moses arrived at the Masonic Temple just in time to be whisked off to the first mass meeting in McComb's history, following its first sit-in arrests. In his absence, Charles Sherrod and others from the influx of Freedom Riders had been conducting classes in nonviolent discipline, much like James Lawson's Nashville workshops, and the young Mc-Comb students—too young to vote, and frustrated by the passivity of the elders they canvassed—had been seized with enthusiasm to do something themselves, like the Freedom Riders. Marion Barry had urged the McComb students to demonstrate against the town library, which did not admit Negroes. During the sit-in, the McComb police had arrested Moses' two volunteers, Hollis Watkins and Curtis Hayes, for breach of the peace.

They were in the Pike County jail when Moses came back to McComb with his head wounds, and the furor among the town's Negroes was such that James Bevel came down from Jackson to address a mass meeting of some two hundred people. With his high-pitched voice and shooting-star images, Bevel preached the fire of nonviolent witness. Moses, in telling of the day's events in Liberty, spoke reluctantly and almost inaudibly, as always, but the core of his message was the same: that the important thing was to keep going. His offhand announcement that he intended to return to the Liberty courthouse the next day swept the crowd no less than Bevel's hot gospel. A white reporter from the local newspaper warned his readers that the Negroes might be serious.

In his reflections later that night, Moses decided that it was imperative for him to act as though he and other Negroes enjoyed the same legal rights as Mississippi white people. Accordingly, he drove back to the Liberty courthouse the next day and told the Amite County attorney that he wanted to swear out a complaint against Billy Jack Caston for criminal assault. This statement unsettled the prosecutor as thoroughly as Moses' appearance had shocked the registrar the day before. As the seriousness of the request registered, the prosecutor said that of course he had heard about the beating, and it was a terrible thing. He seemed to become more troubled as he talked about his legal duties and Moses' theoretical rights, and finally he said that, yes, he would put the case to a jury in the name of Amite County. But he stressed the practical reality that if Moses followed through on his complaint, no one could guarantee Moses' life—or his own legal career—against the wrath of the local white people. He recommended a night's sleep on the decision, and Moses left the office with the impression that the county attorney was a decent man.

At Steptoe's that night, Moses was surprised to learn that although the beating had put a severe fright into nearly all their registration candidates, there was one old farmer named Weathersbee who suddenly was determined to go to the courthouse. Possessed of some choleric defiance that pointed him in the opposite direction from his fearful neighbors, Weathersbee wanted to register the next day if Moses would go with him. Steptoe was less surprised by Weathersbee than by the idea of pressing charges against Caston. With no chance of success, it would enrage every white person in the county and was the sort of notion that did not even occur to sane Negroes.

The county attorney, who seemed to have braced himself for the appearance of Moses and his two witnesses the next day, arranged with the justice of the peace for a country-style prosecution. They summoned Billy Jack Caston by telephone, impaneled a six-man jury, and put out the word in the courthouse. By the time the trial commenced two hours later, white citizens had driven into town from all across the county, many of them in pickups with shotgun racks. Some were amused by the thought of seeing someone so prominent as Billy Jack Caston in the dock on the word of a nigger. Some were angry, and many were a little of both. Their numbers swamped the tiny courtroom, so that they overflowed onto the courthouse lawn outside. When Moses, Dawson, and Preacher Knox finished testifying for the prosecution, they found more than a hundred white men in a surly mood, inflamed partly by a simultaneous affront on the other side of the courthouse.

Weathersbee was trying to register. Travis Britt, a Freedom Rider from New York, had come over from McComb to be with Weathersbee while Moses testified. The registrar had ordered Britt to wait outside, alone and beleaguered under a shower of taunts, and as Moses moved through the crowd to join him the blast of several gunshots sent everyone ducking. No one was hit. It may have been a malicious prank, but it was enough to make the sheriff notify Moses that he and his friends were due for an emergency police escort to the county line. They read in the next day's newspaper that the jury had acquitted Caston.

Back in McComb, there was a fever of commotion on both the white and Negro sides of town. The local students, further inspired by James Bevel's invitations to nonviolent direct action, had staged a sit-in the day before at the Greyhound lunch counter. Police had arrested three of them, and what stirred much of the controversy within both races was the particular fact that one of them, Brenda Travis, was a sixteen-year-old girl. Whites were saying that it was irresponsible of the Negroes to allow a mere child to bear the brunt of such dangerous, illegal business, and Negroes were furious that the white authorities put Travis in the Pike County jail with adult criminals. Unable to make bail, she served thirty days there and missed the first month of school.

Her trial in McComb and Caston's in nearby Liberty occurred on the last day of August. These events marked the end of Moses' first month in Mississippi. There still were no registered Negro voters in Amite County, and only a few new ones in Pike County, but Moses was no longer alone. Already his name, borrowed from the most famous figure in the Old Testament, was acquiring a Christlike ring within SNCC, where the story was repeated that he had clasped his hands and looked heavenward during the Caston assault, saying "Forgive them." This apocryphal story was within the realm of belief, as his solitary, mystical, stubborn meekness had nicked the heart of Mississippi. Wondrous things were happening fast on the fringes of the impossible. Among the freshly legendary Freedom Riders, Moses himself was a budding legend.

Isolated jail-ins and confrontations erupted simultaneously across the South, including a particularly messy skirmish in Monroe, North Carolina. Wyatt Walker broke away from Monroe in time to meet King at the end of his vacation on Martha's Vineyard. The church crisis was upon them. King was scheduled to nominate Gardner Taylor against J. H. Jackson at Kansas City. He and his fellow conspirators had spent a year recruiting preachers to come to Kansas City as Taylor men, pledged to uphold the validity of Taylor's election in Philadelphia, and they had printed their own "official" credentials and literature, parallel to Jackson's. The idea was that they would bring their claim of legitimacy to Kansas City and then bargain with Jackson over the rules of election and the distribution of offices. The Taylor people spared no effort to make an impressive display of strength on the convention floor. One of King's colleagues on the SCLC board raised a cash "flash bundle" of $25,000 to advertise the health of the Taylorites' treasury.

For all this, the strategy was flawed. A head count showed that while about half the preachers said they would vote for Taylor, less than a thousand of them were willing to contest Jackson's right to run the convention as the incumbent. This was not enough, and the irony of his predicament drove King to despair. He was snared in the same trap that had plagued his larger ambitions in the segregated South since his "Give Us the Ballot" speech of 1957: he knew the votes were there to effect a political revolution, but the votes were useless without a prior revolution to make them count. His dream of mobilizing the power of the Negro church to break the hegemony of white segregationist voters was now hostage to the church hegemony of his father's dear old friend, J. H. Jackson.

King faced choices so cruel that he delayed going to Kansas City and stunned his friends by hinting that he might not go at all. When the convention opened on Tuesday, September 5, Gardner Taylor and his advisers tacitly surrendered their challenge for physical control of the convention. They sent their lawyers into Judge Richard H. Koenigsdorf's courtroom to ask for an injunction barring both J. H. Jackson *and* Gardner Taylor from the election. In a contest of rival popes, this conciliatory move was viewed as a sign of weakness. The most Judge Koenigsdorf would do for Taylor was to appoint an eighty-four-year-old preacher to supervise the counting of the ballots.

King's heart was with Taylor, and for the rest of his life he would mourn the failure to acquire this institutional base for the civil rights movement, but the realist in him knew that the more publicly he aligned himself with Taylor's last charge, the more his reputation would suffer from the certain defeat. On the other hand, he worried that if he did not make the nominating speech for Taylor, his friends would think he had made a deal with J. H. Jackson. From this notion grew the haunting fear that if they thought so—if they thought his refusal was selfishly motivated—nothing would etch their suspicions more permanently than his absence from the convention. Therefore, the more convinced he became that he should refrain from nominating Taylor, the more convinced he became that he must be with Taylor and his friends in spite of the personal discomfort. This calculus made no sense to Wyatt Walker, who, satisfied by telephone reports that Taylor would lose, had no desire to be present for the galling moment of Jackson's victory. He stayed behind in Atlanta as King flew after midnight into Kansas City, where the Jackson and Taylor forces were headquartered on opposite sides of the Missouri River.

King's confederates at least pretended to understand his explanation. As a last desperate gamble, their plan was to implant Gardner Taylor on

the speaker's platform—in plain view, near the microphone—before
J. H. Jackson delivered his annual President's Address. Jackson's reelection would most likely come in the emotional afterglow of that sermon,
with a motion to suspend the rules and a quick gavel of acclamation, and
if Taylor did not rise instantly to make his challenge—to demand a head
count by the court-appointed monitor—the moment would not come
again. Tests of convention security established that the invasion could
not be done by stealth, because there were too many Jackson people at
the doors. Therefore, with as much surprise as possible, the Taylorites
tucked Gardner Taylor into a "flying wedge" of several hundred preachers and stormed through the largest entrance to the convention floor.
Pushing aside the officials who objected to their improper credentials,
they shouted the name of their deposed president as they headed for the
podium in a thundering mass. King remained outside.

The flying wedge electrified the auditorium, but it failed to catch J. H.
Jackson completely off guard. He had seated several hundred of his most
loyal followers protectively around him, and as the Taylor people
charged, scores of Jacksonites jumped forward to barricade the ap-
proaches. Above the din of shouting spectators, the two masses of preachers collided at the foot of the platform. There followed at first a struggle
of shoulders, like a giant rugby scrum, then scuffling broke out. Along
the crush of the dividing line, the opposing preachers shoved, wrestled,
and slugged each other out of the way.

When the Taylor wedge gained a few feet of territory, the force of the
advance ran by conduction through the Jackson defenders until it com-
pressed those on the far side of the platform. Rev. Ben F. Paxton of
Chicago was among those who stumbled in retreat against a row of
Jackson dignitaries seated along the edge. He hit the chair of Rev. A. G.
Wright of Detroit, member of the national board and close friend of
J. H. Jackson. Wright leaned back to steady himself against the wall, but
the wall turned out to be merely a curtain. "Hold me!" Wright shouted
in a panic, grabbing Paxton's arm as he tumbled backward into space.
Paxton tumbled after him, flailing at the air and landing with his full
weight on Wright just after Wright's head struck the auditorium floor
some four feet below, fracturing his skull.

Cries for an ambulance brought Kansas City policemen on the run, but
they failed to quiet the escalating conflict on the opposite side of the
platform. On the contrary, screams that Wright was badly hurt only
spurred both sides. The battle went on for nearly an hour, long after
Wright was wheeled away to emergency surgery at Menorah Medical
Center. A staircase to the platform collapsed under the weight of the
antagonists jammed on it, scattering and bruising dozens of people but

halting the struggle only momentarily. A preacher lost three teeth in one of many fistfights along the battle line. Eighty Kansas City riot police finally pushed their way around the platform in a protective cordon, but order was not restored until police cleared a wide path for H. Roe Bartle, Kansas City's three-hundred-pound mayor. From the microphone, Bartle pleaded for calm in what eventually became a fairly respectable layman's sermon invoking the love of God toward the peaceful settlement of disputes. Musicians then sustained the truce with sedate background spirituals.

Surgeons at Menorah labored for two hours to stop the hemorrhage in Reverend Wright's brain. Wright, like Daddy King, was a recognized pillar of the National Baptist Convention, a commanding figure known for his huge congregation as well as a small business empire. Wright's attorney valued his Detroit real estate holdings in excess of $500,000 and his other investments in like amount. He was a model Jackson lieutenant—a strong, hulking emigrant from the South, clad in a dark suit and suspenders, with a gold watch chain—but Wright and all his vitality slipped into a coma that afternoon.

In Liberty, Mississippi, on the day the Kansas City convention opened, Bob Moses and Freedom Rider Travis Britt returned to the courthouse. Ordered to wait outside while four Negroes tried to register, they soon drew a crowd of a dozen whites shouting hostile questions about why niggers from New York would come all the way down there to stir up trouble. Moses lapsed into a silent depression under the barrage, almost anticipating the separation again of mind from body as he fell under attack, but a thin old man in a shaking, uncontrollable rage began to pummel Britt instead. Moses tried to summon the sheriff, but the bystanders blocked his path. Then Moses pulled Britt around the waist, trying to maneuver him out of the beating. The old man kept swinging, possessed of a hatred so intense that it seemed to consume what strength he had. Britt finally escaped in the grasp of Moses, having absorbed some twenty blows that did no worse than puff up and bruise his face. They jumped in their borrowed car and retreated eastward to McComb, leaving the four Negroes to get home on their own after their applications were refused. This third beating in a row paralyzed the would-be registrants from Moses' Amite County registration school.

Two days later, Nashville Freedom Rider John Hardy made his fourth trip to the courthouse in Tylertown, on the opposite side of McComb from Liberty. It was the seat of the other outlying county from which Negroes had come to petition Moses for a registration school. Hardy, the volunteer teacher, had quickly become a conspicuous, controversial figure in Tylertown, where he arrived wearing his usual khaki safari shorts and knee-high black dress socks over his skinny legs. A fastidious, bookish student, Hardy was known for courage rooted in his study of the principles of freedom. On this particular Thursday, he brought with him Edith Peters and Lucius Wilson, both in their sixties, who as owners of sizable farms were among the relatively prosperous Negro yeomen of the county.

Registrar John Q. Wood refused to give registration applications to Peters and Wilson. When Hardy stepped forward to ask why, Wood cut him off abruptly. "I want to see you, John," said Wood as he walked briskly to his desk and pulled a revolver from the drawer. The appearance of the gun froze the room in silence. Wood ordered Hardy to leave the office, and as Hardy was walking out the door, he struck a roundhouse blow to the back of his head with the butt of the gun.

Peters and Wilson rushed past Wood to support the staggering, bleeding Hardy, and the three Negroes made their way out of the courthouse. A white man advised them to see a doctor, but Hardy, mindful of Moses' example after the Caston beating, said he wanted to report the assault to the local sheriff. He had scarcely decided to do so when Sheriff Edd Craft came running to meet him in the middle of the street. The sheriff, confronted by Hardy's demand that he arrest the registrar—which threatened to undermine the fundamental political structure of the county—denounced Hardy bitterly and almost piteously for bringing down such a situation on Mississippi. Then, instead of arresting Wood for assault, Craft arrested Hardy for disturbing the peace. By nightfall, swirling rumors of lynch parties worried the sheriff enough to transfer his prisoner to the Pike County jail in Magnolia, where Hardy was placed in a cell next to the students from the McComb sit-ins.

Reverend Wright died in Kansas City two days after his injury, on the morning John Hardy was beaten. News of the unprecedented fatality imposed a sedative pall upon the hosts of preachers, choristers, and lay worshippers. Its immediate effect was to concentrate hopes of surmounting the shameful internecine warfare upon D. A. Holmes, the special election monitor, who, dressed in formal black suit and white tie, soon entered the auditorium under full police escort. Leaning on the arms of court-appointed assistants, one of whom was a municipal judge, the stern octogenarian made his way to the podium and laid down edicts of compromise procedure. To the Jackson forces went the technical recognition of incumbency: Kansas City police would admit to the floor only those

Taylor delegates who exchanged their credentials for those issued by Jackson, and Jackson would be recognized to deliver the traditional President's Address. To the Taylor forces went Holmes's assurances that he would use tellers, ballot-box watchers, and anything else necessary to insure a fair election, no matter how long it took. "We are going to behave," he declared, "and we are going to be honest from A to Z."

Jackson returned to preach. Ten thousand Baptists filled the auditorium, and many of them, eager for a sermon that would lift them above the unpleasantries of earthly politics, responded more positively than ever. When Holmes called for the delegates to be qualified for voting, Jackson delegates from the entire nation stood up to be counted with those from the first state called, which was Alabama, a Taylor stronghold because of King and Shuttlesworth. Jackson, by such obfuscatory tactics, forced Holmes to qualify the delegates one by one instead of state by state, in a laborious tally that went on into the night. Then Jackson had his delegates place on record a nonbinding resolution that the Holmes rules were usurpations of the president's authority, and that they were participating in the election under protest. The Taylor delegates booed. King and other Taylor leaders believed that Jackson was laying down a pretext for a walkout or a coup against Holmes, should the election go badly.

Nevertheless, King decided at the last moment not to nominate Taylor, nor to make a seconding speech. He mustered all his courage to explain to Taylor that he thought his presence might be too inflammatory in the wake of Reverend Wright's death. Taylor asked Abernathy to make a seconding speech in King's place, after which Taylor and Jackson solemnly took seats no more than three feet apart on the stage, each flanked by a half-dozen retainers. The long procession of preachers filed past the ballot boxes until nearly dawn, with Abernathy and Benjamin Mays standing by vigilantly as official poll watchers for Taylor.

There was no argument with the results: Jackson won by a vote of 2,732 to 1,519. His ensuing retribution was swift. Assuming extraordinary powers of appointment by voice vote, Jackson stripped King of his prestigious title as vice president of the Convention's Sunday School Board. This was the most severe punishment available to him, carrying the sting of a summary court-martial or excommunication. Applied to someone as prominent as King, whose name meant far more out in the white world than that of any preacher in the hall, Jackson included, the rebuke spread an awed hush through the convention. A numb King went to see Gardner Taylor. "Can you believe what he just did?" he asked.

Jackson was not finished. At his victory press conference, he interpreted the week's tragedy for reporters who were baffled by such violent chaos among preachers. The coroner may have been technically correct in ruling Reverend Wright's death an accident, he said, but in his opinion the real cause was a planned insurrection. Absolving Gardner Taylor as the figurehead, he charged that it was Martin Luther King who "master-minded the invasion of the convention floor Wednesday which resulted in the death of a delegate." With that, he left for Detroit to sharpen the attack at Wright's mammoth funeral. "The disrespect for law in the move for freedom has opened the way for criminals to come in their midst . . ." he declared. "Too many preachers have the cloth on the outside but don't have the Gospel on the inside. There are hoodlums and crooks in the pulpits today."

By naming King publicly as the culprit in what he all but called a murder, Jackson framed an accusation so clear and compelling that it threatened to leap across the chasm of race. The story moved on the news wires and had already surfaced as a tiny item on a back page of *The New York Times.* For King, this lit the fuse of disaster. If the white newspapers of the South noticed, they could fashion a lasting multiple scandal: homicide and riot by the champion of nonviolence, plus rejection of King's integration agenda by his fellow Negro ministers. King retreated to Atlanta for emergency consultations with a panel of lawyers and SCLC advisers. Wyatt Walker set up a nationwide communications network to poll influential Taylorites. King wanted to force Jackson to retract his charges, but like most potential libel plaintiffs he realized that he might only draw attention to the original allegation. Even worse, he realized that any public controversy initiated by him was almost automatic news within the white press, whereas most white reporters had never heard of J. H. Jackson.

All these factors militated against a lawsuit, but King could not bring himself to let Jackson's remarks go unchallenged. From Atlanta, he sent a telegram to Jackson that hinted of a libel suit and also exposed King's sensitivity to publicity. "As you know," King told Jackson, "my whole philosophy of life and social action is one of love and nonviolence and for one to give the nation the impression that I am little more than a hoodlum with a reckless disregard of the lives and safety of persons is both libelous and injurious to my public image. I, therefore, ask you in a Christian spirit to retract this statement immediately and urge the press to give as much attention to the retraction as it gave to the original accusation. Please send a copy of the retraction to me."

Anticipating that Jackson would not reply, King and his allies worked frantically by telephone to recruit Negro Baptist leaders from twenty-five states to lend their names to a joint telegram similar to King's. The final version asserted that Jackson's statements "will only serve the purposes of the segregationist forces in America" and concluded: "If this character assassination is not righted, it will be a disservice to the Baptists, the Christian family, to the Negro community in America and to God." Benjamin Mays signed on, as did Gardner Taylor himself. The King camp's most prized signatory was Rev. D. A. Holmes, who had supervised the Kansas City election. The telegram opened a line of compromise for Jackson by suggesting that perhaps the reporters had misquoted him.

The crafted nuance was wasted, however, as Jackson retracted nothing. His victory was complete. Unlike King, Jackson had no image to protect beyond the confines of the Convention. The most sordid controversy involving his name would receive little more attention in the white world than a knife fight among hoboes.

King was left with the painful irony that the same racial barriers he was battling to destroy now protected him from scandal in his first major failure. He was obliged to deny complicity in the Wright death with an alibi based on something he was not proud of—his last-minute retreat from the forefront of Taylor support—and he concealed the true motive for that retreat in a bit of disingenuous rhetoric: ". . . my overcrowded schedule made it impossible for me to attend a single strategy session of the Taylor team," he had said in his telegram to Jackson. Both his moral crusade and his expedient calculations came to grief. The bitter result of the long campaign against tyranny was to cleanse Jackson with a democratic victory. It was on this last point that King's regrets eventually came to settle. He reproached himself for having surrendered to the logic of coups and intrigue. "I never thought Jack would allow a fair vote," he sighed repeatedly.

All the Kings were now ostracized from an institution that had been near the center of the family's church identity since before Daddy King was born. Neither King nor his father would address the Convention again in their lifetimes, and J. H. Jackson stood as a colossus against all King's hopes of using the organized national church in the civil rights movement. "The smoke has cleared," Wyatt Walker wrote a friend, "and evil is once more strongly entrenched upon the throne."

The Kennedy Justice Department intervened to block John Hardy's state trial, which was scheduled for September 22. This was a historic move. To challenge the right of a state to bring a criminal prosecution under its own laws was both legally and politically extreme, not least because the circumstances required the federal government to endorse the testimony of Negro witnesses against that of white elected officials. But the lawyers of the Civil Rights Division found the federal voting rights connection to be so egregious—the beating of Hardy by the registrar, inside the registrar's office—and the subsequent state indictment of Hardy so perverse that the case made a mockery of the federal government's powers to enforce voting rights. John Doar put the case for emergency action before Burke Marshall, who authorized him to seek a temporary restraining order against Mississippi, on behalf of Hardy and the United States.

Unfortunately for the Justice Department, Doar wound up in the Federal District Court of Judge Harold Cox, the Kennedy Administration's first judicial appointment in the South. Cox was the son of the sheriff in Sunflower County, home of his powerful sponsor, Senate Judiciary Committee chairman James Eastland. As a segregationist who was to make himself notorious with remarks from the bench in which he called Negroes "baboons," he was not favorably disposed toward the Justice Department's audacious motion. He denied it, whereupon Burke Marshall flew to Atlanta to seek review by the Fifth Circuit Court of Appeals.

There the issue was technical. Under federal rules of procedure, the denial of a motion for a temporary restraining order was not considered "final" enough to merit judicial review. Marshall, knowing that the issue would be moot before a hostile Judge Cox got around to hearings on a permanent injunction, argued that this extraordinary situation justified a reversal. In what became a pattern of the civil rights movement, two Eisenhower judges agreed with the Justice Department against one of the Administration's own Democratic judges. They issued an order that effectively forestalled Hardy's state trial. Mississippi appealed to the U.S. Supreme Court.

Two of the Civil Rights Division's staff lawyers returned to Washington with a scouting report. One of them was a protégé of John Doar, from the same hometown in Wisconsin, and his first field trip affected him no less deeply than had Doar's own trip to Tennessee a year earlier. Around the courthouse in Jackson and on visits to Tylertown, McComb, and Liberty, Doar's friend felt the climate of fear as a prickly sensation under his collar. Like Doar, he drove out to Negro country churches to meet those making the registration complaints, and he was moved by the courage of those who persevered without protections. His dominant impression of Moses was that he was hauntingly peaceful.

Doar flew to Mississippi to investigate for himself. On September 24 —a Sunday when King was introducing the illustrious Mordecai Johnson as special guest preacher at Ebenezer—Doar drove out to Steptoe's farm and met Moses in person, some five weeks after accepting his collect call from the Pike County jail. What he first noticed were the still-unhealed head wounds from the Caston beating. Because the FBI report on the beating had made no mention of cuts or stitches and had included no photograph, contrary to Bureau procedure in cases of substantial injury, Doar had assumed that Moses had suffered only minor bruises. And because Moses, for all the detail in his letters about the incident, never had set forth the gory specifics, Doar had suspected that Moses as the plaintiff in the case had understandably exaggerated the seriousness of a minor assault. Sight of the fresh scars caused Doar to reevaluate the quality of the FBI reporting as well as his estimate of Moses' character.

After listening to long, careful reports from Moses and Steptoe, Doar was convinced that there were grounds for their forebodings of further violence against voter registration workers in Amite County. Steptoe explained the reasons why he felt particularly menaced by Representative Hurst and the Caston family. He feared reprisals against himself and two other local farmers. One of them, Herbert Lee, had volunteered on occasion to drive Moses around the county. Lee, like Steptoe, had nine children, but he was a younger man, still actively farming. His wife had never attended the registration classes and was fearful for her husband. Lee, a small, wiry man, had attended many of the classes, but he said little and had not yet attempted to register. In trying to account for the threats against Lee, Moses could only speculate that whites were angry because they had seen Moses riding in Lee's car. Or possibly they were angry because Lee had once arrived late for a registration class and come upon a group of whites taking down the license numbers of cars parked outside the church. Moses had reported Lee's discovery to the Justice Department and the FBI, and the word had either seeped back into Amite County from there or spread from someone who recognized Lee at the church. Somehow, Moses reported, Herbert Lee was being singled out for resentment as a detective or "spy" for the Negroes.

Doar took these reports seriously enough to ask Moses and Steptoe to take him out to Lee's farm for a talk. Lee was not there, however, and Doar had to leave for Washington that night. When he walked into his office at the Justice Department the next day, Doar found a phone message that Herbert Lee had been murdered.

The message was from Moses. With SNCC chairman Charles McDew, he had been working at the Masonic Temple that morning when a call came in from Dr. Anderson, the man who had sewed up Moses' head wounds. In a chilled voice, Anderson reported that he was at a McComb funeral home with a mysterious corpse, which had lain amid a crowd for some hours in the parking lot of a cotton gin over in Liberty. No white or Negro in Liberty would touch it. When the McComb hearse arrived from across the county line to fetch the body, summoned by a cryptic message from Amite County authorities, no one at the scene dared to disclose even the victim's name. These circumstances led Anderson to suspect that it was someone from the voter registration classes. Moses soon identified the body as Herbert Lee. It lay on a table with a single bullet wound in the left temple.

At the funeral, the new widow Lee left her children to walk up to Moses and McDew, beating her chest in anguish and shouting, "You killed my husband! You killed my husband!" Her cries echoed in the cold misery of Moses' reflections. He labored to reach a philosophical perspective on his guilt, acknowledging that he was a "participant" in the killing, in the sense that it probably would not have occurred without his registration classes. Still, Moses could not convince himself that he should have acted differently unless he also accepted the reality of Amite County as permanent—that Negroes could always be gunned down with impunity for showing interest in the ballot.

There was no doubt about the identity of the actual killer. Representative E. H. Hurst, driving Billy Jack Caston's pickup truck, had followed Herbert Lee to the cotton gin and pulled up beside him. Lee slid away from Hurst, across the front seat of his own pickup and out the passenger door. Hurst ran around the trucks to confront him. According to Hurst, Lee then moved to attack him with a tire iron, whereupon Hurst struck Lee on the head with his pistol, which went off accidentally. Sheriff Caston and the town marshal arrived quickly on the scene and said they found a tire iron under Lee's body. Two eyewitnesses, one white and one Negro, told the same thing to a coroner's jury that same day, after which the killing was ruled an act of justifiable homicide.

Moses finally located the Negro witness at a small house in the country. Louis Allen was a forty-two-year-old logger with a seventh-grade education. He had a wife and three children; a fourth child had died of what Allen described as epilepsy. During World War II service in New Guinea, he had come down with ulcers, which had made the arduous work of cutting and hauling raw timber difficult ever since, but Allen did better with logs than with farming. Because he lacked capital and access to any of the three Negro lawyers in Mississippi, Allen relied on white men to "fix up the papers" for his equipment loans and to buy or lease timber tracts for him to cut. He had logged for Mr. Jewel Sugarman until Sugarman broke his back. Now he was logging for Mr. Roy Newman. His lawyer was Mr. Joe Gordon.

Allen related such details about himself openly, and was equally frank with Moses about what he had seen at the cotton gin. Lee didn't have a tire iron or anything else, he said. Lee had told Hurst that he wouldn't talk to him as long as Hurst had a gun out, and Lee had jumped out of his truck near where Allen had been standing. Hurst then had run around the truck and shouted, "I'm not playing with you this morning!" Then he shot Lee in the head from a few feet away. Allen had testified about the tire iron because that's what he was told to say, and he went along to protect his own life and his family. But he hated to lie about Lee, whom he knew to be an upstanding Negro farmer in the county. Allen told Moses what he had told his wife: "I didn't want to tell no story about the dead, because you can't ask the dead for forgiveness."

Moses had no doubt that Louis Allen was telling the truth, just as he knew that the prudent Herbert Lee would never have dreamed of attacking one of the county's most powerful white men, in public on a Monday morning. Yet Moses also realized that truth was worth little in obtaining justice in the Lee homicide. Trapped between victim and executioner, Moses realized that to push Allen forward might be to kill him. Yet to counsel silence would be to add his own complicity to the injustice of the Lee homicide.

From Washington, John Doar sought to obtain evidence that did not depend on the credibility of human witnesses, Negro or white. "Please examine Lee's body and photograph the wounds before burial," he instructed the FBI on the day after the murder. ". . . Perhaps the angle of the bullet's entry and the nature and location of the powder burns will confirm or refute the witnesses' descriptions." Dr. Anderson told Moses there were no powder burns at all. Confirmation of this fact would provide objective grounds for opening a full FBI investigation. There was no FBI office in the state of Mississippi, however, and by the time Doar's instruction got from FBI headquarters down to the New Orleans office and from there to the lone FBI agent in Natchez, the corpse was buried. Doar never received an official report on Lee's wounds. This left him with no independent evidence that Lee's killing was anything but the routine dispatch of a crazed Negro, as it was presented in the local newspaper.

Steptoe continued to let Moses stay with him in his house across the highway from the Hurst home, but Moses felt uncomfortable there because of the guns. The Steptoe farm always had been a minor arsenal, and Steptoe had a reputation as a magician who knew how to conceal an extra pistol or two. Now, after the Lee murder, Moses kept finding new guns under pillows and in bedside tables. The atmosphere was thick with the anticipation of a frontier shoot-out. Moses, not wishing to impose his own nonviolence on Steptoe, nor to have his own presence ignite the violence, retreated briefly to McComb. The aftershock of the Lee murder was pervasive there too, and it added to the tension that was building over the continued jailing of the four young sit-in students.

Moses had much to answer for with C. C. Bryant, who was upset that the civil rights campaign had strayed so far from the accepted plan. Bryant reminded him tersely that he had been invited to register voters in McComb. Now a farmer was dead in the wilderness of Amite County, and the McComb registration campaign was stalled anyway, because of the sit-ins. Moses confessed to Bryant's charges, but he exercised little control over events. On the morning of October 4, two of the newly released sit-in students returned to high school only to be informed by the august principal, Commodore Dewey Higgins, that they were suspended from classes because of their scrape with the law. This announcement caused an explosion of resentment against Higgins. Negro principals in segregated school systems were towering figures who controlled scarce, precious commodities such as teaching jobs, diplomas, and college recommendations. Often they converted the school system into an economic fiefdom as well—personally collecting the ticket receipts at school sporting events, and other emoluments—under franchise from the white school boards, on the condition that they stifle racial agitation in the schools. When Principal Higgins turned Brenda Travis and Ike Lewis away that morning, rebellion swept through the classrooms. More than a hundred students walked out behind them.

The students made a spontaneous march to the voter registration office at the Masonic Temple. Several of the Freedom Riders still in town urged them to mount a protest march that would draw attention to the injustice of the Lee killing as well as the sit-in punishments. Moses and SNCC chairman McDew spoke against the march, arguing that the suspensions were probably a pro forma move by Higgins, which could be revoked quietly in a few days, but that a march would flush out more vigorous opposition from the whites. Such caution was overwhelmed by the general enthusiasm of the students, however. When they resolved to march to the Pike County Courthouse in Magnolia, Moses and McDew felt obliged to go along in support.

They set off that afternoon for Magnolia, eight miles away, but they had barely passed the city limits when the late hour and the bleak highway ahead caused them to turn back toward the McComb city hall. They arrived on its steps to be greeted by a crowd of whites that had gathered to discuss where the Negroes were going. With police and bystanders looking on, gazing at the makeshift placards, a student spokesman went to the top step and began to pray. Police officers interrupted his first words with warnings that such prayers were not authorized on the steps. They arrested the student when he persisted. Another student then stepped up to pray and was arrested after the first few words—then another and another, including Brenda Travis, in what became a lengthy ritual. The police officers, apprehensive of a riot, finally cut short the procedure and placed the remaining marchers under mass arrest.

As they moved off toward the jail, several civilians darted in to attack Bob Zellner, a SNCC student newly arrived from Atlanta. As the only white person among the marchers, Zellner was a conspicuous target. One man was choking him before Moses and McDew reached his side and pressed themselves against him in an ad hoc maneuver of nonviolent protection. They absorbed some of the blows meant for him. When the attackers tried to pull them out of the way, McDew clutched Zellner around the chest and Moses clung to his waist. Zellner dropped his Bible, trying to hold on to the metal railing of the city hall steps. One attacker reached over the railing to gouge his eyes, and another kicked him squarely in the face. Knocked down in a heap, the three of them were dragged and kicked down the steps until policemen came up to shoo away the attackers. Then the officers jailed the SNCC trio along with 119 students.

This spectacle so aroused the authorities of the sleepy little farm town that they went to the Illinois Central railroad yards the next morning to arrest C. C. Bryant on a warrant signed by the police chief, who reasoned that as NAACP president Bryant was "behind some of this racial trouble." Police also arrested Cordell Reagon, a teenage Freedom Rider from Nashville, and Charles Sherrod. The only SNCC leader who remained free in McComb was Charles Jones, Sherrod's cellmate from the Rock Hill jail-in. Petrified, Jones put on a blood-smeared white smock and crouched in a corner of the shop beneath the Masonic Temple, hoping to pass for a butcher. On a pay phone, Jones alerted outside news services to the first civil rights mass arrest in the history of Mississippi. Fearing that Moses and the others could be dragged out of jail to a lynching at any time, he also called Harry Belafonte and John Doar for help. Doar went immediately to McComb, slipped into the butcher shop by night, and whispered that Jones should draw all the shades. When Jones recovered from this introduction to the mighty federal government, he counted it as a significant moment in his political and racial education to realize that its boldest representative was almost as apprehensive about Klan surveillance as he was.

C. C. Bryant had not attended or even known about the student march. If he had known, he would have disapproved strongly, but the sting of his own arrest nullified some of his tactical arguments about maneuvering to keep the goodwill of white people. Such things didn't matter in a crunch, he decided, and he was surprised to discover that many parents rallied behind their arrested sons and daughters. Hollis Watkins' father delivered a moving speech of support at the first mass meeting. Some parents expressed new interest in registration classes. At an NAACP meeting after he obtained bail, a changed Bryant declared, "Where the students lead, we will follow." His new outspokenness as an NAACP leader, plus the arbitrariness of his arrest, made him the news focus for the reporters who began to trickle into McComb. To a *Time* correspondent, Sheriff Clyde Simmons attributed the crackdown frankly to Bryant's attitude, saying he "puts himself in the class of the white people."

In court, Judge Hansford Simmons sentenced Brenda Travis indefinitely to reform school, released a hundred of the younger students to their parents, and ordered Moses, McDew, Zellner, and a score of the older students held pending trial on disturbing the peace charges. Guards transported the prisoners to the Amite County jail in Liberty, across county jurisdiction, in a move that was explained as something to make them think about the fate of Herbert Lee before they got into more trouble. Harry Belafonte sent them $5,000 in bail money a few days later.

Moses and the newly freed SNCC workers drove to Atlanta for an emergency staff meeting to discuss whether they could continue tactics that posed such enormous legal costs and immobilized nearly all SNCC's national leadership. The sleepy omniscience of rural communities was attuned by then to the tension buried around McComb. The Negroes seemed to have an idea of what was being discussed at the White Citizens Council meetings, and whites were vaguely aware of SNCC's movements. On the morning after the leaders departed for Atlanta, a hand-lettered victory proclamation was found taped to the front window of the Masonic Temple in McComb: "SNCC Done Snuck."

On September 26, the day after Herbert Lee was murdered, King went to Nashville for the SCLC's annual three-day conference. The killing and other sacrifices of the Moses project tempered the congratulatory spirit of the Freedom Ride summer. Neither James Farmer nor James Lawson called for extending the rides into Mississippi. Farmer vaguely predicted that Negroes someday might have to withhold income taxes from states that enforced segregation. Lawson declared that the Freedom Riders, for all their success, had been too few in number to pack the Jackson jails. Tacitly, he was rejecting the notion that nonviolent direct action could be enlarged to attack all segregation in the core state of Mississippi. The cost was too high, and repression would be so harsh as to crush rather than encourage a movement. After the heavy sentences meted out to James Bevel and Diane Nash, young people were shying away from demonstrations, just as they were falling away from registration classes after the Herbert Lee murder. For that reason Lawson disappointed those who hoped that he would move his workshops to Mississippi and spend years re-creating the Nashville experience. Without his guiding discipline, nonviolent direct action stood no chance of sustained application there. As events turned out, direct action never did rise to the supreme test in

Mississippi, leaving voter registration specialists like Moses to wonder whether Lawson could have made a difference.

The SCLC leaders confessed their worries more freely among themselves than in public. They wanted time to consolidate the gains of the Freedom Rides and to recuperate financially. The SCLC was already burdened by legal debts from demonstrations in North Carolina as well as the defense of the Freedom Riders. Most pressing of all was the *New York Times* v. *Sullivan* libel judgment, which was still making its way upward through the appeals courts of Alabama. To raise money to pay all these lawyers, they rented the Grand Ol' Opry for a "Salute to the Freedom Riders" fund-raising concert. Harry Belafonte, the headline performer, recruited Miriam Makeba, the Chad Mitchell Trio, and several other popular entertainers to back him up as the "Belafonte Troupe." Unfortunately, Belafonte himself fell ill before the concert. Public announcement of his cancellation stifled ticket sales, and the SCLC wound up losing a large sum on the venture.

Financial straits complicated King's delicate, multilayered diplomacy with the Kennedy Administration. Burke Marshall, Harris Wofford, and other Kennedy officials remained important people in the complex arrangements to create the Voter Education Project, from which the SCLC stood to gain enormous grants of tax-free money for voter registration. The Administration's demand for strict secrecy meant that King had to be careful about discussing the VEP negotiations even in the SCLC's closed board meeting at Nashville. Wyatt Walker's report on the SCLC's voter registration plans for 1962 did not mention the subject, and the Nashville board meeting drifted into what King's friend Lawrence Reddick feared it would be: a ceremonial procession of preachers' speeches, "in which every 'dignitary' present has to have his say." The official minutes recorded a "very, very lengthy discussion on what the Conference [SCLC] should do to show its appreciation to the President, Dr. King, Jr." Eventually, on the motion of Ralph Abernathy, the board asked King to appoint a committee on resolutions to formulate a presentation for King. Someone amended the motion to include Coretta. Abernathy later moved that the board issue a proclamation to let J. H. Jackson know that it would not back away from King. After a nonpreacher on the board objected that a personal attack on Jackson would be a mistake, Abernathy's motion also was referred to a committee.

King sent Robert Kennedy an immediate telegram of protest over the rash of events in Mississippi—the beatings, the Lee murder, and the mass arrest—calling them "an apparent reign of terror." Even so direct a request was swallowed up, however, by overriding questions of political etiquette. What registered in Washington was that Robert Kennedy first heard about King's Mississippi telegram from a reporter. This insult undercut Kennedy's confidence that he and King could do business privately. King surrendered the point. Wyatt Walker sent Kennedy an abject follow-up telegram accepting blame for the earlier one as "my own personal administrative error." He advised Kennedy that "it is never Dr. King's or SCLC's practice to release the text of any message to the press without it first being transmitted."

King soon received what he thought was an opportunity to repair his political relations with the Kennedy Administration. Harris Wofford invited him to meet privately with the President. Again, like the spring luncheon with Robert Kennedy at the Mayflower Hotel, the session was to be completely off the record. Implicitly, at least, it was another test of King's willingness to play by the rules, after the public controversies over the Freedom Rides. King welcomed the chance, but he knew something else was afoot as soon as he saw Wofford's uncommonly grave face at the White House. Wofford said he had been instructed by the President and the Attorney General to deliver an official message about Stanley Levison.

The genesis of the message lay in FBI Director Hoover's memo notation ("Why not?") during the Freedom Rides in May, demanding to know why the FBI had not thoroughly investigated the troublemaker King. That question had reverberated among his subordinates, who gleaned from Bureau files the information that both King and Harry Belafonte were close friends of Levison. Summary comments about Levison had sounded so ominous to Burke Marshall in the Justice Department that he requested to see all the Bureau's files on Levison. The FBI responded that the files were too sensitive to be shared with Marshall but that Levison was an important operative of the Soviet espionage network in the United States. Soon thereafter, Marshall had lingered in Harris Wofford's office following one of the interagency meetings to raise the matter in strict privacy.

For Wofford, the charges against Levison were an unwelcome return of McCarthyism. He resisted Marshall's argument that King was tainted by association. In response to his request for proof, Marshall obtained FBI briefings on exactly what he could and could not say about the evidence against Levison. Essentially, he could say nothing, because the evidence was classified to protect the FBI's intelligence sources. By the inverted logic of spy cases, the more important the charge, the more closely held was the evidence and the more constrained was the government in taking action.

An unhappy Wofford told King, in words he said had been carefully chosen by his superiors, that the United States government considered

Stanley Levison a prime security threat. It was not a matter of leftist beliefs or Communist sympathies, Wofford added, or even of membership in the Communist Party, but that Levison had been identified at the highest levels of the U.S. government as a key element of the Soviet espionage network, a "direct link to Moscow." The Kennedy Administration was warning King confidentially, but in the strongest terms, to cease all contact with Levison.

King was stunned. He replied that he found it almost impossible to believe such a thing about Levison, who had worked tirelessly and selflessly in King's behalf for nearly five years. King asked Wofford how the government knew such a thing. Had FBI agents caught Levison taking rubles from the Soviets or sending secret messages to spies? Wofford, who had asked those same questions of Marshall but was now on the other side of the table, could reply only that the evidence was secret. Unlike Marshall, Wofford advised King that his own experience made him doubt the accuracy of the FBI's suspicions, but he conceded that his doubts counted for little against the word of the FBI Director.

King eventually fell silent in Wofford's office. The government made it a question of trust, he said finally, and he had far more reason to trust Levison than he did to trust J. Edgar Hoover. King felt ambushed—diverted, perhaps deliberately, from the hopeful agenda he had brought to the White House. To him the new charges were yet another extraneous issue bedeviling his efforts to raise the central moralities of the race question, and it was especially bitter for him to feel so personally the sting of anti-Communist suspicion. The Levison burden was being passed along to him by a chain of people each claiming to be personally removed from the mysterious grievance, each explaining basically underhanded requests in the language of honorable intentions. For King it boiled down to the fact that his best friend in the government was telling him to shun a friend as an alien being, for reasons no more tangible or convincing than suspicion itself.

Deeply depressed, King told Wofford he did not know how he would respond to the warning. He composed himself for his meeting with President Kennedy, which turned out to be a private luncheon in the White House living quarters with Jacqueline Kennedy as well as the President. There was an edge to the arrangements, especially after the delivery of Wofford's message, in that such privacy could be either an honor or a means of concealing King's off-the-record presence, and Mrs. Kennedy's presence could be either a kind social gesture toward King or a signal that business talk was unwelcome. King was accustomed to this sort of ambivalence, and the charm of the Kennedys made for an engaging meal with the First Family. Afterward the three of them went for a tour of the newly renovated White House, featuring Mrs. Kennedy's cultured tastes and acquisitions, which were the subject of much front-page journalism at the time.

When they passed through the Lincoln Room, King saw a way to break through the pleasantries without offending the President—in a request that was at once casual and significant, and which might appeal to Kennedy's sense of history. As they passed by a framed copy of Lincoln's Emancipation Proclamation on a mantel, King said, "Mr. President, I'd like to see you stand in this room and sign a Second Emancipation Proclamation outlawing segregation, one hundred years after Lincoln's. You could base it on the Fourteenth Amendment." Kennedy responded positively enough to ask King to prepare a draft proclamation for him to consider. King said he would be happy to submit one. This exchange allowed him to leave with a presidential mandate that partially offset the imperious demand for Levison's head.

Moses said very little during the Atlanta SNCC meeting, where he joined about a score of younger students from across the South. They carried with them in fledgling form the institutionalized memory of the sit-ins and the Freedom Rides, interpreted in the context of prior generations by their ever-present mentor, Ella Baker. What they had was literally embodied in themselves, and they were in a transfused state. Advanced far beyond their years, most of them were star students who recently had seen more than one jail from the inside. They had seen their own names in the newspapers, and they had felt both the concentrated fears and the most extravagant praise of their elders. They were becoming self-consciously aware of the historical present. James Lawson was just then writing a magazine article entitled "Eve of Nonviolent Revolution?"

Each person was asked to make a short statement of belief and to discuss why he or she wanted to work full time for SNCC. Prayers and dramatic testimonies were offered up until Moses halted the proceedings suddenly by declining to speak on the subject. He said only that he was anxious to get back to Mississippi. He thought the students were grandstanding, trying to surpass one another in eloquence, but he would not say so, any more than he would pressure Mississippi farmers to register, because he recoiled from seeking to dominate others with his presence. Moses was a mystical purist. He valued SNCC for the succor it provided to like-minded people, but he remained aloof from the more pragmatic functions of an organization, such as fund-raising, discipline, and publicity. His experience in Mississippi had left him more suspicious of command, more preoccupied with moral leadership by example.

His silence probably had a greater effect than any speech he could have made. It signaled that he was positively eager to get back to the wasteland of Mississippi. Whereas the consciences of movement people previously had sustained only forays into danger, Moses seemed to require such exposure constantly and to be oppressed by the trivia of ordinary life. He reversed the psychic balance between tension and relief. He was a predominant force within SNCC in spite of himself. One immediate effect of his silence was to dampen the internal power struggle by making its issues seem petty or moot.

Ironically, it was Moses, so mindless of image and self-advancement, who shaped the public perception of the early SNCC. The image of SNCC came to be not so much a sit-in student or Freedom Rider but rather a kind of priest who chose to isolate himself deep behind the lines of segregation for years at a time, armed only with nonviolence. The SNCC worker came to be heralded as a figure of relentless sacrifice, against all conventional ambitions. SNCC mythology, borrowing from that of the early Christians as well as from the labor movement, would focus upon the "organizer" who cared nothing for comfort or recognition, who would meet rejection by cheerfully shaking the dust from his feet and moving on to another outpost. This description, amplified partly as an antipode to the more regal leadership image of Martin Luther King, made "grassroots" a popular term of political discourse in the 1960s.

Returning from Atlanta with a carload of his Mississippi veterans, Moses quickly established that SNCC had not yet snuck from McComb. Their most immediate crisis was that Principal Higgins was refusing to allow the hundred students arrested on October 4 to resume high school classes unless they first signed pledges to refrain from any further racial agitation. The students were holding Higgins to a standoff in daily marches to the school, always with speeches, negotiations, and a march home again after a mass refusal to sign such a pledge. Negro teachers feared that the unprecedented student strike threatened their jobs. There was a nearly continuous danger of violence—both between the opposing Negro factions and from whites hostile to the entire dispute.

To protect student morale from erosion over time, the SNCC leaders created an emergency school of their own, which they called Nonviolent High. Many of the SNCC teachers possessed qualifications more advanced than the regular teachers, and this fact itself touched off one of the countless subtopics of controversy. The excitement warded off much of the normal classroom boredom, and the teachers found themselves learning as much as the students. In the history class, a young boy rose to ask Charles McDew whether the course would cover "the War for Southern Independence."

"The war for what?" McDew replied. He was puzzled until he realized that this was one of the diehard Confederate terms for the Civil War, and that even the young Negro crusaders in his class had absorbed unconsciously a great deal of the Southern point of view. Moses, McDew, and the other teachers knew they faced obstacles as subtle as they were enormous. They also realized that Nonviolent High owed its beginning partly to the grace of white authorities who had not yet bothered to concentrate their opposition.

One night during the chaotic first week of the makeshift school, an extremely nervous visitor called on Moses at the Masonic Temple. Louis Allen told Moses that he had been summoned before a grand jury that was to consider the coroner's findings in the Herbert Lee murder. Allen said he did not want to lie again. He wanted to know if Moses could arrange for the federal government to protect his life if he testified against E. H. Hurst. Admiration welled up in Moses, along with the bittersweet thrill of a murder solved and the joyful hope that some justice might be done in spite of Amite County's blanket of fear. Moses advised Allen to keep silent until he could make inquiries in Washington.

He relayed Allen's offer to John Doar, setting off a round of bureaucratic wrangling. Doar had taken a personal interest in the Lee murder since finding the note on his desk three weeks earlier. On October 19, he had filed his third investigative request on the case with the FBI, asking the Bureau to reinterview the witnesses, to question Sheriff Caston about the discovery of the alleged tire iron, and to obtain the minutes of the coroner's jury testimony. The Bureau had resisted the instruction, arguing that it was fruitless to reopen a civil rights murder inquiry against Hurst in view of the fact that all the county authorities and witnesses agreed that it was self-defense. Doar disclosed to the Bureau that the case was different now because Allen was prepared to change his testimony.

FBI agents eventually returned to Liberty to comply with Doar's request. Louis Allen took the fateful step and told them officially that he had seen no tire iron and that Hurst had simply shot Herbert Lee in a rage. The agents also reinterviewed the only other witness, a white man who had testified that he saw Herbert Lee raise a tire iron against Hurst. Now this witness conceded that he never saw the tire iron until "it was removed" from beneath Lee's body. The passive construction "was removed" appeared four times in the FBI interview report, without any sign that the interviewing agent ever asked who it was that had removed the tire iron. Such neglect of logical, urgent investigative leads drove Doar to despair. The judge who had presided at the coroner's inquest was interviewed, as Doar requested, but the interviewing agent did not obtain the minutes of the inquest, nor even report that he had asked for them.

Doar reported only a summary of this to Moses, leading to the decision that the Justice Department would file no indictment in the Herbert Lee case. This cruel finality compounded the moral conundrum haunting both of them. They knew that without a federal indictment there would be no effective protection for Louis Allen. Therefore it would be almost pointless, as well as dangerous, for Allen to testify against Hurst in the grand jury. Moses and Doar found themselves in the miserable position of cautioning Allen against the consequences of telling the truth—warning him in effect that he should lie again. For Moses it was a betrayal of Allen's courage and of his own philosophical approach to his mission in Mississippi.

Even worse, it was too late to pull back. Nearly everyone in the county, it seemed, already knew of the renewed FBI investigation and of Allen's willingness to accuse Hurst before the grand jury. Allen was a marked man even after he declined to do so. Whites who had bought his loads of pine logs for years began to say they did not need them. Donis Hawkins' gas station cut off his credit, and so did Daryl Blaelock's. Allen's ominous plight left Doar and Moses with the worst of both worlds: they had exposed him to mortal risk without gaining even a chance of justice. From the standpoint of Allen's well-being, it would have been better had they advised him from the beginning to lie or keep silent—to follow the rules for good niggers in Mississippi. Louis Allen had perceived this clearly on the day of the murder, but the movement philosopher and the minister of U.S. justice came around only after they had coaxed Allen fatefully toward a different truth.

Doar tried to restrain Moses in his criticisms of the FBI, arguing that Moses never could hope to make headway by fighting both the segregationist powers of Mississippi and the Bureau. The key to the FBI lay in its name—*Bureau*. Buried within its labyrinthine bureaucratic ways and its extraordinary domination by the personality of J. Edgar Hoover were levers that might be used for civil rights. The FBI abhorred embarrassment and public failure, for example. Most of its agents were Northern Catholics, not Southerners. The Bureau's traditional cooperation with local authorities was nearly always undercut by rivalry—with sheriffs and policemen resenting the high and mighty Bureau, and the FBI agents looking down on the provincial ways of the locals. Doar stressed that it was a practical imperative to study and cajole the Bureau, and to fasten the FBI's vast institutional pride to the new job of enforcing the civil rights laws.

Although it was not easy to say such things to Moses, Doar persisted in his usual terse manner. He had to do so—not only to keep functioning himself but to signal to Moses that the fault was not entirely with the

FBI. What Doar could not say was that he and his colleagues had prepared a powerful "b-suit" based on the Lee murder and a number of the lesser plagues in southwest Mississippi. Doar had come to like Louis Allen personally, and he believed that Allen's plainspoken, fearful honesty could make him a convincing witness. He also knew that it could have a sobering effect on segregationist officials just to see Hurst arrested and tried, regardless of whether a jury convicted him. Following Justice Department rules, Doar kept all this to himself because he did not want to confess that Burke Marshall had rejected the case. Marshall feared chaos, and felt a need to maintain the government's posture of control. Doar grudgingly accepted the judgment, but some of his assistants—especially those few who had worked in Mississippi—remained in a state of open dissent. Among other objections, they argued that the policy made a perversion of the Justice Department's ongoing effort to convince civil rights groups that the federal government would protect them in voter registration. Doar told them that nowhere else could they make their case as freely as under Marshall. Nowhere else were line prosecutors so close to the top. They should keep plugging.

In McComb, some of the students surrendered to Principal Higgins' pledge. The SNCC leaders arranged hurriedly for scores of others to be taken in by a Negro college that offered high school courses. All this was accomplished by October 31, when nearly the entire faculty of Nonviolent High went on trial for the October 4 protest march. After a quick trial, Moses, McDew, Zellner, and fifteen others were taken in handcuffs to the drunk tank of the county jail in Magnolia, to begin serving prison terms of four to six months. On smuggled paper, Moses wrote that Judge Brumfield, while imposing sentence, had scolded him for leading the Negro children to slaughter: " 'Robert,' he was addressing me, 'haven't some of the people from your school been able to go down and register without violence here in Pike County?' I thought to myself that Southerners are exposed the most, when they boast."

The prisoners became objects of curiosity among local whites who had business near the county jail, and some went so far as to make special trips to take a look at them. It was generally accepted that the twelve special ones crammed into one cell were Communists, and few Magnolians had seen a real Communist before. Some asked the guards to point out Moses, whose name was being circulated as their leader. A businessman remarked soberly that they should keep Moses and the others in jail just as long as the Russians imprisoned Francis Gary Powers, the American U-2 pilot. A young girl was thrilled when Charles McDew, yielding to her pleas to hear them "say something in Communist," gave her a few words of Yiddish.

These zoolike diversions at the expense of innocently or ignorantly hostile visitors were rare. For the most part, the cramped prisoners had to stave off boredom and despair on their own. They exchanged advanced Nonviolent High lectures among themselves. Moses and McDew played chess with pieces made of matchsticks. "It's mealtime now," Moses wrote. "We have rice and gravy in a flat pan, dry bread and a 'big town cake'; we lack eating and drinking utensils. Water comes from a faucet and goes into a hole.

"This is Mississippi, the middle of the iceberg. Hollis [Watkins] is leading off with his tenor, 'Michael row the boat ashore, Alleluja; Christian brothers don't be slow, Alleluja; Mississippi next to go, Alleluja.' This is a tremor in the middle of the iceberg . . ."

FOURTEEN

ALMOST CHRISTMAS
IN ALBANY

Charles Sherrod and Cordell Reagon made a special bus trip to attend the Moses trial in McComb. They watched their friends being led off to jail, then they returned to their new outpost in Albany, Georgia. Since criminal charges arising from their own McComb arrests had been dropped in mid-October, they had been working to re-create the Mississippi registration project in the cotton, pecan, and peanut region of southwest Georgia around Albany. They had arrived there full of zeal and empty of nearly everything else, sleeping at times in parked cars or on porches. Having spent the summer in Mississippi, they thought of Albany as a slightly larger version of McComb, and of Terrell County as a forsaken plantation of violence, like Amite County.

From the Southern Regional Council in Atlanta, Sherrod had obtained the name of C. W. King, a prosperous Albany Negro who was a supporter of liberal causes. Patriarch of a remarkable family, C. W. King had seven sons, all highly educated, many of whom had studied abroad. The eldest, Clennon, was the professor who had been declared insane in 1958 because he was crazy enough to apply for admission to the University of Mississippi. The youngest, Preston, was an expatriate professor of philosophy at the University of South Wales, in Australia. Of the five middle brothers, two remained in Albany as pillars of the young Negro establishment. Slater King was a builder and real estate broker, like his father.

C. B. King was one of only three Negro lawyers in all of Georgia outside Atlanta. (He had secured his brother Clennon's release from Whitfield Asylum in Mississippi.) He wore a neatly trimmed beard and tailored suits, and he discussed all subjects in a melodious, polysyllabic stream. Yet with all his affectations, C. B. King remained in Albany to press the legal claims of maids, mechanics, and drunkards. Local white lawyers did not quite know what to make of him.

The eccentric senior King allowed Sherrod and Reagon to occupy an empty room in one of his buildings. The two young SNCC workers seemed a scruffy and unlikely pair of political leaders. Reagon was only eighteen. As a high school student in Nashville, he had so resented James Lawson's rule barring him from the nonviolence workshops as too young that he had crashed some of the Nashville demonstrations. By his own account the seriousness of the movement had not sunk in until he arrived at Parchman Penitentiary in a truck with the first Freedom Riders and saw the guards there beat, shock, and strip the two prostrate Chicago pacifists. Reagon was fearless, but most of his SNCC elders regarded him as a kid who was a little too eager to keep up.

Sherrod was the only SNCC veteran who tolerated his company, and to the Albany Kings, Sherrod himself was a young man of mixed qualities. There had always been something about him that was dangerous as well as innocent. When as a teenager he had announced his intention to locate and introduce himself to his white relatives around Petersburg, Virginia, horrified Negro relatives throttled this violation of taboo. When he returned from his first racially mixed discussion group, he expressed amazement at his discovery that there were things white people did not know. In equal extremes, he seemed both shy and touchy, lazy and driven, a man of the cloth and of the street. Sherrod and Reagon spent their first days simply playing basketball on the playgrounds of the Negro high schools, answering questions as they came. Reagon developed quickly as a star attraction among his age peers, many of whom were agog over his tales about the Freedom Rides. After a week of playground bull sessions, more than a dozen of the students responded positively to the idea of attending a church meeting. They accepted the assertion that they could not understand the sit-ins and Freedom Rides without knowing how nonviolent resistance came straight from the Bible.

Sherrod conducted the first meetings outdoors. He introduced himself as a fellow preacher to the pastors of the churches within walking distance of the high schools, and one of them, Rev. H. C. Boyd of Shiloh Baptist, agreed to let Sherrod use a room in the church. Boyd, attending the first few sessions himself, heard chapter and verse from the Bible on brotherhood and justice. He later came to believe that Sherrod deceived him by emphasizing Christian virtues and a better Albany, while making only passing references to jail or protest, but at the time Boyd soothed himself with the thought that Sherrod was accomplishing what no Albany pastor, including himself, could do—he was attracting a growing number of eager teenagers into church two, three, four times a week.

The first of Albany's Negro leaders to react strongly against Sherrod and Reagon was Tom Chatmon, adult supervisor of the local NAACP Youth Council. A Morehouse graduate in his early thirties, Chatmon already had manifested business skills that would win him several fortunes as a distributor of Negro cosmetics, and also a compulsive gambling habit that would devour more than one of those fortunes. Possessed of a gambler's humor, Chatmon was a popular man in Albany's Negro establishment. His position within the NAACP corresponded roughly to the presidency of the white Jaycees—a stepping-stone toward senior leadership—and as the adult most closely in touch with Albany's young people, Chatmon learned early that the two vagabond outsiders were stealing the enthusiasm of his best Youth Council members. Defensively, he concluded that the SNCC pair might be Communists.

Chatmon's worries unsettled even the boldest and most restless of Albany's Negro leaders. Some members of the prestigious Criterion Club suggested that they be run out of town, or, as C. B. King put it to Sherrod, "have opined that the community might be well advised to divest itself of your presence." A prominent Albany Negro placed "an urgent and distressing call" to NAACP regional headquarters in Atlanta, warning that the two young SNCC activists were about to seduce the local youth into suicidal demonstrations. Three NAACP officials rushed down to Albany to try to restore discipline against such a possibility.

As November 1 approached, Chatmon found it increasingly difficult to resist his Youth Council members who wanted to test the white waiting room of the Trailways bus station on the effective date of the new ICC desegregation rule. Chatmon did not deny that it had cost the Freedom Riders much more pain to obtain this rule than it would cost Albany's youth to test it, and he heartily agreed that both justice and federal law supported any Negro's right to fair treatment at the station. Still, he belabored himself with limits. If he sought approval within the NAACP, he was likely to be refused and almost certain to be accused of bending to the SNCC line. If he went ahead without approval, he invited censure within the hierarchical NAACP. If he did nothing, his Youth Council charges would follow Sherrod to the bus station and discredit Chatmon as the figurehead leader of a timid, inert NAACP. Chatmon reluctantly began negotiations with Sherrod toward a "test" at the bus station on November 1. High school students from the Youth Council would carry it out, but they would not act in the name of the NAACP and they would avoid arrest. A tentative, secret agreement was reached before Sherrod left for the Moses trial in Mississippi.

Word of it seeped back across race lines to the city authorities, prompting Mayor Asa Kelley to call a special meeting of the Albany City Commission on October 30. In closed session, Police Chief Laurie Pritchett reported that "certain demonstrations were expected to occur." Pritchett was a studious, farsighted police officer, notwithstanding his hulking ex-football player's frame and his ever-present cigar. In anticipation of such a crisis, he had studied the performance of Alabama authorities during the Freedom Rides. Concluding that their chief error had been to permit violence, which drew publicity and forced federal intervention, he had lectured his officers on how to enforce the race laws without nightsticks or guns. To the City Commission, Pritchett announced that he had instructed his men to make no arrests under the segregation laws themselves, which were vulnerable to legal attack, but to defend segregation under laws protecting the public order. He said he had put the entire Albany police force on alert status "during the period of expected tension." All vacation time was canceled. The commissioners thanked him for his sophisticated preparations.

When Cordell Reagon and Charles Sherrod approached Albany in a Trailways bus on the morning of November 1, they were about to make Albany one of scores of cities across the South to be tested that day as a follow-up to the Freedom Rides. Gordon Carey of CORE had sent instructions to more than seven hundred volunteers in seven states. The plan for Albany was a kind of pincers maneuver: Sherrod and Reagon were to test the Trailways facilities as passengers, while a group of Chatmon's Youth Council students was to meet them, testing the bus station facilities from the outside. When Sherrod and Reagon walked into the white waiting room, however, no students were in sight. Their greeting party was composed instead of a half-dozen or so grim-faced Albany policemen. Chilled with disappointment, the two SNCC workers left the station quickly to find that paranoia was loose among the Negroes, who had warned of beatings and even massacres at the station. It took all day for them to rally the spirits of the Youth Council members enough for nine of them to venture to the Trailways station that same afternoon. Sherrod and Reagon waited outside as the students entered the white waiting room. When police ordered them to leave, they retreated in compliance.

Although this was the tamest of demonstrations by Freedom Ride standards, Sherrod reported that "from that moment on, segregation was dead." Word flashed through Negro Albany that "the children" had dared to confront Laurie Pritchett's men at the bus station. All but the most

conservative of the local NAACP leaders came quickly to agree that
someone would have to get arrested at the station, if only to establish
grounds for a test case on police violations of the new ICC order. Sherrod
preached Lawson's theme that Supreme Court edicts piled high as the
clouds were irrelevant so long as Albany's Negroes enforced segregation
upon themselves by cowering before the police. High school students
flocked to his meetings in greater numbers, bringing with them older
relatives. College students turned up, as did a few preachers and even a
schoolteacher or two. Sherrod and Reagon were also holding voter registration workshops every Saturday, but the town was consumed with
interest in what would happen next at the bus station.

C. B. King was working on a criminal case that touched the rawest
passions of race. Violence had erupted in the county of the notorious
Screws case—"Bad" Baker County, one of the plantation areas that
ringed Albany. High finance in Baker County was dominated by an illiterate multimillionaire cattle breeder, who wrote checks on scraps of
grocery bags and signed them with an "X," and by Coca-Cola chairman
Robert Woodruff, who owned a 30,000-acre resort plantation called
Ichuaway.

Every Fourth of July, Woodruff's plantation overseer presided at a giant
free barbecue for Negroes only. Three thousand had attended that year's
festivities, during which a Negro field hand named Charlie Ware made
the mistake of flirting with the white overseer's Negro mistress. The
overseer complained to the sheriff, L. Warren Johnson, who fawned upon
the powerful overseer almost as deferentially as the county's Negroes
fawned upon the sheriff. Both Ware and Sheriff Johnson had a fifth-grade
education and a fondness for drink. "Gator" Johnson also had a reputation for meanness, as he was alleged to have killed four or more Negroes
under his custody. As successor to the infamous Sheriff Claude Screws,
he was from the "old school." On the night of the 1961 barbecue, Johnson
drove to Charlie Ware's house and proceeded to beat his wife intermittently until Ware came home. Then Johnson beat Ware on the head,
arrested and searched him, and drove to Newton, a town so tiny it could
not support a restaurant. Parked outside the Baker County jail, with
Ware handcuffed beside him on the front seat, Johnson picked up his
radio transmitter and said, "This nigger's coming on me with a knife!
I'm gonna have to shoot him." He fired two .32-caliber bullets into
Ware's neck. "He's still coming on! I'm gonna have to shoot him again,"
said Johnson, and fired a third time.

This, at any rate, was the account of the FBI agent who investigated the shooting after doctors later brought Ware miraculously back to life, with no permanent injuries except those caused by vertebra fragments that seeped into his spinal fluid. The FBI agent supported Charlie Ware's version almost completely, but his conclusions counted for very little in Baker County. A grand jury promptly indicted Ware for felonious assault upon Sheriff Johnson. Later in July, officers transported Ware from the hospital to the jail. He was still there in November, when C. B. King appealed to a judge to free him on the grounds that Ware was not a risk to flee and that he suffered both mental and physical aftereffects of the shooting, with blood still dripping from his ears. The judge refused to lower the bail bond, forcing the impoverished Ware to remain in jail more than a year until trial, but in the meantime C. B. King filed a civil suit against Sheriff Johnson in federal court, arguing that Johnson's story was preposterous on its face. The sheriff was a full head taller than Ware, outweighed him by more than a hundred pounds, and possessed all the psychological advantages of a white sheriff in a Black Belt county where the air of feudalism still mingled with the heat. King alleged that the sheriff had committed a monstrous violation of Ware's civil rights.

What was new for southwest Georgia was Charlie Ware's refusal to plead guilty to whatever charge pleased Sheriff Johnson. By all previous standards, he and C. B. King were leaping into deep caves with only a single match. But the news of their crusade fanned the incipient rebellion in Albany. A week after C. B. King filed his bail motion for Charlie Ware in Baker County, more than twenty people crowded into Slater King's home for a tense Friday-night summit conference. Representatives of seven Negro organizations in Albany, plus SNCC, gathered in an atmosphere of charged anticipation, undercut by rivalry and suspicion. Anxieties caused them to stress their points of agreement. All the representatives, from the Federated Women's Clubs to the Ministerial Alliance, subscribed to the NAACP's official goal of ending all segregation in Albany. They also agreed that it was preferable to achieve these goals by negotiation rather than demonstrations, which they called by the euphemism "positive actions," but they split over the crucial question of who should decide when positive actions were required. No organization welcomed such responsibility, especially in the pregnant knowledge that Sherrod's youth cadres were burning to go ahead, but none trusted the others, either. Almost inevitably, by a process reminiscent of the bus boycott's first days in Montgomery, they decided to create a new organization called the Albany Movement.

Slater King recommended as president a doctor named William G. Anderson, who had come to Albany from his hometown of Americus, Georgia, only four years earlier. In the elite Criterion Club, Anderson had distinguished himself for persistence and diplomacy. He was hand-some, well-spoken, ambitious, and unscarred. The founding members of the Albany Movement elected him president that night. Slater King be-came vice president. Before adjourning, the members adopted a cautious declaration of method. In language that bore signs of C. B. King's drafts-manship, the document concluded: "It has been our vicarious experi-ence, that when positive actions in matters of this kind have become necessary in order to implement the achievement of these constitution-ally guaranteed rights, it has been detrimental to the best interests of the communities involved, economically, socially, and morally. In view of the threat of such detriment, it is our hope that such positive actions will not be necessary in the city of Albany." A copy soon found its way into the hands of Mayor Kelley and Police Chief Pritchett.

Sherrod and Reagon had reason to be pleased. After about two months' work, they were being incorporated into a leadership organization much broader than anything ever created in McComb. Expected SNCC dem-onstrations were the unspoken cause of unity, and the qualms of the local leaders were so feeble against the tide of student sentiment that the first of the "positive actions" took place on November 22, only five days after the founding of the Albany Movement. Three high school students from Chatmon's Youth Council walked into the white sections of the bus station to confront the officers stationed there during the continuous "alert." After they refused orders to move on, even in the commanding presence of Chief Pritchett himself, they were hauled off to jail under the fixed gaze of several dozen bystanders. Tom Chatmon bailed them out within an hour, but Albany had its first arrests on the day before Thanksgiving.

Late that same afternoon, Albany State College dismissed its students for the holiday weekend. Hundreds of Negro students walked or rode across the Flint River bridge to the Trailways station in downtown Al-bany, bound for their hometowns. Because of the earlier arrests and the persistent rumors of race trouble, the dean of students went ahead of them. He took up a post outside the station, from which he directed the herd of students toward the colored waiting room. All obeyed him except two, Blanton Hall and Bertha Gober. They broke away to "go clean-sided," which was the local Negro slang for entering the white waiting room. The distraught dean, forbidden to pursue them there, peeked in from the outside along with gaggles of awestruck students. A policeman quickly approached Hall and Gober in the line at the white ticket win-dow and said, "You'll never get your ticket there." The two students asked why, nervously and politely standing their ground. A detective laid the groundwork for arrest by advising them that their presence was "tending to create a disturbance," and when they still did not move from the line, Laurie Pritchett ordered them to jail. Word had flashed through Negro Albany by suppertime: two groups to jail in a single day. By morning, nearly everyone knew that two Albany State students were spending their Thanksgiving away from home, behind bars. Although they were almost completely unknown, being from out of town, their plight drew sympathy eclipsing that for the three Youth Council members. Strangers took plates of turkey down to the jail.

The two students stayed in jail through Thanksgiving night, receiving more food and visitors. Frequent bulletins about their condition pulsed outward by telephone and word of mouth. As in McComb, the sentiments of parents and other adults fell heavily to their support, so that the leaders of the new Albany Movement determined on Friday to call their first mass meeting for Saturday night. With a campus crisis, a high school crisis, and a growing fear of violence over segregation, they had a compelling opportunity to introduce their organization to the general public. Anderson and Slater King obtained permission from Rev. E. James Grant to use Mount Zion Baptist Church. This was a breakthrough in itself, as Mount Zion was the church of the Baptist elite.

On Saturday morning, Blanton Hall and Bertha Gober each received in jail an official notice from Albany State, that "as a result of your being apprehended and arrested . . . you are hereby suspended indefinitely as a student." If the mass meeting was not already a guaranteed success, it became one as soon as the leafleters and runners spread word that President Dennis had decided to stand with the white segregationists. Rumors flew—that the students were in tears, that Reverend Grant had resisted pressure to withdraw his permission to use Mount Zion, that Dennis would not dare show his face at his own church.

Dr. Anderson presided at the meeting. Slater King made a speech, as did C. B. King and several others. A. C. Searles, editor of the local Negro weekly, reported on his emergency conference that afternoon with President Dennis. To all his arguments that the student suspensions were not only wrong but improper—handed down without any notice or hearing, in advance of any conviction in the courts—Dennis had replied tersely that the students would be suspended "forever." Dennis had been overwrought, Searles declared, and Searles himself was upset enough to call Dennis—his old friend, fellow deacon and Criterion Club member—"the blackest white man I ever saw." Sharp words ostracized Dennis, and stirring words called for unity against segregation. Long-standing patterns were turned upside down, with age and conciliation giving way to youth and confrontational witness.

Cordell Reagon, an extroverted performer with a clear tenor voice, had discovered in the SNCC workshops two gifted singers, Rutha Harris and Bernice Johnson, both of them preachers' daughters studying voice in the hope of becoming opera stars. The trio had been singing freedom songs together for weeks, and that night they climbed into the Mount Zion pulpit to lead the singing. By prearrangement, no one played the piano or organ for either the freedom songs or the church hymns. The harmonies and intensities of naked voices became a trademark of the Albany Movement. All sounds, from the soaring gospel descants of the soprano soloists to the thunderous hand-clapping of the congregation, were created by human flesh. The songs harked back to the moods of the slavery spirituals. There were tragic, sweet songs like "Oh, Freedom" and rollicking ones like "This Little Light of Mine." At first, the SNCC leaders accepted the songleader role because of their appreciation for movement singing, and the elders conceded them the role because music was of marginal importance to the normal church program. But the SNCC leaders soon developed a manipulative guile about the music. Their *a capella* singing took the service away from established control by either the preachers or the organist. The spirit of the songs could sweep up the crowd, and the young leaders realized that through song they could induce humble people to say and feel things that otherwise were beyond them. Into the defiant spiritual "Ain't Gonna Let Nobody Turn Me Around," Sherrod and Reagon called out verses of "Ain't gonna let Chief Pritchett turn me around." It amazed them to see people who had inched tentatively into the church take up the verse in full voice, setting themselves against feared authority.

Between songs, Anderson invited the five arrested students to tell the congregation why they had decided to defy segregation at the bus station, and what had happened to them. One by one they spoke, with the last student in the pulpit being Bertha Gober, a diminutive young woman with the small voice of a child. She described her arrest, her jailers, the sordid details of her cell. "I felt it was necessary to show the people that human dignity must be obtained even if through suffering or maltreatment," she said. ". . . I'd do it again anytime . . . After spending those two nights in jail for a worthy cause, I feel that I have gained a feeling of decency and self-respect, a feeling of cleanliness that even the dirtiest walls of Albany's jail nor the actions of my institution cannot take away from me." The trembling simplicity of her speech washed over the audience. "There was nothing left to say," Sherrod wrote. He and everyone else were reduced to tears, including the "hard, grown men." They all swayed to the closing song, "We Shall Overcome," and about a third of them stayed on after the benediction to keep singing on their own. Dr. Anderson sang a solo, as did Sherrod and people rising from the audience. The singers stayed on well past midnight, not wanting to let the moment end.

More than five hundred people gathered outside city hall the following Monday for the swift trial and conviction of the five arrested students. Previously, Sherrod had introduced the milling crowd outside to Charles Jones, his SNCC colleague and former Rock Hill cellmate, who was newly arrived from Atlanta, and during the trial Jones marched the crowd slowly back to Shiloh Baptist Church. Chief Pritchett, moving alongside them, wavered between good-natured jokes and orders to disperse— seemingly on the verge of making arrests. The next day, when Sherrod ventured onto the turbulent Albany State campus to address a student gathering, police arrested him on a trespassing warrant signed by President Dennis and two professors. Sherrod spent the night in jail before bonding out.

Sherrod, Reagon, and Jones found themselves hanging on a ledge. Support for them as catalysts had waxed strongly in the recent public meetings, but they sensed that it was unstable. If they engineered another challenge to segregation, the new adults in the movement were likely to turn against them as provocateurs. If they did nothing, however, the movement would dissipate during its recuperation. To break through the impasse, they hit upon the idea of inviting a spark from Atlanta. This would enable them to rekindle the movement with minimal risk of backlash. Accordingly, they called James Forman, the new executive secretary of SNCC, and suggested that he organize a group of Freedom Riders to test the Albany train station.

Forman liked the idea. He was a publicist who had come South from Chicago to write stories about the movement. Forman could be abrasive —he had been thrown out of the sharecroppers' "tent cities" in Fayette County, Tennessee, on charges of "factionalism"—and he had brought to SNCC's autumn meeting a taste for apocalyptic heroics that had struck Bob Moses as amusing. But Forman's aggressive competence filled a vacuum in SNCC. He raised money to pay overdue bills. Through phone calls and press releases, he expanded SNCC's role as a press agent just as reporters were looking for ways to keep up with the unpredictable student demonstrations across the South. Having been active in the predominantly white National Student Association, Forman helped make minor news by encouraging the students of exclusive Sarah Lawrence College in New York to send a telegram of support to Brenda Travis at her Mississippi reform school. He had helped recruit Tom Hayden, a white activist from the NSA, for a publicity trip to McComb, during which Hayden was dragged from a car and beaten.

Inasmuch as SNCC headquarters was too poor to do much administration anyway, Forman decided that little would be lost if he cleared the place out for a Freedom Ride to Albany. He assembled a motley group that included himself, his new office manager, a student volunteer, a touring Danish writer, Nashville Freedom Rider Selyn McCollum, and three whites who had emerged from ordeals in McComb: Bob Zellner and newlyweds Tom and Casey Hayden. All they lacked was money for the train tickets, and for that Forman sounded out Bernard "Jelly" Lee. Since drifting away from SNCC during its summer infighting, Lee had modeled himself more closely than ever on Martin Luther King. Having left his wife, children, and two colleges, he had been taken into the household of Wyatt Walker more or less as a ward. Lee took Forman's idea straight to Walker, who agreed to subsidize the cost of a few train tickets. Lee joined the ride. Forman advised Sherrod of their itinerary. Sherrod alerted the Albany Movement, and someone in turn alerted Chief Pritchett.

The train pulled into Albany's Union Railway Terminal on Sunday afternoon, December 10. Chief Pritchett allowed only Charles Jones and Bertha Gober to meet the train, along with Negro editor A. C. Searles, who claimed status as a media observer. Searles, fidgeting with a camera and a press ID, tried to cut the tension by making nervous jokes with Pritchett, saying, "You wouldn't arrest a newsman like me, would you, Chief?" Forman, Lee, and the other seven Freedom Riders emerged to this dampened reception. Ahead of them was a nearly vacant station, as a squadron of police had sealed off and occupied the white areas. When Pritchett and a few officers tried to escort the integrated group hurriedly through the station, the riders veered off to sit down in the white waiting room. Pritchett tersely ordered them to leave. They complied, hustling toward the white exit as pointed out by Gober and Jones.

At the moment the mixed group of riders stepped unharmed through the door, several hundred waiting partisans of the Albany Movement sent up a cry of relief and triumph. Chief Pritchett became instantly perturbed. With hugs, handshakes, and cheers breaking out all around his porous line of officers, he tried to shout above the noise that they should clear the sidewalks. The intertwined mass moved slowly toward the waiting cars of a small motorcade. It would be impossible to convince the gawking white bystanders and their representatives on the City Commission that this joyous spectacle did no serious damage to segregation.

Pritchett's temper snapped. "Officers, move out!" he shouted to his reserves, and to the celebrants he thundered, "Don't move! You're under arrest." He waded into the crowd to point out the culprits he wanted: the nine Freedom Riders, plus Gober and Jones. Some of them already were inside the waiting cars, with others strewn among people suddenly frozen in surprise. The arresting officers made only one mistake: in the confusion, they seized an Albany State student and missed one Freedom Rider. Eleven prisoners quickly found themselves in a paddy wagon, headed for city hall to be booked on charges of disorderly conduct, obstructing the flow of traffic, and failure to obey an officer. The motorcade left behind was transformed into a dirge recessional to Shiloh Baptist Church.

This time there was no need to organize a summons. More than two hundred eyewitnesses formed a ready-made mass meeting, and their relatives and friends poured into the church by the minute. As their songs swelled up with fervor, everyone knew this was big, that it would sweep the Albany Movement into unknown regions. Back at city hall, Laurie Pritchett tried to explain his action to reporters, saying, "The situation was tense and there could have been general disorder at any time."

On Monday morning, as the leaders of the Albany Movement huddled to frame a negotiating strategy around the crisis, Marion King, wife of Slater King, joined a small group of those who decided they could not let the day go by without doing something. They went downtown to offer a prayer for justice outside city hall, and soon found themselves in jail on the same charges as the Freedom Riders. Although by police code citations these two episodes were essentially the same, those back at Shiloh perceived a jolting difference between a demonstration by young outsiders and a prayer vigil by some of Albany's most respectable Negroes. The very idea of jailing Marion King—a Spelman graduate, a physical therapist who helped rehabilitate people with crippling injuries—shocked more conservative Negroes into attending that night's mass meeting, which overflowed from Shiloh across the street into Mount Zion. The Albany Movement voted to march downtown again in the morning to support the defendants.

Sherrod ducked out of the singing that night for smaller meetings with what he called his "ace group" of young high school students, mostly girls. The police seemed to be arresting anyone who refused to disperse, he said, and that meant they had a chance to fill up the jails. It was time for them all to go. "Now, you're not going in just to get right back out," he added. "You've got to stay and make a sacrifice. You're gonna be heroes to everybody in this town." Privately, Sherrod told Cordell Reagon that he would go to jail himself to help shore up their resolve to stay, and Reagon should stay outside to build up the next group until either Sherrod or Charles Jones came back out. Sherrod was excited. The student movement had been working almost two years toward a chance to fill up the jails, and now in Albany they finally might do it. When Reagon doubted that even such a feat could make segregation crumble, Sherrod laughed. "My uncle always told me that *enough* pressure can make a monkey eat pepper," he said.

In spite of a steady December rain, about four hundred Negroes formed at Shiloh the next morning and, three abreast behind Sherrod, marched to city hall. As the trial of the Freedom Riders commenced inside, the long line circled the block singing "We Are Not Afraid." They went twice around, trailed by police squad cars, while an enormous crowd of both races—at least three times the number of the marchers—accumulated on the perimeter, most of them holding umbrellas. Chief Pritchett halted the march in the third lap. Instead of picking out the leaders, as was expected, he ordered his men to fan out and then herd the entire mass of marchers into a blind alley behind the jail. One line of officers stood guard at the mouth of the alley; others took marchers a few dozen at a time to be booked and jailed. As soon as he realized that they were all being arrested, an ecstatic Charles Sherrod cried out, "We are going to *stay* in jail! We shall overcome!" It took more than two rain-soaked hours to clear the alley.

Page 51 of *The New York Times* of Wednesday, December 13, contained an AP story headlined "Albany, Ga. Jails 267 Negro Youths." About a hundred of the prisoners had bailed out by the time the newspaper reached the streets of Manhattan, but some 150 stayed inside with Sherrod, swamping not only the thirty-person city jail but also the county jail and the work farm. Chief Pritchett had stayed up late the previous night making rental arrangements with the sheriffs of the plantation counties, and at dawn a makeshift fleet of vehicles began to scatter the overload into rural southwest Georgia. Marion King was terrified to learn that she was in a truck with forty women headed for Sheriff Johnson's Baker County jail. Sherrod, on his way to the Terrell County jail, tried to console himself with the ironic thought that he had finally found a place to stay in his original target county, where Negroes had been too frightened to let him spend the night.

At Shiloh, the first panic of the morning rippled outward from the earliest rumors that the prisoners had been moved to the notorious badland counties. The Albany Movement strategists, eyeing the pattern of sharp reaction by the white officials, fluctuated between moves that would send conciliatory signals and hard ones. A similar chemistry was operating at city hall, where Chief Pritchett and Mayor Kelley were moving in and out of an almost continuous session of the City Commission. Pritchett argued that mass arrests might well backfire by recruiting new demonstrators for the Albany Movement, but the commissioners replied that unswerving toughness eventually would crush the rebellion. Pritchett told reporters that once he might have entertained some of the Albany

Movement's new settlement demands, such as hiring Negro policemen, but the City Commission's anger over the marches now made it "vain and useless" even to discuss them. Still, Pritchett enjoyed the confidence of the commissioners, and when a relatively small group of seventy-five showed up that morning to kneel in prayer outside the trial of the Freedom Riders, he decided not to arrest them all. In fact, he accosted only the leader, Slater King, and took him inside to explain openly to the trial judge why they were praying outside his courtroom. Slater King's recitation of the Albany Movement's grievances did not favorably impress Judge Abner Israel, who sentenced him to five days for contempt of court. Defense counsel C. B. King watched the bailiff haul his brother off to jail.

The psychology of the combatants tumbled again, like a pair of wrestlers rolling downhill. At Shiloh, news of Slater King's fate inflamed substantial numbers of people who had preferred a mass march to a prayer vigil in the first place, and more conservative Negroes came to agree that the white people might not respond well to prayer after all. Cordell Reagon decided to activate his clandestine communications system. On his word, volunteers called their sisters and cousins among the few schoolteachers cooperating with SNCC, and the teachers quietly advised trusted groups of students to slip away at a certain hour. They reached Shiloh in great numbers just in time to reinforce the group stepping off behind Reagon to city hall. Chief Pritchett allowed them to march around once. Then, under fire from the city commissioners, who believed this march was the city's sour reward for its leniency earlier that day, he ordered his men to herd them into the alley.

With 202 more marchers in jail by nightfall, Pritchett and Mayor Kelley faced questions from the growing number of national reporters flying into town. Kelley announced that the City Commission saw "no area of possible agreement" with the Albany Movement on integration or prisoner release. Pritchett said Albany "could erupt into violence at any minute," sparked either by angry Negroes or by Klansmen. He vowed to put demonstrators "in jails all over Georgia" if he had to. "We can't tolerate the NAACP or the Student Nonviolent Committee or any other nigger organization to take over this town with mass demonstrations," he said.

In court that afternoon, Judge Israel bound over the eleven people arrested after the Sunday Freedom Ride for trial on new state charges of unlawful assembly. Forman, Bob Zellner, and six others remained in jail. Three bailed out. Tom Hayden left to make a speech to a student group in New York; Charles Jones came out to replace Cordell Reagon; and Bernard Lee was eager to report to Wyatt Walker in Atlanta. Lee told Walker he had never heard of anything like Albany. Negro maids were going to jail under false names, to conceal the arrests from their white mistresses; kids were going to jail two and three times. The people of the Albany Movement were discovering miracles in themselves every day, Lee reported, and at the peak of their fervor they invoked the name of Martin Luther King. The adulation was astonishing. Lee found that whenever he identified himself as youth field secretary for the SCLC, people almost fainted with recognition and clutched him in hopeful wonder, saying, "You're with Martin Luther King?" He thought King should consider coming to Albany, but he warned Walker that a few of the local leaders spoke poorly of King and would probably oppose it. Walker asked crisply for their names.

During the six-week gestation of the Albany Movement, King unwittingly approached the Albany jail on an airborne path of exhaustion. He arrived home from London just as the November 1 ICC ruling went into effect. There seemed to be a bus crisis in nearly every Southern city that day, including Atlanta. In Tennessee, state auctioneers were selling off Highlander's land, buildings, and all confiscated property, including the books from Myles Horton's library. King, leaving the protest telegrams to Wyatt Walker, stayed mostly in transit between airport and rostrum. He returned to Montgomery as a surprise guest speaker at a huge "Testimonial Service of Loyalty and Devotion," marking Ralph Abernathy's departure from the First Baptist Church there. He went to Seattle, Portland, to Mankato College in Minnesota, to Cleveland, and shortly after that into a hospital for tests and two days of rest. From there he went to California for three days and then on to address the Fourth Constitutional Convention of the AFL-CIO in Bal Harbour, Florida.

The speech before the enormous assembly of AFL-CIO delegates fulfilled several complementary objectives of King's recent past. It was a coup for him—an honored forum at the pinnacle of the labor movement —and a welcome sign of recovery from his private disaster at Kansas City. The Alabama libel case against the SCLC and *The New York Times* lent an urgent practicality to King's speeches to organized labor. Having spent more than $27,000 in the early appeals stage of that case, with much larger expenses ahead, he stressed to labor groups that a loss in the Supreme Court would threaten to cripple union organizing as well as civil rights. If the judgment was sustained, he warned, no union leaflet or fund-raising appeal would be safe from a libel suit, especially in the hostile South. Using this theme of common defense, King had recruited a group of labor specialists headed by New York lawyer Theodore Kheel. Stanley Levison, who hoped that King could begin to join the power of a rejuvenated labor movement to the cause of civil rights, was excited enough to write King's speech for him and then follow him to Miami to witness the result.

"Negroes are almost entirely a working people," King said. "There are pitifully few Negro millionaires and few Negro employers." He likened the sit-ins to the pioneer sit-down strikes of the 1930s. Chiding the labor delegates gently for their persecution of Randolph, he summoned them to "admit these shameful conditions" of segregation within unions and to "root out vigorously every manifestation of discrimination. . . . I am aware that this is not easy nor popular," he conceded, "but the eight-hour day was not popular nor easy to achieve" either. Nor were child labor acts or minimum wage laws. "Out of such struggle for democratic rights you own both economic gains and the respect of the country," said King, "and you will win both again if you make Negro rights a great crusade."

It was a "white" speech, restrained and formal, but by then he had long since disarmed a skeptical, even hostile audience. The huge assembly of meatcutters, pipefitters, carpenters, and steelworkers came to their feet as in the old days. Gone for a moment were the dull pension plan reports and the wage increase targets, replaced by an orator who revived the energy of a less bureaucratic era. Some of the Negro unionists, who had quarreled bitterly with George Meany earlier that day, wept openly in the hall. Everyone knew instantly that this was not the ordinary beer chaser of a speech; King had budged the center of gravity of organized labor, with all its political tonnage. Among professional politicians, the AFL-CIO speech was received as the most important development concerning King since his *Time* cover in 1957 and his Atlanta arrest just before the 1960 election. Such events stretched King's influence beyond his given constituency. Even those analysts inclined to minimize the significance of the Negro vote now had to consider King's demonstrable impact on organized labor.

His speech was a minor news item of the day, far behind Eichmann's conviction in Jerusalem, President Kennedy's departure for South America, riots in the Congo, and Zulu chief Albert Luthuli's acceptance of the Nobel Peace Prize in Stockholm.* Also that day, two U.S. Army helicopter units landed in South Vietnam as the first overt American partici-

---

* "It is not necessary for me to speak at length about South Africa," Luthuli said of his native land. "It is a museum piece in our time, a hangover from the dark past of mankind, a relic of an age which everywhere else is dead or dying." He lamented that "the golden age of Africa's independence is also the dark age of South Africa's decline and retrogression."

pants in that country's war against Viet Minh guerrillas. For King, none of these events matched the immediacy of a news story that appeared on his television the night he returned home from the Bal Harbour convention: he saw long lines of Negroes marching through the rain in Albany, Georgia, two hundred miles south of Atlanta. He immediately called Ralph Abernathy, who was freshly reunited with him in Atlanta, installed at his church across town on the prestigious West Side. Knowing that Abernathy was a friend of Rev. E. James Grant (who had grown up a member of First Baptist in Montgomery, and had joined King as a speaker for Abernathy's testimonial in November), King asked whether Abernathy could find out what was behind the events in Albany. Abernathy was already talking with Grant, and also with Albany Movement president William G. Anderson, who had been a college friend at Alabama State. Anderson had been an aspiring disc jockey in those days, Abernathy recalled, but he was a good talker. Abernathy promised to scout Albany by phone.

Late Wednesday night, those leaders of the Albany Movement who were not in jail gathered in a private home following the mass meeting. After two consecutive days of mass arrests, the strain showed beneath their excitement as they discussed what to do next. Of the three hundred still in jail, every leader knew at least a dozen who were desperate to get out to preserve their jobs, their sanity, or the cohesion of their families. But the two hundred already released on $100 cash bonds had soaked up nearly all the loose cash in Negro Albany. No one knew how to get the others out. On another front, an effective boycott of both the downtown merchants and the city bus line now supported the Albany Movement's demands, but the leaders doubted their ability to organize alternative transportation during a money crisis. In short, many of them confessed that they were amateurs in the protest business, and they proposed to seek the help of those who had engineered the legendary victories. Dr. Anderson, seconded enthusiastically by Bernard Lee, suggested Martin Luther King and the SCLC. The local NAACP president suggested Roy Wilkins and the NAACP. No one thought to suggest SNCC, because much of SNCC's national staff was already there. Besides, everyone knew that SNCC lacked the money to keep its volunteers in regular bus fare and doughnut money.

Under pressure of this dilemma, the Albany Movement that night began to twist into political knots. James Forman, recently bailed out of jail, spoke against the idea of inviting King to Albany, saying they already had a strong "people's movement" that could only be weakened by a preacher of such renown. People would look to King as a messiah, and less to themselves. Charles Jones remained silent, knowing that such objections to King would sound petty and arcane to this group of fervent admirers. He also sensed a sharp edge of competitiveness against King glinting through Forman's speech. C. B. King chided Forman for exactly that reason, saying that the real question was not King's alleged demerits but whether the Albany leaders were in over their heads, as he believed. Albany Movement secretary Marion Page spoke up to say that he was against inviting King or any other outsiders to town. This was the same argument that Page still used against the SNCC workers, but now Page joined Forman to oppose King as a newer newcomer than SNCC. A sturdy, conservative retired railroad postman, Page told the group that it took a long time to learn how to grow the distinctively flavored Albany potato, and that they should be patient with their own soil. Over his objections, a motion to appeal for King's help by telegram passed overwhelmingly.

Mayor Kelley summoned his courage the next morning to ride out into the fields of a Baker County plantation in search of Governor Vandiver. Apologizing profusely for barging in on the gubernatorial bird-hunting party, Kelley said that the emergency left him no choice but to ask for the immediate dispatch of a National Guard unit to deter or quell race rioting in his city. More confidentially, he asked Vandiver to send in undercover revenue agents—the whiskey boys—to infiltrate the angry white groups known to be meeting in the outlying counties. If one of them shot a demonstrator, Kelley warned, it might set off the powder keg. When Vandiver reluctantly agreed, the mayor stopped by his house and told his wife to go with their children up to their weekend place on Lake Blackshear, and to stay there until advised that it was safe to come home. From city hall, Kelley introduced himself by telephone to Burke Marshall at the Justice Department in Washington. The two men exchanged anxious variations on the same theme—no violence, no federal intervention.

At Shiloh, where committees of women were working to send food caravans to the various jails, rumors of violence climaxed with a visitor's report that Sheriff Z. T. "Zeke" Mathews had beaten Charles Sherrod in the Terrell County jail. This news caused a panic, on top of five consecutive days of arrests. Emissaries of the Albany Movement took their alarm to Chief Pritchett, who surprised them with an offer to exhibit Sherrod to them in person. The Thursday mass meeting swelled to a large crowd by late afternoon. This was the heart of the movement, pumping spirit and information through Negro Albany. A constant flow of runners moved in and out of the church, and speakers and singers streamed to the front in an endless series. One burly layman stood among his family to speak out loud from his pew:

We pray, oh Lord
That oppression will end
That domination will end
That prejudice will cease.
Thou who
Overruled the Pharaohs
Overruled the Babylonians
Overruled the Greeks and Romans
You alone is God
Always have been God
God in man
God in love.
May our suffering help us.
For the Lord is my shepherd
I shall not want
He maketh me to lie down . . .

The crowd joined spontaneously to complete the Twenty-third Psalm. Then someone rose to sing a hymn, followed by young people with stories of joyous suffering in jail. Suddenly, a muffled commotion interrupted the proceedings. Charles Sherrod appeared in the back of the church, then was hustled solicitously to the front.

"Did they beat you up?" called a voice that spoke for the crowd.

"No. They slapped me a couple of times," said Sherrod, answered by groans of relief mixed with pain. "It cut my lip. A man named Zeke . . . [wanted] no singing or demonstrations in that jail."

"Did you pray?" someone called.

"I prayed to myself," Sherrod replied, to murmurs of approval. "I answered him 'yes' and 'no.' I didn't put a handle on it. He wanted me to say 'yes, sir' and 'no, sir.' I was not badly beaten. I was struck twice in the face while under arrest."

The crowd learned that Sherrod had appeared on a gentleman's agreement with Chief Pritchett. Soon he left for the Albany jail in the custody of the officers who had been waiting outside. When he was gone, a man in the crowd was moved to speak. "It is a funny thing," he said. "As much hell as we've caught here in Albany, I still love it. It's home. I love to fish, to pick the magnolias, to pick blueberries. I love peanuts. I like pecans."

Elsewhere in the city, some 150 National Guardsmen gathered in the armory on stand-by alert that night, and indirect negotiations continued by caucus and messenger relay. City officials, who refused to bargain directly with Negroes, worked through the buffer of three white private citizens, who themselves refused the social risk of sitting down in the same room with the Negroes. Other factors impeding this cumbersome arrangement included a pronounced slipperiness of language. To the Albany Movement's demand for compliance with the ICC desegregation ruling, the white negotiators replied that the city already respected the ruling and had made arrests only under laws protecting the public order. From there, the two sides debated riddles of definition, precedent, and jurisdiction before adjourning late in the night. Marion Page announced that there would be no further demonstrations "as long as the other side keeps the faith."

Friday, December 16, brought the first morning in a week without marches or arrests. The Albany Movement leaders found that the spirit of the mass meeting was difficult to preserve. Their people were in jail, losing jobs. Reaching for a settlement, they sent through their negotiators the mildest four-part proposal they could tolerate: (1) free, unfettered use of the bus and train facilities by Negroes beginning thirty days hence; (2) acceptance by the city of property bonds instead of cash, which would enable those already out of jail to get refunds, and would make it possible to secure the release of the others; (3) appointment by the city of a biracial commission to discuss, without precondition, other aspects of segregation in Albany; (4) a permanent moratorium on demonstrations. As time dragged on without a response to this package, fears grew that it was so weak as to encourage the whites to filibuster in the hope that the Albany Movement would collapse.

Into these anxieties arrived midday news that Slater King had been beaten in the Albany jail. Songs went up for him at Shiloh. The Albany Movement pulled its trio from the negotiations pending inquiry, and the roving corps of reporters soon intercepted Chief Pritchett as he darted between Shiloh and city hall. It seemed that Slater King had refused his food, Pritchett reported, whereupon the jailer had shoved him so roughly back into his cell as to bang his head into the bars. The injury was not serious, Pritchett added, but he had recommended that the jailer be fired. "I don't want a man like that in my jail," he said. Negotiations resumed after he allowed Albany Movement representatives to verify his story with Slater King, but the mood at Shiloh stiffened in spite of some kind words for Pritchett as an honorable adversary. Everyone knew Slater King. No one could understand exactly why the Albany Movement's settlement proposal did not insist upon his release. Nor, on reflection, could anyone satisfactorily explain why their settlement would acquiesce in the permanent suspension of the two Albany State students.

Their proposal now seemed supine, and the negotiators amended it by letter that day to include college reinstatements and a pardon for Slater King.

Albany Movement president Anderson perceived that his biggest enemy was not the chaos at hand but the heavy silence of time. Pressure kept driving him to call his friend Abernathy in Atlanta. They urgently needed a commitment from Dr. King, he said. Their movement would stand or fall on their ability to convince official Albany that the Negroes had the will to sustain even more arrests if their settlement conditions were spurned. King's presence, like nothing else, could lift the Negroes and shake some sense into the whites. Anderson made his case to Abernathy and to King himself when King returned from a speech in New Orleans, stressing that it had to be that day, that night, or it would be too late.

McCree Harris made her decision as soon as the rumor reached her inside Monroe High School. She dismissed her Latin class early and slipped into Shiloh just after three o'clock, making sure she would have a seat when Martin Luther King appeared at eight.

The ensuing clash lasted only seventy-two hours. A little more than a year after flying north from Reidsville State Prison on the eve of the Kennedy-Nixon election, King headed south from Atlanta toward Albany. Abernathy and Wyatt Walker were with him again, along with the regional NAACP director, Ruby Hurley. In Albany, congestion slowed their approach to the mass meeting. More than fifteen hundred people packed both Shiloh and Mount Zion to the rafters. Because the speakers of the hastily rigged sound system had been placed facing Mount Zion, everyone knew that King would first appear at Shiloh, and some of the Mount Zion congregation were hanging out the windows to catch sight of him. Parked cars were jammed up on the curbs for blocks around. A small fleet of police cars occupied a parking lot next to Shiloh. The officers were not directing traffic or providing any obvious service, although their presence may have deterred a few carloads of hostile whites circling the area. To the congregations, the police seemed to be lurking in surveillance. Any Negro who responded to the occasional beckonings from the police officers drew suspicion as a possible informant.

The singing held everything together, even the two churches, which swayed in time to the same song, sending only a heartbeat of an echo back and forth across Whitney Avenue. King's progress through the nearby streets seemed to pass by conduction upstream through a river of sound. When his group emerged from the cars, the singing was a free-form spiritual chant to the tune of "Amen":

FREE—DOM
FREE—DOM
FREE—DOM, FREE—DOM, FREE—DOM!

As the party entered the church and King was sighted on his way down to the pulpit, the sound exploded into cascades of rapture:

Martin King says freedom
Martin King says freedom
Martin King says FREE—DOM
FREE—DOM FREE—DOM!

Let the white man say freedom
Let the white man say freedom
Let the white man say FREE —DOM
FREE—DOM FREE—DOM!

Then, toward the end of a verse, Rutha Harris of the Freedom Singers, the group formed in Sherrod's workshops, moved to the center of the platform and the din ceased abruptly, just in time for her overpowering contralto to switch songs:

I woke up this morning with my mind

And above the faint echo of Mount Zion, which could be heard making the transition in the background, the crowd finished her line:

SET ON FREEDOM.
I woke up this morning with my mind
SET ON FREEDOM.

Three times she led them in this call and response, and then they all raised the one-word chorus:

HALLELU—HALLELU—HALLELUJAH!

The verses kept rolling forth until without signal the sound collapsed all at once into silence. Pious souls would maintain long afterward that they thought the Lord Himself had arrived, so awed were they. More skeptical observers were hardly less stupefied. Pat Watters, a newly arrived Atlanta *Journal* reporter, was so undone by his first exposure to a Negro mass meeting that he scribbled notes furiously to keep hold of himself. For posterity, he later wrote on the cover of his notebook: "Includes the night Dr. King entered the church."

King began slowly and sonorously with points about the relevance of the concurrent independence movement in Africa. He told the crowd that time was neutral to the history of moral causes. They could not sit back and wait for an inevitable march of progress—it was possible for race relations to hurtle backward, as Chief Luthuli said South Africa had done since the creation of apartheid in 1948. Democratic morality was nothing more or less than what they made of it, and it was an internal as well as an external state. He went on to draw his usual distinctions between love and justice, between changed hearts and regulated behavior, and then to describe nonviolence as the application of Christian ethics to worldly politics. The lecture had the effect of dampening the mood of the crowd. It established a sober atmosphere of history and great responsibility before King wound to the purpose of the suffering in Albany. "They can put you in a dungeon and transform you to glory," he said. "If they try to kill you, develop a willingness to die."

Then a quickening pace of oratory consumed the distance between King and the crowd. When he spoke of going to jail "without hating the white folks," they answered with a clap of applause. "Say to the white man, 'We will win you with the power of our capacity to endure,' " he urged. "How long will we have to suffer injustices?" he cried. A deep bass voice shouted back "God Almighty!" and reporter Watters quickly looked up and saw that it belonged to an old man with a very black face. The old man's cries kept punctuating King's rising "How long . . . Not long" litany, and Watters lost ground in his desperate efforts to jot down each spoken word. King was soaring now, as he spoke of redemptive suffering, the possibility of martyrdom. "But we shall overcome," he cried, and both churches shouted back, "Shall overcome!"

The song of that title sprouted softly here and there beneath his oratorical descent. "Don't stop now," King admonished them. "Keep moving. Walk together, children. Don't ya get weary. There's a great camp meeting coming . . ." Suddenly, without the usual cries of jubilation from a hymn or a prophet, his voice trailed off. King stepped away from the pulpit, as though even he had been overwhelmed by the powers he elicited from the congregations. They sang "We Shall Overcome," swaying gently back and forth in the pews as they waved aloft their white handkerchiefs, whose flutter made the church look like a cotton field in cross-cutting breezes. After a number of verses, a clearly transported Dr. Anderson raised his arms for silence. He thanked King profusely for his appearance and pledged that the Albany Movement indeed would keep moving. And then, crowning the moment, he invited King himself to walk together with them against the bastions of segregation.

As the crowd rocked in approval of the suggestion, the leaders huddled on the platform to discuss this departure from the schedule. Unable to hear one another, they retired to Reverend Boyd's study for a brief conference. Anderson argued that King's continued presence alone might produce a settlement, which would make another march unnecessary.

King agreed to stay, notwithstanding other commitments, including an obligation to preach for Daddy King on Sunday. That being decided, someone expressed reservations about advertising Dr. King's whereabouts in advance, given the rumors that redneck whites or stoolie Negroes might try to kill him. Hastily, the leaders devised an announcement designed to encourage the congregations while minimizing the security risk. Then they stepped back out into the music. First sight of Anderson's beaming face told the crowd that King had agreed to stay. When he gained enough silence, he announced in a winking, joyful code, "Be here at seven o'clock in the morning. Eat a good breakfast. Wear your warm clothes and wear your walking shoes."

Shiloh and Mount Zion remained open all night for prayer. After midnight, with King safely ensconced in his home, Anderson sent a telegram to Mayor Kelley: "We waited the night of the 15th of December for an acceptable response, but it was not forthcoming. We shall prayerfully await an acceptable response by 10 A.M. this morning at Shiloh Baptist Church."

The telegram backfired. Kelley and the other commissioners, not being accustomed to city business early on a Saturday morning, opened it only shortly before the deadline. They took offense, especially when Chief Pritchett delivered intelligence reports on the King and Anderson speeches of the previous evening, indicating that the Negroes intended to march again if rebuffed. Mayor Kelley addressed a terse letter of rejection to Marion Page instead of Anderson, perhaps to underscore the commission's disapproval of Anderson's recent conduct. He summoned reporters to announce that Albany was breaking off negotiations.

A forlorn Anderson returned to the Shiloh pulpit after a last desperate trip to city hall. "We found no common ground for discussion," he reported gravely. "We will kneel and pray until God comes and helps to show us and the world the way to take a step toward freedom." Wyatt Walker stepped forward to say that it was time to get down to business. When he asked for a show of hands of those prepared to march to city hall behind Dr. King, about 150 people responded. "That is not enough," Walker said sharply. Quick speeches of exhortation produced few additional volunteers, as the most dedicated people were in jail already. The hand count stalled far below the number of the two big marches earlier that week, made without King.

Walker retired gloomily to the pastor's study, where King had been socializing with the pastors of the twin churches on Whitney Avenue. Like King, Boyd and Grant were Morehouse men, the former a college contemporary of King's brother A.D. and the latter a schoolmate of Daddy King's, back in the late 1920s. King teased them both for supporting J. H. Jackson at Kansas City. Socially, their congregations in Albany were paired much like Dexter and First Baptist in Montgomery, or like Ebenezer and Abernathy's new West Hunter Street Baptist in Atlanta. Abernathy relished pointing out that in Atlanta he and King had reversed their social positions from Montgomery, with Abernathy now holding the more prestigious West Side congregation, "out-doctoring" and "out-professoring" his friend King. When Walker delivered his gloomy news about the scarce volunteers, the preachers turned painfully to business, and decided to go with one last appeal.

Claude Sitton of *The New York Times* noted that it was 4:16 P.M. when King and Anderson came out of the church arm in arm, with Abernathy and Mrs. Anderson the first of 265 others marching two by two behind them. There were a hundred youths below the age of seventeen, including some thirty on bail from previous arrests that week, and a few older people who had trouble keeping up. There was a lone white person, a student from the University of Georgia. (Reporters, pawing for any explanation of his singular presence, seized upon his statement that he had recently visited Ohio.) Now the white student was a conspicuous fleck in the long column moving through Harlem, Albany's Negro business district. They walked past the joints and pool halls, which were gearing up for Saturday night, past gas stations and food stores. Everyone stared at the procession—grizzled drinkers and young children alike. A few of the marchers tried to recruit reinforcements from the spectators, but for the most part they were silent.

It was a chilly December day for Albany, and threatening to rain, so that when the marchers turned toward city hall on Jackson Street the slickered troopers heading toward them appeared to be a mass of yellow in the distance. A number of the Negroes clutched tightly at Bibles under their arms, and among those uttering prayers, the tall, handsome Dr. Anderson drew attention because he spoke with a furtive chipperness that clashed with his normal executive composure. "God bless you," he kept saying to no one in particular. "God bless each of you. Strike me first. God bless you."

The opposing lines converged on either side of Oglethorpe Street, which divided downtown from the Negro section. Two motorcycle policemen pulled up to the curb to block the path across the border. They did not move when King led the Negro column around to their rear, but Chief Pritchett then stepped forward with his amplified megaphone to meet them in no-man's-land. "Do you have a written permit to parade or demonstrate?" he asked, his voice crackling through the drizzle.

"We are simply going to pray at the City Hall," King replied, adding that he did not believe a parade permit was necessary for that purpose.

Pritchett disagreed, ordered the marchers to disperse, and then announced that they were all under arrest. His men—a composite force of policemen, sheriff's deputies, and state troopers—marched across the intersection to herd the procession into the street. Motorcycle officers stopped traffic in all directions; others already had sealed off the area around the city jail. The march resumed in a new formation, down the middle of Jackson Street into downtown, with yellow-slickered lawmen scattered along both flanks. Photographers walked backward to snap shots of King, who was singing "We Shall Overcome" with the others. The entire panorama puzzled, angered, or entertained bystanders according to their perceptions. Its meaning was not obvious to all strangers, including the young white couples who came blinking out of the movie theater's matinee performance of *Come September*, starring Rock Hudson and Gina Lollobrigida. The procession seemed to be combustible and yet orderly, almost rehearsed, with both the Negroes and the officers looking solemn but not grim. At first glance, it could have been anything from a Mardi Gras parade to a mass execution.

After the officers steered the column into the sealed-off alley behind the jail, the true character of the event revealed itself. Moans and prayers went up when King and the other leaders disappeared among the first batch into the jail. One marcher shouted out above the others: "The blessed Son of God was born about this time of the year two thousand years ago to bring peace to this world. And here we stand two thousand years later." Suddenly, somewhere in the midst of the huddled marchers, the sounds intensified into hysteria as about a dozen men pushed their way out of the alley. They were carrying a young woman who was gasping and writhing, with a spoon jammed between her teeth. Police guards responded to desperate cries for water merely by parting to let the men rush frantically down the street with their stricken cargo. Gawking bystanders parted too, until, some distance down the street, the young woman's seizure abated. When her bearers had assured themselves that she was fully recovered, they dutifully retraced their steps to the alley to await admission to jail. Groups being herded inside for booking passed those coming out for transport to prisons in the outlying counties. Pat Watters was struck by the sound of their song, "We Are Not Afraid," and how it seemed steadfast even when muffled behind the doors of a departing paddy wagon. He included this detail in a vivid dose of surrealism that landed on page 10 of the next day's Atlanta *Journal*, between Senator Henry "Scoop" Jackson's wedding photograph and a plane crash story from Iowa.

Chief Pritchett closed all liquor stores and cocktail lounges that night, and doubled police patrols. Military sound trucks roamed the streets

blaring the announcement that all soldiers on leave should return to the
Marine Corps Supply Depot or Turner Air Force Base. City hall was
emptied except for a few straggling bystanders and the main body of
reporters, who waited to find out what was happening to King. Along
with Anderson and Abernathy, he first was hauled from the crowded
holding cell to Pritchett's office. Later, these three ranking prisoners
emerged dramatically in the midst of an armed police escort. One plainclothes officer carried a Thompson submachine gun. They all piled into
the chief's shiny new Buick Roadmaster. Then they were gone—headed
north, Pritchett disclosed, for the Sumter County jail in Americus. Then
and later, white citizens complained bitterly about the Roadmaster and
all the special protection for King, saying that he was receiving privileges
far beyond the due of a white prisoner, let alone a Negro. Pritchett defended his measures as enlightened segregation. If King were to be killed
in Albany, he said, "the fires would never cease."

Fred Chappell was a tough, independent sheriff, who said "nigger" to and
about any person of color, famous or not. He did so with a half-smile of
defiant assurance, as though to emphasize his disregard for polite convention. With his deputies, Chappell slammed a cell door on King's first full
day in the Albany Movement. King became one of some 750 demonstrators arrested there in the past week, one of more than 400 still in jail.
Nothing approaching such magnitude had ever occurred in the civil
rights movement. Albany now combined the dimensions and the tactical
advances of all its recent predecessors, from Montgomery through the
Freedom Rides, including—now that King was in jail—nationwide headlines.
    Anderson had been shaky even before the march. His mumbling had
been a sign of slippage. Now, having been taken to the jail in his own
hometown of Americus, where his father had first achieved prominence
as a traveling salesman for one of the pioneer Negro insurance companies, the experience was so intense for him that it had to be salvation
itself, or the abyss. "Thank you, Jesus," he told King. He prowled the
dingy cell until claustrophobia and the malice of Sheriff Chappell rubbed
a thin spot in his psyche, and then he greeted King again. "You are Jesus,"
he said, as though it should have been obvious all along. Anderson knew
his Bible—the descent of the spirit upon the anointed one at Shiloh,
which everyone could feel, the march into Jerusalem, the dungeons and
revilement. "And we are the saints," he cried, looking not just at his
fellow prisoners but out upon a great assembly of their comrades that
appeared only to him. "The hosts which no man can number."
    For King, this behavior at first may have seemed no more than another

instance of the messianic adulation showered upon him for years, and for Anderson it may have begun as a lapse into a common, ecstatic church persona. In confinement, however, fervid eccentricity could intensify into mania. King tried to calm Anderson, as did Abernathy and Bernard Lee from the next cell. Anderson's passions were almost incandescent with energy, however. He kept jumping up to proclaim the thrill of fresh visions. Even late into the night, nervous exhaustion allowed him only a light, fitful sleep, which was interrupted frequently by Abernathy's extraordinary snoring. On this, Abernathy's first night in jail with King, the piercing volume of his nasal trumpet created a lasting legend. The humor was lost that night to apprehension about Anderson's condition. Each time Abernathy startled him back into full consciousness, it turned out that supernatural realities still were more vivid to him than his jail bunk, dashing the hopes of his fellow prisoners that sleep might restore him to normal.

It was a groggy King who announced his plans through the bars the next morning. "I will not accept bond," he told visiting reporters. "If convicted, I will refuse to pay the fine. I expect to spend Christmas in jail. I hope thousands will join me." A Negro reporter quoted him as pledging to remain in jail "as long as necessary" to force change in Albany's segregation. The strain of incarceration emerged in King's lofty but plaintive comments about the Sumter County jailers. They had pushed his dignity into its final refuge: the pulpit. "I wish some people could be a little more courteous," he said. "The guards in this jail call me 'boy.' I might note that I am the pastor of a church with four thousand members."

Abernathy was gone—bailed out early to make Sunday services in Atlanta and to "rally the nation" from outside. Hopes that daylight would improve Anderson's condition were sadly unfounded. He began to hallucinate about extraterrestrial events, so deep in his own world that King and Bernard Lee discussed their worries in front of him. They were haunted by the memory of a Negro Episcopal priest who had come unhinged during the big Sunday march on the capitol in Montgomery during the early sit-ins of 1960. Firemen had pointed a hose at the priest to move him back, and although they did not turn on the water, something in the sight made the priest snap. His mind went away somewhere and never came back. Abernathy had seen it happen that day, along with Lee and Ella Baker, and King had arrived later to encounter the husk of an old friend. Now it frightened him and Lee to think that Anderson might be having a similar breakdown. They approached him about bailing out ahead of them, but the proposal horrified Anderson as a betrayal of King. He would not be like Simon Peter.

Wyatt Walker swept into the Americus jail late that day, almost quivering with adrenaline. Substituting for King as the main speaker at the previous night's mass meeting, Walker had preached and exhorted, prayed and ducked out to take scores of phone calls. "The SCLC has thrown its full resources behind the Albany Movement," he had announced. His telegrams were summoning Daddy King, James Lawson, and the other SCLC board members to an extraordinary meeting in Albany on Monday night. He had barely slept before stepping up the pace that Sunday—dictating a nationwide fund-raising appeal to be sent over King's signature, giving press statements, making travel arrangements for the board members, allocating some of the SCLC's limited treasury to prisoners making the most desperate pleas for bail, while telling other supplicants that their relatives had to hang on in their cells. Now was the time to strike, he told them, because King was drawing the pressure of world opinion to Albany. They should be thinking about putting more people into jail, not taking any out.

All these matters were compressed into the briefing Walker had prepared for King. Inside the Sumter County jail, King punctured Walker's kinetic strategems. "Wyatt, you've got to get us out of here," he said. "Andy's not going to make it."

These words spun Walker's mind backward, toward visions of disaster. Early release would break the will of the movement, waste all Walker's labors at coordinating support, touch off howls from people demanding to follow King out of jail, and severely damage the credibility of King, who had just promised to stay in jail until Christmas. King thought Anderson could make it through one more night, perhaps.

Walker headed back to Albany with all his grand plans collapsed into one imperative: bluff toward a quick settlement. A second shock greeted him before he adjusted to the first. This time it was a rebellion. Walker's imperious manner had alienated some Albany Movement leaders even before he had assumed command of the last mass meeting. Then, at Shiloh that day, just as C. B. King and some of the locals had been frowning at the news that Walker's solicitation letter called for contributions to be sent to the SCLC in Atlanta, rather than to the Albany Movement, someone rushed in to tell them that Ralph Abernathy was appearing on television from Atlanta. They all rushed in to hear Abernathy tell the viewers of his night in the Sumter County jail and how the SCLC was calling for a nationwide "pilgrimage" to Albany. The conjunction of these two events had soured a number of the Albanians. Having naïvely measured King's treasury by his image, they had expected him to come to town with ample funds to bail out their emergency cases. It was a blow to discover that the money had to be raised first, compounded by the news that it would be siphoned through Atlanta. As for

Abernathy, they had thought he was in jail in Americus, only to see with their own eyes that he had vanished to Atlanta already, and was taking charge of Albany from there. Suddenly they saw Abernathy and Walker as movement "pros" in a less exalted sense—as those who trafficked in the ordeals of innocents. They felt like hayseeds.

No one had voiced these resentments to Walker's face; he was too intimidating a presence as he jerked and crackled across Shiloh's floor like a downed power line. No sooner did Walker leave to visit Martin Luther King in Americus, however, than Charles Jones organized a special SNCC press conference. Jones knew many of the reporters personally, from earlier civil rights protests that year, and he promised them a big story. He and other SNCC leaders stood discreetly in the background as Marion Page read a statement drafted mostly by Ella Baker. It denied as "an unfortunate misrepresentation of fact" the news that the SCLC was in command of Albany. "Mr. Walker or no one else is assuming leadership of Albany," said Page. He renounced nationwide "pilgrimages" and all further demonstrations in Albany, saying that he hoped to renew negotiations with the city's white leaders. When one of the startled reporters asked whether this meant that the Albany Movement was breaking away from the SCLC, Page replied, "We've never been united."

The fresh public feud ambushed Wyatt Walker as soon as he returned from the Americus jail. Reeling under a barrage of press inquiries, Walker was shrewd enough to recognize tactical advantages even in this stinging rebuke to his authority. Had the press conference not taken place, Walker himself would have been forced to propose concessions in order to get King and Anderson out of jail. Since King had forbidden him to mention Anderson's condition to anyone—it became a subject of hushed gossip within the Albany Movement's inner circles—Walker would have been obliged to invent some pretext for retreat. Now he did not have to. Instead, he bit his lip, sent out a flurry of telegrams canceling the SCLC board meeting, and advised the Albanians to seek the best terms their divided ranks could command. For Walker, the SNCC-Page mutiny was a detestable affront that could not have come at a better time.

Far-flung reporters still were checking into Albany that Sunday night when James Gray delivered a television address to southwest Georgia. As Albany's first citizen, he spoke to local viewers much the way modern Presidents had come to address the nation. Gray owned controlling stock in the only television station in town, from whose studios his image was beamed that night, and he owned the region's dominant newspaper, the Albany Herald. He had grown up in Stockbridge, Massachusetts, three

doors down from Norman Rockwell, and played basketball for Dart-
mouth College in the 1930s. At a dance after a game he had struck up a
friendship with one of the opposing players from Harvard, Joseph P. Kennedy, Jr. The two of them roved together enough for Gray to visit the
Kennedy vacation home in Palm Beach several times before Joe Jr. was
killed in World War II. After that, and after Gray had moved South to
marry the daughter of the *Herald's* owner, he maintained a friendship
with the next Kennedy son, Jack.

Over the next dozen years, Jack had changed from Joe's kid brother
into the dashing senator who wanted to be President, and Gray's media
empire made him into something of a potentate in the small markets of
southwest Georgia. In 1958, Gray sent his private plane to fetch Senator
and Mrs. Kennedy to Albany for a weekend of barbecue, golf, and country-style politicking, during which Gray himself proved that it was possible for a Yankee to be popular among Southerners. Now that Kennedy
was President, a great many prominent citizens of Albany had on their
office walls a framed photograph of themselves shaking hands with Kennedy at Gray's reception, and everybody knew that Gray still called the
President "Jack" in private. As chairman of the Georgia Democratic
Party, Gray had been scheduled to debate Martin Luther King on television in late 1960, but the President-elect, reacting to the startling evidence that the Negro vote had supplied the margin of his victory, had
asked his friend to withdraw in favor of James J. Kilpatrick.

This time Gray decided that he could not duck King and the segregation issue. He told his viewers that a "cell of professional agitators" was
mounting a rebellion that "smacks more of Lenin and Stalin than of
George Washington, Thomas Jefferson, and Abraham Lincoln." He knew
enough about the internal splits in the Albany Movement to refer to its
weaknesses, but he also subscribed to the white folklore that any Negro
rebellion was necessarily the work of the NAACP. As for King, Gray saw
nothing but shallow opportunism: "He has learned that martyrdom can
be a highly productive practice for the acquisition of a buck." He closed
with a tribute to segregation as "a system that has proved over the years
to be peaceful and rewarding," and a call for an end to disruption. "What
we need is tolerance," said Gray, "not tantrum."

Privately, Gray advised Mayor Kelley and Chief Pritchett to make any
deal that would get King and the protesters out of jail without surrender.
Simultaneously, Gray was telling his friends in Washington that any
intervention by the federal government would make it harder rather than
easier for the Georgia whites to end the crisis. His argument landed on
receptive ears, as Robert Kennedy was wary of jumping into quicksand
in Albany. This was the political lesson of his baptism in civil rights

earlier that year, when he had been green and impetuous. The Attorney General called in Douglas Kiker and other trusted reporters to announce that he had adopted a "hands off" policy after the spring Freedom Rides. "Real progress" in race relations, he said, required that "local leaders talk it out."

Before dawn on Monday, December 18, Wyatt Walker sent off a plaintive telegram to the White House in King's name, requesting that President Kennedy "issue at once by Executive Order a Second Emancipation Proclamation to free all Negroes from second-class citizenship." That morning, as headlines told New York readers that "Negro Groups Split on Georgia Protest," Robert Kennedy huddled with Byron White and Burke Marshall at the Justice Department, sending out a stream of messages that he was in close touch with events in Albany, that the issue was "number one" on his agenda, and that he stood ready to give advice if requested by either side.

From Americus, King left by prison transport for trial in Albany along with Anderson, whom reporters described as "haggard." The courtroom was a mass of confusion, with reporters jostling spectators and officials bustling in and out with whispered messages. Judge Abner Israel recessed the proceedings even before they began. Bailiffs put King and Anderson in a holding cell, where women's committees from the Albany Movement tried to reach them with gifts of food and cologne. Upstairs, a rumor circulated that negotiations were resuming. Marion Page and his lawyer C. B. King huddled in the mayor's office along with Donald Hollowell, representing SNCC, while Mayor Kelley and other city officials kept their distance in a separate room. Chief Pritchett shuttled between them with refinements on the truce conditions.

By ten thirty that morning, the whites had dropped their feigned inability to interfere with the operations of the courts and offered to release all local Albany Movement prisoners without any bond at all, provided that King leave town and demonstrations cease. But they held firm on high bail for the Freedom Riders, whom they considered professional agitators, and they refused to commit to writing any agreement with the Negro representatives. C. B. King and Hollowell—the same legal team that was still seeking Charlie Ware's release so that he could receive medical treatment for the neck wounds he suffered in July—bargained all day for binding statements of City Commission policy, but the most they could get was an unsigned note authorizing Chief Pritchett to speak for the commission on certain matters. Late that afternoon, Mayor Kelley summoned Judge Israel to ratify the new understanding, and the judge then announced from the bench a host of new rulings, including a sixty-day postponement of King's trial.

King appeared suddenly on the courthouse steps, freed after forty-eight hours of custody. Anderson, still unstable in the midst of his visions, was protectively ushered aside by Walker as King told the assembled reporters that he would leave Albany in spite of his dissatisfaction with the verbal truce. "I would not want to stand in the way of meaningful negotiations," he said, in his only allusion to his own departure as one of the conditions.

Prisoners began to spill forth from the jails of southwest Georgia. It would take until nearly dawn to empty them, by which time contending assessments of their week-long travail were on their way to interested readers across the nation. King himself put the most positive face on the deal, telling a cheering Shiloh crowd that "it wasn't necessary" for him to stay in jail, as promised. The bus and rail terminals had been "thoroughly integrated," he said. Bail requirements had been swept away to free hundreds of unjustly arrested protesters, and the City Commission had promised to appoint a biracial commission to address the segregation issue as a whole. Even as King spoke, however, Chief Pritchett was denying that the city had granted a single point. He insisted that Albany had obeyed all laws, including the ICC desegregation ruling. All charges against the demonstrators, including Slater King and the suspended students, remained in place pending trial. As for the biracial commission, Pritchett insisted that the City Commission had agreed only to entertain such a proposal, as it would do for any timely and proper recommendation from local citizens. At the Shiloh mass meeting, Marion Page told his listeners to disregard white victory claims and pay attention to "official" announcements from the Albany Movement.

"In appreciation for the accurate coverage of Albany's difficulties," as they announced it, Albany leaders treated white members of "the national and international press corps" to a steak dinner Monday night at the Radium Springs club where James Gray had played golf with John Kennedy. Mayor Kelley announced that Attorney General Kennedy had called within an hour of that afternoon's truce to congratulate the city for preventing an outbreak of violence. Perhaps the city's shrewd hospitality helped set the tone for news reports that described Albany's crisis as having been safely navigated by wise restraint, and that criticized King's protest methods for stirring up a dangerous but ineffectual discontent. Journalists had spiteful reason to fault King for nondelivery. Many of them had just traveled to Albany at considerable expense on King's promise of a protracted, newsworthy confrontation, only to have the story fizzle almost upon their arrival. Elsewhere, too, there was lingering disgruntlement over King: Page, Charles Jones, and other leaders of the Albany Movement privately blamed him for the meager settlement.

The New York *Herald Tribune* called the Albany truce "a devastating loss of face" for King, "one of the most stunning defeats" of his career. Most reporters took a sportswriter's approach and billed the week's events essentially as Segregation 1, King 0. More thorough press reflections focused on the discovery in Albany of bureaucratic divisions within the Negro movement. NAACP officials supplied much of the confidential information, but they were careful not to reveal the parochial motivation that dominated their own internal communications. Privately admitting that the Albany branch of the NAACP was "almost defunct," and had been so for nearly a decade, they had maneuvered singlemindedly to disparage any competing organization. They offered to make William Anderson president of the local branch if he would dissolve the Albany Movement as unnecessary. They made similar overtures to Slater King. They tried to stop demonstrations and fumed over the popularity of the movement songs. This starkly self-interested perspective extended to Mississippi, where field secretary Medgar Evers boasted to his superiors that strong NAACP chapters had prevented student registration projects from making any headway. Evers assured headquarters that King had raised very little money for the Freedom Riders in Mississippi, and he strongly implied that Moses, John Hardy, and other registration workers had brought persecution on themselves when they "became involved with some hoodlums, law enforcement officers, and voter registrars."

To some degree, Evers and other NAACP employees tailored their reports to the expectations of their superiors, but the antagonisms were real. NAACP sources openly derided student activists and then subtly confirmed those same activists in their criticisms of King. The outlines of such quarrels escaped to the white press. Claude Sitton's reprise on Albany in the next Sunday's *New York Times*, headed "Rivalries Beset Integration Campaign," traced the quarrels to the sit-ins of 1960. In a more sensational article entitled "Confused Crusade," *Time* quoted Roy Wilkins in scathing appraisal of SNCC: "They don't take orders from anybody; they don't consult anybody. They operate in a kind of vacuum: parade, protest, sit-in . . . When the headlines are gone, the issues still have to be settled in court." King's gingerly reply—"I think it would be a mistake to try, as some civil rights leaders want to, to throw the students out of the movement. The little conflicts are inevitable"—was barely heard amid cross-firing attacks from anonymous SNCC leaders, who criticized King for status-seeking, for whirlwind speech-making, and for "meekly" shirking his jail time in Albany. Such attacks in *Time* brought SNCC a public identity more than all its previous campaigns. James Forman, who resented King's bourgeois habits and his quest for media recognition, was featured as one of the four established national leaders. He posed for the *Time* photographer in a starched white shirt and tie, with a pipe.

All this bilious contention was too much for Stanley Levison, who promptly wrote a letter protesting the lack of "ordinary fairness" in *Time*'s presentation. "Status seekers do not generally go to jail, even for limited periods," he wrote. ". . . Ironically, there are those who have argued that Dr. King is so extraordinarily self-sacrificing that he must be seeking martyrdom, while now a new voice charges that he avoids sacrifice. He is indeed damned if he does and damned if he does not." *Time* did not publish Levison's letter.

In Albany, Charles Jones and Cordell Reagon were more abrasive than Sherrod in their judgment of King. They called him "De Lawd," a SNCC nickname mocking both King's pomposity and the submissiveness of ordinary church folk. They also intimated that they had orchestrated the Albany negotiations toward precisely the result that followed: King's removal from Albany, bearing the onus of a weak settlement. This remained their secret almost as much as Anderson's mental crisis remained King's. They privately endorsed a weak settlement in order to promote a strong movement, privately sought King's release from jail and then criticized him for not staying there. They justified competitive maneuvers on the theory that their goals could not be advanced or protected without influence to offset King's. This was SNCC's classical revolutionary dilemma. To oppose their ally, they became more like what they said they opposed, beginning a cycle of imitation and rejection.

In later years, Wyatt Walker conceded that his manner toward the SNCC students was perhaps too "flint-faced," but at the time he blamed their jealous insubordination for damaging the Albany Movement. He did not bother to address their grievances against him until Charles Jones made some headway in convincing Harry Belafonte that Walker's autocratic style was dividing the movement. This seized Walker's attention because he knew that Belafonte commanded King's attention, but even then he complained that Jones had "brainwashed" Belafonte with false tales about Albany. Belafonte, for his part, took the dispute privately to King and found him to be almost blithely philosophical. Walker and the students were not as different as they might appear, King replied.

To mitigate Walker's abrasiveness toward the SNCC students, King had hoped to use Bernard Lee, but it was now clear that Lee identified too closely with King to be effective in that role. Lee already had come to dress like King, walk like King, and even to imitate King's long, measured phrases. After talking with Belafonte, King called James Bevel and asked him to mediate between the SCLC and SNCC.

Bevel was in Mississippi, living on his small stipend from the SCLC. Still struggling to turn Jackson into Nashville, he was the foremost preacher among the SNCC students, and among the most unpredictable of their free spirits. A case in point was his recent marriage to Diane Nash. This union of SNCC leaders matched social opposites. Nash had been runner-up in Chicago's "Miss America" trials. Poised and proper, so light-skinned that she could pass for white, she had been raised in a middle-class Catholic family. Now she confronted a wild man from Itta Bena, Mississippi, a self-described example of the legendary "chicken-eating, liquor-drinking, woman-chasing Baptist preacher." Their tempestuous romance, held together by the passion of the movement, had elements of Shakespearean richness to it, rearranged along lines of Negro American culture: she as an upper-class Kate and he as a vagabond Prince Hal.

Bob Moses found the newlyweds at Amzie Moore's house in Cleveland, north of Jackson. He had obtained release from the Pike County jail on a $1,000 appeal bond on December 6, having served thirty-seven days for disturbing the peace during the McComb student prayer march back in October. Moses emerged to find that time and fear had made him a relative stranger. Jerome Smith, one of the New Orleans students who had responded to James Farmer's plea to take up the first Freedom Ride, had been so inspired by reports of the outpost in McComb that he organized a Freedom Ride to the McComb Greyhound station in November, shortly after finishing his sentence at Parchman.* After a white mob beat them severely at the station, a bloodied Smith vowed to send another team of riders, and the next attempt, on December 1, attracted forty FBI agents, a squadron of police, a score of reporters, and a white mob of five hundred. The cordon of officers allowed the Negro riders to achieve the first-known peaceful integration of a bus-station waiting room in Mississippi history—it lasted three minutes, while their bags were being unloaded—but the mob took out some of its anger on the white reporters observing in the background. Simmons Fentress, *Time*'s Atlanta bureau chief, was thrown into a plate-glass window, and several others were bruised or cut. The attack on the reporters prompted an outraged editorial in *The New York Times*, whose correspondent, Claude Sitton, believed he escaped a beating because the mob had mistaken him for an FBI agent. Sitton had moved on to cover King in Albany.

Meanwhile, U.S. District Court judge Sidney Mize effectively canceled

---

* Smith had taken one of the most militantly nonviolent positions among CORE staff members. Against James Farmer's directions, he and Doris Castle checked back into Parchman to complete their full sentences. Later, Smith became the central figure in a dramatic 1963 confrontation with Attorney General Kennedy.

the integration at McComb by banning further Freedom Rides. Judge Harold Cox upheld and extended the order, ruling that it did not conflict with federal law because the ICC ruling applied to Negroes whereas the injunction applied only to agitators. Burke Marshall was obliged to seek reversal of such blatant sophistry.

All this racial violence had subdued Negro McComb by the time Moses emerged from jail a few days after the attack on the reporters. John Hardy, one of his registration colleagues, had just survived a shotgun blast into a bedroom of the house where he was lodged in downtown McComb. Neither Hardy nor Moses could persuade people to attend the registration classes. The Masonic Temple was closed to SNCC. Moses, finding that Steptoe and the others wanted to rest for a time, decided that it was pointless to continue work in southwest Mississippi. With Hardy, Curtis Hayes, Hollis Watkins, and several other young people, he decamped for Amzie Moore's house in the Mississippi Delta. There he found Bevel and Nash, who, like himself, were freshly out of jail on appeal.

Although the three of them had vastly different personalities, they groped together toward a revised plan. Because the state was even tougher than they had thought, they decided to abandon hopes for alliances with Negro churches or businessmen and with white liberals. They resolved instead to scale down—to depend only on tiny cadres of proven young workers. Bevel's idea was to run Negro candidates for Congress in two Delta districts. He did not dream that they could win—indeed, part of the idea was that whites would not harass such a ludicrous effort—but he hoped that the campaigns would plant the very idea of voting in the minds of Negro citizens, 90 percent of whom were unregistered. The cadres then could build upon that idea in their registration classes, using live candidates and new dreams. Moses agreed to stay in Jackson as the unofficial campaign manager for Rev. R. L. T. Smith. Bevel went north into the Delta to Greenwood, near his hometown of Itta Bena, to work for Rev. Theodore Trammell. "We can't lose," Smith declared when Mississippi whites allowed him, more or less as a novelty, to announce his candidacy on television.

Starting over in a new area, Moses was as philosophical about his tribulations around McComb as was Martin Luther King about Albany. "We had, to put it mildly, got our feet wet," Moses wrote. "We now knew something of what it took to run a voter registration campaign in Mississippi."

In Atlanta, Wyatt Walker recuperated quickly enough from the tangled passions of Albany to send to the Afro-American Newspapers his personal evaluation of the year gone by. Despite his frequent, vociferous criticisms of those in and around the civil rights struggle, Walker had developed in his first full year at SCLC a professional's detached eye for the political center. For American of the Year in 1961, Walker nominated the Attorney General. "Moved with decisiveness in Montgomery violence," Walker wrote of Robert Kennedy. "Petitioned ICC for new ruling with teeth. . . . has given clear evidence that his department means business."

Walker acknowledged few peers in composure, but he did humble himself before King's phenomenal personal ballast. Even as they returned together from their first ordeal in Albany, King was joking about the intense, conflicting pressures that had bombarded him there. "I had the displeasure of meeting the meanest man in the world," he said drolly of Sheriff Chappell. Although stung by press criticism, the infighting among his allies, and the disintegration of friends (a fragile, recuperating Dr. Anderson was practically barricaded in his home, which renegade Albany Movement students pelted with tomatoes because of his failure to resume marching), King still was able to look amiably to a future of pain and glory coming at him almost randomly. What stuck in his throat more than Albany was the debacle in Kansas City. Less than forty-eight hours after leaving the Americus jail, King sat down to write a long letter to one of his family mentors in New York. Rev. O. Clay Maxwell was national president of the NBC's Sunday School Congress, from which King had just been removed as vice president. Having had made his own pained choice to stay with the National Baptist Convention, Maxwell wanted to know whether King intended to fight the banishment edict of the triumphant J. H. Jackson, who was away on a European tour that included a private meeting with Pope John XXIII.

King had been considering lawsuits against Jackson and protest marches inside the convention hall, because he believed that "Dr. Jackson will continue his un-Christian, unethical and dictatorial tactics as long as no-one openly oposes [sic] him." But, on reflection, he had decided that he would spare both Maxwell and himself the ordeal of further rebellion. "I do not feel that I am of the temperament to put up a struggle at this point," he wrote. "I think it may give the impression that I am fighting to maintain an office. . . . It would make me look little rather than big, and my involvement in the struggle for the rights of my people must always keep me above the level of littleness."

FIFTEEN

HOOVER'S TRIANGLE AND KING'S MACHINE

Then came the last year of postwar innocence. "What can you say," John Glenn exclaimed after orbiting the globe, "about a day when you have seen four beautiful sunsets?" Mickey Mantle won the Most Valuable Player award; John Steinbeck won the Nobel Prize for Literature. Intellectuals and Hollywood directors still showcased cigarette smoke as a positive image, paying little attention to obscure health warnings from Britain's Royal College of Physicians. The first of the baby-boom children turned sixteen, snatched up their driver's licenses, and created a new stage of life within Detroit's shiny creations. The Ford Motor Company designed tiny cars to compete with the German Volks-wagen, but Henry Ford publicly dropped the idea as un-American.

America was king, though some of its newly powerful citizens ached for the settled refinements of Europe. Cardinal Spellman announced that he had arranged to bring Michelangelo's *Pietà* to New York for exhibition, whereupon potentates in Washington, not to be outdone, borrowed Leonardo's *Mona Lisa* for the National Gallery. On television, a new show called "The Beverly Hillbillies" unexpectedly broke the hegemony of the Westerns atop the ratings charts, replacing frontier adventure with social satire that blended the extremes of gushing wealth and heartwarming naïveté. Through John and Jacqueline Kennedy, declared a story in *The New York Times*, "the average American has a much clearer idea of what it must be like to have everything." Future writers chose 1962 as the year of nostalgia, the perfect setting for surf comedies and carefree romances. Still, forebodings of ideological dislocation ran beneath popular enthusiasms for achievement, new dance steps, gadgets, and peaceful change.

On October 1, 1961, W. E. B. Du Bois applied for membership in the Communist Party of the U.S.A. "I have been long and slow in coming to this conclusion," Du Bois wrote in a public statement, "but at last my mind is settled." He was ninety-three. Born a year before Mohandas Gandhi, during the Andrew Johnson impeachment trial of 1868, he was a year younger than the historic First Baptist Church (Colored) of Montgomery. More than sixty years after breaking the color line on Harvard doctorates, fifty after founding the NAACP, thirty after surrendering his beloved *Crisis* magazine to a "sportswriter" named Roy Wilkins, and ten after being hauled manacled into federal court for advocating peace talks in Korea, the old man decided that "capitalism cannot reform itself; it is doomed to self-destruction. No universal selfishness can bring social good to all." Still haughty in manner and freethinking in scholarship, Du Bois was an unlikely candidate for the discipline of a working-class party. In his membership application, he reviewed for party chairman Gus Hall his lifelong disagreements with the Communists.

His statement found its way into King's files as well as J. Edgar Hoover's. King cited the defection by "one of the most brilliant Negro scholars in America" in one of his warnings about the limits of Negro patience: "There can be no doubt that if the problem of racial discrimination is not solved in the not too distant future, some Negroes, out of frustration, discontent, and despair, will turn to some other ideology." He did not speak publicly of Du Bois again for six years.

Hoover might have hailed the Du Bois statement as a vindication of the FBI's long-standing diagnosis of subversive tendencies, but he took no public notice of it. This supreme rebuke to Du Bois—that his last insult to American values failed to draw even recognition in mainstream politics—starkly illustrated his insignificance in the white culture. Although Hoover was waging a major battle over the security threat posed by the American Communist Party, the Du Bois defection was peripheral to him because he needed examples that would register with Attorney General Kennedy and with the public at large. Du Bois did not.

The running battle between Kennedy and Hoover took place on different ground. Kennedy wanted to shift the Bureau's priorities drastically from domestic intelligence to organized crime. Citing the FBI's own private figures that the American Communist Party had shriveled further since its collapse in 1956—until some fifteen hundred FBI informants within the party supplied a hefty part of its budget and membership—he insisted that the Bureau's vast domestic security network was a wasteful bureaucratic appendix from the McCarthy era. Kennedy was appalled to learn that there were only a dozen FBI agents targeted against organized crime, as opposed to more than a thousand in political security work. He would have preferred something close to a reversal, and it annoyed him almost beyond endurance that the FBI still denied the very existence of organized crime.

By the end of Robert Kennedy's first year as Hoover's nominal boss, worn edges were beginning to show. In December, Kennedy told a British journalist that the U.S. Communist Party "couldn't be more feeble and less of a threat, and besides its membership consists largely of FBI agents." In sharp but indirect rebuttal, Hoover told a House committee the next month that the U.S. Communist Party was "a Trojan Horse of rigidly disciplined fanatics unalterably committed to bring this free nation under the yoke of international communism." Hoover substantiated this ringing alarm by disclosing confidentially to the congressmen, and to selected senators as well, that a New York lawyer named Stanley Levison was both a secret member of the Communist Party, subject to orders from the Kremlin, and a guiding adviser to Martin Luther King. The message was clear: that the troublesome Negro revolution was Moscow's skirmish line, and that only the omniscient Hoover knew the full details. "The threat from without should not blind us to the threat from within," he wrote. More pointedly, in a January 8 classified memo to Robert Kennedy, Hoover extended the reach of suspicion. Not only did the Communists have influence upon King through Levison, he warned, but through King, in turn, Levison and the Communists had "access" to the Attorney General himself and to the White House. Because King had met personally with both Kennedy brothers—even taken a meal recently with the President—there was a specter of Communist influence at the highest levels.

Kennedy made no recorded response, perhaps because he dismissed the notion that he was personally vulnerable to Communist manipulation. Not everyone in the Justice Department felt secure from the threat, however, as became evident as soon as Kennedy left on February 1 for a month-long goodwill trip around the world. The next day, Acting Attorney General Byron White called in the FBI liaison officer specifically to discuss Hoover's January 8 warning about Levison. "It is White's feeling that definitely some action should be taken," the liaison officer reported afterward to the Bureau. White wanted to review Levison's FBI file for ammunition that might awaken the Kennedy Administration to the danger.

For the Bureau's purposes, White's enthusiastic initiative was too much of a good thing. His request for the Levison file raised thorny problems. For one thing, nearly all the intelligence information about Levison's Communist allegiance was at least five years old, and it came from two brothers, Jack and Morris Childs, who had infiltrated the party as FBI informants after having been purged in the factional turmoil of the late 1940s. Worse, the Levison record would show that the FBI itself twice had attempted to recruit Levison since then, which would make it difficult to explain why the Bureau now considered him so sinister. Finally, while the Bureau could show that Levison and King were close friends in the civil rights movement, there was no evidence as yet to show that either one of them followed the orders or even the wishes of the American Communist Party, let alone the Kremlin. In short, the January 8 memo had exaggerated the subversive linkages in order to get a message through to Kennedy, and Byron White's sudden embrace of the alarm now called for the Bureau to show its hand. This potential embarrassment rose instantly to J. Edgar Hoover for decision. "King is no good any way," he scrawled on the memo outlining the problem. "Under no circumstances should our informant be endangered."

By this, his first written assessment of King, Hoover marked him for FBI hostility in advance of any investigation. The terse comment, while crudely put, effectively guided FBI subordinates in their dealings with White. The important signal to get across was that King was tainted by his association with Levison. As to White's request for evidence, Hoover transformed weakness into strength: the information could not be revealed, he ordered, because it was too important. The Levison file must remain secret in all its details.

Courtney Evans, the FBI liaison, took Hoover's answer to White a few days later. White replied that he fully appreciated the reasons why he could not see the Levison dossier. Still, to restrain White, Evans went so far as to tone down Hoover's January 8 memo. It was not Levison himself who was talking to the Attorney General and the White House, Evans reminded White, but King. The Communist access was indirect rather than direct. Such assurance drew out White's sarcasm. "White said from the character of some of the people over at the White House he would not have been surprised if it were reported that Levison actually did have such a contact," Evans wrote, transmitting to FBI headquarters a barb doubtless aimed at Harris Wofford.

From the FBI's point of view, Evans achieved an ideal understanding with Byron White, in that the Acting Attorney General seemed to embrace the Bureau's suspicions of King and Levison on Hoover's word alone. Moreover, the incident helped Hoover reestablish direct commu-

nications with the White House. Robert Kennedy had been able to cut
the Director's cherished access to the President's office by insisting that
FBI messages be cleared through channels at the Justice Department. On
February 14, Hoover sent Byron White a file summary on King's miscellaneous contacts with supporters of left-wing causes. Simultaneously, he
sent a similar report to Kenneth O'Donnell at the White House, delivered
by hand in an important-looking FBI pouch. "My dear Mr. O'Donnell,"
he began. "I thought you would be interested in the following concerning
the Reverend Martin Luther King, Jr., prominent southern Negro
leader . . ."

Meanwhile, Robert Kennedy circled the globe on his extraordinary
tour, speaking confidently for the Administration on foreign policy and
other subjects far afield from the Justice Department, traveling with
legions of reporters who speculated that such trips foretold a Kennedy
dynasty in which Robert would follow his brother into the White House.
In poorer countries, Kennedy was bedeviled by persistent questions about
the American stand on colonialism. Indonesians in particular refused to
accept his neutral comments about their negotiations for the independence of New Guinea from the Netherlands. Kennedy, trying not to
offend a NATO ally, took essentially the same position he maintained
during the conflict in Albany, Georgia: that it was a matter for the local
parties to decide for themselves. This earned him a barrage of criticism
for his implied recognition of merit in the Dutch colonial claims. With
his shy humor and dogged grit, Kennedy gamely faced hecklers in more
than one country. Later he reflected that no amount of East-West debate
on the claims of democracy against communism would dispel the global
preoccupation with race and economics. "There wasn't one area of the
world that I visited," he said later, ". . . that I wasn't asked about the
question of civil rights."

J. Edgar Hoover welcomed the Attorney General home on February 27
with a dose of scandal so fantastic in those days that even the most
credulous readers of supermarket tabloids would have dismissed it as
lurid fantasy. Hoover's memo was the result of an investigation that had
begun sometime earlier, when FBI agents in Las Vegas arrested private
parties for placing illegal wiretaps on the home of singer Phyllis Mc-
Guire. Preliminary development of the wiretap prosecution had shown
that the wiretappers were in the employ of Robert Maheu, a former FBI
agent working for Howard Hughes, and Sam "Momo" Giancana, Al Capone's mobster heir in Chicago. That much was good news to the entire
Justice Department—Hoover loathed Maheu as a Bureau renegade, and

Kennedy had sought the conviction of Giancana almost as diligently as that of Jimmy Hoffa. The first of the bad news was that Maheu and Giancana claimed immunity from prosecution on the grounds that their wiretap was sanctioned by the CIA. Officials from the CIA, in turn, had confirmed through gritted teeth that Maheu and Giancana indeed had been working for them in a series of top-secret attempts to assassinate Cuban premier Fidel Castro by means of Giancana's gangster connections. Giancana, while plotting these missions, had asked Maheu and the CIA to make sure that his mistress, Phyllis McGuire, was not two-timing him while he was away, and the agency officials had decided that they were in no position to refuse.

All this was only the beginning. Further investigation, plus the wiretaps themselves, had revealed that Phyllis McGuire nursed her own complaints about the relationship, including the fact that Giancana maintained a second mistress, in California, named Judith Campbell. Singer Frank Sinatra had introduced Campbell to Giancana and to other gangsters with whom he socialized. Sinatra also had introduced Judith Campbell to John Kennedy, it turned out, and both John and Robert Kennedy to Marilyn Monroe, among others, in a serial exchange of lovers. In fact, it seemed that Sinatra did as much introducing as singing, and that his libertine social network included glittering figures of many kinds—from politics, gangsterdom, and show business. Giancana, for his part, was an old-school gangster, not merely in the assumption of his prerogative to wiretap one lady friend while carrying on himself with another, but also in his practical view of social matters. His affair with Campbell was strictly business, bestowing enormous hidden power upon him because he shared a mistress with the President of the United States.

It required all of J. Edgar Hoover's genius to boil down such steaming pulp into the dignified drone of policy: phone records confirmed that Judith Campbell had placed some seventy calls to the White House in the year since Kennedy moved in; CIA officials opposed criminal prosecution of Giancana or Maheu, for fear of compromising the national security operations against Castro. The ramifications of this one Las Vegas arrest could spell disaster for the Administration. It meant that the CIA and the Kennedy brothers had poisoned the U.S. government's chances of prosecuting Giancana and associated gangsters for any of their crimes. They had exposed the U.S. government to disgrace as one that pursued murder in partnership with gangsters, and exposed the President to blackmail as a consort of gangster women. Hoover summarized the whole package with professional detachment, but private satisfactions converged from many directions. This was the CIA that had driven his Bureau out of foreign intelligence work since World War II? These were the Kennedys who were pressuring him to declare war on gangsters such as Giancana? These were the people who belittled his far-flung vigilance against domestic subversion?

With little fear of rebuke, Hoover continued to rebuild his direct White House channel by sending an identical copy of his February 27 memo to Kenneth O'Donnell. That same day he ordered the New York and Atlanta FBI offices to search their files thoroughly for information on Martin Luther King. A week later, Hoover formally requested Attorney General Kennedy's authorization to place wiretaps in the office of Stanley Levison. Kennedy approved. By an odd custom that Justice Department executives preferred not to discuss, Hoover himself assumed the authority to place room listening devices—bugs, as opposed to wiretaps —and he moved swiftly on bugs even before Kennedy authorized the wiretap.* On the night of March 15, New York FBI agents broke into Levison's office to plant the bugs, which were called "misurs" in the bureau's standard abbreviation for "microphone surveillances." Technicians hooked up the telephone wiretaps on the afternoon of March 20.

The complete Levison coverage was in place just before Director Hoover's private luncheon at the White House on March 22, when he reported to President Kennedy on the FBI's discovery of the Sinatra-Mafia-Castro-mistress tangle. Personally, Hoover was not a man who enjoyed personal confrontation. He leaned heavily on the soothing theme that he was the President's loyal servant, doing his duty by bringing private warning of possible dangers ahead. Also, in confronting the President about his sexual escapades, Hoover was fortified by the experience of having done so twenty years earlier. During World War II, FBI agents watching a Danish reporter named Inga Arvad (who was suspected as a spy because she had known Hitler, Goebbels, Goering, and other top Nazis) had discovered that she was having an affair with Kennedy, then a Navy lieutenant. Acting on FBI accusations, the Navy had punished Kennedy with a transfer, and Hoover had denied Kennedy a written ab-

---

* There is no kind way to describe the process by which the nation's leaders came to regard FBI microphone surveillances—bugs—to be legal on Hoover's authority alone. The only written justification for the practice was a private 1954 memorandum in which Attorney General Herbert Brownell effectively advised Hoover to disregard a unanimous Supreme Court decision outlawing such bugs. In practice, no Attorney General for the next generation tried to hold Hoover accountable to any law or review. When this record came to light during the intelligence scandals of the 1970s, congressional authorities found it too embarrassing to acknowledge an official history of blatant illegality or supine ignorance. Instead, they simply accepted Brownell's 1954 memorandum as a permanent "policy" that conferred legal authority for Hoover to bug at will.

solution from suspicions of disloyalty, refusing even personal appeals from his friend Ambassador Joseph Kennedy. Afterward, when Lieutenant Kennedy continued the affair, FBI agents had bugged their trysts to obtain tape recordings of Navy talk mixed with pillow talk. Hoover did not forget the episode. Upon Kennedy's election to the presidency in 1960, he asked his assistant Cartha "Deke" DeLoach to retrieve the Kennedy-Arvad tape recordings from the FBI files for review. DeLoach, who had heard only rumors about the tapes, recalled them as involving Joseph Kennedy, not his son, but the Director said firmly, "No, it was the boy."

Now the boy was President. A conversation between President Kennedy and J. Edgar Hoover touching the topic of sex was a remarkable event, as Hoover came from a different galaxy. In 1941, the same year that Kennedy began squiring Inga Arvad, Hoover warned America that if motels were allowed to proliferate along the highways, citizens would sleep unwittingly on mattresses still warm from "illicit relations." A generation later, motels having sprung up everywhere, this same Hoover went to the White House for a discussion that would have made a Borgia or Medici feel at home. When it was over, President Kennedy buzzed Kenneth O'Donnell. "Get rid of that bastard," he commanded. "He's the biggest bore."

There is no record of what Hoover actually told Kennedy, but the results suggest strongly that he emphasized the dangers of the Sinatra connection. Hoover's agents had overheard Giancana and other "hoodlums" plotting to ask the government for favors through Sinatra, and Sinatra was a point of contact not only for some of the mistresses but also for gangsters who would not shrink from blackmailing the President. On these points, Hoover had a strong case. That same afternoon, the President had his last known phone conversation with Judith Campbell, apparently a sign-off, and Kennedy also decided not to stay with Frank Sinatra during his upcoming visit to Palm Springs. Instead, he would stay with Sinatra's rival, Bing Crosby, and break off social contact with Sinatra altogether.

Meanwhile, FBI technicians in New York first turned on the receivers for the newly implanted Levison bugs at 10:10 on the morning of March 16. Thereafter, the ear of the U.S. government would remain surreptitiously close to Levison and King throughout the remainder of King's life.

For King, the year had begun as it would end: being dragged toward Birmingham. While Hoover and the Kennedys sparred over communism,

King was beseeching the Administration to keep Fred Shuttlesworth out of jail.

On January 8, Shuttlesworth flew into Birmingham from his new home in Cincinnati. One of a score of prosecutions from his past had come to an unfavorable end that day, when the U.S. Supreme Court declined to review his conviction for riding in the front of a Birmingham bus in 1958. Although the courts had struck down the segregation ordinance involved, the Justices denied Shuttlesworth's appeal as technically flawed. His lawyers had failed to file a copy of the trial transcript within sixty days of his original conviction, as required by Alabama law. Lean, blunt, and eloquent as ever, Shuttlesworth stood before the regular mass meeting in Birmingham to castigate his own lawyers, Arthur Shores and Orzell Billingsley, who were two of the most distinguished Negro lawyers in Alabama. "My Calhouns," he called them acidly, after the polysyllabic bumbler on the "Amos 'n' Andy" show. "From now on, I am telling the lawyers how to fight my cases."

King wired Attorney General Kennedy on January 15, requesting an appointment to discuss emergency intervention by the Justice Department. Burke Marshall responded by phone with what was becoming known as Marshall's theory of federalist limitation. Because the Constitution severely curtailed the powers of the federal government in the fields of police action and law enforcement, Marshall wrote in a follow-up letter, he had "not been able to discern any basis upon which this Department might possibly intervene in the cases." Marshall also deflected the lesser steps King had in mind, such as arranging for Shuttlesworth to be confined outside Birmingham. Most likely these would be ineffective, and Marshall wanted to conserve the Justice Department's public authority for more advantageous cases. Attorney General Kennedy would not talk with King on the subject, lest he raise false expectations.

Collateral events only punctuated King's disappointment with this response. The day after King's talk with Marshall, federal judge Hobart Grooms pronounced sentence in Birmingham on six men who admitted FBI charges of mayhem and assault in the destruction of the first Freedom Rider bus outside Anniston the previous May. Grooms gave five of the men a year's probation. He allowed the sixth to serve a term concurrent with a prior burglary sentence. The news emanating from the courtroom was that none of the defendants would spend a single day in jail for their vicious attacks on one bus, whereas Shuttlesworth would serve ninety days merely for sitting in another.

That night, dynamite bombs severely damaged three Birmingham churches that recently had hosted mass meetings, including Shuttlesworth's former church. A policeman, responding to emergency broadcasts about the first two blasts, happened to be driving by the third targeted church when the last bomb went off. Concussion shattered the windows of his squad car from a distance of a hundred yards, sending him to the hospital with lacerations. Bull Connor first denied that the bombings were racially inspired, then later tersely declared, "We know that Negroes did it." Connor also announced his candidacy for governor in that year's election. One of his first steps in office, he pledged, would be to buy a hundred new police dogs to sic on any Freedom Riders who ventured into Alabama.

On January 25, as Shuttlesworth surrendered at the Birmingham city jail along with his companion from the 1958 bus test, Rev. J. S. Phifer, King appealed to Robert Kennedy for protection. "It is clear that hundreds of segregationists, in and out of jail, would like nothing better than to do bodily harm to the Rev. Mr. Shuttlesworth," he wrote. King sent Wyatt Walker immediately to Birmingham, and by the next morning they had secured the endorsement of twenty-eight civil rights organizations for a joint telegram to Kennedy. High fees and new legal bills drove King to send out a desperate plea to his most trusted friends in the Negro clergy:

> None of us ever dreamed he [Shuttlesworth] would actually have to serve time. We had to secure additional counsel to perfect the legal steps we are taking to free him. William Kunstler, Esq., of New York City is now in our employ on this matter. Mrs. Shuttlesworth is not well; to relieve both her and Fred of unnecessary anxiety, we have committed ourselves to fill his pulpit in Cincinnati in his absence. SCLC is responsible for all these expenses. Trial costs for the Freedom Ride along with attorney's fees still remain to be met. The three million dollar libel suits continue against Ralph Abernathy, Fred Shuttlesworth, Joseph Lowery and S. S. Seay, Sr. The day-to-day operation must continue, but with this sudden drain on us, we cannot keep pace . . . Would you possibl[y] arrange to take an after offering this coming Sunday?

"Dear Mike," replied Rev. O. Clay Maxwell, with whom King had just exchanged such painful correspondence over the schism in the Negro Baptist church, "I was a bit distressed by the letter I received from you the latter part of last week in which you requested that I lift an offering of one hundred dollars for you . . . I don't know what others may be able to do but I did know that we at Mount Olive were able to do better than one hundred dollars." Maxwell sent five hundred.

"Maintenance of law and order in any locality is the primary responsibility of local officials," Marshall wrote King later that month. He sent a similar reply when King called for a federal investigation of the bombing that demolished the home of C. O. Simpkins, the SCLC board member from Shreveport. King's appeals seemed to have less effect than public criticism. To Negro reporters who wanted to know why the Justice Department did not authorize the FBI to investigate the triple church bombing in Birmingham, Marshall conceded that the Justice Department did not permit the FBI to take the initiative in such cases. Uncomfortably, Marshall said he was reviewing this policy, which, he added, he had inherited from the Eisenhower Administration. King chafed at the Administration's aloofness but was unwilling to risk a break. "While the President has not yet earned unqualified confidence and support," he wrote in *The Nation*, "neither has he earned rejection and withdrawal of support."

On Lincoln's Birthday, King flew to Birmingham for a mass meeting in support of the jailed preachers, Shuttlesworth and Phifer. The crowd at the Sixteenth Street Baptist Church overflowed into the basement and then into the street, growing so large that it required fully a half hour just to collect the offering. Although President Lucius Pitts of Miles College considered Shuttlesworth a martinet, and dangerously provocative, he too came to the mass meeting. Just as he was telling the crowd that Negro youth would never get anywhere in life if they kept wearing sharp-pointed, odd-colored shoes and tight, short skirts, or if they kept doing vulgar new dances instead of studying, King made his entrance.

He spoke glowingly of economic discipline and scholarship, but warned that these would not be enough to win freedom in Birmingham. "I wish I could tell you our road ahead is easy," he said. "That we are in the promised land, that we won't have to suffer and sacrifice any more, but it is not so. We have got to be prepared. The time is coming when the police won't protect us, the mayor and [police] commissioner won't think with clear minds. Then we can expect the worst. We want to be free." To offset these clairvoyant forebodings, he told the crowd of his unpublicized visit to President and Mrs. Kennedy—how the Kennedys had shared a wonderful meal with him and given him a tour of the White House, and how in the Lincoln Room he had asked the President to sign a Second Emancipation Proclamation. Faced with implacable and determined opponents in Birmingham, King emphasized his hopes for the Kennedy Administration rather than his frustrations.

Two weeks later, the U.S. Supreme Court unanimously ordered Judge Grooms to free Shuttlesworth on appeal bond if the Alabama courts failed to do so within five days. "Whites can't stop us now," declared a triumphant Shuttlesworth upon his March 1 release. "Negroes are beginning to realize Birmingham is not so powerful after all—not in the face of a federal edict." Wyatt Walker came into town to address the next mass meeting, saying, "The world situation for the Negro will be straightened out by the three K's: Kennedy, Khrushchev, and King." Roy Wilkins followed Walker the next week. By then, students and Shuttlesworth supporters had seized upon the anger generated by the incarceration to begin a boycott of the segregated stores in downtown Birmingham. Leaflets appeared bearing the slogan "Wear Your Old Clothes for Freedom." Reverend Phifer told the next mass meeting that they should all wear old jeans to church on Easter Sunday as a sign of their commitment. "Bull and Old Art's [Mayor Arthur Hanes] days are numbered," he said. Phifer became so ecstatic in his sermon that scores of shouters joined him spontaneously on the rostrum, and several preachers labored to restore calm.

Bull Connor noticed the boycott. "I don't intend to sit here and take it with a smile," he said at a City Commission meeting on April 3. Connor then moved to cut off city distributions to the needy from the federal government's surplus food program, reasoning that most of the recipients were Negroes. The next day, his officers found Shuttlesworth and Phifer walking down the street and arrested them for blocking the sidewalk. On making bail, Shuttlesworth declared that Connor's reprisals would increase rather than decrease support for the new campaign. With defiant relish, he described the boycott as "like Ivory Soap—99 and 44/100ths percent pure."

Birmingham was not yet the main focus of King's activities. He spent less time there than in many other cities, and he stayed nowhere very long. If there was anything new in his chaotic pursuits, it was a steady accumulation of evidence that there was life after all in the dreams of the past five years. The breakthroughs came in several areas almost at once—fund-raising, voter registration, the recruitment of professional cadres. Where there had formerly been pennies, fruitless committees, and pitiful delays, there suddenly sprang up a well-financed registration operation. Roughly speaking, the spark came from King. The fuel came from the new Voter Education Project grants, as supervised by a newcomer named Andrew Young. The payload came from Septima Clark's citizenship schools, which were training registration workers. And the indispensable mechanics came from Jack O'Dell, who was the manager of Stanley Levison's direct-mail operation in the New York SCLC office.

O'Dell soon became significant to the Kennedy Administration because of his Communist background. Five years King's senior, he had been left as a child to grow up in the home of his grandfather, a janitor in a Detroit public library, and grandmother, who raised him as a strict Catholic—so devout that O'Dell remained an altar boy even in college, at Xavier in New Orleans. During World War II, he ferried war cargoes under destroyer escort for the Coast Guard merchant marine, and, like Harry Belafonte, first encountered political history through Negro sailors who introduced him to the works of W. E. B. Du Bois. For nearly six years, he killed long hours below decks reading Du Bois on Reconstruction, world history, the NAACP, and the subjugation of Africa. Then he went back to New Orleans and found work as an organizer for his union, the National Maritime Union. It was renowned among Negroes as the first seamen's international to break the color line. Shipping jobs were not posted by race. One of its international executives was the first Negro to hold such a position in any trade union. In its racial advances, the NMU followed the policy of the Communist International. When an anti-Communist faction purged the union in 1950, O'Dell was expelled for circulating peace petitions.

He had found work selling burial insurance in Birmingham. By 1957, O'Dell's skill with numbers earned him a promotion to manager of the company's Montgomery office, and there, as a lapsed Catholic, he went several times to hear the newly famous Martin Luther King preach at Dexter Avenue Baptist Church. Later, while doing graduate work in New York, he volunteered to work under Bayard Rustin on the 1959 Youth March for integrated schools. Through Rustin, O'Dell met Stanley Levison, who later asked him to promote the 1961 Sammy Davis–Frank Sinatra benefit concert for the SCLC at Carnegie Hall, just after the Kennedy inauguration. That evening was a high point in the life of O'Dell, who was a most unusual man. He still retained his Communist friends, as well as his deep appreciation for the Communist Party's efforts in behalf of Negro sailors. At the same time he kept up his fraternity contacts, still felt the tugs of the Catholic faith, and treasured the memory of hearing Frank Sinatra sing "Moonlight in Vermont" at Carnegie Hall.

O'Dell had first met King as a colleague rather than a celebrity when Levison took him to present a report on the net receipts from the Carnegie Hall event. Financial success made it a festive occasion, and Levison pressed King to establish a more permanent fund-raising structure. He recommended O'Dell, with his experience in business management, as the ideal supervisor for an experimental program of fund-raising by mass mailings. King approved Levison's plan, and the mail solicitation proved successful beyond all expectation. O'Dell soon was working full time as director of the SCLC mail room in Harlem, drawing a small salary from the proceeds. He saw so much potential in the newfangled techniques that he took advanced marketing classes at the NYU Business School. By August 1961, Levison and O'Dell reported proudly to King that their little operation had raised $80,000 for the SCLC in the past year—more than half the SCLC budget—above expenses of less than $10,000. In the parlance of direct mail, they reported to King that they were adding every day to a "master list" of 12,000 "proven contributors."

The New York SCLC office was a beehive of efficiency. Experience there as a typist and envelope stuffer had led Bob Moses to expect something similar at SCLC's Atlanta headquarters, where he found instead the languid atmosphere of a church social. The discrepancy discouraged Levison as well as Moses, and finally King himself concluded that the organization of the Atlanta office was critically flawed. In January 1962, anticipating large voter registration grants on the establishment of the VEP, King asked O'Dell to begin commuting between New York and Atlanta. His new assignment was to apply the lessons of his fund-raising project to voter registration. Wearing two hats, O'Dell became in effect the SCLC's first quartermaster. He was keeper of lists, statistician of votes, designer of systems.

Just before O'Dell started commuting, Andrew Young went South as the Field Foundation's new supervisor for Septima Clark's citizenship schools. Young was charged with the vital task of connecting New York philanthropy to the civil rights movement by steering tax-exempt money into voter registration. For the better part of a year, Young had vacillated over a career decision: should he leave the expense-account comforts of his job as associate director of the Department of Youth Work in the National Council of Churches for the risks and hardships of civil rights work in the segregated South? "Now I am forced to make a choice," he had written in a letter to King, seeking advice. Never having met Young, King had asked Levison to meet and evaluate Young in New York. Levison found him competent but unfocused. Gardner Taylor gave King a more personal report, as Taylor had known the Youngs as one of the most distinguished Negro families in New Orleans. They were wealthy Congregationalists, from the highest and "lightest" of the churches, and a number of Young cousins were so light-skinned and respectable that they had passed over into the white world. Andrew Young, three years King's junior, had first thought he might join the idealism of the Southern movement by tutoring the unlettered preachers of the SCLC. "The Southern Christian Leadership Conference is made up largely of Baptist Churches and lower class Negroes," he wrote a New York friend. "These clergy do not have the respect of the educated Negro, and there is almost no way for them to get together. They need each other desperately, though. This would be one of my objectives."

Months of adjustment had followed, running parallel to the creation of the Voter Education Project. From Highlander, Myles Horton apologized to Young for the delays. Young apologized to philanthropists for the conceptual fuzziness of the voter education scheme, and confessed to Wyatt Walker that "we get more chicken about moving back to the center of the struggle." The final arrangements between Young, the SCLC, the foundations, and the National Council of Churches amounted to an elaborate exchange of titles and obligations, comprehensible only to foundation experts. Young went on the Field Foundation payroll, but the SCLC paid his travel expenses and other budget items. Myles Horton helped weave a third institution into the patchwork by securing through the National Council of Churches an abandoned Congregationalist missionary school as a site for citizenship classes.

At Dorchester, the missionary school, not far from Savannah, Georgia, Young merged the old citizenship education program with voter registration, accepting Septima Clark as the undisputed schoolmistress of both. She took in adult students by the busload, a week at a time, and used the practical methods she had been developing for more than forty years. In math class, she taught her pupils how to figure out seed and fertilizer allotments. In literacy classes, she worked upward from street signs and newspapers to the portions of the state constitutions required for voter registration. Although her pedagogy commanded the attention of professionals like Young, her gift lay in recognizing natural leaders among the poorly educated yeomanry—midwives, old farmers and draymen, grandmothers who had pushed children and grandchildren through school—and imparting to them her unshakable confidence and respect. There was an invisible edge to her. Still touchy about being the daughter of a slave, she was quick to notice what she called pridefulness among her own people—taking it personally, for instance, that Mother King never invited her into the "drawing room" of the King home in Atlanta, and noting that powerful preachers of the movement were given to vainglory and often oblivious to the contributions of women.

At first, Clark treated her new boss almost as a pupil—all the more so since Andrew Young had accomplished nearly all his grant-knitting wizardry before she had even met him. Once, when a new busload arrived at Dorchester, Young flew in by chartered airplane for the opening ceremonies, and Clark intercepted him on the way to the pantry. He should not eat unless he shared the food with all the new arrivals, she said patiently, because they had been on a bus all night and were hungry. Young blinked. There was no money for a communal breakfast in the budget, he said, and besides, no one had complained about what was due him as the director. Clark said he must bear in mind that these were people who put sand in Coke bottles just to prove to the folks back home that they had seen the ocean. They would never dream of attending church at Ebenezer, let alone Young's elite congregation, because the worshippers there dressed up too much and were too refined for them, and if the recruits could not feel comfortable doing such simple things, how could they feel worthy to vote against the wishes of the white man? Clark said that the recruits noticed everything. Young's budget priorities and his lack of eagerness to mingle with his recruits spoke as eloquently as his speeches. "If you can pay all that money that the Marshall Field Foundation has sent us to rent a plane, why can't you give them two or three dollars to buy breakfast?" she asked. Failing that, he could share their discomfort.

"Septima, you are a saint," said Young.

"No, I'm not a saint," she replied. "I don't consider myself a saint. But I do know that what you are doing is not wise."

"There are saints in hell, you know," said Young, who was agile in theological debate.

"Well, then, I might be one of them," said Clark. She already had ruined Young's appetite, and eventually the foundation director from New York found himself loosening his tie and eating bag lunches with citizenship students.

Such working adjustments were well under way by February—not only for Clark and Young but also for Jack O'Dell and Wiley Branton, the incoming director of the Voter Education Project. On February 2, 1962, all these people gathered at a meeting of SCLC affiliates in Atlanta. King made a speech. Septima Clark and Dorothy Cotton were introduced as the new citizenship teachers. James Lawson conducted workshops in nonviolence. Andrew Young attended as the representative of the Field Foundation. And Jack O'Dell, as director of SCLC voter registration, conducted the business sessions. O'Dell described a new flow chart for registration. First, King would speak on tour, using the power of his name and his message to solicit new volunteers. Then O'Dell and Young would send selected volunteers to Dorchester for citizenship training with Septima Clark. The most gifted trainees would take her methods back to their home areas as teachers. Finally, O'Dell would submit the records of trained, functioning workers to Wiley Branton for VEP funding as ongoing SCLC registration projects.

King left immediately on what he called variously a "People-to-People" tour, a "Southwide" tour, and a "Freedom Corps" drive. Beginning with a traditional rally in the First Baptist Church of Clarksdale, Mississippi, he spent three days whirling through the Delta's Third Congressional District, where James Bevel was working. To drive home the point that he was after more than big audiences and heavy collection plates, King held meetings at country stores as well as churches, and stopped at the smallest hamlets as well as the ones with paved roads.

While James Lawson held nonviolence workshops at Tougaloo College, King preached registration politics to awed farmers in Jonestown. In tiny Sherard, he gave a pep talk to an audience of exactly one old man, who proudly claimed to have walked thirteen miles to meet King. With Wyatt Walker and Dorothy Cotton, King recruited in three days some 150 people willing to make the long journey to Septima Clark's citizenship school in Georgia.

He went on to new tours through South Carolina and Georgia. By February 22, when Wiley Branton announced that at long last the Voter Education Project was "open for business," the SCLC hit the ground running for the newly available funds. More than a thousand people quickly signed up for the Freedom Corps. Hundreds of them passed through Septima Clark's training program at Dorchester. The Voter Education Project secured three initial grants totaling $162,000 from the Taconic, Field, and Stern foundations, with the promise of much more to come, and the SCLC almost instantly received an advance of $11,000 against its first-year request of $60,000. *Jet* magazine, the largest Negro weekly, published a story entitled "Dr. King Uniting Greatest Force Since Reconstruction," observing that King was touring the South "in a manner more familiar to an office-seeker than a man of the cloth . . . in the best traditions of a political machine."

Other civil rights groups did not fail to notice the SCLC's head start, and King tried to repair relations with SNCC as well as the NAACP. In March, he agreed to speak at a private SNCC fund-raiser in New York, hosted by Harry Belafonte. SNCC's financial distress was such that Bob Moses made one of his rare trips out of Mississippi for the event. Jones and Sherrod came up from Albany. Tim Jenkins came down from Yale Law School. SNCC chairman Charles McDew arrived at the last minute from Louisiana, where, on a visit to a jailed SNCC colleague, he had been imprisoned for a month himself on a manifestly contrived charge of vagrancy. Before King arrived, Belafonte had a long session in his living room with the SNCC delegation, trying to convince them that their criticisms of King's leadership were misguided. The students complained generally that King was too far above the battle, too cautious, too distracted by his fame. Moses said very little, but his immersion into Mississippi stood as the prime counterexample to King. Among themselves, the SNCC leaders grumbled that Belafonte's allegiance to King was grounded in an entertainer's rule that every show must have a star. To Belafonte's arguments that the real King was much less bourgeois than he might seem, they snickered about Coretta's pearls and pillbox hats, Daddy King's self-centered bluster, King's vacations and silk pajamas. "If it looks like it, acts like it, tastes like it, smells like it, and feels like it, you know, at some point you've got to say it *is*," one joked.

They spoke with the conviction of those who had purged themselves of status attachments, but they did not press their sarcasm too openly upon Belafonte. They respected him as one of SNCC's prime benefactors, and they conceded his point that no other leader would tolerate their effrontery. At that night's cocktail party, King mingled briefly with the crowd, then stood next to Belafonte to make a glowing speech about what he himself had learned from the sacrifices of SNCC students. He introduced each of them for a statement about the nature of SNCC's ongoing work, urged the guests to support them, and departed without mentioning his own organization.

King plunged into another "People-to-People" tour on March 24. "Let's pull it, doctor!" Wyatt Walker shouted to his wife as their alarm clock sounded before dawn, and they pushed King's schedule up a notch to the frantic pace of a political campaign. By midmorning, Walker, King, Abernathy, Dorothy Cotton, and Bernard Lee had flown from Atlanta to Richmond, held a press conference, greeted a host of Negro dignitaries, and raced by motorcade to Petersburg for a luncheon speech. They canvassed door-to-door that afternoon, then drove a hundred miles west to a mass meeting of nearly three thousand people. The tour went on through Virginia, dragging behind schedule despite the prodding of Walker and his clipboard, so that some audiences were left waiting two and three hours. Walker dispatched preachers ahead to hold the crowds.

News of the VEP and the new registration drives did not escape into the white press at all. VEP officials actively discouraged publicity for fear of inciting a political storm against their tax arrangements. Whitney Young of the Urban League refused to join in a public announcement because he was dissatisfied with the anticipated allotment of funds. For diplomatic reasons, King urged that Roy Wilkins be the focus of any VEP announcements, but Wilkins declined to participate. These inhibiting factors kept the early successes of the registration drive a secret even from activists in the civil rights movement. Stanley Levison was shocked to hear Wyatt Walker report that Dorchester trainees already had founded 61 small citizenship schools across the South. This was fantastic, cried Levison, but where was the news? Press clips were vital to his fund-raising letters, which generated money to build the entire program. By the time King agreed to issue a low-key press release on the SCLC drive, the number of schools had grown to 95 and the Dorchester trainees to 930. The release attracted little attention among reporters, who had grown skeptical of drum rolls for Negro registration.

Levison was preoccupied with the SCLC's running battle against extinction. On March 9, he traveled to Atlanta for an emergency meeting about the *Sullivan* case. Prospects were grim. The Supreme Court, by rejecting a request that the case be transferred to federal court, had just killed the desperate hope of the four SCLC defendants to postpone the confiscation of their assets. As a result, the automobiles of Shuttlesworth, Abernathy, and Joseph Lowery had been sold at a state-ordered auction. Some of S. S. Seay's real estate was attached for quick sale. Sullivan had placed a lien on the land Abernathy had inherited from his father, and lawyers were moving to discover other property that could be seized. Fred Shuttlesworth, still growling about the incompetence of his lawyers in his Birmingham sit-in case, walked into the emergency meeting almost directly from the Birmingham jail. As King's appointed secretary for the occasion, he noted drily in the minutes that the discussion "centered on lawyers and their efficiency."

There was subdued panic among the four SCLC defendants, for whom ruin was no longer merely a theoretical possibility. Mayor James of Montgomery had another $500,000 judgment in the appeals courts behind Sullivan; Governor Patterson had a bigger one after that. It was fine for them to portray themselves in fund-raising appeals as four lowly Negro preachers being crushed by state repression, but at stake were the family treasures of relatively prosperous men. Lowery disclosed to his colleagues that he stood to lose between $150,000 and $200,000. This was real money, the new birthright of preachers who had succeeded despite the millstone of a segregated economy. Together with jail and violence, such financial persecution was driving the SCLC's leadership from the toughest parts of the South. Shuttlesworth had moved to Cincinnati. Phifer, his cellmate, was taking a church in New York, and the recent bombing of his home had convinced C. O. Simpkins to move from Shreveport to Chicago. Adapting to harsh realities, King handled the delicate diplomacy of bringing in Northern white lawyers to supersede Southern Negro ones. Stanley Levison, sharp-eyed and practical as always, strongly supported the move on the grounds that the Southern lawyers were overpaid and ineffective, which made it more difficult for Levison to raise money. The crisis sent him back to New York with a renewed mandate.

From the beginning, Levison had seen the *Sullivan* case as both a threat and an opportunity. Because the lawsuit gravely jeopardized newspaper advertising as a fund-raising mechanism, Levison had helped pioneer the direct-mail method. Because the issues in the lawsuit threatened labor organizers in the South as well as Negroes, he and King slowly had built union support. The labor interest in turn helped King enlist labor lawyers and constitutional experts, and this, like the AFL-CIO speech, attracted the attention of professional politicians. When Theodore Kheel hosted a

New York lawyers' luncheon in February, Nelson Rockefeller heard about it and sent King a friendly note "to assure you of my personal support."

After the Kheel luncheon, King found himself alone in a hotel room with a Wall Street lawyer who had a large cigar in his mouth but remorse on his face. At forty-four, Harry Wachtel had made a name for himself as the legal architect for an Israeli immigrant named Meshulam Riklis, one of the inventors of the modern conglomerate. By perfecting a technique called the leveraged buy-out, through which he essentially bought companies with their own assets, Riklis had built a $500 million empire from what seemed to be an irrational combination of firms, ranging from the Playtex brassiere company to the Schenley distillery. Wachtel's reputation as a business predator made him an unlikely sympathizer for King, but he disgorged a capsule life history in a confessional tone. He was a Jewish shopkeeper's son, he said, and as a college radical in the late 1930s had vowed to use his law degree for the downtrodden. But things had not turned out that way, and he had worked, as he put it, "not on the side of the angels." The cruelest irony for him was that his conglomerate, Rapid-American, owned several of the chains whose segregated lunch counters still were the targets of sit-ins in the South—Greene's, McCrory's, McClellan's. Wachtel's daughter had pummeled his conscience relentlessly, wanting to know what good was all his money and power if he was helpless to create elementary justice in the Riklis company.

Tormented, Wachtel said he had always admired King, but now, having heard him speak, he was resolved to recapture the idealism of his youth and the respect of his daughter: he would resign from Rapid-American. And he would make a splash. He would give a public statement denouncing the hypocrisy of the Northern variety-store owners. "If you say the word," he told King emotionally, "I will fall on my sword."

King hesitated only a moment. "I don't think you should do that," he said quietly. "You can't leave a spot like that for a flare." He said he was sure Wachtel could help the civil rights movement more where he was than out on the street, and Wachtel, immensely relieved to be spared from career suicide, soon offered as a first step to give King some money. "I'd like to make a contribution of $7,000," he said, pulling out his checkbook. He asked for the name of the SCLC's tax-exempt branch.

"We don't have one," King admitted. "We ask people who are worried to give through my church."

Wachtel frowned in surprise. He explained why he thought this was dangerous, and listed some people he knew in Washington who could help King get an exemption. It would be easy. King should form a foundation to promote the less controversial aspects of the SCLC's work.

Before Wachtel got very far, King asked whether Wachtel himself might undertake such a project. Not only would he be happy to do so, Wachtel replied, but he did not think any lawyer could do it better.

"You see there?" said a smiling King. "You've already found something you can do." Wachtel fairly exploded with enthusiasm as he and King fell into discussion of the newly born project, talking of "the foundation" as though it existed already. When King asked whether it might safely raise funds for the *Sullivan* appeal, which he said was "floating between nowhere," Wachtel replied that this would be an ideal purpose. In fact, he added, he had some ideas about the *Sullivan* defense as well, and if King agreed, he would be happy to have his firm work on the case.

Wachtel jumped swiftly into King's acquaintance. He and Levison were destined to be paired for years as King's twin Jewish lawyers. In later years, it became a running joke among the SCLC's Southern staff that no one could tell them apart. They went in and out of harmony with each other, but Levison actively encouraged Wachtel's relationship with King because he knew that Wachtel opened new and larger worlds. Whereas Levison knew a host of union officials, ideologues, and activists from the American Jewish Congress, Wachtel knew how to get high government officials on the phone and how to touch corporate officers for five-figure donations to B'nai B'rith. He was big time.

Twenty-four hours after Levison praised Wachtel in an April 10 talk with King, a summary of the wiretapped conversation was placed on the desk of FBI Director Hoover. "Who is he?" Hoover asked tersely about Wachtel, and his curiosity sent Bureau officials scrambling to investigate. This question and all that brought it to being—the wiretaps, the investigations, the acute political sensitivity that caused the FBI Director himself to spend time scanning these wiretap summaries—were products of a side to King's life that was clandestine even to him.

From the point of view of the technicians and supervisors on the Levison surveillance, the operation of the bugs in particular was a painful chore. Unlike wiretaps, for which recorders could be activated automatically by phone calls, the bugs required continuous human monitoring. The sounds could be loud or maddeningly faint, depending on how far away Levison happened to be from the microphones in his wall, and the monitors faced the disadvantage that his visitors, being in each other's physical presence, did not identify themselves the way callers tended to do on the telephone. It was tedious work. The Bureau's stringent reporting rules obliged the monitors to make time-keyed notations of every sound they heard—even coughs, rustling papers, and chairs scraping across the floor. If the office was silent, this fact itself had to be recorded at regular intervals. Nothing could be overlooked, as someone might find it to be a clue. Each shift of monitors had to distinguish the various voices customarily heard in Levison's office. They quickly learned to recognize Levison, his secretary, and the regular run of business visitors and gossipers. In time they learned that the "Clarence" who stopped in to talk politics on many afternoons was Clarence Jones, who had grown close to Levison in King's service since moving back to New York from California. They discovered that "Jack" was Jack O'Dell. The supervisors expressed special interest in what these two discussed with Levison, as Bureau records showed that Jones had a suspicious political background and that O'Dell was an outright Communist. These two names were investigative coups. Their conversations with Levison went to FBI head-quarters by red-flag express for analysis of Communist Party influence.

The results were almost entirely disappointing along that dimension. Levison's conversations were full of real estate talk about ground leases, rental payments, and city tax appeals. What he discussed endlessly with both O'Dell and Jones was the SCLC's fund-raising. He talked of unions that might contribute to the *Sullivan* defense, of donor lists, test mailings, and other refinements of solicitation. With O'Dell, Levison lamented the inefficiencies and personnel shortcomings of the Atlanta SCLC office. With Jones, he debated how best to cultivate wealthy new supporters such as Harry Wachtel—not dreaming that within two days these comments would prompt action by J. Edgar Hoover himself—and he batted around the names of celebrities who might be willing to serve on the board of Wachtel's proposed tax-exempt foundation. The foundation had become a priority objective, and was tentatively to be named in honor of Mahatma Gandhi. The FBI monitors heard Levison telling Jones that he objected to the proposed name, Gandhi Foundation, on the grounds that potential union sponsors might find the word "foundation" too corporate in tone. It became the Gandhi Society.

Levison's work in King's behalf, while intense to the point of obsession, turned out to be mundane stuff for an alleged Communist agent. The lack of a Kremlin-style conspiracy did not mean that the surveillance was barren of use to the FBI, however, as it generated usable political intelligence. On March 30, for instance, both the microphone and the wiretap picked up Levison's incoming phone call from Wyatt Walker, who said that King wanted his opinion about the vacancy on the Supreme Court. Justice Charles Evans Whittaker had resigned the day before, and the morning newspapers said that President Kennedy was considering a Negro appeals judge, William Henry Hastie, as his replacement. King admired Hastie, and wanted advice as to whether he should lobby for him by public statement or "through channels," by private phone calls.

"My tendency is for Martin to issue a statement on it, and speak of

this as a superb opportunity coming at a critical juncture in our history,"
Levison told Walker. King should put President Kennedy on the spot a
little bit, especially since Negroes would expect a leader to step forward
on the issue. Walker said he was inclined to agree, as King had not gained
much by being nice to the Administration. What little pressure he had
applied had been directed at Robert Kennedy, not the President, and this
was an opportunity to change. Still, Walker said, King was troubled by
the thought that a public statement would make him seem to be endorsing Hastie just because Hastie was a Negro. Levison argued that Hastie
was "far superior to any of the other candidates" being mentioned in the
newspapers. "[Abraham] Ribicoff is a farce," he said. "He's no lawyer.
[Arthur] Goldberg has been in federal areas a limited time only, and is
not of judicial temperament. Here is a man [Hastie] who has been on the
court of appeals, is competent and qualified. There is no strain to show
he's qualified . . . I don't understand Martin's point . . . Hastie is the man
even if he were purple."

The microphone and wiretap monitors sounded immediate alarms in
the New York FBI office when this conversation ended about four o'clock
that afternoon. The monitors commandeered stenographers and wired a
partial transcript to Washington so fast that an action memorandum
landed high in the Bureau that same evening, recommending that Attorney General Kennedy be advised. This was lightning work, but it arrived
hours too late: the White House had already announced President Kennedy's choice of Byron White to fill the Whittaker vacancy on the Court.
Hoover and his top aides were among the few people in the world who
could appreciate the irony that the same Byron White who facilitated
their interception of King's thoughts on the Supreme Court appointment
(by encouraging FBI action on Levison) rendered those thoughts moot by
getting himself named to the Court.

FBI executives decided to make use of the intercepted material "even
tho White's appointment has been announced." With Hoover's approval,
a report promptly reminded the Attorney General that Judge Hastie had
been "connected" with ten organizations cited as Communist fronts
on various lists of subversives, including that of the House Un-American
Activities Committee. It went on to advise that King had asked Levison
for strategy "in attempting to influence the President to appoint Judge
Hastie to the Supreme Court." Levison's salty characterizations and
other human effects were whittled away to leave a bare spike of danger:
that Communist agent Levison had advised Negro leader King to urge
upon the President a Negro judge of questionable loyalty.

The Levison coverage was an instant boon to the FBI's political intelligence function, allowing Hoover to appear omniscient. He seemed to

know what King had done, and to predict uncannily what King would do. Upon learning that Vice President Johnson had joined King at a Justice Department meeting in April, Hoover promptly dispatched by courier a "My dear Mr. Vice President" letter, advising Johnson that the FBI knew all about it. "I thought you would be interested in knowing that King is a close associate of Levison and . . . O'Dell," Hoover wrote. To this he appended a capsule summary of the Bureau's dossiers on the two advisers.

A week later, Hoover's courier delivered another "My dear Mr. O'Donnell" letter to the White House. It too was couched in language suggesting both gossip and statecraft. "I thought you would be interested in additional information concerning the influence of Stanley David Levison, a secret member of the Communist Party, on King," Hoover wrote. He disclosed that the Bureau had learned through "a confidential source" —the surveillance—that Levison was working to create for King a new organization "to be known as the Ghandi [sic] Society for Human Rights." Hoover added that King and Levison were planning to announce the existence of the Gandhi Society at a high-profile luncheon in Washington on May 17, the eighth anniversary of the *Brown* decision, and he warned O'Donnell that they might invite Attorney General Kennedy, the President, and numerous other dignitaries. These were the names being tossed around by Clarence Jones and Levison, as picked up by the bug in Levison's office.

Any politician so warned about the Gandhi Society might greet King's invitation with wariness, knowing that the FBI was watching. King did obtain a dismal response to his invitations—getting regrets from Robert Kennedy, Lyndon Johnson, Chief Justice Warren, Senator Hubert Humphrey, and a host of others—but the FBI influence most likely was not decisive. In the official Washington of that season, King was hardly a commanding political presence even for his admirers in high places. The pace was quick, the mood vibrant, and the focus international. King's moralism went against the prevailing tides of the middle Cold War period. In this atmosphere, Hoover found it necessary to warn against the rise of King more than to campaign against him. In fact, the FBI sometimes acted as a restraining force.

Certainly, FBI officials were unhappy when the Senate Internal Security Subcommittee subpoenaed Stanley Levison on April 24 for summary appearance three days later. Some of them grumbled among themselves that the "old man" had talked too freely about Levison in his January appearances before Congress, overly stimulating the segregationists who ran the Senate Internal Security Committee—Senators James Eastland and John McClellan. FBI officials objected that the subpoena was dangerous as well as premature. It telegraphed a warning that the government was targeting Levison, which might drive him into hiding before the Bureau's eavesdropping had uncovered any damning information on his activities. Nevertheless, the committee issued the subpoena, hoping that Levison would spill out his Communist convictions and a detailed history of his partnership with King, which together might be publicized so as to eliminate King as a threat to Southern institutions.

The most that FBI officials could salvage from their Senate allies was a promise of strict secrecy and a three-day postponement for consultations, during which the senators agreed not to ask Levison anything about King at least until Levison admitted something subversive. As it turned out, however, the most the committee members could pry out of Levison was nothing. Facing his inquisitors at the classified Senate hearing, Levison made a one-sentence statement: "To dispose of a question causing current apprehension, I am a loyal American, and I am not now and never have been a member of the Communist Party." After that, he invoked the Fifth Amendment to protect his silence. His refusals to answer enraged the senators, who were loath to admit to the FBI that they had taken the risk for no return.

The FBI's eavesdropping devices, having already recorded Levison's surprised reaction when the deputy marshal handed him his subpoena, and later his consultations with his attorney in preparation for the hearing, now picked up Levison's relief when it was over. Back in his New York office the next afternoon, Levison told callers how thankful he was that King's name had not been mentioned at all, and how funny the hostile old senators had looked when they were angry. "I wasn't as much bothered as McClellan," he said, recalling how the senator had branded him the worst witness ever to pass through the chamber. "That means I was worse than Jimmy Hoffa," Levison added wryly.

Harris Wofford was on his way out of the White House. His status alone was enough to convince King that the opposition in Washington was not confined to the segregationist fringe of the government, as the nerve center of the Kennedy Administration had grown more rather than less wary of civil rights. For Wofford, this meant that the meetings of his subcabinet civil rights group had become listless affairs. Participants quickly realized that Wofford's White House address did not mean he spoke for the President, because the President left nearly all civil rights decisions to the Justice Department. Power at the subcabinet level flowed inexorably to Burke Marshall.

Wofford became the custodian of the thousands of pens arriving steadily by mail in the "Ink for Jack" protest. With President Kennedy into the second year of postponement on his campaign pledge to eliminate housing discrimination with the "stroke of a pen," civil rights lobbyists were urging their followers to mail "Ink for Jack" pens to the White House. They hoped to appeal to the witty President, but the White House courtiers did not take well to the humor. Seeing their President as the butt of a joke, they responded in kind toward Wofford: he became the man to see when anyone ran out of pens. Eventually it was arranged to have the surplus donated to a home for the mentally retarded.

President Kennedy endorsed all the items on Wofford's agenda, but he consistently drew back from their execution. Far from engaging him, they caused discomfort in a man who customarily relied on his charm and composure. With other White House aides, he fell into animated, spontaneous political discussions, but to Wofford he habitually tossed a passing wave and a glancing smile, asking, "Are your constituents happy?" Wofford was far too earnest about racial segregation to enjoy the repartee, and by the spring of 1962 the more congenial atmosphere of Sargent Shriver's Peace Corps was worth more to him than the opportunities at the White House. "The spirit of your administration and your spirit make me want to go and work on a frontier of my own," he wrote President Kennedy on resigning to take a job in Ethiopia. Wofford could make such parting remarks in good conscience, as he believed that Kennedy "will continue to make history in civil rights," but the capital's power experts saw only that the White House specialist on civil rights was going off to oblivion in Africa. President Kennedy resisted a request orchestrated by Wofford, King, Roy Wilkins, and others that he appoint the popular Louis Martin as a replacement. Instead, he abolished the post and assigned Wofford's duties to Lee White, an oil and gas lawyer on Sorensen's staff. Wofford had been much more of a civil rights man than Eisenhower's Rocco Siciliano, but their jobs met an equal fate.

King welcomed thirteen of his thirty-one SCLC board members to the annual board meeting, held in Chattanooga on May 15 and 16. As Shuttlesworth was among them, King reminded everyone of their determination to challenge the grim city of Birmingham by taking the SCLC's mass convention there in September. Afterward, he called on his staff to give reports on the SCLC's new projects. Wyatt Walker described the "People-to-People" tours. Jack O'Dell gave facts and figures on the new VEP grants and the numbers of newly registered voters in the scattered SCLC target areas. Praising the Supreme Court's recent *Baker* v. *Carr* decision, which mandated "one man/one vote" apportionment of political representation, O'Dell predicted that the ruling would prove to be as much of a godsend to their cause in voting as was *Brown* in education.

Septima Clark, Andrew Young, and Dorothy Cotton told how they took the raw recruits from the "People-to-People" tours and later fed them into the registration projects. They showed a film on Clark's classes at Dorchester, including a segment showing a group of middle-aged Negroes learning to write their names. After the film, board member Aaron Henry rose to say that the citizenship program already had spawned six small schools in his area of Mississippi, and that it was heartwarming to see people rise so quickly from illiteracy to full-fledged registration work.

When the floor was opened for general discussion, Rev. Roland Smith shifted attention to King. "Now if you get the best out of a man, you ought to pay him better," he declared. Smith went on to fashion a tribute into a motion for a salary increase for King. The motion was properly seconded, but during the clamor that followed King rose to oppose it. Smith interrupted him. "Are you killing what we are trying to do?" he asked.

"No," replied King. "I am just stating my philosophy."

Smith did not back down. "I stand and speak from the vantage point of a man getting old," he said. "You are now where your Papa used to be —you have the advantage of youth. The public will not love you always. You must keep in mind the law of diminishing returns. Keep your philosophy. Let folks do for you when they want to do. Whenever my church wants to show its appreciation to me, I have nothing to do with it. I know if you were head of a white foundation, *they* would pay you."

King tried to make a joke of it, saying that he already drew a salary from the SCLC: one dollar a year, so that he could qualify for the health plan. But this was no laughing matter for the assembled preachers, and King, sobering quickly, observed that money was one of the "defeating points" of Negro leadership and all other leadership. "All of us have our shortcomings," he said. "I always ask God to help me. One of my shortcomings, I feel, is not in the realm of money."

Daddy King stood somberly to speak. "I agree with my son in part," he said. He made his points emphatically and with great feeling, although the thrust of them shifted erratically. "He is not going to change. I think some of these things ought to be pointed up. We should put it in writing so that the world will know it. He has a family—three children and a wife . . . My sons can get anything that I have. I am going down with them no matter what . . . I know that sometimes you draft folk and override them. So I think this ought to be overridden."

There was some tension in the room, as Daddy King had wound around to oppose his son openly. The issue was touchy, not just because the Ebenezer budget could have used some relief from the SCLC, but also because King's ascetic concept of leadership put his father and all the other SCLC preachers on the defensive. When the board members fell silent, King referred the whole matter to a committee. Then he proposed the election of several "young people" to the SCLC board. They included thirty-six-year-old Hosea Williams of Savannah, who, though three years older than King himself, was considered young because he had no church and was not firmly established in a career. King also nominated John Lewis, who he said was transforming the face of Nashville. Steady and thorough, Lewis had returned to Nashville to lead successful student demonstrations against one segregated establishment after another—churches, department stores, libraries, restaurants, theaters. He was marching through Nashville's yellow pages.

Daddy King rose to make sure these people would not embarrass the SCLC by refusing election to the board. A debate over the proper role of young people struck another nerve touching on money and authority, which calmed only when Abernathy moved that the whole matter be studied by a committee. The board meeting ended on that note. King, having negotiated slow passage among the titans, left immediately for the founding luncheon of the Gandhi Society for Human Rights, held in Washington the next day.

"Non-violence is now woven into the fabric of American life in hundreds of boycotts across the South," he declared in his speech. "It is marked on the jail walls of thousands of cells of Freedom Riders . . . Non-violent protest is no longer a bizarre or alien concept." Speaking of the Southern representatives in Congress, King argued that segregation was an obsession that penalized the whites of the region economically as well as morally. "Indeed, let us say it bluntly and candidly . . ." he said. "Many Southern leaders are pathetically trapped by their own devices. They . . . know that the perpetuation of this archaic, dying order is hindering the rapid growth of the South. Yet they cannot speak this truth—they are imprisoned by their own lies. It is history's wry paradox that when Negroes win their struggle to be free, those who have held them down will themselves be freed for the first time."

To add spice to what was otherwise an occasion for fund-raising, King announced that he had delivered to the White House that morning his draft of a Second Emancipation Proclamation. Bound in fine leather, with its pages carefully wrapped to protect the anticipated historical value, the document carried ambitions far greater than a ceremonial tribute to the memory of Lincoln. Instead, King described a proclamation designed to adapt the boldness of Lincoln's war measure to conditions a century later. He wanted President Kennedy to break segregation in much the same way Lincoln had abolished slavery: by an electric, symbolic act that reached beyond the authority or control of the White House. "We ask," said King, "that he proclaim all segregation statutes of all southern states to be contrary to the Constitution, and that the full powers of his office be employed to avoid their enforcement."

Such a proclamation would shake American politics and reverberate throughout the world. For King, it was so logical and compelling a short cut to racial justice that he had had his volunteer lawyers—Clarence Jones, Theodore Kheel, Harry Wachtel, and Stanley Levison—spend more than six months drafting the document, and he had long since asked the Secretary of the Interior to reserve the Lincoln Memorial for ceremonies at midnight of the next New Year's Eve, which would mark the passage of one hundred years since the effective date of Lincoln's proclamation.

Unfortunately for King, the Gandhi Society speech attracted almost no publicity. He still lacked the stature to define public issues so clearly that others had to respond to his terms. Those who heard about the speech at all tended to be those who admired King already, and their reactions sometimes struck him from a blind side. His friends at the *Christian Century*, for instance, saw the Gandhi Society as a sectarian departure from King's Christian base in America. Their sharp, public criticisms obliged King to write one of his pained, multi-page letters of defense. "You have the impression that the Gandhi Society is made up of Christian leaders who have deserted Christ and the church," he added. "Nothing could be further from the truth." Tortuously, King defended his Christianity to his own followers, while simultaneously defending Gandhi as a non-Christian of Christian essence. He realized too late that the Gandhi Society was fatally flawed as a rallying point for public support. Most of its contributors would be labor unions whose leaders knew that the foundation was a vehicle for fighting the *Sullivan* case with tax-exempt funds.

President Kennedy was celebrating his forty-fifth birthday with a fund-raiser attended by fifteen thousand people at Madison Square Garden, highlighted by Marilyn Monroe's surprise solo of "Happy Birthday, Mr. President." The President did not respond to King's draft proclamation even by private letter, but he did invite him soon afterward to a White House luncheon honoring Archbishop Makarios of Cyprus. King declined, pleading other commitments.

It had been a trying year for Nelson Rockefeller. The previous November, he had shocked political and social New York with the announcement that he was leaving his wife of thirty-two years, and the front pages had chronicled the juicy divorce story ever since. Rockefeller insisted that the divorce would not harm his chances of gaining the White House. As political reporters doubted such claims in print, legal specialists explored the governor's prickly dilemma: he could obtain a divorce in New York only on grounds of adultery, which would mean political suicide; he could obtain a valid divorce outside New York only if he established residence in another state, which under New York law would require him to relinquish the governorship. Rockefeller eventually solved the problem by persuading his wife to move to Nevada and seek divorce on grounds of "extreme cruelty," to which she dutifully agreed, though stating that it was very much against her will. Newspaper accounts contrasted her composure with his political manipulations and harshness— noting that he ordered all mention of his ex-wife and their children deleted from his official state biography.

In the midst of these difficulties, Rockefeller's son Michael drowned off the coast of New Guinea. The governor was a battered man when he arrived in Atlanta on June 4 to deliver the commencement address at Spelman College. Calamity seemed to follow him South, as he arrived just behind the news of Atlanta's deadliest single-day disaster since the Civil War. An Air France jetliner crash near Paris killed more than one hundred of Atlanta's leading citizens as they were ending a chartered tour of European art capitals. The sudden extinction of a generation of art patrons cast a pall over all Atlanta, including its Negro cocoon, where an otherwise grand celebration was proceeding. While Rockefeller addressed Spelman, Eleanor Roosevelt spoke at the sister campus of Atlanta University, and the president of Harvard received an honorary degree from Morehouse. "Demand and get the equal chance that is your birthright as Americans," Rockefeller told the Spelman graduates. New York reporters noted his criticism of President Kennedy and the Democrats as civil rights charlatans—full of election promises but "found wanting in the courage, the profound and true belief that must back promises with action."

Rockefeller went off to a college presidents' luncheon, where he sat next to King, and then attended a political dinner honoring Edward Smith, the Republican candidate for governor of Georgia. He urged Smith to persevere in the quest for two-party democracy in Georgia, but Smith promptly died in a car crash on the way home. Georgia Republicans despaired of finding another sacrificial candidate, as their party remained something of a political joke in many Southern states. The chairman of the Republican Party in North Carolina was disgraced that summer upon the revelation that, under a fictitious identity, he maintained a second family in Virginia.

•   •   •

Harry Belafonte arrived in Atlanta as Rockefeller departed, and the singer attracted by far the greater news attention. Rockefeller was only a rich governor who slipped in and out of the city's obscure circles (Republicans, Negroes, and Negro Republicans), but Belafonte was an international star who had not toured the South since the year of the *Brown* decision. Vice Mayor Sam Massell presented him with the keys to the city. Belafonte and his racially mixed troupe of entertainers went from a press conference to the Atlanta Cabana Motel, the finest of the city's new downtown inns, where they registered without incident. This extremely public breach of hotel segregation fulfilled one of the many goals set by King and Belafonte.

Just before the Belafonte concert, King privately asked the new mayor, Ivan Allen, to help remove the restriction against racially mixed audiences at the Municipal Auditorium. Allen did, and down went another barrier. Since ordering the removal of "Colored" and "White" signs from city hall drinking fountains on his first day in office, Allen had gone on to throw out the first ball at the first integrated baseball game at Ponce de Leon ball park. In Birmingham, by contrast, the color signs were still up, the parks were all closed, and the Birmingham Barons had dissolved that spring rather than comply with integration in baseball's Southern Association. King hoped to send a message that through enlightenment Atlanta got baseball, Belafonte, and prosperity, whereas Birmingham was forfeiting all three.

The Atlanta FBI office anticipated trouble, however: managers of the Atlanta Cabana's plush restaurant, the King's Inn, intended to refuse service to any Negroes who tried to eat there, celebrities or not. Warning cables flashed to headquarters and from there to Burke Marshall in the Justice Department, and Marshall, unbeknown to King and Belafonte, called the restaurant owner to urge him not to bar them. Failing at that, Marshall launched a private lobbying campaign to prevent the arrest of such visible leaders and the inevitable publicity that would follow. "It was arranged that the police would not make any arrests unless it became absolutely unavoidable," Marshall reported to Attorney General Kennedy. "Dr. King and Belafonte left the restaurant after a fairly short time, so that no police action was necessary."

The confrontation at the King's Inn came as a stinging surprise to King and Belafonte, who had arrived for a festive pre-concert luncheon in full confidence that all was arranged. At a hastily organized press conference, King announced that ordinarily he would have called for sit-ins against the King's Inn, but that in view of Atlanta's grief over the Air France disaster he was postponing demonstrations "until a more propitious moment." This diplomatic gesture allowed him to minimize the damage to the positive spirit of the Belafonte concert. The embarrassed hotel manager also tried to make the best of the insult, by inviting the Kings, the Abernathys, and all the members of the Belafonte troupe to crowd into his office for a free lunch. "I cannot get too excited or upset," remarked singer Miriam Makeba. "I'm from South Africa, which makes Atlanta look like the cradle of democracy."

Evaluations of the Belafonte visit rested heavily upon perspective—as to whether it was a success or a failure, whether or not it was noticed, whether the treatment of Negro stars by fancy white restaurants was a weighty or trivial matter. King considered the rejection at the King's Inn to be of enormous symbolic importance, affecting the willingness of masses of Negroes to risk similar humiliation. For King, the incident was both a point of defeat and of mobilization, worthy of press conferences and public statements. In sharp contrast, he made no public statement at all when he received direct threats from the Ku Klux Klan that the "nigger King" would be assassinated in Shreveport, Louisiana, his next stop after the Belafonte concert. Death threats were too inflammatory for public discussion. By the peculiar logic of racial politics, King raised a cry about restaurant courtesies while accepting death threats quietly as a hazard of his work.

Wyatt Walker did call Burke Marshall about the Shreveport death threats, and Marshall responded immediately by making phone calls to the Shreveport police commissioner and the parish sheriff. Their blunt responses put Marshall in the awkward position of knowing in advance that local law enforcement officers intended to ignore a serious threat to a civil rights leader. Diligently, Marshall canvassed judges in the Shreveport area until he found two who agreed to intercede. The judges eventually assured Marshall that the police officers did promise to do their duty, though they could not bring themselves to say so directly to a Washington official. Meanwhile, King and Walker flew to Shreveport against the wishes of the SCLC's Shreveport leaders, who urged King to cancel the appearance.

Local Negroes packed the Little Union Baptist Church, turning out to show support for their voter registration project in the face of the bombings that had driven C. O. Simpkins out of town. Wyatt Walker found a police squadron surrounding the church, for which he gave thanks to Burke Marshall. As the hymns gave way to the serial introductions of King, Walker went outside to talk with Police Commissioner Earl

Downs, with whom Marshall had conducted an unpleasant discussion that afternoon. Downs ordered Walker back inside. "All right, Commissioner," Walker replied, "but I'd like to establish that the rear of the church is going to be covered." Walker's executive manner, and possibly the detail-laden clipboard he carried, so incensed Downs that he ordered his men to arrest him for loitering on the church steps. The meeting inside continued as Walker disappeared. Held incommunicado all that night and most of the next day, he received macabre notification that he would be allowed outside contact only with Dr. Stuart DeLee, the parish coroner. DeLee appeared twice to interrogate the prisoner with the announced purpose of assessing his sanity. He asked Walker exactly how long he had believed in integration and whether he thought people were out to get him.

Upon his release, Walker had no time for protest or reflection. He flew to Chicago for two days of exploratory talks with representatives of Billy Graham. These private negotiations no doubt would have surprised most experts in politics or religion, as the famous white evangelist and the Negro movement occupied separate regions of the public mind. During the clamor over segregation since the *Brown* decision, Graham had preserved his attendance records and a relatively undisturbed ministry, adapting in religion much the way Vice President Nixon adapted in politics. Indeed, Graham and Nixon became more closely identified with each other in the late 1950s, appearing on each other's platforms in the kind of symbiotic cooperation that King once hoped to achieve with each of them, especially Graham. But Graham had not broken with King as completely as Nixon. He regarded King's gospel as his own, and King respected Graham's course professionally if not in doctrine. Although the two of them did not work together in public, they cooperated privately through their lieutenants.

King sent Walker and Chauncey Eskridge to pose some difficult questions: how did Graham maintain such a favorable public image outside the church world, and how did he keep his huge operation solvent while making relatively few public appearances? At the Civic Opera Building, which was headquarters for an upcoming Chicago Crusade, Graham's media adviser Walter Bennett told them candidly that King's entire approach was faulty. Whereas Graham reduced his annual exposure to a few crusades that were so enormous as to command news attention outside the religious press, King dissipated his strength in countless speeches before relatively small audiences. Therefore, said Bennett, King's favorable publicity depended almost entirely upon sympathetic reporters who were quick enough to catch him as he dashed through town. This was too small a publicity base for any preacher, especially a

Negro. By Bennett's diagnosis, King's constant pursuit of the next convert and the next small budget transfusion was shortsighted, because it
kept King from breaking through a media threshold. Bennett offered the
professional opinion that his current pace would kill King within five
years by heart attack or exhaustion. Walker and Eskridge highlighted
this dire prediction in their report to King.

Billy Graham's chief of staff, Walter Smyth, gave Walker and Eskridge
more mechanical advice the next morning, dissecting Graham's historic
innovations in evangelical tradecraft. Smyth's staff had begun preparation for the Chicago Crusade a year in advance, he advised. They had
built up a list of some eight thousand preachers within traveling distance
of Chicago, and the responses to successive mailings had helped the staff
select a Crusade steering committee of ten preacher "captains," each one
supported by five preacher "lieutenants." A parallel organization of
churchwomen canvassed Chicago households to recruit audiences for the
Crusade, timing their visits to coincide with Graham's specially produced radio devotionals. Simultaneously, other Graham workers arranged what amounted to a small municipal bus system to get them all
to and from the nightly meetings. Smyth explained that a successful
crusade was the result of nearly a million man-hours of unseen preparation. He designated one of his own assistants to begin transmitting to
the SCLC the Graham team's accumulated store of specialized knowledge. None of this explained how to surmount the central obstacle of
race, but Walker took a full load of practical guidelines back to King,
anyway.

Fitfully, at times, King still hoped that by emulating Graham's evangelical methods he could somehow escape the path which had been beckoning since the Montgomery boycott. Just as Wyatt Walker was sitting
down with Graham's representatives in Chicago, King flew to New York
and took a cab to 39th Street near Fifth Avenue. The FBI eavesdroppers
must have jumped out of their headsets when their transmitters first
picked up in Stanley Levison's office the unmistakable voice of Martin
Luther King himself.

Arriving unannounced, King fell into conversation with Levison as
though they worked together every day.* What they talked about was
business—fund-raisers, speeches, personnel problems in the SCLC. King

---

* King and Levison did in fact talk several times a week, but the FBI did not learn
of this pattern until later taps on Levison's home phones picked up the regular,
post-midnight calls between them.

told Levison that one staff member was continually at loggerheads with
Wyatt Walker. He said that late expenses from the Belafonte concert had
reduced the SCLC's net profit to $9,600, and he asked whether Levison
thought $25 per plate was too much to charge for a dinner featuring
Count Basie. Levison replied that $25 was "pretty steep," but that the
NAACP pulled in $50 per plate at its annual dinner. Levison said he was
pleased that King had accepted his advice not to protest the King's Inn
affront out of respect for Atlanta's crash victims. King agreed that this
had been wise.

In contrast to the florid praise he customarily heaped on new or potential supporters, King offered Levison only brief comments of assent or
criticism. When Levison asked whether he liked his draft of the speech
King would give at the National Press Club in July, King said that it was
fine. The two of them spoke in shorthand, not mentioning dangers or
traumas or motivating beliefs, as these were understood. They spoke
frankly of the need for King to achieve greater public recognition. King
remarked hopefully that he might get on television, and Levison inquired
whether the *Newsweek* reporter had interviewed him again. They were
like two preacher friends in the pastor's study, except with the businesslike Levison there was no banter or pulpit tales.

To the FBI, the significance here was the confirmation that King was
under the influence of a Communist. The next day, Director Hoover
ordered his offices in New York, Georgia, and Alabama to determine
whether the SCLC had met all the legal registration requirements for a
charitable organization. He also ordered them to find out whether Levison or O'Dell appeared on SCLC stationery, and he instructed the New
York office "to advise if the door to the SCLC office has O'Dell's name
printed thereon." From the beginning, Hoover showed practically no
interest in proving the substance of the case against Levison or O'Dell—
in documenting their alleged submission to the discipline of Soviet
agents, or in gathering legal evidence that they were engaged in treason-
ous, violent, or clearly malevolent conspiracies against the United States.
Also from the beginning, Hoover laid down admonitions of secrecy in
language suggesting that, over the decades, his sense of democratic duty
had given way to the sly vanity of a monarch. "All investigation conducted in this matter must be handled in a most discreet manner," Hoover ordered, "to preclude the possibility of disclosing the identities of
informants or causing embarrassment to the Bureau."

That spring, Levison's steady subject was Wyatt Walker. The FBI monitors picked up Levison telling Clarence Jones that Walker was "more
advanced than Martin," meaning that Walker was ready for showdown
and suffering, and less concerned than King with paralyzing ramifica-

tions. Levison paid tribute to Walker's nerve by recalling to Jones that when Levison and King had decided that Walker needed to go to jail during the Freedom Rides, they had known that Walker would comply without a second thought. For all that, however, Levison kept saying that Walker was a poor executive director for the SCLC, because he was "emotionally immature even though he is brilliant." Walker was so egocentric, he added, that he was "in conflict with the organization all the time." Others who talked with Levison agreed: Walker was too mercurial and unstable, while Jack O'Dell was a worker of painstaking miracles.

Levison suggested to King that Walker be shifted to a job as King's publicist and traveling assistant—where, King agreed, Walker's gifts lay —and that O'Dell take on the responsibility of running the Atlanta office. Levison, having just passed through a Senate loyalty hearing himself, said he did not want to see O'Dell in such a visible position in view of his Communist associations, but there was no one else at the SCLC who could do the job. The FBI was dutifully listening in when Levison told O'Dell that King was favorably disposed to the proposal. King took a moral approach to Communist associations and the danger of McCarthy-style attack, Levison added, quoting King's words that "no matter what a man was, if he could stand up now and say he is not connected, then as far as I am concerned, he is eligible to work for me."

Such tolerance for communism was anathema to Hoover, who promptly sent an account of the intercepted conversation to Attorney General Kennedy. Omitting all Levison's personal assessments of O'Dell and Walker, Hoover implied that Levison was maneuvering O'Dell into King's confidence solely to further Communist influence. On its face, Hoover's memo was nothing more than good intelligence work, but it closed with a warning that carried extra dimensions. "Levison also said," Hoover wrote, "that if O'Dell and King should reach an agreement, it would be possible for King to see you and say 'lay off this guy' [O'Dell]." This last line made the Attorney General both the beneficiary and the subject of FBI intelligence about Communist intentions. If Kennedy did indeed "lay off" O'Dell upon request, he would become, like King, at least a partially witting dupe in Levison's manipulations. In the spy's world, as opposed to the courtroom, Levison could corrupt Kennedy without knowing it, and Kennedy could become vulnerable to charges of conspiring with, or coddling, a man he had never met. Hoover classified his memo "Top Secret."

Early in July, Roy Wilkins brought the NAACP convention to Atlanta for the first time since 1951, the year King graduated from Crozer. More

than a thousand delegates from forty-two states came to town a month
after Harry Belafonte. There was some picketing—delegates picketed
"Johnny Reb's" restaurant, and orderly groups carried signs reading "12
Southern Cities Have 'Open' Hotels. Why Not Atlanta? NAACP"—but
Wilkins set the tone for what *Crisis* would nickname the "Hard-Working
Convention." "I would like to emphasize that what we came to Atlanta
to do was conduct a convention, with a full agenda of business . . ." he
told reporters, "and while a sit-in in a restaurant may be psychologically
important . . . this is not the main business of this convention."

James Meredith was presented to the convention as a young man who
might become the first Negro to enter the University of Mississippi.
James Nabrit, president of Howard University, delivered the main address at a Fourth of July barbecue. King appeared as one of the off-night
speakers. As always, his photograph was conspicuously absent from
C. A. Scott's *Daily World*, which published dozens of convention shots,
and he would be the only major speaker not shown in the *Crisis* issue
devoted to the week's events. These were among the signs—subtle to
some, blatant to others—that King remained a thorn to his elders in
leadership. But there were limits to such discouragements. King was a
phenomenon who had to be accorded at least a platform, and a platform
was all he needed. Comedian Dick Gregory introduced him as America's
"only celebrity who gives out more fingerprints than he does auto-
graphs."

"True peace is not merely the absence of tension, but it is the presence
of justice," King told the audience. "And I think this is what Jesus meant
when he looked at his disciples one day and said, 'I come not to bring
peace but a sword.' Now certainly he didn't mean he came to bring a
physical sword. Certainly he didn't mean that he did not come to bring
true peace. But Jesus was saying this in substance: that . . . whenever I
come, a conflict is precipitated between the old and the new. Whenever
I come, tension sets in between justice and injustice . . . The tension
which we see in the South today is the necessary tension that comes
when the oppressed rise up and start to move forward toward a permanent, positive peace."

Moments later, King shifted to the theme of internal tension, saying
that "the time has come" for public discussion of the bickering within
the civil rights movement. Almost plaintively, he recalled for the delegates that he had "addressed NAACP chapters in more than twenty
states." Many of his SCLC officers also were NAACP officials, he said.
Marchers and boycotters "should not minimize work through the courts.
But . . . legislation and court orders can only declare rights. They can
never thoroughly deliver them. Only when the people themselves begin
to act are rights on paper given life blood."

Then King tried to burn up all the divisions among them in the heat of his own personal belief. He portrayed nonviolence as the way out. It was the transcendent key, the bridger of gaps. "This is the beauty of nonviolence," he said. "It says you can struggle without hating. You can fight war without violence. This is where we find the essence of love, standing at the center of this movement." His method was open. It was democratic because it respected the democratic faith that all persons were created with equal standing. "I submit to you that any individual who decides to break a law that conscience tells him is unjust and willingly accepts the penalty for it is at that moment expressing the very highest respect for law. There is nothing new about this. Go back with me if you will to the Old Testament. See Shadrach, Meschach, and Abednego as they stand before King Nebuchadnezzar. They made it clear: 'We cannot bow.' Come if you will to Plato's Dialogues. Open the Credo or the Apology. See Socrates practicing civil disobedience. Academic freedom is a reality today because Socrates practiced civil disobedience. Come to the early Christians. See them practicing civil disobedience to the point that they were willing to be thrown to the lions to stand up for what they believed. Listen to Peter as he says, 'We must obey God rather than man.' Come up to the modern world. Never forget that everything that Hitler did in Germany was legal. It was illegal to aid and comfort a Jew in the day of Hitler's Germany. And I believe that if I had lived there with my present attitude I would have disobeyed that law, and I would have encouraged people to aid and comfort our Jewish brothers. If I lived in South Africa today, I would join Chief Luthuli as he says to his people, 'Break this law. Don't take this unjust pass system where you must have passes. Take them and tear them up and throw them away.' "

Now he rushed feverishly to a closing, four-word slogan: "All. Here. And now." Rhythmic applause allowed him to speak only one sentence between bursts of mass emotion. "We want *all* of our rights," he shouted. ". . . We want our freedom *here* in America, here in the black belt of Mississippi, here behind the cotton curtain of Alabama, here on the red clay of Georgia . . . We have lived with gradualism, and we know that it is nothing but do-nothingism and escapism which ends up in standstillism!" This pseudo-pedantic Negroism added laughter to the shouting. "No, we are not willing to wait any longer," King cried. "We want freedom now!" This set off a pandemonium that King stilled only with a solemn reprise on the likelihood of persecution and death, and he closed with a flourish of inspiration from the prophets. He had done it again— come into the NAACP's own house and stolen a crowd. Although his summons was objectionable to NAACP leaders in spirit and direction, it contained too much power and too little specific heresy to be challenged.

His NAACP speech did not register in the white world. As with many sensational scenes from his life, it remained a matter of journalistic whimsy whether interest crossed the racial line, and the only kind of event almost guaranteed to command an audience on both sides was the drama of white force seizing personally on King's body. Even followers of civil rights had hazy memories about whether King had been involved in the Freedom Rides, as he had never been arrested then, but plain citizens and every cub reporter knew about King's manacled trip to Reidsville. It was news when he went to jail.

It could have happened at Shreveport or at any stop on the "People-to-People" registration tours, but King expected the pinch in Albany. Among the court dates circled on his calendar was the July 10 sentencing from his arrest on Albany's streets the previous December. For such a minor misdemeanor by a gainfully employed person, Judge Durden might ordinarily have dismissed the case or suspended sentence—if not for mercy, then to spare Albany the publicity of having King in its jail. This did not seem likely, however, in light of the harsh mood that had descended upon Albany's politics in the past seven months. Not long before King's sentencing, Georgia Democratic Party chairman James Gray wrote a special front-page editorial in his Albany *Herald*, in which he denounced Albany Negroes' complaints as "the Hitlerian tactic of the 'Big Lie' . . . The Negroes are lying. The Department of Justice knows they are lying. . . . This sordid effort will fail, as all of the craft and cunning the Negro agitators have employed in their plottings for months have failed. . . . It will fail because its motivation is essentially evil."

King had little reason to hope for enlightened leniency in such a city. Before he and Walker and Abernathy drove down for the hearing—back to the dirt side streets and the *a capella* hymns at Shiloh—King told his secretary, Dora McDonald, that most likely he would have to cancel his engagement at Washington's National Press Club. Judge Durden proved him correct by sentencing King and Abernathy to pay a $178 fine or serve forty-five days in jail. Both said they would serve the time rather than cooperate with injustice, and by the time they had been searched and processed into their green jail fatigues, Dora McDonald in Atlanta was composing her daily report on the phone calls that had swamped King's office since the first news bulletins. One Washington reporter, she wrote, was "shocked beyond words" to hear that King was in jail, while an official of the National Press Club only wanted to know why King had not waited until after his speech there on July 19. McDonald advised King that she had already arranged for him to receive the Atlanta *Constitution* at the jail, and for Abernathy to get *The New York Times*. "Rev. Abernathy and you would be very proud of me today," she wrote. "I have not cried—not even a little bit."

SIXTEEN

THE FIREMAN'S
LAST REPRIEVE

King and Abernathy went to jail on the historic day when live television pictures first leaped across an ocean, via Telstar satellite. All three television networks broke into their evening programs with a picture that appeared simultaneously on French and American screens: Vice President Lyndon Johnson was shown huddling with excited scientists, all watching themselves on television in the act of watching themselves, in the infinite regression of the media age. For the return transmission, French authorities selected a simple head shot of actor Yves Montand singing "The Little Song." The content of the beams was trivial in comparison with the feat itself, which the *Times* hailed as "rivaling in significance the first telegraphed transmission by Samuel F. B. Morse more than a century ago."

Such frontier technology did not yet reach to Albany, Georgia. There, television reporters still had to break off by early afternoon so that they could fly with their exposed film by charter airplane to Atlanta, where facilities existed for "feeding" news footage to New York in time for possible use on the evening news. Only extraordinary events justified such expensive effort, which meant that developments in remote areas had to reach high levels of visual drama. The King jailing was not a television news story.

But it did set off tremors along more traditional lines. The news played on the front page of the Albany *Herald*, under the sarcastic head-line "King Languishes in Bastille," and it also played just under the Telstar story in papers across the country. The account in *The New York Times* reminded readers that a previous jailing of King had proved critical to the outcome of the 1960 presidential election. Both the *Herald* and the *Times* noted significantly that Governor Nelson Rockefeller, a presidential aspirant, had released a telegram urging Attorney General Kennedy "to assure the physical safety of Dr. King and his companions," and to "investigate whether constitutional rights of peaceable assembly have been violated." Early the next morning, Harvey Shapiro of *The New York Times Magazine* became the first of several newspaper editors calling the SCLC in the hope of publishing a "letter from prison" by King. Dora McDonald immediately relayed Shapiro's proposal to Chauncey Eskridge, and by noon Eskridge was analyzing it with Billy Graham's public relations specialist. His advice—"Nothing should be published while you are in prison . . . hold everything until released"—postponed a notion that would reappear within a year as King's "Letter from Birmingham Jail."

Dr. Anderson summoned Albany Movement supporters back to Shiloh that morning to prepare for what he called a "now or never effort" to break segregation. His speech met with little enthusiasm. The emotions of the previous year's marches had cooled over months of waiting, and perhaps his listeners were numbed by the harsh realization that the city had dared to jail a celebrity like King on charges which still hung over some seven hundred of them too. In any case, only thirty-two people stepped forward, and they came only upon exhortation by King's friend and colleague C. K. Steele, who had led a bus boycott in Tallahassee parallel to King's in Montgomery. The diminutive Reverend Steele offered a final prayer in the church:

> *We feel much akin*
> *To those who went out*
> *Two by two*
> *In the days of old.*
> *We will march around*
> *Those jail house walls*
> *That symbolize segregation.*
> *We will walk around them*
> *Like unto Joshua*
> *Until the walls*
> *Come tumblin' down.*
> *Take care of us*

Take care of the policemen
Take care of Chief Pritchett
Take care of the mayor
And the city council.
We pray that as they see
A prayerful and peaceful people
Their hearts will be moved.
Consecrate, dear God,
This whole community.

At 10:53 A.M., they marched out behind Steele toward the city jail, where King and Abernathy were on cell-scrubbing detail, and while they were being arrested under the gaze of reporters and bystanders they sang "We Shall Overcome," in the hope that the prisoners already inside would take heart.

In Washington, reporters were questioning White House press secretary Pierre Salinger at the morning briefing about what the President would do on King's behalf. The news angle was obvious: would Kennedy do more or less as President than he had done as a candidate in 1960? By the end of the day, Salinger announced that President Kennedy had asked the Attorney General to prepare a full report on the King situation. Privately, the President called Burke Marshall at his vacation fishing pond in the Pocono Mountains of Pennsylvania. For Marshall, this rare contact with the President was bracing, but Kennedy was worried. In several calls that day, he instructed Marshall to speak with Coretta in Atlanta and with public officials in Albany. Essentially, the strategy was for Marshall to assume the sympathetic campaign posture of 1960, leaving the Kennedys themselves in reserve.

President Kennedy also took a phone call from James Gray, his old college acquaintance who was now chairman of the Georgia Democratic Party. Gray said he was calling with Mayor Kelley standing there in his office. "Jack, we've got Martin Luther King in jail," he said, stating the obvious. "The damn media is having a field day. We don't want him in jail, but what can we do? He violated our law. I'll tell you. It would be very nice if you sent somebody down here to pick him up."

The President agreed that it was very bad to have King in jail, but he did not embrace the idea of having him released for some presidential purpose. They faced an impasse that was politically delicate. King refused to compromise with segregation. Albany refused to compromise with integration. And the Administration was determined to maintain an image of masterful control without intervening forcefully on either side. These constraints called for trust and stealthy maneuver. President

Kennedy promised to send someone to Albany, and he advised Gray to consult immediately with the Attorney General. By midday, a hastily recruited Gray emissary was on a flight to Washington.

B. C. Gardner, a senior partner in Mayor Kelley's three-man law firm, represented nearby Baker County, the Ichuaway plantation, and most major interests not represented by his partners. His father was a judge. In his office he kept a picture of himself shaking Senator John F. Kennedy's hand at Gray's private party in 1958. As the city's unofficial ambassador, Gardner brought a message that Robert Kennedy heartily seconded. King's jailing, they agreed, was an embarrassment to everybody—to Albany, to the Kennedys, to Georgia, and to the entire United States in the court of world opinion. Therefore, it must be terminated by any means necessary. Gardner flew home that same night with a plan.

There was a mass meeting at Shiloh. A crowd of six hundred began to recapture the emotion of the December meetings, and now in the summer heat the people waved hand fans painted with Bible scenes and mopped their brows with handkerchiefs. Outside, a smaller crowd of juke-joint Negroes and early-evening drinkers took it upon themselves to drive the police observers out of the Harlem section of town. They lofted bricks and bottles at the squad cars. The first loud noises of dented metal attracted a sizable crowd from the surrounding neighborhood. By unspoken rules, the authorities had allowed the city's Negroes certain license inside Harlem—King and other marchers had been arrested only when they reached the boundary of white Albany—but now spontaneous hostilities erupted against the very presence of the police on Negro territory. Heavily armed but also heavily outnumbered, officers sought shelter against random bombardment. The shouts and thuds of the violence pulled people out of Shiloh in droves, with the church people shouting at the others for calm.

Chief Pritchett huddled with his besieged men, who were in a war mood. Ordering them to refrain from retaliation, he asked his most trusted officer, Captain Ed Friend, to follow him into the hostile Negro crowd. "If you get hit, don't stop," Pritchett told Friend, then pushed his way to the closed front door of the church and shouted, "Bo, I'm coming in." Emmanuel "Bo" Jackson, the unofficial sergeant-at-arms for the Albany Movement, shouted back, "Come on in!" and the two policemen entered the sanctum of the opposition in full uniform, with guns on their hips. Slater King called out over the commotion, "I notice we have in our presence Chief Pritchett!" When he offered the chief Shiloh's pulpit, the crowd fell into a dead silence. Then, as Pritchett made his way forward to speak, someone shouted, "Let's give him a hand!" and an ovation rolled on for fully half a minute. Those outside who had expected to hear angry words, perhaps even gunshots, could only stare at each other in wonder.

Pritchett reached the pulpit with his neck, face, and ears flushed deep red. "I appreciate the opportunity to be here," he said, half smiling. "I have often been told I would be welcome. I didn't know whether I would or not." Reporter Pat Watters, while marveling at the chief's bravery, perceived a rich mixture of tone in his voice. There was some gratitude and respect, even some fellowship, he thought, combined with an edge of half-humorous sarcasm that Watters saw as the protective coating for Pritchett's racial authority. "I never have interrupted your peaceful assemblies," Pritchett told the crowd. ". . . Many people misunderstand your philosophy of nonviolence, but we respect your policy. I ask your cooperation in keeping Albany peaceful. This business of throwing rocks is not good." The crowd applauded again. Pritchett contained his relief until he reached the police huddle outside. Captain Friend confessed to wobbly legs. "Don't take me back in there, Chief," he said, trying to grin. "Nobody but the laundry man will know how scared I was."

Once the rock throwers had melted away, Slater King returned to the Shiloh pulpit to lay bare a conflicted appraisal. On the one hand, he praised the congregation for welcoming Chief Pritchett in the charitable spirit of nonviolence, and for proving that the movement people inside were not like the hoodlums outside. On the other hand, he lamented the signs of sycophantic admiration for Pritchett. These were deep roots of segregation, he said. After all, the very purpose of their meeting had been to exhort people to challenge Pritchett's authority by offering up their bodies to his jail. "We want to give him respect," said Slater King, "but not like he's some kind of God. Maybe I am guilty of this myself. It's the system we've been conditioned by—like we've been brainwashed."

Later that night, Pritchett and Albany's leading white citizens did some soul-searching of their own. B. C. Gardner was back from Washington with a stark proposal: they should pay Martin Luther King's fine surreptitiously and then expel him from the jail. There was no other way, he explained, and they must be prepared to lie about it. If it became known that the city fathers of Albany had imprisoned King and then paid to free him, they would become a laughingstock. For men who prided themselves on their Southern code of honor, the lying part was a sour requirement indeed —all the more so because it was a Negro who forced the awful choice upon them. Still, they could not very well pressure the Kennedys to spring King, as it would look like a defeat for Albany at federal hands. Besides, the Kennedys were doing all they could. They had refrained from intervening or speaking out on King's behalf; they had tacitly endorsed the scheme, and promised not to expose it. Robert Kennedy had impressed on them that the national security and prestige of the United States suffered every day that King was in jail. This provided a patriotic salve, making their hoax certainly bearable and almost noble. Chief Pritchett consulted Mayor Kelley about how to reduce the elements of outright falsehood in the scheme. Then he summoned his desk sergeant to give him stern instructions on how Martin Luther King was to be released from jail.

At dawn the next morning, July 12, B. C. Gardner appeared at the deserted jail desk with $356 in cash. "Here's Martin Luther King's fine," he said "Turn him out." By prearrangement, the desk sergeant made out the receipt not to Gardner but to King and Abernathy. Gardner then disappeared, his part completed. At 7:30 A.M., Pritchett sent to the cell-block for King and Abernathy, instructing them to change into their own clothes for a meeting in his office. When they arrived there, thinking the clothes were for the benefit of some important intermediary, Pritchett informed them that their fines had been paid and they were free to go. In fact, they had to go.

The two stunned preachers demanded an explanation, whereupon Pritchett gave them what was to be his stock response through the ensuing publicity storm. All he knew, he said, was that the jailer had told him that "an unidentified, well-dressed Negro male" had paid the fines, asking not to be identified, and Pritchett did not want to question the jailer further about it, for fear of subjecting him to reprisal. Two of Pritchett's detectives drove King and Abernathy to Dr. Anderson's house, where Wyatt Walker slammed the door against the reporters who came just behind. The reporters overheard spirited arguments about what had happened. Was it possible that the Albany whites had an accomplice among the city's professional Negroes? If Pritchett was lying, how could they prove it?

King emerged to hold a news conference at Shiloh late that morning. "This is one time I'm out of jail that I'm not happy to be out," he declared. He denounced the "subtle and conniving tactics" used to engineer his release. He did say, by way of consolation, that Chief Pritchett had all but assured them that the cases against the other seven hundred demonstrators from the previous December would be dropped, and that a biracial commission would be appointed to settle the larger disputes. Across town, however, Pritchett was telling his own news conference that "there has been nothing of a settlement in reference to anything." Mayor Kelley said he did not know who paid the fines. Then, possibly to make himself more comfortable, he modified his position to say he had "no communicable information on that subject." Kelley held tenaciously to the pact of silence for decades thereafter.

In Washington, Robert Kennedy told reporters that "Dr. King's release should make it possible for the citizens of Albany to resolve their differences in this situation in a less tense atmosphere. Therefore, I am very glad that Dr. King has been released." His phrasing subtly endorsed the perspective of leading Albany whites, who saw segregation as a local matter. Ed Guthman, Kennedy's press spokesman, assured reporters that Robert Kennedy had not paid King's fine—nor had President Kennedy, nor any other official of the federal government. To stress the parallel with the Kennedy performance after King's 1960 jailing, Guthman did disclose that Burke Marshall had made phone calls to Mrs. King and others, which he said might have facilitated the outcome.

In Albany, King's release surprised all but the most cynical observers. The *Herald* declared that rumors of an impending negotiated settlement were false ("City Will Not Back Down on Negro Issue"). To dispel suspicions of collusion with Washington, Mayor Kelley publicly denounced the Justice Department for "collaborating and conspiring with the leaders of the Albany Movement . . . to violate existing ordinances of the City of Albany." His accusations produced a flurry of denials from the Justice Department. Privately, Justice officials were consumed by bureaucratic spats with the FBI over appearances and lines of command.

Out of jail, King swiftly lost his leverage. He appeared to be a stranger to the Kennedy Administration and, having been snookered, became fair game for barbs long stored by his critics. *The New York Times* published a profile suggesting that King was out of his league in politics. He was "woefully inadequate in organizational ability," stated a *Times* source, and the correspondent added that King's "chief problem" was his determination to establish the SCLC as an organization independent of the NAACP. The nation's news outlets made sport of the mystery of King's anonymous benefactor. *Newsweek* called the case a "Georgia Whodunit." The Albany *Herald* chortled over the rascally maneuver behind headlines such as "Mayor Stays Mum" and "Who Got King Out?" Most newspapers accepted the official version of the transaction itself and then proceeded to speculate about possible accomplices of the "well-dressed Negro male." No one bothered to scrutinize the official stories. B. C. Gardner's name never surfaced, and Chief Pritchett's account survived as the working draft of the truth.

It took King two weeks to get back into jail. He regarded it as imperative that he return, not least because most of the thirty-two who had marched with him were still locked up. It appeared that he had led them into a trap and then escaped himself. But he did not seek jail immediately, as his Albany supporters were too numb to follow. A six-month lull in demonstrations had been followed by a sharp defeat, and local whites seemed tougher and less compromising than ever. The Albany Movement, James Gray declared, had done nothing more than to bankrupt the city bus system, cancel the Christmas parade, "cost Negroes jobs and money," and cause "the jailing of nearly 800 persons, many of them children of long-established and honorable citizens of the Negro community. . . . They now have criminal records. Is this the way to teach the young about their America?" Some Albany Negroes, in the grip of discouragement or fear, were swayed by Gray's argument that King himself was the problem.

To recover lost momentum, the leaders of the Albany Movement first issued a document called the "Albany Manifesto," declaring that during the past six months the Albany officials had dealt with them in bad faith. By day, the Albany Movement leaders sent small groups to test segregation at the city library and parks. All of them met a police blockade, and many were arrested. Each incident demonstrated to wavering Negroes that race relations were not as sweet as Gray and his colleagues claimed. The nighttime crowds grew toward the overflow numbers of the previous December.

King flew to Washington on July 19 to address the National Press Club. Reporters recorded the exact moment—12:35 P.M.—at which he entered the fifty-four-year-old press club to become its first Negro American speaker. The capacity audience rose a second time, and then a third, in spontaneous ovations. Many of the members were proud to have broken the race barrier, and although King gave them a rather stiff speech on the merits of nonviolence, they were proud, too, to sponsor such lofty oratory. This was King's ironic trap up close: he could bring inspiration even to the National Press Club, but he could force his movement into the news columns only by bloodshed or political miracle. News accounts of the speech were spare, as there was little news in King's message itself. One story noted that not a single press club member had resigned in protest of King's appearance.

Cutting short a Northern fund-raising tour, King found Albany in a tense chess game, commingled of silliness and hate. A white man dressed as an exterminator had sprayed pesticide on Negroes testing the segregation of city picnic tables. Charles Jones had outwitted the police patrols who were trying to keep Negroes out of the whites' restrooms in city parks. And the air thickened with rumors that city officials aimed to stifle the movement with a court order. "I understand that the city attorney has gone to Atlanta to get an injunction to get the undesirables out," King declared at the mass meeting on July 20. "Now I assume by the undesirables he's speaking of Ralph Abernathy, James Bevel, Bernard

Lee, Andrew Young, Wyatt Tee Walker, Charles Jones, Sherrod, and I could name many others." He told the crowd that the obstructions did not matter—not the courts, nor the mayor, nor the governor, nor even the federal government. None of these mattered, said King, if the people of Albany acted upon rights that were theirs: "The salvation of the Negro in Albany, Georgia, is within the hands and the soul of the Negro himself." He told his favorite story from India: Gandhi's Salt March, of Gandhi beginning alone but ending with a million people by the sea, and how he changed history by the simple act of holding aloft a pinch of free, untaxed sea salt. "And the minute that happened," cried King, "it seemed I could hear the boys at Number Ten Downing Street in London, England, say, 'It's all over now'!" This run of oratory put the church into pandemonium. King joined to these emotions memories of another famous march to the sea, by Union General W. T. Sherman, whose fiery swath through Georgia had emancipated the direct ancestors of many in King's audience. "And so let's get our marchin' shoes ready," King told them. ". . . For we are goin' to Albany's March to the Sea."

They planned a march for the next afternoon, a Saturday, but that morning deputy U.S. marshals began knocking on doors with court papers signed by U.S. District Court judge J. Robert Elliott, a strident segregationist recently appointed by President Kennedy. Accepting the novel—critical lawyers said fantastical—arguments of Albany officials, Judge Elliott turned upside down the civil rights movement's cherished stand on the Fourteenth Amendment. Instead of ruling that segregation was a denial of Negroes' rights to equal protection under the law, Elliott ruled that Negro protest marches denied Albany's *white* people equal protection by draining police manpower and other public resources out of white neighborhoods. Therefore, pending a hearing on the city's request for a permanent injunction, the judge ordered Albany's protest leaders to desist from further marches.

A deputy marshal knocked that morning at the home of Dr. Anderson. He was promptly shown to the master bedroom, which was crammed with Albany Movement leaders in the midst of emergency consultations. There he served an order on Dr. Anderson, whom he knew by sight, after which he pulled another order from his sheaf of papers and asked whether Martin Luther King was present. An awkward silence followed. King was sitting on the bed in plain view, but the marshal did not recognize him. King and the others remained frozen in silence, so great was their panic over the consequences of the order. When the marshal withdrew to take up station outside Anderson's house, King and other named defendants escaped through a window and down a back alley. They soon reconsidered their instinctive flight. Although they shied from the order as a catastrophe for their cause—it put the Justice Department, the FBI, and the authority of the federal judiciary squarely in opposition to their protests against segregation—they decided on reflection that it did them no credit to hide. King drove to the courthouse early that afternoon and volunteered to be served.

Whether he should obey the order was a different and more difficult question, which was debated all afternoon and into the night. William Kunstler advised King that the restraining order was manifestly illegal. But should he act on that assumption or wait respectfully for a higher court to vacate it? To disregard the order risked a confrontation with federal judges—even those who agreed with King on the merits of desegregation—over the deference due to federal edicts, whereas to obey the order risked a permanent surrender on the critical issue of timing. The latter was a point hammered home by Charles Jones, Charles Sherrod, and James Forman of SNCC. Any federal judge could issue a restraining order, they said, and with a Democratic president now naming judges on the recommendations of segregationist, home-state U.S. senators, white officials would have restraining orders at their bidding. The SNCC leaders argued that it would take time, perhaps weeks or months, to overturn such orders, during which a ripe protest inevitably would decay. If the movement leaders conceded to the white opponents the power to quash protests at moments of disadvantage, they never would find an offsetting weapon. Protest was all they had.

These arguments were persuasive to King. As the expectant marchers began to trickle into Shiloh that afternoon, he told Robert Kennedy from Anderson's house that he felt "impelled" to march. Kennedy, who had initiated the call, was shocked to hear that the rumors were true. The Attorney General remained prickly on the subject of civil disobedience. How could King even think of violating this court order, he demanded to know, when governors and school officials across the South were praying for an excuse not to obey federal school desegregation orders?

King held his ground. While acknowledging the validity of Kennedy's points, he said that the whole point of the movement was to rise up against blatantly unconstitutional, segregationist laws. Always, King protested, somebody would find a way to make protest unreasonable and segregation reasonable for the moment. "We're tired, very tired," he said. "I'm tired. We're sick of it." Kennedy kept pounding home the argument that King could not afford to risk the goodwill of the federal courts, where the movement was winning its greatest victories. Contrasting King's recklessness with the Administration's steady progress in securing compliance with desegregation orders, Kennedy pressed the point too far for King. "Some of these problems you have created yourself," King replied, "by appointing these segregationist federal judges." By implication, King was painting the Administration rather than himself as the trouble-maker. Annoyed, Kennedy had the presence of mind to quell the shouting match by turning the telephone over to Burke Marshall.

Marshall debated King for nearly two hours that Saturday afternoon, with both sides breaking frequently for consultations with seconds. Marshall's strength was his patience and command of detail. He pointed out that if King marched in defiance of Elliott's order, he would go to jail for contempt of court. The segregation issue would be lost. King would put himself in a difficult corner—precisely where the Administration was trying to put Governor Barnett of Mississippi in the James Meredith case. To all this, King responded with some technical points of his own. Barnett's First Amendment rights were not being violated, he said, whereas the Elliott order plainly stifled his. Barnett faced an order that had been tested through many hearings and appeals, and which was consistent with both justice and Supreme Court law, whereas King faced a contrary order slapped together by one judge. Marshall, while granting many legal weaknesses in Elliott's order, stressed that the segregationists were watching, and if King were allowed to violate the first federal ruling he didn't like, "then the whole credibility of our even-handed position— that this is the law—goes out the window."

They argued to an exhausted stalemate, by which time runners from Shiloh were bringing King urgent messages that the crowd was growing restive. King closeted himself briefly and then sent Clarence Jones circulating through the Anderson house with his decision: he would obey the order until the lawyers could get it overturned. Then he began to agonize over the fresh question of what he should say to the crowd at Shiloh. He knew from experience that their cheering would raise the roof the moment he showed his face, and it was painful to think of deflating their enthusiasm—so painful in fact that he began to reconsider his concession to Marshall. But no, he must stick to his best judgment, so perhaps he should stay away from the church altogether. Then again, no, he could not bear to have the mass meeting go on without him. With his thoughts lurching about, King took a walk in the night air and then decided to go to Shiloh after all, without knowing exactly how to inform the crowd of the postponement. Surrounded by lawyers, the Albany Movement leaders, and the SNCC students, he made his way into Reverend Boyd's study.

They could hear seven hundred people singing freedom songs and spirituals in the church. Whenever the singing died down, a speaker gave them a dose of rhetoric and something to pass for an update on the delays. Because most of the regular leadership was huddled around King, the speaking task fell most often to Rev. Samuel B. "Benny" Wells, a stocky, coal-black man of little education. He had immensely broad shoulders, which he used in his regular job as a freight loader at the U.S. Marine depot. On weekends, he pastored a tiny country church called Blue Spring Baptist out in Worth County, some twenty-five miles from Albany. Wells felt out of place in the councils of the city preachers. His strengths were a coarse eloquence and an earthy, forceful presence, plus a lack of inhibiting career goals.

"Take us up!" someone shouted from the congregation, and Wells did his best to oblige. Never had he faced such a crowd. He preached them to an emotional peak, hoping that the bedlam would entice King to make his entrance, but when nothing happened he was obliged to preach them back down again toward a prayer and a new song. Then Wells hastened to the wings for consultations. Once he made his way inside the study and said, "Dr. King, the world is waiting for a message. They are looking and listening for a message tonight." King nodded. His aides told Wells to hold the crowd because they were not yet certain of the next move. Obliging, Wells stalled until the crowd grew restless, and then he preached them to another peak, and down again. After three or four times through the cycle, Wells could stand it no longer. "I've heard about an injunction, but I haven't seen one! I heard a few names, but my name hasn't been called!" he cried. "But I do know where my name *is* being called. My name is being called on the road to freedom. I can hear the blood of Emmett Till as it calls from the ground!" At this the church erupted in throaty courage that refused to die down until Wells proposed to march out with them. "We will go down to the City Hall," he said, "and we will protest peacefully the evils that have been grinding the life out of our spirits for ninety-nine years."

Nearly two hundred people, mostly teenagers, followed Wells out of the church and down the familiar route to the border of the white business district. When Chief Pritchett and a police squadron blocked them at the bus station, Wells fell to his knees in the street. Sweaty, overwrought, and plainly frightened, he prayed aloud for courage until Pritchett could take it no longer. Standing directly over Wells, the police chief said sourly, "All right, Rev, come on and get up, goddamn it. Let's go to jail." One hundred thirteen people followed Wells into the cell blocks. Others retreated, but a burst of fervor soon moved another fifty to file across Oglethorpe Avenue to join them.

Inside Dr. Anderson's station wagon, King observed from a distance. Although he tried to avoid the note-taking FBI agents, lest they charge that he had violated Judge Elliott's injunction by encouraging the demonstration, he was overjoyed that the ordinary folk of the Albany Movement had marched on their own. "They can stop the leaders," King said happily, "but they can't stop the people." Albany's white officials, on the other hand, figured that the enjoined leaders must have connived in the march somehow, in violation of the injunction. They asked the FBI to investigate. Director Hoover shrewdly insisted upon direct orders from the Justice Department. Then FBI headquarters instructed agents to tell each Negro being questioned—including King—that a criminal contempt investigation was being conducted specifically for the Attorney General.

From the perspective of national politics, the main story was that King and the other named defendants had not defied the order. A legal crisis was averted. King was not in jail, and the Wells march was a minor event that the Administration could overlook because it raised no legal challenge or public clamor. "The Negroes finally decided to obey this injunction," Burke Marshall reported simply to the Attorney General. Similarly, a *New York Times* editorial focused exclusively on King's confrontation with Judge Elliott. "We are glad he [King] is not . . . leading the Negroes of Albany, Ga., in defiance of a Federal court injunction," the *Times* declared. "Whatever the shortcomings of local justice in the Deep South, certainly no one knows better than Dr. King that the Federal judiciary is a pillar of the constitutional safeguards his followers have so often been denied."

On Sunday, with the new prisoners farmed out to jails in the surrounding counties, King and Anderson held a press conference. Describing Judge Elliott's injunction as "unjust and unconstitutional," they told reporters that their lawyers were working to have it vacated by the federal appeals court, headed by Judge Elbert Tuttle, an Eisenhower appointee. It was an uncomfortable session for King. He could denounce the injunction all he wanted, but he felt constrained to say he respected it. He could not advocate any demonstrations or urge his followers to do anything but wait, lest he be found in contempt of Judge Elliott's court. White reporters from Albany pressed him to explain why he had not done more to stop the Wells march.

King began a far more harrowing ordeal late that afternoon when he agreed to sit for a private gripe session with the SNCC leaders in Albany —Sherrod, Jones, Reagon, and Forman, plus Yale Law School student Tim Jenkins, who had flown in for the crisis. It began politely enough in Slater King's backyard, with the students restating their reasons why King had erred in submitting to Judge Elliott's injunction. This was familiar ground for King, as he half agreed with them, but the criticism escalated rapidly into a general attack on King's character and methods.

The SNCC leaders were in a bind. They wanted a "people's movement," like SNCC itself, and yet without King, the Wells march had had
little impact on the outside world, and without such impact it was nearly
impossible to inspire more of Albany's ordinary people to take up the
crusade. What they needed was the use of King's influence without his
suffocating glory, and it was all the more galling that they were obliged
to ask King to reform himself accordingly. To these political differences,
each of the SNCC leaders added an acute, private complaint against King.
For Charles Sherrod, it was King's pragmatism, his habit of second-guessing the great mystical tide of the movement. For Tim Jenkins, it was
King's aura of religion and suffering, which Jenkins thought stigmatized
Negroes as an emotional people unequipped for the rigors of politics. For
James Forman, it was being older than King and yet dwarfed like a child
by his heavily credentialed fame.

The students said King was too dreamy to have the cunning that the
movement required, but they also said he was too attached to his worldly
status to lose himself in zealous commitment. They told him they resented his control of the press—how much they hated it when reporters
in Albany would phone King in Chicago or New York for an interpretation of events in Albany. Forman attacked his caution in the face of the
Elliott injunction, saying that King only wanted to protect his "fund-
raising base" among the white people who read *The New York Times*.
They recounted their grievances over the division of movement funds,
arguing that the money should be controlled by the Albany Movement instead of the SCLC. They denounced Wyatt Walker as Iago or a
martinet, and King for hiring him. Above all, they said King was too
middle-class. Using a favorite term of opprobrium among aristocrats and
proletarians alike, they called him "bourgeois."

It went on hour after hour, into the night. King flinched defensively
but never flashed in anger. When indignant staff aides jumped in to
defend him, King waved them aside. Marion King, Slater King's wife,
kept bringing trays of food to sustain them through the argument, and
each time she came outside from the kitchen she winced and nearly cried
out against the scathing names she heard being heaped upon King. She
held back, however, as did her husband and the other observers. King and
the students had created their own charged space. Ironically, the confrontation gradually took on a kind of intimacy. As tempers and political
labels gave way to introspection, King talked increasingly to Charles
Jones, the student most like himself. Jones moved so near King's chair in
the yard that he spoke nearly in a whisper.

"Martin, you are the symbol of spiritual integrity," Jones said. "If *you*
say this injunction is a tactical move to co-opt the movement, then
everybody will listen and follow you to jail. And you then change the

rules. You have done this before, and now we are at a point where you have to provide the leadership even for the Kennedys, as well as the movement. So let's go to jail, bro'. I'm gonna be going. We'll be there together."

King smiled. "Chuck, do I have to?" he asked. He joked about how difficult it was even to shave in jail—he used an acrid powder to soften his tough beard—and how as a pastor he was accustomed to having his things laid out for him. He and Jones chatted about their experiences in jail, but they seemed to be speaking also of a symbolic level of surrender. Jones had just decided to give up the pulpit. Paradoxically, as only a young Brahmin preacher could do, he kept saying King had to choose his cross over his career.

"Even you have got to grow a little bit more," Jones told King. "Please listen to me. I love you. You know that. Whenever you've called, I've been there. But now I'm saying this is ahead of you. You've got to accept it." In the end, exhausted, Jones and King smiled silently at each other. Tim Jenkins later snapped Jones from a kind of trance by complaining that his pitch had been too religious.

King retired late Sunday night to the counsel of his lawyers at the Anderson house, across the street, where Coretta had come for a visit. Battered by criticism and stalemated by the injunction, he was tired. In later years, he jokingly gave thanks for the stamina that allowed him to accomplish something positive in Albany that weekend, when his fourth child, Bernice, was conceived.

On the following afternoon, Marion King drove through the country outside Albany to the Mitchell County jail in Camilla, where the daughter of her maid was among those incarcerated from Saturday's Wells march. Arriving at the hulking, whitewashed jail with plates of freshly baked food, she stood outside the chain-link fence in a throng of other Negroes from Albany, waiting for visitors' hour. They all sang freedom songs and scanned the jailhouse windows for familiar faces. Nothing about the crowd pleased the Mitchell County sheriff and his deputies, who were accustomed to a grimmer atmosphere. (Among their regular prisoners they counted the miserable Charlie Ware, still awaiting trial on attempted murder charges more than a year after the Baker County sheriff shot him three times in the neck.) The mass singing outside foretold another unbearable visitors' period in which the officers would be lost in a sea of Negroes fretting over mail privileges and lost pocketbooks. Irritably, to cut down on the noise and bother, the deputies shooed the waiting visitors away from the fence. All skittered backward except for a woman with two small children, who backed up slowly and silently, seemingly unaware of the commotion.

Marion King did not move fast enough. Something about her prompted the sheriff and one uniformed deputy to walk briskly outside. "I mean you!" one shouted. King retreated steadily. She had seen Ella Mae in the jail window and did not want to set an example of cowering in fear. A split second later, the sheriff slapped her sharply across the face. Three-year-old Abena went sprawling from her arms to the pavement. One-year-old DuBois shrieked. As the sheriff slapped her again, the deputy kicked her in the shins, knocking her feet from beneath her, and then kicked her several times more on the ground. She lost an instant to blackout or shock, as the next thing she knew was the sharp pain in her knees, which had struck the pavement. The officers were going back through the gate, and the crowd behind was gasping in horror.

Slater King broke down and cried like a baby that night, so great was his rage at being helpless in the wake of the attack. To complete his frustration, his own brother, C.B., refused to bring a civil action against the assaulting officers. A year's suffering in the Ware case, he said, had convinced him that Negro lawsuits against rural sheriffs were a form of self-torture. Sometime after midnight, an FBI agent arrived to begin investigation of their complaint under the federal police brutality statutes. Marion Cheek, a native Atlantan even larger than Chief Pritchett, began asking questions of Marion King. His detached tone and his insistence on verifiable detail met with wounded outbursts from King and her relatives, who doubted that the federal government would take action in their behalf. Martin Luther King came to Cheek's defense. "Now this gentleman is just trying to do his job," he said. "Tell him what happened."

That night King sent off additions to his growing pile of telegrams at the Justice Department. These gained him only two more pro forma responses from Burke Marshall, one pledging to take "appropriate action" and the other stating that "the internal administration of a state penal institution is not a matter over which this Department would have any jurisdiction in the absence of an indication of a violation of federal law."

In Atlanta, Judge Elbert Tuttle vacated Judge Elliott's temporary restraining order the next day, leaving the leaders of the Albany Movement free to demonstrate at least until Elliott held a proper hearing. Mayor Kelley called Tuttle's ruling "incredible." The Albany *Herald* proclaimed shock at the betrayal ("Judge Tuttle Rules with Negro Leaders"), and editor Gray wrote a somber, front-page editorial entitled "Albany Will Stand." King and Dr. Anderson, for the other side, sent Mayor Kelley a telegram that fairly dripped with graciousness. "We do not consider the lifting of the injunction a victory," they wrote. "We . . . beg you once more, in the name of democracy, human decency and the welfare of Albany, to give us an opportunity to present our grievances to the City Commission immediately."

In Albany's Harlem, the joyous news from Atlanta collided with the reports of what had happened to Marion King in Camilla. The latter news carried more voltage. One story was about distant lawyers arguing over complicated things, while the other was about the brazen public beating of a very special woman in Albany. Marion King was regal but cheerful, accomplished but without airs—just the sort to drive all the way out to a country jail to visit her maid's daughter. It had been her surprise jailing that touched off the first mass marches the previous December. Everyone knew she was in maternity clothes, more than six months pregnant.* Every detail—the fact that she was hit while pregnant, and that her little girl was literally knocked from her arms—magnified the hideousness of the affront. The effect of the news was so potent that the Negro leaders of Albany instinctively hushed it up. Normally, stories of brutality or intimidation were told and retold at the mass meetings to stir solidarity, but that night, to the dense crowds that overflowed from Shiloh to Mount Zion, only Abernathy even mentioned the Marion King beating. For Anderson, Martin King, and Slater King, the subject was too raw, passions too inflamed.

The leaders postponed plans for an immediate march. They wanted to give Mayor Kelley time to respond to their invitation to negotiate, they said, and among themselves they acknowledged that the crowd was disorganized, distracted, and extremely volatile. No sooner had they departed to seek an audience at city hall, however, than a prominent white visitor from New York, Marvin Rich of CORE, exhorted the crowd to embark on a night march of protest. Forty people followed him. As they walked along the familiar route through Harlem, they picked up stragglers and onlookers in large numbers, anticipating a showdown. And as the demonstrators filed across Oglethorpe Avenue to be arrested, some of the angry Negro bystanders flung beer bottles at the distant policemen.

What quickly followed, if not a riot, was a near riot. There was no fighting, looting, or gunfire, but flying rocks and bricks soon joined the bottles in a sustained pelting. The contagious excitement of sirens, battle cries, and breaking glass emptied the Negro beer joints and pool halls, while police reinforcements hustled up from the opposite side. Reporters

---

* King miscarried some weeks later, and although she herself was never sure enough to say that the Camilla officers had killed the unborn baby, that assumption was more than reasonable enough for the creators of Albany Movement lore.

converged from all directions, and from the churches, panicky and nearly sickened Albany Movement leaders plunged in among the swarming rock throwers, trying desperately to stop the attack. Andrew Young pleaded with them not to give the movement a bad name, not to ruin everything. When that failed to work, he taunted them almost hysterically, crying, "You're too yellow to march!" Other well-dressed church people joined Young in a thin line along the fringes, trying to push the skirmishers back out of range.

Chief Pritchett was a roving commander, sending squadrons of police and state troopers to clear the streets of Harlem block by block, under strict orders to use no clubs or guns unless attacked with such weapons. Behind his advancing men, Pritchett ordered Negro night spots closed and posted guard details. He, not King, was the master of nonviolence that night, and he made sure no slow-witted reporter missed the point. "Judge Tuttle ought to see this," he quipped, and as the missiles flew he called out to reporters, "Did you see them nonviolent rocks?" When it was over, he announced at a hasty press conference that "there was no violence on our part—the officers never took their nightsticks from their belts." One of his men had been struck by a bottle but not injured, he said, and a rock had knocked out two of state trooper Claude Hill's teeth. A photograph of Hill holding the rock appeared the next day on the front page of the Albany *Herald*. By then Governor Vandiver, from whom it had been difficult to pry any statement so long as Albany's whites were on the defensive, had all but taken to the rooftops. "I want all trouble-makers to know that I will do whatever is necessary to prevent violence at Albany, Georgia," he announced. Vandiver pledged to send in all 12,000 National Guard troops if necessary.

A chastened King held a press conference too. "We declare a day of penance beginning at twelve noon today," he said, calling for "all supporters of the Albany Movement to pray for our Negro brothers who have not yet learned the nonviolent way." It was a public ritual of contrition and purification that echoed Gandhi's cancellation of huge protests in 1919 and 1922, and it proved no less controversial among King's colleagues. James Forman in particular was incensed that King was blaming Negroes, dividing their natural constituency, pulling back from the struggle. He argued that King should place the blame for the violence on the officers who had beaten Marion King, and on the stubborn city officials who maintained segregation by arresting nonviolent protesters. King replied that this was not good enough, and that the violence drowned out such explanations.

The grip of crisis on the Albany Movement was so strong that some SNCC leaders resolved to stand publicly behind King's day of penance.

With Abernathy, Bernard Lee, and a clutch of reporters, Charles Jones set off behind King on a peacemaker's tour of Albany's Negro dives. Jones in blue jeans and the others in business suits, they popped into pool halls and beer joints such as the Beehive and the South Grand Terrace, like space travelers from another planet. "I have brought you the symbol of nonviolence," Abernathy announced to startled, surly customers, and King labored to overcome the pompous effect. "I hate to hold up your pool game," he said. "I used to be a pool shark myself." Loosening his tie and taking a pool cue, King showed them a few of the shots he had learned at Crozer. Over this icebreaker, he told them that bottle-throwing played into the hands of the segregationists. "We don't need guns and ammunition, just the power of souls," he said. Charles Jones took a more conspiratorial, low-down approach. He was well aware, he claimed, that whites had slipped money to Negro snitches to provoke the fight, and he warned against the treason of whispered deals. As he spoke, collapsing nerves told Jones that he was nearing his end in the movement. Still dazed from his intimate wrestling match over King's identity, he soon made arrangements for a long trip to Mexico.

That night of July 25, during the forced idleness of the twenty-four-hour penance in Albany, Charles Sherrod drove far out into the backwoods of nearby "Terrible" Terrell County to attend a voter registration meeting in a tiny wooden church called Mount Olive Baptist. The event attracted only thirty-eight Negroes and two white SNCC workers, but it produced perhaps the most remarkable news dispatch of the entire civil rights generation. Landing two days later on the front page of *The New York Times*, correspondent Claude Sitton's story began: " 'We want our colored people to go on living like they have for the last hundred years,' said Sheriff Z. T. Mathews of Terrell County." Sitton went on to describe how Mathews had burst into the church ahead of several armed deputies, and then, while the deputies scowled and rubbed their guns and tapped their heavy flashlights menacingly in their palms, had lectured from the pulpit on why no more than the current 51 Negroes, out of the county's 8,209, need be registered to vote.

Almost entirely in narrative, Sitton's story interspersed the continuing hymns and prayers of the frightened registration workers with the threats of the lawmen. The car doors of a gathering posse were heard slamming outside in the darkness. Inside, Sherrod steadfastly prayed: "Give us the wisdom to try to understand this world." Sheriff Mathews announced that he was closing registration until December. Sitton recorded snatches of dialogue: " 'I know you,' said one officer to a Negro.

'We're going to get some of you.' " Veiled threats followed professions of friendship in a scene Sitton painted rich with foreboding. "Overhead," he wrote, "swarms of gnats circled the three light globes and now and then one of the audience would look up from the pine floor to steal a fearful glance at the door. Mr. Sherrod then read from the Scriptures." When Sitton and the other reporters finally pushed their way out of the church, they found that someone had slashed a tire on their car and spiked the gas tank with sand.

President Kennedy read the story, as did the Attorney General. The story was an outrage, splashed across the pages of the *Times*, and it made a mockery of the voting rights protections in the civil rights acts. This touched Robert Kennedy in two tender spots. He began shouting "Move!" at his chief lawsuit coordinator, John Doar. Within hours, a task force of Justice Department lawyers and FBI agents descended on Terrell County. They worked so rapidly and relentlessly, Burke Marshall soon reported to Kennedy, that the Justice Department filed a voting rights complaint against Sheriff Mathews "in less than two weeks after Claude Sitton's story."

That Thursday morning in Albany, however—as Sitton returned from his ordeal, and as the day of penance came to its end—the political state of affairs was anything but vivid. None of the major news stories about the "nonviolent rocks" riot so much as mentioned the Marion King beating, or any other precipitating cause. To many readers, it appeared that the Negroes who should have been celebrating the victory they had gained in Judge Tuttle's courtroom had rioted instead. The leadership muddle only made things more puzzling: of the two marches in the past week, Martin Luther King had sat out the first and opposed—or not known of—the second. Now he was apologizing for the violence, and *The New York Times* published a laudatory profile of Chief Pritchett.

Ebenezer deacon C. A. Scott chose that Thursday to publish a scolding editorial in the South's only Negro daily. "Dr. King and others might help relieve the situation by gracefully retiring from the scene there . . ." he wrote, "and we hope no third party will allow his presence to delay or complicate matters in Albany." At Shiloh, movement veterans were so emotionally gnarled that when Albany Movement leaders announced on Friday that city officials had flatly refused to negotiate any issue of segregation, and then called dramatically for volunteers to line up for a protest march to jail, practically no one responded. Exhortations failed. Andrew Young begged them, holding up a stack of pledge cards signed by volunteers for jail. Charles Sherrod shamed them for choosing comfort over freedom, and Reverend Wells tried his thunder: "Everybody that's got religion that'll do when the world's on fire, raise your hand!" But still they sat snugly in the pews.

Lacking the power to be heard over the babble of contrary emotions, King had only the hope that his image still spoke more forcefully than his tongue. At 2:15 P.M. on July 27, by Claude Sitton's watch, he arrived at the sidewalk outside city hall with Abernathy, Anderson, Slater King, and seven female supporters to pray for negotiations. Wyatt Walker handed out press releases explaining King's decision, while Chief Pritchett said the tiny number of demonstrators proved that King lacked the support of Albany's Negroes. When a runner took Pritchett's grave charge back to Shiloh, Charles Jones managed to scrounge up fifteen volunteers for a small second wave of jail marchers. King was gone before they arrived. Two weeks after the intervention of the "well-dressed Negro male," he reached the end of the long twisting path back to his cell, and the doors of Laurie Pritchett's jail clanged shut on him for the third time in eight months.

The arrest seeded cloudbursts in national politics before nightfall. Governor Rockefeller sent a telegram urging Attorney General Kennedy to "take immediate steps to assure the physical safety of Dr. King . . . and investigate whether Constitutional rights of peaceable assembly have been violated." White House reporters badgered Press Secretary Pierre Salinger for a presidential response—what would Kennedy do now that King was arrested for praying against segregation?

King and Abernathy were leading inmates in freedom songs and personal statements of witness that night when Chief Pritchett unlocked the door and beckoned to King. Saying that King had a long-distance phone call from Lawrence Spivak, creator of NBC's "Meet the Press," he promised King that this was no trick to eject him from jail. King soon found himself in a heated discussion with Spivak, who wanted King on "Meet the Press" that Sunday morning. Spivak was at first dumbfounded, then provoked to a sputtering rage, by King's reply that he might have to stay in jail rather than bond out for the program. Most public figures begged for the chance to appear on the most prestigious network interview show, and Spivak did not relish being turned down in favor of a jail cell. Only the bizarre contortions of racial politics explained King's modesty: he seized more of the limelight, and made a more powerful statement, by remaining hidden in jail than he could hope to make before millions on television. Chief Pritchett, who wanted King out of jail almost as badly as Spivak, kept promising that King could check back into jail easily, without hitch or chicanery, but King insisted that there were too many risks. Besides, to leave jail so soon after making such an effort to get in would make him look like some sort of luxury guest. These and other considerations recommended an ingenious solution: King would ask Spivak to accept Dr. Anderson in his stead. This would allow King to stay in jail, and he would be able to get Anderson out quickly with an unimpeachable excuse. The switch idea grew on King's advisers as a godsend, and Spivak, with the utmost reluctance, accepted Anderson as the only way to get the hot issue of Kennedy and King on the air.

Anderson bonded out the next day and went swiftly into emergency rehearsal for "Meet the Press." Walker, Clarence Jones, C. B. King, and others, impersonating the panelists, bombarded him with hostile questions. For C. B. King this emergency was superseded by another when runners came from the county jail with word that inmates had beaten one of the Albany Movement supporters during the night. The victim was William Hansen of SNCC, the only white person who had gone to jail in the previous day's marches. All the runners knew was that cries were coming from the jail windows about a broken jaw and other grave injuries. No one had been allowed to visit Hansen.

C. B. King speedily presented himself at the county jail as Hansen's lawyer and asked to see his client. The sheriff, seventy-six-year-old D. C. "Cull" Campbell, contemplated the legal request sourly, knowing what the lawyer would find, and then ordered King to leave. When he did not retreat rapidly enough, Campbell chased him out. Inside the door was a rack of wooden canes that had been carved by a blind man, and a cigar box of coins from purchases on the honor system. As the enraged sheriff passed the rack, he grabbed a cane and struck C. B. King full force on the head, then again from behind as King fled. Reeling, with blood running down in a stream that quickly soaked his shirt to the waist, King made a startling sight for the full complement of reporters and police officials who just then were presiding over the arrest of another small band of marchers from the Albany Movement. "C.B., who did this?" shouted Chief Pritchett, and King replied with strained dignity, "The sheriff of Dougherty County, D. C. Campbell." As the newsmen swarmed, Campbell himself emerged from the courthouse wearing a white Panama hat and did not deny King's charges. Campbell was old-school Albany. His son had served as deputy clerk of the U.S. District Court since 1937, and his own career went back to World War I.

An obviously distressed Chief Pritchett ordered a police car to take C. B. King to the hospital. "This is exactly what we've been trying to prevent," he told reporters. Campbell allowed officers to check on Hansen, who went to the hospital for treatment of a broken jaw, facial lacerations, and several broken ribs, and then was transferred that night to a cell in the city jail, near Martin Luther King. Before that, on the courthouse lawn, FBI agent Marion Cheek interviewed Campbell for his official report on the incident. "Yeah, I hit him in the head," Campbell told

Cheek. "I told the son of a bitch to get out of my office, and he didn't get out." Cheek sent the interview to Washington.

Word of the Hansen and C. B. King beatings rocketed through Negro Albany with mixed reactions. There was an outpouring of sympathy from an enormous overflow crowd that night at the mass meeting, but only five people came forward to march the next day, despite stirring songs and emotion-drenched sermons on the cumulative outrages of recent days. "You can't fight a war without soldiers," pleaded Wyatt Walker. When the five marchers presented themselves on the sidewalk outside city hall, Chief Pritchett told them they could pray all they wanted, night and day. Shrewdly, against the urging of some angry whites, Pritchett refused to order arrests. He told reporters that the marchers were too few to disturb anyone.

A gory photograph of C. B. King appeared on the front page of the Sunday Atlanta *Journal-Constitution.* Claude Sitton's account ran on the front page of the Sunday *Times.* Even the Albany *Herald* featured a rare indictment of official behavior, albeit under the sporting headline "Sheriff Campbell Whacks C. B. King." The sporadic violence in Albany was registering ominously in the news media, creating a vibrant atmosphere for Dr. Anderson's appearance on "Meet the Press." Spivak bore in relentlessly with questions suggesting that the Negroes lacked support, had achieved nothing, were run by outsiders, were ruining their chances to make friends with Albany's white people, and were not negotiating in good faith. Other panelists raised the central news angle of national politics: was the Kennedy Administration doing enough? Anderson said no. Although "there has been sufficient indication of violation of constitutional rights," he declared, the federal government had taken no action in Albany. The President had asked the Attorney General for a report after the last King jailing, but so far nothing had been heard of it. "Moreover," said Anderson, "I feel as though the President can make a firm statement himself as regards the matter." The FBI was investigating instances of violence and illegal arrest, he added, but the President had directed no response "as a result of this cumulative material."

President Kennedy was on holiday that Sunday, sailing in his sloop *Victura* off Hyannis Port—not far from Martha's Vineyard, where King had planned to spend the entire month of August. It was Jacqueline Kennedy's birthday. With most of his family and in-laws aboard, the President ran aground near port and suffered the indignity of watching his mainsail collapse into Lewis Bay. Family members teased him unmercifully. No response to Friday's King arrest had yet pushed its way into the President's schedule, but the issue stalked him.

On Monday, Wyatt Walker was talking on two telephones at once when someone interrupted him to say that Governor Rockefeller wanted to speak with him on the third phone. "Me?" said Walker. He said, "Hello, Governor. This is Wyatt Walker, executive assistant to Dr. King." Rockefeller said he was worried about King and wanted to know what he could do to help. "Governor, you called at a propitious moment," Walker replied. He said there was staggering press demand from the last few days, more marches to run, and the crush of personal needs from the people already in jail, who numbered nearly three hundred. "I'm really up against it for bail money," said Walker. When Rockefeller asked briskly how much he needed, Walker closed his eyes, tripled his hopes, and said, "Well, twenty-five thousand dollars would do nicely." Rockefeller said it would be there in the morning, and that he planned in addition to make a like contribution to the general work of the SCLC. Walker hung up in dazed joy. Hints of Rockefeller's concrete "interest" in the movement found their way to reporters.

At a Tuesday-morning press conference, devoted mostly to the thalidomide drug scandal and underground testing of nuclear weapons, a reporter asked President Kennedy what he proposed to do about Albany. Kennedy stumbled at first in his response, saying that care was needed because of the confused tangle of local and federal jurisdictions. He paused and then added a thought as though getting it off his chest: "Let me say that I find it wholly inexplicable why the city council of Albany will not sit down with the citizens of Albany, who may be Negroes, and attempt to secure them, in a peaceful way, their rights. The United States Government is involved in sitting down at Geneva with the Soviet Union. I can't understand why the government of Albany, the city council of Albany, cannot do the same for American citizens."

Dr. Anderson instantly seized upon Kennedy's call for negotiations. "We earnestly desire reconciliation in the Albany community, not victory," he told Mayor Kelley in another telegram asking for a meeting. Kelley declined to talk with "lawbreakers," and branded President Kennedy's statement "incredible." Because Kennedy spoke in rebuke of the Albany officials, his remarks raised a howl of protest from Southern congressmen. In the Senate, Richard Russell lamented that the President had given the nation's highest "stamp of approval" to the Negro lawbreakers, saying his statement would "encourage the importation of many other professionals and notoriety seekers and worsen an already bad situation." Russell speculated that Kennedy's real motive was to win votes for his brother Edward in the upcoming Massachusetts election. Senator Talmadge denounced King for leading "a violent, calculated campaign to damage the United States in foreign affairs and to set race against race." Picking up on the fact that the President had called for

Albany to negotiate with its local citizens, not with King, he declared that the city's racial troubles could be solved if "outside agitators" left town.

In the Albany *Herald*, James Gray eulogized the "Negro-wooing Government," and wryly mourned the political demise of his friends the Kennedy brothers as "two ambitious Bostonians, who have been as practically connected with the American Negro in their lifetimes as Eskimos are to the Congo Democrats." Officials of the Kennedy Administration, for their part, believed that King's rivals in the civil rights movement were putting on a show of lukewarm support for him. Just before Roy Wilkins led a group into the Attorney General's office for a summit meeting, Burke Marshall told Robert Kennedy that Wilkins and the others needed to be able to say they were doing something about Albany. Marshall assured Kennedy that they cared very little for the Albany demonstrations, which were "not Roy's style." The meeting fulfilled Marshall's predictions until the NAACP's Washington lobbyist, Clarence Mitchell, said he was disturbed by posturing within the government. Mitchell called for the Justice Department to take some action in Albany —arrest somebody, file a suit, protect a march, anything. His unexpected bluntness provoked Robert Kennedy. "You know as well as I do, Clarence, that we have done what we can do under existing law," he said. "We could do a great deal more if our hands weren't tied."

Stanley Levison, just back from his annual vacation in South America, was sending draft statements to King's cell by mail. The FBI's wiretap overheard him saying that the Wilkins meeting was a substitute for action on both sides. It was "very possible," he told a friend, that "the NAACP and the Administration would like to see Martin King kill himself. And the tactic, of course, is to let him languish in jail, and then if it doesn't arouse a lot of support, then gradually people will get discouraged and they will win, the city officials will win." King's job, he added, was to keep the heat on, to make it plain that "this is not the time for the federal government to be weak." King's strength also was the antidote for NAACP-flavored criticisms appearing in the skeptical white press. *Time* was reporting that King "has failed to convince Albany's Negroes" of the value of nonviolent protest. Suggesting that "too much success has drained him of the captivating fervor that made him famous," *Time* quoted one anonymous Negro saying that King "doesn't even speak for the Baptist ministry, let alone 20 million Negroes," and another saying that marching to jail was not an intelligent way to desegregate Albany: "Some of us think we can do the job less wastefully."

King remained isolated in his cell. Chief Pritchett kept King and Abernathy off work details for security reasons, and allowed them extra food and visiting privileges. Every morning a women's committee of the Albany Movement brought each of them a clean pair of silk pajamas and plates of food to supplement the wretched jail diet. Abernathy relished a lemon pie. The idea of King in silk pajamas was especially galling to *Herald* editor James Gray, but, deciding that any protest against the luxury might belittle him among the whites and enlarge King among the Negroes, he held the information in his craw.

King held devotional services among the prisoners, often reading from the Book of Job. On some days Pritchett's men took them blinking into the sunlight to attend Judge Elliott's hearings on the city's request for an injunction, which had been mandated by Judge Tuttle. Other days King stayed in the cell and tried to work on a new book of sermons, later published as *Strength to Love*. By the end of his first week in jail, Albany's political and judicial authorities began to accept the unpleasant reality that he was not likely to bail out. As it was unfeasible to expel him again surreptitiously, or delay much longer his trial on the charges of obstructing the sidewalk, time dragged them along inexorably toward a grim choice. They could convict King and sentence him to jail. This course risked renewed mass demonstrations and the embarrassment of possible reversal in appeals court. Worst of all, it kept King not only in town but inside their jail, drawing pressure from distant quarters. Or they could let King go, publicly, and take the chance that this breach might crumble the entire wall of segregation.

Chief Pritchett was just as happy that such decisions were beyond his province. On Saturday, August 4, another cluster of brave but trembling marchers approached city hall from Shiloh—nine women and four men. They confronted the police at the usual spot, while the regular reporters watched from their assigned press section on the sidewalk. Pritchett, appearing relaxed, allowed the marchers to hold a vigil for nearly half an hour before he dryly advised them that their repertoire was exhausted. They were just about sung out and prayed out, he said, and when they failed to disperse, he led them off to jail like a tour guide. It was dusk. Inside, for the benefit of the newest prisoners, Pritchett called out for the regular prisoners to sing one of the freedom songs they had modified in his honor, "Ain't Gonna Let Chief Pritchett Turn Me Around." "I think he really enjoyed hearing it," King wrote in his diary.

Marilyn Monroe died on the night of August 4 in her bedroom across the country. Attorney General Kennedy attended Mass the next morning at the Church of St. Mary in Gilroy, California, outside San Francisco. Already there were reports of mysterious phone calls and gaps in Monroe's last hours, and subsequent decades lent more credence to the Hollywood gossip. Following later disclosures about President Kennedy's associations with Frank Sinatra's friends, as intercepted by J. Edgar Hoover, investigators of various quality unearthed glimpses of Monroe's star-crossed liaisons with both Kennedys.

Kennedy left San Francisco after Mass for the World's Fair in Seattle. At a press conference there, reporters asked him about a scathing think-tank report that accused J. Edgar Hoover of using "sententious poppy-cock" to exaggerate the threat of the tiny U.S. Communist Party. Although the report accurately expressed Kennedy's own private views, he parried the question in defense of Hoover. The reason the Communist Party was so small, he replied, was precisely that Hoover had been so skillful in controlling it. "I hope he will serve the country for many, many years to come," Kennedy added.

At the White House, a stunned Arthur Schlesinger wrote in his journal of his vivid memories of Monroe from the Kennedy birthday party in May: "I do not think I have seen anyone so beautiful; I was enchanted by her manner and her wit, at once so masked, so ingenuous and so penetrating. But one felt a terrible unreality about her—as if talking to someone under water. Bobby and I engaged in mock competition for her; she was most agreeable to him and pleasant to me—but then she receded into her own glittering mist." From Atlanta, Dora McDonald sent her thoughts to King at the Albany jail. "Poor Marilyn Monroe," she wrote. "She needed something to live for. It's a pity for anyone to feel that life is not worth living at 36."

There were no marches in Albany that week, as no one could squeeze new volunteers out of the Shiloh mass meetings. With the reinforcements dried up, King's presence in jail carried a larger share of the pressure on Albany officials. William Kunstler prepared a habeas corpus motion to force the city to vacate its charges or bring him swiftly to trial, and when the recorder's court set the trial date for Friday, Anderson and Wyatt Walker fixed that day as the target for a renewed campaign. They would either celebrate King's victory in court or stage a protest march against his conviction.

With the showdown set, the triangular negotiations between the Albany Movement, the city, and the Justice Department intensified, and on Wednesday the Justice Department took its first public action in the protracted controversy. Jerry Heilbron, the mild-mannered Arkansan who was supposed to charm the Southerners out of segregation, went into Judge Elliott's court and filed an amicus brief in support of the

Albany Movement, saying that the city of Albany did not come into court "with clean hands." City officials already were using police power and local ordinances to negate federal court orders, Heilbron argued, and they should not be granted the additional weapon of a federal ban on "demonstrations seeking to introduce constitutional rights into Albany."

Robert Kennedy felt strong practical incentives for making such a move. After all, if a federal injunction was granted and upheld, he and not Laurie Pritchett would become responsible for repressing demonstrations against segregation. Kennedy did not want that. Still, for all its care, the amicus brief spoke loudly to the press. "U.S. Intervenes on Negroes' Side," announced the *Times.* King issued a statement hailing the Administration's "legal and moral support" for the Albany Movement. Volunteers raised their hands at the Shiloh mass meetings, which were full of spirit again. Wyatt Walker planned a Mothers' March in which the wives of the leaders—Coretta King, Juanita Abernathy, Jean Young, Norma Anderson, Ann Walker, Lotte Kunstler, Marion King, Carol (Mrs. C. B.) King, and even Diane Nash Bevel, with her infant daughter—would effect another dramatic change in the clientele of Laurie Pritchett's jail. All these fresh enthusiasms weighed on the calculations of the city officials.

Police guards escorted King and Abernathy from jail to the local recorder's court on Friday morning, August 10. It was the first day of the third week of their latest stretch in jail, and exactly one month since they had stepped into the same courtroom for sentencing on their original Albany arrests of the past December. The trial before Judge Durden did not last long. C. B. King, his head still wrapped in bandages, raised the defense that his clients had not been disorderly, and that the charges were a subterfuge for the city's actual purpose: to enforce segregation. He was encouraged by the city attorney's announcement that Albany no longer enforced any segregation laws against contrary federal rulings, but Judge Durden soon delivered a verdict that straddled the entrenched lines of the political siege. Finding King, Abernathy, Anderson, and Slater King guilty as charged, he imposed upon each of them a $200 fine and sixty days in jail. Then he suspended the sentences on condition that the defendants violate no laws.

Elated but wary, C. B. King spoke up to ask whether this condition meant that the defendants must obey the city's segregation ordinances. No, replied Judge Durden, because the Supreme Court had expressly overruled those ordinances. After this, the defendants filed out to celebrate. Two pillars of Albany politics had just renounced segregation. King announced that he would go home to preach at Ebenezer that Sunday, and Mayor Kelley all but acknowledged that his departure was part of a compromise package, offsetting the concessions. "I think the Attorney General's intervention . . . has given Dr. King plenty of reason to leave," he told reporters. "He's accomplished his purpose."

That afternoon, the FBI wiretap on Stanley Levison's office phone picked up a call to Levison at his home. His secretary, sounding uncomfortable, told her boss that she did not want to ruin his weekend, but a court summons had just arrived in connection with a financial dispute at one of his rental properties. Levison replied that nothing could spoil his weekend, "because they suspended sentence on Martin." This was a "real victory," he said, and not just in Albany, because King's stature now cast its shadow across the South. King's opponents only recently had thought he had overreached himself, Levison added, and that nobody would raise much of a fuss if they let him rot in jail. Now even Albany had admitted that it could not contain the "tornado" of locking King away in defense of segregation. Levison told his secretary not to fret over money or the summons. His analysis of the Albany verdict was one piece of Levison intelligence that Director Hoover did not see fit to pass on to the Attorney General.

Levison's long-range optimism about King's personal influence did not guarantee the success of the Albany Movement itself, which immediately began to sputter. When teams fanned out through the city on Saturday to test the city's sworn cancellation of the segregation laws, Laurie Pritchett and his police units scrambled after them. True to their promise, the city officials made no arrests under the segregation laws, but neither did they permit the slightest breach of the custom. They closed the city library to prevent the first Negro from checking out a book. They closed the white parks when integrated groups attempted to play tennis. When a doubles match retreated to the all-Negro George Washington Carver Park, city employees raced up to cut the nets just before the first integrated point could be played. Thwarted, William Kunstler angrily smashed a tennis ball high into the air. The racial dispute came to approximate a kindergarten standoff. "King or No King," declared the *Herald*, "City Avows No Compromise."

King was back in Atlanta, preaching at Ebenezer. The morning crowd spilled out of the church down into the basement auditorium. Daddy King presided happily. His good mood bubbled up repeatedly during his son's sermon, as he rapped his cane on the floor in agreement and shouted out a gruff command, "You hear that, deacons!" The younger King announced that he must return to Albany in light of the latest reversal.

He appeared the next night at Shiloh, while James Bevel preached to the spillover mass meeting across the street at Mount Zion. They delayed renewed demonstrations for two days, because the City Commission had granted them a major concession: the commission would receive its first delegation of local Negroes that Wednesday night for the presentation of grievances. Expectations of the historic occasion were justifiably low. At the appointed hour, with thick clusters of Albany Movement people waiting outside city hall in a rainstorm, Mayor Kelley recognized Marion Page. "I am M. S. Page, a law-abiding citizen of Albany," Page began, emphasizing the fact that he had refrained from joining the protest marches. He read a petition urging the commission to consider the Albany Movement's original demands. When he finished, the mayor politely but firmly announced that such racial matters remained in litigation before Judge Elliott. Therefore, Kelley said, the commission deemed it improper to discuss or comment upon them. Page was excused.

At the same hour, King was returning from nearby Lee County, where the first jolt of late-summer violence hastened the decline of the Albany Movement. Arsonists had just firebombed the Shady Grove Baptist Church, in which SNCC volunteers had conducted a registration meeting four days earlier. The Lee County sheriff completed his investigation within two hours, speculating that an electrical storm might have started the fire, but FBI agents pursued leads pointing clearly to political sabotage. All that remained of the tiny church was a lonely chimney, and the charred remains of the clapboard walls and pine benches still were smoldering when King, wearing his customary suit and dress shoes, stepped gingerly across a dirt field off the remote stretch of Highway 195 to join a mournful group of church members at an impromptu memorial service.

Back in Albany, he faced gloomy tactical realities. It was obvious that the city officials, having made the compromises necessary to relieve the public pressure of King's imprisonment, were laying down a stern challenge to the Albany Movement. The whites were demonstrating that they too could be galvanized by humiliation and pain, and in the face of their raw power the Negroes found their options much reduced. Mass marches were out of the question, as the wrung-out souls at the mass meetings no longer volunteered for jail. King alone could retrieve headlines by marching back to jail, but the most he could hope to gain was another suspended sentence, with greatly diminished effect. King called for reinforcements, announcing a nationwide appeal to clergymen.

Two weeks later, seventy-four of them, including nine rabbis, eight Catholic laymen from Chicago, and more than forty Protestant ministers, followed the route from Shiloh to face Laurie Pritchett and his men. Their arrest sparked only minor interest, however, as everyone knew it was only a one-day jailing in the wake of much greater dramas. The mass arrest inspired the headline writers of the Albany *Herald* to merry alliteration: "Crowd Cheers as Cops Clap Clerical Crowd in Calaboose." And it provoked a churlish debate on the floor of the United States Senate, where Georgia's senators told New York's senators that Albany-style law enforcement had made Albany safer than Central Park, preacher arrests or not.

Reviews of King's performance in Albany were harsh. Laurie Pritchett announced publicly that he knew—and that King knew—the cause of integration was set back "at least ten years" by events in Albany. The NAACP's Ruby Hurley observed tartly that "Albany was successful only if the objective was to go to jail." Slater King concluded that the Albany Movement had spread its demands too broadly, and movement critics compiled a catalog of King's tactical mistakes. The NAACP's *Crisis* magazine was preparing an article by two movement professors at Spelman, Staughton Lynd and Vincent Harding, which encompassed nearly all the conflicting criticisms: King's shortcomings as an absentee media star, his failure to rely more heavily on the courts, his insensitivity to local whites, his reluctance to go to jail more frequently, errors in handling the bus strike, and so on. While the movement critics wrote from the urgent conviction that the Albany Movement might have succeeded with better leadership, the major press critics simply observed that King had lost and Albany had won. *The New York Times*, noting that "the public life of Albany remains segregated," asserted that King's most exhaustive campaign had failed because of Pritchett's skillful opposition, "internal rivalries" among the Negroes, "tactical errors" by the Negroes, and the growing unity of hostile whites.

More burdensome to King than the multiplicity of his critics was their detachment. Since he viewed Albany as part of a universal moral issue, with only one clear and just resolution that ought to be as compelling to a white reporter in Iowa as to himself, it nettled him to see people of all opinions stand aside to analyze the results as though segregation might be vindicated, or nonviolence falsified, by his performance in Albany. King felt victimized at the hands of bystanders. He did not believe that the continued enforcement of segregation in Albany lessened the justice of his claims any more than a second-place finish by Jesse Owens would have ennobled Hitler's ideas. Still, he knew better than to stand completely on righteousness. The world tested causes by combat, and King had known since Montgomery that a movement even of the purest spirit cannot survive without victories.

In Birmingham, some six weeks after leaving the Albany jail, he reached for the politic view of Albany, insisting that the struggle already was a success. Negro voter registration had more than doubled there in 1962, King told his audience in Birmingham, and had risen by some 30,000 in all of Georgia. One result, he declared, was the victory of the racial moderate Carl Sanders in the recent governor's race. He said the movement already had won over Pritchett and other leading whites of Albany, who were going through the motions of defending a system they believed was, and ought to be, doomed. Fundamental issues were laid bare, hearts changed, backs straightened.

Having strained to put a positive face on Albany (Pritchett was obliged to deny that moderation had crossed his mind), King retired to analyze shortcomings of the Albany Movement by his own lights. Much of his appraisal was implicit in his conception of the next campaign. In strategy sessions, he said he wanted the SCLC in "on the ground floor." Having learned that it took time to seize the attention of the outside world, he wanted to control the timing and rhythm of the next campaign. In Albany he had been a latecomer, arriving after the mass arrests had peaked, but he was drawing most of the criticism anyway. Nobody was calling Albany a tactical failure for SNCC or the NAACP.

From the bus boycott through the Freedom Rides and on into Albany, King always had entered popular movements more or less haphazardly. Now, since his public stature made anything he did a referendum on his principles, pragmatism demanded that he design his own test. He needed advance planning, training, and mobilization on a specific rather than a general target area. In short, he needed control of a concentrated effort, maximizing both his risk and his chances for spectacular success. To his staff, King announced his resolve to swear off spontaneous rescue missions. "I don't want to be a fireman anymore."

SEVENTEEN

THE FALL OF OLE MISS

New spasms of violence plagued the registration campaign as Moses began his second year in Mississippi, and by uncanny coincidence each periodic incident was echoed by an outburst around Albany, more than three hundred miles to the east. On the Saturday of the false victory in Albany, when the city was closing the tennis courts and swimming pools, Moses and Sam Block took their first large group of would-be registrants to the courthouse in Greenwood, Mississippi—twenty-five of them. This was an unprecedented event in LeFlore County, made all the more shocking by the presence of a CBS film crew and a number of reporters. On the following Monday, three angry white men grabbed Block as he stepped from Moses' car in the downtown business district and beat him severely.

Tension thickened in Greenwood, becoming so dense that when two young volunteer teachers arrived on Wednesday, August 14—the day Shady Grove Baptist Church was burning in Georgia—they found the shades drawn at the SNCC office off Broad Street. Inside, the few Negroes who arrived for classes chose their places carefully, whispering of sniper angles. Moses left for a registration drive in nearby Bolivar County, but the following midnight Sam Block called him there in hushed panic, to report that several carloads of armed men were staking out the office. What coiled the fear most tightly was the stark awareness that it was absurd to hope for police protection—Block had seen police cars pull out just ahead of the posse. Hushed emergency calls followed—to the FBI's local resident agent, to John Doar and Burke Marshall at their homes in Washington. After the next call from Block, who said the men were getting out of their cars, some holding guns and others swinging chains, Moses set off in the night for Greenwood. Arriving before dawn, he found the door broken open and the office ransacked. He had no way of finding out that Block and the two new volunteers had escaped through a window leading across the roofs of adjacent buildings, then had shinnied down a television antenna to a back alley. They crept back the next morning to discover Moses asleep. To Moses it had been a natural choice —he was tired, with nowhere to go and no way to find his missing co-workers—but to others his presence at the site of the terror added to the legend of his nonviolent composure. "I just didn't understand what kind of guy this Bob Moses is, that could walk into a place where a lynch mob had just left and make up a bed and prepare to go to sleep, as if the situation was normal," wrote one of the new SNCC workers. "So I guess I was learning." Block and the two volunteers stayed on in Greenwood, but fear cost them their office. It took them five months to find another one.

Since the spring of that year, Moses had labored to implant tiny registration projects in the core counties of the Mississippi Delta, north of Jackson. It was plantation country, where most of the potential Negro voters lived on scattered farms amid unspeakable poverty and illiteracy, in a state of semifeudal dependence on the white planters. In June, he had taken his colleagues to Highlander Folk School for an intensive workshop tailored to the challenge of nonviolent registration work in remote places. Since then the volunteers had struggled to hold classes in six Delta counties, while Moses searched for support money. The SCLC's voter registration director, Jack O'Dell, whom Moses had met in New York through Bayard Rustin, was offering to bring Mississippi recruits by bus all the way across the Black Belt to Septima Clark's citizenship classes at Dorchester, and he was flooding Mississippi with SCLC registration pamphlets—"Crusade for the South: Vote," "Why Vote?"—and literacy materials. "We are using the Workshop Booklets, and the old people think the world of them," wrote Sam Block to the SCLC that July. "They tell the others, 'this is my school book.'" To help with Moses' registration campaign, O'Dell urged James Bevel to return to Mississippi from Albany, with his wife Diane and their new daughter.

Shortly after the raid on the Greenwood SNCC office, a summit meeting was convened on the issue of registration funds for Mississippi. VEP director Wiley Branton came in from Atlanta. James Bevel represented the SCLC. David Dennis represented CORE. Aaron Henry, Amzie Moore, and others represented the Mississippi NAACP. James Forman represented the national office of SNCC, and Moses brought his handful of Mississippi organizers. They all gathered in a church basement at Clarksdale, about an hour's drive northwest of Greenwood, and Branton candidly outlined his political dilemma. As director of the VEP, he was responsible to the foundation donors of the money, who were closely associated with the Kennedy Administration. He was also responsible to the heads of the major civil rights organizations, each of whom owned what amounted to a veto over the operations of the politically delicate, legally vulnerable VEP. Many of those people did not favor spending registration money in Mississippi at all. Aside from that, Roy Wilkins did not want to spend money through SNCC, which he considered irresponsible, and certainly not through SNCC in Mississippi, which he considered an NAACP state.

These obstacles easily would have eliminated registration funds for Mississippi had not Wiley Branton emerged as a most unusual bureaucrat. He and everyone else in the church basement knew that to mount anything more than a ceremonial registration campaign, the VEP would have to support the students who were daring to recruit and train pioneer voters. Most of them worked for SNCC, through Moses. To circumvent the opposition of the NAACP, Branton agreed to channel funds through a new smokescreen organization, in the tradition of the MIA and the Albany Movement. It would allow those in the church to act on their mutual trust while protecting them from political rivalries among distant national leaders. That night in Clarksdale, they founded COFO—the Council of Federated Organizations. They wrote rules, drew territories, allotted future funds. The NAACP's Aaron Henry was elected president, an honor that was intended to help soften any opposition from Wilkins. Moses became director of voter registration.

It was a sophisticated piece of political work, but then they stepped into the night air of Mississippi. No such number of strange Negroes could come into a Delta town without attracting notice, especially since the registration projects had raised tension to the threshold of violence. A sheriff's deputy stopped Forman's car outside of town, but let him off with an order to leave the county. One police patrol arrested David Dennis for a traffic violation. Another arrested Sam Block and five others for loitering. Wiley Branton, who had made it out of town unmolested, was obliged to return to Clarksdale the next day to convince the authorities that it was frivolous to charge anyone with loitering in a moving automobile, whereupon he was presented a grossly inflated bill for towing the car from the scene of the arrest. Resigned, Branton paid the bill out of VEP funds. That same day, on his way to the Jackson airport, Branton learned that Block had been rearrested in Sunflower County with Moses and three other SNCC workers. They went to jail on a criminal charge of distributing literature (a leaflet announcing a voter registration meeting) without a permit. This arrest, while legally indefensible, was not quite flimsy enough for a lawyer like Branton to beat down with words. James Bevel showed up at the jail to bail them out.

Moses resolved to avoid Sunflower County for a while, but he felt an overriding obligation to the Ruleville Negroes. The first eighteen people from the registration classes around Ruleville, a plantation town in northern Sunflower County, were scheduled to register in Indianola the next day. Most of them were semiliterate sharecroppers, and Moses had thought their courage so important that SNCC had rented a bus from an out-of-county driver. Rather than disappoint them, Moses went along on the bus ride from Ruleville to the county seat at Indianola. All eighteen endured the registration tests without crisis, though none was accepted as a new voter, but on the way back to Ruleville a highway patrolman stopped the bus. Moses was arrested once again. The unsuccessful registrants went on back to Ruleville behind the news of their attempt, which swept through the county. That night, the owner of the Marlowe plantation drove to the house of sharecropper Fannie Lou Hamer, a stout woman of forty-four from a family of twenty children, and told her that the Klan and the White Citizens Council were sure to harass him because his field hands had been messing in politics. Sounding as beleaguered as he was angry, the owner told Hamer that she must renounce her registration application or leave his plantation, where she had lived for eighteen years. Hamer fled immediately to the home of a couple who had sheltered teachers for the SNCC registration classes.

This was the last day of August. That same night, vigilantes poured gunshots into four homes in Lee County, Georgia, outside Albany. All four belonged to supporters of the SNCC voter registration drive. State investigators counted twenty-four bullet holes in the frame house where the chairman of the Lee County Movement lived with his extended family of twenty. No one was hit. Claude Sitton of *The New York Times* made sure to point out that the chairman was the same man he and Pat Watters had heard sheriff's deputies threaten at the Shady Grove church in July. Four nights later, vigilantes fired three shotgun blasts into the home of a Terrell County woman who boarded summer volunteers in the registration drive. The shots missed Charles Sherrod, who was asleep in a bunk, but wounded a white student in the arm and grazed two others.

.   .   .

By then the pilgrimage of rabbis and ministers had come and gone in the Albany jail. King stayed out of Albany. At first he did so on the slim chance that negotiations might be more productive and less rancorous in his absence, as critics ranging from Governor Vandiver to Attorney General Kennedy and C. A. Scott maintained. When the talks collapsed, however, he continued to stay away for lack of a constructive alternative. He did not have the support "to turn the city upside down and right side up," as he had promised to do. He knew the movement's striking power was in decline. Besides, King felt besieged by pressures from other quarters. His two-month diversion in Albany had cost him not only his vacation but also the revenues from SCLC fund-raisers that were essential to expand the voter registration campaign across the South.

He was giving a fund-raising speech in New York when the phones brought news of two fresh burnings of country churches: Mount Mary Baptist and Mount Olive Baptist in Terrell County, both of them sites for registration meetings and both completely destroyed. Judge Elliott already had denied the Justice Department's request for an injunction based on Sheriff Mathews' highly publicized raid at Mount Olive in July, and Mathews now said there was no evidence of arson at the two churches. FBI agents found plenty of evidence. Poking around in the ruins, wearing their standard FBI business suits, they enraged white bystanders who had gathered to view the destruction. Virgil Puckett went berserk, taking a wild drunken swing at one of the agents and knocking off his glasses. He was arrested for assault.

The next night, in Ruleville, Mississippi, night riders fired shots into two of the three homes providing shelter for volunteers in the SNCC registration campaign. Herman and Hattie Sisson were talking with their granddaughter and a friend, who were spending the night there on their way back to college, when a series of popping noises startled them. "That sounded like a rifle to me," Sisson observed calmly, but in the next instant both college girls tumbled from the couch to the floor, writhing. As Mrs. Sisson described it later, everyone in the house fell to the floor and began hollering, as other shots came spitting though the walls. By the time the two girls went to the hospital—one wounded critically in the neck and head, the other in the leg and arm—there were large pools of blood on the floor and Mayor Dorrough of Ruleville had arrived and was pacing about, clearly upset, talking incessantly. He ordered his men to take Mrs. Sisson to the hospital for treatment of glass cuts, then looked at the bullet holes. "I'm so glad Hattie didn't get shot," he said. Then, calling the sheriff of Sunflower County, the mayor said, "Bob Moses is the cause of all of it. I knowed something like this was going to happen. That's how come I been riding day and night." One of SNCC's summer volunteers rushed in, made a hysterical phone call to Moses in

Jackson, and then composed himself enough to make notes and talk to people, as Moses had instructed. His presence so annoyed Mayor Dorrough at the hospital that he ordered him arrested on the charge of doing the shooting himself as a publicity stunt to raise money for SNCC. He was in jail the next morning when Moses arrived, his car having broken down on the way.

Moses compiled his usual detailed report, running to nine single-spaced pages, and sent copies to SNCC, the FBI, the Justice Department, the news media, and Martin Luther King, anticipating correctly that white officials would move to consolidate the advantages gained by terror. The local newspaper in Ruleville published the names of all the Negroes who had tried to register. Mayor Dorrough ordered city water service cut off at Ruleville's Williams Chapel, the only church in the area that dared to host registration meetings. When U.S. Fidelity and Guaranty canceled the church's casualty insurance from faraway Baltimore, Moses tried vainly to persuade the company to reinstate the coverage. Driven finally from the church, the SNCC volunteers tried to hold classes in homes or in tents, but no one would come. They chopped wood and helped run errands, holding on. "Because it's very important that the Negroes in the community feel that you're . . . going to ride through whatever trouble arrives," Moses explained. "And in general, the deeper the fear, the deeper the problems in the community, the longer you have to stay to convince them."

President Kennedy held a news conference shortly after the shootings in Ruleville. In an opening statement, he denounced Soviet military shipments to Cuba and dismissed Fidel Castro's public claims that Cuba was only trying to protect itself against "imminent invasion" by the United States.* Later, in response to a question about King's telegrams protesting violence against voter registration workers, the President turned just as forcefully on the terrorists in the South: "I don't know any more outrageous action which I've seen occur in this country for a good many months or years than the burning of a church—two churches—because of the effort, made by Negroes, to be registered to vote." He went on to mention the Ruleville shootings as well, and to brand the attacks "cow-

---

* Kennedy ascribed some of Castro's difficulties to the U.S. boycott on trade with the island, but of course he did not mention the highly secret campaign of protracted economic and military sabotage, code-named Operation Mongoose, that the CIA had been conducting under his orders for the previous ten months. Its secrecy, plus the secrecy of Cuba's dealings with the Soviet Union, severely restricted the vision of historians trying to explain the origins of the Cuban missile crisis.

ardly as well as outrageous." "I commend those who are making the effort to register every citizen," he added. "They deserve the protection of the United States Government, the protection of the states . . . And if it requires extra legislation, and extra force, we shall do that."

This was President Kennedy's strongest statement on civil rights to date. Given a shining opportunity to address the issues at the center of the Administration's civil rights strategy—violence and voting rights— Kennedy responded unequivocally. "We appreciate the strong and forthright words from the President of our nation," King said the next night. "We need his moral support. We are praying that these words will be translated into powerful action." He spoke at a prayer service at the ruins of Mount Olive Baptist Church, having led a nighttime car caravan out into Terrell County from Albany. The caravan itself was a daring act, inconceivable before the transformations of the Albany Movement. King announced that Nelson Rockefeller had pledged $10,000 to rebuild the three burned churches, and he presented each of the three pastors with a $1,000 check from the SCLC toward the same purpose.

The Kennedy and King statements proved to be no more than a rhetorical interlude between church burnings, as the I Hope Baptist Church of Terrell County was consumed by flame three nights later, torched by a kerosene bomb. This time, four of the arsonists were so brazen that the first FBI agents on the scene found them still there watching the blaze, drinking beer. Arrested, the four suspects confessed to the FBI. Justice Department lawyers, scrutinizing their statements as to motive, found them difficult to translate in the idiom of the Supreme Court's opaque ruling in the 1944 *Screws* case, but in general they had more to do with hating Negroes than with voting rights. At any rate, this was the interpretation placed upon them in Washington when the Attorney General revealed that the federal government, having solved the case in one day, was surrendering the suspects to Sheriff Mathews for trial in state court. The Justice Department's announcement explained the move as follows: "The evidence in this case was given to local authorities because the FBI investigation established that the persons responsible did not burn the church specifically to intimidate Negroes from registering to vote, Attorney General Kennedy said. . . . The Attorney General personally called Mr. Hoover and commended the quick, decisive action by FBI agents involved in the investigation of this case." Ironically, the four defendants in the arson would be convicted by a state jury—the only conviction in the many such cases in Georgia. All the major cases were "solved," in the sense that the FBI produced a report naming the responsible parties, but few went to trial in federal court and there were no convictions, in part because of obstacles such as Judge Elliott in the federal trial courts.

The Justice Department and the FBI both faced extremely hostile conditions in Southern courts and Klan counties. Both performed poorly at times. In general, two years in office had made Justice officials more rather than less timid about criminal prosecutions in their showcase area of voting rights. Burke Marshall said as much in a private meeting with Fred Shuttlesworth and other civil rights leaders that September, when he warned that the Justice Department offered no "protection guarantees" to those running registration programs in the South. Federal powers were limited, he told them, and so essentially they must look out for themselves. Hearing this, the Negroes complained bitterly that Marshall and others had steered them into voter registration precisely because it was the area of clearest federal authority.

Four more Negro churches were burned in Georgia within ten days after the fire at I Hope Baptist. King was in New York at the time, accepting the death of his hopes for a Second Emancipation Proclamation from President Kennedy. This was difficult for him, as the idea of a great symbolic presidential stroke against segregation long had been dear not only to him but to officials within the Kennedy Administration. USIA Director Edward R. Murrow, for example, had urged the proposal on Kennedy since his first days in office. He said the centennial of Lincoln's attack on slavery offered an ideal opportunity to invoke the full authority of the White House against segregation.

In the summer of 1862, Lincoln had surprised his cabinet with a private reading of his original draft proclamation, which abolished slavery in the areas under Confederate rebellion. He defended it as a war measure that would weaken the Southern economy and force Jefferson Davis to divert more soldiers to security against slave rebellion. Moreover, Lincoln argued, the measure would give the Union war effort a public purpose that would make it impossible for European powers to intervene on the side of the Confederacy. For these reasons and others, Lincoln ignored the objections of some of his cabinet members, saying that he would make public his proclamation as soon as the Union Army achieved a victory in battle. Timing was important to Lincoln, because he did not want the proclamation to be seen as a desperate act. The humiliations of the second battle of Bull Run forced him to wait a month, but only days after the slaughterous stalemate at Antietam forced Robert E. Lee to retreat back to Virginia, Lincoln made good on his word.

Now, one hundred Septembers later, the debate within the Kennedy Administration had nothing to do with a new proclamation but whether President Kennedy should show up at the official ceremony honoring the last one. At a White House meeting, Kenneth O'Donnell startled planners of the event by announcing that he had never heard of plans for Kennedy to make the major address, and had in fact scheduled the President to make a speech outside Washington. "We were amazed," responded a congressman from the delegation, in a letter listing no fewer than a dozen White House commitments made earlier that year, including two conversations with the President himself. Copies of the letter went to the three presidential aides most involved in planning for the centennial—Arthur Schlesinger, Ted Sorensen, and Lee White. A final round of internal lobbying ensued, but O'Donnell held his ground. For the President to appear was to draw attention to the occasion, and thus invite comparisons between Kennedy's performance and Lincoln's.

In New York, raising funds to rebuild the burned churches in Georgia, King had to balance Kennedy's coolness to the Emancipation celebration against Nelson Rockefeller's ardor. This was Rockefeller's day, honoring a president of his Republican Party and summoning up nearly a century of Rockefeller family interest in the welfare of the former slaves. Fittingly, Rockefeller possessed the original parchment of Lincoln's Proclamation. When he invited King to appear with him at the Emancipation dinner of the New York State Civil War Centennial Commission, King's advisers discussed the drawbacks at length. Kennedy still held the power, they said, and was notoriously sensitive about Rockefeller's presidential ambitions. If King embraced Rockefeller too closely, he risked driving Kennedy toward Southern Democrats.

The FBI wiretap on Stanley Levison picked up discussions of the Rockefeller invitation. Was the New York dinner too "Republican," asked the advisers. Soothed by Clarence Jones's discovery that there were Democrats on the New York centennial commission, they turned to the delicate, complicating issue of money. So far, Nelson Rockefeller had delivered only $5,000 of the $50,000 that Wyatt Walker said he had promised to deliver to the SCLC and the Gandhi Society. Now Rockefeller had pledged another $10,000 toward the burned churches. His invitation to King conflicted with a scheduled fund-raiser in New York, so that in effect King was being asked to give up hard funds in part to cultivate the maker of delinquent pledges. This presented a dilemma common to those dependent on philanthropy: whether to call a rich man on his promises. They also debated whether they could safely push to solicit the Emancipation dinner guests—Rockefeller's political friends. Legally, they could not pass the hat at the dinner itself, which was a state function, but could they ask for the mailing list, or perhaps even invite the guests to an SCLC reception across the street? "I don't think . . . this choice [is] as hard as you are making it," Levison advised them. "Governor Rockefeller is a sophisticated man. He knows the need for funds, that that money is in that crowd and it would be a pity not to get it. There isn't a multi-millionaire I know that didn't want to see other people contributing when he contributed. Anything they hate is for them to contribute alone. I don't think it would sit badly unless it was said crudely that Dr. King would not come unless he is assured [of funds]."

At the Emancipation dinner, King criticized President Kennedy's sluggishness on civil rights, pointing among other things to his unfulfilled "stroke of the pen" campaign promise on housing discrimination. Rockefeller followed King with similar criticisms of Kennedy, then packed up the Emancipation Proclamation and headed for the centennial celebration in Washington on Saturday, September 22. He joined a fervent but relatively small crowd on the steps of the Lincoln Memorial. Archibald MacLeish read a poem on Lincoln. Adlai Stevenson eulogized the Emancipator as the pride of Illinois. Robert Kennedy represented the Administration but did not speak; instead a tape-recorded message came over the loudspeakers from President Kennedy himself, who was spending the weekend in Newport, Rhode Island. The tape-recorded speech—final product of all the lobbying—was a skillful address, stirring in its evocations of history. Only specialists in civil rights bridled at the President's summary of events since Lincoln's Proclamation, which consigned race problems generally to the past. "A structure of segregation divided the Negro from his fellow American citizen," Kennedy's voice told the crowd. "He was denied equal opportunity in education and employment. In many places he could not vote. For a long time, he was exposed to violence and to terror. These were bitter years of humiliation and deprivation. Looking back at this period . . . it can be said, I believe, that Abraham Lincoln emancipated the slaves, but that in this century since, our Negro citizens have emancipated themselves." Rockefeller then made a brief speech on the Proclamation itself. Partisan rivalries among the politicians were subdued by the state occasion, then washed completely aside by Mahalia Jackson's performance of "The Battle Hymn of the Republic."

King did not appear at the Lincoln Memorial. He had gone to jail twice more since handing President Kennedy his own dream proclamation, and now he turned with chastened expectations to January 1, 1963—the centennial of the Proclamation's effective date, the Day of Jubilee itself. He hoped Kennedy could be persuaded to do something more dramatic then. More immediately, King was headed for Birmingham, where President Kennedy sent him a warm telegram "on the occasion of the sixth annual convention of the Southern Christian Leadership Conference." Kennedy praised King's "personal conduct and your dynamic leadership," which had gained "the respect and admiration of the great majority of the people of the United States." This telegram was a trophy of the convention, read publicly to the four hundred delegates gathering that September in the heartland of segregation.

The balmy shower of official telegrams was becoming a welcome staple at SCLC conventions. What was new in Birmingham was an undercurrent of impending collision that belied the surface calm of the gala banquets and the usual long-winded committee meetings. For the first time, FBI agents planted informants inside the SCLC convention and sent daily reports to headquarters. And for the first time, the mere fact that King was scheduled to visit a segregated city already had led to an unprecedented—and tentatively productive—round of negotiations with white leaders. In this respect, King achieved more in Birmingham before his plane touched the ground than he had during all the months of battering in Albany.

The tension was the result of two currents that had been eating slowly at the stability of Bull Connor's segregation—one uniting the city's Negroes for protest, the other dividing its whites. Birmingham's parks had been closed all year. Its baseball team was gone. Sporadic Klan violence continued. Since the jailing of Fred Shuttlesworth in January, Negroes had supported what began as a student boycott of downtown stores; at its peak the boycott caused some merchants to complain of a 40 percent decline in sales. And King had planned all year to come to Birmingham —not just with his convention's business but with its manpower, to support Shuttlesworth in his long-awaited showdown with Connor. Moreover, King planned to return in 1963 "for a real mobilization of our civil rights forces," he wrote William Shortridge early in September. Shortridge was Shuttlesworth's treasurer and "connectional man," a whirlwind funeral director of Daddy King's generation, Howard '23, and King Jr.'s fraternity, Alpha Phi Alpha. When night riders sprayed his home with gunfire the previous March, Shortridge had dived safely for cover behind the wall of his front porch as the first slug zipped through the front wall and knocked the telephone receiver from his wife's hand. Since then, Shortridge had erected a small extra bedroom on the side of his porch to house the volunteers who guarded his house every night.

On the whites' side, Chamber of Commerce president Sidney Smyer had been groping slowly for eighteen months—since the shock of seeing front-page photographs in Japanese newspapers of the Birmingham mob attacking the Freedom Riders—toward a solution of the cliffhanger riddle: how to get rid of Bull Connor without so much as mentioning his name. Conceding that Connor was politically untouchable as the elected, independent police commissioner, Smyer and his allies hatched a circuitous plan to remove the office instead of the man. Over months of meetings with lawyers, teachers, civics professors, and assorted do-gooder groups, they developed the idea that Birmingham urgently needed a modern, "mayor–city council" form of government, such as Atlanta and other prosperous cities possessed.

There was realpolitik behind the façade of reform. People could campaign for the new structure without overtly challenging Connor or segregation; they could even tout him for the new office of mayor. If the new city government was ratified, however, the reformers could hope that the marginal Birmingham voter might look for more polish in a mayor than in a police commissioner.* To implement the plan, Smyer first tried to recruit a committee of twenty-five "silk-stocking people" to head a public committee, but the nominees all declined with regret, knowing that Smyer's sleight of hand would not fool Connor. Then Smyer had settled for a committee of five hundred "anybodies," headed by a house painter named William A. Jenkins. There were small businessmen, disc jockeys, union stewards, and even the head of the local Nixon campaign from the last election. Early that September, the committee achieved its first miracle by filing a petition signed by some 12,000 citizens, more than enough to trigger a special election on the proposal for a new city constitution.

The reformers were waiting for a judge to verify the petition and set a special election date when someone reminded them that Martin Luther King was about to come to Birmingham. Under the circumstances, they regarded his visit with such foreboding that they sent an emissary secretly to Atlanta to ask King to cancel the convention. The situation was critical, said the emissary. It was no small task to abolish the office of Bull Connor, who had just received 61 percent of the votes for reelection as police commissioner, and nothing would drive the marginal voters behind Connor more decisively than a racial confrontation. King listened politely and referred the emissary back to Shuttlesworth.

These pressures generated Shuttlesworth's introduction to Sidney Smyer. Never before—in more than six years of sit-ins, boycotts, lawsuits, bombings, and Freedom Rides—had he been granted a meeting

---

* Connor's image problems predated the civil rights movement. In 1951, a rival police officer had raided a Birmingham hotel and arrested the police commissioner for having an extramarital affair with his secretary. Convicted on a morals charge and driven from office, Connor had taken advantage of the school desegregation crisis to make his political comeback. In 1957, running as a bareknuckled segregationist who could protect whites more effectively than candidates from polite society, which he scorned, Connor had regained his old office by the slim margin of 108 votes. Since then he had consolidated his power, to the discomfort of many respected leaders in Birmingham.

with the local "power structure," or, for that matter, with Birmingham's leading white clergy. But a few days before the SCLC convention, A. G. Gaston, the city's top Negro businessman, guided Shuttlesworth to a secret conclave. As they went inside, Shuttlesworth joked that even Gaston with all his money never before had been permitted inside a white hotel in Birmingham. When they arrived, Smyer shook Shuttlesworth's hand, calling him "Doctor." Alluding to the precarious reform movement in Birmingham, Smyer first asked Shuttlesworth to persuade King to stay away, and when Shuttlesworth turned that notion aside, he asked for assurances that there would be no trouble. Shuttlesworth could not help making a speech about how long and how much he had suffered to attract the honor of such a request, but then he denied that the honor itself was worth a truce. He said he had to show the city's Negroes deeds instead of words. So how much segregation would the downtown stores give up to avoid demonstrations? When Smyer parried this question by saying that he couldn't speak for the downtown merchants, Shuttlesworth headed for the door and said, "You all called me to the wrong meeting."

Smyer reconvened them the very next morning, this time in the presence of grim-faced representatives from the major stores: Sears, Loveman's, Newberry's, Greene's, Woolworth's, Pitzitz. It began with an awkward silence, which was broken when Shuttlesworth said he was there to hear what they had to say. After another silence, the man from Loveman's said, "I don't mind desegregating my water [fountains]."

"Oh, no, gentlemen," Shuttlesworth replied. "We're past water now. We have to have toilets. Women have to be able to refresh themselves in your stores."

After pained silences, separated by terse outbursts on both sides, A. G. Gaston attempted to break the stalemate. "You know, your daddy and I got started in business about the same time," he told Loveman. "And you know you got your start among the Negroes like I did. We got our money together. And most of our customers are Negroes. And it looks like you could do something. We don't want demonstrations either, but I don't have the power. I can't stop it. But this man here can stop it." He said Shuttlesworth had the marbles.

Shuttlesworth stood up after another silence, saying they should all go pray that the best would come out of this. As he was leaving, he turned to Louis Pitzitz, owner of Birmingham's largest department store. "Mr. Pitzitz," he said, "the last time, they arrested two students in your store. This time it's gonna be different. Martin Luther King and I are gonna sit on your stool, and we aren't gonna walk out. They're gonna have to drag us out. And the press will be there. And you'll be out of business all over Alabama. That's just the way it is."

As Shuttlesworth and Pitzitz glowered at each other, Loveman rose hastily to his feet. "Wait a minute," he said. "I can just call the maintenance man and just paint over that sign in the restroom." He was referring to the "Whites Only" sign.

This was the beginning of a breakthrough. In exchange for integrated water fountains and restrooms, Shuttlesworth agreed to hold a convention without demonstrations. There was much backsliding and quibbling over seemingly trivial details. For example, the "Whites Only" signs must be painted over rather than removed, so that the store owners might more easily disclaim responsibility if Bull Connor thundered down upon them for violating the local segregation laws. In the end, a fragile bargain was struck. Each side worried that the other would renege.

Pressure was also building inside the FBI. Bureau officials, clearly alarmed by the repeated phenomenon of mass arrests in Albany, took note of a report from the Savannah office that the Negroes from the summer jailings "were all trained" at Septima Clark's Dorchester retreat. The report was grossly exaggerated, in that only a tiny fraction of the Albany demonstrators had been to Dorchester, and also misleading, in that Clark's classes focused on literacy and voter registration, not protest. Nevertheless, Bureau officials were inclined to credit the report, in the belief that such unprecedented upheavals must be fomented by cadres. This was the view of people far away, steeped in conspiratorial intelligence work, who never had gone near a mass meeting. It stripped the demonstrators of appreciable human motivation, leaving them more like robots and yet somehow more fanatical. In short, they became more like Communists to the Bureau, and it was seen as no small confirmation on that score that the man in charge of Dorchester was Jack O'Dell.

Bureau officials took word to Attorney General Kennedy that O'Dell, linked to Levison by the wiretaps, was a threat to Birmingham, and Kennedy undertook to handle the problem privately, through his aide John Seigenthaler. As former editor of the Nashville *Tennessean*, Seigenthaler had come to know Rev. Kelly Miller Smith, from whose church James Lawson, Diane Nash, and John Lewis had organized the first of the Nashville sit-ins. Smith sat on King's SCLC board. Before he left for the Birmingham convention, Smith received an official but confidential contact from Seigenthaler, who told him the government was gravely concerned about King's alliance with a man of known Communist associations. King should sever all contact with O'Dell, and in no case should he allow him in Birmingham.

Smith promptly relayed the message to King, who treated the matter as an intriguing nuisance. In context, King decided, the indirect warning meant that the Kennedy Administration was accommodating its own internal McCarthyite forces while hinting to King that there was a relatively painless way out: O'Dell should not go to Birmingham. He called O'Dell in to inform him personally. O'Dell chafed at the news. He was scheduled to lead several workshops at the Birmingham convention— indeed, he was at the center of the SCLC's voter registration drive, as well as its collaborative efforts with COFO and other groups, which were by far the biggest hidden successes of the past year. O'Dell grumbled that it was a ridiculous compromise to admit that he might be a threat to the nation's security and then respond by grounding him for a conference. King said he had seen much sillier things in politics.

O'Dell remained behind in Atlanta when the SCLC convention opened that Monday, September 24. Birmingham's downtown merchants delayed painting over their "Whites Only" signs until the last moment, but they did it, causing amazement among the Negroes. Adhering to the agreement, neither side trumpeted the change to the press, for fear of provoking Bull Connor. Still, the victory put Shuttlesworth into higher spirits than usual. At the Monday-night mass meeting in St. John's Church, he gave such a rousing introduction to Wyatt Walker as King's advance guard that Walker seized the pulpit and cried, "I have come to Birmingham to ride the Bull!" Jackie Robinson, recently elected to the Baseball Hall of Fame, also arrived for the convention that night, but the Birmingham police refused to allow him a motorcade to the church. Shuttlesworth told the packed crowd to obey the police. "No one knows what's going to happen the next few days," he said.

Publicly, the SCLC convention in Birmingham caused about as much stir as a Rotary luncheon. There were no demonstrations. The news was drenched that week with events in Mississippi, as J. H. Meredith's quest to enter Ole Miss reached its climactic stages. Already Governor Ross Barnett once had blocked Meredith in a dramatic physical confrontation. (The Mississippi legislature had made Barnett himself the emergency university registrar, in a ruse to circumvent the court order binding the regular registrar.) Promptly after that, the full Fifth Circuit Court of Appeals hauled the registrar and the university trustees into a hearing, threatened them with contempt, and secured a promise that they would register Meredith.

On Tuesday, September 25, as King was arriving in Birmingham, Chief U.S. Marshal James McShane and John Doar picked Meredith up at Dillard University in New Orleans. Doar was a volunteer courier for a sheaf of the Fifth Circuit's latest orders against evasion and obstruction. Meredith said good-bye to his wife and to Medgar Evers, who had been counseling him for his lonely walk into the maw of Ole Miss. At the New

Orleans airport, Doar and McShane waited awkwardly while Meredith
went downstairs to the colored snack bar and restroom. Then the three
of them flew to Jackson, Mississippi, in a Cessna 220 owned by the U.S.
Border Patrol. Mississippi Highway Patrol aircraft flew alongside them
the whole way. In Washington, Al Rosen fed Burke Marshall a stream of
FBI reports on the intentions of Barnett, the trustees, and a few local
sheriffs who were threatening to arrest Meredith on any convenient
charge.

The trio proceeded by car to the Federal Building in downtown Jackson,
where Registrar Robert Ellis had agreed to perform his loathsome duty of
admitting Meredith. They found no state officials present, however.
When Doar reported this newest wrinkle to Washington, Marshall
tracked them down by telephone at the Woolfolk State Office Building,
some blocks away. The president of the trustees told him they were
trying to comply with the order but were restrained—being practically
in the custody of Barnett and the legislature, which had summoned them
to testify about the university crisis. Another trustee told Marshall that
the Fifth Circuit order no longer applied, because Meredith had been late
reaching the Federal Building. Marshall short-circuited the dispute with
phone calls to Judge Tuttle in New Orleans, by which he obtained a
phone-relayed extension of the deadline. The trustees eventually relented on the time but held fast on the place, insisting that the extension
did not apply to the part of the order that specified the Federal Building.
By then it was almost dark. Robert Kennedy decided to give in and send
Meredith to the Woolfolk Building.

"Can you clear the crowds so we don't make a big circus?" Kennedy
asked Governor Barnett.

"You would have a big space," Barnett replied. "They're not going to
bother him."

Soon the long wait was over. Doar, McShane, and Meredith pushed
their way through a jeering crowd of two thousand outside the Woolfolk
Building, then up the elevator to the tenth floor and through another
crowd in the corridor. Barnett, bathed in television lights, blocked the
threshold of Room 1007. Legislators inside climbed atop chairs and tables
to obtain a better view. As Doar moved forward to explain the Fifth
Circuit's orders to Barnett, television and radio stations transmitted the
confrontation to Mississippians across the state. Barnett "interposed"
Mississippi's sovereignty, as embodied in his own person, between Meredith and the university officials, who maintained an outward willingness to obey the orders.

"Which one is Meredith?" Barnett inquired, sparking titters of laughter, as the familiar and well-known Meredith, standing in front of Bar-

nett, was the only Negro in sight. Barnett read to Meredith his second proclamation of interposition, ending that he did "hereby finally deny you admission to the University of Mississippi." A Rebel yell went up from the crowds gathered around transistor radios ten floors below. When Barnett refused Doar's request to enter, some legislators chanted, "Get going! Get going!" One cried, "Three cheers for the governor!" They hooted the Meredith trio along its path of retreat, then filed back to their chambers in triumph. One state senator hailed Barnett's stand as "the most brilliant piece of statesmanship ever displayed in Mississippi." Another vowed to persevere "regardless of the cost in time, effort, money, and in human lives."

An angry Robert Kennedy called a cheerful Barnett as Meredith was heading for Memphis that evening. "He is going to show up for classes tomorrow," said Kennedy.

"At Ole Miss?" replied the startled governor. "How can you do that without registering?"

". . . I think they arranged it," said Kennedy. ". . . It is all understood."

"I don't see how they can," said Barnett. "They're going to give him special treatment? They can't do that, General."

Ten minutes later, Kennedy called Barnett again, after Marshall and the other Justice officials in his office convinced him that he must give Barnett precise notice of Meredith's arrival on the Ole Miss campus. Otherwise, Barnett could disclaim responsibility for any violence against him. Kennedy relayed the notice along with a stern lecture on the supremacy of federal law. He pointed out that all the judges of the Fifth Circuit were Southerners. "But anyway, Governor," he added, "they will be down there at ten o'clock."

"Ten o'clock will be all right," Barnett said politely. Later that night, three judges of the Fifth Circuit signed an order commanding Barnett to appear before them on Friday in New Orleans for a hearing on whether Barnett should be held in contempt of court. The impending collision of races, and perhaps even armed forces, dominated the next day's news. *The New York Times* published three Meredith stories on its front page beneath a banner headline: U.S. IS PREPARED TO SEND TROOPS AS MISSISSIPPI GOVERNOR DEFIES COURT AND BARS NEGRO STUDENT.

Doar, McShane, and Meredith flew back to Mississippi the next morning in the same Cessna, this time to Oxford. They arrived without troops or any other support force, as Robert Kennedy wished to avoid any appearance that the federal government required abnormal measures to obtain compliance with the law. When an escort of Mississippi highway patrolmen unexpectedly abandoned them near the campus gates, the three of them stepped forward alone to confront Lieutenant Governor

Paul Johnson, who was backed by formidable rows of state troopers and sheriffs. This third standoff ended much like the others, except that Chief Marshal McShane, having heard through the telephone maze that the Mississippians might yield to a face-saving show of force, tried to push his way by. "Governor," he told Johnson, "I think it's my duty to try to go through and get Mr. Meredith in there."

"You are not going in," Lieutenant Governor Johnson replied.

"I'm sorry, Governor, that I have to do this, but I'm going in," said McShane. After a few physical rebuffs, he had to conclude that the rumors of capitulation were false. He and Doar sounded Meredith's third retreat, which pushed euphoria still higher in Mississippi.

King addressed the SCLC convention that night, defending the Albany Movement as a political success even though friend and foe alike were branding it a failure. Behind a merciful curtain of media disinterest, he spent most of his time planning a coordinated assault that would avoid the errors of Albany. With Shuttlesworth, he assembled special caucuses of the Alabama leaders. They scheduled a People-to-People recruitment tour early in the new year, plus a voter registration drive with VEP funds. The plan was to build toward a Christmas shopping boycott as the first stage of a planned confrontation "somewhere in Alabama." King remained coy about the target city, knowing that the meetings were infiltrated. Also, he worried about attacking Birmingham as long as negotiations finally were producing results. On this point Shuttlesworth had no such doubts. "They took those signs down because you were coming to town," he told King, "and they'll put 'em up again just as soon as you leave."

With Governor Barnett vowing to scorn the Fifth Circuit's orders and the federal government threatening openly to back Meredith with soldiers, commentators compared the confrontation to the events preceding Little Rock or even Fort Sumter. Robert Kennedy took advantage of the pressure to bear down on Barnett in nearly continuous telephone negotiations. By their voices, two Americans scarcely could have sounded more foreign to each other. Kennedy spoke a high-pitched, nasal Bostonian, brimming with energy but often garbled by pauses and staccato asides. Barnett, in a low Mississippi drawl, fashioned sentences of cleaner syntax, masking his nerves behind homespun amiability. What united them was the fraternal belief that politicians weathered crises best by accommodating the interests of other politicians—by skirting public controversies to take care of each other. Accordingly, Kennedy never pressured Barnett with the prospect of jail or overwhelming military force. He did not vow to "convert the state of Mississippi into a frog pond," as the Chicago *Tribune* threatened to do in 1865 when the legislature tried to impose onerous Black Codes on the newly freed slaves. Nor did Barnett swear to block the schoolhouse door or die the fire-breathing death of a Rebel martyr. Instead, Barnett focused on Kennedy's need to get Meredith into Ole Miss with the least possible public display of federal power, while Kennedy addressed Barnett's need to defend segregation as vigorously as any Mississippi rival might claim to have done.

Drifting inexorably into public relations, they fashioned an agreement to stage a fake showdown at the gates of the campus. Two dozen armed U.S. marshals would support Meredith, and Barnett, yielding reluctantly to superior force, would retire to the new task of getting Meredith out of Ole Miss. Ironically, this solution faltered when Kennedy's desire to appear accommodating did not quite satisfy Barnett's desire to look as though he was being pushed around.

"Hello, General," said Barnett that afternoon. "I was under the impression that they were *all* going to pull their guns. This could be very embarrassing. We got a big crowd here, and if one pulls his gun and we all turn, it would be very embarrassing. Isn't it possible to have them all pull their guns?"

"I hate to have them all draw their guns," Kennedy replied, "as I think it could create harsh feelings. Isn't it sufficient if I have one man draw his gun and the others keep their hands on their holsters?"

"They must all draw their guns," Barnett insisted. "Then they should point their guns at us and then we could step aside."

By late afternoon, as Doar and McShane were preparing to escort Meredith into Mississippi on his fourth attempt to register—traveling this time by car from Memphis—Barnett and Kennedy were still fashioning the scene. Barnett was afraid that Kennedy might let on that there was a deal, which would finish Barnett in Mississippi politics. Kennedy, having reduced Meredith's military support to a level that made Barnett uncomfortable, was assuring Barnett that he would portray their pretend showdown as a real one.

"You understand we have had no agreement," said Barnett.

"That's correct," Kennedy replied.

"I am just telling you—everybody thinks we're compromising," said Barnett.

Kennedy assured Barnett there would be no appearance of a compromise. "I am just telling you that we are arriving and we are arriving with force," he said.

Actually, they both knew that Meredith would be arriving with practically no federal force, and this aspect of the plan began to look less promising as ominous reports reached Kennedy about the size of the mob gathering in Oxford. Mississippi was caught up in a defiant holiday mood. Horns blared in the streets. Confederate flags flew. Radio stations, on emergency programming, filled the time between Ole Miss bulletins with recordings of "Dixie." The FBI relayed stories of vigilantes converging from distant states with rifles and beer coolers, swearing to defend Mississippi. As Meredith's small caravan left Memphis, Kennedy feared that the federal escort, though small enough for him and large enough for Barnett, might be too small to handle a riot. He wanted Barnett's assurance that state authorities would protect Meredith once the marshals left the campus, but by then Barnett preferred to think of the state forces as weak and submissive. "After he gets in," he told Kennedy, "you certainly don't expect us to guard him all the time. . . ."

"Whatever is necessary, Governor," said Kennedy. "Whatever is necessary to preserve law and order."

"But, General," protested Barnett, "I declare I don't think I could agree to guarantee the man after he gets in. When he gets in he is just one boy."

"I had better call it off, Governor," Kennedy said sharply, but he let the caravan proceed.

An hour later, after touring the crowded, gun-laden streets of Oxford, Barnett called Kennedy again. Fear stripped most of the artifice from his voice. "There are several thousand people here in cars, trucks," he said. ". . . There is liable to be a hundred people killed here. It would ruin all of us. Please believe me . . . a lot of people are going to get killed. It would be embarrassing to me."

"I don't know if it would be embarrassing," Kennedy replied. "That would not be the feeling." Barnett's bluntly selfish comment seemed to snap Kennedy out of his scriptwriter's perspective.

"It would be bad all over the nation," Barnett said.

"I'll send them back," said Kennedy. His order flashed from the Justice Department through military channels to a communications plane. From there it was beamed down to Doar in the Meredith caravan, which was hurtling down one of Mississippi's new interstate highways at nearly a hundred miles per hour. They pulled into a filling station in Batesville, Mississippi, just west of Oxford, so that Doar and McShane could call Robert Kennedy personally to confirm the retreat. To the stoically apprehensive Meredith, sitting in the car, Batesville seemed deserted— stripped of its population, who, from the sound of the radio reports, had motored ahead to join all of Mississippi in defending against him. He was relieved when they turned back toward Memphis.

Events raced at collision speed. THOUSANDS SAID READY TO FIGHT FOR MISSISSIPPI, announced the Jackson *Daily News,* which urged readers to learn a resistance song titled "Never, No Never." Outside Mississippi, the news centered on the challenge to the Kennedy Administration. In the third set of triple-tier headlines that week, *The New York Times* blared: U.S., TO AVERT VIOLENCE, CALLS OFF NEW EFFORT TO ENROLL MEREDITH; SENDS HUNDREDS MORE MARSHALS. In New Orleans, on Friday, a Fifth Circuit panel tried Governor Barnett in absentia and found him guilty of contempt. Lieutenant Governor Johnson promptly received the same verdict. The three judges sentenced them to indefinite prison terms beginning on Tuesday, unless they purged themselves by securing Meredith's registration before then. Robert Kennedy, charged with executing this sentence, faced a new political dilemma. Barnett called Kennedy after lunch and secured a promise that no Negro marshals would be used on the next registration attempt.

Although days earlier Kennedy had branded Barnett a "loony," citing a report that he had been struck on the head by an airplane propeller, and although he now saw Barnett's followers as mad, latter-day brownshirts, still he shrank from using force to support Meredith, because to do so would not only reveal an exhaustion of domestic authority but blot America's reputation in the world. His only alternative was to collaborate privately with Barnett to produce an inspired theatrical effect, worthy of Shakespeare. None but a genius could hope to orchestrate the desired illusion of normalcy and control, especially since Kennedy and Barnett simultaneously sounded public war trumpets that attracted hordes to overrun their stage. The threat of a jailed governor stimulated no new ideas for the script, and by five o'clock the Pentagon was flashing a DEFCON 3 alert to units from Texas to New Jersey: prepare to move within four hours.

King's convention was dull by comparison, as the three hundred SCLC delegates passed resolutions at a closing session late that Friday afternoon. One called upon the Justice Department to correct lapses in the protection of constitutional rights around Albany, Georgia. Another commended James Meredith for courage in seeking to enroll at Ole Miss. King, in the lolling drone of closing announcements, was reminding his audience of major SCLC events ahead—such as Mrs. William Kunstler's gala December fund-raiser in suburban New York, starring Sammy Davis, Jr., and Peter Lawford—when one of the white men in the audience walked to the stage and lashed out with his right fist. The blow made a loud popping sound as it landed on King's left cheek. He staggered backward and spun half around.

The entire crowd observed in silent, addled awe. Some people thought King had been introducing the man as one of the white dignitaries so conspicuously welcome at Birmingham's first fully integrated convention. Others thought the attack might be a staged demonstration from the nonviolence workshops. But now the man was hitting King again, this time on the side of his face from behind, and twice more in the back. Shrieks and gasps went up from the crowd, which, as one delegate wrote, "surged for a moment as one person" toward the stage. People recalled feeling physically jolted by the force of the violence—from both the attack on King and the flash of hatred through the auditorium.

The assailant slowed rather than quickened the pace of his blows, expecting, as he said later, to be torn to pieces by the crowd. But he struck powerfully. After being knocked backward by one of the last blows, King turned to face him while dropping his hands. It was the look on his face that many would not forget. Septima Clark, who nursed many private complaints about the strutting ways of the SCLC preachers and would not have been shocked to see the unloosed rage of an exalted leader, marveled instead at King's transcendent calm. King dropped his hands "like a newborn baby," she said, and from then on she never doubted that his nonviolence was more than the heat of his oratory or the result of his slow calculation. It was the response of his quickest instincts. This impression struck a number of others, including perhaps the assailant himself, who stared at King long enough for Wyatt Walker and some of the others to jump between them.

"Don't touch him!" cried King. "Don't touch him. We have to pray for him." His words, signaling an end to the immediate crisis, released a flood of noise, some delegates loudly repeating King's instructions, others shrieking hatred at the attacker. Several preachers moved to enclose the assailant in a protective circle. Walker, Andrew Young, Bernard Lee, and Birmingham's Rev. Edwin Gardner consulted furtively about what to do. One of them jumped to the microphone to hold back the crowd, saying, "We can handle this on the stage." Others, seeing that people were bolting outside with the news, gave orders that all the doors should be locked, fearing a lynch mob of Negroes or a second wave of attackers. King kept talking quietly to the white man, saying no one was going to hurt him, and the man said very little except to mumble that he believed in white supremacy and that Sammy Davis, Jr., was married to a white woman. As King and the preachers escorted him slowly offstage to a private office, a hastily organized quartet of singers moved to the microphone to hold the crowd, singing "I Want Jesus to Walk with Me" and the somber slave spiritual "Steal Away to Jesus." James Bevel interrupted to say this was no funeral—Dr. King was all right, and they had weathered a stern test of nonviolence. It was a joyful occasion, he declared, as he started them off in a rendition of "I'm on My Way to Freedom Land," which gathered volume until the auditorium shook.

King hushed them when he returned, holding an ice-filled handkerchief to his face. Rosa Parks, mother of the bus boycott, stopped him briefly to administer her favorite remedy for headache: two aspirin and a Coca-Cola. King then announced that he and the assailant had been able to talk calmly in the office, and that the man had presented himself as a soldier on a mission for the American Nazi Party. His refusal to press charges infuriated the Birmingham police officers who arrived at the auditorium, as it put their boss, Bull Connor, into a perverse predicament. Having breached his fundamental political rule—which he had enforced against First Lady Eleanor Roosevelt herself, among many others—to allow an integrated SCLC convention in Birmingham at all, Connor did not hesitate to point out that a white man could not have attacked King at a lawfully segregated meeting of Negroes. Under duress, Connor had permitted the integration, just as he had permitted the signs to come down in the stores, in the hope of holding business support against the new city constitution. For all his strained tolerance, he reaped only a crazed "Nazi" and the prospect of unwelcome publicity. With King refusing to press charges, Connor had no choice but to have the department bring them itself. The Birmingham police persuaded Roy James to plead guilty and hustled him off to serve thirty days.

Wyatt Walker, trying to get the news out, was stymied temporarily because the few major reporters who had come to Birmingham long since had departed to cover Ole Miss. Finally he tracked down a young *New York Times* reporter who was sympathetic and trusting enough to write a story datelined Birmingham, as though he had been there. The reporter, being at risk himself for the deception, could do no more than identify the attacker as a "self-styled Nazi." No firmer description reached the news world, but FBI agents advised headquarters within hours that James was a member of the American Nazi Party, and that his home address was a Nazi "dormitory" outside Washington, D.C. His FBI rap sheet showed previous arrests for violence in New Orleans and his native New York. Almost immediately, police intercepted a letter from Nazi Party commander George Lincoln Rockwell, who wrote "Lieutenant" James that "your heroic deed has put new heart into hundreds of people who . . . have protested the outrage of sending a white American to jail for punching a communist-nigger agitator." Adding, "I know how much you hate jails, Roy," Rockwell promised to secure James's prompt release and closed with "Heil Hitler!" His letter, along with other reports of organized violence against King, lay buried in the files.

When the SCLC convention left town, a Birmingham judge ordered a November referendum on the new city constitution. Bull Connor, having tarnished his segregationist credentials for no political reward, lost patience with the blandishments of reform politics. He promptly sent his men to notify the downtown store owners that they were in violation of city ordinances, and the "Whites Only" signs reappeared one by one.

From his home in Atlanta, with a swollen jaw and a bruised back, King watched the conclusion of the Ole Miss saga on television. On September 29, the day after the James attack in Birmingham, the screen showed the arrival in Oxford of former Major General Edwin Walker, who, disciplined for insubordination, had resigned from the U.S. Army in flaming public protest against what he called the Kennedy Administration's "collaboration and collusion with the international Communist conspiracy." Walker already had gone on the radio to rally volunteers, confessing that he had been "on the wrong side" when he carried out Eisenhower's orders to integrate Little Rock's Central High School five years earlier. "Barnett yes, Castro no!" he declared. "Bring your flags, your tents and your skillets! It is time! Now or never!" Other cameras showed trucks and cars already cruising the streets of Oxford. Intelligence reports picked up Klan Klaverns mobilizing from as far away as Florida. Barnett's desk was stacked with telegrams offering services to the defense of Mississippi.

That Saturday afternoon, Robert Kennedy concluded that the situation was grave enough for him to bring the President himself into the confidential talks with Barnett. In the Oval Office, historian Arthur Schlesinger joined Kennedy, Burke Marshall, and Kenneth O'Donnell, all seated expectantly around the President as the call to Barnett went through. "Go get him, Johnny boy," the Attorney General told his brother with a tight smile, as though spurring on a champion boxer. The President responded with a breezier levity, rehearsing a fake greeting that went, "Governor, this is the President of the United States—not Bobby, not Teddy, not Princess Radziwill." Then Barnett came on the line and President Kennedy, turning serious, was promptly deflected. Barnett asked whether he had talked with the Attorney General that morning about the Attorney General's latest talk with one of Barnett's aides, Tom Watkins, and the President, despite frequent asides with his brother, could not catch up with the third-hand conversation. This gave Barnett an opening to suggest that Kennedy wait for the Barnett aide—"really an A-1 lawyer," said the governor—to bring his unspecified idea personally to Washington. Kennedy agreed to have the Attorney General receive him, but asked what Barnett intended to do about the Tuesday deadline.

"I want to think it over a few days," Barnett replied.

"Well, of course," said Kennedy. "The problem is, Governor, that I got my responsibility just like you have yours."

"I realize that," said Barnett. "And I appreciate that *so much.*" He spoke the last two words with a long earnest drawl, stopping the conversation. Reemphasizing his hope that Watkins could find a way out, Barnett started to sign off. Then abruptly, and sincerely, he said, "I appreciate your interest in our poultry program and all those things."

President Kennedy stifled a laugh until the phone connection was broken, then chuckled in wonder that Barnett could mention livestock in the midst of the constitutional crisis. "You've been fighting a sofa pillow all week," he told the Attorney General. By this he seemed to mean that Barnett's warm, simple manner made him an easy mark, but by the objective results the governor was no pushover for anyone. The President's personal authority—carefully reserved until now—had just come to bear in the emergency with no effect except to ratify a postponement. Segregationists were streaming into Oxford more rapidly than Justice Department officials could reassemble their Freedom Ride–style civilian force of prison guards, Border Patrol agents, and deputy marshals. That force was gathering at the naval air base outside Memphis, having stripped three prisons and the Mexican border of federal manpower, but it numbered only five hundred at maximum strength.

The White House conferees decided that something stronger than words was required to force a change in Barnett. They resolved to nationalize the Mississippi National Guard, though there was some doubt as to whether its units would fight other Mississippians in behalf of James Meredith and the Kennedy White House. The Attorney General immediately set lawyers to work on the necessary presidential proclamations, and the President himself called his chief speechwriter, Ted Sorensen, in the hospital, where he was recovering from a case of White House ulcers. Kennedy asked Sorensen to rouse himself to write a speech for him to deliver on television. Sorensen agreed, saying he would craft some ideas in light of the fact that "the Republicans are taking the straight Ross Barnett line."

"Except Eisenhower," laughed Kennedy. He appreciated the irony of looking more favorably now upon the Little Rock precedent. "Eisenhower's taking a little away from 'em," he said.

"No, I mean the Republicans in Alabama," said Sorensen, making the point that Kennedy would be safe from partisan attack at least in the Deep South: both parties would attack him.

A second call to Barnett went out from the Oval Office an hour after the first. This time Robert Kennedy prepared the way by telling Barnett that they need not wait for Watkins to come all the way to Washington,

as Watkins "would be wasting his time. . . . He doesn't have any suggestions," said Kennedy. "He just told me, Mr. Governor."

"I thought he did have," said Barnett, sounding puzzled.

"Well, he didn't," said Kennedy. "I mean he said something about
sending the, Meredith, uh, sneaking him into Jackson and getting him
registered while all of you were up at . . ."

"Yeah?" said Barnett.

". . . at Oxford. But that doesn't make much sense, does it?"

"Well, I don't know," drawled Barnett. "Why? Why doesn't it? That's
where they ordered him to go at first, you know." The idea was that
Barnett would continue to lead the charge of segregationists up to the
Ole Miss campus at Oxford for the scheduled confrontation; meanwhile
the Kennedys would sneak Meredith into deserted Jackson and register
him there in accordance with the court order from one of the earlier
registration attempts. By this devious plan, Barnett could swear to the
people of Mississippi that he had not given an inch on segregation, and
that Meredith had been registered only by the conniving tricks of the
Kennedys.

Not surprisingly, Barnett had stalled until he heard this idea come out
of Kennedy's mouth rather than his own, but then he embraced it as a
mighty fine suggestion. His enthusiasm led Kennedy to reconsider the
scheme. Its obvious drawback was that while Meredith might leap the
great hurdle of registration, he would wind up an hour's drive from
the Oxford campus, and in the meantime the federal government would
have allowed Barnett to gather Mississippi's army of resistance to prevent him from setting foot there. Perhaps registration was only fool's
gold. In this light, Kennedy pushed Barnett to guarantee that state forces
would maintain order in Oxford. The President came back on the line to
press the same question.

"Oh, they'll do that," Barnett assured him. He said his 220 highway
patrolmen, backing up the local police, would "take positive action, Mr.
President, to maintain law and order as best we can . . . and they'll absolutely be unarmed."

Kennedy stumbled over this surprise twist: "I understa—"

"Not a one of 'em'll be armed," Barnett said proudly.

But the problem was, said the President, "what can they do to maintain
law and order and prevent the gathering of a mob . . . What can they do?"
Kennedy wanted the state forces armed to the teeth when it came to
quelling the mob, and nonviolent only in confronting Meredith, but Barnett refused to be so discerning. He stuck blithely to the previous negotiating scenarios in which Robert Kennedy had addressed the reality
being screamed in the headlines—that the state forces were lining up

against Meredith. The President found himself in the backwash of earlier deals, and the demands of secrecy made his predicament the more vexing. He was like a farmer trying to convince a sly mule that the way to the feed house went through the plow fields. Nevertheless, Kennedy and his advisers concluded that Barnett's ruse promised a step forward. Once Meredith was registered, the game would shift in their direction. When Barnett's next call came in, the President undertook again to move him off the nonviolence idea as applied to the mob at Oxford.

There were rumblings of movement at the White House soon thereafter. Pierre Salinger called the television networks to cancel President Kennedy's scheduled address that night. Burke Marshall called the Justice Department to tell the lawyers to stop drafting the emergency proclamations. "We've got a deal with Barnett," he said. As happy as the draftsmen were to hear that they could go home on a Saturday evening, Marshall's glad news left them with doubts. Norbert Schlei's premonition was so strong that he kept his secretary there until nearly midnight typing up the required presidential documents, just in case. Meanwhile, Ross Barnett went to see the Ole Miss Rebels play the Kentucky Wildcats at Jackson's Memorial Stadium. The war fever of the political crisis boosted the normal emotions of the football rite to the heights of pandemonium, and by halftime the crowd was shouting "We want Ross!" in a deafening roar. Barnett made his way to the fifty-yard line, where he raised a fist of defiance and cried out over the loudspeakers: "I love Mississippi!" The roar intensified, and Barnett, nearly overcome, rose above it to let loose another shout: "I love her people!" Then at the peak: "I love our customs!" These three short sentences were enough to ignite pre-battle ecstasy. People were ready to die. This was as close to, and yet as far from, the fervor of a Negro mass meeting as segregationists came. No one could know that this football game would be the last militant race rally among respectable whites for at least a generation.

In Washington, Norbert Schlei had just gotten home when Burke Marshall called to say that the deal was off again. Barnett could not go through with it. "The President wants to sign those documents," said Marshall. Schlei made it down to the White House and upstairs into the residential quarters by midnight Saturday. President Kennedy, looking over the proclamations necessary to call out the troops, asked, "Is this pretty much what Ike signed in 1957 with the Little Rock thing?" Told it was, Kennedy signed, handed the documents back to Schlei, and rapped the table as he stood up. The moment engaged his sense of history. "You know," he remarked, "that's General Grant's table." He said goodnight, but then stopped Schlei on his way down to face the White House press corps with the documents. "Don't tell them about General Grant's

table," Kennedy cautioned. He did not want to antagonize the South any
further with reminders of the Civil War.

Robert Kennedy and Barnett resumed the search for a way out on
Sunday, while the Pentagon was relaying notice to Mississippi Guard
units that they had been placed under the President's command. It was
difficult to tell whether the great swell of segregationist sentiment had
fortified or encumbered Barnett, who told Robert Kennedy that now he
required a truly spectacular show of force to camouflage a retreat. He
proposed a large-scale version of the gun-drawing plan, this time with
some three hundred Mississippi lawmen and three hundred "soldiers"
(apparently some sort of honor guard drawn from the volunteer vigilantes) arrayed in three lines at the Ole Miss gate to block Meredith.
Barnett would stand at their head. If Kennedy would send a superior force
of federal agents to confront them with guns, he said, he could order
them to step aside without losing face.

Now Kennedy balked. Barnett was talking troop numbers larger than
the garrison at Fort Sumter in 1861, and he was maneuvering so that
Kennedy, unlike Lincoln, would appear to be the aggressor. The governor
kept saying that all the Mississippians would be harmlessly unarmed,
but there was a limit to what Kennedy would believe. He told Barnett
that the grand surrender scheme was unacceptably dangerous. According
to Burke Marshall's record of the conversation, the Attorney General
"said that he thought the matter had gone beyond the stage of politics."

What Kennedy meant was that it had gone beyond the stage of political
courtesy, as he promptly fired a well-aimed dart at Barnett's political
nerve center. The President, he told Barnett, was committed to address
the nation that night, and he would be forced to say that he had called
out the troops because Governor Ross Barnett had broken yesterday's
agreement to register Meredith.

"That won't do at all!" Barnett roared.

"You broke your word to him," Kennedy insisted.

Shocked into disbelief, Barnett asked, "You don't mean the President
is going to say that tonight?"

"Of course he is," said Kennedy. He said they had a complete record of
the times of the phone calls, the circumstances, the words. "We have it
all down," he declared, springing the threat of phone intercepts he had
compiled surreptitiously.

Barnett fairly howled in pain. It got him nowhere to protest that the
Kennedys had given him solemn promises of secrecy, as the Attorney
General only replied that Barnett had lied too, and that a lie canceled a
promise. Barnett pleaded. Couldn't the feds at least storm fences and
barricades around the campus? Couldn't the Attorney General keep the

President from mentioning the prior agreements? Kennedy said no, pressing his advantage. He knew that millions of Americans would consider it a grievous misdeed to lie to a President. He also knew that the governor's fear was precisely the opposite: Barnett was petrified of the revelation that he had *agreed* with the President in a secret integrationist deal. He would have welcomed a thousand lies to keep this one truth hidden.

A new idea popped up from the depths of Barnett's misery. "Why don't you fly him in this afternoon?" he asked suddenly. As a variation on the trick place idea, he suggested that they register Meredith at a trick time. They could sneak Meredith onto the Oxford campus while Barnett continued to rally all of Mississippi for the expected showdown on Monday or Tuesday. Then Barnett could claim he had been hoodwinked. This idea became the heart of a new bargain, although arguments erupted sporadically over lies that were told and lies that were ruined. Burke Marshall and Tom Watkins came on the line to soothe tempers and piece together a detailed plan. Kennedy agreed to keep Barnett well posted on all Meredith's movements. Barnett, in return, agreed to let Kennedy clear the language of the statement in which Barnett, crying foul tyranny and pledging to fight on against integration, would recognize Meredith's registration as a *fait accompli.*

The Justice Department boiled immediately into action, having rehearsed this drill during the Freedom Rides. Any lawyer who happened to be strolling the hallways that Sunday was in danger of being flung aboard a military transport plane. Within hours, the head of the Tax Division found himself commanding a "communications center" in the basement of the post office in Oxford, Mississippi. Press spokesman Ed Guthman shuttled between telephones and troop bivouacs, as did legal draftsman Norbert Schlei. Airborne, the legal shock troops discovered among themselves even an old Harvard football chum of Robert Kennedy's, who had been in Washington that weekend for a White House conference on narcotics. When they landed, Nicholas Katzenbach assumed the role of field commander of the combined civilian forces. Kennedy had stopped him on his way out of the Justice Department to say, "Hey, Nick. Don't worry if you get shot . . . 'cause the President needs a moral issue." Katzenbach laughed at the warm irony and the taut grin. This was the Kennedy panache—bright amateurs dashing cavalierly into semi-war.

James Meredith, plucked from the professional football game he was watching on television at the Memphis air station, flew south with Doar and McShane. At six o'clock that afternoon they looked down from their Cessna to behold the stunning transformation of the little Oxford airport. The field was lined with Army trucks, buses, jeeps, cars, and assorted government planes, plus piles of tents and riot equipment. Other supplies included dramatic items like giant searchlights. Katzenbach and Guthman met the plane when it landed, their Jetstar having cruised in from Washington two hours earlier. By then they had already posted the main body of three hundred marshals around the university's administration building, known as the Lyceum. Katzenbach had assumed that Meredith would be registered there, but he advised Doar that university officials had talked Burke Marshall out of registering on Sunday, for religious reasons. This change confronted Katzenbach with the unhappy decision of whether to leave the marshals all night at the Lyceum, pending registration the next morning, or to move them. Nothing would be easy, he reported, as downtown Oxford was jammed and tense. The first sightings of the marshals, with their white helmets and yellow armbands, had touched off alarms by radio bulletin and word of mouth. A hostile crowd swelled across the tree-dotted lawn called the Grove, outside the Lyceum. Students chanted "Go to hell, JFK!" and other unfriendly slogans.

The only good news was that Barnett, true to the deal, had provided escorts of sullen but cooperative highway patrolmen. Some were helping to hold off the crowds at the Lyceum, while others escorted the prize onto the campus by a back road. By six thirty Sunday evening, little more than a half-hour after his plane landed, Meredith had picked out a room at deserted Baxter Hall. Katzenbach called Robert Kennedy to report the success, then posted marshals with orders to shoot anyone who tried to break into Meredith's room. As he and Doar returned to the Lyceum to negotiate with university officials over the logistics of the next morning's registration, Meredith pulled books from his briefcase and began to study.

President Kennedy had postponed his national address until ten o'clock Washington time—eight o'clock in Mississippi—wanting to make sure that Meredith was safely at Ole Miss. There was nearly an hour and a half to spare when Robert Kennedy called Governor Barnett in Jackson to report that Meredith was safely installed in the dorm. The only deviation from the plan was that he had arrived by car instead of helicopter, and Kennedy advised the governor to revise his draft statement accordingly. Barnett replied glumly that it was too late to correct the minor error. He had no secretary to retype the press release. Within minutes, Barnett stunned Mississippi with his rueful announcement that the state's defenders had been "physically overpowered" at Oxford.

From this last smooth click of the complicated plan, events tumbled toward the abyss. By the time Katzenbach and Doar reached the Lyceum, the crowd outside had reached a thousand in number, mostly students. Anger was rising among them as dusk fell. While some shouted the rhythmic cheer "Go to Cuba, nigger lovers, go to Cuba!" others lobbed pebbles, then rocks, at the lines of marshals standing outside. Worst of all, a Mississippi state senator was inside the Lyceum with a proclamation, signed by Governor Barnett, authorizing him to take command of the highway patrol. Senator George Yarbrough was making no secret of his intention to withdraw the highway patrolmen from the scene. Now that the federal government had "invaded" Ole Miss and defiled it with Meredith, he told Doar and Katzenbach, the feds could defend themselves. Some of the highway patrolmen milling around were only too glad to hear it, but Doar and Katzenbach knew from the crowd's ugly mood that withdrawal would invite disaster. Students were slashing the tires of the Army trucks parked outside. Somebody sprayed a truck driver in the face with a fire extinguisher. The darkness was making it harder for the marshals to dodge the flying rocks.

Doar pleaded for time. Vainly hoping that the students would get tired, he asked Yarbrough to hold the highway patrol until nine, but Yarbrough said no. Each panicky report from outside made Doar desperate for more time and Yarbrough itchy for less. Meanwhile, Katzenbach relayed word of the emergency to Robert Kennedy in the White House Cabinet Room, and Kennedy leaped to the phone with the only proven threat he had: that a withdrawal by the highway patrol would break Mississippi's promise to maintain order, in which case President Kennedy, who was preparing to go on national television, would announce that Mississippi leaders had made and then reneged on a deal. With raw warnings both to the Mississippi officials in the Lyceum and to Barnett in Jackson, he finally induced Barnett to order the highway patrol to stay. Doar and the others were masking their relief, so as not to provoke the mortified and rebellious Mississippians, when marshals burst in shouting that the patrolmen were drifting away. Now it was the Mississippians who masked their satisfaction, saying this could not be true. They pointed to some patrolmen still on duty.

By this time the federal officials and the Mississippians no longer trusted their own eyes, let alone each other, and dozens of contradictory rumors flew at once. At first, Doar and Katzenbach preferred to believe the telephone reports over what they thought they saw happening outside the Lyceum, because the telephones connected them with those in authority. Eyewitness accounts of the withdrawal flew from the bank of pay phones inside the Lyceum to Robert Kennedy or Burke Marshall in the Cabinet Room, or to Ramsey Clark in the Justice Department command center, only to be refuted by those talking simultaneously to distant authorities such as Barnett or an Ole Miss trustee. Under the circumstances, the facts of the incipient riot fought their way up the pecking order in remarkably good time. Historian Walter Lord later pieced together files showing that FBI agents first overheard the withdrawal order on the highway patrol radio frequency at 7:25. Within nine minutes the startling news was being shouted from the post office "communications center" to the Lyceum and up to the White House, steadily beating back contrary reports. By 7:40, it was generally established that most of the highway patrolmen had vanished.

It was 9:40 Washington time, twenty minutes before President Kennedy went on the air. Network technicians were adjusting their equipment in the Oval Office. In the Cabinet Room, Ted Sorensen went over the speech with the President, while Robert Kennedy reacted to the mounting apprehension coming over the wire from the Lyceum. When Ed Guthman told him the marshals might have to use tear gas, Kennedy said he still hoped to avoid it. Guthman scrambled to fetch Senator Yarbrough and Colonel Birdsong of the highway patrol, who argued directly with Kennedy about how many patrol officers had received Barnett's order to stay at the Lyceum. By now each minute was crammed with shouts, fresh advances by the mob, new injuries, and new forms of chaos.

The first flesh-to-flesh violence victimized newsmen, as in the Freedom Rides. Beaten by students, a television cameraman from Dallas struggled to what he thought was refuge inside his car, only to have the windows and fenders kicked in. As the contagion spread across the Lyceum lawn, students attacked two other reporters. An Ole Miss professor tried to rescue one of them but was himself beaten to the ground. Molotov cocktails—gasoline in Coke bottles—spread flames at the feet of several marshals. Senator Yarbrough, racing outside from his phone call with the Attorney General, was horrified to see that the marshals had put on their gas masks. The whole idea of dressing the marshals in civilian clothes had been to make them appear less military, less antagonizing to the Ole Miss students, but now they looked like ghoulish space warriors. Chief Marshal McShane ordered the men to remove their masks in exchange for Yarbrough's desperate promise to make personal pleas for an end to the violence. Yarbrough plunged out into the swirling mob, but his shouts had no greater effect than any other loud noise. The students, darting closer and closer to the Lyceum, added bricks to their projectiles, and when the first big piece of lead pipe felled a marshal, McShane shouted for the tear gas. Cannisters were fired into the crowd from the marshals' line all around the perimeter of the Lyceum. Battle chaos curled backward, as some choking marshals had forgotten or lost their gas masks. And because there had been no warning to the few remaining highway patrolmen struggling against the mob, these most dutiful of the Mississippi officers were rewarded with a dose of gas from behind at point-blank range. A casing knocked one patrolman unconscious and the gas nearly killed him. Mississippi officials screamed with rage at their federal allies.

Inside the Lyceum, Colonel Birdsong was still on the phone with Robert Kennedy, who did not think well of his suggestion that Governor Barnett fly in from Jackson to make a speech to the mob. Ed Guthman, standing next to Birdsong, grabbed the telephone when he heard the thumping report of the first tear gas grenades. "Bob, I'm very sorry to report we've had to fire tear gas," he said. "We had no choice."

It was 7:58 in Oxford. A minute later, Burke Marshall left the Cabinet Room for the Oval Office with news that Ole Miss had deteriorated into a full-scale riot, but the President was frozen in the commanding glare of the television lights. "Good evening, my fellow citizens," he began, facing the cameras from behind his desk. "The orders of the court in the case of *Meredith* v. *Fair* are beginning to be carried out." Meredith was safely on campus, he said. National Guard units had not been used. The rule of law was prevailing, and students and professors alike could return to their normal activities. "This is as it should be," said the President. Twice he emphasized to the nation that the federal government had not been party to the Meredith case. He announced the name and home state of each Fifth Circuit judge who had voted to send Meredith to Ole Miss, adding that his responsibility to carry out their order was "inescapable." "I accept it," he said.

The speech was written on a tight line, crafted to reach undecided white Southerners. Not mentioning Governor Barnett, he neither criticized segregationists nor embraced Meredith's cause. He praised Mississippi specifically as the home of Lucius Lamar, of "four Medal of Honor winners in the Korean War alone," and of Sergeant Jake Lindsay, who in 1945 "was honored by an unusual joint session of the Congress." Then he spoke directly to Ole Miss: "You have a great tradition to uphold, a tradition of honor and courage, won on the field of battle, and on the gridiron, as well as the university campus . . . The eyes of the nation and all the world are upon you and upon all of us . . . I am certain the great majority of the students will uphold that honor. There is, in short, no reason why the books on this case cannot now be quickly closed in the manner directed by the court."

President Kennedy's speech disposed of the Meredith case so convincingly that some troop commanders in Memphis released their men from DEFCON 2 alert (prepare to move immediately). Desire and pronouncement were being overrun by fact, however, as the President quickly discovered. Back in the Cabinet Room, he joined the Attorney General, Sorensen, O'Donnell, Marshall, and congressional adviser Larry O'Brien for a grim siege watch that was destined to last all night. Two or three of them talked on telephones at once, pausing to relay reports to the others. "They're throwing iron spikes," Robert Kennedy told the President. "And they're throwing Coke bottles, and they're throwing rocks." The huddled leaders absorbed erroneous reports that the gassed highway patrolman had died, and accurate ones that it was almost impossible to get injured marshals through the mob to a hospital. One early idea was to enlist football coach Johnny Vaught, a sainted figure at Ole Miss, to make a speech urging the students to disperse. Periodic bulletins on this effort punctuated the early reports that the great cloud of tear gas was only spurring on the rioters: "He [Vaught] said he wants to keep this, all the football squad out of it . . . It's a hell of a squad . . . His wife says he's out . . . Listen, why don't we get Bob to try to call him from here? . . . His wife may be lying to you . . . ."

Within an hour of the President's speech, the first shotgun blasts rang out at Oxford. One marshal was bleeding profusely from a neck wound, and his colleagues, lacking either first-aid equipment or an ambulance, despaired for his life. A few minutes later the first high-powered rifle shot hit a border patrolman in the leg. As casualties mounted, the marshals placed their wounded along the wall inside the Lyceum. Outside, many of the student rioters fled the gunfire, giving way to the adult roughnecks who had converged on Ole Miss. The mob grew above two thousand around the Lyceum, with untold others roaming the campus on foot and in cars.

Gallows humor prevailed at the White House, where the President quipped that he remembered "riots like this at Harvard." During lulls in the incoming calls, the leaders fidgeted glumly. They discussed what to do about a tip that James Reston intended to write a column in *The New York Times* suggesting that the Kennedy Administration was more anxious to meet with the Soviets than were the Soviets to meet with Kennedy. The President attacked the story, ticking off Soviet invitations from memory. "We ought to knock it down tonight," he said. "That's just kicking Reston right in the balls, isn't it . . . Do you want to call him up? Or is that just gonna make him mad?"

The besieged Katzenbach called in again. Those in the Cabinet Room could hear only Robert Kennedy's end of the conversation: "Do you want these troops in there? . . . He got hit by what? . . . Is he gonna live? . . . The state police have left?" Marshall broke in to announce that he had just had a talk with Barnett, who said the troopers "*can't* have pulled out." They *had* pulled out, Kennedy replied. Then Marshall repeated Barnett's assurance that he had just talked with the highway patrol and that everything was under control. Frustrated, the leaders in the Cabinet Room began denouncing the insurrectionist harangues of General Walker, which led them into a discussion of the novel *Seven Days in May*, about a military coup in the United States. President Kennedy remarked that the book's president seemed "awfully vague" to him, but that the coup-plotting general was "a pretty good character." On the phone, Marshall almost plaintively asked someone whether Coach Vaught was "doing any good." On another phone, the Attorney General quietly consoled John Doar, saying he knew Ole Miss was "a long way from Wisconsin."

"I haven't had such an interesting time since the Bay of Pigs," sighed President Kennedy. His brother, assigning himself comparable responsibility for this new disaster, wryly composed a press release for his own sacking: "The Attorney General announced today, he's joining Allen Dulles at Princeton Univ—" Nervous laughter cut him off.

When they ran out of tear gas at the Lyceum, and the volunteer who tried to drive through the mob to fetch new supplies was delayed—feared lost—the leaders in the Cabinet Room decided to move the regular Army units down from Memphis by air, and to move a Mississippi National Guard unit to the campus from the local armory in Oxford. Waiting anxiously for confirmation of troop movements by military officers of unproven loyalty, the President thought of the Shah of Iran. "This is what they must do every night in Teheran," he remarked dryly. Then came a maddening disparity of communications: the cries of desperation arrived instantly from Katzenbach's pay phone inside the Lyceum, but responding orders for help seemed to vanish into a maze of radio hook-ups. "Well, they have to call the Attorney General's office to get the Attorney General's office to call the Secretary of the Army," Marshall explained in exasperation, "and the Secretary of the Army to call to Memphis, and then . . ." When he reported that one unit was known to be forming to receive orders, Sorensen objected that the unit had formed ten or twelve hours earlier. "I saw them form on television," he said. Marshall said they must be forming again.

Robert Kennedy's voice chilled the room shortly before midnight. "They're storming where Meredith is," he said. "They're storming where Meredith is." Bands of rioters had discovered Meredith at Baxter Hall, and the battered marshals at the Lyceum were in no position to move across the campus to help protect him. The men in Washington clung to their telephones, scrambling for ideas. O'Donnell said he feared the riot might turn into a lynching. The President placed an urgent call to Barnett in Jackson. Robert Kennedy tried to reach Katzenbach on the pay phone, but Katzenbach was out rallying his men in the face of new shootings. The Attorney General wound up speaking with his old Harvard football friend, Dean Markham, who told him the marshals could not defend themselves with tear gas alone. O'Donnell, listening in, broke the news to the Cabinet Room that "the marshals are now going to start firing." They had sidearms, he said.

President Kennedy returned to report that Barnett had parried his demand for highway patrolmen, saying the best way to rescue Meredith was to remove him from Ole Miss.

"I *can't* get him out," Robert Kennedy said miserably, hearing the President. "How am I gonna get him out?"

"That's what I said to him," the President replied. "Now the problem is, if he can get law and order restored . . ." He paused, then said, "Okay, we'll move him out of there if he can get order restored."

The decision to withdraw Meredith was impossible to carry out, which rendered it easier for Kennedy to make. And now fresh waves of chaos superseded the Barnett negotiations. Three more marshals had just been shot, Larry O'Brien announced. Listening in on the line, Ken O'Donnell remarked that Ed Guthman was "so scared he can't talk." Robert Kennedy tried to talk Katzenbach out of authorizing the marshals to return gunfire. "Can you hold out if you have gas?" he asked. ". . . Is there any way you could figure a way to *scare* 'em off?" Katzenbach's anguished reply made the Attorney General back off this last suggestion. "Sorry," he said sheepishly, but the marshals held their fire.

About that time a call came in from one of Guthman's assistants. When busy men declined to accept an underling's call, Evelyn Lincoln, President Kennedy's secretary, agreed to take a message for the Attorney General, whereupon she heard the assistant say in a precise, disembodied monotone that "a reporter for the London *Daily Sketch*, whose name is Paul Guihard, G-U-I-H-A-R-D, was killed in Oxford just now. His body was found with a bullet in the back, next to a women's dormitory."

At midnight in Washington, Katzenbach told Robert Kennedy that he needed regular troops—as many as possible. Like Guthman, he spoke with soldierly remorse, blaming himself for failing Kennedy in his prolonged effort to avoid using soldiers. Kennedy took the blame, sent the troops, and summoned Guthman back to the phone to discuss what they would say to the press. "We're gonna have a hell of a problem about why we didn't handle the situation better," he said.

The riot went on all night, as the mob showed astonishing persistence. Rioters sent a bulldozer, then a car, crashing toward the Lyceum as a battering ram. They wounded 160 of the marshals—28 by gunfire—and sent a stray bullet into the head of a local juke-box repairman, killing him. In the Cabinet Room, the leaders absorbed the reports of injury one by one until dawn. They heard that flying wedges of students were attacking Baxter Hall, that flying wedges of marshals were trying to break out with wounded men. Robert Kennedy stressed "how important it is to keep Meredith alive." The leaders adjusted stoically to the two deaths. O'Donnell suggested that the Administration "hit the London papers" with the death of Guihard, who, as a reporter, guaranteed widespread news coverage. "A good story over in Europe," someone said.

What nearly broke them was the waiting. Robert Kennedy, who blamed himself for waiting too long to summon the military, alternately joked, whimpered, seethed, and cursed when the night dragged on past the arrival times promised by the generals. Army Secretary Cyrus Vance* and Division Commander Creighton Abrams† had assured the White House that they could airlift soldiers from Memphis to Ole Miss within an hour, but it took that long for the sixty-five-man Mississippi National Guard unit‡ to reach the campus from the local armory in Oxford. After false sightings and interminable delays, the National Guard trotted loyally up to the Lyceum to stand alongside the battered marshals. ("One of them was just wounded," Larry O'Brien finally announced to the Cabinet Room, "so they know they're there.") No more reinforcements arrived for some three hours, during which time most of the night's injuries were sustained. Both Kennedys spoke sharply to the brass. "I have a hunch that Khrushchev would get those troops in fast enough," O'Donnell sighed. "That's what worries *me* about the whole thing."

A bone-weary Katzenbach was talking with President Kennedy when joyous shouts went up that regular troops had been sighted outside the Lyceum. "Just a minute, Mr. President," said Katzenbach. "They may be here now. Please stay on the line while I confirm it." Katzenbach dashed off, shouting back orders not to let anyone touch the phone because the President was waiting. Returning seconds later, Katzenbach was mortified to discover that the man holding the receiver was not his aide but a reporter. Far from seizing his scoop, however, the reporter was so awed by the thought that the President of the United States was on the other end of the line that he had been unable to move or speak, much less ask a question. Katzenbach grabbed the phone to say, "They're here, Mr. President."

---

* Later Secretary of State under President Carter.
† Later commander of U.S. military forces in South Vietnam.
‡ Commanded by Captain Murry Faulkner, the novelist's cousin.

Meredith's room smelled of tear gas a few hours later when Doar came to pick him up. With Guthman and McShane, they climbed into the same Border Patrol car that had carried them to the first registration attempt eleven days earlier. Then shiny and new, its doors now were pockmarked with bullet holes, its windows shattered by bricks. McShane put army blankets on the backseat to protect them from the shards of glass as they rode to the Lyceum for registration. Soldiers stood on the Grove, holding back students who had gathered to witness the surrender. Meredith—unknown and withdrawn, temperamental, practical, of military bearing and yet erratically sentimental—said it was then that he heard Mississippi whites call him "nigger" for the first time in his life. An hour later, escorted by marshals, he attended his first class in Colonial American history.

The soldiers, once marching, proved even more difficult to stop than to start. Long after the campus had quieted to Meredith-taunting and petty vandalism, new units piled in on top of each other until there were some 23,000 soldiers—three times the population of Oxford. The Marines got in on it; so did the Air Force. No fewer than 10,000 troops scrambled for a riot alarm on the night of October 11, surrounding what turned out to be a pre-engagement "pinning" serenade on the porch of a sorority house. Ordinary soldiers, while dodging a few rocks and grinning at the blistering obscenities they received from otherwise demure coeds, found enough humor to relieve the tedium. They named their tents "Andersonville" and "KKK HQ." A giant sign proclaimed one latrine the "Governor's Mansion."

Political ramifications helped pin the troops down in Mississippi, as neither the generals nor the politicians wanted to look as though they were backing down from Governor Barnett's torrent of indignant rage. All official Mississippi joined the governor in blaming the riot entirely on "trigger-happy marshals" and other federal intruders. Senator Eastland charged that the marshals had "provoked the students and others." Lieutenant Governor Johnson, in a private complaint forwarded to Burke Marshall, charged that the tear gas "affected my lungs and my throat and caused, as the doctor put it, a blood clot upon my lungs." The Mississippi senate passed a resolution expressing its "complete, entire and utter contempt for the Kennedy Administration and its puppet courts." A Lafayette County grand jury indicted Chief Marshal McShane for inciting the riot. The Mississippi legislature's official report, oozing with self-pity and trampled virtue, charged the marshals with "planned physical torture" and other atrocities against Ole Miss students. This document caught the attention of President Kennedy, who lamented that such a brazenly fantastic inversion might one day be taken seriously by historians. Firsthand experience with Ole Miss made the President doubt his old Harvard professors, who taught that Northern fanatics trampled upon an innocent South after the Civil War. "It makes me wonder," Kennedy said privately to Sorensen, "whether everything I learned about the evils of Reconstruction was really true."

President Kennedy, while insightful about the effects of racial passions upon the perception of history itself, took steps toward a renewed mythology. To protect the racial sensibilities of Mississippi, he stripped Negro soldiers out of the military units at Ole Miss. Like Governor Barnett, he went out of his way to avoid mentioning that Meredith was a Negro. The President and his brother ignored most of Governor Barnett's slanderous accusations, and in fact they tasked the best legal minds in the Justice Department to find a way *not* to collect the contempt fines imposed on Barnett and Johnson. There might have been persuasive tactical reasons, as they did not want to renew the constitutional crisis, but such small steps consistently beckoned the Administration to minimize both the significance and the racial texture of the Ole Miss crisis.

President Kennedy's most effective political response to the Ole Miss riot was to move on to other things. Almost never did he mention the subject in speeches, nor did he exercise his famous aptitude for reviewing and interpreting political events during informal interviews. His power to define what was news consigned the Ole Miss story quickly to the back pages. The soldiers remained practically unnoticed at Ole Miss until the last five hundred departed late in the summer of 1963, after Meredith received his degree. The climate of the times helped contain the story. Had the riot occurred later, in the era of the "live network feed," synchronized scenes of the Ole Miss rioting before, during, and after President Kennedy's national address might have been broadcast with jarring effect, making the President appear Pollyannish or incompetent. As it was, however, the sequence of events was blurred to his advantage, making the riot appear to be a rude answer to Kennedy's timely appeal. Friendly newspapers went to great lengths to adjust the speech to the riot. *The New York Times* went so far as to report that Kennedy "qualified his optimism most carefully" in his address, "and indeed made clear that the Government was waiting anxiously to see how Mississippi officials and citizens behaved."

The Ole Miss crisis left people feeling victimized on all sides. Mississippians and other Southern leaders howled against the invasion. The formerly deputized marshals recovered from their wounds and went back to regular duty at prisons and border crossings. Kennedy's political advisers, realizing that all their efforts to accommodate Mississippi had served only to blanket the South with bumper stickers screaming FEDERALLY OCCUPIED MISSISSIPPI and KENNEDY'S HUNGARY, were reinforced in their belief that taking risks for integration invited political suicide. As for Negro leaders, all of whom praised President Kennedy in public for doing what was necessary to get Meredith registered, the sense of victory was hollow. NAACP lawyers, who had handled Meredith's case alone for nearly two years, felt shunted aside by Justice Department lawyers who had taken control of their case and even physical custody of Meredith.

Martin Luther King complained privately that President Kennedy had summoned the nation to nothing more positive than a grim obedience to law. In Kennedy's nationwide address there had been talk of burdens and closed books but not a word of freedom, fresh beginnings, or renewed hope. For King, by contrast, the issue went far beyond his identification with Meredith to touch his core conviction that human beings could transcend enemy-thinking. At stake was nothing less than the capacity to lighten the stain of evil and demonstrate the possibility of justice in the world's design, which for King was the realization of God's presence. His moral intensity in this regard struck President Kennedy as narrow and stifling. King, on the other hand, had heard enough glowing talk of Mississippi's gridiron traditions—and read enough of the political dickering between Mississippi and the Administration—to sink into profound depression. As much as he admired President Kennedy for his stylish command of the modern world, King knew that Kennedy and Barnett still had more in common with each other than either had with him. Their performance at Oxford, he wrote, "made Negroes feel like pawns in a white man's political game." He blended this lament into a bleak assessment of 1962 as the year civil rights lost ground in national politics. No longer the "dominant issue" of domestic debate, it had receded since the year of the Freedom Rides and of the Kennedy Administration's early cry, "We will move!" King too had receded, as measured by his ineffectiveness in Albany, and his criticism of the Administration no doubt reflected his fear that no matter how mightily he shouted and sacrificed, he remained a cork in Kennedy's ocean, left to rise and fall with its tides.

EIGHTEEN

TO BIRMINGHAM

In October 1962, CIA officials obtained photographic intelligence that Soviet nuclear missiles were being shipped to Cuba. "Can they hit Oxford, Mississippi?" asked the President, facetiously suggesting that Fidel Castro and the Russians could do worse than to obliterate the site of his recent vexations. The President kept his nerve during the crisis, if not always his humor. He convened his war chiefs to debate whether to bomb, invade, or quarantine Cuba to root out the missiles, and when it came time to brief congressional leaders, the fever of emergency was so high that Air Force planes retrieved Congressman Hale Boggs from his fishing boat in the Gulf of Mexico, first dropping him an SOS in a plastic bottle.

C. B. King was in Washington, pleading unsuccessfully for federal prosecution of Sheriff Campbell for caning him in July. When President Kennedy announced the naval quarantine of Cuba, King rushed homeward, driving down the East Coast past closed businesses and deserted towns, listening to bulletins on military movements and prayer services, and on his door found a note from his wife saying she had moved the entire family to Clarence Jordan's Koinania Farm for fear that the military bases near Albany would make prime targets for Soviet missiles. Hundreds of millions of people in scores of countries shared similar apprehensions. Certainly not since World War II, and perhaps never, had so many people experienced world politics so vividly at once.

On Sunday, October 28, Premier Khrushchev agreed that the Soviet missiles would be withdrawn from Cuba. In Birmingham, Bull Connor and the other two city commissioners were holding a secret negotiating session with leaders of the fire department. While greatly relieved that the world had not blown up, they quickly turned to gritty local politics: the city commissioners promised the firemen a million-dollar raise if they would vote against the referendum on the new city charter. Bargaining went on in blissful ignorance that a reform sympathizer among them was operating a clandestine tape recorder. The result was an extraordinary series of radio ads, in which a firefighter was heard asking, "Do we get the raise regardless of how the election comes out next Tuesday?" and the voice of Mayor Arthur Hanes replying, "Absolutely not. You don't get your raises unless *we* are here to give it to you." An announcer then came on the air urging Birmingham to "stop corruption in city hall" by voting for the new charter. The ads exposed the stuff of dirty patronage —and the inevitable higher taxes to pay for it. This civic embarrassment was exactly the sort of shock the reformers needed to bury the segregation factor in the referendum, and on election day the voters unexpectedly approved the mayor–city council proposal. The miracle seeded by the Mother's Day beatings of the original Freedom Riders advanced another stage, as Bull Connor's job was abolished. If he wanted to keep ruling Birmingham, he would have to run for mayor in a special election the next March. Connor was teetering in power, making the city a slightly weaker colossus of segregation against the campaign being plotted by Shuttlesworth and King.

Elsewhere, people made glowing new resolutions, as though granted a rebirth. Political analysts, while groping for the secret arrangements through which Khrushchev's retreat had been secured, freely acknowledged that President Kennedy had faced down Armageddon. The Oval Office became even more of a hallowed shrine, and the Camelot mood returned. By lucky coincidence, a talented Kennedy mimic named Vaughn Meader taped a comedy album called *The First Family* on the very day Kennedy announced the quarantine of Cuba. The album quickly sold a million copies, pushing past the debut album of folk trio Peter, Paul and Mary to the top of the pop charts, alongside "He's a Rebel" by the Crystals and "You Are My Sunshine" by Ray Charles. In the afterglow of the missile crisis, presidential humor became a national fad. Even political detractors, outside Mississippi, laughed at Meader's parody of the Kennedy foibles: the President's flat-palate accent, his speedreading, his chasing daughter Caroline around the Oval Office, his remarks on snuggling down in a bed full of Kennedys ("Goodnight, Jackie . . . Goodnight, Bobby . . . "). By paradox at the extreme reaches of fame, humor helped make the Kennedy legend both human and supernatural.

Spectacular success gave the President freer rein to pursue his own interests, which were decidedly international rather than domestic, and the very nature of the missile crisis underscored his point that the global contest was of paramount importance. The tonic of national relief made it easier for people to slough off the troublesome, entrenched dilemmas of race. Civil rights "no longer commanded the conscience of the nation," wrote King, who discovered that while fickle conscience did not operate well in an atmosphere of fear or ignorance, neither did it flower on abundant zest. The white world became too happy for civil rights. Such misalignments of perspective exasperated King in his struggle to lead whites and Negroes to see the same truths. Even the bitterest Negro, he said, must study cross-racial vision. This was the "added demon" necessary to survive in a predominantly white world. Trying at once to explain whites to Negroes and Negroes to whites, King felt all the more acutely the "anxieties and sensitivities" that "make each day of life a turmoil . . . another emotional battle in a never-ending war." The Negro, he said, "is shackled in his waking moments to tip-toe stance, never quite knowing what to expect next, and in his subconscious he wrestles with this added demon."

On October 26, a New Orleans newspaper published a story flatly declaring that Jack O'Dell was a "Communist who has infiltrated to the top administrative post in the Rev. Martin Luther King's Southern Christian Leadership Conference." Citing "a highly authoritative source," the unsigned article identified O'Dell as a "concealed member" of the party's national committee who for years had been "carrying out his Communist party assignments" in civil rights work.

This surprise attack caused dissension to erupt within King's own camp. King already knew that O'Dell had been expelled from the National Maritime Union, and that he had lost his insurance job in Montgomery after being called before the House Un-American Activities Committee as a suspected Communist. He wanted to make sure there was nothing deeper within O'Dell's past, nothing violent or sinister. Wearily, O'Dell told King that he was not a party member, as the article alleged, much less a member of the party's national committee, but he knew people who were. In the past, he had attended their meetings, and in 1956 he had written an article on Louisiana racial politics for a Communist publication. O'Dell traced his HUAC subpoena to such associations. Only four years earlier, congressional investigators had branded O'Dell a fiendish automaton, "part and parcel of the communist conspiracy," scorning not only his professions of idealism but his Negro identity.

HUAC COUNSEL: Do you honestly feel, and are you trying to make this committee and the people of this country believe, that you, a member of the Communist conspiracy, responsive to the will of the Kremlin, are in truth and in fact, concerned with the welfare of the Negro people of this country?

O'DELL: I wouldn't try to make you believe anything.

King did not doubt that O'Dell's labor for the SCLC was sincere. All that was understood, but it was also irrelevant. O'Dell, by his guileless insistence that the Communist program ought to be debated like any other, as in France or Italy, ignored the savage realities of Cold War politics in a white culture, where one brand of enemy-thinking was easily hitched to another. Politically, what mattered about the newspaper article was its public impact. Where did it come from? What did it mean? King saw the story as the second "signal" in two months—first the friendly warning from Washington through Kelly Miller Smith and now a hostile attack in print. These were detailed, official-sounding charges of subversion. The embattled SCLC could scarcely hope to survive a sustained barrage of such propaganda. King told O'Dell the entire SCLC board was upset. "What can I do?" he asked.

O'Dell analyzed the article as a likely plant by police or HUAC investigators in New Orleans. It mentioned the fact that his home in New Orleans had been raided. His recommendation to King was to ignore the attack. Only one small paper seemed to have picked up the story, and the matter would probably die out. To accept the challenge of satisfying segregationists of the purity of one's ideology was to lose in advance, O'Dell warned. If King felt compelled to answer the article, O'Dell would swear that he did not owe allegiance to any foreign power, nor advocate the overthrow of the U.S. government by force, but otherwise he would refuse all interrogations about his political beliefs. He would refuse to renounce the Communist Party or his Communist friends, even so far as the facts allowed. "I have nothing to apologize for," he said.

Although King agreed with O'Dell that a free society betrayed itself by policing beliefs, he could not bring himself to leave the article unanswered. To break the chain of public suspicion, he decided that he must refute the connection between O'Dell and the SCLC rather than the one between O'Dell and the Communists. On November 1, without seeking to publicize it, he made available on request a statement of defense. "It is totally inaccurate and false to state that Mr. O'Dell is Southeastern Director of the SCLC," he declared. "He has not only never been director but was never considered for the position." From there, King minimized his association with O'Dell to the point of falsehood, stating that O'Dell "has functioned purely as a technician with 90 percent of his work taking place in the north, where he resides, and involving the mechanization of our mailing procedures. He was briefly and temporarily filling in in some areas of voter registration, but ceased functioning there long before this publicity appeared." O'Dell had resigned "to avoid embarrassment to SCLC," the statement went on, and King had "accepted it pending further inquiry and clarification."

Privately, King assured O'Dell that all this was only for public consumption, that the "further inquiry" was already over and O'Dell was back on the staff. He never left for a moment, in fact. O'Dell submitted as gracefully as he could, but he was a proud and independent sort. It only weakened King to allow himself to be drawn into the game of denial and half-truth, he grumbled, and it hurt to be the one denied. Between the New York mail-room staff and the people processing VEP paperwork, O'Dell figured he had more people reporting to him than did Wyatt Walker. Yet King pretended barely to know him.

The New Orleans article was an extremely unpleasant distraction for King, who hoped fervently that the issue would fade away. Political fears caused him to dissemble and equivocate. Indeed, his behavior paralleled President Kennedy's course on civil rights. Painful as it was for King to hurt his own colleague, more than a few of his allies wished he had treated O'Dell more severely. When a lawyer in New Orleans sent the news clipping to Lotte Kunstler in New York, for instance, Kunstler's immediate reaction was to fear that this one charge of Communist infiltration might ruin her Sammy Davis fund-raiser for the SCLC on December 11. She did not consider such apprehensions farfetched or paranoid. On the contrary, she had seen two Scarsdale women wreck a benefit for the Freedom Riders earlier that same year on far weaker allegations. The women, wives of stockbrokers affiliated with the American Legion, had filed suit to stop the benefit as subversive, and failing in that, had recruited pickets with signs saying "Turn Left for Scarsdale" and "Doing the Moscow Twist."

Her worries built steadily in early November, as O'Dell continued to handle many of the financial preparations for the Sammy Davis benefit. He signed rental agreements and insurance bonds in behalf of the SCLC and kept track of advance ticket sales. When Kunstler heard that O'Dell was supposed to have resigned from the SCLC, she demanded an explanation. Stanley Levison kept telling her that the story was a distortion of O'Dell's past, and was unlikely to surface, but Kunstler insisted that "this thing might bounce back on us," and that rich people "would tell me to go fly a kite" if they suspected Communist involvement in the SCLC. When Levison suggested that she simply stop referring to O'Dell as the man in charge, she objected that "up to this point there has been no reason for us to use subterfuge, if you want to call it that." She said her own integrity was at stake, because "many people may come back to me and say that I pulled the wool over their eyes." They were dealing in mysteries of character and imagination, she told Levison: "Some people would laugh at this, but others might be terribly hurt . . . That spotlight is a powerful thing."

FBI wiretappers intercepted these emotional exchanges over Levison's office lines in New York and forwarded transcripts to headquarters, where Levison's defense of O'Dell doubtless made perfect sense as one Communist vouching for another. The internal strife at the SCLC also was ample proof that the Bureau's first active blow against King had landed with telling effect. FBI agents had planted the unsigned New Orleans article, along with virtually identical ones in four other newspapers scattered from St. Louis to Long Island.

Hoover launched a full-scale investigation of King at the same time. While it may have seemed illogical for the Bureau to punish King even before gathering evidence of alleged misdeeds, Hoover shrewdly seized his chance to give both orders during the week when the whole country was huddling in fear of extinction by Soviet missiles. The missile crisis inspired and justified emergency measures such as the newspaper attacks on King for employing O'Dell. Because such activities were forbidden within the United States, Bureau officials undertook the operation in the utmost secrecy, knowing they could rely on the discreet collaboration of trusted press contacts. To carry out the first secret strike against King, ironically, they called in the Washington representatives of five American newspapers.

Cartha "Deke" DeLoach, who supervised the dissemination of the five articles, was at the same time lobbying to fend off Robert Kennedy's latest proposal for a government "white paper" on the U.S. Communist Party, which would reveal that the American Communists posed at most a minuscule threat of subversion. The Attorney General wanted to issue the document as a first step toward reducing the FBI's domestic security apparatus—the background checkers, wiretap transcribers, subversive thought specialists, Red squad handlers, and the like—which he considered a gigantic misapplication of manpower. On November 7, however, DeLoach flatly refused Kennedy's latest demand for a white paper. There was a "grave danger," he wrote, that any such description of the Communist network "would compromise FBI informants." Kennedy was caught in a classic spy trap: he could not reduce the mission of the informants without endangering them; therefore he must maintain the mission.

The running battle between Hoover and Kennedy defined the larger political context for the escalation of activity against King, as FBI officials were protecting their anti-Communist intelligence apparatus. Enmity toward King was a driving force. O'Dell was a fresh rationale. The missile crisis was a spur and an opportunity. Finally, the original Levison wiretap was up for six-month renewal, which generated bureaucratic pressures to justify past surveillance by extending it. Whatever the mix of these originating factors, the first King operations were highly satisfying from the Bureau's point of view. Not only did its clandestine newspaper attacks cause reverberating psychological distress, as documented by the wiretaps, but the taps also showed that King had no idea who was behind them. Neither King nor anyone else at the SCLC realized that the New Orleans story was merely one of five. Their suspicions of foul play centered on local police forces. King, like everyone else in the civil rights movement, thought of the FBI as an ally—a most reluctant one at times, and certainly the conservative wing of the federal presence, but nevertheless a force that made segregationists nervous. King sought a more active FBI intervention in the South.

That November, Robert Kennedy signed a request from J. Edgar Hoover authorizing the Bureau to add a fourth wiretap on Stanley Levison. This one covered Levison's home, and fulfilled the agents' hopes of intercepting conversations with King late at night. Such blanket eavesdropping was beyond the reach of King's vision. Even at "tip-toe stance," he would not have been prepared for it. What he saw was a very different document signed that same day by a different Kennedy: President Kennedy issued his long-delayed executive order on racial discrimination in housing. King knew very well that it had been whittled down so that it barely resembled Kennedy's "stroke of a pen" promise from the 1960 campaign. The anti-discrimination order excluded all existing housing, and all new housing except that owned or financed directly by the federal government. King also knew that the order was issued as quietly as possible on the eve of Thanksgiving—"deliberately sandwiched," as Ted Sorensen later wrote, between dramatic presidential announcements on Soviet bombers and the China-India border war. The White House excluded reporters from the signing ceremony, and restricted the event to civil rights staff people. Still, for all these drawbacks, King saw that Kennedy was more of a potential ally than enemy. Publicly, King praised the new order as a step that "carries the whole nation forward to the realization of the American dream."

That Thanksgiving weekend, students gathered for SNCC's Southwide conference in Nashville, where James Lawson's movement was completing its third year of nonviolent demonstrations. After the conference, students from distant regions joined wave after wave of sit-ins against diehard segregationist establishments. The owner of the Tic-Toc Restaurant sprayed a fire extinguisher into the face of Sam Block, who was visiting from his voter registration project with Bob Moses in Greenwood, Mississippi. Two policemen dragged John Lewis to jail from the same restaurant a week later, as the daily demonstrations continued to draw headlines and huge crowds. Privately, there was gossip about a cultural divide along the picket lines. Lewis worried about a breakdown in nonviolent discipline, as evidenced by the casual dress, cigarette-smoking, and overall lack of reverence on the part of some guest demonstrators. In reply, some of the more sophisticated Northern students snickered at Nashville's schoolmarmish regimen, calling Lewis a "square." Still, they all went to jail together.

The movement gossip about King focused upon his performance in Albany. It was a year since the formation of the Albany Movement, and the anniversary was honored by a week-long series of nightly mass meetings, patterned after a church revival. King, addressing the meeting at Third Kiokee Baptist Church, seemed ill at ease as he announced his intention to organize a boycott of segregated businesses "on the national economic level." This proposal was no more than embryonic at the time, and destined to be rejected as impractical, but feelings of pride and delicate sentiment urged King to create the impression of something big. After all that had been said and done in Albany, he could not bring himself to tell those people that he was leaving them for another city, such as Birmingham. Nor could he admit that he had abandoned hopes of a breakthrough in Albany. Instead, he retreated behind a cloud of grandiose but vague plans. "I am willing to come back to Albany and go to jail, if necessary," he assured them.

To coincide with the Albany Movement anniversary, the Southern Regional Council published a study that Claude Sitton summarized accurately in a *New York Times* story headlined "President Chided Over Albany, Ga.: Fails to Guard Negro Rights." While the study criticized nearly every major party to Albany's year-long crisis—the Justice Department, the local police, the FBI, and the Negro leaders themselves—it laid primary responsibility upon President Kennedy for his Administration's failure to protect constitutional rights. Sitton quoted the study's assertion that the federal government " 'has hovered about Albany from the beginning. Incredibly, in this whole time, it has not acted.' " The record, contrasting sharply with President Kennedy's campaign promises of bold action, showed clearly that "the Government will not move in racial controversies unless there is uncontrolled violence." Sitton's story, which played on the front page, lit a fuse of skittering, unbalanced racial perceptions.

King left Albany to preach at New York's Riverside Church on the Sunday before Thanksgiving, three days after the Sitton story was published. After the service, a *Times* reporter approached King while he was removing his clerical robes in the pastor's chambers and asked for comments on the Southern Regional Council's Albany study. In the story, which appeared the next day, King was depicted as endorsing the study in all its particulars, including the criticisms of his own strategic short-comings. But the headline trumpeted a radical change of interpretation: "Dr. King Says F.B.I. in Albany, Ga., Favors Segregationists." Suddenly the critic was King instead of the Southern Regional Council. More important, the target was the FBI instead of President Kennedy.

King might as well have hurled lightning bolts into J. Edgar Hoover's office. Hoover's top assistants immediately exchanged a flurry of indignant memos, as they did whenever the Bureau was criticized publicly. Assistant Director Alex Rosen interpreted the remarks attributed to King as further evidence that he was under Communist "domination." Proposals for retaliation rose up through the Bureau's third-highest and second-highest officials, Alan Belmont and Clyde Tolson, to Hoover himself. Significantly, they chose to let the story stand in the white world, where public challenge risked upsetting segregationist whites as well as the Kennedy Administration. For tactical reasons, the Bureau channeled a vengeful response into the Negro world. As King well knew, the FBI did not lack friendly contacts in the upper reaches of the Negro press. Bureau officials prevailed on representatives of *Jet* and *Ebony*, on the publisher of the four *Afro-American* newspapers, and on John Sengstacke, Robert Abbott's heir at the Chicago *Defender*. The prompt result was a series of rejoinders to King in the nation's largest Negro journals. All the articles focused on one statement the *Times* attributed to King: "One of the great problems we face with the FBI in the South is that the agents are white Southerners who have been influenced by the mores of the community. To maintain their status, they have to be friendly with the local police and people who are promoting segregation. Every time I saw FBI men in Albany, they were with the local police force."

From this complaint the FBI-inspired stories plucked the issue of birth: they pointed out that four of the five regular FBI agents in Albany were Northerners. Then, having refuted King on an issue of fact, the stories denied that the FBI had erred in the slightest. *Jet* declared accurately that the Justice Department, not the FBI, was holding up prosecution of Sheriff Campbell for beating C. B. King. The editors warned King against making the FBI a "scapegoat," and advised him to "take the matter up

with the President and the Attorney General, bub." More stridently, the
Chicago *Defender* story quoted Deke DeLoach's charge that the "statements by Dr. King reveal a total ignorance, not only of the true character
of FBI Director J. Edgar Hoover, but also of the FBI record in protecting
civil rights."

The Bureau was correct that four of the five Albany agents were Northerners, but it was also true that Marion Cheek, the only Southerner, took
personal charge of civil rights complaints. This proved very little in itself,
as Cheek was proud of his record in cases of violent excesses by segregationists. As a key witness in the upcoming Charlie Ware lawsuit, he
would tick off facts supporting his conclusion that Sheriff Johnson had
shot Ware in cold blood, and would scoff at the respectable Albany segregationists who proclaimed Gator Johnson's innocence. At worst Cheek
was a modified segregationist, who had gotten along fairly well with
King. Now King's remarks embittered him, not just for the aspersions
against his professional integrity but also for the affront to the Director.
Cheek nearly worshipped Hoover, telling everyone how the old man had
once granted him a station transfer when his wife was sick.

King made a mistake about the birthplaces of the agents. It was a less
trivial mistake to be drawn into a dispute about whether Hoover or the
Kennedy Administration was more to blame in Albany. On instructions
from Hoover, DeLoach called King's office to seek an immediate appointment so that he and William Sullivan, head of the intelligence division,
could set King straight on the facts. When Dora McDonald put him off,
saying that King was secluded at work on a book of sermons, DeLoach
asked the Atlanta SAC to set up the appointment for him. The SAC
reported the next day that he had had no better luck—King was busy
traveling. Although the request was presented as an informal one, not
connected to any official FBI investigation, DeLoach huffily resented
King's failure to schedule the interview. He never called King again. He
did not write King a letter setting forth the Bureau's objections to the
Times article. DeLoach did not attempt to verify the accuracy or balance
of the story, nor consider that King had any but the basest motives for
his comments. Instead, two months later, he closed the matter so suddenly and with such scalding prose as to suggest that he was content to
preserve the purest grievance against King. "It would appear obvious that
Rev. King does not desire to be told the true facts," DeLoach wrote to
his superiors. "He obviously uses deceit, lies and treachery as propaganda to further his own causes." In the two remaining paragraphs of
his memo, DeLoach used variants of the word "lie" five times in reference to King.

All this took place within the bowels of the government, precipitated by one newspaper article and two unreturned phone calls. This secret fury, in turn, was partially the result of the Southern Regional Council's hidden role in brokering the Voter Education Project. During that long process, Leslie Dunbar and other SRC officials had passed along to civil rights leaders the Kennedy Administration's assurances that voter registration would be a haven of federal protection. Now Dunbar, though a Kennedy supporter and a cautious man by nature, felt personally responsible for the unanswered violence coming down on the Moses project in Mississippi and the SNCC registration projects around Albany. His own frustrations with the Administration helped drive the Albany study to public light, but Dunbar could not refer explicitly to the broken promises without compromising the shaky tax arrangements on which VEP rested. Here again the public face of racial politics was fatefully disingenuous: everything seemed as obvious as black and white—tediously so—and yet the central dramas remained invisible.

From different worlds, King, Hoover, and the Kennedys took the measure of one another as they spun toward the new year. Each of them saw things that were concealed from the others, and ignored things that were plain. King alone knew they were heading for Birmingham; he could choose his ground so as to draw attention to freedom as he defined it. In December, he sent Wyatt Walker and Andrew Young there to recruit, plan, and prepare. King himself preached in Birmingham on Sunday, December 9, before flying to New York for a highly successful Sammy Davis fund-raiser—which came off without picket lines against Jack O'Dell—and then a board meeting of the Gandhi Society. On Friday, a bomb detonated outside Birmingham's Bethel Baptist, rattling the church so that the stained glass and all other breakables shattered and jagged fault lines ran up the walls. The concussion tore the roof off the parsonage next door, destroyed the pastor's car, knocked out power and telephone lines, and ripped holes in three other houses, sending two infants to the hospital with severe glass cuts. Bull Connor, now gearing up to run for mayor, arrived with firemen, detectives, and police dogs to take charge of the investigation, which accomplished nothing. "Dammit, they ought to be hung when they're caught," Connor told reporters. The Birmingham *News* noted that Bethel Baptist was renowned as Shuttlesworth's church, the place of refuge for the battered Freedom Riders in May of 1961. It had been bombed twice before, but both the newspaper and Connor puzzled over why anyone would want to bomb it nearly a year after Shuttlesworth had departed for Cincinnati. The new pastor, dazed and shaken, was puzzled too, as he had permitted no civil rights meetings to be held there. "Once more we have been shocked by the bombing of Bethel Baptist Church," King wired President Kennedy. He appealed for help in Birmingham, which he described as "by far the worst big city in race relations in the United States. Much of what has gone on has had the tacit consent of high public officials."

Three nights later, on December 17, King and several other leaders conferred with President Kennedy about Africa. The Negro leaders requested a "Marshall Plan" of economic aid for the impoverished, newly independent nations there. They also pressed for American sanctions against South Africa's apartheid system and for greater diplomatic pressure to free the remaining colonies on the continent. Particularly at issue was a recent United Nations proposal to curtail armed suppression by Portugal of independence movements in its colonies of Mozambique, Angola, and Portuguese Guinea. The United States had cast one of only seven votes against the resolution, joining South Africa and five European nations.

President Kennedy put his guests at ease by sharing their sensibilities. NATO obligations made impossible a simple cutoff of arms shipments to Portugal, the President explained, but he was skeptical of Portugal's promises not to divert NATO arms shipments to suppress anti-colonial movements in Africa. In fact, Kennedy assured the Negro leaders that he did not trust Portugal's word on this point any more than they did. The task of effective government was to design safeguards that would support NATO without allowing Portugal to prop up its colonies by force. These were complexities that absorbed the President in every detail. Although his private conference with the Negro leaders was scheduled to last only half an hour, he slipped out briefly to light the White House Christmas tree and returned for another half-hour—then two more hours. For once, presidential aides found themselves juggling the schedule to benefit civil rights leaders, lopping off or abbreviating appointments with other dignitaries. The Negro press hailed the event as "the longest conference ever held by Negroes with a U.S. President in the White House."

That night, President Kennedy taped a freewheeling interview with correspondents from the three major networks. He was at his best—candid, articulate, and witty. Repeatedly, and with obvious relish, he discussed turning points of the Cuban missile crisis. He stressed the vagaries of decision-making at the pinnacle of government, ticking off the historical "misjudgments" that had brought on each of the twentieth century's major wars. Only once did he bring up the race issue, in complaining that the Ole Miss crisis made it more difficult to pass an education bill.

The President was acutely conscious that his nation had dominated world politics since the war against the Axis. "I think it's a fantastic story," he said. "We have one million Americans today serving outside the United States. There's no other country in history that's carried this kind of a burden ... since the beginning of the world. Greece, Rome, Napoleon and all the rest always had conquest. We have a million men outside, and we're trying to defend these countries." The American empire was coming of age as measured against its most awesome predecessors, and like those predecessors it conceived of its power as a benevolent force. Twice the United States had served as "the great means of defending the world," he said—first against the Nazis, then against the Soviets. "Now I think that's a pretty good record for a country with six percent of the world's population, which is very reluctant to take on these burdens. I think we ought to be rather pleased with ourselves this Christmas."

Early in December, *The Nation* had published an excerpt of the Southern Regional Council's Albany report in an article entitled "Kennedy: The Reluctant Emancipator." This was a small public hint of the linkage between Kennedy and Lincoln that had been on King's mind throughout the disappointing year. On New Year's Eve, the descendants of slavery were to celebrate one hundred years of freedom. By proclaiming the slaves within the Confederacy "forever free," Lincoln had made the Civil War a war of emancipation. Now more than ever, King wanted Kennedy to say something similar about segregation. It would give the movement a moral club to take to Birmingham.

He lobbied privately all month for a Second Emancipation Proclamation, together with organizations such as the African-American Heritage Association. Early prospects looked bleak, as the Civil War Centennial Commission declined to schedule any ceremonies honoring Emancipation Day. For "practical considerations," which almost certainly centered upon the threat of protest by the Southern State Centennial Commissions, the Administration's Bureau of the Budget concluded that it would be "undesirable to use the Civil War Centennial Commission as a vehicle for the observance." This omission—perhaps the most glaring of the government's withdrawals from the four-year centennial—left King without an occasion that beckoned for a presidential appearance. White House interest in his proposal seemed so puny that William Kunstler advised him to march to the White House on New Year's Day, to deliver his Second Emancipation Proclamation to President Kennedy a second time, through the gates if necessary. Kunstler thought he might persuade Lincoln historian Carl Sandburg to go along, but King had no

taste for emancipation as a protest event.* After his Africa meeting at
the White House on December 17, he bubbled with renewed optimism,
because he found the President sympathetic, obviously well briefed, and
"so well informed." King and his aides talked almost daily with Louis
Martin, Lee White, Arthur Schlesinger, and Berl Bernhard of the Civil
Rights Commission.

As usual, the decision bounced around inside the White House until
the last minute. The Administration was preoccupied with Robert Kennedy's frantic efforts to raise Fidel Castro's ransom price of $62 million
for the return of the Bay of Pigs prisoners from Cuba. In another marathon of wild renaissance government, Kennedy was sending his assistants scurrying in all directions at all hours, bending the tax laws,
commandeering airplanes, amassing pharmaceuticals and medical supplies to Castro's satisfaction. An emergency call from the Attorney General to Boston's Cardinal Richard Cushing secured a last million dollars
when the banks were closed for the weekend, and the 1,100 prisoners left
Cuban jails in time to spend Christmas in Miami. Lee White submitted
the draft proclamation to Pierre Salinger the next day, for final decision
by the President in Palm Beach. King's frontal assault on segregation was
gone, as were his suggested flourishes and frills, but the kernel of a new
presidential commitment was preserved in the heart of the short document:

> WHEREAS Negro citizens are still being denied rights guaranteed by the
> Constitution and laws of the United States, and the securing of these rights
> is one of the great unfinished tasks of our democracy:
> NOW, THEREFORE, I, JOHN F. KENNEDY, President of the United States of
> America, do hereby proclaim that the Emancipation Proclamation ex-
> presses our Nation's policy, founded on justice and morality, and that it is
> therefore fitting and proper to commemorate the centennial of the historic
> Emancipation Proclamation throughout the year 1963.

White advised Salinger of staff opinion that "not to issue some statement
would be regarded as a minor disaster."

In Washington, the civil rights cabal gathered in Berl Bernhard's office
to discuss the reservations filtering back from Palm Beach. Those closer
to the President were saying that something so historic as a Second
Emancipation Proclamation was impossible to do halfway. Far better to
do nothing at all, they said, especially since public expectations of Civil
War commemoratives were practically nonexistent. Facing this reason-

---

* When the FBI's Levison wiretaps picked up talk of Kunstler's idea, Hoover
promptly dispatched warnings to Robert Kennedy and Kenneth O'Donnell.

ing, the advisers in Bernhard's office groped for an idea that would salvage something from their year's efforts, knowing that O'Donnell and the others with the President felt some residual sense of obligation. They trotted out and discarded many ideas before Louis Martin began musing that the key was to think of something that made President Kennedy feel that he was taking advantage of his personal strengths. In Martin's view, these were social more than political. Shackled to the Southern Democrats, President Kennedy shrank from the political implications of the draft proclamation. On the other hand, he and Mrs. Kennedy felt completely relaxed at social gatherings of Negroes. Here the contrast between Kennedy and his predecessor, Eisenhower, was stark. In no other aspect relating to race did he compare more favorably, Martin argued. They should think of something like a White House reception for Negro dignitaries.

Arthur Schlesinger perked up as Martin worked through his idea. "I think Louie's got something," he said. They fashioned a proposal for a gala White House reception to be held on February 12—Lincoln's Birthday. The timing would head off much of the possible white criticism from both political parties by casting the event in honor of the hallowed Republican president. Martin was confident that such a reception would redound to President Kennedy's credit among Negroes—to whom the White House had been socially off limits except in token numbers. The presence of Negro celebrities in the White House would attract banner coverage in the Negro press—probably more than the proclamation would have. On this reasoning, Martin and the others struck a bargain with the Palm Beach White House to trade the proclamation for a reception.

President Kennedy visited the Orange Bowl in Miami twice over the next few days. On December 29, he and Mrs. Kennedy reviewed the newly freed soldiers of the Bay of Pigs brigade there. Mrs. Kennedy saluted them in Spanish, and the President delivered an emotional promise to return their tattered battle flag to them "in a free Havana." On New Year's Day, the President was back at the Orange Bowl for a football game, puffing on a cigar as he watched young quarterback Joe Namath lead the University of Alabama to victory over Oklahoma.* The President granted Tom Wicker of *The New York Times* a long New Year's interview in which, anticipating the overthrow of the Castro regime, he said the United States would impose no preconditions on the next government in Cuba.

---

* Ole Miss defeated Arkansas in a Sugar Bowl contest between the two states in which federal troops had been used to enforce school integration.

In Havana, Castro attacked Kennedy's Orange Bowl pledge as the words of a "vulgar pirate chief." Boasting of the Bay of Pigs ransom, he declared that "for the first time in history, imperialism paid an indemnification of war." Che Guevara gave a much more sober speech on economic discipline, charging Cuba's managers to run their operations more profitably. Also that New Year's Day, North Vietnamese gunners shot down eight of fifteen U.S. helicopters in a troop transport convoy, and Nelson Rockefeller was sworn in for his second term as governor of New York. "This is an historic anniversary," he began his address. "Just 100 years ago, on January 1, 1863, the Emancipation Proclamation became law."

King moved immediately after New Year's, as there was nothing left to wait for. First he called in Wyatt Walker to ask if the blueprint for the Birmingham campaign was drafted. Assured that it was, King asked Walker to help him compile a small list for a secret planning meeting. For the first time in his career, King excluded the SCLC board, knowing that they would talk it to death. He did not invite Daddy King, nor any of the off-staff preachers except two whose Alabama experience was vital, Shuttlesworth and Joseph Lowery. Shuttlesworth was indispensable; it was his campaign as much as King's. In addition to three top SCLC officers from Atlanta—Abernathy, Andy Young, and Dorothy Cotton—he selected only four others: Clarence Jones, Jack O'Dell, Stanley Levison, and James Lawson. That made eleven in all, counting King and Walker. King called Clarence Jones to say it was time. He wanted Jones to arrange for the three New Yorkers to come to a retreat at Dorchester on January 10. Jones did not have to be told what it was about. Unwittingly, he alerted J. Edgar Hoover with his call to Levison.

After converging upon Atlanta, they all flew to Savannah on an early morning flight. The mood of the occasion was grimly practical, but the preachers among them appreciated that the Savannah region was a fitting site for revolutions grounded in religion. From Savannah, in 1738, the British revivalist George Whitefield had launched his first phenomenal tour of the American colonies, creating a mass intoxication—known as the Great Awakening—that swept from Georgia to New Hampshire. He drew 30,000 people to the Boston Common in 1740, when the city's entire population was less than two-thirds that number. From Savannah, where John Wesley first landed from England with his Anglican theology shaken by Whitefield's preaching on the voyage, Whitefield's influence spawned Baptist congregations and later Wesleyan (Methodist) ones. The small, malaria-infested seaport in Georgia became mother to the two mass-based Protestant denominations that captured early American

46

SCLC's "Mother Conscience," Septima Clark (46, left), with Rosa Parks at the
Highlander Center. Charles Sherrod (47) canvasses for potential voters in Southwest Georgia, near Albany.

47

48

In Albany, King joined his first mass march to jail (48) and was arrested along with a shaky W. G. Anderson by Police Chief Laurie Pritchett (49). The Albany movement produced music of unparalleled spirit (50), and further mass jailings followed a wildcat march led by Rev. S. B. Wells (51). By the fall of 1962, the Ole Miss crisis had seized national attention (52).

50

49

51

"All the News That's Fit to Print"

The New York Times.

LATE CITY EDITION
U. S. Weather Bureau Report (Page 77) forecast:
Mostly sunny today, fair tonight and tomorrow.
Temp. range: 75—54; yesterday: 74—52.

VOL. CXII. No. 38,237.
© 1962 by The New York Times Company.
Times Square, New York 36, N. Y.

NEW YORK, TUESDAY, OCTOBER 2, 1962.

10 cents beyond 50-mile zone from New York City
except on Long Island, Higher in air delivery cities.

FIVE CENTS

3,000 TROOPS PUT DOWN MISSISSIPPI RIOTING AND SEIZE 200 AS NEGRO ATTENDS CLASSES; EX-GEN. WALKER IS HELD FOR INSURRECTION

SENATE REJECTS AID CUTS AND BAN ON HELP FOR REDS

Upholds Kennedy's Authority to Assist Nations That Do Business With Cuba

By FELIX BELAIR Jr.
Special to The New York Times.

WASHINGTON, Oct. 1—The Senate decided for the Administration today in preliminary votes on the foreign aid appropriation bill, due for passage tomorrow.

It voted, 47 to 28, against cutting $785,000,000 from the $709,400,000 of military and economic aid funds that its Appropriations Committee restored to the bill the House had cut heavily.

The effect of the vote was to hold the appropriation at $4,422,800,000, as recommended by its Appropriations Committee. The Administration had requested the full amount of the authorized ceiling of $4,-754,800,000 but the House cut this back to $3,630,400,000.

On a later vote, the Senate confirmed this action by rejecting a proposal by Senator Allen J. Ellender, Democrat of Louisiana, to adopt the House cut of $150,000,000 for military aid.

Vote Becomes Narrow

By increasingly narrow margins, however, it supported other Administration pleas. For instance, it voted, 38-36 to continue the President's discretion to aid countries doing business with Cuba. Then it decided, 39-37, to give the President similar discretion to waive the ban on aiding Communist nations such as Yugoslavia and Poland.

All three proposals were sponsored by Senator William Proxmire, Democrat of Wisconsin.

They were intended, first, to cut back the separate money items in the bill to the levels voted by the House. Second, they would have approved the House's ban on aiding any Communist countries or free nations that help the Castro regime or allow their ships to deliver any cargo to Cuba.

Only with the help of Republican members was the Democratic leadership able to turn back the Proxmire attack on the President's discretionary powers. On the proposal to ban aid to nations shipping to Cuba, 12 Republicans voted with 27 Democrats to defeat the move, while 22 Democrats and 14 Re-

Continued on Page 16, Column 4

MOSCOW FOCUSING ON BLOC IN EUROPE

Rift With Chinese Believed Behind New Emphasis

By SEYMOUR TOPPING
Special to The New York Times.

MOSCOW, Oct. 1—The Soviet Union has decided to pursue its program of rapprochement with Yugoslavia even at the risk of a further deterioration in relations with Communist China.

Diplomatic officials here have found evidence of this development in a comparative study of Soviet and Chinese Communist documents.

These officials believe that the ideological quarrel with Peking has caused Moscow to resolve to concentrate its resources on the consolidation of the European Communist economic bloc.

Pravda, the Communist party newspaper, published today an edited version of this communiqué issued by the Central Committee of the Chinese Communist party at the conclusion of its plenary session Friday.

The Soviet summary, which covered half a page in Pravda, omitted the strong attacks on President Tito of Yugoslavia by the pro-Communist members of the

Continued on Page 3, Column 1

PRISONERS ARE MARCHED TO ARMORY IN OXFORD: Army men escort a group of prisoners to National Guard Armory. The group had participated in a disturbance and was apprehended after the soldiers were ordered to fire at the feet of the rioters.

WALKER IS STOPPED BY TROOPS: Former Maj. Gen. Edwin A. Walker is stopped by soldiers near the courthouse in Oxford. He was turned over to U.S. marshals and is being held in $100,000 bail on charges stemming from his role in Sunday's campus riots.

SHOTS QUELL MOB

Enrolling of Meredith Ends Segregation in State Schools

By CLAUDE SITTON
Special to The New York Times.

OXFORD, Miss., Oct. 1—James H. Meredith, a Negro, enrolled in the University of Mississippi today and began classes as Federal troops and federalized units of the Mississippi National Guard quelled a 15-hour riot.

A force of more than 3,000 soldiers and guardsmen and 400 deputy United States marshals fired rifles and hurled tear-gas grenades to stop the violent demonstrations.

Throughout the day more troops streamed into Oxford. Tonight a force approaching 5,000 soldiers and guardsmen, along with the Federal marshals, maintained an uneasy peace in this town of 6,500 in the northern Mississippi hills.

[There were two flareups tonight in which tear gas was used. United Press International reported. A small crowd of students began throwing bottles at marshals outside Baxter Hall where Mr. Meredith was housed. They were quickly dispersed by tear gas. Soldiers also broke up a minor demonstration at a downtown intersection.]

200 Are Seized

The troops seized approximately 200 persons.

They were seized in the streets of Oxford and adults that besieged the university's administration building last night and attacked troops on the town square this morning.

Among those arrested was former Maj. Gen. Edwin A. Walker, who resigned his commission after having been reprimanded for his ultra-rightwing political activity. He was charged with insurrection.

The university's acceptance of Mr. Meredith, a 29-year-old Air Force veteran, followed Gov. Ross R. Barnett's retreat from his defiance of Federal court orders that the Negro be enrolled.

The 64-year-old official, a member of the militantly segregationist Citizens Councils, had vowed he would go to jail if necessary to prevent university desegregation.

Mr. Meredith's admission marked the first desegregation of a public educational institution in Mississippi. It reduced the Deep South bloc of massive-resistance states to two —

Continued on Page 21, Column 6

Home Urges West to Help East's Coexistence Moves

By ARNOLD H. LUBASCH

The Earl of Home, Britain's Foreign Secretary, urged last night that the West pursue policies designed to help the Soviet bloc move toward genuine coexistence. He suggested that nuclear war was not the only instrument of policy, that Communist doctrine was changing because of this and that Soviet society was changing even faster.

The West also, he recognized these facts, he said, and adapt its policies to them.

Lord Home's remarks were made at a dinner in the Waldorf - Astoria Hotel. The main theme of the strike would imperil the national health and safety, the President issued an Executive order naming a three-man board of inquiry to investigate the dispute and to report to him by Thursday.

[Meanwhile in New York, leaders of the nation's seven major maritime unions abandoned inter-union battling to plan support for the striking longshoremen. American seamen and officers started leaving their ships, while other unions made plans to avoid servicing foreign-flag ships entering Atlantic and Gulf ports.]

The strike, which began at 12:01 A.M. today, has tied up all ports from Searsport, Me., to Brownsville, Tex. About 75,-000 members of the International-

Continued on Page 78, Column 5

SPAAK REASSURES AFRICA ON TRADE

Tells Newer U.N. Members That Common Market Will Aid Their Development

By THOMAS J. HAMILTON
Special to The New York Times.

UNITED NATIONS, N. Y., Oct. 1—Paul-Henri Spaak, the Foreign Minister of Belgium, assured underdeveloped countries today that they could count on the cooperation of the members of the European Economic Community in the fight for economic advancement.

In addition, Mr. Spaak appealed to the entire world to understand the "new Europe" and its goal of "world cooperation."

Mr. Spaak's policy statement in the General Assembly was addressed in the first instance to 18 newly independent African states, all former possessions of France, Belgium or Italy.

Some of the states have asked the European Economic Community, or Common Market, for status as associates.

The six members of the market—Belgium, France, West Germany, Italy, the Netherlands and Luxembourg—are negotiating with the African states in Brussels.

Success Is Predicted

Mr. Spaak predicted that these talks would be concluded successfully by the end of 1962.

He also predicted that the negotiations with Britain for her admission to the market would be successful. He said the market would then have about the same productive capacity as the United States, and more than the Soviet Union.

The Belgian Foreign Minister, who was one of the leaders in the formation of the Common Market, defended it against two charges: that it is a manifestation of "neo-colonialism," and that it is merely intended to provide economic support for the North Atlantic Treaty Organisation.

Mr. Spaak devoted almost his entire speech to his explanation of the market's program. He received an ovation at the end. With African and Asian members joining.

The Belgian Foreign Minister said that the exports of African associate members would be admitted duty-free to his capital of Bulgawage. A United Nations spokesman

Continued on Page 5, Column 2

KENNEDY MOVING TO END PIER TIE-UP

He Names Board of Inquiry as First Step in Obtaining Taft-Hartley Injunction

By JOHN D. POMFRET
Special to The New York Times.

WASHINGTON, Oct. 1—President Kennedy took the first step today toward getting an injunction to end the Atlantic and Gulf Coast longshoremen's strike for 80 days.

Declaring that continuation of the strike would imperil the national health and safety, the President issued an Executive order naming a three-man board of inquiry to investigate the dispute and to report to him by Thursday.

[Meanwhile in New York, leaders of the nation's seven major maritime unions abandoned inter-union battling to plan support for the striking longshoremen. American seamen and officers started leaving their ships, while other unions made plans to avoid servicing foreign-flag ships entering Atlantic and Gulf ports.]

The strike, which began at 12:01 A.M. today, has tied up all ports from Searsport, Me., to Brownsville, Tex. About 75,-000 members of the International-

Continued on Page 78, Column 5

WALKER IS FACING 4 FEDERAL COUNTS

Flown to Medical Center in Missouri to Await Trial— Bail Put at $100,000

Special to The New York Times.

OXFORD, Miss., Oct. 1 —Former Maj. Gen. Edwin A. Walker was arrested today on charges, including insurrection, for his role in last night's rioting at the University of Mississippi.

The man who commanded Federal forces during the school integration crisis at Little Rock in 1957 was held in $100,000 bail.

Unable to put up the bail, he was flown to the United States Medical Center for Federal Prisoners in Springfield, Mo., to await his trial.

[Mr. Walker, accompanied by marshals, arrived at the medical center Monday night. The Associated Press said.]

"They don't have a ring on me," Mr. Walker said after his arrest. He dictated a message to Gov. Ross R. Barnett, which said:

"Mr. Walker began his career in your behalf and in behalf of the stand for freedom everywhere. Do nothing based on my status that is not in support of your own objectives.

Continued on Page 27, Column 4

Mississippi Aides Blamed By U.S. Officials for Riot

By ANTHONY LEWIS
Special to The New York Times.

WASHINGTON, Oct. 1 — The Federal Government asserted today that the failure of Mississippi officials to keep their word led to the bloody rioting in Oxford, Miss., last night. Attorney General Robert F. Kennedy and other spokesmen said that Gov. Ross R. Barnett and his aides had repeatedly given as-

Statements by Robert Kennedy and Eastland, Page 25.

surances that they could and would maintain order when James H. Meredith, a Negro, entered the University of Mississippi last night.

Instead, the Federal spokesmen said, the state police were withdrawn at the crucial moment of the developing mob scene. Federal troops were then called in, but two men were dead and many were injured by the time they arrived.

Senator James O. Eastland, Democrat of Mississippi, read on the Senate floor this morning a report on the rioting. He said the report had been prepared by officials of the University of Mississippi.

Eastland Opens Inquiry

Tonight, Senator Eastland obtained authorization for his Judiciary Committee, which he heads, to make an investigation of "all events at the University of Mississippi since U.S. marshals and Army troops moved in."

The report read by Mr. Eastland this morning sought to put the blame for the rioting on "amateurism by untrained marshals." It said that the 300 marshals at the university last night had "provoked" the crowd and had "incited violence"

Continued on Page 25, Column 1

BARNETT CHARGES MARSHALS ERRED

Says 'Trigger-Happy' U. S. Officers Are Responsible for Campus Bloodshed

Text of statement appears on Page 25.

By HEDRICK SMITH
Special to The New York Times.

JACKSON, Miss., Oct. 1—Gov. Ross R. Barnett tonight attributed the fatal rioting at the University of Mississippi last night to "inexperienced, nervous and trigger-happy Federal marshals."

The Governor said the statement at a recorded broadcast carried by the National Broadcasting Company. In a later recorded broadcast, carried by the Columbia Broadcasting System, Mr. Barnett directly assailed President Kennedy.

"The responsibility for this unwarranted breach of the peace and violence in Mississippi rests directly with the President of the United States," he said. "He ordered armed forces to invade Mississippi and their actions were directly responsible for violence, bloodshed and death."

People Are 'Enraged'

In his earlier statement, the Governor said that the people of Mississippi "are enraged, as the kind of treatment Mississippians received," he said.

The Governor also said that the only solution to the Mississippi integration crisis was for the Federal Government to remove James H. Meredith, a 29-year-old Negro student, from the university.

The Federal authorities alone have the power to stop bloodshed in Mississippi," he said.

Continued on Page 25, Column 5

CAMPUS A BIVOUAC AS NEGRO ENTERS

2,000 Troops Stand Guard —Meredith Eats Alone

By McCANDLISH PHILLIPS
Special to The New York Times.

OXFORD, Miss., Oct. 1—The University of Mississippi campus today had the look of an armed camp. Mr. Meredith, its first Negro student, attended two classes.

Two thousand of the more than 3,000 Army and National Guard troops here made the campus look like a cross between a bivouac and a prison-of-war camp. More olive drab uniforms were evident on campus than khaki ones.

Mr. Meredith, who did not get his first meal on campus until this afternoon, ate his first meal—breakfast—in his privately tonight, was housed in an end room in Baxter Hall, a residence dormitory. The room next door was occupied by several Federal marshals.

The 29-year-old Negro was taken from his dormitory under guard at 1:45 A. M. and marched to the Lyceum main administration building. He was registered in 45 minutes.

Continued on Page 26, Column 1

Columbia Study Scores Doctors; Says Quality of Care Lags Here

Financial Sanctions Under Blue Shield Suggested in Trussell Report

By FARNSWORTH FOWLE

The medical profession in "do little" about the quality of medical care in the metropolitan area, the state said yesterday in an experts' report.

The report warned that the first reaction of many laymen to poor medical care "is to demand that medical care "is to be dangerous and criticism." A government leadership must be asserted in the public interest." It said that "strong medical, hospital, community and government leadership must be asserted in the public interest."

"The organized purchasers of medical and hospital care can be the strongest arm of the community in upgrading standards, and it is to the best interest of hospital officials and hospitals to work with them,"

Continued on Page 42, Column 1

Congo Flies Troops To End Kasai Revolt

By Reuters.

LEOPOLDVILLE, The Congo, Oct. 1—Reliable sources said today that the central Congolese troops to Luluabourg to put down a new revolt by supporters of Albert Kalonji in South Kasai, following the Government army base nearest to the diamond-rich province.

The troop movement followed the declaration by the Government of a state of emergency in South Kasai. No immediate action was planned by the United Nations.

Mr. Kalonji, self-styled "king," virtually seceded from the central Government short of troops for the Congo became independent two years ago. He escaped recently from a prison near Leopoldville and returned to his capital of Bukwanga while the Africans would make a

Continued on Page 9, Column 8

Bidwell's Tax Trial Ends in Hung Jury

By DAVID ANDERSON

The tax-evasion trial of J. Truman Bidwell, former chairman of the New York Stock Exchange, ended early today with a hung jury.

The jury, which had been deliberating since 1 P.M., filed into the courtroom shortly after midnight and told Federal Judge Thomas F. Murphy that it was hopelessly deadlocked.

Judge Murphy, who two hours earlier had received a similar report and had instructed the jurors to try once more, rein-

Continued on Page 18, Column 5

Dr. Ray E. Trussell

rent officers of management and labor toward improving medical care.

"The proposed purchasers of medical and hospital care can be the strongest arm of the community in upgrading standards, and it is to the best interest of hospital officials and hospitals to work with them,"

Continued on Page 42, Column 1

NEWS INDEX

	Page		Page
Books	31	Music	33-34
Bridge	34	Obituaries	33
Business	43-54	Real Estate	54
Buyers	62	Screen	32-39
Crossword	35	Ships and Air	77
Editorial	36	Society	30
Fashions	47	Sports	42-46
Financial	43-54	Theatres	32-39
Food	47	TV and Radio	79
Letters	36	U. N. Proceedings	11
Man in News	25	Wash. Proceedings	25
Markets	43-54	Weather	77

News Summary and Index, Page 39

Continued on Page 26, Column 1

52

54

A national address by President Kennedy and weeks of political maneuvering between the administration and Governor Ross Barnett (53) failed to ensure the peaceful enrollment of James Meredith, the first black student at the University of Mississippi. A night of tear gas and riots outside the Lyceum (54) forced the Kennedys, shown here (55) with Vice President Lyndon Johnson, to send more than 10,000 U.S. soldiers (56) to guarantee the safety of Meredith, seen here (57) on his first day of classes.

55

56

53

57

59

In Birmingham, Bull Connor (58) and Rev. Fred Shuttlesworth (59) sparred for seven years before the 1963 demonstrations, when marchers climbed into the paddywagons (60) to protest segregation. Later, with the campaign's energy fading, King and his colleagues (61), Ralph Abernathy (seated with King), Wyatt Walker (standing between King and Abernathy), and Bernard Lee (behind Abernathy), faced a court order to desist. On April 12 King defied the order and entered the Birmingham jail (62).

58

63

64

65

When King's imprisonment gained no results, James Bevel (63) organized mass marches of young school children (64), who filled the city jails. After skirmishes with protesters in early May, Birmingham authorities used dogs and high-pressure fire hoses (65, 66) to repulse, rather than imprison, demonstraters, but the emotions that swept outward from the Sixteenth Street Baptist Church (67) overwhelmed the defenders of segregation.

66

67

68

Birmingham fever swept scores of American cities in May, creating a national crisis for Justice Department officials John Doar, Burke Marshall, and Robert Kennedy (68). In Jackson, Mississippi, a lunch counter sit-in on May 28 (69) touched off mass demonstrations.

69

70

Assassinated at the height of the fury, NAACP leader Medgar Evers lay in state (70), mourned by millions including his widow, Myrlie (71). John Doar (72) calmed an incipient riot after the Evers funeral in Jackson on June 15.

71

72

73

Just before a tense White House meeting on June 22 with Robert Kennedy, Roy Wilkins, and A. Philip Randolph (73), President Kennedy warned King that his movement was infiltrated by Communists. The next day, as the President left to proclaim his idea of freedom before the Berlin Wall, King made his own triumphant freedom march in Detroit (74).

74

76   75

Sensing a national break-
through, King joined with
Bayard Rustin and Randolph
(75) to plan a March on Washington for August 28. The
great march filled the VIP
section at the Lincoln
Memorial (76) and attracted a
planeload of Hollywood
celebrities (77).

77

79

The March on Washington will be remembered for King's "I Have a Dream" speech (78) and the crowd's hopeful jubilation (79). On a Sunday morning, less than three weeks later, a bomb struck Birmingham's Sixteenth Street Baptist Church. Bayonet-bearing Alabama troopers guarded the scene of the bombing (80), which critically injured ten-year-old Sarah Collins (81) and killed four young girls, including her sister. Mourners at the funeral were overcome by grief (82), a mood echoed by the nation itself just a few weeks later at the funeral of President John F. Kennedy (83).

78

80

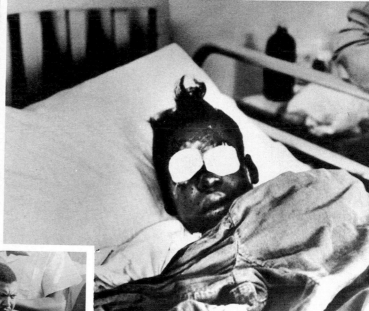

81

82

83

84

85

churchgoers. In Savannah itself, the spirit of conversion was so strong that many of the whites accepted the idea of promoting religion among the slaves. First African Baptist was established there in 1788 as one of the first Negro congregations on the North American continent. A pastor of First African led the slave preachers who parleyed with General Sherman when his March to the Sea reached Savannah. Nearly a century later, Martin Luther King welcomed the honor of preaching the Emancipation Day sermon at First African. To the history-laden congregation, he had delivered an early version of his "I Have a Dream" speech just before the Kennedy inauguration.

The King party proceeded from Savannah to the old Congregationalist retreat at Dorchester, a town imbued with a peculiar variation on Savannah's rich history. It had survived for many decades as the only known Puritan enclave in the slave South, transplanted in 1752 by way of Dorchester, Massachusetts, after the original Puritan flight from Dorchester, England, during the reign of the Stuart kings. The town had retained such disciplined piety that post–Civil War visitors had been amazed to find not a single mulatto among the newly freed slaves. Northern families kept ties to Dorchester even after the plantations shriveled up. Theodore Roosevelt's mother was a native of Dorchester. The fathers of Oliver Wendell Holmes and Samuel F. B. Morse pastored the Midway Congregational Church there. Among the Southern pastors at Midway was the theologian C. C. Jones. A wealthy planter who conducted a lifelong ministry among the slaves, Jones was famous for his doctrines attempting to reconcile slavery with Christianity. He eventually became a tragic figure of American religious history. As a liberal slaveholder, he came under withering attack from Frederick Douglass. Their 1840s duel over the respectability of slavery as opposed to abolition foreshadowed the civil rights debates in both flesh and spirit. Jones's great-grandson, the Episcopal bishop of Alabama, lay across King's path in Birmingham.

King presided over the business sessions at Dorchester, but the initial presentation belonged to Walker. He handed out a blueprint for a campaign in four stages. First, they would launch small-scale sit-ins to draw attention to their desegregation platform, while building strength through nightly mass meetings. Second, they would organize a generalized boycott of the downtown business section, and move to slightly larger demonstrations. Third, they would move up to mass marches— both to enforce the boycott and to fill the jails. Finally, if necessary, they would call on outsiders to descend on Birmingham from across the country, as in the Freedom Rides, to cripple the city under the combined pressure of publicity, economic boycott, and the burden of overflowing jails.

As a general principle, Walker asserted that everything must build. If they showed strength, then outside support would grow more than proportionately. Once started, however, they could not fall back without suffering letdown and depression, which in Birmingham risked a fatal outbreak of Negro violence. In no case, said Walker, could the Birmingham campaign be smaller than Albany. That meant they must be prepared to put upwards of a thousand people in jail at one time, maybe more. They had to keep the average jailgoer inside at least five or six days at a time before bailing out. Walker projected various bail costs to the SCLC against jail costs to the city. Given the estimated value of the weekly Negro shopping power, he calculated the dollar and percentage losses to the downtown merchants from the boycott at various degrees of success. To work, the plan required extensive preparation, perfect timing, and loads of money.

Walker had a flair for the dramatic. He called his entire blueprint Project C—for Confrontation. Assuming that Bull Connor would tap the phones, he assigned to the major leaders protective code names that reflected his aching respect for white authority. King would be "JFK," said Walker. Abernathy would be "Dean Rusk" (which was not much to Abernathy's liking). Walker himself would be "RFK." John Drew, the Birmingham insurance man in whose home King would be staying, would be "Pope John." Shuttlesworth, the movement's war chief, would be "Mac," after Secretary of Defense Robert McNamara. Walker's presentation was at once breathtaking and quixotic. It envisioned a precisely organized march into history by an organization that had taken four years to find a mimeograph machine.

Still, it was Walker's finest hour at the SCLC. Not a comma of the blueprint was altered when he finished. Instead, the conclave spent nearly two days talking and praying that it would work. Among their advantages was the relative vacuum of competition in Birmingham. The NAACP, still outlawed in Alabama, was not a factor, and SNCC had no projects in Birmingham. Shuttlesworth was the unquestioned master of the Alabama Christian Movement for Human Rights (ACMHR), which had not missed a Monday mass meeting in nearly seven years. So long as King and Shuttlesworth got along, there would be no paralyzing schisms. Another potential advantage was Birmingham's economic structure. It remained largely a Carpetbagger city, answerable to steel interests and other corporate power in the North. Walker and O'Dell had been making lists of the companies, so that SCLC supporters could exert leverage on their home bases.

On the other side, the ACMHR could provide only a fraction of the manpower they would need, and they acknowledged that their support was spotty at best among the bulk of Birmingham's Negro leaders. A. G.

Gaston might well oppose them. The pastor of the Sixteenth Street Baptist Church had been badgering the SCLC to pay for the cost of burning the church lights for two nights during the previous September convention—hardly a sign of wholehearted support. Andrew Young said his canvass of the Birmingham preachers had not been encouraging, and Walker admitted that the conservative Negro Ministerial Association might actively oppose them. They ran through the preachers, name by name, until Shuttlesworth interrupted them. "Don't worry, Martin," he said. "I can handle the preachers."

King managed a smile. "You better be right," he replied.

Bull Connor loomed over the discussion. He had made Birmingham into his private fiefdom of segregation, with bareknuckled police tactics that had done nothing to discourage a tradition of vigilante violence. Negro Birmingham was dotted with bomb sites to prove it. The prospect of violence posed no ethical problems for King. "If it comes, we will surface it for the world to see," he said. The issue was whether Project C could withstand systematic repression. Most of the eleven said they needed to move quickly, while the Birmingham reform movement had the whites divided and Connor on the defensive.

Toward the end of the second day, King turned solemnly to O'Dell. "Jack, tell me about the money," he said. "If we run dry again in the next few months, the press will say we went into Birmingham just to get out of debt."

O'Dell was ready with his projections. The SCLC had earned a net profit of $25,000 in the last quarter of 1962, he said, not counting the $12,000 realized from the Sammy Davis fund-raiser, and mass appeals from the New York office promised to double or triple the 1962 revenues. "We are mailing now in lots of 200,000," he reported, to lists of proven return rates. Based on the mailings already out from the New York office and those in the works, O'Dell predicted confidently that direct-mail income would more than pay for the SCLC's regular expenses through the first six months of the year.

On O'Dell's word, King stopped talking about postponing Birmingham for a grand fund-raising tour. Instead, he went around the table asking his colleagues for closing thoughts. Some gave chipper speeches; others passed. Stanley Levison reminded them of Bull Connor's formative political experiences in the 1930s, when he had broken Birmingham's labor movement as a steel company employee. Relatively speaking, he said, the labor movement of the thirties was more powerful than the civil rights movement of the present. Therefore, they could make no mistakes now. They were in for a rough fight.

King closed the meeting somberly. "There are eleven people here as-

sessing the type of enemy we're going to face," he said. "I have to tell
you that in my judgment, some of the people sitting here today will not
come back alive from this campaign. And I want you to think about it."

Shortly thereafter, FBI agents from the Savannah office filmed a deeply
preoccupied group of eleven as they filed into the airport. In a bureaucracy such as the FBI, it was no casual matter to arrange this surveillance
on short notice—to pull agents from other duties, to carry out the security liaison work with the airport managers, to process intelligence on
the whereabouts of the subjects, to secure, place, and operate a hidden
camera. All this was the product of peremptory orders from Director
Hoover himself. His progress reports on the retreat already had landed
on Attorney General Kennedy's desk. A quick survey of the Bureau's
Negro informants turned up no one who knew anything about the meeting, and the Bureau had no idea what had been discussed. This very
secrecy would have made the Dorchester retreat seem sinister to Hoover
even if Levison and O'Dell had not been present. As it was, Hoover saw
King meeting surreptitiously with two Communists, including one who
was supposed to have resigned. On this point, his reports attracted the
Attorney General's suspicion. "Burke—this is not getting any better,"
Kennedy wrote on one of Hoover's memos.

Kennedy's attention reinforced a surge of triumphant indignation in
the Bureau. They had ensnared King in a nest of spies; the Dorchester
meeting might as well have occurred in Red Square. It was then that
Deke DeLoach, who had made a career of reading the shifting moods
within Hoover's FBI, composed his inflamed memo on King's failure to
respond to his phone message in November. "I see no further need to
contacting Rev. King inasmuch as he obviously does not desire to be
given the truth," DeLoach concluded. "The fact that he is a vicious liar
is amply demonstrated by the fact he constantly associates with and
takes instructions from Stanley Levison who is a hidden member of the
Communist Party in New York."

"I concur," Hoover scrawled at the bottom of the memo. With that, on
King's thirty-fourth birthday, the FBI officially wrote him off as unfit for
mediation or negotiation. Thereafter, upon receiving intelligence that
someone was trying to kill him, the Bureau would refuse to warn King
as it routinely warned other potential targets, such as Shuttlesworth.
The FBI assigned full enemy status to King, who had staked his life and
his religion on the chance that enemy-thinking might be overcome. That
an intelligence agency took such a step in the belief that King was an
enemy of freedom, ignorant of the reality that King had just set in motion
the greatest firestorm of domestic liberty in a hundred years, was one of
the saddest ironies of American history.

It took King three months of delay and foreboding to reach Birmingham. Early in the new year, he went to Washington for a private, unpublicized conference with Attorney General Kennedy. No record survives, but circumstances indicate that Robert Kennedy was moving deeper into his middle-man role between King and J. Edgar Hoover, accommodating each one while emphasizing the faults of the other. King came away in grudging awareness that he could not finesse the O'Dell accusations so easily as he had tried in the fall. Reluctantly, he notified O'Dell that he needed a "paper record" to show that he had taken seriously the allegations that O'Dell was a Communist agent. He asked for a written record of O'Dell's Communist associations, along with a restatement of his commitment to nonviolence and a pledge of loyalty to the American form of government. When O'Dell complied, King asked Clarence Jones to write a letter to Attorney General Kennedy using O'Dell's statements to justify King's decision to retain him on the SCLC staff. Jones, reflecting fresh paranoia around King and the charged secrecy of the Kennedy officials, blanked out O'Dell's name wherever it appeared in his draft.

King protected O'Dell at a relatively small cost, but to him the character examination was a skulking, undignified diversion, and the Kennedy Administration's preoccupation with it a sign of growing distance from the movement in tone and substance. President Kennedy, in a background interview with the Negro press, advanced the opinion that the country faced no "serious division" on racial matters, and that the problems of Negroes could be subsumed in the Administration's overall approach to education and economic growth. Lee White, his civil rights aide, told the President what he wanted to hear—that the Negro population "was pretty much at peace." King, speaking directly to President Kennedy by phone from the Attorney General's office, pleaded with him to include civil rights legislation in his State of the Union address, which would mark the beginning of Kennedy's third year in the White House. Thus far, Kennedy had asked for none of the legislation promised by the Democratic platform of 1960, and once again he had decided to postpone civil rights legislation. It would never pass, said the President, who maintained that he could do more for civil rights by appointment and executive order than by the futile, costly gesture of sending unpassable bills to Congress.

The mention of executive orders only deepened King's disappointment, because he knew that President Kennedy was implicitly rejecting any Lincolnesque proclamation against segregation laws. The last symbolic chance for that historic step had just passed by, and the Administration was preparing instead for Louis Martin's White House reception on Lincoln's Birthday. Martin and his allies sent a thousand invitations to a large cross-section of the Negro elite. President Nabrit of Howard University would be there among the college presidents, and J. H. Jackson atop the preachers. The list included Langston Hughes among the surviving literati of the Harlem Renaissance. In his enthusiasm, Martin was boasting that President Kennedy would host on one evening more Negro guests than had assembled in the cumulative history of the White House.

At the same time, the White House strictly reserved all press announcements to itself. The gala event was being planned deliberately to maximize the personal flattery of the Negro guests while minimizing the political exposure everywhere else, especially among whites. Most of the guests did not begrudge the public relations. They saw their invitations as both a personal and political boon—an evening in Camelot to mark a confidential alliance with Kennedy. The Negro press throttled its boosterism to downplay the event, and even the chatty *Jet* magazine scolded nightclub celebrity Dick Gregory for trying to take professional advantage of his invitation: "Baby, you don't send out advance publicity on meeting President Kennedy when you're a social guest."

Only a half-dozen years earlier, King had connived artfully to get himself invited to the Eisenhower White House, and his subsequent speeches revealed an acute hunger for swirling gowns and royal palaces. Now he was among the very few who harbored doubts about going to the White House at all. Still undecided on February 4, he and Walker drove down to the country wilderness of "Terrible" Terrell County to speak at groundbreaking ceremonies for the reconstruction of one of the churches burned down the previous summer. From south Georgia, King flew to New York to address the American Jewish Congress. This was an important speech for him, because Stanley Levison had helped make the AJC a leading supporter in the *Sullivan* libel case. The U.S. Supreme Court had just accepted for review the $500,000 state verdict—the first of several punishments administered along with King's perjury indictment at the dawn of the 1960 sit-ins—and the Court's pending action brought *Sullivan* to widespread attention among constitutional scholars for its potential impact on First Amendment law.

While huddling with Levison before the AJC fund-raiser, King decided to boycott Kennedy's Lincoln's Birthday reception. His rejection coincided with a last-minute change that made the affair all but irresistible by Washington standards. Letitia Baldrige, Kennedy's social secretary, was notifying guests that they were to report not to the East Gate for the reception itself, as their invitations instructed, but to the Southwest

Gate so that they first could be "specially presented" to President and Mrs. Kennedy in the intimacy of the upstairs living quarters at the White House. King sent his regrets in a polite but disingenuous telegram. It was true that Coretta was "expecting our fourth child" and that King had a speech to make "out of the country." But the baby was not due for nearly two months, and King's important-sounding overseas speech was merely the pretext for his escape. After preaching for Adam Clayton Powell in New York and speaking at several fund-raisers, he flew off for a vacation in Jamaica.

He became a brooding, pensive man as he contemplated the leap ahead. In speeches before Birmingham, King returned to some of the formative influences on his beliefs, as though seeking reassurance. From Harry Emerson Fosdick, the surviving founder of Rockefeller's Riverside Church, he cited the distinction between enforceable and unforceable obligations: "Man-made laws assure justice, but a higher law produces love. No code of conduct ever compelled a father to love his children." He quoted Frederick Douglass and Martin Buber. On the necessity of religious and psychological freedom for the human character, he referred to Tillich: "Man is man because he is free." On the social and religious imperatives of freedom, he marshaled Kant's categorical imperative and then added a dictum of his own: "Two segregated souls never meet in God." He quoted St. Augustine's warning: "Those that sit at rest while others take pains are tender turtles, and buy their quiet with disgrace." In handwritten additions to his standard speeches, King begged the churches to abandon their silence during the crisis of freedom, so as to save themselves from "what Reinhold Niebuhr has recently called the 'sin of triviality.' "

King's irritation with the established church had been percolating for months. At a historic Chicago conference on religion and race, just after the Dorchester strategy session, he informed eight hundred distinguished clergymen that "noble pronouncements filter down too slowly." He called for preachers willing to sacrifice, saying, "We are gravely mistaken if we think that religion protects us from the pain and agony of mortal existence." This was his message to the entire clergy, high and low, black and white. He preached it to the liberal white clergy in Chicago, and he preached it with blunt anger to his congregation back home at Ebenezer. "I'm sick and tired of seeing Negro preachers riding around in big cars and living in big houses and not concerned about the problems of the people who made it possible for them to get these things," he said from his pulpit. "It seems that I can hear the almighty God say, 'Stop preaching your loud sermons and whooping your irrelevant mess in my face, for your hands are full of tar. For the people that I sent you to serve are

in need, and you are doing nothing but being concerned about yourself.'
Seems that I can hear God saying that it's time to rise up now and make
it clear that the evils of the universe must be removed. And that God
isn't going to do all of it by himself. The church that overlooks this is a
dangerously irrelevant church."

These internal tempests went with King to Jamaica, where Wyatt
Walker had taught him to play golf only a couple of years earlier. After
the Freedom Rides, King began to criticize golf as too bourgeois, too
frivolous, and Walker, who cultivated the banker's habit of saying that
Wednesday afternoon was his "golf day," kept up a running argument
about whether King was letting the movement interfere too much with
his private life. Increasingly preoccupied, King welcomed the escape to
Jamaica, but urgent distractions followed him across the water. Dooto
Records of Los Angeles, whose recordings of Redd Foxx and other come-
dians had made it the first nationwide, Negro-owned recording company,
was selling a pirated album of King's speeches. King feared that filing a
lawsuit would make him look greedy and also poison his chances of
gaining a contract with Dooto, but Walker convinced him that he had no
choice if he wanted to protect his capacity to earn money for the movement. King decided to sue for $200,000, pledging any proceeds to the
SCLC. Then from Fifth Avenue in New York came an elegant letter from
Stephen Currier, telling King that his Taconic Foundation was "reviewing our major commitments," such as its grants to the VEP and the
citizenship school at Dorchester. Currier invited King to join the Taconic
trustees and other selected philanthropists for a round-table "evaluation of Negro gains up to the present . . . together with an equally well-
informed and sophisticated discussion of what can be anticipated in the
foreseeable future." King did not enjoy the role of supplicant, but he had
to endure the vagaries of money managers—whether they played as
loosely as Dooto or as stiffly as the Taconic trustees.

On February 8, while King was in Jamaica, J. Walter Yeagley, Robert
Kennedy's assistant in charge of the Internal Security Division, startled
J. Edgar Hoover with a memorandum stating that Internal Security
wished to consider criminal prosecution of Stanley Levison as a member
of a subversive organization. This was an extraordinary suggestion, as
the Justice Department long since had severely restricted "membership"
prosecutions on constitutional grounds. Smith Act cases, which had
made Herbert ("I Led Three Lives") Philbrick nationally famous as an
FBI informant in the Communist show trials of the late 1940s, had been
nearly extinct since 1956, when Attorney General Herbert Brownell

ruled that the department would decline to seek indictment without evidence that the target was acting upon "an actual plan for a violent revolution." Under the McCarran Act of 1950, the department generally authorized prosecution only of those who failed to register as national officers of the Communist Party. Although Levison met neither of these standards, even by the FBI's description of him, Yeagley was declaring in effect that if he was as dangerous a Communist operative as Hoover kept saying in his classified bulletins, then the Justice Department was prepared to waive the restrictions. It would be worth the political heat to put Levison out of business, if not in prison, by indictment and trial. In his memorandum, Yeagley asked Hoover for a "current prosecutive summary report."

In the FBI, notwithstanding that Hoover and DeLoach had all but formally declared war on King in January, Yeagley's resolve was far from welcome. It meant that the Bureau would have to corroborate its allegations against Levison. Alternatively, admitting that the allegations came only from the Childs brothers, Hoover would have to make his prized informants available for cross-examination in court. Neither prospect was attractive, as Hoover much preferred the license of political intelligence to the rigors and risks of law enforcement. Hoping to find another way, he ordered agents from the New York office to seek other Communist informants who might testify against Levison. Scrambling, the agents interviewed their best fourteen informants, only to find that not a single one recognized Levison's name or photograph. They told Hoover it was useless. As a last hope, Hoover directed Rhode Island agents to interview Louis Budenz, a contemporary with Morris Childs at the *Daily Worker* in the 1940s, who, along with Philbrick, had been a star witness in the most prominent Smith Act trial. Budenz did not know Levison either.

Once again Hoover used the spy's escape hatch: the reason for the absence of corroborating evidence was precisely that Levison's work was secret even among Communist functionaries. On February 12, the day of President Kennedy's Lincoln's Birthday reception, Hoover wrote Yeagley that the FBI could furnish no "prosecutive summary" on Levison, because the information came from "a highly sensitive source who is not available for interview or testimony." This was the last, naked bluff. Yeagley's choice was to blink or protest bluntly that the emperor wore no clothes, and, faced with the authority of J. Edgar Hoover himself, he blinked. The Levison-King investigation remained in the confines of political intelligence, where Hoover wanted it. Shortly thereafter, the Bureau's internal report on the unsuccessful effort at corroboration was filed away, marked DO NOT DISSEMINATE.

At the White House, the Kennedys' party was going well until the President spotted Sammy Davis, Jr., among the guests milling around the upstairs living quarters. Kennedy was aghast—"absolutely feathered," as his aide Lee White put it a year later. He had nothing against Davis personally, and in fact had socialized with him in the company of Frank Sinatra and Peter Lawford. But that was in California. What galvanized the President now was the fact that Davis, as half of the most famous interracial couple in the United States, was sure to draw the concentrated attention of the press corps photographers waiting downstairs. Kennedy feared that shots of him with the Davises would make deadly smear material in a close campaign. Moreover, as a gifted observer of the press, he sensed that White House photos of Sammy Davis would draw enough press interest to break through Pierre Salinger's carefully planned media snooze on the reception.

Kennedy snatched his aides into various side rooms and closets, demanding to know how Sammy Davis got through the gates. None of the aides, including Louis Martin, owned up to the knowledge that Martin himself had tenaciously reinserted Davis' name on the clearance list every time it disappeared. Everyone shrugged dumbly over the mysteries of bureaucracy, until the President calmed down to address the practical question of how to keep Davis out of the photographs without provoking his anger or the press's interest. They debated the problem furtively while Kennedy continued to greet the guests. One strategy called for Mrs. Kennedy to draw Davis aside for some private discussion just as the photographers were admitted. Shortly after Mrs. Kennedy was given instructions, however, panicky word spread that the plan offended her as an insult to White House manners, or to Davis, or to Mrs. Davis—the aides were not sure which. In any case, the First Lady was refusing to come downstairs for the reception. President Kennedy himself had to patch that up before the operation could proceed.

For Lee White, Louis Martin, and other Kennedy assistants, the President's anger over the Davis presence produced an unforgettable jolt, but the evening went off smoothly on the surface. Sammy Davis' face went unrecorded. At Lincoln's Birthday celebrations all around the country, Republicans had to do without the best-known Negro speakers—a collateral, partisan benefit of the White House evening that did not go unappreciated. Salinger's press office managed to cast the reception as a minor event in President Kennedy's day, subsidiary to his receiving a Lincoln centennial report from the Civil Rights Commission. Salinger led the reporters to focus on the less threatening aspects of the report, such as the overcrowding of Negro students in urban schools. The *New York Times* account, headed "Civil Rights Fight Shifting to North," noted the reception in passing as a gathering of "civil rights leaders and Government officials," and of the guests mentioned only Vice President Johnson by name. To Louis Martin, such dissembling was the price of crashing the White House social barrier against Negroes. Hints of recognition escaped the privacy of Negro society—*Newsweek* called the casual acceptance of the reception a "milestone" in itself—but even as a secret, Martin prized the historic accomplishment of securing admission for an entire generation of leadership. He went off to recuperate in Miami about the time King returned from Jamaica.

Those who joined King in boycotting President Kennedy's party were few but highly significant. A. Philip Randolph and Clarence Mitchell refused to come, and each was more explicit than King in letting it be known that he did so in protest of Kennedy's timidity. Randolph's impatience was such that for months he had been talking with Bayard Rustin about reviving his 1942 plans for a march on Washington, with which he had bluffed President Roosevelt into integrating the nation's war industries. Mitchell, the NAACP's chief lobbyist in Washington, stayed home because Kennedy had given him nothing to lobby for in Congress. He regarded the New Frontier much less favorably than did his old colleague Roy Wilkins—so much so that there were rumors of a feud between them. For months, Mitchell had been dropping veiled warnings that the NAACP might do well to defect to the Republicans. He argued that the Republicans in Congress already had introduced bills to attack segregation, job discrimination, and voter intimidation—acting on all the promises made by both political parties in 1960.

Late in February, President Kennedy reacted to the warnings of revolt by introducing a voting rights bill. His decision came so unexpectedly that Lee White and others stayed up all night drafting the legislation. The bill, hustled up to Congress with a written message, attracted modest applause at best. Liberal Republicans said their legislation was much better. Disappointed civil rights leaders suggested that it was a narrow and limited afterthought, albeit a worthy one. Even those who had basked in the glow of the Lincoln's Birthday reception could not bring themselves to praise the initiative with much enthusiasm. President Kennedy, bound by his own inclinations and by the Southerners of his party, had worked himself into a corner where on all sides he received less criticism for doing nothing substantive in civil rights than for doing a little bit.

Governor Rockefeller seized the moment to attack Kennedy's civil rights record. At an NAACP rally in upstate New York, he proclaimed what Clarence Mitchell had been saying in private. Trenchantly, Rockefeller attacked Kennedy's much-publicized plan to make racial progress through presidential appointments, charging that the President's most critical appointments had been four Southern judges of well-known segregationist views. This pointed attack by a leading presidential rival for 1964 stimulated the only civil rights question at Kennedy's next press conference. The President replied by commending his four judges for "a remarkable job in fulfilling their oaths of office." He compared them favorably with Eisenhower's appointments in the South, then moved on to a question about the Cuban missile crisis.

The next day, Kennedy called Nicholas Katzenbach at the Justice Department. "Is it real bad?" he asked, putting Katzenbach in an awkward spot. On one hand, Katzenbach knew full well that Rockefeller's attack actually had understated the Republican case against the Kennedy judges. The best civil rights judges in the South, and indeed the department's only hopes for racial justice through the courts, were Eisenhower appointees; the most egregious segregationists were Kennedy's, and they were more than four in number. On the other hand, Katzenbach was a subordinate officer whose boss, the President of the United States—who was probably staring at the front page of the morning *New York Times*, where his "remarkable job" quotation was splashed alongside unsavory descriptions of the judges—wanted reassurance that the dangerous Nelson Rockefeller had not made a fool of him. Katzenbach waffled, saying that one Kennedy appointment "hasn't been impossible." Bravely he forced out some of the worst news—that Judge Cox of Mississippi "has not been good"—but when the President almost plaintively remarked that "our other appointments have, uh, uh, have done pretty well," and then waited for a comment, Katzenbach turned bitter truth to sweetness. "I don't think we have anything to be embarrassed about on that," he said.

This controversy over the Kennedy judges flared up in the beginning of March 1963. King preached at Ebenezer those first two Sundays. There was always a private, cocoon-like quality to his sermons before the home congregation. Now, having disappeared from public sight to purify himself for Birmingham, his tone was even more self-absorbed than usual. He preached on his lifelong preoccupation with the nature of evil in the world, using as his standard text the story from Matthew 17 about the disciples who were shaken because they could not exorcise the evil spirit from a madman. "Why could we not cast him out?" they asked.

In his sermon, King replied that evil was beyond the responsibility of God as well as beyond the reach of man. He ridiculed as hypocrites those who supinely left the cause of righteousness to supernatural beings.

These were the "big Negro preachers" in Cadillacs and all the timid souls of false piety who allowed comfort or habit to subvert the demands of conscience. Hammering on his theme, King showed the passion that was driving him into Birmingham, but related passions were just as strong. They could not cast the demon out, he told the congregation, because evil was too deeply rooted in human character. No human faculty, known or unknown, developed or undeveloped, could touch it—not the liberal reason of a dozen Enlightenments, nor all the wildest dreams of scientific progress fulfilled. "The humanist hope is an illusion," King said.

Then, to illustrate his point, he did not turn outward to the usual depravities of slavery, the Holocaust, or the atomic bomb. Instead, he invited the congregation to look inward with him at addictions that seemed simple at first but then grew slowly more tenacious until finally, overcoming all goodwill, they emerged almost innocently as invincible evil—alien, yet human as a toothache. "Many of you here know something of what it is to struggle with sin":

> Year by year you became aware of the terrible sin that was taking posses-
> sion of your life. It may have been slavery to drink, un-truthfulness, the
> impurity of selfishness or sexual promiscuity. And as the years unfolded
> the vice grew bolder and bolder. You knew all along that it was an unnatu-
> ral intrusion. Never could you adjust to the fact. You knew all along that it
> was wrong and that it had invaded your life as an unnatural intruder. You
> said to yourself, "One day I'm going to rise up and drive this evil out. I
> know it is wrong. It is destroying my character and embarrassing my fam-
> ily." At last the day came and you made a New Year's resolution that would
> get rid of the whole base evil. And then the next year came around and you
> were doing the same old evil thing. Can you remember the surprise and
> disappointment that gripped you when you discovered that after all of your
> sincere effort—you discovered that after all that you had done through your
> resolutions to get rid of it—the old habit was still there? And out of amaze-
> ment you found yourself asking, "Why could I not cast it out?" And in this
> moment of despair you decided to take your problem to God . . . You dis-
> covered that the evil was still with you. God would not cast it out.

King expressed another passion all too real—an empathy with evil that became relentless self-abasement, a cry for penance. Low and leveling, yielding to no one in keenness of feeling, this raging humility collided with high righteousness to produce a synthetic passion that was uniquely King's.

On one level, he resolved the conflict simply for the congregation. Neither God nor human beings would transform human nature alone; human beings must allow God to attack evil through them. "This is the only way to be delivered from the accumulated weight of evil," he said.

"It can only be done when we allow the energy of God to be let loose in our souls. May we go out today big in faith." From there he began to fashion a closing based on the conventional theology of mankind's need to invite partnership with the divine. The humblest Ebenezer member could understand it, and the most devout fundamentalist could not object to the conclusion. Still, most members knew that this was no ordinary Baptist sermon. King's fiery attacks on the Cadillac preachers carried a frightening promise of true controversy; his meditations on evil conveyed authentic despair.

The examples of hope that King rolled out came not from the struggles of everyday life but from the pantheon of immortals. He spoke of "Simon of Sand" converted into "Peter of Rock," of "persecuting Saul into an Apostle Paul," and of "the lust-infested Augustine into a Saint Augustine." He quoted Tolstoy's claim of utter transformation: " 'What was good and bad changed places . . . The things I used to do, I don't do them now. The places I used to go, I don't go there now. The thoughts I used to think, I don't think them now.' " King referred to legendary sinners who had redirected the torment of their inner confessions to produce historical miracles. The evidence of their conversions was a changed world. As King himself contemplated a historical miracle in Birmingham, his sermons revealed a turbulent conflict over the relationship between the public and private person. Perhaps it was possible by extraordinary feats and sacrifices for the public man to redeem the private man. Perhaps it was possible for private demons not only to drive the public man but also to help him—to leaven his hubris, allow him to see opponents instead of enemies. If King felt fury, it was not against Bull Connor or the most virulent of racists, as there were more unfathomable sins than theirs, but against the aloof moderates and blind pietists who refused to see that King was offering them a way out of a maddeningly obvious and relatively *easy* evil—the sins against brotherhood.

Here was direction for King, but not comfort or clarity. It was never comfortable for a man who spoke all his life of consuming guilt to be held up as a public saint. And his course made a paradox of King's fundamental conception of evil. In the manner of the nineteenth-century dialecticians, King seemed to be turning Reinhold Niebuhr on his head: the evil within individual people was more intractable than the injustices of society, not less. If a sinner like King could produce a miracle of public morality in Birmingham, what became of *Moral Man and Immoral Society?* What then became of Niebuhr's theology? Worshippers at Ebenezer often saw through such muddles. When King seemed depressed and out of sorts, they came out of his sermons shaking their heads over his powerful rumblings, remarking that he was a "God-troubled" man, surely on the verge of shaking up the white man's world.

After his sermon on evil, King hurried to preach that same day in Birmingham for Shuttlesworth's chief assistant in the ACMHR, Rev. Nelson "Fireball" Smith. Birmingham's special election fell on Tuesday of that week. By Wyatt Walker's original plans for Project C, the demonstrations were to have commenced the following day, March 6, but complaints from Birmingham Negroes already had forced a postponement until March 14. The idea was that they needed at least a week or two after the election to prepare for the campaign, and also to find out whether the election produced a more favorable political climate in Birmingham. The compromise target of March 14 left exactly one month in what Walker called the "prime shopping season" before Easter, during which the combination of an economic boycott and escalating demonstrations would have the maximum chance to break segregation in the city.

No clear winner emerged from the March 5 election, however, and a runoff between Bull Connor and Albert Boutwell was scheduled for April 2. With the limbo in Birmingham politics thus extended for another four weeks, the arguments for delay resurfaced within the King-Shuttlesworth alliance. All Birmingham was alive to the fateful choice on whether or not to end the Bull Connor era. Connor, by making himself the chief obstacle to the Chamber of Commerce as well as the civil rights movement, had united the downtrodden with the elite. Inside the unlikely, unspoken coalition against him—Negroes, labor unions, white newspapers, reformers, and image-conscious businessmen such as Sidney Smyer—everyone was compulsively on his best behavior. By their reckoning, the spring of 1963 suddenly became the worst possible time to launch racial demonstrations in Birmingham. A. G. Gaston strenuously opposed the campaign. Rev. J. L. Ware, president of the Baptist Ministers' Alliance, almost broke public silence on King's plans with near passage of a resolution that warned King to stay out of the city. Private opinion among Negro leaders ran so strongly that even Shuttlesworth—who normally belittled the difference between the runoff candidates, calling Boutwell merely a "dignified Connor"—hesitated to leap in against the tide. After all, he was in exile from Birmingham, living in Cincinnati.

James Lawson was prominent among the few who argued against postponement. Since the January retreat at Dorchester, he had been making periodic forays into Birmingham from his church in Memphis, conducting workshops in nonviolent methods for members of Shuttlesworth's ACMHR. Lawson's job was to train the foot soldiers for Project C, as he had trained those for the prolonged campaigns against segregation in Nashville and other cities. Meeting in church basements and private homes, often introduced by Wyatt Walker, Lawson had been recruiting, teaching, proselytizing for nonviolence. His goal was to find as many volunteers as possible who were willing to endure ten days in the Birmingham jail. If their initial inspiration survived the practice tests staged in the workshops, they signed the nonviolence pledge cards Lawson had designed. By March, Walker had some two hundred cards in his "jail file," and Lawson opposed postponement on the grounds that these two hundred people—not the whims of Birmingham politics—should guide decisions. Their readiness and their morale were what mattered.

Walker heard people quoting his earlier exhortations on the vital importance of the Easter shopping season. But, since they now had to wait until after the April 2 runoff, they said, and since there wouldn't be enough time after that to build a good campaign before Easter, and since Birmingham's Negroes then would have spent all their money and therefore would not be able to boycott effectively until the Christmas shopping season, perhaps they should postpone until the end of 1963. The drift of such comments drove home Lawson's point that all these professed practicalities were nothing more than an outward sign of the fears that inhibited any mass protest. There was always good reason to postpone. But the stark realities of Birmingham so concentrated these inhibitions that they threatened to strip away the support of local Negro leaders, and this was a loss that King could not ignore. While he granted Lawson's point that it would be twice as difficult to re-recruit jailgoers after a long postponement, he also saw that recriminations were bubbling up with the arguments for postponement. Preachers were letting loose their resentments against Shuttlesworth, calling him an absentee autocrat. Even John Porter, King's protégé and former assistant pastor at Dexter Avenue, whom King had just installed personally in a Birmingham pulpit, was holding back from Project C. He said Shuttlesworth was an unstable dictator.

They teetered back and forth between the urge to go ahead and the pressure to postpone. On Saturday, March 9, the FBI monitors picked up an extremely guarded phone conversation between Jack O'Dell and Stanley Levison, in which Levison asked whether the campaign "in the unnamed city" was still scheduled as planned. O'Dell replied that it was. The next day, however, King himself told Levison that he had decided to "postpone that thing until the day after the election, because Bull Connor is in the runoff, and we feel that if we make a move before that time, he could use that to his advantage." Another factor holding him back, King confessed to Levison, was his assumption that Birmingham whites would "do everything they can to destroy the image of the SCLC." He mentioned specifically the Birmingham *News* and its published accusations that King employed Communist subversives such as O'Dell.

This intercepted conversation was the FBI's first notice that King was contemplating a new campaign, and the Bureau circulated an internal appeal for information on "King's purpose in going to Birmingham." Meanwhile, at Ebenezer that Sunday, King preached his own version of Vernon Johns's "Segregation After Death" sermon on the parable of Lazarus and Dives. He did not go to Birmingham the next day for the regular mass meeting, but Shuttlesworth flew in from Cincinnati. Despite the runoff and despite King's wishes, the idea of an immediate launch was still alive in his mind. That night's meeting revealed a mixture of anticipation and coyness. "There will be no nigger any more," one speaker promised. "It will be *mister* nigger." Shuttlesworth, without disclosing any details to Connor's detectives in the audience, told the crowd that Attorney General Kennedy would protect them in the dangers ahead. The next day, Wyatt Walker and the Birmingham leaders continued to debate the wisdom of postponement, and not until that Friday did Shuttlesworth finally concur in the delay, which ran against his entire persona—his promises, famed bravado, and grand assurances of control over Birmingham's Negro preachers. His letter to King and Walker masked concessions to nerves or adversity behind a thick screen of vagueness.

The extent of King's commitment was sinking in: he must change Birmingham, for otherwise Birmingham's past would be his future, in which case he was finished. To meet this challenge, he now seemed to have less than minimal support, plus a run of bad luck and more internal problems than usual. Various factions of lawyers were squabbling over the anticipated legal cases for Project C, and one disgruntled former staff member, who quit upon being chastised for unauthorized use of SCLC travel expenses, was making nasty public charges that King had "sold out to Governor Rockefeller" for personal gain. In short, nothing was falling easily into place, and all these deficiencies put King so much on edge that he spent the last two weeks of March exploring a backup amendment to the plan: if all else failed in Birmingham and the movement's momentum collapsed, he would appeal to outsiders to pour into Birmingham to help fill the jails. King felt the need for such a contingency force so strongly that he went as far away as Washington, D.C., asking trusted friends to recruit secret cadres of volunteers. Walter Fauntroy, Walker's old seminary friend, accepted the assignment. His reports on a growing list of reserves in the capital soon established him in King's mind as a figure of comfort.

From Washington, King flew home to Atlanta on March 27, just in time to take Coretta to the hospital for the birth of their fourth child, Bernice Albertine—the one conceived in Albany. He paused long enough to pose with the mother and infant for a photographer from *Jet*, then slipped back into Birmingham on March 29. From there he flew to New

York City on the thirty-first. The secret meeting was partly Harry Belafonte's idea and partly Levison's. Noting King's habit of running to his
Northern supporters in the midst of a crisis, they suggested that it might
be wiser for King to take these supporters into his confidence by giving
them advance notice of Project C. That way King would look more organized, and the supporters, feeling more a part of the drama, might
respond more readily to appeals for help. Wyatt Walker, who stayed behind in Birmingham, belittled the plan as a "stroking session" for the
celebrities, "a little razzmatazz," but King was sparing no courtesy. With
Shuttlesworth, Abernathy, Levison, and Clarence Jones, he pushed his
way into Belafonte's jammed apartment past actors Anthony Quinn and
Fredric March, past William and Lotte Kunstler, Governor Rockefeller's
press man Hugh Morrow, James Wechsler of the New York *Post* and
some seventy other reporters, dignitaries, friends, and strangers—all
sworn to secrecy. King functioned well for his own speech that evening,
but during Shuttlesworth's emotional description of the dangers before
them in Birmingham his head jerked ever so slightly. Belafonte thought
it was a nervous tic brought on by tension. He had not seen such physical
signs of stress in King before.

It was not until almost morning, when everyone except Abernathy had
gone home, that King began to relax. Julie Belafonte brought out his
personal bottle of Harvey's Bristol Cream. Ever since she had introduced
him to the sherry, King had kept up a running joke about how much he
savored the nightcap of the most elegant New Yorkers. Whenever he
came to the Belafonte home, he made a great show of inspecting the
bottle to make sure that the sherry had not fallen below the line he had
marked carefully on the label at the end of his last visit. That night,
sipping his Harvey's, he conquered Birmingham by teasing his comrade.
"Let me be sure to get arrested with people who don't snore," he intoned,
eyeing Abernathy.

Abernathy protested vehemently that he did no such thing.

King's eyes went wide with delight. "You are *torture*," he declared.
"White folks ain't *invented* anything that can get to me like you do.
Anything they want me to admit to, I will, if they'll just get you and your
snoring out of my cell."

He and Abernathy guffawed and pantomimed until sleep came, as they
had done back in Montgomery. Then they flew back to Atlanta, where
waiting for King was a notice that all tickets for the newly integrated
Metropolitan Opera tour in Atlanta were sold out. He brought Coretta
and the baby home from the hospital on Tuesday, April 2, and left that
same afternoon for Birmingham. Slipping into a city whose attention was
riveted on the ballot-counting from that day's runoff election, King went

unnoticed to the Gaston Motel to find Wyatt Walker waiting with his clipboard and all his lists—the jail list, the phone volunteer list, the transportation committee list, the food list, the mail-room list, plus his layout charts of the targeted downtown lunch counters and his street maps of the best routes to get there. To the second, Walker knew precisely how much longer it would take the average old person to walk to McCrory's for a sit-in than the average teenager, but all his mountain of lists and calculations seemed pitifully small next to the core identity of an American city. In the end, Project C was no social science formula, approximation of political risks, or rational exercise of any kind, not even one touched by genius. It was a cold plunge.

NINETEEN

GREENWOOD AND BIRMINGHAM JAIL

A transit strike made Birmingham quieter than usual on Wednesday, April 3, or "B-Day," as Walker mobilized his telephone list to call his jail list—350 by his count, 250 by King's later memory—and of these, some sixty-five showed up to fulfill their pledge. In the basement of A. D. King's church, Walker briefed them like an air commander before a bombing mission, with the logistics sketched out on a blackboard. King and James Lawson followed with a final reprise on the philosophy of nonviolence. Then they set off to meet Shuttlesworth at the Sixteenth Street Baptist Church, which sat just across Kelly Ingram Park from King's headquarters at the Gaston Motel. Shuttlesworth already had dispatched two of his sturdiest ACMHR officers to ask for a demonstration permit, face to face with Bull Connor himself, and they reported that Connor had thrown them out of his office, roaring, "I will picket you over to the City Jail!" Shuttlesworth himself distributed copies of his "Birmingham Manifesto" to reporters. "The patience of an oppressed people cannot endure forever," it began. ". . . The absence of justice and progress in Birmingham demands that we make a moral witness to give our community a chance to survive."

Then, stepping through the pane of normalcy, the sixty-five moved off in five groups to lunch counters at Loveman's, Pizitz, Kress, Woolworth's, and Britt's. They had steeled themselves for arrest, but well-rehearsed waitresses at the first four counters simply advised the white customers that they were closing and turned out the lights, leaving the Negroes debating what to do next. Only at Britt's did the management call in the police, who hauled off twenty-one demonstrators in paddy wagons. Bull Connor came out of his office, where, brooding over his defeat by Albert Boutwell, he was formulating a desperate plan to hang on to his job in spite of the election results. In public, Connor castigated the owners of the four closed lunch counters for failing to cooperate with his plan to incarcerate every Negro who challenged segregation. He repeated his public promise to "fill that jail full."

King shared Connor's disappointment with the small number of people jailed. He had hoped to begin more impressively, especially now that the Easter deadline was so near. He and his aides perceived an alarming tide of opposition among activist Negroes, many of whom preferred to celebrate Connor's defeat than to talk of jail. At that night's special mass meeting, Shuttlesworth announced that they would meet every night until the end of the campaign. Abernathy joked with a crowd of four hundred about the urgency of time. "The white man can learn to do the Twist and the Slop in two weeks," he said, "but it has taken us two hundred years to learn to live with each other. . . . Are you ready? Are you ready to make the challenge?" He coaxed some seventy-five new volunteers to come forward to join the jail list, but they managed to get only four of them into jail the next day. Everything seemed to be going wrong. The few reporters who were paying attention puzzled over the gaping difference between these meager results and King's promise of a "full-scale assault" on segregation. Of the handicaps early in the Birmingham crisis, perhaps the most serious was King's image as a reluctant and losing crusader. He had been largely out of the public eye for eight months, since his retreat from Albany. His name had faded. He appeared to be a worthy symbol from the 1950s who had overreached himself trying to operate as a full-fledged political leader.

It was like starting over. King had planned to go to jail himself by the third day, but he decided instead to shore up the internal strength of the movement. In painstaking remedial work, he met almost constantly with groups of ministers, preaching to them, answering skeptical and even hostile questions. With the sit-in plans complicated by the defensive tactics of the store owners, movement leaders switched to protest marches on city hall. Fred Shuttlesworth led the first one on Saturday, April 6, taking more than forty people with him into jail. This was a respectable number. Walker decided that what had been lost in clarity— the plain connection between the demonstration and the demands for lunch-counter integration—was more than offset by signs of life in the campaign. In the private strategy session, however, they had some difficulty finding preachers of stature to follow Shuttlesworth into jail the next day. King had been seeking volunteers from his own SCLC board since January, but the only one who was there and willing was James Lawson, who could not be spared from his workshops. Cutting through the dilatory talk of preaching obligations, King turned to "Fireball" Smith, Shuttlesworth's vice president in the ACMHR, and said, "Smith, I want you to go to jail." He reluctantly agreed. King asked his brother A.D. to join Smith, and then he recruited John Porter to round out the team of preachers leading the next day's march toward city hall.

Bull Connor and his K-9 corps confronted the marchers on the sidewalk before a large crowd of bystanders. Unnerved by the sight of the dogs, a nineteen-year-old demonstrator named Leroy Allen pulled a clay pipe out of his pocket, whereupon two dogs swarmed over him, felling him to the pavement. When officers managed to pull the dogs off, they led Allen into the paddy wagon along with more than twenty other marchers and the three preachers. Primal tales of the police dogs raced through Negro Birmingham that night, contrasting sharply with stories about how grand the three preachers looked being led off to jail in their Palm Sunday robes.

Still, jail volunteers were scarce. All of Walker's cherished details did not save the campaign from the appearance of haphazard spontaneity. Compared with King's previous ventures, Birmingham was mired in a relative news vacuum. Even the local Negro biweekly treated King's campaign as a disturbing rumor and provided no firsthand coverage of the demonstrations. In an editorial, it attacked direct action as "wasteful and worthless" and looked to Mayor-elect Boutwell for solace. Some days later, with more than a hundred demonstrators in the Birmingham jail, the paper headlined a luncheon speech by Roy Wilkins in Kentucky. Walker and King expected such treatment from the Birmingham *World*, which, as a sister paper to the Atlanta *Daily World*, was owned by King's Ebenezer nemesis, C. A. Scott.

They did no better in other media. King launched Project C just as the city was bursting with optimism and civic renewal. Editorial cartoons showed the incoming city leaders eagerly rolling up their sleeves, and the white newspapers shut out the segregationists and King alike as blemishes on the civic reform movement. When Bull Connor and the other two city commissioners announced that they would refuse to leave office on April 15—thus posing the threat of a putsch, or a war between rival governments—they were obliged to buy an advertisement in the *News* to get their intentions published. Almost proudly, the *News* ran a small story about how both Governor George Wallace and Fred Shuttlesworth were complaining of a "blackout of news" on the sit-ins. Approvingly, the white newspapers passed along Mayor-elect Boutwell's declared policy toward King: "I urge everyone, white and Negro, calmly to ignore what is now being attempted in Birmingham."

Notwithstanding King's name and the city's public image as the Bastille of segregation, outside observers ignored the showdown too. President Kennedy made no statement about the demonstrations, and answered no questions because Washington reporters asked none. The Administration's only move was a phone call from Burke Marshall, who, acting on a request from the publisher of the Birmingham *News*, called King to urge delay. Marshall told Walker that Robert Kennedy himself opposed the demonstrations as an "ill-timed" ambush on a reform city government that was not yet in office. National publications reflected the mood of the White House. Birmingham news played in the back pages of *The New York Times*, which headlined its first Project C stories "Integration Drive Slows . . . Sit-Ins and a Demonstration Plan Fail to Materialize . . . Demonstrations Fail to Develop." King complained that never had his work received such negative press in the North.

Most people were in no mood for Birmingham, anyway. During the first exuberant spring since the brush with Armageddon in Cuba, established organs of the mass culture promoted almost anything that was optimistic. *Life* magazine celebrated the government's plans for using hydrogen bombs to blast out new harbors and a copy of the Panama Canal, and predicted that LSD, peyote, and other hallucinogens soon would be harnessed to make people "more productive and generally effective." There was infectious awe over miracles—both profound ones such as the discovery of the DNA molecule, the "key to life itself," and prosaic ones such as the invention of the pop-top beer can. Young Jack Nicklaus challenged Arnold Palmer in the Masters tournament, and the most popular song that April was the Chiffons' bubbly "He's So Fine."

By the time King's volunteers finally began to trickle forward, a meager press appetite for civil rights had settled elsewhere. In the Mississippi Delta, SNCC registration leaders had managed almost unconsciously what King hoped to do by careful design: build a movement that could seize national attention. They succeeded so well that the Kennedy Administration's internal messages on civil rights focused on Mississippi, not Birmingham, even after King's followers began filling Bull Connor's jail. The dreamy grit of the Mississippi students framed an irresistible story of violence and innocence, such that Claude Sitton and other leading reporters stayed with Bob Moses in Greenwood.

To Hollis Watkins and Curtis Hayes, his initial recruits from McComb, Moses added some fifteen SNCC workers to a voter registration project now scattered over six counties of the rich plantation country of the Delta, between the loops of the Mississippi and Yazoo rivers. Group labels mattered little to the workers. Diane Nash Bevel worked for SNCC. Her husband James drew a semi-regular paycheck from the SCLC in Atlanta, which excited mild envy but no scorn. Amzie Moore and Aaron Henry, both of the NAACP, frequently joined their night councils as father figures.

After the discouragements of 1962, their realistic goals for 1963 did not extend much beyond survival. The ruling whites of Mississippi had demonstrated that they were hardly complacent about Negro voting, even in counties where less than 5 percent of eligible Negroes had registered. Ever sensitive to political danger, the Mississippi legislature added a requirement that names of new voter applicants be published in the newspapers for two weeks prior to acceptance. Another new law allowed current voters to object to the "moral character" of applicants. Facing these laws, plus the shootings and padlocked churches, no Mississippi Negro could hope to slip quietly in or out of the courthouse.

The registration movement lived in a tiny glass house. SNCC staff members commonly had no more than thirty dollars a month to cover all personal and office expenses for a county-wide pilot project. Payroll checks, which were sent out sporadically at best, often went to the wrong place or the wrong person. Poverty and internal disorganization severely curtailed movement operations, and, with the post office, the phone company, and all other public facilities in hostile hands, logistical frustrations reached humorous extremes. Sending a message was an art; getting a ride was an ordeal; finding a meeting place was a saga. Even when the volunteers could move and speak, fear among Negroes shut most doors to them. A turnout of twenty sharecroppers was considered a mass meeting. In December 1962, Moses conceded to the Voter Education Project that "we are powerless to register people in significant numbers anywhere in the state." He listed three conditions for change: (1) the removal of the White Citizens Council from control of Mississippi politics; (2) action by the Justice Department to secure safe registration for Negroes; and (3) a mass uprising of the unlettered, fearful Negroes, demanding the immediate right to vote. "Very likely all three will be necessary before a breakthrough can be obtained," wrote Moses.

Desperation drove him to take wild gambles. On January 1, with the endorsement of Martin Luther King and the support of the Gandhi Society, Moses filed a federal suit in Washington against Robert Kennedy and J. Edgar Hoover. Joining Sam Block, Hollis Watkins, and other young

SNCC plaintiffs, he sought an injunction ordering Kennedy and Hoover to enforce six different sections of the federal code that made it a crime to harass or intimidate those trying to vote. They wanted examples to break patterns. Whether or not convictions ensued, they wanted white children to ask their parents why the FBI was arresting a sheriff or a registrar. Such enforcement would signal a marked change from the current practice in which FBI agents were asked only to gather information for possible use in civil suits that may or may not, some years later, result in a court order.

Naïvely, or perhaps disingenuously, Moses characterized the suit as a friendly demonstration for the benefit of its targets, Hoover and Kennedy. The litigation "does not reflect any antipathy toward the defendants or any lack of appreciation of the two-year record of the Civil Rights Division of the Department of Justice," he said in a statement. Instead, taking at face value all the Justice Department's disclaimers about the restraints of federalism, the plaintiffs sought to prove to Kennedy and Hoover that "their powers are immeasurably greater than they possibly realize." Not surprisingly, Kennedy saw the lawsuit as a threat to the prestige of the entire Administration, founded as it was on the explicit premise that the Justice Department had "systematically refused to take action." Justice Department lawyers maneuvered successfully to block the lawsuit as a crank scheme.

Mississippi authorities attacked the registration project more actively by shutting off distribution of federal food surpluses in two Delta counties. COFO workers, confronted with a famine in the heart of their registration area, sent out nationwide appeals for emergency relief. At first only restricted circles responded—Freedom Ride veterans, members of civil rights groups, students who drove South with carloads of donated canned goods—but the project grew over a bitter winter as grim facts reinforced Mississippi's unsavory reputation. The cutoff affected Sunflower County, home of Senator James Eastland, and adjacent LeFlore County, where Emmett Till had been lynched and where the White Citizens Councils of Mississippi had their headquarters. In LeFlore County, the cutoff stopped food relief to some 22,000 people—nearly half the county population, mostly Negroes, fully a third of whom had an annual income of less than $500. At SNCC's first major fund-raiser, on February 1, the relief appeal dominated a Carnegie Hall evening headlined by Harry Belafonte and the Albany Freedom Singers. A few days later, in Chicago, comedian Dick Gregory announced that the stories had moved him to pay for a charter plane that took seven tons of food into Mississippi.

More than six thousand sharecroppers stood in line outside the Wesley

Chapel in Greenwood, hoping for some of the supplies. A smattering of
American Indians among the Negroes bore witness to the Delta's lingering Indian heritage. (LeFlore County and its principal town, Greenwood,
were named for the last high chief of the Choctaw nation, Greenwood
LeFlore.) Even after some thirty tons came in by plane and truck, there
were enough cheese and blankets only for about a seventh of those in
line, more than 90 percent of them illiterate. As the Negroes least likely
to take or pass the registration test, these destitute sharecroppers seemed
a poor choice of clientele to the COFO registration workers. But the
registration campaign was moribund anyway, with only fifty Negroes
having taken the test in the preceding eight months, and sharecroppers
had begun to trickle into the nighttime registration meetings. By Delta
standards it was a great event when seventy-five of them showed up on
February 11 to hear James Bevel. He sang freedom songs, then preached
on the connection between the voter registration effort and the cutoff of
food. "Don't let the white man do your children as he has done you," he
pleaded.

The next day, far away in the White House, the sufferings of the Mississippi sharecroppers intruded upon the ceremonies at the Lincoln's
Birthday reception. Members of the Civil Rights Commission took advantage of their private moment with President Kennedy to say that they
felt an urgent duty to investigate racial conditions in Mississippi. Chairman John Hannah said he was embarrassed that never in its five-year
history had the commission held hearings in the one state that, more
than any other, cried out for the commissioners to fulfill their purpose
of fact-gathering and public education. Hannah knew he was raising a
sensitive topic, as the Justice Department had lobbied to keep the commission *out* of Mississippi. Kennedy told him that he thought hearings
in Mississippi would serve no purpose and might ruin what little chance
the Justice Department had for success in its county-by-county litigation.

Private contentions over Mississippi reached Wiley Branton by a different route. Having sent some of his Voter Education Project grant money
into the COFO registration projects, Branton was shocked when Bob
Moses listed in his official reports numerous purchases of food and clothing made with VEP money. Branton demanded to know the meaning of
this blatant violation of VEP rules. Any half-intelligent IRS auditor could
look at those reports and know that the VEP had gone beyond its stated,
tax-exempt purpose, he sternly told Moses.

"I know, Wiley," Moses replied. "But what can you do when you're
faced with all those people standing in line?"

His description of the relief lines first drew the reproach out of Branton, then turned him around. "All right, but don't document it!" he told Moses. "Don't put it in the reports." Branton had second thoughts as soon as he put down the phone. He knew he was partial to the Mississippi project. The students were a refreshing contrast to projects elsewhere, in which adult leaders often haggled over the portion of grant money they could keep for expenses, and Branton's harrowing experiences at COFO's founding meeting the previous August had given him a firsthand appreciation of the ceaseless threats hanging over the Mississippi registration workers. Still, he was a stickler by nature, and had not come as far as he had in the treacherous field of Negro law by giving in easily to sentiment. The strategic side of his brain told him that Roy Wilkins was correct—that the marginal voter registration dollar was wasted in Mississippi. Branton realized that he must either put a lot more money into Mississippi or none at all. He sent his VEP field director, Randolph Blackwell, to investigate.

Greenwood erupted before Blackwell could get there. Early on February 20, an anonymous caller told a SNCC volunteer that she would not be working in Greenwood anymore, because the office "has been taken care of." She rushed downtown to find four Negro businesses near the SNCC office being destroyed by fire. Although the SNCC office escaped damage, many local Negroes believed that the fire was a bungled arson attempt against the registration campaign or the relief project, and when Sam Block said as much to a small public gathering two days later, Greenwood police arrested him for "statements calculated to breach the peace."

As the one SNCC student who had lived continuously in Greenwood during the nine months of the registration project, Block had acquired a local reputation as a stubborn, lonely figure among the strange new breed of devout daredevils. He had handed out food to six hundred people on the day of the fire. For months he had accompanied the few would-be registrants to the courthouse, and for that he bore the brunt of official retaliations. His seventh arrest in Greenwood was a compelling topic of conversation while he stayed in jail over the weekend. Some people had been won over by his sheer persistence, others by his performances in the tiny mass meetings, where he led call-and-response spirituals in a distinctively jaunty tenor, marked by a hint of calypso syncopation. Something about his latest arrest caused an unprecedented phenomenon on Monday: more than a hundred Greenwood Negroes crowded into the police court for Sam Block's trial.

After finding him guilty, the judge offered to suspend sentence if the defendant agreed to stop working for the SNCC office, give up the voter registration project, and leave town. "Judge," Block replied, "I ain't

gonna do none of that." A murmur of awe passed through the crowd as
Block accepted a sentence of six months plus a $500 fine, and that night
a record 250 people jammed into the Greenwood mass meeting. Bob
Moses held up both Block's cheerful suffering and the relief food campaign as inspirations for those who wanted to be free. And the minimum
requirement for being free, he added, was to be able to vote.

Events and emotions had rolled over each other and swelled, with the
result that Moses counted more than fifty of Greenwood's poorest Negroes lined up outside the registrar's office early in the morning. Another
150 joined them before the close of business. By delay and avoidance, the
registrar managed to test only a handful, and most of these eventually
would learn that they had been rejected, but nearly all of them held their
ground even when the police told them to go home. Such assertiveness
by Mississippi Negroes had been extinguished from reality, and largely
from the imagination, for nearly a hundred years. The wonder of it moved
Moses to write a letter to Chicago supporters the next day, February 27.
"We don't know this plateau at all . . ." he confided. "We were relieved
at the absence of immediate violence at the courthouse, but who knows
what's to come next."

It was then that the VEP's Randolph Blackwell arrived to investigate
registration prospects in the Delta. On the night of February 28, he held
a council in the Greenwood SNCC office. Although Blackwell was something of a dandy—a sociology professor in his mid-thirties, an author of
textbooks on economics and business whom Branton had hired on the
strength of his commanding personality and his spare degree in law—his
formalities failed to deter the excited, grant-hungry registration workers,
and their passion flushed out the daring conspirator in him. County by
county, they discussed the needs of the associated projects deep into the
night, until Jimmy Travis interrupted to warn that three white men were
staking out the office from a Buick with no license plates.

The response had become almost a drill. Moses announced that they
had best break up the meeting so as not to be too concentrated a target.
Then they scattered toward their home counties, with Blackwell accompanying Moses to his lodgings some forty miles away across Sunflower
County. Travis, a twenty-year-old SNCC volunteer who was serving as a
driver for Blackwell, had learned a great deal about traveling the Mississippi roads at night. With Blackwell and Moses beside him, he followed
James Bevel's car slowly out of town, watching closely for ambushes or
police. Seeing the suspicious Buick in his rearview mirror, Travis first
stopped at a gasoline station in hopes that it would pass by. When instead
the car simply waited across the street for him to fill up, Travis turned
off his headlights and pulled out a rear exit from the station into dark,

unlit side streets. A few minutes' evasive driving lost both the Buick and Bevel, who turned off toward his temporary quarters in Shaw.

Travis made his way back to Highway 82, toward Sunflower County, and felt somewhat relieved until the Buick suddenly reappeared, headed in the opposite direction, and executed a sharp U-turn to fall in behind them again. Then Travis faced a breathless choice: he could try to outrun the Buick, slow down in the slim hope it would pass, or stop to confront the three men. He chose the middle course. The two cars moved in tandem until, some seven miles outside Greenwood, the Buick finally made a move to pass. Stabs of hope and fear were battling inside Travis and his two passengers when their car windows exploded.

"I'm hit!" cried Travis. Letting go of the steering wheel, he slumped over into Moses' lap. The car swerved off the highway.

"Hit the brakes!" yelled Blackwell. "Hit the brakes!" Moses grabbed the steering wheel with one hand, held Travis with the other, and groped with his foot for the brake.

The Buick was gone by the time Moses brought the car to a stop. The terrifying din of gunfire and squealing tires gave way to the crunch of broken glass as they squirmed to check themselves for wounds. The windshield and all the windows lay shattered in thousands of pieces. Travis had been shot twice, once in the shoulder and once in the back of his neck. When they had laid him gingerly across the backseat, Moses drove the open-air car in search of a hospital that would treat an injured pariah Negro. Two days later, in Jackson, doctors removed a .45-caliber bullet from Travis' neck.

The shooting of Jimmy Travis touched off a chain reaction. The SNCC staff voted to converge on Greenwood so as to prove that terror could not dislodge the registration project. They also decided that the miraculous new courage of illiterate Negroes cried out for citizenship classes. An appeal to Bernice Robinson, Septima Clark's original teaching partner at Highlander, brought her into Mississippi. Although Andrew Young rejected as suicidal a proposal to establish another SCLC citizenship training center in Mississippi,* he did agree to allow Annell Ponder, a newly trained assistant to Septima Clark at Dorchester, to take up residence in Greenwood. She arrived within a week of the shooting, just as Negro churches in the Delta first opened their doors to registration classes, and

---

* "It is quite possible that there will never be anything to show for your stay in Mississippi, not in a material sense anyway," Young wrote James and Diane Nash Bevel, in a sad letter of what Young called "bureaucratic daydreams."

James Bevel soon went to Dorchester with the first busload of Greenwood citizens who, having learned basic reading in a week, signed up for a week of "advanced" teacher training.

Greenwood burst upon the front pages of Negro newspapers across the country, and *The New York Times* published excerpts from Wiley Branton's telegram to President Kennedy. "This can no longer be tolerated," Branton declared. "We are accordingly today announcing a concentrated, saturation campaign to register every qualified Negro in LeFlore County." Branton also sent appeals to Attorney General Kennedy and to John Hannah of the Civil Rights Commission, touching sore points within the government. Hannah risked an open feud with Robert Kennedy by hastening preparation of a Mississippi report. Kennedy sent lawyers into Greenwood to investigate the local suspension of food relief, which he considered the immediate cause of the flare-up.

News from Greenwood echoed not only through the Kennedy Administration but also through the growing civil rights subculture. From the New York coffeehouses, folk singer Pete Seeger soon took Bob Dylan on his first pilgrimage to the South. By then, Birmingham and a hundred other cities would have erupted in demonstrations, but Dylan appeared only before a small Negro crowd in Greenwood, singing his "Blowin' in the Wind." This song, as recorded by Peter, Paul and Mary, had just displaced puppy love atop the pop charts.

From the beginning, the white authorities of LeFlore County denounced the outside attention. Under pressure from the FBI, they arrested three well-known whites for shooting Travis, but they postponed trial indefinitely in the face of vociferous local support for the vigilantes. Officials remained steadfastly hostile to the registration project. With Negroes outnumbering whites three to two, anything approaching fair registration raised at least the threat of a Negro "swing" vote, and possibly even the Reconstruction specter of Negro political control. A white voter explained his gut appraisal to reporters: "We killed two-month-old Indian babies to take this country, and now they want us to give it away to the niggers."

Greenwood politicians, while accommodating the white vigilantes who kept them in office, also tried to project an image of sovereign control. Their dissimulations toward this impossible goal reached the level of blatant contortion, of a kind that would be seen from afar as the trademark of ignorant Southern racists. When night riders fired a shotgun into a car occupied by Sam Block and Willie Peacock on March 6, Mayor Charles Sampson of Greenwood condemned both the shooting and the Negroes in the only way he could: he suggested that SNCC must have shot at its own workers to stimulate more publicity. He maintained this double-jointed conspiracy theory as the violence escalated through March. Arsonists destroyed the Greenwood SNCC office on March 24.* Two nights later, attackers fired a shotgun at Dewey Greene, Sr., just as he was entering his home.

A sturdy, middle-aged paperhanger, Greene was a volunteer in the daily registration lines, and his son had applied to succeed James Meredith as the second Negro student at Ole Miss. Feelings for him ran so deep among Greenwood Negroes that a large crowd gathered outside Wesley Chapel early the next morning. "We sang and we sang and we sang," Moses recalled. Finally, they all gathered in a huge circle to sing "We Shall Overcome," and then Moses addressed them. "We are not stopping now," he said. "We had a mass meeting last night and it was packed." For the quiet-spoken Moses, this was tantamount to a tirade. He told the crowd that since they were all there anyway, they might as well honor Dewey Greene by walking as a group to see the county registrar down at the courthouse. Some 150 people fell in behind him.

Before they could leave, James Forman intervened to suggest that first they march to city hall to protest the absence of basic police protections. The crowd cheered Forman's idea too, which precipitated a brief leadership huddle. Moses saw Forman's protest march as a diversion from the singleminded business of registration, as well as a provocation that Greenwood's white authorities would not fail to meet. Forman replied that the people must be allowed an outlet for their grievances over the violence. Under pressure of the hundreds of moving feet, Moses and Forman engineered a hasty compromise: they would walk by city hall on the way to the county courthouse. Rumor raced ahead of them, so that when the column approached city hall, Mayor Sampson and a dozen policemen came outside to square off against them. One of the policemen held a German shepherd on a taut leash. Mayor Sampson shouted out to the crowd that they must go home at once. "If you don't," he said, "we are going to turn the dog loose."

When Moses called out that he wanted to talk with the police chief, there was no reply except an order to move forward in a line. As the policemen surged into the crowd of marchers, the German shepherd snapped and tore at Moses' pants leg, ripping it to the thigh. The dog next seized the leg of a marcher named Matthew Hughes, tearing the flesh badly enough that Hughes had to be hospitalized. By then, the crowd was retreating in bedlam. One woman later remembered that a

* "We must get [white photographer] Marion Palfi out of Mississippi tonight," Bernice Robinson wrote Myles Horton. "It is dangerous for her to stay here and take pictures."

policeman kept shouting "Kennedy is your God!" The leaders shouted out that they must not run, that they must go about their business at the courthouse.

Moses helped turn the retreat back to Wesley Chapel. Singing broke out again. As mass relief bathed their determination, the SNCC staff leaders began helping people into cars for a less vulnerable trip down to the registrar's line at the courthouse. But the police, who had followed the retreat all the way to the church, countered this move by wading into the crowd to arrest Moses and seven others whom they recognized as workers in the Delta registration project. Soon they were all reunited in cells of the Greenwood city jail, where Forman talked excitedly about having smuggled a roll of film to one of his confederates. The whole world would see that snarling police dog, he said.

Word of the morning police attack flew so fast on the phone wires that Claude Sitton of *The New York Times* rushed into the state in time to file from Greenwood that same day. Other national reporters joined him on the hunch that the story promised something big. Their instincts were rewarded the next day when the police—reinforced by more dogs and by nearly a hundred lawmen from surrounding counties—confronted a line of forty-two Negroes as they marched back to Wesley Chapel from the courthouse. As white bystanders shouted "Sic 'em! Sic 'em!" a dog bounded into the column in full view of a half-dozen photographers and bit the pastor of the Wesley Chapel, drawing blood. Some of the marchers carried him away while others scattered in terror. Officers confiscated the film of a CBS cameraman and otherwise menaced the astonished assembly of reporters, who soon cornered Mayor Sampson to ask why the police had attacked unarmed Negroes who were on their way home. "They had a report up there that them niggers was going to the Alice Café for a sit-in," the mayor replied. It seemed more likely that the Greenwood police, having called in their colleagues as reserves against an enormous threat of insurrection, simply could not allow the quiet insult of a registration attempt to go unpunished.

By morning Greenwood was a crossover news flash, playing that Friday on the front pages of both white and Negro newspapers. The Chicago *Defender* rolled out a Pearl Harbor typeface for a two-tier proclamation: DOGS AGAIN ROUT VOTERS IN MISS. CITY, BITE PASTOR. Somewhat more restrained, the front-page headline in *The New York Times* read "Police Loose a Dog on Negroes' Group, Minister Is Bitten," but the *Times* also published a photograph of the Greenwood policemen charging behind their dog. Worse, from the standpoint of the Kennedy Administration, the picture of the dog ran just below a shot of the entire Republican leadership in Congress, assembled to promote their own new package of strong civil rights legislation. Senator Jacob Javits of New York said the Republicans no longer could wait for leadership from President Kennedy.

For Burke Marshall at the Justice Department, March 29 was a miserable Friday. President Kennedy already had asked what could be done about the dogs in Mississippi. Marshall bargained ceaselessly for a truce. He threatened to bring suit for a federal injunction ordering Greenwood officials to respect the basic constitutional protections due the would-be voters, but his leverage was reduced because he was running a bluff. Marshall knew the suit would not succeed, at least initially, because it would go before a federal judge in Mississippi whom Marshall already had described to Robert Kennedy as an unscrupulous segregationist. And even if the suit could be won, Marshall and Kennedy did not want responsibility for effecting a revolution in race relations with military or police power. This was their political lesson from the Freedom Rides and Ole Miss. It was one reason they had reacted so icily to the Moses lawsuit asking them to do just that.

Marshall was hit by a simultaneous rearguard action from the Civil Rights Commission, whose members sent word that they must issue an immediate statement on Mississippi. The six commissioners were incensed that their silent submission to the Administration had stretched into a shameful record of complicity. It was all Marshall could do to extract a promise that the commissioners would do nothing publicly without giving the President another chance to meet with them in the White House. "At least four members are very doubtful, however, for the long pull," he wrote Robert Kennedy that night, "and we may at some point have to face resignations from [John] Hannah, [Theodore] Hesburgh, [Erwin] Griswold, and [Robert] Storey."

Civil rights leaders poured into Greenwood all weekend—Medgar Evers of the NAACP, James Farmer and David Dennis of CORE, Charles McDew of SNCC. Wiley Branton flew in from Atlanta to represent Moses, Forman, and six other SNCC registration workers at their trial that Friday. When all eight were quickly convicted of disorderly conduct and given the maximum sentence of four months, Branton announced to the court that his clients elected to serve the time rather than appeal. By their continued presence in jail, the eight prisoners maintained a focal point for pressure on the federal government to bring elemental justice to Greenwood. Moses felt the buzz reaching into his jail cell, and the potential of all this clashing power moved him begrudgingly toward the view that the federal government responded more readily to discomfort than to cooperation, law, or logic.

On Tuesday, April 2, comedian Dick Gregory joined the fifth consecutive business day of registration marches in Greenwood. "I can't tell you how heartbroken I was last week as I sat in New York City and read the reports coming out of Greenwood," he told a pre-march mass meeting in Wesley Chapel. "If Russia aggravated West Berlin half as much as you was aggravated last week," he joked, "we would be there." Three times that day he walked to the courthouse, only to be forcibly driven away by police. As the first nationally known celebrity to march in Greenwood, he turned each confrontation into a performance with commentaries so daring as to be touched by madness or sublime inspiration. "There's your story!" he shouted to the national reporters. "Guns and sticks for old women who want to register!" He waved his hands toward the motley squad of police who were pushing the Negroes away from the courthouse. "Look at them," he said loudly. "A bunch of illiterate whites who couldn't even pass the test themselves." Later, when Mayor Sampson was holding forth gravely on the character deficiencies that made the Negroes unqualified to vote, Gregory pushed through the reporters on the sidewalk. "Well, now, Mr. Mayor," he interrupted with a beaming smile. "You really took your nigger pills last night, didn't you?" His utter lack of inhibition amazed the LeFlore County Negroes, as did the passive response of the white officials. Such effrontery was unheard of—no local Negro could get away with it—but Gregory's star quality seemed to make him untouchable. He drew thunderous applause that night for a short speech of earnest passion laced with humor. "We will march through your dogs!" he cried. "And if you get some elephants, we'll march through them. And bring on your tigers and we'll march through them!"

Three days of Gregory publicity pushed the Justice Department forward. John Doar visited Moses and the other prisoners the next morning, on their eighth day in the Greenwood jail. He announced that they must look their best the next day for a hearing in the courtroom of federal judge Claude Clayton. Doar was about to ask for an injunction ordering Greenwood officials to do three things: (1) vacate the convictions of the eight SNCC leaders as illegal interferences with the right to vote; (2) cease harassing or intimidating Negro citizens wishing to register; and (3) provide fair and adequate police protection at the courthouse registration office. Failure to obey such an order inevitably would bring in the U.S. marshals, and Doar expressed confidence that he could win in a higher court, though not from Judge Clayton.

This was Wednesday, April 3, when nervous volunteers were moving off for the first sit-ins at Birmingham's lunch counters. In Greenwood, the fire department tried to help the police quell that day's registration march by putting a fire truck across the route to the courthouse. Fear of being injured by high-powered fire hoses paralyzed the march line until

James Bevel walked boldly to the fire chief and said, "There's a fire going on inside of us, baby, but you can't put it out." In New York, a large photograph of Dick Gregory appeared on the front page of the morning *Times*, his arms twisted behind his back by Greenwood policemen. In Washington, the Greenwood story surfaced at President Kennedy's press conference. Asked whether the Justice Department could do more for the voter registration drive, Kennedy replied that the department already had filed a new voting rights suit in Greenwood "that's due for a hearing very shortly—perhaps this week." He said he hoped Doar's action would show that "there has been a denial of rights, which seems to me evident, but which the court must decide."

There was euphoria among the new U.S. clients inside the Greenwood jail. Having been briefed by Doar in the morning, they learned that President Kennedy himself specifically endorsed their case on national television later that day. That evening, U.S. marshals came to take them away from state authorities, which seemed another step toward victory until the marshals proceeded to manacle and chain them together at the waist. Although they were merely being transferred to federal custody for the next day's hearing, this treatment seemed excessively harsh for the government's allies. Several of the manacled students made sarcastic comments about how their protectors were playing to the sympathies of the Greenwood segregationists. As always, Forman's reaction was at once less subtle and more subtle than the others. While furiously demanding to speak with the sheriff or the senior marshal, he also conspired to get a publicity photograph taken of the SNCC prisoners in the "federal chains." Moses and several of the other students could only shake their heads in amusement at Forman as the irrepressibly scheming, imperious victim. Forman also demanded to see the sheriff about their many legitimate grievances—medical treatment, the lack of towels, and the quality of prison food. "There is no justification for not feeding prisoners a balanced diet," he said.

The ironic twists of jailhouse politics were trivial to Moses, who, after nearly two solid years under the heel of Mississippi, finally glimpsed an opening in the larger paradox: how Negroes could obtain freedom without power and power without freedom. By the next morning, before the hearing, Moses had shed his usual reticence to rejoice out loud in his cell. He was "in rare form, standing behind the bars, singing alone," said Forman. Urged on by the regular prisoners, Moses began a chant: "Do you want your freedom? Are you ready to go to jail?" and even the thieves and vagrants around him understood the chant to be a revelation of hope. Then, suddenly, the jailers opened their cells, and they received the miraculous news that Greenwood had caved in during the pre-trial negotiations, so that their sentences were suspended and the papers signed—they were free! Singing "This Little Light of Mine," the eight SNCC workers walked outside the jail to a triumphant press conference. "We stood eyeball to eyeball and the other side just blinked," one of them told reporters, echoing Secretary of State Rusk's famous boast after the Cuban missile crisis.

The celebration went on long after Moses began falling into gloom. He learned that there would be no hearing that day on the other two objectives of Doar's lawsuit—the federal orders to desist from harassing and to provide protection for people in the Greenwood registration lines. Doar first told reporters he needed more time to prepare his case. Then he said he thought it was more important to get Moses and the others out of jail than to proceed hastily with the lawsuit. Finally, reporters confirmed rumors that Doar's superiors in Washington had set aside the lawsuit in exchange for release of the eight prisoners. The reporters did not find out about another bargain: to get relief assistance resumed in LeFlore County, the federal government agreed to pick up the county's distribution costs. This part of the settlement allowed LeFlore County leaders to say that they had stood up to Washington without restoring a dime of local tax money for the distribution of food to rebellious Negroes. In effect, they were making the federal government pay them for having shut off food relief.

Doar searched for Moses in the Negro neighborhoods of Greenwood. As the official most personally torn by the brutalities of civil rights politics, he wanted to try to explain. Doar's respect for Burke Marshall and Robert Kennedy was so strong that he had accepted their reasoning for the deal, which was that the government could not place its authority behind civil rights in voter registration without being prepared to assume far-flung police responsibilities—not just in LeFlore County but possibly across the entire South. If they won the injunction, Marshall reasoned, then local police might simply abdicate their responsibilities, which would leave the federal government no choice but to intervene in force. U.S. Border Patrol officers might find themselves directing traffic in Greenwood, answering fire alarms, and riding shotgun for a thousand endangered registration workers like Jimmy Travis.

Doar understood why Kennedy and Marshall refused to take a step in that direction, but he also knew what an effort Moses had made to cooperate with the federal government—how conscientiously he had followed the Administration's advice to pursue registration instead of demonstrations, how meticulously he had filed detailed reports on beatings, shootings, and lesser harassments. He knew Moses would be profoundly disappointed to see Washington maneuvering to get *out* of, rather than into, Greenwood, but still he was not prepared for the look of depression on Moses' face when he finally located him on a back street, isolated among Negroes still celebrating the release from jail. To Doar, it seemed as though Moses, already having intuited the strategic reasoning behind the bargain with Greenwood, was lost in despairing thoughts about the implications for the Mississippi movement. The look was so penetrating that Doar could not bring himself to present his explanations, and when Moses did not raise the subject himself, they said good-bye with numb pleasantries. Thereafter, a barrier of formality came between Doar the government man and Moses the wary supplicant.

Abundant signs indicated what Moses already knew: that the Greenwood movement was collapsing. Dick Gregory left town. The mass meetings shriveled. Heading home to Atlanta, James Forman stopped off in Birmingham with urgent ideas for invigorating the sagging movement there as a joint project of SNCC and the SCLC, only to be rudely expelled by Wyatt Walker as a pretentious, panhandling nuisance. ("If I ever cut anybody's throat," Walker recalled, "that was it.") In a dramatic about-face, Greenwood's Mayor Sampson provided a city bus to transport those Negroes who really did want to take the registration test. This gesture was the result of ceaseless prodding by federal officials, who finally convinced the politicians of LeFlore County that it was more important to maintain political control than to flaunt it. In return for putting away their police dogs, they retained their post-Reconstruction prerogative of determining who was eligible to vote. Over the next six months, the tireless workers of the LeFlore County registration project brought 1,500 Negroes to take the registration test, and of these only fifty were accepted. Although Negroes outnumbered whites, Negro registered voters tallied only 300 against 10,000. On election day they were still invisible.

Claude Sitton, for once letting his sympathies outrun his devotion to fact, told readers of The New York Times that the registration movement "has picked up momentum." He proclaimed LeFlore County a "major battleground" of civil rights, but this was his last important dispatch from Greenwood. An evaporation of news soon forced him to leave town. In Atlanta, Wiley Branton was fuming. He blamed the sudden demise of the Greenwood movement not on tepid federal support or the resilience of Mississippi but on Martin Luther King. Complaining bitterly to his colleagues, he charged that an envious King, seeing Mississippi rise up without him as the main chance to break segregation, had launched a quick diversion in Birmingham.

On B-Day, April 3, clairvoyance or the example of Greenwood had inspired King to proclaim, "They may set the mad dogs on us!" Six days later, preoccupied with less dramatic threats, he faced more than a hundred skeptical Negro businessmen at a special meeting. In an atmosphere that King recalled as "tense and chilly," the men peppered him with criticisms of the movement. Some said they didn't need outsiders to solve their problems. Some said King had not given Boutwell a fair chance. Nearly all expressed a preference for cooperation over the dangerous, distasteful business of handcuffed picketers and angry policemen. King responded with all his rhetorical powers, preaching with his career on the line. He tried to overwhelm them with descriptions of his comprehensive planning. He tried to seduce them with visions of celebrities, promising to bring Jackie Robinson and Sammy Davis, Jr., to town.

They applauded when it was over, allowing King to say that he had at least neutralized them. A. G. Gaston released a statement afterward that King's supporters claimed as an endorsement of the movement. Segregationists also praised Gaston, however, and white newspapers published his call for "all the citizens of Birmingham to work harmoniously together in a spirit of brotherly love to solve the problems of our city, giving due recognition to the local colored leadership among us." Gaston's statement took no notice of King or the demonstrations. King knew that his own impact upon the businessmen would be short-lived, and that some of those who had applauded him to his face already were grumbling that he should leave town. At the mass meeting that night, he announced that he had postponed plans to go to jail himself. Having hoped that his own jailing would add a last surge of momentum to a great mass movement, he now faced jail instead as a last resort, to ward off the movement's extinction.

King's extinction was precisely what Alabama's white officials were plotting with Governor Wallace that same day in Montgomery. Knowing that bail funds already were low, they drafted a bill to raise the maximum appeal bond in misdemeanor cases from $300 to $2,500, applicable only in Birmingham. They added a resolution proclaiming that Birmingham "has been invaded by foreigners who would by force and violence attempt to overthrow laws which may not be to their liking." With these measures dispatched to the legislature, the white politicians quarreled over police tactics. Bull Connor and Governor Wallace wanted to send in a conspicuous force of one hundred tough-looking state troopers to crush or intimidate the Negro demonstrators, but the reform faction of the Birmingham establishment—the sheriff, the newspapers, the leading businessmen, and the Boutwell administration—endorsed the "velvet fist" tactics of Albany's police chief Laurie Pritchett, with whom they had been consulting. Any step to make the conflict more violent or dramatic would backfire, they argued.

Politics saturated these backroom disputes. Both sides played to the

Alabama judges who would rule on Bull Connor's lawsuit to overturn or delay the new city charter, which would invalidate the recent city election. Connor needed racial drama if he was to be seen as the indispensable strong man, a latter-day Stonewall Jackson. The establishment needed a smothering quiet if they were to remain guarantors of civic dignity. The two sides compromised on Tuesday: no state troopers for now, but Connor would obtain an Albany-style court order banning Negro protest. Such an injunction either would cripple the movement or give a more statesmanlike purpose to Bull Connor's mass arrests.

The impending injunction was an open secret all day Wednesday, as city attorneys scrambled to prepare affidavits. King heard it was coming. The only good news was that Connor was applying to state court instead of federal court, the better to secure a reliable judge. This was a welcome distinction to King, as now he would face the order of a segregationist state, Alabama, rather than of the United States. "Everyone in the movement must live a sacrificial life," King told the mass meeting that night, but his predicament put him in a snappish mood. He denounced the people breaking the downtown shopping boycott as "traitors to the Negro race." Abernathy followed with an emotional pledge to go to jail on Good Friday, and then the leaders resumed their strategy sessions late into the night, receiving minute-by-minute reports on the progress of the emergency injunction. Judge William A. Jenkins signed the papers about nine o'clock. Shortly after one o'clock the next morning, a deputy sheriff walked into the restaurant of the Gaston Motel for what amounted to a staged ceremony of war. Receiving him at a table, flanked by Abernathy and Shuttlesworth, King silently read the court order while a full contingent of reporters waited behind cameras and microphones for his response. King was the first-named object of a sweeping injunction. To preserve public order and to prevent anticipated "bloodshed and violence," Judge Jenkins specifically ordered 133 people not to engage in or encourage a host of protest activities: "parading, demonstrating, boycotting, trespassing and picketing," even "conduct customarily known as 'kneel-ins' in churches."

It was easy for the three Negro leaders to denounce the injunction as flagrantly unconstitutional. It was relatively easy for them to announce the next day that they "cannot in all good conscience obey such an injunction," and that the movement would not stop. The final step was far more difficult: to envision a plan that would relieve the certain pain of defying the injunction with the promise of positive accomplishment. Their grand Birmingham campaign showed signs of terminal weakness. In eight days, they had put fewer than 150 people in jail. By comparison, nearly twice that number had gone to jail in tiny Albany on the first day of mass protest alone. Even after the supporters hanging over the Gaston balconies cheered the pledge of the three leaders to lead a Good Friday march to jail, only seven volunteers stepped forward for the demonstrations on Thursday, April 11. Less than fifty signed up for the privilege of accompanying King to jail.

By staying away from the Thursday-night mass meeting at the Sixth Avenue Baptist Church, King avoided making any more promises. In the crisis, Daddy King rushed over from Atlanta to preach in his place, just as a new development promised to keep his son out of jail after all. The city notified the movement's bail bondsman that he had reached the limit of established credit, which amounted to a bankruptcy notice for the jail project. No longer could volunteers be assured that the movement would provide bail, and now the poorest of them might wind up in jail for six months instead of six days. Until late in the night, King and his advisers paddled around among a hundred ramifications. Could they warn potential jailgoers of this sad state without ruining what spirit remained? Was King's first obligation to fulfill his promise of going to jail, or should he, as the SCLC's only proven fund-raiser, tour the country to recharge the bail funds? If he took the latter course, would there be any movement left when he returned to Birmingham?

"Let's think it through," King kept saying, but the more kinetic Wyatt Walker often darted out of the nonstop discussion to supervise his projects. He had one group of volunteers stuffing 1,500 letters, another distributing 50,000 leaflets in support of the downtown boycott. Walker seemed to lose himself more than ever in organizational details, as though to avoid the more general impotence of the campaign. All over Birmingham, Negroes were doing their wash, sitting on porches, playing on ballfields, stubbornly in neglect of the master plan. Walker's diagrams could not levitate an entire city. When King had sent a runner to fetch him one too many times, Walker slammed his clipboard furiously on the table. "I can't be everywhere at one time!" he shouted at King. A shocked King tried to calm him, saying, "Wait a minute, wait a minute."

Norman Amaker, an NAACP lawyer from New York, briefed King and some two dozen movement leaders early on Good Friday morning, April 12. Crowded into the sitting room of King's Room 30, the only suite in the Gaston Motel, they heard Amaker say that the Jenkins injunction was probably unconstitutional, but that anyone who violated it would probably be punished regardless. Whatever King decided to do, Amaker said in closing, the NAACP's Legal Defense Fund would stand behind him in court. King himself set a gloomy tone for what followed, saying he did not want to spend the rest of his life in jail. He did not know what to do, and felt trapped between conflicting obligations. While he did not want to let the injunction make him renege on his promises to carry on the Birmingham movement, neither did he want to lead new people blindly into jail, especially since he did not know how the movement could make bond for those already there. Then he called on his friends for suggestions. After a silence, one said that King could not go to jail, because the movement would die without new money. Daddy King recommended that his son not break the injunction. A lawyer boasted implausibly that if King went to jail, he would spring him by getting the injunction quashed. Andrew Young and several others said they would support whatever King decided. Significantly, no one, including Shuttlesworth and Abernathy, suggested that other leaders go to jail in King's place. They were in a downward spiral; King recalled that "our most dedicated and devoted leaders were overwhelmed by a feeling of hopelessness."

He did not reply to any of the suggestions. When they died out, he simply withdrew into the bedroom and shut the door, acutely conscious that at the moment his closest associates formed an inert mass. Before him in one direction was the abyss of jail, with exaggerated martyr's hopes that his arrest would ignite both the Kennedy White House and Birmingham's Negroes. In the other direction were press conferences and elaborate explanations why a fund-raising detour was necessary for a sounder movement, with exaggerated hopes of a triumphant return—and silent fears that this was the end, that a leader could not duck out behind his followers. When King stepped back into the other room a few minutes later, he wore a work shirt, blue jeans that were crisply new and rolled up at the cuffs, and a new pair of "clodhopper" walking shoes. It was a startling sight, as some of those in the room had never seen King wear anything but a dark business suit.

This first glimpse of him announced that he would go to jail, which hushed the room. "I don't know what will happen," he said. "I don't know where the money will come from. But I have to make a faith act."

He turned to Abernathy, who, despite his speeches about going to jail for Easter, still planned to be home at West Hunter for the most important event of the church calendar. He had been grumbling privately that it was easier for King to arrange for Easter services in his absence than it was for him, as Abernathy was alone at West Hunter whereas King had his father as an ever-present stand-in. What kind of preacher would be available to substitute for Abernathy on two days' notice at Easter? King fell upon these excuses with the weight of an open request. "I know you want to be in your pulpit on Easter Sunday, Ralph," he said. "But I am asking you to go with me."

Abernathy did not reply, leading Daddy King to interpret the impasse as a sign that the decision was not yet final. He spoke up once again to recommend that his son not violate the injunction "at this time." Exposed and plainly waffling, he covered himself by adding that he supposed King would do what he wanted to do, anyway.

King replied firmly that he had to march. "If we obey this injunction, we are out of business," he said.

Daddy King sagged visibly and shifted in his seat, as though pawing the floor. "Well, you didn't get this nonviolence from me," he said. "You must have got it from your Mama."

"I have to go," King repeated softly. "I am going to march if I have to march by myself."

"Wait a minute," said Abernathy, rising to his feet. "Let me see if I can get in touch with my deacons, because I'm gonna spend Easter in the Birmingham jail."

Abernathy's commitment put the gathering to silence. With nothing left to say, they sang "We Shall Overcome" and filed out to a multitude of tasks, leaving Daddy King alone in Room 30.

For Wyatt Walker, one serendipitous discovery stood out among the strategic disappointments of the campaign: he learned that newspaper estimates of the numbers involved in demonstrations tended to lump together all Negroes near the scene. In effect, the reporters gave the movement credit for bystanders as well as marchers and picketers. This trait of the news business overjoyed Walker, all the more so because it made a virtue of the movement's customary tardiness. A corollary rule of his media strategy held that the later an event dragged behind schedule, the more onlookers would gather.

The rule worked to perfection on Good Friday. When King and Abernathy finally stepped off from the Sixteenth Street Baptist Church nearly three hours after the announced starting time for the march, they led only about forty jailgoers, as emotion-drenched exhortations had failed to persuade more to join. But midday crowds of Negroes built up along the expected route, talking excitedly about whether it was true that King would face Bull Connor. The long-awaited first sight of King touched off shouts of celebration and encouragement, which grew louder as the marchers pushed their way down the sidewalks for several blocks. By the time the line ran up against the police blockade, reported the next morning's New York Times, "more than a thousand shouting, singing Negroes had joined in the demonstration." When King made an unexpected turn, the police scrambled in a wild blur of U-turns by motorcycles and squad cars, with reporters and white pedestrians in hot pursuit. With the police

line re-formed across King's path on Fifth Avenue, the pageantry of confrontation played out abruptly. Giving no warning, a detective seized
King by the back of his belt, lifted him to his toes, and shoved him toward
a paddy wagon. A motorcycle officer pushed Abernathy in the same
direction, grabbing a handful of his shirt. Photographers snapped their
shutters in a clicking chorus. Negro bystanders, shouting out in rage or
prayer at the sight of the arrests, melted in so closely among the marchers
that the officers were not sure which ones to arrest. Stragglers and spontaneous protesters wound up among the fifty-two people who landed in
jail behind King and Abernathy. Bull Connor told reporters that King was
getting what he wanted.

Connor had different ideas than Laurie Pritchett about special jailhouse treatment for King. There were no newspaper subscriptions or silk
pajamas in Birmingham, where the jailers singled him out instead for
isolation. After lock-up, they separated him from everyone else and refused his requests to make phone calls or talk with his lawyers. King
disappeared into solitary confinement, "the hole," sealed off from his
fellow prisoners and the outside world alike. Silence made the tumult of
his arrest fade into memory, and a man accustomed to an intense bombardment of news and emotion passed over into a vacuum where day and
night were indistinct. The only clues he had about the continuing crisis
of the Birmingham movement were those he imagined filtering in with
the stripes of light above the door of his cell.

Other events of hidden significance occurred elsewhere that day. In
Rome, Pope John XXIII interrupted a Good Friday service at St. Peter's to
order that a reference to "perfidious Jews" be stricken from the liturgy.
The Pope had issued his visionary encyclical *Pacem in Terris* only the
day before. Of late he had been acting boldly—almost recklessly, some
said—battling to put ecumenical reforms through the hidebound Vatican
bureaucracy before cancer killed him.

In Columbus, Georgia, a jury took less than ninety minutes to clear
Sheriff L. Warren Johnson of civil liability for having beaten and shot
Charlie Ware in 1961, while Ware was a prisoner in the sheriff's car. The
swift acquittal shocked Ware's lawyer, C. B. King, who believed that the
case against Johnson was impregnable, even to an all-white jury. He
asked for a poll of the jurors, and when Carl Smith stood up in the jury
box to confirm the verdict, he attracted the special attention of several
Negroes who had driven up from Albany for the five-day trial. Smith was
the proprietor of one of the three white-owned grocery stores in Harlem,
the Negro section of Albany, all of which the Albany Movement had

been picketing for their refusal to hire Negro clerks and cashiers. Now he declared under oath that Sheriff Johnson had not deprived Charlie Ware of his civil rights or inflicted actionable injury upon him, and at that moment two separate streams of outrage converged.

Students from the Albany Movement set up another Saturday picket line outside Carl Smith's store eight days after the verdict. They carried their regular picket signs, urging Smith's all-Negro clientele not to patronize a store that denied jobs to Negroes, and as usual they lasted only an hour before Laurie Pritchett's police dispersed their line by making several arrests. Nevertheless, this brief effort was destined to become the most significant single picket line of the entire civil rights movement. It polarized racial politics, spreading far and wide to engage people who never heard of Charlie Ware or Carl Smith. Passions traceable to Smith's service on the Ware jury nearly wrecked the great March on Washington the following August.

B. C. Gardner set the white reaction in motion. On Smith's behalf, he filed a civil suit against the leaders of the Albany Movement, charging that they had driven Smith out of business with an illegal boycott. In a parallel attack, Gardner contacted the local bar association, his FBI acquaintances, the trial judge, and Burke Marshall in Washington, alleging that the Negroes had obstructed justice by punishing Smith for his vote on the Ware v. Johnson jury. Suddenly the pattern was reversed—a white man was presented as the victim of criminal action by the civil rights movement—and law enforcement officials who had been stalling, bickering, or neutralizing each other now found themselves working in concert. Preliminary results landed on Attorney General Kennedy's desk only ten days after the Saturday picket line. "In Albany, Georgia, we received complaints of an organized Negro boycott against a grocery store owned by a white man who had sat on a jury . . ." Burke Marshall wrote Kennedy. "It appears that the matter will be presented to a grand jury, that indictments will be returned, and that one of the persons indicted will be Dr. W. G. Anderson, the leader of the Albany Movement."

More than thirty FBI agents were detailed to interview scores of Albany Negroes. Law enforcement officials at all levels saw a chance to win, to settle personal or racial grudges, or to demonstrate the evenhandedness of the system. Their targets, however, saw the dragnet as proof that the entire federal system had sunk to the level of Baker County. Against Negroes, justice was a fast waterslide to jail; for Negroes, it was a tarpit of evasions.

Charles Sherrod did not attend the trial in Columbus. That Good Friday, he took several of his most promising Albany students to Atlanta for SNCC's fourth general conference. There he declared his determination to keep the Albany Movement going in spite of the letdown from the previous year's mass demonstrations. To hang on through adversity and national obscurity, Sherrod pledged, "we are willing to pick cotton, scrub floors, wash cars and windows, babysit, etcetera, for food and lodging."

In the featured speech of the conference, Bob Moses gently prepared his audience for the decline of the Greenwood movement, remarking that "what you need is not five hundred but five thousand going down." Then he began meandering into the self-critical abstractions by which he had thought through his own state of depression. They must seek universal suffrage, he said, beginning what became SNCC's "One man/ one vote" campaign. In pushing for universal suffrage, they must acknowledge that they were

> asking all white people in the Delta to do something which they don't ask of any white people any place . . . And that is to allow Negroes to vote in an area where they are educationally inferior but yet outnumber the white people and hence constitute a serious political threat. Because in every other area of the country, the Negro votes are ghettoized—the Negroes elect their leaders, but they don't elect leaders to preside over what we could call a numerically inferior but educationally superior white elite. I don't for one minute think that the country is in a position or is willing to push this down the throats of white people in the Delta, and it will have to be pushed down their throats because they are determined not to have it done.

As Moses relentlessly pursued the difficulties of universal suffrage, the enemy no longer appeared to be ignorant rednecks so much as universal forces of politics, and the purpose of the civil rights movement not so much Christian enlightenment—teaching people to be charitable and fair—as political revolution. While Moses could not see how to achieve universal suffrage, neither could he back down from its necessity. To seek anything less, he said, was to exclude an enormous mass of Southern Negroes and to leave political relations largely intact, which meant that the movement would gain at most symbolic privileges. In a warning to SNCC's advocates of direct action, and very likely with King's Birmingham campaign in mind, Moses said, "I think we are in danger of fighting for some things" that would wind up helping only "the black bourgeoisie."

Stress and confusion erupted intermittently among the 350 students at the Atlanta conference. In some of the workshops, participants sang freedom songs of sunny optimism, while in others, shared stories of beatings, isolation, and fears built to cries of anguish and rebellion. Some students broke out of their nonviolent serenity by throwing chairs. One put his fist through a window. While many welcomed the idea that SNCC ought to be "challenging the political structure of the country," as Forman put it, others mourned a loss of essential simplicity. In a confessional organization such as SNCC, students urged each other to dig deeper. What they found was that behind the shared vision of racial brotherhood, they were a diverse lot of saints, hustlers, intellectuals, and runaway farmers, who, cut loose from conventional moorings, had been tiptoeing around the gaping cultural and racial differences between them. Many of the leaders had come into the movement confident that their shining idealism could reorient the outside world, but now their own identities were in flux, too.

Charles Sherrod walked out onto the grounds of the Gammon Theological Seminary and grabbed hold of a tree. Suddenly he hated the dark color of his arms. His kinky hair repulsed him, as did everything else about him, including the way words came out of his mouth. Shame ate him alive. Ashamed of his mother, he became again the waif who peeked into a white world of perfection and longed for his white ancestors. This very shame shamed him again, and then yet again when he thought of all the years he had been teaching young Negroes differently, mouthing the movement's phrases about accepting yourself. Having sent trusting young Negroes to jail on convictions that now seemed to rest on fantasy and hypocrisy, Sherrod felt utterly unclean. When he recovered, he could only liken the ordeal to one of the graphic Old Testament conversions. He felt stronger for it, but never again did he talk so glibly about slipping into a new racial attitude.

Summoned by King, James Bevel arrived from Greenwood just in time to preach at the Birmingham mass meeting on Friday night, April 12, a few hours after King went to jail. He said he had heard about Birmingham and Bull Connor all his life. Birmingham was sick, he said. Its white people were sick with blind hatred, and its Negroes were sick because they would not take the step to freedom. Bevel looked out over three hundred people, who seemed lost in the cavernous Sixteenth Street Baptist Church, and pronounced it a pitifully small crowd for so momentous a day. He pointed an accusing finger at the two white police detectives who were sitting in the audience with their tape-recording equipment. "The police can come to our meeting, bring their guns and their badges and little microphones to church," Bevel declared, "but if you want to be free, there is nothing they can do about it."

The crowd stirred as Bevel began to preach with his usual abandon. Both races must stop worrying about their conveniences, he cried ("If

God can feed the cockroach, he can feed the Negro"), and open their eyes to spiritual healing. It was easy to be whole, he declared. Freedom was there for the taking. Quoting the words of Jesus to the lame man at the pool of Bethesda ("Rise, take up thy bed, and walk!"), Bevel began a cascade of oratory. To heal themselves with freedom, he cried, all they had to do was walk—walk to the mass meetings, walk to the courthouse, walk to jail. On this theme he "worked himself and the congregation into such a frenzie [sic] that we were unable to understand what he was saying," the police detectives later confessed to Bull Connor. The crowd understood. Bevel was a spiritual kamikaze, shaking them loose. "The Negro has been sitting here dead for three hundred years," he declared. "It is time he got up and walked."

On Monday afternoon, King was overjoyed to see the handsome face of Clarence Jones at his cell door. Jones, hoping to ward off hostile treatment from the Birmingham jailers, was decked out in his finest New York lawyer clothes. He greeted King with the words he most wanted to hear: "Harry has been able to raise fifty thousand dollars for bail bonds." And Belafonte had said he was good for more, for "whatever else you need." King wrote later that these few words from Jones "lifted a thousand pounds from my heart." They meant that those who wanted out of jail could get out, and that King could not now be second-guessed for going to jail instead of raising money.

Jones also told King that Belafonte and Walker were organizing a phone and telegram campaign to pressure the Kennedy Administration to seek decent treatment for King in the jail. So far King remained isolated in his cell, allowed no phone calls. He had no mattress or linen, and was sleeping on metal slats. Hearing of these conditions from Wyatt Walker, Belafonte had called Robert Kennedy. As King knew, the Attorney General strongly opposed the entire Birmingham campaign, let alone King's going to jail, and Kennedy had further reason to feel put upon because he knew that King could relieve his suffering at any time by posting bond and walking out of jail. Under these circumstances, Jones reported, Kennedy's response to Belafonte had been testy, but leavened with humor. "Tell Reverend King we're doing all we can," Kennedy had told Belafonte, "but I'm not sure we can get into prison reform at this moment."

After Jones departed, the jailers led King out of his cell to the prisoners' pay phone, saying it was time for him to call his wife. King, who had enough jail experience to know that guards normally do not nurture an inmate's family communications, suspected correctly that the sudden kindness was really for the convenience of the police department's wiretap stenographers. When Coretta promptly informed him that the President had just called her, King did not reply. Stalling—caught between his hunger for her news and his reluctance to let Bull Connor know what President Kennedy was doing—King made small talk with his two older children. His evasive manner alerted Coretta.

"Are you being guarded?" she asked.

"Yes," he replied.

"Did they give you a time limit?"

"Not exactly, but hear everything, you know," King said pointedly. "Who did you say called you?"

"Kennedy," said Coretta. "The President."

"Did he call you direct?"

"Yes. And he told me you were going to call in a few minutes. It was about thirty minutes ago."

This was significant news, potentially a replay of President Kennedy's famous phone call before the 1960 election. "Let Wyatt know," King instructed. ". . . Do that right now."

Coretta recounted her conversation with President Kennedy, saying, "He told me the FBI talked with you last night. Is that right?"

"No, no," said King. He told her again to get word of Kennedy's phone call to Walker so that Walker could issue a statement. Coretta did not agree to do so outright, sensing perhaps that she was in a bind because she had issued her own statement to *The New York Times*, whereas King wanted Walker to handle the matter. She kept adding details of President Kennedy's expressed concern, and of two earlier phone calls from Robert Kennedy, while King kept asking her to tell it all to Walker.

When the news did reach Birmingham, Walker seized hopefully on the White House involvement to proclaim the beginning of phase two in Birmingham—the national phase. Responses outside the mass meeting proved to be far less enthusiastic. News stories pointed out that President Kennedy had not initiated the phone contact, as he had done during the 1960 campaign. Instead, Kennedy had returned Coretta's urgent phone calls to the White House switchboard. This made Kennedy seem less resolutely sympathetic to King, and therefore made King's cause seem less worthy. Other, less subtle discrepancies appeared. With the Birmingham police department denying that FBI agents had visited King or that President Kennedy's influence had produced better treatment for King— and Chief Moore going so far as to declare that it had been his idea for King to call his wife, because he, Moore, was concerned about Coretta's postnatal condition—most newspapers concentrated their skepticism on the least authoritative party: Coretta. Reports tended to portray her as an anxious new mother who may have confused her White House fantasies with reality. She bore the brunt of condescension even though her version of the episode was closest to the truth. In Washington, the *Star* dismissed her entire story in a lead editorial entitled "Just a Bit Phony."

General press reaction to the Birmingham campaign was no more favorable. *Time* called it a "poorly timed protest": "To many Birmingham Negroes, King's drive inflamed tensions at a time when the city seemed to be making some progress, however small, in race relations." A Washington *Post* editorial attacked King's Birmingham strategy as one of "doubtful utility," and speculated that it was "prompted more by leadership rivalry than by the real need of the situation." *The New York Times*, while playing down President Kennedy's phone call to Coretta, devoted a great deal of space to a press conference in which Burke Marshall said the federal government had no authority to take action in Birmingham. By contrast, the *Times* was almost gushingly optimistic about Birmingham's prospects under its new mayor, Albert Boutwell, who was sworn in on April 15 as Clarence Jones was visiting King in jail. "A warm sun was shining," the *Times* reported. The swearing-in ceremony was "like a picnic," with the "giggles of little girls" making a pleasant change from "the sounds of demonstrations carried on in the last 13 days," and most Birmingham citizens of both races were looking to Boutwell for "a diminution, if not an end, to racial tensions that have grown alarmingly the last few days." In an editorial declaring that it did not expect enlightenment to come to Birmingham "overnight," the *Times* added that Martin Luther King "ought not to expect it either."

For white Birmingham, the tone of Northern news coverage was a refreshing change, hailed that week in local news stories such as "Washington Liberals Ponder Wisdom of Demonstrations" and "Birmingham Image Gets Better Press." All sides seemed to be converging upon a common ground of forward-looking vagueness, which the *Times* called "mutual respect and equality of opportunity" and Mayor Boutwell called "mutual respect and understanding." Such a view rejected King and Bull Connor alike as dangerous, polar extremists.

King read these press reactions as fast as Clarence Jones could smuggle newspapers into his cell. They caused him the utmost dismay, especially since a diverse assortment of friends and enemies were using the same critical phrases almost interchangeably. King could have addressed his "Letter from Birmingham Jail" to almost any of these—to Mayor Boutwell or Burke Marshall or A. G. Gaston, to the Birmingham *News* or *The New York Times*. He gave no thought to secular targets, however, after he saw page 2 of the April 13 Birmingham *News*. There, beneath two photographs of him and Abernathy on their Good Friday march to jail, appeared a story headlined "White Clergymen Urge Local Negroes to Withdraw from Demonstrations." After attacking the Birmingham demonstrations as "unwise and untimely," and commending the news media and the police for "the calm manner in which these demonstrations have been handled," the clergymen invoked their religious authority against civil disobedience. "Just as we formerly pointed out that 'hatred and violence have no sanction in our religious and political traditions,' " they wrote, "we also point out that such actions as incite hatred and violence, however technically peaceful those actions may be, have not contributed to the resolution of our local problems. We do not believe that these days of new hope are days when extreme measures are justified in Birmingham."

The thirteen short paragraphs transfixed King. He was being rebuked on his own chosen ground. And these were liberal clergymen. Most of them had risked their reputations by criticizing Governor Wallace's "Segregation Forever!" inauguration speech in January. They were among the minority of white preachers who of late had admitted Andrew Young and other Negroes to specially roped off areas of their Sunday congregations. Yet to King, these preachers never had risked themselves for true morality through all the years when Shuttlesworth was being bombed, stabbed, and arrested, and even now could not make themselves state forthrightly what was just. Instead, they stood behind the injunction and the jailers to dismiss his spirit along with his body. King could not let it go. He sat down and began scribbling around the margins of the newspaper. "Seldom, if ever, do I pause to answer criticism of my work and ideas," he began.

By the time Clarence Jones visited the jail again that Tuesday, King had pushed a wandering skein of ink into every vacant corner. He surprised Jones by pulling the newspaper surreptitiously out of his shirt. "I'm writing this letter," he said. "I want you to try to get it out, if you can." To Jones, the "letter" was an indistinct jumble of biblical phrases wrapped around pest control ads and garden club news. He regarded the surprise as a distraction from the stack of urgent business he had brought with him—legal questions about King's upcoming criminal trials, plus money problems, Belafonte and Kennedy reports, and a host of movement grievances assembled by Walker. Waving these away, King spent most of the visit showing a nonplussed Jones how to follow the arrows and loops from dead ends to new starts. "I'm not finished yet," King said. He borrowed a number of sheets of note paper from Jones, who left with a concealed newspaper and precious few answers for those awaiting King's dispositions at the Gaston Motel.

King wrote several scattered passages in response to the criticism that his demonstrations were "untimely." He told the white clergymen that "time is neutral," that waiting never produced inevitable progress, and that "we must use time creatively, and forever realize that the time is always ripe to do right." He feared that "the people of ill-will have used time much more effectively than the people of good will," and pointed out that Negroes already had waited more than three hundred years for justice. "I guess it is easy for those who have never felt the stinging darts of segregation to say, 'Wait.' " Then, in a sentence of more than three hundred words, he tried to convey to the white preachers a feeling of time built upon a different alignment of emotions:

But when you have seen vicious mobs lynch your mothers and fathers at will and drown your sisters and brothers at whim; when you have seen hate-filled policemen curse, kick, brutalize and even kill your black brothers and sisters with impunity; when you see the vast majority of your twenty million Negro brothers smothering in an air-tight cage of poverty in the midst of an affluent society; when you suddenly find your tongue twisted and your speech stammering as you seek to explain to your six-year-old daughter why she can't go to the public amusement park that has just been advertised on television, and see tears welling up in her little eyes when she is told that Funtown is closed to colored children, and see the depressing clouds of inferiority begin to form in her little mental sky, and see her begin to distort her little personality by unconsciously developing a bitterness toward white people; when you have to concoct an answer for a five-year-old son asking in agonizing pathos: "Daddy, why do white people treat colored people so mean?"; when you take a cross-country drive and find it necessary to sleep night after night in the uncomfortable corners of your automobile because no motel will accept you; when you are humiliated day in and day out by nagging signs reading "white" and "colored"; when your first name becomes "nigger" and your middle name becomes "boy" (however old you are) and your last name becomes "John," and when you wife and mother are never given the respected title "Mrs."; when you are harried by day and haunted by night by the fact that you are a Negro, living constantly at a tip-toe stance, never quite knowing what to expect next, and plagued with inner fears and outer resentments; when you are forever fighting a degenerating sense of "nobodiness"; then you will understand why we find it difficult to wait.

King assumed a multitude of perspectives, often changing voice from one phrase to the next. He expressed empathy with the lives of millions over eons, and with the life of a particular child at a single moment. He tried to look not only at white preachers through the eyes of Negroes, but also at Negroes through the eyes of white preachers ("The Negro has many pent-up resentments and latent frustrations . . . So let him march sometime, let him have his prayer pilgrimages"). To the white preachers, he presented himself variously as a "haunted," suffering Negro ("What else is there to do when you are alone for days in the dull monotony of a narrow jail cell other than write long letters, think strange thoughts, and pray long prayers?"), a pontificator ("Injustice anywhere is a threat to

justice everywhere"), a supplicant ("I hope, sirs, you can understand . . ."), and a fellow bigshot ("If I sought to answer all of the criticisms that cross my desk, my secretaries would be engaged in little
else"). He spoke also as a teacher: "How does one determine when a law
is just or unjust? . . . To put it in the terms of Saint Thomas Aquinas, an
unjust law is a human law that is not rooted in eternal and natural law.
. . . All segregation statutes are unjust because segregation distorts the
soul and damages the personality . . . Let me give another explanation . . ." And he spoke as a gracious fellow student, seeking common
ground: "You are exactly right in your call for negotiation . . . I am not
unmindful of the fact that each of you has taken some significant stands
on this issue."

By degrees, King established a kind of universal voice, beyond time,
beyond race. As both humble prisoner and mighty prophet, as father,
harried traveler, and cornered leader, he projected a character of nearly
unassailable breadth. When he reached the heart of his case, he adopted
an authentic tone of intimacy toward the very targets of his wrath—
toward men who had condemned him without mentioning his name.
Almost whispering on the page, he presented his most scathing accusations as a confession:

> I must make two honest confessions to you, my Christian and Jewish broth-
> ers. First, I must confess that over the last few years I have been gravely
> disappointed with the white moderate. I have almost reached the regretta-
> ble conclusion that the Negro's great stumblingblock is not the White
> Citizen's Council-er or the Ku Klux Klanner, but the white moderate who
> is more devoted to "order" than to justice, who prefers a negative peace
> which is the absence of tension to a positive peace which is the presence of
> justice, who constantly says "I agree with you in the goal you seek, but I
> can't agree with your methods of direct action," who paternalistically be-
> lieves that he can set the timetable for another man's freedom . . .

Back at the Gaston Motel, deciphering what he called King's "chicken-
scratch handwriting," Wyatt Walker became visibly excited by these
passages. "His cup has really run over with those white preachers!"
Walker exclaimed. Long frustrated by what seemed to him King's excessive forbearance, Walker thrilled to see such stinging wrath let loose. He
knew that the history of the early Christian church made jail the appropriate setting for spiritual judgments—that buried within most religious
Americans was an inchoate belief in persecuted spirituality as the natural price of their faith. Here was the early church reincarnate, with King
rebuking the empire for its hatred, for its fearful defense of worldly attachments. For this, Walker put aside his clipboard. Long into the night,
he dictated King's words to his secretary for typing.

•   •   •

King was aiming at a tender spot in political and religious culture. The church had been central to Negro politics since 1441, when Prince Henry the Navigator brought the first recorded slaves out of sub-Sahara Africa and presented all ten of them as a gift to Pope Eugenius IV. Four hundred years later, the two largest Protestant churches in America divided not on some scholastic twist of theology—though there were plenty of these, too—but pointedly over the personal respect due two slaveholding preachers from Georgia. When Northerners raised doubts about their Christian fitness, Southern Baptists and Methodists indignantly marched out to form their own sectional churches. All through the 1840s and 1850s, the eminent Rev. C. C. Jones of Savannah labored to stave off a parallel schism within the Presbyterian Church. Haunted by the personal implications of slavery ("How often do I think of the number of hands employed to furnish me with the conveniences of life," he had written in the 1820s, "of which they are in consequence deprived—how many intellects, how many souls perhaps, withered and blasted forever for this very purpose!"), he had dedicated his life to the controversial proposition that the first duty of Christians was to extend the benefits of religion to Negroes. Having convinced himself that "the salvation of one soul will more than outweigh all the pain and woe of their capture and transportation, and subsequent residence among us," Jones expanded a slave mission from the Puritan congregation at Dorchester. He nurtured the Negro church in infancy, only to be blasted himself by some of the abolitionist Frederick Douglass' most withering oratory. "Oh, the artful dodger!" cried Douglass. "Well may the thief be glad, the robber sing, and the adulterer clap his hands for joy." Boring in against Jones's trademark distinction between the evil system and the conscientious, Christian slaveholder, Douglass insisted that slavery existed only because it was respectable, and that it was respectable because men such as Jones were wrongly accorded the gentlemanly respect due Christians. Jones came to defend his life's mission with embittered contempt, calling abolitionists "fanatics of the worse sort, setting at defiance all laws human and divine." When the Southern Presbyterians finally split away during the Civil War, Jones urged the church to adopt the religious instruction of slaves as a high calling.

A century later, religious respectability remained the crux of the issue that incensed King as he wrote Jones's great-grandson and namesake, Bishop C. C. Jones Carpenter. As instigator and first signatory, Carpenter had hand-carried the clerical letter attacking the Negro demonstrations to the Birmingham newspapers, exercising great care against interception or editorial changes. Explosive racial tension added gravity to every word, all the more so because of Carpenter's reputation as the senior Episcopal bishop in the United States. He was a sophisticated critic of segregation and a lifelong correspondent of Reinhold Niebuhr's best friend, Bishop Will Scarlett, who regularly pleaded with Carpenter to hurl his immense prestige against segregation.* However, Carpenter needed to pick only the slightest difference with King in program or emphasis to stand aside, leaving the weight of his reputation to fall against the movement. King sought a revolution to reverse the burden of inertia. Carpenter chided King on the grounds that protest lacked Christian respectability, unaware of the countervailing storm within King against the Christian respectability of clergymen such as Carpenter himself.

"I need more paper," King told Clarence Jones. Sometimes directly, and sometimes with the clandestine help of an old Negro trusty in the jail, he exchanged the new handwritten original for the typed draft. By then the smuggling relay was exasperating Jones, for whom the letter was a toothless appeal to white clergymen who did not matter. But he saw the letter-writing as a mental health exercise for King. "I figured he was entitled to it—you know, a man in jail," Jones later recalled. "But Lord have mercy, I thought he had lost his perspective." Among the few business decisions Jones managed to wrest from King was an order to evict Hosea Williams from the Gaston Motel. Williams had responded to King's request for help by driving over from Savannah with a carload of assistants, who were running up a motel bill on the SCLC's tab. Walker found this not only expensive but unseemly, as the outside staff people far outnumbered the Birmingham volunteers going to jail every day. King agreed.

The two confessions filled the second half of what turned out to be a twenty-page letter. At first King formally denounced the white preachers for their shortcomings, as though speaking from a pulpit. "I have heard numerous religious leaders of the South call upon their worshippers to comply with a desegregation decision because it is the *law*," he wrote, "but I have longed to hear white ministers say, 'follow this decree because integration is morally *right* and the Negro is your brother.' " As he continued with his usual themes on the failures of the church, his wrath

---

* "This is in line with my suggestion years ago that the sight of the great Bishop of Alabama ridden out of his State on a rail because of courageous and enlightened speech, would be one of the greatest events of many years," Scarlett wrote Carpenter. "I still think so: I think you have an opportunity of a hundred years."

turned slowly into a lament: " I have wept over the laxity of the church. But be assured that my tears have been tears of love." In supreme irony, the prisoner in the hole mourned over the most respectable clergymen in Alabama as lost sheep who were unable to find the most obvious tenets of their faith.

"Maybe again, I have been too optimistic," King added, as though it may have been folly to expect better. ". . . Maybe I must turn my faith to the inner spiritual church, the church within the church, as the true *ecclesia* and the hope of the world." Even if the prelates excluded themselves and all their authority from the cause of justice, King said he would not despair, because for him the inner church was a stream of belief intermingled with the religious core of the American creed. If all men were created equal, then all were brothers and sisters, and these fundamental beliefs tilted history toward the affirming conclusion that the universe was on the side of justice. "We will reach the goal of freedom in Birmingham and all over the nation," wrote King, "because the goal of America is freedom . . . If the inexpressible cruelties of slavery could not stop us, the opposition we now face will surely fail. We will win our freedom because the sacred heritage of our nation and the eternal will of God are embodied in our echoing demands."

In this letter, as in his sermons, King pulled back from an initial peroration. Almost as an aside, he mentioned the part of the Carpenter statement that expressed thanks to the Birmingham authorities for downplaying the demonstrations with muffling restraint. "I don't believe you would so quickly commend the policemen if you would observe their ugly and inhuman treatment of Negroes here in the city jail," King wrote. Conceding that the police had performed with professional discipline in public, King raised the question he thought should have occurred to the white preachers. "But for what purpose?" he asked them, and he answered his own question: "To preserve the evil system of segregation." For all his nonviolent preaching about how it was wrong to use immoral means to attain moral ends, King wrote, "it is just as wrong, or even more so, to use moral means to preserve immoral ends." He quoted T. S. Eliot to that effect.

Then he returned soulfully to his lament. "I wish you had commended the Negro sit-inners and demonstrators of Birmingham for their sublime courage, their willingness to suffer and their amazing discipline in the midst of the most inhuman provocation," he wrote. "One day the South will recognize its real heroes . . . One day the South will know that when these disinherited children of God sat down at lunch counters, they were in reality standing up for the best in the American dream and the most sacred values in our Judeo-Christian heritage, and thusly, carrying our whole nation back to those great wells of democracy which were dug deep by the founding fathers."

Late at night, an exhausted Willie Pearl Mackey literally fell asleep over her typewriter. Failing to revive her, Wyatt Walker lifted his secretary by the arms, placed her in another chair, and sat down at the typewriter himself. Against his sharply defined sense of executive hierarchy, only the rarest emergency could compel the descent into clerical duty, but this time Walker pecked to the end. He could not bear to leave undone so exquisite a blend of New Testament grace and Old Testament wrath. Near his closing, King groped consciously toward the mixture. "If I have said anything in this letter that is an overstatement of the truth and is indicative of an unreasonable impatience, I beg you to forgive me," he wrote to Bishop Carpenter and the others. "If I have said anything in this letter that is an understatement of the truth and is indicative of my having a patience that makes me patient with anything less than brotherhood, I beg God to forgive me."

The "Letter from Birmingham Jail" did not spring quickly to acclaim. It remained essentially a private communication for some time, in spite of Wyatt Walker's labors to attract the attention of the passing world. Its Gandhian themes did impress some of James Lawson's contacts, who offered to publish the letter in the June issue of *Friends*, the Quaker journal, but ordinary reporters saw no news in what appeared to be an especially long-winded King sermon. Not a single mention of the letter reached white or Negro news media for a month. In hindsight, it appeared that King had rescued the beleaguered Birmingham movement with his pen, but the reverse was true: unexpected miracles of the Birmingham movement later transformed King's letter from a silent cry of desperate hope to a famous pronouncement of moral triumph.

Wyatt Walker sorely needed a glimpse of this future. In the absence of swelling expectations, his mechanical genius was being ground to bits. For the first time in the decade, physical persecution of King aroused no whirlwind of political pressures. The Kennedy Administration, after responding circumspectly to Coretta's initiatives, preferred to remain silent. Its officials reacted no better than neutrally toward King if pressed, and in private criticized his movement as a nuisance. Four days after King went to jail, Walker tacitly acknowledged that King's name had lost some of its symbolic power. In a letter to Burke Marshall he notified the Justice Department that henceforth the Birmingham campaign "would be channeling the enthusiasms built up into voter registration efforts." Although Walker casually presented the change as "the second phase of our campaign," it actually meant scrapping all the solemn resolve to break segregation in Birmingham by concerted direct action. Walker's notice to Marshall anticipated an Albany-style retreat from Birmingham. It also signaled to the Kennedy people that King needed their support badly enough to adopt their preferred methods.

Bishop Carpenter sat down in his study with a copy of King's mammoth reply. He read the letter through to the end, then turned to his bishop coadjutor, George Murray, with a sigh of resignation. "This is what you get when you try to do something," he said. "You get it from both sides. George, you just have to live with that." Carpenter felt abused and misunderstood for his efforts to act as a progressive force in race relations. The clash of emotion turned him, like his great-grandfather, into a more strident Confederate.

For the Kennedy Administration, King's incarceration in Birmingham coincided with a climax of the intramural struggle over Mississippi. When the Civil Rights Commission submitted an advance draft of its special report, Burke Marshall rebutted selected phrases from the report in a memorandum to President Kennedy. Of the finding that Negroes in registration lines had been "set upon by vicious dogs," Marshall reported that a single dog had bitten a single preacher in Greenwood. "The use of police dogs is not a prohibited activity," he added. Of the finding that Mississippi Negroes had been "beaten and otherwise terrorized because they sought to vote," Marshall told Kennedy that he did "not know what specific instances are referred to" but that one Negro registration worker indeed had been "pistol-whipped by the registrar of Walthall County." Then, having reduced the charge of statewide voter intimidation to one incident, Marshall assured Kennedy that the Justice Department "brought a successful case in that instance." He did not mention the bizarre limits of the success: the federal government had stopped Mississippi from prosecuting John Hardy for disturbing the peace while getting pistol-whipped. The Kafkaesque reality of Mississippi was that this was indeed a bold and notable first step from madness. The altered reality of Marshall's memo created the impression for President Kennedy that Justice had punished the pistol-whipper and set things right for would-be Negro voters.

At the White House, Lee White turned Marshall's summary a few degrees into an outright attack on the Civil Rights Commission. For each "Charge" of injustice he listed an "Answer" cribbed from Marshall, leading to the conclusion that the report was wholly irresponsible. "Implicit is the suggestion that the President and the Administration have not done all that could be done for the Mississippi situation," he wrote President Kennedy. "This, of course, is manifestly wrong." White went on to suggest a number of "harmful effects" that the President might point out in urging the commission to withdraw or amend its report. Some of them amounted to threats: the report could "kill the bill to extend the life of the Commission," said White, and "destroy the Commission's reputation for reasonableness and that of its individual members."

President Kennedy summoned the commission's staff director, Berl Bernhard, for a one-sided series of questions, many laced with sardonic disbelief. How in the world could various commissioners with such bad judgment have been appointed in the first place, he wanted to know, and why didn't they understand that the report would "poison an atmosphere that is already pretty bad?" Armed with White's memo, the President disputed the commission's allegations of attacks on the Moses registration projects. As to a collateral finding of the commission that the federal government was subsidizing segregated programs in Mississippi, Kennedy told Bernhard that his information indicated otherwise. He said the Federal Aviation Administration had specifically denied that the new airport in Jackson would have segregated rest rooms and lunch counters.

Bernhard feinted and dodged his way out of Kennedy's office, not wishing to contradict the President to his face. The good news, he reported back to the commissioners, was that the President had not ordered them to withdraw the special report. Kennedy was basing his stand on the facts, where the unanimity of commissioners was most solid. Over the next few days, they gradually disclosed to the Justice Department one of their secret weapons: they had the architect's drawings for the new Jackson airport, which clearly showed a partitioned lunch room and dual sets of rest rooms for whites and Negroes. By the time Chairman John Hannah accompanied Bernhard to the White House for a final showdown over the report, Administration officials conceded that there was to be segregation in the rest rooms and lunch counters, but said there would be none in those parts of the airport subsidized by the federal government —the runways and the control tower. Therefore, the Administration would not be supporting segregation directly.

By respectful persistence, Hannah and Bernhard won what they thought was a complete victory. President Kennedy reserved his quibbles of fact and ordered no changes. He asked only for the right to handle press announcements, but through this opening he sprang a trap that more than offset the commission's airport blueprints. On Tuesday, April 16—while King was working feverishly on his letter in the Birmingham jail, and as Wyatt Walker was notifying Marshall of plans to fall back into voter registration—President Kennedy himself spoke privately with White House reporters upon release of the commission report. He drew attention to the final section, in which the commissioners "concluded unanimously that only further steps by the Federal Government can arrest the subversion of the Constitution in Mississippi." One possible step was for President Kennedy to "explore his legal authority" to use federal spending as leverage against segregation. Here was the news, said the President, hinting strongly that this was a crackpot proposal, ensuring that the report came to light with emphasis on its most inflammatory ideas. "President Urged to Cut Off Funds for Mississippi," announced *The New York Times.*

White House aides fanned out among reporters to make sure they grasped the breadth of official disdain. Cutting off funds to punish racial abuses was impractical as well as unconstitutional, they said, and the very idea of singling out Mississippi implied that similar abuses were acceptable in other states. Even worse, the proposal was cruel to Mississippi Negroes, who would be the most severely punished by any curtailment of federal support. These objections took root everywhere in the press, including the outlets most supportive of civil rights. Such a public reception enabled President Kennedy safely to dismiss the commission three days later. "With regard to the incidents referred to in the Commission's report," he told Chairman Hannah in a public letter, "I am advised that every case, but one, has been successfully resolved." At the Civil Rights Commission, which had submitted its grand declaration of conscience only to be hooted out of Washington, a miserable shock set in over this demonstration of the Administration's power to control the tone of public discussion.

When King and Abernathy bonded out that Saturday, after nearly nine days in the Birmingham jail, King appeared at an impromptu press conference wearing a heavy beard for the first and only time in his life, as there had been no shaving allowed in solitary. He explained that he had come out to confer with his lawyers about the contempt trial that was beginning on Monday. (He did not mention his long letter, but he did say he had managed to read two smuggled books, Ralph McGill's *The South and the Southerner* and Du Bois's *The Souls of Black Folk.*) Three of the first four prosecution witnesses against him turned out to be news reporters, who testified that they had heard King and other defendants urging Negroes to demonstrate in defiance of the injunction. At the mass meeting that Monday night King predicted freedom in a defiant speech that concluded with a full recitation of "The Star-Spangled Banner." Practically unnoticed, he seemed to be darting through a refracted reality, like a kook.

By eerie coincidence, a more obscure kook was on a parallel trek. As

King was leaving jail on Saturday, a white postman from Baltimore was presenting himself at the White House gate with a letter notifying President Kennedy that he intended to take ten days' vacation to walk all the way from Chattanooga to Mississippi wearing two signboards, END SEGREGATION IN AMERICA and EQUAL RIGHTS FOR ALL MEN. "If I may deliver any letters from you to those on my line of travel, I would be most happy to do so," offered the postman, William Moore. Rebuffed, his letter refused by the guards, Moore scribbled a handwritten P.S. to President Kennedy: "Keep up your fight against the Cuban war hawks. And read over your Senate speeches on Vietnam!" Then Moore, wearing his signs and pushing his personal effects in a two-wheeled postal cart, picketed on the White House sidewalk for a while before dropping his letter into a mailbox on his way to the bus station. He added "Mississippi or Bust" to one of his signboards.

By Monday night, when King was reciting "The Star-Spangled Banner," Moore was on the road, writing in his diary about his adventures thus far. He had adopted a dog and given it away to a small boy, he wrote, and a Negro in Chattanooga had ripped the word "black" out of his new signboard, EAT AT JOE'S, BOTH BLACK AND WHITE, saying angrily that the word should be "colored." * Moore also wrote that he had drawn angry epithets and a few tossed rocks from roadside segregationists, as well as requests for interviews by feature reporters. He was indeed an odd sight as he pushed his cart down highways from Tennessee through a corner of Georgia and into Alabama. Blistered, swollen feet forced him to walk barefoot except when he went into stores to buy food.

Moore had covered some seventy miles by Tuesday evening, when a reporter from radio station WGAD in Gadsden stopped him on the road for an interview. Asked his purpose, Moore said, "I intend to walk right up to the governor's mansion in Mississippi and ring his doorbell. Then I'll hand him my letter." The letter was a civil rights plea asking Barnett to "be gracious and give more than is immediately demanded of you." Of shouted threats that he would never make it alive, Moore said that he had grown up in Mississippi. "I don't believe the people in the South are that way. I think a lot of this stuff is just made up."

The reporter left Moore on a remote stretch of U.S. Highway 11, near Attala. A passing motorist discovered the body a mile down the road, shot twice through the head at close range. A call from a farmhouse

---

* Though jarring by later standards, the word "black" was usually taken as an insult in the pivotal year of 1963. In Toledo, Ohio, high school students staged a mass protest after an assistant principal referred to them as "black students" over the intercom.

telephone brought sirens and reporters upon the murder scene. Moore lay face up in the grass, still wearing his signboards. In his pockets were $51, his letter to Governor Barnett, his diary, and postal receipts for expense money he had mailed ahead to himself at Birmingham and other towns along his route. Next to him was the postal cart containing his shoes, his extra clothes, and copies of his letter to President Kennedy.

During Moore's last moments on the road toward Birmingham, the nightly mass meeting there was advertising to Negroes the support of young people, especially whites. Fred Shuttlesworth dramatically introduced three white students from Birmingham Southern College, who walked sheepishly onto the platform to thunderous applause. King announced that two of the three were the children of preachers. When Shuttlesworth put his arms around the two female students, most of the audience bolted to its feet to cheer this astonishing public display of cross-racial, cross-sexual friendship. Police observers were correspondingly galled and disgusted. Two detectives met the next day with officials of Birmingham Southern, who promised swift disciplinary action against the two females for their conduct at the Negro church. Sam Shirah, they said with relief, had flunked out already.

News of the roadside execution was flashing across the country that Wednesday. It did not take reporters long to discover that Moore, a hulking ex-Marine with a family in Binghamton, New York, had been confined for more than a year in a New York mental hospital, after which he had published a book in 1955 called *The Mind in Chains*. "I took my teachings literally," he wrote of his Mississippi childhood, "and where the world was not like the ideal, I believed the world was wrong and so did not adjust my behavior to reality." Stories told of Moore's treatment for schizophrenia, his identification with Don Quixote, his sit-in arrest in Baltimore, his reputation among fellow postal workers as a likable screwball. They quoted from the conclusion of his book: "So the dream which led me to the State Hospital still has possession of me. . . . My whole future is in your hands. I can only give my life. And you must make it or break it for me."

In Washington, Moore's letter to President Kennedy had been delivered into the hands of Lee White, who made sure to brief his boss on the strange horror before that day's televised press conference. No one asked about Moore, however. Nor did reporters ask a single question about King and the twenty-one consecutive days of demonstrations in Birmingham. Most of the questions had to do with great-power tensions over Laos and Cuba. In the only civil rights matter raised, a reporter asked if there was not some merit in the case for more federal action to establish the rights of Negroes in Mississippi. "Well," President Kennedy replied, "in every case that the Civil Rights Commission described, the United States Government has instituted legal action in order to provide a remedy." After several more comments in this vein, the President himself mentioned the previous night's shooting of William Moore, perhaps to reach stronger and more truthful ground. "Now it's very difficult," he said. "We had an outrageous crime, from all accounts, in the State of Alabama in the shooting of the postman who was attempting, in a very traditional way, to dramatize the plight of some of our citizens. I think being assassinated on the road—" He paused in midsentence, then started again in a more official tone: "We have offered to the State of Alabama the services of the FBI . . ."

These presidential remarks about William Moore spurred press discussion about whether the childlike postman had been crazier or saner than the accepted world. Within the movement, the stunning news of his tragic "Freedom Walk" rekindled the sacrificial energies of two years earlier, when the first Freedom Riders suffered savage beatings at the Birmingham bus station. From the Fisk Chapel, John Lewis led an integrated march of 125 students to the Federal Building in Nashville. They carried signs reading "William Moore. Who Will Be Next?" and "Moore Died for Love. Let's Live and Act in Love." Paul Brooks, one of Lewis' fellow Freedom Riders, announced that he was leaving to take up the walk where Moore had been shot down, saying he could not allow violence to win. In New York, James Farmer convened the CORE steering committee to plan a response to this first slaying of a CORE member.* From Atlanta, SNCC's James Forman called Moore's widow in Binghamton to ask whether she thought her husband would have wanted students to take up his march. From Birmingham, Diane Nash reactivated her telephone network. She was with her husband, James Bevel, recalling the picnic of 1961 when they heard about the burning of the Freedom Ride bus outside Anniston.

Bevel's afternoon workshops for students had grown so large that they outnumbered the regular mass meetings. That afternoon, following the Kennedy press conference, Bevel and Andrew Young invited the workshop students to stay on into the night. The result was a mass meeting so jammed with people that a fire marshal entered the St. James Baptist Church to try to enforce occupancy regulations. Fred Shuttlesworth ban-

---

* It was an acutely awkward tragedy for CORE's national leaders. Privately, they hesitated to lionize Moore, because they had summarily refused his request for CORE sponsorship of his walk, and had disparaged him among themselves as a kook. More pragmatically, they qualified their support for the memorial marches, having not yet recovered from the near bankruptcy of the Freedom Rides.

tered merrily with him, and the heightened spirit of the meeting inspired Shuttlesworth to vow that all Negroes attending the next day's session of the contempt trial would use the "whites only" water fountains at city hall. A tumultuous roar of approval went up. Tributes to William Moore made tears flow, and the movement choir rocked the church with freedom songs. When the call came for the next day's jail-going volunteers, however, the spirit all but evaporated. It took King more than half an hour to coax a score of volunteers from the huge crowd. Significantly, many of these came from the workshops—students from high schools and even elementary schools. King repeatedly explained that while he deeply appreciated their willingness to suffer, and while he hoped their noble example would inspire their parents, the Birmingham jail was no place for children. In spite of King, some of the third- and fourth-graders refused to sit down.

Robert Kennedy and Burke Marshall were in Montgomery the next day for a tense special meeting with Governor Wallace. At the Sixteenth Street Baptist Church, Fred Shuttlesworth told a packed mass meeting he was "glad Bobby came down." "I wish he would come to Birmingham," he added, "but he can hear the noise we are making one hundred miles away." Shuttlesworth preached with gleeful, improvised mirth on the water battle at city hall, reporting that the desperate city fathers had shut off both the white and Negro water fountains. "And all the toilets were locked up," he said. "So if the judge was ill at ease, he wasn't no worse off than anybody in the court." Above peals of laughter, Shuttlesworth told how he had been obliged to walk over to the bus station to relieve himself, and how he had found white policemen in the rest room there too, and how they had suffered together for lack of water. "Segregation is a silly thing!" he cried. ". . . Here we are—arguing over something that's free!" To illustrate why they were persisting, he told the story of the little boy who said, " 'Daddy, what makes a lightnin' bug light?' " Shuttlesworth described how the father had stalled, stammered, and scratched his head until finally, pressed for an answer, he said, " 'Well, I'll tell you the truth, boy. The stuff is just in him, that's all.' " To howls of laughter and a chorus of cheers, Shuttlesworth added, "And for the spirit that these Negroes be free, well, *the stuff is just in 'em!*"

On Friday, April 26, Judge Jenkins announced that he found King, Shuttlesworth, Walker, Abernathy, and seven Birmingham leaders guilty of criminal contempt. He sentenced each of them to serve the maximum penalty of five days, holding open the threat that further violations of his injunction might lead to more severe penalties under the civil contempt laws, which provided that a judge might jail defendants indefinitely until they "purged" themselves by apology and recantation. To the defendants, the verdict was less daunting than the burden of the movement's response. Now that the interlude necessitated by the trial was concluded, there could be no more entertainments over the water fountains at city hall. The next move fell to the leaders at a time when there was an acute disparity between the enthusiasm of the mass meetings and the scarcity of jail-going volunteers. The leaders could not predict exactly how an uprising would lead to victory instead of further pain, but they did recognize that they were lost without some decisive move. Accordingly, on the very day of the verdict, Shuttlesworth petitioned the city fathers of Birmingham for permission to stage a mass protest march on the following Thursday, May 2.

This gave the leaders five days to prepare. From the beginning, it was no secret that their model was the 1960 march at the climax of James Lawson's sit-ins in Nashville. This three-year-old event had become a new inspiration in Birmingham, since Bevel had been showing his film copy of an NBC special report on Nashville, narrated by Chet Huntley and David Brinkley. "Four thousand Negroes marched on the City Hall in Nashville, Tennessee," Andrew Young announced at the mass meeting. "We would like to have that many here in Birmingham." In their private strategy sessions, however, the leaders recognized that they faced crippling disadvantages. Nashville had jailed none of its marchers, whereas Birmingham had a consistent record of jailing them all. There had been no injunction against demonstrations in Nashville, nor any Bull Connor. Most critically, the Nashville march line had been formed mostly of students, whereas the Birmingham movement had been a grim war waged by Negro adults.

Bevel wanted to change that. Young people were the ones watching the Nashville film at the workshops every day. In Birmingham, where a scarcity of adult volunteers forced King's colleagues to devise alibis and side projects, the only hope for a march rested on a mass infusion of students. As in Mississippi, Bevel and Diane Nash had begun by recruiting the elite students—basketball stars, Miss Parker High School—and within two weeks the workshops had become a contagion. An entire new echelon of student leaders had distinguished themselves by their ability to slip in and out of schools. Every day younger and younger students popped up in the workshops, full of bravado, ready to march to jail, and every night King presided over debates about which ones they should permit to go. John and Deenie Drew, A. G. Gaston, and Rev. John Porter stoutly opposed allowing students younger than college age, as did nearly every Birmingham leader consulted. School records and lifetime hopes could be ruined, young lives scarred by exposure to rapes, beatings, and the unmentionable ugliness of the jailhouse. Far from allowing their own children to march, the Drews sent their eleven-year-old son off to a distant prep school, to protect him from dangers created by their house-guest, "Mike" King. No self-respecting adult could use their children for battle fodder, they said, as even the early Christians had not encouraged their children to face the lions at the Colosseum.

Birmingham's white leadership grew more confident that its united, noninflammatory toughness was subduing the Negro protest. The *News* published an instructive article entitled "Greenwood Rolled with Punch —And Won." Meanwhile, the two city governments of Birmingham maintained a remarkable truce as they waited for the Alabama courts to decide which of them was legitimate. The rivals shared everything from memo pads to parking spaces, and every Tuesday they acted out a cere-mony of parallel sovereignty. When Bull Connor and his fellow commis-sioners filed out of city hall, Mayor Boutwell and the new city council filed in to take up the same business anew. At the third set of dual meetings, on April 30, both bodies denied Shuttlesworth's request for a parade permit that Thursday.

At the Gaston Motel, King and his aides faced the implications of the denial. It meant that anyone who marched would be subject to arrest, and that the leaders could be reimprisoned for violating Judge Jenkins' injunction. Furthermore, anyone who urged children to make the march would be subject to prosecution for contributing to the delinquency of a minor, and King believed that the circumstances gave Birmingham a good chance to make criminal convictions stick on appeal. Nervously, he kidded Bevel about the possibility that the great gamble would only make them all long-term inmates. "Well, Bevel, you already got about eighty counts of contributing to the delinquency of minors pending in Jackson," he said.

"Well, that's the problem," Bevel replied. "I didn't get enough. If I had had eight thousand, they wouldn't have bothered me."

This was not the first time that young veterans of the Freedom Rides had pressed King to jump off the cliff, but none of them had been quite like Bevel. He had returned from Mississippi wearing a yarmulke atop his shaven head, which he explained sometimes as a token of his affec-tion for the Hebrew prophets and other times as a protective device to keep himself out of jail, saying Mississippi sheriffs were so mystified by the sight of a Negro preacher in a "Jewish beenie" that they preferred to let him alone. Bevel possessed the unique charm of a spellbinding eccen-tric, a junior Vernon Johns. For King, who was far surer of his judgment than of his innate creativity, Bevel had the appeal of a free spirit, a madcap Aristotelian. He even respected the "voices" Bevel claimed to hear. In moments of stress, Bevel served as a reminder that there was an essential element of craziness to the movement, as did the murder of William Moore. When deciding whether to send children into Bull Connor's jails, King could not get away with the rational repose of Solomon.

With King's permission, Bevel addressed the mass meeting a few hours after the parade permit was denied on Tuesday. To the crowd, and to the police detectives conspicuously among them, he announced that there would be a mass march on Thursday with or without a permit. It would be a special march of high school students on what Bevel and Walker called D-Day. Almost as an aside, Bevel added that his wife Diane was leaving that night to take up the Freedom Walk of the slain William Moore.

Two separate Moore marches stepped off on Wednesday morning, the first of May. Not surprisingly, both groups drew heavy press coverage. Walking in the footsteps of a dead man, having been threatened by Klansmen as well as Alabama officials, and having been denied protection by the Justice Department, the small bands of walkers were a guaranteed suspense story. Claude Sitton of *The New York Times* left Birmingham to cover one group of ten volunteers who, after protracted negotiations between CORE and SNCC, had been selected to make the walk along Moore's entire route from Chattanooga to Jackson. This group included Bob Zellner and Bill Hansen of SNCC, Jesse Harris of the Greenwood movement, and Sam Shirah, the white Birmingham Southern student who had caused such a stir at a Birmingham mass meeting. James Forman went along as an observer. Simultaneously, Foster Hailey of the *Times* left Birmingham to cover the smaller group of Diane Nash Bevel, Paul Brooks, and six others, who began walking toward Birmingham from the spot where Moore's body had fallen. Alabama state troopers soon arrested all eighteen in both groups, plus Forman.

In Birmingham, the partial evacuation of reporters handed King a verbal shield for the internal politics of the D-Day march. To John Porter and others who were upset by the decision to use high school children, King said he had to do something dramatic in Birmingham because the press was losing interest. These words seemed shocking and cynical to Porter, who with each step into the movement had been swept toward dilemmas more unsettling to his temperament. For King's purposes, however, the press argument obscured the central debate over sending children to jail, where the drift of King's inclinations would have driven Porter and others to near apoplexy. In private talks with Walker, Shuttlesworth, Bevel, and others closest to him, King was allowing the minimum age of jail volunteers to drift steadily downward.

From his workshops, where hundreds of Birmingham's children were pressing themselves forward for the D-Day march, Bevel brought to King a simple formula: any child old enough to belong to a church should be eligible to march to jail. Nearly all the young volunteers were Baptists, like King and himself, and Baptist doctrine required only a conscious acceptance of the Christian faith as a condition of both church membership and personal salvation. By common practice, churches allowed the youngest school-age children to become members. That settled it right there, Bevel insisted. How could he and King tell six-year-old church members that they were old enough to decide their eternal destiny but too young to march against segregation? How could they keep church members out of a nonviolent movement that embodied Christian teachings?

King knew that Bevel was overwrought for good reason, as his wife was at that moment out on William Moore's route down Highway 11. He also knew that it was absurd to form a jail march based on church teachings as addressed to the afterlife. Still, he felt the truth of what Bevel was saying, as well as its hope of transformation. The church had paved the way for the movement by swallowing up not only the fear of death but also distinctions of race and age and all the compromises of everyday sanity. Bevel made it plain: if they could, they should send volunteers to jail over the objections of their parents. "Against your Mama," he told King, "you have a right to make this witness."

By then the Birmingham police department had received an FBI intelligence report that leaflets were circulating in the Negro high schools urging all students to leave school at noon on Thursday. This threat of mass truancy was only a hint of the rumblings in Negro Birmingham. "Meatball" and other Bevel recruits were sounding the call in the elementary schools too. "Tall Paul," a rock 'n' roll disc jockey, was broadcasting a jived-up announcement about the "big party" Thursday at Kelly Ingram Park, and nearly every Negro kid in Birmingham knew what he meant. The night was filled with anguish and excitement, as some young people wrestled with plans to sneak in or out of the march, while others confided bravely to relatives that Martin Luther King wanted them to march to jail.

For King, too, the moment brimmed with tension. Eight years after the bus boycott, he was on the brink of holding nothing back. Eight long months after the SCLC convention in Birmingham, he was contemplating an action of more drastic, lasting impact than jumping off the roof of city hall or assassinating Bull Connor. Having submitted his prestige and his body to jail, and having hurled his innermost passions against the aloof respectability of white American clergymen, all without noticeable effect, King committed his cause to the witness of schoolchildren.

TWENTY

THE CHILDREN'S MIRACLE

Birmingham police squads, anticipating a "D-Day" youth march on Thursday, May 2, reinforced their daily roadblocks along the routes downtown from the Sixteenth Street Baptist Church. The usual crowds of Negro bystanders gathered directly across from the church in Kelly Ingram Park, watching the police officers. Both groups listened to freedom songs wafting outward through the brick walls and stained glass windows. When the front doors opened shortly after one o'clock, fifty teenagers emerged two abreast. Their high-spirited singing and clapping transformed "We Shall Overcome" from a wistful dirge into a ragtime march.

Jumping wearily to duty, the officers halted the line, gave notice of the court injunction against demonstrations, warned of arrest, and started directing the teenagers into the paddy wagons. Except for the absence of adults in the line, it seemed to be another day in the month-long siege until a second double line of marchers spilled out through the church's front doors. Shortly after them came another group, followed by another and another. Wyatt Walker, speaking to assistants by walkie-talkie, sent some groups veering off by different routes. Police radios crackled with requests for more paddy wagons. The dispatchers, swallowing the department's pride, called on Sheriff Bailey to send in county deputies. Still the marchers kept spilling forth, outnumbering and enveloping the officers so that one group of twenty teenagers was able to slip around the clogged arrest lines toward city hall. They had almost disappeared into the down-town business district before a police detachment took off in pursuit.

From the swirling mass of Negro children, blue uniforms, and picket signs, an anxious policeman spotted a familiar figure across the Sixteenth Street truce line. "Hey, Fred," he called. "How many more have you got?"

"At least a thousand!" shouted Shuttlesworth.

"God Almighty," said the policeman.

Reporters saw things they had never seen before. George Wall, a tough-looking police captain, confronted a group of thirty-eight elementary-school children and did his best to cajole or intimidate them into leaving the lines, but they all said they knew what they were doing. Asked her age as she climbed into a paddy wagon, a tiny girl called out that she was six. When city firemen came up to help contain the demonstration, one group of marchers dissolved in panic at the sight of high-pressure hoses being spread across Fourth Avenue; then they managed to re-form. An elderly woman broke away from the cheering observers in Ingram Park and ran along the arrest lines, ecstatically shouting "Sing, children, sing!" Four blocks away, police overtook the twenty students who had circumvented the blockade. They carried signs that read "Segregation Is a Sin" and "No Eat, No Dollars." The very sight of them was a blow to the city's goal of confining the unsettling disturbances to the Negro sections of town.

On running out of paddy wagons and sheriff's patrol cars, police com-manders called in school buses to take load after load of hookey-playing students away. It was all over by four o'clock. With the streets cleared, the energy that had created the extraordinary sights disappeared into the jails, where as many as seventy-five students were crammed into cells built for eight. And almost as soon as the lines stopped coming out of Sixteenth Street Baptist, early birds began filing into the mass meeting at Fred Shuttlesworth's old church some blocks distant. Rev. Edwin Gardner, the warm-up preacher, directed their overflow emotions into songs, prayers, and an offering. "If you are dead broke, see me after the meeting," he said. There were a thousand people in the church by the time surveillance detectives took their seats at six, and nearly twice that number when Shuttlesworth and King arrived. "The whole world is watching Birmingham tonight," said Shuttlesworth.

Like all the other preachers, Shuttlesworth was too distracted to give a normal speech. The church buzzed with rumors. The crowd's fervor rose with the disintegration of the usual program, as the loss of normalcy itself heralded a spectacular surge of emotion. "I have been inspired and moved today," declared King. "I have never seen anything like it." Using figures from Wyatt Walker's jail registry, he announced that precisely 958 children had signed up for jail that day, and that of these some 600 were in custody. For tactical reasons, he kept to himself the news that a flood of new young people was replenishing the jailed volunteers several times over. "If they think today is the end of this," he said, "they will be badly mistaken." He introduced CORE chairman James Farmer, who had flown into Birmingham for the CORE-SNCC Freedom Walk in honor of William Moore. "We are prepared and ready to unite behind you," Farmer told the Birmingham crowd.

King revealed that Dick Gregory had just agreed to join the Birmingham movement on Sunday. Cheers went up for the comedian who had drawn national publicity to Greenwood. King also announced that Diane Nash and the other members of the Moore march had been arrested. Finally, he introduced James Bevel, who fairly sprang into the pulpit. "There ain't gonna be no meeting Monday night," he shouted, "because every Negro is gonna be in jail by Sunday night." In wild, boundless bravado, Bevel vowed to finish off segregation in Birmingham fast enough to be "back in Mississippi chopping cotton" by Tuesday. Preaching on the courage of the children, he burst into the freedom songs they had sung on their way into the paddy wagons. Some three hundred people rose spontaneously in anticipation of a march to jail. Unable to wait for the next day, they walked up and down the aisles as the church thundered in song.

The contest resumed with greater intensity on Friday, May 3. By noon, an audience of anxious parents and curious onlookers jammed Kelly Ingram Park, while more than a thousand young people received marching orders inside the Sixteenth Street Baptist Church. Across from them, blocking the eastbound cross streets, Birmingham's uniformed authorities massed in front of school buses, fire equipment, and police cruisers. When the first group of sixty singing students marched out of the church, Captain G. V. Evans confronted them at the corner of Fifth Avenue and Seventeenth Street. This time there was no talk of arrest. With both the city and county jails bulging already, the goal was to keep the demonstrators out of the downtown business section without making arrests. On the orders of Bull Connor, Captain Evans pointed to the fire hoses behind him and told the sixty students to disperse "or you're going to get wet."

The students kept singing, whereupon Captain Evans signaled the firemen to douse them with spray through fogging nozzles. Wetness shocked

nearly all the marchers into retreat. Behind them, the bystanders in Ingram Park recoiled instinctively from the threat of being drenched.
Through his bullhorn, Evans ordered an evacuation of the area, and the
water seemed to enforce his commands effectively, until he and everyone
else began to notice the holdout students. About ten of the original sixty
stood their ground. Already soaked beyond any worry of lost dignity, they
sang one word, "freedom," to the tune of "Amen." As the firemen concentrated the hoses upon the singers, the crowd surged back toward the
contested borders. Then the firemen advanced toward the holdouts,
pounding them with water at close range. The holdouts sat down on the
sidewalk to stabilize themselves. It was a moment of baptism for the
civil rights movement, and Birmingham's last effort to wash away the
stain of dissent against segregation. For Captain Evans and the firemen,
it was a mechanical problem of increasing the water pressure enough to
overcome physical resistance on the pavement. Ideally suited for the task
were special monitor guns that forced water from two hoses through a
single nozzle, mounted on a tripod. The fire department advertised these
attachments as miracles of long-range firefighting, capable of knocking
bricks loose from mortar or stripping bark from trees at a distance of one
hundred feet.

A. G. Gaston was among the first of millions to be converted by the
monitor guns. The city's leading Negro businessman was talking on the
telephone with David Vann, one of the architects of the city charter
campaign against Bull Connor. As they often did, the two were singing a
hymn of complaint against King's street demonstrations for undermining
their delicate, mostly secret, reform alliance just at its moment of opportunity. If successful, King would force Gaston and other established
Negro leaders to endorse his tactics, which would alienate the city's
nervous white moderates. If unsuccessful, King would strengthen segregationists. Either way, the demonstrations were a curse to Vann and
Gaston, who had been groping for a way to maneuver King out of town
gently, so as not to give comfort to Bull Connor. That Friday afternoon,
Gaston suddenly asked Vann to excuse him. Staring down from the window of his office in the Gaston Building, which overlooked Ingram Park,
he saw something that yanked out the roots of his millionaire's bluster.

"But lawyer Vann!" Gaston gasped. "They've turned the fire hoses on
a little black girl. And they're rolling that girl right down the middle of
the street."

The monitor guns made limbs jerk weightlessly and tumbled whole
bodies like scraps of refuse in a high wind. One look made Gaston sign
off the telephone. Outside, brave songs turned to screams, and bystanders
threw bricks and rocks at the hoses. When the water drove them back

out of range, some of them sneaked into buildings so they could lob their projectiles from above. Eventually, they hit two firemen and *Life* photographer Charles Moore.

During the noisy, sporadic duel of rocks and hoses, young marchers continued to spill out of the Sixteenth Street Baptist Church. Walker, Bevel, Andrew Young, and other supervisors directed the lines away from the conflict, avoiding both the hoses and the contaminating association with violence. Their maneuver confronted police commanders with a dilemma: the hoses were pinned down by darting, rock-throwing bystanders while the marchers escaped toward downtown from the other end of Ingram Park. There were not enough hoses to cover both flanks, especially when the monitor guns halved their number. Police detachments did manage to intercept the marchers and load them into jail-bound school buses, but this meant that the authorities were failing in their plan to repulse rather than arrest the demonstrators. Worse, from the commanders' point of view, the concentrated city forces were being split apart. In consultation with Bull Connor, they decided that they had to drive the Negroes back together. To do that, they needed an intimidating weapon more mobile than the hoses.

The police commanders deployed eight K-9 units at the corner of Ingram Park farthest from the church. First sight of the dogs brought shouts of fright and rage from the milling crowds. Many fled instantly; some threw rocks at the dogs and their handlers; a few reckless teenagers waved waterlogged shirts like bullfighters. On command, the officers handling the dogs rushed forward to gain close quarters. Where the crowd was too tightly massed to flee cleanly, the growling German shepherds lunged toward stumbling, cowering stragglers. They bit three teenagers severely enough to require hospital treatment. Other targets, screaming with terror and turning in confusion, either disappeared into the Negro section to the west or took refuge in the church. Most of the K-9 units kept up pursuit, but a few veered back to chase away clumps of Negroes who had drifted back into the vacant spaces to gaze on the full panoply of ambulances, billyclubs, paddy wagons, arrest scenes, distant marchers, and the thick ropes of water from the monitor guns.

On a street corner outside the Jockey Boy restaurant, two dog teams came up behind a group of awed spectators who did not notice them until one of the handlers seized a fifteen-year-old boy and whirled him around into the jaws of a German shepherd. An AP photographer standing nearby caught the sight that came to symbolize Birmingham: a white policeman in dark sunglasses grasping a Negro boy by the front of the shirt as his other hand gave just enough slack in the leash for the dog to spring upward and bury its teeth in the boy's abdomen. And most compelling was the boy himself, who was tall, thin, and well dressed, leaning *into* the attacking dog with an arm dropped submissively at his side and a straight-ahead look of dead calm on his face. The graphic power of the picture concealed a supreme irony. The victim, young Walter Gadsden, was not steeped in nonviolent discipline, nor had he intended to become part of the demonstration. His handsome cardigan sweater was an emblem of his standing in the prosperous family of C. A. Scott, who so scorned King's demonstrations that his *World* papers in both Atlanta and Birmingham still ignored Project C more resolutely even than Birmingham's white newspapers. Although the image of the savage attack struck like lightning in the American mind, the reaction of Walter Gadsden lay buried in the deeper convolutions of race. True to his family, he later said the German shepherd had shocked him into the realization that he had been "mixing with a bad crowd" of Negroes when he went to observe the demonstration. He resolved to get off the streets and prepare for college.

At three o'clock, a police inspector ventured inside the church to negotiate. From a military tactician's point of view, the engagement thus far was confined to a relatively mild skirmish in which the K-9 units had rotated on the controlling vector of the fire hoses, sweeping Negroes out of Ingram Park or across it into the church. Only half the Negro groups had stepped off on their jail marches, of whom some 250 were being arrested. The dogs and police units had reconcentrated outside, bottling up scores of wet, angry bystanders amid the five hundred demonstrators who were still trying to form their lines. In that precarious situation, King was only too happy to accept a truce for the day, as he knew that the political tremors had been set loose already. Seizing a moment in the chaos, he called Clarence Jones in New York with a long list of people who should be told personally of the day's events. At 3:57 P.M. by the FBI wiretapper's log, Jones gave Stanley Levison a breathless summary and an emergency request from King that Levison draft telegrams for President Kennedy and Robert Kennedy "within the hour." Levison, whose qualms about the decision to use child marchers had put him on edge already, became so rattled that he wrote an awkward, overly erudite telegram that King could not use, ending, "Will you permit this recrudescence of violence in Birmingham to threaten our lives and deny us our rights?"

Birmingham's white leaders scrambled to head off a swell of public sympathy for King by denouncing his use of children. Mayor Boutwell told the city that "irresponsible and unthinking agitators" had made "tools" of children to threaten lives and property. "The respectable people of Birmingham, white or colored, did not create this danger," he declared. "We are not contributing to it. We are innocent victims . . . I cannot condone, and you cannot condone, the use of children to these ends." Judge Talbot Ellis, whose juvenile court was inundated with young Negro defendants, said that those who "misled these kids" into demonstrations "ought to be put under the jail." In Washington, Robert Kennedy issued a statement of more balanced tone. "Continued refusal to grant equal rights and opportunities to Negroes makes increasing turmoil inevitable," he announced. "However, the timing of the present demonstrations is open to question. School children participating in street demonstrations is a dangerous business. An injured, maimed or dead child is a price that none of us can afford to pay." Kennedy stressed that the injustices of Birmingham were a local rather than a federal responsibility, to be resolved "in good faith negotiations, and not in the streets." These attacks came too late to faze King. In caustic remarks, he and his fellow preachers noted that this tender solicitude for Negro children had never produced much concern over their consignment to miserable schools or other injuries of segregation.

Burke Marshall, who had called that morning to request that the demonstrations be suspended, called again more urgently, arguing on behalf of the Kennedy Administration that King must call a halt now because the rock-throwing by Negroes had contributed to the violence. King refused. Although he resented Marshall's attitude, he also sensed more pain in Marshall's voice than conviction. King interpreted this pain as the forerunner of enormous political pressure in Washington, which confirmed that the Birmingham movement was taking off. The burden of inertia was shifting. Marshall, having caught an earful from A. G. Gaston about the little girl being squirted down the street, was not far behind in perceiving that dissent against King was evaporating in Negro Birmingham. Hard upon this surge of internal strength radiated the national news that a thousand Negro children had marched to jail in two days, and before the far-flung American public could begin to absorb such a troubling novelty, violence, the universal messenger, was racing toward their living rooms with pictures of water hoses and dogs loosed on children. Marshall's pain, like the stridency of Birmingham's white leaders, revealed an underlying defensiveness, and their appeals to the welfare of Negro children drew them toward King's ground. To anticipate and experience these complex shifts of emotion was the essence of historic movement; to have caused them raised the sweet thrill of legend.

King knew that the people who cared most about the children were the mothers and fathers streaming all afternoon into the Sixteenth Street Baptist Church to join hundreds of marchers and onlookers who simply stayed on for the mass meeting. The big church was packed long before evening. Passing the collection plates took a full hour, and the spirit of the congregation ran so high that Andrew Young came out to make a cautionary speech. "We have a nonviolent movement," he said, "but it's not nonviolent enough." He warned that no amount of provocation justified rock-throwing. "We must not boo the police when they bring up the dogs," he added. ". . . We must praise them. The police don't know how to handle the situation governed by love, and the power of God. During these demonstrations we must tell the crowd to behave."

A tumultuous cheer went up when King made his entrance. He too preached nonviolence, but at first his address was unusually informal and frisky. He told preacher jokes about the futility of trying to defeat Negro Baptists with water hoses, predicting that even Bull Connor would come to admit that "not only did they stand up in the water, they went UNDER the water!" "And dogs?" he asked. "Well, I'll tell you. When I was growing up, I was dog bitten"—he paused, as a horrified cry rose up —"for NOTHING! So I don't mind being bitten by a dog for standing up for freedom!"

He told them that not all whites were hostile, and that their movement was reaching people far away. "No, we are not alone in this," he assured them. "Don't let anybody make you feel we are alone." Birmingham had made the Huntley-Brinkley news show on NBC, he said. Help was on the way; they were moving. Then, in a single sentence, he swept aside the pressures for a moratorium on the demonstrations: "Now yesterday was D-Day, and tomorrow will be Double-D Day!"

The announcement that the jail marches would continue over the weekend drew deafening applause. Then King moved on almost quietly, dispensing with oratorical surges. He repeated his willingness to negotiate over the movement's four basic demands, which he reviewed at length. Only at the end did he mention the little catalysts who had ignited the city. "Now, finally, your children," he said, "your daughters and sons are in jail, many of them, and I'm sure many of the parents are here tonight." Then he said simply, "Don't worry about them." That alone smothered some of the desperate fears and skittering rumors— tales true and false about rats, beatings, concrete beds, overflowing latrines, jailhouse assaults, and crude examinations for venereal disease. "They are suffering for what they believe," he said, "and they are suffering to make this nation a better nation." The crowd seemed soothed not just by his words but by his calmness. Having committed everything, holding nothing back, he touched the faith at his core. In fact, his great gamble looked so promising that he slipped almost into a reverie, assuring the parents that the Birmingham jail was not only bearable for their children but a "spiritual experience" to be welcomed, even longed for.

"Jail helps you to rise above the miasma of everyday life," he said. A thought distracted him. "If they want some books, we will get them," he promised. "I catch up on my reading every time I go to jail."

King and his advisers stayed up long past midnight plotting strategy for Saturday's march. Blessed with an abundance of volunteers, they devised schemes to divide or circumvent Bull Connor's blockading forces. Their goal was to put at least another five hundred young people in jail. All that night, the attention of the outside world gathered forcefully upon them. Irate Birmingham citizens strung up an effigy of King in the court-yard of a Catholic church, and news presses across the country mass-produced photographs of Friday's violence. The morning *New York Times* featured three of them stacked two columns wide on the front page: on the bottom, state troopers dragging the CORE-SNCC "freedom walkers" to jail in Fort Payne, Alabama; in the middle, Birmingham firemen straining to aim a monitor gun at demonstrators; on top, the police dog sinking its teeth into Walter Gadsden's midriff. The visual power of the Gadsden photograph was so profound that President Kennedy, like millions of readers, could see nothing else. The picture made him "sick," he told a morning audience of ADA liberals at the White House. Although he lacked legal authority to do anything about Birmingham, Kennedy added, he was dispatching Burke Marshall and Joe Dolan as mediators that very day. This presidential mission, plus the established threat of violence, conferred a status on the Birmingham confrontations that greatly stimulated the influx of reporters. Claude Sitton of the *Times* abandoned the William Moore march in favor of Birmingham, as did Pat Watters of the Atlanta *Journal.* For Sitton, who had been in Greenwood, this marked the second time in a month that the Birmingham campaign had deflated an ongoing story. Watters came to Birmingham reluctantly; his fresh sympathy for the lonely students on the William Moore death trek, along with his glimpses of movement rivalries, convinced him that the children's marches were another attempt by a cynical or capricious King to undercut CORE and SNCC.

On Saturday afternoon, as tense police lines awaited the first sally from the Sixteenth Street Baptist Church, Wyatt Walker engineered a surprise five blocks away. On a signal, several groups of ordinary-looking young pedestrians merged just outside city hall, and only then did a girl display a banner reading "Love God and Thy Neighbor." Bull Connor emerged personally to investigate and, incensed by the trickery, ordered all twenty-five Negroes hauled off to jail. Almost immediately, a woman and a small girl without banners knelt on the steps of city hall to pray.

They went off to jail too, whereupon Connor ordered his men to arrest or disperse all groups of "strolling Negroes" near city hall, with or without picket signs. In so doing he not only failed to keep Negroes from swamping his jails but also created a racial dragnet that went far beyond the limits of Judge Jenkins' court order.

King's strategists had achieved a tactical advantage by switching to guerrilla concealment, but Connor swiftly retaliated. When his men discovered that young demonstrators were slipping out of two different churches in twos and threes, he sent his men to seal off both churches. When, after some 150 arrests, the lock-in dried up the supply of volunteers headed toward city hall, the confrontation shifted across the street from Sixteenth Street Baptist to Kelly Ingram Park. There the adult Negro spectators watched policemen guard the exits to trap the young demonstrators inside, and rage spread among them as the monitor guns swept away the few young marchers who escaped. A cascade of rocks soon rained down on the uniformed officers.

Now the advantage shifted against the movement, whose leaders realized that their young marchers, schooled in nonviolence, were locked up inside the churches while adults armed with rocks, knives, and guns moved freely on the perimeter. James Bevel, alarmed that a riot would undo all their efforts to arouse public opinion against segregation, managed to talk a police lieutenant into lending him his bullhorn. "Everybody get off this corner!" he shouted. "If you're not going to demonstrate in a nonviolent way, then leave!" Bevel darted about like a sheepdog, effectively dispersing the troublemakers, some of whom recognized him as the madcap young preacher who had mobilized the youth demonstrations. When the anger subsided, he grandly announced that he was suspending all marches for the following day too, so that the movement could purify itself for a giant push on Monday. Later that day, hot words passed privately between Bevel and Wyatt Walker, who considered Bevel an insubordinate grandstander. It fell to King to arrange a truce between his two hot-tempered aides. While supporting Walker on procedure, he approved Bevel's one-day moratorium as a wise emergency move. Then King escaped the tension by flying home to preach at Ebenezer.

Birmingham swelled over the weekend. Along with Burke Marshall and scores of reporters, activists of all kinds arrived in the wake of the stunning children's marches. Ella Baker flew in from New York, as did pacifist Dave Dellinger. SNCC's James Forman, arrested on the William Moore march, bailed out and headed straight for Birmingham, as he had done a month earlier upon leaving jail in Greenwood. Dick Gregory made his way down from Chicago, and among the miscellaneous newcomers that Sunday were two folk singers, Guy Carawan and Joan Baez. Carawan came expressly to record a mass meeting for Folkways Records, Baez to give a concert, and they happened upon each other in the Gaston Motel. Baez was burning with curiosity about the civil rights movement, which was why she had booked a concert tour of Negro colleges in the South, but she was more than a little apprehensive about crossing the race barrier in a city poised for war. Even though Sunday was the truce day, helmeted police units patrolled the streets in force and hovered around the Negro test groups who sought to worship in white churches.

Baez was only too happy to accept Carawan's escort into the morning worship service and the afternoon mass meeting at New Pilgrim Church. There, as one of a handful of whites among two thousand Negroes, Baez first encountered soul music. The Birmingham movement's choir was a polished group in comparison with the spontaneous, *a capella* singers of Albany. It had a director, Carlton Reese, an organist, and established stars such as Mamie Brown and Cleo Kennedy. But its freedom music still astonished a folk purist such as Baez. There were sweet spirituals, arrhythmic blues solos, and thundering gospel numbers—all intensified by the imminent surrender to jail—and the power of it melted Baez's alien separateness so that she shouted and cried, and looked close enough to a happy seizure that she came briefly to the attention of the roving ushers. When a driver whisked her away to the haven of all-Negro Miles College, Baez was astonished again to discover that her concert audience maintained a steadfast disinterest in the cauldron of protest across town. The Birmingham *World*, which was not covering the demonstrations, sent its own reporter to this first concert by a white celebrity on the Miles campus, and the reviewer praised the performance, though noting tartly that the singer felt free to remove her shoes on stage.

Back at the mass meeting, a distraught Andrew Young interrupted to announce that the Birmingham police had just arrested Guy Carawan and his wife Candie on the steps of the church. "They are the ones who taught us many of the songs that we sing in the movement," Young lamented, adding that the police were getting nervous, nasty, and unpredictable. Perhaps Bull Connor, interpreting the truce as a sign of weakness in the movement, was trying to intimidate the Negroes into submission. As the police hauled the Carawans off to jail, an angry-looking James Bevel strode swiftly to the pulpit with Bernard Lee. "We're tired of this mess!" he shouted. "Let's all get up!" Waving his arms, he directed the packed congregation to march around inside the church and then down to the city jail a few blocks away. They would encourage the movement prisoners inside, while showing the police that they were not afraid. Almost cackling, Bevel suggested that this spontaneous demonstration would not violate the conditions of his self-imposed truce. "Let's not march," he called out. "Let's just walk."

The music soared as the congregation rose without noticeable dissent. Off in the wings, the preachers huddled to argue. Wyatt Walker fumed against this latest maverick surprise from Bevel, who had called off that day's demonstration and was now calling it back on. Walker saw every circumstance as unfavorable: King was out of town; the congregation was mostly adults, in their Sunday clothes, unprepared for jail; and rough treatment by Connor's police might puncture morale before the climactic jail marches the next day. Worst of all from a personal point of view, Bevel had swept along Bernard Lee into his renegade spontaneity, and since Lee had been practically Walker's ward for the past two years, this reflected poorly on Walker's discipline. Bevel kept saying they must not allow the police to plant fear in a nonviolent movement, and all the while the surrounding preachers urged them to set aside the dispute for the pressing reality that the congregation was about to exit leaderless through the church doors. Walker salvaged some authority by decreeing that Bevel could not lead the column—he could not risk being jailed before Monday's youth march. From the volunteer preachers he selected Charles Billups, a Shuttlesworth colleague of many years, and Billups ran ahead to catch up.

They spilled out of New Pilgrim past the startled police officers, who retreated before them up Sixth Avenue, waiting for orders. Sirens sounded. Curious porch-sitters watched the solemn marchers go by for five long blocks through a Negro section of town. Paddy wagons and fire equipment converged ahead, just short of the city jail. Firemen rushed to hook up, while some police units stopped traffic and others roughly cleared the area of all bystanders, including indignant reporters. Before the head of the Negro column reached the barricade, Bull Connor himself walked out into the tangle of fire hoses to confront them.

Drawing close, Billups knelt on the pavement, and many of the two thousand behind followed his lead, like a line of falling dominoes stretching all the way back to New Pilgrim. After a brief prayer, Billups stood up and shouted loudly enough for the distant reporters to hear: "Turn on your water! Turn loose your dogs! We will stand here 'til we die!" Many of the Negroes within range trembled, and a woman keeled over in a faint, but after a few seconds some noticed that the fireman remained paralyzed at his tripod, unable to blast the preacher at point-blank range. To save face, Connor repeated his order to fire in a hushed, angry growl. Some heard him say "Dammit! Turn on the hoses" before the silence swallowed him up too. After a few more seconds, Wyatt Walker gingerly approached the two police captains standing near Connor and whispered that the Negroes need not march into white Birmingham nor even to the city jail. He suggested that they be allowed to gather for a prayer service just across the street in a Negro-only public park.

"Let us proceed," intoned Billups, who walked forward as though in a trance. Watching from afar, the puzzled reporters felt the tension evaporate, and then they saw Bull Connor walking toward them. He explained breezily that he had granted a routine request to let the marchers pray in a segregated park, but to the marchers themselves it was nothing short of a miracle. Billups led the column past the water pumpers and the dreaded monitor guns, stepping over the hoses. As disbelief turned to joy behind him, shouts of "Hallelujah!" raced back along the line. Nonviolence had touched the fireman's heart, they said, and had tamed Bull Connor's hatred as surely as Moses had parted the Red Sea.

Across two hectic and furtive days, Burke Marshall had taken soundings across the racial divide. Fred Shuttlesworth, while glorying in the attention from Washington, objected that Marshall's practice of shuttling back and forth between whites and Negroes helped the whites maintain segregated negotiations. On the other side of town, Marshall found the city's leading whites boiling with internal conflict. They were desperate to remove the stigma of racial ignorance and violence, to restore the city's prosperity and reputation on their own initiative. This was the white power structure's "whole desire," Marshall told President Kennedy. "They want Birmingham to look like Atlanta." However, another side of their pride made them deeply resent the Negro demonstrators as the proximate cause of their troubles. The idea of negotiating under the pressure of street demonstrations was offensive to all the city's leading merchants and politicians. Conservatives refused to talk with any Negroes at all, Marshall found, and liberals refused to sit down with "outsiders," most especially King.

The best Marshall could do that Sunday night was to patch together scouting groups of moderate whites and conservative Negroes. Reform leaders Sidney Smyer and David Vann, plus several white merchants, met downtown with Negroes led by Arthur Shores and A. G. Gaston. Both sides lamented the dangers of demonstrations, but the Negroes stood by King's original four-point program as a necessary condition of stopping them. In the end, the whites rejected all four points. But at least it was a beginning, and Burke Marshall followed up on all sides with his most telling and persistent argument: they should keep talking, he said, because only then could they sort out King's confused, irrational demands. He said King did not know what he wanted. In the aftershock of the D-Day publicity, this perspective served Marshall's tactical need to promote consideration of King's aims, and balanced his criticisms of segregation with a parallel attack on King. Politically, it supplied a dignified role for the Kennedy Administration. By casting Birmingham as a failure of articulation on King's part, Marshall projected the sovereign understanding of a problem solver without risking any government authority.

Partly because the characterization so sharply patronized King, it appealed to those who recoiled from the protests as nearly unfathomable outbursts of Negro passion. It was particularly welcome in Washington, as the leaders of the Free World did not enjoy professing helplessness on a stark issue of freedom that was commanding attention around the world. Even privately, Marshall and his colleagues clung to a portrayal of themselves as facilitators cutting through the fog of King's unhappiness. Some days later at the White House, Robert Kennedy emphasized the brainpower gap to the full cabinet, saying that "the Negro leadership didn't know what they were demonstrating about. They didn't know whether they were demonstrating to get rid of Bull Connor or whether they were demonstrating about the stores . . . I think some of the people who were demonstrating certainly didn't know what they were demonstrating about, and none of the white community knew what they were demonstrating about." A year later, in a joint oral history with Kennedy, Marshall said that when he went to Birmingham, "I talked to King and I asked him what he was after. He really didn't know." Twenty years later, Marshall recalled that it was "hard to negotiate with King because he had no specifics. What he wanted was something."

At John Drew's house on Monday morning, May 6, Marshall spent two and a half hours trying to convince King that the afternoon demonstrations would hinder rather than help the negotiations now under way. It was true, Marshall conceded, that the white merchants could grant some of King's demands on their own authority, but it was also true that the city could prosecute the merchants under the segregation ordinances if they did. Therefore, on this and every other matter at stake, the merchants were justifiably reluctant, not knowing which of the pretender governments would be recognized as legitimate. Until the courts decided between Boutwell and Connor, which would be only a few days now, all parties, including the federal government, would be partially blind, and demonstrations in the interim could only raise tempers at substantial risk of violence. To all this, King replied that he believed Birmingham's merchants had the power to prevail upon any city government, including Connor's. One of his mistakes in Albany had been to aim his marches at politicians, who didn't need Negro votes, instead of merchants, who did need Negro trade. Now that the demonstrations were better focused, he would negotiate at any time, but he would not shut down the Birmingham movement on the mere promise of later negotiations. Every time

Marshall cited the logic driving the merchants' position, King replied that pressure, even fear, had been improving their reason. When Marshall left Drew's house about noon, reporters pried out comments that the meeting had been instructive but essentially fruitless.

The red pumper trucks and the monitor guns were in position when King pulled up at Sixteenth Street Baptist, but the police deployments otherwise revealed that Bull Connor had changed his tactics. To reduce the chance of conflict with riotous, non-movement Negroes, he had ordered his men to seal off the war zone of Kelly Ingram Park, which was now an empty square block of trampled grass surrounded by helmeted police. Almost politely, by way of compensation, Connor had permitted a crowd of some two thousand Negro spectators to gather on the sidewalks near the church. Though the rows of stand-by school buses indicated that Connor was going to try the Laurie Pritchett, welcome-to-jail strategy, no one knew what would happen. With King preaching nonviolence to the forming lines inside the church, James Bevel stepped outside for a final parley. Extending his hand to shake on the bargain, Bevel publicly asked a police captain to confirm that he would not use the hoses on the marchers if they kept good order. The captain, who by this time had built up a cross-trench acquaintance with Bevel, smiled tightly as he contemplated the dark outstretched hand. He replied that the police would not use excessive force, but no, he could not go so far as to shake on it.

On signal, Dick Gregory led the first nineteen children out of the church. The captain called for the paddy wagon after the standard warning of arrest, whereupon the young people behind Gregory broke into a song of spirited relief. To the tune of "The Old Grey Mare," they sang "I ain't scared of your jail / 'cause I want my freedom / want my freedom / want my freedom . . ." Some of them snake-danced into the wagon as the next group spilled from the church. After that they came so continuously, and sang so loudly, that the police commanders merely waved them toward the paddy wagons and buses, dispensing with the dialogue.

Older people joined in significant numbers for the first time since D-Day, comprising more than half the demonstrators. Some parents went to jail with their children. Others were so overcome by fear or disapproval that they snatched their children from the lines by force. At first, isolated outbursts of grief or anger were among the few indications that the procession between rows of nightsticks was no parade, but the festivity gradually wore off among the spectators. Watching friends and relatives walk to jail at the rate of ten per minute for nearly two hours, a number of them grew sullen and angry, perhaps compounded by guilt that they were not willing to submit to the jailers themselves. A few bottles and rocks landed on the pavement near officers who, laboring in the heat under orders of restraint, lost snappish tempers more than once. In front of news photographers, five of them threw an overwrought Negro woman to the pavement and subdued her with knees to the throat and limbs.

King's aides, fearing that a riot soon would tarnish the largest single day of nonviolent arrests in American history, raced outside at 2:40 P.M. to call a halt. "That's it for today!" one shouted, urging both Negroes and policemen to go home. Nearly eight hundred people had marched to jail from the church; more than two hundred reached the same destination from surprise picket lines in the downtown business district. With the next day's headlines secured by midafternoon—BIGGEST MARCH STUNS BIRMINGHAM! the Chicago *Defender* would say—King's aides began to harvest the newcomers who surged forward to replace the jailed ones many times over. Bevel said they would have six thousand ready for the next day. He and the other leaders directed the crowds into the mass meeting at St. James Baptist Church, which was swamped long before nightfall. The movement was becoming a tempest. A foretide of one event churned into the backwash of others, and mass communications spread the ripples far and wide.

In New York, Stanley Levison worked to place the first newspaper fund-raiser since the 1960 ad that had brought the crippling *Sullivan* v. *New York Times* libel suit. In the forty-eight hours since he first saw the *Times* photograph of the police dog attacking Walter Gadsden, Levison had talked constantly with Jack O'Dell about how to capitalize on the opportunity to make money for the SCLC. O'Dell said that his mass mailings were already showing a fantastic shift in public opinion. Mailing lists were yielding many times the expected return. Ten-dollar contributions suddenly were giving way to big ones. A woman from Queens had sent $3,000. One list had money pouring in from Canada. These early signs put the New York mail room in chaos and O'Dell in awe. With his concurrence, Levison had prepared an ad, but on Monday afternoon—minutes before the first marchers went to jail in Birmingham—the man at the advertising agency called Levison to say that "the bastards at the *Times* wouldn't print the ad."

Levison brought Clarence Jones in for phone negotiations, and Jones, after talking with some of the *Times* lawyers he knew from the *Sullivan* case, reported that "they want to take out references to brutality and all strong references to segregation and discrimination in Birmingham." Although the deletions included headlines and copy that had been published in the *Times'* own news stories, Levison was too pragmatic to waste time fighting. He said the lawyers' business was to be conservative, and that the *Times* was fearful of being sued again over a controversial King ad. The important task was to get an ad out, he said—almost any ad that mentioned King, Birmingham, and an address to which to send contributions. Not long after the arrests ended that afternoon, Levison was back on the phone with the *Times* lawyers, negotiating a compromise ad that referred to Birmingham simply as "one of the largest segregated cities in the Western Hemisphere." FBI wiretap clerks laboriously transcribed all this, together with his intermittent conversations about stock prices. While the business side of the *Times* dickered with Levison, the news editors agreed to publish on the next day's front page another gripping dispatch from Claude Sitton, headlined "Birmingham Jails 1,000 More Negroes."

In Birmingham, the Monday mass meeting overflowed from St. James Baptist into Thurgood Church, from there to St. Luke's, and finally to St. Paul's. Five to ten thousand people packed the four churches simultaneously, buoyed by songs and testimonials from jail. Birmingham preachers circulated among them with impromptu performances, as did soloists and movement treasurer William Shortridge, whose assistants staggered off under the weight of a record $40,000 offering. Much of the sum came from celebrity Negro preachers who had "lifted" a special Birmingham gift at Sunday services as far away as Pittsburgh and Los Angeles. That evening, Fred Shuttlesworth was attending a second negotiating session with the whites, led by Smyer and Vann, with Burke Marshall hovering in the background. Meanwhile, distraught relatives bombarded the leaders with horror stories about the children penned up outdoors at the fairgrounds. In a rainstorm, James Forman burst in upon King and insisted that he personally inspect the conditions at the camp. King saw crowds of relatives throwing blankets and candy bars over the chain-link fences to the wet young prisoners. He asked police commanders to shelter them, called Burke Marshall to press for federal attention to these "political prisoners," as he called them, and then broke away to the mass meetings.

With Abernathy, surrounded by a throng of message-bearers and supplicants, King pushed his way into all four churches. At St. Luke's, the movement choir's rendition of "Rock Me, Lord" drove one woman into screeches so unworldly that the preachers on the platform whispered among themselves about whether something should be done. She quieted when Abernathy took the pulpit for King, who was closeted offstage among the telephones. Abernathy, always the salty sidekick, proclaimed that he could tell they were "on the threshold of freedom in Birmingham" by how nervous Burke Marshall was. "Today," he declared, "I sat in a room with one of the top men in the Justice Department, who paced the floor, couldn't sit down, changed from chair to chair." In a voice of pride tinged with merriment, Abernathy assured them that they had the white folks tied in knots. "Day before yesterday we filled up the jail," he said. "Today, we filled up the jail *yard*. And tomorrow, when they look up and see that number coming, I don't know *what* they're gonna do!" The congregation clapped and chuckled in the comic expanse of Abernathy's ego. He told them not to worry about their relatives in jail, because he was going to call Burke Marshall about their safety. "And if he doesn't do anything about it, I'm gonna call *Bobby*," he declared, to peals of laughter, "and if Bobby doesn't do anything about it, I'm gonna call *Jack*." By the time he saw King approaching from the wings, Abernathy had the crowd laughing at all the perils of the movement, including death itself. "The problem with us is that we are too afraid of dying," he said, "and too afraid of going places that will *cause* us to die." Instead of worrying about the Birmingham jail, he advised the fearful, "when you go home tonight you better stand up in the corner and not go to bed, because more folk have died in the *bed* than any place I know."

King spoke of the jail marches with joyous respect, of mass meetings packed inside and out so that "you can't get near the church," of experiences that day beyond any he had known. "There are those who write history," he said. "There are those who make history. There are those who experience history. I don't know how many historians we have in Birmingham tonight. I don't know how many of you would be able to write a history book. But you are certainly making history, and you are experiencing history. And you will make it possible for the historians of the future to write a marvelous chapter. Never in the history of this nation have so many people been arrested for the cause of freedom and human dignity!" When the cheers died down, he said, almost in disbelief, "You know, there are approximately twenty-five hundred people in jail right now."

Earnestly, almost gingerly, he wound to the subject of love. "Now we say in this nonviolent movement that you've got to love this white man," he told them. Above a cry of "Yes!" he said, "And God knows, he needs our love. . . . And let me say to you that I'm not talking about emotional bosh when I talk about love." Begging their indulgence, he recited again the distinctions among the three Greek words for "love." This time he added a small new twist by stating that there was something mundane, even debased, about *eros* and *filia*. "Romantic love is inevitably a little selfish," he declared. "You move your lover because there is something about your lover that *moves you*." Titters punctuated his coy description until he moved on to *agape*. "And when you rise to love on *this* level," he declared, "you love those who don't move you.

You love those that you don't like. You love those whose ways are distasteful to you. You love every man because God loves him!"

   A few seconds later, as King left hurriedly for the last mass meeting,
the choir sprinted into a runaway version of "Ninety-nine and a Half
Won't Do." To round off the moment, and to cover King's exit, Abernathy took the pulpit again to tease King for presuming to teach native
Alabamans such as himself about love. "I had been telling him that we
know the meaning of that word he calls 'eros,' " said Abernathy, pronouncing the Greek with pompous exaggeration. "He says that 'eros' is
that type of love that *moves ya.*" Abernathy spoke the words so seduc-
tively that skitters of laughter replaced the gospel fervor in the audience.
"And he went on to say what it *might* be," he impishly reminded them.
"It *might* be the way your lover walks. And it *might be* the way your
lover talks. I was glad that he didn't tell you what it *really is!*" Then,
with the crowd convulsed in laughter, Abernathy gave a deadpan shrug.
"But that's the way people *talk* from Georgia. In Alabama, we'll take the
'might be' out, and let you know just plainly *what it is.*" He hastened off
after King, leaving the crowd bubbling with satisfaction that the movement had everything: religion, music, drama, tender fellowship, Greek
lessons, cataclysms of history, and a full range of entertainment that
included sexy humor from preachers.

King's strategy talks lasted the balance of the night at the Gaston Motel.
From the negotiating front, Shuttlesworth and his colleagues reported
modest progress at best. On the demonstration front, however, they were
encouraged by a huge and nearly flawless day's march to jail, and beyond
that, some of them had noticed a critical sign: the downtown business
district had been practically a ghost town, empty not only of Negro
shoppers but also of white ones. They were not sure what had caused
this phenomenon—whether it was the sight of the two hundred young
pickets or merely the cumulative awareness of the daily "Negro trouble"
downtown—but in any case the white women were staying home. To
King's strategists, this was economic leverage beyond their fondest
hopes. It was also serendipity, as even Wyatt Walker admitted that Project C never contemplated a boycott by whites as well as Negroes. Seizing
the new possibility of a complete, biracial shutdown of Birmingham's
retail trade, they decided it was less important to march people to jail or
to picket certain stores than to flood the business district with masses of
protesting Negroes. To do that, they needed to get around the fire hoses
and paddy wagons. The planners hatched schemes all night, and at 6:00
A.M. on Tuesday, May 7—just as Shortridge and his assistants finished

sorting the record offering in a neighboring motel room, which they had rented especially for that pleasant labor—the youth leaders began to fan out to homes and schools, rousting their most trusted recruits.

Across town, the white negotiators met early. They knew that the Negroes would mount another onslaught that afternoon, that Bull Connor had no room to imprison more demonstrators, and that nationwide sensitivity to the racial conflict in Birmingham soon would force either President Kennedy or Governor Wallace to send troops into the city. They were not sure which would be the greater calamity, but they foresaw that all paths led within a matter of hours to economic and social catastrophe, which Sidney Smyer referred to as a humiliating "black eye" for Birmingham. Recognizing that they lacked the power among themselves to avert disaster, they resolved to sound an alarm to the entire white business establishment—to all the "big mules" of the semi-secret Senior Citizens Committee, which had pushed through the reform against Bull Connor. The negotiators rushed to the telephone to summon all members to an emergency session that very morning at the Chamber of Commerce.

At ten o'clock, King held a news conference at the Gaston Motel. "Ladies and gentlemen," he told the huge assembly of reporters, "I would like to say briefly that the activities which have taken place in Birmingham over the last few days to my mind mark the nonviolent movement's coming of age. This is the first time in the history of our struggle that we have been able literally to fill the jails." Even as he spoke, young demonstrators made their way unobtrusively toward a dozen rendezvous points scattered around the business district. Volunteers stowed picket signs inside car trunks. Dorothy Cotton, Isaac Reynolds, and others delivered final instructions to vanguard groups of fifty or less, while Bevel, Walker, and the better-known leaders made a show of gathering as usual at the Sixteenth Street Baptist Church.

At the Chamber of Commerce, seventy of the "big mules" assembled before noon in a banquet room. On call from Chairman Smyer, Sheriff Bailey delivered a grim briefing on the state of law enforcement: stuffed jailhouses with rebellious staffs and budgets already overspent for the year; street officers on the point of cracking from relentless stress, helpless to make further arrests but caught between taunting demonstrators, omnipresent news cameras, and the conflicting orders of an unstable and divided high command that included Bull Connor. An old ex-governor, chairman of a Chamber of Commerce committee to attract new industry to Birmingham, stood up to announce gravely that if it was that bad, they should call up Governor Wallace right then, tell him to declare martial law to "suppress this whole business," and be done with it. A wave of seconding speeches rolled forth in support of his opinion, during which the noise of sirens began to penetrate the walls.

Shortly after noon, a group of fourteen Negro children, some carrying schoolbooks and lunch bags, marched out of the Sixteenth Street Baptist Church toward downtown. Sight of them surprised the police commanders, as the demonstrations never had started before one o'clock. Many police units were still at lunch, others not due to report until twelve thirty, but the available officers managed to carry out their orders. They blocked the line of students, confiscated their picket signs, and directed them back toward the Negro section, saying they could march there all they wanted. From across the street, movement leaders studied this police response as they sent forth more "decoy" lines and waited for pandemonium to erupt. Blocks away, vanguard groups of the best-trained nonviolent students already were in motion, running double-time along the sidewalks from all four points of the compass. Within minutes, they retrieved their signs from movement cars at corners near their designated sites and threw up lines totaling six hundred pickets in the heart of the business district.

Police radios crackled with strange sightings of trotting Negroes at unusual places. At the church, where reporters were massed and police units still converging, it was some time before it was fully accepted that these rampaging bands had anything to do with Martin Luther King's mannerly troops, who were still coming out of the church. Even then, with headquarters angrily squawking that a dastardly surprise attack had concentrated behind their rear lines, the commanders were reluctant to believe that the main contest could be elsewhere, but finally they sent units peeling off downtown under siren.

From his observation post in the Smith Building, Wyatt Walker watched the police blockade thin out until there were far too few officers to arrest or disperse his marchers, and then he called by walkie-talkie for a general charge. Suddenly, all the doors of Sixteenth Street Baptist flew open to disgorge a dozen lines of young Negroes who bolted into full sprint past the decoys, across the street, and around the police. Ignoring crosswalks and traffic signals, endless streams of them pushed past gaping white pedestrians and blocked what little traffic had not been halted already by the police. Bevel called it their "freedom dash." The next day's Birmingham *News* gave the bedlam a lyrical cast: SIRENS WAIL, HORNS BLOW, NEGROES SING.

Inside the Chamber of Commerce, talk of martial law had chilling real-life accompaniment from outside. Smyer gravely called upon President Kennedy's representative to speak. His many talks in Birmingham had convinced him, Burke Marshall said, that martial law under Governor

Wallace's troops offered at best a dangerous truce. He thought the Negroes would keep marching, then or later, because the "central problem" and the "root of the demonstrations" was a denial of basic constitutional rights. Marshall spoke softly, and the more softly he spoke the louder were the intruding sounds of chaos. It seemed to him that a pressing responsibility fell to the Senior Citizens themselves, he said, as they had the power to bring about a lasting solution. All they had to do was to stand behind the retail merchants in their efforts to reach a negotiated settlement with the Negroes. Marshall sat down after the brief but courageous speech, which, at the very least, checked the stampede of the Alabamans toward martial law. Some voices still spoke up for that option, a few for Marshall, and with the issue thus joined, Smyer thought it prudent to recess for lunch.

No executive repast was ever like this one. As the big mules descended toward their favorite downtown restaurants, choruses of "We Shall Overcome" first blasted their cars, and then they were swallowed up by what amounted to Birmingham's nonviolent Bastille Day. Not only had the young Negroes broken into the downtown enclave, they had jammed the sidewalks and streets in a wild celebration of triumph and possession, paying little attention to the august businessmen who were obliged to go around them or, coming upon a patch of sidewalk literally carpeted with sit-ins, to step over them. Turning the first corner, the Senior Citizens beheld what King proudly called "square blocks of Negroes, a veritable sea of black faces." Newspaper estimates of their number would run upward from three thousand. Joyous, weaving processions burst out of segregated stores, then back in again. Here and there a policeman lamely tore up a picket sign or two. Wincing commanders explained to the business leaders that they were making no arrests because the jails would hold no more, and they could not otherwise clear the area without teargassing or shooting up the downtown sanctum itself, including the Chamber of Commerce.

All these sensations struck the mules with revolutionary force. One of them, publisher Clarence B. Hanson of the Birmingham *News*, rushed back to his office to compose a telegram to President Kennedy. Although he clung even then to the amazing local cabal of journalistic restraint—burying on inside pages a host of news stories, such as "Negro Mobs Break Through Police: Swarm Over Downtown Area"—Hanson splashed the crisis telegram across the top of that afternoon's final edition. His extraordinary appeal to Kennedy, which broke the five-week embargo against front-page mention of King, revealed that even powerful American whites conceived of themselves as helpless victims of race: "Mr. President, if these were white marches . . . we believe your Administra-

tion would have taken vigorous action to discourage them." Hanson
objected to Burke Marshall's call for self-responsibility on the grounds
that it conveniently exempted President Kennedy himself. Having encouraged the aspirations of King and other Negroes, said Hanson, Kennedy was obliged to stop their demonstrations: "If there is to be order,
and respect for law . . . you, sir, must be the one to bring it."

A number of the shaken business leaders unburdened themselves as
freely as the publisher that day, but when they reassembled at the Chamber of Commerce they thought better of his call for intervention by
President Kennedy. Inevitably, that would mean federal occupation,
force-fed integration, and protracted strife with Governor Wallace. Besides, how could the Army itself dry up the rivers of Negroes they had
seen? As the emergency session consumed the afternoon, Burke Marshall
kept supplying Robert Kennedy with the names of key executives to be
lobbied by cabinet members or by President Kennedy himself. The President made several calls, arguing that there was no way out except settlement. These efforts remained private. While the President worked
continuously on Birmingham—meeting at the White House with Ted
Sorensen, Nicholas Katzenbach, Lee White, John Doar, Berl Bernhard,
and Louis Martin—he instructed his press officers to stress that his powers were not engaged. The President was "closely monitoring events,"
they announced, and "continues to hope the situation can be resolved by
the people of Birmingham themselves." The White House received the
Hanson telegram as "part of our study of this thing." "We are not sitting
idly by," said Assistant Press Secretary Andrew Hatcher. "We just can't
say anything."

At the Gaston Motel, King experienced the terrible exultation of a commander whose troops had just charged over the hill. Where were they,
and what now? As always, the point of breakthrough was the moment of
maximum danger. The emblems of the victory, such as the inability of
the police to make arrests, shifted the burden of good behavior to the
movement just as the dispersed, pell-mell attack severely reduced King's
control. Worse, he knew that half or more of the Negroes now paralyzing
the retail district were bystanders who had joined spontaneously upon
seeing the demonstrators run wild without getting arrested. Many did
not have the slightest training or interest in nonviolent discipline. How
long could such a huge, motley crowd celebrate downtown, loosed from
the fears of Bull Connor and segregation, without fights breaking out
with police or each other—or riots, looting, or vandalism? On the other
hand, if King tried to pull them out, only the nonviolent ones might
follow his lieutenants, leaving the others more likely to run amok.

Chaos overran King's hopes of salvaging a complete, nonviolent triumph. Hundreds of demonstrators made their way back to Ingram Park when they ran out of adrenaline or nerve, and within an hour leaders and followers were chasing each other in all directions. Fred Shuttlesworth burst into King's room shouting, "Martin, this is it!" One more foray downtown would break the city's will, Shuttlesworth insisted. Just after he rushed off to lead a "second wave," Forman burst in shouting that further demonstrations would be foolish and suicidally cruel. King reluctantly supported Shuttlesworth, but plans to retreat from downtown so as to return in better order were too complicated. Orders were modified, lost, delayed, disbelieved, or ignored. Miraculously, there was almost no violence from or upon the remnant who maintained the occupation downtown, but a pitched battle back near the church vindicated the news judgment of the stubbornest reporters, who had ignored the downtown stampede. Somewhere in the middle of the confusion, Wyatt Walker desperately tried to clear a path for the "second wave" by means of underhanded tactics that he had concealed from King. First swearing them to secrecy, Walker dispatched trusted runners to sound false fire alarms in distant corners of the city. Walker himself, in an unsuccessful attempt to drive off the intimidating K-9 corps, sneaked into an alley and blew on high-pitched dog whistles he had imported from the North.

Among the Negroes, thousands of joyful newcomers were in no mood to resubmit to the amassing phalanx of white firemen and police officers, who in turn were in no mood to suffer the Negro celebration or to allow another breach of their ranks. A duel of rocks and fire hoses escalated by three o'clock to what the reporters agreed was a riot. Firemen worked the hoses with such furious abandon that they accidentally cracked the ribs of a policeman. When Shuttlesworth appeared with his line of singing children, the firemen used a monitor gun to slam him against the wall of Sixteenth Street Baptist, pinning him there until he collapsed. An ambulance took him to the hospital, whereupon Bull Connor declared, "I wish they had carried him away in a hearse." For another hour, the hoses battered not only rock-throwers in the park but also lines of children who sallied forth from the church under the gleeful urging of James Bevel. Wyatt Walker fumed that Bevel's madness had turned his climactic demonstration into a "Roman holiday," but Bevel insisted that the playful submission to punishment represented a sublime and contagious form of nonviolence. "We intend to have the fire department pumping water tomorrow," he announced from the pulpit that night. "Wear your swimsuit if you want to."

At a three-church mass meeting, the day's fury at last subsided into the gentler passions of speeches and organ music. "This is a great movement," said King. "We are not going to stop this movement until we have *moved* segregation from this city." He preached nonviolence, as always, and pledged not to flinch even though "the Governor—bless his heart" was moving Alabama state troopers into Birmingham that very hour. Still, there was a hint of melancholy in his voice. Weary, King discarded his morning excitement about the ripe powers of the movement and spoke instead of a need for earthly help. "The hour has come for the Federal Government to take a forthright stand on segregation in the United States," he said. "I am not criticizing the President, but we are going to have to help him." Almost plaintively, King recalled his long, futile campaign to persuade President Kennedy to issue a Lincoln-esque proclamation. He told the congregation of his encounter with the Kennedys in the Lincoln Room of the White House, and said that once he thought Kennedy "*wanted* to sign." Although the sentimental opportunity of the Emancipation Day centennial was long past, King drifted back to his yearning for a simpler way. "We need to call on the President to sign a paper saying that segregation is unconstitutional," he said.

Robert Kennedy joined his brother for dinner that night in the White House, where they anxiously awaited word on the "big mules" debate. When the call finally came through at eight o'clock, an aide considered the moment important enough to make notes on Burke Marshall's first, exhausted words to President Kennedy: "The meeting worked. The meeting of all the businessmen worked. Now if [it] holds w/ Negroes, we're over the hump. They've had a hell of a day—& we've got to make it stick." With only a handful of dissenting votes, Marshall added, the Senior Citizens had empowered a committee to negotiate a settlement with the Negroes in their name.

The white committee, led by the board chairman of Royal Crown Cola, pitched immediately into negotiations with the Negroes, led by Arthur Shores, A. G. Gaston, and President L. H. Pitts of Miles College. At midnight, abandoning the fiction that they could perfect a compromise without the informed consent of King, they retired under cloak of secrecy to seek him out at the Drews' house. Mayor Boutwell's chief assistant, Billy Hamilton, was among the whites who dropped out at this critical stage; Boutwell simply could not risk public disclosure that his man had gone into a Negro neighborhood at night to barter away segregation face to face with the arch-villain himself. For the others, the midnight meeting was a personal and political watershed, such that the gruffly irreverent Sidney Smyer, who regularly boasted that he had been "called a son of a bitch plenty of times," led the group in a prayer for divine guidance. Then they grappled with the details of segregation's demise. Generally, the whites wanted vagueness and delay in order to minimize the danger of reprisal, while the Negroes wanted precision and immediacy in order to minimize the likelihood of dispute or betrayal. As the night dragged on, both sides tended to credit the mild, unflappable Andrew Young with ideas that achieved overall balance by proceeding in mixed stages. For the Negroes, there would be immediate desegregation of downtown dressing rooms, which was relatively easy for the whites because there were few left. For the whites, the linchpin segregation of the lunch counters would be surrendered at the end of sixty days or upon the integration of the public schools, whichever came first. By 4:00 A.M., King, Smyer, Marshall, and all the others agreed that they had at least a blueprint for a settlement, and could do no more without sleep.

At almost exactly that pre-dawn hour, two firebombs crashed into Hartman Turnbow's farmhouse outside Mileston, Mississippi, between Jackson and Greenwood. Turnbow jumped from bed and tried to put out the fires, until his wife and daughter shouted to him that they could not escape because there were armed white men outside. Turnbow grabbed one of his rifles and drove away the intruders in a spirited gunfight.

Bob Moses arrived shortly after daybreak. The attack endangered his rural registration projects because Turnbow, only a few days earlier, had become the first Negro in the twentieth century known to have tried to register in Holmes County. Turnbow was a yeoman farmer like E. W. Steptoe, stout as an oak and owner of seventy acres "free and clear." In return for his courageous, colorful folk wisdom, SNCC workers cheerfully overlooked the arsenal of firearms that he had concealed in at least a dozen places on his property and person. ("This nonviolent stuff ain't no good," Turnbow later told "Martin Lufus King," as he called him. "It'll getcha killed.")

By the time Sheriff Andrew P. Smith arrived at the farmhouse that afternoon, Moses was taking photographs of the fire damage for his report, having taken his own statements from the witnesses. ("They come by here and shot all in my kitchen," Mrs. Turnbow declared.) An FBI agent, dispatched by John Doar at Moses' urgent request, was pulling slugs from the clapboard walls. This sort of meticulous investigation put Sheriff Smith into a nearly insoluble political dilemma. If he accepted the Turnbow account and went after the white firebombers, he would be doomed as sheriff in Holmes County. If he stalled, or pronounced himself unable to solve the case, he would have to turn the investigation over to the FBI. These choices being unacceptable, Sheriff Smith accused Turnbow of firebombing his own house and shooting it full of holes to build sympathy for the Moses registration campaign.

Turnbow defended himself with a squirrel hunter's knowledge of ballistics. "Why, I ain't never owned a forty-five in my life," he protested, pointing to the holes in his house. "Them's forty-five bullets and forty-five holes, and I never owned nary'un."

Nevertheless, Sheriff Smith, his conspiracy theory reinforced by intense feelings of scorn and frustration, arrested Turnbow, Moses, and three SNCC workers for arson and related crimes. A jury promptly found them guilty. Moses was fined $50 on a separate charge of impeding Smith's investigation by taking pictures. The overall predicament, which was at once logical and patently absurd, obliged Doar to launch a protracted effort to void the state prosecutions. All this took place in the quiet obscurity of the Mississippi countryside, markedly in contrast with the tumult that had left Greenwood only a month earlier and passed on to Birmingham.

Fred Shuttlesworth exploded in dissent as soon as King sent word on Wednesday morning of a proposed one-day moratorium on demonstrations. From his hospital bed, though groggy from "three hypos" of sedation, as he said, Shuttlesworth reared up to tell his loyal preachers of Birmingham that the softhearted King was giving away their chance to finish off Bull Connor. "Ain't no use scalding the hog on one side!" he thundered. "While the water is hot, scald him on both sides and get him clean. If the water gets cold, you ain't *never* gonna clean off that hog!" Aside from this policy disagreement, Shuttlesworth made it clear that he was affronted as King's co-equal prince of the church. King should have visited him in the hospital. On something as important as this first break in their avalanche of street pressure, King should have convened the Negro hierarchy around Shuttlesworth's bed to make the decision.

By the time he burst into Drew's house, still wearing hospital tags, Shuttlesworth was a cauldron of steam. He peppered King's explanations of the truce with mordant comments: "Say that again. . . . Did I hear you right? . . . Well, Martin, *who* decided? . . . You're in a hell of a fix, young man." As King tried vainly to calm him, an aide pointed out that the matter was moot because King already had scheduled a press conference. This only inflamed Shuttlesworth's sarcasm. "Oh, you've got a *press conference?*" he asked in mock wonder. "I thought we were going to make joint statements." Daring King to announce a truce, he promised to nullify it by leading the kids right back into the streets.

Of the mortified bystanders in the Drew living room, Shuttlesworth's threat most sorely alarmed Burke Marshall, who had been assuring Washington almost minute by minute that President Kennedy could announce a Birmingham truce to the nation at his televised press conference that day. Only such a dire emergency forced Marshall to interject his professorial voice into the raging distemper among the Negro preachers. He warned Shuttlesworth that a historic agreement was at stake, that promises had been given and commitments made. "What promises?" shouted Shuttlesworth. The reference to unknown understandings backfired, as did Abernathy's soothing suggestion that perhaps Shuttlesworth was sick after all and should go back to the hospital. He was leaving all right, Shuttlesworth stormed, but they had better understand that neither King nor President Kennedy himself could call off the afternoon march.

"Wait a minute, Fred," King said softly. Over his shoulder to Marshall, he stressed the obvious vulnerabilities facing leaders of a small national minority. "We've got to have unity, Burke," he said. "We've just got to have unity."

Shuttlesworth bridled at hearing the call of unity imposed for once upon him. "I'll be damned if you'll have it like this!" he roared at King. "You're Mister Big, but you're going to be Mister S-H-I-T!"

No one knew exactly what King told Shuttlesworth when they retired to a back room. Most likely he stressed that the boycott was still on, that the white negotiators had given in on many points, that a day off from the previous day's nearly tragic explosions might be healthy. And perhaps he just passed time to let him settle down, believing as he did that it was difficult for Shuttlesworth to find himself ignored by the hordes of reporters—178 of them, by Wyatt Walker's latest count, from as far away as Japan and the Soviet Union—who came into town knowing little of Shuttlesworth's history in Birmingham. Whatever King said, it appeared to work, as the two leaders emerged in a sunny, performing mood. At the press conference shortly thereafter, Shuttlesworth took the lead in announcing the truce he had denounced so violently in private. "We do believe that honest efforts to negotiate in good faith are under way," he told reporters.

Burke Marshall, who had warned Washington of a snag, now passed along the Justice Department's equivalent of a huge sigh, and President Kennedy stepped before the cameras half an hour later. "Good afternoon," he said. "I'm gratified to note the progress in the efforts by white and Negro citizens to end an ugly situation in Birmingham, Alabama." He praised Marshall for his tireless mediation effort to "halt a spectacle which was seriously damaging the reputation of both Birmingham and the country." Noting that the Negro leaders had stopped the demonstrations, and that the incoming Boutwell administration had "committed itself wholeheartedly to continuing progress in this area," the President said he hoped for a final settlement within a day.

President Kennedy had scarcely completed his masterly performance
at the press conference—his first to be dominated by the subject of race
—when a new snag imperiled the truce from the opposite direction. This
time it was Governor Wallace, who announced that *he* certainly did not
know of any negotiations to compromise segregation, nor did he think
that Arthur Hanes and Bull Connor could approve of such. Hanes
promptly challenged the "other" mayor, Boutwell, to admit that he was
somehow involved in negotiations with Negroes. Governor Wallace's
state troopers began military drills in Kelly Ingram Park, and Bull Connor
sent his men to padlock the Sixteenth Street Baptist Church. The most
decisive blow of the hard-line segregationists fell upon King and Abernathy: at a hearing on their unlawful-parade convictions from the Good
Friday march, a local judge unexpectedly set their appeal bonds at the
new legal maximum of $2,500 apiece. Before a shocked courtroom audi-
ence, the defendants pronounced themselves both unwilling and unable
to pay, whereupon guards hauled them off to the Birmingham jail, shortly
after President Kennedy's optimistic press conference.

Now a furious A. D. King jumped before the Birmingham press corps
to declare that this betrayal voided the truce. He predicted huge demonstrations by the end of the day, the padlocked church notwithstanding,
and Wyatt Walker said much of the same. Only the personal intercession
of Attorney General Kennedy deflected Shuttlesworth from leading Bevel's reserves on a march downtown. Kennedy's theory was that Bull
Connor was trying to provoke a riot as a pretext for martial law under
his political ally, Governor Wallace, which would scuttle prospects for a
settlement. Kennedy did not have to say that such an immediate and
violent rebuttal of the President's position would be a disaster for the
Administration. He felt obliged to defend the settlement, and he knew
that King's imprisonment would stiffen the Negro terms just when the
President was trying to soften both sides. Moreover, as Marshall had seen
in the vivid confrontation with Shuttlesworth, the arrest removed the
one presence that was indispensable for sustained Negro unity behind
any settlement.

Once again, more urgently than ever, Robert Kennedy needed to get
King out of jail. He called Harry Belafonte in New York with an emergency request: could Belafonte protect the movement, the country, and
Dr. King all at once by raising $5,000 bond money—in cash, that same
day, as every hour was precious? Belafonte agreed to try. The New York
banks were closed, but he mobilized wealthy friends to pluck up loose
cash in the city. By evening, Belafonte called Kennedy to say that the
money soon would be on its way to the airport. In a telling aside, however, Belafonte added that he was still waiting to get confirmation from

Wyatt Walker that Dr. King actually wanted to come out of jail. This was a clinker for Robert Kennedy. Of all the surprise twists of the day, the most vexing were the signals reaching Marshall that King wanted to stay locked up.

For King, the most difficult of the unresolved issues was the fate of some two thousand movement prisoners still jailed in Birmingham. He thought Bull Connor had made a mistake by arresting him, because the public stir strengthened his leverage to demand that all his fellow demonstrators leave jail with him, with the charges dropped as unjust, or, at a minimum, that bail be dropped so that they could gain release on personal recognizance. Robert Kennedy, for his part, was irked by the very idea that King wanted to use himself as a hostage. As stupid as it was for Connor to have engineered King's incarceration, Kennedy thought it was irresponsible of King to risk an explosion of racial violence in Birmingham over what Kennedy saw as a side issue to the segregation dispute. He told Belafonte to stand by with the money, and secretly pursued alternative methods to free King.

In Birmingham, the negotiating teams met into the night, the afterglow of President Kennedy's public endorsement spurring on their eagerness to finish. However, that same national spotlight made the businessmen instinctively wary, and the Negro strategists remained divided in King's absence. At the mass meeting, only James Bevel addressed the crowd, and, as though to demonstrate that anything could happen once people surrendered to the movement, a procession of nineteen white people entered the church, some of them wearing beards and rabbinical garb. They marched down the aisles of Sixth Avenue Baptist and up to the rostrum, where they embraced the preachers and the choir. "We came to applaud your courage and dignity in your struggle for everyone," said a rabbi from New Jersey, introducing colleagues from as near as Memphis and as far away as Nova Scotia, saying they had been elected at a rabbinical conference to make a spontaneous pilgrimage in response to publicity about Birmingham. "I have never been moved more deeply in my life," declared Rabbi Alex Shapiro, who said that as Jews who had seen the Germans overrun Europe, they hoped always to lend succor against oppression anywhere. "We shall do what you ask," he said. "Our people are your people." From the pulpit a cantor taught them a simple song of brotherhood in Hebrew, then directed the swaying congregation to embrace one another in the pews. For the ever-present Birmingham police detectives, this joyful hugging was the worst part of the night's surveillance. "Of course Officer Watkins and myself were sitting between two negroes," Officer Allison reported to Bull Connor, "and they really gave us the treatment."

A number of the Negro negotiators believed that King was wrong to stay in jail. With the active encouragement of Attorney General Kennedy, they prevailed upon A. G. Gaston to show up at the jail with $5,000 cash from his own bank. As in Albany ten months earlier, King and Abernathy found themselves ejected from their cells. This time there was no mystery, and the demands of unity prevented King from complaining publicly about the deception. Still, it was an unhappy King who returned to the Gaston Motel that night. He believed that his own misguided allies had deprived him of an advantage supplied by the cooperative foe, Bull Connor. Fittingly, a day that had begun with an enraged Shuttlesworth escaping from the hospital ended with an angry King trying to barricade himself in jail, and in between, the contending parties had zigzagged through a baffling series of press statements. After dark, farmer Shuttlesworth wound up talking urbanely about holding the course, while citified King wound up wanting to scald the other side of the hog. Late that night, King told reporters that if there was no settlement by eleven o'clock Thursday morning, the movement would mount its largest demonstration yet.

The deadline slid by without result. It was Thursday, May 9, 1963, one extraordinary week since the gamble of the D-Day children's march. In Moscow, *Pravda* ran a story headlined "Monstrous Crimes Among Racists in the United States." Less vitriolic stories had become staples throughout Europe, and *The New York Times* reported that Birmingham was competing daily with an insurrection in Haiti for top news billing across non-Communist Asia. A majority of the news outlets, taking the merits of the Negro cause to be obvious, wondered why the Kennedy Administration failed to hasten a solution with a public assertion of authority.

In Birmingham, with negotiations still deadlocked on the issue of the demonstrators still in jail, the whites pointed out that in return for King's one-day moratorium they had quietly engineered the release pending trial of the five hundred youngest prisoners. Moreover, they said that after the settlement, and certainly upon the confirmation of the Boutwell administration, they could get the remaining bonds reduced drastically, perhaps even the charges dropped. But they were only businessmen, they insisted, and even if they could make puppets of the city courts and prosecutors, they could not boast of such powers in a public settlement. Surely King could understand that. The best they could do was to include a promise of concerted effort to get the demonstrators released.

This was not good enough for King. He recoiled from the thought of the great mass meeting at which he would tell the mothers and fathers that while they had cracked segregation in Birmingham, their children must stay in jail. Those people should not have been arrested in the first place, he insisted. On principle, and personal honor, King refused to settle. If the Senior Citizens could not get the prisoners released outright, then perhaps they could raise $250,000 to get them freed on bond. If they could not or would not do it, then perhaps the federal government could raise the money. After all, Robert Kennedy had raised more than $60 *million* for the Bay of Pigs prisoners. To Kennedy's protestations, through Marshall, that the government role here was peacemaker and mediator, not bondsman, King replied that if the federal government had not already been a party to the conflict before President Kennedy's press conference, and before Robert Kennedy has pressured Gaston to bail him out against his will, then surely it was now, and ought to be more so.

These were prickly talks, laced with innuendo. To Kennedy's urgent warnings that the Negroes should settle before Governor Wallace's troopers crushed their hopes under martial law, King hinted that Governor Rockefeller might help with the bond funds if Kennedy refused. The threat of partisan revolt touched Kennedy where he was vulnerable, not only in presidential politics but even in the Democratic House, where hearings had opened only the previous day on Republican bills to outlaw segregation. Some days later, in a White House presentation before the entire cabinet, Robert Kennedy said he had told King repeatedly that his stubbornness "doesn't really make a lot of sense."

King returned Kennedy's annoyance. At the Thursday press conference, at which he extended the truce another day, King publicly contradicted the Administration for the first time in Birmingham. "The President said that there were no federal statutes involved in most aspects of this struggle," he said, "but I feel that there have been blatant violations of basic constitutional principles. I think also that we must recognize that some persons who have been arrested were arrested for going down to register to vote, and the federal government has done nothing about that. And some persons have been arrested in the Federal Building, at the lunch counter there. Nothing has been done." He went on to assert that several other existing statutes plainly justified federal intervention.

Perhaps intentionally, King gave no more than this hint that the heat of his negotiations had shifted from the Senior Citizens to the Kennedy Administration, and only a few people, such as Stanley Levison, were privy to the friction. FBI wiretaps picked up Levison's candid agreement with Robert Kennedy's position that the prisoners were a "secondary issue." It was a "pity," said Levison, that King wanted so much not to

look like a privileged leader—he should take the deal and then worry
about the prisoners. "Even if the people have to go to jail," Levison said,
"the other things that are won will just make them martyrs and make
the victory even clearer. And I'm damn sure that for the kind of victory
this represents, people will be delighted to serve a term, because this is
the big victory. No question, if this comes, this is the big one." On the
other hand, Levison said he was pleased that King had scolded the Kennedy Administration for its aloofness. Levison figured that the Kennedys
were adopting a "new policy" of private maneuver behind a public stance
of sympathetic neutrality. "It's right, and it's wrong," he said. While the
movement "has to be prepared to do a job without relying on Washington," it was "impermissible for Washington not to be involved." In another call, Levison told Clarence Jones that he thought "the
Administration made a mistake by not intervening" more forcefully in
Birmingham.

King and Kennedy muttered about each other to their respective aides,
who in turn muttered more harshly. But the Birmingham emergency did
not allow either side to give in completely to hostility, as political disaster menaced them both. Kennedy, accepting that King would march
again rather than leave people in jail, resolved to find the bail money.
King, accepting that Kennedy's help offered the only way out, gave up
hopes for immediate bail reduction or release. Together, they resolved to
buy their way out of the impasse, and the tacit alliance spawned a frenzy
of hidden cooperation. King called Harry Belafonte to say that he needed
some $90,000 in cash, and that this time he was working with the Attor-
ney General without reservation. Kennedy's first call was to Walter
Reuther of the United Auto Workers, who was soon barking orders from
Detroit to his Washington lawyer, Joseph Rauh. "Joe," he said, "we need
to get a hundred and sixty thousand dollars to Birmingham by morning."
Rauh laughed; then he gulped.

Robert Kennedy went to dinner that night at the White House, where
the President pried out of his guest, *Newsweek* bureau chief Ben Bradlee,
a tip that the subject of the next cover story would be Senator Barry
Goldwater's chances to become the Republican presidential nominee in
1964. "I can't believe we'll be that lucky," said Kennedy, who hoped to
run against Goldwater. "I can't believe Barry will be that lucky, either."
The Attorney General missed nearly all the dinner gossip, being closeted
with the telephone. From ALF-CIO president George Meany, he secured
a promise for half the $160,000 out of two of Meany's departmental
accounts. He obtained a quarter-share of $40,000 directly from David
McDonald of the Steelworkers, and, with Walter Reuther's promise to
send the final share out of Auto Workers funds, Kennedy turned to the

feat of instant delivery. It was a matter of slush funds and satchels, of the sort that Kennedy himself had publicized in his war against unsavory union practices. No less than a national security crisis legitimized the transactions, and Kennedy discussed the logistics with Secretary of Labor Arthur Goldberg.

The Attorney General was counting minutes, waiting for confirmations of cash in hand. Fretfully, he called Harry Belafonte to make sure that the settlement was not falling through on King's end. While he was pressing for reassurance, Belafonte's doorbell rang, and when Belafonte said it might be a delivery right then, Kennedy anxiously insisted that Belafonte find out while he waited on the line. Obliging, Belafonte put the phone down and opened his door to behold a uniformed Negro deliveryman, who handed him a small black satchel containing $50,000 in cash from his boss, Michael Quill of the New York transportation workers' union. For King, this favor was in part a return on a speech he had delivered before Quill's workers several years earlier. For Belafonte, the quick circuit between Robert Kennedy's voice and the deliveryman's face remained a salient memory of his political life.

Racing home to New York, Jones followed King's instructions to report to Harry Belafonte, and then followed Belafonte's instructions to meet Governor Rockefeller's assistant Hugh Morrow at Rockefeller Plaza. By then the New York banks had closed for the weekend, but Jones soon found himself standing with Morrow and a punctilious vice president inside a cavernous vault of Chase Manhattan, the Rockefeller bank. Governor Rockefeller himself was in Venezuela, having just married Happy Murphy so swiftly on the heels of their respective divorces that the minister who performed the ceremony was subjected to ecclesiastical reprimand by Presbyterian superiors. In the Gallup poll on Republican presidential contenders, Rockefeller dropped thirteen points within a week of his marriage, instantly boosting the prospects of his rival, Barry Goldwater. These circumstances contributed to the atmosphere of secrecy inside the bank vault. Rockefeller wanted to avoid public charges that he had tried to "buy" the Negro vote, and King wanted to avoid publicity about Rockefeller's contribution to protect his relations with the Kennedys. For the bank itself, customs of confidentiality dignified the irregular transaction. In return for a promissory note by which Jones numbly promised to repay the full sum instantly upon demand, the vice president handed over a briefcase full of cash. Jones, feeling like a character in a spy novel, walked out of the vault to Belafonte's apartment, before heading back to Birmingham. On his return, he found in the mail a "blind" receipt notifying him that his loan had been repaid in full.

At the Gaston Motel, where the army of reporters had been promised a major announcement by noon, King stalled well into Friday afternoon. He was waiting first for confirmation that Joe Rauh had wired the union money from the UAW bank in Washington, then for the whites in Birmingham to fulfill their pledge to pay the money to city bond clerks, thereby setting free a steady stream of demonstrators. He was also waiting for word from Belafonte that Jones was heading South with more than enough money to free the last prisoners. With Burke Marshall and the white negotiators, King was exchanging last-minute modifications on how the various parties would behave when the great moment came —what they would sign, what they would say publicly, what they would truly mean. All the while, King was composing and rehearsing the performance on the Negro side. When finally the reporters threatened mutiny, King, Abernathy, and Shuttlesworth marched solemnly before the cameras. For reasons of internal diplomacy, King made sure who spoke the first words. Shuttlesworth said, "The City of Birmingham has reached an accord with its conscience."

Although Shuttlesworth announced the terms of the settlement, the reporters would not be satisfied until they heard it from King himself, as most of their readers knew nothing of Shuttlesworth. King stepped forward to speak. Through his cautionary remarks—"there is still a strenuous task before us, and some of it is yet uncharted"—shone his first euphoric predictions of a national contagion. While he was speaking, Shuttlesworth collapsed in a dead faint. Shrieks went up about his exhaustion and his fire-hose bruises. Even so, the medical crisis diverted attention only briefly to Shuttlesworth, and the press conference resumed as soon as ambulance attendants bore him off to Holy Family Hospital.

At St. John's Church, a crowd of some two thousand people broke off a rollicking version of "Oh Freedom" when the preachers made their entrance to the first mass meeting that Friday night. Triumph inspired Abernathy to a rhapsody on leadership. "Amen!" he shouted. "Give me a big hand! Tonight is victory night, and you ought to stand up for me!" He said that if he were dying, he wanted King to be holding one hand and Shuttlesworth the other while his wife cradled his head. "All these preachers are great men," Abernathy proclaimed, "but there isn't but one Martin Luther King! God sent him to lead us to freedom. Are you going to follow him? Is he our leader?" To great rhythmic shouts of "Yes!" Abernathy cried, "Then say 'King'!" This served as the introduction for King, who took the pulpit amid a deafening chant of his name.

He quelled the adulation by reading the formal statement he had made at the press conference. Then, to establish a tone of intimacy, he gave the crowd an exclusive tidbit of the written agreement, details of which were being withheld so as not to alert the Klan. "The sitting rooms will be integrated by Monday," King announced. He went on through the timetable of the phases: a biracial committee in fifteen days, integrated rest rooms and water fountains in thirty days, lunch counters and up-graded Negro clerks in sixty. All movement prisoners were "either out of jail or on the way out of jail," he promised, and he told them "off the record" that the white businessmen planned to move faster than the timetable specified.

He warned them that the world would try to minimize, negate, and forget their achievement. Indeed, Mayor Boutwell already was announc-ing that he would not be bound by the settlement. Mayor Hanes was calling it a "capitulation by certain weak-kneed white people under threats of violence by the rabble-rousing Negro, King." The Birmingham *News* was publishing a slanted farewell story, "Negroes End Desegrega-tion Campaign: Not Able to Get Charges Dropped," and, almost pathet-ically, the editors placed alongside it a graphic summary of spring rampages at Princeton, Brown, Brandeis, and Yale, strongly implying that the local upheaval was of no greater moment than panty raids up North. "Now don't let anybody fool you . . ." King told the crowd. "Do not underestimate the power of this movement! These things would *not* have been granted without your presenting your bodies and your very lives before the dogs and the tanks and the water hoses of this city! . . ."

"Then another thing," he said, his voice now quivering with emotion. "The United States is concerned about its image. When things started happening down here, Mr. Kennedy got disturbed. For Mr. Kennedy . . . is battling for the minds and the hearts of men in Asia and Africa—some one billion men in the neutralist sector of the world—and they aren't gonna respect the United States of America if she deprives men and women of the basic rights of life because of the color of their skin. Mr. Kennedy *knows* that." The President's worries gave the movement le-verage to change the reality of a segregated bastion like Birmingham, King said, and now they had touched a nerve connecting conscience with power. He told them he had been flooded with phone calls offering sup-port—not just from the rabbis and the most powerful Negro preachers, but planeloads from Denver and Los Angeles and Pittsburgh, and the head of the American Baptists, and Jackie Robinson and Floyd Patterson. And Harry Belafonte had called that morning to say that three thousand New Yorkers were ready to picket the White House if necessary to gain an agreement. "Now this is an *amazing* thing!" King cried. "And it should make all of us feel happy."

As always, since the Montgomery bus boycott, the greatest danger followed closely upon a victory for civil rights, and the true measure of national support for the movement lagged well behind the early swells of enthusiasm. King knew this even before he reached home on Saturday. In Atlanta, both white and Negro newspapers sneered at the Birmingham settlement as a standoff of troublemakers. The *Journal* focused biliously upon King "and his flamboyant policy of inciting riot in the name of justice . . . Now having created a deadlock and enough ill will to last a generation, the time has come for him to hit the road and pass the hat once more." On Auburn Avenue, C. A. Scott wrote a scorching editorial entitled "The Tragic Cost at Birmingham," in which he dismissed the tenuous gains of the settlement against the "calamity," the "terrible price," and the "ugly picture before the nation and the world. . . . Not soon will the wounds be healed nor the tragic era forgotten."

Elsewhere in the South's only Negro daily, Scott promoted an extraordinary event: that week in Atlanta, "Supersonic Attractions" featured in one concert a dazzling collection of Negro musicians, including Jimmy Reed, Dionne Warwick, Dee Clark, Hank Ballard and the Midnighters, Solomon Burke, the Drifters, Little Ester ("Release Me") Phillips, the Crystals, Jerry Butler, and Sam Cooke—all for a two-dollar ticket. Ponce de Leon Park would be jammed not only with Negro fans but also with young white people, for whom the best Negro pop music reached beneath formal and worldly preoccupations to release elemental emotions of sex, frivolity, love, and sadness. The stars of soul music and blues stood with King as exemplars of the mysterious Negro church—nearly all of them had been gospel singers—but they were still ahead of him in crossing over to a mass white audience. They unlocked the shared feelings, if not the understanding, that he longed to reach.

The catalytic rise from Birmingham required a final jolt of chaos. Uncannily, two earnest young religious reporters from Radio Riverside, a station owned by the storied New York church of Harry Emerson Fosdick and John D. Rockefeller, Jr., drifted just ahead of each outburst. On Saturday night, they ventured boldly with microphones into a Ku Klux Klan rally at Moose Club Park, on the outskirts of Birmingham. More than a thousand hooded Klansmen burned a giant cross and raised a halfhearted cry of "Fight the niggers! Fight the niggers." The Grand Dragon of Georgia revealed that Atlanta University was producing a stage play in which a Negro Cleopatra "gets kissed by a white boy at the end." "That's what's happening," he said gravely. The Grand Dragon of Mississippi denounced the federal government as "Hersheytown—ninety percent black and ten percent nuts. . . . We're with you. Don't worry about that." The host Klansman, Imperial Wizard Robert Shelton of Alabama, exclaimed that

"Martin Luther King has not gained *one thing* in Birmingham, because the white people are not going to tolerate the meddlesome, conniving, manipulating moves of these *professional businessmen!*" Like all the Klan speakers, Shelton spat out the word "businessmen" as a foul epithet. He introduced an anonymous Klan Kagle, evidently a kind of paramilitary chieftain, who shouted that they would prevail over "the greatest darkness that this nation has ever faced" by relying upon "the power of God along with some good stiff-backed men who is willing to shoulder the load and willing to go out to fight the battle for the Lord Jesus." The Kagle led practice shrieks of the famed Rebel yell, which came out rusty and anemic.

Back in Birmingham, commanders of law enforcement huddled apprehensively at Kelly Ingram Park. Among them was Chief Laurie Pritchett, who had driven over from Georgia partly to find out whether King truly intended to return to Albany, and partly to warn his fellow officers against the deadly combination of Negro celebrations and Klan rallies. He urgently recommended that Chief Moore station all-night police units prominently around King's headquarters at the Gaston Motel, across the street from the park. Bull Connor vetoed the suggestion, however, saying he refused to "guard that nigger son-of-a-bitch." With that, Moore took Pritchett aside for a heated argument. As Pritchett's main confidant on the Birmingham force, Moore tried to explain that he was in no position to press a direct confrontation with Connor, since Connor had hired all the subordinate commanders including himself. Pritchett huffily replied that Moore was not fit to be chief if he lacked the authority to deploy his own men. Then he stalked off. By the time the Riverside reporters returned from the Klan rally, Kelly Ingram Park was nearly empty.

Rev. A. D. King, home from a mass meeting at which Bevel had been the principal speaker, was in bed at his parsonage when the first bomb struck at about 10:45 P.M. He ran through the smoke to find his wife Naomi dazed but unhurt in the living room, and together they were evacuating their five children through the back door when a second, larger dynamite bomb blew a hole eight feet high in the brick façade and sent the front door flying in chunks against the back wall of the living room. The fire department later calculated the damage at one-third of the parsonage value, but the Kings' immediate worry was the fear of more bombs. By the time police and fire officials pronounced the area free of undetonated explosives, upwards of a thousand Negroes had gathered, in various stages of undress. A number of them threatened retaliation against whites, especially against the policemen who were ordering them to go home, but A. D. King grabbed a megaphone and preached nonviolence. He sent some of his church deacons through the crowd to start up freedom songs, and when he went inside to notify his Atlanta relatives of the bombings, he held up the telephone to let his brother Martin hear the reassuring sounds of "We Shall Overcome" in the background.

From somewhere within A. D. King—temperamental, hard-drinking, insecure in the shadow of his famous brother—the shocks of the night drew out his finest moments of the movement years. Just before midnight, the crack of another explosion reached the parsonage all the way from downtown Birmingham, several miles away. This time it was the Gaston Motel, and as the news spread, the crowd around A. D. King's parsonage swelled again until it neared two thousand. Resentment of the bombings boiled into rage. Stones rained down on the police vehicles, and a brick struck one detective. The Riverside reporters got close enough to record a megaphone voice above the shouting: "This is Reverend A. D. King speaking to you! Please put your bricks down!" A trailing voice came behind: "That's your leader! Put 'em down!"

Driving back downtown, the Riverside reporters pushed their way into Kelly Ingram Park. Ambulances were leaving with four Negroes injured by the bomb, none seriously. People strained against the police lines to get a view of the damage: a door-sized hole blasted into the reception area of the Gaston Motel beneath Martin Luther King's second-floor suite, knocking out the main water and electrical lines, and, in a vacant lot across the street, three house trailers twisted and buckled from an explosive that evidently landed farther from the motel than intended. With more than two thousand Negroes jamming the park, the scene was reminiscent of the massive confrontations there over the past nine days, except that now all the Negroes came from the taverns and dance halls of the surrounding commercial district, which had been emptied of their Saturday-night customers. "Eye for an eye, tooth for a tooth!" shouted one. Rocks flew, and soon a car parked outside the Sixteenth Street Baptist Church was overturned and set on fire.

Bricks shattered glass storefronts near the park. Inside the motel, Wyatt Walker realized that the danger of further bombs was superseded by the threat of violence that might wipe out the precious gains of the Birmingham movement. He grabbed a megaphone, telling Bernard Lee they had to go out to disperse the crowd. Lee balked after a few steps into the hail of bottles and stones. "We can't do nothing!" he protested, but he followed Walker into the park. "Please do not throw any of the bricks any more!" cried Walker. A brick struck him in the ankle, after which he hobbled back and forth on the sidewalk. Police K-9 units scrambled out of cars to the head of the police lines, and these creatures, made infamous by the mass demonstrations, attracted a hail of missiles. Angry policemen chased rock-throwers into dark alleys; after one foray, an officer staggered back out with three knife wounds in his back. Police commanders and Negro preachers maintained a desperate liaison in the middle zones. They agreed that the preachers should labor to disperse the rioters while the commanders tried to hold back their police lines, but they had more sense than control. A burning grocery store lit up the park, and sporadic looting broke out.

By then the Riverside reporters, stranded amid fire, sirens, rocks, and rioters, were hostages rather than observers. They held their microphone aloft like a torch in a hurricane, and above the megaphone pleas for calm it picked up the voice of a hysterical man nearby, shouting, "How come *we* have to go home every time *they* start violence?" The voices of the Riverside reporters themselves, sounding hollow and stripped of radio polish, could be heard insisting that they were there only to get the news. "Ain't nobody gonna bother you!" someone kept telling them. When the roof of the grocery store collapsed in flames, a male voice moaned, "Aw, man, now see we gone too far." Another man said, "We gone too far because they don't know *what* to do," and an angry woman said, "Yeah, but they were *led* to do it."

A. D. King arrived at the Gaston Motel about 1:30 A.M., the uprising near his home having finally died down. He rushed into Kelly Ingram Park with the loudest megaphone, and soon could be heard above the other preachers: "Our *home* was just bombed . . . Now if we who were in jeopardy of being killed, if we have gone away *not* angry, *not* throwing bricks, if we could do that and we were in danger, why must *you* rise up to hurt our cause? You are *hurting* us! You are *not* helping! Now won't you *please* clear this park." King's initiative, along with the fatigue of the rioters and the relative restraint of the police, allowed the phalanx of Negro preachers to make headway in dispersing the crowd. Wyatt Walker had limped back to the motel to see his wife, Ann, who had flown in from Atlanta that night with two of their children, then returned to the park. He and the others dispersed nearly all the crowd within the hour.

A. D. King, having lured nearly three hundred unruly laggards into a parking lot, was singing "We Shall Overcome" from atop a parked Cadillac when Colonel Al Lingo landed like the Marines. Leading a force of 250 state troopers and irregular volunteers from state agencies across Alabama, Lingo saw disaster: blazing fires, scores of Negroes throwing rocks from alleys, and brick attacks against the monitor guns that firemen had brought up for their designed purpose. Chief Moore, on the other hand, saw renewed disaster in Lingo's men, who were brandishing carbines and billy clubs. "If you'd leave, Mr. Lingo, I'd appreciate it," he said as politely as he could.

Lingo replied that he was there on the higher authority of Governor Wallace.

"Those guns are not needed," Moore said tightly. "Will you please put them up? Somebody's going to get killed."

"You're damned right it'll get somebody killed!" Lingo exploded in battle heat, raising his repeater shotgun. Within minutes, he led the first group of state troopers in a charge down the street. As police officers shouted ahead that everyone had better get inside, troopers clubbed any Negroes who did not. They beat a begging man to the ground outside a door that he shrieked was locked, then kicked the door open, tossed him inside, and moved on. From the Gaston Motel, some of the Negro preachers cried out that the troopers did not need their guns, and the response was a stampede of Lingo's irregulars into the motel compound itself. Claude Sitton of the *Times* wrote that "the 'thonk' of clubs striking heads could be heard across the street." Karl Flemming of *Newsweek* called the violence more sickening than the worst of the Ole Miss riot. Wyatt Walker found his wife on the floor, felled by a trooper's rifle butt.

Lingo's savage attacks swiftly produced the most wanton destruction of the night, as hundreds of Negroes who had been dispersed toward their homes vented renewed rage against targets across a wide area. In Washington, alerted by frantic calls relayed from FBI observers, John Doar decided at 2:30 A.M. that the crisis was serious enough to begin waking up Robert Kennedy's aides. By dawn, when the riot had spent itself, six businesses, several houses, and a two-story apartment building were burned to the ground, several dozen cars were destroyed, and nearly seventy people had been taken to University Hospital. On leaving his wife's bedside, a distraught Wyatt Walker made the mistake of trying to retrieve her clothing from the Gaston Motel before sending her and the children back to Atlanta. Stopped at a roadblock, he offered to go in on foot, whereupon two state troopers and an irregular beat him, fractured a wrist throwing him into a cruiser, slammed the door on his leg, and dumped him at the motel, which troopers kept sealed off without water, phone, or electricity. Hours later at midday, Walker remained among the disappeared. In Washington, a White House helicopter flew off to fetch Burke Marshall from his farm, where he had just gone to recuperate from the Birmingham ordeal.

Emergency strategy sessions consumed Sunday at the Pentagon and Justice Department. As King flew back to Birmingham from Atlanta, Robert Kennedy arrived at the White House in the open air of his Ford Galaxie convertible, accompanied by Burke Marshall, Ed Guthman, Nick Katzenbach, and his dog Brummus. President Kennedy, having just flown in from a weekend at Camp David, waited there in his rocking chair, flanked by Defense Secretary Robert McNamara, Army Secretary Cyrus Vance, and General Earle Wheeler, the Army Chief of Staff. The Attorney General accurately summarized a treacherously complex political dilemma. After bombings and riots had shaken the goodwill of the movement Negroes, the local police, and the moderate whites alike, he said, the Wallace-Connor forces had moved into the confusion with a decisive show of anti-Negro violence. Their objective was to sabotage the Birmingham settlement in one of three ways: (1) by direct intimidation of the white businessmen who had authorized it; (2) by provoking the Negroes to riot against the state troopers, or to demonstrate, or to renounce the agreement themselves; or (3) by forcing the federal government to intervene, which would put the Birmingham businessmen in a politically untenable alliance with Yankee soldiers as well as Negroes.

"The argument for sending troops in is what's gonna happen in the future," said Kennedy. ". . . The governor has virtually taken over the state. You're going to have his people around sticking bayonets in people and hitting people with the clubs, guns, etcetera. You're going to have rallies all over the country . . . people calling on the President to take forceful action." However, among the arguments against sending troops was the difficulty of explanation. Unless the Administration was willing to brand the state troopers as the threat to public order—in effect, to declare war on Alabama—it would have to justify the use of federal troops as a means of quelling the Negroes, not the whites. Racially, this would be the reverse of Ole Miss and the Freedom Rides, and with Army troops patrolling the Negro neighborhoods, the reluctant white moderates in Birmingham might take advantage of the federal shield.

President Kennedy did not need to be told the grim conclusion. "They might tear up that paper agreement that they made," he interrupted quickly. "Therefore, you'd have the Negroes knocked down again without getting an agreement."

This prospect caused Burke Marshall to speak up. "If that agreement blows up," he said wearily, "the Negroes will be, uh . . ." His voice faded away.

"Uncontrollable," suggested the President.

Marshall nodded. "And I think not only in Birmingham," he added, as one of the few white people who shared King's premonitions about the outward ripples from Project C.

They drifted toward a preliminary deployment of U.S. Army troops near, but not in, Birmingham. This maneuver would give the nation's liberals the appearance of movement in support of the agreement, while positioning the troops to intervene if, as President Kennedy feared, "there is going to be violence there tonight—that's obviously what Governor Wallace wants." The maneuver would also warn the Wallace forces without giving them the political leverage to cancel the settlement. For President Kennedy, the principal unknown of these close calculations was Martin Luther King. He was presumed to have enormous influence over the Negroes on the streets of Birmingham, and, to millions of Americans now intently following media accounts of the crisis, his public utterances on the Administration's performance might be crucial. The mystery of King so preoccupied President Kennedy that he interrupted General Wheeler to ask Burke Marshall, "How freely do you talk to King?"

"I talk to him freely," Marshall replied. "I'll tell you what he intends to do, Mr. President. He intends to go to this church and call upon the people to [stay off the streets], as the Attorney General says, and then tomorrow, he intends to go around the city and visit pool halls, saloons, and talk to the Negroes, and preach against violence. Those are his intentions."

This report hung in the air, lacking handles for incisive comment. After a few seconds President Kennedy said that King must have political expectations because he had called upon the Administration to make a statement. Rustling a newspaper, scanning King's quotes, the President wanted to know whether King expected him to send troops, and whether King might attack him for failure to do so, but Robert Kennedy warned that they could not put such questions to King, even confidentially, for fear that King would say publicly that the Administration had asked his opinion, in which case partisan wags might pillory the commanders of the Free World for soliciting the advice of a nonviolent Negro on military decisions. To preclude such risk, President Kennedy asked Marshall to call King right then from the Oval Office, "like you're just talking on your own." Without mentioning troops, Marshall was to probe for King's expectations.

While Marshall stepped outside to place the call, Press Secretary Salinger darted out to pacify the reporters, who had been promised a statement on the crisis by President Kennedy himself, and General Wheeler came forth with his shopping list of forts and attack routes. "Tell you what I can do, Mr. President," he said. "I've got a Battle Group over at Fort Benning, which is overland—takes six hours and thirty minutes to make Birmingham." The civilians wanted to know why it took so long to cover a hundred miles, and some time later, during Wheeler's foggy explanations why there were no transport planes at the Fort Benning air station, Marshall returned.

"What did he say?" asked President Kennedy, cutting off General Wheeler.

"Well," said Marshall, "he says that if there are no other incidents he thinks he can control his people. Of course, he just got there, and he's . . . going to try to organize the Negroes to go around into the communities. He said a lot of those people were drunk last night. It being Saturday night."

"Yeah," said the President. "He didn't say anything about troops, did he?"

"No, he didn't," Marshall replied. "Well, I didn't raise that, and he didn't." Official reticence thus kept the government from learning that King had told reporters explicitly that he was not calling for federal troops. His unstated purpose was to protect the fragile desegregation agreement at all costs by not antagonizing the Birmingham businessmen. On this objective, King and the Kennedy Administration were more firmly allied than they realized. To Marshall, King did stress that the settlement was the ultimate hostage to the violence. "If it causes the businessmen to go back on their agreement," Marshall reported to President Kennedy, "he said the game is over. And I think that's absolutely right." The specter of open racial warfare invaded the Oval Office.

Recognizing the supreme importance of the settlement, Marshall ducked out again to take a phone call from Sidney Smyer. As the only Senior Citizen to acknowledge his role publicly, Smyer was under relentless attack from local segregationists demanding that the names of the other "traitors" be made known. Mayor Hanes was vilifying other parties "implicated" in the settlement as provocatively as he could—announcing that "the nigger King ought to be investigated" as a "revolutionary," deriding Chief Moore as fainthearted, and stating of Robert Kennedy that "I hope that every drop of blood that's spilled he tastes in his throat, and I hope he chokes on it." In the face of all this, Smyer hazarded a promise to Marshall that the Senior Citizens would hold up. They would lie low for a few more days, he said, because many of them were worried for the safety of themselves and their families, but they would stick by their agreement with King. His steadfastness relieved Marshall. Soon afterward, Smyer called in Birmingham reporters to reveal, behind smokescreen denunciations of Negro rioters, that prominent people in the city were actively promoting racial turbulence "to shove the city into martial law." Under anybody's martial law, Wallace's or Kennedy's, Smyer warned, "the community is under the heel of the military. No longer can we solve anything ourselves."

At the White House, General Wheeler resumed: "Well, Mr. President, I got another Battle Group alerted up in Fort Campbell, Kentucky."

President Kennedy took notes on which Army units would move where, and shortly after Marshall returned he dispatched Wheeler and Vance to get three thousand soldiers moving in Operation Oak Tree. As soon as they were out of earshot, he led a round of chuckling over the military bureaucracy's precision. "When they say the flying time's an hour," quipped the President, "the mistake you always make is that's what you think—that they'll be there in an hour."

McNamara, Katzenbach, Marshall, and Guthman retired to the Cabinet Room to draft a presidential statement. While justifying the troop movements in the name of public order, it strongly implied that their mission was to protect the desegregation agreement as well. They fed the statement one page at a time to the President's secretary Evelyn Lincoln for typing, but latecomer Ted Sorensen and President Kennedy objected that it "leaned too much on the side of the Negroes." Even so, when President Kennedy stepped out at 8:48 P.M. to face hordes of reporters and live broadcast coverage, the version he read cemented his commitment to the landmark settlement. "The Birmingham agreement was and is a fair and just accord," he declared. ". . . The federal government will not permit it to be sabotaged by a few extremists on either side."

Ralph Abernathy heard President Kennedy's statement on a car radio as he made his way to the New Pilgrim Baptist Church in Birmingham. The meeting could not be held downtown, because the state troopers had sealed off a twenty-eight-block area around the Gaston Motel, where Wyatt Walker and a score of occupants remained incommunicado. Even out at New Pilgrim, the fear of trigger-happy troopers or nighttime riot was so strong that Negroes who ventured outdoors wore their best clothes and stepped gingerly. It was a long meeting, and through most of it Andrew Young was stuck with the task of squiring the visiting dignitaries, who, having come to celebrate the victory, found themselves instead in a war zone. Among them were Dorothy Height and a delegation from the National Council of Negro Women. Holding themselves primly above the renewed strife, they made speeches about their organization's mission "to strengthen in every way that we could the moral fiber of our country," and in praising their founder, Mary McLeod Bethune, they quoted at length "the wonderful words of her last will and testament."

Bursting into the church, Abernathy obliterated this contrived decorum. He announced President Kennedy's support for the settlement. But, he shouted above prolonged cheers, he was resting his hopes on even greater powers than the U.S. Army or the White House. He was looking to the Almighty God who had listened to Paul and Silas in the Philippi jail, to Daniel in the lions' den, to the three devout Jews in Nebuchadnezzar's fiery furnace. Between rhythmic shouts from the congregation, Abernathy cried out that he was looking to the God who had sought out Moses in the land of Midan and Martin Luther King "in the sophisticated, well-endowed Ebenezer Baptist Church of Atlanta, Georgia . . . He is the leader! He is the Moses! . . . We are going to listen now to our leader."

King's Sunday speech was recorded by the indefatigable pilgrims from Radio Riverside, who had filled nearly five reels of tape since the previous night's Klan rally. On Monday, they followed him on a tour of Negro taverns and billiard rooms, during which a drubbing from a riffraff pool shark left King fretting once again that his skills had atrophied since Crozer. As the Riverside reporters walked the tense streets outside, they recorded a frustrated diatribe from Bull Connor himself. "Well, the son of a bitch," Connor sneered. "He's the only one that's caused any violence. You can quote me as saying that if you put 'son of a bitch' in front of it . . . The biggest racketeer that ever hit America. Shakedown artist . . . He's down there in the pool room now, preaching nonviolence."

That Monday night, the Riverside reporters followed King again to the mass meeting. The relief of two days' shaky peace, plus the presence of celebrities, packed the Sixth Avenue Baptist Church. Former heavyweight champion Floyd Patterson, who was preparing for a July rematch with the awesome new champion, Sonny Liston, told them with expressive humility how the televised news footage of Birmingham had moved him. "And I've got my training camp," he said, "and I felt very guilty . . . that here I was sitting in camp watching you people, my people, go through this . . . And I would like to thank you from the bottom of my heart." When Patterson sat down, a bandaged but dapper Wyatt Walker came forward. "It does not take long to introduce Jackie Robinson," he said snappily. "You can do it as quick as you can say Jackie Robinson." And the gray-haired baseball immortal drew a river of sighs and cheers that eclipsed even King's.

"I don't think you realize down here in Birmingham what you mean to us up there in New York," said Robinson. "And I don't think white Americans understand what Birmingham means to all of us throughout the country." Normally a facile public speaker, Robinson said haltingly that he could not express himself, could not explain it, that the only thing he could think to tell them was that when he left New York his three children had wanted to come with him to go to jail too, because they had seen Birmingham children going to jail for what they believed in. "I can't help getting emotional about this thing," he said. ". . . And I wish that this same kind of enthusiasm that has shown right here in this church tonight could be shown to Negroes through America."

"I am convinced that the agreements that have been made will be met," King told the congregation. With the Alabama troopers and the Army soldiers locked in a stalemate, the movement's followers could hope again, but the long trail of ordeal had honed King's optimism down to a fierce determination. "We *must* have faith in our movement," he declared with all his passion. "And another thing we must realize—this is not a racial conflict basically. I want you to understand me here. We are *not* going to allow this conflict in Birmingham to deteriorate into a struggle between black people and white people. The tension in Birmingham is between justice and injustice." Their goal was to enlist "consciences," not skin colors, he said, as their cause was as broad as religion and democracy. He insisted that some white people in Birmingham were with them secretly, or in spirit. One had even called with an offer to rebuild A. D. King's parsonage. "I do not know," King intoned. "They may try to bomb a little more." He drew gasps by announcing that a Negro pedestrian named Prince Green, of Coosa Street, was in the hospital after being shot from a passing car that evening. They would keep going through bombings and shootings. "I'm sorry," King cried out, "but I will *never* teach any of you to hate white people."

Ralph Abernathy coaxed from the congregation a "love offering" of $600 for Fred Shuttlesworth, who was still in bed since Friday's collapse at the victory press conference. Shuttlesworth did not reappear until after King left town, but on Wednesday he made an entrance leaning on the arms of two retainers, and spoke with his old vigor. "I have just about de-bulled ol' Bull!" he roared. "I didn't know it would take me seven years." By then King was in Cleveland. It was May 15—"some six or seven weeks," as he put it, since the birth of his daughter at the commencement of Project C, and nearly two weeks since the first children's march of May 2. Only after he emerged from Birmingham's long dark tunnel did he begin to see how drastically everything, including his own life, had changed.

TWENTY-ONE

FIRESTORM

Mobbed at the airport, King motorcaded like an astronaut through the streets of Cleveland to St. Paul's Episcopal Church for what amounted to the first white mass meeting of the civil rights movement. His separate constituencies suddenly blended into jumbled hordes. In a whirlwind twelve hours, he gave six speeches and a television interview. After posing with the Episcopal bishop of Ohio, he complied with Negro photographers who insisted that Wyatt Walker lift his shirt so that King could point solemnly to his rib bruises. At his second stop in Cleveland, traffic was jammed for twenty blocks around Cory Methodist Church, a converted Jewish synagogue, where churchwomen with picnic baskets had been encamped for as long as nine hours. Finding it impossible to squeeze King through the crush of bodies, the sponsors diverted the over-flow to three Negro churches nearby, and squadrons of Cleveland police shuttled King among the congregations while Abernathy and Walker held off the crowds. An enterprising man ran extension cords out of one church and sold hookups to those who wanted to record King's address. The evening's live audience exceeded ten thousand, and the SCLC netted $15,000 from the offerings. "I've never seen a more aroused response," King exclaimed from one pulpit.

It was as though the Birmingham movement had been transplanted magically to Cleveland. Scarcely pausing, King spent a day holding the truce in Birmingham and then a night in New York with Harry Belafonte, who told him that Hollywood and Los Angeles were mobilizing to top Cleveland's welcome. From Chicago, Mahalia Jackson said people were so worked up over Birmingham that she could turn out the entire city to hear King. She vowed to do just that within a week.

That Sunday, the New York *Post* discovered King's month-old "Letter from Birmingham Jail." Much to Stanley Levison's regret, the two-page scoop killed interest in the "Letter" at the *Times*, where the editors had just told King and Levison that they had it "cut down and ready to be put in type" for the Sunday *Magazine*. Although the *Times* quickly yanked the excerpt from the publishing schedule, lesser journals were not so put off by the competitive staleness, and the "Letter" sprouted on the covers of *Liberation, Christian Century, The Witness, Friends,* and *The Mennonite,* among others. Within days, Levison sold reprint rights to the *Atlantic Monthly* for $600, and Clarence Jones soon mounted a campaign to stop wildcat circulation in order to protect King's copyright for book negotiations. William Kunstler took the initiative for a book to be written jointly by King and himself, but Stanley Levison maneuvered Kunstler aside as an "opportunist." The feverish excitement over Birmingham penetrated even the New York literary establishment, where a publisher suggested to Levison the eventual title of King's third book, *Why We Can't Wait.*

In Birmingham, King helped foil a churlish attempt by the Connor forces to expel two thousand child marchers from school, then flew off the next weekend to a rally of nearly fifty thousand in Los Angeles. The audience, clutching programs that bore pictures of snarling Birmingham police dogs, filled the seats and aisles of the old Wrigley Field and then spilled across the field and out into the parking lot. The largest civil rights rally to date was also the first integrated mass meeting, and self-consciousness hung beneath the excitement. Whites and Negroes were shy or excessively polite to each other, like strangers at a freshman dance. With awkward sincerity, Paul Newman read a list of actors and California politicians "who have evinced concern and interest." A soprano drew nervous coughs when she trilled heroic r's through "Right On, King Jesus." Wyatt Walker quickly sat down after his early pronouncements—"I am America's *new* black Joe"—fell flat. SNCC's Sam Block tried to make a short speech about Greenwood, but stage fright reduced him to cardboard words about "trying to make the world safe for democracy."

Of all the speakers, only King was at home. He personified Birmingham to nearly everyone there, and he did not have to change his delivery much to suit an integrated audience. Having always aimed his speeches

at the common spine, he opened quietly with the trigger line from his
first speech of the Montgomery bus boycott: "There comes a time when
people get tired of being trampled over by the iron feet of oppression."
The crowd rose with him through three perorations. Near the end, one
ecstatic woman could be heard shrieking in the tones of a wolf whistle.
"Now the Governor of Alabama has said that he will stand in the door
to try to prevent a Negro from entering the University on June the
tenth," King declared. "And I think that if the Governor of Alabama will
present his body by standing in the door to preserve an evil system, then
President Kennedy ought to go to Tuscaloosa and personally escort the
student into the university with *his* body! And I think that would be a
magnificent witness for what this nation stands for." He kept the crowd
near a roar through his final run from "The Battle Hymn of the Republic."

After the rally, Burt and Norma Lancaster hosted a reception in Beverly
Hills, for which California governor Edmund G. Brown had sent out the
invitations. A brassy Hollywood lawyer got down to business by announcing that it took $1,000 in hard cash to run the SCLC movement
each day. Paul Newman wrote the first $1,000 check, singer Polly Bergen
the second, actor Tony Franciosa the third. Actors John Forsythe and
Lloyd Bridges contributed, as did the wife of basketball star Elgin Baylor.
Marlon Brando mumbled a warning against "what-we-have-doneism"
and bought a week of the movement for $5,000. Sammy Davis, Jr.,
matched the reception's total receipts with his own pledge of $20,000.
Together with Wrigley Field contributions of $35,000, the evening
brought the SCLC $75,000. Awed by the glitter and money, a *Jet* reporter
wrote that "We Shall Overcome" rang out from the Lancaster home "like
Wings Over Jordan in Beverly Hills."

Then King flew to a different kind of awe in the heartland: riding in an
open car amid a fleet of limousines, rushing through the streets of Chicago behind the roar of police motorcycles and the wail of sirens to city
hall for an official welcome by Mayor Daley. The mayor, looking only
slightly uncomfortable, joined the motorcade to the city-owned Mc-
Cormick Place on the shore of Lake Michigan, where for nearly an hour
he stood backstage with King as Mahalia Jackson fussed over them,
straightening their ties and thundering at the stagehands and musicians
who were delaying her big night. Then, finally, Mayor Daley welcomed
the heroes of Birmingham. In his own speech King was hard-pressed to
match the dueling headliners—Mahalia Jackson, queen of gospel, appearing for once with her archrival Dinah Washington, queen of the blues.
The three of them held the overflow crowd until two o'clock in the
morning, when young Aretha Franklin topped them all with her closing

hymn. Only twenty-one, already a battered wife and the mother of two
children aged six and four, she had seen the underside of church glamour
as the daughter of big-time singing preacher C. L. Franklin ("The Man
with the Million-Dollar Voice"). Aretha Franklin still remained four
years away from crossover stardom as Lady Soul, but she gave the whites
in her audience a glimpse of the future. She wrung them all inside out
with the Thomas Dorsey classic "Precious Lord, Take My Hand," and by
the time she finished few doubted that for one night they had held the
most favored spot on earth. Franklin herself was so moved by the privilege of singing at King's rally that she slipped four $100 bills into Mahalia
Jackson's hand on stage.

Wyatt Walker stayed behind in Chicago to help count the evening's
receipts, which netted the SCLC $40,000. King himself went ahead to
Kentucky, where the mayor of Louisville led an escort to the Civic Auditorium, then on to St. Louis for yet another giant rally, always calling
upon President Kennedy to issue a Second Emancipation Proclamation
against segregation. A single week's events had brought some $150,000
to the SCLC, which went a long way toward repaying the portion of the
Birmingham bond money that had been advanced as loans. Financially,
the movement was reaping a bonanza. Stanley Levison pronounced himself "flabbergasted" that the one, neutered ad in *The New York Times*
had generated ten times its cost in revenue, with responses still coming
in weeks after publication.

King's associates were fanning out to help meet the demand for
speeches about Birmingham. Atlantic City wanted King, was promised
Abernathy, and finally got Fireball Smith. Wyatt Walker darted off to
speeches as far apart as Albany and San Francisco. In the latter city,
Bernard Lee came behind Walker to lead an integrated march of some
20,000 people to a rally at the Civic Center, where Police Chief Thomas
Cahill donated the first five dollars "to help the people of Birmingham."
Lee also made a speech to the embattled movement in Greenwood, Mis-
sissippi. "He whooped," Annell Ponder wrote thankfully to King, saying
Greenwood needed the boost.

Birmingham had suddenly changed King from a tireless drone on the
speaking circuit to the star of a swarming hive. And beyond the rallies of
support as far away as Birmingham, England, and Havana, Cuba, a host
of spontaneous actions made news. Clergymen in the manicured white
suburb of Greenwich, Connecticut, united to fight segregation. Duke
University announced the admission of its first Negro students. Demonstrations spread arrests to a new city almost every day in May: 34
arrested in Raleigh, nearly 100 in Albany, 400 in Greensboro, 1,000 in
Durham, North Carolina.

•   •   •

The same winds that lifted King from behind struck the Kennedy Administration in the face. Intelligence reports noted that the Soviet Union
broadcast 1,420 anti-U.S. commentaries about the Birmingham crisis
during the two weeks following the settlement—seven times more than
at the worst of the Ole Miss–Meredith crisis, nine times the peak during
the Freedom Rides. When President Kennedy sent a message on May 21
to a summit conference of the independent African nations, stressing the
importance of unity in the free world, Prime Minister Milton Obote of
Uganda replied with an official protest against the fire hoses and "snarling dogs" of Birmingham. President Kennedy saw that even one of his
own soldiers was allowed to march in support of the Birmingham movement at a remote Air Force base in South Dakota, and that such a pid-
dling event made the news. "How the hell did this happen?" he
demanded of Lee White.

On May 20 and 21, President Kennedy privately consulted his government on the repercussions from Birmingham. One problem, the Attorney
General told the full cabinet, was that the federal government itself
maintained a largely segregated work force. In Birmingham, "there
weren't any Negroes that held any positions where anybody could see
them," and the businessmen had demanded to know, " 'Why should we
hire Negroes? *You* don't hire Negroes.' " Kennedy introduced Civil Service Commission chairman John Macy for a quick summary of the numbers elsewhere: of 405 U.S. Treasury employees in Nashville, there were
four Negroes, all clerks; of 249 Agriculture Department employees in
Nashville, two Negro clerks; of 114 employees at Labor and Commerce,
no Negroes at all. Rolling out similar statistics for other Southern cities,
Macy endorsed the Attorney General's view that it was better to address
them early than "just wait until they flare up."

More privately, with Burke Marshall and his closest political advisers,
President Kennedy assessed the threat of serial, Birmingham-style eruptions. "There must be a dozen places where we're having major problems
today," said the Attorney General, adding that the mood of Birmingham
was spreading among Northern Negroes too. Only the day before, he
reported, Mayor Daley of Chicago had predicted "a lot of trouble," saying
that Negroes in underworld bars suddenly were snickering, not running,
when a white police captain walked in. Daley had said, "The Negroes
are all mad for no reason at all," Kennedy reported, "and they want to
fight . . . He says you can't have a moderate Negro any more." On this
point, Lawrence O'Brien remarked that Adam Clayton Powell had told
him candidly that the new militancy of Negro leadership was "very

simple": "He said, 'I'm not going to watch the parade pass me by. I'm gonna lead it.' " From confidential sessions with Dick Gregory, Marshall and Robert Kennedy reported that competition and ill will among Negro leaders made it impossible for them to be reasonable. "Roy Wilkins hates Martin Luther King," said the Attorney General. He recalled Gregory's quip that even his maid was sassing him, and joked that he had advised Gregory to fire her.

The Kennedy advisers isolated their dilemma: if the uprising would not die down among the Negro masses, and could not be dampened by Negro leaders, how could they avoid a nightmarish string of Birminghams? President Kennedy toyed briefly with legislating "a reasonable limitation of the right to demonstrate," but switched quickly to the idea of civil rights legislation. All his aides recognized that legislation on some of the basic Negro demands offered the advantage of "biting the bullet"—of getting past the dilemma with one difficult but sweeping move. However, they were split on what such a bill should include. Sorensen, O'Brien, and Kenneth O'Donnell stressed the political liabilities of an accommodations law that would explicitly integrate public facilities such as lunch counters. They favored instead Title III, the famous provision stricken from the 1957 Civil Rights Act, which would give the Justice Department broad powers to initiate suits for equal protection under the law. But, the very features that made Title III palatable to the political advisers made the Justice Department cringe: it was piecemeal, discretionary, and vague. Pressures would concentrate on the Attorney General, who would be charged with protecting every Negro demonstration and seeking the integration of every swimming pool. Having denied such authority in the Bob Moses lawsuit, Marshall told President Kennedy that he did not *want* that authority, either. Robert Kennedy agreed. With Title III, he said, Negroes would be "lining up outside . . . Everybody would have a suit, and we'd be the ones who would be doing it." He said Title III would be "unhelpful . . . just awful."

When O'Donnell and the others said Title III was vital because it was the established litmus test of civil rights legislation, President Kennedy asked, "How will we get away with *not* sending any Title III?" On the other hand, he agreed with Marshall that whereas Title III was messy, a public accommodations law would appeal to Negroes because it would have "a personal impact on their daily lives." He asked pointedly whether such a law would include movie theaters. Told that it would, he said brusquely, "Well, we've got to get that one by. I mean, that's just a basic. We've got to have it." On matters like integrated movie theaters, President Kennedy was inclined to dismiss the pangs of white Southerners. To him, school integration was a tough issue because it touched real fears of class and status, as did jobs and voting. But sitting with Negroes was at worst a requirement of public civility in the modern world. He doubted that Southerners were as "sore" about public accommodations as they claimed. "And I don't care if they're sore on that," he said. "I mean, we can't go around saying you can't demonstrate . . . and they can't get a solution."

By the end of the meeting, President Kennedy leaned toward proposing a civil rights bill. Nearly everything about it was in flux, however, and his own political people were far from reconciled to a public accommodations section. For the immediate future, Robert Kennedy was in a rush to hold a series of off-the-record meetings at the White House with governors, mayors, theater owners, chain-store owners, lawyers, preachers, civil rights leaders, and others—both to lobby for national action and to take soundings on their course. The President agreed, stipulating only that any meeting with Martin Luther King come late in the series. "Otherwise, it will look like he got me to do it," said the President. "The trouble with King is that everybody thinks he's our boy, anyway. So everything he does, everybody says we stuck him in there. We ought to have him well surrounded . . . King is so hot these days that it's like Marx coming to the White House. I'd like to have some Southern governors, or mayors, or businessmen first. And my program should have gone up to the Hill first."

Publicly, the Administration continued to dwell on more comfortable business such as the splashdown of astronaut Gordon Cooper. When pressed for comment about racial demonstrations, officials confined their remarks to calls for sensible progress. The scruffy odyssey of the actual deliberations remained unknown until the disclosure a generation later of a hidden recording system in the Kennedy White House, and the only contemporary hint of the jittery nerves and psychic dramas was Robert Kennedy's painful encounter with author James Baldwin, as leaked to *The New York Times*. Dick Gregory had suggested in his confidential briefings that Robert Kennedy consult Baldwin, and Kennedy, needing shortcuts, introduced himself to Baldwin with a spontaneous request that he assemble a group of deep thinkers to explain both the new anger of the masses and the inability of Negro leaders to dampen it. The next day, May 24, Baldwin produced a haphazard assortment that included his brother, his lawyer, his secretary, his literary agent, a television producer, a white woman who worked for the NAACP, and the director of the Chicago Urban League, who had brought with him a young friend from CORE. Kenneth Clark appeared as the reigning academic, and lu-

minaries from the arts included Harry Belafonte, Lena Horne, and play-
wright Lorraine Hansberry, author of *A Raisin in the Sun*. As the guests
gathered secretly in Joseph Kennedy's family apartment near the Plaza
Hotel, a mystified Belafonte wondered why, in the political crisis after
Birmingham, Robert Kennedy wanted an emergency meeting with such
a menagerie rather than with the Negro civil rights leaders themselves.

Robert Kennedy arrived with Burke Marshall and his press aide Ed
Guthman, straight from a secret meeting with Harry Wachtel's nervous
cabal of Northern chain-store owners. The Baldwin session began innocently enough with a review by the Attorney General of the Administration's unprecedented commitment to civil rights, and with mild
challenges from guests who said that Kennedy must do more. The Attorney General replied that impatience in the Negro community seemed to
be rising independently of his efforts—that while every conceivable measure was being considered, and more action was in the works, Negroes
were listening to dangerous extremists such as the Black Muslims, which
could cause real trouble. Then the young CORE man shattered the parlor
mood like an eggshell. "You don't have no idea what trouble is," he told
Kennedy. "Because I'm close to the moment where I'm ready to take up
a gun."

This was Jerome Smith, who with Doris Castle had answered James
Farmer's desperate call for CORE volunteers on the first Freedom Ride
from Montgomery into Mississippi. Upon release from Parchman Penitentiary, he had endured a series of beatings for attempting to integrate
bus facilities in McComb, Mississippi, after even Bob Moses abandoned
the region as too violent, and since then he had worked as a sometimes-
paid CORE worker across the South, most recently in North Carolina.
The particulars of Smith's work were not well known to most of the
Negroes in the room, let alone to Kennedy. Smith had a speech impediment that thickened when he was upset, and now, stammering with
emotion, he told the Attorney General that the Black Muslims were no
threat to anyone, because they risked nothing. In Birmingham, Jeremiah
X had stood on the side and watched while children faced the dogs and
fire hoses. The Negro masses knew who was on the line, said Smith, and
the real trouble would come if those who had been willing to die became
disgusted with nonviolence. "When *I* pull the trigger," he said, "kiss it
goodbye."

The meeting never recovered. When Kennedy tried to skip past Smith's
rawness as a hobo's intrusion, Baldwin asked Smith whether he could
imagine fighting for the United States. "Never! Never!" cried Smith.
Baldwin hoped that this exchange would demonstrate to Kennedy the
seriousness of Smith's pacifism and the depth of his anguish, but the

Attorney General reacted instead to a lack of patriotism. "How can you say that?" he demanded. Smith and Kennedy talked past each other, with Smith ranting about prisons and beatings while Kennedy tried to put him straight about the seriousness of military obligations. Finally, Smith said that sitting there with Kennedy made him want to vomit. Baldwin saw this as a poetic statement of Smith's despair over the necessity of being there at all, of having to dramatize for the Attorney General the portent of such injustice; Kennedy saw it as an insult to himself and his office, and turned away to dismiss him. This brought Lorraine Hansberry to her feet to say that being there made her sick too. "You've got a great many very, very accomplished people in this room, Mr. Attorney General," she said archly, "but the only man who should be listened to is that man over there."

Belafonte, who had arrived worrying that Kennedy would take advantage of the entertainers in some scheme to undercut Negro protest or win the 1964 election, suddenly worried that the diatribes would make a permanent enemy of Kennedy. He tried to dispel the poison by recalling out loud the many hours he had spent around the pool at the Attorney General's home on Hickory Hill, discussing these same explosive issues without rancor. Clarence Jones, who was there as Baldwin's lawyer, picked up on Belafonte's lead by raising some suggestions he knew were dear to Martin Luther King, such as presidential "fireside chats" on race and an executive order on segregation. But it was too late. Kennedy scoffed at them all as impractical or silly. He laughed out loud when Jones mentioned King's idea that President Kennedy should fight segregation with the kind of dramatic gesture that Gandhi had employed against untouchability in India—with a new Emancipation Proclamation or by personally escorting the first Negro students past Governor Wallace's avowed blockade at the schoolhouse door. Burke Marshall laughed too. The Negroes, for their part, laughed when Kennedy defended Harold Cox and other segregationist appointees as upright jurists, and again when Marshall spoke of the "special men" from the Justice Department who helped the FBI protect civil rights workers. Kennedy considered the Negroes hopelessly naïve about big-time politics; they considered him just as naïve about race. The two sides jerked apart, past frustration and disbelief to drained hysteria, laughing at each other. Hansberry ended it by leading a walk-out from what Kenneth Clark called "*the* most dramatic experience I have ever had."

In the aftermath, Clarence Jones tried to apply a professional glaze to the abrasions by introducing himself to Kennedy with the easy warmth of an opposing lawyer on lunch break. Shaking Kennedy's hand, Jones said he knew Marshall from Birmingham, where as King's lawyer he was aware of some of the Justice Department's labors. "I wish you had spoken up and said something about that," Kennedy replied. These parting words hardened fatefully. When he heard from Marshall that the Attorney General considered him a weak hypocrite for failing to defend the Administration, Jones complained to Stanley Levison of Kennedy's arrogance in assuming that the Administration's secret role in Birmingham had been wholly positive, and that Jones could have offset the statements from Kennedy's own mouth. "Each time he said something, it merely underlined the deep gulf," Jones told Levison, who replied that Kennedy and Marshall were under the "mad illusion that they and not the Negroes won the Birmingham battle."

To Kennedy, on the other hand, Clarence Jones made a first impression of cowardly defection. When James Baldwin leaked word of the disastrous meeting to *The New York Times*—"Robert Kennedy Fails to Sway Negroes at Secret Talks Here"—the Attorney General countered by featuring Jones in leaks to the *Times*'s James Reston and others about how Negro "moderates" were bailing out under pressure, leaving the Kennedy Administration alone between the extremists of both races. When Jones defended himself in a letter to the *Times*, Kennedy scratched a caustic note to Burke Marshall across his copy: "He is a nice fellow & you have swell friends." From reports on the Baldwin guests supplied swiftly by the FBI, Kennedy seized upon the fact that Jones was among three Negroes married to whites,* and he grumbled that they must be suffering from psychological "complexes" about living so comfortably apart from their race. Almost certainly, Kennedy's personal enmity contributed to his decision some weeks later to authorize FBI wiretaps on Jones's home. By quirk of timing, this wiretap first opened to J. Edgar Hoover the details of Martin Luther King's private life.

In other respects, Robert Kennedy's reaction to the Baldwin meeting was more fluid. Only days after leaving in a cold fury, he told Guthman that perhaps he would feel that strongly against his country if he had grown up a Negro. His anger had at first frightened Arthur Schlesinger, but the historian saw him change quickly. Perhaps Kennedy's most characteristic and telling response was an intermediate one: he channeled the rage toward others. Within days, he began to erupt at sleepy inter-

---

* Clarence Jones had married Ann Norton, daughter of the founder of the prestigious W. W. Norton publishing company, in 1956. Jones's father, still a Lippincott chauffeur, hosted the Waldorf reception after one of New York high society's first interracial weddings. For the groom, the most lasting irony was that his widowed new mother-in-law married the financial adviser to President Hendrik Verwoerd, the architect of apartheid.

agency meetings on Negro hiring. His tongue-lashings on the lack of action were so startling and personal that they humiliated the targets, most frequently Lyndon Johnson. The Vice President chaired the President's Committee on Equal Employment Opportunity, carrying out a task which, like most of his assignments, did not engage the President. Johnson's exclusion from the Administration's inner core was so complete that he had not been consulted even about how to get emergency civil rights legislation past his fellow Southerners in the Senate, and Lawrence O'Brien reported to President Kennedy that Johnson was alarmingly meek in legislative meetings. Later, when asked directly for an opinion by President Kennedy, the Vice President almost whispered that inasmuch as he had seen none of the drafts of the bill and knew only about the general race problem "from what I've read in the press . . . I'm not competent to counsel you." For the once-mighty Johnson, the semipublic scoldings added to a store of grievances against the younger Kennedy.

As an authentic disaster, the Baldwin meeting made Robert Kennedy a pioneer in the raw, interracial encounters of the 1960s. Hard upon Birmingham and his previous ordeals in civil rights, the experience knocked the Attorney General off balance. What was intensely personal no longer seemed so distinct from policy, nor public from private. The drive to hire Negroes in the federal government became an obsession to him, but it could not be publicly mentioned without drawing attention to embarrassing realities. For Kennedy, it required a new gyroscope to learn what was appropriate for what audiences at what times, when to "feel" like a Negro and when not. Ironically, these anxieties gave Kennedy a dose of Du Bois's "twoness" and King's "tip-toe stance" just as King himself was having a taste of Camelot.

Unexpectedly, the next major storm came by way of Jackson, Mississippi, where conflicting pressures were nearly tearing Medgar Evers apart. Only two days after King had announced the settlement victory in Birmingham, Evers spoke for the NAACP in publicly demanding that the city of Jackson appoint a biracial committee to negotiate the same grievances. Mayor Allen Thompson rejected the idea so vehemently that a local television station granted Evers air time for a response, and the novelty of a direct broadcast from a Negro ("In the racial picture things will never be as they once were," Evers said. "History has reached a turning point, here and over the world") made him the focal point of tensions between the races. Just then he received a set of shackling, paranoid instructions from his immediate boss in New York, Gloster B.

Current. "I suspect that Jackson, Mississippi, will be the next scene of attack by the King forces," warned the NAACP's director of branches, "... but whatever target is selected next, it will make it that much harder for the NAACP to carry on its work effectively." Current instructed his Southern representatives to "hit hard" and quickly, "as soon as the Birmingham crisis is past." For Evers, these were unenviable orders. He was to reproduce the jail-battered, tentative miracle of Birmingham independently—without mass marches, nonviolent oratory, or other methods that smacked of King.

At mass meetings through the rest of May, Evers spearheaded a quest for negotiations. When Mayor Thompson easily dodged—once by announcing that he would meet with a biracial committee of his own choosing, specifying Negro members who had praised his stand on segregation—Evers tried to tighten the NAACP boycott against selected local companies that advertised their support of the White Citizens Councils. Finally, on May 28, the Negroes of Jackson erupted joyfully over news that Mayor Thompson has agreed to appoint a legitimate biracial committee and to desegregate public facilities and city jobs, including the police force. It was almost the entire Birmingham package, except for the integration of lunch counters, but Thompson squelched the celebration within a few hours by disowning the agreement as a misunderstanding. Under the sting of this disappointment, pressure for direct action broke loose that same day.

Four students and a white professor from Tougaloo College staged a sit-in at the Woolworth's lunch counter in Jackson. It lasted for three hours, which gave converging reporters plenty of time to record the details. A mob of young whites took turns slathering the demonstrators with ketchup, mustard, and sugar—a scene graphically depicted in the next issue of *Newsweek*. After dragging them off the stools only to watch them return, the whites doused them with spray paint and then, growing annoyed, began sporadically to beat them. The tormentors darted forward to pour salt into the professor's head wound after someone clubbed him to the floor. An ex-policeman named Benny Oliver brazenly kicked demonstrator Memphis Norman's face bloody until a policeman emerged to arrest them both. A photograph of the kicking appeared on the front page of the next morning's *New York Times*.

In Jackson, the flash of emotion was such that one shoeless, begrimed demonstrator found herself being rushed ahead of waiting customers at a nearby beauty shop, where fluttering attendants washed her hair and stockings and almost sacramentally wiped dried mustard from her legs, just so she would be presentable for the mass meeting. An overflow crowd gave Medgar Evers one standing ovation when he entered the Pearl

Street A.M.E. Church that night, then another when he introduced the heroes of Woolworth's. Finally, a standing ovation that seemed endless —perhaps twenty minutes or more—greeted his announcement that the NAACP was officially launched upon a "massive offensive" against segregation in Jackson. Evers himself remained skewered between inspiration and misgiving. He had not endorsed the sit-in, much less planned it. Aside from his own private doubts about the discipline of the young people, and his worries about suicidal violence in the crucible of Mississippi, he was burdened by the heavy oversight of his superiors. Although he could claim credit for the demonstrators as active members of his NAACP Youth Council, he knew that the critical motivation for their sit-in came from their peers. Some of them had been shuttling to Greenwood on weekends since March. The one who had received the emergency beauty treatment confessed to near worship of Bob Moses, who that week was holding voter registration workshops at Tougaloo College. Such people could not be content with the NAACP boycott of Barq's soft drinks and Hart's bread.

Evers straddled the divide. In his speeches, he mixed the NAACP's tactics ("Don't shop for anything on Capitol Street!") with the spirit of the students ("We'll be demonstrating here until freedom comes"). Privately, he used the standard NAACP arguments to discourage the students from further demonstrations: they had not realistically defined their goals, and they could not expect others to pick up the cost of their defense. But when a group of students returned downtown the next day in spite of his counsel, and nineteen were thrown in jail off picket lines, Evers rose in the mass meeting to praise their courage. He did not object when David Dennis of CORE and other youth leaders told the young Negroes of Jackson to "bring your toothbrushes" to the next day's demonstration, nor did he resist the advice of a high school junior who took the pulpit: "To our parents we say we wish you'd come along with us, but if you won't, at least don't try to stop us." At the march on May 31, Evers watched policemen take some six hundred schoolchildren to a makeshift jail at the state fairgrounds, hauling many of them in garbage trucks.

Few students begrudged his role. Evers was likable, less abrupt than most adult leaders, and he had been there without flinching since the cold days of Emmett Till. He was the acknowledged leader—the one who stood up personally to Mayor Thompson, who negotiated their bail, who received nearly all the death threats. Moreover, the students could see his identification with their cause etched deeply in his face, as Evers was a man of guile but not hypocrisy or cowardice. He was in revolt against his artificial role as spokesman aloof from strategy. Because the

Jackson movement had exploded so obviously as a clone of Birmingham, he consulted Martin Luther King covertly about what to do. And he called Roy Wilkins. With more than six hundred Negroes in jail, and all Jackson aroused because of them, they could no longer pretend that direct action was incidental to the struggle. Wilkins recognized that the student sit-ins, not the boycott, had made Jackson into front-page news for four straight days. He made it five on June 1, by flying to Jackson to be arrested with Evers off a picket line outside Woolworth's.

On May 30, King sent telegrams to President Kennedy and the Attorney General requesting a personal audience with them "to avert an unnecessary national calamity." What King hoped was that now, with the worldwide protest over Birmingham, he could finally persuade President Kennedy to issue the executive order against segregation. Stanley Levison endorsed King's strategy with the observation that no Administration had ever been so worried about the Negro problem as the Kennedys were now. FBI wiretaps on Stanley Levison's home phone enabled J. Edgar Hoover to dispatch his couriers with advance warning of King's telegrams—of King's expressed hope "to put so much pressure on the President that he will have to sign an Executive Order"—and to note that King was formulating such plans with a "secret member of the Communist Party." King, of course, did not know of the wiretap, nor of Kennedy's earlier resolve not to receive him while he was so "hot." All he knew was that Lee White declined his request on the grounds that President Kennedy was too busy.

It was almost midnight on June 1 when King placed a conference call to Levison and Clarence Jones to discuss his response. He opened with a bit of news for the New Yorkers, telling them that Roy Wilkins was in jail in Jackson, Mississippi. Medgar Evers had called again, he said, but had disclosed none of his plans because he believed the Jackson police were tapping his phone. For King, Wilkins' first arrest in nearly thirty years was a sober but hopeful development. "We've baptized brother Wilkins," he said. Levison said they could expect new things like that to spread through the Southern cities, and he suggested a special SCLC meeting to discuss how to respond. Jones talked of mobilization discussions he had attended with New York church groups.

King cut them off. "We are on a breakthrough," he said gravely. "We need a mass protest." They must take advantage of the fever he felt sweeping ahead of them. What he had in mind was a "mass march" on Washington "and also a unified demonstration all over America." He said Paul Newman and Marlon Brando, both "Kennedy men," had offered to help, and so had trade unions across the country. Levison caught the rush of King's thought and chimed in that Phil Randolph would join too. To influence President Kennedy to "really push" civil rights legislation, they agreed that a march of "possibly a hundred thousand people" on Washington was needed, and that such a monstrosity could not be organized before August.

King told them to contact Philip Randolph and signed off, leaving Jones and Levison to soar away in appreciation of his sudden audacity. For days they treasured this one phone call among thousands. In an uncharacteristic gush, Levison told Jones's wife Ann that "you tingled" when King talked that way about historical opportunity, and he confessed that his own ideas were "a step behind Martin." Jones kept saying he was "thrilled by the conversation." "We both know that Martin is a very cautious and thoughtful person," declared Jones, "and he is saying the hour is now." The FBI's wiretap stenographer summarized their glowing reprise: "They agree that all sorts of very exciting things are happening."

When Wilkins flew back to New York from the Jackson jail, he left behind negotiating demands identical to King's in Birmingham, but a modified strategy. While Evers and other NAACP spokesmen announced a "second phase" of smaller demonstrations, a battery of the NAACP Legal Defense Fund's best lawyers filed lawsuits in support of the demands. To keep up spirits at the nightly mass meetings, Wilkins recruited celebrities such as Lena Horne, who had volunteered her services after the traumatic challenge of the James Baldwin–Robert Kennedy meeting. Mayor Thompson kept them off balance by extending and withdrawing concessions. One day Evers announced that Thompson had promised to hire the first twelve Negro policemen within thirty days. Then the promise vanished, and Thompson announced instead that he had secured a court order banning further demonstrations. While opposing lawyers quarreled over its legality, students went defiantly to jail in wildcat demonstrations. The strain so eroded Medgar Evers' nerves that one night, hearing a noise, he stalked through his house with his rifle, only to come upon his nine-year-old son in the bathroom.

The stalemate dropped Jackson out of the headlines during the first week of June, when Pope John XXIII died in Rome and President Kennedy made a political trip to Honolulu. Political commentators speculated intensely about the Administration's internal debate over what kind of civil rights legislation to propose. Tear gas and 257 arrests made news of continuing demonstrations against segregated movie theaters in Tallahassee, Florida. In North Carolina alone, major demonstrations continued in half a dozen cities, including Lexington and Greensboro, where on June 6 police arrested 278 students led by Jesse Jackson, student-body president at North Carolina A&T.* Fresh racial dramas diverted attention as far away as Newfoundland, where forty Negro soldiers protested their exclusion from Charlie's Snack Bar, near their Strategic Air Command flight station. Still, events were drawing a wide variety of movement characters back to Mississippi, as though to assemble them all for the assassination of Medgar Evers.

John Doar was already there. Since leaving his wife and newborn son at a hospital delivery room on May 14, he had not been back to Washington and scarcely had time to call home. His emergency cases included the attempted expulsion of the Birmingham schoolchildren and the charges that Hartman Turnbow and Bob Moses had conspired to bomb Turnbow's home, plus a host of legal/military preparations for anticipated battles over university integration. The latter issue kept him shuttling between Alabama and Mississippi. On June 5, Doar successfully escorted the first Negro student into the law school at Ole Miss.

By then Bob Moses, free on another bail bond, was returning from a trip North. During the eruptions in Jackson, he testified with Charles Sherrod and Timothy Jenkins before a hearing of the House Judiciary Committee. In a New York speech on June 3, Moses remarked that if the Justice Department had not dropped its protective lawsuit in Greenwood, "Negroes would still be marching downtown to the courthouse today." He qualified himself almost in the next sentence, however, not wishing to make self-serving or exaggerated claims. "The Negro community at that time—before Birmingham—was not ready to demonstrate *en masse*," he conceded. "The thinking was that adults should be going down, and not children. And so we didn't have sustained marches of people." Nearly two years before King would launch huge marches at Selma, Moses envisioned applying the pressures of mass direct action to voter registration. "Now, after Birmingham, it may be possible to launch this kind of thing," he told his tiny audience. "I'm not sure. Of course, Birmingham is directly responsible for what's going on in Jackson now." Moses made his way back to Mississippi in time for a week-long training workshop on Monday, June 10. Its leaders were to be Bernice Robinson of Highlander and Annell Ponder of the SCLC, but Ponder disappeared that Sunday morning.

---

* Jackson already had attracted notice in the Negro press as a sports star and precocious social leader. He had been elected second vice grand basileus of the national Omega Psi Phi fraternity. In these first political stories, he appeared in a snap-brim hat, telling his followers, "I'll go to jail and I'll go to the chain gang if necessary."

Ponder got as far as Winona by Trailways bus. With five recent graduates of her literacy school, she had made another run to Septima Clark's school. They had gone through a week's teacher-training classes—complete with a menu offering "Freedom Fighting Hot Rolls," "Full Citizenship Barbecued Chicken," "Literacy Potato Salad," and "Brotherhood Punch"—and then made the long journey back across Georgia and Alabama to the last rest stop before Greenwood, less than thirty miles away. The sight of Ponder walking into the whites' waiting room of the Winona bus station caused the waitress behind the counter to wad up her check pad and fling it at the wall in disgust, crying out, "I can't take no more." Police officers and a highway patrolman promptly came over and threw the Negroes out, notwithstanding Ponder's reminders of the pertinent ICC ruling of 1961. Standing outside on the pavement, humiliated in front of people she had just packed full of freedom songs and leadership lessons, Ponder decided to take down the license numbers of the police cruisers in order to file a complaint. This was too much for the senior officer, who ordered Ponder and her students arrested.

The assorted officers interrogated the prisoners one by one in the station-house booking room. First they asked June Johnson, a sixteen-year-old from Greenwood, whether she was a member of the NAACP, and when she admitted it, one officer started slapping her around. They asked who paid her and what kind of trouble her bosses were planning for Winona, and in the rising heat of the cuffings another officer hit her on the back of the head with a blackjack. They took the wailing Johnson back to a cell and brought out Annell Ponder—tall, schoolmarmish, and fatefully dignified. She said she and her friends did not hate them, she steadfastly refused their demands to say "sir" to them so long as they called her "nigger" and "bitch," and she admitted straightforwardly to the highway patrolman that she had been writing down his license number for a complaint to the federal government. All these answers enraged men who already had stepped over the line of violence. Cursing the name Bobby Kennedy, they kept beating Ponder to the floor and pulling her to her feet until her head was swollen and bloody, a tooth chipped, and one eye seemed knocked off line. Ponder held unsteadily to the corridor walls as they pushed her back toward the cells. She made a terrifying sight to her students, including Fannie Lou Hamer, who was next. By then vengeance had consumed her captors. They dragged Hamer into an empty cell, threw her face-down on a cot, and ordered a young Negro prisoner to beat her with a blackjack. When she screamed, they answered with taunts about whether she had seen Martin Luther King that day. They brought a second prisoner to sit on her legs, then to switch places with the first one when he got tired. Hamer was beaten until the fingers protecting her head were blue and the skin on her back swelled up hard

as a bone. Then the officers shut not only the cells but the station-house
doors, and began figuring out how to protect themselves against inquiries
that were sure to come.

At midnight, some twelve hours after the first blows in the Winona
station house, Wyatt Walker convened a conference call for King and his
closest advisers, who were scattered around the country. King solicited
advice about the proposed march on Washington. Was it feasible? Would
Philip Randolph agree to merge his October march for jobs with an August march for freedom? He introduced the questions in a way that left
no doubt about his own inclinations, saying "something dramatic must
be done" to support the civil rights bill that President Kennedy was
expected to introduce any day. "I don't think it will pass otherwise," said
King. "It will get him off the hook—he can use this thing politically by
saying he *tried* to get it, knowing all the time it can't pass."

For King, the primary question was whether to "center" the march on
President Kennedy or Congress. "I've had mixed emotions about the
President," he said. "I'm just not sure." A lengthy debate produced two
agreements.* First, they would aim the march against the clear and cer-
tain opposition of a Southern filibuster in the Senate. On this point only
Clarence Jones dissented, saying it would be impossible to match the
complex logistics of a huge march with the unpredictable timetable of
Congress. Second, they decided not to seek an advance alliance with Roy
Wilkins, for fear that Wilkins would stall or even preempt them with
public announcement of a conflicting NAACP conference, as he had
done to Randolph's plan for a June march against Negro unemployment.
Instead, they would secure a private agreement with Randolph and then
announce the march publicly to force Wilkins to go along. Stanley Levison urged King to make at least a preliminary announcement that week
in New York. As they were signing off, Andrew Young interjected the
news that Annell Ponder may have been arrested. "I got it second-hand
twenty minutes ago," he said. "I'm trying to get the FBI to investigate."

.   .   .

---

* Only Abernathy said nothing. Always quiet in such political discussions, he
was perhaps more preoccupied than usual, as that day he had basked at West
Hunter in a gala service of "Tribute to Our Pastor and First Lady," opening a
week-long celebration of Abernathy's second anniversary in that pulpit. The
panegyrics were lavishly detailed and slavishly fawning, extravagant even by the
standards common to preachers of his station.

The Winona mystery deepened when Lawrence Guyot, one of the SNCC students who had been jailed with Bob Moses in Greenwood, drove to the jail and disappeared himself, arrested and beaten when he asked the sheriff what had happened to his friends. While no outsider yet knew that Winona was a flytrap of violence, panic began to spread among movement insiders who knew that silence was an ominous sign. Wiley Branton tried desperately from Atlanta to find out what had happened, but he was told that he could get no information unless he had a client, and he could obtain no clients without coming to the jail. The FBI promised to investigate, but the Bureau maintained no field office in the state and its stringer agents were busy in Jackson. No agents reached Winona all of Monday, and John Doar, the federal official most likely to have responded personally to the crisis, had left Mississippi for Alabama, where on Tuesday Governor Wallace fulfilled his pledge to block integration by "standing in the schoolhouse door."

For weeks, Wallace and the Kennedy Administration had attracted national publicity as they maneuvered for the showdown. Kennedy had the leverage of the Army troops already mobilized in Alabama to support the Birmingham settlement, plus the benefit of his experience the previous fall at Ole Miss. Wallace, for his part, ensconced himself in a makeshift office on campus, near the designated registration spot, and there, behind a host of troopers and the hum of newly installed air-conditioners, he concealed his plans. In the end, Nicholas Katzenbach proceeded alone to meet Wallace, who stood at a lectern behind a line that his media advisers had painted on the ground as the symbolic threshold of segregation. Katzenbach announced that he had a proclamation from President Kennedy ordering Wallace to cease his illegal resistance to the federal court order on integration, and Wallace responded by reading a defiant proclamation of his own. "There can be no submission to the theory that the central government is anything but a servant of the people," he declared. "We are God-fearing people, not government-fearing people. We practice today the free heritage bequested to us by the Founding Fathers." When he finished, Katzenbach made Wallace physically bar the door by bumping ceremoniously toward him four times, and then Katzenbach retreated. Meanwhile, away from the cameras, the two Negro students proceeded quietly to their dormitory rooms, and Wallace did not oppose the National Guard units that later moved onto campus to defend them.

The tacit bargain between Wallace and the Administration contained hidden elements of some consequence. By holding the two Negro students back from the public confrontation—sending Katzenbach alone rather than in the usual escort role—Robert Kennedy ensured that Wallace did not actually block the two students he had been ordered to let through, which spared Kennedy the vexing "Mississippi" problem of prosecuting a sitting governor for contempt of court. The price was that Wallace was allowed to make his contemptuous nationwide address while looking upward at a representative of the federal government rather than downward upon the two Negroes whose rights were at issue. This difference helped elevate Wallace from the marginal stature of a Ross Barnett into a presidential contender. His stand against Washington and do-gooder bureaucrats planted a conservative standard which, further rinsed of overtly racial content, came to dominate American politics for more than a generation.

A lesser consequence was that President Kennedy felt pressure to deliver some compensatory showmanship. Just the night before, at American University, he had given a major address on the need to take risks toward a reduction in worldwide nuclear armaments. He announced a temporary suspension of nuclear tests in the atmosphere, a renewed effort to secure a test-ban treaty with the Soviet Union, and a conviction that "no government or social system is so evil that its people must be considered as lacking in virtue." Now on Tuesday the speech was an instant success, hailed as a step away from the Cold War and as a gesture of peace in the spirit of the late Pope John's *Pacem in Terris.* Yet the same front pages also told of the newest racial collisions—of twenty-five arrests outside the courthouse in Cambridge, Maryland, and of attacks worse than Bull Connor's in Danville, Virginia, where fire hoses and nightsticks sent to the hospital forty-eight of sixty-five Negroes protesting downtown segregation. ("We will hose down the demonstrators and fill every available stockade," proclaimed Mayor Julian Stinson of Danville.)

As President Kennedy and the Attorney General had anxiously awaited the outcome of the showdown with Governor Wallace, a telegram came in from Martin Luther King on the "beastly conduct of law enforcement officers at Danville." Asserting once again that "the Negro's endurance may be at the breaking point," King implored the Administration to seek a "just and moral" solution. "I ask you in the name of decency and Christian brotherhood to creatively grapple with Danville's and the nation's most grievous problem." There was a rougher, public message from King on the front page of *The New York Times.* Warning that the historic new legislation would be wasted if President Kennedy merely introduced it and then left for Europe, as he was planning to do, King said that supporters of the bill were prepared to stage a march on Washington. The *Times* highlighted King's assessment that its passage would require the "total weight of the President and his prestige," and quoted his plea that, above all, President Kennedy must begin speaking of race as a moral issue, in terms "we seldom if ever hear" from the White House.

Given his recent sensitivity to King's opinions, these urgings may have influenced President Kennedy's extraordinary decision to make what amounted to an extemporaneous civil rights address on national television. The causes were uncertain because the notion of a speech came so suddenly from the President himself, without a trace of the usual gestation within the government. When he startled his advisers on Tuesday with the thought that he might announce his civil rights legislation on television that night, no one liked the idea. Political advisers Kenneth O'Donnell and Lawrence O'Brien objected that the civil rights bill itself would carry more than enough political danger; they said the President should not magnify his risk with a personal commitment. To speechwriter Ted Sorensen, what made these drawbacks more compelling was Kennedy's precipitate haste. There was no speech draft. There had been no consultations with Congress or anyone else on what the President planned to say. To make a naked dash that very night on so sensitive an issue seemed like the worst sort of presidential whim, but Kennedy refused to let it go. Burke Marshall later remembered that Robert Kennedy alone had encouraged the speech idea, but the Attorney General himself remembered that his brother "just decided that day . . . He called me up on the phone and said that he was going to go on that night." Toward six o'clock that evening, President Kennedy ordered fifteen minutes of network time at eight. He gave Sorensen some general ideas and some scraps he liked from Louis Martin, then sent him off to write a speech within two hours.

Minutes before eight, Sorensen came into the Cabinet Room with a draft that President Kennedy found workable but stiff. He began tinkering to add paragraphs of fervor and rhetoric, dictating to Evelyn Lincoln while Sorensen cross-dictated to Gloria Liftman. They retyped pages and fragments, inserting them here or there in the stack as opinions changed in the mad fit of purpose. Everyone else in the room was aghast with the realization that there would be no finished text—that the leader of the free world was about to ad-lib on national television—but as the seconds ticked away the President was at his best, wired both hot and cool. "Come on now, Burke," he prompted. "You must have some ideas."

The President's first peroration before the cameras was a bit awkward, on the refrain "it ought to be possible," but then he broke through with a sketch from Louis Martin contrasting the life chances of two newborn American babies, one white and one Negro. "We are confronted primarily with a moral issue," he declared. "It is as old as the Scriptures and is as clear as the American Constitution. The heart of the question is whether all Americans are to be afforded equal rights and equal opportunities, whether we are going to treat our fellow Americans as we want to be treated."

These words brushed along a religious course that was starkly out of character for the worldly President. Their flow transformed even his approach to the global struggle:

> We preach freedom around the world, and we mean it. And we cherish our freedom here at home. But are we to say to the world—and much more importantly, to each other—that this is the land of the free, except for Negroes, that we have no second-class citizens, except Negroes, that we have no class or caste system, no ghettos, no master race, except with respect to Negroes?
>
> Now the time has come for this nation to fulfill its promise. The events in Birmingham and elsewhere have so increased the cries for equality that no city or state or legislative body can prudently choose to ignore them. . . . We face, therefore, a moral crisis as a country and a people . . . A great change is at hand, and our task, our obligation, is to make that revolution, that change, peaceful and constructive for all.

Kennedy wandered on and off his text, outlining his forthcoming legislation. He kept inserting parenthetical phrases signaling that race was no longer an issue of external charity or deflection: "We owe them, and we owe ourselves, a better country." When he ran out of text, he coasted unevenly to the end. By then, it didn't matter.

In Atlanta, King drafted an instant response, with errors characteristic of his own uncertain typing and spelling. "I have just listened to your speech to the nation," he wrote. "It was one of the most eloquent[,] profound and unequiv[oc]al pleas for Justice and the Freedom of all men ever made by any President. You spoke passionately to the moral issues involved in the integration struggle." An equally excited Stanley Levison called King that night to say that President Kennedy had done "what you have been asking him to do." To Levison, the historic speech underscored the importance of their decision to make Congress, not President Kennedy, the focus of the Washington demonstration.

In Jackson, all three Evers children, including toddler Van Dyke, tumbled in their parents' bed, arguing over which television program to watch. Their mother had allowed them to stay up past midnight to find out what their father thought of the President's wonderful speech, and they all rushed for the door when they heard his car. Medgar Evers was returning from a glum strategy session. All but nine of the seven hundred Jackson demonstrators were out of jail. Local white officials were claiming victory untainted by concession. Both the white and Negro press portrayed the Jackson movement as shrunken, listless, riddled by dissension. Privately, Evers had asked for permission to invite Martin Luther King to join forces, but his NAACP bosses ignored the heretical idea. Finally home, Evers stepped out of his Oldsmobile carrying a stack of NAACP sweatshirts stenciled "Jim Crow Must Go," which had made poor sales items in Mississippi's sweltering June. His own white dress shirt made a perfect target for the killer waiting in a fragrant stand of honeysuckle across the street. One loud crack sent a bullet from a .30-'06 deer rifle exploding through his back, out the front of his chest, and on through his living room window to spend itself against the kitchen refrigerator. True to their rigorous training in civil rights preparedness, the four people inside dived to the floor like soldiers in a foxhole, but when no more shots came, they all ran outside to find him lying face-down near the door. "Please, Daddy, please get up!" cried the children, and then everything fell away to bloodsmeared, primal hysteria. The victim said nothing until neighbors and police hoisted the mess of him onto a mattress and into a station wagon. "Sit me up!" he ordered sharply, then, "Turn me loose!" These were the last words of Medgar Evers, who was pronounced dead an hour later.

The Evers murder came at the midpoint of a ten-week period after the Birmingham settlement when statisticians counted 758 racial demonstrations and 14,733 arrests in 186 American cities. Two men demanding integration chained themselves to the gallery of the Ohio legislature. An Alabama mob stoned the home of a white preacher who suggested that Negroes be allowed to worship in his church. Ironically, one of the few places that was quiet for a time was Greenwood, Mississippi, where Bob Moses and Bernice Robinson held their training workshops "in spite of the chaos all around us," which included the four-day disappearance of their friends, who finally were sprung from the Winona jail on the day Evers was shot. "They were a horrible sight," Robinson reported to Myles Horton. "Annell Ponder's eyes were swollen and bloodshot from the beatings, and one hip was swollen twice the size of the other. Mrs. Hamer had bruises all over her head, and her hips were bruised." They closed the week's session a little early so that everyone could go down to the Evers funeral in Jackson, but these intimidations caused no one to drop out, and twelve more people around Greenwood came forward to become registration teachers. By the time Robinson's report reached Highlander, Horton had abundant troubles of his own: a posse of ten sheriff's deputies had staged a blitzkrieg raid on his relocated camp near Knoxville and arrested all twenty-seven members of the weekly workshop for unchap-

eroned interracial conduct. The local sheriff announced that he had authorized the raid to forestall vigilante action by angry, fearful
constituents, including one who had threatened to "take shotguns and
there will be Negro blood running down the mountain." The sheriff
padlocked the Highlander camp, which arsonists burned to the ground
four days later.

In Winona alone, John Doar worked on no fewer than three federal
suits: one to order local officials not to interfere with integration at the
bus station, another to overturn the criminal convictions of the Negroes,
and a third, futile one to punish the officers who had administered the
jailhouse beatings. Doar snatched a private moment to attend the funeral
in Jackson—he had considered Medgar Evers a friend and ally since his
clandestine scouting trip two years earlier—but emergency duties followed him even there. At the end of a silent memorial march through
town, the dignitaries disappeared inside the Collins Funeral Home for a
small private service, leaving most of the huge crowd of five thousand
marchers outside to disperse. Of these, some one hundred young people
defied the court order that made public silence a condition of their gathering. They sang "Oh Freedom" as a dirge, and then, when someone
broke into an up-tempo version of "This Little Light of Mine," a hand-
clapping mass edged back into the street. "Now they're making their
way downtown," an apprehensive radio announcer told his listeners in
San Francisco, "and my guess is that a demonstration is under way."

The noise of sirens and screams broke out over the singing, as the
Negroes marched to a halt, nose to nose with a gathering phalanx of fire
trucks and policemen armed with shotguns. The temperature was 103
degrees. Some of the Negroes shouted, "We want the killer! We want
freedom!" These were the young movement people who had been forbidden to march for two weeks now, since the children's march of June 1.
Even on Flag Day, June 14, pairs of them had been arrested off the streets
for carrying little American flags, as Jackson's white officials allowed
Negroes no public display of any kind. The police regarded the spontaneous demonstration as the bitter but predictable result of the city's
decision to allow the Negroes to memorialize Medgar Evers. They
brought up pumper trucks and dogs, and they charged when some of the
young marchers began to throw rocks at them. They had clubbed several
and arrested nearly thirty when, suddenly, the man who talked like Gary
Cooper appeared in a showdown scene from one of his movies.

An astonished Claude Sitton wrote in The New York Times that Doar
walked into the flashpoint of a riot, hands raised above his head "with
bottles and bricks crashing around him." Shouting his name, he told
them this was not the way, and the very sight of him stilled the crowd

so that he could be heard. An angry young woman came up to him. "We get our rumps shot up!" she yelled in his face, and then, stammering with disgust, "And what are *they* gonna do . . . and what are *we*, are we gonna wait for the *Justice Department?*" "Aw, give us a break," pleaded Doar. One of the Jackson officers, looking to the uncertain Negroes behind, shouted that Doar should make sure they all knew who he was. "My name is John Doar!" he yelled. "D-O-A-R. I'm in the Justice Department in Washington. And anybody around here knows that I stand for what's right!" He walked forward, calling out the names of Dave Dennis and other movement leaders he knew and how many times they had been arrested, saying they too wanted the crowd to disperse. Miraculously, they did. Doar scarcely paused after his famous "stroll" that day. His month-old son back in Washington was still nameless, and remained so for another two weeks until Doar's colleagues made him take time literally to pull a name from a hat.

In Jackson, the unburied corpse of Medgar Evers already was a shrine to the altered state of American race relations. His murder was eerie and providential, so flushed with history as to seem perversely proper—shot in the back on the very night President Kennedy embraced racial democracy as a moral cause. This was a mythical event of race, the first national one since Emmett Till's death trip into the Tallahatchie River. In a subtle but important turn of perception, people referred to the killing as a political assassination instead of a lynching, adding both personal and historical connotations. White people who had never heard of Medgar Evers spoke his name over and over, as though the words themselves had the ring of legend. It seemed fitting that the casket was placed on a slow train through the South, bound for Washington so that the body could lie in state. In death, Evers inspired reappraisals, conversions, and heroics on a grand scale, but the extraordinary emotions also produced raw adjustments among the leaders. Some of them were at each other's throats before the funeral train left Jackson.

On the morning after the Evers murder, Majority Leader Carl Albert called President Kennedy to apologize for the Democratic defectors who unexpectedly rejected a $450 million section of the Administration's public works bill. "I couldn't do a damn thing with them, you know," said Albert, and the President instantly understood. "Civil rights did it," Kennedy replied. Albert expressed amazement that even committee chairmen, "some of the top men in the House," had deserted the Administration to support toughening or weakening amendments on racial policy. The issue split the Democrats. "I'm awfully sorry," Albert said sheepishly, and the President tried to console him. "Just events are making our problems," Kennedy said wearily. "Christ, you know, it's like they shoot this guy in Mississippi . . . I mean, it's just in everything. I mean, this has become everything." Albert agreed that the civil rights uproar was "overwhelming the whole program." He told the President it would be nearly impossible to pass farm bills or mass-transit funding. On every close question from foreign aid to the space budget, civil rights loomed as the margin of defeat.

Robert Kennedy reached a point of overload the next day, when three thousand anti-segregation pickets showed up outside his office on Pennsylvania Avenue. He tried to win them over with a speech about how demonstrations were unnecessary because the Administration was on their side, as evidenced by the President's television speech. But this was a brash crowd, and the more vociferous ones shouted questions at Kennedy about the Greenwood shootings and the Winona beatings. What especially annoyed the Attorney General was his inability to refute the placards that accused the Justice Department of racial discrimination in its own hiring. Kennedy knew how hard he had worked on this issue. He had ordered internal surveys and recruitment drives, exploded in tantrums over the slowness of the bureaucracy. However, disclosure of such efforts would lead to painful facts—Burke Marshall had just reported that the Civil Rights Division itself had hired almost a dozen Negro clerks but not a single lawyer or administrator above Civil Service grade 11. Worse, the facts would invite harsh questions about Kennedy's command of his own department. Inevitably, it seemed, a politician in confession was a politician without power, and the prestige of his office was not served by the Attorney General scrapping with street demonstrators. When he tried to finesse the hiring issue with boasts of percentage gains over the Eisenhower record, a shouting picketer retorted that he saw precious few Negroes coming out the Justice Department's doors. Kennedy snapped, preferring to scorn than to bend to such critics. "Individuals will be hired according to their ability, not their color," he said icily, provoking loud jeers from the crowd.

King was attending the Gandhi Society's first-anniversary fund-raiser at New York's Americana Hotel when reports confirmed the death of Medgar Evers. Among the messages that reached him through Clarence Jones was a suggestion relayed from the Jackson movement that the Gandhi Society should name its bail fund for Evers. After all, Evers had given his life in a crusade that had brought nonviolent direct action to the heart of the beast—Mississippi—with six hundred Mississippians arrested in one day. King liked the idea, especially since one of his own Gandhian mentors, Mordecai Johnson, was present at the fund-raiser and

pronounced himself pleased to head such a project. Together, they announced the Gandhi Society's new "Medgar Evers Memorial Bail Fund"
after the luncheon that same day.

To Roy Wilkins, King might as well have stolen Evers' body. It was
bad enough that King had practically killed Evers—sending demonstration fever from Birmingham into Mississippi, forcing Evers to accommodate tactics that led swiftly to violent white retribution, as Wilkins
had predicted. It was worse that King tried to make an NAACP man into
a symbol of direct action with a bail fund, of all things. And it was worse
still that King was rushing in to raise money off his intrusions. Other
Evers funds were springing up independently of the NAACP—including
one at the Chicago *Defender*, which solicited on its front page—but it
was King's fund that brought down the wrath of the NAACP hierarchy.
Wilkins instructed his aides to contact the widow that first evening after
the murder. They secured her written agreement that funds honoring her
husband should be controlled by the NAACP rather than by "King's
organization."*

The Gandhi Society surrendered instantly to this demand, but resentments had been unleashed. In an otherwise unctuous letter of capitulation, president Theodore Kheel of the Gandhi Society subtly tweaked
Wilkins for carrying on a vendetta through the newspapers. When Stanley Levison first heard the rumbles, he told his friend Frank Montero that
"the furor that you are talking about has long and very much deeper
roots. The antagonism towards Martin at NAA[CP] has been a disgrace
for a long time." Montero, who was both an old friend of Wilkins and the
man who had presented Mordecai Johnson at King's Gandhi Society luncheon, tried to pass off the dispute as the result of hypercompetition by
underlings on both sides. No, Levison insisted, the malice and backbiting
were "all on one side, although I admit that this will sound very unusual." To the startled Montero, Levison poured out a long tale of grievance against Wilkins. "Roy and every single member of his staff except
John Morsell . . . have carried on against Martin," he said. For years they
had conducted a "dirty campaign" of gossip about King—for instance,
spreading the "hair-raising" rumor that King moved to Atlanta in 1960
only because the Negro insurance companies paid him $1 million a
month to "hold the Negroes back." Through it all, said Levison, King
kept speaking at NAACP functions, opening NAACP branches, and
praising the NAACP in speeches. He did not understand how King had

---

* With more difficulty, they also gained the widow's permission to have Evers
buried at Arlington Cemetery instead of the family plot in Jackson, where she
had been telling friends that he would lie.

been "so patient with the amount of garbage that's heaped on him." In fact, Levison said, King's patience "infuriates me." This went on to be the longest and most emotional outburst from Levison ever picked up by the FBI wiretaps.

King himself nearly skipped the Evers funeral in Jackson for fear that his very presence would exacerbate the tensions. In the end, he went but made no speeches or statements. At the public service, he endured eulogies that trivialized his methods as pointedly as funereal dignity allowed. "Lest we forget, and it does appear that some people have forgotten, it was right here in Mississippi back in 1952 that the first statewide nonviolent protest was carried out," declared T. R. M. Howard. ". . . We put out some 40,000 fluorescent bumper signs on cars, saying Don't Buy Gas Where You Can't Use the Restroom. Our martyred hero, Medgar Evers, was one of the individuals who participated in this first campaign, four years *before* Dr. King marched at Montgomery." From the Masonic Temple, King marched through the Jackson heat beside Roy Wilkins in a show of unity, then ducked out to the airport. He was gone before John Doar's one-man performance at the spontaneous march downtown that Saturday, June 15.

King's discretion did him little good, perhaps because the very nature of the Jackson stalemate made him a continuous, galling challenge to the NAACP leaders filling in for Medgar Evers. Having stalled demonstrations until his death, and then postponed them pending his funeral, they were back in the vise. Mayor Thompson was offering no concessions on lunch counter segregation or other issues. The assassination created more movement pressure than ever to secure Birmingham-style results through Birmingham-style mass marches, but the NAACP leaders viewed such tactics as a suicidal obeisance to King—the more so, since they might adopt King's nonviolence and still fail to budge white Jackson. Their dilemma was so painfully obvious that the ever-independent James Meredith stepped forward to suggest a compromise—a general strike or work stoppage in honor of Medgar Evers. He thought the tactic might add pressure to the NAACP-sanctioned boycott, but his attempted diplomacy earned him only a scathing dismissal from Gloster Current. "We couldn't comment on any idea a student has . . ." said Current. "We're in a titanic struggle here, and it's not a struggle in which an amateur has to give advice to those who know what it's all about." This was empty bravado, as Current was unable to say either that they would or would not resume demonstrations. He and the other national officers left for Washington the day after the Evers funeral.

Wilkins was met there by his nephew Roger, a lawyer in the State Department, who was struck by a change in his uncle's lifelong demeanor. Roy Wilkins had always been a man of formal, laconic reserve, who showed little of himself to anyone and practically nothing to his juniors, but now he could not stop unburdening himself of his troubles, most especially of his torture by King. "Can you imagine it?" he asked his nephew. "Medgar was an NAACP man all the way, and King comes in and tries to take the money." The younger Wilkins had never seen his uncle so angry or so raw. Grief, pressure, and the ghoulish turf war had worn the polish off the fierce institutional pride of Wilkins' thirty years with the NAACP. While the Medgar Evers funeral train was chugging toward Washington, he lashed out in a public speech. "The other organizations furnish the noise and get the publicity," he said, "while the NAACP furnishes the manpower and pays the bills. . . . They are here today and gone tomorrow. There is only one organization that can handle a long, sustained fight—the NAACP." Belittling the small memberships of the other groups, Wilkins urged the crowd not to stray. "Don't go giving them your money when it should be given to us," he admonished. "Don't get so excited."

While in Washington, Wilkins pressed upon the Kennedy Administration his view that no civil rights crisis was more important than the one in Evers' hometown, where failure to reach a negotiated settlement on segregation would encourage extremists of both races toward violence or demonstrations. Kennedy officials agreed. With the NAACP leaders, they sought answers to the tactical conundrum of Jackson: how to use federal leverage without attracting attention. Their best answer was to walk a tightrope. Robert Kennedy and then the President received the NAACP preachers from Jackson for White House conferences that raised their stature as successors to Medgar Evers. Simultaneously the Attorney General pressured Mayor Thompson, saying that unless he made concessions to the Negro preachers, he would not long be able to contain the young people who were straining to march. Finally, President Kennedy himself made two phone calls to Mayor Thompson.

Thompson was a garrulous and optimistic sort who kept telling the President he was wonderful and not to "get your feelings hurt" by the nasty things Thompson might have to say on political occasions, such as the rally he was attending with Governor Wallace that day, "because I think the world of you." Kennedy laughed and gave Thompson "full permission to denounce me in public as long as you don't in private." As to the negotiations, Thompson managed to pass off his refusal to seek desegregation of the downtown stores as a positive achievement: "I told the merchants . . . it's entirely up to them—if they want to sell to whites, sell to Negroes, or fish, or anything in the world, it's up to them, and I'm going to protect them with every force that's in my command."

He told Kennedy he had "answered every other thing" on the Negro preachers' list "except the biracial committee, and I just can't do that right now." When the President asked about one of the items on the list —hiring the city's first Negro policemen—Thompson nearly purred over the wire. "Oh, I've got that!" he exclaimed. He was planning to take that step and several other big ones, he assured the President, but stressed that "we *have* to do it *our* way."

Thompson asked President Kennedy to help things along by trying to persuade the Negroes to "go through the courts, and not have marches and intimidation." He said Jackson was in an "explosive situation" because of the young Negroes "being used as shields, and they have just gone wild. They have got it in their system, and the people can't control them or anything." On this point, President Kennedy asked for Mayor Thompson's evaluation of the Jackson preachers who had come to the White House—which one should he talk to, who had most control, was Rev. R. L. T. Smith "the stud duck down there?" Thompson replied that "the power" was not Smith but a Rev. G. R. Haughton, who "is the one that causes problems, and he's real smart and they look to him a lot."

The next night, Reverend Haughton rose to present the final result of the negotiations to a mass meeting in his own Pearl Street A.M.E. Church. Groans and hoots rose up from the crowd even before he finished reading the four-point package: (1) six Negro policemen "to be used in the Negro areas," (2) eight Negro school-crossing guards at Negro schools, (3) eight Negro promotions in the city sanitation department, and (4) "the city will continue to hear Negro grievances." Why was there no biracial committee? someone asked. Why were the Negro policemen to be segregated? Why was there no mention of segregation in the downtown stores? Against the onslaught, Haughton defended the settlement as a starting place. He preached, invoked the approval of Attorney General Kennedy, and finally offered up his pastoral honor. "I'm not getting one penny," he cried. "My hair's getting whiter every day. I'm missing my meals. My family is worried about me, here and elsewhere. Some of us want to make a big noise and that's all, but we're here for *business!*"

Large numbers of supporters cheered Haughton. Another preacher pressed his advantage by challenging anyone to say that the steering committee would betray the movement. Then Arthur Jones rose as the authorized NAACP spokesman to say that the settlement honored Medgar Evers, who was just then being buried in Washington. He reminded the crowd that Evers had said from the beginning that he did not want another Birmingham in Jackson, and "if we want freedom for Medgar's sake, we *still* don't want a Birmingham."

The patchy settlement held against all discontents. On Thursday, the

Negro preachers and the city fathers applauded each other at a ceremony in which Mayor Thompson swore in Jackson's first Negro policeman, stressing as assets his 250-pound weight and his trustworthy record. This was a mawkishly empty victory to most of the young activists who had gone to jail, but they bowed to it, retreating to their workshops and registration projects in the Mississippi countryside. CORE's David Dennis told a gathering why they had not challenged the settlement with demonstrations: "I think everyone can see that a split between the organizations at this particular point could do us no good," he said. Tim Jenkins, down from Yale Law School, declared in a speech that organizational rivalries were no more fatal in civil rights than in the Pentagon or the peace movement. Jerome Smith, less than a month after his parlor confrontation with Robert Kennedy in New York, brought his battering intensity back to his CORE project in Canton, one of Mississippi's toughest towns. "Our religion must not just become empty prayers," he told a mass meeting, "but our religion must become a living vote, you see, because if the church was right, and if the church would not conform to the whims of a sick society . . . we would not be here and Medgar would not be there."

In Washington, integrated troops fired a last salute and buried Medgar Evers with full military honors on June 19, eight days after the assassination. Twenty-five thousand people had viewed the body in a two-day processional, and the burial service at Arlington Cemetery was the largest since that of John Foster Dulles. President Kennedy did not attend, but afterward he sent a limousine for the widow and her two older children. He gave them kind words of condolence, and for the kids there were PT-109 souvenirs plus a scoot across the bed on which Queen Elizabeth had slept.

For President Kennedy and Martin Luther King, the alternating doses of euphoria and rude shock built toward a profound, historic climax. On the very morning after the Evers assassination, Kennedy invited King to join him for a discussion of civil rights at the White House the following Monday, June 17. King eagerly agreed, then abruptly rescinded his acceptance by telegram the next day. In the brief interim, the ugly feud over the Evers Bail Fund erupted, and King, with the march on Washington at issue, wanted to delay meeting the President until he at least had a chance to patch up the internal wounds. Also, he learned that he was to be only one of some 250 religious leaders received by the President in the East Room. Discovery of this mass audience punctured hopes for a working alliance. Put down, King rejected Kennedy's invitation, ending his telegram with the pointed suggestion: "I hope we will be able to talk privately in the not too distant future."

King and Kennedy were like a pair of ill-fated lovers, with similar interests but mismatched passions. Having embraced, even imitated, King's message on television, Kennedy now was pulling back. Entrenched Southerners were revolting against him in Congress. Everett Dirksen, the windy Republican leader of the Senate, proclaimed himself against the public accommodations centerpiece of Kennedy's new bill as a violation of property rights. Kennedy's speech had failed to check the epidemic of Negro protest, and scattered campaigns ripened into new mass protest nearly every day. Hosea Williams sent more than 200 children to jail in Savannah, then joined them. In Gadsden, Alabama, police arrested 450 students trying to renew the William Moore memorial march. Police in Danville broke down church doors to seize protest leaders. In Albany, Laurie Pritchett's men arrested nearly 150 over the next week. Negroes threw up picket lines around police stations in Kansas City, and New York's front pages showed local politicians scrambling to head off marches against segregated housing and employment. All this was distressing to Kennedy. Through Secretary of State Rusk, he secretly ordered all U.S. ambassadors to mount a concerted diplomatic effort to counter the "extremely negative reactions" overseas. (John Kenneth Galbraith, ambassador to India, replied tartly that "such crash effort would be wholly devoid of conviction," and advised the Administration not to panic.) Meanwhile, the President did his best to concentrate public attention elsewhere.

King was slogging through enervating distractions in his own world— a money quarrel in Birmingham, the closing of Atlanta's Funtown to thwart an integrated handful of patrons, the publication of a *Saturday Evening Post* profile accusing King of "arrogance and opportunism," which wounded him to the brink of filing a libel action. He was still the outsider. But he could not long be denied a White House meeting now that the President had invited no fewer than 1,500 national leaders to discuss civil rights in the month since the Birmingham settlement. Kennedy aides finally scheduled King's private audience with the President, early on a weekend morning. Then, having secured King's acceptance, they sandwiched him between an even earlier presidential meeting with Roy Wilkins and a later one with all the major civil rights leaders, plus UAW president Walter Reuther. Only then did Kenneth O'Donnell notify King that he was expected to stay on for the larger meeting, which White House press officials presented publicly as the major story—the paired sessions with King and Wilkins being a kind of administrative preparation. All these pains reflected his leverage as well as the aroused

opposition among his allies. Taking the best he could get, King kept his
White House appointment on Saturday, June 22.

While Roy Wilkins met first with President Kennedy, Burke Marshall
gathered privately with King and several SCLC aides, including Andrew
Young and Walter Fauntroy. Marshall took King aside for one of those
urgently confidential government discussions, which turned out to be
the first whispered ambush of the day. King could no longer defer the
threat of Communist infiltration in the SCLC, Marshall warned. Specifically, he must sever relations with Stanley Levison, who was a Communist functionary, and with Jack O'Dell, whom Levison had "planted"
inside the SCLC to influence the civil rights movement. King's first
reaction was to shrug in amused disbelief. He was nonplussed, caught
between the utter gravity of Marshall's tone and his own instinctive
dismissal of the claims. No doubt he felt disoriented by whiplash: having
come at last to make his case that the glory of the national freedom
movement was at hand, King met instead the preemptive charge that he
was harboring the most sinister enemies of peace and freedom. When he
tried to tell Marshall that there must be some mistake, some confusion
perhaps between an outright Communist and a person who had sympathized with Marxist tenets, Marshall contradicted him. This was not
paranoid mush, he said, but hard intelligence from the very pinnacle of
the U.S. government. Levison was something much more dangerous than
an old New York radical; he was "a paid agent of the Soviet Communist
apparatus." Marshall told King that he was authorized to say no more.
When King asked to see proof, the point Marshall stressed was that
neither he nor King was in a position to second-guess the highest U.S.
national security experts, and even if they were, the politics of the moment rendered their doubts irrelevant. The controlling fact was that President Kennedy was about to "put his whole political life on the line"
with the civil rights bill, and the President simply could not make himself vulnerable to charges of Communist association.

Seeing from King's face that he was not convinced, Marshall was
obliged to deliver him straightaway to Robert Kennedy for another round
on the same subject. The initiative for these confrontations had come
from the Attorney General, who had called J. Edgar Hoover the previous
Monday to arrange a special FBI briefing on just how dramatic and explicit he could make the new warning to King without endangering the
Bureau's sources, principally the Childs brothers. Hoover was only too
happy to comply, knowing that such favors weakened Kennedy's case for
shifting Bureau manpower out of the internal security field. For once,
Kennedy was pushing Hoover about the threat of domestic subversion
instead of vice versa. Now the Attorney General found it worth paying

tribute to Hoover in order to gain a measure of control over King. Here was a man who was boring in on the White House, threatening to transform or destroy its domestic political base, and yet he held no public office, displayed no personal ambitions that could be traded on, succeeded by methods such as going to jail, and thrived on the very upheavals that most unsettled the Administration. These qualities, on top of the prosaic fact that at first sight King would be mistaken for a waiter at most Washington establishments, put him beyond the reach of the Kennedys' political and social language. With King talking of a demonstration that might turn the capital into a giant Birmingham, Robert Kennedy sought to check his momentum. He would gain a bargaining hold if King admitted that his movement was poisoned. He would gain the upper hand if King conceded to the government the unilateral right to define what was poisonous.

But King shrugged off Robert Kennedy too. He kept asking for proof, saying that these terrible spy terms did not ring true of the men he had known so well, that he could not very well throw them out of the movement on unsupported allegations. Everybody he knew in the movement had been called a Communist for years, himself included. People across the South were calling even Robert Kennedy a Communist, and a reporter had recently asked the Attorney General to his face if he was a member of the party. Kennedy insisted that this was different. He buttressed his claim by pounding on two themes: first, that Levison's true nature was even more fiendish than he was being allowed to tell King, and second, that the evidence came from the highest and most sophisticated machinery of American espionage, the James Bond stuff, where secrets were true beyond doubt. Hinting at things Hoover had forbidden him to disclose to King, Kennedy intimated that Levison was working on Soviet orders to weaken the United States by manipulating the civil rights movement. To King, however, these state secrets only fed the spiral of disbelief. The higher Kennedy reached for authority, the less his descriptions sounded like the Levison whom King knew. The more Kennedy evoked the omniscience of the government's central brain, the more that brain sounded like an ordinary segregationist.

Kennedy saw that he was not getting through. In the oral history he gave jointly with Burke Marshall the next year, on condition of secrecy, he recalled the crux of the impasse as King's stubborn refusal to take the charges seriously. He said King was "always sort of dismissing the whole idea." Kennedy could not understand it. "Well, he's just got some other side to him," he remarked. "So he sort of laughs about a lot of those things, makes fun of it." In the oral history, Burke Marshall said that King "must have believed it," especially after they passed him up the ladder to President Kennedy that same day to receive the ultimate warning. After that, Marshall concluded, "I think he was probably just weak about it." Beyond King's unfathomable temerity, what astonished the oral-history interviewer was hearing the disclosure that President Kennedy himself had bothered to lobby a civil rights leader on the national security dangers posed by particular Communists. "The President talked to King?" he asked in disbelief. When Robert Kennedy replied "Yes," the interviewer gasped, "My God! And what was King's reaction?"

King must have been at least that dumbfounded as it was happening. Part of the psychological battle was his own uncertainty about whether the Kennedys themselves really believed that Stanley Levison was a danger to the United States, or whether they were merely saying so to get a hook into King. His doubts intensified in the heat of their serial performance. When King walked into the Oval Office, President Kennedy asked him to take a private stroll outdoors in the White House Rose Garden. When they were alone he said, "I assume you know you're under very close surveillance." King said little in reply. He was trying to figure out whether this amazing precaution meant that the President feared that he himself was bugged, or whether he meant that the surveillance of King extended even into the White House. Whatever the case, the President's Rose Garden manner employed the most potent combination of power and intimacy to warn that King could have no secrets. Conservatives in Congress were denouncing the idea of a march on Washington as a Communist tactic, Kennedy confided. J. Edgar Hoover had similar worries and would not hesitate to leak them, especially since the Bureau knew that King had two Communists working for him.

What King later remembered most vividly was that the President put a hand on his shoulder and almost whispered that he had to "get rid of" Levison and O'Dell. "They're Communists," Kennedy said. When King replied that he was not sure what that meant, as Hoover considered a great many people Communists, President Kennedy came back instantly with specifics: Jack O'Dell was a ranking member of the national committee of the American Communist Party. Stanley Levison's position was too highly classified for him to give details, but the President could say that Levison was O'Dell's "handler," and King could draw his conclusions about Levison from that. These were the hard facts, said Kennedy. O'Dell was fully engaged in conspiracy as the "number five Communist in the United States."

King tried to soften the pressure. "I don't know how he's got time to do all that," he managed to reply. "He's got *two* jobs with me." He laughed weakly, but his attempted humor failed to lighten the President's mood. Kennedy stressed the international implications of the threat by declaring that both Levison and O'Dell were "agents of a foreign power." This pushed King over the line of rebellion. He wanted to deny it vehemently on his own personal conviction, but the best he could muster to the President's face was a gentle rejoinder that he didn't think so. He said he would need to see proof before he could believe such things of these men.

President Kennedy took another tack. "You've read about Profumo in the papers?" he asked. King said he had. John Profumo, the British Secretary of State for War, had given his name to a sensational scandal by first denying, then admitting, that he had carried on an extramarital affair with a gorgeous lady of the night named Christine Keeler, who was simultaneously romancing a Soviet diplomat among many others.* The ongoing revelations obsessed President Kennedy to the point that he had ordered all State Department cables on the Profumo case sent to him at full length, without summary. Now, not fully aware how soon or how fatefully the example might apply to King as well as to himself, Kennedy warned King that sudden explosions from the underworld of sex and spying could ruin public men. "[Prime Minister Harold] Macmillan is likely to lose his government because he has been loyal to a friend [Profumo]," said the President. "You must be careful not to lose your cause for the same reason." Truth was only part of the equation. In England, once the tawdry question reached the tabloids, it quickly became irrelevant whether or not British military secrets really had passed from Profumo across Keeler's pillow to the Soviet diplomat. Kennedy's point was that King must not let his personal esteem for Levison blind him to the enormous stakes he was playing for, or to the fact that ruthless opponents could turn a spark of truth into a blaze of scandal. "If they shoot *you* down, they'll shoot *us* down, too," Kennedy told King. "So we're asking you to be careful."

The heads of two men, Levison and O'Dell, seemed a small enough price to insure something so vitally important as a full partnership between the White House and the civil rights movement, but King said he still would like to see some proof, especially on Levison, just for the sake of fairness. President Kennedy said of course, that was no problem. Rather than extend further appeals to King's trust, he broke off the discussion and led the way back inside from the Rose Garden.

---

* Readers of the Negro press in the United States received early notice of the scandal because of its racial origins. Christine Keeler had first attracted attention in London by failing to appear at the trial of Johnny Edgecombe, a West Indian charged with shooting at her in a jealous rage and also rumored to have slashed the face of another of Keeler's West Indian lovers. Press inquiries about these violent passions had uncovered Keeler's affair with Profumo.

There was quiet coughing in the Cabinet Room, where the milling civil rights leaders whispered protocol questions about who should sit in what chairs when President Kennedy arrived. Some of them snickered at the diminutive Walter Fauntroy for cheekily claiming the empty one next to the President's, and then, when King came in at the last minute, beckoning him over to take the prize. Of those looking on, Joe Rauh realized that such childish musical chairs might have lasting political effect. Perhaps the most important practical competition to be decided that day was the selection of a White House liaison for lobbying on the civil rights bill. Rauh knew that Walter Reuther coveted that role, as did Roy Wilkins, both of whom had asked him to help them jockey for first recognition from the President, on the theory that Kennedy would grant the lobbying power to the first supplicant rather than immerse himself in a catfight. Rauh grudgingly admired the King forces for seizing the tactical advantage of the chair on Kennedy's immediate right.

John Lewis, the newly elected chairman of SNCC, was among those oblivious to the parliamentary jostling. He would remember his first sight of President Kennedy in the flesh—the big smile and the choppy "Hello, hello, hello" as he hurriedly shook hands around the table. Robert Kennedy observed from a chair on the perimeter of the room, holding one of his daughters in his lap, as the President made welcoming remarks about the partnership behind the historic new civil rights bill. Now their great challenge was to get it through Congress, he said, plunging into a detailed analysis of the obstacles—the tangled committees, the sectional and personal complications of key legislators, the formidable muck of a Southern filibuster in the Senate. In closing, President Kennedy pulled out a scrap of paper. He said it was the latest poll, showing that his national support had plunged from 60 to 47 percent in the few days since he came out strongly for civil rights. None of those in the room ever could locate this dire poll—the President was famous for pulling fresh ones from his pocket for dramatic effect—but they had no doubt that the fight in Congress would be desperate. "I may lose the next election because of this," said Kennedy. "I don't care." He was committed, and he needed their help.

At this signal, the Cabinet Room came alive like a classroom or a presidential press conference, with a flock of hands shooting into the air. The President heeded several people who were chanting "Call on Roy," and Wilkins, after appropriate reminders of his dedication, declared that the Leadership Conference on Civil Rights stood ready to work with the White House in mobilizing support. This was a shrewd choice, as Wilkins headed the venerable umbrella group and the other leaders, being board members, could not protest their exclusion. President Kennedy merely nodded, and the lobbying role was fixed. Then Whitney Young of the Urban League gained recognition to ask whether the President in fact opposed the idea of a march on Washington, as indicated by press reports. His question invited the President to plant himself firmly against the idea, which offered him the best chance to scuttle the march but left no dignified avenue of retreat if the Negroes marched anyway. "We want success in the Congress," he replied, "not a big show on the Capitol."

A. Philip Randolph was the first to speak up on the other side. "The Negroes are already in the streets," he declared, and he told why he thought it was rightly so. To Randolph, this made the question academic. He said the situation was different from his near-march of 1941. "There *will* be a march," he announced with his booming bass voice and clipped accent. The only question was what form it would take, whether it would be violent or nonviolent, well or poorly led. James Farmer spoke up for Randolph, as did others who had been caucusing in New York. In reply, Vice President Johnson told them why he thought the President had a better approach to the same goal. He knew congressmen, he said, and the way to move them was by methods they understood: arm-twisting, deal-making, nose-rubbing, flesh-hammering corridor politics. Anything else might backfire. Johnson's was an outburst of great effect; some were saying that this series of civil rights meetings had brought him to life again. Only then, near the end of the two-hour session, did King speak up for the first time, arguing that the march and the traditional politics were not antagonistic alternatives. He thought they were complementary. The march, said King, could dramatize the civil rights issue positively, "mobilizing support in parts of the country that don't know the problem firsthand. I think it will serve a purpose," King added. "It may seem ill-timed. Frankly, I have never engaged in a direct-action movement that did not seem ill-timed. Some people thought Birmingham was ill-timed."

"Including the Attorney General," quipped the President.

Others spoke up for the march on the basis of the internal politics within their own organizations, saying they would face leadership challenges from aroused supporters if they did *not* march. President Kennedy appropriated this theme for his exit. "Well, we all have our problems," he said, rising to his feet. "You have your problems, I have my problems." The President said his problems included Congress, the Russians, NATO, and President de Gaulle, which reminded him that he was late for a final briefing before flying off to Europe. They should help each other and by all means keep in touch, he said, and his guests were soon facing the reporters gathered outside the White House. King's description of the meeting gave their news stories a slant that nettled the Administration: "Negroes Inform Kennedy of Plan for New Protests," said the

Times. "If there is a filibuster in Congress, we will have a nonviolent, peaceful demonstration in Washington," said King, adding that the President had not explicitly opposed the idea. Roy Wilkins drew less attention with a qualified demurral that he was "not involved at the present time." Of the march he said, "That little baby does not belong to me."

As they spoke, President Kennedy left the South Lawn by helicopter, heading for a stopover at Camp David and then on to Germany that night aboard Air Force One. King was flying to Detroit. This was to be a life-shaping trip for each of them. King, like Kennedy, hoped to escape the shackles of everyday politics and show that he stood for an idea of awesome, sustaining power. Kennedy, like King, hoped to prove that his message transcended all barriers of culture, language, and race. Each left Washington with the other prominently in mind, and each promptly broke through to success of frightening dimensions. It was as though they had sprinkled magic dust on one another. The similarities between their miracles were striking enough, but the contrast gave them depth. King and Kennedy were at odds over the innermost meanings of freedom. Having wrestled to a secret, preliminary draw in the Rose Garden, they acted out their differences in gargantuan public spectacles of haunting, providential aptness, like a thunderclap after confession.

President Kennedy went to Europe over strong, bipartisan objections. Senators and press critics pointed out that he was leaving a nation racked with crisis to visit three countries—Germany, Italy, and Great Britain—where no substantive presidential talks were scheduled, nor could there be, inasmuch as all three governments had fallen or were falling, and as yet there was no new Pope in Rome. National Security Adviser McGeorge Bundy defended the journey as best he could, saying on television that cancellation would bring down "quite serious consequences with respect to American clarity of purpose." Privately, President Kennedy told his staff that the trip was important precisely because it was a diversion from the intractable problems of the United States, which discouraged foreigners as well as Americans. Seeking to touch peoples, not governments, he landed in Germany as the conqueror turned protector. A staggering one million people hailed his motorcade in Frankfurt. Similar crowds saluted the American President across Germany, as he vowed that he would risk sacrificing his own cities in order to deliver theirs from nuclear war. In West Berlin—Hitler's capital, a city haunted by the last holocaust and literally torn apart by threat of the next—150,000 Germans shouted his name at the foot of the Berlin Wall as Kennedy gave the speech of his life:

Two thousand years ago the proudest boast was *Civis Romanus sum.* Today, in the world of freedom, the proudest boast is *Ich bin ein Berliner.*

There are many people in the world who really don't understand, or say they don't, what is the great issue between the free world and the Communist world. Let them come to Berlin! There are those who say that communism is the wave of the future. Let them come to Berlin!

. . . All free men, wherever they may live, are citizens of Berlin, and, therefore, as a free man, I take pride in the words, *Ich bin ein Berliner.*

If a speech could be said to shake the world, this one did. The ear-crushing response thrilled Kennedy to the point of dread. Upon a word from him, or perhaps merely a raised arm, the hysterical crowd might have torn down the Berlin Wall with bare hands, and for an instant the thought chilled him as power gone mad again in Germany. As he climbed aboard Air Force One to leave, Kennedy said, "We'll never have another day like this one as long as we live."

Deeply shaken by the triple ambush in Washington, King ordered Jack O'Dell and his staff to prepare for what amounted to a summary trial within forty-eight hours—as soon as King could get to New York. He then flew with Walter Fauntroy to Detroit for a grand march, which had been plagued by ominous contention. The rally already had been postponed once, partly because of leadership resentment against King's closest ally there, Rev. C. L. Franklin, and the Evers Bail Fund feud had exacerbated local rivalries to the point of open feud. Franklin's people levied charges that the NAACP leaders were "a bunch of Uncle Toms," and were answered by public claims that the NAACP was "the real and only voice of the Negro community." In marked contrast with the organizational cooperation that had made the Los Angeles event a giant success in May, Detroit's NAACP hierarchy was boycotting the King rally. Negro congressman Charles Diggs, who was to introduce King in Detroit, was about to demand that King conjure up a "graceful withdrawal" from the whole idea of a march on Washington. Given such hostilities, King faced a chance of being scolded again in public, this time at his own event.

The first breath of Detroit blew away all such worries. The police commissioner greeted King at the airplane door with a promise that "you'll see no dogs and fire hoses here," and delivered the first reports that the downtown march was getting magnificently out of hand. The advance crowd, packed so densely that the city's mounted police could not reach their parade escort stations, spilled out of a twenty-one-block staging area and headed downtown without King and the other leaders. An endless stream of marchers filled almost the full breadth of Woodward Avenue, the city's main thoroughfare. In a holiday spirit, they raised spontaneous choruses of "We Shall Overcome" and "Battle Hymn of the Republic." One woman wore a gaudy hat in the shape of a birdbath, with a sign saying "Birds of any color can bathe here." To bystanders, strutting marchers shouted, "Come on, get out here. You ain't in Mississippi. Let's walk!" There were countless placards honoring Medgar Evers, and one group of whites carried a banner reading "I'm Ashamed I Live in Dearborn," a wealthy, all-white suburb. When King's motorcade finally intercepted the head of the line at Cadillac Plaza, his name was cried out and the people swarmed forward, knocking aside the police cordon around him. In a deafening chaos, with angry warnings and claustrophobic squeals of terror amid the joyful roar, King linked arms in a line with C. L. Franklin, Walter Reuther, and Mayor Jerome Cavanagh to keep from being swallowed up and crushed by his own admirers. The tide of people pushed around them with such force that the leaders' legs churned and their bodies moved rapidly down the street without their feet touching the ground. Mayor Cavenaugh recalled that the only words he exchanged with King were "Hang on, hang on."

Crowd estimates ranged upward from 125,000. Parents recovered twenty-six children from the lost-and-found. Reporters wrote VJ-Day-style stories that saturated Detroit's Negro and white newspapers almost equally. At Cobo Hall, a breathless King pronounced it "the largest and greatest demonstration for freedom ever held in the United States." He spoke for forty-eight minutes on his standard themes, so magnified by the occasion that cheers followed nearly every sentence. Among the few insertions to fit the time and place was a new call for a "march to Washington more than a hundred thousand strong" in support of the civil rights bill. "Let's not fool ourselves," said King. "This bill isn't going to get through if we don't put some work in it and some determined pressure." In a veiled reference, possibly to Stanley Levison, he warned that people in the movement would be "misunderstood and called bad names," even killed like Medgar Evers, and he urged them not to allow a "magnificent new militancy" to sour into mistrust. "There are some white people in this country who are as determined to see the Negro free as we are to be free," he declared. In his final peroration, he delivered a longer and richer version of the "Dream" sequence that became famous two months later in Washington. He quoted Amos' vision of justice, Jefferson's democratic intuition, and finally the epiphany of Isaiah, ending: "I have a dream that one day 'every valley shall be exalted, every hill and mountain shall be made low, the rough places will be made plain and the crooked places will be made straight, and the glory of the Lord shall be revealed and all flesh shall see it together.' I have a dream this afternoon that the brotherhood of man will become a reality . . ."

In those few days, a president of Irish descent went abroad to Germany while a preacher of African descent went inland to Detroit, both to stir the divided core of American identity. The proconsul defended the empire of freedom while the prophet proclaimed its soul. They inspired millions of the same people while acknowledging no fundamental differences in public. Together, they traced a sharp line of history. Where their interpretations of freedom overlapped, they inspired the clear hope of the decade. Where incompatible, they produced conflict as gaping as the Vietnam War.

King felt the blade at his neck. The next night he received Jack O'Dell, Wyatt Walker, Andrew Young, Thomas Kilgore, Clarence Jones, and Walter Fauntroy in his New York hotel room, in an atmosphere that was as stone cold as the great rally had been tumultuous. It was Monday, June 24, fifty-four days after Bevel's first children's march in Birmingham, twelve days after the assassination of Medgar Evers. Stanley Levison missed the tribunal, having left the previous week for his annual vacation month in Ecuador. Some ventured jokes about what kind of Soviet agent would duck out just when his minions had the capitalists on the run, but the jokes fell flat. King somberly framed the dilemma. "I have just come out of Detroit, and it's clear that the masses of people are with this movement," he said. "But I'm dialectical enough to know that it's your moment of greatest heights that could also be the beginning of your undoing." Then he described the three wrenching conversations in Washington, recalling that he had endured everything except President Kennedy's final statement in the Rose Garden that Levison and O'Dell were agents of a foreign power. "I checked him on that," King said stoutly. "I told him that can't be true, and he just turned red and shook."

King laughed as he told them how the three Administration officials had tried to impress him with all sorts of spooky code names. Whenever he had asked for proof—evidence that Levison and O'Dell were under Communist control, or that they wanted to make him do something he didn't want to do—the Kennedys had dodged and danced around with more fancy words. This amused King—these big white folks acted like country preachers promising to pay back some money. What it really meant, King accurately guessed, was that J. Edgar Hoover was hoarding whatever evidence there was, if there was any. On this point, Andrew Young said he had gotten the impression that Burke Marshall did not expect to see what the FBI had. Marshall had suggested to him, Young recalled, that Levison and O'Dell should sue the FBI for defamation and force the Bureau's evidence out in court, if they dared.

"*Sue?* Why should I sue?" interjected O'Dell, who had been brooding like a prisoner on death row. "I don't consider it a slander!" He said he was proud of his association with Communists who had dedicated themselves to fighting racism. All of the people in the room knew most of them—they were some of Du Bois's people, and Ben Davis, the hard-line vice chairman of the party, now sick with terminal cancer. O'Dell said he had never done anything to betray Dr. King. As the only one there who did not call King by his first name, he already felt less a colleague than a defendant, and soon he sputtered into rage. "Hoover can kiss my ass!" he said. "I am not the issue!" The issue was control of the movement, he said, and whatever Dr. King decided, he should not kid himself into believing that Hoover and the Kennedys would be satisfied with this one execution.

Others spoke up in agreement. This was a classic purge. It was beginning with two of King's most indispensable people—O'Dell, the heart of both direct-mail fund-raising and voter registration records, and Levison, King's closest confessor and sounding board in the white world. What would keep the government from coming after any of them, including King, once he accepted their terms with a tacit admission that he had subversive ties? Clarence Jones said this was what already was eating at Harry Belafonte, who was as close to Levison as any of them. Belafonte was saying you could not allow a witch-hunt into the movement—that's how you self-destructed, piece by piece, that's how Hitler came into power.

King kept saying the principle was not in doubt. The problem was that the government was trying to force them to sacrifice one principle to realize others, such as the civil rights bill. If they refused, the likely price would be an avalanche of propaganda and a severance of relations. King recalled that on Saturday morning Marshall and the Kennedys had kept up such a barrage that he could not even discuss any other subject. He decided to seek other advice, talk to Belafonte, prolong the agony, but the pressure was already slashing his nerves. "You know, it's one thing to have the head of the Civil Rights Division of the Justice Department come down on you," he mused. "I can handle that. And even the Attorney General. But when Burke Marshall, the Attorney General, *and* the President of the United States all come down on you in *one day*, you have to consider that. You have to give it some weight."

TWENTY-TWO

THE MARCH ON
WASHINGTON

Age had begun to work on Bayard Rustin's daredevil composure. At fifty-three, he had managed a long life as a globe-trotting pacifist while never making more than $25 per week. Now at last, in the national upheaval over civil rights he saw a chance to turn his past as a misfit hobo into a recognized credential, but the rumors against him were so unnerving that the phone call came almost as a relief. "Look, Bayard," said Roy Wilkins, "I want you to know that I'm not in favor of your organizing the March on Washington."

"Well, Roy, I can understand that," Rustin replied, "but I'd like to know why."

Wilkins spoke calmly, without an accusing edge. "There are several reasons," he said. "First of all, I know that you were a sincere conscientious objector during the war, but you have been called a draft dodger over and over again on the floor of the Senate and House. Second, you are a socialist, and many people think that socialism and communism are basically the same thing. Thirdly, you admit that you belonged to the Young Communist League. And then there's the whole business of your having been arrested in California on a sex charge. Now, do you think we ought to bring all that into the March on Washington? Because it's gonna come out, you know."

"I know, I know," Rustin said defensively. He hesitated, as though the recitation made his life sound tawdry even to him. "But what happens depends on you people who are the main leaders. If you stand up and have some courage, it will do no damage."

"Randolph may be prepared to do that," said Wilkins. "But I'm not. I just wanted you to know."

"Okay, Roy." Rustin, though shaken, respected Wilkins for having the decency to warn him personally of his opposition. There was a dutiful, straightforward side to Wilkins' cunning, which Rustin considered a character strength corresponding to one of Martin Luther King's weaknesses—an exasperating instinct of avoidance. Rustin had been estranged from King for more than three years, since Adam Clayton Powell's threat to use Rustin's homosexuality to blackmail King. King had never spoken to Rustin about the breach—not then, nor in the excited caucuses of the past few weeks, when the idea of the great march had renewed their association.

When the nation's major civil rights leaders gathered at New York's Roosevelt Hotel a few days later, on July 2, Roy Wilkins made an entrance that indelibly stamped the event. Taking one look at the private dining room with place settings for some fifteen people, he announced that this would never do. He had come for a chiefs-only meeting, he said, and began literally to tap the men on the shoulders, saying, "This one stays. This one goes." A. Philip Randolph could stay but not Rustin, who had come as his deputy. Among the others Wilkins marked for ejection were Fred Shuttlesworth, James Forman, Norman Hill of CORE, and Cleveland Robinson, the New York labor leader who had helped subsidize the march preparations by giving Bayard Rustin a union office and a stipend. Wilkins cut through the group like a scythe. It was no small tribute to his stature that he could command obedience from such people as Shuttlesworth and Forman, who had come great distances for the summit meeting but soon retreated sullenly into the hallway. (The rebuke so stung Forman that he later claimed to have conceived the chiefs-only idea and to have disinvited himself accordingly.) Grumbling furiously among themselves, some of the expelled ones said this power play by Wilkins surely foretold an effort to scuttle the entire march, perhaps at the behest of the Kennedys. Rumors to that effect spread among the scores of representatives of the Leadership Conference on Civil Rights, who were to meet in the downstairs ballroom that afternoon.

Only six chiefs remained: Wilkins of the NAACP, Randolph of the Brotherhood of Sleeping Car Porters, King of the SCLC, Farmer of CORE, John Lewis of SNCC, and Whitney Young of the Urban League. Randolph opened the business by declaring that a march on Washington had been his obsession for more than twenty years, and that he wanted Bayard Rustin to make it a reality. Wilkins said he wanted no part of Rustin. Farmer and King defended Rustin's superior abilities but conceded that political attacks on Rustin might harm the march. Young supported Wilkins, who refused to yield, and finally someone asked whether Randolph himself should lead the march instead of Rustin.

"Yes, Phil, you should lead it," said Wilkins. Randolph promptly reached for a compromise, telling Wilkins that if he did, he would insist upon the right to choose his own deputy, and it would be Rustin. Wilkins replied that he would not quarrel with such an arrangement. "You can take that on if you want," he told Randolph, "but don't expect me to do anything about it when the trouble starts." King joined a chorus of approval for the compromise. He thought the histrionics by Wilkins camouflaged what was essentially a surrender of the NAACP's traditional claim to preeminence.

Wilkins did not have to wait long to feel confident that his adjustment to the march was prudent. He flew to Chicago that same day for the NAACP's fifty-fourth annual convention, which Mayor Daley already had pitched into controversy by declaring at an opening ceremony that "there are no ghettos in Chicago." Daley, a conservative ally of the NAACP, led ten thousand convention delegates down State Street in a Fourth of July freedom march, but when he tried to make a speech to them in Grant Park he met a solid wall of catcalls. Loud, continuous boos forced Daley to step back from the microphone so that Wilkins and other NAACP dignitaries could plead for courtesy—if not for a friend, or for Daley's right to speak, then at least for the convention's official host. Their pleas only added to the noise of the hecklers, who roared on for twenty minutes, driving the furious mayor in retreat to his limousine. Red-faced and tear-streaked, but partisan to the quick, Daley blamed the insult on "the Republicans."

J. H. Jackson, King's conqueror in the National Baptist Convention, had the temerity to come forward on the platform, only to receive a greeting that might have made him envy Daley's. Jackson had just issued a statement denouncing the March on Washington as a dangerous, unwarranted protest, and now he endured the first public booing of his life. Jackson stared in disbelief. When he too stepped down without speaking, the crowd's ugly mood materialized in the form of hecklers who pinned him against a wall, shouting, "Kill him! Kill him!" until police escorts plucked him to safety.

These two incidents amounted to a public relations disaster for the NAACP. To make matters worse, James Meredith set off an embarrassing quarrel the next day when he addressed the convention's Youth Freedom Fund banquet. The hero of Ole Miss, still smarting from Gloster Current's dismissive remarks after the Medgar Evers funeral, gave a deliberately provocative speech in which he dressed down the NAACP Youth Council members for lack of discipline. He also denounced the proposed march on Washington as a lay intrusion in political matters that should be left strictly to the five Negro congressmen. An already frosty audience booed Meredith for this iconoclastic suggestion, whereupon Meredith lost his temper and scolded them as immature "burrheads." This fiasco left Wilkins with few things to be thankful for in Chicago, but the same convention delegates who three times had turned into a mob cheered heartily when Wilkins summoned them all to Washington, saying, "We propose to use the capital as a parade ground for human rights."

A public alliance seasoned the personal relationship between Wilkins and King. They began to appear jointly on television to promote the march, and neither knowledgeable nor hostile interviewers could break down their harmony on the air. King praised Wilkins as the senior statesman and legislative strategist; Wilkins told viewers that King had "triggered" the national crisis that had forced President Kennedy to introduce the civil rights bill. "What Martin Luther King and his associates did in Birmingham made the nation realize that at last the crisis had arrived," said Wilkins. In private, the eight-year rivalry did not disappear so quickly. From the low point of the Medgar Evers dispute, the two men improved to a kind of barbed repartee, approximating the preacher banter by which King's closest friends vented their tensions and petty jealousies. Wilkins still reminded King that he owed his early fame to the NAACP lawsuit that had settled the Montgomery bus boycott, and he still taunted King for being young, naïve, and ineffectual, saying that King's methods had not integrated a single classroom in Albany or Birmingham. Wilkins tended to smile slyly for such remarks. "In fact, Martin, if you have desegregated *anything* by your efforts, kindly enlighten me."

"Well," King replied, "I guess about the only thing I've desegregated so far is a few human hearts."

King smiled too, and Wilkins nodded in a tribute to the nimble, Socratic reply. "Yes, I'm sure you have done that, and that's important. So, keep on doing it. I'm sure it will help the cause in the long run."

In Harlem, Bayard Rustin moved into a battered stucco building owned by the Friendship Baptist Church of the Rev. Thomas Kilgore—Ella Baker's pastor, a King family friend almost from the time of King's birth. Rustin hung a giant banner from the third-story window on West 130th Street: "March on Washington for Jobs and Freedom—August 28." There was no elevator. A hand-lettered sign directed visitors to walk upstairs to the office, where Rustin, in a cloud of cigarette smoke, raced incessantly between telephones and borrowed typewriters. He had less than sixty days to mobilize, transport, service, and control some 100,000 human bodies, but within two weeks he had distributed his *Organizing Manual No. 1* to two thousand interested leaders. Still affecting the screechy, pompous West Indian accent he had acquired in his youth, he insisted that a great redemption lay within reach.

Four days after his Rose Garden meeting of June 22, King sent word to O'Dell that he should begin looking for another job. He saw the purge as the price of alliance with the Administration, and he felt less capable of resisting demands for O'Dell's head than Levison's, because O'Dell was on the SCLC payroll. This was a miserably painful accommodation for King, who was notoriously slow to fire people for the best of reasons. Had he not suffered another sharp-spurred kick from the Administration, O'Dell likely would have enjoyed a protracted severance period from a regretful employer.

On June 30, the Birmingham *News* for the first time used King's name in a front-page headline: "King's SCLC Pays O'Dell Despite Denial." The article, which was a direct feed from FBI files, included surveillance and wiretap information on events such as O'Dell's trip to Dorchester the previous January to plan the Birmingham movement. King could scarcely believe it. The public attack came only eight days after his meeting with President Kennedy in the Rose Garden, a week after his triumphant march in Detroit, six days after his solemn meeting with advisers on the Kennedy ultimatum, and four days after he had given O'Dell his notice.

King thought he had been moving at lightning speed through ugly and unprincipled business, but he soon learned from Burke Marshall that the Administration saw it differently. The message essentially was that you do not trifle with the President of the United States. When President Kennedy told King that the national interest required him to get rid of O'Dell, he meant now, *immediately*, without second thoughts or tender farewells. On other occasions, the FBI might have initiated this sort of press whipping, perhaps even in disagreement with the Administration, but this story was written by James Free, one of Robert Kennedy's most favored reporters, who had been given almost free run of his office in the Justice Department and had sat in on several of the critical meetings during the Birmingham crisis.

King absorbed a cruel fact: once he agreed to fire O'Dell as a poisonous subversive, he lacked the standing even to set his own timetable for the deed. On July 3, as soon as he returned from the Wilkins-Rustin summit meeting on the Washington march, he sent Marshall a copy of a letter of dismissal to O'Dell. This accomplished King's formal submission, but he still refused to accept the Administration's tone or rationale. His "Dear Jack" letter blamed O'Dell's plight on the lingering power of the Mc-Carthyite blacklist, and the wording of his conclusion left no doubt that he saw O'Dell as a noble witness against injustice. "Certainly, yours is a significant sacrifice commensurate with the sufferings in jail and through loss of jobs under racist intimidation," he wrote O'Dell. "We all pray for the day when our nation may be truly the land of the free. May God bless you and continue to inspire you in the service of your fellow-man." O'Dell vanished from the SCLC office to join the staff of *Freedomways*, a New York journal recently founded by followers of W. E. B. Du Bois, including several prominent Negro Communists.

With O'Dell gone, the pressure shifted to Levison, who was still down in Ecuador on his annual sojourn. Ostensibly he was looking after Secomatico, his dry-cleaning investment in Quito, but he used this tax-deductible purpose to subsidize vacation treks through the Andes. This year he had taken his teenaged son Andy with him for a trip that featured the added excitement of a revolution. President Carlos Arosemena had become so intoxicated during a reception for the American ambassador that he had urinated in the punch bowl—or so it was told in Quito, with such effect that Army tanks soon rumbled through the streets to rescue the national honor by military coup. While witnessing these peculiarly Ecuadorian events, Levison was the star in absentia of a drama at home that was similarly fantastic. In many respects it was an American echo of the Alfred Dreyfus scandal in France, with the crucial distinction that the hysteria played out behind a wall of government secrecy.

King was determined to resist President Kennedy's personal order to banish Levison. Clearly, since he could not fire someone who did not work for him, Kennedy's demand meant that the Administration laid claim to govern not only King's hiring practices but also his friendships and contacts—even the advice he could seek and the words he could hear. This amounted to thought control, managed by the obsessively narrow-minded J. Edgar Hoover. For King, who labored to maintain a receptive spirit of *agape* toward his bitterest enemies in civil rights, few prospects were more repugnant than shunning a dear friend as unfit for human contact.

His first line of defense was the proof. In July, King sent word that he would take no action until the Administration delivered the evidence promised by President Kennedy in the Rose Garden. This notice put Robert Kennedy and Burke Marshall into a stall, as they could not fulfill the promise to King without violating their duty to protect Hoover's secrets. Paralyzed, having to accept Hoover's word themselves, they expected King to accept it too, but finally, after several postponements, Burke Marshall agreed to meet Andrew Young at the Federal Courthouse in New Orleans. When Young arrived, Marshall guided him into a hallway for security against unseen spies, then delivered an earnest question in place of the long-awaited evidence. "Do you know who Colonel Rudolf Abel is?" asked Marshall. He explained that Abel was the highest-ranking KGB officer ever convicted of espionage.* If Young knew who Abel was, Marshall added significantly, then he knew Stanley Levison. Marshall said he could divulge no more, but that the message to Dr. King was clear: Levison was a man like Colonel Abel.

King and his advisers were not sure how to interpret this communication. Could Marshall really be saying that Stanley Levison was a Russian, insinuated into the United States years ago by Stalin or Beria? If so, why was the government negotiating his "punishment" with Martin Luther King? Could Marshall really believe such a thing himself? For King, who had received an escalating series of excuses and hair-raising new charges for more than two years, this round cracked any lingering faith in the oracles of national security. If Stalin had invented a puppet named Stanley Levison, joked King and his aides, the monstrous dictator should be credited with a service to humanity. Later, Harry Wachtel and others gave Levison the private nickname "Colonel," in mock tribute to the superspy Colonel Abel.

This was hardly the first time that something ridiculous from the white world had caused pain or obliged King to devise a soberly respectful strategy in opposition. What the "Colonel Abel" message meant, it seemed, was that the Kennedys either believed J. Edgar Hoover or felt they had no choice but to submit to him. King preferred to concentrate on the latter interpretation, recalling President Kennedy's talk of omniscient surveillance and his hints of political blackmail. On this theory, he fashioned a tactical compromise that he hoped the Kennedys could use to mollify the FBI Director.

King sent Clarence Jones to present his plan to the Administration on July 16. Privately, in Burke Marshall's office, Jones gave a lawyerly cast

---

* A highly trained Russian officer, Abel had been infiltrated into the United States many years earlier to develop a cover identity as a struggling artist in Brooklyn. Although it was never clear how Abel managed to extract U.S. nuclear secrets under such disguise, FBI agents did seize his code book, microfilm, hollow pencils, and other spy paraphernalia when they arrested him, and Soviet officials considered the deeply planted KGB agent to be of such value that they traded their captured American U-2 pilot, Francis Gary Powers, for Abel in a celebrated spy exchange of 1962.

to what was essentially a groping response. He said he was assuming that the root of the problem was political, because otherwise the government's criminal prosecutors and espionage experts could take care of it themselves. Therefore, said Jones, King was willing to take steps to reduce the Administration's political vulnerability to segregationists and others who might distort the Communist issue. Specifically, King would stop communicating directly with Stanley Levison. That way, whoever was eavesdropping on the movement would not pick up the conversations which, by President Kennedy's account to Dr. King, were triggering the accusations of subversion. While he was willing to impose this sacrifice upon Levison and himself, Jones continued, King wanted the Administration to understand that he had received no legitimate reason to stop communicating altogether with Levison, toward whom he maintained full confidence and affection. King reserved the right to exchange ideas with Levison indirectly, through intermediaries such as Jones.

Jones intimated to Marshall that the plan would work better if the government could suggest which indirect channels might be used safely. Specifically, Jones said he had reservations about talking on the telephone with Levison. Marshall, correctly interpreting this as an effort to find out which telephones were wiretapped, ignored the hints and merely stressed that all parties "had no choice" but to make sure that King broke off contact with Levison. Jones took Marshall's enigmatic pronouncements as a grudging acceptance of the compromise, but this reading proved to be woefully optimistic. When Marshall told Robert Kennedy that Jones expected him to conspire with King to circumvent the FBI, Kennedy responded with calculated fury. That very afternoon, Kennedy told the FBI he wanted to supplement the Levison surveillance with wiretaps on Martin Luther King *and* Clarence Jones.

Kennedy's resentments overflowed for at least three reasons. First, Jones's timing could not have been worse. Over the past four days, Governors Barnett and Wallace had attracted national headlines by attacking the Administration on the subversion issue: "Barnett Charges Kennedys Assist Red Racial Plot," announced *The New York Times*. In Senate testimony against the new civil rights bill, both governors had displayed a poster-sized photograph of King addressing the 1957 convention at Highlander Folk School, which they identified as a "Communist training school." Barnett said he knew that the FBI had information on "the real motivation" of civil rights leaders, and he challenged the senators to ask the FBI about the photograph. Wallace introduced for the Senate record a news article quoting Karl Prussion, a self-described "FBI counterspy of 22 years' experience," to the effect that King belonged to more Communist organizations than any man in the United States.

Just that morning, Kennedy and Burke Marshall had made an emergency call to their FBI liaison, Courtney Evans, giving him less than an hour to identify Myles Horton and several others who appeared with King in the Highlander picture. Senators were asking whether the Highlander photograph really proved that King had been trained as a Communist, and the Attorney General urgently needed the information in time for a scheduled appearance on Capitol Hill. The Bureau had met the deadline with a factually truthful report. Highlander was not a Communist training school, Evans told Kennedy, but it advocated racial brotherhood and at times had allowed individual Communists on the premises. King had not been "trained" at Highlander—he had visited there only once, to make a speech. As to the photograph, Evans reported that none of those shown with King was a Communist except for Abner Berry, a Negro correspondent for the old *Daily Worker*. Evans left to Kennedy the unenviable task of explaining to senators and reporters whether all this meant that King was mixed up with Communists or not. This siege put Kennedy in no mood to hear from Marshall that King wanted his permission to keep associating indirectly with Stanley Levison, a man Hoover flatly described as a top-echelon Communist agent.

A second negative factor was the intermediary. Kennedy remembered Clarence Jones as the one who, though he could have come to his defense, had sat silently through his verbal stoning at the James Baldwin meeting in May. That experience, plus the FBI report he had since received, fixed Jones in Kennedy's mind as a suspicious character—elegant, manipulative, married to a wealthy white woman. In his subsequent oral history, Kennedy stressed the mixed marriage as a sign of instability, describing both Jones and Harry Belafonte as questionable types animated by guilt and beguiled by celebrity glitter and wealth. Having marked Jones as a clan enemy, Kennedy rewarded his overture with a wiretap instead of a favor.

A third inflammatory reality lay coiled in Marshall's report: Clarence Jones was letting it be known that President Kennedy had warned King of FBI surveillance. The spread of such information could endanger the President himself. Already Jones knew, and had told Marshall. If Jones talked to Levison over the FBI wiretap, then reports of President Kennedy's warning to King would circle back into the FBI's files. No doubt the Attorney General realized that his brother had mentioned the surveillance for good reason on that Saturday in the Rose Garden, meaning to intimidate King with the powers of an omniscient FBI. Still, the President's disclosure might be construed as a serious breach of security that compromised the FBI's effort to control subversion. This was the last thing Robert Kennedy wanted, now that leaks and innuendo from FBI files already were tilting the unstable center of public opinion on civil rights. The Attorney General did not seriously worry that Hoover would accuse a sitting President of treachery, as he once had accused ex-president Truman, but it was not farfetched to imagine a defter, less confrontational leak ("President Told King to Ditch Reds") that would undermine the Administration.

Kennedy did not advertise this political danger even to Marshall, in whom he placed full trust. In this Machiavellian intrigue, the Attorney General saw his core function as the protection of his brother, and this was best done alone. He waited until Marshall left to call Courtney Evans, and never afterward did he tell Marshall of his fateful step. By ordering wiretaps on Jones and King, Kennedy signaled Hoover that he was standing with the FBI's interpretation of the Levison matter rather than King's. He told Evans that the new surveillance would help ensure that King had no contact whatsoever with Levison, direct or indirect.

The order stunned Evans. Normally wiretap requests were initiated within the Bureau and forwarded to the Attorney General for disposition. This one came suddenly the other way. "I told the AG," Evans reported back to the Bureau,

> that I was not at all acquainted with Jones, but that, in so far as King was concerned, it was obvious from the reports that he was in a travel status practically all the time, and it was, therefore, doubtful that a technical surveillance [wiretap] on his office or home would be very productive. I also raised the question as to the repercussions if it should ever become known that such a surveillance had been put on King.
>
> The AG said this did not concern him at all; that in view of the racial situation, he thought it advisable to have as complete coverage as possible.

Hoover's formal requests for the two wiretap authorizations went to Attorney General Kennedy within a week. This was fast, eager work by the Bureau. Upon completion of security checks and a small mound of paperwork, Hoover notified Kennedy on July 22 that the FBI could wiretap Clarence Jones at his law firm, his home, and at the Gandhi Society. Early the next morning, FBI couriers rushed the wiretap request on King to the Attorney General, although headquarters had received only preliminary assurance from the Atlanta office that the taps were technically feasible. What required the extra day after the Jones request, most likely, was deliberation over a unique loophole phrase. Hoover asked for written authority to wiretap King "at his current residence or at any future address to which he may move." The key word here was "address." An "address" was not necessarily a residence, nor a "move" more permanent than an overnight stay. If the Attorney General truly wanted "complete coverage" on a moving target such as King, then perhaps he would authorize the FBI to install short-order surveillances in hotel rooms and guest houses—wherever King went.

Kennedy signed the authorization for the three taps on Jones, but he brooded over the King request for the better part of two days. He was wavering. In a decision of this magnitude, he had to consider not only his relations with Hoover and King but also the risk of public revelation. Externally, the political equation was shifting every day. In the short time since the Attorney General had set this tap in motion, President Kennedy had refuted charges of racial subversion by the "few remaining Communists" at a televised news conference, labeling such talk a "scapegoat" search by fearful segregationists, and *Newsweek* had published a bold special issue entitled "The Negro in America." Among its splashy revelations was a feature entitled "The Big Man Is Martin Luther King," and a nationwide poll showing that King commanded the support of 88 percent of American Negroes. Similarly, the *Newsweek* poll revealed that since the introduction of the civil rights bill, Negro voters favored President Kennedy by an astonishing 30 to 1 over any Republican opponent.

The Attorney General was straddling a thin line. On the one hand, he wanted to protect the Administration against charges of being soft on communism. On the other hand, he did not want to give the FBI license to attack the civil rights bill and the Administration's base of Negro support. No one knows how candidly Courtney Evans spoke to him about the dangerous wording of the King authorization. (In later years, almost visibly crushed by the open hostility between the Kennedy and FBI forces, Evans would give testimony of zombielike vagueness on these issues, altogether avoiding the thick layers of innuendo.) By now, Kennedy knew that no move in this tangle was simple or discrete; each caused a host of adjustments, none more than this one. If he signed the line marked "Approved" and returned the King authorization to the FBI, he would give Hoover an irrevocable, written endorsement of the suspicions Hoover had lodged against King's civil rights movement.

On July 25, Kennedy released a letter in response to the public charges of communism in the civil rights movement. He invoked the authority of the FBI files behind his assertion that no leader, including King, was a Communist or "Communist controlled." By careful wording, he did not rule out Communist influence or inspiration, as such assurance might have pushed Hoover to public revolt. Kennedy may have concluded that it made no sense to exonerate King and order his phones tapped on the same day. For whatever combination of reasons, the Attorney General decided that the Jones wiretap was enough for now. He returned the King authorization unsigned, which set off a silent wail of disappointment in the Bureau.

•   •   •

Stanley Levison returned from Ecuador on July 21—earlier than expected, his wife said, because their son had suffered nosebleeds in the
heights of the Andes. His home country had been sunnily transformed
from the cauldron he had left a month earlier, with Medgar Evers freshly
buried. For the first time in his presidency, Kennedy discussed race issues
regularly at his press conferences, and was doing his best to advertise the
March on Washington as a wholesome expression rather than a threat.
King and Wilkins seemed reconciled. Atlanta's Mayor Ivan Allen
stunned the political world by publicly endorsing the new civil rights
bill, becoming the first and only elected Southern official to do so. Pounding the witness table, Allen spoke with a tempered anguish that brought
tears to some of the spectators in the jammed hearing room. The civil
rights issue seeped into the media culture beyond politics, as thinkers of
all kinds came forward with discoveries about race.

Yet Levison the insider ran smack into an undertow that was stronger
than all these excitements. Sober men—the very ones guiding the destiny of the free world—were looking at the daily record of his long service
to King, and in place of his avuncular, steady advice and his absorption
with tedious practicalities such as mailing lists, they saw a surreptitious
invasion of the United States by a one-man vanguard of the Red Army.
The shocking news had a magical quality, like a peasant crowned king
or a president elected overnight from the cornfields, except that Levison's
anointment was all sinister and secret. At first the FBI wiretap caught
Levison chuckling over the irony that President Kennedy himself could
perceive him as such a danger, given the fact that Levison had been
arguing so recently to King that Kennedy was improving his civil rights
performance and ought not to be the target of the March on Washington.
Such musings vanished the very next day, July 25, as the FBI brought
down a new sledgehammer of media punishment on King: "Onetime
Communist Organizer Heads Rev. King's Office in N.Y." This was another attack on Jack O'Dell, appearing on the front page of the Atlanta
Constitution. The newspaper's executives had the nerve to copyright the
story ostentatiously and otherwise promote it as an exclusive, even
though much the same information had been published almost a month
earlier in the Birmingham News, which in turn had been fed most of its
salient facts by the FBI.

The new attack sunk King into a state of stunned befuddlement. Technically speaking, the O'Dell story was not news, but it was an unmistakable declaration of war on King in his hometown, by a newspaper—Ralph
McGill's Constitution—that was regarded as a beacon of liberalism in
the South. Alarmed by the political magnitude of the crisis, King imme-

858 PARTING THE WATERS

diately issued a public statement refuting the *Constitution* story as
"packed with half truths and vicious innuendos." He held a press conference in Atlanta to amplify his defense, and summoned Chauncey Eskridge from Chicago to fend off a parallel attack by Eugene Cook, the
attorney general of Georgia. Cook, boring inward under sanction of state
subversion laws, demanded to know the names of all King's associates
who had recommended or worked with O'Dell. He announced publicly
that his office—"and to my certain knowledge the Attorney General of
the United States"—possessed files on Communist activity within the
SCLC.

Privately, that same day, King initiated an emergency round of telephone conferences with the Justice Department and with his advisers in
New York, in which he wondered out loud what more he must do to end
these crippling attacks. King's grievances ran headlong into Kennedy's,
just as the Attorney General was deciding not to sign his own request for
a wiretap on King. Kennedy used King's distress calls to clarify the warning about O'Dell and Levison: King should break off all contact, direct
and indirect, and it was only upon assurance of strict compliance by King
that the Attorney General publicly defended the movement as free of
Communist taint. This was "the treaty," as Clarence Jones called it.

Fear invaded King's councils during these discussions. In Atlanta, he
circulated a special bulletin and required SCLC employees to sign it as
proof of comprehension. "All staff members should be informed of the
fact that the office phones, and some home phones, are tapped," it starkly
declared, "so we should be extremely careful of anything said on the
telephone." In New York, FBI wiretaps recorded that Clarence Jones,
fearing wiretaps, began referring opaquely to Hoover as "the other person," and to King or Levison as "our friend." The code words made his
reports on the complicated Kennedy talks so impenetrable that Levison
often said he could not follow them. "Well," Jones once explained, "if
they [the Kennedys] didn't have the assurances [that King would shun
Levison and O'Dell], then they wouldn't have made that statement
[clearing King of Communist domination]." Levison replied, "Oh, now
I see."

For Levison, this jolt of political vertigo drove home the depth of the
predicament. Kennedy had promised Hoover more than he had let on to
King, and King in turn had promised Kennedy more than he was willing
to deliver. The gaps left all parties ample room to feel betrayed, and King
still was vacillating over his obligations of principle and affection to
Levison. Levison knew King well enough to perceive the paralyzing force
of his dilemma, and within a few days he took the initiative himself.
"I'm not going to let Martin make that decision," he told Jones and

Belafonte, among others. Instead, Levison resolved to withdraw from King's counsel, sparing King the pain of severing their association. This was the only logical solution, he insisted, as no one person should become the stumbling block for the entire movement.

Levison broke off direct contact with King. He explained that he was inextricably involved in only one short-term project—the creation and publication of King's book about Birmingham—and even there his work was mostly on the business side as King's established representative with publicists, agents, and publishers. He transferred to Clarence Jones the editorial work that required dealing with King, and Levison could fade completely from King's affairs as soon as the book was published. In early August, while in New York to work on the manuscript, King told Clarence Jones that he wanted to call Levison to tell him how sorry he was, or to share his latest thoughts on the mysterious duel with the Kennedys. More than once, King asked Jones if he was sure Levison understood why he did not call. "Oh, yes," Jones replied. "In fact, he would be rather upset if you did."

One of the first fruits of the wiretap on Clarence Jones was an intercepted conversation in which King spoke of moving into Jones's home two days later as a house guest. By this extraordinary coincidence, the eavesdroppers soon netted King accidentally. For the next three weeks, the tap meant for Jones overheard King instead, bringing delighted FBI executives their first intercepts of King's salty conversations with people other than Levison. Although King and Levison spoke freely of rogues and weaknesses, never a cussword or a ribald comment passed between them. They spoke as blood brothers in the rush of a great cause, too busy for foolishness. Unmistakably, Levison defined a side of King, but the new wiretaps revealed a different facet, of wild preacher gossip and the night-life of Negro princes. Beneath King's sturdiest qualities there was an opposing release of instability, fury, wanton merriment, and profane despair.

King was in a rare family mode, as Coretta accompanied him for the entire visit. While enjoying what she described as the Joneses' "large, comfortable and well-appointed home" in Riverdale, they took sightseeing trips in an effort to squeeze in part of the vacation they had lost to the movement for three Augusts running. King slipped away on occasional speech runs, as always, or to frenzied planning sessions for the Washington march. He was preoccupied also by the continuing bombardment of post-Birmingham demands, including the determined harassment of the Georgia attorney general and the tug of demonstration crises in a half-dozen cities. Still, he managed to escape almost every day to the nearby Riverdale Motor Inn, where Clarence Jones had ensconced a writer named Al Duckett to help with crash production of the Birmingham book. A Negro publicist of broad Rockefeller and Republican connections—serving among other roles as ghostwriter for Jackie Robinson's newspaper column—Duckett was living proof that Stanley Levison had relinquished his editorial hand in the book project, as Levison considered Duckett to be a public relations type of negligible skills and shallow character. He bluntly bemoaned Jones's choice when he learned of it.

By this time, King had lowered his personal barriers to Jones, offering him the essential secrets of his private life. Unerringly, King chose to reveal himself to men and women who could absorb the news without developing blisters of uneasiness between themselves and him. They did not scorn him as a fallen preacher, nor lapse into paralyzing discomfort. These were people who tolerated or even applauded King's demon delights as a humanizing revelation that bonded them even closer to him and his public purpose. Often they accepted King more easily than he accepted himself. They saw sexual adventure as a natural condition of manhood, or of great preachers obsessed by love, or of success, or of Negroes otherwise constrained by the white world, and they objected to King's mistresses no more than to the scores of concubines who had soothed King David during the composition of his Psalms. Some of them grew tired of King's insistence that it was a sin, and of his endless cycles from hedonism to self-recrimination and back. In any case, they adjusted —whether by sigh, sly wink, or eager imitation—and such adjustment defined an innermost circle around him: Abernathy, Walker, Young, Jones, Bernard Lee, and a small network of others, mostly preachers. These were his road buddies, the people he could travel with and let go. King and Levison alone had formed a separate inner circle.

Clarence Jones was privy to the secret, and he knew that a requirement of his trust was a sensitive instinct for protection. Astutely, by degrees, he had to gauge who was suspicious, who was vulnerable, who was dangerous. Already he sensed that his own wife, Ann, idealized King in such a way that she might not be able to handle the slightest knowledge. In this he proved tragically correct when hints from other sources later precipitated a crisis between them. "If the rumors are true, I never want to see Martin again," she said at first, and in the divorce, depression, alcohol, and untimely death that followed her, King's affairs distressed her nearly as much as her own husband's. All this remained merely a risk to Jones in August 1963. Although he knew King's regular mistress in the New York area, and helped arrange their meetings, he stayed carefully with his wife and contacted the Riverdale Motor Inn only by telephone.

Although the FBI eavesdroppers picked up only the hints that passed over Jones's phone wires, King's language was startling enough for the FBI, which seized upon even the political conversations as a coup. They revealed for the first time King's talk of sex and his Negro vernacular, proving to Hoover that he was not the high-minded moralist he claimed to be. Hoover had no trouble seeing King as both a bloodless Communist puppet and a sybarite of unbridled desire—a "tom cat," as Hoover called him. The Director sent a confidential two-page summary to Nicholas Katzenbach on August 13. (This became the first item in a mountain of personal material that in 1977 federal judge John Lewis Smith would order locked away under seal for fifty years.) The summary was a racy, secret communication that shot upward to the Attorney General and on to President Kennedy himself. "I thought you would be interested in the attached memorandum," a droll Robert Kennedy privately wrote his brother.

Small indiscretions opened new opportunities for the Bureau. In one intercepted conversation about the advance anxieties of the March on Washington, a friend told King that "your boy Burke Marshall is scared to death, and so is the Attorney General."

King agreed, then added his own worry that the enemies of the march were moving to expose Bayard Rustin's background. "They are going to make a hell of a mess of it," King said, predicting that the Southerners would employ a "combination" attack on Rustin's Communist connections and his "morals charge."

"I hope Bayard don't take a drink before the march," the friend knowingly fretted.

"Yes," King said. "And grab one little brother. 'Cause he will grab one when he has a drink."

Wiretap stenographers speedily transmitted King's remarks to John Malone, Special Agent in Charge (SAC) of the New York office. Malone stood out within the hierarchy as a kind of good-natured galoot—his Bureau nickname was "Cement Head"—but he was smart enough to send a verbatim Teletype straight to Hoover, who immediately incorporated King's "grab one little brother" comment into a confidential memorandum for the Attorney General. Already the Bureau had collected more than a dozen reports on Rustin's Communist associations—his party service in the late 1930s, his attendance as an observer at the 1957 convention of the CPUSA—parts of which found their way into speeches by Strom Thurmond. Now King's comments prompted an emphasis on Rustin's sodomy case in California. On August 13, the day after Hoover disseminated the "little brother" remark, Thurmond rose in the Senate to denounce Rustin for sexual perversion, vagrancy, and lewdness, inserting a copy of his police booking slip into the *Congressional Record*.

When Thurmond's attack attracted little notice in the news media, perhaps because it was distasteful and too obviously political, the Bureau reached for more explicitly shocking evidence. Two days later, the Los Angeles office notified headquarters that the 1953 incident involved oral sodomy upon two white men, "with Rustin taking the active part." After that, no aspect of this one case was too vulgar, stale, or obscure for transmission by urgent Teletype, and headquarters badgered the field offices for new details well into November.

From the FBI's point of view, the hidden events of early August were satisfying in spite of Kennedy's refusal to authorize the King wiretaps. While losing that skirmish, Hoover had shifted the terms of debate. No longer was the Bureau expected to prove that the KGB or the American Communists were controlling Stanley Levison, as King first demanded. Nor was it even required to show that Levison or O'Dell was conspiring with King to commit a criminal or subversive act. Those standards had vanished in concession to Hoover. Worn down by the FBI's commanding persistence and by corrosive uncertainty, King and the Kennedys gradually yielded to a new, simpler definition: the slightest contact between King and the banned people threatened U.S. national security. The FBI sought to follow up its advantage with a stream of new reports seeking to establish that King was receiving messages from Levison. On August 7, Burke Marshall wrote the Attorney General of one such report: "I think this is inconclusive to show any continuing relationship. The Bureau should keep on it, and we should wait."

The issue became one of associations rather than crimes or deeds, in a world of contamination by word of mouth. Then the Jones tap picked up tantalizing hints of King's hidden sex life, enabling Hoover to suggest more strongly that the Administration was in league with a pack of guttersnipes. One character issue joined another, and the associations raised taboos that were chilling to most Americans, especially white ones, of Negro back alleys and cutthroats and faceless subversives and hellish perversions. For the FBI, the true nature of King's movement reduced to the issue of whether he did or did not have contact with undesirables—an elementary question suited to the Bureau's skills and tastes. All it needed to prove or disprove these associations was comprehensive surveillance of King. For Robert Kennedy, the test soon became whether previous retreats before Hoover left any ground to defend.

Reinhold Niebuhr perceived an entirely different sex scandal simply by reading the newspapers. "Your former choir boy, Barry Goldwater, is cutting a wide swath," he wrote Bishop Will Scarlett. "Interesting how

Rockefeller's lack of private morality has made him a dead duck and given Barry his chance." Niebuhr thought Rockefeller's spicy divorce and remarriage might have the political effect of turning the Republicans into "a reactionary party" built upon white voters in the South and West. Jackie Robinson expressed similar fears in a newspaper column headed "Is the GOP Going Lily White?" So did King, who told Clarence Jones privately that "the Goldwater surge pushes Kennedy more and more to the right." Although Niebuhr and King never became friends—never overcame disparities of age and stature, nor the barrier of Niebuhr's Cold Warrior phase—they were beginning to sound alike in their private communications. The civil rights movement helped revive the seventy-one-year-old theologian, who, despite severe depressions and failing health, was beginning a reprise on his pre-Depression days as a race radical in Detroit.

The racial crisis also helped lift Lyndon Johnson from the torpor of the vice presidency. For the first time since his formative experience as a New Deal congressman, an Administration was fighting for survival against domestic rather than foreign crisis. The fate of the Kennedy Administration unexpectedly hinged on a legislative program for the downtrodden, and Johnson, who had felt so superfluous and insecure among the fast-track Kennedy globalists, responded as though to a shot of adrenaline. Instead of cultivating the resistance among his fellow Southerners, he seemed to relish the chance to slough off his past as a regional politician. Suddenly he was in demand again as the Senate architect of the only two successful civil rights bills since Reconstruction. In private White House meetings, the Vice President changed from a sullen lump of self-pity into the gleefully rapacious arm-twister of the Johnson legend.

Johnson told President Kennedy how he had reacted when the city of Houston shut off dockside electricity to protest the Navy's new policies on off-base segregation. "The head of Houston Power and Light Company is [Senator] Eastland's cousin," he said. "So I called up Albert Thomas and I said, 'Shall I tell the President that you cannot supply power to a Navy installation there because of the Negro question? And . . . what are you gonna do about space?' " Thomas had gotten the message that his nasty little protest endangered millions of dollars in new federal contracts for a NASA tracking station in Houston, Johnson reported, and the Navy had got its power back immediately. When Kennedy suggested that it might be unwise to force showdowns with entire Southern states, Johnson said, "Yeah, but I want the governor of Texas and the governor of Arkansas and the governor of Georgia . . . to know that when they stand up there and come out for segregation, it may cost them the economy of that state. And they ought to think about it a good deal." Johnson advocated a Southern-style program of bareknuckled sweet talk to condition Southern politicians to new realities, saying he knew why they were howling in public about segregation, and there were ways to make them un-howl. President Kennedy was wary of such Machiavellian zeal. "You could do all that on the phone?" he asked.

By early August, Johnson's enthusiasm for the civil rights scrap was attracting public notice, which vexed electoral strategists for the 1964 campaign. Newspaper stories suggested that President Kennedy was so worried that he planned to send Johnson on a tour of Scandinavia during the March on Washington. By exiling the Vice President to the blondest part of the globe, far from the anticipated convergence of Negro unrest, strategists hoped to preserve enough of LBJ's Southern image to salvage Texas and perhaps North Carolina for the Democrats. Such desperate schemes reflected the unsettled nerves within the Administration. Its officials were like sailors who, having leaned far overboard to grasp a new mooring, felt their ship slipping away to the rear.

With palpable relief, President Kennedy announced on August 1 that the long season of racial demonstrations was subsiding at last. He embraced this prognosis so firmly that he warned the nation not to "go to sleep and forget the problem." Almost as he spoke, however, Chicago police arrested a racially mixed band of one hundred demonstrators, and the next day authorities in Gadsden, Alabama, conducted a mass arrest of nearly seven hundred young people who were trying to renew the William Moore march. Picketers went to jail that same weekend in places as far apart as Torrance, California, and Athens, Georgia. Upstaged again, the Administration groped for political balance. In a complicated, partisan maneuver at the National Governors Conference, it managed to abolish the resolutions committee in order to forestall a ringing endorsement of civil rights. Such a vote of the assembled governors would have dramatized the sharp splits among the Democrats while showcasing Republican unity behind Nelson Rockefeller, and under these special circumstances the Kennedy strategists decided to duck rather than to win. Meanwhile, in the Justice Department, Robert Kennedy made two difficult choices that comforted Southern politicians in their campaign to suppress racial dissent. Both choices involved Charles Sherrod's ongoing SNCC project in southwest Georgia.

In Americus, two counties north of Albany, a team of SNCC students had struggled through the spring to register Negro voters, and since the national outburst of direct action they also had tried to integrate the town's Martin Theater by pickets and sit-ins in the lobby. Nearly a hundred local teenagers went to jail in July. On the night of August 8, after a mass meeting at the Friendship Baptist Church, an overflow of energy and bravado led to a spontaneous one-block march through the Negro section of town by more than two hundred young people. The march irritated the Americus policemen on monitor duty. Their orders to disperse achieved nothing but a tight huddle of students and louder choruses of "We Shall Overcome." Police reinforcements buttressed the white side of a standoff between authority and song, until Sheriff Fred B. Chappell finally issued orders to arrest them. This was easier said than done, as the officers were heavily outnumbered. They fired warning shots to scatter as many of the protesters as possible, then closed in on the holdouts, who braced themselves for arrest by lying down on the sidewalk. Sheriff Chappell stood over SNCC field worker Don Harris, a Negro graduate of Rutgers, and tried to make him get up by jabbing him with an electric cattle prod, known locally as a "hot shot." The sheriff later testified that Harris lay "wiggling and twisting" on the ground but refused to tell his followers to stop singing. This vivid duel between the opposing leaders provoked anger on both sides. White officers fired more shots as they wielded their clubs; some Negroes threw bricks and broke windows. Seventy-seven demonstrators went to jail on the first night of a siege that soon left seven officers and twenty-eight demonstrators wounded. A state trooper broke one Negro's leg with a baseball bat, and a policeman shot another fatally in the back as he walked through a white neighborhood.

What raised the primitive dispute to the Attorney General's desk was a unique decision by local authorities to charge four SNCC leaders— Harris, two white students from the North, and a young Negro from Americus—with seditious conspiracy against local laws. The charges were grounded in what was known as the "Angelo Herndon statute," after the famous communism/integration show trial of the 1930s, which had started Herndon's lawyer, Ben Davis, toward his career in the Communist Party. The statute made sedition a capital crime, and the Sumter County solicitor all but openly declared that he had filed these particular charges in order to jail the demonstration leaders indefinitely by fiat, as Georgia law permitted no pre-trial release in capital cases.

For his murmurs of dissent against the crudely injudicious prosecution, the Sumter County attorney was hounded out of his church and eventually out of the county. Most of the local white leaders kept silence, and from Washington the Attorney General swiftly closed off hope of federal intervention in the case. His press office announced on August 13 that the FBI had found no merit in complaints of police brutality. Kennedy also declined to challenge the sedition prosecutions on behalf of the United States. Until November, when a team of defense lawyers

won a federal court order aborting the sedition charges as an unconstitutional abuse of police power—the first such order ever won by a private
litigant under the 1957 Civil Rights Act—the four SNCC workers languished in jail under threat of execution.

Kennedy's second tack against the civil rights movement was more
confrontational. He held a special press conference on August 9—the day
after the sedition arrests in Americus, and only hours after his nephew,
the President's newborn son Patrick, had died in a Boston hospital—to
announce federal criminal indictments against nine members of the Albany Movement. To disinterested observers, this was an obscure though
troubling case, illustrating perhaps that civil rights leaders could make
errors just like cruel sheriffs. To those closer to the movement, however,
"the Albany Nine" became almost a watchword for bitterness, a stark
refutation of Pollyannish Camelot, and within the government the nice-
ties of legal language masked ferocious internal struggles. This was the
case that harked back to the gruesome, landmark *Screws* lynching case
in Baker County, and to the point-blank shooting of another Negro prisoner by Sheriff Screws's successor, "Gator" Johnson, on a night clouded
by alcohol and cross-racial sex at the annual barbecue on the Coca-Cola
plantation, and to the miraculous survival of the prisoner, Charlie Ware,
and to Ware's audacious civil suit against Sheriff Johnson that had been
lost on the Good Friday, April 12, that Martin Luther King was locked
up in the Birmingham jail.

Since April, special detachments of FBI agents had swarmed over Albany trying to establish that movement Negroes had picketed Carl
Smith's grocery store in retaliation for his jury vote to acquit Sheriff
Johnson. This had been no easy assignment, as there had been only a few
hours of picketing on a single day, and the Albany Movement undeniably
had been picketing that grocery and many other stores before the Ware
verdict. Without hard evidence isolating vengeance as the picketers' motivation, the white prosecutors from the U.S. Attorney's office found
themselves in the uncomfortable position of Negro plaintiffs who long
had struggled to prove subjective realities as obvious as intimidation or
voter discrimination. As a last resort, the prosecutors brought to bear the
full weight of their authority: they had a special federal grand jury impaneled to investigate the Albany Movement and sent U.S. marshals
swooping through the Negro section of town to serve nearly sixty sub-
poenas, spreading panic in their wake. "These ain't no crackers now,"
declared Sherrod. "This is the *federal government.*" C. B. King hastily
scheduled a meeting in his law office to brief the subpoena recipients on
their rights and duties as grand jury witnesses, but then he was called
away to another county for a quickie mass trial of young people arrested

at a library sit-in. In his absence, the meeting was a haphazard affair conducted by Elizabeth Holtzman,* a summer law clerk who had come South from New York to gain experience in civil rights litigation. Holtzman nearly got indicted herself.

The grand jury grillings turned up dry on the picketing itself, but the prosecutors forged success on a collateral issue. When one of the witnesses mentioned the legal briefing conducted by C. B. King, the prosecutors craftily recalled selected leaders of the Albany Movement and asked them if they had "attended any mass meeting or meeting where one or more people were in attendance, where it was being discussed about the fact that certain ones were going to have to appear before the grand jury?" Slater King and several others replied, "I don't recall." Thus they met their downfall. When C. B. King learned of their testimony, he was distraught that they had equivocated about something so innocent and defensible as a meeting with their attorney. The chagrined witnesses could only explain that they had panicked, fearing a trap to indict C. B. King or to make the meeting part of some conspiracy.

The proposed indictments also caused distress in the Justice Department. Even the steeliest review attorneys felt qualms about charges that intruded so closely on lawyer-client privilege. Both the questions and answers at issue were vague, making perjury difficult to prove, and there were numerous quirks in the indictment package. Joni Rabinowitz, the only proposed white defendant, was a young SNCC volunteer whose father, Victor Rabinowitz, was a New York lawyer of an alleged Communist past, and for that reason she was being cast as a ringleader of the entire Albany Movement, acting on orders that may have come from Moscow. This was a J. Edgar Hoover twist designed to appeal to white segregationist juries, but it was highly implausible to lawyers who knew anything about the Albany Movement. Also among the defendants was an unconnected, miscellaneous Negro who was rumored to have angered FBI agents by telling them they had no right to conduct interviews in his barber shop. Only two of the nine defendants—Rabinowitz and Dr. W. G. Anderson—actually were alleged to have conspired against Carl Smith, the juror from the *Ware* v. *Johnson* case. Only Rabinowitz was alleged actually to have picketed the grocery store, and witnesses were divided on that elementary point. Other defendants appeared to have been singled out for political reasons. These included Rev. Samuel Wells, who had led one of the most spectacular jail marches of the previous summer, and Thomas Chatmon, the NAACP Youth Council leader who

---

* Later U.S. Representative and Brooklyn District Attorney.

had suffered so many misgivings about letting his members join the original Albany Movement.

Inside a divided Justice Department, lawyers from the Criminal Division conceded flaws in the package but argued that the rash of equivocation over the legal meeting indicated that the defendants had guilty minds over the picketing of Smith. The U.S. Attorney's team was comforted by the excellent chances of obtaining convictions before a Georgia jury. Lawyers from the Civil Rights Division, on the other hand, argued strenuously against bringing such marginal charges against Albany Negroes while failing to indict the jailer who had beaten Slater King or the officers who had kicked Slater King's pregnant wife to the ground. When the conflict reached Robert Kennedy for decision, he realized that there was no subtle way to shelve the case. Only his explicit order to the U.S. Attorney could abort the indictments. Such an order would infuriate a number of government officials who had invested much labor in the prosecution, including the U.S. prosecutors in Georgia and Kennedy-appointed District Court judge Robert Elliott, who had pushed the investigation from the start. Once the Attorney General resolved not to block the indictments, it was politically expedient to be as noisy about the decision as he was quiet about civil rights enforcements on behalf of Negroes. Accepting an inevitable torrent of criticism from the civil rights movement, Kennedy moved boldly to capture the attention of those on the other side. As he was announcing the indictments at his press conference in Washington, U.S. marshals and FBI agents were hauling the nine defendants to jail in Georgia. Deputy Attorney General Katzenbach told reporters that the Albany Movement's picketing of Smith's grocery store "must become a matter of serious Federal legal concern." The department further signaled the Administration's unwavering support by dispatching senior prosecutors to assist the U.S. Attorney in Georgia, where the first convictions would be recorded in November. The Washington *Star* congratulated Attorney General Kennedy for proving in the Albany Nine case that he did not stand "with the Negro against the white man."

All through August, little pinpricks of back-page news joined the running stories from Americus and Albany. In Birmingham, a tear-gas cannister sent twenty shoppers to the hospital from Loveman's just after the store complied with integration conditions of the spring settlement, and a few days later a bomb demolished the entrance to the home of Arthur Shores, the city's best-known Negro lawyer. In Plaquemine Parish, Louisiana, James Farmer of CORE led a march of two hundred to jail, where he stayed all month through a sustained siege of mounted patrolmen and house searches and night riders so menacing that he eventually escaped the region concealed in the back of a hearse. These and other threatening episodes ran counter to the larger mood of a nation that was just adapting to the moral challenge of the civil rights bill, and in which the same Kennedys who were prosecuting the Albany Nine were widely disparaged as nigger-lovers. Perhaps no American felt the ragged edges of these contradictions more acutely than John Lewis, who spent the summer shuttling between Southern jails and luxurious salons of power. Don Harris, the most threatened and abused sedition defendant in the Americus jail, was his closest friend in SNCC. Lewis knew several of the Albany Nine personally, and scores of other prisoners were as real to him as freedom songs or the rattle of handcuffs. He identified with their latest ordeals even as he was rising to personal acquaintance with the President and the Attorney General.

Lewis was a gifted mimic. During the last executive planning sessions for the March on Washington, he was the guest of a wealthy family in Westchester County, New York, where in off hours he entertained sophisticated Northern students with his droll imitations of Robert Kennedy's choppy, distracted discourse and of King's pulpit cadences. Lewis beguiled the students as the irresistible Negro man-child, awed by everything and nothing. He radiated with the belief that power and luxury were immoral, and yet this conviction, filtered through James Lawson's teaching that there was virtue in all people, came out in Lewis as a gentle parody on the distractions of worldly success. On the Saturday before the march, he climbed into a tanning chair and floated out into the Westchester swimming pool. From this perch, he was holding forth on the vicissitudes of the movement when an emergency phone call came in from one of the Southern jails. As Lewis could not swim and the others were fully dressed, the task of fishing him out brought a few seconds of addled, crisis hilarity. Scrambling students tossed off jokes that the national chairman of SNCC would save the day just as soon as they could tow his chair to a poolside phone.

Lewis laughed too, but he soon took leave of his guests to prepare his speech for the March on Washington. Although the prospect was daunting for a young man with a speech impediment, Lewis had no trouble deciding what aspects of this historic moment he would try to highlight for a crowd that might be larger than the population of Idaho. He drafted a simple speech about the Americus prisoners and the Plaquemine cavalry charges. He invoked the plight of Slater King by name, summoning his audience to look more sharply for complicity in ostensible goodwill. "Do you know," he asked, "that in Albany, Georgia, nine of our leaders have been indicted not by the Dixiecrats but by the Federal Government for peaceful protest?" He turned charges of equivocation and fuzzy purpose back upon the Administration. "I want to know," he wrote, "which side is the Federal Government on?"

A week before the march, Clarence Jones ducked out of his office to call Stanley Levison from a pay phone. Dispensing with greeting or introduction, he said, "The only reason that I'm hounding you is that I would like to get what you have, and start getting it transcribed."

"Well, I have to go over it," Levison replied. He promised to "have something" by that night.

"Okay, but time runneth on," said Jones.

Inside the New York FBI office, the Levison wiretappers decided that this cryptic caller must be Jones. They contacted the Jones wiretappers, who reported that Jones had been in his law firm just minutes before but that the Levison call had not gone out over Jones's office lines. Once the technicians confirmed by voice identification that the caller indeed was Jones, they noted the suspicious circumstances for their superiors: Jones and Levison clearly were taking precautions against wiretaps. For the Bureau, this gave a sinister cast even to Levison's effort to complete the crash book project on Birmingham. He was drafting passages to submit to King and the ghostwriter, Al Duckett, who were holed up at the Riverdale Motor Inn.

King broke away from Riverdale that night to give a speech in Chicago before the National Insurance Association. This was a big money event for the SCLC, as the NIA executives had guaranteed a minimum collection of $10,000 and Wyatt Walker had wangled free use of their mailing list. The event also carried personal and political significance for King, who greeted his audience as "the economic power structure of the Negro community." These were the heirs of the pioneers who had forged the first major Negro business markets by writing dime-a-week life insurance and burial policies, often doubling as morticians and bill collectors or working in collaboration with preachers, such as Daddy King, to collect on pledges to the church coffers. "You know as well as I know that these vast economic resources that you've gained through pooled resources have come by and large from the masses of the Negro people," King told them. "And you owe it to them to pour some of these resources back into the struggle." The mood of the crowd was so bright that they burst into applause at this blunt assessment, and they applauded again when King warned that they could not have both integration and a protected Negro market. "Now if you have the illusion at any point that our job will be merely to compete with Negroes in this new age that is emerging," he said, "you're sleeping through a revolution . . . We must set out to do our jobs so well that the living, the dead, or the unborn couldn't do them any better."

Having admonished the Negro capitalists, King turned to easier targets. He denounced the white politicians in Congress for "playing around with one of the vital issues facing our nation and . . . our world." Already those politicians were maneuvering to weaken the civil rights bill and delay its consideration at least into the next year, and King drew cheers from the insurance executives by vowing not to let it happen. A surge of emotion carried him through rather abstract remarks on the power of nonviolence. Almost defiantly, he invited them to contemplate the potential of a system that embraced no inherently repugnant means. "I believe that one of the weaknesses of communism is found right here," King declared, citing Lenin's defense of deceit and violence toward the goal of a classless society. "And this is where nonviolence breaks with communism or any other system that would argue that the end justifies the means, for in the long run the end is pre-existent in the means, and the means represents the ideal in the making and the end in process." As his content grew more technical and remote, King compensated with nearly desperate passion. "I have come to see *even more*," he cried in a choking voice, "that as we move on toward the goal of justice, hatred must *never* be our motive."

"I refuse to become bitter," he said, then moved to a final peroration on a theme that had inspired the multitude at his Detroit speech in June. "And so tonight I say to you, as I have said before, I have a dream, a dream deeply rooted in the American dream," he began. "I have a dream that one day, right down in Birmingham, Alabama, where the home of my good friend Arthur Shores was bombed just last night, white men and Negro men, white women and Negro women, will be able to walk together as brothers and sisters. I have a dream . . ." During the ovation that followed, the dapper Chicago emcee shouted that he wished he had King's eloquence in order to express his appreciation for the speech. "I don't have that eloquence, so you'll have to have another dream," he quipped.

King returned to New York to join Roy Wilkins for a guest appearance on "Meet the Press." In the first question, Lawrence Spivak spoke of the numerous authorities who "believe it would be impossible to bring more than 100,000 militant Negroes into Washington without incidents and possibly rioting," and he asked Wilkins sourly what the country could possibly learn about civil rights that could justify such risks. Spivak asked no questions of King—perhaps still fuming over King's refusal to come out of jail for the show the previous summer—but the next panelist promptly asked King three times how the march's leadership could tolerate Bayard Rustin's background of subversion and character defects. The friendliest reporter, Robert MacNeil of NBC News, sparred with King over the meaning of "social equality" and wanted to know how the civil rights movement could survive the "psychological climax" of the march without either disbanding to rest or pushing on into violence. The fourth panelist pressed King to admit that the movement needed to eliminate extremism and "rowdyism," such as the public booing of Mayor Daley and J. H. Jackson. "I wouldn't say that I condone every action that is taking place at this time," King replied. "I think we must see that we are in the midst of a great social revolution, and no social revolution can be neat and tidy at every point."

Wilkins and King did their cooperative best to project the march in a positive light—there was not a shaving's difference between them in tone or substance—but public expectations brimmed with apprehension. In Washington, authorities from all sectors guarded against the possibility that marauding Negroes might sack the capital like Moors or Visigoths reincarnate. The city banned liquor sales for the first time since Prohibition. President Kennedy and his military chiefs were poised with pre-drafted proclamations that would trigger suppression by 4,000 troops assembled in the suburbs, backed by 15,000 paratroopers on alert in North Carolina. Washington hospitals canceled elective surgery. Some storekeepers transferred merchandise to warehouses to safeguard against looting. Chief Judge John Lewis Smith, Jr., notified his fifteen colleagues to be prepared for all-night criminal hearings,* and practically no baseball fans protested when the Washington Senators postponed two days' games until Thursday, when the march would be safely over.

Similar fears penetrated the movement itself. Bayard Rustin spent countless hours arranging police security and imported a supplementary force of four thousand volunteer marshals from New York. From his new headquarters tent near the Washington Monument, he announced that the psychology of peace was fragile and that there was no telling what might happen if attackers burned one of the two thousand buses headed toward Washington, as they had burned the Freedom Ride bus, or if any bombs were detonated, as in Birmingham. It was Rustin's obsession to make sure that no flaw in the arrangements permitted claustrophobia or discomfort to flare up into violence. He drove his core staff of two

---

* Less than fourteen years later, after elevation to federal District Court, Smith would order all tapes, transcripts, and other FBI intercepts of King's private life to be impounded for fifty years under seal of secrecy.

hundred volunteers to pepper the Mall with several hundred portable toilets, twenty-one temporary drinking fountains, twenty-four first-aid stations, and even a check-cashing facility. Meanwhile, in the great hall of New York's Riverside Church, volunteers worked in shifts to prepare 80,000 cheese-sandwich bag lunches for overnight transport to Washington—to feed growling stomachs, and thereby to prevent growling people. Over the vast march area, Rustin had signs posted high enough to be read by someone jammed in a crowd. "If you want to organize anything," he kept saying, "assume that everybody is absolutely stupid. And assume yourself that you're stupid."

As to the program, Rustin notified all speakers that a hook-man would unceremoniously yank them from the podium if their speeches exceeded seven minutes. He was determined to move the huge mass of people into Washington after dawn and out again before dusk, and therefore he could not tolerate the usual stretch of performers' egos. Strict discipline would allow timely evacuation, which would reduce the chances of violence by or upon Negroes wandering strange city streets at night. It would also refute the racial stereotype of imprecision and inbred, self-indulgent tardiness. The planners wrestled not only with logistics but with the weight of perceptions that had accumulated over centuries. Never before had white America accepted a prescheduled Negro political event for national attention. By guilt or aversion, many of the most sympathetic whites retained a subliminal belief pairing Negroes with violence, such that even innocent beating victims were implicated to some degree in their fate.

These stakes prompted the leadership to turn outward—to emphasize their goals and common grievances rather than their particular enemies. Once again, this self-conscious political diplomacy conflicted with the self-conscious foot-soldiery of SNCC leaders. A number of them labored to turn attention to the jailhouse door, where they were. Huddling with John Lewis, each of them added a line or two to the draft of his speech. Courtland Cox helped sharpen the politics by pointing out that nothing in the Administration's civil rights bill would protect Negroes seeking to vote or protest segregation, nor "the hundreds and thousands of people who have been arrested upon trumped-up charges." Tom Kahn, a young white socialist who had attended Howard University with Cox, helped add language to make the speech more overtly ideological: "If any radical social, political and economic changes are to take place in our society, the people, the masses, must bring them about." James Forman inserted references to specific outrages, such as the caning of C. B. King by the Albany sheriff, and in his swashbuckling style contributed a vision of conquest: "We will march through the South, through the heart of Dixie, the way Sherman did. We shall pursue our own 'scorched earth' policy and burn Jim Crow to the ground—nonviolently. We shall crack the South into a thousand pieces and put them back together in the image of democracy." After polishing by Julian Bond and Eleanor Holmes, among others, the final draft of the Lewis speech became a collective manifesto of SNCC's early years. Courtland Cox was so proud of it that when he saw a pile of advance copies of Whitney Young's speech sitting on the press table at the Statler-Hilton Hotel, he mimeographed a stack of Lewis speeches for equal distribution.

Trouble over the speech began on Tuesday afternoon, the day before the march. A Catholic prelate took the Lewis draft to Washington's Archbishop Patrick O'Boyle, who was scheduled to deliver the opening invocation at the march. O'Boyle found Lewis' remarks incendiary, and his complaints soon spread to Burke Marshall, Walter Reuther, and to other white clergymen who had agreed to participate. Within hours, Bayard Rustin was obliged to convene an emergency mediation session at the Statler-Hilton. Lewis stoutly defended his speech against censorship by the elders, who argued in rejoinder that its content—particularly the statement that the civil rights bill came "too little, too late" and was unworthy of SNCC support—was incompatible with the general purpose of the march. This triggered a heated debate on what exactly the purpose was. Word of the dispute filtered downstairs to the hotel lobby, where Malcolm X was fielding questions from reporters, and the Black Muslim leader adroitly cited the reports to buttress his thesis that powerful white forces had made puppets of the Negroes and turned the protest into a Kennedy pep rally, which Malcolm later ridiculed as the "Farce on Washington." Word of his stinging comments filtered back upstairs to the SNCC contingent. Lewis and several others had met Malcolm that day. They admired him for slinging darts of uncomfortable truth, and yet they also wanted to prove that at least some Negroes were not puppets.

Several blocks away, Bob Moses led a crew of pickets on the sidewalks outside the Justice Department. Ever aloof from public speeches and political deals, even those of his closest SNCC colleagues, Moses remained fixed upon the deeds that he saw as the essence of good faith. If the federal government would fulfill its duty to protect would-be voters and lawful demonstrators, he insisted, the movement could accomplish the rest by hard work. To him, all else was political vapor. No march could make these underlying realities more or less compelling, and part of him rebelled against conniving with federal authorities to create a public climate for recognizing responsibilities that already were obvious. Together with supporters of the Americus prisoners and the Albany Nine, he attacked the Justice Department for retreating shamefully into politics. Moses himself carried a picket sign that caused more than a few pedestrians to brush by him as a doomsday kook: "When There Is No Justice, What Is the State but a Robber Band Enlarged?"

Late that night, King returned to Washington from two days on the road. Sealing himself off in his suite at the Willard Hotel, he began to outline his speech for the next day. His opening sentence bowed to Lincoln: "Five score years ago, a great American, in whose shadow we stand today, signed the Emancipation Proclamation." King would have liked to stamp the moment with his cry for a Second Emancipation Proclamation, but he knew he would reap confusion or worse by introducing a strange alternative to the civil rights bill. Instead he conjured up the safer notion that Lincoln and the Founding Fathers had issued all Americans a "promissory note" guaranteeing basic democratic freedoms. From there he developed an opening run on the clanking, dissonant metaphor of a "bad check" of liberty for Negroes—"a check which has come back marked 'insufficient funds.' But we refuse to believe that the bank of justice is bankrupt . . . So we have come to cash this check . . ."

King wrote new language for one of his standard refrains, "*Now* is the time," ending with a rebuttal of the rumors that the movement was being tamed by success or by the Kennedy Administration. "Those who hope that the Negro needed to blow off steam and will now be content will have a rude awakening if the nation returns to business as usual," he wrote. He turned aside briefly in a paragraph addressed to incipient Negro separatism within the movement—not only from Malcolm X but also from King's exasperating colleague Adam Clayton Powell, who of late had been sounding off about how Negroes needed to purge the civil rights organizations of white influence. King blended a plea for renewed nonviolence with a call for a "biracial army." "The marvelous new militancy which has engulfed the Negro community must not lead us to a distrust of all white people," he wrote. It was a measure of the extraordinary national shift since spring that King felt obliged to nurture white allies rather than to scold them desperately, as in his "Letter from Birmingham Jail." This was a complicated, delicate line of racial politics, and he returned to urgency in a third paragraph on a cumbersome new refrain: "We cannot be satisfied . . . we can never be satisfied . . . we cannot be satisfied as long as a Negro in Mississippi cannot vote and a Negro in New York believes he has nothing for which to vote."

These few themes exhausted the seven minutes. All night long King pared his language so that he could squeeze in a run on his common refrain, "With *this* faith . . . With *this* faith . . ." His final result was a mixture of truncated oratory and fresh composition. The speech was politically sound but far from historic, nimble in some streaks while

club-footed through others. King gave his handwritten draft to Wyatt
Walker for typing and reproduction just as the Moses picket line was
ending its all-night vigil at the Justice Department. Also that morning,
Robert Kennedy was calling Archbishop O'Boyle to renew the stalemated
discussions over the acceptability of the John Lewis speech, and FBI
agents, on order from Hoover, were calling Charlton Heston and other
celebrities in their Washington hotel rooms, warning them to stay in-
doors because the government expected violence. None of these contending parties had yet found a formula to shape or define the March on
Washington. This privilege fell to the anonymous people who had spent
the night on trains and buses.

It was the first—and essentially the last—mass meeting ever to reach
the national airwaves. Relatively few Negroes and almost no whites had
experienced the mood of that central institution—not during the bus
boycott or the Freedom Rides, nor since then from the churches of Albany, Birmingham, or Greenwood. As a result, the term "mass meeting"
meant very little when the pilgrims spilled out singing freedom songs. A
trainload that had boarded in Savannah singing "We Shall Not Be
Moved" arrived at Washington's Union Station singing "We Shall Overcome." Andrew Young was there when hundreds of movement people
from another city stepped through the train doors singing, "Woke up this
morning with my mind set on freedom. Hallelu, hallelu, hallelujah!"

According to march historian Thomas Gentile, twenty-one charter
trains pulled in that morning, and buses poured south through the Baltimore tunnel at the rate of one hundred per hour. A jaunty young Negro
finished a week-long journey on skates, having rolled all the way from
Chicago wearing a bright sash that read "Freedom." An eighty-two-
year-old bicycled from Ohio, and a younger man pedaled in from South
Dakota. Small high school bands improvised on corners of the Mall.
Determined high spirits converged from all directions in a kind of giant
New Orleans funeral—except that here there was hope of removing the
cause of the underlying pain, and here the vast acreage between the
Capitol and the Washington Monument muffled the excitement with
the dignity of open space. Among the tens of thousands of inpouring
whites, plainspoken workers from the UAW and other unions mingled
with students and over-earnest intellectuals. Few of them were completely at ease in a swelling sea of dark faces, but nearly all of them forgot
their apprehensions. They were swept away by what in fact was the
ordinary transport of countless mass meetings, while movement veterans absorbed revelatory homage from palpable symbols of white prestige

—the television cameras, movie stars, and dearest edifices of American democracy. A chorus of news cameras clicked as James Garner pushed through the crowd hand in hand with Negro actress Diahann Carroll; they were among dozens who had arrived on the Hollywood "celebrity plane" organized by Harry Belafonte and Clarence Jones. Even those who had attended a hundred mass meetings never had witnessed anything like Marlon Brando on the giant stage, holding up for the world an actual cattle prod from Gadsden as an indictment of segregationist hatred.

At the Washington Monument staging area, a public address system came alive shortly after ten o'clock with the voice of Joan Baez, who entertained the early-bird crowd by singing "Oh Freedom," a spiritual that Odetta had made popular. Odetta herself came on next, singing "I'm On My Way," and her mountainous voice prompted Josh White to jump up beside her out of turn. White, whose career reached back into the 1920s and 1930s, when young Communist Bayard Rustin had been one of his sidemen, asked Baez to join them during a number, and soon Peter, Paul and Mary stepped in among them. The trio took the lead on one of their new hits, Bob Dylan's "Blowin' in the Wind," and then Dylan himself stepped out among them. He had just written a ballad about the death of Medgar Evers. It was a rare moment for folk music, as the performers on the stage had gained celebrity status for themselves and celebrity for their overtly cross-racial tradition. To underscore their respect for the movement, they brought on the SNCC Freedom Singers from Albany. Baez had just persuaded one of them, Bernice Johnson, to give up the study of opera for what became a luminous career as a performer and student of music derived from Africa; Rutha Harris, much to her eventual regret, was about to turn down a recording contract because she had promised her mother she would finish school in Albany. A potpourri of Americana filled the interludes between songs. The first Negro airline stewardess led cheers. Norman Thomas, the old patrician Socialist, looked tearfully over the huge crowd and said, "I'm glad I lived long enough to see this day."

The warm-up music did not appeal to everybody, and great masses of people stepped off toward the Lincoln Memorial long ahead of schedule. Some sought good seats for the afternoon rally. Others were simply eager to march. Teenagers from Danville wore white sweatshirts and black armbands to signify racial injustice in their hometown, and another young group danced down Constitution Avenue with signs saying they had been arrested in Plaquemine Parish, Louisiana. Rustin's crowd-control marshals lacked the numbers or the heart to hold them back. The streams of early marchers grew so thick that it required almost a military operation to create the illusion for posterity that King and the other sponsors had gone ahead of them all. Marshals waded in from the flanks in sufficient force to open a temporary wedge of space. The leaders squeezed in, locking arms against the dammed tide behind them, which held just long enough for news photographers to catch the scene from a flatbed truck.

Mounted in the eagle's eye of the Washington Monument, a CBS television camera showed viewers a thick carpet of people on both sides of the half-mile reflecting pool and all around the base of the Lincoln Memorial. At noon, nearly two hours before the rally began, the police estimated the crowd at more than 200,000. From this official number, friendly observers argued plausibly that late arrivals and high density justified talk of 300,000, and the usual effusions ran it upward to 500,000. By whatever count, the numbers reduced observers to monosyllabic joy. Within the movement, the gathering sea of placards and faces produced the most brain-numbing sight since the first ghost fleet of empty buses chugged through Montgomery.

An ancient man reached halfway around the world to fix the historical moment: W. E. B. Du Bois had died in Ghana. In making the announcement over the huge loudspeakers at the march, Roy Wilkins had the grace to downplay the Communist apostasy of his old tormentor: "Now, regardless of the fact that in his later years Dr. Du Bois chose another path, it is incontrovertible that at the dawn of the twentieth century his was the voice that was calling to you to gather here today in this cause." For those who revered Du Bois, news of his death that very morning came as a shockingly appropriate transition. Gone finally was the father of pan-Africanism, the NAACP, and the Negro intelligentsia. Taking his life's jumbled status to the grave, Du Bois would receive a state funeral in Accra, a Marxist eulogy, and burial outside Christianborg Castle.

Prosaic crises distracted the march leaders. King was preoccupied with the sensitivities of Fred Shuttlesworth, who, along with James Baldwin and other notables, was upset over his exclusion from the list of speakers. Once the leaders pushed their way up the steps of the Lincoln Memorial, they confronted renewed brushfires over the latest draft of John Lewis' speech. Walter Reuther was furious, saying that while Lewis was right to prod the Kennedy Administration, he was foolish to belittle the civil rights bill. Burke Marshall rushed from the Justice Department in the sidecar of a police motorcycle, bearing a revised draft that blunted Lewis' criticisms of the government. Archbishop O'Boyle did not care so much about the Kennedy image, but he did consider the "scorched earth" language to be unacceptably violent in tone, and he refused to give the opening invocation unless changes were made.

Bayard Rustin improvised with music to cover the chaotic dispute backstage, where rumors were flying and Ralph Abernathy kept running around telling everybody to be calm. Peacemakers shuttled between clumps of aggrieved speakers with compromise wordings. In the central huddle, Lewis and Roy Wilkins wound up shaking fingers angrily in each other's faces until Rustin jumped in to appoint an emergency truce committee of Randolph, King, Lewis, and the Rev. Eugene Carson Blake, a prominent white clergyman from the National Council of Churches. While the committee retired for deliberations inside a guard station beneath the giant seat of the Lincoln statue, Rustin persuaded O'Boyle to go ahead with the invocation on the assurance that he would be shown the final Lewis text in time to walk off the platform if he found it unacceptable. Much to King's relief, Rustin hustled Shuttlesworth out for an impromptu filler speech.

Reverend Blake's arrest in Baltimore gave him special status as the march's only white speaker who had gone to jail in a civil rights demonstration, and to stress his commitment he submitted abjectly to the indictment that King had hurled at the white church from Birmingham ("We come late, late we come, in the reconciling and repentant spirit," Blake declared that day to the marchers). Still, Blake was a forceful man —Eisenhower's personal pastor—and no amount of contrition could make him a pushover. In the huddle, he objected vehemently to Lewis' use of "revolution" and "the masses," calling them terms of an alien dogma. When Randolph defended the words as perfectly proper, saying he had used them regularly for forty years, Blake shifted his attack to the "Sherman's march" passage, which he insisted was contrary to the spirit of the entire march. Here he had better success. Lewis retreated to a defense of his right to choose his own words. King took this opening to doubt, correctly, that the "scorched earth" language was in fact Lewis'. "John, I know you as well as anybody," he said. "That doesn't *sound* like you." The salvaged agreement was a bundle of irony. King changed a few words while insisting that it was merely an adjustment of style and context, not substance. James Forman, pecking furiously at a portable typewriter, deleted phrases he himself had added. Textual changes were trivial relative to the contention they spawned.

The secret battle under Lincoln's seat became a cherished, bitter legend within SNCC, full of accusations against those who had acquiesced in the demands for unity and "emasculated" Lewis' speech. Some SNCC partisans nursed a commanding sense of separation, snickering at optimism that was miles wide and inches deep, like a desert lake. Essentially, the argument was about the proper mix of emotion to project to the world at this opportunity—anger, love, sadness, hope. Under pressure of time, extraordinary virtues were turning sour, as though human nature were demanding recompense for the saintly maturity of young movement people since the early sit-ins and freedom rides. Professing to be bored by the vapid emotions of the march, the students turned inward, alienated from hopes they themselves had largely created.

Very little of the new undertow touched Lewis himself. When his turn came to face the vast host, he stepped forward to a long rumble of applause in tribute to the students of the movement. He began nervously, and in places he inserted a hint of a British accent to cover a slow, Alabama farm tongue, but the crowd soon warmed up his cadence. Even those who had never heard of C. B. King or James Farmer could tell by the way he spoke their names that Lewis was personally acquainted with those being beaten and jailed. His authenticity stirred a crowd that was sleepy from a long afternoon's drone of self-conscious speeches. From him, talk of living "in constant fear of a police state" did not seem extreme, and his refrain, "What did the federal government *do*?" came as a bracing dose of realism. Prophetically, he did not use the word "Negro," and alone of the speakers talked of "black people" and "the black masses." Crowd response swept him through difficult rhetoric of scolding, cold-eyed idealism:

> My friends, let us not forget that we are involved in a serious social revolution. By and large, American politics is dominated by politicians who build their careers on immoral compromises and ally themselves with open forms of political, economic, and social exploitation.
> There are exceptions, of course. We salute those. But what political leader can stand up and say, "My party is the party of principles"? For the party of Kennedy is also the party of Eastland. The party of Javits is also the party of Goldwater. Where is *our* party? Where is the political party that will make it unnecessary to march on Washington? Where is the political party that will make it unnecessary to march in the streets of Birmingham?

Summoning up the will for a continuing march "until true freedom comes, until the revolution of 1776 is complete," Lewis called off a long list of marching cities, and in doing so he achieved a preaching rhythm that he had practiced with barnyard chickens only a few years earlier.

In a harbinger of a separate movement to come, there had been muffled contention over the role of women in the march. Without noticeable dissent, the planning committee barred Coretta King and the other wives of the male leaders from marching with their husbands. Diverting them to a separate procession down Independence Avenue, the committee scheduled no female speakers during the entire three-hour program. Yet women provided much of the afternoon's historical resonance. In a "Tribute to Women," Randolph introduced for bows what amounted to a women's roll call of the movement: Rosa Parks, Daisy Bates, Diane

Nash Bevel, Gloria Richardson of Cambridge, Maryland. Few in the audience recognized the shy widow of Herbert Lee, who had been slain two years earlier during SNCC's first registration drive in Mississippi, but those who did cheered her all the more. Randolph also presented Josephine Baker, the expatriate singer who had flown in from Paris for the march wearing her Free French uniform. He introduced Marian Anderson to sing "He's Got the Whole World in His Hands," and finally, when the long procession of speakers had reduced the sun-drenched crowd to restless fatigue, he brought out Mahalia Jackson. Her first notes were a cry from the deepest wellsprings of culture. The song was "I Been 'Buked and I Been Scorned," a spiritual born of the slave experience, but Jackson managed also to stir emotions irresistible to whites. People fumbled for handkerchiefs, and responsive cries chased the echoes of her *a cappella* voice through the cavernous outdoors.

Rabbi Joachim Prinz of the American Jewish Congress received a smattering of polite applause when he followed Jackson to the microphone. There were scattered cries for King, who was next and last. Although the program was running nearly a half-hour *ahead* of schedule, by a miracle from Bayard Rustin, people ached to stretch limbs and escape sunstroke. They were ready to go home. When Randolph introduced King as "the moral leader of our nation," small waves of applause lapped forward for nearly a minute in tribute to the best-known leader among them as well as to the end of a joyous day. Then the crowd fell silent.

It was a formal speech, as demanded by the occasion and the nature of the audience. By then, ABC and NBC had cut away from afternoon soap operas to join the continuous live coverage by CBS. King faced also a giant press corps and listeners as diverse as the most ardent supporters of the movement and the stubborn Congress at the other end of the Mall, where by quorum calls sullen legislators "spread upon the Journal" the names of the ninety-two absent members who might have let the march distract them from regular business. For all these King delivered his address in his clearest diction and stateliest baritone. Ovations interrupted him in the cracks of infrequent oratorical flourish, and in difficult passages small voices cried "Yes!" and "Right on!" as though grateful and proud to hear such talk. From the front, a woman could be heard to laugh and shout "Sho 'nuff!" when King told them about the freedom checks that had bounced. Five minutes later, when King declared that the movement would not stop "as long as our bodies, heavy with the fatigue of travel, cannot gain lodging in the motels of the highways and hotels of the cities," a shout went up from a pocket of the crowd so distant that the sound did not reach King for a second or two.

He recited his text verbatim until a short run near the end: "We will not be satisfied until justice runs down like waters and righteousness like a mighty stream." The crowd responded to the pulsating emotion transmitted from the prophet Amos, and King could not bring himself to deliver the next line of his prepared text, which by contrast opened its lamest and most pretentious section ("And so today, let us go back to our communities as members of the international association for the advancement of creative dissatisfaction"). Instead, extemporaneously, he urged them to return to their struggles ("Go back to Mississippi. Go back to Alabama . . ."), to believe that change would come "somehow" and that they could not "wallow in the valley of despair."

There was no alternative but to preach. Knowing that he had wandered completely off his text, some of those behind him on the platform urged him on, and Mahalia Jackson piped up as though in church, "Tell 'em about the dream, Martin." Whether her words reached him is not known. Later, King said only that he forgot the rest of the speech and took up the first run of oratory that "came to me." After the word "despair," he temporized for an instant: "I say to you today, my friends, and so even though we face the difficulties of today and tomorrow, I still have a dream. It is a dream deeply rooted in the American dream . . ."

Mindful of his audience, he held himself to a far more deliberate pace than in Detroit, or in Chicago the week before. Here he did not shout or smile, and there was no chance to build upon cascading rhythms of response, as in a mass meeting. The slow determination of his cadence exposed all the more clearly the passion that overshadowed the content of the dream. It went beyond the limitations of language and culture to express something that was neither pure rage nor pure joy, but a universal transport of the kind that makes the blues sweet. Seven times he threw the extremities of black and white against each other, and each time he came back with a riveting, ecstatic dignity.

The "Dream" sequence took him from Amos to Isaiah, ending, "I have a dream that one day, every valley shall be exalted . . ." Then he spoke a few sentences from the prepared conclusion, but within seconds he was off again, reciting the first stanza of "My Country 'Tis of Thee," ending, " 'from every mountainside, let freedom ring.' " After an interlude of merely one sentence—"And if America is to be a great nation, this must become true"—he took it up again: "So let freedom ring." By then, Mahalia Jackson was happy, chanting "My Lord! My Lord!" As King tolled the freedom bells from New Hampshire to California and back across Mississippi, his solid, square frame shook and his stateliness barely contained the push to an end that was old to King but new to the world: "And when *this* happens . . . we will be able to speed up that day when *all* God's children, black men and white men, Jews and Gentiles, Protestants and Catholics, will be able to join hands and sing in the words of the old Negro spiritual, 'Free at last! Free at last! Thank God Almighty, we are free at last!' " With that King stepped suddenly aside, and the March tumbled swiftly to benediction from Benjamin Mays.

Like most television viewers, President Kennedy was witnessing a complete King speech for the first time. "He's damn good," the President remarked to his aides at the White House. Kennedy was especially impressed with King's ad lib off the prepared text, and he was quick to pick out the most original refrain. As the principal leaders filed into the Cabinet Room from the march, he greeted King with a smiling "I have a dream," as a fellow speechmaker who valued a good line. The compliment made King feel slightly uncomfortable, as he alone had been showered with hosannas all the way over from the Lincoln Memorial. Deflectively, King asked President Kennedy if he had heard the excellent speech of Walter Reuther. The latter indeed had delivered a fiery oration containing the day's most pointed barbs at President Kennedy ("We cannot *defend* freedom in Berlin so long as we *deny* freedom in Birmingham!"), and the President in turn deflected mention of Reuther. "Oh, I've heard him plenty of times," he replied.

The President and King lacked the chemistry for small talk. Roy Wilkins was better. Once Kennedy had shaken hands all around, Wilkins embarked on a folksy monologue, craftily pointing out that the glowing success of the march could shift the heavy center of American opinion by diluting suspicions that the Negro and his cause were somehow inherently flawed. Wilkins employed flattery of the President—"If you will permit me to say so, sir, you're politically astute"—and toward the end he wove in a strand of self-pity: "It fell to my lot, sir, in this afternoon of superlative oratory, to be the one to deal rather pedantically and pedestrianly with the hard business of legislation. And the other gentlemen were free to soar in the wild blue yonder. And they did so soar." Only then did he ease into his argument that the Kennedy Administration should strengthen its civil rights bill. The House was ready to pass better legislation, he asserted, and was only waiting for assent from the White House.

Randolph's booming British accent quickly seconded Wilkins. At a minimum, the President should agree to add a section banning racial exclusions in employment, he said, stressing the rising threats of automation and joblessness. Inner-city teenagers, seeing no jobs ahead, were dropping out of school in epidemic numbers. "I may suggest to you that they present almost an alarming problem," Randolph told Kennedy, "be-

cause they have no faith in anybody white. They have no faith in the
Negro leadership. They have no faith in God. They have no faith in the
government. In other words, they believe the hand of the society is
against them."

Walter Reuther spoke up for a second desired amendment: the old Title
III section stripped from the 1957 act, which would empower the Attorney General to initiate lawsuits to correct egregious denials of civil
rights. The Kennedy bill provided such power only for school desegregation cases, and only then if private litigants had initiated a suit and were
found to be indigent. To expand that power was urgently necessary and
eminently fair, said Reuther. Now they had the muscle to do so, he
added, as one practical effect of the march was that "we've put together
the broadest working legislative coalition we've ever had."

President Kennedy interrupted to check the momentum of the concerted appeal. On the problem of jobs and school dropouts, he said, he
and the Attorney General had been talking about Harlem and Southside
Chicago, and they thought that in the coming months Negro leaders
might do well to follow the Jewish example. "This doesn't have anything
to do with what we've been talking about," he said. "But it seems to me,
with all the influence that all you gentlemen have in the Negro community, that we could emphasize . . . which I think the Jewish community has done, on educating their children, on making them study,
making them stay in school and all the rest." From there, Kennedy listed
the difficulties his own bill already faced. State by state in the House
and person by person in the Senate, he read off Lawrence O'Brien's predicted vote count. Prospects looked close in the House and grim in the
Senate. Besides, the current bill would be more palatable to the Senate,
where it must somehow overcome a filibuster.

Wilkins had presented far more optimistic numbers, including a private assurance from Speaker John McCormack that a much stronger bill
could pass the House to gain leverage against the Senate. A weaker bill
would earn no gratitude in the Senate, where the arch-defenders of segregation were poised to slice any bill down to nothing. Randolph rose to
say that if the obstacles were as great as President Kennedy indicated,
"it's obvious that it's going to take nothing less than a crusade to win
approval for these civil rights measures." When Kennedy agreed, Randolph told him, "Nobody can lead this crusade but you," and he urged
him to take the crusade directly to the voters, over the heads of Congress.

President Kennedy squirmed in the trap. "Well, we're doing the, uh,
we're, uh, I think it would be helpful if you gentlemen indicated as you
would here that this is a matter that, uh, that, uh, involves both parties,"
he replied. "And are confident, which I said at the press conference, that

I'm confident that the Republican Party is for the . . . Lincoln all the way down . . . just treat it as if you *anticipate* their support." When one of the leaders asked directly if this meant the President thought the march had made no impression, Kennedy spoke more frankly of his political misgivings. What the Republicans were "trying to do is to play to the South—with some success, these days." Nationally, they had nothing to lose, as the Democrats already had most of the Negro vote, and if they could push the President into a crusade, then they could be safely for civil rights and still hang blame for Negro excess on the Democrats. Then and later, President Kennedy alluded to treacherous political games being played—segregationist Democrats maneuvering for pro-Negro amendments to make it easier for moderates to vote against the entire bill, liberal Republicans threatening to vote against the bill because it was too weak. Exasperated, the President argued that the civil rights forces needed to push for a bipartisan consensus instead of a Democratic crusade. It was hard enough to get most Republicans to be for civil rights at all, he declared, citing his White House meeting with "all the golden names of American business." The businessmen "sat on their tails" and fretted about demonstrations, Kennedy complained. "That's all we could get out of them."

Reuther jumped in to correct the President's approach. "You gotta get small groups of these fellows," he said urgently. In Detroit, he had picked key auto executives. "And I said, 'Look, you can't escape this problem, and there are two ways of resolving it: either by reason or riots. Now the civil war that this is gonna trigger is not gonna be fought at Gettysburg, it's gonna be fought in your backyard, in your plant, where your kids are growing up.' " Reuther claimed to have organized an emergency management/labor group to integrate the auto industry. He commended his method—Lyndon Johnson–style conspiratorial jawboning—as the only way to get difficult things done, and all but rebuked President Kennedy for his seminar appeals. "You call a big meeting," said Reuther, "and you haven't got a little group organized that will give it a sense of direction, a little push, and nothing will happen."

King remained silent through the politely contentious debate of the post-march summit. Near the end, he asked whether a private moral appeal might induce former President Eisenhower to exert influence on Minority Leader Charles Halleck, the most critical of the House Republicans.

"No, it won't," President Kennedy replied quickly. "No, it won't."

To correct any impression that he wanted to undertake such a mission himself, King told Kennedy that he meant "some groups" should do it, as Ike "happens to be in the other denomination." Chuckles broke out

over this play on religion and race. King continued his improbable role
as Cabinet Room jester by adding a partisan twist. There must be some
way to enlist Eisenhower, he quipped. "Isn't he a Democrat when he
goes to church?"

Reverend Blake, Eisenhower's pastor, waded out of the ensuing laughter to declare that in fact Ike "can be got at on that ground." However,
Blake counseled against a one-on-one pastoral appeal, warning that the
former president could get testy "if he thinks I'm trying to push him."
Blake thought it better to send a blue-ribbon ecumenical delegation to
make the moral case to Eisenhower less personally. President Kennedy
seized on the idea and urged Blake to organize a secret pilgrimage to
Eisenhower's Gettysburg farm as soon as possible. He recommended that
Blake include a Catholic, "and maybe a businessman or two." Smiling at
the firebrand Reuther, he added, "And keep Walter in the background."

At 6:12 P.M., after a meeting of seventy-two minutes, President Kennedy excused the leaders on this light note, promising to keep in touch
on the legislative head counts. By then, Rustin had volunteer crews
sweeping up the debris from an emptied Mall, and news organizations
were rushing to meet evening deadlines on one of the world's leading
stories. Heavy coverage stressed the unprecedented size and utter peacefulness of the march, with a strong subliminal message that the first
whiff of mass political integration had been remarkably pleasant. Not all
white newspapers were attuned at first to the depth of the impression
King had made. The Washington *Post*, for example, highlighted Randolph's speech and made no mention of King's. By contrast, *The New
York Times* featured a story headlined " 'I Have a Dream . . .' Peroration
by Dr. King Sums Up a Day the Capital Will Remember," by James
Reston, on a front page containing no fewer than five different stories on
the march, arranged in a collage around two large crowd photographs. It
was perhaps the zenith of the *Times*'s pioneer devotion to the civil rights
movement. Negro press coverage amounted to a proud rhapsody. Even
the Atlanta *Daily World* announced that the rally "forever" changed
racial perceptions, and the paper relaxed its rules against picturing King
on the front page (though only in a group shot with President Kennedy).
Motown Records released an album within weeks, followed swiftly by
bootleg recordings of "I Have a Dream" by Mr. Maestro Records and
Twentieth Century–Fox Records. Clarence Jones soon brought suit
against the bootleggers on King's behalf.

Among the instant commentators, only Stanley Levison paid much
attention to the political nuances of King's speech. Bursting with pride
over the success of the day, Levison told callers that "it was marvelous
in Martin's speech the way he handled the white and Negro question,

completely repudiating this kind of nonsense of Adam Powell and the Muslims and everybody else in a way that was so positive." He praised King as "the man of the hour for everybody," and said he was "bowled over" by the public generosity of Roy Wilkins, who once had refused to invite King to the NAACP's fiftieth anniversary dinner.

What quickly swept the press of both races was the "Dream" sequence, which stamped King's public identity. Critics would point out that the dream was ethereal, and people who yearned for simple justice would object that the content was too simple. Still, precious few among millions detected lightness or naïveté in the speech. On the contrary, the emotional command of his oratory gave King authority to reinterpret the core intuition of democratic justice. More than his words, the timbre of his voice projected him across the racial divide and planted him as a new founding father. It was a fitting joke on the races that he achieved such statesmanship by setting aside his lofty text to let loose and jam, as he did regularly from two hundred podiums a year.

TWENTY-THREE

CROSSING OVER:
NIGHTMARES AND
DREAMS

That September, Birmingham faced a federal court order to admit the first five Negro students to three different public schools. Governor Wallace threw up a public cloud of resistance, citing the threat of violence. Mayor Boutwell maneuvered furtively between Wallace and Burke Marshall, telling each that he wanted to keep the other's troops out of the city. In a last-minute compromise, Boutwell sought a delay for the court to consider new evidence of "inherent differences in the races." That night another dynamite bomb struck the home of Arthur Shores, touching off another long night of swarming demonstrations, sorties by the police riot tank, rock-throwing, and finally armed suppression that killed one Negro and sent twenty-one others to the hospital. By the next morning, Wallace had persuaded Boutwell to close the schools targeted for integration. King sent another protest telegram to President Kennedy.

On September 9—the date on which President Kennedy appeared exclusively on NBC's "Huntley-Brinkley Report," inaugurating the network's jump from fifteen to thirty minutes of nightly news—the three Birmingham schools finally opened, but Wallace sent National Guard troops in to bar the Negro students. By some oversight, Wallace neglected to surround one school in a parallel case across the state in Huntsville, with the result that Alabama's first Negro elementary-school student, six-year-old Sonnie W. Hereford IV, attended a previously all-white school that day. By morning, President Kennedy had federalized and withdrawn the Alabama guard troops in Birmingham, allowing the five Negro students to attend classes there, whereupon a majority of the white students filed out in protest. A crazily inverted pattern of tension developed across the balance of the week. At West End High, white cheerleaders and football players organized a movement to support integrated classes against fellow students who marched and threw rocks to enforce a segregationist school strike. Other white students staged a sit-in at Mayor Boutwell's office to protest integration. Governor Wallace denounced federal intervention. On Friday, September 13, he flew to Baltimore and declared his intention to run in the 1964 Maryland presidential primary.

That Sunday was the annual Youth Day at the Sixteenth Street Baptist Church. Mamie H. Grier, superintendent of the Sunday school, stopped in at the basement ladies' room to find four young girls who had left Bible classes early and were talking excitedly about the beginning of the school year. All four were dressed in white from head to toe, as this was their day to run the main service for the adults at eleven o'clock. Grier urged them to hurry along and then went upstairs to sit in on her own women's Sunday-school class. They were engaged in a lively debate on the lesson topic, "The Love That Forgives," when a loud earthquake shook the entire church and showered the classroom with plaster and debris. Grier's first thought was that it was like a ticker-tape parade. Maxine McNair, a schoolteacher sitting next to her, reflexively went stiff and was the only one to speak. "Oh, my goodness!" she said. She escaped with Grier, but the stairs down to the basement were blocked and the large stone staircase on the outside literally had vanished. They stumbled through the church to the front door and then made their way around outside through the gathering noise of moans and sirens. A hysterical church member shouted to Grier that her husband had already gone to the hospital in the first ambulance. McNair searched desperately for her only child until finally she came upon a sobbing old man and screamed, "Daddy, I can't find Denise!" The man helplessly replied, "She's dead, baby. I've got one of her shoes." He held a girl's white dress shoe, and the look on his daughter's face made him scream out, "I'd like to blow the whole town up!"

By then, ten-year-old Sarah Collins had staggered out through the gaping hole in the wall where the stone staircase had been. She was partially blinded, bleeding through the nose and ears from concussion. Her brother ran around screaming that his sister was dead, and in the addled shock it was some time before anyone understood he did not mean Sarah but older sister Addie Mae, fourteen. Ambulance medics scooped up Sarah

Collins among some twenty others and headed for University Hospital. It registered dimly on Mamie Grier that Denise McNair and Addie Mae Collins were two of the four girls she had seen in the ladies' room minutes earlier. Grier took a chance that her car would start even though its windows were shattered, fenders curled, and part of a door blown off. She drove unsteadily away until stopped at one of the police roadblocks being thrown up around the city. Officers recruited a white man off the street to drive her car to the hospital, where she found her husband among the less seriously wounded. The hospital was a noisy blur of shrieks, hymns, television cameras, and shouted orders from crowd-control guards. Comforting stories circulated about how the pastor's injured daughter, four-year-old Susan Cross, had smiled so bravely when they wheeled her through a nearby corridor. Grier could say little more than "Those poor girls," a phrase she would repeat vacantly under sedation for the next two weeks.

Claude Wesley, principal of Lewis Elementary School, did not often subject himself to Sunday-school classes. He had dropped his adopted daughter Cynthia at the church and then escaped to the errands of a pleasant Sunday morning. When the noise of the blast interrupted his shoeshine, he had made his way to the church, the hospital, and finally the morgue, where he and his wife identified their daughter's remains by the feet and a ring on her finger. Chris McNair made the same desperate trip to the morgue. A Lutheran, schoolteacher, and freelance photographer, McNair had heard the bomb from his own church some blocks distant. He had stopped to pick up his camera on the way to investigate, but the horrible procession of clues left the camera dangling uselessly by the time he found his wife Maxine and her father at the hospital. In his grief, the grandfather switched numbly from rage to religion. "Maybe the kid's death will do some good," he said. Chris McNair soon reeled away back downtown, seeking refuge in objects and details, searching for items the family would need for the funeral ordeal. Everywhere he went, white sales clerks burst into tears, saying they had seen him on television. Odd novelties of emotion burned through his daze, leaving senseless impressions of pain and balm. McNair was sure that some white people had just killed his daughter in church, but that same afternoon dignified, over-wrought white strangers knocked at his door to express their condolences. Some of them arrived in cars bearing Confederate license plates.

Secondary effects of the church bombing churned madly through the white population of Birmingham. A preacher cut short a segregationist rally at a Go Kart track. Heading home from the rally, a pair of Eagle Scouts fired their new pistol at two Negro boys riding double on a bicycle, killing a thirteen-year-old perched on the handlebars; the Eagle

Scouts told police they had no idea what made them shoot. By late afternoon, the polite remorse that had prevailed among policemen at the bomb site had hardened against real and anticipated reprisals from angry Negroes in the streets. Governor Wallace sent in the dreaded Colonel Lingo with three hundred state troopers. Typically, when officers came upon rock battles between young whites and Negroes, the Negroes ran while the whites welcomed the relief. Officers killed one fleeing Negro by shooting him in the back of the head. Among civilian whites in general, reactions wound more softly in the same coil: a stab of sympathy and generalized remorse, followed quickly by resentment of exaggerated accusations and then a growing sense of innocence. White attorney Charles Morgan passionately declared that he and all other whites shared guilt for the bombing because they had tolerated or encouraged racial hatred. "We all did it," he said. For this he became a pariah among whites, and his speech itself fed a tide of aggrieved self-vindication. "All of us are victims," insisted Mayor Boutwell.

As revulsion at the church bombing spread swiftly around the world, President Kennedy retrieved Burke Marshall from his weekend farm by helicopter and dispatched him once again to Birmingham. Marshall found a city literally glutted with firearms, openly displayed. Businesses remained closed. White officers barricaded Negroes in the Negro neighborhoods, while roving bands of Negroes expelled white intruders by brandishing shotguns and clubs. The police and local FBI agents both refused to risk taking Marshall to meet King at John Drew's house. Finally, an intrepid team of Negroes wearing homemade "Civil Defense" uniforms fetched Marshall from the Federal Building, slapped him facedown in the back of a car with a white helmet on his head, and ran the gauntlet up to Dynamite Hill, where hired bodyguards were protecting the homes of wealthy Negroes against follow-up bombers. Marshall found King in a seething mass of preachers, advisers, and local Birmingham leaders. Urgent clues from the last bombing competed with threats of the next, and both overlapped with other emergencies, such as hourly checks on the well-being of the five young Negroes in white schools. King, refuting the implications of A. G. Gaston and other Birmingham conservatives, maintained that the bombing was the result of too little daring in civil rights, not too much. He blurted out a hint of this debate to reporters: "What murdered these four girls? The apathy and the complacency of many Negroes who will sit down on their stools and do nothing and not engage in creative protest to get rid of this evil." Marshall, relieved to learn that King planned no immediate demonstrations, gave assurances that the Attorney General had ordered the FBI full force into the church bombing investigation, ignoring the previously cited legalisms and jurisdictional obstacles. From firsthand observation, Marshall agreed with King's fear that open racial warfare could erupt any hour.

When Marshall returned to Washington, King stayed behind to bury the dead. Unlike military commanders, he could not limit contact with the survivors to telegrams or belated ceremonies. As a preacher, he was obliged instead to face the families in funeral homes and to speak out directly over the open caskets. Although King was falling into tactical paralysis, lacking any practical idea of what he might do to restore progress in Birmingham, he made no effort to distance himself from the bombing, or to portray these deaths as incidental to the movement. On the contrary, he claimed the mangled bodies. On hearing of plans for separate funerals, he demanded an explanation from John Cross, pastor of Sixteenth Street Baptist. "Why didn't you try to have a mass funeral?" King asked.

"Well, Martin, I did," Cross replied. "I tried to have a mass funeral, but one family wouldn't agree."

Unsatisfied, King went personally to the grieving parents of Carole Robertson. For an hour he pleaded with them to permit their daughter to be eulogized jointly with the others. In doing so, he proved to the point of callousness that he was anything but squeamish about confronting the human costs of his leadership. Still, he could not budge the Robertsons, both schoolteachers, who stoutly resisted the "grandstand play" of a mass funeral. "We realize Carole lost her life because of the movement," said Mrs. Robertson, "but we feel her loss was personal to us." She allowed Shuttlesworth to preach at her daughter's funeral.

King spoke over but three of the four coffins from the Birmingham church bombing. "At times, life is hard," he said, "as hard as crucible steel." Eight thousand people braved the vigilantes and jeep patrols to attend the giant funeral that overflowed Rev. John Porter's church. No elected officials attended. Among the mourners were eight hundred Birmingham pastors of both races, making them many times over the largest interracial gathering of clergy in the city's history. They assembled on Wednesday, September 18, exactly three weeks after the March on Washington. In conjunction, the two events etched a conflict of mythological clarity: purpose and suffering of blinding purity against a monstrous evil. Such extremes of reality were inherently unstable, but they opened new eyes.

That night, Diane Nash presented to King the germ of what became his Selma voting rights campaign in 1965. She was angry. Privately, she told

King that he could not arouse a battered people for nonviolent action and then give them nothing to do. After the church bombing, she and Bevel had realized that a crime so heinous pushed even nonviolent zealots like themselves to the edge of murder. They resolved to do one of two things: solve the crime and kill the bombers, or drive Wallace and Lingo from office by winning the right for Negroes to vote across Alabama. In the few days since, Nash had drawn up a written plan to accomplish the latter with a rigorously trained nonviolent host, organized at brigade and division strength, that would surround Wallace's government in Montgomery with a sea of bodies, "severing communication from state capitol bldg . . . Lying on railroad tracks, runways, and bus driveways . . . Close down the power company." Her plan amounted to a protracted sit-in on the scale of the March on Washington. "This is an army," she wrote King. "Develop a flag and an insignia or pin or button." When she argued for the plan that night, King could barely take it seriously. He had just come from the funeral. His problem was what could be done in Birmingham tomorrow, not in Montgomery six months hence. Besides, Wallace would love to be attacked by such an army. King stopped short of dismissing Nash, or John Lewis, who was there and thought well of her idea, but he sloughed off her plea for a special strategy session. His lack of interest annoyed Nash, who thought King was too eager to get to Washington for empty talks with politicians.

By the time King reached Washington the next afternoon, his options had been chopped away both to the front and rear. He brought no independent plan for action, such as a march or demonstrations toward specific demands. He traveled with A. G. Gaston, Rev. J. L. Ware, and other pillars of Negro Birmingham who had dragged against his demonstrations all spring and now felt burdened with the cruel aftermath. They would not hear of big demonstrations, because they saw their city as on the brink of annihilation. All King brought to Washington was a plea for federal assistance, but the Kennedy Administration, warned by Marshall, foreclosed such hopes. Early in the day, Robert Kennedy announced that he saw no legal basis for sending marshals or troops to Birmingham. And just before five o'clock that afternoon, Pierre Salinger announced that President Kennedy had appointed two personal emissaries to mediate the racial crisis in Birmingham: former Army Secretary Kenneth Royall and former West Point football coach Earl Blaik. The Administration publicly set its response to the Birmingham bombing only minutes before the King group arrived at the White House.

A pall hung over the private discussion in the Cabinet Room. King opened with a gloomy monologue on the twenty-eight unsolved bombings in Birmingham and the current tinderbox of segregationist martial law. "There is a great deal of frustration and despair and confusion in the Negro community," he told the President. "And there is a feeling of being alone and not being protected. If you walk the street, you're unsafe. If you stay at home, you're unsafe—there's a danger of a bombing. If you're in church, now it isn't safe. So that the Negro feels that everywhere he goes, or if he remains stationary, he's in danger of some physical violence." President Kennedy said nothing until A. G. Gaston interrupted King to complain that insurance companies were canceling commercial policies on Negro businesses, and President Pitts of Miles College pointed out that he had been unable to secure insurance coverage for his new student union building. At this, Kennedy perked up to say here was a problem they could take care of. "I'll get it, Mr. President," Burke Marshall said confidently.

But the President fell silent again when Shuttlesworth renewed King's argument for sending federal troops to replace the state troopers in Birmingham. He wanted to know why a city that was 40 percent Negro should live under the bayonets of an all-white force with a record of stark brutality and unsolved crimes. Ware took up the case, saying the local police had sunk almost to the level of Wallace's troopers. President Kennedy did not contest these assertions, but to him they only proved the implacable hatred toward Negroes by a powerful white majority. He interrupted Ware with marked irritation. "Well, if the local police are there and the State Police are there, what's the hope in Birmingham?" he asked. When Ware mumbled something about martial law, the President sternly pressed his point: "What is the long-range hope for Birmingham?"

The audience shrank from President Kennedy's distemper. King rose quietly to surrender the troop argument. "I still have faith in the vast possibilities of Birmingham," he said. "There are many white people of good will in Birmingham. They need help. I think the situation that we are presenting now is an emergency crisis . . . Troops cannot solve the problem. And we know that. The problem with the mayor is that he's a weak man."

President Kennedy said he understood their frustration. "Now it's tough for the Negro community," he said. ". . . And I know that this bombing is particularly difficult. But if you look at any, as you know, of these struggles over a period, across the world, it's a very dangerous effort. So everybody just has to keep their nerve." He commended his two new emissaries, saying their reputations gave them a chance to open communication between the races. "Royall is an outstanding fellow," he said, "and Colonel Blaik's one of the finest men I've ever met."

King soon faced the huge White House press corps outside. "This is the kind of federal concern needed," he said. *The New York Times* and other major newspapers played the day's developments straight: "Kennedy Names 2 . . . Negroes Applaud Move, Drop Appeal for Troops and Accept Panel." However, dissent sprouted even during King's press conference. Reporters, especially the few Negro ones, asked pointedly if he really thought a "study team" was an appropriate response to the carnage at the Sixteenth Street Baptist Church. Did he think a "segregated" pair of white Army retirees was a sensible way to promote racial harmony? Did King know that Royall was a corporate lawyer from North Carolina, or that no Negro ever played for "Red" Blaik's famous teams at West Point? Did King know these men, or anything about them? Did he think the appointments had been timed deliberately to show he had played no role in the decision? King defended himself lamely and escaped to the seclusion of the Justice Department, where the next day he protested the Albany Nine prosecutions without success. Clarence Jones warned King that James Baldwin and a group of New York intellectuals were furious that he had allowed President Kennedy to outmaneuver him so shamefully. Still, the Baldwin group's more "militant" response of a Christmas shopping boycott fizzled almost as quickly as it was announced. King was cornered between realism and ridicule.

That Sunday marked one week since the Birmingham church bombing. By then, news stories circulated symbolic details of the tragedy—the church clock stopped at 10:22 A.M., the face of Jesus was knocked cleanly from the only surviving stained-glass window in the east wall. On a New York television program, James Baldwin discussed the "missing face of Christ" with Reinhold Niebuhr. Their talk was suffused with the gathering emotion of the civil rights movement, which Niebuhr called a "revolution" that was bringing him out of retirement. Baldwin contended that suffering made Negroes "the only hope this country has," not because of their race or inherent virtue but because only in extremity do people "discover what they really live by." Most Americans, he added, "don't have any longer a real sense of what they live by. I really think it may be Coca-Cola." Niebuhr, saying "history throws a light on this," endorsed Baldwin's idea. "We are in a revolutionary situation," he said, "and all through history, it was a despised minority—the proletarians, the peasants, the poor—who recaptured the heights and depths of faith. And the country itself choked in its own fat, as we are inclined to choke in our own fat."

It was an extraordinary bit of television—a spontaneous, passionate, unlikely alliance between the plodding old Germanic theologian and the tormented young ghetto artist. The one crack of difference between them was a pregnant conundrum on nonviolence. Baldwin chafed at the limits

of nonviolence, which he criticized as a psychological affliction peculiar
to Negroes, saying that through all American history, "the only time
that nonviolence has been admired is when the Negroes practice it." In
reply, Niebuhr gently chided Baldwin for adopting the prevailing condescension toward nonviolence as a ghetto of the weak. "People ask me,"
said Niebuhr, "since I am such a strong anti-pacifist, how I can have this
admiration for a pacifist? Well, I have a simple answer . . . King's doctrine
of nonviolent resistance is not pacifism. Pacifism of really the classical
kind is where you are concerned about your own purity and not responsibility. And the great ethical divide is between people who want to be
pure and those who want to be responsible. And I think King has shown
this difference."

The spirit of resistance already seemed aroused among King's respectable
opponents. On Monday, September 23, a five-man delegation of Birmingham officials marched into President Kennedy's office to present their
side of the dispute, showing no trace of doubt or defensiveness. "Mr.
President, we came here, sir, with big chips on our shoulder," began
Mayor Boutwell's spokesman, William Hamilton. He said the responsible whites of Birmingham deeply resented implications that they were
somehow tarnished by the church bombing, that on the contrary they
already had taken steps to solve racial problems but "have not, in a great
many instances, been given credit for them," and finally that what was
holding back their progress was the lack of a peaceful working atmosphere, most especially a respite from Northern critics and outside agitators such as Martin Luther King.
    President Kennedy doggedly followed the briefing agenda he had re-
ceived from the Attorney General and Burke Marshall. He pressed the
officials to take even one of three minimal, concrete steps that would
ease national pressures since the bombing: (1) hire at least some of the
Negro sales clerks promised in the May agreement, (2) begin biracial
negotiations with *local* Negro leaders, or (3) hire at least one Negro
policeman, as even Jackson, Mississippi, had done. "I'd like to see what
steps you could take," said the President, "even though you may feel
that what you've done is enough." The Birmingham delegates parried
each salvo. As to a Negro policeman, Hamilton said Kennedy had no idea
what personal abuse they were taking just for replacing Bull Connor. "I
would say fifty percent of the morning force when I walk into City Hall,
and when the mayor walks into City Hall, if I hold out my hand, they
refuse to shake hands," said Hamilton. "If I speak, they refuse to speak."
He said at least a third of the police force would quit rather than serve

with a Negro. Rev. Dr. Landon Miller, president of the Birmingham Council of Ministers, told Kennedy that the moderates already were "branded." "When we left the airport yesterday, there were signs over our heads saying these liberals do not represent us," he said.

President Kennedy expressed sympathy, saying people were calling him names too, but that this was the price of public life in difficult times and that things would get worse if they did not do something. Every few minutes he ventured forth on his refrain: "Now isn't it possible to do something? . . . Is there anything that can be done? . . . I'm just trying to think of two or three things that could be done . . . Is there anything that you can do now?" He finally prodded Frank Newton, vice president of the telephone company, into what Newton called "a straightforward answer, but a respectful answer," that such steps would only encourage "those people," and that in fact "a lot of people . . . think *you've* been giving those people encouragement."

"I understand that," replied the President, his voice rising defensively. He told them he had not encouraged any agitation in Birmingham, but on the other hand he did not think all the agitation was unwarranted. "Let me make it clear that I regard getting a police force as legitimate," he said. "And I regard people working as clerks in the stores as legitimate. And I don't think that you can take any other position from a national point of view. And my opinion is that if you can integrate the armed forces, where you have to live together, eat together, use the same john, and all the rest, you can in these cases work together. . . . We're talking about some things which are rather limited." When Newton rejoined that in his opinion the Kennedy public accommodations bill was not so limited, President Kennedy fairly exploded. "Oh, public accommodations is nothing!" he said, launching a passionate monologue on the theme that public accommodations was minimal justice compared with the wrenching problem of the public schools. "Nobody here is naïve about it," he said, "or doesn't understand it, or doesn't see what's happening in Washington, where you've got fifty-four percent Negro and eighty-five percent in the schools, the whites just *running* out of Washington. Nobody wants that. Public accommodations is nothing! My God, it's whether you can go into a store or a hotel. They don't go into the Statler . . . and they won't be coming into the hotel in Birmingham." He wound up his exhortation by telling them he hated to argue with the state of Alabama, "but isn't there something that you can now do, given the problem as it is? . . . You ought to be able to turn that situation around."

"We think we *have* turned it around," Newton replied with cheerful obstinance. After that, President Kennedy hazarded no more emotional pleas. He did warn them not to pin their hopes on getting King out of Birmingham, saying that SNCC and far more radical groups would come behind him. "King has got a . . . terrific investment in nonviolence," said the President, "and SNCC has got an investment in violence, and that's the struggle." But Kennedy himself made no threats, offered no deals, sold no bargains. He resumed the plaintive theme of a rather helpless president in a representative democracy, saying no fewer than twenty-five times that he wished they could take just one step, "even a public relations action . . . anything that gives a hook that suggests that the prospects are better." Out of sheer exhaustion, President Kennedy collapsed toward the only positive step available: support for the Blaik-Royall advisory mission. Grasping the gesture, the Birmingham leaders said they were ready to do just that and already felt better for the exchange of views.

King, while not privy to the internal dynamics of the White House meeting, saw the public result on the front page of the *Times*: "Kennedy Says Birmingham Can Solve Its Own Problems." Such news fed the anxieties gnawing at him that week in Richmond, where the SCLC assembled for its seventh annual convention. The giant four-day affair drew five hundred delegates for what was meant to be a celebration of the movement's breakthrough. Rosa Parks gave a short speech, as did Francis Griffin, the preacher who twelve years earlier had first supported Barbara Johns's student strike in Farmville. The Birmingham movement choir gave nightly concerts of freedom songs. A panel discussion on "The Power of Nonviolence" featured organizers now acquiring an aura of legend—Bayard Rustin, James Bevel, James Lawson, and C. T. Vivian. The convention heard reports from Gadsden, Danville, and ten other cities in the grip of showdowns inspired by Birmingham. Celebrity speakers included Dick Gregory, Roy Wilkins, Adam Clayton Powell, and two U.S. senators.

They all crowded into Richmond's Hotel John Marshall, a proud old facility that bent to its first integrated convention with strained civility. For the delegates, a different strain of dissension rippled in all directions on the supercharged emotions of the church bombing, making it difficult to maintain even the façade of movement idealism. For King, at the center of a tempest, the underside of success collided with the topside of failure. Wyatt Walker demanded nearly a threefold salary increase based on the SCLC's stupendous growth, while diverse critics charged that King's paralysis had put the SCLC out of business. King's "I Have a Dream" fame caused Ralph Abernathy's long-simmering jealousy to spill

over into indignant complaints that his hotel room was not appointed as
finely as King's, and finally into an inebriated elevator scuffle with a
white man who did not share his low opinion of the room service. Septima Clark followed Abernathy to his room to tell him bluntly that he
was a spoiled man, full of unseemly spite, and while she was at it, she
also reproached him for his habit of being deliberately late to church
services in order to flaunt his mastery over the common people of
the congregation. In particular, she reminded him of the time when she
spoke in his church and he insisted on showing her his garden while
sending word that the congregation should keep singing hymns until he
got there. Abernathy retorted lamely that Clark did not know everything,
but very likely he would have tolerated no such scolding from anyone
other than the SCLC's mother conscience. (Clark refused the pay raise
offered her at the convention, writing King that she "couldn't accept it
and feel perfectly free inside.") Meanwhile, out on the convention floor,
the rakish Adam Clayton Powell renewed his attack on Wilkins and the
NAACP as "white-controlled," and he spiked hopes for passage of the
civil rights bill, saying that the white man already had given Negroes
more than he wanted to.

The scheduled three-hour board meeting stretched over the full four
days. All the preachers believed that King desperately needed to launch
a new campaign in order to recover from the trauma of the church bombing. The rub was how and where. Most had favored Danville, but now
some argued that it would be fatal to abandon Birmingham. As they
spoke, news flashed from Birmingham that Mayor Boutwell had spirited
Blaik and Royall away from an all-white airport ceremony into seclusion,
that Boutwell had arranged which local Negroes they were to see, that
Blaik and Royall had agreed to conduct only secret, segregated meetings,
and finally that Pitts and other leading Negroes were furious because
they had not heard from President Kennedy's envoys and had no way of
contacting them.

All this poured bane on King's humiliation for his hasty endorsement
of the Kennedy response to the bombing. William Shortridge, Shuttlesworth's treasurer, told the board that Birmingham Negroes were collecting arms, whereupon the board swung heavily in favor of renewed
nonviolent demonstrations for Negro clerks and policemen. King agreed,
but expressed caution on three counts: (1) many Birmingham Negroes
would oppose them ferociously, (2) Birmingham officials were still holding some $300,000 of SCLC bail money from the previous spring, and (3)
the demonstrations could not be effective unless they were even larger
than those in May. Benjamin Hooks argued instead for a march on Montgomery, a modified version of Diane Nash's plan. This possessed the

advantage of militancy aimed at Governor Wallace and the voting franchise, but it was a new direction, and King knew well from his years in
Montgomery that the MIA was far from a smooth machine. As they
debated, fresh news came of a double bombing on Dynamite Hill in
Birmingham, and then of John Lewis' arrest in Selma, Alabama, for carrying a "One Man/One Vote" sign outside the courthouse. Nearly two
hundred followers joined Lewis while the SCLC board was meeting in
Richmond. In jail, SNCC leaders planned a Selma "Freedom Day" campaign, which was a cross between Nash's new idea and Bob Moses' plan
for a Freedom Vote in Mississippi.

As the SCLC board spun dizzily between alternative plans, indecision
did nothing to improve morale. King had hired Harry Boyte, an executive
of long experience with the Red Cross, and Boyte's crash campaign to
reduce spelling errors, gossip, and other defects of what he called a poorly
educated, unprofessional SCLC work force had run headlong into Wyatt
Walker, who denied that any white office manager could be more exact-
ing than he. Staff resentment against the imperious Walker surfaced in
nasty chain-of-command struggles. Walker fought back by dismissing
four top SCLC employees for "irresponsibility and insubordination" at
the convention. King later talked him into docking their pay instead.
Walker conceded, partly because the hide he really wanted was Bevel's.
When King's inner circle suggested that he make amends with Bevel too,
Walker exploded with his first resignation. "This is intolerable," he said.
"I'm gone."

King tried to calm Walker down, and to soothe him on the money
question. Late at night, they still had the cathartic of fraternal preaching.
Gathering in a suite with cigarettes and a few bottles, the top-ranking
SCLC preachers teased each other about what hurt most—death, feuds,
the day's persecutions, and, always, their racial insecurities. Nearly every
punch line evoked appropriate lines of Scripture, and someone would
soar off on a run of preaching. They passed around improvised solos like
jazz musicians in a late-night cutting session, showing off their operatic
voices and their inexhaustible supply of metaphors, fables, and allegories.
Bevel and Walker preached to each other on the meaning of famous blood
feuds. Walker promised to buy "Chubby" Abernathy a diamond ring
when he earned his first million dollars, which drew forth sermonettes
on vanity and the love of money. They teased King about his liver lips
and rhinoceros ears, Andrew Young about his nappy hair and fuzzy
"white man's" shoes, Walker about his satin ties and high-yaller cheek-
bones, Bernard Lee about his wandering eye.

But morning brought no easy escape from the movement's predicament. King wanted desperately to revive the nonviolent campaign, and
thereby to preserve hopes for its deepest influences upon both races, but

he knew that the next Birmingham bombing might well touch off a race war that would obliterate nonviolence, perhaps leaving the civil rights movement as vulnerable as the Communists and CIO organizers who dashed themselves against segregation after the war. He thought he should go to Danville, but he could not stay out of Birmingham. Logically, he could not risk breaking with a Kennedy Administration that commanded 90 percent support among Negroes, and which already was vulnerable to white backlash against civil rights. Yet he could no longer profess faith in the Blaik-Royall mission.

"I have kept silence," he admitted in his closing speech to the convention on September 27. ". . . In doing so, I have acted contrary to the wishes and the frustrations of those who have marched with me in the dangerous campaigns for freedom . . . I did this because I was naïve enough to believe that the proof of good faith would emerge. It is now obvious to me that this was a mistake." He talked of the unsolved bombings, the evasions of the Administration, and the elusive goodwill of the March on Washington. He accused the Administration of wanting to believe that a quiet march meant the revolution was over. "They could have made no bigger mistake," he said. ". . . We are more determined than ever before that nonviolence is the way. Let them bring on their bombs. Let them sabotage us with the evil of cooperation with segregation. We intend to be free." In conclusion, King delivered a hastily composed new dictum: "When General of the Armies Douglas MacArthur was repelled in a just campaign during World War II, he fell back—just as your humble servant fell back at the White House that day when the President sent two men to do the job of reconciliation. But I serve notice tonight, that *I will return* to Birmingham, unless, by a certain date . . . " and he listed essentially the same minimal conditions that President Kennedy had tried to sell the Hamilton group in the White House.

The White House ignored the speech, but A. G. Gaston and Arthur Shores immediately denounced King from Birmingham. Breaking with Pitts and the other conservative Negro leaders, they issued a public statement declaring faith in the Blaik-Royall team and implacable opposition to demonstrations or "outside interference." Both the white and Negro newspapers in Birmingham splashed the Gaston-Shores statement on the front pages. As a result, King was left with a threat of open schism in Birmingham if he acted, silence from Washington until he did, and the tinny echo of his own grandiose pledge to regroup as triumphantly as MacArthur. Feeling demoralized and stale, King asked Chauncey Eskridge to undertake a secret mission to Petersburg, Virginia.

•   •   •

Eskridge could tell the errand was important to King, and anyway he was delighted by the adventure of trying to locate Vernon Johns. Since meeting King in 1960, Eskridge had acquired a trove of Vernon Johns stories. Knowing that the old preacher was in another vagabond phase and had not lived regularly with Altona Johns in some years, Eskridge was not surprised to hear King say that he was not reachable by telephone, lived "somewhere around Petersburg," some thirty miles from Richmond, and that the recommended detective approach was to go to a church or street corner and ask any Negro. Still, Eskridge was not prepared for the husk he found on the vacant lot of an abandoned gasoline station. It was cordoned off by rope to keep cars from parking there, or from miring in the red mud. Inside, tending a squatter's vegetable stand, was a silver-stubbled old relic in brogans without socks or shoelaces. Eskridge suspected that a prankster had directed him to one of the local winos.

Vernon Johns was no less taken aback by the message he received from the impeccably tailored Chicago attorney. "Dr. King sent you to me for that?" he asked, speaking every word in disbelief.

Eskridge insisted that indeed King was hungry for some of Johns's ideas —hungry enough to give Eskridge expense money out of his own pocket, along with an urgent plea to track him down. "He wants you to give me all your notebooks for your Sunday sermons," Eskridge repeated.

It took some time for Johns to adjust to the gravity of the request. When he did, he began ticking off sermon titles, then reciting snatches of sermons, and finally he began preaching in full animation on the dangers of drinking Pharaoh's wine. Eskridge stood there in the mud for the better part of an hour, deeply moved. Later he recovered enough of his legal skepticism to suspect correctly that the notebooks Johns promised to send did not exist—always his sermons returned to the air from which they had come. King did not easily accept the lonely reality of such a conclusion. He insisted that there must be notebooks. Even after Johns died months later,* he asked Eskridge whether any had arrived in the mail.

Beyond King's knowledge, layers of intrigue were piling up against him within the secret chambers of the federal government. Just before the March on Washington, the FBI's intelligence chief had informed Director Hoover that an exhaustive analysis revealed little or no Communist

---

* Shortly after delivering one of his most famous lectures, "The Romance of Death," at Howard University, Johns himself dropped dead, in a sequence his admirers swore Johns had prearranged with God.

involvement in the march. The Communist Party's most sensible members had long since quit by the tens of thousands, and those remaining were largely ineffectual misfits, damaged by years of persecution and welded to psychosis, Soviet dogma, and dreams of cataclysm. There was a note of triumph in Assistant Director William Sullivan's appraisal of the march as a home-grown American protest.

Fatefully, Hoover challenged the intelligence assessment with the full weight of his authority. "This memo reminds me vividly of those I received when Castro took over Cuba," he scratched across Sullivan's letter. ". . . I for one can't ignore the memos re King, O'Dell, Levison, Rustin." Hoover did not welcome a giant march for freedom by a race he had known over a long lifetime as maids, chauffeurs, and criminal suspects, led by a preacher he loathed. More pragmatically, he also faced a dire institutional question: if there was no subversion here—with several hundred thousand Negroes and white sympathizers descending upon the capital with demands for revolutionary change in all American institutions, including the all-white FBI—then where might the subversion be? If Communists were not powerful among these Negroes, then they must be negligible indeed, and if so, Hoover could not long deploy the Bureau so heavily against the threat of internal subversion. The Director instantly forgot that he had remarked favorably on Sullivan's qualifications as an eventual successor.

For Sullivan, Hoover's comments signaled a failed gamble and hence a career emergency. Down through the ranks of the Bureau, where officials were conditioned to send the Director only what they knew he agreed with (and usually in the exact words he preferred), the heresy only proved that "Crazy Billy" Sullivan was nuts. Sullivan tried to save himself by blatantly reversing his position. "The Director is correct," he wrote just after the march. "We were completely wrong." While even conservative commentators were acknowledging the patriotic merits of the "I Have a Dream" speech, Sullivan told Hoover that "in light of King's powerful demagogic speech yesterday he stands head and shoulders over all other Negro leaders . . . We must mark him now, if we have not done so before, as the most dangerous Negro of the future in this nation from the standpoint of communism, the Negro and national security."

Hoover did not let the chastened intelligence chief off with surrender. At first, when Sullivan proposed that the Bureau go so far as to unleash its COINTELPRO covert warfare against King's movement, Hoover pretended that he could not understand "how you can so agilely switch your thinking . . . Now you want to load down the Field with more coverage in spite of your recent memo depreciating CP influence in racial movement. I don't intend to waste time and money until you can make up your minds." In effect, Hoover demanded that Sullivan grovel, and Sullivan abjectly complied. By example, Hoover enforced discipline within the entire FBI intelligence apparatus. Two days after the march, Hoover ordered the New York office to find out whether a wiretap could be added safely to the telephone of Stanley Levison's teenaged son. A week later, he ordered preparations for wiretaps on the SCLC offices in New York and Atlanta, and also on King's home. Just as the march was introducing the movement to millions of Americans as a legitimate cause—if not a compelling one against the rights and feelings of segregationists—Hoover targeted it as a full-fledged national security enemy.

Justice Department officials perceived that the FBI was rumbling ominously again on King's Communist connections. Politically, the threat was that a leak might allow hostile congressional investigators to discredit King and the civil rights bill, and through them the Administration. To close off exploitable gaps between the FBI and Justice, Burke Marshall composed a summary record of the Attorney General's vigilance against O'Dell. It was a delicate task. Marshall had to portray the Attorney General as acting in full appreciation of the danger but without exposing any FBI secrets, and as having eliminated the threat without subsequently relaxing. He delivered a confidential draft personally to Robert Kennedy. After a week's consideration, interrupted by the trauma of the Birmingham church bombing, Kennedy concluded that Marshall himself should seek a truce with Hoover. To do so, Marshall sent the draft to Hoover's aides with a request that Hoover agree to receive it as worded. Thus, without directly exposing Attorney General Kennedy to repudiation, Marshall tacitly asked Hoover to bless the department's performance on O'Dell. Bureau officials groused that Marshall's summary was incomplete and somewhat soft, but not enough so to pick a fight on this ground. With Hoover's consent, they archly notified Marshall that he "should feel free, of course, to submit the memorandum as he drafted it."

One effect of Sullivan's reeducation was to sharpen the selectivity of perception in his Intelligence Division. Officials had no trouble interpreting Hoover's instructions to keep pecking away at Kennedy with anything new on O'Dell or Levison. When surveillance agents once spotted O'Dell walking into the New York SCLC office, the Bureau rocketed this discovery to the Justice Department as proof of "King's duplicity" and O'Dell's continuing subversion. On the other hand, the Bureau did not report at all the wiretapped conversations of King's aides complaining that a wounded, rejected O'Dell had left the SCLC "high and dry," taking with him mailing lists and files, with the result that the SCLC's direct-mail fund-raising effectively ceased.

These extraordinary bureaucratic exchanges signified an atmosphere of groping suspicion between the Bureau and the Justice Department. Mistrust and miscommunication were most pronounced over the hot issue of King, but they also intensified along at least two parallel tracks. One was organized crime. That fall, differences were personified in a crew-cut contract killer named Joe Valachi, who for his own reasons was willing to testify publicly about the inner workings of crime syndicates. For Kennedy, Valachi's proposed firsthand revelations about "capos" and "consiglieres" would prove that the old legends of Capone were alive, enlarged, and modernized into an established criminal conspiracy of enormous power. However, such revelations threatened to contradict Director Hoover's public position that organized crime theories were "baloney." From a different angle, Valachi's testimony raised the same danger as Sullivan's short-lived declaration of victory over the Communists. If he publicly described the vast operations of the five New York crime families, Hoover could not long hold out against Kennedy's demand for new priorities within the Bureau.

When by adroit news leaks and prearranged congressional demands, Robert Kennedy assured that Valachi would deliver his confessions in public, Hoover tried to cover his retreat. Two days after the March on Washington, he issued an "FBI Bulletin" to law enforcement officers across the country, claiming that the FBI had long since established "a successful penetration . . . into the innermost sanctum of the criminal deity." Just as Kennedy was advertising Valachi's impending testimony as a historic breakthrough, Hoover minimized information he said "corroborated and embellished the facts developed by the FBI as early as 1961." Going a step further, Hoover wrote that public appearances by informants "serve, in a larger degree, to magnify the enormous task which lies ahead." Reporters seized upon the word "magnify" as a veiled charge that Robert Kennedy was making the FBI's job more difficult. Kennedy asked Hoover to issue a clarifying statement, but Hoover refused, saying his language spoke for itself.

Joe Valachi, surrounded by heavily armed U.S. marshals, first appeared before a Senate committee and a nationally televised audience on September 27. His tales of comic terror, godfathers, snags in the heroin business, and Mafia manners ("How can I 'splain that to you, Senator?") were the gripping originals for a later generation of entertainment. Because of Valachi, Kennedy said privately, "the FBI changed their whole concept of crime in the United States." *The New York Times* published an "underworld glossary" of terms Valachi introduced. Opening-day coverage overshadowed all contemporary events, including President Kennedy's schedule and King's anguished "MacArthur speech" to the

Richmond SCLC convention, and Valachi dominated the news for much of the next month. Robert Kennedy published a national summons to war against "the private government of organized crime," in which he praised the IRS and the Bureau of Narcotics but mentioned the FBI only in passing. This was a momentary departure from Kennedy's patient cultivation of Hoover, most likely owing to pride or irritation. The Attorney General quickly resumed his courtier's campaign of flattery and encouragement.

Kennedy had special reason to be gentle in victory over Hoover and his prized internal security apparatus: he knew they held the balance in a quivering scandal that might well ruin President Kennedy. FBI agents had discovered that among the President's mistresses was a woman named Ellen Rometsch, who had fled her native East Germany in 1955 and made her way to Washington in 1961 as the wife of a soldier stationed in the West German Embassy. To the Bureau, this made Rometsch suspect as a possible East German spy. Even so, the scandalous implications might easily have been buried because of the President's privacy in such matters, except that Rometsch was part of a collateral scandal that could not be contained. She was one of many courtesans and party girls associated with Bobby Baker, an old Lyndon Johnson protégé on the Senate staff.

Baker's anonymity was about to be shattered by a disgruntled vending machine contractor angling to sue Baker for default on bought favors. That triggering event eventually sent Baker to prison. Long before then, it promised to open many lurid avenues of revelation about him as a one-man backroom marketplace who assiduously arranged contracts, cash, and backrubs. Robert Kennedy knew that one of those avenues led through Ellen Rometsch to President Kennedy. He had her quietly deported in August, but all through September, as lawyers and investigators circled Baker in private, the information left behind was a threat of the utmost sensitivity. Essentially, it was a reprise on John Kennedy's unknown Inga Arvad affair of the 1940s. Both these exotic romances with foreign women lay within Hoover's dreaded files, and Hoover, more than any other person, had the power to determine whether the Rometsch affair stayed as quiet as Arvad or became as noisy as the Profumo scandal in England, which was lurching toward a conclusion marked by suicide and political disgrace.

Far from public view, the King wiretap and the Baker scandal began in lockstep. On Friday, October 4, William Sullivan formally recommended that Hoover once again seek Kennedy's approval for a wiretap on King's home in Atlanta, "because of the communist influence in the racial movement shown by activities of Stanley Levison as well as King's connection with him." The proposal was a watershed for Hoover, especially since Kennedy had turned him down once already in July. "I hope you don't change your minds on this," he scribbled to Sullivan in an acid reminder of his brief apostasy. Possibly he was warning Sullivan to prepare for blame if Kennedy again crossed the Bureau on this vital question.

Bobby Baker went into hiding that same Friday, ducking a command summons from his Senate boss, Majority Leader Mike Mansfield. With Minority Leader Everett Dirksen and Senator Richard Russell of Georgia, Mansfield waited much of the afternoon, joined by Senator John Williams of Delaware, a conservative, abstemious Republican who, through scandals dating back to the Truman Administration, had earned a reputation as an independent "watchdog" of Senate ethics. By diligent research into the rumors flying between Capitol Hill and the FBI, Williams had gained results so alarming that he wanted to confront Baker with them in the presence of the Senate leadership. When Baker failed to appear, Mansfield promised to reconvene the meeting as soon as he could be located.

Hoover took Sullivan's draft of the new King wiretap request home for a final weekend of thought, then sent it to the Attorney General on Monday. That afternoon, Senator Mansfield told his private leadership group that an inebriated Baker had shown up to resign his Senate position rather than face Senator Williams. Baker had shouted that it was all a partisan witch-hunt designed to injure Vice President Johnson because of their close association. Rumors already circulated that Robert Kennedy was encouraging the Baker investigation surreptitiously, because of his dislike for Johnson, but Baker, Williams, and Hoover were among those who already knew that the Attorney General had his own reason to fear a scandal.

On Thursday, amid early ripples of publicity about Baker's resignation, the Senate unanimously ordered a Rules Committee investigation of Baker's conduct. That afternoon, having sent a terse note—"Courtney, speak to me"—Robert Kennedy met privately with Courtney Evans, his FBI liaison. He still had not signed the King wiretap authorization. To Evans, Kennedy stressed the political delicacy of the issue, saying that any public discovery of such a tap would be a disaster of the highest order. Logically, there was no more reason to tap King now than in July. The way to get at the contact between Levison and King was to monitor Levison, which the Bureau was doing already by every available means, including bugging. The results had failed for two years to corroborate the primary allegation of conspiracy between Levison and any Communists, let alone the Soviets. Moreover, the substance of the communication between Levison and King had been deemed dangerous only by FBI axiom that Levison was sinister. From any less rigid perspective, Levison appeared to be more or less as sensible as the civil rights movement itself.

Politically, there was *less* reason to tap King than in July. Since then, King's speech at the March on Washington had established him as a national spokesman for a significant minority of whites as well as the vast majority of Negroes. Also, the Birmingham church bombing had caused a perceptible increase in national sympathy for the Negro cause, and indirectly for King. If word of the wiretap got out, Kennedy could not hope to gain public support for an action that added to King's persecution. No law enforcement official could easily accept responsibility for tapping King when so many crimes against King's movement remained unsolved. That very day, Burke Marshall informed Robert Kennedy that Wallace's state troopers had arrested three men believed to have done the church bombing and charged them with minor offenses—deliberately, said Marshall, to protect them from imminent arrest on capital murder charges. Marshall's information came directly from Floyd Mann in Alabama, in secret. By his own high standards of crusading against criminal corruption, Kennedy had far more reason to slap a wiretap on Governor Wallace than on King.

Although neither Kennedy nor Courtney Evans spoke so plainly in their private memos, the best arguments for a wiretap on King had to do with obtaining political intelligence. Ironically, much of that information had been shut off by Kennedy's insistence that King stop talking to Levison, which had reduced the take from the Levison wiretaps. More than ever, Kennedy needed to know exactly what King intended. Congress was aflame over the civil rights bill. A surprise demonstration or a denunciation of the Administration could be calamitous from Kennedy's point of view. To deal with King—to court, control, or, in a dire emergency, renounce him entirely—he needed to know every possible detail. This was the unspoken bait from Hoover, who was not above larding his intelligence reports with political gossip.

On the other hand, it was a trap. If Kennedy handed Hoover a signed wiretap authorization on Martin Luther King, the precarious balance of their relationship would shift. Hoover would possess a club to offset Kennedy's special relationship with the President. Thereafter, it would become more difficult for Kennedy to restrain Hoover from any action he proposed against King. For that matter, it would become more difficult to suggest practically anything to Hoover. How could Kennedy hope to control Hoover once he had agreed to wiretap King? There was a Faustian undertow to Kennedy's dilemma, and he did not feel strong enough to resist. Some time later, after holding the matter entirely to himself, he told an aide tersely that there would have been "no living with the Bureau" if he had not signed.*

King tried to sort out his dead ends after the Richmond convention. Heavy bail indebtedness and other obstacles meant that demonstrations were "an absolute last resort," he concluded, especially in Birmingham. "Our challenge now," he wrote his staff, "is to be ingenious enough to keep the threat of demonstrations alive so as to give the local and national public a picture of our determination and continued militancy, and yet constantly find face-saving retreats in order to avoid demonstrations if possible." He embarked on a circuit-riding tour of escalating bluster, fully conscious that he was racing his engine while braked.

He made four passes through Birmingham in October, once hitching a ride with Nelson "Fireball" Smith down to Selma. Mrs. Amelia Boynton, the local woman whose "honor roll" of would-be registrants had prompted John Doar to file voting suits there, had invited King to give a boost to her beleaguered registration campaign. By the time he addressed a mass meeting there, went on to Montgomery, and circled back to Birmingham, Alabama investigators had established that the car in which King made one leg of his journey had been rented by an observer from the Justice Department. Governor Wallace angrily denounced the federal government for subsidizing King's conspiracy against state laws. Two state grand juries and the U.S. Fifth Circuit Court of Appeals eventually entered a swelling controversy that obliged King to issue several public statements. Congressional inquiries and contradictory evidence forced Burke Marshall to apologize for an earlier firm denial. Marshall fired the young Negro staff attorney who had been in charge of the car† for his panicky coverup, and very nearly fired John Doar for lax supervision.

Hypersensitivity infected public discourse about civil rights and King in particular. At the White House, emissaries Blaik and Royall promised to divulge at least a summary of their report to President Kennedy on events in Birmingham since the church bombing, but they never came

---

* Hoover would leak word of the taps when Robert Kennedy was running for president in 1968, after King's death, and John Seigenthaler, seeing the stricken look on Kennedy's face when asked about the rumors during a practice debate, knew instantly that he did not need to ask whether it was true, nor could he bear to ask why. Instead, after Kennedy himself was killed that year, Seigenthaler wrote a letter of apology to Stanley Levison.
† Thelton Henderson, later a District Court judge in California.

close to formulating a report to summarize. Their prescription for Birmingham was calm. Anything they said or did about the state of race relations was certain to cause turmoil. Therefore, they said nothing. Privately with the Kennedys, they talked about football. Their evasiveness became so blatant that some moderate whites in Birmingham sent secret protest notes to the Justice Department, and Earl Blaik himself complained privately to Marshall that his partner, Royall, was "never interested in any of my reports" and favored a "bland, PR approach" to Birmingham. In time, the two soldiers asked for and received permission to dissolve their assignment without report, recommendation, or public comment, as though it never happened.

While King was in Selma, Robert Kennedy went before the full House Judiciary Committee to ask for the deletion of strengthening amendments that had been added to the civil rights bill in subcommittee. For this he was roundly denounced not only by Roy Wilkins but by liberal Republicans, who complained that Kennedy, unable to deliver the votes of his own party, was pleading for bipartisan support while stripping out the few amendments for which Republicans could claim credit. The legislative tangle was a cartoonist's cloud of flying fists. Politicians claimed they needed a weaker bill now to get a stronger one later, and vice versa. Jujitsu effects were calculated out to the third and fourth degree, as charges of posturing competed with pronouncements of political genius. "For an understanding of this bizarre battle," declared *The New York Times*, "it is helpful to look both backward and forward."

Stanley Levison gradually deepened his involvement in King's Birmingham book. At first he had made awkward excuses when King's agent and publishers asked why he had dropped out of the editing process, but when they complained that Al Duckett's revisions were unsatisfactory, Levison found another writer. Upon new complaints about the revisions, Levison agreed that the second writer made the "fatal mistake" of "talking down to the readers." By then, the publishers were exerting pressure to get the book done quickly, fearing that public appreciation for the Birmingham story had faded already. King's agent, Joan Daves, told Levison that Clarence Jones was ineffective as King's editorial go-between. Levison worked on the manuscript himself while finding a third writer. Through Jones, he sent word to King that the book was hostage to continuing events in the movement. If King pulled out of Birmingham for Danville, Levison warned, he could not expect readers to get excited about the watershed events of the previous spring. King would come off "like a child who can't finish something and moves on to some other game." By October, Levison had had more than one direct talk with King about the manuscript. He stopped telling friends that he was out of touch with King and began saying he had to "finish off this book thing that was started."

All this came through on the FBI wiretaps, but the Bureau was less excited about such contact after Robert Kennedy approved the wiretap on King's home and New York office. Long before any results could be obtained, Hoover made a supplementary request to wiretap all four telephone lines at King's SCLC headquarters in Atlanta. On Monday, October 21, Courtney Evans found the Attorney General upset, vacillating. He approved this further request but reserved the right to review all the King wiretaps in thirty days. That Friday, Kennedy called Evans in again, this time "obviously irritated." He had just learned that the Bureau was disseminating within the government a scalding report on King as "an unprincipled man," one who "is knowingly, willingly, and regularly taking guidance from communists."

Full of sarcasm and wrath, Kennedy said people all through the Pentagon were talking about the report. "The Attorney General asked what responsibilities the Army had in relation to the communist background of Martin Luther King," Evans reported, adding that his technical explanation about the Army's security functions "seemed to serve no purpose." Dismissing Evans, Kennedy called Hoover. He extracted a promise that Hoover would recall the report to prevent leaks, but he threatened no discipline. The damage had been done. "I have talked to A.G. & he is satisfied," scrawled Hoover, sounding satisfied himself.

That weekend Kennedy scrambled to plug two rumbling volcanoes at once. While the rebellious FBI was painting the Administration as an ally of a Communist Negro movement, the Ellen Rometsch scandal suddenly threatened to erupt. A reporter working with Senator Williams wrote the first exclusive story—"U.S. Expels Girl Linked to Officials"—which revealed that Rometsch had been "associating with congressional leaders and some prominent New Frontiersmen." It said Rometsch's name had surfaced in the Bobby Baker investigation, and that there was some concern about security risks, even espionage, "because of the high rank of her male companions." Senator Williams, who wanted to know why she had been expelled from the country if she was not a security risk, and what it meant if she was, had scheduled an appearance before a closed session of the Senate Rules Committee on Tuesday. The newspaper story referred to Rometsch as a "party girl" and stressed her sex appeal: "Those acquainted with the woman class her as 'stunning,' and in general appearance comparable to movie actress Elizabeth Taylor."

For Robert Kennedy, the only solace in this calamity was that the story appeared in an Iowa newspaper. This obscure origin gave a brief reprieve, as the story would not take hold in the national press until after the weekend. Kennedy had a little time. Among his first acts was an emergency call to La Vern Duffy, a close friend and Senate investigator, who had just finished work on the Valachi hearings. The Attorney General gravely asked him to jump on the first plane to West Germany and stay there. His assignment was to find Rometsch, calm her down, and keep her from talking. One foreboding detail of the Iowa story made Duffy's mission all the more vital: Rometsch was rumored to be angry that her "important friends" had allowed her to be shipped out of the United States. Duffy took off like James Bond. Kennedy then called the President. They agreed that the only way to control Williams by Tuesday was through the influence of the Senate leadership. Unfortunately,the only way to move the Senate leadership on something like this was through J. Edgar Hoover.

By early Monday morning, October 28, Robert Kennedy had alerted the Senate leaders, Dirksen and Mansfield. Then he called in Courtney Evans to declare that he and President Kennedy were greatly concerned about the Ellen Rometsch allegations. They could harm the United States. To emphasize his battleship mood, he telephoned the President in front of Evans and exchanged words to the same effect. Then he sent Evans to forewarn Director Hoover of an imminent conference.

Almost immediately, Kennedy appeared at Hoover's door, and the Director, pleased that the upstart Attorney General had made the humble journey rather than summoning him, dismissed his aides. Alone, Kennedy told Hoover that he and the President urgently wanted him to brief Mansfield and Dirksen on the larger dangers of the Rometsch case. If the case blew open, it could hurt so many officials inside *and* outside the executive branch of government as to damage the integrity of the United States.

Hoover let Kennedy suffer a bit. Implying that the whole business was distasteful to him, he said that the Bureau already had furnished him a complete memorandum on the personal aspects of the case. The Attorney General could read it to the senators himself if he wished. Kennedy could only reply that the senators were primarily interested in the security aspects, and that Hoover's personal authority was essential. What he meant was that only Hoover could convince the senators that there would be no partisan profit or duty in a Profumo-style attack on the President. He must say that an attack would bring down retaliation in kind upon Republican and Democratic senators alike, supported by Hoover himself.

Hoover did not give a direct response. He said only that he already had a phone message from Senator Mansfield, and would speak with him. Kennedy changed the subject to the Birmingham church bombing and King. His words suggested a kind of wistful reproach, of pride mixed with a plea that Hoover recognize what he had risked to accommodate the FBI. Kennedy said he was sorry they had not been able to solve the church bombing; Hoover replied that the Bureau would have cracked the case if not for the obstruction of Alabama, but had not given up. As for King, Kennedy explained why he had been so upset on Friday about the new FBI report on King and communism. Hoover did not give an inch. When Kennedy mentioned the flak and gossip still coming from the Pentagon, Hoover replied that the report had been disseminated to the CIA and the State Department too, among others. When Kennedy said he was worried because, although the report did not say so explicitly, most readers would quickly conclude that King was a Communist, Hoover replied that every statement in the report was "accurate and supported by facts."

Hoover called Senator Mansfield at eleven o'clock, just after the Attorney General withdrew. The Majority Leader said he and Dirksen badly needed a meeting with the Director alone within the next few hours. Capitol Hill was swarming with reporters working on the story out of Iowa, he warned, and any unscheduled sighting of the three of them would attract attention. Therefore, Mansfield suggested that they meet at his home, and Hoover agreed.

Afterward, Hoover called the Attorney General. Almost simultaneously, President Kennedy obtained his first report from Senator Mansfield, who said he was badly shocked by what Hoover had laid out, complete with names, dates, and places: Rometsch, Bobby Baker's other party girls, senators from both sides of the aisle, foreign women, Negro mistresses, cruises, quarrels, deals. Mansfield's battered state suggested that an emergency silence might be imposed on the seething mess, but the first true test came the next morning at one of the rare hearings of the Senate Rules Committee that made the front pages. Before appearing as the committee's sole witness, Senator Williams issued a statement that the Iowa story was not on his agenda. Inside the closed hearing, he told the senators that he would not speak on the Rometsch issue. They could ask for pertinent FBI information if they wished. Then Williams began detailed, sworn testimony on Baker's financial irregularities. When it was over, the committee chairman faced the waiting reporters and said, "We didn't go into West Germany."

Three days later, on November 1, Robert Kennedy approved an FBI request to wiretap Bayard Rustin. The Administration had lost much of its control over Hoover, but the danger of a Profumo scandal receded from the brink. Already the investigation was settling upon Capitol Hill, and specifically upon Bobby Baker's finances. Living close to the edge, President Kennedy felt confident enough to tease reporters with hints of what Hoover knew about Ellen Rometsch. "Boy, the dirt he has on those senators," he said brashly. "You wouldn't believe it."

Rebel troops overthrew the South Vietnamese government in Saigon that same November 1, assassinating President Diem and his brother who had commanded the secret police. The bloody coup shocked many Americans into an unsettling first awareness of the Vietnam War, as news accounts speculated delicately but persistently about clandestine U.S. support for the revolt. All through the breakthrough year of 1963, the Vietnam crisis had built as a haunting foreign echo of civil rights. On May 8, during the peak of Bevel's children's marches in Birmingham, Vietnamese soldiers had killed monks and civilians in Hue to enforce a government order prohibiting the display of Buddhist colors on Buddha's birthday. Buddhist protest had seized world attention a month later, on the day of the Medgar Evers assassination in Mississippi, when a monk named Trich Quan Duc publicly immolated himself in downtown Saigon. Vietnam's Catholic rulers contemptuously dismissed a string of later suicides as "Buddhist barbecues" inspired by the Communist enemy.

Americans awakening to the Vietnam crisis puzzled over the conduct on both sides. Given the overwhelmingly Buddhist population, it was as though a Jewish U.S. president had forcibly suppressed Christmas as a Communist conspiracy. Uncomfortable barriers of religion and race plagued Kennedy Administration officials most responsible for U.S. war policy in Vietnam, so that they "decided long ago," wrote Max Frankel in the *Times*, "to discuss it as little as possible." Privately, however, they split over the most divisive internal question of the entire Administration: whether it was moral, democratic, or necessary to overthrow Diem in order to preserve a war against tyranny in Vietnam. "My government's coming apart!" President Kennedy had exclaimed on the day before the March on Washington. Two days later, his ambassador in Saigon cabled that the course was set toward a coup: "There is no turning back." All through September and October, the secret cable traffic had flopped erratically between excited hopes of imminent success and bouts of bloody remorse, like speeches from *Macbeth*. When it was over, U.S. officials tried to make the best of a fresh start with a new Vietnamese regime of French-educated, Catholic generals.

In Atlanta, another subterranean track remained entirely hidden. Agent R. R. Nichols, posing as the owner of an electrical engineering firm, rented a large office on West Peachtree Street to house the King surveillance equipment. Normally, wiretap lines ran from the phone company to the local FBI office, but this operation was so secret that some agents thought Hoover might not have the Attorney General's approval. Nichols hated the assignment. His frustrations were typical of a typical FBI career. After a first assignment to Birmingham's Communist squad in 1947, Nichols had been shipped to Washington to work in the giant new loyalty program. It was tedious background work, the worst of it being a long investigation of foreign-born government carpenters.

By the time of his transfer to Atlanta in 1955, Nichols had been tagged as a security specialist, which meant that he was shut out of criminal work. A few top security officials enjoyed prestige at headquarters, but the regular agents commanded very little status in the field offices. Nichols spent years hiring Negro college students to take notes on speeches inside the new Black Muslim temple in Atlanta. The students kept quitting because the speeches were repetitive and dull. Eventually, Nichols slacked off on the only real activity permitted him—suggesting to employers that Muslims be fired from their jobs or evicted from their quarters—because success only meant that he would have to locate them again. He developed a creeping insecurity about his abilities, having never worked on what he considered an interesting case. Criminal agents scorned his assignments, including the top-secret new King detail. There was no hope of making arrests. Even interviews with King or King's people were strictly forbidden because of potential controversy. It was all busy work—training extra shifts of headphone monitors and supervising stenographers. Although Nichols held no unorthodox opinions for an agent—saying that King was a communist of the kind who thought he was a liberal and didn't understand the danger of people like himself— he wished someone else had the job that stretched years ahead of him. On November 8, he notified his superiors that the King taps were up and running.

At first the taps missed King, who was enduring a new leadership schism in Detroit. Rev. C. L. Franklin had scheduled a two-day convention at Cobo Hall, scene of King's triumphant speech in June, for the purpose of forming a Northern organization comparable to the SCLC in the South. But the conference barely survived its planning sessions. Fistfights broke out between Franklin and other preachers, many of whom had resented his highhanded ways since the struggles within the National Baptist Convention. An unlikely combination of Muslims, militants, and J. H. Jackson loyalists walked out to convene an alternative Grass Roots Leadership Conference. What united them against Franklin was an aversion to nonviolence and to King's eagerness for fellowship with white people. "I'm sick and tired of singing 'We Shall Overcome,'" declared one preacher. Conservative Baptists preached racial pride, SNCC veterans such as Gloria Richardson wondered what virtue of integration could induce black people to give up the right of self-defense, and keynote speaker Malcolm X declared that integration was a training exercise for Negroes, run by whites. "You bleed when the white man says bleed," he said, scolding a delighted crowd.

At Grass Roots, a new sense of power ran into an old sense of injury, foreshadowing the separatist reaction a few years ahead. Much of the emotion was still personal and evanescent, but Malcolm X did preach one line that drove a deep wedge between King's movement and his church heritage. Malcolm revered Moses as a common prophet of Islam and Judaism, and also as the father figure of the Negro Christian church. "Nowhere in that Bible can you show me where Moses went to his people and said, believe in the same god that your slavemaster believes in, or seek integration with the slavemaster," Malcolm said often. "Moses' one doctrine was separation. He told Pharaoh, '. . . Let my people go.'" Malcolm X challenged King to prove how he could reconcile the ecumenical spirit of integration with the tribal cohesion of a Negro culture that was joined at the hip to Moses.

After huddling with C. L. Franklin, King decided to duck an appearance at the fracas in Detroit. Back in Georgia for the second anniversary of the Albany Movement, he criticized the Justice Department for "unjust blows" and fired off another telegram urging Robert Kennedy to stop the prosecution of the Albany Nine. By then, a large staff was trying to "work up on a movement in Danville," as Andrew Young put it, and Shuttlesworth was urging a renewed push in Birmingham. Frictions among local Negroes made King reluctant to go to either place, but he had no better idea how to overcome the battle-weary lull in the movement. He told Clarence Jones on November 16 that he was suffering from a case of perpetual hiccoughs.

At New American Library, King's editors were frantic about the fired writers and other messy delays on the Birmingham manuscript. King's literary agent in turn was "terribly uncomfortable," and her anxiety fell mostly upon Stanley Levison, who was far more accessible than Jones or King. Levison and Jones finally arranged a crisis meeting at New York's Idlewild Airport, when King passed through on his way home from a conference of Reform and Conservative Jews. The various FBI wiretaps intercepted the plans well enough in advance to cover the airport rendezvous in heavy numbers, on a cold, rainy Wednesday. Agents managed to overhear some of the conversation, which indeed concerned the Birmingham book. Among other things, King asked Levison to try to rehire the woman who had worked on *Stride Toward Freedom*. Of far greater importance to the Bureau was an achievement that the Intelligence Division quickly trumpeted at headquarters: "Notwithstanding trying circumstances, both from a climatic and security standpoint, our New York Agents were able to secure a photograph of the aforementioned three individuals." One of Sullivan's deputies, harking back to the Smith Act heresy convictions, speculated that the picture might one day become evidence in a Communist conspiracy trial.

That same day, Robert Kennedy was celebrating his birthday at a small party in the Justice Department. He stood on his desk amid joking friends and delivered a chipper little talk about how the fight would go on even if his own days on the job were numbered. At the White House, President Kennedy had called in Lee White to make sure that the local Washington barbers quit complaining about serving Negro customers, as was reported in the newspaper. Another, nastier bit of racial politics had reached his desk. Congressman John L. Pilcher, of Albany, Georgia, was lobbying to create wily new pork-barrel opportunities from segregation. If civilian hospitals near Turner Air Force Base remained segregated, and were thus unserviceable under new Pentagon regulations on equal opportunity, did that mean Turner would become eligible for construction of a new military hospital? Budget officials, keen to the ramifications of Pilcher's game, insisted that such an interpretation of the regulation would require presidential approval, but Kennedy made no final decision before leaving on a trip to make peace between quarrelsome Democratic factions in Texas. As soon as he left, an army of White House craftsmen stripped the Oval Office for a quick remodeling in his absence.

Stanley Levison rode the train to Washington for the Kennedy funeral. He came back talking of "a whole city in which no one talked in a normal tone of voice." People were whispering, moving in slow motion. In all the eerie mass pain he saw only one hopeful turn of emotion: the news commentators were not hysterical, but instead were talking about how much hatred there had been. "A feeling like that covering a country can be more important than anything else," Levison told his secretary. He called King's literary agent to say that the Birmingham book must be postponed yet again. "This book always seems to be in the shadow of tragic deaths," he said—Medgar Evers, the four girls, and now President Kennedy. At times Levison gushed, calling Kennedy the first intellectual president since Jefferson, and he offered wobbly speculations on the murder of the assassin by Jack Ruby. Once he said that Ruby was a Communist who killed Lee Harvey Oswald because he thought Oswald was a right-winger discrediting the left. Another time he said Oswald himself must have been from the "Chinese wing of the ultra-left." Then he said Oswald was the sort of person who could be influenced by extremists from either side. Struggling to regain his political realism, he remarked that he was "not at all pessimistic" about Lyndon Johnson on civil rights, because he saw Johnson as a liberal New Dealer at heart. King liked Johnson, which was good, and in certain areas Johnson had more ability than Kennedy.

King also attended the funeral, though neither he nor Levison was aware of the other. He traveled alone, without even his constant road man Bernard Lee, and stood unnoticed on the street. Like Roy Wilkins, he was deeply hurt not to have been invited to the funeral Mass at St. Matthew's. King still identified with both Kennedys, especially the President. They had many things in common, such as coarsely overbearing fathers and a penchant for noble romance. Each was a closet smoker, catnapper, and skirt-chaser. Between them they delivered most of the memorable American oratory of the postwar period.

What King had envied in President Kennedy was his self-esteem and his lack of perceptible angst. Although politically on the defensive nearly every time King communicated with him, Kennedy always possessed an independent sense of well-being. By contrast, King was personally self-conscious. He worried about his looks, his tough skin, about what people thought of him and whether they might find out that he had ghostwriters for his books. Race accounted for much of the difference, but President Johnson was a worrier like King, and for that reason King never looked up to him personally. From their first meeting in the White House, when the new President nervously refused to be photographed with King, Johnson seemed to be insecure in ways that aroused only occasional sympathy and no admiration from King.

Kennedy's best qualities remained his alone, untransferable to King, but the reverse was not true. In death, the late President gained credit for much of the purpose that King's movement had forced upon him in life. No death had ever been like his—Niebuhr called him "an elected monarch." In a mass purgative of hatred, bigotry, and violence, the martyred President became a symbol of the healing opposites, King's qualities, which had been much too earnest for the living man. President Johnson told the nation that the most fitting eulogy would be swift passage of his civil rights bill. By this and other effects of mourning, Kennedy acquired the Lincolnesque mantle of a unifying crusader who had bled against the thorn of race. Honest biographers later found it impossible to trace an engaged personality in proportion to the honor. Because the best spirit of Kennedy was largely absent from the racial deliberations of his presidency, the issue remained an exogenous factor to the most intimate, admiring accounts of his life. In his seminal history, *A Thousand Days,* which was written and published during the peak of the national movement, Arthur Schlesinger, Jr., introduced civil rights in the thirty-fifth of thirty-seven chapters.

As for Robert Kennedy, King's travail with him was largely over. The two of them had stumbled through relations from camaraderie to contempt. Kennedy had been more of an ally to the movement during the Freedom Rides than during Birmingham, which contradicted common notions of steady growth in his character. His experience as Attorney General, and specifically with King, may well have begun to reverse his theory that the way to engineer social change was to minimize the discomfort of politicians, but for the time being he was simply too dispirited. His admirable, underappreciated campaign to reform the fundamental structure and purpose of the FBI came largely to grief, and Kennedy suffered much for that. Hoover abruptly severed all but the barest pretense of professional obligation or courtesy on the very day of the assassination in Dallas. Without the intervening power of President Kennedy, a state of mutual hatred quickly set in. From the standpoint of personal injury to King, Robert Kennedy did perhaps his greatest disservice by remaining a caretaker Attorney General for another ten months, when the FBI ran unchecked.

The Bureau wasted no time describing its target as "King's unholy alliance with the Communist Party, USA," and King as "an unprincipled opportunistic individual." Sullivan summoned Agent Nichols and others to Washington for a nine-hour war council, the result of which was a six-point plan to "expose King as an immoral opportunist who is not a sincere person but is exploiting the racial situation for personal gain." All the top officials signed a ringing declaration of resolve laced with four of the usual pledges to proceed "without embarrassment to the Bureau." The underlying hostility did not make the officials that unusual among Americans of their station. Nor was it unusual that an odd man such as Hoover would run aground in his obsession with normalcy. Race, like power, blinds before it corrupts, and Hoover saw not a shred of merit in either King or Levison. Most unforgivable was that a nation founded on Madisonian principles allowed secret police powers to accrue over forty years, until real and imagined heresies alike could be punished by methods less open to correction than the Salem witch trials. The hidden spectacle was the more grotesque because King and Levison both in fact were the rarest heroes of freedom, but the undercover state persecution would have violated democratic principles even if they had been common thieves.

For King, the rise of American liberalism was both a gain and a loss.

Many of his admirers were quick to thank the movement for bringing religious homilies to national attention, and just as quick to dismiss him now as a Baptist preacher out of his depth. He reaped recognition and condescension hard upon each other. As a result, newcomers to derivative freedom movements programmed themselves to run amok, because they grossly underestimated the complexity, the restraint, and the grounding respect for opponents that had sustained King, Moses, and countless others through the difficult years. The antiwar movement and others would be child's play compared with the politics of lifting a despised minority from oblivion.

SNCC's annual conference was held in Washington in the week following the Kennedy assassination. Innocence thought lost was lost again many times over. John Lewis was among those who wanted to lead an official SNCC processional to the grave at Arlington Cemetery, but the idea was voted down. Some objected that such tribute would be hypocritical, given their differences with the late President. Others said they should pay their respects through the movement.

More so than usual, Bob Moses spoke as though in a trance. "The white people in the country, by and large, have not as yet made up their minds whether they're willing to grant freedom to Negroes," he said. That month's Freedom Vote had been designed to give Negroes a means of building the movement without threatening whites unduly—a mock vote parallel to the official election, a full-scale pretend vote with ballot boxes and live candidates, just to implant the *feel* of what it would be like to vote, together with a hint that the exclusionary regular election was illegitimate. Some 90,000 Mississippi Negroes had "voted." Many of them had since expressed interest in trying to register, and national publicity about the Freedom Vote had spread the idea that Negroes would vote in great numbers if allowed. Still, said Moses, the only hope was to force a confrontation between federal and state authority, in which the states would have to give ground toward equal rights. "It is true, the Negroes are blackmailing the Federal Government," he said in a partly confessional tone.

One way to force the confrontation was to extend the notion of the Freedom Vote to a parallel school system, Freedom Schools, which could teach literacy skills and constitutional rights on a mass scale. Eighty Yale and Stanford students had come down as volunteers for the Freedom Vote, and if they returned for the summer in greater numbers, they could help staff the schools. This proposal nearly tore SNCC asunder. Projects outside Mississippi complained that it would drain resources from them.

Most Negro Mississippians were enthusiastic about any help, including that of Northern white students, but veteran SNCC staff workers objected vehemently to the deference and attention the white students inescapably would command. Across weeks of raw debate, Moses himself refused to express a firm opinion for or against the summer project. Always opposed to fiat by leaders, he added that this idea also carried special responsibilities. White volunteers would be beaten severely or killed, he said, and their race and status would magnify the national reaction. To the extent that SNCC consciously used the students as white lambs of sacrifice, they must bear the burden of that moral and political choice.

A messenger interrupted one of the marathon debates in Hattiesburg with news that Louis Allen had been found under his logging truck in Amite County, dead of three shotgun wounds to the head. Guilt ate at Moses even before he found the stricken widow. He had been out of touch. It had been more than a year since his last letter to John Doar, after a deputy sheriff had broken Allen's jaw with a flashlight: "They are after him in Amite . . ." Allen had been a marked man ever since telling Moses he had seen the state legislator shoot Herbert Lee in cold blood. The potshots and threats had so frightened him that Louis Allen had tried repeatedly to leave the state, once saying "Thank you, Jesus" when he crossed the line into Louisiana, but he simply did not have the wherewithal to live outside Mississippi. Lost away from his family and his logging work, Allen had returned to a series of half-finished escape plans, including one that fell through when his mother got sick and died in his last week. Moses knew none of this last pathos, but he did realize that he had failed to reach Camus' ideal of being neither a victim nor an executioner. He was both, and he was also a political leader in spite of his obsession for consensus. He had led Louis Allen to where he was now, and it would make utterly no difference unless he led others.

Moses returned straight to Hattiesburg. "We can't protect our own people," he said bluntly. With that he threw his influence and reputation behind an expanded plan to bring at least a thousand Northern volunteers to Mississippi in the summer of 1964.

Back home after the Kennedy funeral, King felt the wide range of his life's journey. He had to cancel the SCLC's credit cards because Abernathy and others were spending too much and the treasury was bare again. Robert Kennedy dismissed his objections to the Albany Nine prosecutions in a terse letter. From Selma, Mrs. Boynton asked him to help in the desperate case of forty elderly Negro women who had been locked out of a rest home for protesting when one of them was beaten in the registration line; Boynton wanted to buy a sewing machine so that some of the women could earn their keep in private homes. King mediated a dispute over a dentist bill for Mahalia Jackson, made more speeches, and sat alone with President Johnson for an hour in the close embrace of noble dreams as big as Texas. Back home, sick in bed, he received the first white graduate student pursuing a doctorate on King's oratory. The children were running wild through the house. "I think we're gonna have to let Dexter go out," King said. "He doesn't have the restraint, uh, the virtue of quietness . . . I'll call mama downstairs." When the student asked about the effects of Kennedy's death, King said it was a blessing for civil rights. "Because I'm convinced that had he lived, there would have been continual delays, and attempts to evade it at every point, and water it down at every point," he said, almost brightly. "But I think his memory and the fact that he stood up for this civil rights bill will cause many people to see the necessity for working passionately . . . So I do think we have some very hopeful days ahead."

The reaction to Kennedy's assassination pushed deep enough and wide enough in the high ground of political emotion to enable the movement to institutionalize its major gains before receding. Legal segregation was doomed. Negroes no longer were invisible, nor those of normal capacity viewed as statistical freaks. In this sense, Kennedy's murder marked the arrival of the freedom surge, just as King's own death four years hence marked its demise. New interior worlds were opened, along with a means of understanding freedom movements all over the globe. King was swelling. Race had taught him hard lessons about the greater witness of sacrifice than truth, but there was more. Nonviolence had come over him for a purpose that far transcended segregation. It touched evils beyond color and addressed needs more human than status or possessions. Having lifted him up among rulers, it would drive him back down to die among garbage workers in Memphis. King had crossed over as a patriarch like Moses into a land less bounded by race. To keep going, he became a pillar of fire.

ACKNOWLEDGMENTS

I am grateful to Alan Morrison of the Public Citizen Litigation Group and to the lead counsel in my case, Katherine Meyer, for patient, skillful pursuit of classified FBI material on Stanley Levison.

My editor, Alice Mayhew, has lifted me through this, our third book together, with her sustaining belief in the project. I thank her, along with at least a few of the people at Simon and Schuster who I know have gone beyond professional duty to help me: Henry Ferris, George Hodgman, Tina Jordan, David Shipley, Marcia Peterson, Eileen Caughlin, Natalie Goldstein, and Lisa Petrusky. Richard Snyder and other executives have financed me generously (but not extravagantly) for more than six years, beyond expectations of commercial return. I thank the John S. Guggenheim Foundation for a grant that subsidized the better part of one year's research. As always, I am grateful to my agent, George Diskant of Los Angeles, for his diligent encouragement of our family's welfare.

Our seven-year-old daughter Macy and five-year-old son Franklin have only gently inquired what their father has been doing upstairs all their lives. My heart's response to them, to Christy, and to other family members belongs privately elsewhere, but I do want to acknowledge the advice, encouragement, and inspiration of a few special friends: Scott Armstrong, Samuel Bonds, Karen De Young, David Eaton, Mary Macy, Bettyjean Murphy, Dan and Becky Okrent, Charles Peters, John and Susan Rothchild, Michele Slung, and Nicholas von Hoffman.

Among the employees of the libraries and archives cited in the notes, I am especially indebted to the following people, some of whom have since moved on to other positions: Louise Cook, Cynthia Lewis, and Diane Ware of the King Archives in Atlanta; Howard Gotlieb of the Mugar Library at Boston University; Martin Teasley of the Eisenhower Library in Abilene; Will Johnson and Ron Whealan of the Kennedy Library in Boston; Linda Hanson and Nancy Smith of the Johnson Library in Austin; Elinor Sinnette and Maricia Bracey from the Moorland-Spingarn Research Center at Howard University; Harold Miller of the State Historical Society of Wisconsin in Madison; Sue Thrasher and Paul DeLeon of the Highlander Research and Education Center in New Market, Tennessee; James H. Hutson of the Manuscript Division of the Library of Congress; Joyce Lee of the Schomburg Center for Research in Black Culture, a division of the New York City Public Library; Joseph Ernst of the Rockefeller Archive Center in Pocantico, New York; Walter Naegle of the A. Philip Randolph Institute in New York; Emil Moschella and Helen Ann Near of the FBI's Records Management Division; Janet Blizzard, James P. Turner, Nelson Hermilla, Curtis Goffe, and William B. Jones of the U. S. Department of Justice; Nancy Angelo of the Pacifica Radio Archive in Los Angeles; and Marvin Whiting and Donald Veasey of the Birmingham Public Library. I am grateful to Archie E. Allen, Edwin Guthman, C. B. King, and Mrs. W. E. "Pinkie" Shortridge for sharing historical materials in their personal possession. Jennifer Bard and Beth Taylor Muskat ably conducted specialized research during 1983.

This book would not have been possible without the cooperation of several hundred people who agreed to share with me their personal knowledge. Their names are scattered throughout the notes. Some, like Ella Baker, Septima Clark, C. B. King, E. D. Nixon, and Bayard Rustin, have since died. Some remain new friends, and I respect others for persisting in our interviews through pain or disagreement. Of those who responded to several inquiries over the years, I owe special thanks to Ralph Abernathy, Harry Belafonte, James Bevel, G. Murray Branch, John Doar, Clarence Jones, Thomas Kilgore, Bernard Lee, Beatrice Levison, Burke Marshall, Robert P. Moses, Kenneth Lee Smith, Harry Wachtel, and Wyatt Tee Walker.

Similarly, I want to pay special tribute to those writers whose work opened new regions of pleasure and investigation to me, for which I am grateful beyond the literal debts cited in the notes: Clayborne Carson, W. E. B. Du Bois, Samuel Gandy, David Garrow, Thomas Gentile, Richard Kluger, Leon Litwack, Walter Lord, Aldon Morris, Pat Watters, Carter G. Woodson, and Lamont Yeakey.

ABBREVIATIONS USED
IN SOURCE NOTES

A/AR	Anne Romaine Oral History Collection, King Library and Archives, The Martin Luther King, Jr., Center for Nonviolent Social Change, Inc.
A/KP	Papers of Dr. Martin Luther King, Jr., King Library and Archives
A/KS	King Speech Collection, King Library and Archives
A/OH	Martin Luther King, Jr., Oral History Collection, King Library and Archives
A/SC	Southern Christian Leadership Conference Records, King Library and Archives
A/SN	Papers of the Student Nonviolent Coordinating Committee, King Library and Archives
AAP	Private papers of Archie E. Allen, Santa Barbara, California
AC	Atlanta *Constitution*
ADW	Atlanta *Daily World*
AH	Albany *Herald*
AJ	Atlanta *Journal*
APR	Papers of A. Philip Randolph, Library of Congress
BIR	Archives Division, Birmingham Public Library, Birmingham, Alabama
BIR/AB	Papers of Albert E. Boutwell, Birmingham Public Library
BIR/BC	Papers of Eugene T. "Bull" Connor, Birmingham Public Library
BIR/C	Papers of Bishop C. C. J. Carpenter, Birmingham Public Library
BN	Birmingham *News*
BUK	Martin Luther King, Jr., Papers, Special Collections Department, Mugar Library, Boston University
BW	Birmingham *World*
CD	Chicago *Defender*
CORE	Papers of the Congress of Racial Equality, Library of Congress
CRA	City Records, Albany, Georgia
CRDPOH	Oral History Collection, Civil Rights Documentation Project, Moorland-Spingarn Research Center, Howard University
CUOH	Oral History Collection, Columbia University Library

DDE	Dwight D. Eisenhower Library, Abilene, Kansas
FA	FBI File #157-6-2 (Racial Matters, Albany, Georgia)
FER	FBI File #105-122316 (Ellen Rometsch)
FHFS	FBI File #61-7511 (Highlander Folk School)
FJ	FBI File #100-407018 (Clarence Jones)
FJNY	FBI File #100-73250 (Clarence Jones, New York Office)
FK	FBI File #100-106670 (Martin Luther King, Jr.)
FL	FBI File #100-392452 (Stanley D. Levison)
FLNY	FBI File #100-111180 (Stanley D. Levison, New York Office)
FR	FBI File #100-158790 (Bayard Rustin)
FSC	FBI File #100-438794 (Southern Christian Leadership Conference)
HOH	Oral History Collection, Harry Lasker Library, Highlander Research and Education Center, New Market, Tennessee
JFK	John F. Kennedy Library, Boston, Massachusetts
LBJ	Lyndon Baines Johnson Library, Austin, Texas
MA	Montgomery *Advertiser*
MC	Michigan *Chronicle*
MVCOH	Oral History, Mississippi Valley Collection, Memphis State University
NAACP	Papers of the National Association for the Advancement of Colored People, Library of Congress
NR	Not Recorded (for serials in FBI files)
NT	Nashville *Tennessean*
OH	Oral History
NYAN	New York *Amsterdam News*
NYT	*New York Times*
PC	Pittsburgh *Courier*
PRA	Pacifica Radio Archive, Los Angeles
RAC	Rockefeller Archive Center, North Tarrytown, New York
RN	Papers of Reinhold Niebuhr, Library of Congress
SHSW/HP	Papers of the Highlander Research and Education Center, State Historical Society of Wisconsin, Madison, Wisconsin
SHSW/SP	Papers of Donald H. Smith, State Historical Society of Wisconsin, Madison, Wisconsin
UAB	University of Alabama in Birmingham, Oral History Research Office
WP	Washington *Post*
WS	Washington *Star*

NOTES

One
FORERUNNER: VERNON JOHNS

1 outdoor sheriff's sales: E. King. *Great South*, p. 333.
2 more dignified access: Int. Dr. Zelia Evans, June 8, 1983.
2 property worth $300,000: Evans, *Dexter Avenue*, p. 14.
3 "on American soil": Du Bois, *Souls*, p. 216.
4 largest Negro church: Int. Rev. Ralph D. Abernathy, March 5, 1984.
4 proceeds to the church: Int. William Beasley, secretary, First Baptist Church, Dec. 20, 1983.
4 exchange for the property: Ibid.
4 "Brick-a-Day Church": Ibid.; program for the Centennial Celebration of the First Baptist Church, Montgomery, 1967.
5 firmly unrepentant: Int. R. D. Nesbitt, Dec. 29, 1983.
6 "God-blessed": Evans, *Dexter Avenue*, p. 62. Trial information, int. R. D. Nesbitt, Dec. 29, 1983.
7 in October 1948: Dexter's official history states that Johns took up the pastorate in 1947, but all the Johns relatives cited below agree that Vernon Johns moved to Montgomery in October 1948, four months after his wife and two months before the rest of his family.
7 the stuff of legend: Sources used below on Vernon Johns generally include Gandy, *Human*, and Boddie, *God's Bad*. On Johns's family background, sources include interviews with the following relatives: Robert Johns (brother), Jan. 11, 1984; Vernon Increase Johns (son), Feb. 14, 1984; Altona Johns Anderson (daughter), Jan. 31, 1984 and Feb. 7, 1984; Enid Johns (daughter), Jan. 24, 1984 and Jan. 30, 1984; Jeanne Johns Adkins (daughter), Jan. 28, 1984; William Trent (wife's brother), Feb. 2, 1984; and Barbara Johns Powell (niece), Dec. 9, 1983. On Johns as a preacher, sources include interviews with Dr. Samuel Gandy, Oct. 19, 1983; Rev. S. S. Seay, Sr., Dec. 20, 1983; Rev. G. Murray Branch, June 7, 1983; Rev. Gardner Taylor, Oct. 25, 1983; Rev. Charles S. Morris, Feb. 3, 1984; Rev. Thomas Kilgore, Nov. 8, 1983; Rev. Vernon Dobson, Oct. 5, 1983 and Dec. 2, 1983; Rev. James L. Moore, Dec. 2,

1983; Dr. E. Evans Crawford, May 31, 1983; Rev. Melvin Watson, Feb. 25, 1983; Rev. David Briddell, Aug. 17, 1983; and Rev. Marcus G. Wood, Oct. 4, 1983. On Vernon Johns in Montgomery, sources include interviews with William Beasley, Dec. 20, 1983; Dr. Zelia Evans, June 8, 1983; Jo Ann Robinson, Nov. 14, 1983; Rufus Lewis, June 8, 1983; E. D. Nixon, Dec. 29, 1983; Richmond Smiley, Dec. 28, 1983; and R. D. Nesbitt, Dec. 29, 1983 and Feb. 16, 1984. Also specific sources as cited below.

7 with a scythe: Yeakey, "Montgomery," p. 110. Also int. Altona Johns Anderson, Jan. 31, 1984, and Jeanne Johns Adkins to author, Feb. 5, 1984.

7 white man named Price: The Price story was repeated to the author in only slightly different forms by all the close relatives of Vernon Johns who gave interviews.

7 "like she was a white woman": Int. Vernon Increase Johns, Feb. 14, 1984.

8 every word from memory: Gandy, *Human*, p. xvi.

8 "or students with brains": Ibid., p. xvii. Also int. Rev. G. Murray Branch, June 7, 1983, and Rev. Charles S. Morris, Feb. 3, 1984.

9 the University of Chicago: Gandy, *Human*, p. xix, and Jeanne Johns Adkins to author, Feb. 5, 1984. The Oberlin stories are repeated in generally the same fashion by the scattered Johns sources cited above.

10 "some mountain-top experience": Gandy, *Human*, p. 51.

10 who married Thurman: Int. Rev. Vernon Dobson, Dec. 2. 1983.

10 selling subscriptions: Int. Rev. Charles S. Morris, Feb. 3, 1984. Morris traveled with Johns for five summers, 1936–40.

11 and a semi-fresh shirt: Int. Dr. Samuel Gandy, Oct. 19, 1983.

11 to change the Dexter hymnal: Int. Enid Johns, Jan. 24, 1984.

11 He beckoned Edna King: Int. R. D. Nesbitt, Dec. 29, 1983.

12 "not a dry eye": Int. Rev. James L. Moore, Dec. 2, 1983.

12 "spinksterinkdum Negroes": Int. Altona Johns Anderson, Feb. 7, 1984.

13 "hesitation pitch": Tygiel, *Baseball's*, p. 227.

13 executive order of July 26: Donovan, *Conflict*, p. 411.

13 silken cords that never broke: Int. William McDonald, Dec. 29, 1983.

13 "Selma needs the water": Ibid.

14 one case against a storekeeper: Int. E. D. Nixon, Dec. 29, 1983. Nixon says he went to Tuskegee with Johns and the victim.

14 against six white policemen: Int. Altona Johns Anderson, Feb. 7, 1984. Anderson says she went to Tuskegee with Johns and the victim.

14 "should know better": Int. Richmond Smiley, Dec. 28, 1983.

15 "hell of a funeral": Int. Rufus Lewis, June 8, 1983.

15 "semi-annual visit to the church": Int. R. D. Nesbitt, Dec. 29, 1983, and many others, as this remark to the august Trenholm was widely heard and seldom forgotten.

15 "murderer in the house": Int. Rev. Ralph D. Abernathy, March 5, 1984. The Adair murder story was mentioned by many other Johns sources.

16 one dentist and three doctors: Yeakey, "Montgomery," p. 17.

16 "important business activity": Gandy, *Human*, p. xv.

16 "some land he owns": Boddie, *God's Bad*, p. 65.

17 it "cheapened" the church: Int. Jo Ann Robinson, Nov. 14, 1983.

18 kept playing the Bach: Int. Enid Johns, Jan. 24, 1984, and Barbara Johns Powell, Dec. 9, 1983.

18 "weren't bought in the store": Int. Richmond Smiley, Dec. 28, 1983.

18 "when Negroes start making them": Int. Rev. James L. Moore, Dec. 2, 1983.

18 arrange a truce: For the deacons' meeting over the fish generally, int. R. D. Nesbitt, Dec. 29, 1983, and Rev. Vernon Dobson, Oct. 5, 1983.

19 them with his fists: Int. Rev. G. Murray Branch, June 8, 1983, and R. D. Nesbitt, Dec. 29, 1983.

20 "all out of here!": B. Smith, *They Closed*, p. 38. This book treats the Prince Edward County school strike and its aftermath. The same subject is covered in Kluger, *Simple Justice*, pp. 451ff.

20 comic book between her knees: Int. Barbara Johns Powell, Dec. 9, 1983.

21 "limb is not a man": Kluger, *Simple Justice*, p. 478.

21 still had no telephones: Int. Barbara Johns Powell, Dec. 9, 1983.

21   so plainly "tickled": Int. Robert Johns, Jan. 11, 1984.
21   quoting all that poetry: Ibid.
21   her astonishing achievement: Int. Barbara Johns Powell, Dec. 9, 1983.
22   to anyone in Montgomery: Ibid.
22   "each other's names!'": Int. Dr. Zelia Evans, June 8, 1983.
22 $1.95 from a white woman: Jeremiah Reeves case. Discussed in King speech of April 6, 1958, BUK 1f11a.
22   with a tire iron: Int. Enid Johns, Jan. 24, 1984.
22   "Safe to Murder Negroes": Int. Altona Johns, Jan. 31, 1984. See also Yeakey, "Montgomery," pp. 104ff, Gandy, *Human*, p. xv, and B. Smith, *They Closed*, p. 78. This incident is one of the most popular of the Johns stories and was mentioned to the author by practically every source who knew him.
23   "his hide is not worth it": B. Smith, *They Closed*, p. 78, and int. Barbara Johns Powell, Dec. 8, 1983.
24   Sherman's memoirs and "When the Rapist Is White": Int. Altona Johns Anderson, Feb. 7, 1984.
24   women of the church were incensed: Int. Rev. G. Murray Branch, June 8, 1983, and R. D. Nesbitt, Dec. 29, 1983.
24   this latest resignation, his fifth: Int. R. D. Nesbitt, Dec. 29, 1983.
25   fault she shared with her uncle: Int. Barbara Johns Powell, Dec. 9, 1983.
26   to meet Martin Luther King, Jr.: Int. R. D. Nesbitt, Dec. 29, 1983 and Feb. 16, 1984. Also Nesbitt, A/OH.

Two
ROCKEFELLER AND EBENEZER

28   first gift: Read, *Spelman*, pp. 64-65.
28   "Paddle My Own Canoe" and "Pleased Although I'm Sad": Flynn, *God's Gold*, pp. 53, 110.
29   never bring reproach: Read, *Spelman*, p. 83.
30   awarded its first three in 1897: Brawley, *Morehouse*, p. 83.
30   October 29, 1899: E. Smith, "Ebenezer."
30   threatening foreclosure: Ibid., p. 1. Also King Sr., *Daddy*, p. 84.
30   Ebenezer was prosperous: Ebenezer bought the Fifth Baptist Church on Bell Street, pursuant to resolution by Fifth Baptist, on Dec. 12, 1900. Fulton County Deed Book 152, p. 76.
30   Ricca & Son: Last Will and Testament of Alberta Williams King, City of Atlanta Estate #97282, Will Book 109. p. 37.
31   "supremacy of the Anglo-Saxon": Andrew Sledd, "The Negro: Another View," *Atlantic Monthly*, July 1902.
31   "did not reflect": NYT, Oct. 20, 1901, p. 1.
31   "wise and just to civilize": NYT, Oct. 27, 1901, p. 11.
31   Atlanta race riot: AC, Sept. 21–25, 1906. See also Golden, *Mr. Kennedy*, p. 48.
32   president of the Atlanta: E. Smith, "Ebenezer," p. 3. Also King Sr., *Daddy*, in the introduction by Benjamin S. Mays.
32   shyness and humility: King Sr., *Daddy*, p. 21. (In this autobiography, Daddy King describes his wife's education and social position in some detail, but says little about her character or appearance.) Also int. Rev. Larry Williams, Dec. 27, 1983.
32   would not be noticed: Mrs. Leathers (local public librarian), April 1, 1970, A/OH.
32   "kind of fearful": Int. Rev. Joel King (Alberta Williams' brother-in-law), Jan. 9, 1984.
33   doctorate upon him in 1914: E. Smith, "Ebenezer," p. 3.
33   children in the flames: Hugh Davis Graham and Ted Robert Gurr, *Violence in America: Historical and Comparative Perspectives. A Staff Report to the National Commission on the Causes and Prevention of Violence*, Vol. I, p. 254.
33   in Ohio to bury her: Flynn, *God's Gold*, p.464.
33   another $50 million: Ibid., p. 443.
33   completed by 1918: Read, *Spelman*, p. 194.
34   "Well, I'se preaching": King Sr., *Daddy*, p. 21.

34 a used Model T Ford: Ibid., p. 60. King says his mother traded one cow for the Ford, but this is unlikely given the relative values of cows and cars about 1918. Unless Mrs. King owned a truly amazing beast, she would have had to swap at least three or four cows for a Model T that would run.

34 whom he had never met: Ibid., pp. 13–15.

36 "father wouldn't allow it": Ibid., p. 69.

36 asked her to court: Ibid.

37 attended Morehouse only: Ibid., p. 75.

37 "just not college material": Ibid., p. 76.

37 bearer to classes: Ibid.

38 Robert E. Lee: Read, *Spelman*, p. 204.

38 Buddha, Lao-Tze: Harry Emerson Fosdick, "Shall the Fundamentalists Win?" as reprinted in *Christian Century*, June 28, 1922, p. 713.

39 John Foster Dulles represented Fosdick: Hoopes, *The Devil*, p. 8.

39 "Jesse James of the theological world": Fosdick, *The Living*, p. 153.

39 "Crowds Tie Up Traffic": NYT, Oct. 27, 1924.

39 "like your frankness": Fosdick, *The Living*, pp. 177–78.

39 razed the apartment buildings: See NYT, Jan. 29, 1926.

39 On October 5, 1930: NYT, Oct. 6, 1930, p. 11. On Rockefeller and Fosdick, see also Ahlstrom, *Religious History*, p. 911.

40 of a heart attack: King Sr., *Daddy*, p. 90.

40 "I am the First Lady": Ibid., p. 92.

40 feelings of his wife: Ibid., pp. 92–93. King twice mentions the sentiment against him among the Ebenezer deacons.

40 padlock on the church's front door: Ibid., p. 93.

41 *about my father's BUSINESS:* As discussed in Ahlstrom, *Religious History*, p. 905.

41 no credit in the ledger: E. Smith, "Ebenezer," p. 5. Daddy King's methods and innovations also discussed in int. Rev. G. Murray Branch, June 7, 1983, Rev. Gardner Taylor, Oct. 25, 1983, Rev. Thomas Kilgore, Nov, 8, 1983, and Rev. Marcus G. Wood, Oct. 4, 1983, among others.

43 one nickel for Atlanta Life: Int. Rev. Thomas Kilgore, Nov. 8, 1983. Kilgore first went to Ebenezer and to the King home in 1931, just before King took over the church. He recalls that Ebenezer members still were talking with approval about how Mrs. Williams was holding herself in the background for the sake of her daughter. In later years, as a nationally prominent minister himself and colleague of King Jr., Kilgore often discussed Daddy King's genius as a church financier at preachers' gatherings.

43 church outreach programs: Ibid. Also E. Smith, "Ebenezer," p. 5.

43 "tell you this morning, Ebenezer": Int. Rev. Larry Williams, Dec. 27, 1983.

43 highest-paid Negro minister: King Sr., *Daddy*, p. 94.

44 glorious trip for King: Ibid., p. 97.

44 "Royally Welcomed on Return": ADW, Aug. 28, 1934, p. 1.

44 from Michael to Martin: Reddick, *Crusader*, pp. 50–51. Also King Sr., *Daddy*, p. 88.

45 freedom to choose a name: See Litwack, *Storm*, pp. 247–55. See also Douglass, *Narrative*, pp.114–15; and Fenderson, *Thurgood*, p. 23.

45 what to call themselves as a race: Litwack, *Storm*, pp. 541ff.

45 *The New York Times:* Kluger, *Simple Justice*, p. 546.

45 Chicago *Defender:* Ottley, *Lonely*, pp. 109–10.

45 Abbott hated the word: Ibid., pp. 110, 213, 221, 287, 288.

46 J. H. Meredith: Meredith, *Three Years*, p. 53. See also Mays, *Born*, pp. 113–16.

46 Air Force: Lord, *The Past*, p. 33.

46 calling himself Martin: Reddick, *Crusader*, pp. 43, 48, 50–51.

46 autobiography, Reverend King: King Sr., *Daddy*, pp. 26, 88.

47 State Department records: Passport application of Martin Luther King, Jr., filed Feb. 12, 1957. The clerk made a note on the passport after inspecting King's birth certificate.

47 "Big Mike": Reddick, *Crusader*, p. 43.

47 "earned" his name: *Time*, Feb. 18, 1957, p. 17.

48 roughly two-thirds: Lewis, *King*, p. 7.

48 "anti-capitalistic feelings": King Jr., "Autobiography."
48 "get ahead of me": Ibid.
48 five fingers: Reddick, *Crusader*, p. 54. Also Clayton, *King*, p. 18.
48 head with a telephone: This story first appeared in Reddick, *Crusader*, p. 59. Also King Sr., *Daddy*, p. 127. Characterizations of the children drawn from the King biographies and from interviews, notably Alberta King's friend Lavata Lightner, Feb. 3, 1972, A/OH, and King Jr.'s high school friend Emmett Proctor, April 15, 1970, A/OH.
48 out the window: Reddick, *Crusader*, p. 60. Also Lewis, *King*, p. 13, and Oates, *Trumpet*, pp. 8–9.
49 reserved the primal "Mama": Reddick, *Crusader*, p. 51. Also Clayton, *King*, p. 27.
49 "was Harvard's": A common folklore, repeated for National Public Radios's 1980 profile of Du Bois. See also Wilkins, *Standing Fast*, p. 93.
49 by their first names: Arthur Spingarn, March 6, 1968, CRDPOH.
50 White had no brains: Ibid.
50 fashion show: Wilkins, *Standing Fast*, pp. 77–81.
50 "finest address in Harlem": Ibid., pp. 106, 117.
50 "tucked among the most august": Ibid.
51 word "nigger": ADW, Jan. 30, 1934.
51 NBC Radio censored: Ross, *Spingarn*, p. 154. Also ADW, Feb. 15, 1934.
51 "embrace Jim Crow": Wilkins, *Standing Fast*, p. 153.
51 "biggest plate-glass window": Ibid.
51 hire him back at Atlanta: Davis, *Leadership*, p. 144.
52 "lick boots": *The Crisis*, June 1934, p. 182.
52 Roy Wilkins first: Ross, *Spingarn*, p. 210.
52 rumors about his sex life: Ibid., p. 212. Also Arthur Spingarn, March 6, 1968, CRDPOH.
52 H. L. Mencken: H. L. Mencken, "Notes on Negro Strategy," *The Crisis*, October 1934, p. 289.
53 led several hundred people: King Sr., *Daddy*, pp. 99–102.
53 King abandoned the project: Ibid., pp.104–7.
53 alleged embezzlement: English, *Prophet*, p. 42.
54 "Seven Minutes at the Mike": Int. William H. Borders, March 7, 1984, and Larry Williams, Dec. 27, 1984.
54 unknown speeches: For examples of some of the better speeches made by Negro leaders during Reconstruction, see Woodson, *Negro Orators*.
55 U.S. Communist Party had to fire him: NYT, Dec. 22, 1939, p. 1, and Dec. 24, 1939, p. 14.
55 The Ebenezer choir: ADW, Dec. 15, 1939, p. 1.
55 ferocious attack: ADW, Dec. 20, 1939, p. 1. Also Raines, *My Soul*, p. 59; int. William H. Borders, March 7, 1984; NYT, Dec.16, 1939, p. 1.
55 35,000 cheering Baptists: ADW, July 27, 1939, p. 1. Also int. Rev. Joel King, Jan. 7, 1984.
56 Reinhold Niebuhr and Paul Tillich: Stone, *Paul Tillich's*, p. 108.
56 offered Mays instead: Int. Benjamin Mays, March 6, 1984. Mays identified the Rockefeller associate as Trevor Arnett.
56 The tenor soloist: Int. Robert Williams, April 3, 1984.
57 and the violin case: Lewis, *King*, p. 16.
57 snatches of the "Moonlight Sonata": Int. Robert Williams, April 3, 1984.
57 his grandmother was dead: King Sr., *Daddy*, p. 109. Also Reddick, *Crusader*, p. 60, Oates, *Trumpet*, p. 13, and King Jr., "Autobiography."
57 could not sleep: King Sr., *Daddy*, p. 109.
57 young man overnight: Clayton, *King*, p. 31.
58 "dreaming about": King Sr., *Daddy*, p. 109. Settlement was on Nov. 1, 1941. Fulton County Deed Book 1872, p. 114.
58 executor and sole heir: Records of the Fulton County Court of Probate, Estate #31740. Also Deed Book 1540, p. 317.
59 "upper upper class": King Jr., "Autobiography."
59 "mostly lower middle class": Reddick, *Crusader*, p. 55.

59 "middle middle class": Emmett Proctor, April 15, 1970, A/OH.

59 penchant for tweed suits: Ibid.

59 "Sack," and "Mole": Reddick, *Crusader*, p. 55.

59 close for the duration: Mays, *Born*, p. 184.

60 Read finally triumphed: Davis, *Leadership*, p. 145.

60 two kinds of students: Int. Robert Williams, April 3, 1984. Such boastful sayings were rather common. Students spoke wryly of "Harvard, Yale, and Morehouse." Also Reddick, *Crusader*, p. 65.

60 "larger than a hamburger": Int. Samuel Du Bois Cook, April 4, 1984.

60 friends King made: Ibid. Also int. Robert Williams, April 3, 1984.

61 "revolutionary stage": Walter McCall, A/OH.

61 "nobody there was afraid": Bennett, *What Manner*, p. 26.

62 first frank discussions: Ibid.

63 dancing and card-playing: Walter McCall, A/OH.

63 "organically quiescent": Oates, *Trumpet*, p. 18.

63 laugh out loud in disbelief: Int. Robert Williams, April 3, 1984.

63 calling him "nigger": Lewis, *King*, p. 21.

63 six Negro war veterans: Grant, *Black Protest*, p. 218.

63 first multiple lynching since 1918: NYT, July 27, 1946, p. 1.

64 180 bullet holes: ADW, July 17, 1946, p. 1.

64 "best people in town": AC, July 28, 1946, p. 1.

64 "My God!": Donovan, *Conflict*, p. 244. Also Wilkins, *Standing Fast*, p. 193.

64 first campus chapter of the NAACP: Int. Samuel Du Bois Cook, April 4, 1984.

64 little interest: Ibid.

64 three Sundays a month: Int. Larry Williams, Dec. 27, 1983, and Rev. William Holmes Borders, March 7, 1984.

64 proof of intrigue: Int. Larry Williams, Dec. 27, 1983.

64 cut off his friendship: Int. Juanita Sellers Stone, March 6, 1984.

65 rejoined the Morehouse: Christine King Farris, "The Young Martin," *Ebony*, Jan. 1986, pp. 56–58.

65 antics culminated: Int. Larry Williams, Dec. 27, 1983.

65 soften the blow: Ibid.

65 later they joked: Reddick, *Crusader*, p. 75.

65 "It won't hold 'em!": Int. Larry Williams, Dec. 27, 1983.

66 oration had been borrowed: Ibid.

66 King became "Shady": Int. Larry Williams, Dec. 27, 1983.

66 "The Wreckers": Int. Emmett Proctor, Nov. 20, 1984; Garrow, *Bearing*, p. 36.

66 closing his sermon folder: Int. Emmett Proctor, Nov. 20, 1984.

66 first American president to address: Donovan, *Conflict*, p. 333.

66 "To Secure These Rights": Released Oct. 27, 1947. Discussed in Kluger, *Simple Justice*, p. 253.

66 call McGill a "weasel": Ashmore, *Hearts*, p. 110.

67 "The Purpose of Education": Bennett, *What Manner*, p. 29.

67 apologize publicly: C. King, *My Life*, p. 99. Also int. Larry Williams, Dec. 27, 1983.

68 among his own: King Sr., *Daddy*, p. 141.

68 "there are moral laws": Int. Samuel Du Bois Cook, April 4, 1984.

Three
NIEBUHR AND THE POOL TABLES

69 possible for Jonah: Int. Rev. George W. Lawrence, Feb. 24, 1984.

69 naked children: Ibid.

69 gold cross: Int. Rev. Edward Spath, Oct. 4, 1983.

70 poolroom beneath: The poolroom was mentioned by all Crozer alumni interviewed for this chapter.

70 full third of the class: Int. Rev. Marcus Wood, Oct. 4, 1983.

70 pagan deities: Int. Rev. Francis Stewart, Dec. 23, 1983.

70 taught Benjamin Mays: Reddick, *Crusader*, p. 78.

70 least intelligent class: Int. Rev. Marcus Wood, Oct. 4, 1983, and Rev. Edward Spath, Oct, 4, 1983.

71 "he that is not against": Mark 9:40 and Matthew 12:30.

72 Jesus and John: Int. Kenneth Lee Smith, Oct. 12, 1983. In spite of Mark 1:9, Matthew 2:13–14, etc.

72 Moses was an uncorroborated: Int. James B. Pritchard, June 25, 1984.

72 The standing joke: Int. Kenneth Lee Smith, Oct, 12, 1983.

72 B− in Pritchard's: Int. James B. Pritchard, June 25, 1984.

72 utterly transformed: Walter McCall, A/OH.

73 "One ever feels his twoness": Du Bois, *Souls*, p. 45.

73 "loud and always laughing" and "grimly serious": King interview in *Redbook* magazine, as cited in Reddick, *Crusader*, p. 86. In this passage, Reddick suggests that the interracial composition of Crozer was the principal cause of King's radically improved scholarship.

73 tear down the students' religious: Int. Rev. Lester Loder, Feb. 27, 1984, and other Crozer classmates.

73 read all night: Walter McCall, A/OH.

73 King would ever cite specifically: Smith and Zepp, *Search*, p. 37. This book, coauthored by one of King's teaches at Crozer, is the primary authority on his intellectual experience during the seminary years.

74 Pittsburgh steel mills: Ibid., p. 22.

74 Davis' personal copy: Ibid., p. 48.

74 King never accepted pacifism: Ibid., Ch. 3 generally. Also King Jr., *Stride*, p. 95.

74 attacking A. J. Muste's: "War and Pacifism," a book review King wrote for Kenneth L. Smith's course in Christian social philosophy in the spring of 1951, BUK.

74 nearly one-third: Smith and Zepp, *Search*, p. 21.

74 "fall in line": King Jr., "Autobiography."

74 his behavior eccentric: Int. James B. Pritchard, June 25, 1984.

75 something of a bigot: Int. Rev. Francis Stewart, Dec. 23, 1983.

75 Enslin would express: Int. Kenneth Lee Smith, Nov. 3, 1983. Smith reviewed the letter among the contents of King's file at Crozer, which authorities at Colgate Rochester Theological Seminary (into which Crozer was merged in 1970) have not released.

75 Joseph Kirkland: The Kirkland portrait is drawn from an interview with Lydia Kirkland (his widow), Dec. 9, 1983, and from Crozer interviews generally.

75 packed the chapel: Int. Rev. George W. Lawrence, Feb. 24, 1984.

76 "have a zeal": Int. Rev. Lester Loder, Feb. 27, 1984. Text taken from Romans 10:2.

76 "Christianity and communism": Int. Rev. Francis Stewart, Dec. 23, 1983.

76 "religious lectures": Crozer interviews generally. The phrase appears in a letter critiquing one of King's sermons, Melvin Watson to King, Aug. 14, 1952, BUK 15f50.

76 no fewer than nine: Int. Larry Greenfield, president of Colgate Rochester Theological Seminary, July 5, 1983. Greenfield counted the courses from the King personnel folder, which is in his custody.

76 as he knew Shakespeare: Int. Rev. George W. Lawrence, Feb. 24, 1984.

76 "clear spring of friendship": Augustine, *Confessions*, Bk. III, Ch. 2.

76 "the three P's": King int. by Smith, Nov. 29, 1963, SHSW/SP.

77 Rabbit in the Bushes: Int. Rev. Marcus Wood, Oct. 4, 1983.

77 countrified parody: Ibid.

77 second-best preacher: Int. Rev. Marcus Wood, Oct. 4, 1983, Rev. Edward Spath, Oct. 4, 1983, and Rev. Francis Stewart, Dec. 23, 1983.

77 J. Pious Barbour: Reddick, *Crusader*, p. 83.

77 "deepest theologian": Barbour to King, July 21, 1955, BUK8f21.

78 Catholic priest: Int. James B. Pritchard, June 25, 1984.

78 "Tillich is all wet": Barbour to King, July 21, 1955, BUK8f21.

78 nowhere to climb: Int. Juanita Sellers Stone, March 6, 1984. The third member of this inner circle of Spelman friends in New York was June Dobbs—sister of opera star Mattawilda, daughter of lecturer and Atlanta Negro society figure John Wesley Dobbs, and aunt of future Atlanta mayor Maynard Jackson.

78 King visited Sellers: Ibid.

78 exercise in ministerial diplomacy: Ibid.

79 permanent pattern of conversation: Int. Rev. Gardner Taylor, Oct. 25, 1983, among many others. Taylor, a friend of Daddy King's for many years, described the conversations he heard between the two Kings as almost invariably a running banter on the modern vs. tradition argument.

79 crushed the lighted cigar: Int. Rev. Joel King, Jan. 9, 1984.

79 Christmas holidays of 1949: King Jr., *Stride*, p. 92, and King Sr., *Daddy*, p. 147.

80 movement had stolen: NYT, April 25, 1949, p. 16.

80 fulminating against: King Sr., *Daddy*, p. 147.

80 "Greek atomists": Watson to King, Aug. 14, 1952, reviewing a King sermon on communism, BUK15f50.

80 made his presence known: Int. Rev. Francis Stewart, Dec. 23, 1983, and Rev. Marcus Wood, Oct. 4, 1983.

81 first choice was Yale: undated letter, King to Dr. Sankey Blanton, president of Crozer, BUK15f49.

81 Edinburgh University: King to Prof. Hugh Watt, Nov. 5, 1950, BUK15f49, and Professor Rankin to King, Dec. 15, 1950, accepting King at Edinburgh, BUK15f50.

81 two schools accepted him: King to Blanton, BUK15f49.

81 playfully appending: Int. Larry Williams, Dec. 27, 1983.

82 beginning of the end: Int. Dr. Kenneth Lee Smith, Oct. 12, 1983, and Dr. John C. Bennett, May 10, 1984. Both for source material and original insight regarding King and Niebuhr, the author is heavily indebted to Smith and Zepp, *Search*, Ch. 4.

82 Henry Hodgkin: Int. Glenn Smiley, Nov. 14, 1983.

82 1935 poll: Manchester, *Glory*, p. 152.

82 Niebuhr ridiculed Dewey's: Niebuhr, *Moral Man*, pp. xii-xvii.

82 "in perfect flight": Reinhold Niebuhr, Feb. 14, 1953, CUOH, p. 38.

82 "love of God in contempt": Augustine, *City of God*, Bk. 4, Ch. 28, as cited in Niebuhr, *Moral Man*, pp. 69–70.

83 "mind which governed the self": Reinhold Niebuhr, Feb. 14, 1953, CUOH, p. 69.

83 always be selfish: Niebuhr, *Moral Man*, p. xi.

83 "speak with a dogmatism": Ibid., p. 253.

83 "apocalyptic vision": Ibid., p. 155.

83 "style of great drama": Ibid., p. 154.

83 "egotism and vindictiveness": Ibid., p. 156.

83 "force and fear": Ibid., p. 157.

83 "naive Christian Marxist": Reinhold Niebuhr, CUOH, p. 91.

84 disturbed by the Marxist themes: Bingham, *Courage*, p. 212.

84 "worse than a thug": Ibid.

84 counteract the influence: Int. John C. Bennett, May 10, 1984.

85 "Resist not evil": Matthew 5:39. Tolstoy described the incident in his 1884 essay "My Religion," as retold in Kaufman, *Religion*, pp. 53ff.

85 "ulterior motive": Ibid.

85 Tolstoy Farm: Fischer, *Gandhi*, pp. 39–41.

86 "type of coercion": Niebuhr, *Moral Man*, pp. 250–52.

86 "larger contribution": Ibid., p.254.

86 "love's message": "Reinhold Niebuhr's Ethical Dualism," King paper written May 9, 1952 for a Boston University seminar on systematic theology, BUK15f20.

87 "disastrous to religion itself": "Karl Barth's Conception of God," King paper written Jan. 2, 1952 at Boston University, BUK15f20.

87 half-dozen books on Gandhi: King Jr., *Stride*, p. 96.

87 his own major books: Smith and Zepp, *Search*, p. 71.

87 "Niebuhr's great contribution": King Jr., *Stride*, p. 96. Also pp. 96–99 generally, in which King presents Gandhi as his major interset and Niebuhr as a minor one. The language that he uses, however, makes the reverse seem true.

87 "Niebuhrian stratagem of power": Wayne H. Cowan (editor of *Christianity and Crisis*) to Niebuhr, April 13, 1970, Box 38, RN. Cowan repeated King's comments as relayed by Andrew Young.

87 pacifism and race to sin: See King papers on Niebuhr in Boston University's Mugar

Library, Drawer 15, including "Reinhold Niebuhr," a biographical sketch in King's hand-writing, "Reinhold Niebuhr," and two versions of "Reinhold Niebuhr's Ethical Dualism."

87 Church History 153: Exam paper, BUK15f27.

88 "author widely known": NYT, Feb. 10, 1951, p. 1.

88 arraigned in handcuffs: Davis, *Leadership*, p. 145.

88 scraggly picket line: Int. Harry Belafonte, March 6–7, 1985.

88 dismissed the case: Ibid., and NYT, Nov. 21, 1951.

88 Wilkins straddled: Donovan, *Tumultuous*, p. 188, and "Negroes Reaffirm Opposition to Reds," NYT, July 1,1951.

88 friend named Snuffy: Int. Kenneth Lee Smith, Oct. 12 and Nov. 3, 1983.

88 daughter of a German: Int. Rev. Marcus Wood, Oct. 4, 1983, Lydia Kirkland, Dec. 9, 1983, and Horace Whitaker, July 31, 1984. David Lewis identified this woman as the daughter of Crozer's superintendent of buildings and grounds in Lewis, *King*, p. 33, but King's Crozer friends remembered only the romance with the daughter of the cook. Their memories of the social discomfort it caused are so vivid, particularly Whitaker's, that I believe Lewis described the same affair with a mistaken identification of the girlfriend. See also Garrow, *Bearing*, p. 30.

88 incipient competition: Int. Kenneth Lee Smith, Nov. 3, 1983. Smith declined to discuss the romance except to say that it was a serious matter. He described King to an early biographer (Lewis, *King*, p. 28) as "reserved and humorless," but later wrote an excellent, favorable book about King's intellectual life at Crozer.

89 face the pain: Int. Horace Whitaker, July 31, 1984.

89 charged him with bastardy: Int. Kenneth Lee Smith, Nov. 3, 1983, and Horace Whitaker, July 31, 1984.

89 all but acknowledged paternity: McCall to King, Aug. 5, 1954, BUK15f49.

90 new green Chevrolet: Reddick, *Crusader*, p. 87.

90 "Power Glide": Int. Horace Whitaker, July 31, 1984.

90 Edgar S. Brightman: See generally Smith and Zepp, *Search*, Ch. 5.

91 described God using only a long list: Augustine, *Confessions*, Bk. I, Ch. 4.

91 "that something of supreme value": As quoted in Lewis, *King*, p. 43.

91 "the mystery of self": *Time*, Feb. 19, 1951, p. 59.

91 first coast-to-coast television: Manchester, *Glory*, p. 717.

91 Willie Mays: Tygiel, *Baseball's*, p. 288.

91 direct long-distance dialing: Manchester, *Glory*, p. 1001.

92 ten of his fifteen: Smith and Zepp, *Search*, pp. 99–100.

92 "McTaggart Under Criticism": BUK15f14.

92 light inside his closet: Int. David Briddell, Aug. 17, 1983.

92 ornate signatures: The practice signatures appear on the back of an exam paper covering the philosophy of Alfred North Whitehead, dated March 16, 1952(?), BUK15f35.

92 fiddled with a pipe: Int. Wilhard Williams, Dec. 8, 1983, and James Jones, Dec. 8, 1983.

92 philosophy department: Int. L. Harold DeWolf, May 9, 1983.

92 "I used the silent conclusion": W. T. Handy, Jr., to King, Nov, 18, 1952, BUK15f50.

92 Spinoza's epistemological theory: Exam paper dated March 21, 1952, BUK15f25.

92 "What Is Man?": Sermon draft, BUK16f17. King delivered this sermon in Chicago on Jan. 12, 1958, in a service broadcast over radio. A/KS.

93 "Answer to a Perplexing Question": Text taken from Matthew 17:19, "Why Could Not We Cast Him Out?" Sermon, BUK16f16.

93 Dialectical Society: Called Philosophical Club in Reddick, *Crusader*, p. 88, Lewis, *King*, p. 38, and in other books. King himself once referred to it as the Theology Club, in a letter to DeWolf of May 15, 1954, BUK15f49. It is possible that the name of the informal group changed over time. Surviving members recall it as the Dialectical Society.

93 "we buried Jim": Int. David Briddell, Aug. 17, 1983.

93 "spiritual cell movements": Int. George Thomas, March 7, 1984, and Douglas Moore, Oct. 24–25, 1984.

93 never landed King himself: Ibid.

93 choose "race-related" topics: Int. E. Evans Crawford, Oct, 5, 1983.

93 "up in the clouds": W. T. Handy, Jr., to King, Nov. 18, 1952, BUK15f50.

94   charges reversed: Int. Wilhard Williams, Dec. 8, 1983.

94   see his son married: Lewis, *King*, p. 42.

94   "amply endowed": Int. Wilhard Williams, Dec. 8, 1983, and James Jones, Dec. 8, 1983.

94   laughed at her endlessly: Int. Douglas Moore, Oct. 24–25, 1984.

94   "I'm at my Waterloo": C. King, *My Life*, p. 67. Lewis, *King*, p. 41, and Reddick, *Crusader*, p. 105.

95   "give my photograph": C. King, *My Life*, p. 69.

95   wound up picking cotton: Ibid., p. 40.

95   "I look for in a wife": Ibid., p. 68.

96   romance and pragmatism: Ibid., pp. 69–77.

96   first ever to be televised: Phillips, *Truman*, p. 420.

96   practically ignored her: C. King, *My Life*, p.78.

96   "final decision": Ibid., p. 76.

96   grade of D +: BUK15f31.

96   three consecutive A's: Ibid.

97   "still galivanting [sic] around Boston": W. T. Handy, Jr., to King, Nov. 18, 1952. BUK15f50.

97   Both elder Kings: Description of the King visit to Boston from C. King, *My Life*, pp. 80–82, and King Sr., *Daddy*, pp. 148–51.

98   lectured for six hours: Class notes for Dec. 2 and 9, 1952, BUK15f26.

99   "baffles the theist": Exam paper, Jan. 9, 1953, BUK15f19.

99   "How a Christian Overcomes Evil": Ibid.

100   shifted his registration: Int. Harold DeWolf, May 10, 1983.

100   German-language: Petition dated Feb. 4, 1953, BUK15f25.

100   "Year of Change": National Archives, Universal Newsreels, Dec. 24, 1953.

100   Easter egg: Donovan, *Eisenhower*, p. 195.

100   "bourgie": Int. David Briddell, Aug. 17, 1983, and George Thomas, March 7, 1984.

100   Scott refused: Int. Wilhard Williams, Dec. 8, 1983, and James Jones, Dec. 8, 1983.

100   "not down with it": Int. David Briddell, Aug. 17, 1983.

101   largest wedding: C. King, *My Life*, pp. 84–87.

101   "I can't help myself": Ibid., p. 85.

101   large cash settlement: Int. Rev. Ralph D. Abernathy, May 30, 1984.

102   preached his way north: King to J. T. Boddie, Nov. 19, 1953, and King to J. L. Henry, Nov. 19, 1953, BUK15f49.

102   criticize both Tillich and Wieman: King dissertation, "A Comparison of the Conceptions of God in the Thinking of Paul Tillich and Henry Nelson Wieman," BUK; discussed in Ansbro, *Making*, pp.60–63.

102   DeWolf pressed him: For instance, on King's paper "Reinhold Niebuhr's Ethical Dualism," DeWolf wrote: "I wish the critical evaluation had been carried further," BUK15f20. The critical evaluation was King's conclusion that Niebuhr had overlooked the "relative perfection of the Christian life" and God's grace. To carry it further would have taken King to the heart of the difference between Niebuhr and Personalism.

102   Tillich replied: Tillich to King, Sept. 22, 1953, BUK15f50.

102   same question to Niebuhr: King to Niebuhr, Dec. 1, 1953, BUK15f49. Niebuhr to King, Dec. 2, 1953, BUK15f50.

103   talk with Dr. Mays: Int. Benjamin Mays, March 6, 1984.

103   Through his friend Melvin: Melvin Watson to King, Nov. 19, 1953, and King to Watson, Nov. 24, 1953, BUK15f50.

103   chapel of Alabama State: King to J. T. Brooks, Nov. 24, 1953, BUK15f49.

103   talked apprehensively: Int. Major Jones, March 7, 1984. Jones, who went on to become president of Gammon Theological Seminary in Atlanta, was one of King's fellow graduate students at Boston University and a traveling companion on the long drives between Boston and Atlanta.

103   friend of theirs packing: Ibid.

103   annual Lynching Letter: NYT, Dec. 31, 1953.

103   Nesbitt into the kitchen: R. D. Nesbitt, Jan. 24, 1972, A/OH.

104   "*big* nigger's church": Int. R. D. Nesbitt, Dec. 29, 1983.

104 "This is Vernon Johns": Int. Rev. Ralph D. Abernathy, March 5, 1984. Abernathy heard the story from both King and Johns that same afternoon in Montgomery.

Four
FIRST TROMBONE

106 *Lucia di Lammermoor:* King Jr., *Stride,* p. 15. King states that he was alone, but Abernathy recalls in some detail that he arrived with Johns. Also Abernathy interview by Smith, Dec. 3, 1963, SHSW/SP.
106 "the prophet's dinner": Int. Rev. Ralph D. Abernathy, March 5, 1984.
106 "food is smelling so good": Ibid., along with description of dinner that follows.
108 "That was you, Brother King": Ibid.
108 "if anybody can pastor": Int. Robert Williams, April 3, 1984.
108 afternoon at the Brooks home: R. D. Nesbitt, Jan. 24, 1972, A/OH.
109 McCall wanted Dexter: Int. R. D. Nesbitt, Dec. 29, 1983, and Larry Williams, Dec. 27, 1983. Both Williams and McCall had been unsuccessful candidates for the pastorate of the Baptist Tabernacle in Augusta, Georgia.
109 Abernathy's for another supper: Int. Rev. Ralph D. Abernathy, March 5, 1984.
110 preacher without a church: Ibid., and int. Rev. Marcus Wood, Oct. 4, 1983.
110 Benjamin Mays's offer: Mays, *Born,* p. 266.
110 "ontologically real": R. D. Crockett to King, Feb. 8. 1954, BUK15f50.
110 succeeding a prophet: Int. David Briddell, Aug. 17, 1983.
110 threatening to hit him: Int. Rev. Marcus Wood, Oct. 4, 1983.
110 "Four Dimensions": Int. Rev. Ralph D. Abernathy, March 5, 1984. McCall preached for Abernathy that Sunday night.
110 "I can't touch King": Int. R. D. Nesbitt, Dec. 29, 1983.
110 still friends: C. King, *My Life,* p. 108. Mrs. King wrote that King had pursued the Dexter pulpit only after McCall had assured him that he did not want to go there. By her account, McCall's disinterest combined with King's chivalry to eliminate all possibility of conflict, but in fact the two friends competed consciously and directly. McCall's remarks to King about not wanting the job were probably more in the nature of a face-saving device, delivered after each man knew the competition was over.
110 Chattanooga passed him over: Int. Major Jones, March, 7, 1984.
111 King moved cautiously: R. D. Nesbitt, Jan. 24, 1972, A/OH.
111 offered a salary of $4,200: King to "Dexter Avenue Baptist Church, R. D. Nesbitt, Clerk," April 14, 1954, BUK15f49.
111 highest-paid Negro: Oates, *Trumpet,* p. 49.
111 On April 14: King to Nesbitt, April 14, 1954, BUK15f49.
111 quick meeting: Nesbitt to King, April 19, 1954, BUK15f50.
111 Lahey Clinic: Medical report, BUK15f50.
111 "Motivos de Son": C. King, *My Life,* p. 102.
111 white Presbyterian church: Int. James Jones, Dec. 8, 1983, and Wilhard Williams, Dec. 8, 1983.
112 resign herself to Montgomery: C. King, *My Life,* pp. 106–12.
112 "run that church": Ibid., p. 114.
112 showed shirtless: National Archives, Universal Newsreels, April 1, 1954.
112 Eisenhower commented: Ahlstrom, *Religious History,* p. 954.
112 percent of Americans: Manchester, *Glory,* p. 897.
112 King's first sermon: Nesbitt to King, April 19, 1954, BUK15f50.
112 bulletin at 12:52 P.M.: Kluger, *Simple Justice,* pp. 700–708.
112 Barbara Johns: Int. Barbara Johns Powell, Dec. 9, 1983.
113 Eisenhower informed: Donovan: *Eisenhower,* p. 162.
113 James Reston: NYT, May 18, 1954, as quoted in Kluger, *Simple Justice,* p. 711.
113 Sherman Adams: Adams, *Firsthand,* p. 331.
113 Voice of America: Kluger, *Simple Justice,* p. 708.
113 Universal Newsreels: National Archives, Universal Newsreels collection.
113 "Angel of Dienbienphu": NYT, May 25, June 7, July 27, and July 30, 1954. Also National Archives, Universal Newsreels, July 26, 1954.

114 "forgotten the Ole boy": McCall to King, Aug. 5, 1954, BUK15f49.
114 too formal for his taste: Int. Rev. Ralph D. Abernathy, March 5, 1984.
114 letter to McCall: King to McCall, Oct. 19,1954, BUK15f49.
114 "Recommendations to the Dexter": Evans, *Dexter Avenue*, pp. 71–79.
117 so far as to consult: See King to Thomas Kilgore, pastor of New York's Friendship Baptist Church, June 24, 1954, in which King wrote that he could see from Kilgore's annual report that "superb organization" is "the secret of your success," BUK15f49.
117 "appropriately formulated": Melvin Watson to King, Oct. 20, 1954, BUK15f50.
117 Another friend wrote: Major Jones to King, undated, BUK15f50.
117 up by five-thirty: C. King, *My Life*, p. 113.
117 played musical chairs: Int. Zelia Evans, June 8, 1983.
117 Morehouse Club: Int. Robert Williams, April 3, 1984.
117 played pool there: Ibid. also int. Elliott Finley, Dec. 28, 1983.
117 his blinding schedule: Evans, *Dexter Avenue*, p. 83.
117 "revolutionized" Dexter: Int. R. D. Nesbitt, Dec. 29, 1983.
117 more than $2,100: King to McCall, Oct, 19, 1954, BUK15f49.
118 Reverend King led: Ibid. Also Evans, *Dexter Avenue*, p. 82.
118 written Paul Tillich: King to Tillich, Oct, 19, 1954, BUK15f49.
118 Tillich replied: Tillich to King, Nov, 3, 1954, BUK15f49.
118 "revise my system": Stone, *Paul Tillich's*, p. 131.
118 "What are you doing?" Alfreida Dean Thomas, Jan. 24, 1972, A/OH.
119 "not a God man": Ibid.
119 "brought down the house": Int. Thomas Kilgore, Nov, 8, 1983, and Gardner Taylor, Oct. 25, 1983. In 1954, King preached twice at Kilgore's Friendship Baptist and once at Taylor's Concord Baptist, both in New York,
119 "devil turns all": King Sr. to King Jr., Dec. 2, 1954, BUK15f50.
120 Claudette Colvin: Account of the Colvin case drawn from various sources, including Yeakey, "Montgomery," Clifford Durr, CRDPOH, and interviews with Jo Ann Robinson, Nov, 14, 1983, and E. D. Nixon, Dec. 29, 1983.
120 Clifford Durr: Durr portrait drawn from Durr, *Outside*, passim; Durr interviews, CRDPOH and CUOH; Durr papers and interviews, LBJ.
121 Highlander Folk School: Highlander sketch from Durr sources, Ibid., plus SHSW/HP; Bledsoe, *All Hang*, passim; Fox, *Niebuhr*, p. 126; FHFS.
122 exploded in rage: NYT, March 21, 1954, p. 1; *Newsweek*, March 29, 1954, p. 26.
122 "nasty polecat": Virginia Durr, LBJOH.
123 Women's Political Council: Virginia Durr, Mrs. Johnnie Carr, and Mrs. A. W. West, A/OH. Also int. Jo Ann Robinson, Nov, 14, 1983.
123 getting his doctorate: Dean Duncan E. Macdonald to King, May 31, 1955, and DeWolf to King, May 28, 1955, BUK15f50.
123 wanted King to become: Dent to King, July 25, 1955, BUK15f50. Also int. Samuel Du Bois Cook (president of Dillard University), April 4, 1984, and Cook to author, May 3, 1984. Howard Thurman dedicated the Lawless Chapel on Oct. 23, 1955.
124 came from Rosa Parks: Parks to King, Aug. 26, 1955, BUK15f50.
124 background and character: Int. Rev. Ralph D. Abernathy, E. D. Nixon, Dec. 29, 1983, Jo Ann Robinson, Nov, 14, 1983, and Rev. Robert Graetz, among others.
125 Trinity Lutheran: Int. Nelson Trout, Jan. 18, 1984, and Robert and Jeannie Graetz, Jan. 18, 1984.
125 acquired the name Martin Luther: Int. Nelson Trout, Jan. 18, 1984.
126 "toward the South": Acts 8:26. Reported in MA, Jan. 10, 1956, p. 4-A.
126 the Graetzes forfeited: Int. Rev. Robert and Jeannie Graetz, Jan. 8,1984.
127 Juliette Morgan: Ibid.
127 see-through clapboard shacks: Int. E. D. Nixon, Dec. 29, 1983. The Smith arrest occurred on Oct. 21, 1955.
127 "leg to stand on": Yeakey, "Montgomery," p. 272.
127 "dollar buy so much": Evans, *Dexter Avenue*, p. 80.
127 big baby girl: C. King, *My Life*, pp. 118–25.
128 Nixon, who called: Int. E. D. Nixon, Dec. 29, 1983, and Rufus Lewis, June 8, 1983.
128 tease his wife and mother: C. King, *My Life*, p. 122.
128 like Mary Jane: Ibid., p. 118.

128 Rosa Parks left the Montgomery Fair: On the Parks arrest, see King Jr., *Stride*, pp. 43–52; Durr, *Outside*, pp. 278–81; Raines, *My Soul*, pp. 31ff; Yeakey, "Montgomery," pp. 273ff; and Norman W. Walton, "The Walking City: A History of the Montgomery Boycott," *Negro History Bulletin*, Pt. I, October-November 1956. Also int. Jo Ann Robinson, Nov, 14,1983, and E. D. Nixon, Dec. 29, 1983.

128 "make it light on yourselves": Raines, *My Soul*, p. 32.

129 "Did they beat you?": Yeakey, "Montgomery."

129 "Go and get her": E. D. Nixon, A/OH.

130 hem dresses: Yeakey, "Montgomery."

131 "kill you, Rosa": Ibid.

131 Robinson had grown up: Int. Jo Ann Robinson, Nov. 14, 1983.

132 marking the origins: King Jr., *Stride*, p. 44; E. D. Nixon, "How It All Started," *Liberation*, December 1956; Reddick, *Crusader*, pp. 124–26; Wilkins, *Standing Fast*, pp. 237ff; Raines, *My Soul*, pp. 33–45; int. E. D. Nixon, Dec. 28, 1983; Nixon, A/OH.

133 "let me think about": E. D. Nixon, A/OH, and other Nixon interviews.

133 "the hottest story": Int. E. D. Nixon.

133 broke up about midnight: King Jr., *Stride*, pp. 47–48.

134 "It was me, Pastor Graetz": Int. Rev. Robert and Jeannie Graetz, Jan. 8, 1984.

134 "mob of Georgia Tech": MA, Dec. 4, 1955, p. 1. See also "Regents Give Georgia Tech 'Green Light,' " MA, Dec. 6, 1955, p. 1.

135 "Negro 'goon squads' ": MA, Dec. 5, 1955, p. 1.

136 rattled even Nixon: E. D. Nixon, A/OH, and int. Nixon.

136 they reassembled that afternoon: Account of afternoon meeting drawn from interviews with E. D. Nixon, Rufus Lewis, S. S. Seay, and Ralph Abernathy. Also E. D. Nixon, A/OH; Virginia Durr, A/OH; Raines, *My Soul*, pp. 40–42; King Jr., *Stride*, pp. 55–58; Reddick, *Crusader*, p. 134; and Oates, *Trumpet*, pp. 67–69.

137 verge of approval: King Jr., *Stride*, p. 58.

138 from his conscience: Ibid., p. 60.

138 "into something big": Int. Elliott Finley, Dec. 28, 1983.

138 "for serious business": Recording and transcript of speech, A/KS1.

141 "runs down like water": Amos 5:24.

Five
THE MONTGOMERY BUS BOYCOTT

143 James Lawson: Lawson, MVCOH. also int. Lawson, Nov. 9 and 14, 1983.

144 Juliette Morgan: King Jr., *Stride*, p. 85; MA, Dec. 12, 1955, p. 4-A. Also int. Jo Ann Robinson, Nov. 14, 1983, and William McDonald, Dec. 29, 1983.

144 simple decent treatment: Cf. letters from Frances P. McLeod, Dec. 9, 1955, MA, p. 4-A; Mrs. J. B. Rutledge, Dec. 9, 1955, p. 4-A; Helen R. Gross, Dec. 15, 1955, p. 4-A; Mrs. E.J.R., Dec. 25, 1955, p. 4-A.

144 One woman correspondent: Mrs. C.S. to MA, Dec. 15, 1955, p. 4-A.

144 first editorial: MA, Dec. 8, 1955, p. 4-A.

145 friend T. J. Jemison: King Jr., *Stride*, p. 57; Yeakey, "Montgomery," pp. 385ff.

145 call him Mike: See Jemison to King, Oct. 27, 1956, BUK8f29.

146 150 car owners: Yeakey, "Montgomery," p. 388.

146 40,000 Negro fares: Ibid., p. 527.

146 boasting of a victory: King Jr., *Stride*, p. 112.

146 "practically rubbing knees": Yeakey, "Montgomery," p. 435.

146 At their next meeting: King Jr., *Stride*, pp. 114–19; Yeakey, "Montgomery," pp. 445–53.

147 "almost godly": Jo Ann Robinson private memoir, cited in Yeakey, "Montgomery," p. 451.

147 from start to finish: Int. W. Thomas Johnson, Dec. 29, 1983.

147 Six days before Christmas: King Jr., *Stride*, pp. 119–22; Yeakey, "Montgomery," pp. 454–60.

148 "terrible sense of guilt": King Jr., *Stride*, p. 121. See also King speech of Dec. 3, 1956, pp. 2–3, BUK1f16.

149 "any queen": BW, Dec. 20, 1955, as quoted in Yeakey, "Montgomery," p. 463.

149 "feets is tired": The story first appeared publicly in Tom Johnson's profile of Graetz, MA, Jan. 10, 1956, p. 4-A. Also King Jr., *Strength*, p. 125. Part of the quotation later became the title of Raines, *My Soul*, derived from an anecdote described therein on p. 56. It is not clear from any of the earlier sources that King was the preacher to whom Mother Pollard spoke. This is doubtful, as King did not say so himself when telling the story.

150 "trade my Southern": MA, Jan. 7. 1956, p. 1.

151 Daddy King's sermon: Dexter church program, Jan. 8, 1956, BUK10f10.

151 Gray's legal presentation: Yeakey, "Montgomery," pp. 468–70.

151 "wear the other down": Minutes of the MIA Executive Board, Jan. 12, 1956, Hazel Gregory Papers, cited in Yeakey, "Montgomery," p. 470.

152 anything but a conventional: Hall portrait drawn from Hollis, *Hall*, passim King Jr., *Stride*, p. 176; Reddick, *Crusader*, pp. 163–65; Yeakey, "Montgomery," pp. 444, 489, 590, 595, 614; int. Jo Ann Robinson, Nov. 14, 1983, W. Thomas Johnson, Dec. 29, 1983, and William McDonald, Dec. 29, 1983.

152 "who is behind the MIA": Int. W. Thomas Johnson, Dec. 29, 1983.

153 nearly $7,000: MA, Jan. 10, 1956, p. 4-A.

153 next Saturday morning: Int. W. Thomas Johnson, Dec. 29, 1983. Also Dexter church program for Jan. 15, 1956, BUK10f10.

154 "sitting by": MA, Jan. 18, 1956, p. 1.

154 rumor campaign: King Jr., *Stride*, pp. 22–24.

154 "tough on us niggers": Int. William McDonald, Dec. 29, 1983.

154 protect them from the goon squads: Virginia Durr, CRDPOH.

155 like the Durrs: Virginia Durr, A/OH; Durr, *Outside*, pp. 282–84.

155 "stays off the buses": Ibid.

155 Carl Rowan: King Jr., *Stride*, pp. 124–26. Also Yeakey, "Montgomery," pp. 482–85, and Rowan, *Go South*, pp. 130–32.

155 betrayed him behind his back: King Jr., *Stride*, p. 125.

156 a Holiness church: Minutes of the MIA Executive Board, Jan. 23, 1956, cited in Yeakey, "Montgomery," p. 484.

156 all three names before midnight: Rev. B. F. Mosely, Baptist; Rev. W. K. Kinds, Presbyterian; and Rev. Bishop Rice, Holiness. Ibid.

157 "no noticeable increase": MA, Jan. 24, 1956, pp. 1, 2-A.

157 "pussyfooted around": Ibid.

157 "laughing at white people": Ibid., p. 1.

158 "bunions and blisters": Ibid.

158 offered his resignation: Minutes of the MIA Executive Board, Jan. 23, 1956, Hazel Gregory Papers, cited in Yeakey, "Montgomery," p. 481.

158 "drink my portion": Int. S. S. Seay, Sr., Dec. 20, 1983.

158 NAACP lawyers in New York: Gray to Robert L. Carter, Dec. 10, 1955, cited in Yeakey, "Montgomery," p. 502.

158 Durr warned Gray: Clifford Durr, CRDPOH.

159 ticketed them anyway: King Jr., *Stride*, p. 127. Also int. Rufus Lewis, Richmond Smiley, and Robert Williams.

159 seventeen tickets: Int. Jo Ann Robinson, Nov, 14, 1983.

159 too dictatorial: Int. Hazel Gregory, Dec. 22, 1983.

160 "Get out, King": King Jr., *Stride*, pp. 127–31.

161 seven mass meetings: King, "Our Struggle," *Liberation*, April 1956, p. 5.

161 corps of drivers: Int. Robert Williams, Elliott Finley, and Richmond Smiley, Jr., Dec. 28, 1983.

162 "Listen, nigger": King Jr., *Stride*, p. 134.

162 "I've come to the point": Ibid.

163 thank Roy Wilkins: King to Wilkins, Jan. 28, 1956, BUK8f14.

163 "transferred them stealthily": Int. E. D. Nixon, Dec. 29, 1983, William Beasley, Dec. 20, 1983, and Rufus Lewis, June 8, 1983. Also King Jr., *Stride*, pp. 83–84. Those interviewed are not certain beyond doubt that the emergency transfer into the church occurred that last Sunday in January, but they remember it as shortly after King's first arrest, as early in the boycott, or as about the time of the bombing.

164 "Come here, son": King Jr., *Strength*, pp. 125–26.

164 raw energy: Ibid.

164 "house has been bombed": King Jr., *Stride*, pp. 136–38. Also C. King, *My Life*, pp. 139–41; MA, Jan. 31, 1956, p. 1; Reddick, *Crusader*, pp. 134–36; N. W. Walton, "The Walking City: A History of the Montgomery Boycott," *Negro History Bulletin*, Pt. I, October-November, 1956, p. 5; int. Richmond Smiley and Robert Williams.
166 "Don't get panicky": King Jr., *Stride*, p. 138, and MA, Jan. 31, 1956, p. 2-A.
167 "better to be a live dog": C. King, *My Life*, p. 142. It is interesting that King's own version of the wake-up after the bombing in *Stride*, pp. 139–40, does not mention Daddy King. He wrote only of a visit from Coretta's father, while she wrote of both fathers.
167 to four cents: Donovan, *Eisenhower*, p. 385.
167 "nothing to do with that mess": MA, Feb. 4, 1956, p. 1.
167 The police car: Rustin, *Down the Line*, p. 56.
167 white students rioted: Woodward, *Strange Career*, p. 155.
167 hundred-dollar bill: Irving Howe, "Reverberations in the North," *Dissent*, Spring 1956, p. 122.
168 "it's oiled, it's greased": Martin, *Deep South*, p. 39.
168 revoked his minister's deferment: MA, Feb. 8, 1956, p. 1.
168 Senator James Eastland: MA, Feb. 11, 1956, p. 1. Also Martin, *Deep South*, pp. 39ff.
168 impaneled a special grand jury: MA, Feb. 14, 1956, p. 1.
168 1921 statute: Yeakey, "Montgomery," p. 516.
168 fingerprinted Fred Gray: MA, Feb, 19, 1956, p. 1.
168 "full scale racial war": MA, Feb, 6, 1956.
168 still in Nashville: Int. Major Jones, March 7, 1984, and Paul Deats, Aug. 1, 1984.
168 Bayard Rustin: Rustin portrait drawn mainly from interviews with Rustin, Nov. 28, 1983, and Feb. 21, 1984. Also Meier and Rudwick, *CORE*, pp. 3–39, and Harrington, *Fragments*, pp. 68–69, 98–103; biographical sketch of Feb. 13, 1957, FR-NR, and other materials from the Rustin FBI file; int. James Farmer, Nov. 18, 1983, Michael Harrington, Oct. 27, 1983, Glenn Smiley, Nov. 14, 1983, and Irving Howe, Nov. 28, 1983.
169 Finn named August Yokinen: Howe, *Communist*, pp. 209–10. Also int. Bayard Rustin, Feb. 21, 1984.
173 "no retaliation whatsoever": Yeakey, "Montgomery," pp. 473–74.
173 "weather is warming up": Ibid.
173 "cut off the head": Int. Rev. Ralph D. Abernathy, March 5, 1984.
173 "let's all go to jail!": Int. S. S. Seay, Sr., Dec. 20, 1983.
174 only two voted to end: Yeakey, "Montgomery," p. 475.
174 Abernathy formally notified: Ibid.
174 Rustin knocked: Rustin, "Montgomery Diary," *Liberation*, April 1956, pp. 6–11.
174 raised the money: Raines, *My Soul*, p. 46.
174 phone to Nashville: King Jr., *Stride*, p. 143.
175 securing a loan: Fulton County Deed Book 3089. p. 326.
175 self-description in church programs: For example, the Dexter church program of Jan. 8, 1956, BUK10f10, which states that Dr. King Sr. "is leading the Ebenezer Baptist Church in an expansion program which will exceed $200,000."
175 opened his attack: King Jr., *Stride*, p. 144.
175 115 Negroes had been indicted: MA, Feb. 22, 1956, p. 1.
175 there in the King home: King, Jr., *Stride*, pp. 144–46.
176 "Well, here I am": Rustin, "Montgomery Diary," p. 8.
176 actually traded jokes: Reddick, *Crusader*, p. 136.
177 "no vaudeville show!": Ibid.
177 loan of $5,000: Rustin to King, May 9, 1956, BUK8f34.
177 second consecutive night walk: Rustin, "Montgomery Diary," pp. 8–9.
177 *Le Figaro*: Int. Rev. Robert Graetz, and Glenn Smiley, Nov, 14, 1983. Also Rustin to King, March 8, 1956, BUK1f29.
177 "wouldn't be alive": "Montgomery Diary," p. 9.
178 twenty-fourth minister: MA, Feb. 24, 1956, p. 1.
178 five prayers: "Montgomery Diary," p. 9.
178 thirty-five reporters: MA, Feb. 24, 1956, p. 1.
179 called John Swomley: Int. Glenn Smiley, Nov. 14, 1984.

179 Rustin attended Dexter: "Montgomery Diary," p. 10.

179 history of the boycott: Rustin prepared an article on the origins of the boycott, which appeared under King's name as "Our Struggle," *Liberation*, April 1956, p. 5. This was the first of many works for which King used collaborators or ghostwriters.

179 Coretta remembered: C. King, *My Life*, p. 148.

179 offering a reward: See Rustin to King, March 8, 1956, BUK1f29.

179 threatening to expose Rustin: Int. Glenn Smiley, Nov. 14, 1984, and Rev. Robert Graetz. Smiley says he heard this story through Swomley and Muste and later again from King. Graetz says he heard it at MIA meetings. Both identify the reporter as Emory Jackson of the Birmingham *World*. Jackson, a powerful figure in the Alabama NAACP, covered the boycott from its inception.

180 rather sad briefing: Int. Glenn Smiley, Nov. 14, 1984.

180 smuggled to Birmingham: Raines, *My Soul*, p. 48.

180 mild-mannered white Methodist: Int. Bayard Rustin, Nov. 28, 1983; James Lawson, Nov. 14, 1983; Glenn Smiley, Nov. 14, 1983.

180 "Don't bother me": Int. Glenn Smiley, Nov. 14, 1983.

180 pig's-ear sandwiches: Ibid., and int. Rev. Robert Graetz.

180 Rabb summoned: Morrow, *Black Man*, p. 33.

181 not be sworn in: Ibid., p. 199.

181 influence was pervasive: Ibid., p. 36.

181 classified briefing: Minutes of cabinet meeting of March 9, 1956, copy of Hoover's briefing paper, and selected quotations of the President, Cabinet Series, Box 6, DDE. Also discussed in Adams, *Firsthand*, pp. 336ff, and Donovan, *Eisenhower*, pp. 390ff.

183 Johnson was saying: Miller, *Lyndon*, p. 228.

183 submitted to Congress: Adams, *Firsthand*, p. 338. The bill went to Congress on April 9, 1956.

183 "the dumbest act": Grover Hall draft article, dated July 16, 1956, BUK5f176. It appears that Hall sent the draft to King, which is interesting in itself.

183 "duenna and Indian guide": Ibid.

184 "cat's-paw": Reddick, *Crusader*, p. 152.

184 "so soree": Hall draft, July 16, 1956, BUK5f76.

184 Eight lawyers: NYT, March 20, 1956, p. 24.

184 could not recall: Yeakey, "Montgomery," pp. 523–25.

184 Graetz testified: Ibid.

184 4:39 P.M.: NYT, March 23, 1956, p. 28.

184 "Behold the King!": Ibid.

184 "King is King!": Reddick, *Crusader*, p. 145.

184 "nailed to the cross": Ibid.

185 "heap on me": NYT, March 23, 1956, p. 28.

185 which he doubted: Reddick, *Crusader*, p. 147.

185 "Modern Moses": *Jet*, April 12, 1956.

185 "particularly well read": NYT, March 21, 1956.

185 "for the Brooklyn Dodgers": NYAN, March 31, 1956, pp. 1, 18–20.

185 first solo album: Shaw, *Belafonte*, p. 228.

185 "I need your help": Int. Harry Belafonte, March 6–7, 1985.

186 "in the name of our movement": King to Wilkins, March 3, 1956, BUK8f14. King's friend Kelly Miller Smith, among others, wrote King that his local NAACP branch was taking up a collection for the MIA. Smith to King, Feb. 25,1956, BUK15f50.

186 "would be fatal": Wilkins to King, March 8, 1956, BUK8f14.

186 droll statement: NYT, March 21, 1956, p. 24.

186 notified King: Wilkins to King, April 12, 1956, BUK8f14.

186 "our dependence": King to Wilkins, May 1, 1956, BUK8f14.

186 Wilkins had invited King: Wilkins to King, May 8, 1956, BUK8f14.

187 eight years and several trips: BN, June 1, 1956, p. 1. Also Yeakey, "Montgomery," pp. 575–85.

187 other Southern states: Wilkins, *Standing Fast*, pp. 241–43.

187 most unusual and significant: Shuttlesworth characterization drawn from Shuttlesworth, A/OH and CRDPOH.

187 running the family still: Ibid. Also Shuttlesworth arrest record dated Oct. 16, 1963, BIR/AB21f23.
188 "too egotistical": MA, June 12, 1956, p. 1.
189 Fields believed: Yeakey, "Montgomery," pp. 550–60; int. Uriah J. Fields, Nov. 12, 1983. Fields has since relocated to Los Angeles, left the Baptist clergy, and opened a California-style personal improvement counseling center. His latest book as of 1983 was *Be the Best, Do It Easy, Do It Now.*
189 strip him of the pastorate: Yeakey, "Montgomery," p. 553. Fields regained his pulpit by going to court and later winning a vote of reinstatement.
189 aborted his California vacation: King Jr., *Stride*, pp. 153–57.
189 elements of truth: Yeakey, "Montgomery," pp. 546–50.
189 Evers invited: Medgar Evers to King, July 31,1956, BUK8f12.
190 annoyed Thurgood Marshall: Reddick, *Crusader*, p. 153. Also Hall draft, July 16, 1956, BUK5f176.
190 "careful consideration": Wilkins, *Standing Fast*, p. 238.
190 Prettiest Baby: *Dexter Echo*, July 18, 1956, BUK10f13.
190 FLASH: *Dexter Echo*, Aug. 6, 1956, BUK10f13.
190 "spotlight off me": Int. E. D. Nixon, Dec. 29, 1983.
190 "supreme moral issues": King statement, Aug. 11, 1956, A/KS1.
190 give enough credit: Int. E. D. Nixon, Dec. 29, 1983.
191 "you bad policemen!": Int. Rev. Robert Graetz.
191 "publicity stunt": MA, Aug. 26, 1956, p. 1.
191 "without protecton of law": King et al. to Eisenhower, WHCF, GF124A, 1956, DDE.
191 Stevenson replied to Wilkins: Wilkins, *Standing Fast*, pp. 232–33.
191 "I support this": Martin, *Adlai*, p. 361.
191 Ebbetts Field: Morrow, *Black Man*, p. 67.
191 Adam Clayton Powell: Bernard M. Shanley, Memorandum of Conversation, Oct. 11,1956, 3:02-3:27 P.M., DDE. Also Coleman, *Adam*, p. 84.
192 "from Dakar": Ibid., p. 331.
192 Fear of war: Manchester, *Glory*, p. 937.
192 carried the city: Ibid., p. 943.
192 Lewis B. Hershey: Yeakey, "Montgomery," pp. 585–91.
192 Negroes had voted Republican: Manchester, *Glory*, p. 943. Also Wofford, *Of Kennedys*, p. 25; Rustin, *Down the Line*, p. 120.
192 "quite bewildered": Martin, *Adlai*, p. 394.
193 "another blunder": MA, Nov. 1, 1956, p. 4-A.
193 surprise city witness: MA, Nov. 14,1956. p. 2-A.
193 off the AP ticker: King Jr., *Stride*, pp. 159–60.
194 "religious ecstasy": MA, Nov. 14, 1956, p. 2-A.
194 force of an epiphany: Int. Rev. Robert Graetz. Also King Jr., *Stride*, p. 161, and "We Are Still Walking," *Liberation*, December 1956.
195 six lessons: King speech of Dec. 3, 1956, BUK1f11b. King was adding to the speech until the last moment, as evident from the handwritten addendum located in BUK10f44.
195 seventy-ninth anniversary: Evans, *Dexter Avenue*, p. 109.
196 eight thousand people: Yeakey, "Montgomery," p. 631.
196 inviting Coretta: Reddick, *Crusader*, p. 177. Also *Dexter Echo*, Oct. 31, 1956, BUK10f13.
196 "evil construction": MA, Dec. 21, 1956, p. 1.
196 "glad to have you": King Jr., *Stride*, p. 173. NYT, Dec. 22, 1956, p. 1.
196 moment of innocence: Int. Glenn Smiley and Rev. Robert Graetz.
196 King asked Bayard Rustin: Int. Bayard Rustin, Feb. 21 and Sept. 24, 1984; King to Rustin, Sept. 20, 1956, enclosed with Rustin to Randolph, n.d., Box 2, APR.
197 Nixon claimed more: E. D. Nixon, "How It All Started," *Liberation*, December 1956, pp. 18–21.
197 face down: Int. Bayard Rustin, Sept. 24, 1984, and Robert Williams, April 3, 1984.
197 shotgun blast: MA, Dec. 24, 1956, p. 12-A.
197 "not come to eat": Int. Bayard Rustin, Nov. 28, 1983 and Sept. 24, 1984.
198 five men jumped: Yeakey, "Montgomery," p. 633.

198 fifteen sticks of dynamite: Shuttlesworth, A/OH and CRDPOH. Also Westin and Mahoney, *Trial*, p. 17, and Raines, *My Soul*, p. 66.

198 bushwhackers fired: Yeakey, "Montgomery," p. 634.

199 "so is the baby": Int. Rev. Ralph D. Abernathy, March 5, 1984.

199 four bombed churches: MA, Jan. 11, 1956, p. 1.

199 Sherman Adams replied: Assistant Attorney General Warren Olney III to King, Jan. 30, 1957, BUK9f16. Also Reddick, *Crusader*, p. 184.

200 "Brother pastor": Int. Rev. Ralph D. Abernathy, March 5, 1984.

200 neighbor snipped: Int. Rev. Robert Graetz. Also MA, Jan. 11, 1956, p. 2-A.

200 mental breakdown: Int. Rev. Robert Graetz, Jan. 8, 1984.

200 "Dear Sir": Nixon to King, June 3, 1957, BUK4f16. Nixon says in the letter that he had advised King several months earlier of his intention to resign.

201 "an adornment of the movement": Reddick, *Crusader*, pp. 126–27.

201 Montgomery airport: Int. Rev. Robert Graetz, Jan. 8, 1984.

201 guilty and miserable: Reddick, *Crusader*, pp. 178–79; King Jr., *Stride*, p. 177.

201 "let it be me!": King Jr., *Stride*, p. 178.

201 "Bob, I think": Int. Robert Williams, April 3, 1984.

201 twelve sticks: MA, Jan. 28. 1957, p. 1.; King Jr., *Stride*, pp. 178–79.

202 "vision in the kitchen": MA, Jan. 28, 1957, p. 2-A. Also Reddick, *Crusader*, p. 166.

202 "Enters Hagiology": Reddick, *Crusader*, pp. 165–66.

202 Gray had missed: Yeakey, "Montgomery," p. 645.

202 twin amnesty: Ibid., pp. 644–46.

203 second inaugural: Morrow, *Black Man*, pp. 84–86.

203 "Italian communists": Luce to King, Jan. 2, 1957, BUK8f6.

203 "Above all": *Time*, Feb. 18, 1957, pp. 17ff.

203 "Meet the Press": Spivak to King, March 4, 1957, BUK8f12. The first Negro to appear had been Roy Wilkins the previous year.

203 "earned our right": *Time*, Feb. 18, 1957, p. 17.

204 himself as James Lawson: Evans, *Dexter Avenue*, p. 110. Also, James Lawson, MYCOH and int. Lawson Nov. 9 and 14, 1983.

Six
A TASTE OF THE WORLD

207 Harris Wofford: Wofford background from Wofford, *Of Kennedys*, passim; also, int. Wofford, June 26 and Aug. 28, 1984, and April 5, 1985.

207 "I hate God!": Wofford, *Of Kennedys*, p. 110.

207 "some of the Gandhian techniques": Wofford to Horton, June 28, 1954, SHSW/HP.

207 "your arm chair strategist": Wofford to King, April 25, 1956, BUK8f33.

207 ran across him: Wofford to King, Aug. 20, 1956, BUK8f33.

207 Omega Psi Phi: Evans, *Dexter Avenue*, p. 110. Also *Dexter Echo*, Oct. 31, 1956, BUK10f13.

208 local Freemasons: Int. Elwood Sockley of Baltimore Omega Psi Phi, Oct. 2, 1984.

208 Stanley Levison: General sources on Levison include Garrow, *FBI*, pp. 26–42, plus interviews and documents cited for p. 209. On the Baltimore story, sources include Levison interview, CRDPOH.

209 prevailing Marxist jargon: Shannon, *Decline*, pp. 58–67.

209 called In Friendship: NYT, March 1, 1956, p. 28; FBI In Friendship file, No. 100-424895. In Levison's own FBI file, there is a long report on In Friendship, NY SAC to Director, Nov. 28, 1956, FL-NR. The FBI launched an investigation of In Friendship as a Communist front, with Hoover urging the utmost secrecy to protect informants. Most FBI information about In Friendship remained classified through 1987. Useful In Friendship papers include A. Philip Randolph to Rabbi Edward Klein, March 15, 1956, Box 23, APR; Agenda for June 20, 1956, Box 23, APR; Minutes of Executive Committee July 19, 1956, Box 23, APR; Ella Baker to Randolph, Aug. 29, 1956, Box 23, APR; Stanley Levison to Randolph, Jan. 2, 1957, Box 2, APR; "A Brief Digest of the Activities of 'In Friendship,'" March 6, 1957, Box 23, APR; Levison to Randolph, April 22, 1958, Box 30, APR.

209 Levison personally had raised: Int. Bayard Rustin, Feb. 21, 1984.

210 "no doubt about it": Watson to King, Aug. 14, 1952, BUK15f50.

210 knew Ben Davis: Int. Bayard Rustin, Feb. 21, 1984. Davis sources include sketches in Scales, *Cause,* and Isserman, *Hammer;* NYT, July 7, 1960, p. 26, and Aug. 24, 1964, p. 27; *Jet,* May 16, 1963, pp. 8–9.

211 Communist Party faced extinction: Howe, *Communist,* pp. 489–93; Isserman, *Hammer,* pp. 3–31.

211 Hoover briefly entertained: Director to SAC Chicago, Nov. 23, 1956, FBI file No. 100-3-104-NR, cited in Powers, *Hoover,* p. 567. On Hoover's response to the demise of CPUSA, Ibid., pp. 336–43.

211 three warring factions: Int. John and Lillian Gates, Nov. 28, 1987; Albert Blumberg, June 29, 1988, Junius Scales June 28, 1988. Blumberg, who went to prison under a Smith Act conviction, as did his wife, says he recalls no such "truce" meeting before the 1957 convention, but the detailed memories of John and Lillian Gates are compelling.

212 national convention gathered: Isserman, *Hammer,* pp. 28–29; Scales, *Cause,* pp. 315–17; Shannon, Decline, pp. 324–28.

212 drafted by Stanley: Levison to King, Feb. 11, 1957, BUK9f16.

213 "have no moral choice": Draft telegram, Feb. 14, 1957, to Thomasville, Ga., BUK9f16.

213 "legislate morality": Golden, *Mr. Kennedy,* p. 73.

213 "nigger jokes": Ambrose, *Eisenhower,* pp. 327, 408.

213 "colored retainers": Ibid., p. 386.

214 into the cockpit: Reddick, *Crusader,* p. 181.

214 three billion people: MA, Oct. 16, 1957, p. 4-A.

214 bonus of $2,500: Reddick, *Crusader,* p. 180.

215 "thing that impressed me": King sermon, "The Birth of a New Nation," April 1957, A/KS1.

216 discussed it in Ghana: Reddick, *Crusader,* p. 186.

216 Administration stalled: Asst. Sec. of Commerce to Maxwell Raab, April 17, 1957, WHCF, GF 124-A-1, DDE.

217 headed off a plan by King: Ibid. Also note to Rabb, April 18, 1957, and Mitchell to Rabb with enclosure from Wilkins, April 24, 1957, WHCF, GF 124-A-1, DDE.

217 "first-rate rabble-rouser": FBI memo, May 9, 1957, FK27.

217 "not be adversely affected": Rabb to Sherman Adams, April 17, 1957, WHCF, OF Box 731, DDE.

217 honed his text: Reddick, *Crusader,* pp. 193–94.

217 "sit right on my tongue": Int. Bayard Rustin, Feb. 21, 1984.

217 high-spirited program: Reddick, *Crusader,* pp. 193ff; C. King, *My Life,* pp. 168ff.

218 "Give us the ballot!": King's handwritten address for May 17, 1957, A/KS1.

218 Rustin decided: Int. Bayard Rustin, Nov. 28, 1983.

218 Reminding Nixon: King to Nixon, May 15, 1957, A/KP18f24.

218 Nixon promptly: Nixon to King, May 23, 1957, and King to Nixon, May 28, 1957, BUK8f14.

218 Eisenhower himself: Rabb memorandum, May 23, 1957, WHCF, GF Box 912, DDE.

218 "non-partisan approach": Rustin and Levison to King, June 1957, BUK1f29.

218 appointment with Vice President Nixon: Reddick, *Crusader,* pp. 199–202. Also int. Bayard Rustin, Feb. 21, 1984.

219 "most dangerous man in America": King to Earl Mazo, Sept. 2, 1958, BUK4f4. This letter, repetitive and dotted with grammatical errors, was written during the Abernathy sex scandal, as described below, which was a time of great stress for King and Abernathy regarding the inner sincerity of preachers.

220 voted Republican: Ambrose, *Eisenhower,* p. 412.

220 Eisenhower would enjoy: Rabb to Adams, June 24, 1957, WHCF, GF Box 912, DDE.

220 consumed 121 hours: Douglass Cater, "How the Senate Passed the Civil Rights Bill," *The Reporter,* Sept. 5, 1957.

220 filibuster record: Morris, *Origins,* p. 107.

221 break into tears: Clarence Mitchell, CRDPOH.

221 worst political losses: Adams, *Firsthand,* p. 342.

221 "this century": Kearns, *Lyndon,* p. 150.

221 Wilkins finally decided: Int. Joseph Rauh, Oct. 17, 1983.

221 King announced later: King to Nixon, Aug. 30, 1957, A/KP18f24.

221 "offers you a spade": Reddick, *Crusader*, p. 203.

222 "What sound reason": Morris, *Origins*, pp. 121–22.

222 twenty-five separate lawsuits: NAACP Annual Report of 1957, cited in Ibid., p. 33.

222 Little Rock: Account drawn generally from Huckaby, *Central High*, Adams, *First-hand*, and Ambrose, *Eisenhower*.

223 on-site news extravaganza: Ashmore, *Hearts*, p.269.

223 sending telegrams: King to Eisenhower, Sept. 9, 1957, A/KP18f24. Also Wilkins, *Standing Fast*, p. 249.

223 Faubus' own father: Ashmore, *Hearts*, p. 260.

224 Shays's Rebellion: Herbert Brownell, Jan. 31, 1968, CUOH, p. 215.

224 "if we have to do this": Ibid., p. 212.

224 before nightfall: Ambrose, *Eisenhower*, p. 420.

224 into the girls' bathrooms: Huckaby, *Central High*, p. 62.

225 than Pearl Harbor: Ambrose, *Eisenhower*, p. 430.

225 "Control of space": Kearns, *Lyndon*, p. 145.

225 780,000 miles: Reddick, *Crusader*, p. 179. Also C. King, *My Life*, p. 169.

225 "All we need is the sponsor": Levison to King, Feb. 11, 1957, BUK9f16.

226 favorable to communism: Oates, *Trumpet*, p. 131.

226 fell badly behind: Marie Rodell to King, Dec. 13, 1957, BUK1f14.

226 pressure built steadily: Reflected in Levison to King, Jan. 24, 1958, BUK1f10.

226 "your soul and body": Eugene Exman to King, Feb. 6, 1958, BUK1f14.

226 pay $2,000: Oates, *Trumpet*, p. 131.

226 editorial network: Exman to King, Feb. 26, 1958, BUK1f14; Popper to King, March 27, 1958, BUK4f32.

226 "most difficult job": King to Levison, March 7, 1958, BUK5f15.

226 "bonds do better": Levison to King, Jan. 17, 1958. BUK1f10.

226 King's tax records: Levison to King, Jan. 17 and April 7, 1958; King to Levison, April 12 and June 30, 1958, all BUK1f10. Also int. Fred Gray, Dec. 21, 1984.

226 favorite lemon pie: Levison to King, Feb. 28, 1958, BUK5f15.

227 weakness for rich men: Int. Bayard Rustin, Nov. 27, 1983, and Harry Wachtel, Oct. 27, 1983.

227 "You don't know it, Stan": Int. Beatrice Levison, Jan. 3, 1984.

227 during the sixty-eight-night: Reddick, *Crusader*, p. 202.

227 "No Color Line": Rev. Howard Jones, in *Ebony*, September 1957. The clipped article is in the King files, BUK14f2.

227 crusade committee: Crusade document, BUK14f20.

227 Gardner Taylor and Thomas Kilgore: Int. Kilgore and Taylor.

227 Graham held three private: Graham biographer John C. Pollack to author, Sept. 10, 1986.

228 "Brother Graham": King to Graham, July 23, 1958, A/SC32f14.

228 first executive board: SCLC Executive Board Minutes, Oct. 18, 1957, BUK6f153.

229 "sought to cut me down": Evans, *Dexter Avenue*, p. 109.

229 women huddled outside: Int. Dr. Zelia Evans, June 8, 1983.

230 "Aristotle's logic": Speech, "Some Things We Must Do," Dec. 5, 1957, A/KS1.

230 "gonna be a Negro": Ibid.

230 described the week unsparingly: Reddick, *Crusader*, p. 211.

230 carefully drafted letters: King to J. H. Jackson, Dec. 17, 1957, BUK8f6, and identical letters to a number of prominent people, all dated Dec. 18, 1957, BUK6f151.

231 "in the public mind": Bunche to King, Dec. 31, 1957, BUK6f151.

231 "pushes the inebriate": Granger to King, Dec. 27, 1957, BUK6f151.

231 "number one activity for 1958": Wilkins to King, Jan. 14, 1958 (two letters), BUK4f23 and BUK6f151.

231 "year of disagreement": Bennett, *What Manner*, p. 80.

231 meet King alone: Int. Bayard Rustin, Feb. 21, 1984.

231 Ella Baker: Ibid., and int. Ella Baker, Oct. 27, 1984. Also Morris, *Origins*, pp. 102–4; M. King, *Freedom*, pp. 42–46.

231 dancing a roundelay: The slow pace of the process is reflected in the minutes of the SCLC administration committee, Dec. 19, 1957, A/SC32f5.

232 married briefly: M. King, *Freedom*, p. 455.

232 to a preacher: Int. Septima Clark, Dec. 16, 1983.

232 faithful member of Kilgore's church: Int. Ella Baker, Oct. 25, 1984. Also Baker to Kilgore, May 22, 1959 (apologizing for church absence and enclosing $160 to cover her regular contributions for the previous seventeen Sundays), A/SC32f33.

232 she resented news: Ella Baker, CRDPOH. Also int. Baker, Oct. 25, 1984, and Bayard Rustin, Feb. 21, 1984.

232 "fed to us in teaspoons": King statement, Feb. 12, 1958, BUK1f11a.

232 Associated Press released: Story dated March 12, 1958, cited in Ella Baker SCLC report, April 3, 1958, BUK8f26.

232 "superfluous printing": Rev. R. Julian Smith to King, Feb. 25, 1958, BUK9f2.

233 sparks flew between them: Int. Ella Baker, Oct. 25, 1984, and Bayard Rustin, Feb. 21, 1984.

233 "a little abrupt": Maude Ballou note to King, May 16, 1958, BUK16f24.

233 remained mired: Baker to King, April 24, 1958, A/SC53f1.

233 to Levison for inclusion: Levison to Baker, April 14, 1958, BUK16f24.

233 half-empty house: Int. James Lawson, Nov. 14, 1983.

233 198-year sentence: Vincent Johnson to King, June 3, 1958, BUK3f28.

233 "is dancing a sin": Lucille Pete to King, June 5, 1958, BUK3f28.

233 application on May 11: Clennon King to King, May 31, 1958, A/SC4f21.

233 King issued: SCLC release, June 12, 1958, BUK6f154.

233 Ella Baker asked: Rev. W. H. Hall to Baker, June 10, 1958, A/SC32f7.

233 "day after tomorrow": Rocco Siciliano, CUOH, pp. 102–3.

233 Siciliano did not welcome: Ibid., p. 101.

234 alone on June 9: Ibid. Also Siciliano to Adams, June 10, 1958, WHCF, OF 731, DDE; and Morrow, *Black Man*, p. 164.

234 King pressed the White House: Memo to Appointments Secretary Stephens, June 13, 1958, WHCF, OF 731, DDE.

234 Morrow left Washington: Morrow, *Black Man*, pp. 165–66.

234 vague but careful: King to "Adam," June 10, 1958, BUK4f31.

234 "cash in an envelope": Powell to "My dear Friend," June 1958, BUK4f31.

235 "help Adam mature": Levison to King, June 10, 1958, BUK1f10.

235 "Well, Siciliano": Rocco Siciliano, CUOH, p. 105.

235 wanted only to listen: Primary source for the meeting is Siciliano's memorandum of June 24, 1958, Diary Series Box 33, DDE. Other sources include Reddick, *Crusader*, pp. 221f; Wilkins, *Standing Fast*, pp. 256f; Morrow, *Black Man*, pp. 169f; Morrow, CUOH; Siciliano, CUOH; Randolph to King *et al.*, June 23, 1958, Box 31, APR; and int. William P. Rogers, June 11, 1984.

236 Rogers dated his own: Int. William P. Rogers, June 11, 1984.

236 "May I say": Excerpts from press conference, June 23, 1958, A/KS1.

236 "built on sand": Siciliano to Eisenhower, June 25, 1958, Diary Series Box 33, DDE.

237 "Rocco Siciliano—Minorities": Rocco Siciliano, CUOH, p.109.

237 group of prominent Indians: Bennett, *What Manner*, p. 97. Also Lewis, *King*, p. 96.

237 Levison wrote him: Levison to King, Aug. 15, 1958, BUK1f10.

237 bomb damage to Abernathy's church: Abernathy to King, May 28, 1958, thanking King for bringing the Dexter congregation to First Baptist for the rededication service on April 27, BUK6f154.

237 Baker was reminding: Baker to Abernathy, August 1958, A/SC53fa.

237 "I have come to kill you": Davis attack on Abernathy based on records of Case #8741, Montgomery Recorder's Court. Also MA, August 30, 1958, p. 1, Aug. 31, p. 2, Sept. 4, p. 1; Nov. 22, p. 1; BW, Dec. 3, 1958, p. 3.

238 "Big Two": Sketch of Edward Davis drawn from interviews with Fred Gray, Nov. 21, 1984, Richmond Smiley, Dec. 28, 1983, Robert Williams, April 3, 1984, and Rufus Lewis, June 8, 1983, among others.

239 confided to a colleague: Int. James Farmer, Nov. 18, 1983.

239 "waiting to see my lawyer": C. King, *My Life*, pp. 171–74. Other accounts of the

September 3 events in Reddick, *Crusader*, pp. 225–26; MA, Sept. 4, 1958, p. 1; BW, Sept. 6, 1958, p. 1.

240   lieutenant he knew: Int. Richmond Smiley, Dec. 28, 1983.

241   serve out the time: King trial and aftermath from Reddick, *Crusader*, pp. 227–29; C. King, *My Life*, pp. 173–74; MA, Sept. 6, 1958, p. 1; MIA Newsletter, Sept. 27, 1958, BUK1f38.

241   Gandhi's famous declaration: Fischer, *Gandhi*, p. 72.

241   "My action is motivated": King statement, Sept. 5, 1958, BUK1f11a.

242   "White women can be lures": J. Raymond Henderson to King, Sept. 17, 1958, BUK4f4.

243   sent autographed books to: Eisenhower to King, Nov. 13, 1958, Nixon to King, Dec. 5, 1958, Truman to King, Dec. 10, 1958, all BUK11f21; Warren to King, Jan. 27, 1959, BUK9f13. Niebuhr's copy in the possession of Mrs. Reinhold Niebuhr, courtesy of Elisabeth Sifton.

243   Levison to send complimentary: King to Levison, Aug. 11, 1958, and Levison to King, Aug. 14, 1958, BUK1f10.

243   Wofford found too tepid: Wofford to King, Sept. 5, 1958, and Wofford to Levison, Sept. 5, 1958, BUK9f13.

243   plunged deep into his chest: New York *Daily News*, Sept. 21, 1958, pp. 1, 3, 64; *New York Age*, Sept. 27, 1958, p. 3; Reddick, *Crusader*, pp. 229–32; Bennett, *What Manner*, p. 99.

245   Magistrate Vincent Rao's: Bennett, *What Manner*, p. 99.

245   slender Japanese penknife: Photo of weapon, BUK5f179.

245   indefinite commitment: Int. Bellevue spokesman James Walsh, Dec. 7, 1984.

245   delivered no speeches: As indicated by the absence of records and by John Tilley to King, Dec. 3, 1958, A/SC53f1.

245   locked twelve thousand: B. Smith, *They Closed*, p. 152.

245   "need now, Mike": Wyatt Tee Walker to King, Nov. 6, 1958, cited in Morris, *Origins*, p. 185.

245   Randolph's Youth March: Int. Bayard Rustin, Nov. 28, 1983, and Michael Harrington, Oct. 27, 1983. Also Morrow, *Black Man*, p. 190.

245   Harry Belafonte: Int. Harry Belafonte, March 7, 1985.

245   "If the young people are aroused": Levison to King, Nov. 3, 1958, BUK1f10.

245   Davis trial: MA, Nov, 2, 1958, p. 1; BW, Dec. 3, 1958, p. 3; int. Richmond Smiley and Robert Williams.

247   proving to be a disappointment: Int. Rev. Ralph D. Abernathy, Nov. 19, 1984.

247   "the secondary functions": Tilley to King, Oct. 17, 1958, BUK16f24.

247   "Well, I don't want to": Ella Baker, CRDPOH. Also int. Baker, Oct. 27, 1984.

247   "guilt-ridden man": C. King, *My Life*, p. 179.

248   "natural turning point": Reddick, *Crusader*, p. 232.

248   nicknamed the Taj Mahal: Evans and Novak, *Johnson*, p. 216.

248   Rogers told a White House: Int. William P. Rogers, June 11, 1984.

249   "setting you up": Ibid., and Ann Whitman diary for Feb. 3, 1959, AWDS Box 10, DDE. Johnson had introduced his own minimal civil rights bill on Jan. 20, 1959, Miller, *Lyndon*, p. 276.

249   "if Lyndon tries": Int. William P. Rogers, June 11, 1984.

249   "haven for socialists": Manchester, *Glory*, p. 1034.

249   "erosion of the middle class": Ambrose, *Eisenhower*, p. 512.

250   stack of materials about India: "Notes for a Conversation Between King and Nehru," BUK1f5.

250   *shanti sena*: Lewis, *King*, p. 101.

250   excess baggage: $88.02, by King's accounting to the AFSC, BUK1f5.

250   old friend Richard Wright: Int. Rudolph Aggrey, Oct. 8, 1986. (Aggrey was present at the Kings' dinner with Wright.) Also King, "My Trip to India," BUK1f5.

250   dense fog: King, "My Trip to India," BUK1f5.

250   gathered at the airport: Int. James Bristol, Oct. 22, 1984.

250   recoiled from the sight: C. King, *My Life*, pp. 181f.

251   small replica: *With the Kings in India*, p. 8. *With the Kings in India* is a pamphlet containing memories of the King journey by Swami Vishwananda and James Bristol, published in New Delhi by the Gandhi National Memorial Fund. King's copy is located in A/KP12f57. Also Lewis, *King*, p. 99.

251 nothing less than a miracle: *With the Kings in India*, p. 8.

251 Prime Minister greeted: C. King, *My Life*, p. 182.

251 other guests: Countess Mountbatten (Lady Brabourne) to author, Nov. 12, 1984. Also King sermon, March 22, 1959, A/KS2.

251 Nehru felt obliged: Lady Pamela Hicks to author, Feb. 8, 1985.

251 Coretta retained: C. King, *My Life*, p. 182.

252 correlate shades of color: Int. James Bristol, Oct. 25, 1984.

252 Kings did not complain: Int. S. K. De, June 18, 1985.

252 Arthur Koestler: Ibid. The Koestler novel was *The Lotus and the Robot*, which contrasted India with imperial Japan.

252 rendezvous with Vinoba: *With the Kings in India*, p. 22.

253 impossibly vague: Int. James Bristol, Oct. 25, 1984.

253 three thirty in the morning: Ibid.

253 "Americanized" walk: Lewis, *King*, p. 104.

253 King put to Vinoba: Int. James Bristol, Jan. 11, 1985.

253 King was careful: Ibid.

254 "India should declare itself": Statement March 9, 1959, A/KS2.

254 Egypt and Greece: Bristol to King, April 16, 1959, BUK3f10b.

254 "palatial apartment": King to Belafonte, March 25, 1959, BUK3f11.

254 private home screening: Int. Harry Belafonte, March 6, 1985.

254 Belafonte offered: King to Belafonte, March 24, 1959, BUK3f11.

254 "absolute self-discipline": Sermon, March 22, 1959, A/KS2.

255 "call thee Allah": Ibid.

255 submarine slipped: Manchester, *Glory*, p. 1001.

255 Joan Baez: Rolling Stone, *Almanac*, p. 47.

255 Kennedy conclave: Sorensen, *Kennedy*, p. 119.

255 Pentagon demonstrated: Manchester, *Glory*, p. 1002.

255 muttering witticisms: Int. Michael Harrington, Oct. 27, 1983, and Bayard Rustin, Nov. 28, 1983.

255 "Do you realize": Speech, April 18, 1959, A/KS2.

256 "direction of the CP": Baumgardner to Belmont, April 22, 1959, FL-NR.

256 "closely associated": Hoover to NY SAC, April 22, 1959, FL-NR.

256 Hoover directed: Ibid.

256 a consummate bureaucrat: Hoover portrait drawn from Powers, *Hoover*; Ungar, *FBI*; Sullivan, *The Bureau*; Garrow, *FBI*; plus Hoover's written comments throughout the FBI files on Levison and King.

256 mushroomed in size: Powers, *Hoover*, pp. 135, 255.

256 set foot outside: Sullivan, *The Bureau*, p. 101.

257 "violently defensive": Powers, *Hoover*, p. 274.

257 assigned four hundred: Ibid., p. 335.

257 buffalo hunters: Ibid., p. 340.

257 recruit Levison as an informant: Garrow, *FBI*, p. 42; SAC NY to Director, Nov. 27, 1959, Feb. 9, 1960, and March 4, 1960, all FL-NR.

257 "mob action was invited": King to Rogers, April 25, 1959, BUK4f40.

257 sixty agents: Doar and Landsberg, "Performance," p. 30ff.

258 "flagrant and calculated": Ibid.

258 ten thousand Negroes: Baker to Tilley, Feb. 7, 1959, A/SC32f8.

258 along well with C. O. Simpkins: Int. Ella Baker, Oct. 27, 1984.

258 registered only fifteen: Baker report, May 15, 1959, BUK6f151.

258 he fired someone: King to Tilley, April 2, 1959, and Tilley to King, April 13, 1959, BUK9f10.

258 "acting" rather than permanent: Int. Ella Baker, Wyatt Tee Walker, and Rev. Ralph D. Abernathy.

258 leaky roof: Baker to Abernathy and King, July 10, 1959, A/SC32f39.

259 "even more keyed up": King to Nelson, April 24, 1959, BUK4f23.

259 registered attendance: Baker to King, July 7, 1959, BUK1f5. As of that date, Baker reported registration of sixty people, including the speakers.

259 virtual absence: Smiley to Baker, A/KP33f7.

259 band of nonviolence leaders: Taken from "Proposed Schedule," BUK1f15, and related correspondence as cited.

260 "balanced with practical": James Lawson evaluation, A/KP33f7.

260 ice cream parlor: Morris, *Origins*, p. 198.

260 "break the backbone": Moore to King, Oct. 24, 1956, BUK8f10, and Maude L. Ballou (for King) to Moore, Dec. 7, 1956, BUK8f10.

260 make the long lonely drives: Int. Rev. Douglas Moore, Oct. 24, 1984.

261 one day that summer: June 13, 1959, per Fred Gray's letter to Lewis, June 9, 1959, AAP.

261 introduced as John Lewis: Lewis material from Archie E. Allen interviews with Lewis, Lewis' parents, and Abernathy, AAP. Also Lewis, CRDPOH, and int. Lewis, May 31, 1984.

262 Glenn Smiley often filled in: Nashville *Banner*, March 24, 1958.

263 refused to attend Lawson's workshops: Int. John Lewis, May 31, 1984.

263 shuttling between a mother: Int. James Bevel, May 16, 1985.

263 shower after his shower: Int. John Lewis, May 31, 1984.

263 like Socrates: Morris, *Origins*, p. 147.

263 "winding around the maypole": Archie E. Allen interview with Septima Clark, Sept. 21, 1968, AAP.

263 Septima Clark: Generally from Clark, HOH, 1983. Also Clark, A/OH, and int. Clark, Dec. 17, 1983.

264 special trip to Highlander: Baker report, Oct. 23, 1959, cited in Morris, *Origins*, pp. 114, 156.

264 "authorized to explore": Ibid.

264 "Honesty impels us": King recommendations, Sept. 29–Oct. 1, 1959, BUK6f151.

264 "not been publicized": Ibid.

265 not mention Rustin's name: Levison to King, Sept. 1, 1959, and Oct. 1, 1959, BUK1f10.

265 "headlines won't do it": *Jet*, Oct. 20, 1959, pp. 10–11.

265 "counteract some false ideas": King recommendations, Oct. 27, 1959, BUK6f151.

265 political caravan: King to Levison, Nov. 19, 1959, BUK1f10, and Levison to King, Dec. 21, 1959, BUK7f25.

266 "I can't wait on you forever": Int. Rev. Ralph D. Abernathy, Nov. 19, 1984.

267 "walk the benches": Ibid.

267 King told Nesbitt: Int. R. D. Nesbitt, Dec. 29, 1983.

267 making the announcement: King to Levison, Nov. 25, 1959, BUK1f10.

267 November 29: C. King, *My Life*, p. 190. Also Lewis, *King*, p. 109; Evans, *Dexter Avenue*, p. 140; *Dexter Echo*, Dec. 9, 1959, BUK10f13; King's handwritten statement, A/KS2.

267 expansive declaration: Statement, Dec. 1, 1959, C. King, *My Life*, p. 191.

267 "not welcome to Georgia": ADW, Dec. 2, 1959, p. 2.

268 "medieval walled cities": Ashmore, *Hearts*, p. 287.

268 1954 Pontiac: ADW, Feb. 18, 1960, p. 4.

268 told Negro reporters: ADW, Dec. 29, 1959, pp. 1, 3.

268 Harvard University: SCLC release, Jan. 6, 1960, BUK4f40.

268 find a babysitter: Gwendolyn Middlebrook (a King babysitter), A/OH.

268 Lawson sent a dozen: John Lewis chronology files, AAP.

269 "appointed you the guardian": Goulden, *Meany*, pp. 311ff.

269 "Castro begins to look": Ambrose, *Eisenhower*, p. 556.

269 "damn near treason": Ibid., p. 561.

269 settled with the IRS: MA, May 28, 1960, p. 7A. Also ADW, May 27, 1960, p. 1.

270 silver tea service: C. King, *My Life*, p. 191.

270 "Testimonial of Love": Program dated Feb. 1, 1960, BUK1f38.

270 "to escort our children": Abernathy speech, Feb. 1, 1960, BUK1f38.

270 official gavel: *Jet*, Feb. 18, 1960, p. 4.

270 box filled with cash: Ibid.
270 money be divided: ADW, Feb. 7, 1960, pp. 1, 3.
270 "every penny of it": PC, Feb. 13, 1960, p. 3.
270 "I cannot claim": Statement, Feb. 1, 1960, BUK1f38.
271 "might as well go now": Ottawa *Citizen*, June 13, 1961. This account of the sit-in by Canadian reporter Tim Creery, though written more than a year later, contains some of the most realistic interviews with the first four sit-in students: Ezell Blair, Jr., Franklin McCain, Joe McNeil, and David Richmond.

Seven
THE QUICKENING

272 sixteen other cities: Morris, *Origins*, p. 188.
272 contacted Floyd McKissick: Ibid., p. 198.
273 National Student Association: Int. Curtis Gans, Jan. 5, 1985.
273 Moore called James Lawson: Morris, *Origins*, p. 205. Also int. Rev. Douglas Moore, Oct. 25, 1984.
273 Carey flew: Morris, *Origins*, p. 200.
273 four hundred students: ADW, Feb. 7, 1960, p. 1.
273 fresh sit-ins broke out: Watters, *Down to Now*, pp. 72–81; Morris, *Origins*, p. 200; ADW, Feb. 13, 1960, p. 1.
273 "You must tell Martin": Morris, *Origins*, p. 201.
274 preacher in Rock Hill: Ibid.
274 arrested forty-one students: ADW, Feb. 13, 1960, p. 1.
274 Lawson presided: Morris, *Origins*, p. 206. Also Viorst, *Fire*, p. 107, and int. John Lewis, May 31, 1984.
275 thirty-one Southern cities: Morris, *Origins*, p. 197.
275 "another panty raid": Ibid., p. 200.
275 extracted from him on January 18: Chauncey Eskridge to Clay Blair, Jr. (editor of the *Saturday Evening Post*), June 24, 1963, A/KP25f25.
275 urgent telegrams: Implied in Belafonte response telegram, Feb. 5, 1960, BUK3f11.
275 Wilkins recommended two: Int. Chauncey Eskridge, Feb. 20, 1985.
275 guarded letter: Implied in Judge Hubert Delaney to King, Feb. 1, 1960, BUK3f20a.
275 visit to the F. W. Woolworth: Photograph of Abernathy and King at Woolworth's in "A Creative Protest," King address of Feb. 16, 1960, A/KS2.
275 "Men are tired": Ibid.
276 reporting the sit-ins cautiously: See for example *Jet*'s report on the sit-ins, March 3, 1960, pp. 4–5.
276 Defense Fund refrained: Morris, *Origins*, p. 198. See also NYAN, March 5, 1960, p. 1.
276 "fill up the jails": Address, "A Creative Protest," Feb. 16, 1960, A/KS2.
276 warrant for King's arrest: ADW, Feb. 18, 1960, p. 1.
277 first citizen in the history: MA, May 29, 1960, p. 2A.
277 "If you dance": ADW, March 1, 1960, p. 1.
277 King so distraught: C. King, *My Life*, p. 192.
277 Roy Wilkins declared: ADW, Feb. 20, 1960, p. 1.
278 tried to recruit: *Jet*, March 3, 1960, p. 8.
278 preachers met to formulate: ADW, Feb. 21, 1960, p. 1.
278 heading off the threat: Meeting described (with differing emphases) in Mays, *Born*, pp. 288ff, and in Lonnie King, CRDPOH, pp. 26ff. Also int. Marian Wright Edelman, March 5, 1985.
278 In Nashville: Nashville sit-ins and Lawson case from James Lawson, MVCOH, and int. Lawson, Nov. 14, 1983; int. John Lewis, May 31, 1984, and John Lewis, CRDPOH; Viorst, *Fire*, pp. 108ff; "Sit-In," Folkways Album No. FH5590; *Christian Century*, March 16, 1960, p. 309, June 8, 1960, pp. 685–86, Aug. 10, 1960, pp. 921–25.
280 planning session in Abernathy's: Int. Bernard Lee, Oct. 17, 1984.
281 "totalitarian in spirit". *Alabama Journal*, Feb. 26, 1960, p. 1.
281 "Boy, they really love you": Int. Bernard Lee, Oct. 27, 1984.

281 moved in perfect concert: Bernard Lee, CRDPOH.
282 photograph with a caption: MA, Feb. 28, 1960, p. 1.
282 "Sullivan's problem": MA, March 2, 1960, p. 4A.
282 King surrendered: ADW, March 1, 1960, p. 1.
282 not to flunk: Int. Robert Williams, April 3, 1984.
282 students all sang: Bernard Lee affidavit, February 1961, A/SC60f10.
283 At Orangeburg: Morris, *Origins*, p. 204.
283 arrested 388: Ibid., p. 209
283 sight of it haunted McDew: Charles McDew, CRDPOH.
283 forty new cities: Morris, *Origins*, p. 197.
283 "flaunting their arrogance": MA, March 6, 1960.
284 "Don't all of you pile": Bernard Lee affidavit, February 1961, A/SC60f10.
284 "Fred, I'm not a dictator": Shuttlesworth, A/OH.
284 suppressed Birmingham's: Report of Lt. George Wall, Feb. 29, 1960, BIR/BC6f14.
284 Connor issued: Connor press release, Feb. 26, 1960, BIR/BC6f14.
284 "Keep your eyes open": Connor to T. H. Cook, March 8, 1960, BIR/BC5f24.
285 offered Ella Baker's SCLC post: King to Walker, March 5, 1960, BUK9f16.
285 Including Wyatt Walker: Int. Rev. Wyatt Tee Walker, Aug. 20, 1984.
285 Walker was a hotspur: Ibid., Dec. 21, 1984; also Walker, CRDPOH, Oct. 11, 1967.
286 Walker asked the librarian: Walker interviews and CRDPOH, Ibid.
286 He sent Walker: King to Walker, March 8, 1960, BUK9f16.
286 telegram to Fred: King to Shuttlesworth, April 4, 1960, BUK6f154.
286 Pat Stephens issued: Meier and Rudwick, *CORE*, pp. 106–7.
286 "nothing more majestic": King to C. K. Steele, March 19, 1960, BUK9f2.
286 "reign of terror": King to Eisenhower, March 9, 1960, BUK1f38.
286 "An Appeal for Human Rights": ADW, March 9, 1960. Also published in AC, AJ, and NYT.
286 seventy-seven students arrested: ADW, March 16, 1960, p. 1.
287 billed King $1,000: Blayton to Judge Hubert Delaney, April 29, 1960, BUK1f24.
287 charged King nearly: Blayton to King, June 8, 1960, BUK1f24, by which time Blayton's fee was listed at $4,610.18.
287 lawyers thought Blayton: Int. Chauncey Eskridge, Feb. 20, 1985. Also int. Clarence Jones, Nov. 21, 1983, and Delaney to Ming, April 15, 1960, BUK1f24. In Delaney to King, May 2, 1960, BUK1f24, Delaney told King he did "not care to make a comment" about Blayton's latest bill, but that he hoped King could persuade Blayton to make an adjustment. He advised King that Stanley Levison was planning to talk to Blayton himself, which Delaney, evidently aware of Levison's blunt manner, believed would be a mistake.
287 He had five of them: King to Ming, Delaney, Gray, Shores, and Seay, March 5, 1960, BUK1f24.
287 Northerners complaining: Int. Chauncey Eskridge, Feb. 20, 1985. Also Levison to King, July 13, 1960, BUK1f10.
287 Southerners complaining: Int. Fred Gray, Nov. 21, 1984.
288 astonished Levison and Harry: Int. Harry Belafonte, March 6, 1985.
288 Committee to Defend: Committee documents in the A. Philip Randolph Papers include "Statement on the Indictment of Martin Luther King, Jr.," March 3, 1960; minutes of board meetings of March 7, March 21, March 28, and April 4, 1960; and Stanley Levison to Randolph, Sept. 2, 1960 (with financial statement enclosed)—all Box 23, APR.
288 sat down with Harry: Int. Bayard Rustin, Feb. 21, 1984.
289 suing the *Times*: Facts on the genesis of the lawsuit taken from petitioners' brief to the U.S. Supreme Court in *The New York Times* v. *Sullivan*, Case No. 40, October Term, 1963, pp. 8, 9, 28.
289 Besides, said Rustin: Int. Bayard Rustin, Feb. 21, 1984.
289 bluster and petty bickering: Int. Bayard Rustin, Rev. Ralph D. Abernathy, and Joseph Lowery.
290 surprise raid: Clark, *Echo*, pp. 3ff.
290 "integrated whorehouse": Bledsoe, *All Hang*, pp. 106–7. Also Nashville *Tennessean*, cited in Clark, *Echo*, p. 10.
290 first padlocked: ADW, Oct. 1, 1959, p. 1, and Feb. 18, 1960, p. 4. Also Clark, *Echo*, p. 229.

290   moonshine laws: Clark, *Echo*, p. 8.

290   Clark hosted the first: Morris, *Origins*, pp. 218–19. Roster and agenda in Harris Wofford correspondence file, SHSW/HP.

290   "You Better Leave Segregation Alone": Int. James Bevel, May 16, 1985; Folkways Album #FH5590.

290   taught them old songs: Carawan report to Myles Horton, c. 1965, Reel 7, SHSW/HP.

290   guarantee the expenses with $800: Carson, *In Struggle*, p. 20.

290 $600 contribution: Abernathy to SCLC board, April 7, 1960, A/SC53f5.

291   The trio agreed: Baker to King and Abernathy, March 23, 1960, A/SC32f39.

291   "Love is the central motif": Carson, *In Struggle*, p. 22.

291   "magazine of the black bourgeoisie": Nashville *Banner*, April 18, 1960, p. 8.

291   unjustly and unwisely exposed: Int. James Lawson, Nov. 8, 1983.

291   "our greatest resource": Carson, *In Struggle*, p. 23.

291   "moving away from tactics": Statement, April 15, 1960, BUK1.

291   vigorous contest: Charles McDew, CRDPOH.

292   wrangled briefly: Int. Bernard Lee, Oct. 25, 1984.

292   Baker "smashed": Forman, *The Making*, p. 215.

292   drafted testimony: Ella Baker, CRDPOH, pp. 48–49.

292   "There is no fight": Nashville *Banner*, April 18, 1960, p. 8.

292   hierarchies were invidious: Int. James Lawson, Nov. 9, 1983.

293   "That's the best news": Ibid. Also int. Rev. Douglas Moore, Oct. 24, 1984.

293   Ming had helped: Hughes, *NAACP*, p. 107.

294   fretting among themselves: Delaney to Ming, April 15, 1960, BUK1f24. Also int. Chauncey Eskridge, Feb. 20, 1985.

294   "some little unintentional": ADW, March 1, 1960, p. 1.

294   Eskridge perked up: Int. Chauncey Eskridge, Feb. 20, 1985.

295   "How about eating": Viorst, *Fire*, p. 116.

295   "Little lady": Ibid.

296   "Dr. King didn't take": Int. Chauncey Eskridge, Feb. 20, 1985.

297   "No lie can live": Nashville *Banner*, April 21, 1960, p. 8.

297   "puzzled and greatly distressed": Wilkins to King, April 27, 1960, A/KP17f5.

298   "no one in the world today": Muste to King, March 23, 1960, BUK4f19.

298   welcomed Kenneth Kaunda: ADW, May 6, 1960, p. 1.

298   "no dealings with SCLC, ever": Int. James Lawson, Nov. 9, 1983.

299   "I think Martin": Ibid.

299   heard the news: Int. Rev. Douglas Moore, Oct. 24, 1984.

299   "I'm just mean enough": Int. Rev. Wyatt Tee Walker, Aug. 20, 1984.

300   two-day meeting early: Ibid. Also int. Bayard Rustin, Feb. 21, 1984. The three-page agenda Walker prepared for the meeting, May 10–11, 1960, is in BUK1f31.

300   "able to pay his salary": E.g., King to Shortridge, July 21, 1960, Shortridge Papers.

300   "Don't you think we need": Int. Robert P. Moses, Aug. 10, 1983.

301   deputies on horseback: NYT, May 17, 1960, p. 19.

301   gathered the next morning: Int. Marian Wright Edelman, March 5, 1985.

302   "that many niggers": ADW, May 18, 1960, p. 4.

303   birth control pill: Enovid story appeared in NYT, May 9, 1960, p. 75, as noted in Manchester, *Glory*, p. 1039.

303   opened fire on a crowd: Hoagland, *South Africa*, p. 132.

303   Africans burning: NYT, March 29, 1960, p. 1.

303   jailed 13,000: Hoagland, *South Africa*, p. 133.

303   secret agents snatched: NYT, May 24, 1960, p. 1.

303   dropped 90 percent: NYT, May 4, 1960, p. 1.

303   On May 5: Ambrose, *Eisenhower*, pp. 563ff. The U-2 account is drawn entirely from Ambrose's authoritative biography of Eisenhower.

303   sign the Civil Rights Act: Miller, *Lyndon*, p. 280.

304   "like to resign": Ambrose, *Eisenhower*, p. 575.

304   wore white collars: Goldman, *Crucial Decade*, p. 298.

304   "Gone for the first time": *Time*, Jan. 10, 1955, quoted in L. Jones, *Great Expectations*, p. 37.

305 "must be smoking opium": NYT, March 29, 1960, p. 1.

305 Only two senators: Muskie of Maine and Jackson of Washington, Evans and Novak, *Johnson*, p. 269.

305 Eleanor Roosevelt: Schlesinger, *Thousand Days*, pp. 22–23; Sorensen, *Kennedy*, pp. 118–19.

305 only Democratic senator: Sorensen, *Kennedy*, pp. 48–49.

305 Adam Clayton Powell: NYT, July 2, 1960, p. 6.

305 "Senator, are you certain": Sorensen, *Kennedy*, pp. 151–52.

306 contact lenses: Evans and Novak, *Johnson*, p. 274.

306 Jackie Robinson refuse: Belford Lawson, JFKOH.

306 "We're in trouble": Wofford, *Of Kennedys*, p. 47.

307 "What can he do?": Int. Harry Belafonte, March 6–7, 1985.

308 "in strictest confidence": Wofford to King, May 3, 1960, BUK7f55.

308 999 exhibits: MA, May 26, 1960, p. 1.

308 took the ultimate risk: Int. Clarence Jones, Nov. 21, 1983, Chauncey Eskridge, Feb. 22, 1985, and Fred Gray, Nov. 21, 1984.

309 geographic-median-airfare: MA, May 28, 1960, p. 7-A.

309 muttered to himself: Int. Chauncey Eskridge, Feb. 22, 1985.

309 "represents great hope": Ibid., p. 1. Also ADW, May 29, 1960, p. 1.

309 "in my 34 years": NYAN, June 4, 1960.

310 "We Shall Overcome": The modern adaptation of the C. A. Tindley song is ascribed to Highlander Folk School, and most often to Zilphia Horton. A thorough description of the song's passage through Highlander appeared in "The Adventures of a Radical Hillbilly," a WNET/New York public television interview of Myles Horton by Bill Moyers, first aired on June 11, 1981. Also NYT, July 23, 1963, p. 21.

310 prime influence on: Walker, *Calling*, pp. 130–31.

310 heard the song for the first time: Int. Chauncey Eskridge, Feb. 22, 1985. King's friend Robert Williams of the Alabama State music department recalled first hearing "We Shall Overcome" earlier during the 1960 student protests in Montgomery.

310 "Autobiography of Suffering": ADW, May 31, 1960, p. 1.

311 "Something happened to the jury": Ibid.

Eight
SHADES OF POLITICS

312 $1,000,000 libel suit: NYT, May 31, 1960, p. 20.

312 a full retraction: NYT, May 16, 1960, p. 22.

312 launched a retribution: ADW, June 16, 1960, p. 1. Also King statement of June 16, 1960, BUK4f40, and int. Robert Williams, April 3, 1984, and Jo Ann Robinson, Nov. 14, 1983.

312 agony of his decision: Battered and discouraged, Trenholm took leave from Alabama State after thirty-eight years as its president. He soon fell ill and died. "He could have survived if he had something to live for," a friend said. *Jet*, March 7, 1963, p. 47.

313 endorsed Kennedy in 1959: Sorensen, *Kennedy*, p. 156.

313 The three of them: Ibid., p. 150; Wofford, *Of Kennedys*, pp. 150ff; Lewis, *King*, p. 123.

313 "house Communist": Wofford, *Of Kennedys*, p. 44.

314 breakfast on June 23: NYT, June 25, 1960, p. 13.

314 hosting a banquet: John Pollock to author, Sept. 10, 1986.

314 King received a nasty: Int. Bayard Rustin, Nov. 28, 1983, and Feb. 21, 1984. Also Rustin, LBJOH; int. Clarence Jones, Nov. 25, 1983; Harrington, *Fragments*, p. 115; James Baldwin, "The Dangerous Road Before Martin Luther King," *Harper's*, February 1961.

314 An emissary: Int. Bayard Rustin, Nov. 28, 1983. Rustin identified the emissary as Ann Arnold Hastings of New York.

315 saved by a hung jury: NYT, April 23, 1960, p. 1.

316 "to grow and learn": Sorensen, *Kennedy*, p. 155.

316 "not for cortisone": Evans and Novak, *Johnson*, p. 289.

316 "Hitler was right": Ibid.

317 At the Shrine Auditorium: Lewis, *King*, pp. 124–25.
317 drafted mostly by Ella Baker: Int. Bernard Lee, Oct. 17, 1984. Also Archie E. Allen interview of Baker, Nov. 7, 1968, A/AP.
317 odd pair: Harrington, *Fragments*, pp. 109–15. Also int. Michael Harrington, Aug. 31, 1983, and Clarence Jones, Nov. 25, 1983.
318 "all the way with the Bowles": Wofford, *Of Kennedys*, p. 52. Also int. Harris Wofford, June 26, 1984.
319 apoplectic indecision: Sketch of LBJ selection from Schlesinger, Jr., *Robert Kennedy*, pp. 222–27. Also Wofford, *Of Kennedys*, pp. 53–58, and Miller, *Lyndon*, pp. 311–20.
320 "troubled, trembling world": NYT, July 16, 1960, p. 7.
320 chastised King: James E. Walker to King, July 27, 1960, BUK9f14. Also Committee for Presenting the Truth About the Name "Negro" to King, May 29, 1960, BUK9f14.
320 Malcolm X: Malcolm X to King, July 21, 1960, and Maude Ballou to Malcolm X, Aug. 10, 1960, BUK2f1.
320 alma mater in Boston: Malcolm X addressed the BU School of Theology on May 24, 1960, during King's perjury trial in Montgomery. Mays, *Born*, p. 307.
321 then to Buffalo: Log, A/SC29; log, BUK6f151.
321 good news that Alabama: ADW, July 19, 1960, p. 1.
321 Rustin had sent: Identified by Bayard Rustin as Norman Hill, a New York socialist and pacifist later prominent in CORE, and Jack O'Dell, a radical organizer who soon brought invaluable skills and paralyzing controversy into King's service, as detailed below. Int. Rustin, Feb. 21, 1984, and O'Dell, July 1, 1986.
321 twice as many people: Minutes of SCLC Board Meeting, Oct. 11, 1960, A/KP29f1.
321 "Munich of the Republican": NYT, July 24, 1960, p. 38.
321 "made a backbone plank": NYT, July 25, 1960, p. 16.
321 "Nixon Says Rights": NYT, July 26, 1960, pp. 1, 16.
321 "Nixon Wins": NYT, July 27, 1960, p. 1.
322 "ceiling on America's security": NYT, July 24, 1960, p. 38.
322 protested to Nixon by telephone: Ambrose, *Eisenhower*, pp. 597–98.
322 weak-minded spendthrift: Ibid., pp. 545–46, 559. Also Eisenhower-Rockefeller telephone call, June 11, 1960, Diary Series, Box 50, DDE.
322 "Job had his boils": NYT, July 27, 1960, p. 17.
322 "Richard E. Nixon": NYT, July 29, 1960, p. 9.
323 Eisenhower criticized: Ambrose, *Eisenhower*, p. 222.
323 "One hundred years ago": Morrow, *Black Man*, p. 212.
323 not much difference: King, JFKOH.
323 "Nixon and Lodge Are Best": ADW, Aug. 5, 1960, p. 4.
323 officials in Durham: ADW, Aug. 2, 1960, p. 1.
324 Wilkins to their shoulders: *The Crisis*, August–September 1960, p. 412.
324 U.S. Attorney General: ADW, Aug. 11, 1960, p. 1.
324 Trailways officials: ADW, Aug. 16, 1960, p. 1.
324 Only nine student delegates: Roster from A/SN1f20. Also A/SC35f10.
324 invited Senator Kennedy: ADW, Aug. 9, 1960, p. 1.
324 might be a Communist: Neary, *Rebel*, p. 142. Also int. Robert P. Moses, Aug. 10–11, 1983, July 30–31, 1984, and March 13, 1988.
325 Moses was only six years: Moses interviews, ibid.
327 Rustin to Ella Baker: Re Moses recommendation in Ernestine Brown to Abernathy, July 11, 1960, A/SC53f10. Also Ella Baker, A/AR; int. Bayard Rustin, Feb. 21, 1984; and Moses interviews, ibid.
328 "I advise against": Moses interviews, ibid.
328 on friendly terms: Ella Baker to Dombrowski, July 26, 1960, A/SC32f25.
329 Deeply wounded, Rustin: Int. Bayard Rustin, Feb. 21, 1984.
329 hounding King: Fred Gray to Kilgore, with copies to King, Abernathy, and Shuttlesworth, among others, Aug. 17, 1960, BUK1f16.
329 evicting the one-woman: Archie E. Allen interview of Ella Baker, Nov. 7, 1968, AAP.
329 got King to send: Draft letters in Walker's handwriting, plus Walker memo to Miss Brown, A/SC35f9.

329 "internationally known": Programs for the Second Statewide Institute on Nonviolence, Aug. 4–5, 1960, A/SC35f10.

329 provided bus tickets: Memo to Walker on Moses' travel funds, Aug. 8, 1960, A/SC.

330 last flurry: ADW, Aug. 9, 1960, p. 1; Stembridge to David Forbes, Aug. 14, 1960, A/SN17.

330 "SNCC now has a Field": Stembridge to Rev. John Collins, Aug. 11, 1960, A/SN17.

330 "plooped on front lawns": Moses to Stembridge, undated, A/SN17.

330 "mucho great job": Stembridge to Moses, Aug. 18, 1960, A/SN17.

330 "capacity in which Bayard": Stembridge to Moses, Aug. 25, 1960, A/SN17.

330 beauty shop was partitioned: Int. Robert P. Moses, July 31, 1984.

330 "Amzie is the best": Moses to Stembridge, "Friday morning" (probably Aug. 19, 1960), A/SN17.

331 "Nobody starry eyed": Ibid.

331 "happened to my kidneys": Stembridge to Moses, Aug. 25, 1960, A/SN17.

331 Nixon was greeted: ADW, Aug. 27, 1960, p. 1. The group, whose photograph appeared on p. 1, included Milton White, C. R. Yates, John Wesley Dobbs, Bishop Wilkes, Q. V. Williamson, C. A. Scott, and T. M. Alexander.

331 paternity suit: Int. John Doar, Oct. 25, 1983.

331 express purpose: Int. William P. Rogers, June 11, 1984.

332 "I'll do it": Int. John Doar, Oct. 25, 1983.

333 Hoover first tried to scuttle: Doar and Landsberg, "Performance," pp. 29–32.

334 nearly two hundred pages: Ibid., p. 15a.

334 Nearly every hand: Ibid., p. 31.

334 fifty affidavits: Ibid.

335 opened a new eye: Int. John Doar, Oct. 25, 1983, and May 16, 1985.

335 more than 35,000: NYAN, Sept. 10, 1960, p. 1.

335 fellow conspirators in January: Int. Rev. Thomas Kilgore, Nov. 8, 1983, Rev. Ralph D. Abernathy, May 30, 1984, and Rev. Gardner Taylor, Oct. 25, 1983.

335 "official auxiliary": Int. Rev. Gardner Taylor, Oct. 25, 1983, Rev. Ralph D. Abernathy, Nov. 19, 1984, and Rev. Wyatt Tee Walker, Dec. 21, 1984.

335 preached to 10,000: NYAN, March 31, 1956, p. 1.

336 preachers off to jail: PC, Sept. 24, 1960, p. 3.

336 cook baby alligators: Mahalia Jackson with Wylie, *Movin'*, p. 26.

336 fallen in with Thomas A. Dorsey: Goreau, *Mahalia*, pp. 55–56.

336 muffled and hidden: Ibid., pp. 95–100.

336 diapered young Aretha: Ibid., p. 107.

336 who was reeling from: Int. Chauncey Eskridge, Feb. 20 and 22, 1985.

336 not trust Secretary Jemison: ADW, Sept. 9, 1960, pp. 1, 6.

336 delivered Lyndon Johnson's: Schlesinger, *Thousand Days*, p. 58.

337 "Negro Baptists Pick": NYT, Sept. 9, 1960, p. 60.

337 The noise began: Account of convention from Kilgore, Abernathy, Taylor, Walker, and Eskridge interviews. Also ADW, Sept. 9, 10, 14, 16, and 18, 1960. NYAN, Sept. 10 and 17 and Oct. 1, 1960; and PC, Sept. 17 and 24, 1960.

338 "The people voted": NYAN, Sept. 24, 1960, p. 35.

340 "drop him down on Friday": Int. Rev. Vernon Dobson, Dec. 2, 1983, and Rev. James L. Moore, Dec. 2, 1983. I have not been able to fix the exact date of the preachers' meeting. No records have been located, and the Maryland Baptist Center no longer exists. The late summer of 1960 represents the best guess of many Vernon Johns sources, and falls within the time Johns is known to have stayed in Baltimore. Both Moore and Dobson attended the disastrous lunch meeting. Moore was to have introduced Johns.

340 Kennedy's Houston speech: Sorensen, *Kennedy*, p. 188; Miller, *Lyndon*, p. 324.

341 White argued: Wofford, *Of Kennedys*, pp. 61–63.

341 unseemly infighting: Int. Sargent Shriver, Nov. 30, 1983, Wofford, June 26, 1984, and April 5, 1985, and Louis Martin, Oct. 14, 1983.

341 Martha's Vineyard: Belford Lawson, JFKOH.

341 Teamsters union: Int. Simeon Booker, Feb. 11, 1985.

341 represented J. H. Jackson: PC, Sept. 24, 1960, p. 3.

341 was seen bringing a white woman: Int. Simeon Booker, Feb. 11, 1985.

341   appeal to Louis Martin: Int. Harris Wofford, April 5, 1985, and Sargent Shriver, Nov. 30, 1983.

342   "pay us some money": Int. Louis Martin, Oct. 14, 1983.

342   Martin was a godsend: Int. Sargent Shriver, Nov. 30, 1983, and Harris Wofford.

343   "Uncle Tom's Cabin": Shriver and Wofford interviews, ibid. Also Wofford, *Of Kennedys*, p. 61.

343   persuade Jackie Robinson: Int. Louis Martin, Oct. 14, 1983. Also NYT, Sept. 3, 1960.

343   hard cash was involved: Int. Louis Martin, Oct. 14, 1983. Also Wofford, *Of Kennedys*, p. 60; Sorensen, *Kennedy*, p. 172 (Sorensen wrote only that there were "high-level negotiations" with Powell); int. Harris Wofford and Sargent Shriver; Robert Kennedy, JFKOH, p. 517. (RFK said Powell "always exacts a price . . . for his support. . . . He wants money.")

343   solved by arranging: Int. Louis Martin, Oct. 14, 1983.

344   opened in Harlem: Wofford, *Of Kennedys*, pp. 63–64.

344   "Careful, Jack": Ibid. Also Sorensen, *Kennedy*, p. 183.

344   announcement of Powell's divorce: NYAN, Oct. 22, 1960, p. 1.

344   delaying the release: Wofford, *Of Kennedys*, p. 27.

344   five bags of chicken feed: Evers, *For Us*, pp. 220ff.

345   address on the philosophy: Carson, *In Struggle*, p. 27. Also King log, A/SC29.

345   The Rustin controversy: Carson, *In Struggle*, p. 29; Forman, *The Making*, p. 219; int. Robert P. Moses and Bayard Rustin.

345   "If history offers": Carson, *In Struggle*, p. 28.

345   cache of two-way radios: Raines, *My Soul*, p. 89.

346   own brother A.D.: Int. Bernard Lee, Oct. 25, 1984.

346   along with Lonnie: Raines, *My Soul*, p. 91.

346   So did Bernard: Int. Bernard Lee, Oct. 25, 1984.

346   he warned them: Ibid.

346   on the verge of tears: Int. Glenn Smiley, Nov. 14, 1983. Also int. Bernard Lee, Oct. 25, 1984. (Lee says he was one of the students at the airport.)

346   "racism at its worst": ADW, Oct. 18, 1960, p. 1. Also WP, Oct. 19, 1960, and NYT, Oct. 21, 1960, p. 14, among many such stories.

347   zone of negotiation: Int. Harris Wofford, June 26, 1984, and April 5, 1985, and Louis Martin, Oct. 25, 1983.

347   Opinion polls showed: WP, Oct. 28, 1960, p. 2.

348   "High Hopes": Sorensen, *Kennedy*, p. 151.

348   Levison joined Belafonte: Int. Harry Belafonte, March 6–7, 1985.

348   "stressed with Sammy": Levison to King, Oct. 13, 1960, BUK1f10.

348   Daddy King burst: Int. Bernard Lee, Oct. 25, 1984.

348   calls from Harris Wofford: Wofford, *Of Kennedys*, pp. 12–13. Also int. Wofford, June 26, 1984, and April 5, 1985.

349   "obliged to issue": Int. Harris Wofford, June 26, 1984, and April 5, 1985.

349   "The hell with that": Ibid.

349   Daddy King joined: ADW, Jan. 19, 1960, p. 1. Also C. A. Scott, A/OH.

350   "retreating under fire": WP, Oct. 19, 1960, p. 1.

350   "meet you on the bridge": Raines, *My Soul*, p. 93.

Nine
A PAWN OF HISTORY

351   "I cannot accept": ADW, Oct. 20, 1960, p. 1.

352   gave way to euphoria: Int. Bernard Lee, Oct. 25, 1984.

352   many as two thousand: PC, Oct. 29, 1960, p. 2. WP, Oct. 21, 1960, p. 14, put the number at only two hundred.

352   "practice what I preached": PC, Oct. 29, 1960, p. 2.

353   "most dangerously irresponsible": WP, Oct. 22, 1960, p. 8.

353   Wofford heard radio: Wofford, *Of Kennedys*, p. 13.

353 attorney named Morris Abram: Ibid. Also Abram, *Day*, pp. 125ff; Stein, *Journey*, pp. 90ff; William B. Hartsfield, JFKOH. In the story of political interventions in King's October arrest cases, there are slight conflicts between the versions of Wofford, Hartsfield, and Abram, which I have resolved insofar as possible through common sense, after interviews with Louis Martin, Bernard Lee, Wofford, and Sargent Shriver.

353 influential Negro leaders: King Sr., *Daddy*, p. 173. Also ADW, Oct. 23, 1960, p. 4.

354 Rich had broken down: Raines, *My Soul*, p. 93.

355 "Why should he be ashamed": Int. Harris Wofford, Aug. 28, 1984, and William B. Hartsfield, JFKOH, p. 4.

355 "I ran with the ball": Wofford, *Of Kennedys*, p. 14.

355 "The Senator is hopeful": Ibid., p. 15.

356 "shortest route to heaven": ADW, Oct. 23, 1960, p. 4.

356 "make love a reality": NYT, Oct. 24, 1960, pp. 1, 12.

356 preached six different sermons: PC, Nov. 3, 1960, p. 2.

356 hold King in jail: C. King, *My Life*, p. 200; Lewis, *King*, p. 126; NYT, Oct. 25, 1960, p. 31.

357 cellmates mutinied: Int. Bernard Lee, Oct. 25, 1984.

357 "intention or desire": ADW, Oct. 25, 1960, p. 3.

357 fuzzy statements: Ibid.

357 "M.L. will be": Int. Bernard Lee, Oct. 25, 1984.

357 white theology students: NYT, Oct. 26, 1960, p. 43.

357 into cold fear: Int. Bernard Lee, Oct. 25, 1984.

357 As for King: Ibid.

358 Judge Mitchell's hearing: Account taken from NYT, Oct. 26, 1960, p. 1; Oates, *Trumpet*, pp. 163–64; C. King, *My Life*, pp. 200–1; NYAN, Oct. 29, 1960, p. 1.

359 Walker spread: Int. Rev. Wyatt Tee Walker, Aug. 20, 1984.

359 Belafonte called: Int. Harry Belafonte, March 6–7, 1985.

359 Wofford responded: Wofford, *Of Kennedys*, p. 16; Schlesinger Jr., *Robert Kennedy*, p. 233.

359 "What we want": Wofford, *Of Kennedys*, pp. 16–17.

360 Bowles readily agreed: Ibid.

360 presence of Negroes: Ibid. Also int. Harris Wofford, June 26, 1984.

360 "King! Get up!": PC, Nov. 3, 1960, p. 2.

360 Hollowell called: Ibid.

361 nearly hysterical: Wofford, *Of Kennedys*, p. 17.

361 safer at Reidsville: Ibid., p. 18.

361 call found Shriver: Ibid. Also int. Harris Wofford, June 26, 1984, and Sargent Shriver, Nov. 30, 1983.

362 "some good numbers": Int. Sargent Shriver, Nov. 30, 1983.

362 "What the hell": Ibid.

362 appointment with Morris Abram: C. King, *My Life*, p. 202; King Sr., *Daddy*, p. 175.

362 "just wanted you to know": C. King, *My Life*, p. 203; *Jet*, Nov. 10, 1960, p. 4.

362 in solitary confinement: PC, Nov. 3, 1960, p. 2.

363 "Hello Darling": King to Coretta King, "Wednesday afternoon" (Oct. 26, 1960), A/KP7f24.

363 Kennedy mentioned casually: Wofford, *Of Kennedys*, p. 19.

363 lawyer who had pried: Sorensen, *Kennedy*, pp. 203–4.

364 "threat to survival": NYT, Oct. 26, 1960, p. 1.

364 game ended abruptly: Wofford, *Of Kennedys*, p. 19.

364 tongue-lashed and belittled: Int. Sargent Shriver, Nov. 30, 1983.

364 "one to tell Bobby": Int. Harris Wofford and Louis Martin.

365 "heard that Jackie Robinson": Louis Martin, CRDPOH, pp. 9–10. Also int. Martin, Oct. 14, 1983. Martin is the source for the dialogue of his meeting with Robert Kennedy.

365 nothing else controversial: Wofford, *Of Kennedys*, p. 20.

365 draw fire away: Schlesinger Jr., *Robert Kennedy*, p. 234.

365 "She is a friend": Wofford, *Of Kennedys*, p. 20.

365 never met Coretta: C. King, *My Life*, p. 245.

366 charter a private plane: Lewis, *King*, p. 128.

366 at 3:46 P.M.: PC, Nov. 3, 1960, p. 2.

366 "look of vulnerability": Watters, *Down to Now*, p. 53.

366 Cadillac limousine: PC, Nov. 3, 1960, p. 2; C. King, *My Life*, p. 204.

366 promised Harris Wofford: Int. Wofford, April 5, 1985; Abram, *Day*, p. 131.

366 "dump them in his lap": Wofford, *Of Kennedys*, p. 23; NYT, Oct. 29, 1960; NYAN, Nov. 5, 1960, p. 5. Both Daddy King and Coretta King democratized this quotation in their respective books some years later, changing it to read, "If I had a suitcase full of votes, I would . . ." The original wording appears in the contemporary accounts.

366 "your Nixon buttons": Oates, *Trumpet*, p. 165.

366 All he said: PC, Nov. 3, 1960, p. 2.

367 "that crazy judge": Stein, *Journey*, p. 93; Schlesinger Jr., *Robert Kennedy*, p. 234.

367 "screwing up my brother's": Wofford, *Of Kennedys*, p. 21.

367 "Can't we just say": Ibid.

367 "honorary brother": Int. Louis Martin. Also Wofford, *Of Kennedys*, p. 22.

368 featured the call: NYT, Oct. 28, 1960, p. 1.

368 "These white folks": PC, Nov. 3, 1960, p. 2.

368 "sea change": Int. Sargent Shriver, Nov. 30, 1983.

368 say nothing of it: Int. Louis Martin, Harris Wofford, and Sargent Shriver.

369 severe criticism: King Sr., *Daddy*, p. 175.

369 "not pay your debt": Int. Harry Belafonte, March 6–7, 1985.

369 flying to Chicago: *Jet*, Nov. 10, 1960, p. 4.

369 "being considered an ingrate": Statement, Nov. 1, 1960, BUK1f11b, A/KS2.

369 "firmly re-endorsing": ADW, Nov. 2, 1960, p. 2.

370 "blue bomb": Wofford, *Of Kennedys*, p. 24.

370 "we all have fathers": Ibid., pp. 27–28. Also Schlesinger, *Thousand Days*, p. 76, and Schlesinger Jr., *Robert Kennedy*, p. 235.

371 bizarre trial: MA, Nov. 2, 3, and 4, 1960, all p. 1.

371 "Senegambian": Ashmore, *Hearts*, p. 21.

371 Ike defended: MA, Nov. 3, 1960, p. 1.

372 "enemy advances": MA, Nov. 3, 1960, p. 1.

372 "must be greater": Ibid., p. 339.

372 two million copies: Wofford, *Of Kennedys*, p. 25.

372 Marshall L. Shepherd: PC, Sept. 24, 1960, p. 3.

373 "racial elevation": *Jet*, Nov. 10, 1960, p. 6.

373 Sargent Shriver and Louis Martin: Int. Shriver, Nov. 30, 1983.

373 fifteen hundred beauticians: ADW, Nov. 6, 1960, p. 2.

374 not permitted to vote: NYT, Nov. 3, 1960, p. 30.

374 Sorensen greeted him: White, *1960*, p. 347; Sorensen, *Kennedy*, p. 212.

374 tiniest of changes: White, *1960*, p. 350.

374 "sticking his nose": Ambrose, *Eisenhower*, p. 604.

374 "couple of phone calls": Wofford, *Of Kennedys*, p. 25.

374 30 percent shift: "Why Nixon Lost the Negro Vote," *The Crisis*, January 1961.

375 Morton declared: Ibid., p. 7.

375 "fundamentally unjust": NYT, Dec. 14, 1960.

375 implored Nixon: Morrow, *Black Man*, p. 213; Int. William P. Rogers, June 11, 1984; Raines, *My Soul*, pp. 97ff.

375 to hide Rogers: "Why Nixon Lost the Negro Vote," *The Crisis*, January 1961, p. 12.

375 Nixon implied: In his 1962 book, *Six Crises*. Also NYT, March 27, 1962, p. 52.

376 not even drafted: Draft statement by Deputy Attorney General Judge Lawrence E. Walsh, Oct. 31, 1960, WHCF, DDE. (King was released on Oct. 27, 1960.)

376 moved by memo: William B. Hartsfield, JFKOH, p. 6.

376 "result of economic issues": Sorensen, *Kennedy*, p. 216.

376 carried the Negro precincts: ADW, Nov. 10, 1960, p. 1.

376 Abram and Daddy King warmed to: Abram, *Day*, pp. 124–32; King Sr., *Daddy*, pp. 175–76.

377 Wilkins, who promptly: Wilkins, *Standing Fast*, pp. 279–80.

377 said with a laugh: Robert Kennedy, JFKOH, p. 514.

377 "Sure I'm glad": Schlesinger Jr., *Robert Kennedy*, p. 235.

377   he verified: White, *1960*, pp. 323, 354.
378   "master stroke": Ibid., p. 354.

Ten
THE KENNEDY TRANSITION

379   Winston Churchill: Schlesinger Jr., *Robert Kennedy*, p. 238.
380   fumigating machine: Nashville *Banner*, Nov. 11, 1960. Also John Lewis interview by Archie E. Allen, Feb. 14, 1969, AAP. Int. Lewis, May 31, 1984, and James Bevel, May 16, 1985.
380   Nebuchadnezzar's fiery furnace: Daniel 3:12ff.
380   behalf of Morris Abram: King interview, March 9, 1964, JFKOH.
380   appoint Benjamin Mays: King to Kennedy, March 1, 1961, BUK9f16. Also int. Louis Martin, June 10, 1985; *Jet*, April 6, 1961, p. 3.
380   Nigerian government: *Jet*, Nov. 17, 1960, p. 9. Also King speech, Jan. 1, 1961, A/KS2.
380   televised debate: "The Nation's Future," NBC-TV debate, Nov. 26, 1960, A/KS2.
381   failed to parry: Oates, *Trumpet*, pp. 168–69.
381   JIM CROW MUST GO!: ADW, Nov. 26, 1960, p. 1; *Jet*, Dec. 15, 1960, p. 37.
381   philanthropists were expanding: Steven Currier (of Taconic Foundation) to King, Jan. 5, 1961, BUK7f50; also a number of letters about a King meeting with Currier on Feb. 3, 1961, BUK7f50.
382   Lee of the Montgomery: Lee to King, Nov. 9, 1960, A/SC36f5.
382   Stokely Carmichael: Receiving $500, per Edwina Smith to J. C. Herrin, Jan. 4, 1961, A/SC36f5.
382   transfer Septima Clark's: Minutes, SCLC Admin. Committee, March 8–9, 1961, A/SC36F11.
382   two major proposals: Ibid.
382   politically cheap: Int. Louis Martin, Oct. 14, 1983, and June 10, 1985.
382   twelve hundred new Negro votes: Forman, *The Making*, p. 130. Also int. Louis Martin, June 10, 1985.
382   "appoint and appoint": Joseph Rauh, JFKOH.
382   "Negro by Negro": Golden, *Mr. Kennedy*, pp. 131ff.
383   each of the three sides: Int. Harris Wofford, Louis Martin, and Burke Marshall.
383   "make things happen": Wofford, Martin, and Marshall interviews, ibid.
383   "We observe today": Sorensen, *Kennedy*, pp. 245ff.
384   "Negro ever played golf": Speech at mass meeting, Jan. 23, 1961, BIR/BC9f24.
384   danced with Negro women: Int. Simeon Booker, Feb. 11, 1985.
384   included Louis Martin: Int. Martin, June 10, 1985.
384   Sinatra produced: *Jet*, Feb. 2, 1961, p. 60. Also *The Kennedy Years and the Negro* (Johnson Publishing Co., 1964), distributed by the Kennedy Library.
385   Sinatra reassembled: Int. Harry Belafonte, March 6–7, 1985, and Louis Martin, June 10, 1985; Stanley Levison to A. Philip Randolph, Jan. 10, 1961, with enclosed progress report on Carnegie Hall receipts, Box 23, APR.
385   "associated in the public eye": Henry Wheatley to Rockefeller, Jan. 4, 1961, RAC. Also Oren Root to Emmet Hughes, Nov. 17, 1960, Hughes to Root, Nov. 17, 1960, Root to Rockefeller, Dec. 29, 1960, Ilene Slater to Hugh Morrow, Jan. 12, 1961, among others, RAC.
385   speeches on successive days: King's report to Ebenezer for the church year 1960–61, A/KP9f6.
385   sing for Pope John: *Jet*, Jan. 19, 1961, p. 60.
385   "name it Mahalia": Goreau, *Mahalia*, pp. 286–87.
385   unusual Saturday meeting: McGeorge Bundy, Memorandum of Discussion on Cuba, Jan. 28, 1961, part of Taylor Report, JFK.
385   ten White House meetings: General David W. Gray, Summary of White House Meetings, May 9, 1961, part of Taylor Report, JFK.
386   "stand-ins at theatres": NYT, Jan. 29, 1961.
386   seized personal property: *Jet*, March 2, 1961, p. 25, and March 9, 1961, p. 8.
386   the land $4,350: *Jet*, April 6, 1961, p. 16.

386 King protested: King public letter, Feb. 2, 1961, A/KP1f6; King to William Kunstler, Feb. 6, 1961, A/KP1f6.
386 first televised press conference: NYT, Jan. 26, 1961, p. 10.
386 J. H. Meredith: Meredith, *Three Years*, pp. 50ff; Schlesinger Jr., *Robert Kennedy*, p. 341.
386 Evers, who felt wounded personally: Evers, *For Us*, p. 224.
386 "tell me what you're doing": Int. John Doar, May 12, 1986.
387 three hundred sharecroppers: Doar and Landsberg, "Performance," pp. 29–32.
387 chronicled daily: Cf. ADW, Dec. 15, 1960, p. 1, and Dec. 31, 1960, p. 1.
387 "Mahalia Jackson Avenue": *Jet*, Jan. 12, 1961, p. 8.
387 "I want to move": Int. John Doar, Oct. 25, 1983.
387 opposition of Byron: Schlesinger Jr., *Robert Kennedy*, p. 310; Wofford, *Of Kennedys*, pp. 92–94; int. Burke Marshall, June 27, 1984.
387 White recommended: Schlesinger Jr., *Robert Kennedy*, p. 310; Navasky, *Justice*, p. 163.
388 "silent interview": Guthman, *Band*, pp. 95–96; John Seigenthaler, JFKOH.
388 Taylor helped King design: King to Harry Emerson Fosdick, April 12, 1961, BUK8f10.
389 $5,000 contribution: *Jet*, May 11, 1961, p. 16.
389 Taylor sponsored Abernathy: Int. Rev. Gardner Taylor, Oct. 25, 1983, and Rev. Ralph D. Abernathy, Nov, 19, 1984.
389 Taylor lost his last: *Jet*, Jan. 19, 1961, p. 45.
389 "veiled dagger": *Jet*, Feb. 2, 1961, p. 48.
389 lining up votes: Int. Rev. Thomas Kilgore, Nov. 8, 1983.
389 new national director: Meier and Rudwick, *CORE*, pp. 130–31; Farmer, *Lay Bare*, p. 194.
389 scenes of his erudite father: Farmer, *When?*, p. xxi.
390 wife had miscarried: Farmer, *Lay Bare*, pp. 161–65.
390 made the official selection: *Jet*, Feb. 16, 1961, p. 9.
390 "listened to Minnie": Farmer, *Lay Bare*, pp. 194–95.
390 Gordon Carey proposed: Ibid., pp. 195–96. Also Meier and Rudwick, *CORE*, pp. 135–44.
391 jury were wearing beards: *Jet*, Feb. 16, 1961, p. 4.
391 Jefferson Davis stand-in: NYT, Feb. 19, 1961, p. 50.
391 Bernard Lee removed: *Alabama Journal*, Feb. 1, 1961, p. 1. Also Bernard Lee affidavit, A/SC60f10.
391 pledge to take the hard labor: Meier and Rudwick, *CORE*, pp. 118–19; Carson, *In Struggle*, pp. 32–33.
391 carried a toothbrush: Peck, *Ride*, p. 78.
391 "Try to understand": Ibid.
392 at the Butler Street YMCA: Minutes of SNCC meetings of Feb. 3–5, 1961, A/SN7; int. Rev. Charles Sherrod, Jan. 23, 1986, and Rev. Charles Jones, Nov, 23, 1986.
392 Tom Gaither: Int. Rev. Charles Sherrod, July 10, 1985.
392 "we have no alternative": Minutes of SNCC meetings of Feb. 3–5, 1961, A/SN7.
393 "explosive trouble spot": Gaither reports to CORE, March–April 1961, cited in Meier and Rudwick, *CORE*, p. 136.
393 church in Cincinnati: Police notes of mass meeting, Feb. 6, 1961, BIR/BC9f24.
393 "name of Jesus": Mass meeting, Feb. 13, 1961, BIR/BC9f24.
393 begging West Hunter: King to J. R. Butts, Feb. 8, 1961, A/KP1f1.
393 he sent a letter: King to Nash and Sherrod, Feb. 17, 1961, BUK7f28.
394 "matter of pride with you": Archie E. Allen interview of Will Campbell, Sept. 1, 1968, AAP.
394 "We're gonna march": Ibid.
394 February 20: Archie E. Allen interview of John Lewis, AAP.
395 saw in the same issue: Int. John Lewis, May 31, 1984.
395 CORE's first advertisement: *Student Voice*, March 1961, A/KP23f16.
395 "give up all if necessary": Meier and Rudwick, *CORE*, p. 136.
395 close more than seventy: ADW, March 1, 1961, pp. 1, 5.

395 Allen hesitated briefly: Allen, *Mayor*, p. 37.
395 Many of the students: Lonnie King, CRDPOH; Raines, *My Soul*, pp. 94–95.
395 made front pages: NYT, March 8, 1961, p. 1.
396 "reinstated in every way": ADW, March 8, 1961, p. 1.
396 "Clarification Mass Meeting": ADW, March 10, 1961, p. 1.
396 "got to give and take": ADW, March 11, 1961, p. 1.
397 "That's what's wrong!": Lonnie King, CRDPOH.
397 "I'm surprised at you": Allen, *Mayor*, p. 41.
397 "cancer of disunity": Raines, *My Soul*, pp. 96–97.
397 Fulbright's segregationist voting: Schlesinger, *Thousand Days*, p. 135.
397 Ernest Vandiver Secretary: AC, Jan. 2, 1961, p. 1.
398 Kennedy received John Hannah: Wofford, *Of Kennedys*, pp. 130ff; Navasky, *Justice*, pp. 160ff.
399 White believed: Navasky, *Justice*, p. 161.
399 Iowa legislature: *Jet*, March 2, 1961, p. 6.
399 annual rash of spring training: *Jet*, March 9, 1961, p. 54.
399 Hank Aaron: Hotel agreement, Feb. 28, 1961, cited in Tygiel, *Baseball's*, p. 319.
400 a Negro delegate: Ibid.
400 letter to General Ulysses: NYT, March 18, 1961, p. 1; *Jet*, March 30, 1961, p. 4.
400 controversy escalated: Cf. NYT, March 22, 1961, p. 34; March 27, p. 25; March 29, p. 25; April 2, p. 41; April 16, p. 72.
400 slurs on the ancestry: NYT, April 13, 1961, pp. 1, 25.
400 upside-down parody: NYT, April 12, 1961, p. 1.
401 Gagarin's first manned: NYT, April 12, 1961, p. 1.
401 gracefully assumed: Schlesinger, *Thousand Days*, p. 271.
401 "quiet landing of patriots": Sorensen, *Kennedy*, p. 302.
401 $17 billion nuclear missile: Ibid., p. 602.
402 twelve thousand new Marines: Collier and Horowitz, *Kennedys*, p. 274.
402 "before this decade is out": Sorensen, *Kennedy*, p. 525.
402 Oriental pageant: Robert Kennedy, JFKOH, passim; int. John Seigenthaler, Dec. 17, 1987, and Edwin Guthman, June 25, 1984.
403 jump through hoops: Int. Cartha DeLoach, June 1, 1984.
403 five Negro retainers: Powers, *Hoover*, pp. 313, 323, 442.
404 FBI were integrated: *Nation*, Feb. 4, 1961, pp. 91ff.
404 "call his hand": M. A. Jones to DeLoach, Feb. 7, 1961, cited in Garrow, *FBI*, p. 24.
404 on March 6: Int. Edwin Guthman, June 25, 1984, and review of Guthman's personal notes of the "meeting with civil rights leaders" on March 6, 1961.
404 appointment with President Kennedy: King to Kennedy, March 16, 1961, BUK9f16.
404 O'Donnell turned him down: O'Donnell to King, March 25, 1961, BUK9f16.
404 The King problem: Interviews with Louis Martin, Harris Wofford, and Burke Marshall, as listed below.
405 Kennedy-style meeting over lunch: Mayflower meeting drawn from interviews with Wofford, June 26, 1984, and April 5, 1985, and Martin, Oct. 14, 1983, and June 10, 1985. Also King, JFKOH; John Seigenthaler, CRDPOH; Wofford, *Of Kennedys*, p. 216; and Garrow, *FBI*, pp. 44, 240. Unfortunately, Burke Marshall (interview of June 27, 1984) had no memory of the Mayflower meeting at all. There is a time discrepancy between the account offered here and Garrow's authoritative work, which has minor ramifications for interpretations of the history of the FBI's campaign against King. Garrow, partly on information that Andrew Young was present, dates the Mayflower meeting in early 1962, but several factors make the spring 1961 setting more likely. Wofford and Martin independently described the meeting as the Administration's first tentative contact with King, undertaken with some trepidation very early in the Kennedy presidency. Martin recalled distinctly that he and King were the only Negroes present, and that Andrew Young was not there. Also, King in his 1964 oral history described his first meeting with Attorney General Kennedy as having taken place between the Bay of Pigs and the Freedom Rides. King talked about Kennedy's strong push for voter registration, but he discreetly omitted any mention of the complex, delicate arrangements that resulted in the creation of the Voter Education Project. The author, based on source recollections as corroborated by various details of internal

consistency, believes that the Mayflower meeting dates to the 1961 period described by King.

407 "colony at Oak Bluff": *Jet*, May 4, 1961, p. 63.
408 "You're the best weapon": Int. John Doar, May 12, 1986.
408 Sheriff Claude Screws: *Screws* v. *United States of America*, 325 U.S. 91–161.
410 wore khaki pants: Int. John Doar, May 12, 1986; Lord, *The Past*, pp. 104–7.
410 assembly line for a-suits: Int. John Doar, May 12, 1986.
411 J. P. Majors: Garrow, *Protest*, p. 31.
411 address the annual convention: A/KS2. Letters praising the speech, which the UAW recorded and distributed as an album, are located in BUK6f119.

Eleven
BAPTISM ON WHEELS

412 Lewis missed his bus: Archie E. Allen interview of John Lewis, Feb. 14, 1969, AAP.
412 motley collection: Peck, *Ride*, p. 89.
412 Dance of 1933: Ibid., p. 30.
412 *Golden Rule:* NYT, May 2, 1958, p. 1, and June 5, 1958, p. 38; Raines, *My Soul*, p. 118.
412 interested only three reporters: Int. Simeon Booker, Feb. 11, 1985.
413 "call me if there is": Ibid. Also John Seigenthaler, CRDPOH.
413 Kennedy promptly forgot: RFK, JFKOH; Guthman, *Band*, p. 167; Marshall, JFKOH, p. 11.
413 signs still guarded: *Jet*, May 25, 1961, p. 10.
413 Walker's former church: Archie E. Allen interview of John Lewis, May 30, 1969, AAP.
413 passed through Farmville: Peck, *Ride*, p. 90.
414 "Western Nations Rejoice": NYT, May 6, 1961, pp. 1, 11, 14.
414 for five weeks: Guthman, *Band*, p. 160.
414 "biggest percentage" to "We will move": NYT, May 7, 1961, p. 62.
415 "resolute speech": Ibid., p. 1.
415 Salinger announced: NYT, May 10, 1961, p. 1.
415 Vandiver was announcing: Ibid., p. 29.
415 "cactus bouquet": NYT, May 11, 1961, p. 24.
415 Greyhound terminal at Rock Hill: Incident described in Peck, *Ride*, pp. 91–92; Raines, *My Soul*, pp. 117–18; Farmer, *Lay Bare*, p. 199; Viorst, *Fire*, pp. 143–44; *Jet*, May 25, 1961, p. 14; Archie E. Allen interview of John Lewis, Feb. 14, 1969, AAP.
416 SCLC board meeting: *Jet*, May 25, 1961, p. 8; Reddick to King, May 9, 1961, BUK7f39; Fauntroy to King, April 26, 1961, BUK8f10.
416 sent a telegram: Unlocated but referred to in Kennedy's reply to King, May 18, 1961, BUK1f48.
416 Shuttlesworth had just: *Jet*, June 1, 1961, p. 12.
416 all but decided: Int. Rev. Ralph D. Abernathy, Nov. 19, 1984.
416 dinner on Saturday night: Farmer, *Lay Bare*, p. 200; int. James Farmer, Nov. 18, 1983. Farmer was mildly annoyed that King did not offer to pick up the tab for dinner.
417 "You will never make it": Int. Simeon Booker, Feb. 11, 1985.
417 "I can outrun": Ibid.; Raines, *My Soul*, p. 119.
417 emergency phone call: Farmer, *Lay Bare*, pp. 200–201.
417 Perkins became group: *Jet*, May 25, 1961, p. 12.
417 plainclothes investigators: Ibid.; Patterson, JFKOH; Raines, *My Soul*, p. 120.
417 warning of a mob: *Jet*, May 25, 1961, p. 12.
417 "White Intrastate Passengers": NYT, May 15, 1961, p. 22.
418 pounding on the bus: Greyhound burning from Peck, *Ride*, p. 96; Raines, *My Soul*, pp. 119ff; *Jet*, May 25, 1961, p. 12; NYT, May 15, 1961, p. 1; BN, May 15, 1961, p. 1; BW, May 17, 1961, p. 1; MA, May 15, 1961, p. 1.
419 Trailways bus pulled into Anniston: *Jet*, June 1, 1961, pp. 14ff; Peck, *Ride*, pp. 97ff; BN, May 15, 1961, p. 10.
420 Shuttlesworth had been telling: Shuttlesworth, CRDPOH; Meier and Rudwick, *CORE*, p. 137.

420　told his FBI handlers: Rowe, *Undercover*, pp. 38ff.

420　FBI's Birmingham office: FBI memos and Rowe Senate testimony cited in Corley, "Quest," pp. 215ff.

420　SAC kept a record: SAC Birmingham to Director, airtel, May 12, 1961 (2:52 P.M.), and airtel, May 13, 1961 (10:55 A.M.), from FBI Gary Thomas Rowe file, #170-9-SF.

420　active collaborator: Informant report, April 25, 1961, FBI file BH 137-698-SF-42; SAC Birmingham to Director, airtel, and Letterhead Memorandum, May 5, 1961, FBI file #157-48; Kemp to SAC Birmingham, May 18, 1961, FBI file #170-9-SF, serial 4.

420　"only man on duty": SAC Birmingham to Director, "Urgent" teletype, May 14, 1961 (9:12 P.M.), FBI file 149-1684-[illegible].

420　Rev. John Rutland: Int. David Vann, Aug. 1, 1986.

421　Rowe learned by telephone: Rowe, *Undercover*, p. 42.

421　designated testers for Birmingham: Account of attack from *Jet*, June 1, 1961, pp. 14ff; Peck, *Ride*, pp. 98ff; NYT, May 15, 1961, p. 1, and May 17, 1961, p. 23; MA, May 15, 1961, p. 1; BN, May 15, 1961, p. 1; int. Simeon Booker, Feb. 11, 1985.

422　distress from Anniston: Raines, *My Soul*, pp. 121–22; Shuttlesworth, CRDPOH.

423　reached John Seigenthaler: Int. Simeon Booker, Feb. 11, 1985.

423　"day is coming": MA, May 15, 1961, p. 1.

424　Peck answered questions: Peck, *Ride*, p. 99; BN, May 15, 1961, p. 10.

424　glorious Sunday picnic: Int. James Bevel, May 16, 1985, and Diane Nash Bevel, Feb. 20, 1985.

424　"keep talking nasty": Int. James Bevel, May 16, 1985.

425　marathon debate: Ibid.; also Archie E. Allen interview of John Lewis, May 30, 1969, AAP.

425　"Where Were the Police?": BN, May 15, 1961, p. 1.

425　businessman told: Corley, "Quest," p. 216.

425　"eyewitness account": NYT, May 15, 1961, p. 10.

425　superimpose that shot: Farmer, *Lay Bare*, p. 203.

425　In faraway Tokyo: Duard LeGrand lecture by David Vann, November 1978, Center for Urban Affairs, University of Alabama at Birmingham; int. David Vann, Aug. 1, 1986.

426　struck at ten o'clock: *Jet*, June 1, 1961, p. 20.

426　case of the mumps: Marshall to Charles Reich, May 3, 1961, Marshall Papers, JFK; Burke Marshall, JFKOH.

426　Kennedy quickly established: Birmingham siege of May 15 drawn from *Jet*, June 1, 1961, pp. 20–21; NYT, May 15, 1961, p. 1; Peck, *Ride*, p. 101; Farmer, *Lay Bare*, p. 203; Guthman, *Band*, pp. 167–68; Meier and Rudwick, *CORE*, p. 173; int. Simeon Booker, Feb. 11, 1985; John Seigenthaler, CRDPOH; Burke Marshall, JFKOH; John Patterson, JFKOH; Fred Shuttlesworth, CRDPOH; report of May 15 mass meeting, BIR/BC9f24.

429　preferred to be called: Burke Marshall, JFKOH, p. 5.

429　"You know Diane Nash": John Seigenthaler, CRDPOH. Burke Marshall, in JFKOH, p. 13, recalled that he learned of Nash's plans from Seigenthaler, not the other way around, but chronology and the placement of people at the time favor Seigenthaler's memory.

430　consumed all of Tuesday: Archie E. Allen interview of John Lewis, May 30, 1969, AAP; int. Lewis, May 31, 1984; int. James Bevel, May 16, 1985; Viorst, *Fire*, p. 149.

430　"Young lady": Fred Shuttlesworth, CRDPOH; int. James Bevel, May 16, 1985; Morris, *Origins*, p. 232.

430　Bevel first chose: Int. James Bevel, May 16, 1985; Archie E. Allen interview of John Lewis, AAP.

432　Monday's siege: Forman, *The Making*, pp. 150ff; John Lewis, A/OH; Archie E. Allen interview of Lewis, AAP; MA, May 18, 1961, p. 1; NYT, May 18, 1961, p. 27.

433　President in his pajamas: Breakfast meeting primarily from Burke Marshall, May 29, 1964, JFKOH. Also John Seigenthaler, CRDPOH; John Patterson, JFKOH; NYT, May 19, 1961, p. 17.

434　Khrushchev in Vienna: MA, May 15, 1961, p. 1; NYT, May 17, 1961, p. 1.

436　"couldn't stand their singing": Burke Marshall, JFKOH.

437　Lewis sat behind Bull: Ardmore journey drawn from John Lewis, A/OH; Archie E. Allen interview of Lewis, May 30, 1969, AAP; Forman, *The Making*, pp. 150ff; Viorst, *Fire*, pp. 150ff.

438 "Many thanks to you": RFK to King, May 18, 1961, BUK1f48.
439 "We do not wish": Marshall to Earl James, May 19, 1961, Marshall Papers, Box 1, JFK.
439 achieved bulletin status: Forman, *The Making*, p. 153; John Lewis, A/OH; int. Lewis, May 31, 1984.
440 third attempt to move: NYT, May 20, 1961, p. 18; MA, May 20, 1961, p. 1; Grant, *Black Protest*, p. 323; Forman, *The Making*, p. 153.
441 "President Can't Reach": NYT, May 20, 1961, p. 1.
441 "speeches at me, John": RFK and Marshall, JFKOH, p. 559; John Patterson, JFKOH.
441 "Glad to see you": John Seigenthaler, CRDPOH.
442 "given me this statement": Ibid. Also MA, May 20, 1961, p. 1; NYT, May 21, 1961, p. 78; Guthman, *Band*, p. 170.
442 obtained from Montgomery's: MA, May 20, 1961, p. 1.
443 "one life to give": Grant, *Black Protest*, p. 323. Also Archie E. Allen interview of John Lewis, AAP; Lewis, A/OH; Raines, *My Soul*, p. 126; Viorst, *Fire*, p. 151. Lewis puts the driver's declaration at a different time during the Birmingham siege.
443 "touch with Mr. Greyhound": Schlesinger Jr., *Robert Kennedy*, p. 318.
444 "I never recovered": RFK, JFKOH, pp. 566–67.
444 Finally, without warning: Grant, *Black Protest*, pp. 318, 323.
444 not believe a word: Burke Marshall, JFKOH, p. 18; Guthman, *Band*, p. 170; NYT, May 21, 1961, p. 78.
444 Seigenthaler finished breakfast: Seigenthaler, CRDPOH, pp. 38ff.
445 ordered Doar to stay clear: Int. John Doar, May 12, 1986.
445 "It doesn't look right": Raines, *My Soul*, p. 128.
445 "Let's all stand together": Forman, *The Making*, pp. 154ff. May 20 Montgomery riot drawn heavily from Stuart Loory's eyewitness account in the New York *Herald Tribune*, May 21, 1961, reprinted in Grant, *Black Protest*, pp. 318ff. Also from John Seigenthaler, CRDPOH; Burke Marshall, JFKOH; John Patterson, JFKOH; John Lewis, A/OH; Archie E. Allen interview of Lewis, May 30, 1969, AAP; Guthman, *Band*, pp. 170–71; Navasky, *Justice*, p. 124; Durr, *Outside*, p. 298; NYT, May 21 and 22, 1961; MA, May 21, 1961; ADW, May 21, 1961; secretary's notes of Doar phone report of May 20, 1961, Ed Guthman Papers.

Twelve
THE SUMMER OF FREEDOM RIDES

451 "How are you doing?": John Seigenthaler, CRDPOH.
452 rumbling ominously: NYT, May 21, 1961, pp. 78–79; MA, May 21, 1961, p. 1, and May 22, 1961, p. 1.
452 Farmer ordered: Farmer, *Lay Bare*, p. 204.
452 then accepted Doar's: NYT, May 22, 1961, p. 1; int. John Doar, May 12, 1986.
453 about fifty of them: John Patterson, JFKOH.
453 "don't need your marshals": NYT, May 22, 1961, p. 26; MA, May 22, 1961, pp. 1, 2; Guthman, *Band*, pp. 172–73.
454 hiding in the basement: Forman, *The Making*, p. 155.
454 White called Washington: Raines, *My Soul*, p. 342.
454 began trickling into: Montgomery siege of May 21 drawn from interviews with John Lewis, May 31, 1984; Diane Nash Bevel, Feb. 20, 1985; James Bevel, May 16, 1985; William Beasley, Dec. 20, 1983; Bernard Lee, June 19, 1985; James Farmer, Nov. 18, 1983; Rev. Ralph D. Abernathy, Nov. 19, 1984; Rev. Wyatt Tee Walker, Aug. 20, 1984; Edwin Guthman, June 26, 1984; Archie E. Allen interview of John Lewis, May 30, 1969, AAP; Lewis, CRDPOH; Lewis, A/OH; John Patterson, JFKOH; RFK and Burke Marshall, JFKOH; Marshall, JFKOH; William Orrick, JFKOH; Shuttlesworth mass meeting of May 22, 1961, BIR/BC9f14; Forman, *The Making*, pp. 155–56; Guthman, *Band*, pp. 175–78; Raines, *My Soul*, pp. 128ff, 334ff; Navasky, *Justice*, pp. 24, 124–25; Farmer, *Lay Bare*, pp. 204–7; Schlesinger Jr., *Robert Kennedy*, pp. 320–21; Viorst, *Fire*, pp. 153ff; Meier and Rudwick, *CORE*, pp. 138–39; NYT, May 22, 1961; MA, May 22, 1961.
458 light of a bonfire: Durr, *Outside*, pp. 300–301. The burned car belonged to Clifford and Virginia Durr. The Durrs had lent their Buick to their houseguest and friend, British author Jessica Mitford, who was researching a humor article for *Esquire* on American class distinctions.

465 Byron White told: MA, May 23, 1961, p. 1.

465 "Alabama Asks": NYT, May 22, 1961, p. 1.

465 stacks of telegrams: MA, May 23, 1961, p. 48, and May 25, 1961, p. 4.

466 "baby-sitting the agitators": MA, May 23, 1961, p. 6.

466 Roy Wilkins . . . told: Jet, June 22, 1961, p. 8.

466 "he's just worried": Int. Diane Nash Bevel, Feb. 20, 1985.

467 Lewis recoiled from Farmer: Archie E. Allen interview of John Lewis, May 30, 1969, AAP.

467 but was not sure: Jet, July 6, 1961, p. 16; int. James Lawson, Nov. 14, 1983, and Bernard Lee, June 19, 1985.

467 "Me, too": Viorst, Fire, p. 156; Raines, My Soul, p. 130; Farmer, Lay Bare, p. 206; int. James Farmer, Nov. 18, 1983.

467 "my Golgotha": Int. James Farmer, Nov. 18, 1983.

467 "He don't have to have": Int. Rev. Wyatt Tee Walker, Aug. 20, 1964.

467 Bevel supported King's: Int. James Bevel, May 16, 1985.

468 "respected him more": Forman, The Making, p. 147.

468 Lewis bridled: Int. John Lewis, May 31, 1984.

468 "Riders must develop": Jet, June 8, 1961, p. 17; NYT, May 24, 1961, p. 1.

468 appeared in front of Orrick: William Orrick, JFKOH.

468 thanked Ben Davis: Scatterday to Rosen, May 22, 1961, cited in Garrow, FBI, p. 24.

469 strongly resembled a report: Sgt. T. H. Cook to Eugene Connor, "Martin Luther King, Jr. and Communism," May 17, 1960, BIR/BC5f24.

469 "difficult decision": Burke Marshall, JFKOH, p. 37.

469 Kennedy then faced: Guthman, Band, p. 176.

470 "That would be a matter": MA, May 23, 1961, p. 1.

470 "in fact, I suppose": RFK, JFKOH, cited in Schlesinger Jr., Robert Kennedy, p. 322.

470 "your baby crib": Burke Marshall, JFKOH, p. 39.

470 reinforcements arrived: John Lewis, A/OH; int. Lewis, May 31, 1984.

470 imperial jade ring: Dietrich to Walker, Aug. 1, 1961, and Walker to Dietrich, Aug. 21, 1961, A/SC33f2.

471 "may be a hazardous journey": Jet, June 8, 1961, p. 15.

471 7:06 A.M.: MA, May 25, 1961, pp. 1, 2, 3.

472 vomited on the side: Burke Marshall, JFKOH, p. 38.

472 "nothing to do": MA, May 25, 1961, p. 1.

473 "I think we should all": NYT, May 25, 1961, p. 24.

473 reported almost continuously: Log of conference call, papers of Ed Guthman, Philadelphia, Pa.

473 "My prayers are with you": Farmer, Lay Bare, p. 3; int. James Farmer, Nov. 18, 1983.

474 "embarrassed all our lives?": Stein, Journey, pp. 98–103.

474 "damn shame": MA, May 25, 1961, p. 2.

475 "cooling-off period": NYT, May 25, 1961, p. 24.

475 "displayed any common sense": MA, May 25, 1961, p. 1.

475 "Our conscience tells us": Guthman, Band, pp. 154–55. This sentence was deleted from the version reported in Schlesinger Jr., Robert Kennedy, p. 322. The conversation was preserved by aides listening in on Kennedy's end of the line, handwritten notes in papers of Ed Guthman.

475 "against the atom bomb?": Wofford, Of Kennedys, p. 156.

475 all but excluded: Int. Harris Wofford, Sept. 26, 1985.

476 "they don't understand": Wofford, Of Kennedys, p. 156.

476 "Do you want to go on?": Stein, Journey, pp.100–101.

476 Sheriff Mack Sim Butler: MA, May 26, 1961, p. 1; NYT, May 26, 1961, p. 1.

476 "so furious": Stein, Journey, p. 101.

476 "took a lot of guts": WP, May 25, 1961, cited in Navasky, Justice, p. 206. Kennedy is not identified in the story as the source of the quotations, but Navasky and the context of the story make it plain that it was he.

477 "we can end segregation": NYT, May 26, 1961, p. 21.

477 King presided: Minutes of meeting, May 26, 1961, A/KP10f39.

477 "I am here to promote": NYT, May 26, 1961, p. 12.

478 tripled draft calls: Manchester, *Glory*, p. 1117; NYT, July 27, 1961, p. 1.

478 approaching two hundred: NYT, June 26, 1961, p. 9.

478 "long-held customs": NYT, May 26, 1961, p. 32.

478 "Dr. King Refuses": Ibid., p. 1.

478 Gallup poll: Wofford, *Of Kennedys*, p. 157.

478 telescoped a process: Guthman, *Band*, p. 175; Schlesinger Jr., *Robert Kennedy*, p. 323.

479 Kennedy himself intervened: RFK, JFKOH, cited in Schlesinger Jr., *Robert Kennedy*, p. 325.

479 Capahosic: Int. Leslie Dunbar, May 12, 1986.

479 "three Charlies": Int. Timothy Jenkins, March 11, 1986.

480 On June 16: Carson, *In Struggle*, p. 39.

480 "You are a public official": Int. Charles Sherrod, July 10, 1985; Farmer, *Lay Bare*, pp. 219–20.

480 draft exemptions: Int. Charles Jones, Nov. 24, 1986.

480 Wofford put the choice: Raines, *My Soul*, pp. 245–46.

480 call the Justice Department collect: Ibid., p. 250; int. Robert P. Moses, Aug. 10, 1983.

481 wedding anniversary: *Jet*, July 13, 1961, p. 13. The Belafonte meeting, like Robert Kennedy's meeting with the SNCC students, was a substitute for Harris Wofford's persistent recommendations that President Kennedy himself meet these leaders: e.g., Wofford to Kenneth O'Donnell, March 20, June 12, and Oct. 4, 1961, all File HU, May 11, 1961–Nov. 15, 1961, Box 358, WHCF, JFK.

481 "Negro Vote Surge": NYT, June 26, 1961, p. 1.

481 Belafonte encouraged: Int. Harry Belafonte, March 6–7, 1985; Carson, *In Struggle*, p. 39.

481 all-day meeting in New York: Meier and Rudwick, *CORE*, pp. 174–75. Letters about King's participation in the July 28 meeting are in BUK7f50.

481 a month later: Telegrams between Walker and Currier, Aug. 15, Aug. 17, and Aug. 17, 1961, A/SC36f23, regarding the meeting on Aug. 23, 1961.

481 a hundred compromises: Wofford, *Of Kennedys*, p. 159; Schlesinger Jr., *Robert Kennedy*, pp. 324–25; Morris, *Origins*, pp. 234–36.

482 "empirical evaluation": Dunbar to Farmer, Wilkins, Young, Walker, McDew, and Jenkins, Sept. 13, 1961, A/SC36f24.

482 Down in Mississippi: Freedom Rider jail account drawn heavily from Farmer, *Lay Bare*, pp. 1–32. Also Meier and Rudwick, *CORE*, pp. 139–42; Peck, *Ride*, pp. 110–17; Raines, *My Soul*, pp. 133–38, 305; int. James Bevel, May 16, 1985; int. John Lewis, May 31, 1985; Lewis, A/OH; C. T. Vivian, 1983, HOH; int. James Farmer, Nov. 18, 8583; *Jet*, June 15, 1961, pp. 12–13, and June 22, 1961, pp. 6–7.

485 "top priority": SNCC minutes, Baltimore meeting, July 14–16, 1961, A/SN7 and A/KP23f18; Carson, *In Struggle*, p. 40.

486 "this is an emergency": Sherrod circular, July 22, 1961, A/KP23f18.

486 Baffled by the intrigue: Int. Robert P. Moses, July 30, 1984.

487 two cooperating wings: Carson, *In Struggle*, pp. 41–42; Charles McDew, CRDPOH, p. 72.

487 "Move on Mississippi": Charles McDew, CRDPOH; int. James Bevel, May 16, 1985.

487 up to three years: *Jet*, Aug. 17, 1961, p. 16; int. James Bevel, May 16, 1985, and Diane Nash Bevel, Feb. 22, 1985.

487 map on the wall: Int. John Doar, Oct. 25, 1983, and Charles Sherrod, July 10, 1985.

488 Sherrod was obliged: Int. Charles Sherrod, July 10, 1985.

488 trying to make peace: NYT, May 26, 1961, p. 1.

488 "Steps have been taken": News Service of the Southern Baptist Convention release, Aug. 9, 1961, BUK7f7.

488 On a single day: NYT, June 17, 1961, p. 10; Peggy Fowler to Wheatley et al., June 12, 1961, RAC; int. Hugh Morrow, Dec. 20, 1984.

489 "interest the television networks": Rockefeller to King, Aug. 22, 1961, responding to King of Aug. 9, 1961, BUK7f39.

489 King flew back: Log, A/KP9f6.

489 ventured into Jackson: *Jet*, July 20, 1961, p. 6.

489 dollar-conscious Benjamin: Mays to King, July 20, 1961, BUK7f26.

489 arranged for him: Levison to King, July 24, 1961, BUK7f25.

490 "before the bank froze": Levison to King, June 20, 1961, BUK7f25.

490 Levison to whom King entrusted: Ibid.

490 "grammar is uncertain": King, " 'The Time for Freedom Has Come,' " *The New York Times Magazine*, Sept. 10, 1961.

490 emergency meeting: Minutes of the Freedom Ride Coordinating Committee, Aug. 3, 1961, A/SC35f2.

491 opened their first: Grant, *Black Protest*, p. 304.

491 day trip to New York: Log, A/KP9f6.

Thirteen
MOSES IN McCOMB, KING IN KANSAS CITY

492 C. C. Bryant: Int. Robert P. Moses, July 30, 1984; *Time*, Oct. 20, 1961, p. 26.

493 Hollis Watkins: Watkins interview by Joe Sinsheimer, student at Duke, Feb. 13, 1985.

494 morning of August 15: Int. Robert P. Moses, July 30, 1984. Also *Liberation*, January 1970, pp. 8ff; Forman, *The Making*, pp. 226–27; Tom Hayden, *Revolution in Mississippi*, Students for a Democratic Society publication reprinted in Grant, *Black Protest*, pp. 303ff; Carson, *In Struggle*, pp. 47–49; New York U.S. Attorney's report "Résumé of the Inquiry Re: Robert Parris Moses, Conscientious Objector," March 21, 1962, pp. 10–11, A/SN17.

497 next morning, August 29: Int. Robert P. Moses, July 30, 1984. Also Doar and Landsberg, *Performance*, pp. 34–35; telegram, SAC New Orleans to Director Hoover, Aug. 29, 1961, FBI file #44-18167, serial 1; Moses statement of Sept. 6, 1961, FBI file #44-1348.

500 "Forgive them": "Résumé of the Inquiry Re: Robert Parris Moses."

500 "flash bundle": Int. Rev. Thomas Kilgore, Nov. 8, 1983.

501 King faced choices: Int. Rev. Gardner Taylor, Oct. 25, 1983, Rev. Wyatt Tee Walker, Dec. 21, 1984, and Rev. Ralph D. Abernathy, May 30, 1984.

501 Koenigsdorf's courtroom: Kansas City *Star*, Sept. 6, 1961; int. Chauncey Eskridge, Feb. 22, 1985.

501 made no sense to Wyatt: Int. Rev. Wyatt Tee Walker, Dec. 21, 1984.

502 "flying wedge": *Jet*, Sept. 21, 1961; Kansas City *Star*, Sept. 7, 1961, p. 1; CD, Sept. 9–15, 1961, p. 1; ADW, Sept. 7, 1961, p. 1; int. Rev. Gardner Taylor, Oct. 25, 1983.

503 Wright's attorney valued: *Jet*, Feb. 1, 1962, p. 46; CD, Sept. 16–22, 1961, p. 1.

503 Britt finally escaped: *Liberation*, January 1970, p. 11; NYT, Oct. 11, 1961, p. 28; Carson, *In Struggle*, p. 48; int. Robert P. Moses, July 30, 1984; Director Hoover to SAC New Orleans, Sept. 7, 1961, FBI file #44-18167-NR (Not Recorded); Burke Marshall to Hoover, Sept. 26, 1961, "Intimidation of Negro Applicants for Registration in Amite County, Mississippi," records of the Civil Rights Division, U.S. Dept. of Justice.

504 khaki safari shorts: Int. John Doar, Oct. 25, 1983.

504 "I want to see you": *U.S.* v. *Wood*, 295 F. 2nd 772, opinion reprinted in Grant, *Black Protest*, pp. 308f.

505 "A to Z": Kansas City *Star*, Sept. 7, 1961, p. 1.

505 Jackson won: Kansas City *Star*, Sept. 8, 1961, p. 1.

505 "Can you believe": Int. Rev. Gardner Taylor, Oct. 25, 1983.

506 "masterminded the invasion": NYT, Sept. 10, 1961, p. 35; *Jet*, Sept. 28, 1961, p. 18.

506 "hoodlums and crooks": CD, Sept. 16–22, 1961.

506 "injurious to my public image": King to Jackson, Sept. 10, 1961, BUK7f19.

507 "is not righted": SCLC release, Sept. 12, 1961, BUK7f19.

507 "Jack would allow": Int. Rev. Wyatt Tee Walker, July 30, 1984.

507 "smoke has cleared": Walker to Reid, Sept. 6, 1961, A/SC129f12.

507 Department intervened: Bass, *Unlikely Heroes*, p. 216; Grant, *Black Protest*, p. 308.

508 Marshall, who authorized: Int. John Doar, May 12, 1986.

508 hauntingly peaceful: Int. Arvid Sather, Nov. 8, 1985.

508 illustrious Mordecai Johnson: Church program, BUK7f23.

508 Moses in person: *Liberation*, January 1970, p. 12; Doar and Landsberg, *Performance*, p. 12.

509 Doar found a phone message: Int. John Doar, Oct. 25, 1983.

510 "You killed my husband!": Charles McDew, CRDPOH, p. 102.

510 perspective on his guilt: *Liberation*, January 1970, p. 12; int. Robert P. Moses, July 30, 1984.

510 the actual killer: Doar and Landsberg, *Performance*, pp. 36f; Grant, *Black Protest*, p. 327; Carson, *In Struggle*, p. 48; Tom Hayden interview, Oct. 27, 1961, "The Children of McComb," Tape #BBO225, PRA; Burke Marshall to Director Hoover, Sept. 26, 1961, "Intimidation of Negro Applicants for Registration in Amite County, Mississippi," records of the Civil Rights Division, U.S. Dept. of Justice.

510 Louis Allen was: Elizabeth Allen affidavit in Council of Federated Organizations, *Mississippi*, pp. 30ff.

511 "I'm not playing with you": Louis Allen affidavit of July 31, 1962, attached to the investigative report of staff attorneys William H. Downs and Jack F. Govan, Aug. 29, 1962, U.S. Civil Rights Commission. Other government documents on Louis Allen's testimony, and the pressures upon him, include the file memo of D. Robert Owen, Oct. 20, 1961, and Burke Marshall to J. Edgar Hoover, Aug. 22, 1962, in the records of the Civil Rights Division, U.S. Dept. of Justice.

511 Trapped between victim: Int. Robert P. Moses, July 30, 1984.

511 "examine Lee's body": Doar and Landsberg, *Performance*, p. 37.

512 Moses confessed to Bryant's: Int. Robert P. Moses, July 30, 1984.

513 along with 119 students: Charles McDew, CRDPOH; Grant, *Black Protest*, p. 307; int. Robert P. Moses, July 30, 1984; *Jet*, Oct. 19, 1961, pp. 4–5; Zellner interview, "The Children of McComb," PRA.

513 "behind some of this racial": NYT, Oct. 7, 1961, p. 47.

513 Jones alerted outside news: Int. Charles Jones, Nov. 24, 1986.

513 "Where the students lead": *Jet*, Nov. 2, 1961, p. 18.

514 "puts himself in the class": *Time*, Oct. 20, 1961, p. 26.

514 Belafonte sent them $5,000: Charles McDew, CRDPOH, pp. 93–94.

514 "SNCC Done Snuck": Ibid., p. 95.

515 Moses to wonder: Int. Robert P. Moses, July 30, 1984.

515 Grand Ol' Opry: Lewis records, AAP; Reddick to King and Walker, Oct. 6, 1961, BUK7f39.

515 "has to have his say": Reddick to King and Walker, Sept. 15, 1961, BUK7f39.

515 "reign of terror": *Jet*, Oct. 19, 1961, p. 5.

516 "my own personal": Walker to Kennedy, Oct. 6, 1961, BUK1f48.

516 privately with the President: Wofford's renewed requests for a King appointment recorded in Wofford to O'Donnell, Oct. 4 and Oct. 9, 1961, File HU May 11, 1961–Nov. 15, 1961, Box 358, WHCF, JFK.

516 ominous to Burke Marshall: Marshall to Hoover, June 9, 1961, FL-130.

516 Marshall had lingered: Int. Harris Wofford, June 26, 1984; Wofford, *Of Kennedys*, p. 216.

516 Marshall's argument: Int. Burke Marshall, June 27, 1984.

517 meeting with President Kennedy: *Jet*, Oct. 26, 1961, p. 4; Wofford, *Of Kennedys*, p. 216; Oates, *Trumpet*, p. 179; King, Birmingham speech, Jan. 20, 1962, BIR/BC6f14. Also mentioned in King to Wachtel, Nov. 7, 1961, BUK7f55.

517 after the delivery: The dating of Wofford's formal warning to King comes partly from Marshall's memo to RFK of Sept. 12, 1963 (Marshall Papers, Box 3, JFK), which placed the warning in 1961. Interviews with Wofford and Marshall, and log records, make the Wofford warning and the Kennedy lunch most likely to have occurred on the same day, as presented here.

518 "Eve of Nonviolent": *Southern Patriot*, November 1961.

518 Moses halted: Forman, *The Making*, p. 235.

520 "war for what?": Charles McDew, CRDPOH.

520 Moses advised Allen: Int. Robert P. Moses, July 30, 1984.

520 On October 19: Doar and Landsberg, *Performance*, pp. 36–39.

521 Moses and Doar found themselves: Int. Robert P. Moses, July 30, 1984.

521 Donis Hawkins': Elizabeth Allen affidavit, in Council of Federated Organizations, *Mississippi*, p. 32.

522 come to like Louis Allen: Int. John Doar, Oct. 25, 1983.

522 open dissent: Int. John Doar, May 12, 1986.

522 few words of Yiddish: Charles McDew, CRDPOH.

523 "middle of the iceberg": Moses note, Nov. 1, 1961, reprinted in Forman, *The Making*, p. 233.

Fourteen
ALMOST CHRISTMAS IN ALBANY

524 full of zeal and empty: Morris, *Origins*, p. 240; int. Charles Sherrod, July 10, 1985, and Jan. 23, 1986.

524 King had seven sons: Int. C. B. King, July 10, 1985.

525 something about him: Charles Sherrod interview by Joe Phister, made available by Sherrod.

525 let Sherrod use a room: Int. H. C. Boyd, July 11, 1985.

526 Tom Chatmon: Int. C. B. King, July 10, 1985.

526 might be Communists: C. B. King, A/OH.

526 "urgent and distressing call": Monthly Report of Vernon E. Jordan, Nov. 10, 1961, File III-A-258, NAACP.

527 "demonstrations were expected": Minutes of Special Meeting of Albany City Commission, Oct. 30, 1961, 4:00 P.M., CRA.

527 seven hundred volunteers: NYT, Nov. 2, 1961, p. 28.

527 plan for Albany: Zinn, *Albany*, p. 10; Carson, *In Struggle*, p. 58; Lewis, *King*, p. 144.

528 giant free barbecue: Guy Touchtone deposition, Jan. 18, 1963, *Georgia* v. *Ware*, indictments #933-35. Touchtone was the Ichuaway overseer.

528 account of the FBI agent: Int. Marion Cheek, July 11, 1985; statement of Charlie Ware, July 23, 1961, C. B. King files.

529 dripping from his ears: Defense motion filed Nov. 10, 1961, in *Georgia* v. *Ware*.

529 Slater King's home: Goldie Jackson and E. D. Hamilton, both A/OH.

529 rivalry and suspicion: Slater King, "Battleground of Albany," *Freedomways* (First Quarter, 1964), p. 95.

530 "vicarious experience": Albany Movement founding document of Nov. 17, 1961, CRA; Morris, *Origins*, pp. 240–41.

530 on November 22: Zinn, *Albany*, pp. 11ff; Forman, *The Making*, pp. 247ff; Carson, *In Struggle*, pp. 56ff.

530 "go clean-sided": Int. McCree Harris, Jan. 24, 1986.

531 "blackest white man": Int. A. C. Searles, July 11, 1985.

532 the songleader role: Int. Rutha Harris, Jan. 23, 1986, A. C. Searles, July 1, 1985, and Charles Jones, Nov. 23, 1986; Watters, *Down to Now*, pp. 158–59; Morris, *Origins*, p. 241.

532 "hard, grown men": Sherrod report to SNCC headquarters, cited in Forman, *The Making*, p. 247.

533 inviting a spark: Int. Charles Sherrod, Jan. 23, 1986.

533 new executive secretary: Forman sketch drawn from Forman, *The Making*, passim.

534 Lee took Forman's idea: Int. Bernard Lee, June 19, 1985.

534 pulled into Albany's: Arrival at station and subsequent arrests from Zinn, *Albany*, pp. 12ff; Watters, *Down to Now*, pp. 157ff; Lewis, *King*, pp. 145–46; Forman, *The Making*, p35 252–53; int. Charles Sherrod, Jan. 23, 1986, Rutha Harris, Jan. 23, 1986, McCree Harris, Jan. 24, 1986, and A. C. Searles, July 1, 1985; NYT, Dec. 11, 1961, p. 40; AC, Dec. 11, 1961, p. 30.

535 jailing Marion King: Watters, *Down to Now*, p. 159; Forman, *The Making*, p. 253.

535 "ace group" to "monkey eat pepper": Int. Charles Sherrod, Jan. 23, 1986, and McCree Harris, Jan. 24, 1986.

536 December rain: March to city hall and mass arrest from Zinn, *Albany*, p. 14; Forman, *The Making*, p. 253; NYT, Dec. 13, 1961, p. 51; AC, Dec. 13, 1961, p. 1; int. Charles Sherrod, Jan. 23, 1986, and McCree Harris, Jan. 24, 1986.

536 Pritchett argued: Int. Asa Kelley, Jan. 22, 1986.
537 "other nigger organization": NYT, Dec. 14, 1961, p. 47.
537 Lee told Walker: Int. Bernard Lee, June 19, 1985.
538 auctioneers were selling: Clark, *Echo*, p. 224; SAC Memphis to FBI Director, Oct. 17, 1961, FBI file #61-7511, serial 276.
538 protest telegrams: King to RFK, Nov. 1, 1961, A/SC 35f1.
538 airport and rostrum: Log, BUK6f151.
538 "Testimonial Service": Speech list, A/KP9f6; testimonial program, A/SC58f14.
538 hospital for tests: NYT, Dec. 2, 1961, p. 25; *Jet*, Dec. 14, 1961, p. 17.
538 spent more than $27,000: Levison and O'Dell budget memo, Aug. 31, 1961, A/SC57f11.
538 Theodore Kheel: Int. Harry Wachtel, Oct. 27, 1983; King to Wachtel, Nov. 7, 1961, BUK7f55.
539 write King's speech: Garrow, *FBI*, p. 26.
539 "Negroes are almost entirely": King AFL-CIO address, Dec. 11, 1961, A/KS2.
539 came to their feet: Oates, *Trumpet*, pp. 185–88.
539 Eichmann's conviction: NYT, Dec. 11, 1961, p. 1.
539 Lithuli's acceptance: Ibid., pp. 1, 12.
539 landed in South Vietnam: NYT, Dec. 12, 1961, p. 21.
540 immediately called Ralph: Int. McCree Harris, Jan. 24, 1986.
540 Late Wednesday night: Forman, *The Making*, p. 255; Morris, *Origins*, pp. 242–43; Lewis, *King*, p. 147; AC, Dec. 15, 1961, p. 10; int. Bernard Lee, June 19, 1985, A. C. Searles, July 11, 1985, C. B. King, July 10, 1985, and Emmanuel "Bo" Jackson, July 10, 1985.
541 asked Vandiver: Int. Asa Kelley, Jan. 22, 1986.
542 "We pray, oh Lord" to "I like pecans": Watters, *Down to Now*, pp. 163–65; also Albany documentary "Freedom in the Air," Tape #BBO270, Sept. 10, 1962, PRA. On the Sherrod beating, FBI agent Marion Cheek recalls that Sheriff Mathews admitted pushing Sherrod around and said he had told the Negro prisoners, "I want it so quiet in this jail that you can hear a flea peeing in a wad of cotton" (int. Cheek, July 11, 1985).
543 "keeps the faith": AC, Dec. 15, 1961, p. 1.
543 Slater King had refused: NYT, Dec. 16, 1961, p. 18.
544 amended it by letter: Solomon Walker to Kelley, Dec. 15, 1961, CRA.
544 dismissed her Latin: Int. McCree Harris, Jan. 24, 1986.
544 The ensuing clash: Watters, *Down to Now*, pp. 11–15; also int. Rutha Harris, Jan. 23, 1986, Charles Jones, Nov. 23, 1986, and other Albany interviews.
545 He told the crowd: NYT, Dec. 16, 1961, p. 18; Lewis, *King*, p. 148.
546 "put you in a dungeon": Watters, *Down to Now*, p. 14.
546 departure from the schedule: Ibid., p. 15; int. C. B. King, July 10, 1985, and McCree Harris, Jan. 24, 1986.
547 "Be here at seven": AJ, Dec. 16, 1961, p. 20; Albany draft restraining order, Dec. 15, 1961 (probably misdated from the 16th), CRA; Oates, *Trumpet*, p. 190.
547 "waited the night": AJ, Dec. 16, 1961, p. 20.
547 Kelley addressed a terse: Kelley to Page, Dec. 16, 1961, CRA.
547 "found no common ground": AJ, Dec. 17, 1961, p. 10.
547 "That is not enough": Ibid.
547 for supporting J. H. Jackson: Int. Rev. H. C. Boyd, July 11, 1985.
548 4:16 P.M.: NYT, Dec. 17, 1961, pp. 1, 46.
548 "God bless you": Lewis, *King*, p. 148.
548 opposing lines converged: NYT, Dec. 17, 1961, p. 1; AJ, Dec. 17, 1961, p. 1; *Newsweek*, Dec. 25, 1961, pp. 17–18; int. McCree Harris, Jan. 24, 1986.
549 dose of surrealism: AJ, Dec. 17, 1961, p. 10.
550 Buick Roadmaster: *Jet*, Dec. 28, 1961, p. 6.
550 "fires would never cease": Raines, *My Soul*, p. 404.
550 "You are Jesus": Int. Bernard Lee, June 19, 1985; also Rev. Wyatt Tee Walker, CRDPOH, p. 33.
551 Abernathy's extraordinary snoring: Ibid.
551 "expect to spend Christmas": AJ, Dec. 18, 1961, p. 10.
551 "long as necessary": *Jet*, Dec. 28, 1961, p. 6.
551 haunted by the memory: Int. Bernard Lee, June 19, 1985.

552 "Andy's not going": Int. Rev. Wyatt Tee Walker, Aug. 20, 1984.

552 manner had alienated: Int. C. B. King, July 10, 1985, and Bo Jackson, July 10, 1985.

553 drafted mostly by Ella Baker: Record of a telephone conversation between NAACP officials Ruby Hurley, Vernon Jordan, and Closter B. Current, Dec. 18, 1961, File III-A-258, NAACP.

553 "unfortunate misrepresentation": NYT, Dec. 18, 1961, p. 1; AJ, Dec. 18, 1961, p. 1.

553 James Gray: Int. Gray, Jan. 24, 1986.

554 "smacks more of Lenin": NYT, Dec. 18, 1961, p. 31.

554 "not tantrum": AJ, Dec. 18, 1961, p. 10.

555 "hands off": AJ, Dec. 19, 1961, p. 7.

555 "Second Emancipation Proclamation": King et al. to JFK, Dec. 18, 1961, Box 1478, Name File, JFK.

555 "Negro Groups Split": NYT, Dec. 18, 1961, p. 1.

555 gifts of food: Int. McCree Harris, Jan. 24, 1986.

555 Pritchett shuttled: AJ, Dec. 18, 1961, pp. 1, 10.

555 ten thirty that morning: Document headed "10:30 A.M., December 18, 1961," CRA.

555 unsigned note: CRA.

556 "I would not want": NYT, Dec. 19, 1961, pp. 1, 24.

556 "it wasn't necessary": AJ, Dec. 19, 1961, pp. 1, 7, 10, 11.

556 "for the accurate coverage": Ibid.

557 "loss of face": New York *Herald Tribune*, Dec. 19, 1961, p. 1.

557 internal communications: (NAACP Georgia field secretary) Vernon Jordan monthly report, Oct. 13, 1961, File III-A-253, and monthly report, Nov. 10, 1961, File III-A-258, NAACP; telephone conversation between Vernon Jordan and Gloster B. Current, Dec. 14, 1961, File III-H-215, NAACP; two telephone conversations between Ruby Hurley, Vernon Jordan, and Gloster Current, Dec. 18, 1961, File III-H-215, NAACP; Current to Hurley, Dec. 20, 1961, File III-H-213, NAACP.

557 "became involved with some hoodlums": Medgar Evers to Roy Wilkins, Gloster B. Current, and Ruby Hurley, Oct. 12, 1961, "Operation of Other Civil Rights Organizations in the State of Mississippi," File III-A-253, NAACP.

557 "Rivalries Beset": NYT, Dec. 24, 1961, p. E5.

557 "Confused Crusade": *Time*, Jan. 12, 1962, p. 15.

558 "damned if he does": Levison to *Time*, Jan. 11, 1962, A/SC36f21.

558 also intimated: Lewis, *King*, pp. 151–54.

558 "flint-faced": Morris, *Origins*, pp. 245–46.

558 "brainwashed" Belafonte: Rev. Wyatt Tee Walker, CRDPOH.

558 took the dispute privately: Int. Harry Belafonte, March 6–7, 1985.

558 Lee identified too closely: Int. C. B. King, July 10, 1985.

558 King called James: Int. James Bevel, May 16, 1985.

559 marriage to Diane Nash: *Jet*, Jan. 11, 1962, p. 23; Chicago *Tribune*, April 17, 1965.

559 runner-up in Chicago's: *Jet*, June 29, 1961, p. 49.

559 $1,000 appeal bond: U.S. Attorney's report, March 21, 1962, A/SN17.

559 Jerome Smith: *Jet*, Dec. 14, 1961, pp. 4ff.

559 checked back into Parchman: *Jet*, Sept. 21, 1961, p. 8.

559 attracted forty FBI: *Time*, Dec. 8, 1961, p. 25; *Newsweek*, Dec. 11, 1961, pp. 30–31; *Jet*, Dec. 21, 1961, p. 6

559 outraged editorial: NYT, Dec. 7, 1961, p. 42.

559 mob had mistaken: Int. Claude Sitton, Dec. 14, 1983.

559 Sidney Mize: NYT, Dec. 23, 1961, p. 26.

560 survived a shotgun: SNCC booklet, *Mississippi: A Chronicle of Violence*, p. 6, A/SN16f15.

560 pointless to continue: Int. Robert Moses, July 30, 1984.

560 "We can't lose": *Jet*, Jan. 25, 1962, pp. 18ff.

560 "got our feet wet": Moses tape of 1962, published in *Liberation*, January 1970, p. 14.

561 Walker nominated: Walker to Arthur M. Carter, Dec. 26, 1961, A/SC33f4.

561 "meanest man": *Jet*, Jan. 4, 1962, p. 46.

561 pelted with tomatoes: Int. A. C. Searles, July 11, 1985.

561 to know whether King: Maxwell to King, Dec. 14, 1961, A/KP15f26.
561 "level of littleness": King to Maxwell, Dec. 20, 1961, A/KP15f26.

Fifteen
HOOVER'S TRIANGLE AND KING'S MACHINE

562 "four beautiful sunsets": Manchester, *Glory*, p. 1140.
562 Royal College: *Nation*, March 31, 1962, pp. 277ff.
562 Ford publicly dropped: NYT, April 11, 1962, p. 1.
562 Spellman announced: NYT, March 29, 1962, p. 24.
562 borrowed Leonardo's: NYT, Dec. 5, 1962, p. 5.
563 "to have everything": NYT, Jan. 20, 1962, p. 14.
563 "my mind is settled": Du Bois to Hall, Oct. 1, 1961, A/KP8f36; also *Jet*, Dec. 7, 1961, p. 5.
563 "some other ideology": King to Edward D. Ball, Dec. 14, 1961, A/KP17f1.
563 Kennedy wanted to shift: RFKOH, pp. 191ff, 634ff.
563 fifteen hundred FBI informants: Jack Levine, "Hoover and the Red Scare," *Nation*, Oct. 20, 1962, pp. 232ff.
564 "couldn't be more feeble": Schlesinger Jr., *Robert Kennedy*, p. 281.
564 "Trojan Horse": NYT, July 3, 1962, p. 27; Navasky, *Justice*, p. 37.
564 "threat from without": Navasky, *Justice*, p. 37.
564 January 8 classified memo: Paraphrased in Bland to Sullivan, Feb. 3, 1962, FL-135.
564 "White's feeling": Evans to Belmont, Feb. 2, 1962, FL-134.
565 came from two brothers: Garrow, *FBI*, pp. 34–44.
565 "King is no good": Notation on Bland to Sullivan, Feb. 3, 1962, FL-135.
565 "White said from the character": Evans to Belmont, Feb. 6, 1962, FL-136.
566 On February 14: Hoover to Attorney General, Feb. 14, 1962, and Hoover to O'Donnell, Feb. 14, 1962, both FL-NR.
566 Kennedy circled the globe: NYT, Feb. 2, 1962, p. 1; Schlesinger Jr., *Robert Kennedy*, pp. 607ff.
566 Indonesians in particular: NYT, Feb. 18, 1962, p. 31.
566 "There wasn't one area": NYT, April 24, 1962, pp. 1, 20.
566 Hoover's memo: U.S. Senate (Church Committee), Report No. 94-465, *Alleged Assassination Plots*, pp. 129–30; Summers, *Goddess*, pp. 256–57; Collier and Horowitz, *Kennedys*, pp. 292–93.
568 search their files thoroughly: Garrow, *FBI*, p. 46.
568 moved swiftly on bugs: Hoover authorized the Levison bugs on March 2, 1962, four days before asking Kennedy to authorize the wiretap. Bland to Sullivan, March 6, 1962, FL-140. Also Hoover to SAC New York, March 6, 1962, FL-NR.
568 no kind way to describe: U.S. Senate (Church Committee), Report No. 94-755, Book III, Vol. 3, pp. 112–15; U.S. House, *Assassinations Report*, p. 573; Schlesinger Jr., *Robert Kennedy*, pp. 293–99.
568 Brownell effectively advised: Brownell to FBI Director, May 20, 1954, reprinted in Macy and Kaplan, *Documents*, pp. 41–43.
568 broke into Levison's office: SAC New York to Director, airtel, March 16, 1962, FL-146.
568 Technicians hooked up: SAC New York to Director, airtel, March 20, 1962, FL-147.
568 Hoover's private luncheon: U.S. Senate (Church Committee), Report No. 94-465, *Alleged Assassination Plots*, p. 130.
569 Inga Arvad: Blair and Blair, *Search*, pp. 138–71.
569 "it was the boy": Int. Cartha D. DeLoach, June 1 and 11, 1984.
569 Hoover warned America: Manchester, *Glory*, p. 293.
569 "the biggest bore": Summers, *Goddess*, pp. 257–58.
569 last known phone conversation: U.S. Senate (Church Committee), Report No. 94-465, *Alleged Assassination Plots*, p. 130.
569 not to stay with Frank: Collier and Horowitz, *Kennedys*, pp. 295, 338; Schlesinger Jr., *Robert Kennedy*, pp. 532–34.
570 declined to review: NYT, Jan. 9, 1962, p. 20; Kunstler, *Deep*, pp. 80–84.

570　"My Calhouns": Police surveillance notes, mass meeting of Jan. 8, 1962, BIR/BC12f17.

570　Marshall responded: Marshall memo to RFK, Jan. 22, 1962, Box 16, Marshall Papers, JFK; Marshall to King, Jan. 22, 1962, A/KP24f18.

570　Grooms pronounced sentence: NYT, Jan. 17, 1962, p. 62.

570　dynamite bombs: NYT, Jan. 17, 1962, p. 15.

571　"Negroes did it": NYT, Feb. 1, 1962, p. 17.

571　new police dogs: *Nation*, May 5, 1962, p. 399.

571　"hundreds of segregationists": King telegram, Jan. 25, 1962, quoted in *Jet*, Feb. 8, 1962, p. 46.

571　joint telegram to Kennedy: Press release, Jan. 26, 1962, A/KP22f30.

571　High fees: Int. Rev. Edward Gardner, Jan. 21, 1986.

571　"None of us ever dreamed": King to "Doctor," Feb. 6, 1962, A/KP1f6.

571　"we at Mount Olive": Maxwell to King, Feb. 12, 1962, A/KP1f6.

571　"Maintenance of law": Marshall to King, Feb, 1, 1962, A/KP24f18.

571　similar reply: King to Marshall, Feb. 19, 1962, A/KP24f18.

572　Marshall said he was reviewing: *Jet*, March 1, 1962, pp. 3f.

572　"While the President": *Nation*, March 3, 1962, p. 190.

572　"I wish I could tell you": Police surveillance notes, King speech, Feb. 12, 1962, BIR/BC12f17.

572　"Whites can't stop": *Jet*, March 22, 1962, pp. 24f; SCLC release, March 1, 1962, ASC125f5.

573　"the three K's": Police surveillance notes, Walker speech, March 5, 1962, BIR/BC12f17.

573　"Bull and Old Art's": Phifer speech, March 28, 1962, ibid.

573　"sit here and take it": "Boycott in Birmingham," *Nation*, May 5, 1962, pp. 397–401.

573　O'Dell soon became: O'Dell background from O'Dell interviews, March 6, 1986, and July 1, 1986; also O'Dell to King, Jan. 29, 1963, AKP18f38. Earliest King-O'Dell correspondence includes O'Dell to King, Aug. 27, 1959, King to O'Dell, Sept. 4, 1959, and O'Dell to King, Jan. 18, 1960, all BUK7.

574　raised $80,000: Levison and O'Dell to King, Aug. 31, 1961, A/SC57f11.

575　"Now I am forced": Young to King, March 24, 1961, BUK7f56.

575　King had asked Levison: King to Levison, King to Young, and King to Myles Horton, all April 25, 1961, cited in Garrow, *FBI*, pp. 28, 237.

575　Taylor gave King: Int. Rev. Gardner Taylor, Oct. 25, 1983.

575　Young cousins: Gardner, *Young*, p. 11.

575　"one of my objectives": Young to Robert Spike, April 25, 1961, Young correspondence folder, SHSW/HP.

575　Months of adjustment: Several dozen documents record the transfer of the citizenship schools from Highlander to the SCLC under the tax sponsorship of the National Council of Churches. Aside from the Horton letters in the Young correspondence folder, SHSW/HP, there are numerous letters and proposals by Myles Horton on the subject, beginning in December 1960, SHSW/HP.

576　"get more chicken": Young to Walker, Aug. 8, 1961, BUK7f56. A similar letter ("The hour cometh . . .") is Young to King and Walker, Sept. 11, 1962, BUK7f56.

576　At Dorchester: Herman H. Long to Horton, May 25, 1961, SHSW/HP. Long was director of the Race Relations Department, American Missionary Association.

576　used the practical: Dorothy Cotton, HOH; int. Cotton, July 6, 1983.

576　before she had even met him: Horton to Young, Sept. 14, 1961, SHSW/HP.

577　"saints in hell": Int. Septima Clark, Dec. 17, 1983; also generally Clark interview, HOH; int. Bernard Lee, Oct. 25, 1984.

577　On February 2: Program, A/KP24f18.

577　three days whirling: Aaron Henry to Walker, Feb. 10, 1962, ASC35f5; King statement, "Nonviolence on Tour," March 17, 1962, AKS2; King column, "Pathos and Hope," for NYAN, March 3, 1962; Hosea Williams to O'Dell, Feb. 8, 1962, and O'Dell to Williams, Feb. 18, 1962, A/KP35f15; O'Dell to Harry Blake, Feb. 22, 1962, A/SC135f7; *Jet*, Feb. 22, 1962, p. 4, and March 8, 1962, pp. 14–16.

578 "open for business": Branton notification letter, Feb. 22, 1962, A/KP22f33.

578 hit the ground running: Minutes of SCLC board meetings, May 15, 1962, A/KP29f1; King and Walker to Branton, May 6, 1962, A/SC36f23.

578 "Dr. King Uniting": *Jet*, March 8, 1962, pp. 14–16.

578 hosted by Harry: Int. Harry Belafonte, March 6–7, 1985; int. Robert Moses, July 30, 1984; int. Timothy Jenkins, March 11, 1986; int. Charles Sherrod, Jan. 23, 1986. The specific date of the 1962 fund-raiser is uncertain. I have placed it with Sherrod's known trip North in March, as Sherrod remembers no other trip that year.

578 "If it looks like it": Int. Timothy Jenkins, March 11, 1986.

579 "pull it, doctor!": Wyatt Walker, "Fifty-three Hours with Martin Luther King," A/SC37f10.

579 discouraged publicity: Dunbar to King, March 27, 1962, A/KP22f33.

579 Urban League refused: Young to Dunbar, Jan. 12, 1962, A/KP22f33.

579 King urged that Roy: King to Dunbar, Jan. 19, 1962, A/KP22f32.

579 fantastic, cried Levison: Handwritten notes from Levison misur (bug), March 26, 1962, FL-NY-5-1-NR.

579 grown to 95: King statement, April 5, 1962, A/KS2.

580 Supreme Court: NYT, Feb. 20, 1962, p. 13.

580 "centered on lawyers": Administrative committee minutes, March 9, 1962, A/SC36f11.

580 Lowery disclosed: Ibid.

580 driving the SCLC's leadership: Int. Wyatt Walker, Aug. 20, 1984.

581 King found himself alone: Int. Clarence Jones, Nov. 25, 1983; King to Wachtel, Nov. 7. 1961, BUK7f55.

581 Meshulam Riklis: Int. Harry Wachtel, Oct. 27, 1983; *Forbes*, Nov. 15, 1976, pp. 29ff; *Newsweek*, Nov. 7, 1977, pp. 81ff.

581 "not on the side of the angels": Int. Harry Wachtel, Oct. 25, 1983; also King to Wachtel, Feb. 12, 1962, A/KP25f24.

582 Levison actively encouraged: Jones-Levison conversation, April 6, 1962, FL-NY-5-1-NR.

582 "Who is he?": Handwritten note on New York SAC to Headquarters, April 11, 1962, FK-NR.

582 scrambling to investigate: Bland to Sullivan, April 13, 1962, FL-NR.

583 Levison's conversations: Handwritten early misur notes in FL-NY Subfile 5, passim, especially for March 26, March 30, and April 11, 1962.

583 too corporate in tone: FBI summary of Levison-Jones conversation, March 26, 1962, FL-NY-5-1-NR.

583 On March 30: Misur notes, March 30, 1962, FL-5-NR; Baumgardner to Sullivan, March 30, 1962, FL-148.

584 "he were purple": Misur notes, March 30, 1962, FL-5-NR.

584 choice of Byron: NYT, March 31, 1962, p. 1.

584 reminded the Attorney: Hoover to RFK, April 2, 1962, FL-NR.

585 "dear Mr. Vice": Hoover to LBJ, April 13, 1962, FK-41 and FL-NR.

585 "dear Mr. O'Donnell": Hoover to O'Donnell, April 20, 1962, FL-NR.

585 dismal response: RFK to King, May 10, 1962, A/KP11f13; other letters, A/KP11f11-12.

585 subpoenaed Stanley Levison: SAC New York to Director, April 26, 1962, FL-152; Garrow, *FBI*, p. 47.

586 "not now and never have been": Ibid., p. 48.

586 "worse than Jimmy Hoffa": Misur log, May 1, 1962, FL-NY-5-NR.

586 Wofford was on his way: Wofford, *Of Kennedys*, pp. 164–67; int. Harris Wofford, June 26, 1984.

587 mentally retarded: Lee White, JFKOH.

587 "a frontier of my own": Wofford, *Of Kennedys*, p. 167.

587 "continue to make history": NYT, May 13, 1962, p. 46.

587 duties to Lee White: Ibid. Also int. White, Dec. 13, 1983; Burke Marshall, RFKOII, p. 29.

588 O'Dell predicted: Int. Jack O'Dell, July 1, 1986.

588 "you ought to pay him better": SCLC board minutes, May 15, 1962, A/KP29f1.

589 "Non-violence is now woven": King speech, May 17, 1962, A/KS3.

589 Second Emancipation Proclamation: "An Appeal to the Honorable John F. Kennedy, President of the United States," May 17, 1962, A/SC27f6.

589 Bound in fine leather: Kunstler, *Deep*, pp. 90–91.

590 reserve the Lincoln Memorial: King to Stewart Udall, Feb. 22, 1962, A/KP24f17.

590 "deserted Christ and the church": King to Fey, June 23, 1962, A/KP6f6.

590 contributors would be labor unions: Discussion between Clarence Jones and Stanley Levison about labor contributions to the Gandhi Society, which took place on the day after the founding luncheon. Handwritten misur notes of May 18, 1962, FL-NY-5-NR.

590 forty-fifth birthday: Summers, *Goddess*, pp. 270f.

590 Archbishop Makarios: Invitation to White House luncheon on June 5, 1962, and King's response by Dora McDonald, A/KP14f4 and A/KP26f6; NYT, June 6, 1962, p. 1.

591 crash near Paris: AC, June 3, 1962, p. 1 (Special Extra Edition), and June 4, 1962, p. 1.

591 "Demand and get": ADW, June 5, 1962, pp. 1, 2; NYT, June 5, 1962, p. 29.

591 Smith promptly died: ADW, June 6, 1962, p. 1.

591 second family in Virginia: *Time*, Aug. 3, 1962, p. 14; AH, July 27, 1962, p. 1.

592 keys to the city: ADW, June 8, 1962, p. 1.

592 privately asked the new mayor: King to Allen, May 31, 1962, A/KP2f9.

592 city hall drinking fountains: Allen, *Mayor*, p. 84.

592 Ponce de Leon ball park: Ibid., p. 85.

592 FBI office anticipated: Rosen to Belmont, June 6, 1962, FSC-115.

592 "arranged that the police": Marshall to RFK, June 1, 1962, Marshall Papers, Box 16, JFK.

593 "more propitious moment": ADW, June 7, 1962, p. 1.

593 Walker did call Burke Marshall: Marshall to RFK, June 11, 1962, Marshall Papers, Box 16, JFK; Walker affidavit, June 11, 1962, A/SC36f7; Marshall to Walker, June 27, 1962, A/SC36f7.

594 representatives of Billy Graham: int. Rev. Wyatt Tee Walker, Dec. 21, 1984; also int. Chauncey Eskridge, Feb. 22, 1985.

595 kill King within five years: Ibid. Also Eskridge to King, June 13, 1962, A/SC9f31.

595 King fell into conversation: Misur record, June 11, 1962, FL Sub. 5-1; report marked "Secret," June 12, 1962, FK-73.

596 "embarrassment to the Bureau": Director to SAC New York, June 12, 1962, FL-NR.

596 "more advanced than Martin": Misur record, March 26, 1962, FL-NY-5-NR.

597 "no matter what a man was": Garrow, *FBI*, pp. 49–50; SAC New York to Hoover, June 21, 1962, FK-80.

597 " 'lay off this guy' ": Hoover to RFK, June 25, 1962, FK-79.

598 "Hard-Working Convention": *Crisis*, August–September 1962, passim; ADW, July 3–7, 1962.

598 "True peace": King address, July 5, 1962, A/KS3.

600 "the Hitlerian tactic": AH, June 28, 1962, p. 1.

600 "I have not cried": McDonald to King, July 10, 1962, A/KP15f9.

Sixteen
THE FIREMAN'S LAST REPRIEVE

601 "rivaling in significance": NYT, July 11, 1962, p. 1. Also AH, July 12, 1962, p. 1.

602 "letter from prison": McDonald to King, A/KP75f9.

602 "now or never effort": AJ, July 12, 1962, p. 1; AH, July 11, 1962, p. 1; NYT, July 12, 1962, p. 18.

602 "We feel much akin": Watters, *Down to Now*, p. 208.

603 Salinger announced: NYT, July 12, 1962, p. 1.

603 pond in the Pocono: Int. Burke Marshall, Sept. 26, 1984.

603 "Jack, we've got Martin": Int. James Gray, Jan. 24, 1986.

604 Gardner brought a message: Int. B. C. Gardner, July 11, 1985.

604 mass meeting at Shiloh: NYT, July 13, 1962, p. 10; AJ, July 12, 1962, pp. 1, 16.

604 asked his most trusted officer: Int. Laurie Pritchett, Nov. 25, 1986.

604 "Bo, I'm coming in": Int. Ed Haggerty (Albany FBI agent), July 11, 1985.

604 "Let's give him a hand!": Watters, *Down to Now*, pp. 204–8.

605 "we've been brainwashed": Ibid.

606 summoned his desk sergeant: Int. Laurie Pritchett, Nov. 25, 1986.

606 "Turn him out": Int. B. C. Gardner, July 11, 1985, and James Gray, Jan. 24, 1986.

606 "well-dressed Negro male": NYT, July 13, 1962, p. 10.

606 Kelley held tenaciously: Int. Asa Kelley, Jan. 22, 1986.

607 Robert Kennedy told reporters: AJ, July 12, 1962, p. 1.

607 "Not Back Down": AH, July 14, 1962, p. 1.

607 "collaborating and conspiring": AH, July 15, 1962, p. 1; NYT, July 15, 1962, p. 28.

607 bureaucratic spats: Katzenbach to Kelley, July 14, 1962, CRA. Also SAC Atlanta to Director, July 15, 1962, FA-423; Hoover to RFK, July 16, 1962, FA-439; McGowan to Rosen, July 17, 1962, FA-459; Evans to Belmont, July 17, 1962, FA-[illegible]. Press secretary Guthman asked the FBI how many agents it had in Albany, and Hoover instructed his agents not to tell the Justice Department. (Apparently, Hoover did not want Robert Kennedy to be able to second-guess his allocation of manpower.) Also, when Katzenbach himself called an FBI SAC to inquire about the state of racial disturbance in Albany, FBI headquarters shuddered over its exclusion from the information loop. Courtney Evans wrote that he "tactfully" advised Katzenbach "that only at Bureau headquarters is information from all field divisions centralized and, accordingly, the only complete check that can be made is here in Washington."

607 "woefully inadequate": NYT, July 16, 1962, p. 47.

607 "Georgia Whodunit": *Newsweek*, July 23, 1962, p. 18.

607 "Mayor Stays Mum": AH, July 12, 1962, p. 1.

607 "Who Got King Out?": AH, July 13, 1962, p. 1.

608 "cost Negroes jobs": AH, July 18, 1962, p. 1.

608 "Albany Manifesto": Dated July 15, 1962, handed to Chief Pritchett "about 1:30 pm, 7/16/62," CRA.

608 National Press Club: *Jet*, Aug. 2, 1962, pp. 6–7; NYT, July 20, 1962, pp. 8, 23; *Congressional Record*, July 20, 1962, p. S14247.

608 "Now I assume": Watters, *Down to Now*, pp. 196–202.

609 escaped through a window: Int. C. B. King, July 10, 1985.

610 King drove to the courthouse: Ibid. Also McGowan to Rosen, July 22, 1962, FA-450.

610 debated all afternoon: King, JFKOH; Levison conversation of Aug. 3, 1962, FL-NY-5-NR; int. Burke Marshall, Sept. 26, 1984; int. Charles Sherrod, Jan. 23, 1986; int. Clarence Jones, May 18, 1986; int. C. B. King, July 10, 1985; int. Laurie Pritchett, Nov. 25, 1986. (Pritchett said he had the conversation wiretapped, and that he was amazed to hear King speak heatedly to the Attorney General as an equal.)

611 walk in the night air: Kunstler, *Deep*, p. 102.

612 Wells felt out of place: Int. S. B. Wells, July 9, 1985.

612 "blood of Emmett Till": Lewis, *King*, p. 161; NYT, July 22, 1962, p. 1; AH, July 22, 1962, p. 1.

612 "get up, goddamn it": Int. Claude Sitton, Dec. 14, 1983.

613 including King: FBI affidavit taken from King on July 24, 1962, acknowledging that "any statement I make may be used in a court of law against me," FA-504.

613 specifically for the Attorney General: Hoover's written note on Rosen to Belmont, July 23, 1962, FA-479; Rosen to Belmont (later on), July 23, 1962, FA-477.

613 "The Negroes finally": Burke, "Monday Report," July 24, 1962, Box 16, Marshall Papers, JFK.

613 "We are glad": NYT, July 23, 1962, p. 20.

613 "unjust and unconstitutional": NYT, July 23, 1962, p. 1; AH, July 23, 1962, p. 1.

613 private gripe session: Forman, *The Making*, pp. 274–75; Lewis, *King*, p. 163; Kunstler, *Deep*, p. 106; int. Charles Jones, Nov. 23, 1986; int. Charles Sherrod, Jan. 23, 1986; int. C. B. King, July 10, 1985; int. Timothy Jenkins, March 11 and April 23, 1986; int. Clarence Jones, Aug. 18, 1986; int. Marion King Smith, July 31, 1986.

615 his fourth child: Int. Clarence Jones, Aug. 18, 1986.

616 "I mean you!": Int. Marion King Smith, July 31, 1986.

616 "trying to do his job": Int. Marion Cheek, July 11, 1985.

616 pro forma responses: Although Agent Cheek recalls a mixture of anger and cooperation on the part of those at Slater King's home on the night of Marion King's beating, the reports out of FBI headquarters emphasized the surliness of the Negroes while glossing over the alleged damage to Mrs. King. This is another illustration of the way FBI information was shaped by sensitivities at headquarters, which in turn affected the Justice Department. See Director Hoover to the Attorney General, "Racial Situation, Albany, Georgia . . . ," July 24, 1962, FA-515.

616 "the internal administration": Marshall to King, two telegrams dated July 26, 1962, both in A/KP24f19 and Marshall Papers, Box 16, JFK.

616 "Rules with Negro": AH, July 24, 1962, p. 1.

616 "Albany Will Stand": AH, July 25, 1962, p. 1.

617 "We . . . beg you": King and Anderson to Kelley, July 24, 1962, 1:46 P.M., CRA.

617 only Abernathy even mentioned: Int. C. B. King, July 10, 1985; int. Charles Jones, Nov. 23, 1986; Rosen to Belmont, "Racial Situation, Albany Georgia . . . ," July 24, 1962, FA-494.

617 a near riot: NYT, July 25, 1962, p. 1, and July 26, 1962, p. 1; AH, July 25, 1962, p. 1; AJ, July 25, 1962, p. 1; Time, Aug. 3, 1962, pp. 12–13; Newsweek, Aug. 3, 1962, p. 19; Watters, Down to Now, pp. 210–12.

619 peacemaker's tour: Watters, Down to Now, pp. 213–15; int. Charles Jones, Nov. 23, 1986.

619 remarkable news dispatch: NYT, July 27, 1962, p. 1. Also described by Pat Watters in Down to Now, pp. 164–68.

620 descended on Terrell County: Int. John Doar, May 12, 1986; Doar, "Monday Report" to RFK, Aug. 7, 1962, and Marshall to RFK, Aug. 29, 1962, Marshall Papers, Box 16, JFK.

620 "by gracefully retiring": ADW, July 26, 1962, p. 4.

620 "when the world's on fire": NYT, July 28, 1962, p. 44; Lewis, King, p. 164.

621 "immediate steps to assure": Rockefeller to RFK, July 27, 1962, RAC; NYT, July 28, 1962, p. 44.

621 discussion with Spivak: King handwritten jail diary, BUK16f9; excerpts of jail diary published in Jet, Aug. 23, 1962, pp. 14–21; int. Rev. Wyatt Tee Walker, Aug. 20, 1984.

622 "C.B., who did this?": NYT, July 29, 1962, p. 1; AJ, July 29, 1962, p. 1.

622 Campbell was old-school: AH, Sept. 15, 1962, p. 10. Former police chief Pritchett recalled that as a young police officer Campbell had been convicted of murder in a nearby county, and that he had worked his way into the sheriff's office from jail (int. Laurie Pritchett, Nov. 25, 1986).

622 "Yeah, I hit him": Int. Marion Cheek, July 11, 1985.

623 Spivak bore in: "Meet the Press" transcript for July 29, 1962; a copy is in King's files, A/KP1f26.

623 Martha's Vineyard, where King: King log, BUK6f151; Jet, Aug. 16, 1962, p. 16.

623 President ran aground: NYT, July 30, 1962, p. 12.

624 "called at a propitious moment": Int. Rev. Wyatt Tee Walker, Aug. 20, 1984.

624 "find it wholly inexplicable": NYT, Aug. 2, 1962, pp. 1, 8.

624 "We earnestly desire": Anderson and Slater King to Kelley, Aug. 2, 1962, 3:41 P.M., CRA.

624 "violent, calculated campaign": AH, Aug. 3, 1962, p. 1; NYT, Aug. 4, 1962, p. 11.

625 "Negro-wooing Government": AH, Aug. 10, 1962, p. 1.

625 "not Roy's style": Int. Burke Marshall, Sept. 26, 1984.

625 "if our hands weren't tied": Kunstler, Deep, pp. 118–19; Doar to RFK, Aug. 7, 1962, Marshall Papers, Box 16, JFK.

625 "Martin King kill himself": Levison intercept, Aug. 3, 1962, 5:03 P.M., FL-NY-5-NR.

625 "let alone 20 million Negroes": Time, Aug. 3, 1962, pp. 12–13.

626 silk pajamas: Int. McCree Harris, Jan. 24, 1986, and James Gray, Jan. 24, 1986; C. King, My Life, p. 211.

626 sung out and prayed out: City Manager S. A. Roos memorandum, Aug. 4, 1962, CRA.

626 wrote in his diary: Jet, Aug. 23, 1962, p. 20.

627 unearthed glimpses: Summers, *Goddess*, passim, esp. pp. 353–56.

627 "sententious poppycock": *Newsweek*, Aug. 20, 1962, p. 29; Seattle *Times*, Aug. 7, 1962, p. 1.

627 "Bobby and I engaged": Schlesinger journal, Aug. 6, 1962; Schlesinger Jr., *Robert Kennedy*, pp. 636–37.

627 "Poor Marilyn Monroe": McDonald to King, Aug. 8, 1962, A/KP15f9.

628 "with clean hands": NYT, Aug. 9, 1962, p. 9.

628 Mothers' March: C. King, *My Life*, p. 212.

628 trial before Judge Durden: NYT, Aug. 11, 1962, p. 1.

629 "suspended sentence on Martin": intercept of Levison conversation with Toni Hamilton, Aug. 10, 1962, 3:28 P.M., FL-NY-7-1440.

629 closed the city library: NYT, Aug. 12, 1962, p. 1.

629 "King or No King": AH, Aug. 11, 1962, p. 1.

629 "You hear that, deacons!": Kunstler, *Deep*, pp. 125–26.

630 "I am M. S. Page": *Newsweek*, Aug. 27, 1962, pp. 25–26; Page statement, Aug. 15, 1962, CRA.

630 charred remains: NYT, Aug. 16, 1962, p. 1; King statement, Aug. 15, 1962, A/KS2.

630 including nine rabbis: NYT, Aug. 17, 1962, p. 8; AH, Aug. 29, 1962, p. 1; NYT, Aug. 30, 1962, p. 17; S. A. Roos memorandum, Aug. 28, 1962, CRA; list of "Religious Arrested August 28, 1962," A/SC1f26.

631 "at least ten years": AH, Aug. 15, 1962, p. 10A.

631 "only if the objective": Lewis, *King*, p. 169.

631 encompassed nearly all: "Albany, Georgia," *Crisis*, February 1963, pp. 69–78.

631 "Albany remains segregated": NYT, Aug. 18, 1962, p. 44.

632 King told his audience in Birmingham: NYT, Sept. 27, 1962, p. 29.

632 "fireman anymore": Int. Rev. Wyatt Tee Walker, Dec. 21, 1984.

Seventeen
THE FALL OF OLE MISS

633 thickened in Greenwood: NYT, Aug. 16, 1962, p. 12; *Liberation*, January 1970, pp. 16–17; Forman, *The Making*, pp. 283–86.

634 "kind of guy this Bob Moses": Forman, *The Making*, p. 286.

634 colleagues to Highlander: Ibid. Also confidential report by Bernice Robinson (Septima Clark's partner at the Highlander citizenship school) dated July 19, 1962, and Robinson to Moses, July 19, 1962, both SHSW/HP.

634 " 'this is my school book' ": Block to SCLC, July 16, 1962, A/SC33f12.

634 O'Dell urged James Bevel: O'Dell to Bevel, Aug. 8, 1962, A/SC135f7.

635 Wiley Branton: Sketch from Branton, CRDPOH; int. Branton, Sept. 28, 1983.

635 they founded COFO: Forman, *The Making*, p. 288; Carson, *In Struggle*, p. 78; Watters and Cleghorn, *Climbing*, p. 64; int. Wiley Branton, Sept. 28, 1983.

636 rearrested in Sunflower County: SNCC booklet, *Mississippi: A Chronicle of Violence*, p. 9, A/SC16f15.

636 classes around Ruleville: *Liberation*, January 1970, p. 17; Forman, *The Making*, p. 91; Robinson to Myles Horton, July 30, 1962, SHSW/HP.

636 Hamer fled: Raines, *My Soul*, pp. 271–74.

636 vigilantes poured gunshots: NYT, Sept. 1, 1962, p. 20.

637 two fresh burnings: NYT, Sept. 10, 1962, p. 1.

637 two girls went to the hospital: NYT, Sept. 11, 1962, p. 20; *Jet*, Sept. 27, 1962, pp. 14–21.

638 usual detailed report: Memo from Bob Moses and Charles Cobb, "Shooting Incident in Ruleville," A/SC141f4. The copy in King's files is marked "Attn: Andy" in King's handwriting, indicating that King assigned the response to Andrew Young.

638 from faraway Baltimore: Watters and Cleghorn, *Climbing*, p. 139.

638 They chopped wood: Carson, *In Struggle*, p. 79.

638 "the deeper the fear": *Liberation*, January 1970, p. 17.

638 Operation Mongoose: U.S. Senate (Church Committee), Report No. 94-755, Book III, pp. 135ff.

638   "any more outrageous action": NYT, Sept. 14, 1962, pp. 1, 12.

639   pledged $10,000: NYT, Sept. 15, 1962, p. 12.

639   I Hope Baptist Church: NYT, Sept. 18, 1962, pp. 1, 26.

639   "specifically to intimidate": Navasky, *Justice*, pp. 119–20.

640   "protection guarantees": *Jet*, Oct. 4, 1962, pp. 3–4.

640   Four more Negro churches: NYT, Sept. 26, 1962, p. 23.

640   USIA Director Edward R. Murrow: Golden, *Mr. Kennedy*, pp. 123–24.

641   "We were amazed": Rep. Fred Schwengel to O'Donnell, Aug. 24, 1962, Lee White Papers, Box 20, JFK. A previous miscommunication is reflected in Lawrence O'Brien to Rep. James Roosevelt, April 7, 1962, Box 1478, Name File, JFK.

641   wiretap on Stanley: Levison intercept, Aug. 14, 1962, FL-NY-7-148a.

642   "Anything they hate": Levison intercept, Aug. 27, 1962, FL-NY 7-161a.

642   centennial celebration: PC, Sept. 22, 1962, p. 4.

642   "A structure of segregation": NYT, Sept. 22, 1962, pp. 1, 50.

642   Kennedy praised King's: JFK to King, Sept. 24, 1962, A/KP14f4.

643   "real mobilization": King to Shortridge, Sept. 4, 1962, Shortridge Papers, in the possession of Mrs. W. E. (Pinkie) Shortridge.

643   "connectional man": Shuttlesworth remarks at Shortridge funeral, May 2, 1964, Shortridge Papers, ibid.

643   Shortridge had dived: Shortridge statement to FBI agents, May 29, 1962, re shooting of March 28, 1962, Shortridge Papers, ibid.

643   small extra bedroom: Int. Pinkie Shortridge, July 29, 1986.

644   Connor's image problems: BN, Dec. 26, 1951, p. 1; BN, Jan. 7, 1952, p. 1; Corley, "The Quest," pp. 159–61.

644   "silk-stocking people": David Vann, Duard LeGrand Lecture of 1978, collected by the University of Alabama in Birmingham, Center for Urban Affairs, pp. 14–15.

644   emissary secretly to Atlanta: Lee E. Bains thesis, BIR, p. 9; int. David Vann, Aug. 1, 1986.

645   "wrong meeting": Fred Shuttlesworth, A/OH; Shuttlesworth, CRDPOH; Raines, *My Soul*, pp. 168–69.

645   "We have to have toilets": Ibid.

646   "were all trained": Savannah office report, Aug. 29, 1962, cited in Garrow, *FBI*, p. 52.

646   confidential contact from Seigenthaler: Int. John Seigenthaler, Dec. 15, 1987, and Jack O'Dell, July 1, 1986.

647   O'Dell chafed at: Int. Jack O'Dell, July 1, 1986.

647   "to ride the Bull!": Police notes of mass meeting, Sept. 24, 1962, BIR/BC6f14.

647   Tuesday, September 25: Meredith confrontation from Lord, *The Past*, pp. 139–43; Meredith, *Three Years*, pp. 193–97; Navasky, *Justice*, pp. 185–92, 199–204; NYT, Sept. 26, 1962, p. 1.

650   Meredith's third retreat: NYT, Sept. 27, 1962, p. 1; Watters and Cleghorn, *Climbing*, pp. 144–45.

650   Christmas shopping boycott: Int. Rev. Wyatt Tee Walker, Dec. 21, 1984.

650   "soon as you leave": Ibid.

651   "Hello, General": Navasky, *Justice*, p. 209; Watters and Cleghorn, *Climbing*, p. 147.

651   "thinks we're compromising": Navasky, *Justice*, p. 215.

652   defiant holiday mood: Watters and Cleghorn, *Climbing*, pp. 150–52.

652   stoically apprehensive Meredith: Meredith, *Three Years*, pp. 205–6.

653   triple-tier headlines: NYT, Sept. 28, 1962, p. 1.

653   "loony": Schlesinger Jr., *Robert Kennedy*, p. 342.

653   DEFCON 3: Charles Vanderburgh, "A Draftee's Diary from the Mississippi Front," *Harper's*, February 1964, p. 37.

653   dull by comparison: NYT, Sept. 28, 1962, p. 23.

653   landed on King's left cheek: Account of attack drawn from int. Septima Clark, Dec. 17, 1983, Edward Gardner, Jan. 21, 1986, and John Drew, Jan. 21, 1986; int. Clark, HOH; Robert Brank Fulton to King and Walker, Oct. 4, 1962, containing Fulton's statement dated Sept. 29, 1962, A/SC33f15; Ann Braden to King and Walker, Oct. 6, 1962, with enclosed draft, A/SC34f15.

655 "self-styled Nazi": NYT, Sept. 29, 1962, p. 9; Peter Kihss to Walker, Oct. 4, 1962, and Walker to Kihss, Oct. 10, 1962, A/SC33f15; int. Rev. Wyatt Tee Walker, Dec. 21, 1984.

655 Nazi "dormitory": Rosen to Belmont, Sept. 28, 1962, FSC-7x6.

655 "Heil Hitler!": Rockwell to James, Sept. 30, 1962, BIR/BC10f6.

656 "Bring your flags": Lord, *The Past*, p. 159.

656 bring the President himself: Guthman, *Band*, p. 199.

656 "Johnny boy": Schlesinger Jr., *Robert Kennedy*, p. 344.

656 "an A-1 lawyer": Presidential Recordings, Integration of the University of Mississippi, Belt 4-A, JFK.

657 he was recovering: Sorensen, *Kennedy*, p. 484.

657 "Except Eisenhower": Belt 4A-2, JFK.

658 "sneaking him into Jackson": Lord, *The Past*, p. 165.

658 "Not a one of 'em'll be armed": Belt 4C, JFK.

659 "We've got a deal": Navasky, *Justice*, p. 230.

659 "I love Mississippi!": Lord, *The Past*, p. 169.

659 "General Grant's table": Schlesinger Jr., *Robert Kennedy*, p. 345.

660 "stage of politics": Navasky, *Justice*, pp. 230–31.

660 "We have it all down": Lord, *The Past*, p. 172.

661 "Hey, Nick": Raines, *My Soul*, p. 374.

661 little Oxford airport: Meredith, *Three Years*, p. 211.

662 "Go to hell, JFK!": Lord, *The Past*, p. 178.

663 Doar pleaded for time: Guthman, *Band*, pp. 201–2.

664 Historian Walter Lord: Lord, *The Past*, pp. 180–84.

665 "Bob, I'm very sorry": Guthman, *Band*, p. 202.

665 "my fellow citizens": NYT, Oct. 1, 1962, p. 22.

666 grim siege watch: Description of riot drawn from Lord, *The Past*, pp. 181–204; Sorensen, *Kennedy*, pp. 485–87; Guthman *Band*, pp. 200–205; Schlesinger Jr., *Robert Kennedy*, pp. 346–49. Also from Presidential Recordings, Integration of the University of Mississippi, JFK, cited below by number.

666 "throwing iron spikes": Audiotape 26, JFK.

666 "wife may be lying": Ibid.

668 Barnett had parried: Dictabelts 4E and 4F, JFK.

668 "Okay, we'll move him": Audiotape 26, JFK.

668 "G-U-I-H-A-R-D": Jack Rosenthal to Evelyn Lincoln, Dictabelt 4F-2, JFK.

668 "hell of a problem": Audiotape 26A, JFK.

669 reporter was so awed: Int. Nicholas Katzenbach, Oct. 22, 1986.

670 army blankets: Meredith, *Three Years*, p. 212.

670 "Andersonville": Vanderburgh, "A Draftee's Diary," *Harper's*, February 1964.

670 "provoked the students": NYT, Oct. 2, 1962, pp. 1, 25.

670 "a blood clot": Johnson to Mrs. George Etz, Jr., Nov. 20, 1962, Marshall Papers, Box 19, JFK.

670 "utter contempt": Lord, *The Past*, p. 206.

670 indicted Chief Marshal McShane: NYT, Nov. 17, 1962, p. 1.

670 "planned physical torture": Silver, *Closed*, pp. 128–32.

671 "evils of Reconstruction": Sorensen, *Kennedy*, p. 4; Schlesinger Jr., *Robert Kennedy*, p. 350.

671 best legal minds: Navasky, *Justice*, pp. 235–36.

671 "qualified his optimism": NYT, Oct. 1, 1962, p. 1.

672 profound depression: William Goldsmith, *The Growth of Presidential Power*, cited in Schlesinger Jr., *Robert Kennedy*, p. 351.

672 "feel like pawns": King, "It's a Difficult Thing to Teach a President," *Look*, Nov. 17, 1964.

Eighteen
TO BIRMINGHAM

673 "hit Oxford": Schlesinger Jr., *Robert Kennedy*, p. 545.

673 retrieved Congressman Hale Boggs: Sorensen, *Kennedy*, p. 702.

673 moved the entire family: Int. C. B. King, July 10, 1985.

674 "Absolutely not": Duard LeGrand lecture by David Vann, Center for Urban Affairs, UAB.

674 *The First Family: Newsweek*, Dec. 3, 1962, p. 29; Rolling Stone, *Almanac*, p. 73.

675 "tip-toe stance": King address, Dec. 27, 1962, A/KS3.

675 "infiltrated to the top": New Orleans *Times-Picayune*, Oct. 26, 1962, p. iv–1.

675 O'Dell told King: Int. Jack O'Dell, July 1, 1986; O'Dell to King, Jan. 29, 1963, A/KP18f33.

675 "communist conspiracy": Testimony, July 30, 1958, HUAC Hearings, pp. 2712–20.

676 "I wouldn't try": Ibid., p. 2716.

676 "What can I do?": Int. Jack O'Dell, July 1, 1986.

676 "totally inaccurate and false": King statement, A/KP18f38.

677 O'Dell figured: Int. Jack O'Dell, July 1, 1986.

677 "Turn Left for Scarsdale": NYT, March 19, p. 31, and March 16, 1962, p. 33.

678 "Some people would laugh": Levison intercept, Nov. 14, 1962, FLNY-7-240a; also FBI headquarters memo, Nov. 15, 1962, FS-NR.

678 agents had planted: FBI headquarters ordered the COMINFIL (Communist infiltration) investigation on Oct. 23, 1962, and planted the five articles the next day, Garrow, *FBI*, p. 53.

678 DeLoach flatly refused: DeLoach to Guthman, Nov. 7, 1962, Edwin Guthman Papers; int. Guthman, June 25, 1984.

679 suspicions of foul play: Int. Jack O'Dell, July 1, 1986.

679 add a fourth wiretap: Garrow, *FBI*, p. 57; the home wiretap was installed on Nov. 29, 1962, FLNY-9-77.

679 "deliberately sandwiched": Sorensen, *Kennedy*, p. 482.

679 "carries the whole nation": *Jet*, Dec. 6, 1962, p. 7.

680 wave after wave: *Jet*, Dec. 20, 1962, pp. 6–7; NT, Nov. 25 and Dec. 2, 1962.

680 cultural divide: Archie E. Allen interviews with Stanley Wise, May 31, 1969, and John Lewis, Aug. 8, 1969, AAP.

680 Third Kiokee: Laurie Pritchett memo, Nov. 10, 1962, CRA.

680 "come back to Albany": AC, Nov. 16, 1962, p. 5.

680 "President Chided": NYT, Nov. 15, 1962.

681 "Dr. King Says": NYT, Nov. 19, 1962, p. 21; reprinted widely, as in PC, Dec. 1, 1962, p. 1.

681 Rosen interpreted: Garrow, *FBI*, p. 55.

681 *Jet* declared: *Jet*, Dec. 6, 1962, p. 12.

682 "reveal a total ignorance": CD, Dec. 6, 1962, p. 4.

682 "deceit, lies and treachery": DeLoach to Mohr, Jan. 15, 1963, FK-NR.

683 Dunbar could not refer: Int. Leslie Dunbar, May 12, 1986.

683 December 9: Documents describing installation sermon for Rev. John Porter, BUK5f83 and A/KP1f17.

683 board meeting: Minutes of board meeting, Dec. 12, 1962, A/KP11f20.

683 rattling the church: BN, Dec. 15, 1962, p. 1.

684 "worst big city": King to JFK, Dec. 15, 1962, Box 1478, Name File, JFK.

684 "Marshall Plan": WP, Dec. 18, 1962, p. 18; also George M. Hauser to King et al., Dec. 14, 1962, A/KP3f5.

684 "longest conference": *Jet*, Jan. 3, 1963, pp. 6–7.

685 "We have a million men": Kennedy interview, Dec. 17, 1962, Tape #BB0443, PRA.

685 "Reluctant Emancipator": Howard Zinn, "Kennedy: The Reluctant Emancipator," *Nation*, Dec. 1, 1962, pp. 373–76.

685 lobbied privately: Ishmael Flory to JFK, Dec. 3, 1962, A/SC33f15.

685 "practical considerations": Budget Director to Lee White, White Papers, Box 20, JFK.

686 dispatched warnings: FBI Letterhead Memorandum of Dec. 5, 1962, FL-NR.

686 "so well informed": Ibid.

686 "Now, THEREFORE": Draft enclosed in White to Salinger, Dec. 26, 1962, White Papers, Box 20, JFK.

686 "minor disaster": Ibid.

687 "Louie's got something": Int. Louis Martin, June 10, 1985; Lee White, JFKOH.

687 "in a free Havana": Schlesinger Jr., *Robert Kennedy*, p. 579.
687 puffing on a cigar: WS, Jan. 2, 1963, p. 1.
688 "vulgar pirate chief": Ibid.
688 Che Guevara: NYT, Jan. 2, 1963, p. 2.
688 "Just 100 years ago": Ibid., p. 7.
688 secret planning meeting: Drawn from Garrow, *FBI*, pp. 57–59; Stein, *Journey*, pp. 112–13; Schlesinger Jr., *Robert Kennedy*, pp. 352–53; Cross to Gardner and Walker, Oct. 29, 1962, A/SC33f15; int. James Lawson, Nov. 14, 1983; int. Rev. Wyatt Tee Walker, Aug. 20, 1984, and Walker, CRDPOH; int. Clarence Jones, Nov. 25, 1983, and Aug. 18, 1986; int. Jack O'Dell, July 1, 1986.
688 Whitefield had launched: Ahlstrom, *Religious History*, pp. 280ff.
689 First African Baptist: Woodson, *Negro Church*, pp. 41ff; int. W. W. Law, Dec. 17, 1983.
689 parleyed with General Sherman: Litwack, *Storm*, p. 400.
689 delivered an early version: King speech, "The Negro and the American Dream," Jan. 1, 1961, A/KS2. (There are many minor errors in the transcription of this speech from the Archives recording.)
689 Congregationalist retreat at Dorchester: American Missionary Association pamphlets A1316, A1429, and A1313, Amistad Research Center, New Orleans.
692 "Burke—this is not": Handwritten note on Hoover to Kennedy, Jan. 10, 1962, FK-107.
692 "vicious liar": DeLoach to Mohr, Jan. 15, 1963, FK-NR.
693 "paper record": Int. Jack O'Dell, July 1, 1986.
693 O'Dell complied: O'Dell to King, Jan. 29, 1963 (two drafts), A/KP18f38.
693 blanked out O'Dell's name: Jones to King, Feb. 20, 1963, A/KP11f21.
693 background interview: *Jet*, Jan. 17, 1963, pp. 6–7.
693 "pretty much at peace": Lee White, JFKOH.
693 pleaded with him to include: King, JFKOH; C. King, *My Life*, pp. 224–25.
694 Martin was boasting: Int. Louis Martin, June 10, 1985.
694 "Baby, you don't send": *Jet*, March 7, 1963, p. 12.
694 AJC a leading supporter: Cf. Shad Polier's eight-page report to the AJC, Jan. 15, 1963, A/SC1f12.
694 U.S. Supreme Court: NYT, Jan. 8, 1963, p. 4.
694 huddling with Levison: FBI wiretap, Feb. 5, 1963, 2:12 P.M., FLNY-7-323a.
695 "specially presented": Baldrige to King, Feb. 5, 1963, A/KP14f4.
695 "expecting our fourth child": King wire to Kennedys, Feb. 6, 1963, A/KP14f4.
695 preaching for Adam: Log, A/SC29; also King to Powell, Feb. 15, 1963, BUK5f7.
695 some of the formative influences: Speech, "An Analysis of the Ethical Demands of Integration," Nashville, Dec. 27, 1962, A/KS3.
695 handwritten additions: Speech, "A Challenge to the Churches and Synagogues," Jan. 17, 1963, A/KS4.
695 "pronouncements filter": Ibid. Also NYT, Jan. 17, 1963; CD, Jan. 19, 1963, p. 1.
695 "I'm sick and tired": Sermon, March 3, 1963, A/KS4.
696 taught him to play golf: Int. Rev. Wyatt Tee Walker, Aug. 20 and Dec. 21, 1984.
696 Dooto Records: PC, Feb. 16, 1963, p. 2; *Jet*, Feb. 14, 1963, p. 60.
696 "evaluation of Negro gains": Currier to King, Feb. 4, 1963, A/KP23f23.
697 "plan for a violent revolution": Powers, *Hoover*, p. 337.
697 "current prosecutive summary": Yeagley to Hoover, Feb. 8, 1963, FL-187.
697 best fourteen informants: NY report to Hoover, Feb. 21, 1963, FL-190.
697 told Hoover it was useless: Ibid.
697 interview Louis Budenz: SAC Boston to Hoover, airtel, Feb. 21, 1963, FL-189.
697 "source who is not available": Hoover to Yeagley, Feb. 12, 1963, FL-187.
698 "absolutely feathered": Lee White, JFKOH.
698 Kennedy snatched his aides: Ibid.; also int. Louis Martin, June 10, 1985.
698 Sammy Davis' face: White and Martin interviews, ibid.; also *Jet*, March 7, 1963, p. 12.
698 "Shifting to North": NYT, Feb. 13, 1963, p. 1.
699 Hints of recognition: *Newsweek*, Feb. 25, 1963, p. 26; *Jet*, Feb. 28, 1963, pp. 12–13.

NOTES

Randolph and Clarence Mitchell refused: *Jet,* March 7, 1963, p. 12.

699 reviving his 1942 plans: Gentile, *March,* pp. 14–15. Early press rumors of a march on Washington spoke of plans to protest the job displacement of Miami blacks by Cuban refugees. Later stories said that lack of union support forced Randolph to postpone his march against unemployment from June to October 1963. *Jet,* March 21, pp. 14–18, May 23, p. 12, and June 6, 1963, p. 12.

699 rumors of a feud: Int. Simeon Booker, Feb. 11, 1985.

699 defect to the Republicans: Joseph Rauh, JFKOH.

699 hustled up to Congress: Lee White, JFKOH.

699 Rockefeller seized: NYT, March 6, 1963, p. 4.

700 "a remarkable job": NYT, March 7, 1963, pp. 1, 4.

700 Katzenbach waffled: Dictabelt of March 7, 1963, Item 11A5, JFK.

701 "The humanist hope": Sermon, March 3, 1963, A/KS4.

702 "the lust-infested Augustine": Ibid.

703 King hurried: BW, Feb. 27, 1963, p. 3.

703 were to have commenced: Lewis, *King,* p. 176.

703 target of March 14: Minutes of executive staff meeting, Jan. 23, 1963, A/SC36f13.

703 "prime shopping season": Int. Rev. Wyatt Tee Walker, Dec. 21, 1984.

703 Gaston strenuously opposed: A. G. Gaston interview for PBS documentary "Eyes on the Prize."

703 near passage of a resolution: Int. Rev. Wyatt Tee Walker, Dec. 21, 1984, and Edwin Gardner, Jan. 21, 1986.

703 "dignified Connor": Police notes on mass meeting, March 11, 1963, BIR/BC13f2.

703 Lawson's job: Int. Rev. James Lawson, Nov. 14, 1983.

704 nonviolence pledge cards: King Jr., *Can't Wait,* pp. 63–64.

704 Even John Porter: Int. Rev. Wyatt Tee Walker, Dec. 21, 1984; Garrow, *Bearing,* p. 238.

704 "the unnamed city": New York SAC to Hoover and SAC Birmingham, airtel, March 13, 1963, FLNY-9-194.

704 "destroy the image": Ibid.

705 "no nigger any more": Police notes on mass meeting, March 11, 1963, BIR/BC13f2.

705 letter to King and Walker: Shuttlesworth to King and Walker, March 15, 1963, A/KP 22f11.

705 factions of lawyers: Int. Mrs. W. E. Shortridge, July 29, 1986, and Rev. Edwin Gardner, Jan. 21, 1986.

705 "sold out to Governor": BW, April 6, 1963, p. 1; AC, April 2, 1963, p. 6.

705 recruit secret cadres: Int. Rev. Wyatt Tee Walker, Dec. 21, 1984; also Westin and Mahoney, *Trial,* p. 51; Levison-Jones conversation, April 10, 1963, FLNY-7-387a.

705 Atlanta on March 27: Garrow, *Bearing,* p. 236.

705 pose with the mother: *Jet,* April 11, 1963, p. 12.

705 slipped back into Birmingham: C. King, *My Life,* p. 225.

706 on the thirty-first: Garrow, *Bearing,* p. 669; Jones-Levison conversation, March 29, 1963, FLNY-7-375a.

706 "razzmatazz": Int. Rev. Wyatt Tee Walker, Dec. 21, 1984.

706 Belafonte's jammed apartment: King Jr., *Can't Wait,* p. 57; Kunstler, *Deep,* pp. 173–75; int. Clarence Jones, Nov. 25, 1983; int. Hugh Morrow, Dec. 20, 1984; Levison-Jones conversation, April 1, 1963, FLNY-9-124a.

706 "You are *torture*": Int. Harry Belafonte, March 6–7, 1985.

706 Opera tour: Jackson P. Dick, Jr., to King, March 29, 1963, A/KP7f5.

706 left that same afternoon: Coretta King interview by Donald H. Smith, Dec. 7, 1963, SHSW/SP; C. King, *My Life,* p. 225.

707 waiting with his clipboard: Int. Rev. Wyatt Tee Walker, Dec. 21, 1984; Walker interview for PBS documentary "Eyes on the Prize."

Nineteen
GREENWOOD AND BIRMINGHAM JAIL

708 350 by his count: Walker interview and speech, May 25, 1963, Tape #0388, PRA.

708 King's later memory: King Jr., *Can't Wait,* p. 58.

708 Walker briefed them: Walker interview by Donald H. Smith, SHSW/SP.
708 "picket you over": Westin and Mahoney, *Trial*, pp. 65–66.
708 "make a moral witness": BW, April 6, 1963, p. 2; *Freedomways*, First Quarter 1964, p. 20.
709 turned out the lights: Rev. A. L. Woods oral history, UAB.
709 hauled off twenty-one: BW, April 4, 1963, p. 7.
709 "do the Twist": Police notes on mass meeting, April 3, 1963, BIR/BC13f2.
709 get only four of them into jail: BN, April 5, 1963, p. 2.
710 "I want you to go": Int. Rev. Edwin Gardner, Jan. 21, 1986.
710 dogs swarmed over him: BW, April 8, 1963, p. 2.
710 "wasteful and worthless": BW, April 10, 1963, p. 6.
710 speech by Roy Wilkins: BW, April 13, 1963, pp. 1, 8.
710 buy an advertisement: BN, April 7, 1963, p. 2.
711 "blackout of news": BN, April 5, 1963, p. 2.
711 "calmly to ignore": BN, April 4, 1963, p. 7.
711 phone call from Burke Marshall: Marshall, JFKOH.
711 "Integration Drive Slows": NYT, April 5, p. 16, and April 6, 1963, p. 20.
711 complained that never had his work: King Jr., *Can't Wait*, pp. 65–66.
711 *Life* magazine celebrated: *Life*, March 15, 1963.
711 "key to life itself": *Newsweek*, May 13, 1963.
711 pop-top beer: *Newsweek*, Aug. 5, 1963, p. 61.
712 added some fifteen: Hearings, House Judiciary Subcommittee No. 5, May 28, 1963, p. 1276.
712 thirty dollars a month: Hollis Watkins interview by Joe Sinsheimer, Feb. 13, 1985.
712 "powerless to register": Watters and Cleghorn, *Climbing*, p. 65.
712 Moses filed a federal suit: Complaint reprinted in hearings, House Judiciary Subcommittee No. 5, May 28, 1963, pp. 1278–81.
713 "antipathy toward the defendants": Plaintiffs' statement of Jan. 1, 1963, A/SC35f17.
713 on February 1: Forman, *The Making*, p. 293; hearings, House Judiciary Subcommittee No. 5, May 28, 1963, p. 1277.
713 Gregory announced: ADW, Feb. 6, 1963, p. 2.
714 thirty tons came: *Newsweek*, March 1, 1963, pp. 30–31.
714 "Don't let the white man": Mass meeting of Feb. 11, 1963, Bevel report, A/SC141f5.
714 Chairman John Hannah said: Berl Bernhard, JFKOH; Lee White, JFKOH; hearings, House Judiciary Subcommittee No. 5, May 8, 1963, pp. 1089–92.
714 "I know, Wiley": Int. Wiley Branton, Sept. 28, 1983.
715 "taken care of": Hearings, House Judiciary Subcommittee No. 5, May 28, 1963, p. 1282.
715 "I ain't gonna do": *Jet*, March 7, 1963, pp. 8–9.
716 "don't know this plateau": Moses letter, Feb. 27, 1963, reprinted in Grant, *Black Protest*, pp. 299–301.
716 Jimmy Travis: Travis affidavit, COFO, *Mississippi*, pp. 8–9; James Bevel, "Field Secretary Report Feb. 28–March 8, 1963," A/SC141f6; int. Robert Moses, July 30, 1984; "Story of Greenwood, Mississippi," Folkways Record FD5593; Carson, *In Struggle*, p. 81; Forman, *The Making*, pp. 284–85; Zinn, *SNCC*, pp. 86–90.
717 Andrew Young rejected: Young to James and Diane Bevel, Feb. 21, 1963, A/SC41f5.
717 Annell Ponder: Ponder report on Mississippi, September 1963, A/SC155f26.
717 opened their doors: Ponder report on Mississippi, March 1963, A/SC41f7.
718 "no longer be tolerated": NYT, March 2, 1963, p. 4.
718 Dylan appeared: NYT, July 6, 1963, p. 7.
718 "Indian babies": NYT, April 6, 1963, p. 20.
719 "out of Mississippi tonight": Robinson to Horton, March 25, 1963, SHSW/HP.
719 "sang and we sang": Moses in "Story of Greenwood, Mississippi," Folkways Record FD5593.
719 "not stopping now": ADW, March 28, 1963, p. 1.
719 Forman intervened: Forman, *The Making*, p. 297; int. Robert Moses, July 30, 1984.
719 retreating in bedlam: NYT, March 28, 1963, p. 4; *Newsweek*, April 8, 1963, pp. 24–

25; "Story of Greenwood, Mississippi," Folkways Record FD5593; hearings, House Judiciary Subcommittee No. 5, May 28, 1963, pp. 1300ff; Zinn, *SNCC*, pp. 91–92.

720   "Sic 'em!'": NYT, March 29, 1963, p. 1; *Newsweek*, April 8, 1963, pp. 24–25; CD, March 30, 1963, p. 1.

721   done about the dogs: Int. John Doar, May 12, 1986.

721   Marshall bargained: Marshall to RFK, March 29, 1963, Marshall Papers, Box 3, JFK.

721   described to Robert Kennedy: Marshall to RFK, March 11, 1963, Marshall Papers, Box 16, JFK.

721   "face resignations": Marshall to RFK, March 29, 1963, Marshall Papers, Box 3, JFK.

722   "how heartbroken I was": "Story of Greenwood, Mississippi," Folkways Record FD5593.

722   "There's your story!'": NYT, April 3, 1963, pp. 1, 40.

722   "your nigger pills": Int. Claude Sitton, Dec. 14, 1983.

722   "bring on your tigers": "Story of Greenwood, Mississippi," Folkways Record FD5593.

722   Doar visited Moses: Grant, *Black Protest*, pp. 329–35; Forman, *The Making*, pp. 299–303.

723   "you can't put it out": *Jet*, April 18, 1963, p. 23.

723   Kennedy replied: NYT, April 4, 1963, p. 10.

723   shake their heads in amusement: Int. Robert Moses, July 30, 1984.

723   "balanced diet": Grant, *Black Protest*, p. 335.

723   "in rare form": Forman, *The Making*, p. 303.

724   "eyeball to eyeball": *Jet*, April 18, 1963, p. 23.

724   Doar first told: Ibid., p. 26; CD, April 5, 1963, p. 1.

724   reporters confirmed rumors: NYT, April 5, 1963, p. 16.

724   get relief assistance resumed: NYT, April 2, 1963, p. 23; Burke Marshall to JFK, April 8, 1963, Box 23, Lee White Papers, JFK.

724   Doar searched for Moses: Int. John Doar, May 12, 1986, and Robert Moses, March 13, 1988.

725   barrier of formality: Doar and Moses interviews, ibid.

725   "cut anybody's throat": Walker, CRDPOH; for Forman's point of view, Forman, *The Making*, pp. 311–12.

725   only fifty were accepted: Annell Ponder, 1963 report on LeFlore County, A/SC155f26.

725   "picked up momentum": NYT, April 6, 1963, p. 20.

725   blamed the sudden demise: Branton, CRDPOH; int. Leslie Dunbar, May 12, 1986.

725   "set the mad dogs": Police notes on mass meeting, April 3, 1963, BIR/BC13f3.

725   more than a hundred: King Jr., *Can't Wait*, p. 67; Kunstler, *Deep*, pp. 182–84.

726   Gaston's statement: BN, April 10, 1963, p. 6.

726   postponed plans: Police notes on mass meeting, April 9, 1963, BIR/BC13f3.

726   plotting with Governor: BN, April 10, 1963, p. 6.

727   "a sacrificial life": Police notes on mass meeting, April 10, 1963, BIR/BC13f3.

727   "parading, demonstrating": Westin and Mahoney, *Trial*, pp. 69–73.

727   "in all good conscience": Ibid., p. 78.

727   fewer than 150 people: Garrow, *Bearing*, p. 241.

728   only seven volunteers: NYT, April 12, 1963, p. 1.

728   Daddy King rushed over: Police notes on mass meeting, April 11, 1963, BIR/BC13f3.

728   bankruptcy notice: King Jr., *Can't Wait*, p. 71.

728   "can't be everywhere": Walker, CRDPOH.

728   Good Friday morning: Account of meeting and arrest from King Jr., *Can't Wait*, pp. 72–74; Westin and Mahoney, *Trial*, pp. 81–84; Walker, CRDPOH; int. Rev. Wyatt Tee Walker, Dec. 21, 1984, and Rev. Edwin Gardner, Jan. 21, 1986; Dorothy Cotton, HOH; police notes on mass meetings, April 11 and April 12, 1963, BIR/BC13f3; C. King, *My Life*, pp. 227–29; Raines, *My Soul*, p. 155; NYT, April 13, 1963, p. 1; CD, April 13, 1963, p. 1; BN, April 13, 1963, p. 2.

731   "perfidious Jews": *Newsweek*, April 22, 1963, pp. 21–22.

731   ecumenical reforms: F. E. Cartus, "Vatican II and the Jews," *Commentary*, January 1965, pp. 19–23.

731 less than ninety minutes: Ware and Albany Nine cases drawn generally from the case files of C. B. King in Albany. Also int. C. B. King, July 10, 1985, Marion Cheek, July 11, 1985, B. C. Gardner, July 11, 1985, and Ed Haggerty, July 11, 1985; Slater King, "Battleground of Albany," *Freedomways*, First Quarter 1964, p. 99; FBI reports on picket lines in Albany, e.g., File 157-6-2, serials 1013 and 1040, and File 157-4-2, serial 165.
732 Marshall wrote Kennedy: Marshall "Monday Report" to RFK, April 30, 1963, Marshall Papers, Box 16, JFK.
733 "willing to pick cotton": Carson, *In Struggle*, p. 81.
733 Moses gently prepared: Ibid., pp. 81–82; Forman, *The Making*, pp. 305–7.
733 Shame ate him alive: Int. Charles Sherrod, Jan. 23, 1986; Sherrod interview by Joe Phister, undated.
734 Bevel began to preach: Police notes on mass meeting, April 12, 1963, BIR/BC13f3; int. Rev. James Bevel, May 16, 1985.
735 pool of Bethesda: John 5:1–9.
735 "Harry has been able": King Jr., *Can't Wait*, p. 75.
735 "lifted a thousand": Ibid.
735 telegram campaign: Int. Clarence Jones, Nov. 25, 1983, and Rev. Wyatt Tee Walker, May 1, 1988; Walker to JFK, April 13 and April 14, 1963, both in Box 1478, Name File, JFK.
735 "get into prison reform": Int. Harry Belafonte, March 6–7, 1985, and Clarence Jones, Nov. 25, 1983.
736 "Are you being guarded?": Police transcript of conversation, April 15, 1963, BIR/BC13f3.
736 she was in a bind: Int. Rev. Wyatt Tee Walker, May 1, 1988. Walker recalls being upset that the news came out of Atlanta rather than Birmingham, with troublesome confusion over the details, but he had no way of knowing what King had told Coretta.
736 Walker seized hopefully: Police notes on mass meeting, April 15, 1963, BIR/BC13f3.
737 General press reaction: WP, April 14, 1963, p. E6; WS, April 17, 1963, p. A20; NYT, April 14, pp. 1, 46, April 15, p. 1, and April 16, 1963, p. 1; AJ, April 16, 1963, p. 5; BN, April 15, p. 2, April 16, p. 2, April 17, p. 5, and April 18, 1963, p. 4; *Time*, April 19, 1963, pp. 30–31; *Newsweek*, April 22, 1963, pp. 28–29.
738 "Seldom, if ever": King to Carpenter et al., April 16, 1963, BIR/AB12f44. The original typed letter was addressed to only seven of the eight signers of the Carpenter statement; Methodist bishop Paul Hardin was omitted, most likely by error. Washington, *Testament*, pp. 289–302.
738 "I'm writing": Int. Clarence Jones, Nov. 25, 1983.
740 "His cup has really": Int. Rev. Wyatt Tee Walker, Dec. 21, 1984.
741 first recorded slaves: Quarles, *The Negro*, p. 19.
741 two particular slaveholding preachers: Methodist Bishop J. O. Andrew and Baptist Rev. James E. Reeves, Ahlstrom, *Religious History*, pp. 661–64.
741 the eminent Rev. C. C. Jones: Charles Colcock Jones was the patriarch of a family whose personal letters were published in the prize-winning six-volume series *The Children of Pride*, edited by Robert M. Myers. Jones family portrait drawn from this work and from Clarke, *Wrestlin' Jacob*.
741 parallel schism within the Presbyterian: Previous Presbyterian compromises on slavery mentioned in Scherer, *Slavery and the Churches*, p. 134 (1797), Ahlstrom, *Religious History*, p. 648, and Woodson, *Negro Church*, p. 110 (1818). Jones's work to hold the Presbyterians together came in the context of abolitionist attacks on the exchanges of support between slaveholders and the Free Church of Scotland, which had seceded from the Church of Scotland. On these complex disputes, see the Cincinnati resolution of May 27, 1845, reprinted in *Free Church of Scotland, Report of the Proceedings of the General Assembly on Saturday, May 30, and Monday, June 1, 1846*, pp. 9–11. Also Woodson, *Negro Church*, p. 113; Clarke, *Wrestlin' Jacob*, pp. 95–145.
741 "withered and blasted": Clarke, *Wrestlin' Jacob*, p. 13.
741 "Oh, the artful dodger!": Douglass speech of May 29, 1846, in Glasgow, Scotland, reprinted from Woodson, *Negro Orators*, pp. 170–77:

Slavery, I hold it to be an indisputable proposition, exists in the United States because it is respectable. The slaveholder is a respectable man in America. All the important offices in the Government and the Church are filled by slaveholders. Slaveholders are Doctors of Divinity; and men are sold to build churches, women to support missionaries, and children to send Bibles to the heathen. Revivals in religion and revivals in the slave trade go on at the same time.

Now what we want to do is to make slavery disrespectable. Whatever tends to make it respectable tends to elevate the slaveholder; and whatever, therefore, proclaims the respectability of the slaveholders, or of slaveholding, tends to perpetuate the existence of this vile system. Now, I hold one of the most direct, one of the most powerful means of making him a respectable man, is to say that he is a Christian, for I hold that of all other men, a Christian is most entitled to my affection and regard.

Well, the Free Church is now proclaiming that these men—all blood-besmeared as they are, with their stripes, gags and thumb-screws, and all the bloody paraphernalia of slaveholding, and who are depriving the slave of the right to learn to read the word of God—that these men are Christians, and ought to be in fellowship as such.

741 "fanatics of the worst sort": Myers, *Children of Pride*, Vol. I, p. 23.

741 high calling: Ibid., Vol. III, p. 299; Ahlstrom, *Religious History*, p. 672; Woodson, *Negro Church*, p. 115.

741 C. C. Jones Carpenter: Carpenter description from Carpenter Papers, Birmingham Public Library; int. Rev. Douglas Carpenter, July 1, 1987, and Bishop George Murray, July 16, 1987.

742 lifelong correspondent: Scarlett-Carpenter correspondence in BIR/C15f16.

742 Niebuhr's best friend: Fox, *Niebuhr*, passim.

742 "opportunity of a hundred years": Scarlett to Carpenter, July 22, 1960, BIR/C15f16.

742 old Negro trusty: Int. Clarence Jones, Nov. 25, 1983. Also int. Rev. Edwin Gardner, Jan. 21, 1986; Kunstler, *Deep*, p. 187.

742 figured he was entitled: Int. Clarence Jones, Nov. 25, 1983.

742 evict Hosea Williams: Int. Rev. Edwin Gardner, Jan. 21, 1986.

744 asleep over her typewriter: Walker, CRDPOH; int. Rev. Wyatt Tee Walker, Dec. 21, 1984.

744 Not a single mention: Garrow, *Bearing*, p. 671n.

744 "channeling the enthusiasms": Walker to Marshall, April 16, 1963, Marshall Papers, Box 16, JFK.

745 "get it from both sides": Int. Bishop George Murray, July 16, 1987.

745 "use of police dogs": Marshall to JFK, April 8, 1963, Lee White Papers, Box 23, JFK.

745 "Implicit is the suggestion": White to JFK, April 10, 1963, Lee White Papers, Box 23, JFK.

746 "poison an atmosphere": Berl Bernhard, JFKOH; Najeeb Halaby, JFKOH.

746 Administration officials conceded: JFK press statement, April 19, 1963, Lee White Papers, Box 23, JFK. Also Najeeb Halaby, JFKOH; Lee White, JFKOH; Nathaniel H. Goodrich to White, April 10, 1963, Lee White Papers, Box 23, JFK.

747 "President Urged": NYT, April 17, 1963, p. 1.

747 took root everywhere in the press: E.g., NYT, April 18, 1963, p. 34, and April 19, 1963, p. 42.

747 dismiss the commission: NYT, April 20, 1963, p. 1.

747 "I am advised": JFK press statement, April 19, 1963, Lee White Papers, Box 23, JFK.

747 hooted out of Washington: Berl Bernhard, JFKOH, p. 29.

747 impromptu press conference: BN, April 20, 1963, p. 2.

747 two smuggled books: *Jet*, May 2, 1963, pp. 17–18.

747 Three of the first four: BN, April 23, 1963.

747 "Star-Spangled Banner": Police notes of mass meetings, April 20 and April 22, 1963, BIR/BC13f3.

748 "read over your Senate speeches": William Moore to Kennedy, March 2, 1963, Lee White Papers, Box 21, JFK.

748 Moore was on the road: Moore reports from *Afro-American*, March 30, p. 2, April 6, p. 1, and May 4, 1963, p. 13; *Jet*, May 9, 1963, pp. 14–19; Baltimore *Evening Sun*, April 24, 1963, p. B40; Baltimore *Sun*, April 26, 1963, pp. C1, 6; NYT, April 24, p. 12, and April 26, 1963, p. 17.

748 Toledo, Ohio: *Jet*, Oct. 3, 1963, p. 48.

749 astonishing public display: Police notes of mass meeting, April 23, 1963, BIR/BC13f4.

749 Two detectives met: O. C. Ellard and O. V. Vance memo, April 24, 1963, BIR/BC13f4.

749 President Kennedy replied: NYT, April 25, 1963, p. 16.

750 John Lewis led: NB, April 26, 1963; NT, April 27, 1963.

750 Farmer convened: Steering committee minutes, April 26, 1963, CORE Reel 16, Folder 5.

750 awkward tragedy: Ibid. Also Moore to Peck, Feb. 24, 1963; Peck to Carey (enclosing draft of letter to Moore), Feb. 27, 1963; and Carey to Moore, March 20, 1963, all in CORE Reel 35, Folder 236.

750 Forman called Moore's widow: Forman, *The Making*, p. 308.

750 Bevel's afternoon workshops: Int. Rev. James Bevel, May 16, 1985.

751 Shuttlesworth to vow: Police notes on mass meeting, April 24, 1963, BIR/BC13f4.

751 special meeting with Governor Wallace: NYT, April 26, p. 1, and April 27, 1963, p. 12; BN, April 25, p. 1, and April 26, 1963, p. 1; Schlesinger Jr., *Robert Kennedy*, pp. 362–65; Golden, *Mr. Kennedy*, pp. 172–73.

751 "glad Bobby came": Police notes on mass meeting, April 25, 1963, BIR/BC13f4.

751 "toilets were locked" to "*stuff is just in 'em!*": Watters, *Down to Now*, pp. 233–37.

751 Jenkins announced: Westin and Mahoney, *Trial*, pp. 141–42.

752 petitioned the city fathers: Shuttlesworth telegrams to Birmingham City Commission, Mayor Boutwell, City Clerk Hodges and Traffic Engineer Robinson, April 26, 1963, BIR/AB21f23.

752 Bevel had been showing: Int. Rev. James Bevel, May 16, 1985.

752 "Four thousand Negroes": Police notes on mass meeting, April 27, 1963, BIR/BC13f4.

752 younger and younger: Meier and Rudwick, *CORE*, p. 219; Isaac Reynolds interview in *New America*, May 31, 1963, p. 1; Reynolds to Farmer, n.d., and Reynolds to Carey, April 26, 1963, CORE Reel 37, Folder 263.

753 off to a distant prep school: Adenie Drew oral history, Alabama Historical Society, BIR.

753 "Greenwood Rolled": BN, April 28, 1963, p. 6.

753 both bodies denied: Council resolution and Boutwell statement of April 30, 1963, BIR/AB21f23.

753 "Well, Bevel": Int. Rev. James Bevel, May 16, 1985.

753 Bevel had the appeal: Int. Rev. Wyatt Tee Walker, Dec. 21, 1984, and Bernard Lee, June 19, 1985.

754 two separate Moore marches: NYT, May 2, 1963, p. 18; Meier and Rudwick, *CORE*, p. 215; Forman, *The Making*, p. 308; Watters, *Down to Now*, pp. 243ff.

754 cynical to Porter: Garrow, *Bearing*, p. 247.

755 "Against your Mama": Int. Rev. James Bevel, May 16–17, 1985.

755 FBI intelligence: Lt. M. H. House memo, April 30, 1963, BIR/BC13f4.

755 "Tall Paul": Int. Rev. Edwin Gardner, Jan. 21, 1986.

Twenty
THE CHILDREN'S MIRACLE

756 fifty teenagers emerged: King Jr., *Can't Wait*, p. 9; Lewis, *King*, pp. 192f; Garrow, *Bearing*, pp. 248f; NYT, May 3, 1962, p. 1; BN, May 3, 1963, p. 2.

757 "Hey, Fred": Police notes on mass meeting, May 2, 1963, BIR/BC13f5.

758 "Mississippi chopping cotton": Ibid.

758 Friday, May 3: The day's events drawn from the sources above, plus NYT, May 4, 1963, p. 1, and BN, May 3, p. 2, and May 4, 1963, pp. 2, 4.

759 "But lawyer Vann!": Gaston and Vann interviews for PBS documentary "Eyes on the Prize," No. 4; also int. David Vann, Aug. 1, 1986.

761 Walter Gadsden: *Jet*, Oct. 10, 1963, pp. 26–27.

761 "permit this recrudescence": Levison intercepts, 3:57 and 4:45 P.M., May 3, 1963, FLNY-7-410a.

763 "We must not boo": Police notes on mass meeting, May 3, 1963, BIR/BC13f5.

763 "UNDER the water" to "catch up on my reading": Ibid. Also tape recording of King's May 3 speech, labeled "Dr. Martin Luther King—Topic Birmingham 1963," BIR.

764 another five hundred: Levison intercept, May 4, 1963, FLNY-9-157a.

764 strung up an effigy: L. H. Baily memo, May 4, 1963, BIR/BC13f5.

764 three of them stacked: NYT, May 4, 1963, p. 1.

764 made him "sick": Schlesinger Jr., *Thousand Days*, p. 875.

764 cynical or capricious King: Watters, *Down to Now*, p. 262.

764 "Love God and Thy Neighbor": Saturday demonstration drawn from NYT, May 5, 1963, p. 1, and BN, May 4, 1963, p. 2.

765 Baker flew in: Forman, *The Making*, p. 312.

765 Carawan and Joan Baez: Carawan to Horton, autobiographical summary, 1965, Reel 7, SHSW/HP; BW, May 4, p. 2, and May 15, 1963, p. 3; Baez, *And a Voice*, pp. 104–6; int. Baez, Jan. 13, 1984.

766 arrested Guy Carawan: Police notes on mass meeting, May 5, 1963, BIR/BC13f5.

766 "tired of this mess": Ibid.

767 preachers huddled to argue: Int. Rev. Wyatt Tee Walker, Dec. 21, 1984, and Rev. James Bevel, May 16, 1985.

767 "Turn on your water!": NYT, May 6, 1963, p. 1; King Jr., *Can't Wait*, p. 101. Also BW, May 8, 1963, p. 1; King speech of May 6, 1963, recorded on Folkways Album 5487; Lewis, *King*, p. 194; Morris, *Origins*, pp. 267–69; Kunstler, *Deep*, pp. 190–91; Forman, *The Making*, p. 312; Wyatt Walker speech of May 25, 1963, Tape 0388, PRA.

768 Marshall had taken soundings: Garrow, *Bearing*, pp. 252–53; NYT, May 7, 1963, pp. 1, 33.

768 "look like Atlanta": White House meeting, May 12, 1963, Audiotape 86.2, JFK.

768 scouting groups of moderate whites: Corley, "Quest," pp. 263–65; Garrow, *Bearing*, pp. 251–52; int. Burke Marshall, June 27, 1984.

769 Robert Kennedy emphasized: Cabinet meeting, May 21, 1963, Audiotape 88.6, JFK.

769 "He really didn't know": Marshall and RFK joint interview, June 20, 1964, p. 97, JFKOH.

769 "had no specifics": Int. Burke Marshall, June 27, 1984.

769 mistakes in Albany: King interview by Smith, December 1963, SHSW/SP.

770 Dick Gregory led: Ibid. Also BN, May 6, 1963, p. 2; Len Holt, "Eyewitness: The Police Terror at Birmingham," Manchester *Guardian*, May 16, 1963.

771 Levison worked to place: FBI wiretaps first picked up Levison's idea for an ad in a conversation with O'Dell on Saturday afternoon, May 4, 1963, FLNY-9-157a.

771 "the bastards at the *Times*": Bill Preston—Levison conversation, 1:45 P.M., May 6, 1963, FLNY-7-413a.

771 "references to brutality": Jones-Levison conversation, 3:49 P.M., May 6, 1963, ibid.

772 negotiating a compromise: Levison—"Mr. Redding(?)" conversation, 5:10 P.M., ibid.

772 mass meeting overflowed: Police notes on mass meeting, May 6, 1963, BIR/BC13f5; also Guy and Candie Carawan, "Birmingham, Alabama, 1963: Mass Meeting," Folkways Record 5487.

772 a record $40,000: Int. Rev. Edwin Gardner, Jan. 21, 1986.

772 Forman burst in: Forman, *The Making*, pp. 312–13.

773 "those who write history" to "way your lover talks": Mass meeting of May 6, 1963, Folkways Record 5487.

774 Wyatt Walker admitted: Int. Rev. Wyatt Tee Walker, Dec. 21, 1984.

775 began to fan out: Ibid. Len Holt, "Eyewitness: The Police Terror at Birmingham," Manchester *Guardian*, May 16, 1963.

775 white negotiators met early: Corley, "Quest," pp. 267–68; Garrow, *Bearing*, p. 253.

775 "Ladies and gentlemen": King statement, May 7, 1963, A/KS4; NYT, May 8, 1963, p. 28.

775 At the Chamber of Commerce: Marshall, JFKOH; Marshall and RFK joint interview, JFKOH; Corley, "Quest," pp. 268–69; Harding, "Beginning," p. 16; Navasky, *Justice*, p. 219.

776 pandemonium to erupt: NYT, May 8, 1963, pp. 1, 28; Len Holt, "Eyewitness: The Police Terror at Birmingham," Manchester *Guardian*, May 16, 1963; Forman, *The Making*, pp. 313–14.

776 SIRENS WAIL: BN, May 7, 1963, p. 2.

777 "square blocks of Negroes": King Jr., *Can't Wait*, p. 104; King also described the lunch break as a turning point at the celebratory mass meeting on May 10, 1963, Tape 4, SHSW/SP.

777 "if these were white marches": BN, May 8, 1963, p. 1.

778 executives to be lobbied: Marshall, JFKOH, pp. 99–101; Robert Kennedy, JFKOH, pp. 760–62.

778 "not sitting idly by": BN, May 8, 1963, p. 1.

779 "Martin, this is it!": Shuttlesworth, A/OH.

779 Forman burst in: Forman, *The Making*, p. 314.

779 false fire alarms: Wyatt Walker, CRDPOH.

779 high-pitched dog whistles: Int. Rev. Wyatt Tee Walker, Dec. 21, 1984.

779 "Wear your swimsuit": Police notes of mass meeting, May 7, 1963, BIR/BC13f5.

780 "bless his heart": Ibid.

780 "The meeting worked": Handwritten note headed "8 pm, May 7," Edwin Guthman Papers; Marshall, JFKOH, p. 102.

780 "called a son of a bitch": Raines, *My Soul*, p. 179.

781 blueprint for a settlement: NYT, May 11, 1963, p. 9; Garrow, *Bearing*, pp. 255–56.

781 Hartman Turnbow's farmhouse: NYT, May 10, 1963, p. 14; Moses testimony before House Judiciary Subcommittee No. 5, May 28, 1963, p. 1253; Silver, *Closed*, p. 95; Watters and Cleghorn, *Climbing*, pp. 135–36; Raines, *My Soul*, pp. 285–95.

782 "three hypos": Raines, *My Soul*, p. 171.

782 "scalding the hog": Int. Rev. Edwin Gardner, Jan. 21, 1986.

782 Shuttlesworth was a cauldron: Garrow, *Bearing*, pp. 256–57. Also Shuttlesworth, A/OH; Raines, *My Soul*, pp. 1700–72; int. Rev. Edwin Gardner, Jan. 21, 1986, and Burke Marshall, June 27, 1984.

783 178 of them: Walker speech, May 25, 1963, Tape 0388, PRA.

783 half an hour later: BN, May 8, 1963, p. 1.

783 "Good afternoon": NYT, May 9, 1963, p. 16.

784 personal intercession: Harding, "Beginning," p. 17.

784 Belafonte called Kennedy: Int. Harry Belafonte, March 6–7, 1985. Also, somewhat differently, Kunstler, *Deep*, p. 192.

785 King wanted to stay locked: Int. Harry Belafonte, March 6–7, 1985. Also Harding, "Beginning," p. 17; Bevel speech at mass meeting, May 8, 1963, BIR/BC13f5; Levison-Kunstler conversation, May 19, 1963, FLNY-9-172a.

785 procession of nineteen: Police notes on mass meeting, May 8, 1963, BIR/BC13f5.

785 "gave us the treatment": Ibid.

786 King told reporters: NYT, May 9, 1963, pp. 1, 17.

786 five hundred youngest: Ibid.

787 prickly talks: Harding, "Beginning," p. 17.

787 "make a lot of sense": Cabinet meeting, May 21, 1963, Audiotape 88.6, JFK.

787 "federal government has done nothing": King statement, May 9, 1963, A/KS4.

788 "I'm damn sure": Levison intercept, 2:17 P.M., May 10, 1963, FLNY-7-417a.

788 "the Administration made a mistake": Levison intercept, 9:50 A.M., May 10, 1963, FLNY-9-163.

788 "to Birmingham by morning": Int. Joseph Rauh, Oct. 17, 1983.

788 "we'll be that lucky": Bradlee, *Conversations*, pp. 189–90.

788 George Meany: Navasky, *Justice*, p. 208.

789 Belafonte's doorbell: Int. Harry Belafonte, March 6–7, 1985.

789 speech he had delivered: On Oct. 5, 1961, King had addressed the annual convention of Quill's union, the Transport Workers Union of America, after which Quill had shouted to his members, "That was the greatest speech I've heard in my twenty-seven years [in the labor movement]," A/KS2.

789 vault of Chase Manhattan: Int. Clarence Jones, Nov. 25, 1983. Also int. Hugh Morrow, Dec. 20, 1984. Jones remembers the sum as $100,000, Morrow as $25,000. The figures could not be reconciled, although it is possible that Rockefeller made two separate contributions to the Birmingham movement that spring.

789 Governor Rockefeller himself: NYT, May 5, p. 1, and May 9, 1963, p. 1; *Life* cover story, May 17, 1963.

789 dropped thirteen points: Chicago *Sun-Times*, May 26, 1963, p. 5.

790 "accord with its conscience": NYT, May 11, 1963, pp. 1, 8; Lewis, *King*, pp. 200–1; Garrow, *Bearing*, p. 259.

790 At St. John's Church: Police notes on mass meeting, May 10, 1963, BIR/BC13f5; also Tape 4, SHSW/SP.

792 "flamboyant policy": AJ, May 10, 1963, p. 26. For hostile reactions of the Birmingham newspapers, see BN, May 10, p. 2, and May 11, 1963, p. 2; Corley, "Quest," p. 273.

792 "Tragic Cost": ADW, May 12, 1963, p. 4.

792 dazzling collection: Ibid., p. 3.

792 "Fight the niggers!": WRVR-FM Radio Series, "Testament of Nonviolence," Parts 2 and 6, SHSW/SP.

793 urgently recommended: Int. Laurie Pritchett, Nov. 25, 1986; also *Jet*, May 2, 1963, pp. 4–5.

793 the first bomb struck: NYT, May 12, 1963, p. 1.

793 calculated the damage: "Bombing Damage," undated memo by Fire Chief John L. Swindle, BIR/C1f37.

794 let his brother Martin: King Jr., *Can't Wait*, p. 107; King sermon in Riverside Church, Aug. 9, 1964, p. 7, A/KS6.

794 "put your bricks down!": Donald Smith, Tape 4, SHSW/SP.

794 view of the damage: NYT, May 12, p. 1, and May 13, 1963, p. 1; BN, May 12, 1963, p. 1.

794 followed Walker into the park: Int. Rev. Wyatt Tee Walker, Aug. 20, 1984.

795 "If you'd leave, Mr. Lingo": NYT, May 13, 1963, p. 1; *Newsweek*, May 20, 1963, pp. 25ff.

796 John Doar decided: Notebook of Edwin Guthman, headed "Mother's Day," 1963, Edwin Guthman Papers.

796 By dawn: NYT, May 13, 1963, p. 1; BN, May 26, 1963, p. 4.

796 Walker made the mistake: Walker speech, May 25, 1963, Tape 0388, PRA.

796 Galaxie convertible: Notebook of Edwin Guthman, headed "Mother's Day," 1963, Edwin Guthman Papers.

797 "sticking bayonets in people": White House meeting, May 12, 1963, Audiotape 86.2, JFK.

799 King had told reporters: NYT, May 13, 1963, p. 24.

799 "the nigger King": Ibid.

799 Smyer hazarded: Notebook of Edwin Guthman, headed "Mother's Day," 1963, Edwin Guthman Papers.

799 "heel of the military": BN, May 13, 1963, p. 3.

800 Operation Oak Tree: Code name cited in General B. E. Powell memo, May 22, 1963, Box 17, Marshall Papers, JFK.

800 "leaned too much": Notebook of Edwin Guthman, headed "Mother's Day," 1963, Edwin Guthman Papers.

800 "the wonderful words": Tapes 4 and 5, SHSW/SP.

801 "You can quote me": Ibid.

801 "got my training camp" to "teach any of you": Selections from mass meeting of May 13, 1963, ibid.

802 "love offering" and "de-bulled": Police notes on mass meeting, May 15, 1963, BIR/BC13f5.

Twenty-one
FIRESTORM

803 he gave six speeches: Cleveland *Plain Dealer*, May 14, p. 10, and May 15, 1963, p. 1; Cleveland *Call and Post*, May 18, 1963, pp. 1, 2, 16; *Jet*, May 30, 1963, pp. 17, 24–25; King-Levison conversation, May 19, 1963, FLNY-9-172.

804 two-page scoop: New York *Post*, May 19, 1963, p. 1.

804 "cut down and ready": L. Bergman to King, May 17, 1963, A/KP18f17. Also Levison conversations with King, May 18, 1963, FLNY-9-171a, and with Harvey Shapiro of the *Times Magazine*, May 19, 1963, FLNY-9-170.

804 *Liberation:* June 1963 issue.

804 *Christian Century:* Issue of June 12, 1963.

804 *Witness*, etc.: Listed in A/KS4, A/SC27f21.

804 Levison sold reprint: King call to Levison, May 31, 1963, FLNY-7-438a.

804 maneuvered Kunstler aside: Levison conversations with Kunstler, King, Jones, and O'Dell, May 18–24, 1963, FLNY-9-171a, 172, 172a, and 174; also FLNY-7-427a and 431a.

804 expel two thousand child: Shuttlesworth et al. to Smyer et al., May 17, 1963, Box 17, Marshall Papers, JFK; police notes on mass meeting, May 20, 1963, BIR/BC13f5; King call to Levison, 1:35 A.M., May 21, 1963, FLNY-9-174.

804 old Wrigley Field: Los Angeles *Sentinel*, May 30, 1963, pp. 1, 6.

804 Paul Newman read: Wrigley Field rally, May 26, 1963, Tape 4745a, PRA.

805 "Wings Over Jordan": *Jet*, June 13, 1963, pp. 54–60.

805 shore of Lake Michigan: Ibid., pp. 62–63; Goreau, *Just Mahalia*, pp. 349–52.

806 battered wife: Guralnick, *Sweet Soul Music*, pp. 332–52.

806 $100 bills: *Jet*, June 13, 1963, p. 43.

806 ahead to Kentucky: Levison-King conversation, May 28, 1963, FLNY-7-435a; Louisville *Defender*, June 6, 1963, p. 1.

806 on to St. Louis: CD, June 1–7, 1963, p. 4.

806 Atlantic City: PC, June 8, 1963, p. 2.

806 Walker darted: Walker in Albany on May 20, 1963, per FA-1069, in San Francisco on May 25, 1963, Tape 0388, PRA.

806 Lee came behind: San Francisco *Chronicle*, May 27, 1963, pp. 1, 4, 5; NYT, May 27, 1963, p. 19; BN, May 27, 1963, p. 2.

806 "He whooped": Ponder to King, May 26, 1963, A/KP34f14.

806 Birmingham, England: CD, May 11, 1963, p. 4. Also on breadth of change, Westin and Mahoney, *Trial*, p. 150, and Lewis, *King*, pp. 200–3.

806 34 arrested in Raleigh: NYT, May 15, 1963, p. 26.

806 100 in Albany: SAC Atlanta to Director, May 31, 1963, FBI File #157-4-2, serial 168.

806 400 in Greensboro: NYT, May 21, 1963, p. 19.

806 1,000 in Durham: Ibid.

807 1,420 anti-U.S.: Thomas L. Hughes memo, June 14, 1963, Box 295, NSF, JFK.

807 Milton Obote: Quoted in Ambassador Korry of Ethiopia to Rusk, May 23, 1963, 3 P.M., Box 295, NSF, JFK.

807 "How the hell": Lee White, third interview (1964), JFKOH.

807 " 'Why should we hire' ": Cabinet meeting of May 21, 1963, Audiotape 88.6, JFK.

807 405 U.S. Treasury employees: Ibid.

807 "a lot of trouble" to "like Marx coming": Presidential meeting of May 20, 1963, Audiotape 88.4, JFK.

809 Gregory had suggested: Marshall and RFK joint interview, pp. 708ff, JFKOH.

809 haphazard assortment: NYT, May 25, p. 1, and May 26, 1963, p. 1; list of those present at Baldwin meeting, Box 8, Marshall Papers, JFK.

810 mystified Belafonte: Int. Harry Belafonte, March 6–7, 1985.

810 "take up a gun": Ibid.

810 in North Carolina: Carey to Jerome Smith, Jan. 4, 1963, Reel 36, File 268, CORE.

810 "kiss it goodbye": *Jet*, June 13, 1963, pp. 6, 7, 12; Stein, *Journey*, pp. 119–22.

811 two sides jerked apart: Baldwin sources above, plus Schlesinger, *Thousand Days*, pp. 878–79; Guthman, *Band*, pp. 219–21; Schlesinger Jr., *Robert Kennedy*, pp. 356–60; *Newsweek*, June 3, 1963, p. 19.

812 "mad illusion": Levison-Jones conversation, May 26, 1963, FLNY-9-179a.

812 "you have swell friends": RFK note on Jones letter to NYT editor of June 7, 1963, Box 8, Marshall Papers, JFK; copy in A/KP13f13.

812 three Negroes married to whites: RFK, April 30, 1964, pp. 427–29, JFKOH.

812 married Ann Norton: Int. Clarence Jones, Oct. 25, 26, Nov. 21, 22, and 25, 1983.

812 told Guthman that perhaps: Int. Edwin Guthman, June 25, 1984.

813 tongue-lashings: Schlesinger Jr., *Robert Kennedy*, pp. 360–61.

813 Johnson's exclusion: White House meeting of May 20, 1963, Audiotape 88.4, JFK; Miller, *Lyndon*, p. 374.

813 "not competent to counsel": White House meeting of June 1, 1963, Audiotape 90.3, JFK.

813 two days after King: Evers, *For Us*, p. 265.

813 "History has reached": Ibid., pp. 267–68.

814 "next scene of attack": Current to Hurley et al., May 13, 1963, III-H-138, NAACP.

814 Thompson squelched: Evers, *For Us*, p. 271.

814 sit-in at the Woolworth's: Moody, *Coming of Age*, pp. 236–40.

814 graphically depicted: *Newsweek*, June 10, 1963, pp. 28–29.

814 kicking appeared: NYT, May 29, 1963, p. 1.

814 nearby beauty shop: Moody, *Coming of Age*, p. 239.

815 critical motivation: Ibid., pp. 224–27.

815 Evers straddled: Evers, *For Us*, pp. 257–58, 262.

815 "Don't shop for anything": Segment 5 of PBS documentary "Eyes on the Prize."

815 David Dennis: NYT, May 31, 1963, p. 1.

815 "To our parents we say": NYT, June 1, 1963, pp. 1, 8.

816 made it five on June 1: NYT, June 2, 1963, p. 70; BW, June 5, 1963, p. 1; Wilkins, *Standing Fast*, pp. 288–89.

816 King sent telegrams: King to JFK and RFK, May 30, 1963, A/KP14f4.

816 dispatch his couriers: Hoover to RFK, May 31, 1963, FK-127; Hoover to O'Donnell, May 31, 1963, FK-129.

816 Lee White declined: White to King, June 1, 1963, A/KP14f4; Garrow, *Bearing*, p. 265.

816 "baptized brother Wilkins": Levison's recollection of June 1 conversation, June 2, 1963, FLNY-9-186a.

816 "We are on a breakthrough": Conference call, 11:31 P.M., June 1, 1963, FLNY-9-185a.

817 "you tingled": Levison conversation with Ann and Clarence Jones, June 2, 1963, FLNY-9-186a; also conversations with Jones and "Alice" [Loewi?], June 3, 1963, FLNY-7-441.

817 "second phase": NYT, June 4, 1963.

817 Lena Horne: NYT, June 8, 1963, p. 14; Buckley, *The Hornes*, pp. 246–47.

817 stalked through his house: Evers, *For Us*, p. 273.

817 speculated intensely: E.g., Anthony Lewis in NYT, June 9, 1963, sec. 4, p. 1.

817 Tallahassee: NYT, May 31, p. 1, and June 1, 1963, p. 8.

818 led by Jesse Jackson: NYT, June 7, 1963, p. 14; Meier and Rudwick, *CORE*, p. 218.

818 grand basileus: BW, Jan. 19, 1963.

818 first political stories: Reynolds, *Jesse Jackson*, p. 37; PC, June 1, 1963, p. 1.

818 Newfoundland: Yarmolinsky to White, June 5, 1963, Lee White Papers, Box 19, JFK.

818 wife and newborn: Int. John Doar, Oct. 25, 1983.

818 successfully escorted: NYT, June 7, 1963, p. 14; BW, June 12, 1963, p. 1.

818 hearing of the House: House Judiciary Subcommittee hearings, No. 5, May 28, 1963, pp. 1246–1322.

818 "Negroes would still be marching": *Southern Patriot*, June 18, 1963, p. 4.

818 "launch this kind of thing": Ibid.

819 Winona bus station: Affidavits of June Johnson, Annell Ponder, and Fannie Lou Hamer in COFO, *Mississippi*, pp. 17–24; Ponder-Hamer interview of June 13, 1963, in Watters and Cleghorn, *Climbing*, pp. 361–75.

820 "get him off the hook": Conference call, 12:01 A.M., June 10, 1963, with King, Abernathy, Levison, Jones, Walker, and Young, FLNY-9-194; preliminary consultations with Randolph discussed in earlier conversations of June 4 and 6, FLNY-7-442a and FLNY-9-190.

820 "Tribute to Our": Appreciation Week program of June 9–16, 1963, A/SC58f21.

821 Winona mystery deepened: Raines, *My Soul*, pp. 295–98.

821 Wallace and the Kennedy: BN, June 11, 1963, p. 1; NYT, June 12, 1963, p. 1; Guthman, *Band*, pp. 214–17; Schlesinger Jr., *Robert Kennedy*, pp. 366–68.

822 step away from the Cold War: *Newsweek*, June 24, 1963, p. 27.

822 forty-eight of sixty-five Negroes: King, *Freedom*, p. 88.

822 "We will hose down": WP, June 1, 1963, p. 1.

822 "beastly conduct of law": King to RFK, 12:35 P.M., June 11, 1963, A/KP31f18.

823 "we seldom if ever hear": NYT, June 10, 1963, pp. 1, 20.

823 no one liked the idea: RFK, April 30, 1964, p. 432, JFKOH; Burke Marshall, JFKOH; Schlesinger Jr., *Robert Kennedy*, pp. 368–69; Sorensen, *Kennedy*, pp. 494–95; *Newsweek*, June 24, 1963, p. 29.

823 scraps he liked from Louis: Int. Lee White, Dec. 13, 1983. ("That was Louie Martin's speech.")

823 tinkering to add: Schlesinger Jr., *Robert Kennedy*, p. 369.

823 no finished text: Int. Lee White, Dec. 13, 1983.

823 "Come on now, Burke": Burke Marshall, pp. 109–110, JFKOH.

823 "as old as the Scriptures": NYT, June 10, 1963, p. 20.

824 "I have just listened": MLK to JFK, undated, A/SC4f20.

824 Levison called King: Levison call to King, June 12, 1963, FLNY-9-196.

824 Jackson movement as shrunken: WP, June 12, 1963, p. 14; CD, June 8–14, 1963; *Jet*, June 20, 1963, pp. 8–10.

825 Evers had asked: Evers, *For Us*, p. 252.

825 Evers stepped out: NYT, June 13, 1963, p. 1; BN, June 12, 1963, p. 1; *Newsweek*, June 24, 1963, pp. 32–33; Evers, *For Us*, pp. 301–3.

825 758 racial demonstrations: Harold C. Fleming, "The Federal Executive and Civil Rights: 1961–1965," *Daedalus*, Fall 1965, p. 942; SRC study cited in Viorst, *Fire*, p. 222, and Morris, *Origins*, p. 274.

825 chained themselves: NYT, June 14, 1963, p. 16.

825 stoned the home: NYT, June 15, 1963, p. 9.

825 "Annell Ponder's eyes": Robinson to Horton, June 15, 1963, Reel 7, SHSW/HP.

825 Horton had abundant troubles: Knoxville *Journal*, June 21, 1963, p. 1; NYT, June 25, 1963, p. 15.

826 three federal suits: NYT, June 18, 1963, p. 23; BW, June 29, 1963, p. 7; Hamer interview by Jack O'Dell, *Freedomways*, Spring 1965, p. 238.

826 Doar snatched: Int. John Doar, May 12, 1986.

826 "my guess is that a demonstration": Tape 4817, PRA.

826 "bottles and bricks crashing": NYT, June 16, 1963, p. 1.

827 name from a hat: Int. John Doar, Oct. 25, 1983. The name came out Burke Doar, after Burke Marshall.

827 "Civil rights did it": JFK–Carl Albert conversation, June 12, 1963, Dictabelt 22A, JFK.

828 when three thousand: *Newsweek*, June 24, 1963, p. 34.

828 Marshall had just reported: Marshall to RFK, June 13, 1963, Box 3, Marshall Papers, JFK.

828 "Individuals will be hired": Jack Newfield, *Robert Kennedy*, as cited in Schlesinger Jr., *Robert Kennedy*, p. 371.

829 "Memorial Bail Fund": NYT, June 13, 1963, p. 13.

829 Other Evers funds: Evers, *For Us*, pp. 342–43; CD, June 15–21, 1963, p. 1.

829 secured her written agreement: Wilkins to Kheel and Wilkins to Johnson, June 13, 1963, A/SC5f33; Wilkins to King, June 13, 1963, A/KP17f7.

829 gained the widow's permission: Evers, *For Us*, p. 322.

829 Gandhi Society surrendered: Kheel to Wilkins, June 14, 1963, and Jones to Wilkins, June 14, 1963, A/SC5f33.

829 "antagonism towards Martin": Levison-Montero conversation, June 14, 1963, FLNY-7-452a.

830 "Lest we forget": Evers memorial service of June 15, 1963, Tape 4817, PRA.

830 "a titanic struggle here": NYT, June 15, 1963, p. 9.

831 "Can you imagine it?": Wilkins, *A Man's Life*, p. 123.

831 "furnish the noise": WP, June 15, p. D6, and June 17, 1963, p. 1; NYT, June 17, 1963, p. 12.

831 "I think the world of you": JFK-Thompson conversations of June 18, 1963 [possibly June 17, 1963], Dictabelts 22A.4, 22B.1, and 22B.3, JFK.

832 present the final result: NYT, June 19, 1963, p. 22.

832 "hair's getting whiter": Mass meeting of June 18, 1963, Tape 4817, PRA.

833 250-pound weight: Jackson *Clarion-Ledger*, June 21, 1963, p. 1.

833 "everyone can see": Tape 4817, PRA.

833 "not just become empty prayers": Ibid.

833 buried Medgar Evers: NYT, June 15, p. 1, June 16, p. 1, and June 21, 1963, p. 14; CD, June 15–21, 1963, p. 1; Evers, *For Us*, pp. 322–28; *Jet*, July 4, 1963, pp. 6–10.

833 rescinded his acceptance: JFK to MLK, June 12, 1963; Abernathy to JFK, June 13, 1963; Walker to JFK, June 13, 1963; MLK to JFK, June 13, 1963, all in A/KP14f4.

834 Everett Dirksen: NYT, June 18, 1963, p. 1.

834 to jail in Savannah: NYT, June 19, p. 22, and June 20, 1963, p. 19.

834 In Gadsden, Alabama: Westin and Mahoney, *Trial*, p. 153.

834 broke down church doors: NYT, June 23, 1963, p. 62; Mary King, *Freedom*, pp. 82–84.

834 Laurie Pritchett's men: SAC Atlanta to Director, July 15, 1963, p. 3, FBI File #157-4-2, serial 174.

834 ordered all U.S. ambassadors: Secretary of State Dean Rusk to "All American Diplomatic and Consular Posts," June 19, 1963, NSF, Box 295, JFK.

834 "wholly devoid of conviction": Galbraith to Rusk, June 20, 1963, NSF, Box 295, JFK.

834 money quarrel in Birmingham: Garrow, *Bearing*, p. 271.

834 closing of Atlanta's Funtown: AC, June 17, 1963, p. 5.

834 "arrogance and opportunism": Reese Cleghorn, "Martin Luther King, Jr.: Apostle of Crisis," *Saturday Evening Post*, June 15, 1963, pp. 15–19.

834 brink of filing: Wachtel to Matthew J. Culligan (president of Curtis Publishing Company), June 20, 1963, and Chauncy Eskridge to Clay Blair, Jr. (editor of the *Saturday Evening Post*), June 24, 1963, A/KP25f25.

834 1,500 national leaders: NYT, June 23, 1963, p. 63.

834 O'Donnell notify King: O'Donnell telegram to King, June 20, 1963, A/KP14f4.

835 "paid agent of the Soviet": Int. Burke Marshall, June 27, 1984.

835 "whole political life": Ibid.

835 these confrontations: Marshall to Hoover, Sept. 20, 1963, FK-3656; Evans to Belmont, Sept. 20, 1963, FL-NR.

835 Kennedy was pushing Hoover: Hoover to Tolson et al., June 17, 1963, FK-150; Garrow, *FBI*, pp. 60–61.

836 destroy its domestic political base: Marshall and RFK joint interview, pp. 797–98, JFKOH.

836 "always sort of dismissing": Ibid., pp. 674–76; also int. Burke Marshall, Sept. 26, 1984.

837 "My God!": Marshall and RFK joint interview, p. 677, JFKOH. The interviewer for this oral history was NYT correspondent Anthony Lewis.

837 in the White House Rose Garden: Schlesinger Jr., *Robert Kennedy*, pp. 384–85; Garrow, *Bearing*, pp. 272–73. White House records show that King met President Kennedy at 10:10 A.M., before the group civil rights meeting at 10:30. Appointments log, JFK.

837 hand on his shoulder: Int. Clarence Jones, Oct. 25, 1983.

837 "time to do all that": Int. Jack O'Dell, July 1, 1986.

838 "Profumo in the papers": Schlesinger Jr., *Robert Kennedy*, p. 384. The Profumo scandal was very much in the news at the time of the JFK-MLK meeting: e.g., NYT, June 14, p. 3, and June 18, 1963, p. 1; *Newsweek*, June 17, 1963, p. 38.

838 Readers of the Negro press: E.g., *Jet*, May 9, 1963, pp. 46–47.

838 obsessed President Kennedy: Bradlee, *Conversations*, p. 230.

839 Joe Rauh realized: Int. Joseph Rauh, Oct. 17, 1983.

839 "Hello, hello, hello": Allen interviews of Rachelle Horowitz, Nov. 8, 1968, and John Lewis, Aug. 8, 1969, AAP.

839 daughters in his lap: Wilkins, *Standing Fast*, p. 291.

839 President made welcoming remarks: Schlesinger, *Thousand Days*, pp. 884–85; Schlesinger Jr., *Robert Kennedy*, pp. 375–76.

839 "lose the next election": Int. Joseph Rauh, Oct. 17, 1983.

839 "Call on Roy": Ibid.

840 *"will* be a march": Allen interview of John Lewis, Aug. 8, 1969, AAP.
840 "all have our problems": Ibid.
840 "Negroes Inform Kennedy": NYT, June 23, 1963, p. 1.
841 "That little baby": Gentile, *March*, p. 39.
841 South Lawn by helicopter: Lee White, third interview, May 28, 1964, JFKOH.
841 McGeorge Bundy defended: NYT, June 17, 1963, p. 1.
841 Kennedy told his staff: Sorensen, *Kennedy*, pp. 503, 579.
841 hailed his motorcade: NYT, June 26, p. 1, and June 27, 1963, p. 1.
842 thrilled Kennedy: Schlesinger, *Thousand Days*, pp. 808–9.
842 "never have another day": Sorensen, *Kennedy*, p. 601.
842 postponed once: MC, May 25, p. 1, and June 22, 1963, p. 1.
842 "bunch of Uncle Toms": Detroit *News*, June 25, 1963, pp. 1, 4.
842 "graceful withdrawal": Diggs to King, June 27, 1963, A/KP24f26.
842 "you'll see no dogs": Detroit *News*, June 24, 1963, pp. 1, 2, 19–20.
843 VJ-Day-style stories: Ibid. Also MC, June 29, 1963, p. 1.
843 "largest and greatest demonstration" to "I have a dream": "The Great March to Freedom," Gordy Records #906, distributed by Motown.
844 King felt the blade: Meeting of June 24, 1963, from int. Jack O'Dell, July 1, 1986, Clarence Jones, Oct. 25, 1983, and Aug. 18, 1986, and Harry Belafonte, March 6–7, 1985.

Twenty-two
THE MARCH ON WASHINGTON

846 "Look, Bayard" to "Okay, Roy": Int. Bayard Rustin, Nov. 28, 1983.
847 at New York's Roosevelt Hotel: July 2 meeting from ibid. Also int. Cleveland Robinson, Oct. 28, 1983; Allen interview of John Lewis, Sept. 23, 1969, AAP; Norman Hill, CRDPOH; NYT, July 3, 1963, p. 10; *Jet*, July 18, 1963, pp. 16–20; Lewis, *King*, p. 215; Wilkins, *Standing Fast*, p. 292; Forman, *The Making*, p. 332; Garrow, *Bearing*, pp. 276–77.
848 fifty-fourth annual convention: *The Crisis*, August–September 1963, pp. 389–400; Chicago *Sun-Times*, July 5, 1963, p. 4; CD, July 6, 1963, p. 1; NYT, July 5, p. 1, and July 6, 1963, p. 1; BW, July 10, 1963, p. 1; *Newsweek*, July 15, 1963, p. 20; *Jet*, July 25, 1963, pp. 50–51; Meredith, *Three Years*, pp. 310–19.
849 Wilkins told viewers: "For Freedom Now," NET interview aired July 22, 1963, A/KS4. By King's log, the show was taped in New York on July 12, A/SC29.
849 "a few human hearts": Farmer, *Lay Bare*, p. 216.
849 battered stucco building: Gentile, *March*, pp. 47–56.
850 *Organizing Manual No. 1*: Gentile, *March*, p. 56; NYT, July 25, 1963, p. 11.
850 sent word to O'Dell: Int. Jack O'Dell, July 1, 1986.
850 "Pays O'Dell Despite": BN, June 30, 1963, p. 1.
850 learned from Burke Marshall: Garrow, *FBI*, p. 63.
850 Kennedy's most favored reporters: Int. Edwin Guthman, June 25, 1984. Free was Washington correspondent for BN.
851 letter of dismissal: King to O'Dell, July 3, 1963, A/KP18f38, with a copy to Marshall: Dora McDonald to Marshall with enclosure, July 3, 1963, A/KP24f20; O'Dell to King, July 12, 1963, A/KP18f39.
851 join the staff of *Freedomways:* Int. Jack O'Dell, July 1, 1986. His first article, "The Negro People in the Southern Economy," appeared in the Fall 1963 issue, pp. 526–48.
851 still down in Ecuador: The Levisons discussed the vacation on the telephone, as picked up regularly by the FBI wiretaps, e.g., FLNY-9-236a, from July 22, 1963.
851 President Carlos Arosemena: NYT, July 12, 1963, p. 1.
851 or so it was told: John Rothchild, *Latin America: Yesterday and Today* (Bantam Books, 1978), p. 283.
852 Courthouse in New Orleans: Garrow, *FBI*, p. 62; int. Roger Wilkins, Dec. 7, 1983.
852 deeply planted KGB agent: NYT, Feb. 10, 1962, p. 1.
852 If Stalin had invented: Int. Harry Wachtel, Oct. 27, 1983, and Harry Belafonte, March 6–7, 1985.
852 tactical compromise: Int. Clarence Jones, Aug. 18, 1986.
852 King sent Clarence: Evans to Belmont, July 16, 1963, FBI #100-3-116-41; U.S. Sen-

ate (Church Committee), Report No. 94-755, Book III, pp. 100–1; Garrow, *FBI*, p. 63; int. Clarence Jones, Oct. 25–26, 1983, and Burke Marshall, June 27, 1984.

853 "Barnett Charges": NYT, July 13, 1963, p. 1; also WS, July 12, 1963, p. 1; WP, July 13, 1963, p. 1.

853 Wallace introduced: NYT, July 16, 1963, p. 1; Baumgardner to Sullivan, July 16, 1963, FK-NR.

853 Just that morning: Evans to Belmont, July 16, 1963, FK-166.

854 Bureau had met the deadline: Jones to DeLoach, July 16, 1963, FK-164, based partly on Bland to Sullivan, July 13, 1963, FK-160.

854 suspicious character: Robert Kennedy, JFKOH; Bland to Sullivan, July 17, 1963, FJ-18.

855 did he tell Marshall: Int. Burke Marshall, June 27, 1984.

855 "I told the AG": Evans to Belmont, July 16, 1963, FBI #100-3-116, serial 41.

855 Hoover's formal requests: Hoover to RFK, July 22, 1963, FJ-NR (on Jones); Hoover to RFK, July 23, 1963, FK-165 (on King). The key backup documents for the wiretap requests are two memos from Baumgardner to Sullivan, July 22, 1963, FJ-21 and FK-168.

855 only preliminary assurance: Director to SAC Atlanta, July 26, 1963, FK-169, notes that Atlanta's final feasibility report was sent on July 24.

856 "few remaining Communists": NYT, July 18, 1963, pp. 1, 8.

856 "The Negro in America": *Newsweek*, July 29, 1963, which reached newsstands on July 22, just as the wiretap requests were making their way to RFK.

856 Kennedy released a letter: NYT, July 26, 1963, p. 1.

857 returned from Ecuador: Wiretap, July 22, 1963, FLNY-9-236a.

857 Mayor Ivan Allen: AJ, July 26, 1963, p. 1; Allen, *Mayor*, pp. 104–15.

857 chuckling over the irony: Wiretap, July 24, 1963, FLNY-9-238a.

857 "Onetime Communist": AC, July 25, 1963, p. 1.

858 issued a public statement: Statement of July 25, 1963, A/KS4.

858 held a press conference: AC, July 26, 1963, p. 1; AJ, July 26, 1963, p. 4; NYT, July 27, 1963, p. 8.

858 attack by Eugene Cook: Cook telegram to King, Aug. 1, 1963, A/KP11f34.

858 "to my certain knowledge": Cook to Walker, Aug. 15, 1963, answered by Walker Aug. 16, 1963, A/KP18f39; AC, Aug. 16, 1963, p. 3.

858 "the treaty": Wiretap, July 28, 1963, FLNY-9-242a.

858 "All staff members": King memo, July 26, 1963, A/KP34f4.

858 "Oh, now I see": Wiretap, July 28, 1963, FLNY-9-242a.

858 Levison resolved to withdraw: Schlesinger Jr., *Robert Kennedy*, p. 385; int. Harry Belafonte, March 6–7, 1985, and Clarence Jones, Oct. 25, 1983.

859 only one short-term project: Wiretap, Sept. 21, 1963, FLNY-9-297a, and Oct. 8, 1963, FLNY-7-610a.

859 "upset if you did": Garrow, *FBI*, p. 70.

859 first fruits: SAC New York to Hoover, Aug. 5, 1963, FJNY-84.

859 "well-appointed home": C. King, *My Life*, p. 240; Garrow, *Bearing*, pp. 280–81.

860 writer named Al Duckett: An FBI log of King's August meetings with Duckett was prepared Sept. 24, 1963, FJ-104. References to Duckett are scattered thinly in King's papers, generally in connection with the promotion of celebrity fund-raising events.

860 lowered his personal barriers: Int. Clarence Jones, Nov. 22 and 25, 1983, and Aug. 18, 1986.

860 "If the rumors are true": Ibid.

861 King's talk of sex: Garrow, *FBI*, p. 67.

861 Katzenbach on August 13: Hoover to Katzenbach, Aug. 13, 1963, FK-180.

861 "thought you would be interested": RFK to JFK, Aug. 20, 1963, Box 2, Marshall Papers, JFK.

861 "your boy Burke": SAC New York to Director, Aug. 11, 1963, FK189.

861 "one little brother": Ibid.

861 confidential memorandum: Hoover to RFK, Aug. 12, 1963, FK-178.

861 more than a dozen: Garrow, *FBI*, p. 250 (note 101).

861 Thurmond rose: *Congressional Record*, Aug. 13, 1963, pp. S14836ff. Thurmond had made previous speeches against Rustin and the march, but none so personal: *Congressional Record*, Aug. 2, 1963, pp. 13968ff, and Aug. 7, 1963, pp. S14455ff.

862 "taking the active part": SAC Los Angeles to Director, Aug. 15, 1963, FR-NR.
862 into November: E.g., [deleted] to SAC Los Angeles, Nov. 20, 1963, FR-NR.
862 "this is inconclusive": Marshall to RFK, Aug. 7, 1963, Box 3, Marshall Papers, JFK.
862 "Your former choir boy": Niebuhr to Scarlett, Nov. 11, 1963, Box 33, RN.
863 "Going Lily White?": CD, Aug. 10, 1963.
863 "the Goldwater surge": Letterhead Memorandum of Oct. 30, 1963, FJ-NR.
863 Niebuhr and King never became friends: There is no available record that Niebuhr and King ever met. King's friend Thomas Kilgore, who was a student of Niebuhr's during the 1950s, says that he often heard King speak of Niebuhr's ideas but never of Niebuhr personally. (Int. Rev. Thomas Kilgore, Feb. 11, 1988.) One possible explanation for the lack of initiative on King's part is that Niebuhr had refused King's written request, just after the Montgomery bus boycott, to sign a statement urging President Eisenhower to meet with a delegation of preachers from King's newly formed organization. In a private letter, Niebuhr explained his refusal to Supreme Court Justice Felix Frankfurter, saying, "I was advised that such a pressure would do more harm than good." (Niebuhr to Frankfurter, Feb. 8, 1957, Box 86, Felix Frankfurter Papers, Library of Congress.)
863 "I called up Albert Thomas": White House meeting of July 9, 1963, Audiotape 96.6, JFK.
864 Johnson's enthusiasm: E.g., NYT, Nov. 1, 1963, p. 1.
864 tour of Scandinavia: NYT, Aug. 5, 1963.
864 announced on August 1: NYT, Aug. 2, 1963, pp. 1, 10.
864 Chicago police arrested: Gentile, *March*, pp. 103–7.
864 authorities in Gadsden: NYT, Aug. 4, 1963, p. 1.
864 abolish the resolutions: NYT, July 23, 1963, p. 1; also two antecedent stories, July 15, 1963, p. 1.
864 In Americus: Whitehead, *Attack*, p. 136; Forman, *The Making*, pp. 338–44; Abram, *Day*, pp. 139–40; NYT, Aug. 14, p. 21, Sept. 28, p. 22, Sept. 29, p. 80, Sept. 30, p. 28, Oct. 18, p. 64, Oct. 22, p. 31, Oct. 31, p. 23, Nov. 1, p. 19, Nov. 2, p. 1, Nov. 27, p. 27, and Dec. 8, 1963, p. 54.
866 "Albany Nine": Generally from case files in possession of C. B. King. Also int. Burke Marshall, Sept. 26, 1984, S. B. Wells, July 9, 1985, C. B. King, July 10, 1985, Marion Cheek, July 11, 1985, and Charles Sherrod, Jan. 23, 1986; *Upside-Down Justice: The Albany Cases*, a pamphlet published by the National Committee for the Albany Defendants, M. L. King, Jr., chairman; Navasky, *Justice*, pp. 121–23; Gentile, *March*, pp. 117–18; FBI #157-6-2, serials 1100–1350.
867 Elizabeth Holtzman: WP, Oct. 27, 1987, p. D1.
868 Katzenbach told reporters: NYT, Aug. 10, 1963, p. 1.
868 *Star* congratulated: WS, Aug. 14, 1963.
868 hospital from Loveman's: NYT, Aug. 16, 1963, p. 8.
868 demolished the entrance: BW, Aug. 24, 1963, p. 1; *Jet*, Sept. 5, 1963, pp. 6–7.
868 he eventually escaped: Meier and Rudwick, *CORE*, pp. 221–22; Farmer, *Lay Bare*, pp. 244–54.
869 closest friend in SNCC: Int. John Lewis, May 31, 1984.
869 into a tanning chair: Allen interviews of Rachelle Horowitz, Nov. 8, 1968, and John Lewis, Sept. 23, 1969, AAP.
869 "which side is the Federal": Schlesinger Jr., *Robert Kennedy*, p. 377; Garrow, *Bearing*, pp. 281–82.
870 "I'm hounding you": Wiretap, Aug. 21, 1963, FLNY-9-266.
870 speech in Chicago: CD, Aug. 24–30, 1963, p. 1; Tape 9, SHSW/SP.
871 Lawrence Spivak spoke: "Meet the Press" transcript for program of Aug. 25, 1963.
872 possibility that marauding Negroes: Gentile, *March*, pp. 127, 148–49.
872 impounded for fifty years: WP, Feb. 1, 1977, p. 5; Opinion of the Court in U.S. District Court (D.C.), Civil Action #76-1185 and #76-1186.
872 peace was fragile: Viorst, *Fire*, p. 225.
873 temporary drinking fountains: *Life*, Sept. 6, 1963, pp. 20–29.
873 80,000 cheese-sandwich: NYT, Aug. 28, 1963, p. 1.
873 "absolutely stupid": Viorst, *Fire*, p. 224.
873 exceeded seven minutes: Gentile, *March*, p. 163.
873 Huddling with John Lewis: Allen interviews of Lewis, Sept. 23, 1969, and Rachelle

Horowitz, Nov. 8, 1968, AAP; Gentile, *March*, pp. 171–75; Forman, *The Making*, pp. 333–34.

875 "Robber Band Enlarged": Gentile, *March*, p. 160.

875 in his suite at the Willard: King interviewed by Donald H. Smith, Nov. 29, 1963, Tape 9, SHSW/SP; C. King, *My Life*, pp. 240–41

875 "Five score years ago": Draft of King's speech appeared in several black newspapers, e.g., CD, Aug. 24–30, 1963, p. 4.

876 Also that morning: Gentile, *March*, pp. 176, 212; *Jet*, Sept. 12, 1963, pp. 14–29.

876 boarded in Savannah: Gentile, *March*, p. 191.

876 "Woke up this morning": AJ, Aug. 21, 1983, pp. D1, 4, 5.

876 historian Thomas Gentile: Gentile, *March*, pp. 135ff.

877 "celebrity plane": There is a good deal of correspondence on the effort to recruit celebrities for the march, e.g., Jones to MLK, Aug. 2, 1963, A/KP11f27.

877 SNCC Freedom Singers: Int. Joan Baez, Jan. 7, 1984, Bernice Johnson Reagon, Dec. 15, 1985, and Rutha Harris, Jan. 23, 1986.

878 "Du Bois chose another path": Tape of march speeches, BUK16f34; Wilkins, *Standing Fast*, p. 293.

878 Christianborg Castle: BW, Sept. 7, 1963, p. 1.

878 sidecar of a police motorcycle: Garrow, *Bearing*, p. 283.

879 shaking fingers: Allen interview of John Lewis, Sept. 23, 1969, AAP.

879 "We come late": Gentile, *March*, pp. 175, 226.

879 "John, I know you": John Lewis, CRDPOH; Lewis interview by Allen, AAP; King interview by Donald H. Smith, Nov. 29, 1963, SHSW/SP.

880 vapid emotions of the march: Forman, *The Making*, pp. 333–37; Mary King, *Freedom*, pp. 183–85.

880 "Where is *our* party?": Tape of march speeches, BUK16f34.

880 role of women: Gentile, *March*, pp. 140–42, 225; C. King, *My Life*, pp. 241–42.

881 "spread upon the Journal": Gentile, *March*, p. 199.

881 delivered his address: "The Great March on Washington," Motown recording #908.

882 "Tell 'em about the dream": Int. Cleveland Robinson, Oct. 28, 1983.

882 "came to me": King interviewed by Donald H. Smith, Nov. 29, 1963, Tape 9, SHSW/SP.

882 Jackson was happy: MC, Sept. 7, 1963, p. 2.

883 "damn good": Int. Lee White, Dec. 13, 1983.

883 greeted King: Ibid. Also Gentile, *March*, p. 253; NYT, Aug. 29, 1963, pp. 1, 16.

883 "soar in the wild blue yonder" to "Walter in the background": Audiotape 108.2, JFK.

886 At 6:12 P.M.: Appointment log, JFK.

886 relaxed its rules: ADW, Sept. 1, 1963, p. 1.

886 bootleg recordings: Complaints and legal proceedings, A/KP13f15, A/KP16f37.

886 "marvelous in Martin's speech": Wiretap, 4:30 P.M., Aug. 28, 1963, FLNY-9-273a.

Twenty-three
CROSSING OVER: NIGHTMARES AND DREAMS

888 Boutwell maneuvered: Memos and phone notes, Sept. 3–7, 1963, BIR/AB20f40.

888 King sent another: MLK to JFK, Sept. 5, 1963, A/SC1f9.

888 "Huntley-Brinkley Report": Manchester, *Glory*, p. 1228; *Newsweek*, Sept. 23, 1963, pp. 62–65.

888 Sonnie W. Hereford IV: BN, Sept. 9, 1963, p. 1.

889 Kennedy had federalized: NYT, Sept. 10 and 11, 1963; memos of Birmingham police contact with Justice Department, Sept. 10, 1963, BIR/AB20f38.

889 declared his intention: BN, Sept. 13, 1963, p. 1.

889 Mamie H. Grier: Mamie Grier oral history, Nov. 19, 1975, UAB.

890 noise of the blast: Church bombing generally from NYT, Sept. 16, 1963, pp. 1, 26; BN, Sept. 16, 1963, p. 1; *Newsweek*, Sept. 30, 1963, pp. 20–25; *Jet*, Oct. 3, 1963, pp. 8–26.

891 attorney Charles Morgan: Raines, *My Soul*, pp. 196–202.

891 risk taking Marshall: Int. Burke Marshall, Sept. 26, 1984.

891 "What murdered these four": MLK statement of Sept. 16, 1963, A/KS5. (King had

sent a telegram to JFK on the day of the church bombing, saying "you must call for legislation" and promising to "plead with my people to remain nonviolent": MLK to JFK, Sept.
15, 1963, Box 1478, Name File, JFK. The next day King sought an "emergency audience"
with Kennedy: King et al. to JFK, telegram, Sept. 16, 1963, A/KP14f4.)

892   "Well, Martin, I did": John Cross, A/OH.
892   "her loss was personal": *Jet*, Oct. 3, 1963, p. 26.
892   allowed Shuttlesworth: BW, Sept. 21, 1963, p. 1.
892   "hard as crucible steel": MLK eulogy, A/KS5; funeral program, BIR/AB5f57.
892   Nash presented: Diane Bevel report, Sept. 17–20, 1963, A/SC41f8; Garrow, *Bearing*,
p. 294.
893   one of two things: Int. Diane Nash Bevel, Feb. 20, 1985.
893   "This is an army": Proposal for Action in Montgomery, A/SC41f8.
893   foreclosed such hopes: NYT, Sept. 20, 1963, p. 1; *Jet*, Oct. 3, pp. 10–11, and Oct.
10, 1963, pp. 8–10.
894   "great deal of frustration" to "men I've ever met": White House meeting of Sept.
19, 1963, Audiotape 112.1, JFK.
895   protested the Albany Nine: NYT, Sept. 21, 1963, p. 18.
895   intellectuals were furious: Letterhead Memorandum, Sept. 20, 1963, FJ-NR and
FL-NR.
895   Christmas shopping boycott: NYT, Sept. 22, 1963, p. 1.
895   "missing face of Christ": Transcript of discussion, Sept. 22, 1963, moderated by
Rev. Thomas Kilgore, supplied by Kilgore to Mrs. Reinhold Niebuhr and to author by
Elisabeth (Niebuhr) Sifton.
896   "big chips on our shoulder" to "anything that gives a hook": White house meeting
of Sept. 23, 1963, Audiotapes 112.6 and 113.1, JFK.
896   followed the briefing agenda: Civil rights briefing of Sept. 23, 1963, Audiotape
112.5, JFK.
898   "Birmingham Can Solve": NYT, Sept. 24, 1963, p. 1.
898   seventh annual convention: Official program, Sept. 24–27, 1963, FSC-NR (Section
2); NYT, Sept. 25, 1963, p. 33.
898   Walker demanded: Wyatt Walker, CRDPOH; int. Walker, Aug. 20, 1984.
899   inebriated elevator scuffle: Int. Septima Clark, Jan. 18, 1984.
899   "perfectly free inside": Clark to King, Nov. 4, 1963, A/SC3f24.
899   Powell renewed: NYT, Sept. 28, p. 22, and Sept. 29, 1963, p. 77.
899   board meeting stretched: Minutes, A/KP29f2.
899   all-white airport ceremony: NYT, Sept. 26, 1963, pp. 1, 29.
899   caution on three counts: MLK confidential memorandum, undated, c. September
1963, A/KP32f6.
900   Lewis' arrest in Selma: NYT, Sept. 25, p. 32, and Sept. 27, 1963, p. 30; Allen
interview of John Lewis, Sept 23, 1969, AAP.
900   SNCC leaders planned: *Jet*, Oct. 17, 1963, pp. 14–17, 20–22; NYT, Jan. 8, p. 37, and
Oct. 13, 1963, p. 77.
900   Boyte's crash campaign: Boyte interview by Donald H. Smith, Dec. 3, 1963,
SHSW/SP; Boyte staff memos, Sept. 20 and Dec. 11, 1963, A/KP29f7.
900   dismissing four top: Walker to MLK re "Staff Discipline," undated, A/KP36f4.
900   Walker exploded: Int. Rev. Wyatt Tee Walker, Aug. 20, 1984; Walker to MLK, Oct.
3, 1963, A/KP36f1.
900   cathartic of fraternal preaching: Int. Rev. Wyatt Tee Walker, Dec. 21, 1984, Marian
Logan, April 24, 1984, Rev. Ralph D. Abernathy, Nov. 19, 1984, and Bernard Lee, June 19,
1984.
901   "I have kept silence": MLK speech, Sept. 27, 1963, A/KS5.
901   immediately denounced King: MC, Sept. 28, 1963, p. 1; NYT, Sept. 29, 1963, p. 79;
BN, Sept. 29, 1963, pp. 1, 11; BW, Oct. 5, 1963, p. 1.
902   trove of Vernon Johns stories: Int. Chauncey Eskridge, Feb. 20, 1985. Eskridge had
gained an acquaintance with the Johns legend from King and also from personal experience.
Recommended by King, Eskridge had represented—and later married—one of Dr. Pettus'
daughters from Montgomery. Her sister still complained about how Vernon Johns had
ruined her life by announcing a watermelon sale during her wedding.

902 "give me all your notebooks": Ibid.

902 "The Romance of Death": Gandy, *Johns Reader*, pp. 115–23. Johns died June 11, 1964, according to a biography supplied by Jeanne Johns Adkins.

903 "when Castro took over": Garrow, *FBI*, p. 68; Powers, *Hoover*, p. 376.

903 "The Director is correct": Sullivan to Belmont, Aug. 30, 1963, FK-NR.

903 "make up your minds": Powers, *Hoover*, p. 377.

904 Levison's teenaged son: Director to SAC New York, Aug. 30, 1963, FL-NR.

904 also on King's home: Bland to Sullivan, Sept. 6, 1963, FK-207; Garrow, *FBI*, p. 69.

904 confidential draft: Marshall to RFK, Sept. 12, 1963, Box 3, Marshall Papers, JFK.

904 tacitly asked Hoover: Marshall to Hoover, Sept. 20, 1963, FK-3656.

904 "feel free, of course": Evans to Belmont, Sept. 20, 1963, FL-NR.

904 "high and dry": Wiretap, Sept. 30, 1963, FLNY-7-560a.

905 "baloney": Powers, *Hoover*, pp. 333, 366.

905 Hoover tried to cover: Schlesinger Jr., *Robert Kennedy*, pp. 288–89.

905 "innermost sanctum": "FBI Bulletin," September 1963, Edwin Guthman papers.

905 Hoover refused: Guthman, *Band*, pp. 264–66; int. Edwin Guthman, June 25, 1984.

905 "underworld glossary": NYT, Sept. 28, 1963, pp. 1, 6.

906 Valachi dominated: E.g., *Newsweek*, Oct. 7, 1963, pp. 34–39.

906 Kennedy published: "Robert Kennedy Defines the Menace," *New York Times Magazine*, Oct. 13, 1963, pp. 15ff.

906 among the President's mistresses: Baker, *Wheeling*, pp. 78–79; int. Clark Mollenhoff, Dec. 7, 1983, and Robert G. Baker, March 31, 1986.

906 woman named Ellen Rometsch: Des Moines *Register*, Oct. 26, 1963, p. 1; NYT, Oct. 29, 1963, p. 17; *Newsweek*, Nov. 11, 1963, pp. 32–33; WS, March 28, 1965, p. 1.

907 "don't change your minds": Bland to Sullivan, Oct. 4, 1963, FK-251.

907 Mansfield promised: Senate Rules Committee hearings, Oct. 29, 1963, pp. 1794–95.

907 sent it to the Attorney: Hoover to RFK, Oct. 7, 1963, FK-250.

907 "Courtney, speak to me": RFK to Evans, Oct. 10, 1963, FK-171.

907 privately with Courtney Evans: Evans to Belmont, Oct. 10, 1963; Garrow, *FBI*, p. 72.

908 directly from Floyd Mann: Marshall to RFK, Oct. 4, 1963, Box 3, Marshall Papers, JFK.

909 "no living with the Bureau": Int. Burke Marshall, Sept. 26, 1984, and Edwin Guthman, June 25, 1984.

909 stricken look: Int. John Seigenthaler, Dec. 15, 1987.

909 "Our challenge now": MLK "Confidential Memorandum," undated, A/KP32f6.

909 Amelia Boynton: Boynton to MLK, Oct. 8, 1963, A/KP21f10; Navasky, *Justice*, p. 128.

909 swelling controversy: NYT, Nov. 7, p. 30, and Nov. 14, 1963, p. 14; New York *Herald Tribune*, Nov. 7, 1963, p. 8; MLK statement, Nov. 6, 1963, A/KS5.

909 Marshall to apologize: Marshall to Rep. George Huddleston, Oct. 28, 1963, and Nov. 6, 1963, Box 18, Marshall Papers, JFK.

909 nearly fired John Doar: Int. Burke Marshall, Sept. 26, 1984.

909 Blaik and Royall promised: NYT, Oct. 11, 1963, p. 25; BW, Oct. 16, 1963, p. 1.

910 talked about football: Earl Blaik, JFKOH; Blaik to RFK, Nov. 18, 1963, Box 18, Marshall Papers, JFK.

910 secret protest notes: R. L. "Red" Holland, Jr., to Edwin Guthman, Oct. 3, 1963, Guthman papers.

910 "bland, PR approach": Blaik to Marshall, Nov. 1, 1963, Box 18, Marshall Papers, JFK.

910 dissolve their assignment: Royall and Blaik to LBJ, Dec. 16, 1963, Box 24, Folder HU2/ST1, LBJ.

910 cloud of flying fists: NYT, Oct. 14, 1963, p. 1; *Newsweek*, Nov. 4, 1963, pp. 27–28; *Jet*, Oct. 31, pp. 6–8, Nov. 7, pp. 6–12, and Nov. 14, 1963, pp. 8–15.

910 "backward and forward": NYT, Oct. 24, 1963, p. 32.

911 All this came through: Wiretaps, Sept. 16, FLNY-9-292a; Sept. 21, FLNY-9-297a; Sept. 23, FLNY-7-553a; Sept. 24, FLNY-7-554b; Oct. 10, FLNY-9-316; Oct. 26, FLNY-9-

332a; Oct. 8, FLNY-7-610a; Oct. 28, 1963, FLNY-7-558a; New York Letterhead Memorandum, Nov. 8, 1963, FJ-NR.

911 upset, vacillating: Evans to Belmont, Oct. 21, 1963, FK-259.

911 "obviously irritated": Evans to Belmont, Oct. 25, 1963, FK-NR; Garrow, *FBI*, p. 73.

911 "U.S. Expels Girl": Clark Mollenhoff in the Des Moines *Register*, Oct. 26, 1963, p. 1.

912 Duffy's mission: Int. Robert G. Baker, March 31, 1986, and John Seigenthaler, Dec. 15, 1987.

912 President in front of Evans: Evans to Belmont, Oct. 28, 1963, FER-22.

912 Alone, Kennedy told Hoover: Hoover to Tolson et al., Nov. 7, 1963, FER-99.

913 Kennedy changed the subject: Hoover to Tolson et al., Nov. 7, 1963, FK-NR. This appears to be a slightly altered version of the previous memo on the same day, in which the Rometsch material appears to be deleted in the copy released.

913 "supported by facts": Ibid.

913 called Senator Mansfield: Hoover to Tolson et al., Oct. 28, 1963, FER-20.

913 swarming with reporters: NYT, Oct. 29, 1963; WP, Oct. 29, 1963, p. 10; New York *Post*, Oct. 29, 1963, p. 5 (underlined in the FBI Rometsch file, with a handwritten note from Hoover: "Get after these angles promptly").

913 Hoover called the Attorney: Hoover to Tolson et al., Oct. 28, 1963, FER-24.

913 President Kennedy obtained: RFK, pp. 645–47, JFKOH.

913 not on his agenda: Senate Rules Committee executive session hearings, Oct. 29, 1963, pp. 1796–99.

913 "go into West Germany": NYT, Oct. 30, 1963, p. 1.

913 wiretap Bayard Rustin: Baumgardner to Sullivan, Oct. 25, 1963, and Oct. 6, 1964, FR-NR.

913 receded from the brink: *Newsweek*, Nov. 11, 1963, pp. 32–33; WS, March 28, 1965, p. 1; Senate Report No. 388, 89th Cong. (1965), Rules Committee, esp. pp. 50–53.

914 "Boy, the dirt": Bradlee, *Conversations*, p. 228.

914 Vietnam crisis had built: As chronicled in the various editions of the *Pentagon Papers* and highlighted by selected NYT stories, e.g., June 15, p. 1, Aug. 25, p. 1, Aug. 28, p. 1, Sept. 3, p. 1, Oct. 6, p. 1, Oct 10, p. 1, and Oct. 27, 1963, p. 1.

914 wrote Max Frankel: NYT, July 3, 1963, p. 8.

914 "government's coming apart!": Schlesinger Jr., *Robert Kennedy*, p. 770.

915 typical FBI career: Int. R. R. Nichols, May 29, 1984.

915 up and running: Garrow, *FBI*, p. 77.

915 schism in Detroit: MC, Nov. 2, p. 1, and Nov. 16, 1963, p. 1; *Jet*, Nov. 7, p. 4, and Nov. 28, 1963, pp. 18–19; PC, Nov. 9, 1963, p. 1.

916 "white man says bleed": Breitman, *Malcolm X Speaks*, p. 4.

916 "Nowhere in that Bible": Malcolm X debate with Bayard Rustin, undated, Tape 3014, PRA.

916 "unjust blows": Albany Letterhead Memorandum, Nov. 12, 1963, FBI 157-6-2-1434.

916 "movement in Danville": Garrow, *Bearing*, p. 306; New York Letterhead Memorandum, Nov. 4, 1963, FK-NR; Wyatt Walker interview by Donald H. Smith, SHSW/SP; Jack Greenberg to King et al., Nov. 7, 1963, A/KP31f18; Chase and King to W. J. Irwin, president of Dan River Mills, Nov. 18, 1963, A/KP31f19.

916 Shuttlesworth was urging: Fred Shuttlesworth to MLK, Nov. 7, 1963, A/KP22f11.

916 perpetual hiccoughs: New York memorandum, Nov. 18, 1963, FJ-246.

916 "terribly uncomfortable": Jones to MLK, Nov. 26, 1963, A/KP27f8; Garrow, *Bearing*, p. 307.

917 "our New York Agents": Baumgardner to Sullivan, Nov. 25, 1963, FL-NR.

917 Kennedy was celebrating: Int. Ramsey Clark, Oct. 28, 1963.

917 Washington barbers: Evelyn Lincoln to Lee White, enclosing WS article, Nov. 10, 1963, Box 19, White Papers, JFK.

917 Pilcher's game: White to JFK, Nov. 20, 1963; McGiffert to Wilson, Nov. 16, 1963; Wilson to White, Nov. 12, 1963; McGiffert to Wilson, Nov. 8, 1963; and Yarmolinsky to White, May 15, 1963, all in Box 19, White Papers, JFK.

917 stripped the Oval Office: Lee White, LBJOH.

917 "normal tone of voice": Wiretap, Nov. 26, 1963, FLNY-9-363.

917 Ruby was a Communist: Wiretap, Nov. 24, 1963, FLNY-9-361a.

918 "Chinese wing": Wiretap, Nov. 26, 1963, FLNY-7-617a.

918 deeply hurt: New York Letterhead Memorandum, Nov. 30, 1963, FL-NR.

918 refused to be photographed: *Jet*, Dec. 19, 1963, pp. 6, 7, 37.

919 "unholy alliance": Baumgardner to Sullivan, Dec. 19, 1963, FK-NR. Also in FBI #100-3-116, serial 711.

919 "expose King as an immoral opportunist": Sullivan to Belmont, Dec. 24, 1963, FK-NR. Also in FBI #100-3-116, serial 684.

920 Lewis was among: Int. John Lewis, May 31, 1984.

920 "made up their minds": "Movement Soul," Folkways Album FD5486.

920 Freedom Vote: Background on the November 1963 Freedom Vote as a precursor of Freedom Summer found in Carson, *In Struggle*, pp. 97–98; Harris, *Dreams Die Hard*, pp. 30–34; Allard Lowenstein speech of Oct. 2, 1963, press conference of Nov. 7, 1963, and Moses speech of April 24, 1964, Stanford University Archive of Recorded Sound; Goodlatte-Bass to Lowenstein, Oct. 29, 1963, A/KP7f29; Robert Moses interview by Ann Romaine, A/AR; SNCC executive committee minutes, Dec. 31, 1963, p. 28, A/SN6.

920 "Negroes are blackmailing": NYT, Nov. 30, 1963, p. 8.

920 Yale and Stanford: NYT, Oct. 30, 1963, p. 24.

921 "after him in Amite": Moses to Doar, Aug. 2, 1962, enclosing press release, files of the Civil Rights Division, Department of Justice.

921 "Thank you, Jesus": Elizabeth Allen affidavit in COFO, *Mississippi*, pp. 30–37.

921 "protect our own people": Int. Robert Moses, July 30, 1984.

921 cancel the SCLC's credit cards: King memos to executive staff, Oct. 30, 1963, Dec. 5, 1963, and undated, A/KP31f6.

921 Robert Kennedy dismissed: RFK to MLK, Dec. 4, 1963, A/KP24f21.

921 forty elderly Negro women: Boynton to MLK, Nov. 30, 1963, A/KP21f10.

922 dentist bill for Mahalia Jackson: Dr. R. C. Bell to Walker, Dec. 10, 1963; Walker to Bell, Dec. 19, 1963, A/SC4f18; MLK to Mahalia Jackson, Jan. 10, 1964, A/KP13f1.

922 "let Dexter go out": MLK interview by Donald H. Smith, SHSW/SP.

MAJOR WORKS
CITED IN NOTES

Abram, Morris B. *The Day Is Short*. Harcourt Brace Jovanovich, 1982.

Adams, Sherman. *Firsthand Report: The Story of the Eisenhower Administration*. Harper & Brothers, 1961.

Ahlstrom, Sidney E. *A Religious History of the American People*. Yale University Press, 1972.

Allen, Ivan, Jr., with Paul Hemphill. *Mayor: Notes on the Sixties*. Simon and Schuster, 1971.

Ambrose, Stephen E. *Eisenhower: The President*. Simon and Schuster, 1984.

Ansbro, John J. *Martin Luther King, Jr.: The Making of a Mind*. Maryknoll, N.Y.: Orbis Books, 1982.

Ashmore, Harry S. *Hearts and Minds: The Anatomy of Racism from Roosevelt to Reagan*. McGraw-Hill, 1982.

Augustine, *The Confessions of Saint Augustine* (ca. 400). Signet, 1963.

Baez, Joan. *And a Voice to Sing With*. Summit Books, 1987.

Bains, Lee E. "Birmingham 1963: Confrontation Over Civil Rights." B.A. thesis, Harvard University, 1977.

Baker, Bobby, with Larry L. King. *Wheeling and Dealing: Confessions of a Capitol Hill Operator*. W. W. Norton, 1978.

Bass, Jack. *Unlikely Heroes*. Simon and Schuster, 1981.

Bennett, Lerone, Jr. *What Manner of Man*. Johnson Publishing Co., 1964.

Bingham, June. *Courage to Change: An Introduction to the Life and Thought of Reinhold Niebuhr*. Charles Scribner's Sons, 1972.

Birmingham, Stephen. *Certain People: America's Black Elite*. Little, Brown, 1977.

Blair, Joan, and Clay Blair, Jr. *The Search for JFK*. Berkley/G. P. Putnam's Sons, 1976.

Bledsoe, Thomas. *Or We'll All Hang Separately: The Highlander Idea*. Beacon Press, 1969.

Boddie, Charles Emerson. *God's Bad Boys*. Valley Forge, Pa.: Judson Press, 1972.

Bradlee, Benjamin C. *Conversations with Kennedy*. W. W. Norton, 1975.

Brawley, Benjamin. *History of Morehouse College*. Atlanta: Morehouse College, 1917.

Breitman, George, ed. *Malcolm X Speaks.* Grove Press, 1966.
Buckley, Gail Lumet. *The Hornes: An American Family.* Alfred A. Knopf, 1986.
Carson, Clayborne. *In Struggle: SNCC and the Black Awakening of the 1960s.* Harvard University Press, 1981.
Clark, Septima. *Echo in My Soul.* E. P. Dutton, 1962.
Clarke, Erskine. *Wrestlin' Jacob.* Atlanta: John Knox Press, 1979.
Clayton, Edward T. *King: The Peaceful Warrior.* Prentice-Hall, 1964. Pocket Books, 1969.
COFO (Council of Federated Organizations). *Mississippi Black Power.* Random House, 1965.
Collier, Peter, and David Horowitz. *The Kennedys.* Summit Books, 1984.
Corley, Robert Gaines. "The Quest for Racial Harmony: Race Relations in Birmingham, Alabama, 1947–1963." Ph.D. dissertation, University of Virginia, 1979.
Davis, Allison. *Leadership, Love, and Aggression.* Harcourt Brace Jovanovich, 1983.
Doar, John, and Dorothy Landsberg. "The Performance of the FBI in Investigating Violations of Federal Laws Protecting the Right to Vote, 1960–67." Unpublished paper, 1971.
Donovan, Robert J. *Eisenhower: The Inside Story.* Harper & Brothers, 1956.
———. *Conflict and Crisis: The Presidency of Harry S Truman, 1945–48.* W. W. Norton, 1977.
———. *Tumultuous Years: The Presidency of Harry S Truman, 1949–53.* W. W. Norton, 1982.
Douglass, Frederick. *Narrative of the Life of Frederick Douglass (Written by Himself)* (1845). Signet, 1968.
Du Bois, W. E. B. *The Souls of Black Folk* (1903). Signet, 1969.
Durr, Virginia Foster. *Outside the Magic Circle: The Autobiography of Virginia Foster Durr,* edited by Hollinger F. Barnard. University of Alabama Press, 1985.
English, James W. *The Prophet of Wheat Street.* Elgin, Ill.: David C. Cook Publishing Co., 1967; paperback edition, 1973.
Evans, Rowland, and Robert Novak. *Lyndon B. Johnson: The Exercise of Power.* New American Library, 1966. Signet, 1968.
Evans, Zelia S., ed. *Dexter Avenue Baptist Church: 1877–1977.* Unpublished paper produced for the Dexter Avenue Baptist Church, Montgomery, Alabama, 1978.
Evers, Mrs. Medgar, with William Peters. *For Us, The Living.* Doubleday, 1967.
Farmer, James. *Freedom—When?* Random House, 1965.
———. *Lay Bare the Heart.* Arbor House, 1985.
Fenderson, Lewis H. *Thurgood Marshall: Fighter for Justice.* McGraw-Hill/Rutledge Books, 1969.
Fischer, Louis. *Gandhi: His Life and Message for the World.* Mentor, 1954.
Flynn, J. T. *God's Gold: John D. Rockefeller and His Times.* Harcourt, Brace and Co., 1932.
Forman, James. *The Making of Black Revolutionaries.* Macmillan, 1972.
Fosdick, Harry Emerson. *The Living of These Days.* Harper & Brothers, 1956.
Fox, Richard. *Reinhold Niebuhr.* Pantheon, 1985.
Gandy, Samuel Lucius. *Human Possibilities: A Vernon Johns Reader.* Washington, D.C.: Hoffman Press, 1977.
Gardner, Carl. *Andrew Young.* New York: Drake Publishers, 1978.
Garrow, David J. *Protest at Selma: Martin Luther King, Jr., and the Voting Rights Act of 1965.* Yale University Press, 1978.
———. *The FBI and Martin Luther King, Jr.,* W. W. Norton, 1981.
———. *Bearing the Cross: Martin Luther King, Jr., and the Southern Christian Leadership Conference.* William Morrow, 1986.
Gentile, Thomas. *March on Washington: August 28, 1963.* Washington, D.C.: Dew Day Publications, 1983.
Golden, Harry. *Mr. Kennedy and the Negroes.* Fawcett World Library, 1964.
Goldman, Eric F. *The Crucial Decade—And After: America, 1945–1960.* Vintage, 1960.
Goreau, Laurraine. *Just Mahalia, Baby.* Waco, Tex.: World Books, 1975.
Goulden, Joseph C. *George Meany: The Unchallenged Strong Man of American Labor.* Atheneum, 1972.
Grant, Joanne. *Black Protest: History, Documents, and Analyses, 1619 to the Present.* Fawcett Premier, 1968.

Guralnick, Peter. *Sweet Soul Music.* Harper & Row, 1986.

Guthman, Edwin. *We Band of Brothers.* Harper & Row, 1971.

Harding, Vincent. "A Beginning in Birmingham." *The Reporter,* June 6, 1963, pp. 13–19.

Harrington, Michael. *Fragments of the Century.* Saturday Review Press, 1973.

Harris, David. *Dreams Die Hard.* St. Martin's Press, 1982.

Haskins, James. *Andrew Young: Man with a Mission.* New York: Lothrop, Lee & Shepard, 1979.

Hoagland, Jim. *South Africa: Civilizations in Conflict.* Houghton Mifflin, 1972.

Hollis, Daniel Webster, III. *An Alabama Newspaper Tradition: Grover C. Hall and the Hall Family.* University of Alabama Press, 1983.

Hoopes, Townsend. *The Devil and John Foster Dulles.* Atlantic–Little, Brown, 1973.

Howe, Irving. *The American Communist Party: A Critical History.* Praeger, 1962.

Huckaby, Elizabeth. *Crisis at Central High: Little Rock, 1957–58.* LSU Press, 1980.

Isserman, Maurice. *If I Had a Hammer: The Death of the Old Left and the Birth of the New Left.* Basic Books, 1987.

Jones, Charles C. *The Religious Instruction of the Negroes in the United States* (1842). Libraries Press, 1971.

Jones, Landon Y. *Great Expectations.* Coward-McCann & Geoghegan, 1980.

Kaufman, Walter, ed. *Religion from Tolstoy to Camus.* Harper & Row, 1961. Torchbook, 1964.

Kearns, Doris. *Lyndon Johnson and the American Dream.* Harper & Row, 1976.

King, Coretta Scott. *My Life with Martin Luther King, Jr.* Holt, Rinehart and Winston, 1969. Avon, 1970.

King, Edward. *The Great South.* LSU Press, 1972.

King, Martin Luther, Jr. "An Autobiography of Religious Development." Unpublished paper written at Boston University, ca. 1951.

———. *Stride Toward Freedom: A Leader of His People Tells the Montgomery Story.* Harper & Brothers, 1958.

———. *Strength to Love.* Harper & Row, 1964. Fortress Press, 1982.

———. *Why We Can't Wait.* Harper & Row, 1963. Signet, 1964.

King, Martin Luther, Sr., with Clayton Riley. *Daddy King: An Autobiography.* William Morrow, 1980.

King, Mary. *Freedom Song.* William Morrow, 1987.

Kluger, Richard. *Simple Justice.* Random House, 1975. Vintage, 1977.

Kunstler, William. *Deep in My Heart.* William Morrow, 1966.

Lewis, David L. *King: A Critical Biography.* University of Illinois Press, 1970. Illini, 1978.

Litwack, Leon F. *Been in the Storm So Long: The Aftermath of Slavery.* Alfred A. Knopf, 1979.

Lord, Walter. *The Past That Would Not Die.* Harper & Row, 1965. Pocket Books, 1967.

Macy, Christy, and Susan Kaplan. *Documents.* Penguin, 1980.

Manchester, William. *The Glory and the Dream: A Narrative History of America,* 2 vols. Little, Brown, 1973.

Martin, John Bartlow. *The Deep South Says Never.* Ballantine, 1957.

———. *Adlai Stevenson and the World.* Doubleday, 1977. Anchor, 1978.

Mays, Benjamin. *Born to Rebel.* Charles Scribner's Sons, 1971.

Meier, August, and Elliott Rudwick. *CORE: A Study in the Civil Rights Movement.* University of Illinois Press, 1973. Illini, 1975.

Meredith, James H. *Three Years in Mississippi.* Indiana University Press, 1966.

Miller, Merle. *Lyndon: An Oral Biography.* G. P. Putnam's Sons, 1980. Ballantine, 1981.

Moody, Anne. *Coming of Age in Mississippi.* Dial Press, 1968.

Morris, Aldon D. *The Origins of the Civil Rights Movement.* Free Press, 1984.

Morrow, E. Frederic. *Black Man in the White House.* Coward-McCann, 1963. MacFadden, 1963.

Moses, Robert P. "Mississippi: 1961–62." *Liberation,* January 1970.

Myers, Robert Manson, ed. *The Children of Pride.* Yale University Press, 1972. Popular Library, 6 vols., 1977.

Navasky, Victor S. *Kennedy Justice.* Atheneum, 1972; paperback, 1977.

Neary, John. *Julian Bond: Black Rebel.* William Morrow, 1971.

Niebuhr, Reinhold. *Moral Man and Immoral Society.* Charles Scribner's Sons, 1932.

Oates, Stephen B. *Let the Trumpet Sound: The Life of Martin Luther King, Jr.* Harper & Row, 1982.

Peck, James. *Freedom Ride.* Simon and Schuster, 1962. Grove Press paperback, undated.

Phillips, Cabell. *The Truman Presidency.* Macmillan, 1966. Penguin, 1969.

Powers, Richard Gid. *Secrecy and Power: The Life of J. Edgar Hoover.* Free Press, 1987.

Quarles, Benjamin. *The Negro in the Making of American Life.* Macmillan, 1964; paperback, 1969.

Raines, Howell. *My Soul Is Rested.* G. P. Putnam's Sons, 1977. Bantam, 1978.

Read, Florence Matilda. *The Story of Spelman College.* Princeton University Press, 1961.

Reddick, Lawrence D. *Crusader Without Violence: A Biography of Martin Luther King, Jr.* Harper & Brothers, 1959.

Reynolds, Barbara. *Jesse Jackson.* Chicago: Nelson-Hall, 1975.

Rolling Stone, the Editors of. *The Rolling Stone Rock Almanac.* Rolling Stone Press, 1973.

Ross, B. Joyce. *J. E. Spingarn and the Rise of the NAACP, 1911–1939.* Atheneum, 1972.

Rowan, Carl T. *Go South to Sorrow.* Random House, 1957.

Rowe, Gary Thomas, Jr. *My Undercover Years with the Ku Klux Klan.* Bantam, 1976.

Rustin, Bayard. "Montgomery Diary," *Liberation,* April 1956.

———. *Down the Line: The Collected Writings of Bayard Rustin.* Quadrangle, 1971.

Scales, Junius, and Richard Nickson. *Cause at Heart: A Former Communist Remembers.* University of Georgia Press, 1987.

Scherer, Lester B. *Slavery and the Churches in Early America, 1619–1819.* Grand Rapids, Mich.: William B. Erdman, 1975.

Schlesinger, Arthur M., Jr. *A Thousand Days: John F. Kennedy in the White House.* Houghton Mifflin, 1965. Fawcett, 1967.

———. *Robert Kennedy and His Times.* Houghton Mifflin, 1978. Ballantine, 1979.

Shannon, David A. *The Decline of the American Communist Party.* Chatham, N.J.: The Chatham Bookseller, 1959.

Shaw, Arnold. *Belafonte.* Chilton, 1960.

Silver, James W. *Mississippi: The Closed Society.* Harcourt, Brace & World, 1963.

Smith, Allene de Shazo. *Greenwood LeFlore and the Choctaw Indians.* Memphis: C. A. Davis Co., 1951.

Smith, Bob. *They Closed Their Schools: Prince Edward County, Virginia, 1951–64.* University of North Carolina Press, 1965.

Smith, Esther. "The History of Ebenezer Baptist Church." Unpublished paper, 1956.

Smith, Kenneth Lee, and Ira Zepp. *Search for the Beloved Community: The Thinking of Martin Luther King, Jr.* Valley Forge, Pa.: Judson Press, 1974.

Sorensen, Theodore C. *Kennedy.* Harper & Row, 1965.

Stein, Jean, with George Plimpton. *American Journey: The Times of Robert Kennedy.* Harcourt Brace Jovanovich, 1970.

Stone, Richard H. *Paul Tillich's Radical Social Thought.* Atlanta: John Knox Press, 1980.

Sullivan, William, with Bill Brown. *The Bureau: My Thirty Years in Hoover's FBI.* W. W. Norton, 1979.

Summers, Anthony. *Goddess: The Secret Lives of Marilyn Monroe.* Macmillan, 1985.

Tygiel, Jules. *Baseball's Great Experiment: Jackie Robinson and His Legacy.* Oxford University Press, 1983.

U.S. House of Representatives. *The Final Assassinations Report: Report of the Select Committee on Assassinations.* Bantam, 1979.

U.S. Senate. Select Committee to Study Governmental Operations with Respect to Intelligence Activities (Church Committee). Report No. 94-465, *Alleged Assassination Plots Involving Foreign Leaders: An Interim Report.* U.S. Government Printing Office, 1975.

———. Report No. 94-755, *Supplementary Detailed Staff Reports on Intelligence Activities and the Rights of Americans. Book III: Final Report.* U.S. Government Printing Office, 1976.

Viorst, Milton. *Fire in the Streets.* Simon and Schuster, 1979. Touchstone, 1981.

Walker, Wyatt Tee. *Somebody's Calling My Name: Black Sacred Music and Social Change.* Valley Forge, Pa.: Judson Press, 1979.

Washington, James M. *A Testament of Hope: The Essential Writing of Martin Luther King, Jr.* Harper & Row, 1986.

Watters, Pat. *Down to Now: Reflections on the Southern Civil Rights Movement.* Random House, 1971.

—— and Reese Cleghorn. *Climbing Jacob's Ladder: The Arrival of Negroes in Southern Politics.* Harcourt, Brace & World, 1967.

Westin, Alan F., and Barry Mahoney. *The Trial of Martin Luther King.* Thomas Y. Crowell, 1974.

White, Theodore S. *The Making of the President, 1960.* Atheneum, 1961.

Whitehead, Don. *Attack on Terror: The FBI Against the Ku Klux Klan.* Funk & Wagnalls, 1970.

Wilkins, Roger. *A Man's Life: An Autobiography.* Simon and Schuster, 1982.

Wilkins, Roy, with Tom Matthews. *Standing Fast: The Autobiography of Roy Wilkins.* Viking Press, 1982.

Williams, Juan. *Eyes on the Prize: America's Civil Rights Years, 1954–65.* Viking Press, 1987. Penguin, 1988.

Wofford, Harris. *Of Kennedys and Kings.* Farrar, Straus & Giroux, 1980.

Woodson, Carter G. *The History of the Negro Church,* 2d ed. Washington, D.C.: Associated Publishers, 1921.

——. *Negro Orators and Their Orations.* Washington, D.C.: Associated Publishers, 1925.

Yeakey, Lamont H. "The Montgomery, Alabama, Bus Boycott, 1955–56." Ph.D. dissertation, Columbia University, 1979.

Zinn, Howard. *Albany: A Study in National Responsibility.* Atlanta: Southern Regional Council, 1962.

——. *SNCC: The New Abolitionists.* Beacon Press, 1965.

INDEX

Negro support for, 349–50, 356, 373–376, 378, 384
racial policy unity of, 864
Reston, James, 113, 666, 812, 886
Reuther, Walter, 411, 788–89, 834
civil rights legislation and, 839, 884–886
Detroit rally and, 843
Lewis's March on Washington speech and, 874, 878, 883
"Rev. King Is Boycott Boss, The" (Johnson), 154
Reynolds, Isaac, 422n, 775
Reynolds, Libby Holman, 208
Ribicoff, Abraham, 584
Rich, Marvin, 617
Rich, Richard, 354, 356
Richardson, Gloria, 881, 916
Richmond, Va.:
New Year's Day march in, 259–60, 273
SCLC convention in, 898–901, 906
Richmond *News Leader*, 380
Rich's:
segregation policy of, 346
sit-in at, 350, 351, 354, 357–58, 373, 467
"Right On, Jesus Christ," 804
Riklis, Meshulam, 581
Ritter, Norman, 445–46
Riverdale Motor Inn, 860, 870
Riverside Church, 66, 80, 197n, 243, 489, 491, 681, 695
construction of, 38–39
March on Washington and, 873
Robertson, Carole, 892
Robeson, Paul, 185, 212, 307
Robinson, Bernice, 717, 719n, 818, 825
Robinson, Cleveland, 847
Robinson, Jackie, 13, 359, 647, 726, 860, 863
Birmingham campaign and, 791, 801
1960 elections and, 306–7, 314, 343, 356, 365
Robinson, Jo Ann, 312
Montgomery bus boycott and, 131–32, 147, 159
Parks's arrest and, 131–32
Robinson, Spottswood, 25
Rockefeller, Happy Murphy, 789
Rockefeller, John D., 34, 57
background of, 28
impact on Negro Atlanta of, 27–29, 33
Ludlow massacre and, 33
Rockefeller, John D., Jr., 28–29, 52, 695, 792
Baptist church projects of, 38–39

Rockefeller, Laura Spelman, 28–29, 33, 38
Rockefeller, Michael, 591
Rockefeller, Nelson, 244, 385, 590–92, 639, 705–6, 860, 864
Birmingham movement and, 787, 789
divorce of, 591, 863
Emancipation Proclamation centennial and, 641–42, 688
J. F. Kennedy criticized by, 489, 591, 699–700
on King's Albany imprisonments, 602, 621, 624
King's relationship with, 488–89
in 1960 elections, 305, 321–22, 356
SCLC libel case and, 581
Spelman address of, 591
Rockefeller Foundation, 33
Rock Hill, S.C.:
Freedom Ride in, 415–16
jail-in in, 391–94
sit-in in, 274
"Rock Me, Lord," 772
Rockwell, George Lincoln, 655
Rockwell, Norman, 554
Rogers, Will, 51
Rogers, William P., 324
civil rights interests of, 236n
civil rights legislation and, 248–49, 331, 333
King-Eisenhower meeting and, 235–236
Little Rock crisis and, 436
Nixon campaign and, 375
Parker lynching and, 257–58
Roldan, Amadeo, 111
"Romance of Death, The" (Johns), 902n
Romans, Book of, 8
Rometsch, Ellen, 906, 911–14
Roosevelt, Eleanor, 84, 121, 191, 328, 591, 655
1960 elections and, 305, 316, 344
Roosevelt, Franklin D., 84, 349–50, 389
discrimination in defense industries banned by, 170–71, 699
presidential campaigns of, 371
Roosevelt, Theodore, 31, 689
Rosen, Alex, 473, 648, 681
Rosenberg, Ethel, 100, 208
Rosenberg, Julius, 100, 208
Rosenwald, Julius, 123
Rowan, Carl, 155–56, 194–95, 324
Rowe, Gary Thomas, 420–21
Royal College of Physicians, 562
Royal Crown Cola, 780
Royall, Kenneth:
Birmingham church bombings and, 893–95

PHOTO CREDITS

23. New York Daily News

25. Courtesy Dexter Avenue King Memorial Baptist Church, Montgomery

26, 27. *The Tennessean*, Nashville

28. Highlander Research and Education Center Archives

31, 55. Jacques Lowe/Woodfin Camp & Associates

32. Charles Bonnay/Black Star

33, 35. John F. Kennedy Memorial Library

36, 37. Courtesy of Mrs. Stanley Levison

38, 39, 58, 80. Department of Archives and Manuscripts, Birmingham Public Library, Birmingham

40. Birmingham News Photo

43, 60. Bruce Davidson/Magnum Photos Inc.

44. Lee Lockwood, Black Star

45. Steve Schapiro, Black Star

46. Photo by Ida Berman, courtesy of Highlander Research and Education Center

47, 59. Danny Lyon, Magnum Photos Inc.

52. © 1962 by The New York Times Company. Reprinted with permission

53. Dan McCoy, Black Star

57, 79. Fred Ward, Black Star

61. Ernest Haas/Magnum Photos Inc.

63. Vernon Merit II/Black Star

74. The Detroit News

77. Dan Rudnick/Woodfin Camp & Associates

81. Frank Dandridge, *Life* Magazine. © 1988 Time Inc.

82. Declan Haun/Black Star

83. John Launois/Black Star

84. © Cornell Capa/Magnum Photos Inc.

85. © Bob Fitch/Black Star

ABOUT THE AUTHOR

Taylor Branch is the award-winning author of *Pillar of Fire*, a novel and four collaborative books of nonfiction. He lives in Baltimore, Maryland.

In the second volume of the Pulitzer Prize–winning monumental saga of the civil rights era, Taylor Branch portrays the movement at its zenith, recounting its climactic struggles as it commanded the national stage.

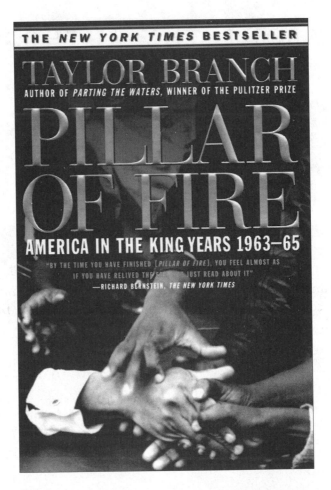

THE NEW YORK TIMES BESTSELLER

TAYLOR BRANCH

AUTHOR OF *PARTING THE WATERS*, WINNER OF THE PULITZER PRIZE

PILLAR OF FIRE

AMERICA IN THE KING YEARS 1963–65

"BY THE TIME YOU HAVE FINISHED [PILLAR OF FIRE], YOU FEEL ALMOST AS IF YOU HAVE RELIVED THE... JUST READ ABOUT IT"
—RICHARD BERNSTEIN, *THE NEW YORK TIMES*

"As he did in *Parting the Waters*, Branch brings to these events both a passion for their detail and a recognition of their larger historical significance."

—*The New York Times Book Review*

"Branch spins an intricate, seamless web of politics and personalities, ambition and imagination, triumph and tragedy."

—*The Washington Post Book World*

"*Pillar of Fire* is a magisterial history of one of the most tumultuous periods in postwar America. . . . Reading Branch, it is easier to see why even the most remarkable revolutions are never complete."

—*Newsweek*

"One part biography, one part history, one part elegy . . . a vast panorama . . . powerful."

—*The Wall Street Journal*

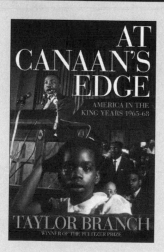